WILLIAM A. HAVILAND

University of Vermont

ANTHROPOLOGY

EIGHTH EDITION

HARCOURT BRACE COLLEGE PUBLISHERS

FORT WORTH PHILADELPHIA SAN DIEGO NEW YORK ORLANDO AUSTIN SAN ANTONIO

TORONTO MONTREAL LONDON SYDNEY TOKYO

DEDICATION

In Memory of David P. Boynton (1921–1995)

Recipient of the American Anthropological Association's
Distinguished Service Award, 1985. The man whose idea this book was,
and who saw it through the first three editions.

A wise soul

Publisher	CHRISTOPHER P. KLEIN
Senior Acquisitions Editor	STEPHEN T. JORDAN
Developmental Editor	AMY HESTER
Project Editor	JEFF BECKHAM
Production Manager	DEBRA A. JENKIN
Art Director	BURL DEAN SLOAN
Picture Editor	SANDRA LORD
Photo Research	CHERI THROOP

Cover Image: Photo by Gary Logan. Photo Layout and Concept: Burl Dean Sloan.

ISBN: 0-15-503578-9

Library of Congress Catalog Card Number: 96-76369

Copyright © 1997 by Harcourt Brace & Company
Copyright © 1994, 1991, 1989, 1985, 1982, 1978, 1974 by Holt, Rinehart and Winston, Inc.

Address for Editorial Correspondence: Harcourt Brace College Publishers, 301 Commerce Street, Suite 3700, Fort Worth, TX 76102.

Address for Orders: Harcourt Brace & Company, 6277 Sea Harbor Drive, Orlando, FL 32887-6777. 1-800-782-4479,
or 1-800-433-0001 (in Florida).

(Copyright Acknowledgments begin on page 798, which constitutes a continuation of this copyright page.)

Harcourt Brace College Publishers may provide complimentary instructional aids and supplements or supplement
packages to those adopters qualified under our adoption policy. Please contact your sales representative for
more information. If as an adopter or potential user you receive supplements you do not need, please return
them to your sales representative or send them to:
Attn: Returns Department
Troy Warehouse
465 South Lincoln Drive
Troy, MO 63379.

Printed in the United States of America
6 7 8 9 0 1 2 3 4 5 048 10 9 8 7 6 5 4 3 2 1

Using ANTHROPOLOGY
A Guide to Learning from Your Textbook

Anthropology, **Eighth Edition,** is designed to give students a thorough introduction at the college level to the principles and processes of anthropology. It covers the basic divisions of anthropology—physical and cultural anthropology, including ethnology, linguistics, and prehistoric archaeology—and presents the key concepts and terminology truly relevant to each.

Anthropology, **Eighth Edition,**

◆ provides a **unifying theme.** Although each chapter has been developed as a self-contained unit of study, a common theme runs through all the chapters: Cultures must produce behavior that is generally adaptive.

◆ ensures **readability.** Using numerous and colorful examples, Dr. Haviland presents even the most difficult concepts in prose that is clear, straightforward, and easy for today's first- and second-year students to understand.

◆ maintains a moderate **length.** The textbook is of sufficient length to avoid superficiality, yet it does not present more material than can reasonably be dealt with in the space of a single semester.

The following pages will introduce you to the many features of *Anthropology,* **Eighth Edition,** and show you how to use the learning aids provided to enhance your study of anthropology.

Original Studies: These unique selections are from case studies and other original works of men and women who have done, or are doing, important anthropological work. Each study sheds additional light on some important anthropological concept or subject area found within the chapter.

Anthropology Applied: These boxed features demonstrate the many "practical" applications of anthropological knowledge, the important work being done by anthropologists outside of academic settings, and the variety of careers pursued by anthropologists.

JANE GOODALL
(b. 1934)

In July 1960 Jane Goodall arrived with her mother at the Gombe Chimpanzee Reserve on the shores of Lake Tanganyika in Tanzania. The first of three women sent out by Kenyan anthropologist Louis Leakey to study great apes in the wild (the others were Dian Fossey and Birute Galdikas, who went to study gorillas and orangutans, respectively), her task was to begin a long-term study of chimpanzees. Little did she realize that, more than 35 years later, she would still be at it.

Though born in London, Jane grew up and was schooled in Bournemouth, England. Upon her graduation at 18, she enrolled in secretarial school, following which she held various jobs in England before the opportunity came to go to Africa. As a child, she had always dreamed of going there to live among animals, so when an invitation arrived to visit a friend in Kenya, she jumped at the opportunity. Quitting her regular job, she worked as a waitress to raise the money for travel, and was then on her way. Once in Kenya, she met Louis Leakey, who gave her a job as an assistant secretary. Before long, she was on her way to Gombe. Within a year, the outside world began to hear the most extraordinary things about this pioneering woman and her work; tales of tool-making apes, cooperative hunts by chimpanzees, and what seemed like exotic chimpanzee rain dances. By the mid-1960s, her work had earned her a Ph.D.

from Cambridge University, and Gombe was on its way to becoming one of the most dynamic field stations for the study of animal behavior anywhere in the world.

Although field studies of primates in their natural habitats had been undertaken prior to 1960, there had been not many of them, and few of those had produced more than extremely limited information. It was Goodall's particular blend of patience and determination that showed what could be achieved, and before long her field station became something of a mecca for aspiring young students interested in primate behavior. The list of those who have worked with her at Gombe, many of them women, reads like a *Who's Who* of eminent scholars in the field of primate behavior.

Although Goodall is still involved with her chimpanzees, she now spends a good deal of time these days lecturing, writing, and overseeing the work of others. She has also become committed to the cause of primate conservation and halting the illegal trafficking in captive chimps. She is also an eloquent champion of humane treatment of captive chimpanzees.

---

reported by primatologist Barbara Smuts are indicative of the care males may invest in their friends' offspring. Two infants of the group she was studying lost their mothers while they were still quite young. In each case, their bond with the

Among gorillas and chimpanzees, the mother-infant bond is especially strong and may last for many years, commonly for the lifetime of the mother. Gorilla infants and young juveniles share their mothers' nests and have been seen sharing ... childless females. Both chim... s males are attentive to juveniles ... parental responsibilities. Male ... ever (as among human food for... er apart from the females and ju... the females who provide stability ... group, whereas it is the domi... ho provides this in the gorilla

Bioboxes: Throughout the textbook, profile boxes provide biographical information about important people in the field of anthropology.

CHAPTER 6
THE EARLIEST HOMININES

PALEOANTHROPOLOGIST DONALD JOHANSON DISCOVERS THE LEG BONE OF AN EARLY HOMININE KNOWN AS *AUSTRALOPITHECUS*. THOUGH THEIR BEHAVIOR PATTERNS WERE MORE APELIKE THAN HUMAN, *AUSTRALOPITHECUS* MOVED AROUND ON THE GROUND ON

Illustrations: Dr. Haviland has chosen numerous four-color photos to make important anthropological points by catching the student's eye and mind. The line drawings, maps, charts, and tables were selected especially for their usefulness in illustrating, emphasizing, or clarifying certain anthropological concepts.

CHAPTER PREVIEW

What Is Culture?

Culture consists of the abstract values, beliefs, and perceptions of the world that lie behind people's behavior and which are reflected in their behavior. These are shared by members of a society, and when acted upon, they produce behavior considered acceptable within that society. Cultures are learned, largely through the medium of language, rather than inherited biologically, and the parts of a culture function as an integrated whole.

How Is Culture Studied?

Anthropologists, like children, learn about a culture by experiencing it and talking about it with those who live by its rules. Of course, ... learn, but are more systematic in the way they learn ... discussion with informants who are particularly k... culture, the anthropologist abstracts a set of rule... behave in a particular s...

Why Do Cultures ...

People maintain cultures to deal with problems ... survive, a culture must satisfy the basic needs of t... for its own continuity, and provide an orderly exist... In doing so, a culture must strike a balance betwe... and the needs of society as a whole. And finally, a ... change in order to adapt to new circumstances ... existing circumstan...

Previews and Summaries: Each chapter begins with a set of "preview" questions, providing a framework for studying the contents of the chapter. At the end of each chapter is a summary containing the kernels of the most important ideas presented in the chapter.

CHAPTER SUMMARY

Culture, to the anthropologist, is a set of rules or standards that, when acted upon by the members of a society, produce behavior that falls within a range of variance the members consider proper and acceptable.

All cultures share certain basic characteristics, study of these sheds light on the nature and function of culture itself. Culture is a set of shared ideals, values, and standards of behavior. It cannot exist without society: a group of people occupying a specific locality who are dependent on each other for survival. Society is held together by relationships determined by social structure or social organization. Culture cannot exist without society, although one can have society, as do creatures like ants and bees, without culture. All is not uniformity within a culture, partly because there is some difference between male and female roles in any human society. Anthropologists use the term *gender* to refer to the elaborations or meanings cultures assign to the biological differences between men and women. Age variation is also universal, and in some cultures there is other subcultural variation as well. A subculture shares certain overarching assumptions of the larger culture, while observing a set of rules that is distinctively different. One example of a subculture in the United States is that of the Amish. Pluralistic societies are those in which cultural variation is particularly marked. They are characterized by a number of groups operating under different sets of rules.

In addition to being shared, all cultures are learned. Individual members of a society learn the accepted norms of social behavior through the process of enculturation. Another characteristic is that culture is based on symbols. It is transmitted through the communication of ideas, emotions, and desires expressed in language. Finally, culture is integrated, so that all aspects of a culture function as an integrated whole. In a properly functioning culture, though, total harmony of all elements is approximated, rather than completely achieved.

The job of the anthropologist is to abstract a set of rules from what he or she observes in order to explain the social behavior of people. To arrive at a realistic description of a culture free from personal and cultural biases, the anthropologist must (1) examine a people's notion of the way their society ought to function, (2) determine how a people think they behave, and (3) compare these with how a people actually do behave. The anthropologist must also be as free as possible of the biases of his or her own culture.

Cultural adaptation has enabled humans, in the course of evolution, to survive and expand in a variety of environments. Sometimes, though, what is adaptive in one set of circumstances, or over the short run, is maladaptive in another set of circumstances, or over the long run.

To survive, a culture must satisfy the basic biological needs of its members, provide for their continuity, and maintain order among its members and between its members as well as outsiders.

All cultures change over time, sometimes because the environment they must cope with has changed, sometimes as the result of the intrusion of outsiders, or because values within the culture have undergone modification. Although cultures must change to adapt to new circumstances, sometimes the unforeseen consequences of change are disastrous for a society.

A society must strike a balance between the self-interest of individuals and the needs of the group. If one or the other becomes paramount, the result may be cultural breakdown.

Ethnocentrism is the belief that one's own culture is superior to all others. To avoid making ethnocentric judgments, anthropologists adopt the approach of cultural relativism, which requires that each culture be examined in its own terms, according to its own standards. The least biased measure of a culture's success, however, employs criteria indicative of its effectiveness at securing the survival of a society in a way that its members see as being reasonably fulfilling.

Suggested Readings and Bibliography: At the conclusion of each chapter is a list of suggested readings that will supply the inquisitive student with further information about specific anthropological points in which they may be interested. A complete bibliography can be found at the end of the book.

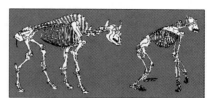

Running Glossary: This textbook has a running glossary that catches the student's eye as he or she reads and reinforces the meaning of each newly introduced term.

Pronunciation Guide: Inside the front and back covers, a pronunciation guide is given to aid students in learning and pronouncing unfamiliar words that appear throughout the textbook.

Putting the World in Perspective: This section, found in the introduction to the book, illustrates for students the many ways in which the globe can be viewed. A discussion of *cartography* and *projections* shows their benefits to anthropology.

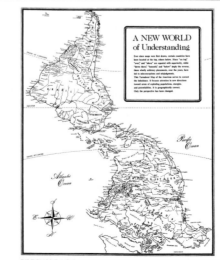

PREFACE

PURPOSE

The aim of *Anthropology* is to give the student a thorough introduction to the principles and processes of anthropology, the basic divisions of anthropology (physical and cultural anthropology, including ethnology, linguistics, and prehistoric archaeology), and the key concepts and terminology germane to each. Because it draws from the research and ideas of a number of schools of anthropological thought, this book will expose students to a mix of such approaches as evolutionism, historical particularism, diffusionism, functionalism, French structuralism, and structural functionalism. Each of these approaches has important things to say about human behavior. Thorough and scholarly in its coverage, the book is simply written and attractively designed to appeal to students. They will find that it pleases as it teaches.

UNIFYING THEME

Although each chapter has been developed as a self-contained unit of study, a common theme runs through all the chapters to convey to students how material in one chapter relates to that in others.

In earlier editions, I referred to this common theme as one of environmental adaptation, although I was never very happy with that phrase. Its principal defect is that it implies a simplistic behavioral response to environmental stimuli. But, of course, people don't just react to an environment as given; rather, they react to it as they perceive it, and different groups of people may perceive the same environment in radically different ways. People also react to things other than the environment: their own biological natures, for one, and their beliefs, attitudes, and the consequences of their own behavior, for others. All of these things present them with problems, and people maintain cultures to deal with problems, or matters that concern them. To be sure, their cultures must produce behavior that is generally adaptive, or at least not maladaptive, but this is not the same as saying that cultural practices necessarily arise because they are adaptive in a particular environment.

OUTSTANDING FEATURES

Readability

A book may be the most elegantly written, most handsomely designed, most lavishly illustrated text available on the subject; but if it is not interesting, clear, and comprehensible to the student, it is valueless as a teaching tool.

This book presents even the most difficult concepts in prose that is clear, straightforward, and easy for today's first- and second-year students to understand, without feeling that they are being "spoken down to." Technical terms appear in boldfaced type, are carefully defined within the text, and are defined again in the glossary in simple, clear language.

Numerous and colorful examples have been utilized to illustrate, emphasize, and clarify anthropological concepts. A cross-cultural perspective, often including the student's own, is introduced wherever appropriate, allowing the student to see comparisons of cultural practices in several different societies.

Original Studies

A unique feature of this textbook is the Original Study that appears in each chapter. These studies consist of selections from case studies and other original works of men and women who have done, or are doing, important anthropological work. Each study sheds additional light on some important anthropological concept or subject area found within the chapter.

The Original Studies help give students a "feel" for how anthropologists actually go about studying humans and their behavior. Because women have always been an important part of the anthropological enterprise, and students need to realize this, women are well-represented as authors of Original Studies in the eighth edition—14 of the 27 studies were written by women.

Illustrations

Another means of appeal is through the use of illustrations and other graphic materials. In this textbook, numerous four-color photos have been used to make important anthropological points. Many are unusual in that they are not the "standard" anthropological textbook photographs; each has been chosen because it complements the text in some distinctive way. The line drawings, maps, charts, and tables were selected especially for their usefulness in illustrating, emphasizing, or clarifying certain anthropological concepts.

Previews and Summaries

Each chapter begins with a set of preview questions, providing a framework for studying the contents of the chapter. At the end of each chapter is a summary containing the kernels of the most important ideas presented in the chapter. The summaries provide handy reviews without being so long and detailed as to seduce the student into thinking that he or she can get by without reading the chapter itself.

Suggested Readings and Bibliography

At the conclusion of each chapter is a list of suggested readings that will supply the inquisitive student with further information about specific anthropological points in which they may be interested. In addition, the bibliography at the end of the book contains a listing of more than 500 books, monographs, and articles from scholarly journals and popular magazines on virtually every topic covered in the text.

Glossary

This textbook has a running glossary that catches the student's eye as he or she reads and reinforces the meaning of each newly introduced term. It is also useful for chapter review.

ADVANTAGES OF THE EIGHTH EDITION

The planning of the eighth edition of *Anthropology* was based on extensive review and criticism by users of the seventh edition as well as users of other textbooks. Many features of the seventh edition were maintained in this new edition, including coverage of gender issues in each and every chapter of the book. Presentation of applied anthropology through boxed features in 20 chapters demonstrates the many "practical" applications of anthropological knowledge, the important work being done by anthropologists outside of academic settings, and the variety of careers pursued by anthropologists.

The major changes from the seventh edition consist of the following:

◆ The old chapter on the earliest hominines has become two separate chapters: Chapter 6 on *Australopithecus*, and Chapter 7 on *Homo sapiens* and cultural origins.

◆ Similarly, the old chapter on *Homo sapiens* has been split into two: Chapter 9 on archaic *sapiens* and the Middle Paleolithic, and Chapter 10 on anatomically modern *sapiens* and the Upper Paleolithic.

This splitting of chapters makes material in what had been two especially concentrated chapters easier for students to grapple with. Other important changes include:

◆ **Chapters 5 and 6:** new discussion of the possible relation of bipedal locomotion to keeping brains cool

◆ **Chapters 7, 8, and 15:** new discussion of language origins

◆ **Chapter 8:** new discussion of evidence for *Homo erectus'* use of fire in Africa

◆ **Chapter 9:** new discussion of evolution of the human birth pattern and its possible significance for the development of empathy

◆ **Chapter 10:** expanded coverage of Upper Paleolithic art, especially in Africa and Europe

◆ **Chapter 11:** expanded coverage of early domestication of plants in Africa and the Americas

◆ **Chapter 12:** new discussion of a Moche tomb

- **Chapter 13:** new discussion of the Bell curve debate
- **Chapter 14:** new discussion of how cultural relativism does not prevent one from being critical of particular practices
- **Chapter 16 (and followed up in Chapters 24 and 25):** new discussion of the meanings of the terms Bushman, San, and Ju/'hoansi for people of the Kalahari Desert and the rest of southern Africa, and new discussion of altered states of consciousness and the question of normal and abnormal behavior
- **Chapter 17:** new discussion of slash-and-burn farming
- **Chapter 18:** new discussion of money
- **Chapter 23:** new discussion of the different popular, legal, and anthropological meanings of "tribe"
- **Chapter 24:** new description of Bushman trance dance
- **Chapter 25:** new reference to the political debate over arts funding in the United States, and new discussion of pictorial art
- **Chapter 27:** revision of material on the human rights situation in Guatemala

In addition, 12 of the 27 Original Studies are new. Their topics include:

- **Chapter 1:** "Tales From the Trukese Taproom" by Mac Marshall
- **Chapter 4:** "The Intellectual Abilities of Orang-utans" by H. Lyn White Miles
- **Chapter 5:** "*Catopithecus* and Anthropoid (Catarrhine and Platyrrhine) Origins" by Elizabeth Culotta
- **Chapter 6:** "The Naked and the Bipedal" by Tim Folger
- **Chapter 10:** "Paleolithic Paint Job" by Roger Lewin
- **Chapter 12:** "Finding the Tomb of a Moche Priestess" by Christopher B. Donan and Luis Jaime Castillo
- **Chapter 13:** "Race Without Color" by Jared Diamond
- **Chapter 17:** "Gardens of the Mekranoti Kayapo" by Dennis Werner
- **Chapter 22:** "Genocide in Rwanda" by Alex de Waal

- **Chapter 24:** "Healing Among the Ju/'hoansi of the Kalahari" by Marjorie Shostak
- **Chapter 25:** "Bushman Rock Art and Political Power" by Thomas A. Dowson and J. D. Lewis-Williams
- **Chapter 27:** The Psychological Impact of Impunity" by Judith Zur

There are two new "Anthropology Applied" features:

- **Chapter 13:** "Studying the Emergence of New Diseases"
- **Chapter 23:** "African Public Defender and Legal Aid Training Exchange"

In addition, there is one new "Biobox" on Jane Goodall in **Chapter 4.**

SUPPLEMENTS TO THE TEXTBOOK

The following supplements were prepared by Cynthia Keppley Mahmood of the University of Maine, Orono.

Study Guide and Workbook

A *Study Guide and Workbook* is provided to aid student comprehension of the textbook material. Each chapter of the Study Guide begins with a synopsis of the corresponding textbook chapter and a concise list of learning objectives. The Study Guide furnishes review sections for key terms and names, review questions, map identification exercises, and practice questions in a variety of formats: fill-in-the-blank, multiple-choice, true/false, matching, and essay. An answer key is supplied with each practice section.

Instructor's Manual

An *Instructor's Manual* is available for teachers. Each chapter of the Instructor's Manual begins with a synopsis of the corresponding textbook chapter and a list of teaching objectives. A review of each chapter provides a more detailed narrative of what is covered in the textbook, including a summary of the Original Study feature and Anthropology Applied feature that appears in the chapter. This section is followed by a listing of the key terms from the textbook. Suggestions are given for exercises, assignments, and research topics related to the chapter. In addition, the Instructor's Manual provides suggestions for other resources that might complement the main text, such as films, transparencies, and ancillary readings.

Test Bank

An extensive *Test Bank* includes multiple-choice, matching, essay, true/false, and short answer questions. The Test Bank contains more than 2,000 questions, approximately 75 per chapter.

Computerized Test Bank

Available in IBM, Macintosh, and Windows formats, *EXAMaster+* software allows you to create tests using fewer keystrokes. Easy-to-follow screen prompts guide you step-by-step through test construction. *EXAMaster+* gives you three ways to create tests:

◆ *EasyTest* lets you create a test from a single screen. It compiles a test using questions you've chosen from the database or randomly selects questions based on the parameters you specify.

◆ *FullTest* gives you a whole range of options for test creation. With *FullTest*, you may:

select questions as you preview them on screen, edit existing questions, or add your own questions; add or edit graphics (in MS-DOS version); link related questions, instructions, and graphics; have questions randomly selected from a wider range of criteria; create your own criteria on two open keys; block specific questions from random selection; print up to 99 different versions of the same test and answer sheet.

◆ *RequesTest* is for the instructor without access to a computer. You may call our Software Support Line and order tests that conform to your criteria. Harcourt Brace will compile the test and either mail or fax it to you within 48 hours.

Overhead Transparencies

A set of 65 color transparencies corresponding to *Anthropology*, Eighth Edition, is also available to instructors.

HARCOURT BRACE VIDEOS AND VIDEODISCS

Anthropology in Focus Video

Harcourt Brace and Films for the Humanities and Sciences have created an exciting new video, *Anthropology in Focus*, to accompany William A. Haviland's anthropology textbooks. Each 10-minute segment on the video directly corresponds to an "Anthropology Applied" box in the textbook. Each segment includes "Ideas and Questions to Focus On," which helps prepare the student for the concepts the video is about to present and shows how the video footage relates to the "Anthropology Applied" boxes in each chapter.

Faces of Culture Telecourse and Study Guide

Valerie L. Lee and Richard T. Searles, *Coast Community College District*

Reflecting the philosophy that culture exists in unique forms as the expression of values, behavior, and social organization, *Faces of Culture* demonstrates the inherent logic of different societies based on problem-solving and adaptation. Twenty-six half-hour programs feature segments filmed under the supervision of anthropologists. Some show people who are seldom filmed; all are handled with great sensitivity. The accompanying *Study Guide* leads students through the course and provides reading and viewing assignments, study activities, and practice test questions.

The Infinite Voyage Video and Videodisc

The Infinite Voyage video series provides four hours of high-interest coverage in anthropology and archaeology. The series contains an exciting compilation of on-location, interview, laboratory, and candid footage. Available on either four one-hour videos or a two-volume set of CLV videodiscs.

The Millennium: Tribal Wisdom and the Modern World Video

Hosted by world-renowned anthropologist David Maybury-Lewis, *The Millennium: Tribal Wisdom and the Modern World* is a video series of ten 60-minute programs presenting a riveting and beautifully photographed exploration of tribal cultures, their lifestyles, and their practices.

Out of the Past Video

Culture, politics, and other fixtures of modern life have been passed down to us by ancient ancestors. In *Out of the Past*, archaeologists examine physical remnants of ancient empires side-by-side with practices of modern societies to trace and understand the evolution of humankind. Each one-hour program includes an excellent introduction to the disciplines of archaeology and anthropology. The programs reveal the scientific detective work that helps scholars build a living picture of a long-dead culture. From the Annenberg/CPB Video Series Collection.

ACKNOWLEDGMENTS

Many people assisted in the preparation of this book, some directly, some indirectly. In the latter category are all of the anthropologists under whom I was privileged to study at the University of Pennsylvania: Robbins Burling, William R. Coe, Carleton S. Coon, Robert Ehrich, Loren Eisley, J. Louis Giddings, Ward H. Goodenough, A. Irving Hallowell, Alfred V. Kidder II, Wilton M. Krogman, Froelich Rainey, Ruben Reina, and Linton Satterthwaite. They may not always recognize the final product, but they all contributed to it in important ways.

A similar debt is owed to all those anthropologists with whom I have worked or discussed research interests and the field in general. There are too many of them to list here, but surely they have had an important impact on my own thinking, and so on this book.

This revision also benefits from my continued association with valued colleagues at the University of Vermont: Robert Gordon, William E. Mitchell, Carroll McC. P. Lewin, Sarah Mahler, Stephen L. Pastner, Marjory Power, Peter A. Thomas, and A. Peter Woolfson. All have responded graciously at one time or another to my requests for sources and advice in their various fields of expertise. We all share freely our successes and failures in trying to teach anthropology to introductory students.

In 1984, I was given the opportunity to participate in a free and open discussion between textbook authors and users at the American Anthropological Association's Annual Meeting (a session organized and chaired by Walter Packard and the Council on Anthropology and Education). From this I got a good sense of what instructors at institutions ranging from community colleges to major universities were looking for in anthropology textbooks; subsequent insights have come from a special symposium on the teaching of anthropology at the University of Vermont in 1986 (organized by A. Peter Woolfson), a meeting of textbook authors with members of the Gender and the Anthropology Curriculum Project at the American Anthropological Association's Annual Meeting in 1988, and (most recently) a special session on Central Themes in the Teaching of Anthropology at the American Anthropological Association's Annual Meeting in 1990 (organized by Richard Furlow). To the organizers and sponsors of all these events, my sincere thanks.

Thanks are also due the anthropologists who made suggestions for this edition. They include the following: James Baenen, Seattle Central Community College; Donna Birdwell-Pheasant, Lamar University; Barbara Butler, University of Wisconsin, Stevens Point; Dennis Choate, Macomb Community College; Bonnie Glass-Coffin, Utah State University; Sandra Gray, University of Kansas; Corwin Hale, Harrisburg Area Community College; Raymond Hames, University of Nebraska, Lincoln; Francis B. Harrold, University of Texas, Arlington; S. Homes Hogue, Mississippi State University; Joe Hollinsworth, Edmonds Community College; Richard Holmer, Idaho State University; Lloyd Miller, Des Moines Area Community College; John Nass, California University of Pennsylvania; Jon Osmundson, Bellevue Community College; James Provinzano, University of Wisconsin, Oshkosh; Laura Putsche, University of Idaho; Bruce D. Roberts, University of Southern Mississippi; Sissel Schroeder, Pennsylvania State

University; Karl Steinen, West Georgia College; Mark A. Tromans, Broward Community College, Davie; William Wedenoja, Southwest Missouri State University; Loy Glenn Westfall, Hillsborough Community College; and Randolph Widmer, University of Houston.

All of their comments were carefully considered; how I have responded to them has been determined by my own perspective of anthropology, as well as my thirty years of experience with undergraduate students. Therefore, neither they nor any of the other anthropologists mentioned here should be held responsible for any shortcomings in this book.

I also wish to acknowledge my debt to a number of non-anthropologists who helped me with this book. The influence of the late David Boynton, winner of the 1985 Distinguished Service Award of the American Anthropological Association and my editor at Holt, Rinehart and

Winston until his retirement in 1983, I am sure lingers on. Helpful in seeing this edition through to publication have been my editors Stephen T. Jordan and Amy Hester; both have been a pleasure to work with. I also wish to thank the skilled production and marketing teams: Jeff Beckham, Debra Jenkin, Sandra Lord, Julie McBurney, and Burl Sloan.

The greatest debt of all is owed my wife, Anita de Laguna Haviland, who has had to put up with my preoccupation with this revision, reminding me when it is time to feed the livestock or play midwife to the sheep in the barn. As if that were not enough, it was she who fed revised text into the word processor. Finally, she has been a source of endless good ideas on things to include and ways to express things. The book has benefited enormously from her involvement.

William A. Haviland

ABOUT THE AUTHOR

Dr. William A. Haviland is professor of anthropology at the University of Vermont, where he has taught since 1965. He holds bachelor's, master's, and doctoral degrees in anthropology from the University of Pennsylvania and has published widely on archaeological, ethnological, and physical anthropological research carried out in Guatemala, Maine, and Vermont. He also has applied experience, having appeared as an expert witness in court on behalf of the aboriginal fishing rights of the Abenaki Indians in Vermont. Dr. Haviland is a member of many professional societies, including the American Anthropological Association and the American Association for the Advancement of Science.

In 1988, Dr. Haviland participated in the project on *Gender and the Anthropology Curriculum* sponsored by the American Anthropological Association. One of his greatest loves is teaching, which originally prompted him to write *Anthropology*. He says he learns something new every year from his students about what they need to get out of their first college course in anthropology. In addition to writing *Anthropology*, Dr. Haviland has authored two other popular Harcourt Brace textbooks for anthropology students.

CONTENTS IN BRIEF

TABLE OF CONTENTS

PART I

PART II

PUTTING THE WORLD IN PERSPECTIVE

Although all humans that we know about are capable of producing accurate sketches of localities and regions with which they are familiar, CARTOGRAPHY (the craft of map-making as we know it today) had its beginnings in 13th-century Europe, and its subsequent development is related to the expansion of Europeans to all parts of the globe. From the beginning, there have been two problems with maps: the technical one of how to depict on a two-dimensional, flat surface a three-dimensional spherical object, and the cultural one of whose world view they reflect. In fact, the two issues are inseparable, for the particular projection one uses inevitably makes a statement about how one views one's own people and their place in the world. Indeed, maps often shape our perception of reality as much as they reflect it.

In cartography, a PROJECTION refers to the system of intersecting lines (of longitude and latitude) by which part or all of the globe is represented on a flat surface. There are more than 100 different projections in use today, ranging from polar perspectives to interrupted "butterflies" to rectangles to heart shapes. Each projection causes distortion in size, shape, or distance in some way or another. A map that shows the shape of land masses correctly will of necessity misrepresent the size. A map that is accurate along the equator will be deceptive at the poles.

Perhaps no projection has had more influence on the way we see the world than that of Gerhardus Mercator, who devised his map in 1569 as a navigational aid for mariners. So well-suited was Mercator's map for this purpose that it continues to be used for navigational charts today. At the same time, the Mercator projection became a standard for depicting land masses, something for which it was never intended. Although an accurate navigational tool, the Mercator projection greatly exaggerates the size of land masses in higher latitudes, giving about two-thirds of the map's surface to the northern hemisphere. Thus, the lands occupied by Europeans and European descendents appear far larger than those of other people. For example, North America (19 million square kilometers) appears almost twice the size of Africa (30 million square kilometers), while Europe is shown as equal in size to South America, which actually has nearly twice the land mass of Europe.

A map developed in 1805 by Karl B. Mollweide was one of the earlier equal-area projections of the world. Equal-area projections portray land masses in correct relative size, but, as a result, distort the shape of contintents more than other projections. They most often compress and warp lands in the higher latitudes and vertically stretch land masses close to the equator. Other equal-area projections include the Lambert Cylindrical

Equal-Area Projection (1772), the Hammer Equal-Area Projection (1892), and the Eckert Equal-Area Projection (1906).

The Van der Grinten Projection (1904) was a compromise aimed at minimizing both the distortions of size in the Mercator and the distortion of shape in equal-area maps such as the Mollweide. Although an improvement, the lands of the northern hemisphere are still emphasized at the expense of the southern. For example, in the Van der Grinten, the Commonwealth of Independent States (the former Soviet Union) and Canada are shown at more than twice their relative size.

The Robinson Projection, which was adopted by the National Geographic Society in 1988 to replace the Van der Grinten, is one of the best compromises to date between the distortion of size and shape. Although an improvement over the Van der Grinten, the Robinson projection still depicts lands in the northern latitudes as proportionally larger at the same time that it depicts lands in the lower latitudes (representing most third-world nations) as proportionally smaller. Like European maps before it, the Robinson projection places Europe at the center of the map with the Atlantic Ocean and the Americas to the left, emphasizing the cultural connection between Europe and North America, while neglecting the geographical closeness of northwestern North America to northeast Asia.

The following pages show four maps that each convey quite different "cultural messages." Included among them is the Peters Projection, an equal-area map that has been adopted as the official map of UNESCO (the United Nations Educational, Scientific, and Cultural Organization), and a map made in Japan, showing us how the world looks from the other side.

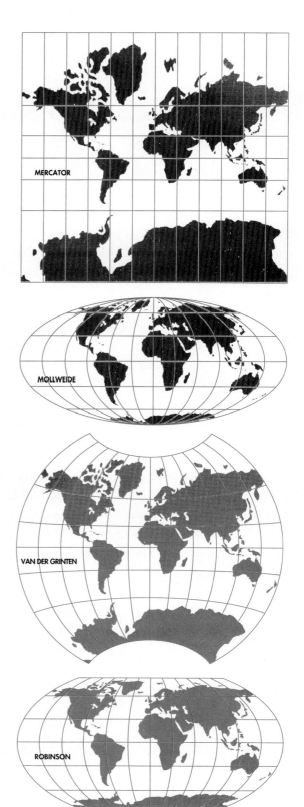

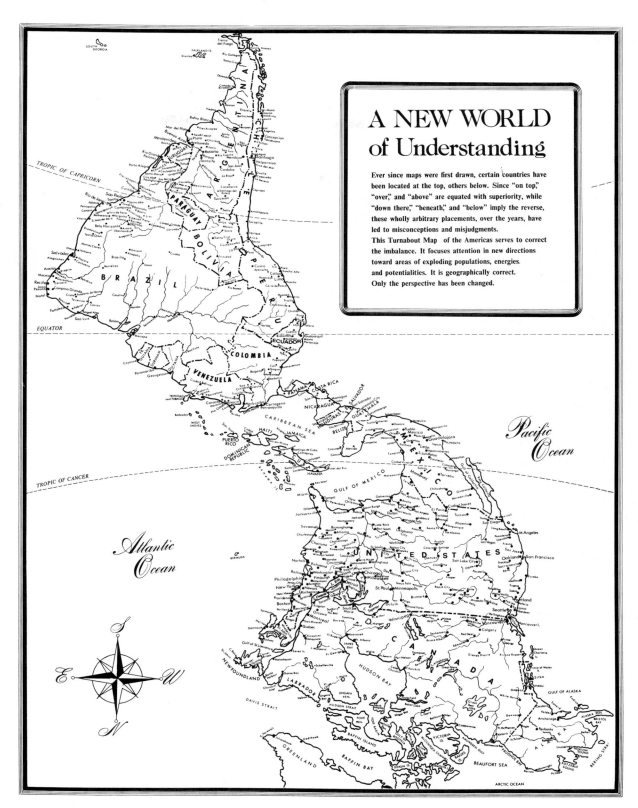

A NEW WORLD of Understanding

Ever since maps were first drawn, certain countries have been located at the top, others below. Since "on top," "over," and "above" are equated with superiority, while "down there," "beneath," and "below" imply the reverse, these wholly arbitrary placements, over the years, have led to misconceptions and misjudgments.

This Turnabout Map of the Americas serves to correct the imbalance. It focuses attention in new directions toward areas of exploding populations, energies and potentialities. It is geographically correct. Only the perspective has been changed.

THE TURNABOUT MAP *The way maps may reflect (and influence) our thinking is exemplified by the "Turnabout Map," which places the South Pole at the top and the North Pole at the bottom. Words and phrases such as "on top," "over," and "above" tend to be equated by some people with superiority. Turning things upside down may cause us to rethink the way North Americans regard themselves in relation to the people of Central and South America.*

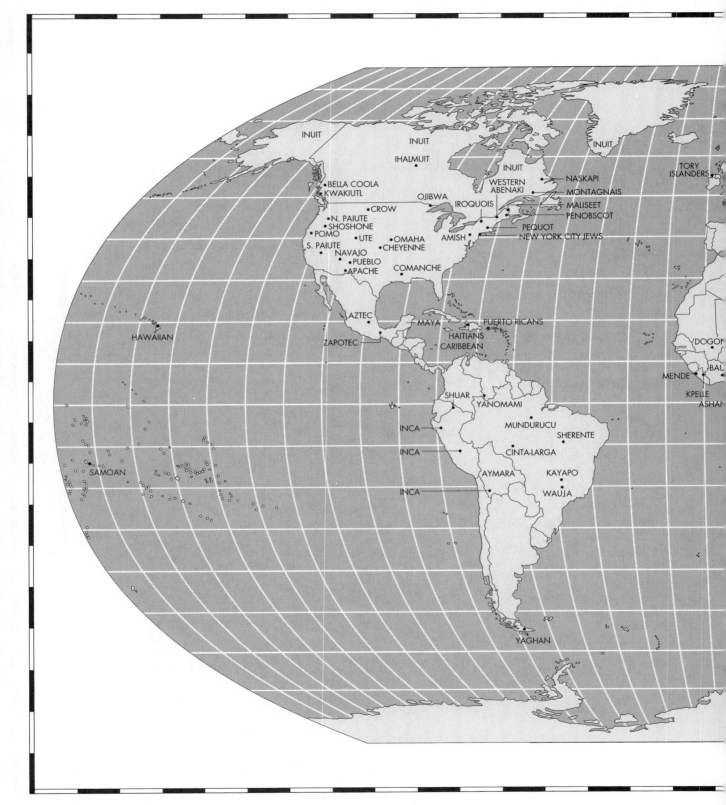

THE ROBINSON PROJECTION *The map above is based on the Robinson Projection, which is used today by the National Geographic Society and Rand McNally. Although the Robinson Projection distorts the relative size of land masses, it does so to a much lesser degree than most other projections. Still, it*

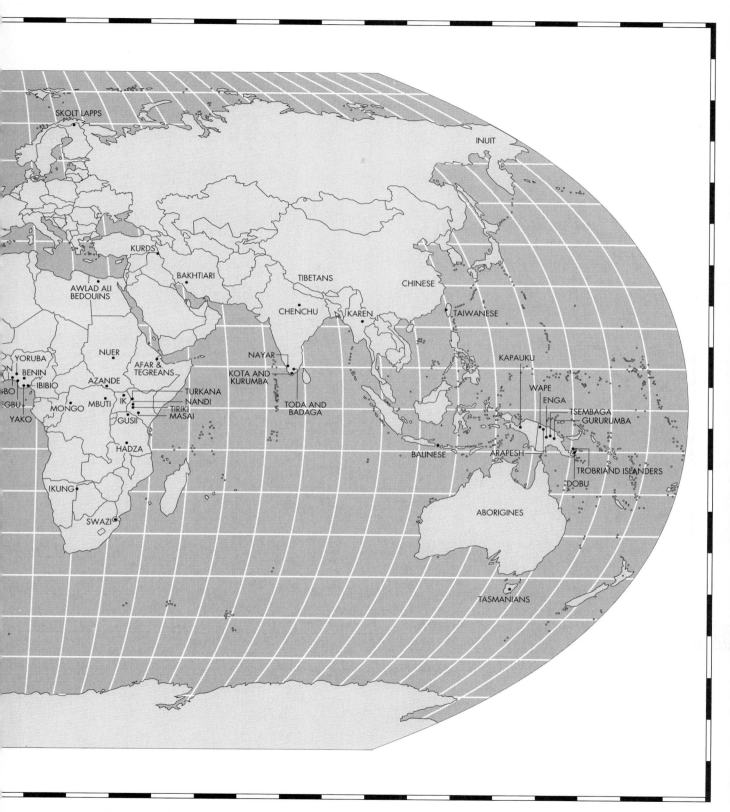

places Europe at the center of the map. This particular view of the world has been used to identify the location of many of the cultures discussed in this text.

THE PETERS PROJECTION *The map above is based on the Peters Projection, which has been adopted as the official map of UNESCO. While it distorts the shape of continents (countries near the equator are vertically elongated by a ratio of two to one), the Peters Projection does show all continents according to*

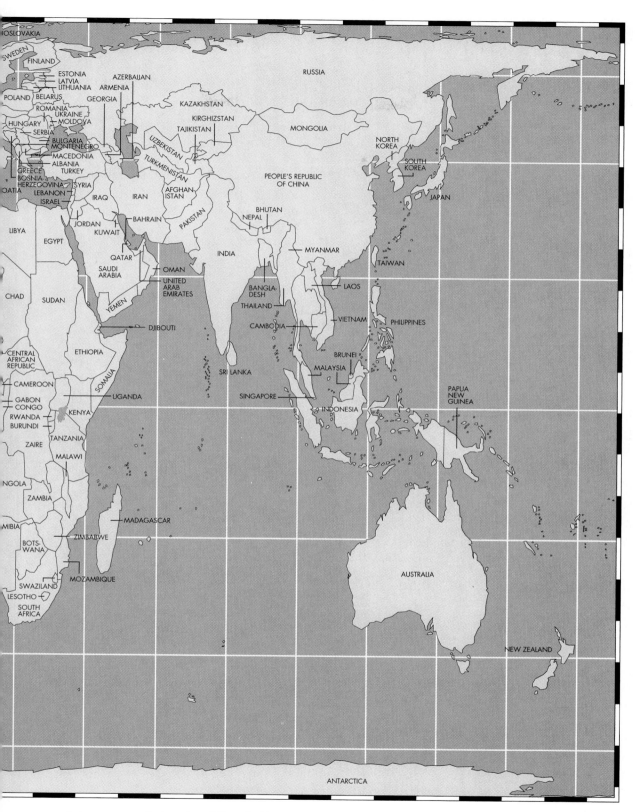

their correct relative size. Though Europe is still at the center, it is not shown as larger and more extensive than the third world.

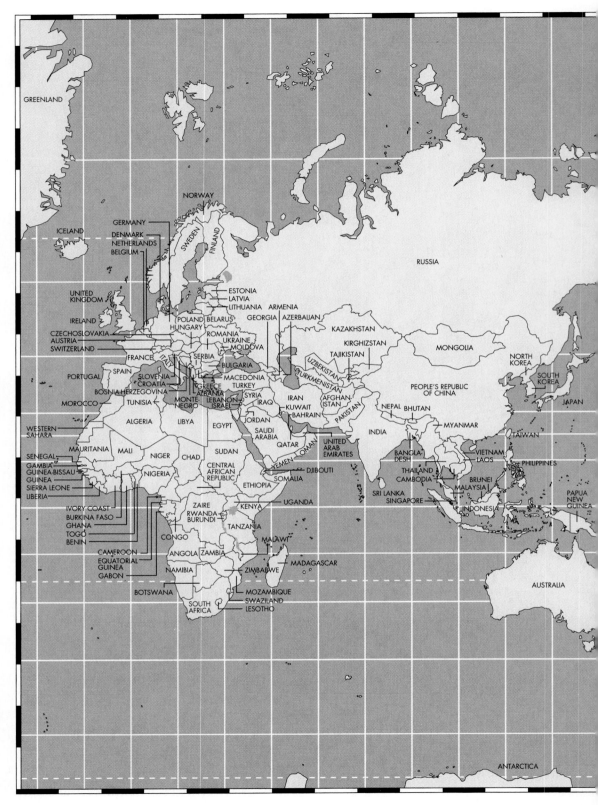

GREENLAND

NORWAY

ICELAND

GERMANY
DENMARK
NETHERLANDS
BELGIUM

SWEDEN

FINLAND

RUSSIA

UNITED
KINGDOM

ESTONIA
LATVIA
LITHUANIA

ARMENIA

KAZAKHSTAN

IRELAND

POLAND BELARUS
HUNGARY

GEORGIA AZERBAIJAN

KIRGHIZSTAN

MONGOLIA

NORTH
KOREA

CZECHOSLOVAKIA
AUSTRIA
SWITZERLAND

ROMANIA
UKRAINE
MOLDOVA

TAJIKISTAN

SOUTH
KOREA

FRANCE

SERBIA

UZBEKISTAN

PEOPLE'S REPUBLIC
OF CHINA

JAPAN

PORTUGAL

SPAIN

BULGARIA

SLOVENIA
CROATIA
BOSNIA HERZEGOVINA

MACEDONIA
TURKEY
GREECE
ALBANIA

TURKMENISTAN

AFGHAN-
ISTAN

SYRIA

IRAN

NEPAL BHUTAN

TAIWAN

MOROCCO

TUNISIA

MONTE-
NEGRO

LEBANON
ISRAEL

IRAQ

PAKISTAN

KUWAIT
BAHRAIN

INDIA

MYANMAR

WESTERN
SAHARA

ALGERIA

LIBYA

EGYPT

JORDAN

SAUDI
ARABIA

QATAR

UNITED
ARAB
EMIRATES

OMAN

BANGLA-
DESH

VIETNAM
LAOS

PHILIPPINES

SENEGAL
GAMBIA
GUINEA-BISSAU
GUINEA
SIERRA LEONE
LIBERIA

MAURITANIA

MALI

NIGER

CHAD

SUDAN

NIGERIA

CENTRAL
AFRICAN
REPUBLIC

YEMEN

DJIBOUTI

SOMALIA

THAILAND
CAMBODIA

BRUNEI
MALAYSIA

PAPUA
NEW
GUINEA

ETHIOPIA

SRI LANKA
SINGAPORE

INDONESIA

IVORY COAST
BURKINA FASO
GHANA
TOGO
BENIN

ZAIRE
RWANDA
BURUNDI

KENYA

UGANDA

CONGO

TANZANIA

CAMEROON
EQUATORIAL
GUINEA
GABON

ANGOLA ZAMBIA

MALAWI

MADAGASCAR

NAMIBIA

ZIMBABWE

AUSTRALIA

BOTSWANA

MOZAMBIQUE
SWAZILAND
LESOTHO

SOUTH
AFRICA

ANTARCTICA

JAPANESE MAP *Not all maps place Europe at the center of the world, as this Japanese map illustrates. Besides reflecting the importance the Japanese attach to themselves in the world, this map has the*

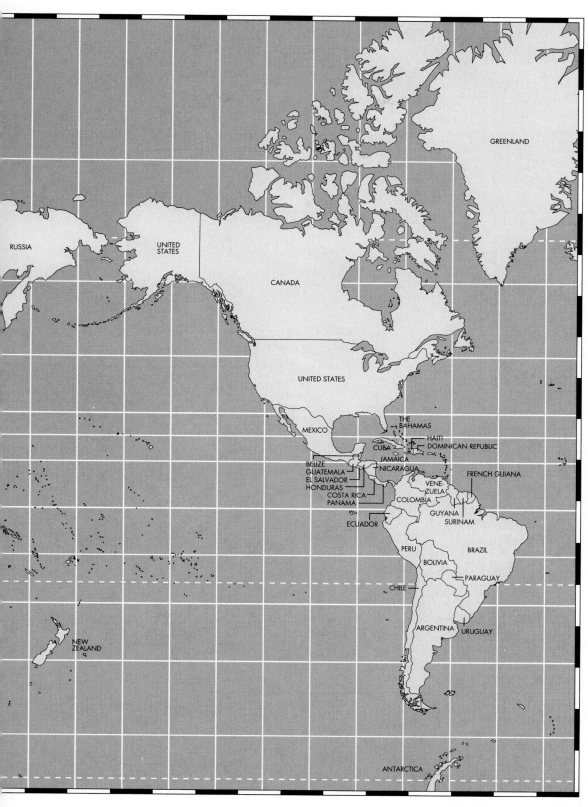

RUSSIA

GREENLAND

UNITED
STATES

CANADA

UNITED STATES

MEXICO

THE
BAHAMAS

CUBA — HAITI
DOMINICAN REPUBLIC

JAMAICA

BELIZE
GUATEMALA — NICARAGUA
EL SALVADOR
HONDURAS
COSTA RICA
PANAMA

VENE-
ZUELA

FRENCH GUIANA

COLOMBIA

GUYANA
SURINAM

ECUADOR

PERU

BRAZIL

BOLIVIA

PARAGUAY

CHILE

ARGENTINA — URUGUAY

NEW
ZEALAND

ANTARCTICA

virtue of showing the geographic proximity of North America to Asia, a fact easily overlooked when maps place Europe at their center.

PART

I

THE STUDY OF HUMANKIND

CHAPTER 1
THE NATURE OF ANTHROPOLOGY

CHAPTER 2
METHODS OF STUDYING THE HUMAN PAST

CHAPTER 3
BIOLOGY AND EVOLUTION

Anthropology is the most liberating of all the sciences. Not only has it exposed the fallacies of racial and cultural superiority, but also its devotion to the study of all peoples, regardless of where and when they lived, has cast more light on human nature than all the reflections of sages or the studies of laboratory scientists. If this sounds like the assertion of an overly enthusiastic anthropologist, it is not; it was all said as long ago as 1941 by the philosopher Grace de Laguna in her presidential address to the Eastern Division of the American Philosophical Association.

The subject matter of anthropology is vast, as we shall see in this book: It includes everything that has to do with human beings, past and present. Of course, many other disciplines are concerned in one way or another with human beings. Some, such as anatomy and physiology, study humans as biological organisms. The social sciences are concerned with the distinctive forms of human relationships, while the humanities examine the great achievements of human culture. Anthropologists are interested in all of these things, too, but they try to deal with them all together, in all places and times. It is this unique, broad perspective that equips

anthropologists so well to deal with that elusive thing called human nature.

Needless to say, no single anthropologist is able to investigate personally everything that has to do with people. For practical purposes, the discipline is divided into various subfields, and individual anthropologists specialize in one or more of these. Whatever their specialization, though, they retain a commitment to a broader, overall perspective on humankind. For example, cultural anthropologists specialize in the study of human behavior, while physical anthropologists specialize in the study of humans as biological organisms. Yet neither can afford to ignore the work of the other, for human behavior and biology are inextricably intertwined, with each affecting the other in important ways. We can see, for example, how biology affects a cultural practice such as color-naming behavior. Human populations differ in the density of pigmentation within the eye itself, which in turn affects people's ability to distinguish the color blue from green, black, or both. Consequently, a number of cultures identify blue with green, black, or both. We can see also how a cultural practice may affect human biology, as exemplified by abnormal forms of hemoglobin, the substance that transports oxygen in the blood. In certain parts of the Old World, when humans took up the practice of farming, they altered the ecology in a way that, by chance, created ideal conditions for the breeding of mosquitos. As a result, malaria became a serious problem (mosquitos carry the malarial parasite), and a biological response to this was the spread of certain genes that, in those people who inherit the gene from only one parent, produced a built-in resistance to the disease. Although those who inherit the gene from both parents contract a potentially lethal anemia, such as sickle-cell anemia, those without the gene are apt to succumb to malaria.

To begin our introduction to the study of anthropology, we will look closely at the nature of the discipline. In Chapter 1 we will see how the field of anthropology is subdivided, how the subdivisions relate to one another, and how they relate to the other sciences and humanities. Chapter 1 introduces us as well to the methods anthropologists use to study human cultures, especially those of today, or the very recent past. However, since the next two parts of the book take us far back into the human past, to see where we came from and how we got to be the way we are today, further discussion of methods used to study contemporary cultures is deferred to Parts Five and Eight (especially Chapter 14). The different methods used to find out about the ancient past are the subject of Chapter 2, which discusses the nature of fossils and archaeological materials, where they are found, how they are (quite literally) unearthed, and how they must be treated once unearthed. From this, one can begin to appreciate both what the evidence can tell us if handled properly, as well as the limitations of its usefulness.

In order to understand what fossils have to tell us about our past, some knowledge of how biological evolution works is necessary. But fossils, unlike flesh and blood people, do not speak for themselves, and so they must be interpreted. If we are to have confidence in an interpretation of a particular fossil, we must be sure the interpretation is consistent with what we know about the workings of evolution; therefore, Chapter 3 is devoted to a discussion of evolution. With this done, we will have set the stage for our detailed look at human biological and cultural evolution in Parts Two, Three, and Four.

THE NATURE OF ANTHROPOLOGY

IN THIS SIXTEENTH-CENTURY DEPICTION, THE NATIVE AMERICAN WOMEN WORKING IN THE FIELD LOOK MORE LIKE A EUROPEAN MALE'S FANTASY OF THE "IDEAL WOMAN" THAN AMERICAN INDIANS. THE TENDENCY TO SEE OTHER PEOPLE AS ONE WANTS TO SEE THEM, RATHER THAN AS THEY ARE, IS STILL A MAJOR PROBLEM THROUGHOUT THE WORLD.

CHAPTER PREVIEW

What Is Anthropology?

Anthropology, the study of humankind everywhere, throughout time, seeks to produce useful generalizations about people and their behavior and to arrive at the fullest possible understanding of human diversity.

What Do Anthropologists Do?

Physical anthropologists study humans as biological organisms, tracing the evolutionary development of the human animal and looking at biological variations within the species, past and present. Cultural anthropologists are concerned with human cultures, or the ways of life in societies. Within the field of cultural anthropology are archaeologists, who seek to explain human behavior by studying material objects, usually from past cultures; linguists, who study languages, by which cultures are maintained and passed on to succeeding generations; and ethnologists, who study cultures as they have been observed, experienced, and discussed with persons whose culture they seek to understand.

How Do Anthropologists Do What They Do?

Anthropologists, in common with other scientists, are concerned with the formulation and testing of hypotheses, or tentative explanations of observed phenomena. In so doing, they hope to arrive at a system of validated hypotheses called a theory, although they recognize that no theory is ever completely beyond challenge. In order to frame hypotheses that are as objective and free of cultural bias as possible, anthropologists typically develop them through a kind of total immersion in the field, becoming so familiar with the minute details of the situation that they can begin to recognize patterns inherent in the data. It is also through fieldwork that anthropologists test existing hypotheses.

common component of the mythology of all peoples is a legend that explains the appearance of humans on earth. Such a myth, for example, is the account of creation recorded in the Bible's Book of Genesis. Another vastly different example, which nonetheless serves the same function, is the Nez Perce (native people of the American Northwest) belief that humanity is the creation of Coyote, one of the animal people that inhabited the earth before humans. Coyote chased the giant beaver monster, Wishpoosh, in an epic chase whose trail formed the Columbia River. When Coyote caught Wishpoosh, he killed him and dragged his body to the river bank. Ella Clark retells the story:

> With his sharp knife Coyote cut up the big body of the monster.
>
> "From your body, mighty Wishpoosh," he said, "I will make a new race of people. They will live near the shores of Big River and along the streams which flow into it."
>
> From the lower part of the animal's body, Coyote made people who were to live along the coast. "You shall live near the mouth of Big River and shall be traders."
>
> "You shall live along the coast," he said to others. "You shall live in villages facing the ocean and shall get your food by spearing salmon and digging clams. You shall always be short and fat and have weak legs."
>
> From the legs of the beaver monster he made the Klickitat Indians. "You shall live along the rivers that flow down from the big white mountain north of Big River. You shall be swift of foot and keen of wit. You shall be famous runners and great horsemen."
>
> From the arms of the monster he made the Cayuse Indians. "You shall be powerful with bow and arrows and with war clubs."
>
> From the ribs he made the Yakima Indians. "You shall live near the new Yakima River, east of the mountains. You shall be the helpers and the protectors of all the poor people."
>
> From the head he created the Nez Perce Indians. "You shall live in the valleys of the Kookooskia and Wallowa rivers. You shall be men of brains, great in council and in speechmaking. You shall also be skillful horsemen and brave warriors."

Then Coyote gathered up the hair and blood and waste. He hurled them far eastward, over the big mountains. "You shall be the Snake River Indians," said Coyote. "You shall be people of blood and violence. You shall be buffalo hunters and shall wander far and wide."[1]

For as long as they have been on earth, people have needed answers to questions about who they are, where they came from, why they act the way they do, and why other people look and act differently. Throughout most of their history, though, people had no extensive and reliable body of data about their own behavior and background, and so they relied on myth and folklore for their answers to these questions. Simply stated, **anthropology** is the study of humankind in all places and throughout time. The anthropologist is concerned primarily with a single species—*Homo sapiens*—the human species, its ancestors, and near relatives. Because anthropologists are members of the species being studied, it is difficult for them to maintain a completely objective, value-free detachment towards those whom they study. But then, neither is natural science value-free and without cultural bias. Nevertheless, a scientific approach does produce useful generalizations about humans and their behavior. With such an approach, anthropologists are able to arrive at a reasonably valid understanding of human diversity, as well as the many things that humans have in common beneath that diversity.

DEVELOPMENT OF ANTHROPOLOGY

Works of anthropological significance have a considerable antiquity, of which two examples are the accounts of other peoples written in the fifth

Anthropology: The study of humankind, in all times and places.

[1]Clark, E. E. (1966). *Indian legends of the Pacific Northwest* (p. 174). Berkeley: University of California Press.

century B.C. by Herodotus the Greek and in the fourteenth century A.D. by the Arab Ibn Khaldun. Yet anthropology as a distinct field of inquiry is a relatively recent invention of Western civilization. In the United States, for example, the first course in general anthropology to carry credit in a college or university (at the University of Rochester) was not offered until 1879. If people have always been concerned about themselves and their origins, why then did it take such a long time for a systematic discipline of anthropology to appear?

The answer to this is as complex as human history. In part, the question of anthropology's late growth may be answered by reference to the limits of human technology. Throughout most of history, people have been restricted in their geographical horizons. Without the means of traveling to distant parts of the world, observation of cultures and peoples far from one's own was a difficult—if not impossible—venture. Extensive travel was usually the exclusive prerogative of a few; the study of foreign peoples and cultures was not likely to flourish until adequate modes of transportation and communication were developed.

This is not to say that people have always been unaware of the existence of others in the world who look and act differently from themselves. Just as the Nez Perce story of Coyote, for example, speaks of other peoples living in the Pacific Northwest whose ways differed from their own, so are the Old and New Testaments of the Bible full of references to diverse peoples, including Jews, Egyptians, Hittites, Babylonians, Ethiopians, Romans, and others. Different though they may have been, however, these peoples were at least familiar to one another, and familiar differences are accounted for in peoples' origin myths. Unfamiliar peoples, however, are another matter. It was the massive encounter with hitherto unknown peoples, which came as Europeans sought to extend their trade and political domination to all parts of the world, that focused attention on human differences in all their glory.

Another significant element that contributed to the slow growth of anthropology was the failure of Europeans to recognize the common humanity that they share with people everywhere. Societies that did not share the fundamental cultural values of Europeans were labeled as "savage" or "barbarian." It was not until the late eighteenth

In the United States, anthropology began in the nineteenth century when a number of dedicated amateurs went into the field to gain a better understanding of so-called "savage" people. Shown here is Frank Hamilton Cushing, in full dress as a war chief of the Zuni Indians, among whom he lived for $4\frac{1}{2}$ years.

century that a significant number of Europeans considered the behavior of such people to be at all relevant to an understanding of themselves. This awareness of human diversity, coming at a time when there were increasing efforts to explain things in terms of natural laws, cast doubts on the traditional biblical mythology, which no longer adequately "explained" human diversity. From the reexamination that followed came the awareness that the study of "savages" is a study of all humankind.

ANTHROPOLOGY AND THE OTHER SCIENCES

It would be incorrect to infer from the foregoing that serious attempts were never made to analyze human diversity before the eighteenth century. Anthropology is not the only discipline that studies people. In this respect it shares its objectives

In the United States, the founders of anthropology included women as well as men. One of these women was Matilda Coxe Stevenson, who did fieldwork among the Zuni and, in 1885, founded the Women's Anthropology Society, the first professional association for women scientists. The tradition of women being active in anthropology continues, and since World War II more than half the presidents of the American Anthropological Association have been women.

with the other social and natural sciences. Anthropologists do not think of their findings as something quite apart from those of psychologists, economists, sociologists, or biologists; rather, they welcome the contributions these other disciplines have to make to the common goal of understanding humanity, and they gladly offer their own findings for the benefit of these other disciplines. Anthropologists do not expect, for example, to know as much about the structure of the human eye as anatomists, or as much about the perception of color as psychologists. As synthesizers, however, they are better prepared to understand these things, such as in analyzing

color-naming behavior in different human societies, than any of their fellow scientists. Because they look for the broad basis of human behavior without limiting themselves to any single social or biological aspect of that behavior, anthropologists can acquire an especially extensive overview of the complex biological and cultural organism that is the human being.

THE DISCIPLINE OF ANTHROPOLOGY

Anthropology is traditionally divided into four fields: physical anthropology and what in reality are three branches of cultural anthropology: archaeology, linguistic anthropology, and ethnology. **Physical anthropology** primarily concerns humans as biological organisms (what humans are), while **cultural anthropology** deals with human behavior (what humans do). Both, of course, are closely related; we cannot understand what people do unless we know what people are, and vice versa. Moreover, we want to know how biology does and does not influence culture, as well as how culture affects biology.

Physical Anthropology

As the branch of anthropology that focuses on humans as biological organisms, physical anthropology (or, alternatively, biological anthropology) has as one of its many interests human evolution. Whatever distinctions people may claim for themselves, they are mammals—specifically, primates—and, as such, they share a common ancestry with other primates, most specifically apes and monkeys. Through the analysis of fossils and observation of living primates, physical anthropologists try

Physical anthropology: The systematic study of humans as biological organisms.

Cultural anthropology: The branch of anthropology that focuses on human behavior.

Anthropology Applied

FORENSIC ANTHROPOLOGY

In the public mind, anthropology is often identified with the recovery of the bones of remote human ancestors, the uncovering of ancient campsites and "lost cities," or the study of present-day tribal peoples whose way of life is erroneously seen as being something "out of the past." What people are often unaware of are the many practical applications of anthropological knowledge. One field of applied anthropology—known as **forensic anthropology**—specializes in the identification of human skeletal remains for legal purposes. Forensic anthropologists are routinely called upon by police and other authorities to identify the remains of murder victims, missing persons, or people who have died in disasters such as plane crashes. From skeletal remains, the forensic anthropologist can establish the age, sex, race, and stature of the deceased, and often whether they were right- or left-handed, exhibited any physical abnormalities, or evidence of trauma (broken bones and the like). In addition, some details of an individual's health and nutritional history can be read from the bones.

One well-known forensic anthropologist is Clyde C. Snow, who has been practicing in this field for 35 years, first for the Federal Aviation Administration and more recently as a freelance consultant. In addition to the usual police work, Snow has studied the remains of George Custer and his men from the battlefield at Little Big Horn, and in 1985, he went to Brazil where he identified the remains of the notorious Nazi war criminal Josef Mengele. He also has been instrumental in establishing the first forensic team devoted to documenting cases of human rights abuses around the world. This began in 1984, when he went to Argentina at the request of a newly elected civilian government as part of a team to help with the identification of remains of the *desapareci-*

dos, or "disappeared ones," the 9000 or more people who were eliminated by government death squads during 7 years of military rule. A year later, he returned to give expert testimony at the trial of nine junta members, and to teach Argentineans how to recover, clean, repair, preserve, photograph, x-ray, and analyze bones.

Besides providing factual accounts of the fate of victims to their surviving kin, and refuting the assertions of "revisionists" that the massacres never happened, the work of Snow and his Argentine associates was crucial in convicting several military officers of kidnapping, torture, and murder. Subsequently, Snow and two of his Argentine associates were invited to the Philippines to look into the disappearance of 600 or more suspected victims of the Marcos regime. Similar requests from other South American countries, from Guatemala to Chile, as well as other parts of the world (Iraqi Kurdistan, for example), in addition to work for regular clients in the United States such as the medical examiners' offices of Cook County, Illinois, the state of Oklahoma, and the FBI, keep Snow busy. Although not all cases he investigates involve abuse of police powers, when this is an issue, it is often the forensic anthropologists who bring the culprits to justice. To quote Snow: "Of all the forms of murder, none is more monstrous than that committed by a state against its own citizens. And of all murder victims, those of the state are the most helpless and vulnerable since the very entity to which they have entrusted their lives and safety becomes their killer."* Thus, it is especially important that states be called to account for their deeds.

*Joyce, C. (1991). *Witnesses from the grave: The stories bones tell.* Boston: Little, Brown.

Forensic anthropology: Field of applied physical anthropology that specializes in the identification of human skeletal remains for legal purposes.

to trace the ancestry of the human species in order to understand how, when, and why we became the kind of animal we are today.

Another major concern of physical anthropology is the study of present-day human variation. Although we are all members of a single species, we differ from each other in many obvious and not

Physical anthropologists do not just study fossil skulls. Shown here is Clyde Snow, whose specialty is forensic anthropology, and who is widely known for his work identifying victims of state-sponsored terrorism. In this photo he holds the skull of a Kurdish youth who was executed by Iraqi security forces.

so obvious ways. We differ not only in such visible traits as the color of our skins or the shape of our noses, but also in such biochemical factors as our blood types and our susceptibility to certain diseases. The physical anthropologist applies all the techniques of modern molecular biology to achieve fuller understanding of human variation and the ways in which it relates to the different environments in which people have lived.

Cultural Anthropology

Because the capacity for culture is rooted in our biological natures, the work of the physical anthropologist provides a necessary background for the cultural anthropologist. In order to understand the work of the cultural anthropologist, we must clarify what we mean when we refer to *culture*. The subject will be taken up in more detail in Chapter 14, but for our purposes here, we may think of culture as the often unconscious standards by which societies—groups of people—operate. These standards are learned rather than acquired through biological inheritance. Since they determine, or at least guide, the day-to-day behavior of the mem-

bers of a society, human behavior is above all cultural behavior. The manifestations of culture may vary considerably from place to place, but no person is "more cultured" in the anthropological sense than any other.

Just as physical anthropology is closely related to the other biological sciences, cultural anthropology is closely related to the other social sciences. The one to which it has most often been compared is sociology, since the business of both is the description and explanation of behavior of people within a social context. Sociologists, however, have concentrated heavily on studies of people living in modern—or at least recent—North American and European (i.e., "Western") societies, thereby increasing the probability that their theories of human behavior will be **culture-bound**—that is, based on assumptions about the world and reality that are part of the Western culture of which

Culture-bound: Theories about the world and reality based on the assumptions and values of one's own culture.

Sociologists conduct structured interviews and administer questionnaires to *respondents*, while psychologists experiment with *subjects*. Anthropologists, by contrast, *learn* from *informants*.

sociology (like anthropology) is a product. Since cultural anthropologists, too, are products of the culture with which they grew up, they are also capable of culture-bound theorizing. However, they constantly seek to minimize the problem by studying the whole of humanity in all times and places and do not limit themselves to the study of recent Western peoples; anthropologists have found that to understand human behavior fully, all humans must be studied. More than any other feature, this unique cross-cultural and evolutionary perspective distinguishes cultural anthropology from the other social sciences. It provides anthropology with a far richer body of data than that of any other social science, and it can also be applied to any current issue. As a case in point, two different anthropologists have tested independently the validity of the argument that a high degree of military sophistication acts as a deterrent to war. By comparing the frequency of war in a number of very different cultures, both found that the more sophisticated a community is militarily, the more frequently it engages in aggressive war and is attacked in turn.[2] This helps us understand why the United States, which has devoted so many resources to the expansion of its arsenal and the development of new weapons systems over the past 50 years, has gone to war more times than any other country since the end of World War II.

The emphasis cultural anthropology places on studies of prehistoric or more recent non-Western cultures has often led to findings that dispute existing beliefs derived from Western studies. Thus, cultural anthropologists were the first to point out

> that the world does not divide into the pious and the superstitious; that there are sculptures in jungles and paintings in deserts; that political order is possible without centralized power and principled justice without codified rules; that the norms of reason were not fixed in Greece, the evolution of morality not consummated in England. . . . We have, with no little success, sought to keep the world off balance; pulling out rugs, upsetting tea tables, setting off firecrackers. It has been the office of others to reassure; ours to unsettle.[3]

Although the findings of cultural anthropologists have often challenged the conclusions of sociologists, psychologists, and economists, anthropology is absolutely indispensable to them as the testing ground for their theories. It is to these disciplines what the laboratory is to physics and chemistry.

Cultural anthropology may be divided into the areas of archaeology, linguistic anthropology, and ethnology (often called sociocultural anthropology;

[2]Bodley, J. H. (1985). *Anthropology and contemporary human problems* (2nd ed., p. 207). Palo Alto, CA: Mayfield.

[3]Geertz, C. (1984). Distinguished lecture: Anti anti-relativism, *American Anthropologist, 86,* 275.

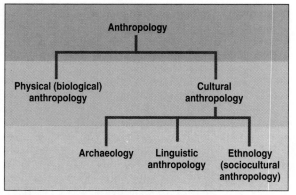

Figure 1.1   The subfields of anthropology.

Fig. 1.1). Although each has its own special interests and methods, all deal with cultural data. The archaeologist, the linguist, and the ethnologist take different approaches to the subject, but each gathers and analyzes data that are useful in explaining similarities and differences between human cultures, as well as the ways that cultures everywhere develop, adapt, and continue to change.

Archaeology

Archaeology is the branch of cultural anthropology that studies material remains in order to describe and explain human behavior. Traditionally, it has focused on the human past, because material products of behavior, rather than behavior itself, are all that survive of that past. The archaeologist studies the tools, pottery, and other enduring relics that remain as the legacy of extinct cultures, some of them as many as 2.5 million years old. Such objects, and the ways they were left in the ground, reflect certain aspects of human behavior. For example, shallow, restricted concentrations of charcoal that include oxidized earth, bone fragments, and charred plant remains as well, and near which are pieces of fire-cracked rock, pottery,

---

Archaeology: The study of material remains, usually from the past, to describe and explain human behavior.

---

and tools suitable for food preparation, are indicative of cooking and associated food processing. From such remains much can be learned about a people's diet and subsistence activities. Thus the archaeologist is able to find out about human behavior in the past, far beyond the mere 5000 years to which historians are limited by their dependence upon written records. By contrast, archaeologists are not limited to the study of prehistoric societies, but may also study those for which historic documents are available to supplement the material remains that people left behind them. In most literate societies, written records are associated with governing elites, rather than with people at the "grass roots." Thus, while they can tell archaeologists much that they might not know from archaeological evidence alone, it is equally true that archaeological remains can tell historians much about a society that is not apparent from its written documents.

Although archaeologists have concentrated on the human past, some of them are concerned with the study of material objects in contemporary settings. One example is the University of Arizona's "Garbage Project," which, by a carefully controlled study of household waste, continues to produce information about contemporary social issues. One aim of this project has been to test the validity of interview-survey techniques upon which sociologists, economists, other social scientists and policy makers rely heavily for their data. The tests clearly show a significant difference between what people

Archaeologists Diane and Arlen Chase exposing a hidden offering made by the ancient Maya at Caracol, Belize.

say they do and what garbage analysis shows they actually do. For example, in 1973, conventional techniques were used to construct and administer a questionnaire to find out about the rate of alcohol consumption in Tucson. In one part of town, 15 percent of respondent households affirmed consumption of beer, but no household reported consumption of more than eight cans a week. Analysis of garbage from the same area, however, demonstrated that some beer was consumed in more than 80 percent of households, and 50 percent discarded more than eight empty cans a week. Another interesting finding of the Garbage Project is that when beef prices reached an all-time high in 1973, so did the amount of beef wasted by households (not just in Tucson, but other parts of the country as well). Although common sense would lead us to suppose just the opposite, high prices and scarcity correlate with more, rather than less, waste. Obviously, such findings are important, for they suggest that ideas about human behavior based on conventional interview-survey techniques alone may be seriously in error.

In 1987, the Garbage Project began a program of test excavations in landfills in various parts of the country. From this work has come the first reliable data on what materials actually go into landfills and what happens to them once there. And once again, we are finding that our existing beliefs are at odds with the actual situation. For example, biodegradable materials, like newspapers, take a much longer time to decay when buried in deep compost landfills than anyone previously expected. Needless to say, this kind of information is vital if the United States is ever to solve its waste disposal problems.

Linguistic Anthropology

Perhaps the most distinctive feature of humanity is its ability to speak. Humans are not alone in the use of symbolic communication. Studies have shown that the sounds and gestures made by some other animals—especially by apes—may serve functions comparable to those of human speech; yet no other animal has developed a system of symbolic communication as complex as that of humans. Ultimately, language is what allows people to preserve and transmit their culture from generation to generation.

The branch of cultural anthropology that studies human languages is called **linguistic anthropology.** Linguistics may deal with the description of a language (the way a sentence is formed or a verb conjugated) or with the history of languages (the way languages develop and influence each other with the passage of time). Both approaches yield valuable information, not only about the ways in which people communicate but also about the ways in which they understand the world around them as well. The "everyday" language of North Americans, for example, includes a number of slang words, such as "dough," "greenback," "dust," "loot," "cash," "bucks," "change," and "bread" to identify what an indigenous native of Papua New Guinea would recognize only as "money." Such phenomena help identify things that are considered of special importance to a culture. Through the study of language in its social setting, the anthropologist is better able to understand how people perceive themselves and the world around them.

Anthropological linguists may also make an important contribution to our understanding of the human past. By working out the genealogical relationships among languages, and examining the distributions of those languages, they may estimate how long the speakers of those languages have lived where they do. By identifying those words in related languages that have survived from an ancient ancestral tongue, they can also suggest both where and how the speakers of the ancestral language lived.

Ethnology

Whereas the archaeologist has traditionally concentrated on cultures of the past, the **ethnologist,** or sociocultural anthropologist, concentrates on recent and contemporary cultures. And unlike the

Linguistic anthropology: The branch of cultural anthropology that studies human language.

Ethnologist: An anthropologist who studies cultures that can be, or have been, observed firsthand from a comparative or historical point of view.

archaeologist, who focuses on the study of material objects to learn about human behavior, the ethnologist concentrates on the study of human behavior as it can be seen, experienced, and discussed with those whose culture is to be understood.

Fundamental to the ethnologist's approach is descriptive **ethnography.** Whenever possible, the ethnologist becomes ethnographer by going to live among the people under study. Through **participant observation**—eating a people's food, speaking their language, and personally experiencing their habits and customs—the ethnographer is able to understand their way of life to a far greater extent than any nonparticipant anthropologist or other social scientist ever could; one learns a culture best by learning how to behave acceptably in the society in which one is doing fieldwork. To become a participant observer in the culture under study does not mean that the ethnographer must join in a people's battles in order to study a culture in which warfare is prominent; but by living among a warlike people, the ethnographer should be able to understand the role of warfare in the overall cultural scheme. He or she must be a meticulous observer in order to get a broad overview of a culture without placing undue emphasis on one of its parts at the expense of another. Only by discovering how all cultural institutions—social, political, economic, religious—relate to one another can the ethnographer begin to understand the cultural system. Anthropologists refer to this as the **holistic perspective,** and it is one of the fundamental principles of anthropology. Robert Gordon, an an-

Ethnographers (like Marjory Shostak, shown here with the Ju/'hoansi of Africa's Kalahari Desert) learn about the cultures of other people by actually living with them.

thropologist from Namibia, speaks of it in this way: "Whereas the sociologist or the political scientist might examine the beauty of a flower petal by petal, the anthropologist is the person that stands on the top of the mountain and looks at the beauty of the field. In other words, we try and go for the wider perspective."[4]

So basic is ethnographic fieldwork to ethnology that the British anthropologist C. G. Seligman once asserted, "Field research in anthropology is what the blood of the martyrs is to the church."[5] Something of its flavor is conveyed by the experience of one young anthropologist working, in this case in relatively comfortable conditions on an island in the western Pacific. In particular, the following Original Study illustrates the impossibility of going into the field free of all naivete, the importance of "the unexpected" in the field, the problems of freeing oneself from the assumptions and biases of one's own culture, and of establishing rapport with those whom one wishes to study.

Ethnography: The systematic description of a culture based on firsthand observation.

Participant observation: In ethnography, the technique of learning a people's culture through direct participation in their everyday life over an extended period of time.

Holistic perspective: A fundamental principle of anthropology positing that things must be viewed in the broadest possible context in order to understand their interconnections and interdependence.

---

[4]Gordon, R. (1981, December). [Interview for Coast Telecourses, Inc.], Los Angeles.
[5]Lewis, I. M. (1976). *Social anthropology in perspective* (p. 27). Harmondsworth, Eng.: Penguin.

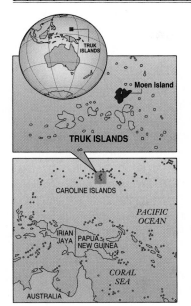

Original Study
Two Tales from the Trukese Taproom[6]

It was nearing sundown in Mwáán Village on Moen Island, Truk, as we bounced slowly along in the Datsun pickup. The landscape glowed, and the Pacific island blues and greens heightened in intensity as the shadows lengthened. The village's daily rhythm slowed, and the moist air was heavy with incompatible aromas: acrid smoke from cooking fires, sweet fragrance of plumeria blossoms, foul stench of the mangrove swamp, and the pleasant warm earth smells of a tropical island at dusk. All was peaceful, somnolent, even stuporous. And then the quiet was shattered by an ear-splitting shout out of nowhere: "Waaaaa Ho!" The horrible roar was repeated, and its source—a muscular young man clad only in blue jeans and zoris—materialized directly in the path of our truck, brandishing a two-foot-long machete.

The three of us in the pickup were all new to Truk. Bill, the driver, was an American anthropologist in his sixties traveling with his wife through Micronesia en route home from Asia, and he'd only been in Truk for a couple of days. Leslie and I, the passengers, had been there for approximately a month awaiting a field-trip ship to take us to our outer island research site on Namoluk Atoll. In the interim she and I were staying in a small guest facility on the grounds of a Protestant church–sponsored high school a couple miles from the town center. We had met Bill and his wife by chance the day before at a local restaurant. The four of us had spent this day voyaging by motorboat to another island in Truk Lagoon to explore the ruins of the former Japanese headquarters that had been destroyed in World War II. On our return we agreed to meet for dinner, and Bill had just come for us in his rented truck to drive back to town for supper. None of us had ever before heard the frightening yell, "Waaaaa Ho!" Nor had any of us been confronted by a young Trukese man built like a fullback and waving a machete over his head.

"What in the hell?" Bill asked, but before I could respond we were nearly upon the young man. Fortunately, the bumpiness of the dirt road limited our speed to perhaps five miles per hour, and Bill avoided hitting our challenger by swerving to the left just in time. As he did so, the young man brought the machete down with all the force he could muster on top of the cab, once again announcing his presence with a loud "Waaaaa Ho!" The machete cut into the edge of the cab approximately half an inch deep right where I had been holding on to the door frame a split second before. As steel hit steel, Bill panicked and floored the truck, but our attacker managed to strike another powerful blow with the knife on the edge of the truck bed before we escaped. We jolted along at fifteen miles per hour the rest of the way to town, the maximum we and the pickup could sustain given road conditions. We were completely shaken by what had just befallen us.

"Why in the hell did he do that?" Bill wanted to know. I was new to Truk, there to study and learn about Trukese society and culture. I had no answer to Bill's question. We literally did not know what had hit us, or more accurately, why we had been attacked. Over dinner we speculated on the possibilities. The young man might have been angry with foreigners and decided to take out his bad feelings on us. No, we rejected that hypothesis because it was clear that the young man would not have been able to tell who was in the truck when he burst out of the bushes and lunged at us. It all happened too fast. A second thought we had was that the young man had it in for someone who owned a blue Datsun pickup, saw our truck approaching, and mistook us for someone else. But this hypothesis failed for the same reason: Because of the dwindling light and the thick brush along the roadside it seemed unlikely our attacker could see the color and make of the truck before he leapt into its path. Finally, based on our collective experience as persons reared in American culture, the four of us concluded either that the young man was emotionally distraught over a recent major trauma in his life or that he was mentally ill and a clear danger to the general public.

We were puzzled and truly frightened. What made the incident all the more bizarre was that Leslie and I had been treated with unfailing kindness by all the Trukese we had met from the moment of our arrival. We had walked through Mwáán Village several times daily for four weeks many times after dark, and always we had been greeted by warm smiles and a cheery "Ran Annim!" What could have provoked this attack? Why in the hell did he do that? Although I could not know it at the time, this incident presaged much of my later research involvement with the people of Truk and directed my attention to a series of questions and puzzles that I continue to pursue.

I can now, with some degree of confidence, provide an answer to why the young man did what he did: He was drunk. The fearsome yell announced that fact immediately to anyone who knew the code surrounding drunken behavior in Truk, but we were ignorant of this as outsiders and novices in the subtleties of Trukese life. When young Trukese men drink, they are perceived to become dangerous, explosive, unpredictably aggressive. Given the option, the received wisdom is to avoid Trukese drunks if at all possible. We, of course, did not have that option and we became yet one more target of the violence associated with alcohol consumption in contemporary Truk. In fact, we were lucky that no one was hurt. Quite often the aggression of Trukese drinkers results in injuries and occasionally deaths.

How long has alcohol been available in the islands? Why do young men drink in Truk and why do women almost uniformly abstain? Why do drinkers so often become violent after consuming alcohol? What happens to the perpetrators of such violence? Questions such as these surrounding the Trukese encounter with alcoholic beverages are legion, and when pursued they open myriad windows into Trukese personality, culture, history, and social organization. Before I came to understand this, however, I had another traumatic experience involving Trukese and alcohol.

By the time this second incident occurred, Leslie and I had been in Truk for four months. We had left the headquarters island of Moen and sailed 130 miles to the southeast to a tiny and remote coral atoll which was to be the focus of my dissertation research. Namoluk was idyllic, an emerald necklace of land surrounding a turquoise lagoon bounded by the deep sapphire blue of the open ocean. Namoluk was a close-knit kin community of 350 persons where people knew one another in terms of "total biography": All the details of one's life and the lives of one's relatives and ancestors were part of local lore and general public knowledge. Everyone had a particular role to play that in some senses seemed almost predestined from childhood onward. Namoluk was fascinating, an integrated yet intricate community with a long history of its own which had been studied only briefly half a century before by a German scholar. I became totally engrossed in my research and in trying to master the local language.

We had taken up residence in a comfortable new cement house with a corrugated iron roof located more or less in the center of the village area. Our house sat at the intersection of two main paths and in between the locations of two of the island's three licensed bingo games. Since bingo was played daily by a large part of the population, a steady stream of islanders strolled past our front door. The family on whose homestead we lived slept in a wooden house next door, but members of the family were in and out of our house continually.

Soon after our arrival in Namoluk I learned that alcohol use was the subject of considerable controversy. Technically the island was dry by local consensus, but the legality of the local prohibition ordinance was questionable because proper procedures for enacting such a law had not been followed. At the time we came on the scene an intergenerational struggle was under way between men over roughly the age of forty or forty-five and younger men for control of the elective municipal government. Alcohol became a central issue in this struggle, with older men supporting prohibition and younger men enthusiastically drinking booze whenever possible. Even so, drinking was certainly not a regular event on Namoluk and when it did take place it often led to nothing more than boisterous singing and loud laughter late at night in the canoe houses. I began to get the impression that drunkenness on Namoluk was categorically different from what we had experienced on Truk a few months before.

And then it happened. Late on a Sunday afternoon we were lolling about our house, just being lazy and chatting with our landlord when suddenly a huge commotion arose in the distance. Sounds of anguish, anger, and anxiety swirled toward us and then, out of the milling mob of men, women, and noise, came that unforgettable yell: "Waaaaa Ho!"

I sprang to my feet, jumped into my zoris, and dashed out the door to find a crowd of twenty to thirty agitated people at the intersection of the two paths, yelling, shouting at one another, and keeping two persons separated. As I took in the pattern of what was happening, I realized that a fight was threatening between two men who had been drinking. Each was being upbraided by female relatives to refrain from fighting, while at the same time men were standing by to make sure that their own male kinsman was not injured. Before I could stop to cooly assess the situation and record it objectively in my data notebook I found myself next to the antagonists. The larger man suddenly jumped on his opponent, wrestling him to the ground. Instantly he began pummeling and pounding the smaller man with his fists. I acted almost instinctively. Before I fully realized what I was doing I had a full nelson on the larger man, had pulled him off of his victim, and was trying to convince him to desist from such behavior.

Though strong enough to protect myself from harm, it occurred to me as I stood there that I had made a terrible mistake. All through graduate school my professors had emphasized the importance of not taking sides or getting involved in local political or interpersonal squabbles in the research community, lest one make enemies, close off potential sources of information, or even get thrown out of the research site. All of those warnings flashed through my mind as I pressed the full nelson on the struggling man. I was convinced that I had blown it and that this whole sorry episode would have nothing but negative repercussions for my work—and just at a time when Leslie and I were beginning to feel like we really fit into the community.

But, oh, how wrong I was.

In learning why I was wrong, I also learned an important lesson about masculinity and how masculinity relates to fighting and to alcohol use in Trukese culture. And I had taken a major step toward what has become the central focus of my research over the past fifteen years: the study of alcohol and culture.

Once tempers calmed and it was clear that the fighting was over I released my hold and returned to my house, shaken and chagrined. How could I have been so stupid as to get involved in a silly drunken brawl? As I sat there feeling sorry for myself, a knock on the door roused me from dejection. It was two of the teenagers on the island, boys of about fourteen years of age, who were among our most loyal and patient language teachers. They asked if they could come in and, though I didn't really feel like company, I said, "Sure." The three of us sat on the woven pandanus mat on the floor and one of them immediately commented, "Wow, you were really strong out there a few minutes ago!" I wasn't sure whether I was being flattered or mocked, but before I gave a snide response I glanced at the boys and recognized the earnestness in their faces. I made some uncommittal answer, and they elaborated. My behavior had been thought impressive and salutory by everyone present: They said it demonstrated strength and bravery or fearlessness. If they only knew, I thought, that it actually demonstrated nothing more than the ignorance of an interloper endeavoring to keep the peace according to the inappropriate canons of his own culture!

Later that evening the man I had restrained, who was among the most influential and important younger men in the community, and on whose bad side I could ill afford to be, knocked on my door, accompanied by an older male relative. My landlord was with me and, while he knew what was about to take place, I was completely in the dark. The older man spoke long and rapidly in the Namoluk language and I understood only a little of what he said. Then the younger man spoke directly to me in English, asking my forgiveness for any problems he may have caused and noting that he would not have acted the way he had if he hadn't been drinking. "It was the alcohol that made me do it," he said. "We Trukese just don't know how to drink like you Americans. We drink and drink until our supply is gone and then we often get into fights." I was enormously relieved that *he* wasn't angry with *me*, and we begged one another's pardon through a mixture of Trukese apology ritual and American-style making up after an unpleasantness.

What I didn't recognize at the time, and only later came to fully understand, was that the incident that upset me so for fear I had botched my community rapport not only improved my rapport (including with the man I had restrained!) but also contributed to the development of my personal reputation on Namoluk. I noted earlier that Namoluk persons know one another in terms of total biography. As a foreigner from outside the system, I was an unknown quantity. Initially, people didn't know whether I was a good or a bad person, whether I would prove disruptive or cooperative, whether I would flaunt local custom or abide by it. Like every Trukese young adult—but especially like young men—I had to prove myself by my actions and deeds. I had to create and sustain an impression, to develop a reputation.

At the time I didn't know this. Luckily for me, and purely by accident, my actions that afternoon accorded closely with core Trukese values that contribute to the image of a good person: respectfulness, bravery, and the humble demonstration of nonbullying strength in thought and deed. What I first believed to have been a colossal blunder turned out to be a fortunate coincidence of impulsive action with deepseated cultural beliefs about desirable masculine behavior. Now I, the unknown outsider, had begun to develop a local biography. But this was something I came to understand only after several more years of fieldwork in Trukese society.

[6]Marshall, M. (1990). Two tales from the Trukese taproom. In P. R. De Vita (Ed.), *The humbled anthropologist* (pp. 12–17). Belmont, CA: Wadsworth.

The popular image of ethnographic fieldwork is that it takes place among far-off, exotic peoples. To be sure, much of ethnographic work has been done in places like Africa, the islands of the Pacific Ocean, the deserts of Australia, and so on. One very good reason for this is that non-Western peoples have been too often ignored by other social scientists. Still, anthropologists have recognized from the start that an understanding of human behavior depends upon knowledge of all cultures and peoples, including their own. During the years of the Great Depression and World War II, for example, many anthropologists in the United States worked in settings ranging from factories to whole communities. One of the landmark studies of this period was W. Lloyd Warner's study of "Yankee City" (Newburyport, Massachusetts). Less well known is that it was an anthropologist, Philleo Nash, who worked at the time in the White House under Presidents Roosevelt and Truman, who was instrumental in desegregating the armed forces and moving the federal government into the field of civil rights.

In the 1950s, the availability of large amounts of money for research in foreign lands diverted attention from work at home. More recently, as political unrest made fieldwork increasingly difficult to carry out, there was renewed awareness of important anthropological problems that need to be dealt with in North American society. Many of these problems involve people that anthropologists have studied in other settings. Thus, as people from South and Central America have moved into the cities of the United States, or as refugees have arrived from southeast Asia, anthropologists have been there not just to study them, but to help them adjust to their new circumstances. Simultaneously, anthropologists are applying the same research techniques that served them so well in the study of non-Western peoples to the study of such diverse things as street gangs, corporate bureaucracies, religious cults, health-care delivery systems, schools, and how people deal with consumer complaints.

An important discovery from such research is that it produces knowledge that usually does not emerge from the kinds of research done by other social scientists. For example, the theory of cultural deprivation arose during the 1960s as a way of explaining the educational failure of many

Anthropologists carry out fieldwork at home as well as abroad. One who is doing this is Dr. Miriam Lee Kaprow of John Jay College, whose work is with New York firefighters.

children of minorities. In order to account for their lack of achievement, some social scientists proposed that such children were "culturally deprived." They then proceeded to "confirm" this idea by studying children, mostly from Native American, African American, and Hispanic populations, interpreting the results through the protective screen of their theory. By contrast, ethnographic research on the cultures of "culturally deprived" children reveals a different story. Far from being culturally deprived, they have elaborate, sophisticated, and adaptive cultures that are simply different from the ones espoused by the educational system. Although some still cling to it, the cultural-deprivation theory is culture-bound and is merely a way of saying that people are "deprived" of "my culture." One cannot argue that such children do not speak adequate Spanish, Black English, or whatever; clearly they do well the things that are considered important in *their* cultures.

Much though it has to offer, the anthropological study of one's own culture is not without its own special problems. Sir Edmund Leach, a major figure in British anthropology, put it in the following way:

> Surprising though it may seem, fieldwork in a cultural context of which you already have intimate first-hand experience seems to be much more difficult than fieldwork which is approached from the naive viewpoint of a total stranger. When anthropologists study facets of their own society their vision seems to become distorted by prejudices which derive from private rather than public experience.[7]

Although the ethnographer strives to get an inside view of another culture, he or she does so self-consciously as an outsider. And the most successful anthropological studies of their own culture by North Americans have been done by those who first worked in some other culture. Lloyd Warner, for example, had studied the Murngin of Australia before he tackled Newburyport. In addition to getting ourselves outside of our own culture before trying to study it ourselves (so that we may see our-

[7]Leach, E. (1982). *Social anthropology* (p. 124). Glasgow: Fontana.

Not only are anthropologists *not* all male, neither are they all European or European-American. Mamphela Ramphele, who is Deputy Vice-Chancellor of the University of Cape Town, is a native South African anthropologist who has studied the migrant labor hostels of Cape Town.

selves as *others* see us), much is to be gained by encouraging anthropologists from Africa, Asia, and South America to do fieldwork in North America. From their outsiders' perspective come insights all too easily overlooked by an insider. Nonetheless, the special difficulties of studying one's own culture can be overcome; what it requires is an acute awareness of those difficulties.

Although ethnographic fieldwork is basic to ethnology, it is not the sole occupation of the ethnologist. What it provides is the basic data the ethnologist may then use to study one particular aspect of a culture by comparing it with that same aspect in others. Anthropologists constantly make such cross-cultural comparisons, which is another hallmark of the discipline. Interesting insights into our own practices may come from cross-cultural comparisons, as when one compares the time that people devote to what we consider to be "house-work." In North American society, there is a wide-spread belief that the ever-increasing output of household appliance consumer goods has resulted in a steady reduction in housework, with a consequent increase in leisure time. Thus, consumer appliances have become principal indicators of a high standard of living. Anthropological research among food foragers (people who rely on wild plant and animal resources for subsistence), however, has shown that they work far less at household tasks, and indeed less at all subsistence pursuits, than do people in industrialized societies. Aboriginal Australian women, for example, devote an average of approximately 20 hours per week to collecting and preparing food, as well as other domestic chores, whereas women in the rural United States in the 1920s, without the benefit of labor-saving appliances, devoted approximately 52 hours a week to their housework. Some 50 years later, contrary to all expectations, urban U.S. women who were not working for wages outside their homes were putting 55 hours a week into their housework, in spite of all their "labor-saving" dish-washers, washing machines, clothes dryers, vacuum cleaners, food processors, and microwave ovens.[8]

Cross-cultural comparisons highlight alternative ways of doing things, and so have much to offer North Americans, large numbers of whom, opinion polls show, have lost confidence in their own ways of doing things. In this sense, one may think of ethnology as the study of alternative ways of doing things. At the same time, by making systematic cross-cultural comparisons of cultures, ethnologists seek to arrive at valid conclusions concerning the nature of culture in all times and places.

ANTHROPOLOGY AND SCIENCE

The primary concern of all anthropologists is the careful and systematic study of humankind. Anthropology has been called a social or a behavioral science by some, a natural science by others, and one of the humanities by still others. Can the work of the anthropologist properly be labeled

[8]Bodley, J. H. (1985). *Anthropology and contemporary human problems* (2nd ed., p. 207). Palo Alto, CA: Mayfield.

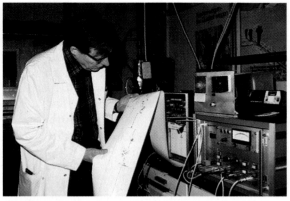

To many people, a scientist is someone (usually a white male) who works in a laboratory, carrying out experiments with the aid of specialized equipment. Contrary to the stereotypical image, not all scientists work in laboratories, nor is experimentation the only technique they use (nor are scientists invariably white males in lab coats).

scientific? What exactly do we mean by the term *science?*

Science is a powerful and elegant way people have hit upon to understand the workings of the visible world and universe. Science seeks testable explanations for observed phenomena, ideally in terms of the workings of hidden but universal and immutable principles, or laws. Two basic ingredients are essential for this: imagination and skepticism. Imagination, though capable of leading us astray, is required in order that we may imagine the ways in which phenomena might be ordered, thinking of old things in new ways. Without it, there can be no science. Skepticism is what allows us to distinguish **fact** from fancy, to test our speculations, and to prevent our imaginations from running away with us.

In their search for explanations, scientists do not assume that things are always as they appear on the surface. After all, what could be more obvious than that the earth is a stable entity, around which the sun travels every day? And yet, it is not so. Supernatural explanations are rejected, as are

Fact: An observation verified by several observers skilled in the necessary techniques of observation.

all explanations and appeals to authority that are not supported by strong empirical (observational) evidence. Because explanations are constantly challenged by new observations and novel ideas, science is self-correcting; that is, inadequate explanations are sooner or later shown up as such and are replaced by more reliable explanations.

The scientist begins with an **hypothesis,** or tentative explanation of the relationship between certain phenomena. By gathering various kinds of data that seem to support such generalizations, and, equally important, by showing why alternative hypotheses may be falsified, or eliminated from consideration, the scientist arrives at a system of validated hypotheses, or **theory.** Thus a theory, contrary to "everyday" use of the term, is much more than mere speculation. Still, although a theory is actually a well-supported body of knowledge, none is acknowledged to be beyond challenge. Truth, in science, is not considered to be absolute, but rather a matter of varying degrees of probability; what is considered to be true is what is most probable. This is true of anthropology, just as it is true of biology or physics. As our knowledge expands, the odds in favor of some theories over others are generally increased, but sometimes old "truths" must be discarded as alternative theories are shown to be more probable.

Difficulties of the Scientific Approach

Straightforward though the scientific approach may appear to be, there are serious difficulties in its application in anthropology. One of them is that once one has stated a hypothesis, one is strongly motivated to verify it, and this can cause one unwittingly to overlook negative evidence, not to mention all sorts of other unexpected things. This is a familiar problem in science; as paleontologist Stephen Jay Gould puts it, "The greatest impedi-

Hypothesis: A tentative explanation of the relation between certain phenomena.

Theory: A system of validated hypotheses that explains phenomena systematically.

ment to scientific innovation is usually a conceptual lock, not a factual lock."[9] In the fields of cultural anthropology there is a further difficulty: In order to arrive at useful theories concerning human behavior, one must begin with hypotheses that are as objective and as little culture-bound as possible. And here lies a major—some people would say insurmountable—problem: It is difficult for someone who has grown up in one culture to frame hypotheses about another that are not culture-bound.

As one example of this sort of problem, we may look at attempts by archaeologists to understand the nature of settlement in the Classic period of Maya civilization. This civilization flourished between A.D. 250 and 900 in what is now northern Guatemala, Belize, and adjacent portions of Mexico and Honduras. Today much of this region is covered by a dense tropical forest of the sort that people of European background find difficult to deal with. In recent times this forest has been inhabited by a few people who sustain themselves through slash-and-burn farming. (After cutting and burning the natural vegetation, crops are grown for two years or so before fertility is exhausted, and a new field must be cleared.) Yet numerous archaeological sites, featuring temples sometimes as tall as a modern 20-story building, other sorts of monumental architecture, and carved stone monuments are to be found there. Because of their cultural bias against tropical forests as places to live, and against slash-and-burn farming as a means of raising food, North American and European archaeologists asked the question: How could the Maya have maintained large, permanent settlements on the basis of slash-and-burn farming? The answer seemed self-evident—they could not; therefore, the great archaeological sites must have been ceremonial centers inhabited by few, if any, people. Periodically a rural peasantry, living scattered in small hamlets over the countryside, must have gathered in these centers for rituals or to provide labor for their construction and maintenance.

This view was the dominant one for several decades, and it was not until 1960 that archaeologists working at Tikal, one of the largest of all Maya sites, decided to ask the simplest and least biased questions they could think of: Did anyone

[9]Gould, S. J. (1989). *Wonderful life* (p. 226). New York: Norton.

The unique character of anthropology in the social sciences in North America owes a great deal to the three men pictured here, all of whom were educated in the natural sciences: Franz Boas in physics, Frederic Ward Putnam in zoology, and John Wesley Powell in geology. Although not the first to teach anthropology, Boas and his students made such courses a common part of college and university curricula. Similarly, Putnam established anthropology in the museum world, as did Powell within government.

live at this particular site on a permanent basis? If so, how many, and how were they supported? Working intensively over the next decade, with as few preconceived notions as possible, the archaeologists were able to establish that Tikal was a huge settlement inhabited by tens of thousands of people who were supported by forms of agriculture more productive than slash-and-burn alone. It was this work at Tikal that paved the way for a new understanding of Classic Maya civilization totally at odds with the older, culture-bound ideas.

Recognizing the problem of framing hypotheses that are not culture-bound, anthropologists have relied heavily on a technique that has proved successful in other fields of the natural sciences. As did the archaeologists working at Tikal, they immerse themselves in the data to the fullest extent possible. By doing so, they become so thoroughly familiar with the minute details that they can begin to see patterns inherent in the data, many of which might otherwise have been overlooked. These patterns are what allow the anthropologist to frame hypotheses, which then may be subjected to further testing.

This approach is most easily seen in ethnographic fieldwork, but it is just as important in archaeology. Unlike many social scientists, the ethnographer usually does not go into the field armed with prefigured questionnaires; rather, the ethnographer recognizes that there are probably all sorts of unguessed things to be found out only

by maintaining as open a mind as one can. This is not to say that anthropologists never use questionnaires, for sometimes they do. Generally, though, they use them as a means of supplementing or clarifying information gained through some other means. As the fieldwork proceeds, ethnographers sort their complex observations into a meaningful whole, sometimes by formulating and testing limited or low-level hypotheses, but as often as not by making use of intuition and playing hunches. What is important is that the results are constantly scrutinized for consistency, for if the parts fail to fit together in a manner that is internally consistent, then the ethnographer knows that a mistake has been made and that further work is necessary.

The contrast between the anthropological and other social science approaches is dramatically illustrated by the following example—one of several—presented by Robert Chambers in his book *Rural Development*. Since Chambers is a highly respected professional in the field of international development, and not an anthropologist, he can scarcely be accused of trying to promote his own discipline at the expense of others.

Sean Conlin lived as a social anthropologist in a village in Peru. While he was there a sociologist came and carried out a survey. According to the sociologist's results, people in the village invariably worked together on each others' individually owned plots of land.

That was what they told him. But in the period of over a year during which Conlin lived in the village, he observed the practice only once. The belief in exchange relations was, he concludes, important for the people's understanding of themselves, but it was not an economic fact.[10]

This does not mean that all sociological research is bad and all anthropological research is good; instead, it means that reliance on questionnaire surveys is a risky business, no matter who does it. Robert Chambers sums up the difficulties:

> Unless careful appraisal precedes drawing up a questionnaire, the survey will embody the concepts and categories of outsiders rather than those of rural people, and thus impose meanings on the social reality. The misfit between the concepts of urban professionals and those of poor rural people is likely to be substantial, and the questions asked may construct artificial chunks of "knowledge" which distort or mutilate the reality which poor people experience. Nor are questionnaire surveys on their own good ways of identifying causal relationships—a correlation alone tells us nothing definite about cause—or of exploring social relationships such as reciprocity, dependence, exploitation and so on. Their penetration is usually shallow, concentrating on what is measurable, answerable, and acceptable as a question, rather than probing less tangible and more qualitative aspects of society. For many reasons—fear, prudence, ignorance, exhaustion, hostility, hope of benefit—poor people give information which is slanted or false.[11]

As Chambers goes on to point out, for the above and numerous other reasons, conventional questionnaire surveys have many drawbacks if the aim is to gain insight into the lives and conditions of poor rural people. Other methods are required, either alone, or together with surveys. The trouble is, extensive questionnaire surveys

preempt resources, capturing staff and finance, thus preventing other approaches.

Yet another problem in scientific anthropology is the matter of replication. In the other physical and natural sciences, replication of observations or experiments is a major means of establishing the reliability of a researcher's conclusions. The problem in ethnology is that observational access is far more limited. As anthropologist Paul Roscoe notes:

> In the natural sciences, the ubiquity of the physical world, coupled with liberal funding, traditionally has furnished a comparatively democratic access to observation and representation: the solar spectrum, for example, is accessible to, and describable by, almost any astronomer with access to the requisite equipment.[12]

Thus, in the natural sciences one can often see for oneself if a colleague has "gotten it right." But, access to a non-Western culture, by contrast, is constrained by the difficulty of getting there and being accepted, the limited number of ethnographers, inadequate funding, the fact that cultures change so that what is observable at one time may not be at another, and so on. Thus, in anthropology one cannot always easily see for oneself whether the ethnographer "got it right." For this reason, an ethnographer bears a special responsibility for accurate reporting.

The end result of archaeological or ethnographic fieldwork, if properly carried out, is a coherent account of a culture, which provides an explanatory framework for understanding the behavior of the people who have been studied. And this, in turn, is what permits the anthropologist to frame broader hypotheses about human behavior. Plausible though such hypotheses may be, however, the consideration of a single society is generally insufficient for their testing. Without some basis for comparison, the hypothesis grounded in a single case may be no more than a historical coincidence. On the other hand, a single case may be adequate to cast doubt on, if not refute, a theory that had previously been held to be valid. The discovery in 1948 that aborigines living in Australia's Arnhem

[10]Chambers, R. (1983). *Rural development: Putting the last first* (p. 51). New York: Longman.
[11]Ibid., p. 51.
[12]Roscoe, P. B. (1995). The perils of "positivism" in cultural anthropology. *American Anthropologist, 97,* 497.

Nagasaki one month after the atomic bomb blast of August 13, 1945. Late in World War II, anthropologists and other social scientists working for the U.S. government predicted a Japanese surrender without the need to drop nuclear bombs. Because this conflicted with preconceived notions, these scientists' prediction was not heeded, but evidence gathered after the war confirmed the prediction's accuracy.

Land put in an average workday of less than 6 hours, while living well above a level of bare sufficiency, was enough to call into question the widely accepted notion that food-foraging peoples are so preoccupied with finding food that they lack time for any of life's more pleasurable activities. Even today, economists are prone to label such peoples as "backward," even though the observations made in the Arnhem Land study have since been confirmed many times over in various parts of the world.

Hypothetical explanations of cultural phenomena may be tested by the comparison of archaeological and ethnographic data for several societies found in a particular region. Nonhistorical, controlled comparison provides a broader context for understanding cultural phenomena than does the study of a single culture. The anthropologist who undertakes such a comparison may be more confident that the conditions believed to be related really are related, at least within the region that is under investigation; however, an explanation that is valid in one region is not necessarily so in another.

Ideally, theories in cultural anthropology are generated from worldwide comparisons. The cross-cultural researcher examines a worldwide sample of societies in order to discover whether hypotheses proposed to explain cultural phenomena seem to be universally applicable. Because the sample is selected at random, it is probable that the conclusions of the cross-cultural researcher will be valid; however, the greater the number of societies being examined, the less likely it is that the investigator will have a detailed understanding of all the societies encompassed by the study. The cross-cultural researcher depends upon other ethnographers for data. It is impossible for any single individual personally to perform in-depth analyses of a broad sample of human cultures throughout the world.

In anthropology, cultural comparisons need not be restricted to ethnographic data. Anthropologists can, for example, turn to archaeological data to test hypotheses about culture change. Cultural characteristics thought to be related to certain specified conditions can be tested archaeologically by investigating situations where such conditions actually occurred. Also useful are data provided by the ethnohistorian. **Ethnohistory** is a kind of historic ethnography that studies cultures of the recent past through the accounts of explorers, missionaries, and traders and through the analysis of such records as land titles, birth and death records, and other archival materials. The ethnohistorical analysis of cultures, like archaeology, is a valuable approach to understanding change. By examining the conditions believed to have caused certain phenomena, we can discover whether those conditions truly precede those phenomena.

Ethnohistorical research, like the field studies of archaeologists, is valuable for testing and confirming hypotheses about culture. And like much of anthropology, it has practical utility as well. In the United States, ethnohistorical research has flourished, for it often provides the key evidence necessary for deciding legal cases involving Native American land claims.

ANTHROPOLOGY AND THE HUMANITIES

Although the sciences and humanities are often thought of as mutually exclusive approaches to learning, they both come together in anthropology. That is why, for example, anthropological research is funded not only by "hard science" agencies like the National Science Foundation, but also by such organizations as the National Endowment for the Humanities. As noted by Roy Rappaport, a past president of the American Anthropological Association, the amalgamation of scientific and humanistic approaches

is and always has been a source of tension. It has been crucial to anthropology because it truly reflects the condition of a species

Ethnohistory: The study of cultures of the recent past through oral histories, accounts left by explorers, missionaries, and traders, and through the analysis of such records as land titles, birth and death records, and other archival materials.

that lives and can only live in terms of meanings that it must construct in a world devoid of intrinsic meaning, yet subject to natural law. . . . Without the continued grounding in the empirical that scientific aspects of our tradition provide, our interpretive efforts may float off into literary criticism and into particularistic forms of history. Without the interpretive tradition, the scientific tradition that grounds us will never get off the ground.[13]

The humanistic side of anthropology is perhaps most immediately evident in its concern with other cultures' languages, values, and achievements in the arts and literature (oral literature, among peoples who lack writing). Beyond this, anthropologists remain committed to the proposition that one cannot fully understand another culture by simply observing it; as the term *participant observation* implies, one must *experience* it as well. Thus, ethnographers spend prolonged periods of time living with the people whom they study, sharing their joys and suffering their deprivations, including sickness and, sometimes, premature death. They are not so naive as to believe that they can be, or even should be, dispassionate about the people whose trials and tribulations they share. As Robin Fox puts it, "our hearts, as well as our brains, should be with our men and women."[14] Nor are anthropologists so self-deceived as to believe that they can avoid dealing with the moral and political consequences of their findings.

Given their intense encounters with other peoples, it should come as no surprise that anthropologists have amassed as much information about human frailty and nobility—the stuff of the humanities—as any other discipline. Small wonder, too, that above all they intend to avoid allowing a "coldly" scientific approach to blind them to the fact that human societies are made up of individuals with rich assortments of emotions and aspirations that demand respect. Anthropology has sometimes been called the most human of the sciences, a designation in which anthropologists take considerable pride.

[13]Rappaport, R. A. (1994, September). [Commentary]. *Anthropology Newsletter, 35*, 76.
[14]Fox, R. (1968). *Encounter with anthropology* (p. 290). New York: Dell.

QUESTIONS OF ETHICS

The kinds of research carried out by anthropologists, and the settings within which they work, raise a number of important questions concerning ethics. Who will make use of the findings of anthropologists, and for what purposes? In the case of a militant minority, for example, will others use anthropological data to suppress that minority? And what of traditional communities around the world? Who is to decide what changes should, or should not, be introduced for community "betterment"? By whose definition is it betterment—the community's, that of some remote national government, or an international agency like the World Bank? Then there is the problem of privacy. Anthropologists deal with people's private and sensitive matters, including things that people would not care to have generally known about them. How does one write about such matters and at the same time protect the privacy of informants? Not surprisingly, because of these and other questions, there has been much discussion among anthropologists over the past two decades on the subject of ethics.

Anthropologists recognize that they have obligations to three sets of people: those whom they study, those who fund the research, and those in the profession who expect us to publish our findings so that they may be used to further our knowledge. Because fieldwork requires a relationship of trust between fieldworkers and informants, the anthropologist's first responsibility clearly is to his or her informants and their people. Everything possible must be done to do them no harm and to honor their dignity and privacy. Although early ethnographers often provided the kind of information needed by colonial administrators to control the "natives," they have long since ceased to be comfortable with such work, regarding as basic people's right to their own culture.

As an example of how the sometimes conflicting interests of the people studied, the profession, and funding agencies may be dealt with, we may turn to a 1981 interview given by Laura Nader:

> In the case of the Zapotec, I was dealing with very sensitive materials about law and disputes and conflicts and so forth. And I was very sensitive about how much of that to report while people were still alive and while things might still be warm, so I waited on that. . . . I feel comfortable now releasing that information. With regard to a funder in that case, it was the Mexican government, and I feel that I have written enough to have paid off the $1200 which they gave me to support that work for a year. So, I've not felt particularly strained for my Zapotec work in those three areas. On energy research that I've done, it's been another story. Much of what people wanted me to do energy research for was . . . to tell people in decision-making positions about American consumers in such a way that they could be manipulated better, and I didn't want to do that. So what I said was I would be willing to study a vertical slice. That is, I would never study the consumer without studying the producer. And once you take a vertical slice like that, then it's fair because you're telling the consumer about the producer and the producer about the consumer. But just to do a study of consumers for producers, I think I would feel uncomfortable.[15]

ANTHROPOLOGY AND CONTEMPORARY LIFE

Anthropology, with its long-standing commitment to understanding people in all parts of the world, coupled with its holistic perspective, is better equipped than any other discipline to grapple with a problem of overriding importance for all of humanity in this last decade of the twentieth century. An inescapable fact of life is that North Americans—a small minority of the world's people—live in a global community in which all of those people are interdependent upon one another. Although there is widespread awareness of this in the business community—which relies on foreign sources for raw materials, sees the non-Western world as its major area for market expansion, and is more and more making its products abroad—citizens of the United States are on the whole as ignorant about the cultures of the rest of the world as they have ever been. As a result, they are poorly equipped to handle the demands of living in the modern world.

Anthropologist Dennis Shaw sums up the implications of this state of affairs:

[15]Nader, L. (1981, December). [Interview for Coast Telecourses, Inc.], Los Angeles.

Ignorance of other cultures can have serious consequences, as the failed United Nations intervention in Somalia shows. Blinded by their own cultures' assumption of the universality of centralized political structure, the powers intervening in Somalia misunderstood the nature of that country's uncentralized, segmentary system.

Such provinciality raises questions about the welfare of our nation and the global context in which it is a major force. We have, as a nation, continued to interpret the political actions of other nations in terms of the cultural and political norms of our own culture and have thus made major misinterpretations of global political affairs. Our economic interests have been pursued from the perspective of our own cultural norms, and thus, we have failed to keep up with other nations that have shown a sensitivity to cultural differences. Domestically, a serious question can be raised about the viability of a democracy in which a major portion of the electorate is basically ignorant of the issues which our political leaders must confront. Internationally, one can speculate about the well-being of a world in which the citizens of one of the most powerful nations are seriously deficient in their ability to evaluate global issues.[16]

Former ambassador Edwin Reischauer once put it more tersely: "Education is not moving rapidly enough in the right directions to produce the knowledge about the outside world and attitudes toward other peoples that may be essential for human survival."[17] What anthropology has to contribute to contemporary life, then, are an understanding of, and way of looking at, the world's peoples, which are nothing less than basic skills for survival in the modern world.

[16]Shaw, D. G. (1984, November). A light at the end of the tunnel: Anthropological contributions towards global competence. *Anthropology Newsletter, 25,* 16.

[17]Quoted in Allen, S. L. (1984, November). Media anthropology: Building a public perspective. *Anthropology Newsletter, 25,* 6.

CHAPTER SUMMARY

Throughout human history, people have needed to know who they are, where they came from, and why they behave as they do. Traditionally, myths and legends provided the answers to these questions. Anthropology, as it has emerged over the last 200 years, offers another approach to answering the questions people ask about themselves.

Anthropology is the study of humankind. In employing a scientific approach, anthropologists seek to produce useful generalizations about humans and their behavior and to arrive at a reasonably objective understanding of human diversity. The two major branches of anthropology are physical and cultural anthropology. Physical anthropology focuses on humans as biological organisms. Particular emphasis is given by physical anthropologists to tracing the evolutionary development of the human animal and studying biological variation within the species today. Cultural anthropologists study humans in terms of their cultures, the often unconscious standards by which societies operate.

Three areas of cultural anthropology are archaeology, anthropological linguistics, and ethnology. Archaeologists study material objects usually from past cultures in order to explain human behavior. Linguists, who study human languages, may deal with the description of a language, with the history of languages, or how they are used in particular social settings. Ethnologists concentrate on cultures of the present or recent past; in doing comparative studies of culture, they may also focus on a particular aspect of culture, such as religious or economic practices, or as ethnographers, they may go into the field to observe and describe human behavior as it can be seen, experienced, and discussed with persons whose culture is to be understood.

Anthropology is unique among the social and natural sciences in that it is concerned with formulating explanations of human diversity based on a study of all aspects of human biology and behavior in all known societies, rather than in European and North American societies alone. Thus anthropologists have devoted much attention to the study of non-Western peoples.

Concerned with the systematic study of humankind, the anthropologist employs the methods of other scientists by developing a hypothesis, or assumed explanation, using other data to test the hypothesis, and ultimately arriving at a theory—a system of validated hypotheses. The data used by the cultural anthropologist may be field data of one society or comparative studies of numerous societies.

In anthropology, the humanities and sciences come together into a genuinely human science. Anthropology's link with the humanities can be seen in its concern with people's values, languages, arts, and literature—oral as well as written—but above all in its attempt to convey the experience of living as other people do. As both science and humanity, anthropology has essential skills to offer the modern world, where understanding the other people with whom we share the globe has become a matter of survival.

SUGGESTED READINGS

De Vita, P. R. (Ed.). (1992). *The naked anthropologist: Tales from around the world.* Belmont, CA: Wadsworth.

For anyone interested in what ethnographic fieldwork can be like, this book and a companion volume, *The Humbled Anthropologist* (1990), are hard to beat. They consist of personal and human accounts of fieldwork, one of which serves as this chapter's Original Study.

Lett, J. (1987). *The human enterprise: A critical introduction to anthropological theory.* Boulder, CO: Westview.

Part 1 examines the philosophical foundations of anthropological theory, paying special attention to the nature of scientific inquiry and the mechanisms of scientific inquiry and the mechanisms of scientific progress. Part 2 deals with the nature of social science as well as the particular features of anthropology.

Peacock, J. L. (1986). *The anthropological lens: Harsh light, soft focus.* New York: Cambridge University Press.

This lively and innovative book gives the reader a good understanding of the diversity of activities undertaken by anthropologists, while at the same time identifying the unifying themes that hold the discipline together.

Spradley, J. P. (1979). *The ethnographic interview.* New York: Holt, Rinehart and Winston.

This contains one of the best discussions of the nature and value of ethnographic research to be found. The bulk of the book is devoted to a step-by-step, easy-to-understand account of how one carries out ethnographic research with the assistance of "informants." Numerous examples drawn from the author's own research in such diverse settings as Skid Row, courtrooms, and bars make for interesting reading. A companion volume, *Participant Observation*, is also highly recommended.

CHAPTER
2

METHODS OF
STUDYING
THE HUMAN PAST

THIS EXCAVATION IS OF THE TOMB OF AN OFFICIAL OF THE
MOCHE KINGDOM THAT HELD SWAY OVER THE NORTH COAST OF
PERU ALMOST 2000 YEARS AGO. (SEE ORIGINAL STUDY FOR
CHAPTER 12.) BECAUSE EXCAVATION OF SUCH FEATURES
DESTROYS THEM, METICULOUS RECORDS MUST BE KEPT.
WITHOUT SUCH RECORDS, THE FINDS TELL US NOTHING ABOUT
THE HUMAN PAST.

CHAPTER PREVIEW

What Are Archaeological Sites and Fossil Localities and How Are They Found?

Archaeological sites are places containing the remains of past human activity. They are revealed by the presence of artifacts—objects fashioned or altered by humans—as well as certain kinds of soil marks, changes in vegetation, irregularities of the surface, and the like. Fossil localities are places containing the actual remains of organisms that lived in the past. They are revealed by the presence of fossils—any trace or impression of an organism of past geological time that has been preserved in the earth. Although fossils are sometimes found in archaeological sites, not all archaeological sites contain fossils, and localities are often found apart from archaeological sites. Though often discovered by accident, sites and localities are generally located by systematically surveying a region.

How Are Sites and Localities Investigated?

Archaeologists and paleoanthropologists face something of a dilemma. The only way to investigate a site or locality thoroughly is by excavation, which results in its destruction. Thus, every attempt is made to excavate in such a way that the location of everything found, no matter how small, is precisely recorded. Without such records little sense can be made of the data, and the potential of the site or locality to contribute to our knowledge of the past would be lost forever.

How Are Archaeological or Fossil Remains Dated?

Remains can be dated in relative terms by noting their stratigraphic position, by measuring the amount of fluorine contained in fossil bones, or by associating them with different floral or faunal remains. More precise dating is achieved by counting the tree rings in wood from archaeological contexts, by measuring the amount of carbon 14 remaining in organic materials, or by measuring the percentage of potassium that has decayed to argon in volcanic materials. Some other techniques are less commonly used, but they are often expensive, are not always as widely available, or else have not yet been proved as reliable.

A common misconception of anthropologists is that they are concerned exclusively with the human past, but as should now be evident, this is not the case. Not even archaeologists and physical anthropologists, those most likely to be engaged in the study of the past, devote all their time to such pursuits. As we have seen, some archaeologists study the refuse of modern peoples, and many physical anthropologists carry out research into such issues as present-day human variation and adaptation. Nevertheless, the study of the human past is an important *part* of anthropology, given its concern with peoples in all places and times. Moreover, an understanding of the human past is essential if we are to understand what it was that made us distinctively human, as well as how the processes of change—both biological and cultural—affect the human species. Indeed, given the radical changes taking place in the world today, one may say that an understanding of the nature of change has never been more important.

Although it is not their exclusive concern, archaeology and physical anthropology are the two branches of anthropology most involved in the study of the human past. Archaeologists (apart from those engaged in the analysis of modern garbage) study things left behind by people who lived in historic or prehistoric times—tools, trash, traces of shelters, and the like. As the British archaeologist Stuart Piggot put it: "Archaeology is the science of rubbish."[1] Most of us are familiar with some kind of archaeological material: the coin dug out of the earth, the fragment of an ancient jar, the spear point used by some ancient hunter. The finding and cataloging of such objects is often thought by nonprofessionals to be the chief goal of archeology. While this was true in the last century, it ceased to be true several decades ago. Today, the aim is to use archaeological remains to reconstruct human societies that can no longer be observed firsthand, in order to understand and explain human behavior. Although it may look as if the archaeologist is digging up *things*, he or she is really digging up human *behavior*.

The actual remains of our ancestors, as opposed to the things they lost or discarded, are the concern of physical anthropologists. Those physical anthropologists engaged in the recovery and study of the fossil evidence for human evolution, as opposed to those who study present-day peoples, are generally known as **paleoanthropologists.** Unlike paleontologists, who study all forms of past life, paleoanthropologists confine their attention to humans, near humans, and other ancient primates, the group to which humans belong. Just as the finding and cataloging of objects was once the chief concern of the archaeologist, so the finding and cataloging of human and other primate fossils was once the chief concern of the paleoanthropologist. But, again, there has been a major change in the field; while recovery, description, and organization of fossil materials are still important, the emphasis since the 1950s has been on what those fossils can tell us about the processes at work in human biological evolution.

In Chapter 1, we surveyed at some length just what it is that anthropologists do and why they do it. We also looked briefly at the ethnographic methods used by anthropologists to study living peoples (we shall touch upon these again in Chapter 14). Other methods are required, however, when studying peoples of the past—especially those of the prehistoric past, before the existence of written records. Since the next two parts of this book are about the prehistoric past, in this chapter, we shall look at how archaeologists and paleoanthropologists go about their study of the human past.

METHODS OF DATA RECOVERY

Archaeologists, one way or another, work with **artifacts,** any object fashioned or altered by humans—a flint chip, a basket, an axe, a pipe, or such nonportable things as house ruins or walls. An artifact expresses a facet of human culture. Because it is something that someone made, archaeologists like to say that an artifact is a product of human behavior or, in more technical words, that it is a material representation of an abstract ideal.

Just as important as the artifacts themselves is the way they were left in the ground. What people

Paleoanthropologist: An anthropologist who studies human evolution from fossil remains.

Artifact: Any object fashioned or altered by humans.

do with the things they have made, how they dispose of them, and how they lose them also reflect important aspects of human behavior. Furthermore, it is the context in which the artifacts were found that tells us which objects were contemporary with which other objects, which are older, and which are younger. Without this information, the archaeologist is in no position at all even to identify, let alone understand, specific cultures of the past. This importance of context cannot be overstated; without context, the archaeologist in effect knows nothing! Unfortunately, such information is easily lost if the materials have been disturbed, whether by bulldozers or by the activities of relic collectors.

While archaeologists work with artifacts, paleoanthropologists work with human or other primate fossils—the remains of past forms of life. And just as the context of a find is as important to the archaeologist as is the find itself, so is the context of a fossil absolutely critical to the paleoanthropologist. Not only does it tell which fossils are earlier or later in time than other fossils, but also by noting the association of human fossils with other

───◦○○───◦○○───

Fossil: The preserved remains of plants and animals that lived in the past.

Unaltered fossil: Remains of plants and animals that lived in the past that have not been altered in any significant way.

───◦○○───◦○○───

nonhuman remains, the paleoanthropologist may also go a long way toward reconstructing the environmental setting in which the human lived.

The Nature of Fossils

Broadly defined, a **fossil** is any trace or impression of an organism of past geologic time that has been preserved in the earth's crust. Fossilization typically involves the hard parts of an organism; bones, teeth, shells, horns, and the woody tissues of plants are the most successfully fossilized materials. Although the soft parts of an organism are rarely fossilized, the casts or impressions of footprints, and even whole bodies, have sometimes been found.

An organism or part of an organism may be preserved in a number of ways. The whole animal may be frozen in ice, like the famous mammoths found in Siberia, safe from the actions of predators, weathering, and bacteria. Or it may be enclosed in a fossil resin such as amber. Specimens of spiders and insects dating back millions of years have been preserved in the Baltic Sea area, which is rich in resin-producing conifers. It may be preserved in the bottoms of lakes and sea basins, where the accumulation of chemicals renders the environment antiseptic. The entire organism may also be mummified or preserved in tarpits, peat, oil, or asphalt bogs, in which the chemical environment prevents the growth of decay-producing bacteria. Such **unaltered fossils,** although not common, are often quite spectacular and may be particularly informative.

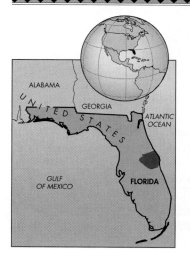

Original Study

Peat Holds Clues to Early American Life[2]

Tenderly buried in a shallow pond in central Florida, the dead of an early American Indian society lay under an ever-deepening shroud of peat for more than 7000 years. Recently resurrected, the bones and artifacts speak poignantly of a little-understood culture and reveal levels of craft previously undocumented in the New World during that era. The site is a genetic gold mine as well—brains preserved in this peat environment have yielded the oldest known human DNA.

Excavation directed by Florida State University began in 1984, two years after a construction crew turned up skulls in a Titusville housing development called Windover Farms. By late 1986 the Windover Archaeological Research Project had uncovered more than a hundred burials dating from

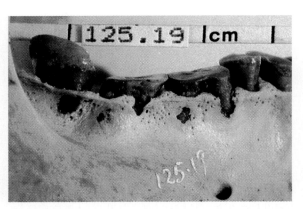

7000 to 8000 years ago. Few sites of this age in the Americas have held so large and diverse a group—nearly equally divided between male and female, adult and subadult.

In life they were hunter-gatherers, making seasonal rounds through this region today known for Walt Disney World and the Kennedy Space Center. At death they were placed in the foot-deep pond. Often laid on their sides in a flexed position, they were wrapped in grass mats, then covered with peat and wood. A frame of branches secured the grave.

Fabric, perhaps from a blanket or poncho, clung to some skeletons. Analysis by Dr. James Adovasio at the University of Pittsburgh has unraveled five distinct types of weaving more sophisticated than any known in the Americas from that time. Made without a loom, one weave is nearly as tight as a modern T-shirt. "There are lots of simpler ways to make durable cloth," says archaeologist Dr. Glen Doran, director of the excavation. "It challenges our traditional model of hunter-gatherer societies. These people had taken care of the basic necessities of life and had enough time to devote to a very complex nonessential activity." Further evidence comes from the skeleton of a teenager who suffered from a degenerative chronic spinal disorder. "It tells us they could support a nonproductive person for a long time," explains archaeologist and codirector Dr. David Dickel.

"They seem to have been oriented toward doing things for children," says Dickel, noting that the most bountiful grave offerings lie with children and teenagers. Artifacts found include a wooden pestle and a paddle, perhaps used to pound plant fibers for weaving. Antler from deer and bone from manatee, rabbit, and fish were shaped into awls and needles, a small hammer, devices to accelerate spear throwing, and tools of unknown function.

Under a tarpaulin shielding the drained pond, field archaeologist John Ricisak (upper left) slices peat from the skeleton of a child who died at about the age of the observing schoolchildren. Even at about 12 years, teeth (upper right) show wear from a diet of rough vegetation such as nuts and cabbage palm.

About ten feet of peat was cleared to reach the burials. Sealed from oxygen and saturated with minerals from Florida peatland waters, the preserved bones contain protein that may reveal diseases this population encountered. Unprotected soft tissue dissolved, but, locked in the skull, a

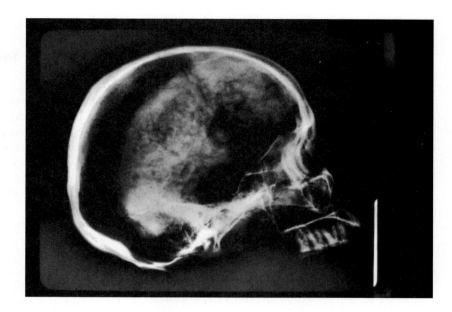

shrunken brain often survived, as seen in this X ray of a middle-aged woman (above). The water's almost neutral pH balance also saved brain DNA. "One of this find's most significant aspects is that human DNA can be preserved," says Dr. William Hauswirth, a microbiologist at the University of Florida who, in collaboration with biochemist Dr. Philip Laipis, has extracted this genetic-coding molecule from the Windover site brains. They are trying to clone it. "There are not many things we can do with it now, but it will be a resource for the future when we understand more about human genes."

In anticipation of such advances, the site was not totally excavated. Reflooded, it awaits archaeologists of another generation.

[2]Levathes, L. E. (1987). Mysteries of the bog. *National Geographic, 171,* 406–407.

Cases in which an entire organism of any sort, let alone a human, is preserved in a relatively unaltered state are rare and comprise possibly less than 1 percent of all fossil finds. The majority of **fossils** have been **altered** in some way. They generally consist of such things as scattered teeth and fragments of bones and are found embedded in the earth's crust as part of rock deposits. Thousands, and even millions, of years ago, the organisms died and were deposited in the earth; they may then have been covered by sediments and silt, or sand. These materials gradually hardened, forming a protective shell around the skeleton of the organism. The internal cavities of bones or teeth and other parts of the skeleton are generally filled in with mineral deposits from the sediment immediately surrounding the specimen. Then the external walls of the bone decay and are replaced by calcium carbonate or silica.

Altered fossils: Remains of plants and animals that lived in the past that have been altered, as by the replacement of organic material by calcium carbonate or silica.

Fossils are not always found in the ground. In this picture, paleoanthropologist Donald Johanson searches for fossils in a gully in Ethiopia. The fossils in the foreground were once buried beneath sediments on an ancient lake bottom, but rains in more recent times have eroded the sediments from around them so that they lie exposed on the surface.

Fossilization is most apt to occur among marine animals and other creatures that live near water, because their remains accumulate on shallow sea or river bottoms, away from waves and tidal action. These concentrations of shells and other parts of organisms are covered and completely enclosed by the soft marine sediments that eventually harden into shale and limestone.

Terrestrial animals, however, are not so successfully fossilized unless they happened to die in a cave or their remains were dragged there by some other meat-eating animal. In caves, conditions are often excellent for fossilization, as minerals contained in water dripping from the ceiling may harden over bones left on the cave floor. In northern China, for example, many fossils of *Homo erectus* (discussed in Chapter 8) and other animals were found in a cave at a place called Zhoukoudian, in deposits consisting of consolidated clays and rock that had fallen from the cave's limestone ceiling. The cave had been frequented by both humans and predatory animals, who left remains of many a meal there.

Outside of caves, the bones of a land dweller, having been picked clean and often broken by predators and scavengers, are then scattered and exposed to the deteriorating influence of the elements. The fossil record for many primates, for example, is poor, because the acid soil of the tropical forests in which they lived decomposes the skeleton rather quickly. The records are much more complete in the case of primates that lived on the grassy plains, or savannas, where conditions are much more favorable to the formation of fossils. This is particularly true in places where ash falls from volcanic eruptions, or waterborne sediments along lakes and streams, could quickly cover over the skeletons of primates that lived there. At several localities in Ethiopia, Kenya, and Tanzania in East Africa, numerous fossils important for our understanding of human evolution have been found near ancient lakes and streams, often "sandwiched" between layers of volcanic ash.

SITES AND FOSSIL LOCALITIES

Places containing archaeological remains of previous human occupation are known as **sites.** There are many kinds of sites, and sometimes it is difficult to define the boundaries of a site, for remains may be strewn over large areas. Some examples of sites are hunting campsites, in which hunters waited for game to pass; kill sites, in which game was killed and butchered; village sites, in which domestic activities took place; and cemeteries, in which the dead, and sometimes their belongings, were buried.

Sometimes human fossil remains are present at archaeological sites, which is the case, for example, at certain early sites in East Africa. Sometimes, though, they are found at other localities. For example, in South Africa the fossil remains of early human

Site: In archaeology, a place containing remains of previous human occupants.

Archaeological remains may be found under water as well as in the soil, giving rise to the specialized field of underwater archaeology.

ancestors have been found in rock fissures, where their remains were dropped by predators. Such places are usually referred to as **fossil localities.**

Site and Locality Identification

Archaeological sites, particularly very old ones, frequently lie buried underground, and therefore the first task for the archaeologist is actually finding sites to investigate. Most sites are revealed by the presence of artifacts. Chance may play a beneficial role in the discovery of artifacts and sites, but usually the archaeologist will have to survey a region in order

to plot the sites available for excavation. A survey can be made from the ground, but nowadays more and more use is being made of remote sensing techniques, many of them by-products of space-age technology. Aerial photographs have been used by archaeologists since the 1920s and are in wide use today. Among other things, they were used for the discovery and interpretation of the huge geometric and zoomorphic markings on the coastal desert of Peru. More recently, use of high-resolution aerial photographs, including satellite imagery, resulted in the astonishing discovery of more than 400 miles of prehistoric roadways connecting sites in the four-corners region (where Arizona, New Mexico, Colorado, and Utah meet) with other sites in ways that archaeologists had never suspected. This has led to a whole new understanding of prehistoric Pueblo Indian economic, social, and political organization. Evidently, large centers like Pueblo Bonito were able to exercise political control over a number of satellite communities, mobilize labor for large public works, and see to the regular redistribution of goods over substantial distances.

On the ground, sites can be spotted by **soil marks,** or stains, that often show up on the surface of recently plowed fields. From soil marks, many Bronze Age burial mounds were discovered in northern Hertfordshire and southwestern Cambridgeshire, England. The mounds hardly rose out of the ground, yet each was circled at its core by chalky soil marks. Sometimes the very presence of certain chalky rock is significant. A search for Stone Age cave sites in Europe would be simplified with the aid of a geological map showing where limestone—a mineral necessary in the formation of caves—is to be found.

Some sites may be spotted by the kind of vegetation they grow. For example, the topsoil of ancient storage and refuse pits is often richer in organic matter than that of the surrounding areas, and so it grows a distinct vegetation. At Tikal, an ancient Maya site in Guatemala (Chapter 12), breadnut trees usually grow near the remains of ancient houses, so that an archaeologist looking for the remains of houses at Tikal would do well to search

Fossil locality: In paleoanthropology, a place where fossils are found.

Soil marks: Stains that show up on the surface of recently plowed fields that reveal an archaeological site.

Some archaeological features are best seen from the air, such as this figure of a hummingbird made in prehistoric times on the Nazca Desert of Peru.

where these trees grow. In England, a wooden monument of the Stonehenge type at Darrington, Wiltshire, was discovered from an aerial photograph showing a distinct pattern of vegetation growing where the ancient structure once stood.

Documents, maps, folklore—ethnohistorical data—are also useful to the archaeologist. Heinrich Schliemann, the famous (and controversial) nineteenth-century German archaeologist, was led to the discovery of Troy after a reading of Homer's *Iliad.* He assumed that the city described by Homer as Ilium was really Troy. Place names and local lore often are an indication that an archaeological site is to be found in the area. Archaeological surveys in North America depend a great deal upon amateur collectors who are usually familiar with local history.

Sometimes sites in eastern North America are exposed by natural agents, such as soil erosion or droughts. Many prehistoric Indian shell refuse mounds have been exposed by the erosion of river banks. A whole village of stone huts was exposed at Skara Brae in the Orkney Islands by the action of wind as it blew away sand. And during the long drought of 1853–1854, a well-preserved prehistoric village was exposed when the water level of Lake Zurich, Switzerland, fell dramatically. In 1991, the mummified body of a late Neolithic man was found in the Tyrolean Alps, where it had been released by glacial melting.

Often, archaeological remains are accidentally discovered in the course of some other human activity. Plowing sometimes turns up bones, fragments of pots, and other archaeological objects. Stone quarrying revealed one of the most important sites of the Old Stone Age in England—at Swanscombe, Kent, in which human remains thought to be about 250,000 years old were found. In 1965, ground breaking for a new apartment complex in Nice, France, uncovered the remains of a campsite of *Homo erectus* (Chapter 8) 400,000 years old. So frequently do construction projects uncover archaeological remains that in many countries, including the United States, projects that require government approval will not be authorized unless measures are first taken to identify and protect archaeological remains on the construction sites. Archaeological surveys in the United States are now regularly carried out as part of the environmental review process for federally funded or licensed construction projects.

Conspicuous sites such as the great mounds or tells of the Middle East are easy to spot, for the country is open. But it is difficult to locate ruins, even those that are well above ground, where there is a dense forest cover. Thus, the discovery of archaeological sites is strongly affected by local geography.

While archaeological sites may be found just about anywhere, the same is not true for fossil localities. One will find fossils only in geological contexts

Shown here is the body of a Neolithic man who froze to death in the Tyrolean Alps; not until 1991 were his remains released by the melting of a glacier.

where conditions are known to have been right for fossilization. Once the paleoanthropologist has identified such regions, specific localities are identified in much the same ways as archaeological sites. Indeed, the discovery of ancient stone tools may lead to the discovery of human fossil remains. For example, it was the presence of very crude stone tools in Olduvai Gorge, East Africa, that prompted Mary and Louis Leakey to search there for the human fossils they eventually found.

Sometimes archaeological sites are marked by dramatic ruins, as shown here. This temple stands at the heart of the ancient Maya city of Tikal. Built by piling up rubble and facing it with limestone blocks held together with mortar, it served as the funerary monument of a king, whose body was placed in a tomb beneath the pyramidal base.

Anthropology Applied
CULTURAL RESOURCE MANAGEMENT

In June 1979, on a knoll next to a river not far from Lake Champlain, a survey crew working for Peter A. Thomas of the University of Vermont's Consulting Archaeology Program discovered archaeological materials unlike any found before in the region. The following June, Thomas returned to the site with a crew of five in order to excavate a portion of it. What they found were the remains of an 8000-year-old hunting and fishing camp that had been occupied for up to a few months in the spring or fall by perhaps one or two families. From the site they recovered a distinctive tool inventory never recognized before, as well as data related to hunting and fishing subsistence practices, butchery or hide processing, cooking, tool manufacture, and a possible shelter. Since many archaeologists had previously believed the region to be devoid of human occupation 8000 years ago, recovery of these data was especially important.

What sets this work apart from conventional archaeological research is that it was conducted as part of cultural resource management activities required by state and federal laws to preserve important aspects of the country's prehistoric and historic heritage. In this case, the Vermont Department of Highways planned to replace an inadequate bridge with a new one. Since the project was partially funded by the U.S. government, steps had to be taken to identify and protect any significant prehistoric or historic resources that might be adversely affected. To do so, the Vermont Agency of Transportation hired Thomas, first to see if such resources existed in the project area, and then to retrieve data from the endangered portions of the one site that was found. As a result, an important contribution was made to our knowledge of the prehistory of northeastern North America.

Since passage of the Historic Preservation Act of 1966, the National Environmental Policy Act of 1969, and the Archaeological and Historical Preservation Act of 1974, the field of cultural resource management has boomed. Consequently, many archaeologists have been employed by such agencies as the National Park Service, the U.S. Forest Service, and the U.S. Soil and Conservation Service to assist in the preservation, restoration, and salvage of archaeological resources. Archaeologists are also employed by state historic preservation agencies. Finally, they do a considerable amount of consulting work for engineering firms to help them prepare environmental impact statements. Some of these archaeologists, like Thomas, operate out of universities and colleges, while others are on the staffs of independent consulting firms.

Site and Locality Excavation

Before the archaeologist or paleoanthropologist plans an excavation, he or she must ask the question: "Why am I digging?" Then must be considered the amount of time, money, and labor that can be committed to the enterprise. The recovery of archaeological and fossil material has long since ceased to be the province of the enlightened amateur, as it once was when any enterprising collector went out to dig for the sake of digging. A modern excavation is carefully planned and rigorously conducted; not only should it shed light on the human past but it should also help us to understand cultural and evolutionary processes in general.

Archaeological Excavation

After a site is chosen for excavation on the basis of its potential contribution to the solution of some important research problem, the land is cleared and the places to be excavated are plotted. This is usually done by means of a **grid system.** The surface of the site is divided into squares, and then each square is numbered and marked with stakes. Each object found may then be located precisely in the square from which it came. (Remember, in archaeology, context is everything!) The starting point of a grid system may be a large rock, the edge of a stone wall, or an iron rod sunk into the ground. The starting point is also known as the reference or **datum point.**

Grid system: A system for recording data from an archaeological excavation.

Datum point: Starting, or reference, point for a grid system.

At a large site covering several square miles, this kind of grid system is not feasible because of the large size of the ruins. In such cases, the plotting may be done in terms of individual structures, numbered accord-ing to the square of a "giant grid" in which they are found (Fig. 2.1).

In a gridded site, each square is dug separately with great care. Trowels are used to scrape the soil, and screens

Figure 2.1   At large sites covering several square miles, a giant grid is constructed, as shown in this map of the center of the ancient Maya city of Tikal. Each square of the grid is one quarter of a square kilometer; individual structures are numbered according to the square in which they are found. The temple shown on page 39 can be located near the center of the map, on the east edge of the Great Plaza.

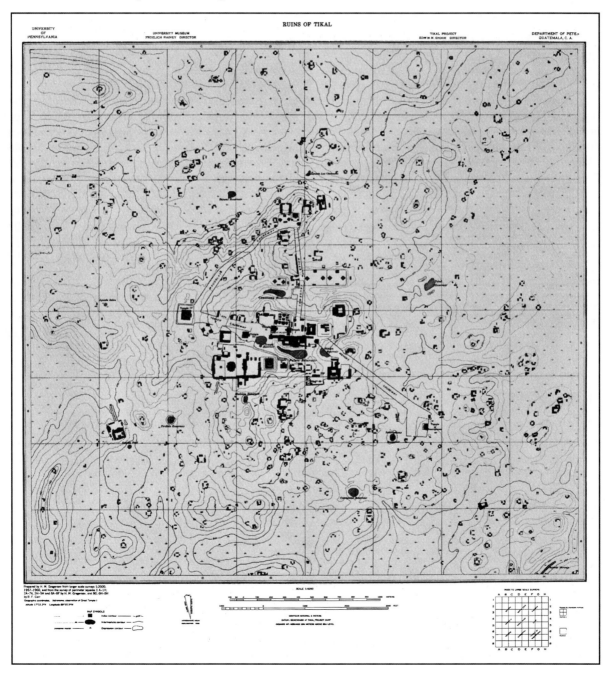

are used to sift all the loose soils so that even the smallest artifacts, such as flint chips or beads, are recovered.

A technique employed when looking for very fine objects, such as fish scales or very small bones, is called **flotation.** Flotation consists of immersing soil in water, causing the particles to separate. Some will float, others will sink to the bottom, and the remains can be easily retrieved. If the site is **stratified**—that is, if the remains lie in layers one upon the other—each layer, or stratum, will be dug separately (see Fig. 2.2 for an example of stratigraphy). Each layer, having been laid down during a particular span of time, will contain artifacts deposited at the same time and belonging to the same culture. Culture change can be traced through the order in which artifacts were deposited. But, say archaeologists Frank Hole and Robert F. Heizer, "because of difficulties in analyzing stratigraphy, archaeologists must use the greatest caution in drawing conclusions. Almost all interpretations of

---

Flotation: An archaeological technique employed to recover very tiny objects by immersion of soil samples in water to separate heavy from light particles.

Stratified: Layered; said of archaeological sites where the remains lie in layers, one upon another.

---

time, space, and culture contexts depend on stratigraphy. The refinements of laboratory techniques for analysis are wasted if archaeologists cannot specify the stratigraphic position of their artifacts."[3] If no stratification is present, then the archaeologist digs by arbitrary levels. Each square must be dug so that its edges and profiles are straight; walls between squares are often left standing to serve as visual correlates of the grid system.

Excavation of Fossils

Excavating for fossils is in many ways like archaeological excavation, although there are some differences. The paleoanthropologist must be particularly skilled in the techniques of geology, or else have ready access to geological expertise, because a fossil is of little use unless its temporal place in the sequence of rocks that contain it can be determined. In addition, the paleoanthropologist must be able to identify the fossil-laden rocks, their deposition, and other geological details. In order to provide all the necessary expertise, paleoanthropological expeditions these days generally are made up of teams of experts in various fields in addition to physical anthropology.

A great deal of skill and caution is required to remove a fossil from its burial place without

[3]Hole, F., & Heizer, R. F. (1969). *An introduction to prehistoric archeology* (p. 113). New York: Holt, Rinehart and Winston.

Figure 2.2   This drawing shows the strata (layers) uncovered on the North Acropolis of Tikal. The remains of at least twenty-two structures were found at this one location. The North Acropolis is shown near the center of the map in Figure 2.1, just north of the Great Plaza.

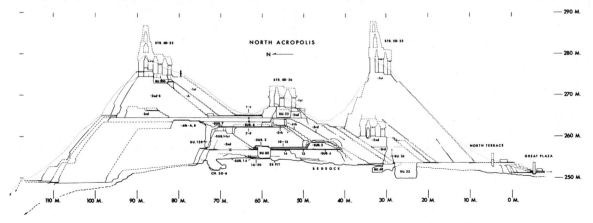

This photo is of the stratigraphy associated with one of the structures (5D-26) shown schematically in Figure 2.2.

damage. An unusual combination of tools and materials is usually contained in the kit of the paleoanthropologist—pickaxes, enamel coating, burlap for bandages, and plaster of paris.

To remove newly discovered bones, the paleoanthropologist begins uncovering the specimen, using pick and shovel for initial excavation, then small camel-hair brushes and dental picks to remove loose and easily detachable debris surrounding the bones. Once the entire specimen has been uncovered (a process that may take days of back-breaking, patient labor), the bones are covered with shellac and tissue paper to prevent cracking and damage during further excavation and handling.

Both the fossil and the earth immediately surrounding it, or the matrix, are prepared for removal as a single block. The bones and matrix are cut out of the earth (but not removed), and more shellac is applied to the entire block to harden it. The bones are covered with burlap bandages dipped in plaster of paris. Then the entire block is enclosed in plaster and burlap bandages, perhaps splinted with tree branches, and allowed to dry overnight. After it has hardened, the entire block is carefully removed from the earth, ready for packing and transport to a laboratory. Before leaving the discovery area, the investigator makes a thorough sketch map of the terrain and pinpoints the find on geological maps to aid future investigators.

State of Preservation of Archaeological and Fossil Evidence

What is recovered in the course of excavation depends upon the nature of the remains as much as upon the excavator's digging skills. Inorganic materials such as stone and metal are more resistant to decay than organic ones such as wood and bone. Often an archaeologist comes upon an assemblage—a collection of artifacts made of durable inorganic materials, such as stone tools, and traces of organic ones long since decomposed, such as woodwork (Fig. 2.3), textiles, or food.

State of preservation is affected by climate; under favorable climatic conditions, even the most perishable objects may survive over vast periods of time. For example, predynastic Egyptian burials consisting of shallow pits in the sand often yield well-preserved corpses. Since these bodies were buried long before mummification was ever practiced, their preservation can be the result only of rapid desiccation in the very warm, dry climate. The tombs of dynastic Egypt often contain wooden

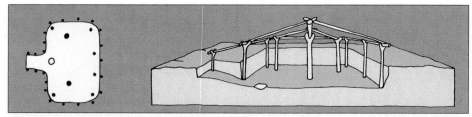

Figure 2.3   Although the wooden posts of a house may have long since decayed, their positions may still be marked by discoloration of the soil. The plan shown on the left, of an ancient posthole pattern and depression at Snaketown, Arizona, permits the hypothetical house reconstruction on the right.

furniture, textiles, flowers, and papyri barely touched by time, seemingly as fresh looking as they were when deposited in the tomb 3000 years ago—a consequence of the dryness of the atmosphere.

The dryness of certain caves is also a factor in the preservation of fossilized human or animal feces. Human feces are a source of information on prehistoric foods and can be analyzed for dietary remains. From such analysis can be determined not only what the inhabitants ate but also how the food was prepared. Because so many sources of food are available only in certain seasons, it is even possible to tell the time of year in which the food was eaten and the excrement deposited.

Certain climates can soon obliterate all evidence of organic remains. Maya ruins found in the very warm and moist tropical rain forests of Mesoamerica are often in a state of collapse—notwithstanding the fact that many are massive structures of stone—as a result of the pressure exerted upon them by the heavy forest vegetation. The rain and humidity soon destroy almost all traces of woodwork, textiles, or basketry. Fortunately, wood, textile, and basketry impressions are sometimes preserved in plaster, and some objects made of these materials are depicted in stone carvings and pottery figurines. Thus, even in the face of complete decay of organic substances, something may still be learned about them.

The cultural practices of ancient humans may also account for the preservation of archaeological remains. The ancient Egyptians believed that eternal life could be achieved only if the dead person were buried with his or her worldly possessions. Hence, their tombs are usually filled with a wealth of artifacts. Many skeletal remains of Neandertals (Chapter 9) are known because they practiced burial, probably because they too believed in some sort of afterlife. By contrast, skeletal remains of pre-Neandertal peoples are rare and when found usually consist of mere fragments rather than complete skeletons.

SORTING OUT THE EVIDENCE

It cannot be stressed too strongly that the value of archaeological materials is virtually destroyed if an accurate and detailed record of the excavations has not been kept.

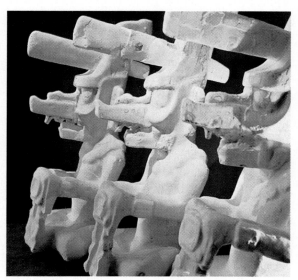

At the Maya site of Tikal, these manikin sceptre figures originally made of wood were recovered from a king's tomb by pouring plaster into a cavity in the soil, left when the original organic material decayed.

The fundamental premise of excavation is that all digging is destructive, even that done by experts. The archaeologist's primary responsibility, therefore, is to record a site for posterity as it is dug because there are no second chances.[4]

The records include a scale map of all the features, the stratification of each excavated square, a description of the exact location and depth of every artifact or bone unearthed, and photographs and scale drawings of the objects. This is the only way archaeological evidence can later be pieced together in order to arrive at a plausible reconstruction of a culture. Although the archaeologist may be interested in only certain kinds of remains, every aspect of the site must be recorded, whether it is relevant to the particular investigation, because such evidence may be useful to others and would otherwise be permanently lost. One must remember that archaeological sites are nonrenewable resources and that their destruction, whether by proper excavation or by looting, is permanent.

After photographs and scale drawings are made, the materials recovered are processed in the laboratory. In the case of fossils, the block in which they have been removed from the field is cut open, and the fossil is separated from the matrix. Like the initial removal from the earth, this is a long, painstaking job involving a great deal of skill and special tools. This task may be done with hammer and chisel, dental drills, rotary grinders or pneumatic chisels, and, in the case of very small pieces, with awls and tiny needles under a microscope.

Chemical means, such as hydrochloric and hydrofluoric acid, are also used in the separation process. Some fossils require processing by other methods. For example, precise identification can be obtained by examining thin, almost transparent strips of some fossils under a microscope. Casts of the insides of skulls are made by filling the skull wall with an acid-resistant material, then removing the wall with acid. A skull may be cleaned out and the inside painted with latex. After the latex hardens, it is removed in a single piece, revealing indirect evidence of brain shape and outer appearance. Such a cast of the skull's interior is helpful in determining the size and complexity of the specimen's brain.

Archaeologists, as a rule of thumb, generally plan on at least 3 hours of laboratory work for each hour of fieldwork. In the lab, artifacts that have been recovered must first be cleaned and cataloged—often a tedious and time-consuming job—before they are ready for analysis. From the shapes of the artifacts and from the traces of manufacture and wear, archaeologists can usually determine their function. For example, the Russian archaeologist S. A. Semenov devoted many years to the study of prehistoric **technology**.[5] In the case of a flint tool used as a scraper, he was able to determine, by examining the wear patterns of the tool under a microscope, that the prehistoric individuals who used it began to scrape from right to left and then scraped from left to right, and in so doing avoided straining the muscles of the hand.

Analysis of vegetable and animal remains provides clues about the environment and the economic activities of the occupants of a site (see Fig. 2.4). Such analysis may help clarify peoples' relationship to their environment and its influence upon the development of their technology—the knowledge they employ to make and use objects. For example, we know that the people responsible for Serpent Mound, in Ontario, Canada (a mound consisting of burials and a shell midden), were there only in the spring and early summer, when they came to collect shellfish and perform their annual burial rites; apparently they moved elsewhere at the beginning of summer to pursue other seasonal subsistence activities. Archaeologists have inferred that the mound was unoccupied in winter, because deer shed their antlers in winter, yet no deer antlers were found on the site. Nor were duck bones found, and so archaeologists conclude that

Technology: The knowledge people employ to make and use objects.

[4]Fagan, B. M. (1995). *People of the earth* (8th ed., p. 19). New York: HarperCollins.

[5]Semenov, A. (1964). *Prehistoric technology*. New York: Barnes & Noble.

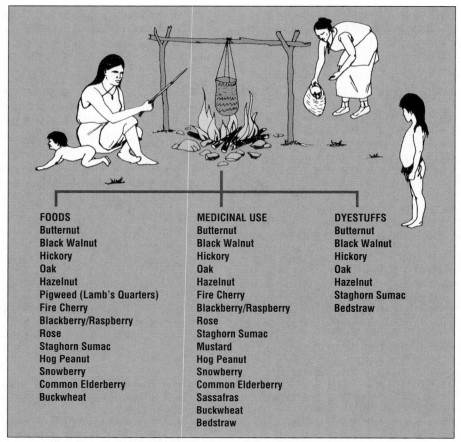

Figure 2.4 Plant remains recovered from hearths used by people between one and two thousand years ago at an archaeological site in Vermont may have been utilized as shown here, based on our knowledge of how some plants were used by Indians in the region when first encountered by Europeans. Occupation of the site must have been in the summer and fall, the seasons when these plants are available.

the mound was also unoccupied in the fall, when ducks stopped on their migratory route southward to feed on the wild rice growing in the region.

Analysis of human skeletal material also provides important insights into ancient peoples' diets. Microscopic wear patterns on teeth, for example, may reveal whether abrasive plants were important foods. Similarly, people who eat more plants than meat will have a higher ratio of strontium to calcium in their bones. At the ancient Maya city of Tikal, analysis of human skeletons showed that elite members of society had access to better diets than lower-ranking members of society, allowing them to reach their full growth potential with greater

regularity. Important insights into life expectancy, mortality, and health status also emerge from the study of human skeletal remains. Unfortunately, such studies have become more difficult to carry out, especially in the United States, as Native American communities demand (and federal law requires) the return of skeletons from archaeological excavations for reburial. Archaeologists find themselves in something of a quandary over this; as scientists, they know the importance of the information that can be gleaned from studies of human skeletons, but as anthropologists, they are bound to respect the feelings of those whose ancestors those skeletons represent.

Currently, archaeologists are working with representatives of Native American communities to work out procedures with which both parties can live.

Dating the Past

Reliable methods of dating objects and events are necessary if archaeologists and paleoanthropologists are to know the sequence of events in the situation under study. But since archaeologists and paleoanthropologists deal mostly with peoples and events in times so far removed from our own, the calendar of historic times is of little use to them. So they must rely on two kinds of dating: relative and "absolute." **Relative dating** consists simply of finding out if an event or object is younger or older than another. **"Absolute"** or (more properly) **chronometric dates** are dates based on solar years and are reckoned in "years before the present" (B.P., with "present" defined as A.D. 1950). Many relative and chronometric techniques are available; here, there is space to discuss only the ones most often used. Ideally, archaeologists try to utilize as many methods as are appropriate, given the materials available to work with and the funds at their disposal. By doing so, they significantly reduce the risk of arriving at erroneous dates.

Methods of Relative Dating

Of the many relative dating techniques available, **stratigraphy** is probably the most reliable.

Relative dating: In archaeology and paleoanthropology, designating an event, object, or fossil as being older or younger than another.

Absolute, or chronometric, dates: In archaeology and paleoanthropology, dates for archaeological materials based on solar years, centuries, or other units of absolute time.

Stratigraphy: In archaeology and paleoanthropology, the most reliable method of relative dating by means of strata.

Stratigraphy is based on the simple principle that the oldest layer, or stratum, was deposited first (it is the deepest) while the newest layer was deposited last (in undisturbed situations, it lies at the top). Therefore, in an archaeological site the evidence is usually deposited in chronological order. The lowest stratum contains the oldest artifacts or fossils, whereas the uppermost stratum contains the most recent ones. Thus, even in the absence of precise dates, one knows the relative age of objects in one stratum compared with the ages of those in other strata.

Some ancient societies devised precise ways of recording dates that archaeologists have been able to correlate with our own calendar. Here is the tomb of the important ruler Stormy Sky, at the ancient Maya city of Tikal. The glyphs painted on the wall give the date of the burial in the Maya calendar, which is the same as March 18, A.D. 457, in our calendar. The tomb, Burial 48, is shown in Figure 2.2 above the 30-meter mark.

Another method of relative dating is the **fluorine test.** It is based on the fact that the amount of fluorine deposited in bones is proportional to their age. The oldest bones contain the greatest amount of fluorine, and vice versa. The fluorine test is useful in dating bones that cannot be ascribed with certainty to any particular stratum and cannot be dated according to the stratigraphic method. A shortcoming of this method is that the rate of fluorine formation is not constant, but varies from region to region.

Relative dating can also be done on the evidence of botanical and animal remains. A common method, known as **palynology,** involves the study of pollen grains. The kind of pollen found in any geologic stratum depends on the kind of vegetation that existed at the time that stratum was deposited. A site or locality can therefore be dated by determining what kind of pollen was found associated with it. In addition, palynology is also an important technique for reconstructing past environments in which people lived.

Another method relies on our knowledge of paleontology. Sites containing the bones of extinct animal species are usually older than sites in which the remains of these animals are absent. Very early North American Indian sites have yielded the remains of mastodons and mammoths—animals now extinct—and on this basis the sites can be dated to a time before these animals died out, roughly 10,000 years ago.

Methods of Chronometric Dating

One of the most widely used methods of "absolute," or chronometric, dating is **radiocarbon analysis.** It is based on the fact that all living organisms absorb radioactive carbon (known as carbon 14), which reaches equilibrium with that in the atmosphere, and that this absorption ceases at the time of death. It is possible to measure in the laboratory the amount of radioactive carbon left in a given organic substance, because radioactive substances break down or decay slowly over a fixed period of time. Carbon 14 begins to disintegrate, returning to nitrogen 14, emitting radioactive (beta) particles in the process. At death, about 15 beta radiations per minute per gram of material are emitted. The rate of decay is known as "half-life,"

and the half-life of carbon 14 is 5730 years. This means that it takes 5730 years for one-half of the original amount of carbon 14 to decay into nitrogen 14. Beta radiation will be about 7.5 counts per minute per gram. In another 5730 years, one-half of this amount of carbon 14 will also have decayed. In other words, after 11,460 years, only one-fourth of the original amount of carbon 14 will be present. Thus the age of an organic substance such as charcoal, wood, shell, or bone can be measured by counting the beta rays emitted by the remaining carbon 14. The radiocarbon method can adequately date organic materials up to 70,000 years old. Of course, one has to be sure that the association between organic remains and archaeological materials is valid. For example, charcoal found on a site may have gotten there from a recent forest fire, rather than more ancient activity, or wood used to make something by the people who lived at a site may have been retrieved from some older context.

Because there is always a certain amount of error involved, radiocarbon dates are not as "absolute" as is sometimes thought. This is why any stated date always has a ± factor attached to it. For example, a date of 5200 ± 120 years ago means that there is a two out of three chance that the true date falls somewhere within the 240 years between 5080 and 5320 radiocarbon years ago. The qualification "radiocarbon years" is necessary, because we have discovered that radiocarbon years are not precisely equivalent to calendar years.

Fluorine test: In archaeology or paleoanthropology, a technique for relative dating based on the fact that the amount of fluorine in bones is proportional to their age.

Palynology: In archaeology and paleoanthropology, a method of relative dating based on changes in fossil pollen over time.

Radiocarbon analysis: In archaeology and paleoanthropology, a technique for chronometric dating based on measuring the amount of radioactive carbon (C-14) left in organic materials found in archaeological sites.

The discovery that radiocarbon years are not precisely equivalent to calendar years was made possible by another method of "absolute" dating, **dendrochronology.** Originally devised for dating Pueblo Indian sites in the North American Southwest, this method is based on the fact that in the right kind of climate, trees add one (and only one) new growth ring to their trunks every year (see Fig. 2.5). The rings vary in thickness, depending upon the amount of rainfall received in a year, so that climatic fluctuation is registered in the growth ring. By taking a sample of wood, such as a beam from a Pueblo Indian house, and by comparing its pattern of rings with those in the trunk of a tree known to be as old as the artifact, archaeologists can date the archaeological material. Dendrochronology is applicable only to wooden objects. Furthermore, it can be used only in regions in which trees of great age, such as the giant sequoias and the bristlecone pine, are known to grow. On the other hand, radiocarbon dating of wood from bristlecone pines that have been dated by dendrochronology allows us to "correct" carbon 14 dates so as to bring them into agreement with calendar dates.

Potassium-argon analysis, another method of absolute dating, is based on a technique similar to that of radiocarbon analysis. Following intense heating, as from a volcanic eruption, radioactive potassium decays at a known rate to form argon, any previously existing argon having been released by the heating. The half-life of radioactive potassium is 1.3 billion years. Deposits that are millions of years old can now be dated by measuring the ratio of potassium to argon in a given rock. Volcanic debris, such as at Olduvai Gorge and other localities in East Africa, can be dated by potassium-argon analysis; thus we know when the volcanic eruption occurred. If fossils or artifacts are found sandwiched between layers of volcanic ash, as they are at Olduvai and other sites in East Africa, they can therefore be dated with some precision. But as with radiocarbon dates, there are

Dendrochronology: In archaeology, a method of chronometric dating based on the number of rings of growth found in a tree trunk.

Potassium-argon analysis: In archaeology and paleoanthropology, a technique for chronometric dating that measures the ratio of radioactive potassium to argon in volcanic debris associated with human remains.

Figure 2.5   Chronometric dating based on tree rings is called dendrochronology. Starting with a sample of known age, ring patterns toward the inner part are matched with those from the outer part of the older sample, and so on, back in time.

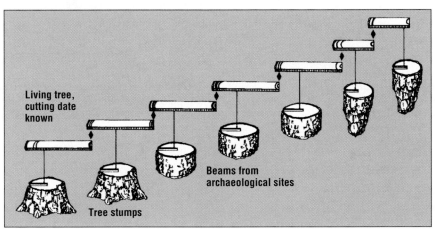

limits to that precision, and potassium-argon dates are always stated with a ± margin of error attached.

Amino acid racemization dating, yet another chronometric technique, is of potential importance because it bridges a time gap between the effective ranges of the radiocarbon and potassium-argon methods. It is based on the fact that amino acids trapped in organic materials gradually change, or "racemize" after death, from left-handed forms to right-handed forms. Thus, the ratio of left- to right-handed forms should indicate the specimen's age. Unfortunately, in substances like bone, moisture and acids in the soil can leach out the amino acids, thereby introducing a serious source of error. However, ostrich eggshells have proven immune to this problem, the amino acids being so effectively locked up in a tight mineral matrix that they are preserved for thousands of years. Because ostrich eggs were widely used as food, and the shells as containers in Africa and the Middle East, they provide a powerful means of dating sites of the Middle Paleolithic, between 40,000 and 180,000 years ago.

Radiocarbon, potassium-argon, and amino acid racemization dating are only three of the several "high-tech" dating methods that have been developed in the past few decades. Radiocarbon and potassium-argon, in particular, are the chronometric methods most heavily relied upon by archaeologists and paleoanthropologists; nevertheless, other methods are increasingly used as a check on the accuracy and to supplement dates determined by other means. To cite one example, a new technique called

electron spin resonance measures the trapped electron population in bone or shell (the number of trapped electrons indicates the specimen's age). Because electron spin resonance dates derived from an important Middle Paleolithic skull from Qafzeh, Israel (discussed in Chapter 9), agree with those based on amino acid racemization, we can have confidence that the dating is correct. Because other methods of chronometric dating are often quite complicated to carry out, they tend to be expensive; many can be carried out only on specific kinds of materials, and in the case of some, are so new that their reliability is not yet unequivocally established. It is for these reasons that they have not been as widely used as radiocarbon and potassium-argon.

Chance and the Study of the Past

It is important to understand the imperfect nature of the archaeological and fossil records. They are imperfect, first of all, because the chance circumstances of preservation have determined what has and what has not survived the ravages of time. Thus, cultures must be reconstructed on the basis of incomplete and, possibly, unrepresentative samples of artifacts. The problems are further compounded by the large role chance continues to play in the discovery of prehistoric remains. Therefore, one must always be cautious when trying to interpret the human past. No matter how elegant a particular theory may be about what happened in the past, new evidence may at any time force its reexamination and modification, or even rejection, in favor of some better theory.

Amino acid racemization dating: In archaeology and paleoanthropology, a technique for chronometic dating that measures the ratio of right- to left-handed amino acids.

Electron spin resonance: In archaeology and paleoanthropology, a technique for chronometric dating that measures the number of trapped electrons in bone or shell.

Shown here is what remains of a 1700-year-old fish weir, for trapping fish, in Maine. Submersion beneath the water preserved the lower portions of wooden stakes, which were revealed by unusually low water levels.

CHAPTER SUMMARY

Archaeology and physical anthropology, though they do not neglect the present, are the two branches of anthropology most involved in the study of the human past. Archaeologists study material remains to describe and explain human behavior; physical anthropologists called paleoanthropologists study fossil remains to understand and explain the processes at work in human biological evolution.

Artifacts are objects fashioned or altered by humans, such as a flint chip, a pottery vessel, or even a house. A fossil is any trace of an organism of past geological time that has been preserved in the earth's crust. Fossilization typically involves the hard parts of an organism and may take place through freezing in ice, preservation in bogs or tarpits, immersion in water, or inclusion in rock deposits. Fossilization is most apt to occur among marine animals and other organisms that live near water because of the favorable chances that their corpses will be buried and preserved on sea and river bottoms. On the land, conditions in caves, or where there is active volcanic activity, may be conducive to fossilization.

Places containing archaeological remains of previous human occupation are known as sites.

Sometimes human fossils are present at archaeological sites, but they may occur by themselves at fossil localities. Sites and localities are generally located by means of a survey of a region. While fossil localities are revealed by the presence of fossils, archaeological sites are revealed by the presence of artifacts. Irregularities of the ground surface, unusual soil discoloration, and unexpected variations in vegetation type and coloring may also indicate the location of a site. Ethnohistorical data—maps, documents, and folklore—may provide further clues to the location of archaeological sites. Sometimes both fossils and archaeological remains are discovered accidentally, for example, in plowing, quarrying, or building construction.

Once a site or locality has been selected for excavation, the area is divided and carefully marked with a grid system; the starting point of the dig is called the datum point. Each square within the grid is carefully excavated, and any archaeological or fossil remains are recovered through employment of various tools and screens; for very fine objects, the method of flotation is employed. The location of each artifact when found must be carefully noted. Once excavated, artifacts and fossils undergo further cleaning and preservation in the laboratory with the use of specialized tools and chemicals.

The durability of archaeological evidence depends upon climate and the nature of the artifacts. Inorganic materials are more resistant to decay than organic ones. However, given a very dry climate, even organic materials may be well preserved. Warm, moist climates as well as thick vegetation act to decompose organic material quickly, and even inorganic material may suffer from the effects of humidity and vegetation

growth. The durability of archaeological evidence is also dependent upon the social customs of ancient people.

Because excavation in fact destroys a site, the archaeologist must maintain a thorough record in the form of maps, descriptions, scale drawings, and photographs of every aspect of the excavation. All artifacts must be cleaned and classified before being sent to the laboratory for analysis. Often the shape and markings of artifacts can determine their function, and the analysis of vegetable and animal remains may provide information.

There are two kinds of methods for dating archaeological and fossil remains. Relative dating is a method of determining the age of objects relative to each other and includes the method of stratigraphy, based upon the position of the artifact or fossil in relation to different layers of soil deposits. The fluorine test is based upon the determination of the amount of fluorine deposited in the bones. The analysis of floral remains (including palynology) and faunal deposits is also widely employed. Methods of "absolute," or chronometric, dating include radiocarbon analysis, which measures the amount of carbon 14 that remains in organic objects; potassium-argon analysis, which measures the percentage of radioactive potassium that has decayed to argon in volcanic material; dendrochronology, dating based upon tree rings; and amino acid racemization, based upon changes from left- to right-handed amino acids in organic materials, especially egg shells. Other chronometric methods exist, such as electron spin resonance, but are not as widely used, owing to limited applicability, difficulty of application, expense, or as yet unproven reliability.

SUGGESTED READINGS

Fagan, B. M. (1995). *People of the earth: An introduction to world prehistory* (8th ed.). New York: HarperCollins.

There are a number of good texts that, like this one, try to summarize the findings of archaeologists on a worldwide scale. This book, being one of the more recent ones, is reasonably up to date.

Joukowsky, M. (1980). *A complete field manual of archaeology: Tools and techniques of field work for archaeologists.* Englewood Cliffs, NJ: Prentice-Hall.

This book, encyclopedic in its coverage, explains for the novice and professional alike all of the methods and techniques used by archaeologists in the field. Two concluding chapters discuss fieldwork opportunities and financial aid for archaeological research.

Sharer, R. J., & Ashmore, W. (1993). *Archaeology: Discovering our past* (2nd ed.). Palo Alto, CA: Mayfield.

One of the best presentations of the body of method, technique, and theory that most archaeologists accept as a foundation for their discipline. The authors confine themselves to the operational modes, guiding strategies, and theoretical orientations of anthropological archaeology in a manner well designed to lead the beginner into the discipline.

Shipman, P. (1981). *Life history of a fossil: An introduction to taphonomy and paleoecology.* Cambridge, MA: Harvard University Press.

In order to understand what a fossil has to tell us, one must know how it came to be where the paleoanthropologist found it. In this book, anthropologist-turned-science-writer Pat Shipman explains how animal remains are acted upon and altered from death to fossilization.

Thomas, D. H. (1989). *Archaeology* (2nd ed.). New York: Holt, Rinehart and Winston.

Some books tell us how to do archaeology, some tell us what archaeologists have found out, but this one tells us why we do archaeology. It does so in a coherent and thorough way, and Thomas's blend of ideas, quotes, biographies, and case studies makes for interesting reading.

White, P. (1976). *The past is human* (2nd ed.). New York: Maplinger.

This book, written for a nonprofessional audience, is a response to those advocating extraterrestrial interference and other mystical "explanations" of the human past.

CHAPTER
3

BIOLOGY AND
EVOLUTION

EVOLUTION HAS PRODUCED A VARIETY OF PRIMATES, RANGING
ALL THE WAY FROM LEMURS TO HUMANS. SUCH VARIETY IS NOT
THE RESULT OF PROGRESSIVE CHANGE, BUT RATHER THE
ADAPTATION OF ORGANISMS TO CONDITIONS AS THEY ARE. ONCE
THOSE CONDITIONS CHANGE, NEW ADAPTATIONS ARE REQUIRED.

CHAPTER PREVIEW

What Forces Are Responsible for the Diversity of Primates in the World Today?

Although all primates—lemurs, lorises, indriids, tarsiers, monkeys, apes, and humans—share a common ancestry, they have come to differ through the operation of evolutionary forces that have permitted them to adapt to a variety of environments in a variety of ways. Although biologists agree upon the fact of evolution, they are still unraveling the details of how it has proceeded.

What Are the Processes of Evolution?

Evolution works through mutation, producing genetic variation, which is then acted upon by drift (accidental changes in gene frequencies in a population), gene flow (the introduction of new genes from other populations), and natural selection. Natural selection is the adaptive mechanism of evolution that works through differential reproduction as individuals with genes for adaptive traits produce more offspring than those without.

How Do These Processes Produce New Forms of Organisms?

Populations may evolve in a linear manner, as small changes from one generation to another improve that population's adaptation. Through the accumulation of such changes over many generations, an older species may evolve into a new one. Or evolution may proceed in a branching manner in response to isolating mechanisms. These serve to separate populations, preventing gene flow between them so that drift and selection may proceed in different ways. This process may lead to the appearance first of divergent races and then of divergent species.

Humans have long had close contact with other animals. Some, such as dogs, horses, and cows, have lived close to people for so long that little attention is paid to their behavior. We are interested only in how well they do what they were bred for—companionship, racing, milk giving, or whatever. Domestic animals are so dependent on humans that they have lost many of the behavioral traits of their wild ancestors. Except to a small child, perhaps, and a dairy farmer, a cow is not a very interesting animal to watch.

By contrast, wild animals, especially exotic ones, have always fascinated people; circuses and zoos attest to this fascination. In cultures very different from those of the industrialized countries of the world, like those of some American Indians, people can have a special relationship with animals, believing themselves to be descended from them; such animals represent their "totems."

A curious feature of this interest is the desire of humans to see animals as mirror images of themselves, a phenomenon known as **anthropomorphism.** Stories in which animals talk, wear clothes, and exhibit human virtues and vices go back to antiquity. Many children today learn of Mickey Mouse, Garfield the Cat, or Kermit the Frog and Miss Piggy; the animals created by Walt Disney, Jim Henson, and others have become an integral part of contemporary North American culture. Occasionally one sees on television trained apes dressed like humans eating at a table, pushing a stroller, or riding a tricycle. They are amusing because they look so "human."

Over the ages, people have trained animals to perform tricks, making them mimic human behavior. But never did people suspect the full extent of the relationship they have with animals. The close biological tie between humans and the other **primates**—the group of animals which, besides

———

Anthropomorphism: The ascription of human attributes to nonhuman beings.

Primate order: The group of mammals that include lemurs, lorises, indriids, tarsiers, monkeys, apes, and humans.

———

humans, includes lemurs, lorises, indriids, tarsiers, monkeys, and apes—is now better understood. The diversity of primates seen today is the result of the operation of evolutionary forces that have permitted them to adapt to environments in a variety of ways. These evolutionary processes are the subject of this chapter.

HEREDITY

In order to understand how evolution works, one must first have some understanding of the mechanisms of heredity, because heritable variation constitutes the raw material for evolution. Our knowledge of the mechanisms of heredity is fairly recent; most of the fruitful research into the molecular level of inheritance has taken place in the past four decades. Although certain aspects remain puzzling, the outlines by now are reasonably clear.

The Transmission of Genes

Biologists call the actual units of heredity **genes,** a term that comes from the Greek word for "birth." The presence and activity of genes were originally deduced rather than observed by an Austrian monk, Gregor Mendel, in the nineteenth century. Working shortly after publication of Darwin's theory of evolution, Mendel sought to answer some of the riddles posed by that theory by experimenting with garden peas to determine how various traits are inherited. Specifically, he discovered what Darwin never knew: how variation, so important to his theory, was passed from one generation to the next. Interestingly, Mendel's work was generally ignored until it was rediscovered at the turn of the century. Since then, the function of genes has been pretty well known, even though no one really knew what genes were until quite recently.

———

Genes: Portions of DNA molecules that direct the development of observable or identifiable traits.

———

Gregor Mendel performed carefully controlled breeding experiments with garden peas that led to the discovery, in 1865, of the basic laws of heredity.

DNA

In 1953, James Watson and Francis Crick discovered that genes are actually portions of molecules of deoxyribonucleic acid, or **DNA.** DNA is a complex molecule with an unusual shape, rather like two strands of a rope twisted around one another (Fig. 3.1). The way that smaller molecules are arranged in this giant molecule is actually a code that contains information to direct the production of proteins. It is at this level that the development of certain traits occurs. The code directs the formation of such things as the protein that colors the iris of the eye (thereby determining eye color) or

---

DNA: The genetic material, deoxyribonucleic acid; a complex molecule with information to direct the synthesis of proteins. DNA molecules have the unique property of being able to produce exact copies of themselves.

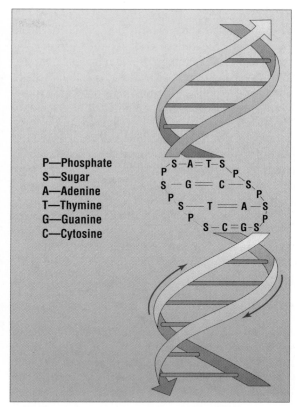

Figure 3.1   This diagrammatic representation of a portion of a deoxyribonucleic acid (DNA) molecule represents the double helix strands and the connecting nitrogenous base pairs. The helix strands are formed by alternating sugar and phosphate groups. The connection is produced by complementary bases—adenine, cytosine, guanine, and thymine—as shown for a section of the molecule.

P—Phosphate
S—Sugar
A—Adenine
T—Thymine
G—Guanine
C—Cytosine

the hemoglobin molecule in red blood cells. Recently there has been great progress in cracking the genetic code, in a series of events as fascinating as any spy story.

DNA molecules have the unique property of being able to produce exact copies of themselves. Thus a copy can be made and passed to another organism; as long as there are no errors made in the replication process, new organisms will contain genetic material exactly like that in ancestral organisms.

Genes

A gene is a segment of the DNA molecule that directs the development of particular observable or identifiable traits. Thus, when we speak of the gene for a human blood type in the A–B–O system, we are referring to the portion of a DNA molecule that contains the genetic code for the proteins that result in the attachment of different sugar molecules to certain other molecules carried on the surface of red blood cells, and which determine one's blood type. A gene, then, is not really a separate structure, as had once been imagined, but a location, like a dot on a map. These genes provide the blueprint for about 60,000 proteins that keep us alive and healthy. Interestingly, only about 10 percent of human DNA encodes proteins. As Jerold Lowenstein puts it, our DNA "like daytime television, is nine-tenths junk."[1] The genes themselves are split by long stretches of this "junk" DNA which, in the course of producing proteins, is metaphorically "snipped out" and left on the "cutting room floor."

Chromosomes

DNA molecules do not float freely about in our bodies; they are located on structures called **chromosomes** found in the nucleus of each cell. Chromosomes are probably nothing more than long strands of DNA combined with protein to produce structures that can actually be seen under a conventional light microscope. Each kind of organism has a characteristic number of chromosomes, which are usually found in pairs. For example, the body cells of the fruit fly each contain 4 pairs of chromosomes; those of humans contain 23 pairs; those of some brine shrimp have as many as 160 pairs. The two chromosomes in each pair contain genes for the same traits. The gene for eye color, for instance, will be found on each chromosome of a particular pair, but there may be variant forms of these genes. One might be for brown and the other for blue eyes. Forms of genes that are located on paired chromosomes and that code for different versions of the same trait are called **alleles.**

──────⊂∘∘⊃────⊂∘∘⊃──────

Chromosome: In the cell nucleus, long strands of DNA combined with a protein that can be seen under the microscope.

──────⊂∘∘⊃────⊂∘∘⊃──────

[1]Lowenstein, J. M. (1992). Genetic surprises. *Discover, 13* (12), 86.

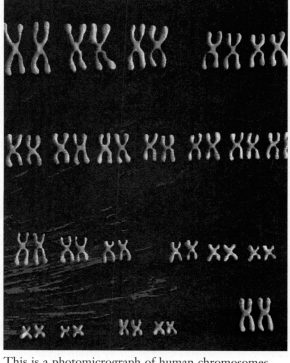

This is a photomicrograph of human chromosomes.

Cell Division

In order to grow and maintain good health, the body cells of an organism must divide and produce new cells. Cell division is initiated when the chromosomes, and hence the genes, replicate, forming a second pair that duplicates the original pair of chromosomes in the nucleus. This new pair then separates from the original pair, is surrounded by a membrane, and becomes the nucleus that directs the activities of a new cell. This kind of cell division is called **mitosis,** and it produces new cells that have exactly the same number of chromosome pairs, and hence genes, as did the parent cell.

──────⊂∘∘⊃────⊂∘∘⊃──────

Alleles: Alternate forms of a single gene.

Mitosis: A kind of cell division that produces new cells having exactly the same number of chromosome pairs, and hence genes, as the parent cell.

──────⊂∘∘⊃────⊂∘∘⊃──────

When new individuals are produced through sexual reproduction, the process involves the merging of two cells, one from each parent. If two regular body cells, each containing 23 pairs of chromosomes, were to merge, the result would be a new individual with 46 pairs of chromosomes; such an individual, if it lived at all, would surely be a monster. But this increase in chromosome number does not occur, because the sex cells that join to form a new individual are the product of a different kind of cell division, called **meiosis.**

Although meiosis begins like mitosis, with the replication and doubling of the original genes and chromosomes, it proceeds to divide that number into four new cells rather than two (Fig. 3.2).

Meiosis: A kind of cell division that produces the sex cells, each of which has half the number of chromosomes, and hence genes, as the parent cell.

Figure 3.2 In cell division both mitosis (a) and meiosis (b) create new cells. However, in mitosis the new cell has the same number of chromosomes as the parent cell, while in meiosis there are half of the chromosomes. Chromosomes in blue originally came from one parent, those in pink from the other.

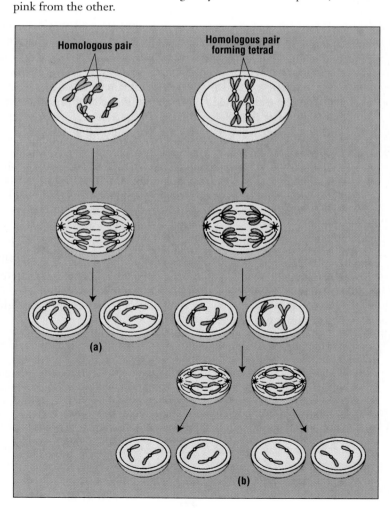

Thus each new cell has only half the number of chromosomes with their genes found in the parent cell. Human eggs and sperm, for example, have only 23 single chromosomes (half of a pair), whereas body cells have 23 pairs, or 46 chromosomes.

The process of meiotic division has important implications for genetics. Since paired chromosomes are separated, two different types of new cells will be formed; two of the four new cells will have one half of a pair of chromosomes, and the other two will have the second half of the original chromosome pair. Of course, this will not make any difference if the original pair was **homozygous,** or identical in genetic material. For example, if in both chromosomes of the original pair the gene for blood type in the A–B–O system was represented by the allele for Type A blood, then all new cells will have the "A" allele. But if the original pair was **heterozygous,** with the "A" allele on one chromosome and the allele for Type O blood on the other, then half of the new cells will contain only the "O" allele; the offspring have a 50–50 chance of getting either one. It is impossible to predict any single individual's genotype, or genetic composition, but statistical probabilities can be established.

What happens when a child inherits the allele for Type O blood from one parent and that for Type A from the other? Will the child have blood of Type A, O, or some mixture of the two? Many of these questions were answered by Mendel's original experiments.

Mendel discovered that certain alleles are able to mask the presence of others; one allele is dominant, whereas the other is recessive. Actually, it is the traits that are dominant or recessive, rather than the alleles themselves; geneticists merely speak of dominant and recessive alleles for the sake of convenience. Thus, one might speak of the allele for Type A blood as being dominant to the one for Type O. An individual whose blood type genes are heterozygous, with one "A" and one "O" al-

lele, will have Type A blood. Thus the heterozygous condition (AO) will show exactly the same physical characteristic, or **phenotype,** as the homozygous AA, even though the two have a somewhat different genetic composition, or **genotype.** Only the homozygous recessive genotype (OO) will show the phenotype of Type O blood.

The dominance of one allele does not mean that the recessive one is lost or in some way blended. A Type A heterozygous parent (AO) will produce sex cells containing both "A" and "O" alleles. Recessive alleles, such as that for albinism in humans, can be handed down for generations before they are matched with another recessive in the process of sexual reproduction and show up in the phenotype. The presence of the dominant allele simply renders the recessive allele inactive.

All of the traits Mendel studied in garden peas showed this dominant-recessive relationship, and so for some years it was believed that this was the only relationship possible. Later studies, however, have indicated that patterns of inheritance are not always so simple. In some cases, neither allele is dominant; they are both codominant. An example of codominance in human heredity can be seen also in the inheritance of blood types. Type A is produced by one allele; Type B by another. A heterozygous individual will have a phenotype of AB, since neither allele can dominate the other.

The inheritance of blood types points out another complexity of heredity. The number of alleles is by no means limited to two; certain traits seem to have three or more allelic genes. Of course, only one allele can appear on each of the pairs of chromosomes, so each individual is limited to two alleles.

Another discovery is the fact that dominance need not always be complete. This is the case with the alleles for normal **hemoglobin** (the protein

---

Homozygous: Refers to a chromosome pair that bears identical alleles for a single gene.

Heterozygous: Refers to a chromosome pair that bears different alleles for a single gene.

Phenotype: The physical appearance of an organism that may or may not reflect its genotype because the latter may or may not include recessive alleles.

Genotype: The actual genetic makeup of an organism.

Hemoglobin: The protein that carries oxygen in the red blood cells.

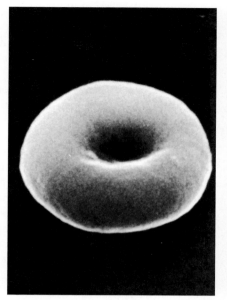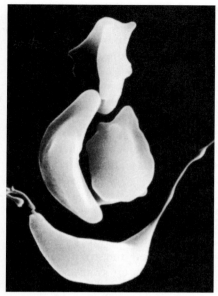

Sickle-cell anemia is caused by an abnormal hemoglobin, called "hemoglobin S." Those afflicted by the disease are homozygous for the allele S; heterozygotes are not afflicted. Shown are a normal red blood cell (left) and the sickle-shaped cells of the abnormal hemoglobin (right).

that carries oxygen in the red blood cells) and the abnormal hemoglobin that is responsible for **sickle-cell anemia** in humans. Sickle-cell anemia occurs in individuals who are homozygous for a particular allele. In those with two such alleles, the red blood cells take on a characteristic sickle shape, which, because they are more rapidly removed from circulation than normal cells, leads to anemia. To compound the problem, the sickle cells tend to clump together, blocking the capillaries and so causing tissue damage. Such individuals normally die before reaching adulthood. The homozygous dominant condition ($Hb^A Hb^A$; normal hemoglobin is known as hemoglobin A, not to be confused with blood type A) produces only normal molecules of hemoglobin while the heterozygous condition ($Hb^A Hb^S$) produces some normal and

some abnormal molecules; except under low-oxygen conditions, such individuals suffer no ill effects. Although the normal seems dominant to the abnormal, the dominance is incomplete, and therefore the other allele is not completely inactive. It is now believed that many instances in which phenotypes appear to indicate complete dominance may show incomplete dominance on the molecular level. We shall return to the sickle-cell condition later, for we now know that under certain conditions the heterozygous condition is actually more advantageous than is the "normal" homozygous condition.

Polygenetic Inheritance

So far, we have spoken as if the traits of organisms are single-gene traits, that is, the alleles of one particular gene determine one particular trait. Certainly this is the case with the A–B–O blood groups and some other things, but in humans, the most obvious traits are usually not single-gene traits. Skin color, for example, is programmed by the action of many genes, each of which produces a small effect. In such cases, we

Sickle-cell anemia: An inherited form of anemia caused by the red blood cells assuming a sickled shape.

speak of **polygenetic inheritance,** where two or more genes (as opposed to just two or more alleles) work together to affect one particular phenotypic character. Because so many genes are involved, each of which may have alternative alleles, it is difficult to unravel the genetic underpinnings of a trait like skin color. Theoretically, the observed range of variation in human skin color seems to require the presence of at least three, if not as many as six, separate genes, each of which produces a small additive effect.

POPULATION GENETICS

At the level of the individual, the study of genetics indicates the way that traits are transmitted from one generation to the next and enables a prediction about the chances that any given individual will display some phenotypic characteristic. At the level of the group, the study of genetics takes on additional significance, revealing mechanisms that support evolutionary interpretations of the diversity of life.

A key concept in genetics is that of the **population,** or a group of individuals within which breeding takes place. It is on the population level that natural selection takes place, as some members of the population produce more than their share of the next generation, while others produce less than their share. Thus, over a period of generations, the population shows a measure of adaptation to its environment due to this evolutionary mechanism.

THE STABILITY OF THE POPULATION

In theory, the characteristics of any given population should remain remarkably stable. And indeed, generation after generation, the bullfrogs in my farm pond, for example, look much alike, have the

Polygenetic inheritance: When two or more genes work together to affect a single phenotypic character.

Population: In biology, a group of similar individuals that can and do interbreed.

same calls, exhibit the same behavior when breeding. Another way to look at this remarkable consistency is to say that the **gene pool** of the population—the total number of different genes and alleles—seems to remain the same.

The theoretical stability of the gene pool of a population is not only easy to observe, it is also easy to understand. Mendel's experiments with garden peas, and all subsequent genetic experiments as well, have shown that, although some alleles may be dominant to others, the recessive alleles are not lost or destroyed. Statistically, a heterozygous individual has a 50 percent chance of passing on to the next generation the dominant allele; he or she also has a 50 percent chance of passing on the recessive allele. The recessive allele may again be masked by the presence of a dominant allele in the next generation, but it is there nonetheless and will be passed on again.

Since alleles are not "lost" in the process of reproduction, the frequency with which certain ones occur in the population should remain exactly the same from one generation to the next. The **Hardy-Weinberg Principle,** named for the English mathematician and German physician who worked it out in 1908, demonstrates algebraically that the percentage of individuals that are homozygous for the dominant allele, homozygous for the recessive allele, and heterozygous will remain the same from one generation to the next provided that these certain specified conditions are met: that mating is entirely random; that the population is sufficiently large for statistical averages to express themselves; that no new variants will be introduced into the population's gene pool; and that all individuals are equally successful at surviving and reproducing. In real life, however, these conditions are rarely met, as geographical, physiological, or behavioral factors may favor matings between certain individuals

Gene pool: The total genes of a population.

Hardy-Weinberg Principle: Demonstrates algebraically that the percentage of individuals that are homozygous for the dominant allele, homozygous for the recessive allele, and heterozygous should remain constant from one generation to the next, provided that certain specified conditions are met.

over others; as populations—on islands, for example—may be quite small; as new genetic variants may be introduced through mutation or gene flow; and as natural selection may favor the carriers of some alleles over others. Thus, changes in the gene pools of populations, without which there could be no evolution, can and do take place. Formally defined, **evolution** is a heritable change in genotype that becomes effective in the gene pool of a population.

FACTORS FOR CHANGE

Mutation

The ultimate source of change is **mutation** of genes. Mutation is an alteration of a gene that produces a new allele—one not inherited from an ancestor, but that is heritable by descendants. The fact is, every second that you read this, the DNA in each cell of your body is being damaged.[2] Fortunately, DNA repair enzymes exist that constantly scan DNA for mistakes, slicing out damaged segments and patching up gaps. Were it not for this repair mechanism, we would have diseases like cancer at a much higher frequency than we do, and we would not get a faithful copy of our parental inheritance. Not only would we not live long, but our species would not live long. But because the repair mechanism itself is not perfect, not all mistakes are corrected; otherwise, there would be no possibility for evolution to occur.

Geneticists have calculated the rate at which various types of mutant genes appear. In human populations, they run from a low of about 5 mutations per million sex cells formed, in the case of a gene abnormality that leads to the absence of an

---

Evolution: A heritable change in genotype that becomes effective in the gene pool of a population.

Mutation: Chemical alteration of a gene that produces a new allele.

---

[2]Culotta, E., & Koshland, Jr., D. E. (1994). DNA repair works its way to the top. *Science, 266,* 1926.

iris in the eye, to a high of about 100 per million, in the case of a gene involved in a form of muscular dystrophy. (Note that the human male ejaculates hundreds of millions of sperm cells at a single time.) The average is about 30 mutants per million. Although mutations sometimes produce marked abnormalities, the great majority of them produce more subtle effects.

Research with a variety of organisms indicates that certain factors increase the rate at which mutations occur. These include certain chemicals, such as some dyes and also some antibiotics; some chemicals used in the preservation of food also have this property. Another important cause of increased mutation rates is irradiation. The ultraviolet rays of sunshine are capable of producing mutations, as are X rays. Radioactive rays have the same mutation-causing effect, as was so sadly demonstrated by the high rates of mutation found in the children of survivors of the bombings of Hiroshima and Nagasaki.

In humans, as in all multicelled animals, the very nature of the genetic material itself ensures that mutations will occur. For instance, the fact that genes are split by stretches of "junk" DNA increases the chances that a simple editing mistake in the process of copying DNA will cause significant gene mutations. To cite one example, the gene for collagen (the main structural protein of the skin, bones, and teeth) is fragmented by no less than 50 segments of "junk" DNA. As a consequence, there are 50 chances for error each time the gene is copied. One result of this seemingly inefficient, if not dangerous situation is that it becomes possible to shuffle the gene segments themselves like a deck of cards, putting together new proteins with new functions. Although individuals may suffer as a result (the French artist Toulouse-Lautrec's growth abnormality resulted from a mutation of the collagen gene), it does make it possible for an evolving species to adapt more quickly to a new environment. Another source of genetic remodeling from within is the movement of whole DNA sequences from one locality or chromosome to another. This may disrupt the function of other genes or, in the case of so-called jumping genes, carry important functional messages of their own.

One recent finding is that humans have longer strings of repetitious DNA within and between genes than do other primates, so it is not surprising

French artist Henri Toulouse-Lautrec, whose growth abnormality resulted from a mutation of the collagen gene.

that we have a higher mutation rate. And a consequence of this is an increased incidence of such genetic diseases as Huntington's disease and Fragile X syndrome (a form of mental retardation).[3]

It is important to realize that mutations do not arise out of need for some new adaptation. Indeed, there is no tendency for the frequency of a particular mutation to correlate with the direction in which a population is evolving. They are purely chance events; what happens once they appear depends on whether they happen (by chance) to enhance the survival and reproductive success of the individuals who carry them.

Genetic Drift

Each individual is subject to a number of chance events that determine life or death. For example, an individual squirrel in good health and possessed of a number of advantageous traits may be killed in a forest fire; a genetically superior baby cougar

may not live longer than a day if its mother gets caught in an avalanche, whereas the weaker offspring of a mother that does not may survive. In a large population, such accidents of nature are unimportant; the accidents that preserve individuals with certain genes will be balanced out by the accidents that destroy them. However, in small populations, such averaging out may not be possible. Since human populations are so large, we might suppose that human beings are unaffected by chance events. While it is true that a rock slide that kills five campers whose home community has a total population of 100,000 is not statistically significant, a rock slide that killed five hunters from a small group of food foragers could significantly alter frequencies of alleles in the local gene pool. The average size of local groups of modern food foragers (people who hunt, fish, and gather other wild foods for subsistence) varies between about 25 and 50.

Another sort of chance event may occur when an existing population splits up into two or more new ones, especially if one of these new populations is founded by a particularly small number of individuals. What this amounts to is a sampling error; in such cases, it is unlikely that the gene frequencies of the smaller population will duplicate those of the larger population.

The effect of chance events on the gene pool of small populations is called **genetic drift.** Genetic drift plays an important role in causing the sometimes bizarre characteristics found in animals

Genetic drift, in the form of "sampling error," is responsible for the appearance of many exotic forms of life on oceanic islands, such as these marine iguanas on the Galapagos Islands.

[3]Glausiusz, J. (1995). Micro gets macro. *Discover, 16* (11), 40.

in isolated island populations. It is also likely to have been an important factor in human evolution, because until 10,000 years ago all humans were food foragers who probably lived in relatively small, self-contained populations.

Gene Flow

Another factor that brings change to the gene pool of a population is **gene flow,** or the introduction of new alleles from nearby populations. Gene flow occurs when previously separated groups are once again able to interbreed, as, for example, when a river that once separated two populations of small

mammals changes course. Migration of individuals or groups into the territory occupied by others may also lead to gene flow. This has been observed in several North American rodents that have been forced to leave their territory due to changes in environmental conditions. Gene flow has been an important factor in human evolution, both in terms of early human or near-human groups and in terms of current racial variation. For example, the last 400 years have seen the establishment of a new phenotype throughout much of Central and South America as a result of the introduction into the gene pool of Indians native to the area of genes from both the Spanish colonists and the Africans whom Europeans imported as slaves.

Genetic drift: Chance fluctuations of allele frequencies in the gene pool of a population.

Gene flow: The introduction of alleles from the gene pool of one population into that of another.

In Central America, gene flow between Native Americans (upper left), Spaniards (upper right), and Africans (lower left) has led to the emergence of a new phenotype (lower right).

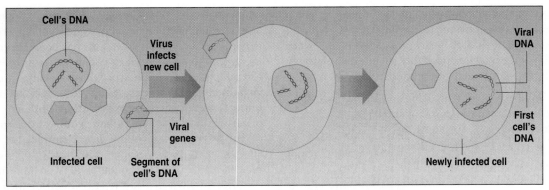

Figure 3.3 How viruses can transfer genetic material from one species to another.

Although we think of gene flow as occurring between populations of related organisms, it has recently become apparent that it can, in fact, occur between unrelated organisms as well. In this case, though, it does not take place by interbreeding, but through other means. Such gene transfer is well known between different kinds of bacteria, but seems to take place even among vertebrate animals. In some cases, the agent of transfer can be a retrovirus, one of the most diverse and widespread infectious entities of vertebrates.[4] How this takes place is illustrated in Fig. 3.3. Retroviruses are responsible for many diseases that affect humans, such as immunodeficiencies (including AIDS), hepatitis, anemias, and some neurological disorders.

Natural Selection

Although the factors listed above may produce change in a population, that change would not necessarily make the population better adapted to its biological and social environment. **Adaptation** is

---

Adaptation: A process by which organisms achieve a beneficial adjustment to an available environment, and the results of that process, the characteristics of organisms that fit them to the particular set of conditions of the environment in which they are generally found.

---

[4]Amábile-Cuevas, C. F., & Chicurel, M. E. (1993). Horizontal gene transfer. *American Scientist, 81,* 338.

both a process, by which organisms achieve a beneficial adjustment to an available environment, and the results of that process, the characteristics of organisms that fit them to the particular set of conditions of the environment in which they are generally found. Genetic drift, for example, often produces strange characteristics that have no survival value; mutant genes may be either helpful or harmful to survival, or simply neutral. It is the action of natural selection that makes evolutionary change adaptive.

Natural selection refers to the evolutionary process through which the environment exerts pressure that selects some individuals and not others to reproduce the next generation of the group. In other words, instead of a completely random selection of individuals whose traits will be passed on to the next generation, there is selection by the forces of nature. In the process, the frequency of genetic variants for harmful or maladaptive traits within the population is reduced while the frequency of genetic variants for adaptive traits is increased.

In popular writing, natural selection is often thought of as "survival of the fittest," the idea being that the physically weak, being unfit, are eliminated from the population by disease, predation,

---

Natural selection: The evolutionary process through which factors in the environment exert pressure that favors some individuals over others to produce the next generation.

CHARLES R. DARWIN

(1809–1882)

Grandson of Erasmus Darwin (a physician, scientist, poet, and originator of a theory of evolution himself), Charles Darwin began the study of medicine at the University of Edinburgh. Finding himself unfitted for this profession, he then went to Christ's College, Cambridge, to study theology. Upon completion of his studies there, he took the position of naturalist and companion to Captain Fitzroy on the *HMS Beagle*, which was about to embark on an expedition to various poorly mapped parts of the world. The voyage lasted for close to 5 years, taking Darwin along the coasts of South America, over to the Galapagos Islands, across the Pacific to Australia, and then across the Indian and Atlantic Oceans back to South America before returning to England. The observations he made on this voyage, and the arguments he had with the orthodox and dogmatic Fitzroy, had a powerful influence on the development of the ideas culminating in Darwin's most famous book, *On the Origin of Species*, which was published in 1859.

Contrary to what many people seem to think, Darwin did not "discover" or "invent" evolution. The general idea of evolution had been put forward by a number of writers, including his grandfather, long before Darwin's time. Nor is evolution a theory, as some people seem to think, any more than gravity is a theory. To be sure, there are competing theories of gravity—the Newtonian and Einsteinian—that seek to explain its workings, but the evidence in favor of gravity is overwhelming. Similarly, the evidence in favor of evolution is overwhelming, even though there have been competing theories that seek to explain how it works.

Darwin's contribution was one such theory—that of evolution through natural selection. His was the theory that was best able to account both for change within species and for the emergence of new species in purely naturalistic terms. As is usually the case with pioneering ventures, there were flaws in Darwin's original theory. Today, we can say that Darwin's basic idea has stood the test of scientific scrutiny remarkably well, and the evidence in its favor is about as good as we had for the theory that the earth is spherical, until we were able to put up an astronaut who could see with his own eyes that this indeed is the case.

---

or starvation. Obviously, survival has some bearing on natural selection; one need hardly point out that the dead do not reproduce. But there are many cases in which individuals survive, and even do quite well, but do not reproduce. They may be incapable of attracting mates, or they may be sterile, or they may produce offspring that do not survive after birth. For example, among the Uganda kob, a kind of antelope native to eastern Africa, males that are unable to attract females form all-male herds in which they live out their lives. As members of a herd, they are reasonably well protected against predators, and so they may survive to relatively old age. They do not, however, pass their genes on to succeeding generations. This is an instance of natural selection at work, leading to different rates of reproduction for different types of individuals within a population. Change brought about by natural selection in the frequency with which certain genetic variants appear in a population is actually a very slow process. For example, the present frequency of the sickle-cell allele is .05 in the entire U.S. population. A 5 percent reduction per generation (about 25 years) would take about 2000 years to reach a frequency of .01, assuming complete selection against those homozygous for the allele. Yet given the great time span involved—life on earth has existed for 3 to 4 billion years—even such small and slow changes will have a significant cumulative impact on both the genotypes and phenotypes of any population.

Natural selection, as it acts to promote change in gene frequencies, is referred to as **directional selection.** Another form it may take is

Directional selection: Natural selection as it acts to promote change in a population's gene pool.

stabilizing selection, in which it acts to promote stability rather than change. This occurs in populations that are already well adapted or where change would be disadvantageous. In humans, for instance, there has been no significant increase in brain size for the last 100,000 years or so. Stabilizing selection seems to be operating here, as the human birth canal is not adequate for the birth of larger-brained offspring. In cases where change is disadvantageous, natural selection will favor the retention of gene frequencies as they are. For this reason, the evolutionary history of most forms of life is not one of constant change, proceeding as a steady, stately progression over vast periods of time; rather, it is one of prolonged periods of stability punctuated by shorter periods of change (or extinction) when altered conditions require new adaptations.

Discussions of the action of natural selection typically focus on anatomical or structural changes, such as the evolutionary change in the types of teeth found in primates; ample evidence (fossilized teeth, for example) exists to interpret such changes. By extrapolation, biologists assume that the same mechanisms work on behavioral traits as well. It seems reasonable that a hive of bees capable of communicating the location of nectar-bearing

---

Stabilizing selection: Natural selection as it acts to promote stability, rather than change, in a population's gene pool.

---

flowers would have a significant survival advantage over those that must search for food by trial and error. Natural selection of behavioral and social traits was probably a particularly important influence on human evolution, since in the primates, social mechanisms began to replace physical structures for food getting, defense, and mate attraction.

ADAPTATION

As a consequence of the process of natural selection, those populations that do not become extinct generally become well adapted to their environments. Anyone who has ever looked carefully at the plants and animals that survive in the deserts of the western United States can cite many instances of adaptation. For example, members of the cactus family have extensive root networks close to the surface of the soil, enabling them to soak up the slightest bit of moisture; they are able to store large quantities of water whenever it is available; they are shaped so as to expose the smallest possible surface to the dry air and are generally leafless as adults, thereby preventing water loss through evaporation; and a covering of spines discourages animals from chewing into the juicy flesh of the plant.

Desert animals are also adapted to their environment. The kangaroo rat can survive without drinking water; many reptiles live in burrows where the temperature is lower; most animals are nocturnal, or active only in the cool of the night.

An example of stabilizing selection: the brain of the modern skull on the left is no bigger than that in the ca. 50,000-year-old skull on the right, even though the outer appearance of the skulls has changed.

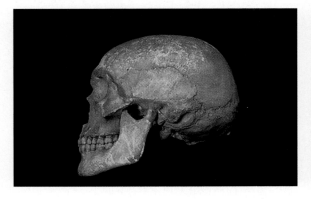
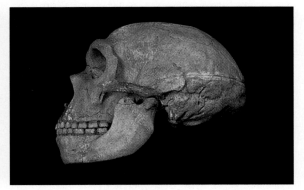

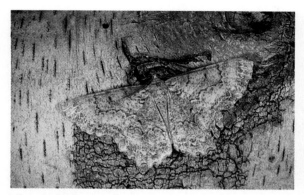 

The moths shown in these two pictures are varieties of a single species. While the mottled brown variant is well-camouflaged on relatively clean tree trunks, it is readily visible on sooty tree trunks. The reverse is true for the black variant, which became especially common when coal fueled British industry.

Many of the stories traditionally offered to explain observable cases of adaptation rely heavily on the purposeful acts of a world creator. The legend of Coyote and Wishpoosh (Chapter 1) is one such example; the belief popular among Europeans early in the nineteenth century that God created each animal separately to occupy a specific place in a hierarchical ladder of being is another.

The adaptability of organic structures and functions, no matter how much a source of wonder and fascination, nevertheless falls short of perfection. This is so because natural selection can only work with what the existing store of genetic variation provides; it cannot create something entirely new. That exquisite design is often not the rule is illustrated by the pains of aching backs, the annoyances of hernias, and problems with hemorrhoids that we humans must endure because the body of a four-footed vertebrate, designed for horizontal posture, has been "jury rigged" to be held vertically above the two hind limbs. Furthermore, the structural alterations that enable us to walk erect have made it more difficult than it is for any other species of mammal to bear offspring. Yet, these defects have been perpetuated by natural selection, because they are outweighed by other aspects of human adaptation that enhance the reproductive success of the species as a whole.

The Case of Sickle-Cell Anemia

Among human beings, a particularly well-studied case of an adaptation paid for by the misery of many individuals brings us back to the case of sickle-cell anemia. Sickle-cell anemia first came to the attention of geneticists when it was observed that most North Americans who suffer from it are "black." Investigation traced the abnormality to populations that live in a clearly defined belt throughout central Africa (although brought to North America from central Africa, the abnormality also exists in some non-African populations, as will be noted below).

Geneticists were curious to know why such a deleterious hereditary disability persisted in these populations. According to the theory of natural selection, any alleles that are harmful will tend to disappear from the group, since the individuals who are homozygous for the abnormality generally die—are "selected out"—before they are able to reproduce. Why, then, had this seemingly harmful condition remained in populations from central Africa?

The answer to this mystery began to emerge when it was noticed that the areas in which sickle-cell anemia is prevalent are also areas in which falciparum malaria is common (Fig. 3.4). This severe form of malaria causes high fevers that significantly interfere with the reproductive abilities of those who do not actually die from the disease. Moreover, it was discovered that the same hemoglobin abnormalities are found in residents of parts of the Arabian Peninsula, Greece, Algeria, and Syria as well as in certain East Indians, all of whom also live in regions where falciparum malaria is common. Further research established that the abnormal hemoglobin was associated with an increased ability to survive the effects of the malarial parasite; it seems that the effects of the abnormal

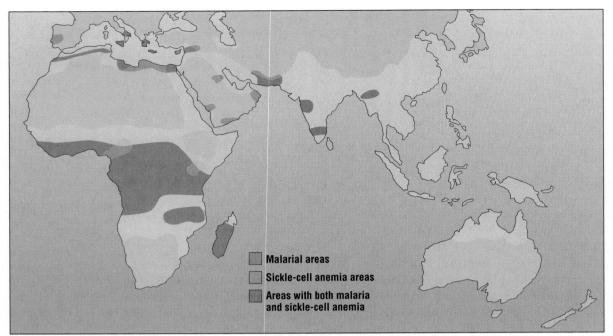

Figure 3.4   The allele that, in homozygotes, causes sickle-cell anemia makes heterozygotes resistant to the ill effects of falciparum malaria. Thus, the allele is most common in populations native to regions where this form of malaria is common.

hemoglobin in limited amounts were less injurious than the effects of the malarial parasite.

Thus, selection favored heterozygous individuals ($Hb^A Hb^S$). The loss of alleles for abnormal hemoglobin caused by the death of those homozygous for it (from sickle-cell anemia) was balanced out by the loss of alleles for normal hemoglobin, as those homozygous for it experienced reproductive failure.

This example also points out how adaptations tend to be specific; the abnormal hemoglobin was an adaptation to the particular parts of the world in which the malarial parasite flourished. When Africans adapted to that region came to North America, where falciparum malaria is unknown, what had been an adaptive characteristic became an injurious one. Where there is no malaria to attack those with normal hemoglobin, the abnormal hemoglobin becomes comparatively disadvantageous. Although the rates of sickle-cell trait are still relatively high among African Americans—about 9 percent show the sickling trait—this represents a significant decline from the approximately 22 percent who are estimated to have shown the trait when the first slaves

were brought from Africa. A further decline over the next several generations is to be expected, as selection pressure continues to work against it.

This example also points out the important role culture may play even with respect to biological adaptation. In West Africa, falciparum malaria was not a significant problem until humans abandoned food foraging for farming a few thousand years ago. In order to farm, they had to clear areas of the natural forest cover. In the forest, decaying vegetation on the forest floor had imparted an absorbent quality to the ground so that the heavy rainfall of the region rapidly soaked into the soil. But once stripped of its natural vegetation, the soil lost this quality. Furthermore, the forest canopy was no longer there to break the force of the rainfall, and so the impact of the heavy rains tended to compact the soil further. The result was that stagnant puddles commonly formed after rains, and these were perfect for the breeding purposes of mosquitos. Mosquitos then began to flourish, and it is mosquitos that carry the malarial parasite and inflict it on humans. Thus, humans unwittingly created the kind of environment that made a hitherto disadvantageous trait, the abnormal hemoglobin associated with sickle-cell anemia, advantageous.

Although it is true that all living organisms have many adaptive characteristics, it is not true that all characteristics are adaptive. All male mammals, for example, possess nipples, even though they serve no useful purpose. To female mammals, however, nipples are essential to reproductive success, which is why males have them. The two sexes are not separate entities, shaped independently by natural selection, but are variants upon a single ground plan, elaborated in later embryology. Precursors of mammary glands are built in all mammalian fetuses, enlarging later in the development of females, but remaining small and without function in males.

Nor is it true that current utility is a reliable guide to historical origin. For one thing, nonadaptive characters may be co-opted for later utility following origins as developmental consequences of changing patterns in embryonic and postnatal growth. The unusually large size of the kiwi egg, for example, enhances the survivability of kiwi chicks, in that they are particularly large and capable when hatched. Nevertheless, kiwi eggs probably did not evolve because they are adaptive. Kiwis evolved from large, moa-sized ancestors, and in birds, egg size reduces at a slower rate than does body size. Therefore, the outsized eggs of kiwi birds seem to be no more than a developmental by-product of a reduction in body size.[5] Similarly, an existing adaptation may come under strong selective pressure for some new purpose, as did insect wings. These did not arise so that insects might fly, but rather as gills that were used to "row," and later skim, across the surface of the water.[6] Later, the larger ones by chance proved useful for purposes of flight.

Evolution of Populations

One consequence of the process of natural selection is that a population may become increasingly well adapted to its environment. This kind of evolutionary change can be thought of as a refinement of the organism. As it moves from the rather generalized prototype to ever more specialized versions, the organism becomes better adapted; each new "model" replaces the old in a process somewhat analogous to the changes that have been made to automobiles since their first appearance. Still, a car remains a car, no matter how "improved" the latest model may have become; it has not been transformed into something radically different. The same principle holds for linear evolution (Fig. 3.5 top). Ultimately, stabilizing selection is likely to take over, as available alleles reach their most adaptive frequencies in a species' gene pool. There will be little change thereafter, so long as the adaptation remains viable.

Ironically, a species may become extinct if it becomes too well adapted. If the environment changes for some reason, those organisms most highly adapted to the old environment will have the greatest difficulty surviving in a new one. Such changes took place a number of times during the course of vertebrate evolution; one of the most dramatic examples was the sudden extinction of the dinosaurs. In such cases, it is usually the more generalized organisms that survive; later they may give rise to new lines of specialists.

But not all evolution is a linear progression from one form to more specialized forms of the same type. Evolution is also **divergent,** or branching

Divergent evolution: An evolutionary process in which an ancestral population gives rise to two or more descendant populations that differ from one another.

This X-ray illustrates the unusually large size of a kiwi's egg.

[5]Gould, S. J. (1991). *Bully for brontosaurus* (pp. 109–123). New York: W. W. Norton.

[6]Kaiser, J. (1994). A new theory of insect wing origins takes off. *Science, 266,* 363.

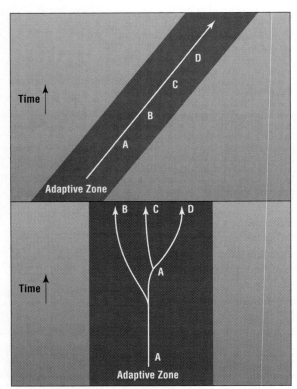

Figure 3.5   Linear evolution (top) occurs when relatively small-scale changes accumulate over time, gradually transforming an old species into a new one. Divergent evolution (bottom) occurs as different populations become reproductively isolated, resulting in an increase in the number of species.

(Fig. 3.5 bottom). This happens when a single ancestral species gives rise to two or more descendant species. Divergent evolution is probably responsible for much of the diversity of life to be observed today. Evolution may also be **convergent,** when two dissimilar forms develop greater similarities—birds and bats, for example. Convergent evolution takes place in circumstances where an environment exerts similar pressures on different organisms, so that unrelated species become more like one another. Because evolution can take many different courses, it is often difficult to reconstruct the sequence of events that led to the

Convergent evolution: A process in which two phylogenetically unrelated organisms develop greater similarities.

emergence of any given group or species, especially when that evidence, such as fossil remains, is often fragmentary and incomplete. We are fortunate, though, in that the fossil record for human evolution is particularly rich.

Speciation

Both linear and divergent evolution can result in the establishment of a new **species.** The term *species* is usually defined as a population or group of populations that is mechanically capable of interbreeding and reproductively isolated from other such populations. Thus the bullfrogs in my farm pond are the same species as those in my neighbor's pond, even though the two populations may never actually interbreed; in theory, they are capable of it if they are brought together. This definition is not altogether satisfactory, because isolated populations may be in the process of evolving into different species, and it is hard to tell exactly when they become separate. For example, all dogs belong to the same species, but a male Saint Bernard and a female Chihuahua are not capable of producing offspring; even if they could somehow manage the feat of copulation, the Chihuahua would die trying to give birth to such large pups. On the other hand, Alaskan sled dogs are able to breed with wolves, even though they are of different species. In nature, however, wolves most often mate with their own kind. Although all species definitions are relative rather than absolute, the modern concept of species puts more stress on the question of whether breeding actually takes place in the wild than on the more academic question of whether breeding is technically feasible.

Populations within species that are capable of interbreeding but may not regularly do so are called **races.** Evolutionary theory suggests that

Species: In biology, a population or group of populations that is capable of interbreeding, but that is reproductively isolated from other such populations.

Race: A population of a species that differs in the frequency of some allele or alleles from other populations of the same species.

species evolve from races through the accumulation of differences in the gene pools of the separated groups. This can happen, however, only in situations where one race is isolated from others of its species for prolonged periods of time. There is nothing inevitable about races evolving into new species; because they are by definition genetically open—that is, members of different races are capable of interbreeding—races are impermanent and subject to reamalgamation.

In the case of humans, as discussed in Chapter 13, the race concept is difficult to apply. For one thing, the human propensity for gene flow makes the definition of biological races particularly arbitrary; for another, there has been a deplorable tendency to mix cultural with biological phenomena under the heading of "race."

Isolating Mechanisms

Certain factors, known as **isolating mechanisms,** separate breeding populations, leading to the appearance first of divergent races and then divergent species. This happens as mutations may appear in one of the isolated populations but not in the other, as genetic drift affects the two populations in different ways, and as selective pressures

may come to differ slightly in the two places. Because isolation prevents gene flow, changes that affect the gene pool of one population cannot be introduced into the gene pool of the other.

Some isolating mechanisms are geographical, preventing gene flow between members of separated populations as a result of traveling individuals or bands. Anatomical structure can also serve as an isolating mechanism, as we saw in the case of the Saint Bernard and the Chihuahua. Other physical isolating factors include early miscarriage of the offspring; weakness or presence of maladaptive traits that cause early death in the offspring; or, as in the case of horses and asses, sterility of the hybrid offspring (mules).

Although physical barriers to reproduction may develop in geographical isolation, as genetic differences accumulate in the gene pools of separate populations, they may also result from accidents as cells undergo meiosis. In the course of such accidents

Isolating mechanisms: Factors that separate breeding populations, creating divergent races and ultimately (if maintained) divergent species.

Although zebras and ponies can produce live offspring like the one shown here, sterility of the offspring maintains the reproductive isolation of the parental species.

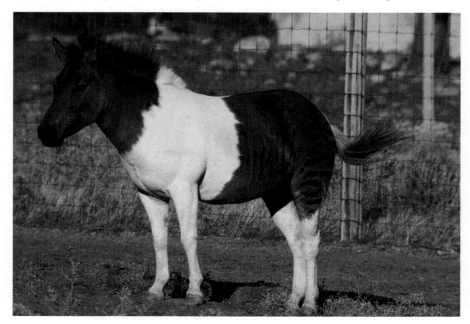

genetic material may be broken off, transposed, or transferred from one chromosome to another. Even a relatively minor mutation, if it involves a gene that regulates the growth and development of an organism, may have a major effect on its adult form.

Isolating mechanisms may also be social rather than physical. Speciation due to this mechanism is particularly common among birds. For example, cuckoos (birds that do not build nests of their own but lay their eggs in other birds' nests) attract mates by mimicking the song of the bird species whose nests they usurp; thus cuckoos that are physically capable of mating may have different courtship behaviors, which effectively isolates them from others of their kind.

Social isolating mechanisms are thought to have been important factors in human evolution. They continue to play a part in the maintenance of so-called racial barriers. Although mating is physically possible between any two mature humans of the opposite sex, the awareness of social and cultural differences often makes the idea dis-tasteful, perhaps even unthinkable; in India, for example, someone of an upper caste would not think of marrying an "untouchable." This isolation results from the culturally implanted concept of a significant difference between "us" and "them." Yet, as evidenced by the blending of human populations that has so often taken place in the world, people are also capable of suspending, or even reasoning away, social isolating mechanisms that would, in the case of other animals, lead separate races to evolve into separate species. Such speciation is very unlikely in *Homo sapiens.*

The Nondirectedness of Evolution

In the popular mind, evolution is often seen as leading in a predictable and determined way from one-celled organisms, through various multicelled forms, to humans, who occupy the top rung of a "ladder of progress." The fallacy of this notion is neatly made clear by paleontologist Stephen Jay Gould.

Original Study
Evolution and the Improbabilities of History[7]

Classical determination and complete predictability may prevail for simple macroscopic objects subject to a few basic laws of motion (balls rolling down inclined planes in high school physics experiments), but complex historical objects do not lend themselves to such easy treatment. In the history of life, all results are products of long series of events, each so intricately dependent upon particular environments and previous histories that we cannot predict their future course with any certainty. The historical sciences try to explain unique situations—immensely complex historical accidents. Evolutionary biologists, as historical scientists, do not expect detailed repetition and cannot use the actual results of history to establish probabilities for recurrence (would a Caesar again die brutally in Rome if we could go back to Australopithecus in Africa and start anew?). Evolutionists view the origin of humans (or any particular butterfly, roach, or starfish) as a historical event of such complexity and improbability that we would never expect to see anything exactly like it again (or elsewhere)—hence our strong opposition to the specific argument about humanoids on other worlds. Consider just two of the many reasons for uniqueness of complex events in the history of life.

1. Mass extinction as a key influence upon the history of life on earth. Dinosaurs died some 65 million years ago in the great worldwide Cretaceous extinction that also snuffed out about half the species of

shallow water marine invertebrates. They had ruled terrestrial environments for 100 million years and would probably reign today if they had survived the debacle. Mammals arose at about the same time and spent their first 100 million years as small creatures inhabiting the nooks and crannies of a dinosaur's world. If the death of dinosaurs had not provided their great opportunity, mammals would still be small and insignificant creatures. We would not be here, and no consciously intelligent life would grace our earth. Evidence gathered since 1980 indicates that the impact of an extraterrestrial body triggered this extinction. What could be more unpredictable and unexpected than comets or asteroids striking the earth literally out of the blue? Yet without such impact, our earth would lack consciously intelligent life. Many great extinctions (several larger than the Cretaceous event) have set basic patterns in the history of life, imparting an essential randomness to our evolutionary pageant.

2.   Each species as a concatenation of improbabilities. Any animal species—human, squid, or coral—is the latest link of an evolutionary chain stretching through thousands of species back to the inception of life. If any of these species had become extinct or evolved in another direction, final results would be markedly different. Each chain of improbable events includes adaptations developed for a local environment and only fortuitously suited to support later changes. Our ancestors among fishes evolved a peculiar fin with a sturdy, central bony axis. Without a structure of this kind, landbound descendants could not have supported themselves in a nonbuoyant terrestrial environment. (Most lineages of fishes did not and could not evolve terrestrial descendants because they lacked fins of this form.) Yet these fins did not evolve in anticipation of future terrestrial needs. They developed as adaptations to a local environment in water, and were luckily suited to permit a new terrestrial direction later on. All evolutionary sequences include such a large set of *sine quibus non* [literally: "without which things it is not possible"], a fortuitous series of accidents with respect to future evolutionary success. Human brains and bodies did not evolve along a direct and inevitable ladder, but by a circuitous and tortuous route carved by adaptations evolved for different reasons, and fortunately suited to later needs.

[7]Gould, S. J. (1985). *The flamingo's smile: Reflections in natural history* (pp. 408–410). New York: W. W. Norton.

The history of life is not one of progressive advancement in complexity; if anything, it is one of proliferation of enormously varied designs that subsequently have been restricted to a few highly successful forms. Even at that, imperfections remain. As Gould so aptly puts it:

Our world is not an optimal place, fine tuned by omnipotent forces of selection. It is a quirky mass of imperfections, working well enough (often admirably); a jury-rigged set of adaptations built of curious parts made available by past histories in different contexts.[8]

[8]Ibid, p. 54.

CHAPTER SUMMARY

Evolution may be defined as a heritable change in genotype that becomes effective in the gene pool of a population. Genes, the actual units of heredity, are portions of molecules of DNA (deoxyribonucleic acid), a complex molecule resembling two strands of rope twisted around one another. The way that smaller molecules are arranged in this giant molecule is actually a code that contains information to direct the synthesis of proteins. DNA molecules have the unique property of being able to produce exact copies of themselves. As long as no errors are made in the process of replication, new organisms will contain genetic material exactly like that in ancestral organisms.

A gene is a unit of the DNA molecule that directs the development of observable traits, for example, blood type. Human DNA provides the blueprint for about 60,000 proteins that keep us alive and healthy.

DNA molecules are located on chromosomes, structures found in the nucleus of each cell. Each kind of organism has a characteristic number of chromosomes, which are usually found in pairs. Humans have 23 pairs. Genes that are located on paired chromosomes and coded for different versions of the same trait are called alleles.

Mitosis, one kind of cell division, begins when the chromosomes (hence the genes) replicate, forming a second pair that duplicates the original pair of chromosomes in the nucleus. It results in new cells with exactly the same number of chromosome pairs as the parent cell. Meiosis, a different kind of cell division, results from sexual reproduction. It begins with the replication of original chromosomes, but these are divided into four cells, each containing 23 single chromosomes.

The Austrian monk Gregor Mendel studied the mechanism of inheritance with garden peas. He discovered that some alleles are able to mask the presence of others. They are called dominant. The allele that is not expressed is recessive. The allele for Type A blood in humans, for example, is dominant to the allele for Type O blood.

Phenotype refers to the physical characteristics of an organism, whereas genotype refers to its genetic composition. Two organisms may have the same phenotype, but different genotypes.

A key concept is that of population, or a group of similar individuls within which most breeding takes place. It is populations, rather than individuals, that evolve. The total number of different genes and alleles available to a population is called its gene pool. The frequency with which certain genes occur in the same gene pool theoretically remains the same from one generation to another; this is known as the Hardy-Weinberg Principle. Nonetheless, change does take place in gene pools as a result of several factors.

The ultimate source of genetic change is mutation. These are accidents that cause changes in sequences of DNA. Although mutations are inevitable given the nature of cellular chemistry, extrinsic factors, such as heat, certain chemicals, or various kinds of radiation can increase the mutation rate.

The effects of chance events (other than mutations) on the gene pool of a small population is called genetic drift. Genetic drift may have been an important factor in human evolution because until 10,000 years ago all humans probably lived in relatively small populations. Another factor that brings change to the gene pool of a population is gene flow, or the introduction of new variants of genes from nearby populations. Gene flow occurs when previously separated groups are once able to breed again. It may also occur as retroviruses transfer DNA from members of one species to another.

Natural selection is the force that makes evolutionary change adaptive. It reduces the frequency of alleles for harmful or maladaptive traits within a population and increases the frequency of alleles for adaptive traits. Adaptation is the process by which organisms achieve a beneficial adjustment to an available environment, and the results of the process are the characteristics of organisms that fit them to the particular set of conditions of the environment in which they are generally found. A well-studied example of adaptation through natural selection in humans is inheritance of the trait for sickling red blood cells. The sickle-cell trait, caused by the inheritance of an abnormal form of hemoglobin, is an adaptation to life in regions in which falciparum malaria is common. In these regions, the sickle-cell trait plays a beneficial role, but in other parts of the world, the sickling trait is no longer advantageous, while the associated sickle-cell anemia remains injurious. Geneticists predict that as malaria is brought under control, within several generations, there will be a decline in the number of individuals who carry the allele responsible for sickle-cell anemia.

Evolution is the process whereby organisms change into a new form from a previous form. Evolution is not necessarily a linear progression. It may be divergent, or branching; or it may be convergent, where two dissimilar forms develop similarities.

A species is a population or a group of populations that is mechanically capable of interbreeding. The concept of species is relative rather than ab-solute; whether breeding takes place in the wild is more important than the academic question of whether it is technically feasible. Populations within species that are capable of interbreeding but do so to a limited extent are called races. While species are reasonably discreet and stable units in nature, races are impermanent and subject to reamalgamation.

Isolating mechanisms serve to separate breeding populations, creating first divergent races and then (if isolation continues) divergent species. Isolating mechanisms can be geographical; physical, as in the differing anatomical structures of the Saint Bernard and Chihuahua; or social, such as in the caste system of India.

Evolution is not a "ladder of progress" leading in a predictable and determined way to ever more complex forms. Rather, it has produced, through a series of accidents, a diversity of enormously varied designs that subsequently have been restricted to a lesser number of still less-than-perfect forms.

SUGGESTED READINGS

Berra, T. M. (1990). *Evolution and the myth of creationism.* Stanford: Stanford University Press.

Written by a zoologist, this book is a basic guide to the facts in the debate over evolution. It is not antireligion, but a successful effort to assist in understanding the scientific basis for evolution.

Cavalli-Sforza, L. L. (1977). *Elements of human genetics.* Menlo Park, CA: Benjamin.

A short book for those who want to know something about genetics and who would like basic genetic principles discussed from a "human" angle.

Edey, M. A., & Johanson, D. (1989). *Blueprints: Solving the mystery of evolution.* Boston: Little, Brown.

This book is about the evolution of the idea of evolution, told as a scientific detective story. As much about the discoverors of evolution as it is about their discoveries, the book provides insights into the workings of science and gives readers the information they need to ponder the significance of our newfound ability, through genetic engineering, to actually direct the evolution of living things, including ourselves.

Gould, S. J. (1991). *Bully for brontosaurus: Reflections in natural history.* New York: Norton.

A collection of Gould's essays from *Natural History* magazine, in which he ranges over various issues in evolutionary biology. No one is better at explaining how evolution works, or exposing common fallacies, than Gould. Collections of his earlier essays, also highly recommended, are *Ever Since Darwin, The Panda's Thumb, Hens' Teeth and Horses' Toes,* and *The Flamingo's Smile.*

Miller, J., & Van Loon, B. (1982). *Darwin for beginners.* New York: Pantheon.

Witty, clever, yet informative and sophisticated, this is a "fun" introduction to Darwin's life and thought.

Woodward, V. (1992). *Human heredity and society.* St. Paul: West.

Written for college students, this book discusses the implications of our knowledge of modern genetics for public policy. Concerned with the rise of interest in genetic engineering for the fixing of social ills, Woodward's premise is that it is as important to know what genes *are not,* as what they are.

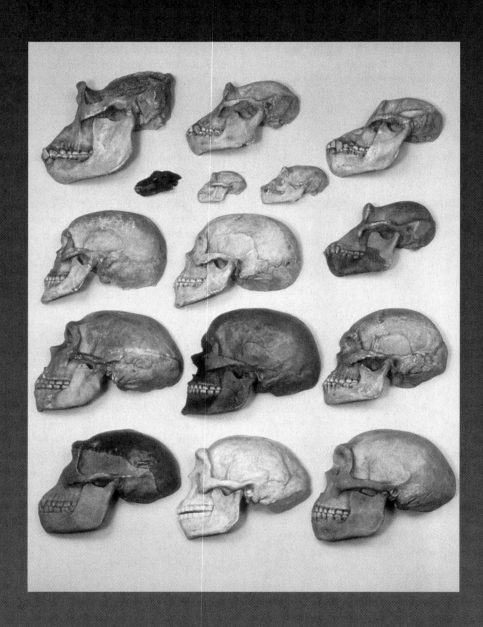

II
PRIMATE EVOLUTION AND THE EMERGENCE OF THE HOMININES

CHAPTER 4
MONKEYS, APES, AND HUMANS: THE MODERN PRIMATES

CHAPTER 5
FOSSIL PRIMATES

CHAPTER 6
THE EARLIEST HOMININES

In Chapter 1, we saw how the Nez Perce Indians of North America explained their existence in the world. Indeed, all human cultures of which we have record have grappled with such age-old questions as where do we come from and what is our place in the overall scheme of things. Each culture has answered these questions in its own way, through bodies of myth and folklore, as did the Nez Perce. It was not until the twentieth century that hard scientific evidence was available to apply to these questions. In particular, as physical anthropologists and archaeologists have unearthed the bones and tools of our earliest ancestors, we have begun to glimpse the outline of a fantastic saga in which a tropical-dwelling apelike creature is transformed into a creative being capable of inventing solutions to problems of existence, rather than passively accepting what the environment and its own biology dictate.

This section of the book discusses developments that set the stage for this transformation. We begin, in Chapter 4, with a review of the modern primates (the zoological order to which primates belong), in order to understand how we humans are like the other primates. In particular, we can begin to appreciate that many of the physical characteristics we think of as distinctively human are simply exaggerated versions of characteristics common to other primates. For example, primate brains tend to be large and heavy relative to body size and weight; in humans, this trait is realized to a greater degree than it is in other primates. We can begin to appreciate as well the kind of behavioral versatility of which present-day members of this order are capable. In the range of modern primate behavior patterns, we find clues to patterns that were characteristic of primates that lived in the past, from which humans were descended.

Knowledge of the modern primates sets the stage for a review of the fossil evidence for primate evolution. In Chapter 5, the important fossils are interpreted in light of evolutionary theory, our understanding of the biological variation of modern primates, and the behavioral correlates of that variation. This brings us to the apelike creatures of 8 to 16 million years ago, from some of which human ancestors evolved. Our early apelike ancestors seem to have spent more time on the ground and probably possessed mental abilities more or less equivalent to those of a modern chimpanzee. Because they were small and vulnerable, we think that the greatest measure of reproductive success came to those that were able to rear up on their hind limbs and scan the savanna, threaten preda-

tors with their forelimbs, transport food to a tree or other place where it could be eaten in relative safety, and transport offspring instead of relying on them to hang on by themselves, all the while managing to keep cool in the heat of the day.

With the appearance by 4 million years ago of *Australopithecus*, one of the earliest true hominines, the stage was set for the human transformation. *Australopithecus* may best be thought of as an apelike human; it walked bipedally in a fully human manner, but its mental abilities do not seem to have differed greatly from those of its ancestors of a few million years earlier. This implies essentially apelike behavior patterns, and it is appropriate to complete this section of the book with a chapter on *Australopithecus*.

MONKEYS, APES, AND HUMANS: THE MODERN PRIMATES

FROM STUDYING THOSE PRIMATES MOST CLOSELY RELATED TO US, AS WELL AS THOSE (LIKE BABOONS) THAT LIVE IN ENVIRONMENTS SIMILAR TO THOSE FACED BY OUR OWN EARLY ANCESTORS, WE CAN RECONSTRUCT MUCH OF WHAT LIFE WAS LIKE FOR OUR ANCESTORS.

CHAPTER PREVIEW

What Is the Place of Humanity Among the Other Animals?

Humans are classified by biologists as belonging to the primate order, a group that also includes lemurs, lorises, tarsiers, monkeys, and apes. They are so classified on the basis of shared characteristics of anatomy, physiology, protein structure, and even the genetic material itself. Among the primates, humans resemble monkeys, but most closely resemble apes.

What Are the Implications of the Shared Characteristics Between Humans and the Other Primates?

The similarities on which the modern classification of animals is based are indicative of evolutionary relationships. Therefore, by studying the anatomy, physiology, and molecular structure of the other primates, we can gain a better understanding of what human characteristics we owe to our general primate ancestry and what traits are uniquely ours as humans. Such studies indicate that many of the differences between apes and humans are differences of degree rather than kind.

Why Do Anthropologists Study the Social Behavior of Monkeys and Apes?

By studying the behavior of apes and monkeys living today—especially those most closely related to us and those that have adapted to life on savannas to which our earliest ancestors adapted—we may find essential clues in the reconstruction of adaptations and behavior patterns involved in the emergence of our earliest ancestors.

All living creatures, be they great or small, fierce or timid, active or inactive, face a fundamental problem in common—that of survival. Simply put, unless they are able to adapt themselves to some available environment, they cannot survive. Adaptation requires the development of behavior patterns that will help an organism to utilize the environment to its advantage—to find food and sustenance, avoid hazards, and, if the species is to survive, reproduce its own kind. In turn, organisms must have the biological equipment that makes possible the development of appropriate patterns of behavior. For the hundreds of millions of years that life has existed on earth, biological adaptation has been the primary means by which the problem of survival has been solved. This is accomplished as those organisms of a particular kind, whose biological equipment is best suited to a particular way of life, produce more offspring than those whose equipment is not. In this way, advantageous characteristics become more common in succeeding generations, while less advantageous ones become less common.

In this chapter, we will look at the biological equipment possessed by the primates, the group of animals to which humans belong. By doing so, we will gain a firmer understanding of those characteristics we share with other primates, as well as those that distinguish us from them and make us distinctively human. We shall also sample the behavior made possible by the biological equipment possessed by primates. The study of that behavior is important to help us understand something of the origins of human culture and the origin of humanity itself.

THE CLASSIFICATION SYSTEM

In order to understand the exact place of humanity among the animals, it is helpful to describe briefly the system used by biologists to classify living things. The basic system was devised by the eighteenth-century Swedish naturalist Karl von Linné. The purpose of the Linnaean system was simply to create order in the great mass of confusing biological data that had accumulated by that time. Von Linné—or Linnaeus, as he is generally

called—classified living things on the basis of overall similarities into small groups, or species. Modern classification has gone a step further by distinguishing superficial similarities between organisms—called **analogies**—from basic ones—called **homologies.** The latter are possessed by organisms that share a common ancestry; even though homologous structures may serve different functions (the arm of a human and the forefoot of a dog, for instance), they arise in similar fashion and pass through similar stages in embryonic development prior to their ultimate differentiation. By contrast, analogous structures look similar and may serve the same purpose (the wings of birds and bats, for example), but they are built from different parts, do not pass through similar stages in embryonic development, nor do the organisms share a common ancestry.

On the basis of homologies, groups of like species are organized into larger, more inclusive groups, called **genera** (the singular term is **genus**). The characteristics on which Linnaeus based his system were the following:

1. *Body structure:* A Guernsey cow and a Holstein cow are of the same species because they have identical body structure. A cow and a horse do not.
2. *Body function:* Cows and horses bear their young in the same way. Although they are of different species, they are closer than either cows or horses are to chickens, which lay eggs and have no mammary glands.
3. *Sequence of bodily growth:* Both cows and chickens give birth to—or hatch out of the

Analogies: In biology, structures that are superficially similar; the result of convergent evolution.

Homologies: In biology, structures possessed by two different organisms that arise in similar fashion and pass through similar stages during embryonic development. They may or may not be similar in adults, but have evolved from a common ancestral stock.

Genera; Genus: In the system of plant and animal classification, a group of like species.

Birds and bats exemplify analogy: Both have wings that are used for flight, but the wings are built differently.

egg—fully formed young. They are therefore more closely related to each other than either one is to the frog, whose tadpoles undergo a series of changes before attaining adult form.

Modern taxonomy (scientific classification) is based on more than body structure, function, and growth. One must also compare chemical reactions of blood, protein structure, and even the genetic material itself. Even comparison of parasites is useful, for they tend to show the same degree of relationship as the forms they infest.

Through careful comparison and analysis, Linnaeus and those who have come after him have been able to classify specific animals into a series of larger and more inclusive groups up to the largest and most inclusive of all, the animal kingdom. In Table 4.1 are the main categories of the

Linnaean system applied to the classification of the human species, with some of the more important distinguishing features noted for each category. (Other categories of primates will be dealt with later in this chapter.)

THE PRIMATE ORDER

The primate order is only one of several mammalian orders, such as rodents, carnivores, ungulates (hoofed mammals), and so on. As such, primates share a number of features with other mammals. Generally speaking, mammals are intelligent animals, having more in the way of brains than reptiles or other kinds of vertebrates. In most species, the young are born live, the egg being retained within the womb of the female until it

An example of homology: Fish have gills but humans do not. Nonetheless, gill structures develop in the human embryo, but are modified to serve other purposes. From the rudimentary structures are built such things as the jaw, bones of the inner ear, thymus, and parathyroid glands.

TABLE 4.1	Classification of Humans	
Kingdom	Animals	Do not make their own food, but depend on intake of living food.
Phylum	Chordata	Have at some stage gill slits as well as **notochord** (a rodlike structure of cartilage) and a nerve chord running along the back of the body.
Subphylum*	Vertebrata	Notochord replaced by vertebral column ("backbone") to form internal skeleton along with skull, ribs, and limb bones.
Class	Mammalia	Maintain constant body temperature; young nourished after birth by milk from mother's mammary glands.
Order	Primates	Hands and feet capable of grasping; tendency to erect posture with head balanced on spinal column; acute development of vision rather than sense of smell; tendency to larger brains.
Family	Hominidae	More rigid bodies, longer arms than other primates, ability to hang vertically from arms; 98 percent identical at the genetic level.
Subfamily	Homininae	Ground-dwelling with bipedal locomotion; more reliance on learned, as opposed to biologically determined, behavior.
Genus	*Homo*	Larger brains; reliance on cultural, as opposed to biological, adaptation.
Species	*sapiens*	Brains of modern size; relatively small faces

*Most categories can be expanded or narrowed by adding the prefix "sub" or "super." A family could thus be part of a super-family, and in turn contain two or more subfamilies.

achieves an advanced state of growth. Once born, the young are nourished by their mothers with milk provided from the mammary glands, from which the class Mammalia gets its name. During this period of infant dependency, young mammals are able to learn some of the things they will need for survival as adults.

Mammals are also active animals. This is made possible by their maintenance of a relatively constant body temperature, an efficient respiratory system featuring a separation between the nasal and mouth cavities, a diaphragm to assist in drawing in and letting out breath, and an efficient four-chambered heart that prevents mixing of oxygenated and deoxygenated blood. It is facilitated as well by a skeleton in which the limbs are positioned beneath the body, rather than out at the sides, for ease and economy of movement. The bones of the limbs have joints that are constructed in such a way as to

permit growth in the young, while at the same time providing strong, hard joint surfaces that will stand up to the stresses of sustained activity.

The skeleton of most mammals is simplified, compared to that of most reptiles, in that it has fewer bones. For example, the lower jaw consists of a single bone, rather than several. The teeth, however, are another matter. Instead of the relatively simple, pointed, peglike teeth of reptiles, mammals have special teeth for special purposes: incisors for nipping, gnawing, and cutting; canines for ripping, tearing, killing, and fighting; premolars

Notochord: A rodlike structure of cartilage that, in vertebrates, is replaced by the vertebral column.

TABLE 4.2		The Primate Order		
ORDER	**SUBORDER**	**INFRAORDER**	**SUPERFAMILY**	**FAMILY**
Primates	Strepsirhini	Lemuriformes	Lemuroidea	Five families of lemurs and lemurlike animals
			Lorisoidea	One family of lorises
	Haplorhini	Tarsii	Tarsioidea	One family, represented solely by Tarsier
		Platyrrhini	Ceboidea	Two families of New World monkeys
		Catarrhini	Cercopithecoidea	Two families of Old World monkeys
			Hominoidea	Hylobatidae (small apes)
				Pongidae (Asian great apes)
				Hominidae (African apes, humans, and near humans)

that may either slice and tear or crush and grind (depending on the kind of animal); and molars for crushing and grinding. This enables mammals to make use of a wide variety of food—an advantage to them, since they require more food than do reptiles to sustain their high activity. But they pay a price: Reptiles have unlimited tooth replacement, whereas mammals are limited to two sets. The first set serves the immature animal and is replaced by the "permanent" or adult dentition.

The primate order is divided into two suborders (Table 4.2), of which one is the **Strepsirhini** (from the Greek for "turned nose"), which includes lemurs and lorises (all members of the infraorder **Lemuriformes**). On the whole, strepsirhines are cat-sized or smaller, although there have been some larger forms in the past. Generally, they do not exhibit the characteristics of their order to as great a degree as do the members of the other suborder, the **Haplorhini** (from the Greek for "simple nose"). The strepsirhines also retain certain features common among nonprimate mammals, such as claws and moist, naked skin on their noses, that have not been retained by the haplorhines.

The haplorhine suborder is divided into three infraorders: the **Tarsii**, or tarsiers; the **Platyrrhini**, or New World monkeys; and the **Catarrhini**, consisting of the superfamilies Cercopithecoidea (Old World monkeys) and Hominoidea. Within the latter are the families Hylobatidae (small apes, like the gibbon), Pongidae, and Hominidae. Although the traditional classification of primates placed all great apes (chimpanzee, gorilla, and orangutan) together in the pongid family and humans alone as

Strepsirhini: A primate suborder that includes the single infraorder Lemuriformes.

Lemuriformes: A strepsirhine infraorder that includes lemurs and lorises.

Haplorhini: A primate suborder that includes tarsiers, monkeys, apes, and humans.

Tarsii: A haplorhine infraorder that includes tarsiers.

Platyrrhini: A haplorhine infraorder that includes the New World monkeys.

Catarrhini: A haplorhine infraorder that includes Old World monkeys, apes, and humans.

hominids, it is now recognized that this way of grouping apes and humans does violence to evolutionary relationships. Since the way we classify is supposed to reflect evolutionary genealogies, recent classifications restrict the Pongidae to orangutans, while chimps and gorillas are included with humans in the Hominidae, as a reflection of their closer relation to each other than to orangs. Unfortunately, old habits die hard, and it is still common to find scientists using the family names in the old way, because that is what they are used to doing. But because it misleads, it is time to abandon obsolete practices; therefore, in this book we shall use classificatory terminology more reflective of evolutionary genealogy. Only at the level of the subfamily will humans (Homininae) be separated from chimps and gorillas, although a case can be made that the separation should be made below even the level of the subfamily.[1]

PRIMATE CHARACTERISTICS

Although the living primates are a varied group of animals, they do share a number of features in common. These features are, however, displayed in varying degree by the different kinds of primate; in some they are barely detectable, while in others they are greatly elaborated. All are useful in one way or another to **arboreal,** or tree-dwelling, animals, although (as any squirrel knows) they are not essential to life in the trees. For animals preying upon the many insects living on the fruit and flowers of trees and shrubs, however, such primate characteristics as manipulative hands and keen vision would have been enormously adaptive. Probably, it was as arboreal animals relying on visual predation of insects that primates got their start in life.

***

Arboreal: Tree dwelling.

***

[1]Goodman, M., Bailey, W. J., Hayasaka, K., Stanhope, M. J., Slighton, J., & Czelusniak, J. (1994). Molecular evidence on primate phylogeny from DNA sequences. *American Journal of Physical Anthropology, 94,* 7.

Primate Sense Organs

The primates' adaptation to their way of life in the trees coincided with changes in the form and function of their sensory apparatus: The senses of sight and touch became highly developed, and the sense of smell declined. When primates took to the trees in search of insects, they no longer needed to live a "nose-to-the-ground" existence, sniffing close to the ground in search of food. The haplorhines especially have the least developed sense of smell of all land animals.

Catching insects in the trees, as the early primates did and many still do, demands quickness of movement and the ability to land in the right place without falling. Thus, they had to be adept at judging depth, direction, distance, and the relationships of objects in space, abilities that remain useful to animals that travel through the trees (as most primates still do today), even though they may have given up most insect eating in favor of fruits and leaves. In the haplorhines, these abilities are provided by their **stereoscopic vision,** the ability to see the world in three dimensions—height, width, and depth. It requires two eyes set apart from one another on the same plane. Each eye thus views an object from a slightly different angle, and the object assumes a three-dimensional appearance, indicating spatial relationships. Stereoscopic vision is one of the most important factors in primate evolution, for it evidently led to increased brain size in the visual area and a great complexity at nerve connections.

Visual acuity, however, varies throughout the primate order. Lemuriformes, for example, are the most visually primitive of the primates. Lacking stereoscopic vision, their eyes look out from either side of their muzzle or snout, much like those of a cow or a rabbit. Nor do they possess color vision. All other primates possess both color and stereoscopic vision, as well as a unique

***

Stereoscopic vision: Three-dimensional vision.

***

Hands that grasp and eyes that see in three dimensions enable primates, like this South American squirrel monkey, to live effectively in the trees.

structure called the **fovea centralis,** or central pit in the retina of each eye. Like a camera lens, this feature enables the animal to focus on a particular object for acutely clear perception, without sacrificing visual contact with the object's surroundings.

Primate sense of touch also became highly developed as a result of arboreal living. Primates found useful an effective feeling and grasping mechanism to grab their insect prey and to prevent them from falling and tumbling while moving through the trees. The primitive mammals from which primates descended possessed tiny tac-

Fovea centralis: A shallow pit in the retina of the eye that enables an animal to focus on an object while maintaining visual contact with its surroundings.

tile hairs that gave them extremely sensitive tactile capacities. In primates, these hairs were replaced by informative pads on the tips of the animals' fingers and toes.

The Primate Brain

By far the most outstanding characteristic of primate evolution has been the enlargement of the brain among members of the order. Primate brains tend to be large, heavy in proportion to body weight, and very complex. The cerebral hemispheres (the areas of conscious thought) have enlarged dramatically and, in catarrhines, completely cover the cerebellum, which is the part of the brain that coordinates the muscles and maintains body equilibrium.

The reasons for this important change in brain size are many, but it likely began as the earliest primates, along with many other mammals, began to carry out their activities in the daylight hours. Prior to 65 million years ago, mammals seem to have been nocturnal in their habits, but with the extinction of the dinosaurs, inconspicuous, nighttime activity was no longer the key to survival. With the change to diurnal, or daytime, activity the sense of vision took on greater importance, and so visual acuity was favored by natural selection. Unlike reptile vision, where the information-processing neurons are in the retina, mammalian vision is processed in the brain, permitting integration with information received by hearing and smelling.

If the evolution of visual acuity began the trend to larger brains, it is likely that the primates' arboreal existence played a major role in furthering that trend. As paleontologist Alfred S. Romer states:

> Locomotion in the trees requires great agility and muscular coordination, which in itself demands development of the brain centers; and it is of interest that much of the higher mental faculties are apparently developed in an area alongside the motor centers of the brain.[2]

An interesting hypothesis that may help account for primate brain development involves the use of the hand as a tactile organ to replace the teeth and jaws or snout. The hands assumed some of the grasping, tearing, and dividing functions of the snout, again requiring development of the brain centers for more complete coordination. Thus, while the skull and brain expanded, the teeth and jaws grew smaller. Certain areas of the brain became more elaborate and intricate. One of these areas is the cortex, considered to be the center of an animal's intelligence; it receives impressions from the animal's various sensory receptors, analyzes them, and sends responses back down the motor nerves to the proper receptor.

An animal living in the trees is constantly acting on and reacting to the environment. Messages from the hands, feet, eyes, and ears, as well as from the sensors of balance, movement, heat, touch, and pain, are relayed to the cortex, individually and simultaneously. The cortex, then, must be developed to a considerable degree of complexity to receive and coordinate these impressions and to transmit

the appropriate responses back. It is assumed that such development must have occurred early in the history of the primates.

The enlarged cortex not only provided the primates with a greater degree of efficiency in the daily struggle for survival, but it also gave them the basis for more sophisticated cerebration or thought. The ability to think probably played a decisive role in the evolution of the primates from which human beings emerged.

Primate Dentition

Although they had added things other than insects to their diets, primates have retained less specialized teeth than other mammals. According to primatologist W. E. LeGros Clark:

> An arboreal life obviates the necessity for developing highly specialized grinding teeth, since the diet available to most tree-living mammals in the tropics, consisting of leaves, shoots, soft fruits and insects, can be adequately masticated by molar teeth of relatively simple structure.[3]

In most primates, on each side of each jaw, in front, are two straight-edged, chisellike broad teeth called incisors (Fig. 4.1). Behind the incisors is a canine, which in many mammals is large, flaring, and fanglike and is used for defense as well as for tearing and shredding food. Among some catarrhines the canine is reduced in size somewhat, especially in females, though it is still large in males. In humans, though, incisors and canines are practically indistinguishable, although the canine has an over-sized root, suggestive of larger canines some time back in our ancestry. Behind the canines are the premolars. Last come the molars, usually with four or five cusps, used mostly for crushing or grinding food. This basic pattern of dentition contrasts sharply with that of nonprimate mammals.

On the evidence of comparative anatomy and the fossil record, LeGros Clark postulated the existence of an early primate ancestor that possessed three incisors, one canine, four premolars, and three molars on each side of the jaw, top and bottom, for

---

[2]Romer, A. S. (1945). *Vertebrate paleontology* (p. 103). Chicago: University of Chicago Press.

[3]Clark, W. E. L. (1966). *History of the primates* (5th ed., p. 271). Chicago: University of Chicago Press.

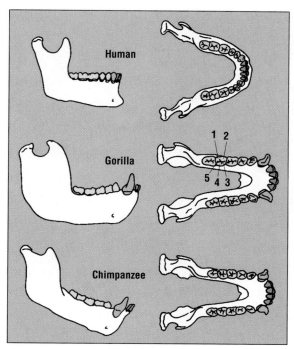

Figure 4.1 In this depiction of the lower jaws of a human, a gorilla, and a chimpanzee, incisors are shown in blue, canines in red, and premolars and molars in yellow. On one of the gorilla molars, the cusps are numbered to enhance their identification.

a total of 44 teeth. In the early stages of primate evolution, four incisors (one on each side of each jaw) were lost. This change differentiated the primates, with their two incisors on each side of each jaw, from other mammals. The canines of most primates develop into long, daggerlike teeth that enable them to rip open tough husks of fruit and other foods. In a combat situation, male baboons, apes, and other primates flash these formidable teeth at their enemies, hoping to scare them off. Only on rare occasions, when this bluffing action fails, are teeth used to inflict bodily harm.

Other evolutionary changes in primate dentition involve the premolar and molar teeth. Over the millennia, the first and second premolars became smaller and eventually disappeared altogether, while the third and fourth premolars grew larger with the addition of a second pointed projection, or cusp, thus becoming "bicuspid." The molars, meanwhile, evolved from a three-cusp pattern to one with four and even five cusps. This kind

of molar economically combined the functions of grasping, cutting, and grinding in one tooth.

The evolutionary trend for primate dentition has generally been toward economy, with fewer, smaller, more efficient teeth doing more work. Thus our own 32 teeth are fewer in number than those of some, and more generalized than those of most, primates. Indeed, the absence of third molars in many individuals indicates that the human dentition is undergoing further reduction.

The Primate Skeleton

The skeleton gives an animal its basic shape or silhouette, supports the soft tissues, and helps protect the vital internal organs. In primates (Fig. 4.2), for example, the skull protects the brain and the eyes. A number of factors are responsible for the shape of the primate skull as compared with those of most other mammals: changes in dentition, changes in the sensory organs of sight and smell, and increased brain size. The primate brain case, or **cranium,** tends to be high and vaulted. A solid partition exists in most primate species between the eye and the temple, affording maximum protection to the eyes in their vulnerable forward position.

The **foramen magnum** (the large opening in the skull through which the spinal cord passes and connects to the brain) is an important clue to evolutionary relationships. In primates, the evolutionary trend has been for this to shift forward, toward the center of the skull's base, so that it faces downward, as in humans, rather than directly backward, as in dogs, horses, and other mammals. Thus, the skull does not project forward from the vertebral column. Instead, the vertebral column joins the skull toward the center of its base, thereby placing the skull in a balanced position in animals that frequently assume upright posture.

Cranium: The brain case of the skull.

Foramen magnum: A large opening in the skull through which the spinal cord passes and connects to the brain.

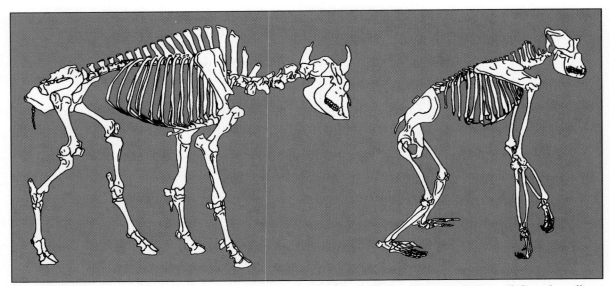

Figure 4.2   Note where the skulls and vertebral columns are joined in these skeletons of a bison (left) and gorilla (right). In the bison (as in most mammals) the skull projects forward from the vertebral column, but in the semierect gorilla, the vertebral column is well down beneath the skull.

In most primates, the snout or muzzle portion of the skull has grown smaller as the acuity of the sense of smell declined. The smaller snout offers less interference with stereoscopic vision; it also enables the eyes to be placed in the frontal position. As a result, primates have more of a humanlike face than other mammals. Below the primate skull and the neck is the **clavicle,** or collarbone, a holdover from primitive mammal ancestors. This serves as a strut that prevents the arm from collapsing inward when brought across the front of the body. It allows greater maneuverability of the arms, permitting them to swing sideways and outward from the trunk of the body. The clavicle also supports the **scapula** and allows for the muscle development that is required for flexible, yet powerful, arm movement. This shoulder and limb structure is associated with considerable acrobatic agility and, in the case of all apes and some New World monkeys, the ability to **brachiate**—use their arms to swing and hang beneath the branches of trees with the body in a vertical (upright) position.

Primates have also retained the characteristic, found in early mammals, of **pentadactyly.** Pentadactyly, which means possessing five digits, is a primitive characteristic found in many nonarboreal animals, but it proved to be of special advantage to tree-dwelling primates. Their grasping feet and hands (Fig. 4.3) have sensitive pads at the tips of their digits, backed up (except in some strepsirhines) by flattened nails. This unique combination of pad and nail provides the animal with an excellent **prehensile** (grasping) device for use when moving from tree to tree. The structural characteristics of the primate foot and hand make grasping possible; the digits are extremely flexible,

Clavicle: The "collarbone."

Scapula: The "shoulder blade."

Brachiate: To use the arms to move from branch to branch, with the body hanging suspended from them.

Pentadactyly: Possessing five digits (fingers and toes).

Prehensile: Having the ability to grasp.

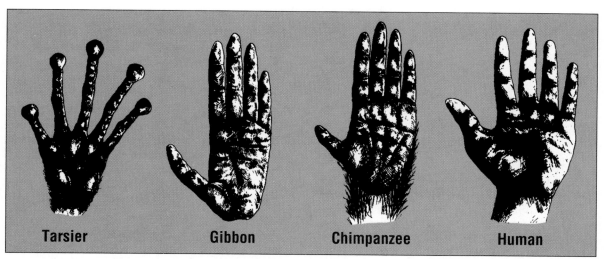

Figure 4.3   The hands of primates are similar. However, human hands are distinguished by well-developed thumbs that can be used in opposition to the fingers. The highly specialized hands of brachiators (gibbons and chimpanzees) are characterized by long fingers and weakly developed thumbs.

the big toe is fully opposable to the other digits in most species, and the thumb is opposable to the other digits to varying degrees.

Hindsight indicates that the flexible, unspecialized primate hand was to prove a valuable asset for future evolution of this group. Had they not had generalized grasping hands, early hominines (members of the human subfamily) would not have been able to manufacture and utilize tools and thus embark on the new and unique evolutionary pathway that led to the revolutionary ability to adapt through culture.

cal, corresponding to her period of estrus, which occurs once each month.

This is not to say that females are receptive regularly each month. Rather, the average adult female monkey or ape spends most of her time either pregnant or nursing, at which times she is not sexually receptive. But after her infant is weaned, she will come into estrus for a few days each month until she becomes pregnant again. Since this can happen at any time, it is advantageous to have males present throughout the year. Thus, sex plays

Reproduction and Care of Young

The breeding of most mammals occurs once or twice a year, but most primate species are able to breed at any time during the course of the year. Generally, the male is ready to engage in sexual activity whenever females are in **estrus**, around the time of ovulation. The female's receptivity is cycli-

Swelling of her sexual skin indicates that this baboon is in estrus. Females of most primates come into estrus once a month until pregnant; thereafter they will not come into estrus until their infant is weaned.

Estrus: In primate females, the time of sexual receptivity during which ovulation takes place.

A young baboon clings to its mother. Since her hands are used in locomotion, she cannot herself carry her infant. Consequently, it must be able to hold on for itself.

a role in keeping both sexes constantly together, except among orangutans, among whom adults come together only when females are in estrus. In most species, however, sex is not the only, or even the most important, cause of males and females remaining together.

One of the most noticeable adaptations to arboreal life among primates is a trend toward reduction in the number of offspring born at one time to a female. The most primitive primates, lemurs and marmosets, produce two or three young at each birth. Catarrhines, however, usually produce only a single offspring at a time. Natural selection may have favored single births among primate tree dwellers because the primate infant, which has a highly developed grasping ability (the grasping reflex can also be seen in human infants), must be transported about by its mother, and more than one clinging infant would seriously encumber her as she moved about the trees. Moreover, a female pregnant with a large litter would be unable to lead an active life as a tree dweller.

Primates bear fewer young at a time, and so they must devote more time and effort to their care if the species is to survive, which usually means a longer period during which the infant is dependent upon its mother. As a general rule, the more closely related to humans the species is, the smaller, more helpless, and more immature the newborn offspring tend to be. For example, a lemur is dependent upon the mother for only a few months after birth; an ape, for four or five years; and a human for more

than a decade. Longer infancy is typically associated with an increase in longevity (see Fig. 4.4). If the breeding life of primates had not extended, the lengthened infancy could have led to a decrease in numbers of individuals. Something approaching this can be seen in the great apes: A female chimpanzee, for example, does not reach sexual maturity until about the age of 10, and once she produces her first live offspring, there is a period of about 5.6 years before she will bear another. Furthermore, a chimpanzee infant cannot survive if its mother dies before it reaches the age of 4 at the very least. Thus, assuming that none of her offspring die before adulthood, a female chimpanzee must survive for at least 20 or 21 years just to maintain the size of chimpanzee populations at their current levels. In fact, chimpanzee infants and juveniles do die from time to time, and all females do not live full reproductive lives, which is one reason why apes are not as abundant in the world today as are monkeys.

Figure 4.4 Primates are born at earlier stages of development than other animals. Humans are born at a particularly early stage because of their larger brain size; later, the baby's head would be too large for the mother's pelvis.

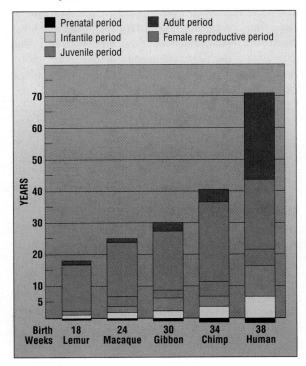

The young of catarrhine, and especially hominoid, species are born with relatively underdeveloped nervous systems; moreover, they lack the social knowledge that guides behavior. Thus they depend upon adults not only for protection but also for instruction, as they must learn how to survive. The longer period of dependence for these primates makes possible a longer period of learning, which appears to be a distinct evolutionary advantage.

Establishing Evolutionary Relationships

Most of the primate characteristics so far discussed are present at least in a rudimentary sort of way in the strepsirhines, but all are seen to a much greater degree in the haplorhines. The differences between humans and the other haplorhines, especially catarrhines, are rather like those between strepsirhines and haplorhines. In humans most of the characteristic primate traits are developed to a degree not realized by any other species. Among some strepsirhines, some of the distinctive primate traits are missing, while others are clearly present, so that the borderline between primate and nonprimate becomes blurred, and the difference is one of degree rather than kind. All of this is fully expectable, given an evolutionary history in which primitive primates having a rough resemblance to today's strepsirhines developed out of some other mammalian order and eventually gave rise to primitive haplorhines; from these emerged the catarrhines and, ultimately, hominids.

Just how close our evolutionary relationship is to other primates is indicated by molecular evidence. There is a striking similarity in blood and protein chemistry among the hominoids especially, indicating close evolutionary relationships. On the basis of tests with blood proteins, it has been shown that the chimpanzee and gorilla are closest to humans; next comes the orangutan; then the smaller apes (gibbons and siamangs); Old World monkeys; New World monkeys; and finally the strepsirhines. Measurements of genetic affinity confirm these findings, providing further evidence of humanity's close kinship to the great apes, especially those of Africa (Fig. 4.5). The classification of humans, chimpanzees, and gorillas together in the family Hominidae, distinct

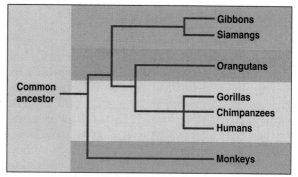

Figure 4.5   Based on molecular similarities and differences, a relationship can be established among various catarrhine primates. It is difficult to take seriously any date in excess of 8 million years for the origin of the separate lineages for chimpanzees and humans.

from the Pongidae, reflects the fact that the three are more closely related to one another than any is to the orangutan.

At the genetic level, humans and chimpanzees are at least 98 percent identical; the only difference is that chimps have an extra pair of chromosomes, and of the others, the 22nd pair shows some difference. With respect to the extra pair, in humans these have fused with another pair to form the single 22nd pair, so even this is not a major difference. Although some studies of molecular similarities have suggested a closer relationship between chimpanzees and humans than either has to gorillas, others disagree, and the safest course at the moment is to regard all three hominids as having an equal degree of relationship.[4]

MODERN PRIMATES

The modern primates are mostly restricted to warm areas of the world. As already noted, they are divided into two suborders, Strepsirhini and Haplorhini. Strepsirhines are small, mostly quadrupedal Old World animals; haplorhines include tarsiers, monkeys, apes, and humans.

[4]Rogers, J. (1994). Levels of the geneaological hierarchy and the problem of hominid phylogeny. *American Journal of Physical Anthropology, 94,* 81.

Strepsirhines

The strepsirhines are considered to be the most primitive primates. They are represented by the single infraorder Lemuriformes, within which are the lemurs and lorises. Although lemurs are restricted to the island of Madagascar, off the east coast of Africa, lorises range from Africa to southern and eastern Asia. All are small, with none larger than a medium-sized dog. In general body outline, they resemble rodents and insectivores, with short pointed snouts, large pointed ears, and big eyes. In the anatomy of the upper lip and snout, lemuriformes resemble nonprimate mammals, in that the upper lip is bound down to the gum and the naked skin on the nose around the nostrils is moist. They also have long tails, with that of a ring-tail lemur somewhat like the tail of a raccoon.

In brain structure, lemuriformes are clearly primates, and they have characteristically primate "hands," which they use in pairs, rather than one at a time. They move on all fours, with the forelimbs in a "palms down" position, and also cling in near vertical positions to branches. Although they retain a claw on their second toe, which they use for scratching and grooming, all other digits are equipped with flattened nails. With their distinctive mix of characteristics, strepsirhine primates appear to occupy a place between the haplorhines and insectivores.

Haplorhines

The suborder Haplorhini is divided into three infraorders: the Tarsii (tarsiers), Platyrrhini (New World monkeys), and Catarrhini (Old World monkeys, apes, and humans). Most haplorhines are bigger than the strepsirhines and are strikingly humanlike in appearance. Actually, it is more accurate to say that humans are remarkably like monkeys, but even more like apes, in appearance. The defining traits of the strepsirhines—large cranium, well-developed brain, acute vision, chisellike incisors, prehensile digits—are even more apparent in the haplorhines. Most haplorhines generally move on all four limbs, but many stand erect to reach fruit hanging in trees: some apes occasionally walk on two feet. Monkeys are often highly arboreal, and New World species have prehensile tails that wrap around tree branches, freeing the forelimbs to grasp food. Some New World monkeys brachiate; Old World monkeys almost never do.

All apes may once have been fully arboreal brachiators, but among modern apes, only the gibbon and siamang still are. The chimpanzee and the gorilla spend most of their time on the ground, but sleep in the trees and may also find food there. Orangutans, too, spend time down on the ground, but are more arboreal than the African apes. When on the ground, they move mostly on all fours.

Tarsiers

Tarsiers are the haplorhine primates most like the lemuriformes, and in the past they were usually classified in the same suborder with them. The head, eyes, and ears of these kitten-sized arboreal creatures are huge in proportion to the body. They have the remarkable ability to turn their heads 180 degrees, so they can see where they have been as

Modern strepsirhines represent highly evolved variants of an early primate model. In them, primate characteristics are not as prominent as they are in monkeys, apes, and humans.

In tarsiers, primate characteristics are somewhat more prominent than among strepsirhines.

well as where they are going. The digits end in platelike, adhesive discs. Tarsiers are named for the elongated tarsal, or foot bone, that provides leverage for jumps of 6 feet or more. Tarsiers are mainly nocturnal insect eaters. In the structure of the nose and lips and the part of the brain governing vision, tarsiers resemble monkeys.

New World Monkeys

New World monkeys live in forests and swamps of South and Central America. They are characterized by flat noses with widely separated, outward flaring nostrils, from which comes their name of platyrrhine monkeys. All are arboreal and some have long, prehensile tails by which they hang from trees. These and the presence of three, rather than two, premolars on each side of each jaw distinguish them from the Old World monkeys, apes, and humans. Platyrrhines walk on all fours with their palms down and scamper along tree branches in search of fruit, which they eat sitting upright. Spider monkeys are accomplished brachiators as well. Although other New World monkeys spend much of their time in the trees, they do not often hang or swing from limb to limb by their arms and have not developed the extremely long forelimbs characteristic of brachiators.

Old World Monkeys

Old World, or catarrhine, monkeys are characterized by noses with closely space, downward-pointing nostrils, the presence of two, rather than three, premolars on each side of each jaw, and their lack of prehensile tails. They may be either arboreal or terrestrial. The arboreal species include the guereza monkey, the Asiatic langur, and the strange-looking proboscis monkey. Some are equally at home on the ground and in the trees, such as the macaques, of which there are some 19 species ranging from Gibraltar (the "Barbary Ape") to Japan.

Several species of baboons are largely terrestrial, living in the savannas, deserts, and highlands of Africa. They have long, fierce faces and move quadrupedally, with all fours in the palms-down position. Their diet consists of leaves, seeds, insects, and lizards, and they live in large, well-organized troops. Because baboons have abandoned trees (except for sleeping) and live in environments like that in which humans may have originated, they are of great interest to primatologists.

Small and Great Apes

The apes are the closest living relatives humans have in the animal world. Their general appearance and way of life are related to their semierect posture. In their body chemistry, the position of their internal organs, and even their diseases, they are remarkably close to humans. They are arboreal to varying degrees, but their generally greater size and weight are obstacles to their swinging and jumping as freely as monkeys. The small, lithe gibbon can both climb and swing freely through the trees and so spends virtually all of its time in them. At the opposite extreme are gorillas, who climb trees, using their prehensile hands and feet to grip the trunk and branches. Their swinging is limited to leaning outward as they reach for fruit, clasping a limb for support. Most of their time is spent on the ground.

The apes, like humans, have no external tail. But, unlike humans, their arms are longer than their legs, indicating that their ancestors remained arboreal brachiators long after our own had become terrestrial. In moving on the ground, the African apes "knuckle-walk" on the backs of their hands, resting their weight on the middle joints of the fingers. They stand erect when reaching for fruit, looking over tall grass, or in any activity where they find the erect position advantageous. The semierect position is natural in apes when on the ground because the curvature of their vertebral column places their center of gravity, which is high in their bodies, in front of their hip joint. Thus, they are both "top heavy" and "front heavy." Furthermore, the structure of the ape pelvis is not well suited to support the weight of the torso and limbs easily. Nor do apes have the arrangement of leg muscles that enables humans to stand erect and swing their legs freely before and behind.

Gibbons and siamangs, which are found in Southeast Asia and Malaya, have compact, slim bodies and disproportionately long arms and short legs, and stand about 3 feet high. Although their usual form of locomotion is brachiation, they can run erect, holding their arms out for balance. Gibbons and siamangs resemble monkeys in size and general appearance more than the other apes.

Orangutans are found in Borneo and Sumatra. They are somewhat taller than gibbons and siamangs and are much heavier, with the bulk characteristic of apes. In the closeness of the eyes and facial prominence, an orangutan looks a little like a chimpanzee, except that its hair is reddish. Orangs walk with their forelimbs in a fists-sideways or a palms-down position. Of the apes, they are the most solitary in their habits and somewhat more arboreal than the African apes.

Gorillas, found in equatorial Africa, are the largest of the apes; an adult male can weigh more than 400 pounds. The body is covered with a thick coat of glossy black hair, and mature males have a

Gibbons and orangutans are Southeast Asian apes. Gibbons are brachiators who use their long arms and hands to swing through the trees. Although orangutans sometimes brachiate, their legs move like arms and their feet are like hands; thus, much of their movement is by "four-handed" climbing.

silvery gray upper back. There is a strikingly human look about the face, and like humans, gorillas focus on things in their fields of vision by directing the eyes rather than moving the head. Gorillas are mostly ground dwellers, but may sleep in trees in carefully constructed nests. Because of their weight, brachiation is limited to raising and lowering themselves among the tree branches when searching for fruit. They "knuckle-walk," using all four limbs with the fingers of the hand flexed, placing the knuckles instead of the palm of the hand on the ground. They will stand erect to reach for fruit, to see something more easily, or to threaten perceived sources of danger with their famous "chest-beating" displays. Although gorillas are gentle and tolerant, bluffing is an important part of their behavioral repertoire.

Chimpanzees are widely distributed throughout Africa. They are probably the best known of the apes and have long been favorites in zoos and circuses. Although thought of as particularly quick and clever, all three great apes are of equal intelligence, despite some differences in cognitive styles. More arboreal than gorillas, but less so than orangs, chimpanzees forage on the ground much of the day, "knuckle-walking" like gorillas. At sunset, they return to the trees, where they build their nests.

THE SOCIAL BEHAVIOR OF PRIMATES

The physical resemblance of human beings to the other catarrhines is striking, but the most startling resemblance is in their social behavior. Because of their highly developed brains, monkeys and apes behave in a manner far more complex than most other animals except humans. Only over the past three decades have primatologists made prolonged close-range observations of catarrhines in their natural habitats, and we are discovering much about social organization, learning ability, and communication among our closest relatives in the animal kingdom. In particular, we are finding that a number of behavioral traits that we used to think of as distinctively human are found to one degree or another among other primates, reminding us once

Chimpanzees and gorillas are African apes.

Anthropology Applied
PRIMATE CONSERVATION

At present, no fewer than 76 species of primates are recognized as being in danger of extinction. Included among them are all of the great apes, as well as such formerly widespread and adaptable species as rhesus macaques. In the wild, they are threatened by destruction of their habitat in the name of "development," by hunting for food and trophies, and by trapping for pets and research. Because monkeys and apes are so closely related to humans, they are regarded as essential for biomedical research in which humans cannot be used. It is ironic that trade in live primates to supply laboratories can be a major factor in their local extinction.

Because of their vulnerability, the conservation of primates has become a matter of urgency. Two approaches to the problem may be taken, both of which require application of knowledge gained from studies of free-ranging animals. One is to maintain some populations in the wild, either by establishing preserves where animals are already living, or by moving populations to localities where suitable habitat exists. In either case, constant monitoring and management are necessary to assure that sufficient space and resources remain available. The other approach is to maintain breeding colonies in captivity, in which

case care must be taken to provide the kind of physical and social environment that will encourage reproductive success. Without such amenities as things to climb, materials to use for nest building, others to socialize with, and places to withdraw not only from humans but from each other, primates in zoos and laboratories do not successfully reproduce.

The value of field studies for effective wild animal management is illustrated by Shirley Strum's relocation in 1984 of three troops of free-ranging baboons in Kenya. The troop she had been studying for 15 years had become a problem, raiding people's crops and garbage. Accordingly, it was decided to move this and two other local troops—130 animals in all—to more sparsely inhabited country 150 miles away. Knowing their habits, Strum was able to trap, tranquilize, and transport the animals to their new home in such a way as not to disrupt their social relationships, cause them to abandon their new home, or block the transfer into their troop of new males, with their all-important knowledge of local resources. The success of her effort, which had never been tried with baboons before, proves that relocation is a realistic technique for saving endangered primate populations.

---

again that many of the differences between us and them are differences of degree, rather than kind.

The range of behavior shown by living primates is great—too great to be adequately surveyed in this book. Instead, we shall look primarily at the behavior of those species most closely related to humans—chimpanzees and gorillas—or that which has adapted to an environment somewhat like the one to which our own ancestors adapted millions of years ago—savanna baboons.

The Group

Primates are social animals, living and traveling in groups that vary in size from species to species. In most species, females and their offspring constitute the core of the social system. Among baboons,

these females are all related, in that they remain for life in the group into which they were born, whereas males generally move to other groups as adolescents. Among chimpanzees, females sometimes leave their natal group to join another, but their sons, and often their daughters, remain in their mother's group for life. Among gorillas, either sex may or may not leave its natal group for another.

Savanna baboons live in large troops that may number more than 100 animals. They have male and female status hierarchies, and males dominate females, unless a female is supported by another male (males are twice as big as females). Each animal knows its place, and the hierarchies are maintained by the self-assertiveness of dominant animals and their success in securing the support of other animals, as well as by the deference of subordinates.

Catarrhine primates, like these baboons, spend a lot of time grooming one another. Such behavior is important in maintaining group cohesion.

High dominance brings with it priority of access to choice food, water, and (sometimes) mates; moreover, high-ranking females are more often groomed by others of their sex as well as by juveniles, and they are less vulnerable to harassment by others when caring for young infants. Although adult females tend to avoid one another when foraging, closely related females sit together and groom each other when at rest. They will also support one another during aggressive encounters with other troop members. Males, by contrast, rarely associate with members of their own sex. Instead, they strike up friendships with one or more females.

Among chimps, the largest organizational unit is the community, composed of 50 or more individuals. Rarely, however, do all these animals come together at a single time. Instead, they are usually found ranging singly or in small subgroups consisting of adult males together, females with their young, or males and females together with their young. In the course of their travels, subgroups may join forces and forage together, but sooner or later these will break up again into smaller units. When they do, members are often exchanged, so that new subunits are different in their composition from the ones that initially came together.

Although relationships between individuals within the community are relatively harmonious, dominance hierarchies do exist. Generally, males outrank females, although high-ranking females may dominate low-ranking males. Physical strength and size help determine an animal's rank, as do the rank of its mother, its effectiveness at enlisting the aid of other individuals, and, in the case of the male, its motivation to achieve high status. Highly motivated males, even though they may not be the biggest in their group, may bring considerable intelligence and ingenuity to bear in their quest for high rank. For example, one chimp in the community studied by Jane Goodall, a pioneer in the study of primate behavior, was able to figure out how to incorporate noisy kerosene cans into his charging displays, thereby intimidating all the other males.[5] As a result, he rose from relatively low status to the number one (alpha) position.

The gorilla group is a "family" of 5 to 20 individuals led by a mature, silverbacked male and includes younger, blackbacked males, females, the

[5]Goodall, J. (1986). *The chimpanzees of Gombe: Patterns of behavior* (p. 424). Cambridge, MA: Belknap Press.

Among chimpanzees, as among most primates, the mother-infant bond is strong. This mother is playfully tickling her offspring.

young, and sometimes other silverbacks. Subordinate males, however, are usually prevented by the dominant male from mating with the group's females, although he may occasionally allow access to lower ranking ones. Thus, young silverbacks often leave their natal family to start their own families by winning outside females. If the dominant male is weakening with age, however, one of his sons may remain with the group to succeed to his father's position. Unlike chimpanzees, gorillas rarely fight over food, territory, or sex, but will fight fiercely to maintain the integrity of the group.

Individual Interaction

One of the most notable primate activities is grooming, the ritual cleaning of another animal's coat to remove parasites, shreds of grass, or other matter. The grooming animal deftly parts the hair of the one being groomed with two fingers, and with the thumb and forefinger of the other hand removes any foreign object, often eating it. Among gorillas, grooming is mainly hygienic; but among chimpanzees and baboons it is a gesture of friendliness, submission, appeasement, or closeness. Embracing, touching, and jumping up and down are forms of greeting behavior among chimpanzees. Touching is also a form of reassurance.

Gorillas, though gentle and tolerant, are also aloof and independent, and individual interaction among adults tends to be quite restrained. Friendship or closeness between adults and infants is more evident. Among baboons, chimpanzees, gorillas, and most other primates, the mother-infant bond is the strongest and most long-lasting in the group. A new infant baboon is an object of tremendous interest to the group, and shortly after birth, mother and infant are surrounded by attention. The adults lipsmack and touch the infant with their fingers or mouths, and young females may even try to take it to practice "mothering" on their own. The new mother aligns herself with a male friend, who protects her from animals that may threaten her or her infant. Two incidents

JANE GOODALL
(b. 1934)

In July 1960 Jane Goodall arrived with her mother at the Gombe Chimpanzee Reserve on the shores of Lake Tanganyika in Tanzania. The first of three women sent out by Kenyan anthropologist Louis Leakey to study great apes in the wild (the others were Dian Fossey and Birute Galdikas, who were to study gorillas and orangutans, respectively), her task was to begin a long-term study of chimpanzees. Little did she realize that, more than 35 years later, she would still be at it.

Though born in London, Jane grew up and was schooled in Bournemouth, England. Upon her graduation at 18, she enrolled in secretarial school, following which she held various jobs in England before the opportunity came to go to Africa. As a child, she had always dreamed of going there to live among animals, so when an invitation arrived to visit a friend in Kenya, she jumped at the opportunity. Quitting her regular job, she worked as a waitress to raise the money for travel, and was then on her way. Once in Kenya, she met Louis Leakey, who gave her a job as an assistant secretary. Before long, she was on her way to Gombe. Within a year, the outside world began to hear the most extraordinary things about this pioneering woman and her work; tales of tool-making apes, cooperative hunts by chimpanzees, and what seemed like exotic chimpanzee rain dances. By the mid-1960s, her work had earned her a Ph.D.

from Cambridge University, and Gombe was on its way to becoming one of the most dynamic field stations for the study of animal behavior anywhere in the world.

Although field studies of primates in their natural habitats had been undertaken prior to 1960, there had been not many of them, and few of those had produced more than extremely limited information. It was Goodall's particular blend of patience and determination that showed what could be achieved, and before long her field station became something of a mecca for aspiring young students interested in primate behavior. The list of those who have worked with her at Gombe, many of them women, reads like a *Who's Who* of eminent scholars in the field of primate behavior.

Although Goodall is still involved with her chimpanzees, she now spends a good deal of time these days lecturing, writing, and overseeing the work of others. She has also become committed to the cause of primate conservation and halting the illegal trafficking in captive chimps. She is also an eloquent champion of humane treatment of captive chimpanzees.

---

reported by primatologist Barbara Smuts are indicative of the care males may invest in their friends' offspring: Two infants of the group she was studying lost their mothers while they were still quite young. In each case, their bond with the mother's male friend intensified and was probably critical in the youngsters' survival.[6] Although such friends are not always the fathers, this grouping of adult males, adult females, and juveniles suggests the kind of situation that may have been a forerunner of human family organization.

[6]Smuts, B. (1987). What are friends for? *Natural History, 96* (2), 41.

Among gorillas and chimpanzees, the mother-infant bond is especially strong and may last for many years; commonly for the lifetime of the mother. Gorilla infants and young juveniles share their mothers' nests and have been seen sharing nests with mature, childless females. Both chimpanzee and gorilla males are attentive to juveniles and may share in parental responsibilities. Male chimpanzees, however (as among human food foragers), may wander apart from the females and juveniles. Thus, it is the females who provide stability in the chimpanzee group, whereas it is the dominant silverback who provides this in the gorilla family.

Sexual Behavior

Among the three foregoing species, as with humans, there is no fixed breeding season. Sexual activity, however—initiated by either the male or the female—occurs only during the period each month when the female is receptive to impregnation. Once impregnated, females are not sexually receptive until their offspring are weaned (at about age 4 among chimps and gorillas; sooner among baboons). Baboon females typically mate with several different males, but exercise choice as to whom they mate with, clearly preferring those with whom they have a prior friendship. Thus, friendship often precedes, rather than follows, a sexual relationship. When they are at the height of estrus, females commonly spend most of their time in proximity to males with whom they maintain exclusive mating relationships.

To a degree, chimps are promiscuous in their sexual behavior, and 12 to 14 males have been observed to have as many as 50 copulations in one day with a single female. Nor do females appear to show preference for known over strange males. Generally, dominant males try to monopolize females in full estrus, although cooperation from the female is usually required for this to succeed. By making herself scarce, she may be able to exercise some choice in the matter. An alpha male, however, is able to monopolize the females to some extent, and some alphas have been seen to monopolize several estrus females at the same time.

In gorilla families, the dominant silverback has exclusive breeding rights with the females, although he may allow a young silverback occasional access to a low-ranking female. Otherwise, the young silverback must leave "home" in order to find sex partners, usually by luring them away from other established groups.

Although the vast majority of primate species are not "monogamous" in their mating habits, many smaller species of New World monkeys, a few island-dwelling populations of leaf-eating Old World monkeys, and all of the smaller apes (gibbons and siamangs) do mate for life with a single individual of the opposite sex. None of these species is closely related to human beings, nor do "monogamous" species ever display the degree of **sexual dimorphism**—anatomical differences between males and females—that is characteristic of our closest primate relatives or that was characteristic of our own ancient ancestors.

Play

Frequent play activity among primate infants and juveniles is a means of learning about the environment, testing strength (rank in dominance hierarchies is based partially—but only partially—on size and strength), and generally learning how to behave as adults. Chimpanzee infants mimic the food-getting activities of their mothers, "attack" dozing adults, and "harass" adolescents.

Observers have watched young gorillas do somersaults, wrestle, and play tug o'war, follow the leader, and king of the mountain. One juvenile, becoming annoyed at repeated harassment by an infant, picked it up, climbed a tree, and deposited it on a branch from which it was unable to get down on its own and its mother had to retrieve it.

Communication

Primates, like many animals, vocalize. They have a great range of calls that are often used together with movements of the face or body to convey a message. Observers have not yet established the meaning of all the sounds, but a good number have been distinguished, such as warning calls, threat calls, defense calls, and gathering calls; the behavioral reactions of other animals hearing the call have also been studied. Among chimpanzees and gorillas, vocalizations are mainly emotional rather than propositional. Much of their communication takes place by the use of specific gestures and postures. Indeed, a number

Sexual dimorphism: Within a single species, the presence of marked anatomical differences between males and females.

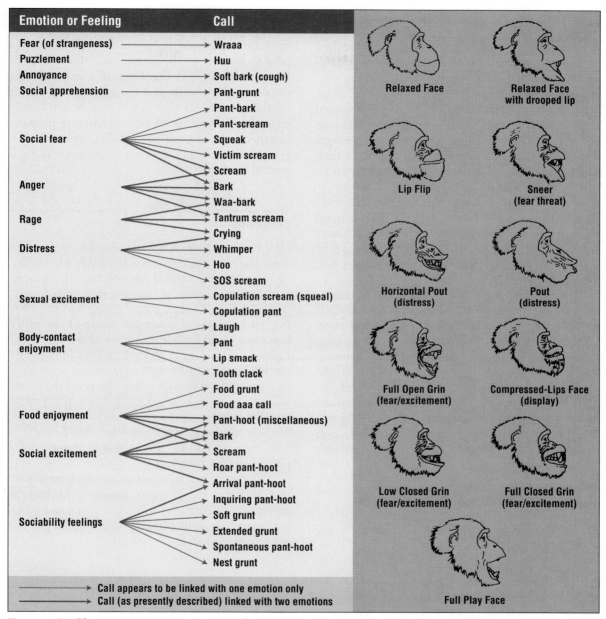

Emotion or Feeling	Call
Fear (of strangeness)	→ Wraaa
Puzzlement	→ Huu
Annoyance	→ Soft bark (cough)
Social apprehension	→ Pant-grunt
Social fear	→ Pant-bark
	→ Pant-scream
	→ Squeak
	→ Victim scream
	→ Scream
Anger	→ Bark
	→ Waa-bark
Rage	→ Tantrum scream
	→ Crying
Distress	→ Whimper
	→ Hoo
	→ SOS scream
Sexual excitement	→ Copulation scream (squeal)
	→ Copulation pant
Body-contact enjoyment	→ Laugh
	→ Pant
	→ Lip smack
	→ Tooth clack
	→ Food grunt
	→ Food aaa call
Food enjoyment	→ Pant-hoot (miscellaneous)
	→ Bark
Social excitement	→ Scream
	→ Roar pant-hoot
	→ Arrival pant-hoot
	→ Inquiring pant-hoot
Sociability feelings	→ Soft grunt
	→ Extended grunt
	→ Spontaneous pant-hoot
	→ Nest grunt

→ Call appears to be linked with one emotion only
→ Call (as presently described) linked with two emotions

Relaxed Face
Relaxed Face with drooped lip
Lip Flip
Sneer (fear threat)
Horizontal Pout (distress)
Pout (distress)
Full Open Grin (fear/excitement)
Compressed-Lips Face (display)
Low Closed Grin (fear/excitement)
Full Closed Grin (fear/excitement)
Full Play Face

Figure 4.6   Chimpanzee communication combines a number of distinctive calls with different facial expressions.

of these, such as kissing and embracing, are in virtually universal use today among humans as well as apes.

Primatologists have classified numerous kinds of chimpanzee vocalization and visual communication (see Fig. 4.6). Together, these facilitate group protection, coordination of group efforts, and social interaction in general. Experiments with captive apes, discussed later in this chapter as well as in Chapters 14 and 15, reveal that their communicative abilities exceed what they make use of in the wild. From such experiments, we may learn something about the origin of human language.

Home Ranges

Primates usually move about within circumscribed areas, or **home ranges,** which are of varying sizes, depending on the size of the group and on ecological factors such as availability of food. Ranges are often moved seasonally. The distance traveled by a group in a day varies; baboons may travel as many as 12 miles in a day. Some areas of a range, known as "core areas," are used more often than others; they may contain water, food sources, resting places, and sleeping trees. The ranges of different groups may overlap, and often a tree-dwelling species will share a range with ground dwellers. In such cases, the two species are not necessarily competing for the same resources; they may be using the range at different times and eating somewhat different foods.

Neither baboons nor gorillas defend their home ranges against incursions of others of their kind, although they certainly will defend their group if it is in any way threatened. Thus, they may be said to be nonterritorial. The chimpanzees studied by Goodall, by contrast, have been observed patrolling their territories to ward off potential trespassers. At one point, she witnessed the destruction of one chimpanzee community by another that had invaded the first one's turf. Although Goodall has interpreted this as territorial behavior another interpretation is possible.[7] In Africa today,

---

Home range: The area within which a group of primates usually moves.

---

[7]Power, M. G. (1995). Gombe revisited: Are chimpanzees violent and hierarchical in the "free" state? *General Anthropology*, 2 (1), 5–9.

human encroachment is squeezing chimpanzees into ever smaller pockets of forest. This places considerable stress on animals whose levels of violence tend to increase in the absence of sufficient space. Perhaps the violence that Goodall witnessed was a response to crowding as a consequence of human encroachment. Another factor may be frustration engendered by artificial feeding. Among primates in general, the clearest territoriality appears in forest species, rather than in those that are more terrestrial in their habits.

Learning

Observation of monkeys and apes has shown that their learning abilities are remarkably humanlike. In an experiment carried out by some Japanese primatologists, a group of Japanese macaques was fed wheat; within 4 hours, wheat eating had spread to the entire group of macaques living in the valley. Inventive behavior has also been observed among Japanese macaques. A group living on an island off the Japanese coast learned to clean sweet potatoes by dipping them in water after observing the young macaque who had first done it. From this youngster, the behavior spread to its playmates and some of their mothers. Once a mother had learned to wash sweet potatoes, this skill was always passed on to her offspring.

The more we learn about catarrhines in general, and apes in particular, the more we become aware of a degree of intelligence and capacity for conceptual thought hitherto unsuspected for any nonhuman primate.

Original Study
The Intellectual Abilities of Orang-utans[8]

Both the fossil data and comparisons of DNA and other biochemical measures suggest that the orang-utan is the most conservative, or primitive, of the great apes. They are most like the ancestral hominoid (ape-like primate) living about twelve million years ago that later gave rise to apes and humans. Orang-utans have retained more of the characteristics of this hominoid than have the African apes. As a result, orang-utans have been labelled a "living fossil," and thus are a kind of time traveller.

Orang-utans have amazing abilities that need wider recognition within both the general population and the scientific community. Cognitive studies with orang-utans have shown that they are at least as intelligent as the African apes, and have revealed a humanlike insightful thinking style characterised by longer attention spans and quiet deliberate action. Susan Essock and Duane Rumbaugh commented: "Chimpanzees are often reputed to be the smartest of the apes, and orang-utans have the reputation of being dull and sluggish. Such tags are unfortunate and contrary to the results of studies."

Orang-utans make shelters and other tools in their natural setting. In captivity, they learn to tie knots, recognise themselves in mirrors, use one tool to make another, and are the most skilled of the apes in manipulating objects. They are the escape artists of zoos because of their ability to cleverly manipulate bolts and wires to get out of their enclosures, a trait with which I have become very familiar. In discussing these tendencies, Benjamin Beck has compared the probable use of a screwdriver by chimpanzees, gorillas and orang-utans. The gorilla would largely ignore it, the chimpanzee would try to use it in a number of ways other than as a screwdriver, and:

> The orang-utan would notice the tool at once but ignore it lest a keeper discover the oversight. If a keeper did notice, the ape would rush to the tool and surrender it only in trade for a quantity of preferred food. If the keeper did not notice, the ape would wait until night and then proceed to use the screwdriver to pick the locks or dismantle the cage and escape.

Wright showed an orang-utan named Abang how to strike flakes from a piece of flint to make a knife, as our hominid ancestors did two million years ago. After Abang learned to make flakes, he opened a box containing food by cutting a string that held it closed.

Finding that orang-utan and human brains are similar in areas specialised for language prompted scientists to speculate that orang-utans could possibly be taught to use gestural signs. Since 1973, I have been doing just that, first with chimpanzees, and, more recently, with an orang-utan named Chantek. Now we do not have to wonder about what might be in the mind of apes, or what emotions they might feel. If we keep our expectations realistic and use human children as our model, we can just ask them. I have learned much about these creatures, and like my colleagues doing similar research, I have found myself unconsciously experiencing them as persons.

Chantek: An Orang-utan Who Uses Sign Language

The similarities between apes and humans seemed in conflict with our behavioral differences, until ape language experiments shifted scientific opinion and began to fill in the gap. Attempts to teach speech to orang-utans have not been very successful because apes lack the flexible right angle bend to their vocal tract that is necessary to make the range of human vocal sounds. After researchers began to use American Sign Language for the deaf to communicate with chimpanzees and gorillas, I began the first longitudinal study of the language ability of an orang-utan named Chantek, who was born at the Yerkes Primate Center in Atlanta, Georgia, USA. There was criticism that symbol-using apes might just be imitating their human care-givers, but there is now growing agreement that orang-utans, gorillas, and both chimpanzee species can develop language skills at the level of a two- to three-year-old human child.

The goal of Project Chantek was to investigate the mind of an orang-utan through a developmental study of his cognitive and linguistic skills. It was a great ethical and emotional responsibility to engage an orang-utan in what anthropologists call "enculturation," since I would not only be teaching a form of communication, I would be teaching aspects of the culture upon which that language was based. If my developmental project was successful, I would create a symbol-using creature which would be somewhere between an ape living under natural conditions and an adult human, which threatened to raise as many questions as I sought to answer.

Beginning at nine months of age, Chantek was raised at the University of Tennessee at Chattanooga by a small group of care-givers who communicated with him by using gestural signs based on the American Sign Language for the deaf. Chantek produced his first signs after one month and eventually learned to use approximately 150 different signs, forming a vocabulary similar to that of a very young child. Chantek learned names for people (LYN, JOHN), places (YARD, BROCK-HALL), things to eat (YOGURT, CHOCOLATE), actions (WORK, HUG), objects (SCREWDRIVER, MONEY), animals (DOG, APE), colours (RED, BLACK), pronouns (YOU, ME), location (UP, POINT), attributes (GOOD, HURT), and emphasis (MORE, TIME-TO-DO). We found that Chantek's signing was spontaneous and nonrepetitious. He did not merely imitate his care-givers as had been claimed for the sign language–trained chimpanzee Nim; rather, Chantek actively used his signs to initiate communications and meet his needs.

Almost immediately, Chantek began to use his signs in combinations and modulated their meanings with slight changes in how he articulated and arranged his signs. He commented "COKE DRINK" after drinking his coke, "PULL BEARD" while pulling a care-giver's hair through a fence, "TIME HUG" while locked in his cage as his care-giver looked at her watch, and "RED BLACK POINT" for a group of coloured paint jars. At first he used signs to manipulate people and objects to meet his needs, rather than to refer to them. He knew the meaning of his signs the way a pet might associate a can of food or a word with feeding time. But, could he use these signs as symbols, that is, more abstractly to represent a person, thing, action or idea, even apart from its context or when it was not present?

One indication of the capacity to use symbolic language in both deaf and hearing human children is the ability to point, which some researchers argued that apes could not do spontaneously. Chantek began to point to objects when he was two years old, somewhat later than human children, as we might expect. First, he showed and gave us objects, and then he began pointing to where he wanted to be tickled and to where he wanted to be carried. Finally, he could answer questions like WHERE HAT? WHICH DIFFERENT? and WHAT WANT? by pointing to the correct object.

As Chantek's vocabulary increased, the ideas that he was expressing became more complex, such as when he signed "BAD BIRD" at noisy birds giving alarm calls, and "WHITE CHEESE FOOD-EAT" for cottage cheese. He understood that things had characteristics or attributes that could be described. He also created combinations of signs that we had never used before. In the way that a child learns language, Chantek began to over or under-extend the meaning of his signs, which gave us insight into his emotions and how he was beginning to classify his world. For example, he used the sign "DOG" for dogs, a picture of a dog in his viewmaster, orang-utans on television, barking noises on the radio, birds, horses, a tiger at the circus, a herd of cows, a picture of a cheetah, and a noisy helicopter that presumably sounded like it was barking. For Chantek, the sign "BUG" included crickets, cockroaches, a picture of a cockroach, beetles, slugs, small moths, spiders, worms, flies, a picture of a graph shaped like a butterfly, tiny brown pieces of cat food, and small bits of faeces. He signed "BREAK" before he broke and shared pieces of crackers, and after he broke his toilet. He signed "BAD" to himself before he grabbed a cat, when he bit into a radish, and for a dead bird.

We also discovered that Chantek could comprehend our spoken English (after the first couple of years we used speech as well as signing). One day when the radio was on, a children's story about a cat was being broadcast. When the narrator said "cat" or made meow sounds, Chantek signed "CAT." We then verbally asked Chantek to sign a number of the words in his vocabulary, which he promptly did, showing that he had developed sign-speech correspondences without intentional training.

Another component of the capacity to use symbols is displacement: the ability to refer to things or events not present. It is an important indicator that symbols are also mental representations that can be held in the mind when the objects to which they refer are not present. This was an extremely important development in the evolution of human language because it freed individuals from the immediate environment and allowed our ancestors to talk about distant times and places. When he was two years old, Chantek began to sign for things that were not present. He frequently asked to go to places in his yard to look for animals, such as his pet squirrel and cat who served as playmates. He also made requests for "ICE CREAM," signing "CAR RIDE" and pulling us toward the parking lot for a trip to a local ice-cream shop.

We learned that an orang-utan can tell lies. Deception is an important indicator of language abilities since it requires a deliberate and intentional misrepresentation of reality. In order to deceive, you must be able to see events from the other persons' perspective and negate his or her perception. Chantek began to deceive from a relatively early age, and we caught him in lies about three times a week. He learned that he could sign "DIRTY" to get into the bathroom to play with the washing machine, dryer, soap, etc., instead of using the toilet. He also used his signs deceptively to gain social advantage in games, to divert attention in social interactions, and to avoid testing situations and coming home after walks on campus. On one occasion, Chantek stole food from my pocket while he simultaneously pulled my hand away in the opposite direction. On another occasion, he stole a pencil eraser, pretended to swallow it and "supported" his case by opening his mouth and signing "FOOD-EAT," as if to say that he had swallowed it. However, he really held the eraser in his cheek, and later it was found in his bedroom where he commonly hid objects.

We carried out tests of Chantek's mental ability using measures developed for human children. Chantek reached a mental age equivalent to that of a two- or three-year-old child, with some skills of even older children. On some tasks done readily by children, such as using one object to represent another and pretend play, Chantek performed as well as children, but less frequently. He engaged in chase games in which he would look over his shoulder as he darted about, although no one was chasing him. He also signed to his toys and offered them food and drink. Like children, Chantek showed evidence of animism, a tendency to endow objects and events with the attributes of living things. Although none of these symbolic play behaviours were as extensive as they would have been in a human child, the difference appears to be one of degree, not kind.

Chantek also experimented in play and problem-solving; for example, he tried vacuuming himself and investigated a number of clever ways to short out the electric fence that surrounded his yard. He learned how to use several tools, such as hammers, nails, and screwdrivers, and he was able to complete tasks using tools with up to twenty-two problem-solving steps. By the time he was two years old, he was imitating signs and actions. We would perform an action and ask him to copy it by signing "DO SAME." He would immediately imitate the behaviour, sometimes with novel twists, as when he winked by moving his eyelid up and down with his finger. Chantek also liked to use paints, and his own free-style drawings resembled those of three-year-old human children. He learned to copy horizontal lines, vertical lines and circles. By four and a half years of age, Chantek could identify himself in the mirror and use it to groom himself. He showed evidence of planning, creative simulation, and the use of objects in novel relations to one another to invent new meanings. For example, he simulated the context for food preparation by giving his care-giver two objects needed to prepare his milk formula and staring at the location of the remaining ingredient.

The above examples show evidence of intentionality, premeditation, taking the perspective of the other, displacement and symbolic use of language. These cognitive processes require that some form of mental image about the outcome of events be created. A further indication that Chantek had mental images is found in his ability to respond to his care-giver's request that he improve the articulation of a sign. When his articulation became careless, we would ask him to "SIGN BETTER." Looking closely at us, he would sign slowly and emphatically, taking one hand to put the other into the proper shape. Evidence for mental images also comes from Chantek's spontaneous execution of signs with his feet, which we did not teach him to do. Chantek even began to use objects in relation to each other to form signs. For example, he used the blades of scissors instead of his hands to make the sign for biting.

Chantek was extremely curious and inventive. When he wanted to know the name of something he offered his hands to be moulded into the shape of the proper sign. But language is a creative process, so we were pleased to see that Chantek began to invent his own signs. He invented: NO-TEETH (to show us that he would not use his teeth during rough play); EYE-DRINK (for contact lens solution used by his care-givers); DAVE-MISSING-FINGER (a name for a favourite university employee who had a hand injury); VIEWMAS-TER (a toy that displays small pictures); and BALLOON. Like our ancestors, Chantek had become a creator of language, the criterion that two hundred years earlier Lord Monboddo had said would define orang-utans as persons.

We had a close relationship with Chantek. He became extremely attached to his care-givers, and began to show empathy and jealousy toward us. He would quickly "protect" us from an "attacking" toy animal or other pretence. He clearly missed favourite care-givers and occasionally asked to see us. When he was eight years old, he became too large to live on campus, and he returned to the Yerkes Center in Atlanta, Georgia, to live. It was a difficult transition, and he missed his familiar companions and activities. One day he sat sadly, and signed "POINT GIVE ANN" while gesturing toward the front door. He watched the door and the different cars and individuals that passed by—waiting for Ann. His loneliness was somewhat relieved when he was introduced to two female orang-utans at the Yerkes Center. Although he impregnated one of them, the offspring died shortly after birth. In the future, not only is it important that Chantek have an opportunity to continue to interact with other orang-utans, but it is also important that his enculturation not be forgotten. My goal is for our interaction to continue, and for Chantek to have an opportunity to use his signs not only with other humans, but with other orang-utans as well.

We have lived day to day with Chantek and have shared common experiences, as if he were a child. We have healed his hurts, comforted his fears of stray cats, played keep-away games, cracked nuts in the woods with stones, watched him sign to himself, felt fooled by his deceptions, and frustrated when he became bored with his tasks. We have dreamed about him, had conversations in our imagination with him and loved him. Through these rare events shared with another species, I have no doubt I was experiencing Chantek as a person.

[8]Miles, H. L. W. (1993). Language and the orang-utan: The old "person" of the forest. In P. Cavalieri & P. Singer (Eds.), *The great ape project* (pp. 45–50). New York: St. Martin's Press.

Use of Objects as Tools

In the wild, neither baboons nor gorillas make or use tools in any significant way, but chimpanzees (like orangutans) do. For our purposes, a **tool** may be defined simply as an object used to facilitate some task or activity. Here, a distinction must be made between simple tool *use*, as when one pounds something with a convenient stone when a hammer is not available, and tool *making*, which involves deliberate modification of some material for its intended use. Thus, otters that use unmodified stones to crack open clams may be tool users, but they are not tool makers. Not only do chimpanzees modify objects to make them suitable for particular purposes, but also chimps can to some extent modify them to regular and set patterns. They can also pick up, and even prepare, objects for future use at some other location, and they can use objects as tools to solve new and novel problems. For example, chimps have been observed using stalks of grass, twigs that they have stripped of leaves, and even sticks up to 3 feet long that they have smoothed down to "fish" for termites. They insert the modified stick into a termite nest, wait a few minutes, pull the stick out, and eat the insects clinging to it, all of which requires considerable dexterity. Chimpanzees are equally deliberate in their nest building. They test the vines and branches to make sure they are usable. If they are not, the animal moves to another site.

Other examples of chimpanzee use of objects as tools involve leaves, used as wipes, or as sponges to get water out of a hollow to drink. Large sticks may serve as clubs or as missiles (as may stones) in aggressive or defensive displays. Stones or rocks are also used as hammers and anvils to open palm nuts and hard fruits. Interestingly, tool use to fish for termites or to crack open nuts is most often exhib-

Tool: An object used to facilitate some task or activity. While tool making involves intentional modification of the material of which it is made, tool use may consist of the use of either made tools or unmodified objects for some particular purpose.

The chimpanzee is using a tool to "fish" for termites.

ited by females, whereas aimed throwing of rocks and sticks is most often exhibited by males. Such tool-using behavior, which young animals learn from their mothers and other adults in their groups, may reflect one of the preliminary adaptations that, in the past, led to human cultural behavior.

Gorillas are the only one of the great apes that have not been observed to make and use tools in the wild. The reason for this is probably not that gorillas lack the intelligence or skill to do so; rather, their easy diet of leaves and nettles makes tools pointless.

Hunting

The hunting, killing, and eating of small- to medium-sized mammals, something that is unusual among primates, has been observed among baboons and chimps, but not among gorillas. Such behavior is exhibited less often by baboons than by chimps, who are less opportunistic in their meat eating. Although chimpanzee females sometimes hunt, males do so far more frequently. When on the hunt, they may spend up to 2 hours watching, following, and chasing intended prey. Moreover, in contrast to the usual primate practice of each animal finding its own food for itself, hunting frequently involves teamwork to trap and kill prey.

The most sophisticated examples of this occur when hunting baboons; once a potential victim has been partially isolated from its troop, three or more adults will carefully position themselves so as to block off escape routes while another climbs toward the prey for the kill. Once a kill has been made, it is common for most of those present to get a share of the meat, either by grabbing a piece as the chance affords, or by sitting and begging for a piece.

Perhaps limited predation is a very old pattern among chimps. Equally possible, it may be a recent development on the part of chimpanzees living at the edge of the savanna; they may just be starting to exploit a food source that our own ancestors tapped in similar circumstances millions of years earlier. Consistent with this behavior, when out on the savanna chimps are known to increase their predation on eggs and vertebrate animals, probably because they cannot so easily satisfy their amino acid requirements (necessary for growth and tissue replacement) from the plants there as they can in the forest.[9] In any case, it is interesting to

[9]Stahl, A. B. (1984). Hominid dietary selection before fire. *Current Anthropology, 25,* 155.

note that, in primates, as among many carnivores, more cooperation seems to go hand in hand with predation and meat eating.

Primate Behavior and Human Evolution

Studies of monkeys and apes living today—especially gorillas and chimpanzees, which are so closely related to us, and baboons, which have adapted to life on savannas like those to which our earliest ancestors adapted—afford essential clues in the reconstruction of adaptations and behavior patterns involved in the emergence of our earliest ancestors. At the same time, we must be careful about how we reconstruct this development. Primates have changed in various ways from earlier times, and undoubtedly certain forms of behavior that they now exhibit were not found among their ancestors. Furthermore, it is important to remember that present-day primate behavior shows considerable variation, not just from one species to another but also from one population to another within a single species. To ignore such variation is to run the risk of faulty generalization—something often seen in the popular literature.

CHAPTER SUMMARY

The Linnaean system classifies living things on the basis of overall similarities into small groups, or species. The characteristics on which Karl von Linné based his system were body structure, body function, and sequence of bodily growth. Modern taxonomy also utilizes such characteristics as chemical reactions of blood, protein structure, and the makeup of the genetic material itself.

The modern primates, like most mammals, are intelligent animals that bear their young live and then nourish them with milk from their mothers. Like other mammals, they maintain constant body temperature and have respiratory and circulatory systems that will sustain high activity. Their skeleton and teeth also resemble those of other mammals, although there are differences of detail.

Modern primates are divided into two suborders. The strepsirhines include lemurs and lorises, which resemble small rodents in body outline. The haplorhines include tarsiers, New and Old World monkeys, apes, and humans. To a greater degree among the haplorhines, and a lesser degree among the strepsirhines, primates show a number of characteristics that developed as adaptations to insect predation in the trees. These adaptive characteristics include a generalized set of teeth, suited for eating insects but also a variety of fruits and leaves as well. These teeth are fewer in number and set in a smaller jaw than in most mammals. Other evolutionary adaptations in the primate line include stereoscopic vision, or depth perception, and an intensified sense of touch. Each of these developments had an effect upon the primate brain, resulting in a general trend toward larger size and greater complexity. There were also changes in the primate skeleton; in particular, a reduction of the snout, larger brain case, and numerous adaptations for upright posture and flexibility of limb movement. In addition, changes in the reproductive pattern took place such that fewer offspring were born to each female, and there was a longer period of infant dependency.

The apes are the closest relatives humans have. These include gibbons, siamangs, orangutans, gorillas, and chimpanzees. In genetic structure, biochemistry, and anatomy, chimpanzees and gorillas are closest to humans and thus must share a common ancestry.

The social life of primates is complex. Primates are social animals, and most species live and travel in groups. Among savanna baboons, females remain for life in the group of their birth, whereas males transfer at adolescence to another. Among chimpanzees, it is females that may transfer, though not all do so; their sons and often their daughters remain with their mothers for life. Among gorillas, either males or females may transfer. In all three species, both males and females are organized into dominance hierarchies. In the case of females, the better food and reduced harassment that are a consequence of high rank enhance reproductive success.

A characteristic primate activity is grooming, which is a sign of closeness between individuals. Among baboons, gorillas, and chimpanzees, sexual interaction generally takes place only when a female is in estrus. Although dominant males try to monopolize females while they are in estrus, the cooperation of the females is usually required for this to succeed. Among baboons, females clearly prefer as sex partners males with whom they already have a friendship. Primates have elaborate systems of communication based on vocalizations and gestures. Usually primates move about within home ranges, rather than defended territories.

The diet of most primates is made up of a variety of fruits, leaves, and insects, but baboons and chimpanzees sometimes hunt, kill, and eat animals as well. Among chimps, most hunting is done by males and may require considerable teamwork. Once a kill is made, most animals present get a share of the meat.

SUGGESTED READINGS

Fossey, D. (1983). *Gorillas in the mist.* Burlington, MA: Houghton Mifflin.

Dian Fossey is to gorillas what Jane Goodall is to chimpanzees. Up until the time of her death, Fossey had devoted years to studying gorilla behavior in the field. This book is about the first 13 years of her study; as well as being readable and informative, it is well illustrated.

Goodall, J. (1990). *Through a window.* Boston: Houghton Mifflin.

This fascinating book is a personal account of Goodall's experience over 35 years of studying wild chimpanzees in Tanzania. A pleasure to read and a fount of information on the behavior of these apes, the book is profusely illustrated as well.

Jolly, A. (1985). *The evolution of primate behavior* (2nd ed.). New York: Macmillan.

The first edition of this book was the standard text on primate behavior for 13 years. In this as in the original edition, the author surveys knowledge about primate behavior and its relevance for human behavior. Though 10 years old, the book is comprehensive, amusing, and well illustrated.

LeGros Clark, W. E. (1966). *History of the primates* (5th ed.). Chicago: University of Chicago Press.

An old classic, this remains a fine introduction to the comparative anatomy of the primates.

Patterson, F., & Linden, E. (1981). *The education of Koko.* New York: Holt, Rinehart and Winston.

Several experiments with captive apes have sought to investigate the full potential of their communicative abilities, and one of the most interesting is that involving Koko the gorilla. This is a particularly readable account of those experiments and their results.

CHAPTER
5
FOSSIL PRIMATES

OUR KNOWLEDGE OF THE EARLIEST CATARRHINE PRIMATES IS
BASED PRIMARILY ON FOSSILS FROM EGYPT'S FAYUM DEPRESSION
IN THE DESERT WEST OF CAIRO. HERE, WINDS AND FLASH
FLOODS HAVE UNCOVERED SEDIMENTS MORE THAN 22 MILLION
YEARS OLD, EXPOSING THE REMAINS OF A TROPICAL RAIN FOREST
THAT WAS HOME TO A VARIETY OF MONKEY-LIKE ANIMALS.

CHAPTER PREVIEW

When Did the First Primates Appear and What Were They Like?

The earliest primates had developed by 60 million years ago and were small, arboreal insect eaters. Their initial adaptation to life in the trees set the stage for the subsequent appearance of other primate models.

When Did the First Monkeys and Apes Appear and What Were They Like?

By the late Eocene Epoch, about 37 million years ago, monkeys and apes about the size of modern house cats were living in Africa. By about 20 million years ago, they had proliferated and soon spread over many parts of the Old World. Some forms remained relatively small, while others became quite large, comparable to present-day chimpanzees and gorillas.

What Group of Primates Gave Rise to the Human Line of Evolution?

Present evidence suggests that our own ancestors are to be found among the "sivapithecines," which were widespread between approximately 17 and 8 million years ago. Small versions of these apelike primates seem to have had the right kind of anatomy, and at least some of them lived in situations in which the right kind of selective pressures existed to transform them into primitive hominines.

A little more than a century ago, Charles Darwin shattered the surface calm of the Victorian world with his startling theory that humans are cousins of the living apes and monkeys and are descended from the same prehistoric ancestors. What would have been the public reaction, one wonders, if they had known, as we do, that even earlier ancestors were small, mouse-sized creatures that subsisted chiefly on insects and worms? Such primitive creatures date back about 60 million years. These ancient forebears of ours evolved over time into different species as mutations produced variation, which was acted upon by natural selection and genetic drift.

Although many of the primates discussed in this chapter no longer exist, their descendants, which were reviewed in Chapter 4, are found living throughout the world. The successful adaptation of the primates is believed to be due largely to their intelligence, a characteristic that reaches its culmination in human beings and which provides for adaptive flexibility. Other physical traits, such as stereoscopic vision and a grasping hand, have also been instrumental in the success of the primates.

What is the justification for studying a form of life whose history is, at best, fragmentary, and which existed millions of years ago? The study of these prehistoric primates tells us something we can use to interpret the evolution of the entire primate line, including ourselves. It gives us a better understanding of the physical forces that caused these primitive creatures to evolve into today's primates. Ultimately, the study of these ancient ancestors gives us a fuller knowledge of the processes through which insect-eating, small-brained animals evolved into a toolmaker and thinker that is recognizably human.

PRIMATE FOSSILS

Considering that primates have shown a tendency through the ages to live in environments where the conditions for fossilization are generally not good, we have a surprising number of fossils with which to work. While some nearly complete skeletons of ancient primates do exist, more often what we have are specimens of teeth and jawbones, because these structures are durable and are often the only remains of an animal to be found. Thus a whole branch of fossil study based on tooth structures, or dentition, has arisen. Dentition is extremely important in helping to identify and classify different fossil forms; often investigators are able to infer a good deal about the total animal on the basis of only a few teeth found lying in the earth. For example, knowledge of the way the teeth fit together indicates much about the operation of the jaws, suggesting the types of muscles needed. This in turn indicates how the skull must have been shaped to provide accommodation for the musculature. The shape of the jaws and details of the teeth also define the type of food that they were suited to deal with, indicating the probable diet of the specimen. Thus a mere jawbone can tell paleoanthropologists a great deal about the animal from which it came.

MAMMALIAN EVOLUTION AND PRIMATE ORIGINS

An interesting fact about the evolution of the mammals is that the diverse forms with which we are familiar today, including the primates, are the products of an **adaptive radiation** that did not begin until after mammals had been present on the earth for more than 100 million years. Actually, the story of mammalian evolution starts as long ago as 230 to 280 million years ago (Fig. 5.1). From deposits of this period, which geologists call the Permian, we have the remains of reptiles with features pointing in a distinctly mammalian direction. These mammal-like reptiles were slimmer than most other reptiles and were flesh eaters. In a series of graded fossils, we can see in them a reduction of bones to a more mammalian number, the shifting of limbs underneath the body, development

Adaptive radiation: Rapid diversification of an evolving population as it adapts to a variety of available niches.

MILLIONS OF YEARS AGO	PERIODS	EPOCHS	LIFE FORMS
2		Pleistocene	
5		Pliocene	First undoubted hominines
23		Miocene	
34		Oligocene	
			First undoubted monkey-ape ancestors
55		Eocene	
65		Paleocene	First undoubted primates
135	Cretaceous		
180	Jurassic		First undoubted mammals
230	Triassic		
280	Permian		Mammal-like reptiles
345	Carboniferous		First reptiles

Figure 5.1 This timeline highlights major "milestones" in the evolution of mammals.

be seen as well in the dark as they can in the light, they can be heard and smelled just as well. Both sound and smell are more complex than sight. If something can be seen, it is right there in the line of vision. By contrast, it is possible to smell and hear things around corners and in other hidden places, and in addition to figuring out what it is that is smelled or heard and how far away it is, the animal must also determine where it is. A further complication is the fact that smells linger, and so the animal must figure out if the cause of an odor is still there or, if not, how old the odor is.

As the hearing and sense of smell of mammals became keener, they lost the ability (possessed by reptiles) to see in color. But the new keener senses and the importance of outwitting both prey and predators served to improve their information-processing capacities and the part of the brain that handles this—the cerebral cortex—over that of reptiles.

Since mammals were developing as such bright, active creatures, it may seem puzzling at first why reptiles continued to be the dominant land animals for more than 100 million years. After all, mammals, with their constant body temperature, can remain active at any time, whereas reptiles become more sluggish unless the surrounding

The appearance of angiosperm plants not only provided highly nutritious fruits and seeds, and flowers but provided as well a host of habitats for numerous edible insects and worms—just the sorts of foods required by mammals with their high metabolism.

of a separation between the mouth and nasal cavity, differentiation of the teeth, and so forth.

By 180 million years ago—the end of what geologists call the Triassic period—true mammals were on the scene. We know these and the mammals from the succeeding Jurassic and Cretaceous periods (180 to 65 million years ago) from hundreds of finds of mostly teeth and jaw parts. All of these creatures were small and flesh eating—such things as insects, worms, and eggs. They seem to have been nocturnal in their habits, which is probably why the senses of smell and hearing became so developed in mammals. Although things cannot

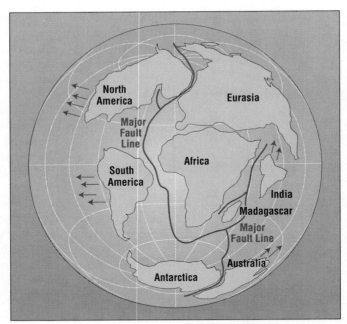

Figure 5.2 The separation of the continents was a result of massive shifting in the plate-like segments of the earth's crust as illustrated by the position of the continents at the end of the Cretaceous period (ca. 65 million years ago).

temperature is just right. Furthermore, mammals provide care for their young, whereas most reptiles leave theirs to fend for themselves. But the mammals were limited by two things. For one, their high activity demanded more in the way of nutrition than did the less constant activity of reptiles. High-quality nutrition is provided by fruits, nuts, and seeds of flowering plants, but these plants did not become common until the end of the Cretaceous period. It is also provided by the flesh of other animals, but the mammals were small and dependent particularly on insects and worms. These were limited in numbers until flowers and fruits provided them with a host of new **ecological niches,** or functional positions in their habitats, to exploit.

The second limitation that affected the mammals was the slight temporal priority enjoyed by the

Ecological niche: A species' way of life considered in the context of its environment, including other species found in that environment.

reptiles—they had preempted most available niches, which therefore were not available to mammals. With the mass extinction of so many reptiles at the end of the Cretaceous, a number of existing niches became available to the mammals; at the same time, whole new niches were opened up as the new grasses provided abundant food in arid places, and other flowering plants provided abundant, high-quality food elsewhere. By chance, the mammals had the necessary biological equipment to take advantage of the new opportunities available to them.

RISE OF THE PRIMATES

The early primates emerged during a time of great change all over the world. The separation of continents was under way as the result of movement of the great platelike segments of the earth's crust on which they rest. Although Europe was still joined to North America, South America and India were isolated, while a narrow body of water separated Africa from Eurasia (Fig. 5.2). On the land itself the great dinosaurs had recently become

The ability to judge depth correctly and grasp branches strongly are of obvious use to animals as active in the trees as this South American squirrel monkey.

extinct, and the mammals were undergoing the great adaptive radiation that ultimately led to the development of the diverse forms with which we are familiar today. At the same time, the newly evolved grasses, ivies, shrubs, and other flowering plants were undergoing an enormous proliferation. This, along with a new, mild climate, favored the spread of dense, lush tropical and subtropical forests over much of the earth, including North and South America, much of Eurasia, and Africa.

With the spread of these huge belts of forest, the stage was set for the evolution of some mammals from a rodentlike ground existence to the arboreal primate condition. Forests would provide our early ancestors with the ecological niches in which they would flourish.

The move to an arboreal existence brought a combination of the problems of earthbound existence with those of flight. In their move into the air, birds developed highly stereotyped behavior; tree-dwelling primates, on the other hand, exhibit flexible behavior in response to decision making. The initial forays into the trees must have produced many misjudgments and errors of coordination, leading to falls that injured or killed the individuals badly adapted to arboreal life. Natural selection favored those that judged depth correctly and gripped the branches strongly. It is quite likely that the early primates that took to the trees were in some measure preadapted, with better vision and more dexterous fingers than their contemporaries.

The relatively small size of the early primates allowed them to make use of the smaller branches of trees; larger, heavier competitors, and most predators, could not follow. The move to the smaller branches also opened up a more abundant food supply; the primates were able to gather insects, leaves, flowers, and fruits directly rather than waiting for them to fall to the ground.

The utilization of a new environment led to an acceleration in the rate of change of primate characteristics. Paradoxically, these changes eventually made possible a return to the ground on the part of some primates, including the ancestors of the genus *Homo*.

Paleocene Primates

Far back in the reaches of geologic time, small, squirrel-like animals resembling today's tree shrews scampered along the branches of trees in tropical forests. Members of the now extinct suborder **Plesiadapiformes,** these creatures appeared during the Paleocene Epoch, about 65 million years ago. They lived mostly on seeds and insects; their muzzles were long and pointed, their ears were small, their wrists and ankles were capable of turning toward each other, enabling them to climb trees, and their digits were flexible and suitable for grasping in spite of the presence of claws.

Since their survival depended on catching live food, these animals had to be quick and intelligent; the latter characteristic was reflected in their brains, which were larger than those of the tree shrews they otherwise resembled. Plesiadapiformes, of which there were a number of species, are known from a series of fossils from North America and Europe. Clearly, they were successful animals in their day, for in North America they account for slightly more than one third of late Paleocene mammalian fossils.

Plesiadapiformes: Now extinct mammals once considered to be primates, now known to be related to colugos (gliding mammals), which share a common ancestry with primates.

Up until 1990, plesiadapiformes were generally considered to be very primitive primates. The recent discovery of a particularly well-preserved fossil from Wyoming, however, has revealed that they were not; rather, they are related to the colugos—gliding mammals that are represented today by two species of "flying lemurs" (which are not lemurs, nor do they fly; like flying squirrels, they glide). Flying lemurs are found today only in Borneo and the Philippines. Since colugos and primates show a close genetic relationship, both likely shared a common ancestry among the insectivores, probably going their separate evolutionary ways by 60 million years ago. Thus, primates would have arisen as part of the great Paleocene adaptive radiation of mammals.

In fact, the earliest surely known primate fossils, 10 teeth from a site in Morocco, are about 60 million years old. These cheek teeth (molars and premolars) are similar to the corresponding teeth of the modern mouse lemur, a tiny strepsirhine primate weighing a mere two ounces.

Eocene Primates

The Eocene Epoch, which lasted from about 55 to 34 million years ago, began with an abrupt warming trend, at which time many older forms of mammals became extinct, to be replaced by recognizable progenitors of many of today's forms. Among the latter were numerous forms of lemurlike and tarsierlike primates, of which over 50 genera are known. Fossils of these creatures have been found in North America, Europe, and Asia, where the warm, wet conditions of the Eocene sustained extensive rain forests.

Eocene primates are usually classified into two families, the **Adapidae** and the **Omomyidae.** The

Adapidae: Extinct family of lemurlike primates.

Omomyidae: Extinct family of tarsierlike primates.

former were mostly diurnal (active during daylight) and generally ate fruit and leaves. Generally small, some were a bit larger than the smallest of today's monkeys. In many ways they were remarkably similar to modern lemurs and lorises, which likely are their descendants. Smaller than adapids are the omomyids, which were nocturnal eaters of fruits and insects. Tarsierlike in their anatomy, they are thought to have given rise to today's tarsier.

What these early primates have in common are somewhat enlarged brain cases, slightly reduced snouts, and a somewhat forward position of the eye orbits, which are surrounded by a complete bony ring (Fig. 5.3 on page 125). Their dentition, however, was primitive and unlike that of modern forms. In their limb skeleton, they were well adapted to grasping, leaping, and perching. Moreover, nails, rather than claws, may be seen on some digits.

A third group of Eocene primates is represented by fossils from late Eocene deposits in Egypt's Fayum depression.[1] Known as *Catopithecus*, these 37-million-year-old fossils include several skulls, jaws, and teeth, clearly revealing them to be catarrhine primates. Whether they are the earliest fossils to represent this group is debated. In 1992, some teeth were discovered in Algeria that could be as many as 46 to 50 million years old, but this is not certain. At least some of the teeth do resemble those of Oligocene hominoids. As for *Catopithecus*, this small creature displays the catarrhine dental formula (two incisors, a canine, two premolars, and three molars on each side of each jaw), a foramen magnum in a somewhat forward position beneath the skull, a completely walled eye orbit, and a brain about 3.1 cubic centimeters in size.[2]

Whether the group of primates that gave rise to *Catopithecus* arose at the same time as the adapids and omomyids, or from some early form of one or the other of these two families, is the subject of lively debate, as illustrated by the following Original Study.

[1]Culatta, E. (1992). A new take on anthropoid origins. *Science, 256,* 1516–1517.
[2]Simons, E. (1995). Skulls and anterior teeth of *Catopithecus* (Primates: Anthropoidea) from the Eocene and anthropoid origins. *Science, 268,* 1885–1888.

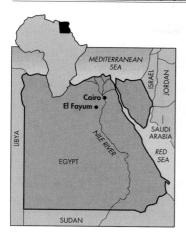

Original Study

Catopithecus and Anthropoid (Catarrhine and Platyrrhine) Origins[3]

When paleontologists disagree, they rarely have the luxury of doing another experiment to see who's right. Instead, they must resort to a more chancy and time-consuming enterprise: returning to the field and unearthing more fossils that prove their point. Paleoanthropologist Elwyn Simons of Duke University claims to have done just that. He presents new fossils from the Fayum Desert in Egypt to help resolve one of the most contentious issues in paleoprimatology: What was the common ancestor of apes, monkeys, and humans?

The new fossils, estimated to be 37 million years old, include rarely-preserved front teeth of the oldest undisputed higher primate, a small leaf- or insect-eating creature called *Catopithecus*. But given the difficulty of proving kinship among ancient primates, the finds are unlikely to forge consensus about this divisive issue. "These are neat specimens, but they don't address all the competing hypotheses. Until we have more complete material from Asia and Egypt, questions will remain," says early primate expert Herbert Covert of the University of Colorado, Boulder.

The problem of the origin of higher primates, also known as anthropoids, has sparked scientific fireworks for decades. Currently, there are at least four competing theories about how, when, and where anthropoids split from lower primates such as the primitive living lemurs. One theory favors an extinct group of primates, the diminutive omomyids, as anthropoid ancestors. Another camp, relying on fragmentary fossils from Africa

Catopithecus is the earliest undoubted catarrhine primate known. It lived in North Africa 37 million years ago.

and Asia, suggests that anthropoids themselves are an ancient group, extending back nearly to the dawn of all primates. And Simons says his new specimens support yet a third idea: Another extinct group, the lemur-like adapids, eventually led to all higher primates, including humans. "The oldest documented anthropoids don't look like omomyids. They look like adapids," he says.

Simons bases this conclusion on newly discovered fossils from an extraordinarily productive area of the Fayum Desert in Egypt where he and his crew have already unearthed 21 different primate species. The new fossils are skulls and jaws of *Catopithecus*, which has held the status of oldest undisputed anthropoid since Simons published the first skull 5 years ago. The new skulls—five or six in all—confirm that this small primate had the accepted anthropoid traits, such as a complete bony cone around the eye socket and forehead bones that are fused together rather than separate.

The new material also preserves incisors and canine teeth in the jaws, a rare find, as front teeth are often broken or lost. These teeth have adapoid traits such as shovel-shaped incisors, says Simons. In contrast, omomyid incisors are pointed, "like carrots," he says.

What's more, *Catopithecus'* upper jaw reveals two big front teeth flanked by smaller ones (just as in humans), while in the lower jaw the lateral incisors are bigger than the central ones. Adapids have exactly the same pattern, but omomyids do not. All in all, according to Simons, *Catopithecus'* teeth look very similar to adapids and nothing like omomyids, suggesting that anthropoids evolved from a branch of the adapid family tree. "The dental resemblances, taken together, show ties between the early anthropoid of the Fayum and one group of adapids, the cercamoniines," he says. He believes early cercamoniines led to higher primates.

Simon gets support from Philip Gingerich of the University of Michigan, who came to similar conclusions in the 1970s. At the time, Gingerich was comparing adapids to later anthropoids because the front teeth of early anthropoids were unknown. "It was a case of waiting for more evidence to catch up with the idea," he says.

But those who favor competing theories question whether the similarities between adapids and *Catopithecus* in fact prove they have a common ancestor. "The front teeth are not necessarily compelling characters," says Covert. "They look the same, but do they indicate shared ancestry?" Covert and others think the answer is probably not. Rather than indicating a common ancestry, some of the similarities may have evolved independently in adapids and anthropoids, says anthropologist Robert D. Martin of the University of Zurich in Switzerland: "I think that there is convergence between late adapids and simians (or anthropoids)." Martin praises the Fayum fossils, but says, "I don't find this adapid argument any more convincing than when it was suggested in the 1920s."

Also, although the Fayum deposits hold the first known anthropoids, the group likely evolved much earlier, so *Catopithecus* may look very different from the first higher primates, says Martin. "The Fayum is simply too late," agrees K. Christopher Beard of the Carnegie Museum of Natural History in Pittsburgh, who has his own candidate for the earliest anthropoid. This is a controversial Chinese primate, about 45 million years old and known from two jaws as well as from unpublished material.

Beard named the fossil *Eosimias*, or "dawn ape," but Simons counters that so far, there's no proof that *Eosimias* or any other older specimens are higher primates. "The trouble with all the other early `anthropoids' is that they are just known from jaw fragments or even teeth. So for them, none of the confirming features of anthropoids can be discerned," he says. "Only the Fayum has certifiable early anthropoids." Simons is not alone in his skepticism about Beard's finds. Says Martin: "About *Eosimias*, I'm on the fence for now."

Still, Beard continues to unearth fragmentary fossils to support his case, most recently a fossil ear bone that he says conflicts with the notion of an adapid ancestor for anthropoids. In an article in press in the *Journal of Human Evolution*, Beard and Ross MacPhee of the American Museum of Natural History show that this ear bone looks much more like an omomyid than an adapid. Thus, although they believe that the anthropoid lineage extends back at least 45 million years, MacPhee and Beard also conclude that anthropoids are more closely related to omomyids than to adapids.

But that argument hasn't won over the skeptics either. The bone was found isolated, so MacPhee and Beard can't prove that it truly belongs to *Eosimias*. And the ear bone looks so much like that of an omomyid that it doesn't boost *Eosimias'* uncertain status as an anthropoid, says paleoanthropologist Richard Kay of Duke. Agrees Gingerich: "That ear bone looks most like an omomyid, which I take to mean that it probably is an omomyid."

These recent volleys of evidence, some promoting an adapid ancestor for anthropoids, others suggesting an ancient link to omomyids, seem unlikely to end the debate. So how to solve the mystery of which early primate group led to our own lineage? On this, even Beard and Simons agree: more field seasons, and more fossils.

[3]Culatta, E. (1995). New finds rekindle debate over anthropoid origins. *Science, 268,* 1851.

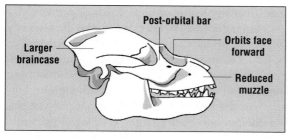

Figure 5.3   The Eocene genus *Adapis* represents the Adapidae.

With the end of the Eocene, substantial changes took place among the primates, as among other mammals. In North America, primates became extinct and elsewhere their range seems to have been reduced considerably. A driving force in all this was probably climatic change. Already, through the late Eocene, climates were becoming somewhat cooler and drier, but at the end temperatures took a sudden dive, sufficient to trigger formation of a substantial ice cap over Antarctica. The result was a marked reduction of the environments to which early primates were adapted. At the same time, some early primate niches may have been more effectively utilized by newly evolved rodent forms. Finally, the precursors of monkeys and apes, up to then overshadowed by adapids and omomyids, may have been able to take over some other niches formerly occupied by the early adapids and omomyids.

Oligocene Monkeys and Apes

The Oligocene Epoch began about 34, and ended about 23, million years ago. Primate fossils that have thus far been discovered and definitely placed in the Oligocene are not common, but enough exist to prove that haplorhines were becoming quite prominent and diverse by this time. The scarcity of Oligocene primate fossils stems from the reduced habitat available to them and from the arboreal nature of primates then living, which restricted them to damp forest environments where conditions are exceedingly poor for fossil formation.

Fortunately, Egypt's Fayum depression has yielded sufficient fossils (more than 1000) to reveal that, by 31 million years ago, haplorhine primates existed in considerable diversity. Moreover, the "cast of characters" is growing, as new fossils continue to be found in the Fayum, as well as in newly discovered localities in Algeria and Oman. At present, we have evidence of at least 60 genera included in two families, **Parapithecidae** and **Propliopithecidae.** Included in the latter is *Catopithecus.* Both families show a combination of monkeylike and apelike features, but the parapithecids are generally smaller than the propliopithecids. The origins of both families probably lie in the third, less numerous group of Eocene primates just discussed, but in the Oligocene the tables have been turned; now lemurlike and tarsierlike forms have become far less prominent than the monkeylike–apelike forms.

Included among the parapithecids may be the ancestors of monkeys. In their dental formula and limb bones, these small primates (about the size of a modern squirrel monkey) resemble platyrrhine monkeys. Some of them could easily have gotten to South America via exposed oceanic ridges and islands between the two continents, which, in the Oligocene, were far closer to each other than they are today. The earliest surely known catarrhine monkey fossil comes from the Miocene Epoch, but its molars look as if they evolved from an earlier pattern much like one seen in parapithecids.

Parapithecidae; Propliopithecidae: Extinct family of haplorhine primates, probably ancestral to hominoids.

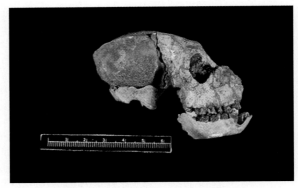

This *Aegyptopithecus* skull dates to the Oligocene Epoch. The enclosed eye sockets and dentition mark it as a catarrhine primate, probably ancestral to *Proconsul.*

More apelike in their dentition are a number of other genera, of which the best known is *Aegyptopithecus* (the "Egyptian ape"). Its lower molars have the five cusps of an ape, and the upper canine and lower first premolar provide a shearing mechanism such as is found in apes. Its skull possesses eye sockets that are in a forward position and completely protected by a bony wall, as is typical of modern monkeys and apes. Evidently *Aegyptopithecus*, and probably the other propliopithecids and parapithecids as well, possessed vision superior to that of the Eocene adapids and omomyids and their descendants, the lemurs and tarsiers. In fact, the inside of the skull of *Aegyptopithecus* reveals that its brain had a larger visual cortex and smaller olfactory lobes than do lemurs or tarsiers. Although the brain of *Aegyptopithecus* was smaller relative to body size than that of more recent catarrhines, this primate seems to have had a larger brain than any lemur or tarsier, past or present.

Aegyptopithecus, besides being the best-known Oligocene primate, is also of particular interest to us, for its teeth suggest that it belongs in the ancestry of those Miocene forms that gave rise to both humans and today's African apes. Although no bigger than a modern house cat, *Aegyptopithecus* was nonetheless one of the larger Oligocene primates. Possessed of a monkeylike skull and body, it evidently moved about in a quadrupedal, monkeylike manner. Differences between males and females include more formidable canine teeth and deeper mandibles (lower jaws) in the males. In modern catarrhines, species with these traits generally live in groups that include several adult females with one or more adult males.

Miocene Apes

The beginning of the Miocene Epoch, which succeeded the Oligocene about 23 million years ago, saw the catarrhine primates still restricted to Africa, where they had originated. Around 17 million years ago, however, Africa came into contact with the Eurasian land mass, permitting the spread and proliferation of apes in the forests that existed in many parts of the Old World.

East Africa is an area particularly rich in the fossils of apes from the early through the middle part of the Miocene. The earliest of these apes, *Proconsul,* is one of the best known, owing to the preservation of almost all elements of its skeleton. Species of *Proconsul* varied considerably in size, the smallest being no larger than a modern female baboon, while the largest was the size of a chimpanzee. That they were apes is clearly

Paleoanthropologist Alan Walker displays bones of *Proconsul,* an unspecialized tree-dwelling, fruit-eating hominoid of the early Miocene.

shown by their dentition, particularly the five-cusped lower molars. Moreover, their skull, compared with that of the Oligocene proto-apes, shows a reduced snout and a fuller, more rounded brain case. Still, some features are reminiscent of monkeys, particularly the forward thrust and narrowness of the face.

Although its overall configuration is not quite like any living monkey or ape, the elbow, hip, knee, and foot anatomy of *Proconsul* is similar to what one sees in living hominoids, while the wrist and pelvis are monkeylike and the lumbar vertebrae and leg bones show features that are intermediate between those of a gibbon and a monkey. Overall, the vertebral column was longer and more flexible, and the torso narrower than in apes, but the hind limb was less monkeylike, being more mobile as are ape hind limbs. The consensus is that *Proconsul* represents an unspecialized tree-dwelling, fruit-eating **hominoid** (the catarrhine superfamily to which modern apes and humans belong). Easily derivable from an animal like *Aegyptopithecus,* it was almost certainly ancestral to the hominoids of the middle Miocene. Like its probable ancestor as well as its descendants, all species of *Proconsul* were sexually dimorphic, the males being the larger sex, with more formidable canine teeth.

Hominoids of the middle and late Miocene (from roughly 16 million to 5 million years ago) can be divided into two broad groups, informally labeled dryopithecines and sivaphithecines. In the former group are several species of forest-dwelling primates having teeth and jaws much like those of the earlier *Proconsul.* They seem to have become somewhat more apelike rather than monkeylike in their overall appearance, however. Dryopithecines ranged over a remarkably wide geographical area: Their fossils have been found in Europe, Asia, and Africa. Such abundance and wide distribution indicates that these primates were very successful animals.

Hominoid: A catarrhine primate superfamily that includes apes and humans.

Sivapithecines

Also living in parts of Africa, Asia, and Europe were the various hominoids lumped together as **sivapithecines** (sometimes called "ramamorphs" and sometimes "ramapithecines," Fig. 5.4). Closely related to the dryopithecines, they too may be descendants of the earlier *Proconsul*. According to David Pilbeam, who has made the study of Miocene hominoids his life work: "Any of [the sivapithecines] would make excellent ancestors for the living hominoids: human bipeds, chimpanzee and gorilla knucklewalkers, Orangutan contortionists.[4] For many years, sivapithecines were known exclusively from the remains of teeth and jaws. Relative to the size of the cheek teeth (premolars and molars), their incisor teeth are comparable in size to those of the dryopithecines, although they are placed a bit more

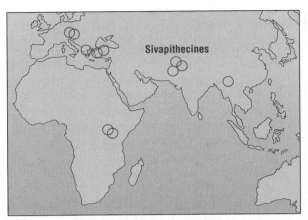

Figure 5.4   Sivapithecine fossils have been found in Central Africa, Europe, and Asia.

vertically in the mouth. The canines are far larger in males than in females, but even in males they are significantly smaller relative to the cheek teeth than the canines of any dryopithecine. Still, they do project beyond adjacent teeth so that, when closed, the jaws of sivapithecines interlock. Furthermore, the shearing function of the upper canine with the first lower premolar is retained. The molars, which show the same five-cusp pattern as the dryopithecines, have noticeably thicker enamel. The shape of the tooth row tends to be slightly V-shaped, while that

---

Sivapithecines: A group of hominoids ancestral to orangutans, and probably to chimpanzees, gorillas, and humans as well.

---

[4]Pilbeam, D. (1986). *Human origins.* David Skamp Distinguished Lecture in Anthropology, Indiana University, 6.

Figure 5.5   The lower jaws of *Dryopithecus* (A), *Sivapithecus* (B), and early *Australopithecus* (C), a hominine who lived nearly 4 million years ago, demonstrate some important similarities and differences between the three hominoids. Relative to the cheek teeth, all have comparably small teeth at the front of the jaw. There is a general similarity between A and B, as well as between B and C. The major difference between *Sivapithecus* and *Australopithecus* is that the rows of cheek teeth are farther apart in the hominine.

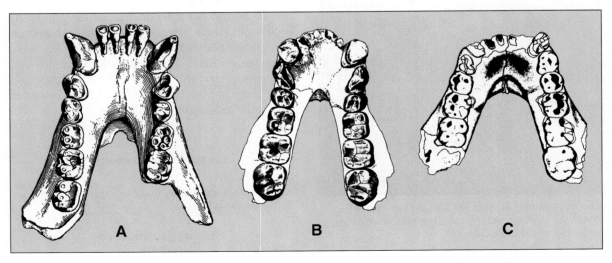

of the dryopithecines is more like a U, with the rows of cheek teeth parallel to one another (Fig. 5.5). The palate, or roof of the mouth, is high and arched. Finally, the lower facial region of the sivapithecines is narrow, short, and deep. Overall, the dental apparatus was built for powerful chewing, especially on the back teeth.

In the past two decades, our dependence on teeth and jaws for our knowledge of the sivapithecines has lessened as a number of their skull and limb bone fragments have been found in China, Hungary, and Pakistan. In many respects, the face is remarkably orangutanlike, even down to small details of the palate. The mandible, however, is only broadly rather than specifically similar to that of an orang, nor are the upper arm bones quite the same.

This *Sivapithecus* skull is remarkably similar to skulls of modern orangutans, so much so that an ancestor–descendant relationship is probable. The last common ancestor of chimpanzees, gorillas, and humans may not have differed greatly from *Sivapithecus*.

Sivapithecines and Human Origins

As long as sivapithecines were known only from fossils of teeth and jaws, it was easy to postulate some sort of relationship between them and ourselves. This was because a number of features—the position of the incisors, the reduced canines, the thick enamel of the molars, and the shape of the tooth row—seemed to point in a somewhat human direction. Some fossils (notably one from Africa) even show a shallow concavity above the position of the canine tooth, a feature not found in any ape, but often found in humans. Indeed, some even went so far as to label sivapithecines as definitely **hominid,** a term then restricted to humans and near humans, excluding all apes (as opposed to newer classifications that place African apes and humans together in the hominid family; humans alone in the subfamily homininae, or hominines). With the discovery of orangutanlike skulls and apelike limb bones, however, it became clear that this could not be so, and many anthropologists concluded that sivapithecines could have nothing to do with human origins. Rather, orangutans were seen as the sole modern survivors of an ancient group from which the line leading to the African apes and humans had branched off some 12 to 18 million years ago.

Recently, opinion has begun to shift back to a middle position. While the link between Miocene sivapithecines and modern orangutans seems undeniable, this does not rule out the possibility of a link with African apes and humans as well.[5] For example, both orangutans and humans have a thick coat of enamel on their molars, whereas the African apes do not. It now appears that humans, like orangs, retain the thick enamel seen in sivapithecines, whereas chimps and gorillas lost it sometime after the separation of hominids from pongids.[6] Then, too, some

Hominid: Hominoid family to which humans alone used to be assigned; now includes African apes and humans, with the latter assigned to the subfamily *Homininae*.

[5]Ciochon, R. L., & Fleagle, J. G. (1987). Ramapithecus and human origins. In R. L. Ciochon & J. G. Fleagle (Eds.), *Primate evolution and human origins* (p. 208). Hawthorne, NY: Aldine de Gruyter.

[6]Lewin, R. (1983). Tooth enamel tells a complex story. *Science, 228,* 707.

Although not identical, the modern ape most like *Sivapithecus* is the orangutan. Chimpanzees and gorillas, like humans, have come to differ more from the ancestral condition than have these Asian apes.

sivapithecines, such as *Ouranopithecus* from northern Greece, seem closer in dental proportions and other features of their teeth to early hominines than do Asian fossils ascribed to this group.[7]

That the ancestry of humans may ultimately be among the apelike sivapithecines, then, is consistent with dental evidence. It is consistent as well with resemblances between the shoulder girdle of the earliest well-known hominine, *Australopithecus* (discussed in the next chapter), and that of orangutans. This suggests that humans evolved from a primate capable of arm movements like those of orangutans, and the sivapithecines were capable of just such arm movements. Finally, the opinion that sivapithecines are ancestral to humans as well as all of today's great apes (Fig. 5.6) is in accord with estimates based on molecular similarities and differences between humans, chimpanzees, and gorillas that they could not have separated from a common ancestral stock more than 10 million years ago. We know from the fossils that the sivapithecines were still on the scene 8 million years ago (indeed, a

form larger than a modern gorilla survived in Asia until about 300,000 years ago) and also that our own human ancestors were going their separate evolutionary way by at least 4.4 million, if not 6 million, years ago.

Sivapithecine Adaptations

Molar teeth like those of the sivapithecines, having low crown relief, thick enamel, and surfaces poorly developed for cutting, are found in a number of modern primates.[8] Some of these species are terrestrial and some are arboreal, but all have one thing in common: They eat very hard nuts, fruits with very tough rinds, and some seeds. This provides them with a rich source of easily digested nutrients that are not accessible to species with thin molar enamel incapable of standing up to the stresses of tough rind removal or nutcracking. Thus the sivapithecines probably ate food similar to that eaten by these latter-day nutcrackers.

[7]Koufos, G. (1993). Mandible of *Ouranopithecus macedoniensis* (Hominidae, Primates) from a new late Miocene locality in Macedonia (Greece). *American Journal of Physical Anthropology, 91,* 232–234.

[8]Kay, R. F. (1981). The nut-crackers—a new theory of the adaptations of the Ramapithecinae. *American Journal of Physical Anthropology, 55,* 141–151.

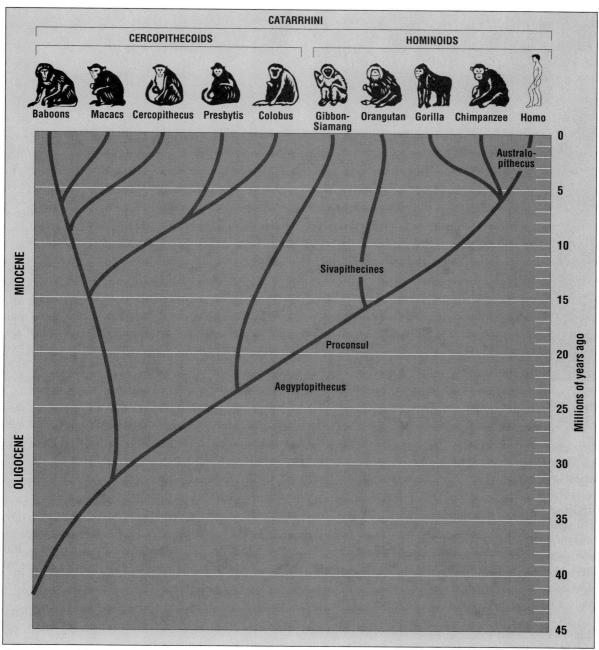

Figure 5.6 Although debate continues over details, this chart presents a reasonable reconstruction of evolutionary relationships among the catarrhine primates.

Analysis of other materials from deposits in which sivapithecine fossils have been found suggests utilization of a broad range of habitats, including tropical rain forests as well as drier bush country. Of particular interest to us, from the standpoint of human origins, are those populations that lived on the edge of open country, where food could be obtained through foraging on the ground out in the open, as well as in the trees of the forests. As it happened, there was a climatic shift under

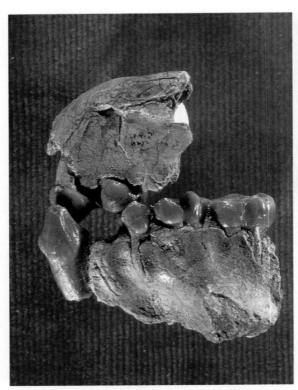

Kenyapithecus, a sivapithecine fossil from east Africa, has relatively small canine teeth and a facial profile suitable for an ancestor of African apes and humans.

Ground-dwelling primates, like this male baboon, depend heavily on their massive canine teeth for protection from other animals. *Sivapithecus*, by contrast, lacked such massive weapons of defense.

way, causing a gradual but persistent breaking up of forested areas, with a consequent expansion of open savanna country. Under such circumstances, it seems likely that those populations of sivapithecines living at the edge of the forests were obliged to supplement food from the forest more and more with other foods readily available on the open savannas. Consistent with this theory, late sivapithecine fossils are typically found in association with greater numbers of the remains of animals adapted to grasslands than are earlier ones.

Because sivapithecines already had large, thickly enameled molars, those that had to were capable of dealing with the tough and abrasive foods available on the savanna. What they lacked, however, were canine teeth of sufficient size to have served as effective "weapons" of defense. By contrast, most modern monkeys and apes that spend much time on the ground rely heavily for defense on the massive, fanglike canines possessed by the males. Since catlike predators were even more numerous on the savanna than now, sivap-

ithecines, especially the smaller ones (which probably weighed no more than about 40 pounds[9]), would seem to have been especially vulnerable primates. Probably the forest fringe was more than just a source of foods different from those of the savanna; its trees would have provided refuge when danger threatened. Yet, with continued expansion of savanna country, trees for refuge would have become fewer and farther between.

Slowly, however, physical and behavioral changes must have improved these primates' chances for survival on the savanna. For one thing, those that were able to gather food on the ground and then carry it to the safety of a tree probably had a better rate of survival than those that did not. Although many species of monkeys have cheek pouches in which to carry food, apes do not. Occasionally, modern apes will assume a bipedal stance in order to transport food in their arms, but they are quite awkward about it. The center of gravity, however, is higher in the body of modern apes than it seems to have been in their earlier ancestors, so that bipedal food transport may not have been quite so awkward for the sivapithecines, especially the smaller ones.

Food may not have been the only thing transported. Among modern primates, infants must be able to cling to their mothers in order to be transported; since the mother is using her forelimbs in locomotion, either to walk or swing by, she cannot

[9]Pilbeam, D. R. (1987). Rethinking human origins. In R. L. Ciochon & J. G. Fleagle, (Eds.), *Primate evolution and human origins* (p. 217). Hawthorne, NY: Aldine de Gruyter.

A young baboon clings to its mother's back. The ability of apes as well as monkeys to carry their infants is limited by their need to use their arms in locomotion.

easily carry her infant. Chimpanzee infants, for example, must cling for themselves to their mothers, and even at the age of 4, they make long journeys on her back. Injuries caused by falling from the mother are a significant cause of infant mortality. Thus, females able to carry their infants would have made a significant contribution to the survivorship of their offspring.

Another advantage of at least the occasional assumption of a bipedal stance would have been the ability to scan the savanna, so that predators could be spotted before they got too close. Such scanning can be seen from time to time among baboons and chimps today when out on the savanna, even though their anatomy is less suited for this than the sivapithecines' was. Bipedalism, too, would have enhanced the ability to use the hands to wield and throw things at predators. Among primates, "threat gestures" typically involve shaking branches and large sticks, while on the ground, chimpanzees have been observed on numerous occasions throwing rocks at leopards. Lacking the large body size and formidable canines of chimps, there is every reason to suppose that the sivapithecines, when away from the trees and faced by a predator, fell back on the same kind of intimidating displays.

Yet another incentive to stand bipedally would be to make use of one of the more abundant food sources on the savanna[10]—the thorn bushes that provide edible seeds, leaves, and pods that would have been too high to pick while standing on four (or three) feet; yet, they are too spiny and are not sturdy enough to be climbed. Moreover, by using two hands (rather than one) to feed on seeds, the time necessary for such feeding would be cut in half, thereby reducing the period of vulnerability.

Another important consideration is the matter of avoiding overheating when out in the open, exposed to the direct rays of the sun. Since all hominoids lack the special physiological mechanisms possessed by most savanna mammals that protect their brains from damaging elevations of temperature, those that ventured out in the open would have been at risk without some other way of dealing with this problem. Bipedalism would have made a significant contribution, for when the sun is directly overhead, the heat load on an upright hominine is only about 40 percent of that received by a same-sized quadruped.[11] Moreover, bipedalism raises the body well above the ground, where heat is most intense and increases exposure to faster-moving air currents for effective heat loss through convection.

[10]Jolly, C. J., & Plog, F. (1986). *Physical anthropology and archaeology* (4th ed., p. 216). New York: Knopf.
[11]Wheeler, P. (1993). Human ancestors walked tall, stayed cool. *Natural History, 102* (8), 66.

EARLY APES AND HUMAN EVOLUTION

Although the sivapithecines display a number of features from which **hominine** characteristics may be derived, and may occasionally have walked bipedally, they were much too apelike to be considered hominines. No matter how much some of them may have resorted to bipedalism, they had not yet developed the anatomical specializations for this mode of locomotion that are seen in the earliest

=====∘∘======∘∘=====

Hominine: Member of the *Homininae*, the subfamily of hominids to which humans belong.

=====∘∘======∘∘=====

known hominines. Nevertheless, existing evidence allows the hypothesis that apes and humans separated from a common evolutionary line sometime during the late Miocene, and some fossils, particularly the smaller African sivapithecines, do possess traits associated with humans. Moreover, the Miocene apes possessed a limb structure less specialized for brachiation than modern apes; this structure could well have provided the basis for the development of human as well as ape limb types.

Clearly not all sivapithecines evolved into hominines. Those that remained in the forests and woodlands continued to develop as arboreal apes, although, ultimately, some of them took up a more terrestrial life. These are the chimpanzees and gorillas, who have changed far more from the ancestral condition than have the still arboreal orangutans.

CHAPTER SUMMARY

Although the study of comparative anatomy and biochemistry of living animals indicates much about their evolution, the most direct evidence comes from fossils. For animals that have often lived where conditions for fossilization are generally poor, we do have a surprisingly large number of primate fossils. Some are relatively complete skeletons, while most are teeth and jaw fragments.

The primates arose as part of a great adaptive radiation that began more than 100 million years after the appearance of the first mammals. The reason for this late diversification of mammals was that most ecological niches they have since occupied were not available until the flowering plants became widespread beginning about 65 million years ago, and the reptiles had already preempted most other niches.

The first primates were arboreal insect eaters, and the characteristics of all primates developed as an adaptation to the initial tree-dwelling environment. While some primates no longer inhabit the trees, it is certain that those adaptations that evolved to a life in the trees were preadaptive to the adaptive zone now occupied by the hominines.

The earliest primates had developed by 60 million years ago in the Paleocene Epoch and were small arboreal creatures. Lemurlike adapids were common in the Eocene, as were species of tarsier-like omomyids. By the late Eocene Epoch, about 37 million years ago, small primates combining features of both monkeys and apes were on the scene. In the Miocene Epoch apes proliferated and spread over many parts of the Old World. Among them were the sivapithecines, which appeared by 16 million years ago and were widespread even as recently as 8 million years ago. Although remarkably similar to orangutans in some respects, details of dentition suggest that hominines, as well as the African apes, arose from the sivapithecines. At least some populations of sivapithecines lived in parts of Africa where the right kind of selective pressures existed to transform a creature just like it into a primitive hominine. Other populations remained in the forests, developing into today's chimpanzee, gorilla, and orangutan. Of these, the orangutan has changed less from the ancestral condition than have the chimp and the gorilla.

SUGGESTED READINGS

Ciochon, R. L., & Fleagle, J. (Eds.). (1987). *Primate evolution and human origins.* Hawthorne, NY: Aldine de Gruyter.

Articles in Part IV of this book summarize current knowledge of early catarrhine evolution, while those in Part V examine the sivapithecines and their possible significance with respect to human origins. Editors' introductions to each section provide the necessary overall perspective on the issues discussed in the articles.

France, D. L., & Horn, A. D. (1992). *Lab manual and workbook for physical anthropology* (2nd ed.). New York: West.

Two chapters of this useful manual are devoted to a review of early primate fossils through the Miocene. Included are excellent drawings and photos.

Lasker, G. W., & Tyzzer, R. (1982). *Physical anthropology.* New York: Holt, Rinehart and Winston.

This is a highly readable textbook in physical anthropology. The chapter on fossil primates is particularly good, with one of the best descriptions of the Fayum deposits from which so many fossils have come.

CHAPTER
6
THE EARLIEST HOMININES

PALEOANTHROPOLOGIST DONALD JOHANSON DISCOVERS THE LEG BONE OF AN EARLY HOMININE KNOWN AS *AUSTRALOPITHECUS*. THOUGH THEIR BEHAVIOR PATTERNS WERE MORE APELIKE THAN HUMAN, *AUSTRALOPITHECUS* MOVED AROUND ON THE GROUND ON TWO LEGS, JUST AS HUMANS DO TODAY.

CHAPTER PREVIEW

When Did the First Hominines Appear and What Were They Like?

By at least 4.4 million years ago, *Ardipithecus*, the first undoubted hominine, had appeared. By 4 million years ago, this gave rise to *Australopithecus*, a hominine remarkably human from the waist down that had become fully adapted for moving about on the open savanna on its hind legs in the distinctive human manner. But from the waist up, *Australopithecus* was still remarkably apelike, with a brain suggesting intellectual abilities roughly comparable to those of a modern-day chimpanzee or gorilla.

What Is the Relation Between the Various Forms of *Australopithecus*?

The earliest forms of *Australopithecus* preserve a number of features indicative of a more apelike ancestor. By 2.5 million years ago, this form gave rise to one whose chewing apparatus had become larger and more massive, at the same time that its brain size remained relatively stable. For a while, this late form coexisted with a less radically altered version of the earlier form.

Why Had *Australopithecus* Become a Bipedal Walker?

Early hominines venturing out on the savanna would have been vulnerable in two ways: to damaging buildup of heat in the brain from direct exposure to the sun, and to the many predators that prowled the savanna. Bipedal locomotion solves the heat problem by reducing the exposure of the body to direct solar radiation and positioning the body for most effective heat loss through convection. It also enabled *Australopithecus* to scan the savanna for danger, carry food to places where it could be consumed in safety, transport offspring, and grab hold of objects with which to threaten predators.

The period between about 7.5 and 4.5 million years ago was one of change; climates became dramatically drier than before and in Africa, as many species of forest or bush-loving mammals became extinct, several new groups made their appearance. Among the latter was the first undoubted hominine, known as **Ardipithecus ramidus**. Discovered in 1994, this species is known so far from 17 fragments of teeth and bone. Much better known is its apparent descendent, **Australopithecus**, the oldest fossils of which date back to between 4.2 and 3.9 million years ago at two sites not far from Lake Turkana in northern Kenya. The earlier fossils of *Ardipithecus* are from deposits 4.4 million years old in Ethiopia. While we do not yet know much about *Ardipithecus*, we do know that *Australopithecus* walked about on the ground on two (rather than four) feet and possessed manipulative and dexterous hands capable of using objects as tools. In spite of its ability to walk in a human manner, its behavior patterns otherwise were probably more apelike than human. Among other things, it spent more time in trees than later hominines, probably even sleeping in them.

For a long time, the fossil evidence of the early stages of human evolution was both sparse and tenuous. In the 1960s, however, there began a rush of paleoanthropologists into the field. Numerous international expeditions, including more than 100 researchers from Belgium, Great Britain, Canada, France, Israel, Kenya, the Netherlands, and the United States, swarmed over parts of East Africa, where they have now unearthed more fossil remains in 30 years than had been unearthed in the previous 40. So much material, coming fast and furiously, has been difficult to digest, and our ideas of early human evolution have had to be constantly revised. Now, there is widespread agreement over the broad outline, even though debate continues over details. What is clear is that the course of human evolution has not been a simple, steady "advance" in the direction of modern humanity. Rather, it appears that at least three divergent hominine lines evolved in the past. In this chapter we will discuss two of them, beginning with the best-known fossils of *Australopithecus*. We will then see how they relate to earlier forms.

AUSTRALOPITHECUS

In 1924, an unusual fossil was brought to the attention of Professor Raymond Dart of the University of Witwatersrand in Johannesburg; it was the cranium of an animal unlike any he had ever seen before in South Africa. Recognizing in this unusual fossil an intriguing mixture of simian and human characteristics, anatomist Dart

Ardipithecus ramidus: The oldest known hominine; lived about 4.4 million years ago.

Australopithecus: The first well-known hominine; lived between 1 and 4.2 million years ago. Characterized by bipedal locomotion when on the ground, but with an apelike brain; includes at least five species: *afarensis, africanus, anamensis, boisei,* and *robustus.*

Raymond Dart, who described the first fossil of *Australopithecus* and correctly diagnosed its bipedal mode of locomotion.

named his discovery *Australopithecus africanus*, or southern ape of Africa. Based on the position of the foramen magnum, the large hole in the skull where the spinal cord enters, Dart claimed that *Australopithecus* was probably a biped.

Since Dart's original find, hundreds of other fossils of *Australopithecus* have been found, first in South Africa and later in Tanzania, Kenya, Ethiopia, and (most recently) Chad (Fig. 6.1). As they were discovered, many were given a number of different specific and generic names, but usually all are now considered to belong to the single genus *Australopithecus*. Most anthropologists recognize at least four species of the genus: *A. afarensis*, *A. africanus*, *A. boisei*, and *A. robustus*. (A fifth species, *A. anamensis*, will be discussed later in the chapter.) The latter two, from eastern and southern Africa respectively, are notable for having jaws that are massive, relative to the size of the braincase. *A. afarensis* and *A. africanus*, also from eastern and southern Africa respectively, are slightly smaller on average and lack such massive jaws.

Figure 6.1 *Australopithecus* fossils have been found in South Africa, Malawi, Tanzania, Kenya, Ethiopia, and Chad.

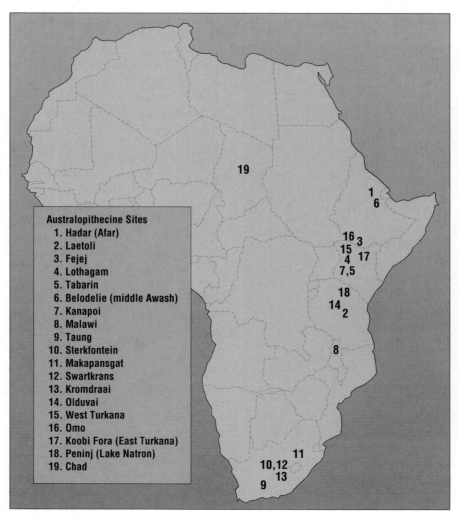

Australopithecine Sites
1. Hadar (Afar)
2. Laetoli
3. Fejej
4. Lothagam
5. Tabarin
6. Belodelie (middle Awash)
7. Kanapoi
8. Malawi
9. Taung
10. Sterkfontein
11. Makapansgat
12. Swartkrans
13. Kromdraai
14. Olduvai
15. West Turkana
16. Omo
17. Koobi Fora (East Turkana)
18. Peninj (Lake Natron)
19. Chad

A. afarensis and africanus

Included in the species *A. africanus* are numerous fossils found in the 1930s and 1940s at Sterkfontein and Makapansgat in South Africa, in addition to Dart's original find from Taung. All date between 3 and 2.3 million years ago (though a partial foot skeleton may be as many as 3.5 million years old). Included in *A. afarensis* are parts of between 35 and 64 individuals who lived between 3.9 and 2.9 million years ago; these were found in the 1970s and 1990s in northern Ethiopia's Afar region. Discovered by Donald Johanson of the United States, these include the famous "Lucy," represented by bones from almost all parts of a single skeleton, and "the First Family," a collection of bones from at least 13 individuals of both sexes, ranging in age from infancy to adulthood, who died together as a result of some single calamity.

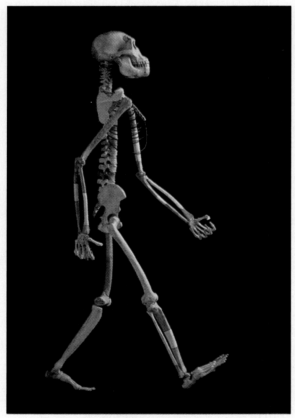

Sufficient parts of the skeleton of "Lucy," a hominine that lived between 2.6 and 3.3 million years ago, survived to permit this reconstruction. Her hip and leg bones reveal that she walked about in a distinctively human manner.

Similar material, close to 4 million years old, found by a team led by Mary Leakey at Laetoli, in Tanzania, is usually assigned to the same species as the Afar fossils. Although some have interpreted the wide variation exhibited by the *afarensis* specimens as indicative of the presence of two separate species, two recent studies support the single-species hypothesis,[1] indicating that *afarensis* was sexually dimorphic, with the males about one and one-half times the size of females. In this respect, they were somewhat like the Miocene apes, with size differences greater than one sees in a modern chimpanzee, but less than one sees in gorillas or orangs.

Other pieces of australopithecines similar to *A. afarensis* or *africanus* have been found at other East African sites that generally are 2 million or more years old. Both species were erect, bipedal hominines about the size of modern pygmies, though far more powerfully built. Their stature ranged between 3.5 and 5 feet, and they are estimated to have weighed between 29 and 45 kilograms.[2] Their physical appearance was unusual by our standards: They may be described as looking like an ape from the waist up (see Fig. 6.2) and like a human from the waist down. Their cranium was relatively low, the forehead sloped backward, and the brow ridge that helps give apes such massive-looking foreheads was also present. The lower half of the face was chinless and accented by jaws that were quite large, relative to the size of the skull.

Much has been written about *Australopithecus* teeth. Speaking generally, both *A. afarensis* and *africanus* possessed small incisors, short canines in line with adjacent teeth, and a rounded dental arch. The molars and premolars are larger in size but similar in form to modern human teeth (Fig. 6.3). The molars are unevenly worn; the upper cheek teeth are worn from the inside, and the lower cheek teeth are worn from the outside. This indicates that

---

Homo erectus: Members of the genus *Homo*, which immediately precede *Homo sapiens*.

---

[1]Leonard, W. R., & Hegman, M. (1987). Evolution of P3 morphology in *Australopithecus afarensis. American Journal of Physical Anthropology, 73*, 60.

[2]McHenry, H. M. (1992). Body size and proportions in early hominids. *American Journal of Physical Anthropology, 87*, 407.

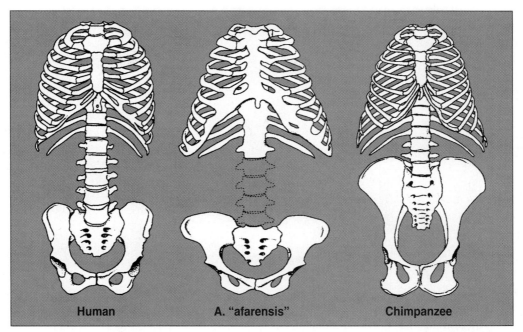

Figure 6.2 Trunk skeletons of modern human, *A. afarensis*, and chimpanzee, compared. In its pelvis, *afarensis* resembles the modern human, but its ribcage shows the pyramidal configuration of the ape.

both species chewed food in a hominine fashion, even though they were probably capable of two to four times the crushing force of modern human beings. Heavy wear indicates that the food chewed was high in tough, fibrous plant substances. There is usually no gap between the canines and the teeth next to them on the upper jaw, a trait common in apes. Further, the large mandible is similar to that of the later hominine **Homo erectus**.

As one might expect, these features are most evident in the fossils of *A. africanus*, the more recent of the two species; the teeth of the earlier

Figure 6.3 The upper jaws of an ape, *Australopithecus*, and modern human show important differences in the dental arch and the spacing between the canines and adjoining teeth. Only in the earliest australopithecines can a diastema (a large gap between the teeth) be seen.

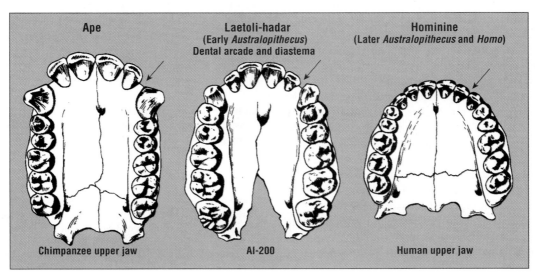

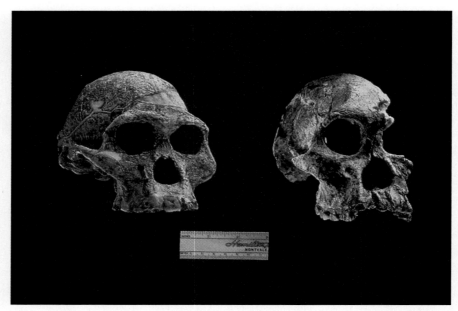

This comparison of two skulls illustrates the degree of sexual dimorphism exhibited by australopithecines about 2 million years ago. The skull on the left is a female and the skull on the right is a male. Earlier australopithecines were equally dimorphic.

afarensis, from Ethiopia but especially from Laetoli, show numerous features reminiscent of the late Miocene sivapithecines that the later ones (of *africanus*) do not (see Fig. 5.5). Generally, the incisors and canines are a bit larger in *afarensis*, there is sometimes a gap between upper lateral incisors and canines, the canines tend to project noticeably, the first lower premolars are less like molars and show more shearing wear, and the dental arch is less rounded. One jaw from Laetoli even shows a partial interlock of upper canines with lower canines and premolars. All of this strongly suggests a sivapithecinelike ancestor for *Australopithecus* back in Miocene times.

In addition to differences in the teeth between earlier *afarensis* and later *africanus*, there were also differences between the sexes. For example, male canines are significantly larger than those of females (Fig. 6.4). There is as well a clear evolutionary trend for the first lower premolar of males to become more molarlike, through development of a second cusp. Those of females, by contrast, do not. Such differences are to be expected if male and female foraging patterns were not quite the same—for example, if females got more of their food from the trees, while males consumed large amounts of lower-quality food

to be found on or near the ground. Consistent with this, some features of the skeleton are somewhat better suited to climbing in females than in males.[3]

Although the brain is small and apelike and the general conformation of the skull seems non-human, the foramen magnum of these australopithecines is placed forward and is downward looking, as it is in later bipedal hominines of the **genus *Homo***. Cranial capacity, commonly used as an index of brain size, varied from 310 to 500 cubic centimeters in *A. afarensis* and 428 to 510 cubic centimeters in *A. africanus*,[4] roughly the size

Genus *Homo*: Hominine genus characterized by expansion of brain and reduction of jaws; includes three species: *habilis*, *erectus*, and *sapiens*.

[3]Simons, E. L. (1989). Human origins. *Science, 245,* 1346.

[4]Grine, F. E. (1993). Australopithecine taxonomy and phylogeny: Historical background and recent interpretation. In R. L. Ciochon & J. G. Fleagle (Eds.), *The human evolution source book* (pp. 201–202). Englewood Cliffs, NJ: Prentice-Hall.

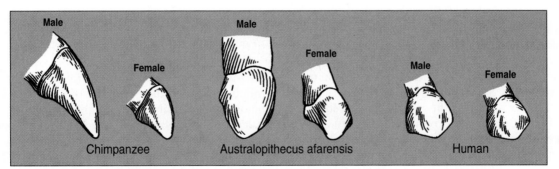

Figure 6.4 Sexual dimorphism in canine teeth.

of a large chimpanzee brain and about one third the size of a modern human brain. Intelligence, however, is not indicated by absolute brain size alone, but is roughly indicated by the ratio of brain to body size. Unfortunately, with such a wide range of adult weights it is not clear whether brain size was larger than an ape's relative to body size. Although some researchers think they see evidence for some expansion of the brain, others vigorously disagree. Moreover, the outside appearance of the brain, as revealed by natural casts of the insides of skulls, is more apelike than human, suggesting that cerebral reorganization toward a human condition had not yet occurred.[5] Consistent with this is the fact that the system for drainage of the blood from the cranium of *A. afarensis* is significantly different from that of the genus *Homo*. At the moment, the weight of the evidence favors mental capabilities on the part of both *afarensis* and *africanus* as being comparable to those of modern great apes.

The fossil remains of *Australopithecus afarensis* and *africanus* have provided anthropology with two striking facts. First, as early as 4 million years ago, this hominine was bipedal, walking erect. This is indicated, first of all, by the curvature of the spine, which is like that of humans and unlike that of apes. This served to place the center of gravity over, rather than in front of, the hip joint. In addition, a forearm bone from "Lucy," which is shorter than that of an ape, suggests that the upper limb was lighter and the center of gravity

lower in the body than in apes. Still, the arms of *A. afarensis* are longer relative to leg length than in *Homo*, the shoulder girdle was more adapted to arboreal performance, and fingers and toes show more curvature. Moreover, a partial foot skeleton between 3 and 3.5 million years old from

Although the Ethiopian government is not releasing photographs of the *A. afarensis* skull discovered in 1994, it confirms the accuracy of this earlier reconstruction based on various fossil fragments.

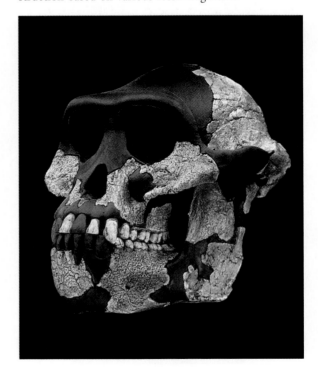

[5]Falk, D. (1989). Ape-like endocast of "ape-man" Taung. *American Journal of Physical Anthropology, 80,* 339.

Sterkfontein, South Africa (Fig. 6.5), shows a long, flexible toe still useful for grabbing onto tree limbs.[6] Such traits indicate that the tree-climbing abilities of *A. afarensis* exceeded those of more recent hominines and that they spent time in trees as well as on the ground.

Bipedal locomotion is also indicated by a number of leg and hip remains (Fig. 6.6). There is general agreement that these are much more human than apelike. In fact, a trait-by-trait comparison of individual bones shows that *Australopithecus* frequently falls within the range of modern *Homo*, even though the overall configuration is not exactly the same. But the most dramatic confirmation of *Australopithecus'* walking ability comes from Laetoli, where, nearly 4 million years ago, two individuals walked across newly fallen volcanic ash. Because it was damp, the ash took the impressions of their feet and these were sealed beneath subsequent ash falls until discovered by Paul Abell in 1978. The shape

of the footprints, the linear distance between the heels where they struck, and the amount of "toe out" are all fully human.

The second striking fact provided by *Australopithecus afarensis* and *africanus* is that hominines acquired their erect bipedal position long before they acquired their highly developed and enlarged brain. Not only is the latter more apelike than human in its size and structure, but also it is now evident that *Australopithecus* did not have prolonged maturation as do modern humans; instead, they grew up rapidly as do apes.[7] Thus, no matter how important bipedal locomotion may have been in setting the stage for the later expansion and elaboration of the human brain, it cannot by itself account for those developments.

A. robustus and A. boisei

The remains of what is now known as *Australopithecus robustus* were first found at Kromdraai and Swartkrans in South Africa by Robert Broom and John Robinson in 1948 in deposits that, unfortunately, cannot be securely dated. Current thinking puts them anywhere from 1.8 to 1 million years ago.

A. robustus shared practically all of the traits listed for the species of *Australopithecus*, just discussed, especially those of *A. africanus* from South Africa. Although similar in size to *A. africanus*, the bones of *robustus'* body were thick for their size, with prominent markings where their muscles attached. The skull of *A. robustus* was thicker and larger than that of *africanus*, with a slightly larger cranial capacity (around 530 cubic centimeters). Its skull also possessed a simianlike sagittal crest running from front to back along the top. This feature provides sufficient area on a relatively small braincase for attachment of the huge temporal muscles required to operate powerful jaws, such as *A. robustus* possessed and gorillas have today; hence, what we have here is an example of convergent evolution in gorillas and hominines.

[6]Oliwenstein, L. (1995). New footsteps into walking debate. *Science, 269,* 476.

Figure 6.5   Drawing of the foot bones of a 3- to 3.5 million-year-old *Australopithecus* from Sterkfontein, as they would have been in the complete foot. Note how long and flexible the first toe (right) is.

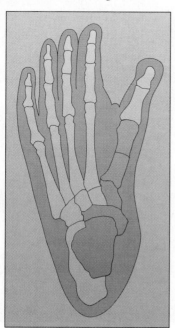

[7]Dean, M. C., Benyon, A. D., Thackeray, J. F., & Macho, G. A. (1993). Histological reconstruction of dental development and age at death of a juvenile *Paranthropus robustus* specimen, SK63, from Swartkrans, South Africa. *American Journal of Physical Anthropology, 91,* 409.

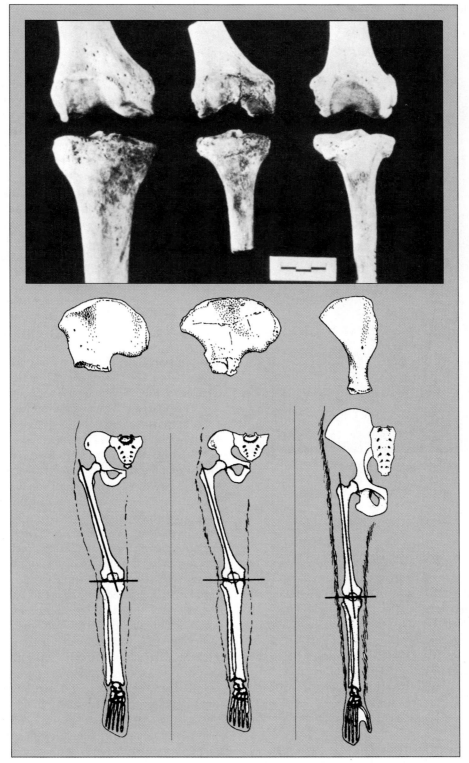

Figure 6.6   Examination of upper hip bones and lower limbs of *Homo sapiens*, *Australopithecus*, and an ape can be used to determine means of locomotion. The similarities of the human and australopithecine bones are striking and are indicative of bipedal locomotion. (The reconstruction of the australopithecine limb is based on the knee joint shown in the photograph.)

These footprints from Laetoli, Tanzania, confirm that australopithecines were fully bipedal.

The first specimen of *Australopithecus boisei* to be found in East Africa was discovered by Mary Leakey in the summer of 1959, the centennial year of the publication of Darwin's *On the Origin of Species*. She found it in Olduvai Gorge, a fossil-rich area near Ngorongoro Crater, on the Serengeti Plain of East Africa. Olduvai, sometimes called the Grand Canyon of East Africa, is a huge gash in the earth, about 25 miles long and 300 feet deep, which cuts through Pleistocene and recent geological strata revealing close to 2 million years of the earth's history.

Mary Leakey's discovery was reconstructed and studied by her husband Louis, who gave it the name "*Zinjanthropus boisei.*" At first, he thought this hominine seemed more humanlike than *Australopithecus* and extremely close to modern hu-

mans in evolutionary development. Further study, however, revealed that "*Zinjanthropus,*" the remains of which consisted of a skull and a few limb bones, was an East African representative of *Australopithecus.* Although similar in many ways to *A. robustus*, most commonly it is referred to as *Australopithecus boisei.* Potassium argon dating places this early hominine at about 1.75 million years old. Since the time of Mary Leakey's original find, numerous other fossils of *A. boisei* have been found at Olduvai, as well as north and east of Lake Turkana in Ethiopia and Kenya. While one (often referred to as the "Black Skull") is known to be as much as 2.5 million years old, some date to as recently as 1.3 million years ago.

The size of the teeth and certain cranial features of *A. boisei* are reminiscent of *A. robustus.* Molars and premolars are enormous, as is the palate. The heavy skull, more massive even than its robust South African relative's, has a sagittal crest and prominent brow ridges; cranial capacity ranges from about 500 to 530 cubic centimeters. Body size, too, is somewhat larger; whereas *robustus* is estimated to have weighed between 32 and 40 kilograms, *boisei* probably weighed from 34 to 49 kilograms.

Because the earliest skull (2.5 million years) in the *boisei* lineage, the so-called Black Skull from Kenya, retains a number of primitive features shared with *A. afarensis*, it is probable that *A. boisei* evolved from *afarensis* ancestors. Whether *A. robustus* represents a southern offshoot of the *boisei* lineage or convergent evolution from an *africanus* ancestor is so far not settled; arguments can be presented in favor of both interpretations. In either case, what happened was that the later australopithecines developed molars and premolars that are both absolutely and relatively larger than those of earlier *afarensis* and *africanus.* Larger teeth require more bone to support them, hence the prominent jaws of *boisei* and *robustus.* Finally, the larger jaws and the chewing of more food require more in the way of jaw musculature that attaches to the skull. The marked crests seen on the skulls of the late australopithecines provide for the attachment of such a musculature on a skull that has increased very little in size. In effect, *boisei* and *robustus* had evolved into highly efficient "chewing machines." Clearly, their immense cheek teeth and powerful chewing muscles bespeak the kind of heavy chewing

LOUIS S. B. LEAKEY   MARY LEAKEY
(1903–1972)   (b. 1913)

Few figures in the history of paleoanthropology have discovered so many key fossils, received so much public acclaim, or stirred up as much controversy as Louis Leakey and his second wife, Mary. Born in Kenya of missionary parents, Louis received his early education from an English governess and subsequently was sent to England for a university education. He returned to Kenya in the 1920s to begin his career there.

It was in 1931 that Louis and Mary began working in their spare time at Olduvai Gorge in Tanzania, searching patiently and persistently for remains of early hominines. It seemed a good place to look, for there were numerous animal fossils, as well as crude stone tools lying scattered on the ground and eroding out of the walls of the gorge. Their patience and persistence were not rewarded until 1959, when Mary found the first hominine fossil. A year later, another skull was found, and Olduvai was on its way to being recognized as one of the most important sources of hominine fossils in all of Africa. While Louis reconstructed, described, and interpreted the fossil material, Mary made the definitive study of the Oldowan tools.

The Leakeys' important discoveries were not limited to those at Olduvai. In the early 1930s, they found the first *Dryopithecus* fossils in Africa at Rusinga Island in Lake Victoria. Also in the 1930s, Louis found a number of skulls at Kanjera, Kenya, that show a mixture of modern and more primitive features. In 1961, at Fort Ternan, Kenya, the Leakeys found the first remains of a sivapithecine in Africa. After Louis' death, a member of an expedition led by Mary Leakey found the first footprints of *Australopithecus*, at Laetoli, Tanzania. In addition to their own work, Louis Leakey promoted a good deal of important work on the part of others. He made it possible for Jane Goodall to begin her landmark field studies of chimpanzees; and later, he was instrumental in getting similar studies started among gorillas and orangutans.

Louis Leakey had a flamboyant personality and a way of making interpretations of fossil materials that frequently did not stand up well to careful scrutiny, but this did not stop him from publicly presenting his views as if they were the "gospel truth." It was this aspect of the Leakeys' work that generated controversy. Nonetheless, the Leakeys accomplished and promoted more work that resulted in the accumulation of knowledge about human origins than anyone before them. Anthropology clearly owes them a great deal.

---

a diet restricted to uncooked plant foods requires. Many anthropologists believe that, by becoming a specialized consumer of plant foods, the late australopithecines avoided competing for the same niche with early *Homo*, with which they were contemporaries (see Chapter 7). In the course of evolution, the **law of competitive exclusion** dictates that when two closely related species compete for the same niche, one will outcompete the other, bringing about the "loser's" extinction. That early *Homo* and late *Australopithecines* did not compete for the same niche seems indicated by their coexistence for something like 1.5 million years.

Australopithecus anamensis and *Ardipithecus ramidus*

As already noted, *A. afarensis* fossils displayed a number of traits suggestive of a sivapithecinelike ancestry. In addition to the features of the teeth, hands, and feet already noted, the skull of *afarensis* is thick boned and has a forward thrust to the face, large, flaring cheek bones, and heavy

Law of competitive exclusion: States that when two closely related species compete for the same niche, one will outcompete the other, bringing about its extinction.

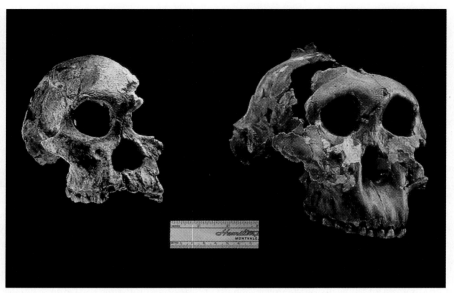

Skulls of *A. africanus* (left) and *A. boisei* (right) show significant differences. Both specimens are male.

cresting. Older than *afarensis* is *A. anamensis*, which dates to between 4.2 and 3.9 million years. Represented by an armbone found in 1965 and two jaws and a shinbone found in 1995, this species had an even more apelike jaw with a shallow palate and large canines. The shinbone, however, is like that of *afarensis* and is the oldest direct evidence so far for bipedalism.

Ardipithecus ramidus, found in Ethiopia in 1994 and represented by pieces of 17 individuals was, as one might expect at 4.4 million years old, even more apelike than *A. anamensis*. Like chimpanzees, *Ardipithecus* had relatively small molars and large canines, but the shape of the canine and vertebral elements are like those of hominines. Unfortunately, we have no foot, leg, or pelvic remains, but since this hominine lived in a somewhat more forested environment than its successors, it undoubtedly spent significant time in the trees. On the other hand, because the fossils of *A. anamensis* fit so neatly in between those of *A. afarensis* on one hand, and *Ardipithecus* on the other, the latter must have had a preference for bipedal locomotion on the ground.

The picture that emerges, then, is the emergence of *Australopithecus*, via *Ardipithecus*, from a sivapithecinelike ancestor around the end of the

These teeth and jaw fragment are from *Ardipithecus*, the earliest known hominine, that lived 4.4 million years ago.

Miocene Epoch. This is not to say that this evolution took place at a steady pace, for it probably did not. For example, fragments of an *afarensis* skull 3.9 million years old are virtually identical to the corresponding parts of one 3 million years old. Evidentally, once the bipedal adaptation was achieved, stabilizing selection took over and there was little change for at least a million years. By 2.5 million years ago, change was again in the works, resulting in the appearance of new forms including *A. boisei* and *A. robustus* (see Fig. 7.4). But again, from about 2.3 million years until the species went extinct around 1 million years ago, *A. boisei*, at least, shows relatively little in the way of change.[8] Evidently, the pattern in early hominine evolution was relatively short periods of marked change separated by prolonged periods of relative stasis.

Environment, Diet, and Australopithecine Origins

Having described the fossil material, we may now consider the evolutionary forces responsible for the appearance of *Australopithecus*. Since a major driving force in evolution is climatic change, in the late Miocene Epoch we must consider the effects of such changes profound enough to cause the temporary drying up of the Mediterranean Sea. On land, tropical forests underwent reduction or, more commonly, broke up into mosaics where patches of forest were interspersed with savanna or other types of open country. The forebears of the hominine line, probably to be found among African sivapithecines, lived in places where there was access to both trees and open country. With the breaking up of forests, these early ancestors of ours found themselves spending more and more time on the ground and had to adapt to this new open environment.

The most obvious problem facing these hominine ancestors in their new situation, other than getting from one patch of trees to another, was food getting. As the forest shrank, the traditional ape-type foods found in trees became less available to them. Therefore, it became more neces-

sary to forage on the ground for foods such as seeds, grasses, and roots. Associated with this change in diet is a change in their dentition; male canines (used by other primates as defensive weapons), not large to begin with, became as small as those of females (Fig. 6.7), leaving both sexes relatively defenseless on the open plain and easy targets for numerous carnivorous predators. Many investigators have concluded that the hands of early hominines took over the weapon functions of the reduced canines, enabling them to threaten predators by using wooden objects as clubs and throwing stones at them. This set the stage for the much later manufacture of more efficient weapons from bone, wood, and stone. Although the hands of the later australopithecines were suitable for

Figure 6.7 This lower jaw from Laetoli, Tanzania, is between 3.6 and 3.8 million years old and belonged to a hominine known as *Australopithecus*. Although its canine tooth projects a bit beyond the other teeth, it is a far cry from the projection seen in most other primates.

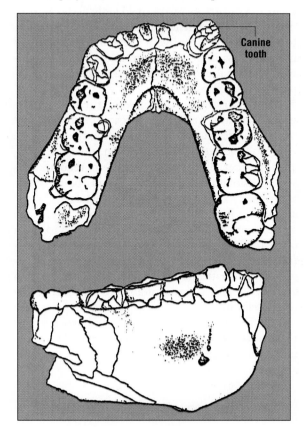

Canine tooth

[8]Wood, B., Wood, C., & Konigsberg, L. (1994). *Paranthropus boisei: An example of evolutionary stasis? American Journal of Physical Anthropology, 95,* 134.

tool making, there is no evidence that any of them ever made stone tools. To illustrate the problem: Experiments with captive chimpanzees have shown that they are capable of making crude chipped-stone tools, but they have never been known to do so under natural conditions. Thus, to have a potential is one thing, but whether it is realized is quite another. In fact, the earliest known stone tools are at least 1.5 million years younger than the oldest undoubted fossils of *Australopithecus*, nor has anyone been able to establish a clear association between stone tools and later *Australopithecus* (as opposed to *Homo*) fossils. Considering the number of sites and fossils known (several hundred), this fact appears to be significant. However, *Australopithecus* certainly had no less intelligence and dexterity than do modern great apes, all of whom are capable of using tools when it is to their advantage to do so. Both orangutans and chimpanzees have been observed in the wild making and using simple tools such as wooden probes to get termites and ants. Gorillas seem not to do so in the wild only because they developed a diet of leaves and nettles that made tools pointless. Most likely, the ability to make and use simple tools goes back to the last common ancestor of the Asian and African apes before the appearance of hominines.

It is reasonable to suppose, then, that australopithecines were tool users, though not tool makers. Unfortunately, few tools that they used are likely to have survived for a million and more years, and any that did would be hard to recognize as such. Although we cannot be certain about this, in addition to clubs and missiles for defense, stout sticks may have been used to dig up edible roots, and convenient stones may have been used to crack open nuts. In fact, some animal bones from australopithecine sites in South Africa show microscopic wear patterns suggesting their use to dig up edible roots from the ground. We may also allow the possibility that, like chimpanzees, females may more often have used tools to get and process food than males, but the latter may more often have made use of tools as weapons.[9]

This bonobo ("pygmy chimpanzee") figured out by himself how to make stone tools like those made by our own ancestors 2.5 million years ago.

Humans Stand on Their Own Two Feet

From an apelike carriage, the early hominines developed a fully erect posture; they became bipedal. Sivapithecines seem to have been primates who combined quadrupedal climbing with at least some brachiation and who, on the ground, were capable of assuming an upright stance, at least on occasion. Since no hominine fossils have been found dating from the period of 2 or more million years between the last known sivapithecines and the first known *Australopithecus*, we may assume that those hominine ancestors who did exist during the period were evolving into fully erect bipeds. *Australopithecus* is the first fully bipedal hominine of which we have a record.

[9]Goodall, J. (1986). *The chimpanzees of Gombe: Patterns of behavior* (pp. 552, 564). Cambridge, MA: Belknap Press.

Just as chimpanzees use wooden probes to "fish" for termites, so do orangutans use probes to extract termites, ants, or honey. Such tool use likely goes back to a time preceding the split between Asian and African hominoids, long before the appearance of hominines.

Bipedalism, as a means of locomotion, has its drawbacks. For example, it makes an animal more visible to predators, exposes its "soft underbelly," or gut, and interferes with the ability to change direction instantly while running. Nor does it make for particularly fast running; quadrupedal chimpanzees and baboons, for example, are 30 to 34 percent faster than we bipeds. For 100-meter distances, our best athletes today may attain speeds of 34–37 kilometers per hour, but the larger African carnivores can attain speeds up to 60–70 kilometers per hour. Other drawbacks include the frequent lower back problems, hernias, hemorrhoids, and other circulatory problems to which humans are prone by virtue of their bipedal specialization. Nor can we overlook the consequences of a serious leg or foot injury; a quadruped can do amazingly well on three legs, but a biped with only one functional leg is seriously hindered. Each of these drawbacks would have placed our early hominine ancestors at risk from predators, and so, we must ask, what made bipedal locomotion worth paying such a high price?

One once popular suggestion is that it allowed males to gather food on the savanna and transport it back to females, who were restricted from doing so by the dependence of their offspring.[10] This is unlikely, however, since female apes, as well as women among food-foraging peoples, routinely combine infant care with foraging for food. Indeed, among food foragers, it is the women who normally supply the bulk of the food eaten by both sexes. Moreover, the pair-bonding (one male attached to one female) required by this model is not characteristic of terrestrial primates, nor of those displaying the degree of sexual dimorphism that was characteristic of *Australopithecus*. Nor is it really characteristic of *Homo sapiens*; in a substantial majority of recent human societies, including those in which people forage in nature for their food, some form of polygamy—marriage to two or more people at the same time—is not only

[10]Lovejoy, C. O. (1981). The origin of man. *Science, 211,* 341–350.

permitted, but preferred. And even in the supposedly monogamous society of the United States, it is relatively common for an individual to marry two or more others (the only requirement is that he or she may not be married to them at one and the same time).

Another suggestion, that bipedal locomotion arose as an adaptation for nonterritorial scavenging of meat,[11] is also unlikely. While it is true that a biped is able to travel long distances without tiring, and that a daily supply of dead animal carcasses would have been available to hominines only if they were capable of ranging over vast areas, there is no evidence that hominines did much in the way of scavenging prior to about 2.5 million years ago. Furthermore, the heavy wear seen on australopithecine teeth is indicative of a diet high in tough, fibrous plant foods. Thus, scavenging was likely an unforeseen by-product of bipedal locomotion, rather than a cause of it.

Yet more recent is the suggestion that our ancestors stood up as a way to cope with heat stress out in the open.

[11]Lewin, R. (1987). Four legs good, two legs bad. *Science, 235,* 969–971.

Original Study

The Naked and the Bipedal[12]

Human beings are a peculiar species. Among other things, we're the only mostly hairless, consistently bipedal primate. Ever since Darwin, evolutionary biologists have wondered how we acquired these unique traits. Not long ago most would have argued that our upright stance evolved as part of a feedback loop that helped free our hands to use tools. But by the early 1980s a series of discoveries in Africa—including fossilized footprints and early hominine bones—made it clear that bipedalism preceded tool use by at least 2 million years. Lately a new theory has been gaining ground: it holds that our forebears reared up on two legs to escape the heat of the African savanna.

"The African savanna is one of the most thermally stressing habitats on the planet as far as large mammals are concerned," says Pete Wheeler, a physiologist at Liverpool John Moores University in England. For several years now Wheeler has been studying just how stressful such an environment would have been for the first primates to venture out of the shade of the forest. Among the apes, our ancestors are the only ones that managed the switch; no other ape today lives on the savanna full-time.

Most savanna animals, says Wheeler, cope with the heat by simply letting their body temperature rise during the day, rather than waste scarce water by sweating. (Some antelope allow their body temperature to climb above 110 degrees.) These animals have evolved elaborate ways of protecting the brain's delicate neural circuitry from overheating. Antelope, for instance, allow venous blood to cool in their large muzzles (the cooling results from water evaporation in the mucous lining), then run that cool blood by the arteries that supply the brain, thereby cooling it too.

"But the interesting thing about humans and other primates," says Wheeler, "is that we lack the mechanisms other savanna animals have. The

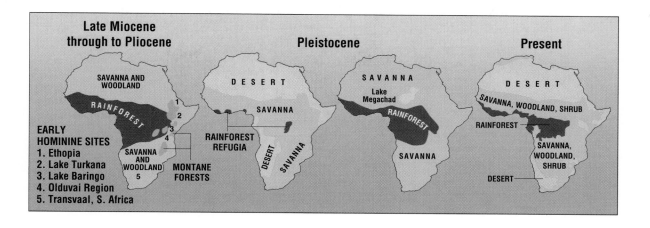

only way an ape wanting to colonize the savanna could protect its brain is by actually keeping the whole body cool. We can't uncouple brain temperature from the rest of the body, the way an antelope does, so we've got to prevent *any* damaging elevations in body temperature. And of course the problem is even more acute for an ape, because in general, the larger and more complex the brain, the more easily it is damaged. So there were incredible selective pressures on early hominines favoring adaptations that would reduce thermal stress—pressures that may have favored bipedalism."

Just how would bipedalism have protected the brain from heat? And why did our ancestors become bipedal rather than evolve some other way to keep cool? Before moving out onto the savanna, says Wheeler, our forebears were preadapted to evolve into bipeds. Swinging from branch to branch in the trees, they had already evolved a body plan that could, under the right environmental pressures, be altered to accommodate an upright stance. Such a posture, says Wheeler, greatly reduces the amount of the body's surface area that is directly exposed to the intense midday sun. It thereby reduces the amount of heat the body absorbs.

Although this observation is not new, Wheeler has done the first careful measurements and calculations of the advantages such a stance would have offered the early hominines. His measurements were rather simple. He took a one-foot-tall scale model of a hominine similar to Lucy—the 3-million-year-old chimp-size australopithecine that is known from the structure of her pelvis and legs to have been at least a part-time biped. Wheeler mounted a camera on an overhead track and moved it in a semicircular arc above the model, mimicking the daily path of the sun. Every five degrees along that path—the equivalent of 20 minutes on a summer day—Wheeler stopped the camera and snapped a photograph of the model. He repeated this process with the model in a variety of postures, both quadrupedal and bipedal.

To determine how much of the hominine's surface area would have been exposed to the sun's rays, Wheeler simply measured how much of the model's surface area was visible in the sun's eye-view photos. He found that a quadrupedal stance would have exposed the hominine to about 60 percent more solar radiation than a bipedal one.

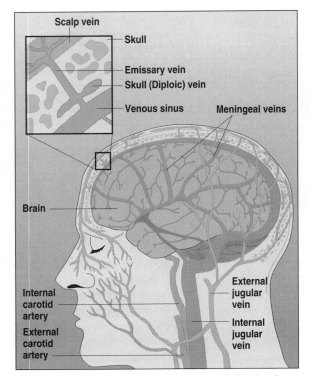

Figure 6.8 How the human brain is cooled: Blood from the face and scalp, instead of returning directly to the heart, may be shunted instead into the braincase, and then to the heart. Already cooled at the surface of the skin, it is able to carry away heat from the brain.

Not only does a biped expose less of its body to the sun, it also exposes more of its body to the cooler breezes a few feet above ground. The bottom line, says Wheeler, is that "on a typical savanna day, a knuckle-walking chimp-size hominine would require something in the region of five pints of water a day. Whereas simply by standing upright you cut that to something like three pints. In addition to that, you can also remain out in the open away from shade for longer, and at higher temperatures. So for an animal that was foraging for scattered resources in these habitats, bipedalism is really an excellent mode of locomotion."

Wheeler suspects that bipedalism also made possible two other uniquely human traits: our naked skin and large brains. "Our work suggests that you can't get a naked skin until you've become bipedal," he says.

"The problem has always been explaining why we don't see naked antelope or cheetahs. The answer appears to be that in those conditions in which animals are exposed to high radiation loads, the body hair acts as a shield. We always think of body hair as keeping heat in, but it also keeps heat out. If you take the fleece off a sheep and stand the animal out in the desert in the outback of Australia, the sheep will end up gaining more heat than you're helping it to dissipate. However, if you do that to a bipedal ape, because the exposure to solar radiation is so much less, it helps the ape lose more heat. Bipedalism, by reducing exposure to the sun, is tipping the balance and turning hair loss, which in quadrupeds would be a disadvantage, into an asset."

We bipeds maximize our heat loss, says Wheeler, by retaining a heat shield only on our most exposed surface—the top of our skull—and by exposing the rest of our body to cooling breezes. And bipedalism and naked skin together, he says, probably allowed us to evolve our oversize brains.

"The brain is one of the most metabolically active tissues in the body," he explains. "In the case of humans it accounts for something like 20 percent of total energy consumption. So you've got an organ producing a lot of heat that you've got to dump. Once we'd become bipedal and naked and achieved this ability to dump heat, that may have allowed the expansion of the brain that took place later in human evolution. It didn't cause it, but you can't have a large brain unless you can cool it."

[12]Adapted from Folger, T. (1993). The naked and the bipedal. *Discover, 14* (11), 34–35.

Persuasive though the "stand up to keep cool" hypothesis may be, we should not overlook other life-or-death considerations. The fact is, the causes of bipedalism are likely to have been multiple. While we may reject the idea of male "breadwinners" provisioning "stay-at-home" females as culture bound, it is true that bipedal locomotion does make food transport possible. A fully erect biped out on the open savanna—whether male or female—has the ability to gather substantial quantities of food for transport back to a tree or other place of safety for consumption; the animal does not have to remain out in the open, exposed and vulnerable, to do all of its eating. But food may not have been the only thing transported. As we saw in Chapter 4, primate infants must be able to cling to their mothers in order to be transported; since the mother is using her forelimbs in locomotion, to either walk or swing by, she cannot very well carry her infant. Chimpanzee infants, for example, must cling for themselves to their mothers, and even at the age of 4, they make long journeys on their mothers' backs. Injuries caused by falling from the mother are a significant cause of infant mortality. Thus, mothers able to carry their infants would have made a significant contribution to the survivorship of their offspring, and the ancestors of *Australopithecus* would have been capable of doing just this.

The ability to transport food, as this chimpanzee is doing with a piece of sugar cane, is not possible for hominoids unless they walk on their hind legs.

Besides making food transport possible, bipedalism could have facilitated the food quest in other ways. With their hands free and body upright, the animals could reach otherwise unobtainable food on savanna thorn trees too flimsy to climb. Furthermore, with both hands free, they could gather food twice as fast. And in times of scarcity, their ability to travel far without tiring would help get them between widely distributed sources of food. Since the head is positioned higher than in a quadrupedal stance, sources of food and

water may be spotted from afar, thereby facilitating their location.

Still other advantages of bipedalism would have enhanced survivability. With their heads up well above the ground, bipeds are able to spot predators before they get too close for safety. Finally, if they did get caught away from a safe place of refuge by a predator, manipulative and dexterous hands freed from locomotion provided hominines with a means of protecting themselves by brandishing and throwing objects at their attackers.

CHAPTER SUMMARY

The course of hominine evolution, we know from fossil finds, has not been a simple, steady "advance" in the direction of modern humans. One early hominine that appeared by at least 4 million years ago was *Australopithecus*, a genus that anthropologists divide into five species. *Australopithecus afarensis* and *africanus* walked erect, they were about the size of a modern human pygmy, they chewed food like humans, and their general appearance was that of an apelike human. The size and outward appearance of their brains suggest a degree of intelligence probably not greatly different from that of a modern chimpanzee or gorilla. Like chimpanzees, *afarensis* and *africanus* may have made some use of objects as tools.

Australopithecus boisei and *robustus* shared practically all of the traits listed for *afarensis* and *africanus*, but were more highly specialized for the consumption of plant foods. *Australopithecus anamensis*, the earliest documented biped, fits neatly between the later *A. afarensis* and the earlier (at 4.4 million years) *Ardipithecus ramidus*. The latter suggests an ancestry among the Miocene sivapithecines of Africa.

During the late Miocene and Pliocene, the climate became markedly cooler and drier; many ar-

eas that had once been heavily forested became woodland and open savanna. The ancestors of hominines found themselves spending more time on the ground; they had to adapt to this altered, more open environment, and food getting became a problem. As their diet changed, so did their dentition. On the whole, teeth became smaller, and many of the defensive functions once performed by the teeth seem to have been taken over by the hands.

Sivapithecines are believed to have been part-time brachiators who may at times have walked erect. *Australopithecus* is the first full biped hominine with erect posture whom we know about. Some disadvantages of bipedalism as a means of locomotion are that it makes an animal more visible to predators, exposes its "soft underbelly," is relatively slow, interferes with the ability to change direction instantly while running, and leaves nothing to fall back on when one leg is injured. Its advantages are that it provides hominines with a means of keeping their brains from overheating, of protecting themselves and holding objects while running, the ability to travel long distances without tiring, and the ability to see farther.

SUGGESTED READINGS

Campbell, B. G., & Loy, J. D. (1996). *Humankind emerging* (7th ed.). New York: HarperCollins.

Several physical anthropology texts have good coverage of the earliest hominines; this one is distinguished by its accessible writing style and well-chosen illustrations.

Ciochon, R. L., & Fleagle, J. G. (Eds.). (1993). *The human evolution source book*. Englewood Cliffs, NJ: Prentice-Hall.

In the first four parts of this book, the editors have assembled articles to present data and survey different theories on the evolution and diversification of the earliest hominines. A short editors' introduction to each section places the various articles in context.

Johanson, D., & Edey, M. (1981). *Lucy: The beginnings of humankind*. New York: Simon and Schuster.

This book tells the story of the discovery of "Lucy" and the other fossils of *Australopithecus afarensis* and why they have enhanced our understanding of the early stages of human evolution. It reads like a first-rate detective story, at the same time giving one of the best descriptions of australopithecines, and one of the best accounts of how paleoanthropologists analyze their fossils, to be found in literature.

PART

III

EVOLUTION OF THE GENUS HOMO AND THE DEVELOPMENT OF EARLY HUMAN CULTURE

By 2.5 million years ago, long after the line of human evolution had branched off from that of apes, a new kind of evolutionary process was set in motion. Early hominines began to manipulate the physical world, inventing solutions to the problems of human existence. With the passage of time, they came to rely more on cultural rather than biological adaptation as a more rapid and effective way of adjusting to environmental pressures. No longer did they have to depend predominately on physical attributes to survive. Moreover, as culture became more efficient at solving the problems of existence, human populations began to spread geographically, inhabiting new and even harsh environments, all of which is illustrated by human habitations of the cold regions of the world. Instead of being dependent on the evolution of humans capable of growing heavy coats of fur, as do other mammals that live in such regions, humans devised forms of clothing and shelter that, coupled with the use of fire, enabled them to overcome the cold. Moreover, once this kind of "cold adaptation" was accomplished, it could readily be changed when circumstances required it. The fact is that cultural equipment and techniques can change rapidly, whereas biological change can be accomplished only over many generations.

The next four chapters discuss how evolving hominines acquired the ability to invent their own solutions to the problems of existence and how this gained primacy over biological change as the human mechanism for adapting to the environment. We begin, in Chapter 7, with the appearance of the genus *Homo*. Although these earliest members of the genus had far smaller brains than ours, they were significantly larger than those of *Australopithecus*. Their appearance is associated with a new way of surviving. Instead of foraging, as do most primates, on a more or less individualistic basis for vegetables and fruits, supplemented by eggs, grubs, lizards, and similar sources of animal protein, early *Homo* invented stone tools with which they could butcher the carcasses of even larger animals. Thus, they were able to increase significantly the amount of meat in their diet. This made possible a degree of economic specialization; males scavenged for meat, and females gathered a wide variety of other wild foods. It also made possible new patterns of social interaction; females and males began sharing the results of their food-getting activities on a regular basis.

Over the next nearly 2.5 million years, a period known as the Paleolithic, or Old Stone Age, the evolving genus *Homo* relied increasingly on improved mental abilities for survival, as we shall see in Chapters 8, 9, and 10. In the process, hunting came to replace scavenging as the main means by which meat was procured, and other improvements of this food-foraging way of life took place. As a consequence, the human species, essentially a tropical one, was able to free itself from its tropical habitat and, through invention, adapt itself to colder climates. By 200,000 years ago, humans had acquired essentially modern brains. Shortly thereafter, they achieved the ability to survive under true Arctic conditions. To invent ways of surviving under such forbidding and difficult conditions ranks as no less an achievement than sending the first man to the moon.

CHAPTER
7

EARLY *HOMO* AND CULTURAL ORIGINS

OLDUVAI GORGE IN TANZANIA IS WHERE THE BONES OF THE EARLIEST TOOL MAKER, *HOMO HABILIS*, WERE FIRST FOUND. A SCAVENGER OF DEAD CARCASSES FOR THEIR MEAT, *H. HABILIS* SHOWS THE FIRST SIGNIFICANT INCREASE OF BRAIN SIZE BEYOND WHAT IS SEEN IN APES.

CHAPTER PREVIEW

When and How Did Human Culture Develop?

Human culture appears to have developed as some populations of early hominines began making stone tools with which they could butcher animals for their meat. Actually, the earliest stone tools and evidence of significant meat eating date to about 2.5 million years ago, just prior to the appearance of the genus *Homo*.

When Did Reorganization and Expansion of the Human Brain Begin?

Reorganization and expansion of the human brain did not begin until at least 1.5 million years after the development of bipedal locomotion. It began in conjunction with scavenging and the making of stone tools. This marks the appearance of the genus *Homo*, an evolutionary offshoot of *Australopithecus*. The two forms appear to have coexisted for a million years or so, during the course of which *Australopithecus* emphasized a vegetarian diet while developing a massive chewing apparatus. In contrast, *Homo* ate more meat and became brainier.

Why Did the Eating of More Meat Lead to Improved Brains?

The making of stone tools, needed to skin, butcher, and crack open the bones of animals for marrow, put a premium on an improved eye-hand coordination and precision grip, both of which selected for better brains. Increased meat eating, too, led to changes in the subsistence activities of both females and males. These changes called for more in the way of thinking and planning for both sexes, which again selected for better brains.

In 1931 when Louis and Mary Leakey began work at Olduvai Gorge, they did so due to the presence of crude stone tools in deposits dating back to very early in the Pleistocene Epoch, which began almost 2 million years ago. When they found the bones of *Australopithecus boisei* in 1959, in association with some of these tools, they thought they had found the remains of one of the toolmakers. They later changed their minds, however, and suggested that these tools were not produced by *A. boisei*, nor were the bones of the birds, reptiles, antelopes, and an extinct kind of pig found with the remains of *A. boisei* the remains of the latter's dinner. Instead, *A. boisei* may have been a victim of a rather different contemporary who created the tools, ate the animals, and possibly had the unfortunate *A. boisei* for dessert. That contemporary was called by the Leakeys *Homo habilis* ("handy man").

EARLY REPRESENTATIVES OF THE GENUS *HOMO*

The Leakeys discovered the remains of this second hominine in 1960, only a few months after their earlier discovery, just a few feet below it. The remains, which were those of more than one individual, consisted of a few cranial bones, a lower jaw, a clavicle, some finger bones (Fig. 7.1), and the nearly complete left foot of an adult (Fig. 7.2). These fossils date from about 1.8 million years ago and represent a hominine with a cranial capacity in the 650 to 690 cubic centimeter range, a skull that lacks noticeable bony crests, and almost modern-looking hands and feet. Subsequent work at Olduvai has unearthed not only more skull fragments, but other parts of the skeleton of *Homo ha-*

bilis as well. These indicated that, in spite of their more modern-looking heads, hands, and feet, the skeleton of this hominine from the neck down does not differ greatly from that of *Australopithecus afarensis* or *africanus*. Overall size was about the same, as was the degree of sexual dimorphism, and they still climbed trees, although perhaps not quite so much as *Australopithecus*.[1] Moreover, dental evidence suggests that, as with *A. afarensis* and *africanus*, the period of infancy and childhood in *H. habilis* was not prolonged, as it is in modern humans, but was more in line with apes.[2]

Since the late 1960s, fossils of the genus *Homo* that are essentially contemporaneous with those from Olduvai have been recognized elsewhere in Africa—in South Africa, in Kenya near Lake Baringo as well as east of Lake Turkana at Koobi Fora, and in Ethiopia just north of Lake Turkana. One of the best of these, known as KNM ER 1470, was discovered by the Leakeys' son Richard (the letters KNM stand for Kenya National Museum, the ER for East Rudolf, the former name for Lake Turkana). The deposits in which it was found are about 1.9 million years old; these deposits, like those at Olduvai, also contain crude stone tools. The KNM ER 1470 skull is more modern in appearance than any *Australopithecus* skull and has a cranial capacity of 752 cubic centimeters. Furthermore, the inside of the skull shows a pattern in the left cerebral hemisphere that, in living people, is associated with a speech area.[3] This is in keeping with indications of brain asymmetry more like that of humans than apes, as well as evidence from wear patterns on tools evidently used by early *Homo* that reveal that these hominines were predominately right-handed. In humans, the speech organs and the right hand are controlled by adjacent areas in the left cerebral hemisphere. While this does not prove that early *Homo* had a spoken language, it does indicate that its brain was not only larger than that of *Australopithecus*, but was reorganized along more human lines.

[1]Lewin, R. (1987). The earliest "humans" were more like apes. *Science, 236,* 106–163.

[2]Lewin, R. (1987). Debate over emergence of human tooth pattern. *Science, 235,* 749.

[3]Falk, D. (1993). Hominid paleoneurology. In R. L. Ciochon & J. G. Fleagle (Eds.), *The human evolution source book* (p. 62). Englewood Cliffs, NJ: Prentice-Hall.

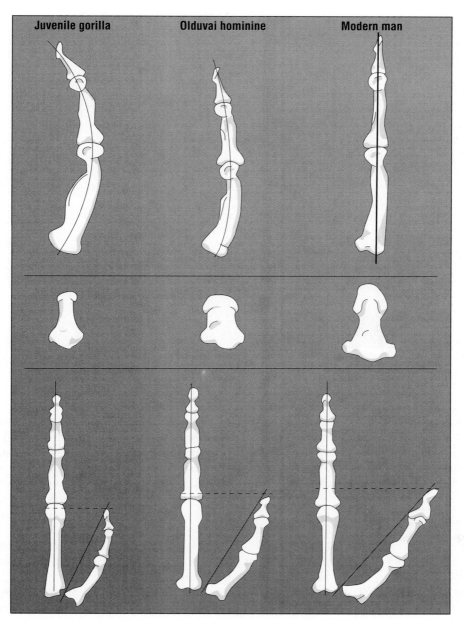

Figure 7.1   A comparison of hand bones of a juvenile gorilla, *Homo habilis* from Olduvai, and a modern human highlights important differences in the structure of the fingers and thumbs. In the top row are fingers and in the second row are terminal thumb bones. The bottom row compares thumb length and angle relative to the index finger.

Although the 1470 skull and other early *Homo* fossils from localities other than Olduvai are frequently assigned to the same species, *H. habilis*, there are those who argue that two distinct species may be present. In favor of this is what appears to be an unusually wide degree of variation; on the other hand, those who suspect that two species are present cannot agree on how to apportion the fossils between them. Nor have they so far been able to demonstrate that they occupied different parts

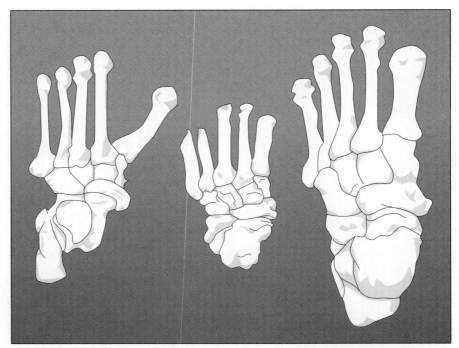

Figure 7.2 A partial foot skeleton of *Homo habilis* (center) is compared with the same bones of a chimpanzee (left) and a modern human (right).

of the paleolandscape. Unless and until these difficulties are overcome, it seems best to regard all of this material as representative of a single species, ***Homo habilis.***

Relations Between *Homo habilis* and *Australopithecus*

A consideration of brain size relative to body size clearly indicates that *Homo habilis* had undergone enlargement of the brain far in excess of values predicted on the basis of body size alone. This means that there was a marked advance in information-processing capacity over that of the aus-

---

Homo habilis: Earliest representative of the genus *Homo*; lived between 2.4 and 1.8 million years ago. Characterized by expansion and reorganization of the brain, compared with *Australopithecus.*

---

tralopithecines. Because larger brains generate more heat, it is not surprising to find that *habilis'* brain was provided with a heat exchanger of a sort not seen in *Australopithecus*, save to a very rudimentary degree in *africanus*.[4] This consists of small openings in the braincase through which veins pass, allowing cooled blood from the face and scalp to be shunted to the brain, from which the blood can then carry off excess heat (see Fig. 6.8). Thus, damage to the brain from excessive heat is prevented.

Although these hominines had teeth that are large by modern standards—or even those of a half million years ago—they are smaller in relation to the size of the skull than those of australopithecines. Since major brain-size increase and tooth-size reduction are important trends in the evolution of the genus *Homo*, but not of *Australopithecus*, it looks as if ER 1470 and similar hominines were evolving in a more human direction. Consistent with this are the indications that

[4]Falk, D. (1993). A good brain is hard to cool. *Natural History, 102* (8), 65.

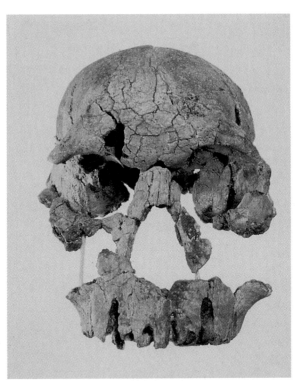

ER 1470: One of the most complete skulls of *Homo habilis* is close to 2 million years old.

the Baringo fossil), soon after the earliest evidence (to be discussed shortly) for stone toolmaking and increased consumption of meat.

As noted earlier, the australopithecine diet seems to have consisted for the most part of plant foods, although *A. afarensis* and *africanus* may have consumed limited amounts of animal protein as well. Later australopithecines (*A. boisei* and *robustus*) evolved into more specialized "grinding machines" as their jaws became markedly larger (Fig. 7.3), while their brain size did not. Nor is there firm evidence that they made stone tools. Thus, in the period between 2.5 and 1 million years ago, two kinds of hominines were headed in very different evolutionary directions.

If neither *Australopithecus boisei* nor *robustus* belong in the direct line of human ancestry, what of earlier species of *Australopithecus?* From the standpoint of anatomy alone, it has long been recognized that either *Australopithecus afarensis* or *africanus* constitutes a good ancestor for the genus *Homo*, and it now seems clear that the body of *Homo habilis* had changed little from that of either species. Precisely which of the two gave rise to *H. habilis* is vigorously debated. Most see *A. afarensis* as sufficiently generalized to have given rise to both the *Homo* and *boisei-robustus* patterns, noting that the earliest skull to show the latter, the so-called Black Skull, nonetheless shows some holdovers from *A. afarensis*. This skull's age (2.5 million

the brain of KNM ER 1470 was less apelike and more human in structure. It is probably no accident that the earliest fossils to exhibit these features appear by 2.4 million years ago (the age of

Figure 7.3 Premolars (left) and molars (right) of *Australopithecus* and *Homo habilis* show significant differences in size. The teeth of *Australopithecus* show a clear tendency to enlarge with time over those of *A. afarensis*, while the teeth of *H. habilis* differ little from those of *A. afarensis*.

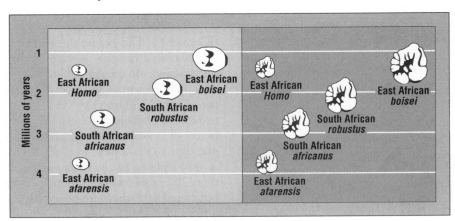

years), is too old for any but the very earliest *africanus* to have figured in its ancestry. Since the earliest *homo habilis* skull is nearly as old, the same must be true for it. Evidently, a three-way split was under way by 2.5 million years ago, with the third line represented by *A. africanus* (Fig. 7.4). This persisted until about 2 million years ago (or later, if *A. robustus* is a descendant of *africanus*, rather than an offshoot of *boisei*), by which time the other two lineages had become widespread in nonforested parts of Africa.

LOWER PALEOLITHIC TOOLS

The earliest tools known to have been made by hominines have been found in the vicinity of Lake Turkana in Kenya and southern Ethiopia, Olduvai Gorge in Tanzania, and Hadar in Ethiopia. Their appearance marks the beginning of the **Lower Paleolithic,** the first part of the Old Stone Age.

These early tools show striking similarities, indicating that they were the results of a cultural tradition of manufacturing tools according to a particular preconceived model or pattern. At Olduvai and Lake Turkana, these tools are close to 2 million years old. The Hadar tools have been found below a deposit dated by potassium argon to about 1.8 million years ago, but above another dated to about 2.8 million years; thus they are estimated to be about 2.5 million years old.

Olduvai Gorge

What is now Olduvai Gorge was once a lake. Almost 2 million years ago, its shores were inhabited not only by numerous wild animals but also by groups of hominines, including *Australopithecus boisei* and *Homo habilis* as well as the later *Homo erectus*

Lower Paleolithic: The first part of the "Old Stone Age"; its beginning is marked by the appearance of Oldowan tools.

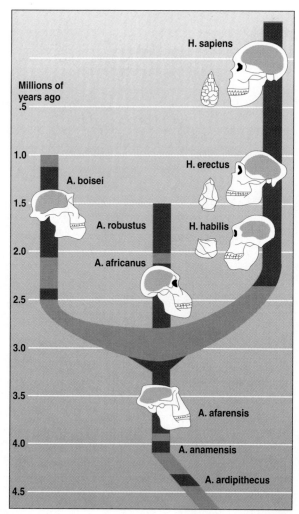

Figure 7.4 This diagram presents one plausible view of early human evolution.

(Chapter 8). The gorge, therefore, is a rich source of Paleolithic remains as well as a key site providing evidence of human evolutionary development. Among the finds are assemblages of stone tools that are about 2 million years old. These lie little disturbed from when they were left, together with the bones of now extinct animals that were eaten. At one spot, in the lowest level of the gorge, the bones of an elephant lay in close association with more than 200 stone tools. Apparently, the animal was butchered here; there are no indications of any other activity. At another spot, on a "living floor" 1.8

million years old, basalt stones were found grouped in small heaps forming a circle. The interior of the circle was practically empty, while numerous tools and food debris littered the ground outside, right up to the edge of the circle. Some interpret this as evidence for some sort of shelter, seeing the stone piles as supports for the framework of a protective fence of thorn branches, or perhaps a hut with a covering of animal skins or grass. Another possibility is that the stones were "stockpiled" ahead of time, to be made into tools as needed, or to be hurled as missiles to hold off other scavengers while the hominines extracted meat, marrow, hide, and sinew from pieces of animal carcass.

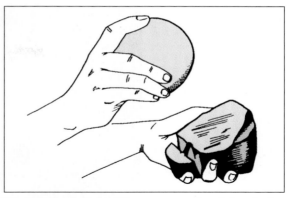

Figure 7.5   By 2.5 million years ago, hominines had invented the percussion method of stone tool manufacture. This technological breakthrough, which is associated with a significant increase in brain size, made possible the butchering of meat from scavenged carcasses.

Oldowan Tools

The oldest tools found at Olduvai Gorge belong to the **Oldowan tool tradition,** which is characterized by an all-purpose generalized chopping tool, produced by removing a few flakes from a stone (often a large, water-worn pebble) either by using another stone as a hammer (hammerstone) or by striking the pebble against a large rock (anvil) to remove the flakes. This system of manufacture is called the **percussion method** (Fig. 7.5). The finished product had a jagged, sharp edge, effective for cutting and chopping. The generalized form of the chopping tool suggests that it served many purposes, such as butchering meat, splitting bones for marrow, and perhaps also defending the owner. Also used were the flakes, which had sharp, useful edges (in fact, many so-called choppers may be no more than by-products of flake manufacture). Some flakes were used "as is" for cutting tools, while others were retouched for use as scrapers.

Oldowan tool tradition: The earliest identifiable stone tools.

Percussion method: A technique of stone tool manufacture by striking the raw material with a hammerstone or by striking raw material against a stone anvil to remove flakes.

Crude as they were, Oldowan choppers and flakes mark an important technological advance for early hominines; previously, they depended on found objects requiring little or no modification, such as bones, sticks, or conveniently shaped stones. Oldowan tools made possible new additions to the diet, because, without such tools, hominines could eat few animals (only those that could be skinned by tooth or nail); therefore, their diet was limited in terms of animal proteins. The advent of Oldowan choppers and flakes meant more than merely saving labor and time—they made possible the addition of meat to the diet on a frequent, rather than occasional, basis. Much of a popular nature has been written about this, often with numerous colorful references to "killer apes." Such references are quite misleading, not only because hominines are not apes but also because killing has been greatly overemphasized. Meat can be obtained, after all, by scavenging or by stealing it from other predators. What is significant is that a dentition such as that possessed by *Australopithecus* and *Homo habilis* is poorly suited for meat eating. What is needed if substantial amounts of meat are to be eaten, in the absence of teeth like those possessed by carnivorous animals, are sharp tools for butchering.

The initial use of tools was probably the result of adaptation to an environment that we know was changing from forests to grasslands. The physical changes that adapted hominines to living in the

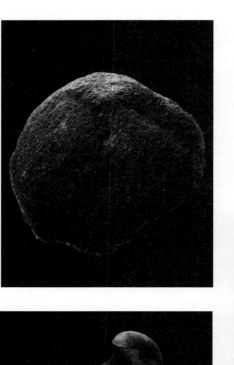

The stone tools used by *Homo habilis* included lava cobbles, choppers, and flakes like these shown here. Most choppers were probably the result of being struck from one cobble by another. These flakes were used to remove meat from bones, leaving cut marks (lower left). The cobbles and choppers were used to break open bones (middle left) to get at the marrow.

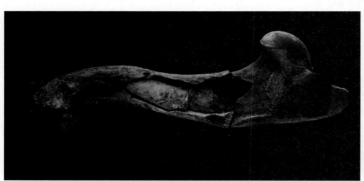

new grassy terrain encouraged toolmaking. It has been observed that monkeys and apes, for example, often use objects, such as sticks and stones, in conjunction with threat displays. The change to a nearly upright bipedal posture, coupled with existing flexibility at the shoulder, arms, and hands, helped hominines to compete with, and survive in spite of, the large predatory carnivores that shared their environment.

What else do these assemblages of Oldowan tools and broken animal bones have to tell us about the life way of early *Homo?* First, they tell us that both *Homo habilis* and large carnivorous animals were active at these locations, for in addition to marks on the bones made by slicing, scraping, and chopping with stone tools, there are tooth marks from gnawing. Some of the gnawing marks overlie the butcher marks, indicating that enough flesh was left on the bones after the hominines were done with them to attract the other carnivores. In other cases, though, the butcher marks overlie the tooth marks of carnivores, indicating that the animals got there first. This is what we would expect if *H. habilis* were scavenging from the kills of other animals, rather than doing its own killing. Consistent with this is the fact that whole carcasses are not represented; evidently, only parts were transported away from the original location where they were obtained, again what we would expect if they were "stolen" from the kill of some other animal. The stone tools, too, were made of raw material procured at some distance from where they were used to process the parts of carcasses. Finally, the incredible density of bones at some of the sites and patterns of weathering indicate that, although *H. habilis* did not linger longer than necessary at any one time (and for good reason—the carnivores attracted by the meat could have made short work of *habilis* as well), the sites were repeatedly used over periods of 5 to 15 years.

All of this is quite unlike the behavior of historically known food-foraging peoples, who bring whole carcasses back to camp, where they are completely processed; neither meat nor marrow is left (as they were at Oldowan sites), and the bones themselves are broken up (as they were not at Oldowan sites) both to get at the marrow and to fabricate tools and other objects of bone. Nor do historically known food foragers normally camp in the midst of so much garbage. The picture that emerges of our Oldowan forebears, then, is of scavengers, getting their meat from the lower Paleolithic equivalent of modern-day roadkills, taking the spoils of their scavenging to particular

Like these modern jackals, *Homo habilis* gained access to meat through scavenging.

places where tools, and the raw materials for making them, had been stockpiled previously for the purpose of butchering. At these sites, the remains were quickly processed, so that those doing the butchering could clear out before their lives were endangered by carnivores attracted by the meat. Thus, the Oldowan sites were not campsites or "home bases" at all. Quite likely, *H. habilis* continued to sleep in trees or rocky cliffs, as do other small-bodied terrestrial or semiterrestrial primates, in order to be safe from predators. However, the advanced preparation for meat processing implied by the caching of stone tools, and the raw materials for making tools, attests to considerable foresight and ability to plan ahead.

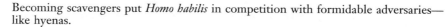

Tools, Meat, and Brains

As we have seen, by 1.5 million years or so after early hominines became fully bipedal, the size and structure of the brain were beginning to change. Up until about 2.5 million years ago, early hominines lived on foods that could be picked or gathered: plants, fruits, invertebrate animals such as ants and termites, and perhaps even an occa-

sional piece of meat scavenged from kills made by other animals. After 2.5 million years ago, meat became more important in their diet, and they began to scavenge for it on a more regular basis.

Since early hominines lacked size and strength to drive off predators, or to compete directly with other scavengers attracted to kills, they must have had to rely on their wit and cunning for success. One may imagine them lurking in the vicinity of a kill, sizing up the situation as the predator ate its fill while hyenas and other scavengers gathered, and devising strategies to outwit them all so as to seize a piece of the carcass. A hominine depending on stereotyped instinctual behavior in such a situation would have been at a competitive disadvantage. One that could anticipate problems, devise distractions, bluff competitors into temporary retreat, and recognize, the instant it came, its opportunity to rush in and grab what it could of the carcass stood a much better chance of surviving, reproducing, and proliferating.

One means by which early hominines gained access to a reasonably steady supply of carcasses while at the same time minimizing the risks involved is suggested by recent field studies of leopards. How this could have worked and the arguments in favor of it are discussed in the following Original Study.

Becoming scavengers put *Homo habilis* in competition with formidable adversaries—like hyenas.

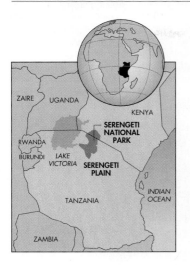

Original Study
Cat in the Human Cradle[5]

Recent evidence, such as marks on some of the Olduvai bones, indicates that animals the size of wildebeests or larger were killed, eaten, and abandoned by large predators such as lions, hyenas, and saber-toothed cats; hominines may have merely scavenged the leftovers. Several specialists now agree that early hominines obtained at least marrow mainly in this way. The picture with regard to the remains of smaller animals, such as gazelle-sized antelopes, is less certain. Paleoanthropologists Henry Bunn and Ellen Kroll believe that the cut-marked upper limb bones of small, medium-sized, and large animals found at Olduvai Gorge demonstrate that hominines were butchering the meaty limbs with cutting tools. Since modern-day lions and hyenas rapidly and completely consume small prey, leaving little or nothing for potential scavengers, Bunn and Kroll conclude that hominines must have acquired the smaller animals by hunting. But another scholar, Kay Behrensmeyer, suggests that a small group of hominines could have obtained these bones, not by hunting, but by driving off timid predators, such as cheetahs or jackals, from their kills.

Since carnivores play a key role in all these scenarios, three years ago I began thinking about studying their behavior and ecology. About the same time, a colleague directed me to a paper on the tree-climbing abilities of early hominines. The authors (anatomists Randall L. Susman, Jack T. Stern, and William L. Jungers) analyzed the limb bones of *Homo habilis* specimens from Olduvai Gorge, as well as those of the early hominine *Australopithecus afarensis* (better known as Lucy). They concluded that early hominines were probably not as efficient as we are at walking on two feet, but they were better than we are at climbing trees and suspending themselves from branches. At the very least, given their apparent lack of fire, early hominines must have used trees as refuges from large predators and as sleeping sites.

One evening, as I watched a documentary film by Hugh Miles about a female leopard and her cubs in Kenya's Masai Mara Reserve, carnivore behavior and early hominine tree climbing suddenly connected for me. In the film, a pack of hyenas attempt to scavenge an antelope that the mother leopard has killed. At the sight of the hyenas, the leopard grabs the prey in her jaws and carries it up a small tree. This striking behavior sparked my curiosity and sent me to the library the next morning to find out more about leopards.

I learned that the leopard differs from other large African carnivores in a variety of ways. Although it occasionally kills large animals, such as adult wildebeests and topi or young giraffes, the leopard preys primarily on smaller antelopes, such as Thomson's gazelles, impala, and Grant's gazelles, and on the young of both large and small species. Unable to defend its kills on the ground from scavenging by lions and spotted hyenas, both of which often forage in groups, the usually solitary leopard stores each kill in a tree, returning to feed but otherwise frequently abandoning it for varying lengths of time.

This leopard has carried part of a Thomson's gazelle up into a tree to prevent other scavengers from consuming what is left. Such tree-stored carcasses may have been the principal source of meat for *Homo habilis*.

Although the leopard may not consume its entire prey immediately, the tree-stored kills are relatively safe from theft. (Even lions, which can climb trees, usually take little notice of this resource.) As a result, a kill can persist in a tree for several days. Also, leopard kills appear to be more predictably located than those of lions and hyenas because leopards tend to maintain a small territorial range for several years and occasionally reuse feeding trees. Finally, leopard kills are usually found in the woodlands near lakes and rivers, the habitat apparently preferred by early hominines. Such circumstances, I reasoned, might have once provided an ideal feeding opportunity for tree-climbing hominines, particularly *Homo habilis*. By scavenging from the leopard's temporarily abandoned larder, early hominines could have obtained the fleshy and marrow-rich bones of small- to medium-sized prey animals in relative safety.

Fossil evidence shows that ancestors of present-day leopards were contemporaneous with early hominines and shared the same habitats. The antiquity of tree-caching behavior is harder to prove, but it is supported by paleoanthropologist C. K. Brain's excavations of ancient caves in southern Africa's Sterkfontein Valley. In these vertical, shaftlike caves, Brain found the fossil remains of hominines, baboons, and antelopes, and of leopards and other large carnivores. The size of the prey animals and the selection of body parts, as well as puncture marks on some of the cranial bones of hominines and baboons, suggested that many of these fossils were the remains of leopard meals. Brain guessed that they had fallen into the caves from leopard feeding trees growing out of the mouths of the caves.

Given its similarities to the ancient environments represented at the early archeological sites—extensive grasslands with wooded lakes, rivers and streams—the Serengeti National Park in northern Tanzania seemed an ideal living laboratory in which to test my hypothesis. I traveled there in July 1987, accompanied by Robert J. Blumenschine, who had conducted an earlier study there on scavenging opportunities provided by lions and hyenas. Along the Wandamu River, a tributary of the Seronera, we were fortunate to find an adult female leopard and her thirteen-month-old (nearly full grown) male cub that tolerated our Land-Rover. We spent a total of about fifty hours, during the day and at night, observing these leopards at three fresh, tree-stored kills of Thomson's gazelles. The leopards frequently left the carcasses unguarded between feedings. On one occasion, a complete young Thomson's gazelle, killed the previous evening, was abandoned for nine daylight hours (we found the leopards resting approximately two miles away). Without directly confronting these predators, therefore, a creature able to climb trees could have easily carried off the same amount of flesh and marrow as it could obtain from hunting.

While Brain's work in South Africa implicates leopards as predators of early hominines, including the genus *Homo,* some hominines may have also benefitted from living near these carnivores. Tree-stored leopard kills could have provided an important resource to early scavenging hominines and the sharp, broken limb bones from the partly eaten prey could have been used to peel back the hide, expose the flesh of the carcasses, and remove large muscle bundles. This activity may even have given early hominines the initial impetus to make and use tools in the extraction of animal nutrients.

Some paleoanthropologists have argued that scavenging was an unlikely subsistence strategy for early hominines, since large predators require expansive home ranges and kills by these carnivores are rare in any particular area. They also contend that very little is left over from such kills after the predator is finished and that hominine competition with large carnivores for these leftovers would be a dangerous activity. My 1988 observations suggest something quite different. During approximately two months in the dry season, I documented sixteen kills of small and medium antelopes made by my adult male and female leopards within an approximately four-by-eight-mile area. The majority of these kills, still retaining abundant flesh and marrow, were temporarily abandoned by the leopard for three to eight and a half hours during a single day.

The tree-stored leopard kills consisted mainly of adult and juvenile Thomson's gazelles. Compared with kills of similar-sized prey made on the ground by Serengeti lions and hyenas, as recorded by Blumenschine, the tree-stored leopard kills lasted longer, offering large quantities of flesh and marrow for two or more days. In part this was because they were not subject to many scavengers. The leopard kills were also more predictably located on the landscape than those of lions in the same area. In modern leopard populations, a male maintains a relatively large territory that overlaps with the usually smaller territories of several females. This pattern often means that several tree-stored kills are available simultaneously during a given period of time within a relatively small area.

An obvious question is how leopards would have responded to repeated theft of their tree-stored kills by early hominines. Would they, perhaps, have abandoned portions of their ranges if such thefts occurred with sufficient regularity? Although I haven't yet tested this, I don't think they would have. According to my observations and those of other researchers, leopards are usually more successful at hunting larger prey, such as gazelles and impala, at night. This gives them the opportunity to consume part of such kills before the arrival of any daytime scavengers. They thus should be able to obtain enough nourishment to warrant remaining in a territory, despite some such losses.

Like modern baboons and chimpanzees, early hominines may have killed some small animals, such as newborn antelopes. But they could have acquired all sizes of animal carcasses without hunting if the prey killed by leopards is taken into account. The wide assortment of animal bones at sites like Olduvai Gorge, which have been attributed to ground-based hunting and scavenging, could instead be attributed to scavenging only, both in trees and on the ground. Leopard kills would then have provided much of the flesh consumed by early hominines, while carcasses abandoned on the ground by other large predators would have yielded primarily bone marrow. Additional flesh may have come from the remains of large kills made by saber-toothed cats or from the carcasses of animals that drowned when herds migrated across ancient lakes.

While we can't observe the behavior of our early ancestors, the present-day interactions between leopards and some other primate species can be instructive. Baboons, for example, often fall victim to leopards while they sleep at night in trees or caves. During the day, however, baboons regularly attack, displace, and according to one account, even kill leopards. In western Tanzania, a park ranger reported that during the day, a group of baboons saw a leopard in a tree with the carcass of an impala. Barking out alarm calls, the adult and adolescent male baboons chased the leopard for about three-tenths of a mile. The females and young baboons stayed with the carcass and began to eat, until the males returned and took possession of the kill.

Similarly, although chimpanzees in western Tanzania are the occasional prey of leopards, there is a report that one day some chimpanzees scavenged what was apparently a tree-stored leopard kill. On a more dramatic occasion, also during the day, a group of chimpanzees was observed noisily surrounding a leopard lair from which an adult leopard was heard growling. A male chimpanzee entered the lair and emerged with a leopard cub, which it and the others killed without reprisal from the adult leopard. This type of shifting day-night, predatory-parasitic relationship may once have existed between leopards and our early hominine ancestors.

[5]Adapted from Cavallo, J. A. (1990). Cat in the human cradle. *Natural History, 2/90,* 54–56, 58–60.

Several lines of evidence suggest it was probably the early hominine males, rather than females, who did most of the scavenging. What predisposed them for this may have been the foraging habits of the earlier australopithecines. As already noted, dental and skeletal differences between males and females suggest that males may have fed on the ground and lower levels of trees more heavily than females, who had a higher proportion of fruit in their diet.[6] Something like this pattern is seen today among orangutans, where it is a response to

[6]Leonard, W. R. & Hegman, M. (1987). Evolution of P3 morphology in *Australopithecus afarensis. American Journal of Physical Anthropology, 73,* 60.

highly dispersed resources. As a consequence, males consume larger amounts of low-quality food such as bark than do females. A major difference, of course, is that orangutan males still forage in the forest, whereas male *Australopithecus* did not. In such a situation, the latter may have been tempted to try supplementary sources of food on the ground, especially if existing sources became scarcer, as they likely did; a markedly cold, dry episode has been identified in the crucial period between 2.6 and 2.3 million years ago.[7] Already bipedal, australopithecines were capable of covering, in an energetically efficient way, the considerable distances (on the order of 32 square miles, based on the Original Study) necessary to ensure a steady supply of meat.

Another consideration is that, without contraceptive devices and formulas that could be bottle fed to infants, females in their prime, when not pregnant, must have had infants to nurse. While this would not have restricted their local mobility, any more than it does a female ape or monkey or women among historically known food-foraging peoples, it would have been less easy for them than for males to range over the vast distances required to search out carcasses. Another necessity for the successful scavenger would have been the ability to mobilize rapidly high bursts of energy in order to elude the many carnivores active on the savanna. Although anatomical and physiological differences between the sexes in humans today are relatively insignificant compared to *H. habilis*, as a general rule, men can still run faster than women (even though some women can certainly run faster than some men). Finally, even for the smartest and swiftest individuals, scavenging would still have been a risky business. To place early *Homo* females at risk would have been to place their offspring, actual and potential, at risk as well. Males, on the other hand, would have been relatively expendable, for, to put the matter bluntly, a very few males are capable of impregnating a large number of females. In evolutionary terms, the population that places its males at risk is less likely to jeopardize its chances for reproductive success than is the one that places its females at risk.

In order to gain access to some of the meat scavenged by males, early hominine females, too, had to "sharpen their wits." For the most part, they continued to gather the same kinds of foods that their ancestors had been eating all along. But instead of consuming all this food themselves as they gathered it (as other primates do), they provided some to the males who, in turn, provided the females with meat. To do this, they had to plan ahead so as to know where food would be found in sufficient quantities, devise means by which it could be transported to some agreed upon location for division at the proper time, while at the same time preventing its loss through spoilage, or to animals such as rats and mice. Thus, female gathering played just as important a role in the development of better brains as did male scavenging.

The new interest in meat on the part of evolving hominines is a point of major importance. Out on the savanna, it is hard for a primate with a digestive system like that of humans to satisfy its amino-acid requirements from available plant resources. Moreover, failure to do so has serious consequences: growth depression, malnutrition, and ultimately death. The most readily accessible plant sources would have been the proteins available in leaves and legumes (nitrogen-fixing plants, familiar modern examples being beans and peas), but these are hard for primates like us to handle digestively unless they are cooked. The problem is that leaves and legumes contain substances that cause the proteins to pass right through the gut without being absorbed.[8]

Chimpanzees have a similar problem when out on the savanna. In such a setting, they spend about 37 percent of their time going after insects like ants and termites on a year-round basis, while at the same time increasing their predation on eggs and vertebrate animals. Such animal foods not only are easily digestible, but they provide high-quality proteins that contain all the essential amino acids, in just the right percentages. No one plant food does this by itself; only if the right combination is consumed can plants provide what meat does by itself in the way of amino acids. Moreover, there is abundant meat to be had on the savanna. All things considered, then, we should not be surprised if our

[7]Skelton, R. R., McHenry, H. M., & Drawhorn, G. M. (1986). Phylogenetic analysis of early hominids. *Current Anthropology, 27*, 31.

[8]Stahl, A. B. (1984). Hominid dietary selection before fire. *Current Anthropology, 25*, 151–168.

ADRIENNE ZIHLMAN
(b. 1940)

Up until the 1970s, the study of human evolution, from its very beginnings, was permeated by a deep-seated bias reflecting the privileged status enjoyed by men in Western society. Beyond the obvious labeling of fossils as particular types of "men," irrespective of the sex of the individual represented, it took the form of portraying males as the active sex in human evolution. Thus, it was males who were seen as providers and innovators, using their wits to become ever more effective providers of food and protection for passive females. The latter were seen as spending their time getting pregnant and caring for offspring, while the men were "getting ahead" by becoming ever smarter. Central to such thinking was the idea of "man the hunter," constantly honing his wits through the pursuit and killing of animals. Thus, hunting by men was seen as the pivotal humanizing activity in evolution.

We now know, of course, that such ideas are culture-bound, reflecting the hopes and expectations of late-nineteenth- and early-twentieth-century European and European-American culture. Recognition of this fact came in the 1970s and was a direct consequence of the entry of a number of highly capable women into the profession of paleoanthropology. Up until the 1960s, there were few women in any field of physical anthropology, but with the expansion of graduate programs and changing attitudes towards the role of women in society, increasing numbers of them went on to earn the Ph.D. One of these was Adrienne

Zihlman, who earned her doctorate at the University of California at Berkeley in 1967. Subsequently, she authored a number of important papers critical of "man the hunter" scenarios. She was not the first to do so; as early as 1971, Sally Linton had published a preliminary paper on "Woman the Gatherer," but it was Zihlman from 1976 on who especially elaborated on the importance of woman's activities for human evolution. Others have joined in the effort, including Zihlman's companion in graduate school and later colleague, Nancy Tanner, who collaborated with Zihlman on some of her papers and has produced important works of her own.

The work of Zihlman and her co-workers was crucial in forcing a reexamination of existing "man the hunter" scenarios, out of which came recognition of the importance of scavenging in early human evolution as well as the importance of female gathering and other activities. While there is still plenty to learn about human evolution, thanks to these women we now know that it was not a case of women being "uplifted" as a consequence of their association with progressively evolving men. Rather, the two sexes evolved together, with each making its own important contribution to the process.

---

own ancestors solved their "protein problem" in somewhat the same way that chimps on the savanna do today.

Increased meat consumption on the part of early hominines did more than merely ensure an adequate intake of essential amino acids, important though this was. Animals that live on plant foods must eat large quantities of vegetation, and obtaining such foods consumes much of their time. Meat eaters, by contrast, have no need to eat so much or so often. Consequently, meat-eating hominines may have had more leisure time available to explore and manipulate their environment; like

lions and leopards, they would have time to spend lying around and playing. Such activity, coupled with the other factors already mentioned, probably was a stimulus to hominine brain development.

The importance of meat eating for early hominine brain development is suggested by the size of their brains: The cranial capacity of the largely plant-eating *Australopithecus* ranged from 310 to 530 cubic centimeters; that of the most primitive known meat eater, *Homo habilis* from East Africa, ranged from 580 to 752 ccs; whereas *Homo erectus*, who eventually hunted as well as scavenged for meat, possessed a cranial capacity of 775 to 1225 ccs.

Meat-eating animals, like these lions, do not have to spend as much time eating as do those that rely on plant foods alone. Consequently, they have more time available for play and exploration.

The Earliest Signs of Culture: Tools

The use of specially made tools of stone appears to have arisen as a result of the need for implements to butcher and prepare meat, because hominine teeth were inadequate for the task. Even chimpanzees, whose canine teeth are far larger and sharper, frequently have trouble tearing through the skin of other animals.[9] Besides overcoming this problem, the manufacturing of stone tools must have played a role in the evolution of the human brain, first by putting a premium on manual dexterity and fine manipulation, as opposed to hand use emphasizing power rather than precision. This in turn put a premium on improved organization of the nervous system. Second, the transformation of a lump of stone into a "chopper," "knife," or "scraper" is a far cry from what a chimpanzee does

[9]Goodall, J. (1986). *The chimpanzees of Gombe: Patterns of behavior* (p. 372). Cambridge, MA: Belknap Press.

when it transforms a stick into a termite probe. While the probe is not unlike the stick, the stone tool is (with the exception of hammerstones) unlike the lump of stone. Thus, the toolmaker must have in mind an abstract idea of the tool to be made, as well as a specific set of steps that will accomplish the transformation from raw materials to finished product. Furthermore, only certain kinds of stone have the flaking properties that will allow the transformation to take place, and the toolmaker must know about these.

Cooperation and Sharing

With an apelike brain and a diet like that of monkeys and apes when out on the savanna, *Australopithecus* probably behaved much like other hominoids. Like apes, adults probably foraged for their own food, which was rarely shared with other adults. Among modern apes, however, there is one

A power grip (left) utilizes more of the hand while the precision grip (right) relies on the fingers for control.

notable exception to this behavior: Although adult chimpanzees rarely share plant food with one another, males almost always share meat, frequently with females.[10] Thus, increased consumption of meat on the part of *Homo habilis* may have promoted even more sharing among adults. Moreover, a regular supply of meat would have required that substantial amounts of time and energy be devoted to the search for carcasses, and food gathered by females and shared with males could have provided the latter with both.

Sharing and cooperation between the sexes need not necessarily have been between mated males and females, but may just as well have been between brothers and sisters and mothers and sons. On the other hand, the capacity of females to engage in sexual activity at any time they deem appropriate may have promoted such activity between a male and one or more sex partners, for among most catarrhine primates, males attempt to monopolize females when the latter are at the height of sexual receptivity. This ability of the human female, alone among primates, to engage in sex at any time seems to be a consequence of bipedal locomotion. The reason for this is that this mode of locomotion requires a higher hormonal output than in other primates, to catalyze the steady release of energy to muscles needed for endurance.[11] Hence, constant sexual activity should go back to the earliest hominines.

Although chimpanzees can and do hunt alone, they frequently cooperate in the task. In the case of *Homo habilis*, cooperation would seem to have been even more crucial to success in scavenging. It is hard to imagine a creature lacking the formidable canines of a chimpanzee competing on an individual basis with carnivores far more powerful than itself.

In summary, then, it seems reasonable to assume that *Homo habilis* engaged in more sharing and cooperative behavior than one sees among

[10]Ibid.

[11]Spuhler, J. N. (1979). Continuities and discontinuities in anthropoid-hominid behavioral evolution: Bipedal locomotion and sexual reception. In N. A. Chagnon & W. Irons (Eds.), *Evolutionary biology and human social behavior* (pp. 454–461). North Scituate, MA: Duxbury Press.

Although adult chimpanzees rarely share plant food with one another, males almost always share meat, frequently with females.

present-day chimpanzees. How much more is certainly not known and probably fell far short of what has been observed among any historically known food-foraging peoples. After all, *Homo habilis* was not just a different sort of hominine from *Australopithecus*; it was different from *Homo sapiens* as well.

Language Origins

The evident importance of cooperation, planning, and foresight in the life of *H. habilis* raises the issue of this species' ability to communicate. Modern apes do this through a combination of calls and gestures, and we humans, in spite of our reliance on spoken language, share this gesture-call system. Like the apes, we have inherited this system from ancient ancestors that predate the evolutionary split between hominids and pongids. After three decades of experiments by several different researchers with captive apes, there is a growing consensus that all great apes share an ability to develop language skills at least to the level of a 2- to 3-year-old human.[12]

(See the Original Study in Chapter 4.) Of course, they do not do so in the wild, even though the potential is there (just as bonobos do not make chipped stone tools in the wild, even though experiments show they are capable of it). Nor do they develop these language skills through speech, but rather through use of gestures. Again, because this linguistic potential is shared, it must be one that the earliest hominines possessed as well.

In view of these considerations, the previously noted features of the brain of *H. habilis* that in modern humans are associated with language take on added interest. Moreover, the speech area is adjacent to that which controls the right hand. Putting this all together, we must at least allow the possibility that *H. habilis* had developed some sort of perhaps quite rudimentary gestural language. With the hands freed from locomotion to do other things, they were certainly more available for purposes of communication than are the hands of apes.

---

[12]Miles, H. L. W. (1993). Language and the orangutan: The old person of the forest. In P. Singer (Ed.), *The great ape project* (p. 46). New York: St. Martin's Press.

CHAPTER SUMMARY

Since 1960 a number of fossils have been found in East Africa at Olduvai Gorge, Lake Baringo and east of Lake Turkana, and in South Africa at Sterkfontein, which have been attributed to *Homo habilis*, the earliest representative of this genus. Among them is the well-known KNM ER 1470 skull, which is more modern in appearance than any *Australopithecus* skull. From the neck on down, however, the skeleton of *Homo habilis* differs little from that of *Australopithecus*. Because they do show a significant increase in brain size, and some reorganization of its structure, their mental abilities must have exceeded those of *Australopithecus*. By 2.4 million years ago, the evolution of *Homo* was proceeding in a direction different from that of *Australopithecus*.

The same geological strata that have produced *Homo habilis* have also produced the earliest known stone tools. These Lower Paleolithic artifacts from Olduvai Gorge, Lake Turkana, and Hadar, Ethiopia, are remarkably similar, suggesting that they were the products of a cultural tradition in which tools were manufactured according to a model.

Finds made at Olduvai Gorge have provided important evidence of human evolutionary development. The oldest Lower Paleolithic tools found at Olduvai are in the Oldowan tool tradition, which is characterized by all-purpose generalized chopping tools and flakes. Lower Paleolithic people used the percussion method to manufacture tools. The simple but effective Oldowan choppers and flakes made possible the addition of meat to the diet on a regular basis because people could now butcher meat, skin any animal, and split bones for marrow. Many Oldowan archaeological sites appear to be where meat was processed, rather than campsites.

Some changes in the brain structure of *Homo habilis* seem to have been the result of the changed diet. Increased consumption of meat, beginning about 2.5 million years ago, made new demands on their coordination and behavior. Successful procurement of meat through scavenging depended on *H. habilis'* ability to outthink far more powerful predators and scavengers. Obtaining animal food presented problems that very often had to be solved on the spot; a small scavenger depending on stereotyped instinctual behavior alone would have been at a competitive disadvantage in such a situation. Moreover, eaters of high-protein foods, such as meats, do not have to eat as often as vegetarians do. Consequently, meat-eating hominines may have had more leisure time available to explore and experiment with their environment.

Toolmaking and use also favored the development of a more efficient brain. To make stone tools, one must have in mind at the beginning a clear vision of the tool to be made, one must know the precise set of steps necessary to transform the raw material into the tool, and one must be able to recognize the kind of stone that can be successfully worked. Advanced eye-hand coordination is also required.

A prime factor in the success of early hominines was the development of some cooperation in the procurement of foods. While the males probably supplied much of the meat, the females continued to gather the sorts of food eaten by other primates; however, instead of consuming what they gathered as they gathered it, they shared a portion with the males in exchange for meat. This required foresight and planning on the part of females, which played as important a role as male scavenging in favoring the development of better brains. Food sharing with a sexual division of labor is characteristic of modern food foragers, and some hint of it can be seen among chimpanzees, among whom meat is frequently shared.

The cooperation, planning, and foresight exhibited by *Homo habilis* suggest the existence of some sort of rudimentary language, as do some features of this species' brain. Experiments with captive apes favor some sort of gestural language.

SUGGESTED READINGS

Campbell, B. G., & Loy, J. D. (1995). *Humankind emerging* (7th ed.). New York: HarperCollins.

As noted at the end of the last chapter, this well written and lavishly illustrated text has excellent coverage of the earliest hominines.

Ciochon, R. L., & Fleagle, J. G. (Eds.). (1993). *The human evolution source book*. Englewood Cliffs, NJ: Prentice-Hall.

This collection of articles by specialists provides a more detailed look at the different theories on early hominine evolution.

Johanson, D., & Shreeve, J. (1989). *Lucy's child: The discovery of a human ancestor*. New York: Avon.

This sequel to *Lucy* is written in the same engaging style. Although it covers some of the same ground with respect to *Australopithecus*, its focus is on *Homo habilis*. Besides giving a good description of this earliest member of the genus *Homo*, it presents one of the best discussions of the issue involved in the arguments over when (and why) *Homo* appeared.

HOMO ERECTUS AND THE EMERGENCE OF HUNTING AND GATHERING

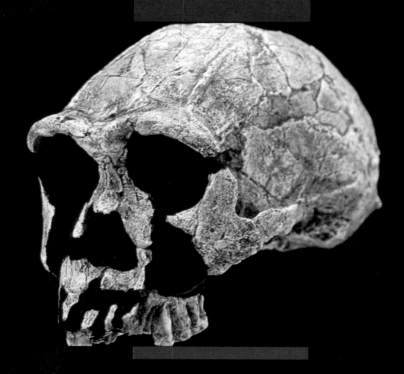

MORE "HUMAN" THAN *HOMO HABILIS*, THOUGH LESS SO THAN *HOMO SAPIENS*, *HOMO ERECTUS* EMERGED ABOUT 1.8 MILLION YEARS AGO, AT WHICH TIME THE GENUS *HOMO* WAS SPREADING TO OTHER PARTS OF THE OLD WORLD. SHOWN HERE IS ONE OF THE OLDEST AND MOST COMPLETE *HOMO ERECTUS* SKULLS FROM KOOBI FORA IN KENYA.

CHAPTER PREVIEW

Who Was *Homo erectus?*

Homo erectus was the direct descendant of earliest members of the genus *Homo*, as have been found in East Africa. Populations of *Homo erectus* were widespread between about 1.8 million and 400,000 years ago, from Africa, and Europe in the West, to Southeast Asia and China in the East.

What Were the Cultural Capabilities of *Homo erectus?*

Having larger brains than its ancestors, *Homo erectus* became better able to adapt to different situations through the medium of culture, which is reflected by better made tools, a greater variety of tool types, regional diversification of tool kits, use of fire, and improved organizational skills.

What Were the Consequences of *Homo erectus'* Improved Abilities to Adapt Through Culture?

As culture became more important as the vehicle through which this species secured its survival, life became somewhat easier than it had been. As a result, selective pressures, other than those favoring increased capacity for culture, were reduced, reproduction became easier, and more offspring survived than before. This allowed populations to grow, causing "spillover" into previously uninhabited regions, which in turn contributed to the further evolution of culture, as populations of *Homo erectus* had to find solutions to new problems of existence in newly inhabited regions.

In 1891, the Dutch army surgeon Eugene Dubois, intent on finding the fossils of a "missing link" between humans and apes, set out for Java, which he considered to have provided a suitable environment for such a creature. At Trinil, Java, Dubois found what he was searching for: the fossil remains of a primitive kind of hominine, consisting of a skull cap, a few teeth, and a thigh bone. Its features seemed to Dubois part ape, part human. Indeed Dubois at first thought the remains did not even belong to the same individual. The flat skull, for example, with its enormous brow ridges and small size, appeared to be like that of an ape; but it possessed a cranial capacity much larger than an ape's. The femur, or thigh bone, was clearly human in shape and proportions and indicated the creature was a biped. Although Dubois called his find *Pithecanthropus erectus*, or "erect ape man," it has since been assigned to the species *Homo erectus*.

These casts of the skull cap and thigh bone of *Homo erectus* were made from the original bones found by Eugene Dubois at Trinil, Java.

analysis and (later) potassium argon dating indicated to be older than Dubois's approximately 500,000- to 700,000-year-old Trinil specimen. Since 1960, additional fossils have been found in Java. A long continuity of *H. erectus* populations in Southeast Asia is indicated, from perhaps as much as 1.8 million years to about 500,000 years ago at least. Interestingly, the teeth and jaws of the earliest Javanese fossils are in many ways quite similar to those of *Homo habilis*.[1]

HOMO ERECTUS FOSSILS

Evidently, *Homo erectus* was the first hominine to extend its range outside of eastern and southern Africa. Fossils of this species are now known from a number of localities, not just in Africa but in China, Europe, Georgia (formerly part of the Soviet Union), and India, as well as Java (Fig. 8.1). In spite of the fact that remains of this species have been found in so many different places on three continents, the remains show very little significant physical variation. Evidence suggests, however, that populations of *H. erectus* in different parts of the world do show some differences from one another on a subspecific level.

Homo erectus from Java

For a long time, the scientific community was reluctant to accept Dubois's claim that his Javanese fossils were of human lineage. It was not until the 1930s, particularly when other fossils of *H. erectus* were discovered by G. H. R. von Koenigswald at Sangiran, Java, in the Early Pleistocene Djetis beds, that scientists almost without exception agreed both discoveries were the remains of an entirely new kind of early hominine. Von Koenigswald found a small skull that fluorine

Homo erectus from China

A second population of *H. erectus* was found in the mid-1920s by Davidson Black, a Canadian anatomist then teaching at Peking Union Medical College. After purchasing in a Peking drugstore a few teeth sold to local inhabitants for their supposed medicinal properties, Black set out for the nearby countryside to discover the owner of the teeth and perhaps the species of early hominine. At a place called Dragon Bone Hill in Zhoukoudian, 30 miles from Beijing, he found one molar tooth on the day before closing camp at the end of his first year of excavation. Subsequently, a skull encased in limestone was found by W. C. Pei, and between 1929 and 1934, the year of his death, Black labored along with Pei in the fossil-rich deposits of Zhoukoudian, uncovering fragment after fragment of the hominine Black had named, on the

[1]Tobias, P. V., & von Konigswald, G. H. R. (1964). A comparison between the Olduvai hominines and those of Java and some implications for hominid phylogeny. *Nature, 204,* 515–518.

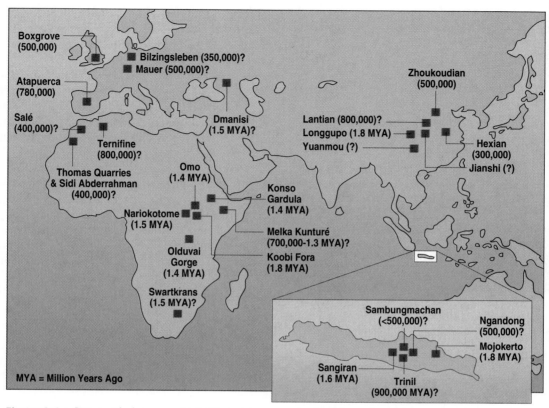

Figure 8.1   Sites, with dates, at which *Homo erectus* remains have been found.

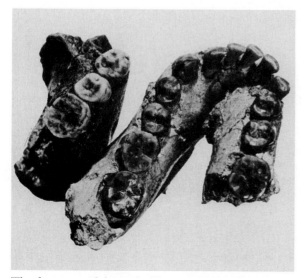

The fragment of the early *Homo erectus* jaw from Java on the left is nearly identical to the jaw of *Homo habilis* from Olduvai Gorge on the right.

basis of that first molar tooth, *Sinanthropus pekinesis*, or "Chinese man of Peking"—now recognized as an East Asian representative of *H. erectus*.

After his death, Black's work was continued by Franz Weidenreich, a Jewish refugee from Nazi Germany. By 1938, the remains of more than 40 individuals, consisting of teeth, jawbones, and incomplete skulls, had been dug out of the limestone. World War II brought a halt to the digging, and the original Zhoukoudian specimens were lost during the Japanese invasion of China. Fortunately, Weidenreich had made superb casts of most of the fossils and sent them to the United States. After the war, other specimens of *H. erectus* were discovered in China, at Zhoukoudian and at a number of other localities. The oldest is a skull about 700,000 to 800,000 years old and comes from Lantian in Shensi Province. Even older is a fragment of lower jaw from a cave in south central China that is as old as the oldest Javanese fossils. Like their Javanese contemporaries, this Chinese fossil is reminiscent of African *H. habilis*. By contrast with these ancient

In Asia, Chinese drug stores are good places to look for fossils—including those of *Homo erectus*—among "dragon" bones and teeth. Actually fossils from many species of animals, these are ground up to make various medicines. This typical assortment of "dragon" teeth, including some from hominine (top row), is accompanied by the formula for converting them into medicine.

remains, the original Zhoukoudian fossils appear to be no more than about 500,000 years old.

Although the two populations overlap in time, the Chinese fossils are, on the whole, not quite as old as those from Java. Not surprisingly, Chinese *H. erectus* is a bit less "primitive" looking. Its average cranial capacity is about 1000 cubic centimeters, compared with 900 cc for Javanese *H. erectus*. The smaller teeth, short jaw, and lack of diastema in the lower dentition—a gap in the teeth to accommodate a large upper canine when the jaws are closed—of the Chinese are further evidence of their more modern status.

Homo erectus from Africa

Although our samples of *H. erectus* from Asia remain among the best, a number of important specimens are now known from Africa. Fossils assigned to this species were discovered there as long ago as 1933, but the better known finds have been made

since 1960 at Olduvai and at Lake Turkana. Among them is the most complete *H. erectus* skeleton ever found, that of a boy who died 1.6 million years ago at about the age of 12. Another partial skeleton, that of an adult, had diseased bones, possibly the result of a massive overdose of Vitamin A. This could have come from eating the livers of carnivorous animals, for they accumulate this vitamin in their livers at levels that are toxic to human beings.

Generally speaking, African *H. erectus* skulls are quite similar to those from Asia; one difference is that their bones are not quite as thick. It may be, too, that individuals living in China were shorter and stockier, on the whole, than those living in Africa. Overall, however, the Africans reveal no more significant physical variations from their Asian counterparts than are seen if modern human populations from East and West are compared. As in Asia, the most recent fossils are less "primitive"

One of the oldest and certainly the most complete *Homo erectus* fossil is the "Strapping Youth" from Lake Turkana. The remains are those of a boy who died in his early teens.

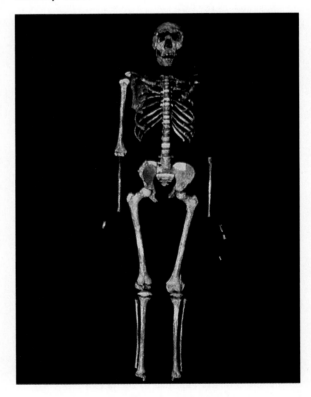

in appearance, and the oldest fossils (up to 1.8 million years old) display features reminiscent of the earlier *Homo habilis*. Indeed, one of the problems is distinguishing early *H. erectus* from late *H. habilis*—precisely what one would expect if the one evolved from the other.

Homo erectus from Europe

Although Europe seems to have been inhabited by at least 780,000 years ago, few fossils attributable to *H. erectus* have so far been found there. A robust shin bone from Boxgrove, England, and a large lower jaw from Mauer, Germany, may be almost a half-million years old. The jaw certainly came from a skull wide at the base, as is that of *H. erectus.* Older yet are fragments of four individuals from Atapuerca

This photo is of a late *H. erectus* skull from Zhoukoudian, China. It may be compared with the earlier African *erectus* skull in the photo at the top right.

This photo is of an early *H. erectus* skull from East Africa. It may be compared with the later *erectus* skull in the photo on the left.

This massive mandible—from Mauer, Germany—is one of the oldest known from Europe. The great space across the back, where it attached to the cranium, bespeaks a skull broad at the base, as is that of *H. erectus.*

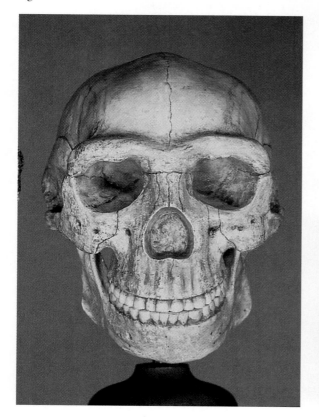

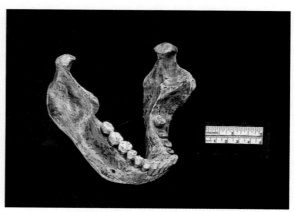

Hill in north central Spain. Other European fossils are not as old as the Mauer jaw, and they display a mosaic of features characteristic of both *H. erectus* and subsequent archaic *H. sapiens*. Here, as in Africa and Asia, a distinction between late *erectus* and early *sapiens* is difficult to make. Until sufficiently old fossils are found, knowledge of *H. erectus* in Europe must remain limited.

Physical Characteristics of *Homo erectus*

Apart from its skull, the skeleton of *H. erectus* differs only subtly from that of modern humans. Although its bodily proportions are like ours, it was more heavily muscled, its rib cage was conical rather than barrel shaped, and its hips were narrower. With a small birth canal, gestation must have been short, with infants born in a relatively immature state. Stature seems to have been in the modern range, as the youth from Lake Turkana was about 5 feet 4 inches tall. Compared with *Homo habilis*, *H. erectus* was significantly larger, but displayed significantly less sexual dimorphism.

Cranial capacity in *H. erectus* ranged from 780 to 1225 cubic centimeters (average about 1000 cc), which compares with 752 cc for the nearly 2-million-year-old ER 1470 skull from East Africa, and 1000 to 2000 cc (average 1300 cc) for modern

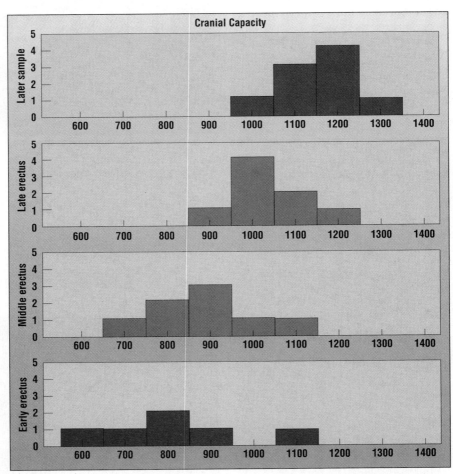

Figure 8.2   Cranial capacity in *Homo erectus* increased over time, as illustrated by the above bar graphs, shown in cubic centimeters. The top graph depicts cranial capacity in skulls transitional from *erectus* to *sapiens*.

human skulls (Fig. 8.2). The cranium itself had a low vault, and the head was long and narrow. When viewed from behind, its width was greater than its height, with its greatest width at the base. The skulls of modern humans, when similarly viewed, are higher than they are wide, with the widest dimension in the region above the ears. Moreover, the shape of the inside of *H. erectus'* braincase showed near-modern development of the brain, especially in the speech area. Although some anthropologists argue that the vocal apparatus was not adequate for speech, others argue that asymmetries of the brain suggest the same pattern of right-handedness with left cerebral dominance that, in modern peoples, is correlated with the capacity for language.[2]

Massive ridges over the eyes gave this early hominine a somewhat simian, "beetle-browed" appearance. *H. erectus* also possessed a sloping forehead and a receding chin. Powerful jaws with large teeth, protruding mouth, and huge neck muscles added to the generally rugged appearance. Nevertheless, the face, teeth, and jaws of this hominine are smaller than those of *Homo habilis*.

Relationship Between *Homo erectus* and *Homo habilis*

The smaller teeth and larger brains of *H. erectus* seem to mark continuation of a trend first seen in *Homo habilis*. What is new is the increased body size, reduced sexual dimorphism, and more "human" body form of *erectus*. Nonetheless, there is some resemblance to *habilis*, for example, in the conical shape of the rib cage, the long neck and low neck angle of the thigh bone, and smaller brain size in the earliest *erectus* fossils. Indeed, as already noted, it is difficult to distinguish between the earliest *erectus* and the latest *habilis* fossils. Presumably the one form evolved from the other, evidently fairly abruptly, in the period between 1.8 and 1.6 million years ago.[3]

[2]Holloway, R. L. (1981). The Indonesian *Homo erectus* brain endocasts revisited. *American Journal of Physical Anthropology, 55,* 521.

[3]Lewin, R. (1987). The earliest "humans" were more like apes. *Science, 236,* 1061.

THE CULTURE OF *HOMO ERECTUS*

As one might expect given its larger brain, *H. erectus* outstripped its predecessors in cultural development. In Africa, Europe, and southwest Asia, there was refinement of the stone toolmaking technology begun by the makers of earlier flake and chopper tools. At some point, fire began to be used for protection, warmth, and cooking, though precisely when is still a matter for debate. Finally, there is indirect evidence that the organizational abilities of *H. erectus*, or at least the later ones, were improved over those of their predecessors.

The Acheulean Tool Tradition

Associated with the remains of *Homo erectus* in Africa, Europe, and southwest Asia are tools of the **Acheulean tradition.** Characteristic of this tradition are hand axes, pear-shaped tools pointed at one end with a sharp cutting edge all around. In East Africa, the earliest hand axes are about 1.4 million years old;

Acheulean tradition: The toolmaking tradition of *Homo erectus* in Africa, Europe, and southwest Asia in which hand axes were developed from the earlier Oldowan chopper.

Homo erectus made a variety of Acheulean hand axes.

those found in Europe and southwest Asia are no older than about 750,000 years. In east Asia, chopping tool traditions reminiscent of the Oldowan, rather than Acheulean and derived traditions, continued through much of the **Paleolithic.** The reason for this is that *Homo erectus* spread from Africa prior to invention of the hand ax, and once in Asia, technological innovation took a different path.

That the Acheulean grew out of the Oldowan tradition is indicated by an examination of the evidence discovered at Olduvai. In Bed I, the lowest level, chopper tools were found along with remains of *Homo habilis*. In lower Bed II, the first crude hand axes were found intermingled with chopper tools. Acheulean hand axes having a more "finished" look about them appear in middle Bed II, together with *H. erectus* remains.

Early Acheulean tools represent a definite step beyond the generalized cutting, chopping, and scraping tools of the Oldowan tradition. Like chopper tools, the hand axes were probably gen-

---

Paleolithic: The Old Stone Age, characterized by manufacture and use of chipped stone tools.

---

eral-purpose implements for food procurement, processing, and defense. However, they were more standardized in form, having been shaped by regular blows rather than by random strikes. In this way, sharper points and more regular cutting edges were produced, and more cutting edge was available from the same amount of stone.

During this period, tool cultures began to diversify (Fig. 8.3). Besides hand axes, *H. erectus* used tools that functioned as cleavers (these were hand axes with a straight edge where the point would otherwise be) and flake tools (generally smaller tools made by hitting a flint core with a hammerstone, thus knocking off flakes with sharp edges). Many flake tools were by-products of hand ax and cleaver manufacture. Their sharp edges made them useful as is, but many were retouched to make points, scrapers, borers, and other sorts of tools. Diversification of tool kits is also indicated by the smaller numbers of hand axes in northern and eastern Europe, where people relied more on simply flaked choppers, a wide variety of unstandardized flakes, and supplementary tools of bone, antler, and wood. Evidently, these people expended less effort in their toolmaking than did their contemporaries living to the south and west. In Eastern Asia, by contrast, many tools may have been made of bamboo and other local woods, from which excellent knives, scrapers, and the like comparable to those of stone can be made.

Figure 8.3   Ten percent of the shaped tools in a typical Acheulean assemblage are of the forms drawn here.

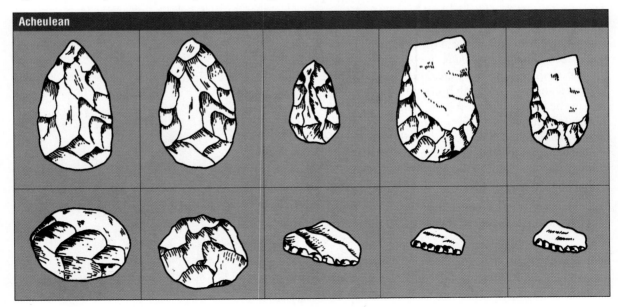

Original Study

Homo erectus and the Use of Bamboo[4]

Bamboo provides, I believe, the solution to a puzzle first raised in 1943, when the late archeologist Hallam Movius of Harvard began to publish his observations on paleolithic (Old Stone Age) cultures of the Far East. In 1937 and 1938 Movius had investigated a number of archeological localities in India, Southeast Asia, and China. Although most of the archeological "cultures" that he recognized are no longer accepted by modern workers, he made another, more lasting contribution. This was the identification of the "Movius line" (which his colleague Carleton Coon named in his honor): a geographical boundary, extending through northern India, that separates two long-lasting paleolithic cultures. West of the line are found collections of tools with a high percentage of symmetrical and consistently proportioned hand axes (these are called Acheulean tools, after the French site of Saint Acheul). More or less similar tool kits also occur in Mongolia and Siberia, but with few exceptions (which are generally relatively late in time), not in eastern China or Southeast Asia, where more crudely made tools known as choppers and chopping tools prevail [Fig. 8.4].

My own research on the Movius line and related questions evolved almost by accident. During the course of my work in Southeast Asia, I excavated many sites, studied a variety of fossil faunal collections, and reviewed the scientific literature dealing with Asia. As part of this research I compared fossil mammals from Asia with those recovered from other parts of the world. In the beginning, my purpose was biostratigraphic—to use the animals to estimate the most likely dates of various sites used by early hominines. On the basis of the associated fauna, for example, I estimate that Kao Pah Nam may be as old as 700,000 years.

After years of looking at fossil collections and faunal lists, I realized that something was very strange about the collections from Southeast Asia: there were no fossil horses of Pleistocene age or for a considerable time before that. The only exceptions were a few horse fossils from one place in southern China, the Yuanmou Basin which was and is a special small grassland habitat in a low, dry valley within the Shan-Yunnan Massif.

To mammalian biostratigraphers this is unusual, since members of the horse family are so common in both the Old and New World that they are a primary means of dating various fossil localities. Fossil horses have been reported from western Burma, but the last one probably lived there some twenty million years ago. Not a single fossil horse turns up later than that in Southeast Asia, although they are known from India to the west and China to the north and every other part of Europe and Asia.

I then began to wonder what other normally common animals might be missing. The answer soon became apparent: camels—even though they too were once widespread throughout the world—and members and relatives of the giraffe family. Pleistocene Southeast Asia was shaping up as a kind of "black hole" for certain fossil mammals! These animals—horses, camels, and giraffids—all dwell in open country. Their absence on the Southeast Asian mainland and islands (all once connected, along with the now inundated Sunda Shelf) is indicative of a forested environment. The

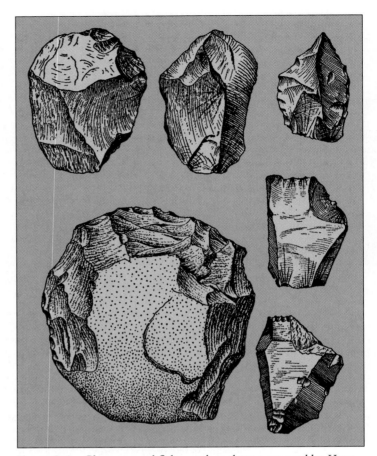

Figure 8.4 Choppers and flakes such as these were used by *Homo erectus* at Zhoukoudian, China.

mammals that are present—orangutans, tapirs, and gibbons—confirm this conclusion.

The significance of this is that most reconstructions of our evolutionary past have emphasized the influence of savanna grassland habitats, so important in Africa, the cradle of hominine evolution. Many anthropologists theorize that shrinking forests and spreading grasslands encouraged our primarily tree-dwelling ancestors to adapt to ground-dwelling conditions, giving rise to the unique bipedal gait that is the hallmark of hominines. Bipedalism, in turn, freed the hands for tool use and ultimately led to the evolution of a large-brained, cultural animal. Tropical Asia, instead, apparently was where early hominines had to readapt to tropical forest.

In studying the record, I noticed that the forested zone—the zone that lacked open-dwelling mammals—coincided generally with the distribution of the chopper-chopping tools. The latter appeared to be the products of a forest adaptation that, for one reason or another, deemphasized the utilization of standardized stone tools. At least this held for Southeast Asia; what at first I could not explain was the existence of similar tools in northern China, where fossil horses, camels, and giraffids were present. Finally, I came upon the arresting fact that the distribution of naturally occurring bamboo coincided almost directly with the distribution of chopper-chopping tools. The only exceptions that may possibly be of real antiquity—certain hand ax collections from Kehe and Dingcun, in China, and Chonggok-Ni, in Korea—fall on the northernmost periphery of the distribution of bamboo and probably can be attributed to fluctuation of the boundary.

Today there are, by various estimates, some 1,000 to 1,200 species of bamboo. This giant grass is distributed worldwide, but more than 60 percent of the species are from Asia. Only 16 percent occur in Africa, and those on the Indian subcontinent—to an unknown extent the product of human importation and cultivation—are discontinuous in distribution and low in diversity. By far, the greatest diversity occurs in East and Southeast Asia.

Based on these observations, I hypothesized that the early Asians relied on bamboo for much of their technology. At first I envisioned bamboo simply as a kind of icon representing all nonlithic technology. I now think bamboo specifically must have been an extremely important resource. This was not, in my opinion, because appropriate rock was scarce but because bamboo tools would have been efficient, durable, and highly portable.

There are few useful tools that cannot be constructed from bamboo. Cooking and storage containers, knives, spears, heavy and light projectile points, elaborate traps, rope, fasteners, clothing, and even entire villages can be manufactured from bamboo. In addition to the stalks, which are a source of raw material for the manufacture of a variety of artifacts, the seeds and shoots of many species can be eaten. In historical times, bamboo has been to Asian civilization what the olive tree was to the Greeks. In the great cities of the Far East, bamboo is still the preferred choice for the scaffolding used in the construction of skyscrapers. This incomparable resource is also highly renewable. One can actually hear some varieties growing, at more than one foot per day.

Some may question how bamboo tools would have been sufficient for killing and processing large and medium-size animals. Lethal projectile and stabbing implements can in fact be fashioned from bamboo, but their importance may be exaggerated. Large game accounts for a relatively small proportion of the diet of many modern hunters and gatherers. Furthermore, animals are frequently trapped, collected, killed, and then thrown on a fire and cooked whole prior to using bare hands to dismember the roasted carcass. There are many ethnographic examples among forest peoples of this practice.

The only implements that cannot be manufactured from bamboo are axes or choppers suitable for the working of hard woods. More than a few archaeologists have suggested that the stone choppers and resultant "waste" flakes of Asia were created with the objective of using them to manufacture and maintain nonlithic tools. Bamboo can be easily worked with stone flakes resulting from the manufacture of choppers (many choppers may have been a throwaway component in the manufacture of flakes).

[4]Adapted from Pope, G. C. (1989). Bamboo and human evolution. *Natural History, 10/89,* 50–54.

The greater variety of tools found in the Acheulean and contemporary traditions is indicative of *H. erectus'* increased ability to deal with the environment. The greater the range of tools used, the greater the range of natural resources capable of being exploited in less time, with less effort, and with a higher degree of efficiency. For example, hand axes may have been used to kill game and dig up roots; cleavers to butcher; scrapers to process hides for bedding and clothes; and flake tools to cut meat and shape wooden objects. As argued in the Original Study, the differences between tool kits for the Far East and West are likely indicative of adaptation to specific regions. The same may be indicated by the differences between the tool kits of northern and eastern Europe on the one hand, and southern and western Europe on the other. One suggested explanation for this is that resources were scarcer in the latter region, which was more heavily forested than the former, and that this scarcity was a spur to increasing the efficiency of technology.[5]

[5]Gamble, C. (1986). *The Paleolithic settlement of Europe* (p. 310). Cambridge: Cambridge University Press.

The improved technological efficiency of *H. erectus* is also evident in the selection of raw materials. While Oldowan toolmakers frequently used coarse-grained stone such as basalt, their Acheulean counterparts generally used such stone only for their heavier implements, preferring flint or other stones with a high silica content for the smaller ones. During later Acheulean times, two techniques were developed that produced thinner, more sophisticated axes with straighter, sharper cutting edges. The **baton method** of percussion manufacture involved using a bone or antler punch to hit the edge of the flint core. This method produced shallow flake scars, rather than the crushed edge that the hammerstone method produced on the earlier Acheulean hand axes. In later Acheulean times, the striking platform method was also used

Baton method: The technique of stone tool manufacture by striking the raw material with a bone or antler "baton" to remove flakes.

Experimentation on an elephant that died of natural causes demonstrates the effectiveness of Acheulean tools. Simple flint flakes easily slice through the thick hide, while hand axes sever large muscles. With such tools, two men can butcher 100 pounds of meat each in an hour.

to create sharper, thinner axes; the toolmakers would often strike off flakes to create a flat surface near the edge. These flat surfaces, or striking platforms, were set up along the edge of the tool perpendicular to its sides, so that the toolmaker could remove long, thin flakes stretching from the edge across each side of the tool.

Use of Fire

Another sign of *H. erectus'* developing technology is evidence of fires and cooking. Compelling evidence comes from the 700,000-year-old Kao Poh Nam rock shelter in Thailand, where a roughly circular arrangement of fire-cracked basalt cobbles has been found in association with artifacts and animal bones. Since such rocks are not native to the rock shelter, and are quite heavy, they probably had to have been carried in by hominines. The reason more readily available limestone rocks were not used for hearths is that when burned, they produce a quicklime, which causes itchy and burning skin rashes.[6] The bones associated with the hearth (which was located near the rock shelter entrance away from the deeper recesses favored by denning animals) show clear evidence of cut marks from butchering as well as burning.

Homo erectus may have been using fire even earlier, based on evidence from Swartkrans, in South Africa. Here, in deposits estimated to date between 1 and 1.3 million years ago, bones have been found that had been heated to temperatures

[6]Pope, G. C. (1989). Bamboo and human evolution. *Natural History, 10/89,* 56.

Archaeologists excavate a hearth at a rock shelter in Kao Poh Nam, Thailand. This hearth testifies to human use of fire 700,000 years ago.

far in excess of what one would expect as the result of natural fires. Natural grass fires in the region will not heat bones above 212 degrees Fahrenheit, whereas coals in campfires reach temperatures from 900 to 1200 degrees. Consequently, bones thrown into such fires reach temperatures higher than 212 degrees. Furthermore, the burned bones do not occur in deeper deposits, even though natural grass fires would have been no less common. South African paleoanthropologists Andrew Sillen and C. K. Brain suggest that the purpose of the Swartkrans fires was protection from predators, as the bones were heated to such high temperatures that any meat on them would have been inedible.[7] Thus, fire may not have been "tamed" initially for cooking or to keep people warm; such uses may have come later.

Whatever the reason for *Homo erectus'* original use of fire, it proved invaluable to populations that spread out of the tropics into regions with cooler climates. Not only did it provide warmth, but it may have assisted in the quest for food. In places like Europe and China, food would have been hard to come by in the long, cold winters, as edible plants were unavailable and the large herds of animals, whose mobility exceeded the potential of humans to maintain contact, dispersed and migrated. One solution would have been to search out the frozen carcasses of animals that had died naturally in the late fall and winter, using long wooden probes to locate them beneath the snow, wooden scoops to dig them out, and fire to thaw them so that they could be butchered and eaten.[8] Furthermore, such fire-assisted scavenging would have made available meat and hides of wooly mammoths, wooly rhinoceroses, and bison, which were probably beyond the ability of *H. erectus* to kill, at least until late in the species' career.

Perhaps it was the use of fire to thaw carcasses that led to the idea of cooking food, thereby altering the forces of natural selection, which previously favored individuals with heavy jaws and large, sharp teeth (food is tougher and needs more chewing when it is uncooked), thus promoting further reduction in tooth size as well as supportive facial architecture. So we find that, between early and late *H. erectus*, chewing-related structures undergo reduction at a rate markedly above the fossil vertebrate average.[9] Cooking did more than soften food, though; because it detoxifies a number of otherwise poisonous plants, alters digestion-inhibiting substances so that important vitamins, minerals, and proteins can be absorbed while in the gut, rather than just passing through it unused, and makes complex carbohydrates like starch—high-energy foods—digestible, the basic resources available to humans were substantially increased and made more secure. The partial predigestion of food by cooking also may have caused a reduction in the size of the digestive tract. Despite its overall similarity of form to those of apes, the digestive tract of modern humans is substantially smaller. The advantage of this gut reduction is that it draws less energy to operate, thereby competing less with the high-energy requirements of a larger brain.

Like tools, then, fire gave people more control over their environment. Possibly, *H. erectus* in Southeast Asia used fire, as have more recent populations living there, to keep areas in the forest clear for foot traffic. Certainly, the resistance to burning characteristic of many hardwood trees in this forest today indicates that fire has for a long time been important in their evolution. Fire may also have been used by *H. erectus*, as it was by subsequent hominines, not just for protection from animals out in the open, but to frighten away cave-dwelling predators so that they might live in the caves themselves; and it could then be used to provide warmth and light in these cold and dark habitations. Even more, it modified the natural succession of day and night, perhaps encouraging *H. erectus* to stay up after dark to review the day's events and plan the next day's activities. That *H. erectus* was capable of at least some planning is implied by the existence of populations in temperate climates, where the ability to anticipate the needs of the winter season by preparing in advance to protect against the cold would have been crucial to survival.[10]

[7]Sillen, A., & Brain, C. K. (1990). Old flame. *Natural History, 4/90,* 10.

[8]Gamble, p. 387.

[9]Wolpoff, M. H. (1993). Evolution in *Homo erectus:* The question of stasis, In R. L. Ciochon & J. G. Fleagle (Eds.), *The human evolution source book* (p. 396). Englewood Cliffs, NJ: Prentice-Hall.

[10]Goodenough, W. H. (1990). Evolution of the human capacity for beliefs. *American Anthropologist, 92,* 601.

OTHER ASPECTS OF *HOMO ERECTUS'* CULTURE

There is no evidence that populations of *H. erectus* lived anywhere outside the Old World tropics prior to a million years ago. Presumably, control of fire was a key element in permitting them to move into cooler regions like Europe and China. In cold winters, however, a fire is of little use without adequate shelter, and *H. erectus'* increased sophistication in the construction of shelters is indicated by the remains of what may be several huts at Terra Amata (Fig. 8.5). Here several huts appear to have been built, probably of saplings. They seem to have been seasonally reoccupied over a number of years, and each apparently had a hearth in the center of its floor.

Keeping warm by the hearth is one thing, but keeping warm away from the hearth when procuring food or other necessities is another. Studies of modern humans indicate that they can remain reasonably comfortable down to 50° F with a minimum of clothing so long as they are active; below that temperature, the extremities cool to the point of pain;[11] thus the dispersal of early humans into regions where winter temperatures regularly went below 50°, as they must have in China and Europe, was probably not possible without more in the way of clothing than hominines had hitherto worn. Unfortunately, we have no direct evidence as to the kind of clothing worn by *H. erectus*; we only know that it must have been more sophisticated than before.

That *H. erectus* became able to organize in order to hunt live animals is suggested by remains such as those from the 400,000-year-old sites of Ambrona and Torralba in Spain. At the latter site, in what was an ancient swamp, were found the remains of several elephants, horses, red deer, wild oxen, and rhinoceroses. Since their skeletons were dismembered, rather than in proper anatomical order, a fact that cannot be explained as a result of any natural geological process, it is clear that these animals did not accidently get mired in a swamp where they simply died and decayed.[12] In fact, the bones are closely associated with a variety of stone tools—a few thousand of them. Furthermore, there is very little evidence of carnivore activity—and none at all for the really big carnivores. Clearly, hominines were involved, not just in butchering the animals, but evidently in killing them as well. In fact, it is likely that the animals were actually driven into the swamp so that they could be easily dispatched. The remains of charcoal and carbon, widely but thinly scattered in the vicinity, raises the possibility that grass fires were used to drive the animals into the swamp. In any event, what we have here is evidence for more than opportunistic scavenging; not only was *H. erectus* able to hunt, but considerable organizational and communicative skills are implied as well.

There is no evidence to indicate that *H. erectus* became an accomplished hunter all at once. Presumably, the most ancient members of this species, like *Homo habilis* before them, got the bulk of their meat through scavenging. As their cultural

Figure 8.5   An artist proposed this reconstruction of a *H. erectus* hut based on remains found at Terra Amata.

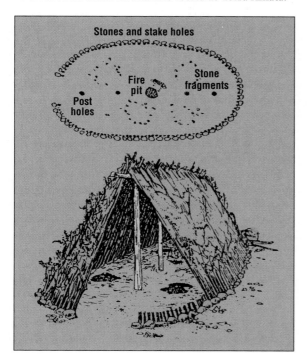

[11]Whiting, J. W. M., Sodergem, J. A., & Stigler, S. M. (1982). Winter temperature as a constraint to the migration of preindustrial peoples. *American Anthropologist, 84,* 289.

[12]Freeman, L. G. (1992). Ambrona and Torralba: New evidence and interpretation. Paper presented at the 91st Annual Meeting, American Anthropological Association.

At some point, *H. erectus* ceased relying on scavenging as a source of meat, in favor of hunting live animals. One of those animals was the elephant hunted at Ambrona, Spain, where the tusk remains.

capabilities increased, however, they could have devised ways of doing their own killing, rather than waiting for animals to die or be killed by other predators. As they became more proficient predators over time, they would have been able to count on a more reliable supply of meat.

Evidence for a developing symbolic life comes from several sites in Europe, where deliberately marked objects of stone, bone, and ivory have been found in Acheulean contexts. These include several objects from a site in Bilzingsleben, Germany, where they occurred in association with remains similar to a *Homo erectus* from eastern Africa. These are among the earliest Paleolithic artifacts that have no obvious utility or model in the natural world. Such apparently symbolic artifacts became more common in later phases of the Paleolithic, as more modern forms of the genus *Homo* appeared on the scene. Similarly, the world's oldest-known rock carvings are associated with Acheulean tools in a cave in India.[13] Alexander Marshack argues that the use of such symbolic images requires some sort of spoken language, not only to assign mean-

ing to the images but also to maintain the tradition.[14] That a symbolic tradition was maintained is suggested by similar motifs on later Paleolithic artifacts. It is also in late Acheulean contexts on three continents that we have our earliest evidence for the use of red ochre, a pigment that more modern forms of *Homo* employed to color symbolic as well as utilitarian artifacts, the bodies of the dead, to paint the bodies of the living, and (ultimately) to make notations and paint pictures.

We do not, of course, know anything definitive about *H. erectus'* linguistic abilities, but this evidence of a developing symbolic life, as well as the need to plan ahead for seasonal changes and to coordinate hunting activities, implies improving linguistic competence. In fact, the vocal tract and brain of *erectus* are intermediate between those of *H. sapiens* and earlier *Australopithecus*. Possibly, a changeover from gestural to spoken language was a driving force in these evolutionary changes. Certainly, the advantages of a spoken language over a gestural one seem to be obvious; not only

[13]Bednarik, R. G. (1995). Concept-mediated marking in the Lower Paleolithic. *Current Anthropology, 36,* 610–611.

[14]Marshack, A. (1976). Some implications of the Paleolithic symbolic evidence for the origin of language. *Current Anthropology, 17,* 280.

This 300,000-year-old ox rib from a site in France is one of several from the Lower Paleolithic that exhibit deliberately engraved designs. The bottom photo shows the engraving in detail.

does one *not* have to stop whatever one is doing with one's hands to "talk" (useful to a species increasingly dependent on tool use), but it is also possible to talk in the dark, past opaque objects, or among people whose gaze is concentrated on something else (potential prey, for example).

With *H. erectus*, then, we find a clearer manifestation of the interplay among cultural, physical, and environmental factors than ever before. However slowly, social organization, technology, and communication developed along with an increase in brain size and complexity. In fact, the cranial capacity of late *H. erectus* is 31 percent greater than the mean for early *erectus*, a rate of increase more rapid than the average fossil vertebrate rate.[15] As a consequence of these, *H. erectus'* resource base was enlarged significantly; the supply of meat could be increased by hunting as well as by scavenging, and the supply of plant foods was increased as cooking allowed the consumption of previously toxic or indigestible vegetables. This, along with an increased ability to modify the environment in advantageous ways—for example, by

using fire to provide warmth—undoubtedly contributed to a population increase and territorial expansion. In humans, as in other mammals, any kind of adaptation that makes life significantly easier than it had been reduces selective pressures, reproduction becomes easier, more offspring survive than before, and so populations grow. This causes fringe populations to "spill over" into neighboring regions previously uninhabited by the species.

Thus, *Homo erectus* was able to move into areas that had never been inhabited by hominines before; first into the warm, southern regions of Asia and ultimately into the cooler regions of China and Europe.

[15]Wolpoff, pp. 392, 396.

CHAPTER SUMMARY

The remains of *Homo erectus* have been found at several sites in Africa, Europe, China, and Java. The earliest is 1.8 million years old, and the species endured until about 400,000 years ago, by which time fossils exhibit a mosaic of features characteristic of both *erectus* and *H. sapiens*. It appears to have evolved, rather abruptly, from *Homo habilis*. From the neck on down, the body of *H. erectus* was essentially modern in appearance. The brain, although small by modern standards, was larger than that of *Homo habilis*. The skull was generally low, with maximum breadth near its base, and massive brow ridges. Powerful teeth and jaws added to a generally rugged appearance.

With *H. erectus* we find a greater interaction among cultural, physical, and environmental factors than ever before. Social organization and improved technology developed along with an increase in brain size. The Oldowan chopper evolved into the Acheulean hand ax. These tools, the earliest of which are about 1.4 million years old, are pear shaped, with pointed ends and sharp cutting edges. Like the chopper, they served a general purpose. During Acheulean times, tool cultures began to diversify. Along with hand axes, tool

kits included cleavers, scrapers, and flakes. Further signs of *H. erectus'* developing technology was the selection of different stone for different tools and the use of fires for protection, warmth, light, thawing frozen carcasses, and cooking. Cooking is a significant cultural adaptation because it took the place of certain physical adaptations such as large heavy jaws and teeth, since cooked food is easier to chew. Since it detoxifies various substances in plants, cooking also increased the food resources available and allowed reduction in the size of the digestive tract. During later Acheulean times, *H. erectus* used the baton and striking platform methods to make thinner axes with straighter, sharper cutting edges. From France comes evidence of the building of huts and the making of nonutilitarian artifacts; from Spain comes evidence of cooperative efforts to kill large amounts of game.

H. erectus' improved organizational, technological, and communicative abilities led to more effective hunting and a greater ability to modify the environment in advantageous ways. As a result, the populations of these early hominines increased and they expanded into new geographic areas.

SUGGESTED READINGS

Campbell, B. G., & Loy, J. D. (1995). *Humankind emerging* (7th ed.). New York: HarperCollins.

This well-illustrated book has three good up-to-date chapters on *Homo erectus* and their way of life.

Ciochon, R. L., & Fleagle, J. G. (Eds.). (1993). *The human evolution source book.* Englewood Cliffs, NJ: Prentice-Hall.

Part V of this book reproduces eight articles that deal with a variety of topics on the history of recovery, diversity, tempo, and mode of evolution and culture of *H. erectus*. An introduction by the editors puts the articles in context.

Gamble, C. (1986). *The Paleolithic settlement of Europe.* Cambridge: Cambridge University Press.

Although it does not deal exclusively with *Homo erectus*, this text does discuss material from Europe associated with this species. In doing so, it takes a critical stance to conventional interpretations and offers new explanations of *H. erectus*' behavior based on a better understanding of the process of archeological site formation.

Rightmire, G. P. (1990). *The evolution of* Homo erectus: *Comparative anatomical studies of an extinct human species.* Cambridge: Cambridge University Press.

This is the standard work on our current understanding of *Homo erectus*.

White, E., Brown, D. et al. (1973). *The first men.* New York: Time-Life.

This magnificently illustrated volume in the Time-Life *Emergence of Man* series deals with *Homo erectus*. Its drawbacks are that it is not up to date, and it portrays early *H. erectus* as too much of a "big game hunter"; nonetheless, it remains a good introduction to many of the fossils, sites, and tools associated with this hominine.

Archaic *Homo Sapiens*
and
the Middle Paleolithic

No examples of archaic *Homo sapiens* are known better than the Neandertals of Europe and western Asia. As this reconstruction in a German museum shows, Neandertals do not differ greatly from modern Europeans, in spite of distinctive facial features. Still, debate continues over how "human" they really were.

CHAPTER PREVIEW

Who Was "Archaic" *Homo sapiens?*

"Archaic" *Homo sapiens* is the name used for members of this species who lived prior to about 35,000 years ago. Included are the Neandertals, descendants of *Homo erectus*, who lived in Europe and western Asia between about 125,000 and 35,000 years ago, and other populations somewhat like them who lived in Africa, China, and Southeast Asia. All had essentially modern-sized brains in skulls that still retained a number of primitive features.

What Was the Culture of Archaic *Homo sapiens* Like?

By 125,000 years ago, the human brain had reached its modern size, and by then human culture had become rich and varied. People not only made a wide variety of tools for special purposes, but they also made objects for purely symbolic purposes, engaged in ceremonial activities, and cared for the old and disabled.

What Became of the Neandertals?

Although there is some debate, the most likely explanation is that their contemporaries, and at least some of the Neandertals, evolved into anatomically modern versions of *Homo sapiens*. This seems to have happened as features of modern anatomy arose in different regional populations and were carried to others through gene flow. Thus, human populations on all three continents of the Old World seem to have contributed to the making of modern humans.

The anthropologist attempting to piece together the innumerable parts of the puzzle of human evolution must be as good a detective as a scholar, for the available evidence is often scant, enigmatic, or full of misleading clues. The quest for the origin of modern humans from more ancient representatives of the genus *Homo* has some of the elements of a detective story, for it contains a number of mysteries concerning the emergence of humanity, none of which has been completely solved to this day. The mysteries involve the appearance of the first fully sapient humans, the identity of the Neandertals, and the relationship of both to more modern forms.

THE APPEARANCE OF *HOMO SAPIENS*

At various sites in Europe and Africa, a number of hominine fossils have been found that seem to date, roughly, between 400,000 and 200,000 years ago. These include skulls and skull fragments from Casablanca and Salé in Morocco, Arago in France, Steinheim and Bilzingsleben in Germany, Swanscombe in England, Vertessöllos

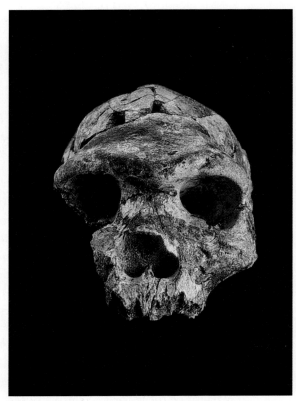

This skull, from Ethiopia, is one of several from Africa indicative of a transition from *Homo erectus* to *Homo sapiens*.

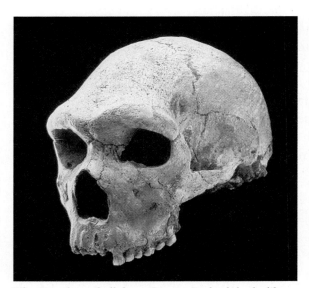

The Petrolona skull from Greece. Its back looks like *Homo erectus*, but at 1220 cc its brain size is in the sapiens range, and its face resembles the European Neandertals.

in Hungary, Petralona in Greece, and Bodo in Ethiopia; jaws and jaw fragments from Casablanca (two sites), Rabat and Temara in Morocco, Arago and Montmaurin in France; and miscellaneous other bones, such as a partial pelvis from Arago. Some of these—most commonly the African fossils, but also the Arago and Bilzingsleben skulls—have been called *H. erectus;* others—most commonly those from Steinheim and Swanscombe—have been called *H. sapiens.* In fact, what they all have in common is a mixture of characteristics of both forms, which is what one would expect of remains transitional between the two. For example, the skulls from Bodo, Steinheim, and Swanscombe had rather large brains for *H. erectus.* The overall appearance of the skulls, however, is different from ours. They are large and robust, with their maximum breadth lower on the skull, and they have more prominent brow ridges, larger faces, and bigger teeth. Similarly, the face

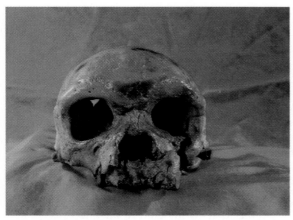

This skull from Dali, China, is representative of archaic *H. sapiens* in East Asia.

of the Petralona skull resembles European Neandertals, but its back looks like *H. erectus*. Conversely, the Salé skull, which had a rather small brain for *H. sapiens* (about 930–960 cc), looks surprisingly modern from the back. Finally, the various jaws from Morocco and France seem to combine features of *H. erectus* with those of the European Neandertals.

A similar situation exists in East Asia, where skulls from Ngandong in Java as well as several fossils from sites in China exhibit the same sort of mix of *erectus* and *sapiens* characteristics. Whether one chooses to call any of these early humans "primitive" *H. sapiens* or "advanced" *H. erectus* seems to be a matter of taste; whichever one calls them does not alter their apparently transitional status. Despite their retention of a number of features of *H. erectus*, their brain size shows a clear increase over that of even late representatives of that species (see Fig. 8.2).

The Levalloisian Technique

The culture of the hominines transitional between *H. erectus* and *H. sapiens* seems little changed from that of their predecessors. Primitive *sapiens* (or advanced *H. erectus*, if that is what one wishes to call them), for example, employed the kinds of heavy-duty tools such as hand axes and smaller flake tools used by *H. erectus* for thousands of years; however, by 200,000 years

ago, the **Levalloisian technique** of tool manufacture had come into use. Levalloisian flake tools have been found widely in Africa, Europe, the Middle East, and even China, where practically no hand axes have been uncovered. This could be a case of independent invention, since eastern Asia is quite distinct culturally from the West. Or, it could represent the spread of ideas from one part of the inhabited world to another. In the Levalloisian technique, the core was shaped by removal of flakes over its surface, following which a striking platform was made by a crosswise blow at one end of the core of stone (Fig. 9.1). Then the platform was struck, removing three or four long flakes, leaving a nodule that looked like a tortoise shell. This method produced a longer edge for the same amount of flint than the previous ones. The edges were sharper and could be produced in less time.

Archaic *Homo sapiens*

The scarcity of *H. sapiens* fossils predating 125,000 years ago is in marked contrast to the situation after that date, by which time the **Neandertals** were becoming widespread in Europe and western Asia, while other representatives of archaic *H. sapiens* are known from East Asia and Africa.

In 1856, three years before publication of Darwin's *On the Origin of Species*, the skeletal remains of an early man were discovered in the Neander Valley—Neandertal in German—near Dusseldorf, Germany. Although the discovery was of considerable interest, the experts were generally at a loss as to what to make of it. Examination of the fossil skull, a few ribs, and some limb bones revealed that the individual was a human being,

Levalloisian technique: Toolmaking technique developed about 200,000 years ago by which three or four long triangular flakes were detached from a specially prepared core.

Neandertals: Representatives of "archaic" *Homo sapiens* in Europe and western Asia, living from about 125,000 years ago to about 35,000 years ago.

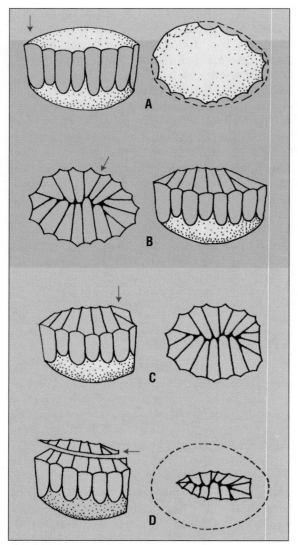

Figure 9.1 These drawings show top and side views of the steps in the Levalloisian technique. Drawing A shows the trimming of the edge of the stone nucleus; B, the trimming of the top surface; C, the striking platform; and D, the final step.

showing primitive and modern characteristics. The cranial capacity had reached modern size, but the skull was still primitive looking. Some people believed the bones were those of a sickly and deformed contemporary. Others thought the skeleton belonged to a soldier who had succumbed to "water on the brain" during the Napoleonic Wars.

A prominent anatomist thought the remains were those of an idiot suffering from malnutrition, whose violent temper had gotten him into many scrapes, flattening his forehead and making his brow ridges bumpy.

The idea that Neandertals were somehow deformed or aberrant was given impetus by an analysis of a Neandertal skeleton found in 1908 near La Chapelle-Aux-Saints in France. The analysis mistakenly concluded that the specimen's brain was apelike and that it walked like an ape. Although a team of North American investigators subsequently proved that this French Neandertal specimen was that of an elderly *H. sapiens* who had suffered from malnutrition, arthritis of the spine, and other deformities, the apelike image has persisted. To many nonanthropologists, Neandertal has become the quintessential "caveman," portrayed by imaginative cartoonists as a slant-headed, stooped, dim-witted individual, clad in animal skins and carrying a big club as he plods across the prehistoric landscape, perhaps dragging behind him an unwilling female or a dead leopard. In a best-selling novel of the 1970s, *Clan of the Cave Bear*, Neandertals were depicted as bow legged and barrel chested with extra long arms, more like those of apes than humans and incapable of the full range of human arm movements, muzzlelike jaws, and a body covering of coarse brown hair—not quite a pelt but not far from it. This brutish image was completed by portraying them as incapable of spoken language, abstract thought, thinking in new ways, or even thinking ahead.

With the discovery that Neandertals were nowhere near as brutish and apelike as originally portrayed, some scholars began to see them as no more than "less finished" versions of the anatomically modern populations that held exclusive sway in Europe and the Middle East 30,000 years ago. For example, Ashley Montagu argued that some faint ancestral Neandertal characteristics may still be seen even in today's Middle Eastern and European populations, with their relatively prominent brow ridges, deep eye sockets, and receding foreheads and chins.[1] Nevertheless, recent work

[1]Montagu, M. F. A. (1969). *Man: His first two million years.* New York: Columbia University Press.

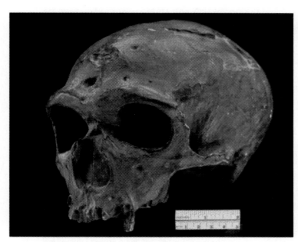

This "classic" Neandertal skull is from La Chapelle Aux Saints, France.

has shown that significant differences do exist between Neandertals and anatomically modern populations. Although they had modern sized brains (average cranial capacity 1400 cc, versus 1300 for modern *H. sapiens*), Neandertal skulls are distinctive in the projection of their noses and teeth and the swollen appearance of the midfacial region. This is due at least in part to the large size of their front teeth, which were heavily used for tasks other than chewing. In many individuals, they were worn down to the stubs of their roots by 35 to 40 years of age. The large noses, for their part, probably were necessary to warm frigid air, preventing damage to the lungs and brain, and to moisten and clean the dry, dusty air of glacial times. The eye-sockets were also positioned well forward, with prominent brow ridges above them. At the back of the skull, a bony mass provided for attachment of powerful neck muscles, needed to counteract the weight of a heavy face.

Both sexes were extraordinarily muscular, with extremely robust and dense limb bones. Details of the shoulder blades indicate the importance of overarm and downward thrusting movements; their arms were exceptionally powerful, and pronounced attachments on their hand bones attest to a remarkably strong grip. Their massive foot and leg bones (their shin bones, for example, were twice as strong as those of any recent human population)

suggests a high level of endurance; evidently, Neandertals spent long hours walking and scrambling about. Since brain size is related to overall bodymass as well as intelligence, the large average size of the Neandertal brain (compared with that of modern humans) is accounted for by their heavy robust bodies.

The Neandertal pelvis, too, shows differences from that of anatomically modern humans, but these do not support suggestions that obstetric requirements were different for Neandertals than they are for modern humans. Although the pelvic outlet is small by modern standards, it is still within the present-day range of variation, and the size of the pelvic inlet is virtually the same.[2] Differences in pelvic shape are easily accounted for as a consequence of posture-related biomechanics and deviation in modern humans from a shape characteristic of earlier hominines. Once born, however, Neandertal infants did mature more rapidly than do our own, as the characteristic Neandertal robustness can be discerned in the bones of children who died even before the age of 5. Furthermore, their teeth erupted earlier, and their brains grew more rapidly after birth than do our own.

African, Chinese, and Javanese Populations

Because Neandertal fossils are so numerous, have been known for so long, and are relatively well dated, they have received much more attention than have other populations of archaic *H. sapiens*. Nevertheless, outside of Europe and western Asia, a number of skulls have been found in Africa, China, and Java that are roughly contemporary with the Neandertals, or at least the earliest ones. They differ from the Neandertals primarily in their lack of midfacial projection and the absence of such massive muscle attachments on the back of their skull. Thus, the Neandertals represent an extreme form of archaic *sapiens*. Elsewhere, the archaics

[2]Togue, R. G. (1992). Sexual dimorphism in the human bony pelvis, with a consideration of the Neanderthal pelvis from Kebara Cave, Israel. *American Journal of Physical Anthropology*, *88*, 1–21.

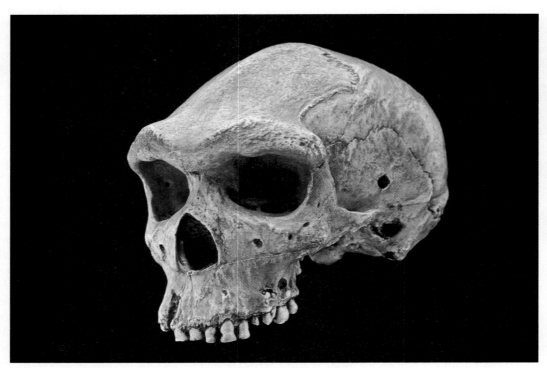

Skull of archaic *Homo sapiens* from Kabwe (Broken Hill), Zambia.

look like robust versions of the early modern populations that lived in the same regions or, if one looks backward, somewhat less primitive versions of the *H. erectus* populations that preceded them. All had fully modern-sized brains.

In China, the Maba skull is the one most like the Neandertals. Its round eye orbits are without precedent in the Far East and suggest admixture with Western populations.

THE CULTURE OF ARCHAIC *HOMO SAPIENS*

As the first hominines to possess brains of modern size, it is not surprising to find that the cultural capabilities of archaic *H. sapiens* were significantly improved over those of earlier hominines. Such a brain made possible an advanced technology as well as conceptual thought of considerable sophistication, and communication was almost surely by speech. In short, Neandertals and others like them were a fully sapient species of human being, relatively successful in surviving and thriving even in environments that would seem to us impossibly cold and hostile.

Middle Paleolithic

The improved toolmaking capabilities of archaic *H. sapiens* are represented by various **Middle Paleolithic** traditions, of which the best known are the Mousterian and Mousterianlike traditions of Europe, western Asia, and North Africa, which date between about 166,000 to 40,000 years ago; they represent a technological advance over Acheulean and even Levalloisian tools. The 16 inches of working edge that an Acheulean flint worker could get from a 2-pound core compares with the 6 feet the Mousterian could get from the same core.

The Mousterian Tradition

The **Mousterian tradition** is named after the Neandertal site of Le Moustier, France. The presence of Acheulean hand axes at Mousterian sites is one indication that this culture was ultimately rooted in the older Acheulean tradition. Neandertals and their contemporaries improved upon Levalloisian techniques; Mousterian flake tools are lighter and smaller than those of the Levalloisian. Whereas Levalloisian toolmakers obtained only two or three flakes from one core, Mousterian toolmakers obtained many more smaller flakes, which were then skillfully retouched and sharpened.

The Mousterian tool kits contained a much greater variety of tool types than the previous traditions: hand axes, flakes, scrapers, borers, gravers, notched flakes for sawing and shredding wood, and many types of points that could be

attached to wooden shafts to form thrusting spears. This variety of tool types indicates that the Mousterian tool kit intensified human utilization of food resources and increased the availability and quality of clothing and shelter. For the first time, people could cope with truly arctic conditions, which became prevalent in Europe beginning about 70,000 years ago.

People likely came to live in cold climates as a result of a slow but steady population increase during the Paleolithic era. As this caused populations to "spill over" into previously uninhabited colder regions, humans developed a series of cold-climate adaptations that increased their cultural variability. Under arctic conditions vegetable foods are only rarely or seasonally available, and meat is the main staple. In particular, animal fats, rather than carbohydrates, become the chief source of energy due to their slower rate of metabolism. Abundant animal fat in the diets of cold-climate meat-eaters provides them with the extra energy needed for full-time hunting as well as needed body heat. Insufficient fat in the diet produces lower resistance to disease, lassitude, and a loss of the will to work. That meat was important to the makers of Mousterian tools is indicated by the following Original Study.

Tools such as these are characteristic of the Mousterian tradition.

Middle Paleolithic: The middle part of the "Old Stone Age" characterized by the emergence of archaic *H. sapiens* and the development of the Mousterian tradition of toolmaking.

Mousterian tradition: Toolmaking tradition of the Neandertals and their contemporaries of Europe, western Asia, and northern Africa, featuring flake tools lighter and smaller than Levalloisian flake tools.

Original Study

Subsistence Practices of Mousterian Peoples[3]

Most of the recent discussions of changes in subsistence strategies across the archaic/modern human transition have focused on a series of generalizations formulated in the recent publications of Binford. In essence, these can be reduced to three basic propositions:

1. Prior to the emergence of anatomically modern populations, the exploitation of animal resources was focused primarily on the scavenging of meat and bone marrow from carnivore kills and included only a relatively minor and secondary component of deliberate hunting of game.
2. Where some hunting was practiced by these archaic populations, it was focused almost entirely on the smaller species of game, especially various species of cervids [deer family] and some of the smaller species of bovids [cattle family].
3. Any deliberate hunting or killing of game by archaic populations was undertaken essentially on an opportunistic or encounter basis and involved little if any deliberate planning, forethought, or "logistical organization" on the part of the human groups.

Binford's interpretations are original and provocative and have undoubtedly served to stimulate more sharply focused research on the problems of Lower and Middle Paleolithic subsistence. Recently, however, they have been challenged from a number of perspectives. In particular, Chase and others have drawn attention to at least three aspects of the current data which would appear to run directly counter to Binford's hypotheses:

1. The faunal assemblages recovered from several Middle Paleolithic sites in Europe reveal a heavy bias in favor of one particular species, which would seem difficult if not impossible to account for by any hypothesis of essentially random or opportunistic exploitation. Examples of these heavily single-species–dominated faunas have been recorded at Staroselje in the Crimea, Ilskaya, Teshik-Tash, and Volgograd in southern Russia, and Ehringsdorf in Germany, as well as at several recently excavated sites in France. One of the most striking illustrations of this single-species orientation has been documented in the recent excavations at Mauran in the French Pyrenees, where (according to preliminary reports) well over 90% of the faunal assemblage (representing at least 108 animals) consists of the remains of large bovids (*Bos/Bison*). As Chase points out, it is difficult to visualize these heavily specialized faunas as the result of either opportunistic scavenging or unstructured encounter hunting on the part of Neanderthal groups. Both of the latter sample the whole range of animal species within the immediate catchment areas of the sites, roughly in proportion to their relative frequencies in the local faunal communities. The fact that the faunal assemblage from Mauran (as well as other sites) consisted almost entirely of very

large game (large bovids, with individual carcass weights of up to 900 kg) runs counter to Binford's hypothesis that hunting was focused exclusively on the smaller species of game.

2. The detailed studies carried out by Chase, Levine, and others of the faunal assemblages from the long Mousterian succession at Combe Grenal (southwestern France) have produced results which conflict in several respects with those reported by Binford from his earlier studies at this site. Thus, Chase has demonstrated that the remains of both horses and large bovids at Combe Grenal (which Binford has maintained were exclusively *scavenged*) are represented more frequently by the major meat-bearing bones from the *upper* parts of the limbs than by the meat-poor bones from the lower limbs and that these bones frequently bear clear cut marks (presumably through fresh flesh) as opposed to indications of heavy chopping through the remains of partially desiccated carcasses. Both these observations are much more consistent with the notion of deliberate hunting of large game than with that of scavenging of remains from natural-death carcasses or abandoned carnivore kills. Similarly, Levine has shown that the age profiles of the horse remains from three separate levels at Combe Grenal appear to indicate an essentially "catastrophic" pattern closely similar to that to be expected in a living herd. This pattern again bears little resemblance to what one would anticipate from the scavenging of carnivore kills, which would be likely to reflect a primary emphasis on the oldest and youngest age-classes, the most vulnerable elements in the animal herds. As Levine points out, these age profiles would conform best to some form of unselective, mass hunting strategies on the part of the Mousterian groups.

3. Finally, the specific character and location of several Middle Paleolithic sites in Europe may well provide some direct insight into the methods by which large game was hunted by Mousterian groups. At the site of La Quina in western France, for example, a dense accumulation of bones of bovids, horses, and reindeer (many with clear indications of butchery marks) occurs immediately at the base of a steep cliff, the only topographic feature of this kind within several kilometres of the site. As Jelinek, Debenath, and Dibble and Chase have pointed out, there would seem to be a strong implication in this case that the site represents a typical jump or cliff-fall hunting site, in which the animals were deliberately driven over the cliff as part of a systematic hunting strategy. A similar situation has been documented in the recent excavations at Mauran, where an accumulation of several thousands of bones of large bovids again occurs immediately at the foot of a steep riverside escarpment. And in a slightly different context, Scott has recently argued that the highly localized and dense accumulations of mammoth and woolly rhinoceros bones at the site of La Cotte de Saint-Brelade (Channel Islands) can only be plausibly explained in terms of some similar strategy of cliff-fall hunting—in this case into a deep coastal ravine. In none of these cases is there any convincing way of explaining the bone accumulations as accidental death assemblages. The strong implication, in other words, is that Middle Paleolithic populations in Europe were practicing some form of organized, systematic cliff-fall hunting in many ways reminiscent of that reflected in the Paleo-Indian bison-jump kill sites

of North America [see p. 241]. As a further indication of the deliberate killing of game in Middle and Lower Paleolithic contexts, one could refer to the well-documented discoveries of wooden spears at the sites of Clacton (England) and Lehringen (Germany) and the recent confirmation from microwear studies that at least certain forms of Mousterian and Levallois points would seem to have functioned as the hafted tips of either thrusting or throwing spears.

The combination of the preceding data leaves little doubt that the Neanderthal populations of Europe *were* practicing a good deal of deliberate hunting of very large game, and in a way that can hardly be described as totally unstructured or opportunistic.

[3]Mellars, P. (1989). Major issues in the emergence of modern humans. *Current Anthropology, 30*, 356–357.

The importance of hunting to Mousterian peoples may also be reflected in their hunting implements, which are more standardized with respect to size and shape than are their domestic and maintenance implements. The complexity of the tool kit needed for survival in a cold climate may have played a role in lessening the mobility of the "owners" of all of these possessions. That they were less mobile is suggested by the greater depth of deposits at Mousterian sites compared with those from the earlier ("lower") paleolithic. Similarly, evidence for long sequences of production, resharpening, and discarding of tools, large-scale butchery and cooking of game, and evidence of efforts to improve accommodations in some caves and rock shelters through pebble paving, construction of simple walls, and the presence of postholes and artificial pits all suggest that Mousterian sites were more than mere stopovers in peoples' constant quest for food. The large number of Mousterian sites uncovered in Europe and western Asia, as well as clear differences between them, is closely related to Neandertal's improved hunting techniques, based on superior technology in weapon manufacture and toolmaking and more efficient social organization than before. These, in turn, were closely related to Neandertal's increased brain size.

Neandertal society had developed even to the point of caring for handicapped members of the group; evidence shows that the disabled were cared for by their companions. For the first time, the remains of "oldsters"—individuals well past their prime—are well represented in the fossil record. Even more dramatic evidence comes from such finds as remains of a blind amputee discovered in Shanidar Cave in Iraq and a man crippled by arthritis unearthed at La Chapelle. Whether this indicates true "compassion" on the part of these early people is not known; what is certain is that culture had become more than barely adequate to ensure survival.

One powerful selective force that might have favored empathy (not to mention cooperation and communication) among Neandertals was childbirth. Earlier in this chapter, we noted that the obstetric requirements for these people were no different than they are for modern humans. This is significant, for among humans, unlike all other primates, childbirth is a difficult business. Because of the remodeling of the pelvis for bipedal locomotion, to get a large-headed fetus down the birth canal, it must enter the canal facing sideways and then rotate so when it emerges, it faces down. In other primates, it enters the canal facing up and exits that way as well. The consequence of this, for humans, is that not only does it take longer to traverse the canal, prolonging the pain, but because babies do not bend backward, mothers cannot pull them out without serious injury. Nor can they clear their newborns' airways if they are in trouble. The upshot is, human mothers need help from others to deliver a baby successfully, so that empathy as well as cooperation and communication would clearly enhance reproductive success. In earlier hominines, the problem may not have been as great, as infants were likely delivered sideways, without need of the final rotation. But as the first hominines with really big heads, Neandertals and other archaic *sapiens* would have had to cope with the full pain and risk.[4]

The Symbolic Life of Neandertals

Although earlier reports of evidence for some sort of "cave bear cult" have turned out to be far-fetched, indications of some sort of symbolic life do exist. At several sites, there is clear evidence for deliberate burial of the dead. This is important, for the intentional positioning of dead hominine bodies by other hominines, whatever the specific reason, nonetheless constitutes evidence of symbolism.[5] To date, about 17 sites in Europe, South Africa, and Southwest Asia include Middle Paleolithic burials. To cite two examples, at Kebara Cave, in Israel, sometime between 64,000 and 59,000 years ago, a Neandertal male aged between 25 and 35 years old was placed in a pit, on his back, with his arms folded over his chest and abdomen. Some time later, after complete decay of attaching ligaments, the grave was reopened and the skull removed (a practice that, interestingly, is sometimes seen in burials in the same region roughly 50,000 years later). Another example is from Shanidar Cave, where evidence was found of a burial accompanied by funeral ceremonies. In the back of the cave a Neandertal was buried in a pit. Pollen analysis of the soil around the skeleton indicated that flowers had been placed below the body and in a wreath about the head. (The possibility that the pollen blew into the cave has been effectively ruled out.) The flowers in question consist solely of varieties valued in historic times for their medicinal properties.

Other evidence for symbolic behavior in Mousterian culture comes from the use of two different pigments: manganese dioxide and red ocher. These show clear evidence of scraping to produce powder, as well as crayonlike facets. Thus, Mousterian peoples were clearly using these for applying color to things. One example is the carved and shaped section of a mammoth tooth pictured on page 216 that was worked by Mousterian peoples about 50,000 years ago. One of a number of carved and engraved objects that may have been made for purely symbolic purposes, it is similar to a number of plaques of bone and ivory made by later Paleolithic peoples, and it is also similar to the "churingas" made of wood by Australian aborigines for ritual purposes. The Mousterian object, which was once smeared with red ocher, has a highly polished face as if from long handling. Microscopic examination reveals that it was never provided with a working edge for any utilitarian purpose. As Alexander Marshack observes: "A number of researchers have indicated that the Neandertals did in fact have conceptual models and maps as well as problem-solving capacities comparable to, if not equal to, those found among anatomically modern humans."[6]

Neandertals and Spoken Language

Among modern humans, the sharing of thoughts and ideas, as well as the transmission of culture from one generation to the next, is dependent upon a spoken language. Since the Neandertals had modern-sized brains and a tool kit comparable to that being used in historic times by Australian aborigines, it might be supposed that they had some form of spoken language. In spite of this, some researchers have tried to argue that the Neandertals lacked the physical features necessary for spoken language. It has been shown, however, that the reconstruction of the Neandertal larynx, on which this argument is partially based, is faulty. In fact, the shape and position in the skeleton from the Kebara Cave burial of the hyoid bone (the "wish bone," associated with the

[4]Fischman, J. (1994). Putting a new spin on the birth of human birth. *Science, 264,* 1082–1083.
[5]Schepartz, L. A. (1993). Language and modern human origins. *Yearbook of Physical Anthropology, 36,* 113.
[6]Marshack, A. (1989). Evolution of the human capacity: The symbolic evidence. *Yearbook of Physical Anthropology, 32,* 22.

This carved symbolic plaque or "churinga" made from a section of a mammoth molar was excavated at the Mousterian site of Tata, Hungary. The edge is rounded and polished from long handling. The plaque has been symbolically smeared with red ocher. The reverse face of the plaque (right) shows the beveling and shaping of the tooth.

larynx) shows that the vocal tract was quite adequate for speech. This is especially noteworthy, for humans pay a high price for the way their vocal tract is positioned; it is far easier for us to choke to death than it is for other mammals. The only advantage worth such a price seems to be the ability to speak.

With respect to the brain, paleoneurologists, working from endocranial casts, are agreed that Neandertals had the neural development necessary for language. Indeed, they argue that the changes associated with speech began even before the appearance of archaic *Homo sapiens*.[7] Finally, arguments that flattening of the skull base would have prevented speech have no merit, as some modern adults show as much flattening as the Neandertals, yet have no trouble talking. Talking Neandertals make a good deal of sense in view of the evidence for the manufacture of objects of apparently symbolic significance. Objects such as the mammoth tooth "churinga" already described would seem to have required some form of lin-

guistic explanation. On the other hand, any language spoken by Neandertals need not have been as complex as those used by their later Paleolithic successors.

ARCHAIC *HOMO SAPIENS* AND MODERN HUMAN ORIGINS

One of the hot debates in paleoanthropology today is over this question: Did populations of archaic *H. sapiens* in most, if not all, parts of the Old World evolve simultaneously into anatomically modern humans, (the "multiregional hypothesis") or was there a single, geographic place of origin, from which anatomically modern *H. sapiens* spread to replace existing populations of the archaic species everywhere else (the "Eve" or "Out of Africa" hypothesis)? Based on the fossil evidence from Africa and some parts of Asia, a good case can be made for the first hypothesis. As several anthropologists have noted, African, Chinese, and Southeast Asian fossils of archaic *H. sapiens* imply local population continuity from *Homo erectus*

[7]Schepartz, p. 98.

FRANZ WEIDENREICH
(1873–1948)

Franz Weidenreich was born and educated in Germany, where he later held professorships in anatomy at Strasburg and Heidelberg. Although his early work was primarily in hematology (the study of blood), his scientific work shifted to the study of bones and related tissues, and in 1926 he published his first study of a human fossil, an archaic *Homo sapiens* cranium from Ehringsdorf. Two years later, he was appointed professor of anthropology at the University of Frankfurt.

In 1935, he was sent by the Rockefeller Foundation to study fossils of *Homo erectus* from Zhoukoudian, China, following the death of their discoverer, Davidson Black. When the Japanese invasion of China forced Weidenreich to leave, he took with him to the United States several painstakingly prepared casts, as well as detailed notes on the actual fossils. From these he was able to prepare a major monograph that set new standards for paleoanthropological reports. For this alone, anthropology owes him a great debt, for the fossils themselves were among the casualties of World War II.

Unlike many physical anthropologists of his time or ours, Weidenreich had an extensive firsthand knowledge of extant human fossils from several parts of the Old World: Europe (where he had worked before going to China), China, and Southeast Asia (he collaborated in the 1930s study of *Homo erectus* and later fossils from Java). What struck him about the fossils in each of these regions was the evident continuity from the earliest to the latest specimens. Out of this observation, he developed his polycentric theory of human evolution, which received its first clear statement in a 1943 publication. In it, he argued the thesis that human populations of common ancestry thereafter evolved in the same direction in four different geographical regions. (Africa was the fourth.) Although he failed adequately to explain this phenomenon, others have since taken up the challenge, and Weidenreich's ideas continue in the modern multiregional theory of human evolution.

---

through archaic to modern *Homo sapiens*,[8] lending strong support to the interpretation that there was genetic continuity in these regions. For example, in China, hominine fossils consistently have flatter faces than their contemporaries elsewhere, as is still true today. Instead of evolving extremely "puffy" faces and massive neck musculature, as did the Neandertals, other archaic *sapiens* populations experienced a reduction in total facial protrusion as facial robusticity decreased, while the backs of their skulls took on a more modern form.

One possible exception to this scenario consists of the Neandertals of Europe. About 40,000 to 35,000 years ago a new technology, known as the **Aurignacian tradition,** spread into Europe from Southwest Asia, where its appearance marks the start of the **Upper Paleolithic** period. In both regions, human skeletons associated with Aurignacian tools are invariably modern in their features. Nevertheless, Neandertals are known to have survived in western Europe until 35,000 to 33,000 years ago, so coexistence between the modern and archaic forms of *sapiens* is indicated. Given the striking anatomical differences between the two, some form of population replacement, rather

Aurignacian tradition: Toolmaking tradition of anatomically modern *H. sapiens* in Europe and western Asia at the beginning of the Upper Paleolithic.

Upper Paleolithic: The last part of the "Old Stone Age" characterized by the emergence of anatomically modern hominines and an emphasis on the blade technique of toolmaking.

[8]Wolpoff, M. H. (1993). Multiregional evolution: The fossil alternative to Eden. In R. L. Ciochon & J. G. Fleagle (Eds.), *The human evolution source book* (pp. 476–497). Englewood Cliffs, NJ: Prentice-Hall.

than simple evolution from one to the other, may have occurred.

How or why this replacement took place remains a mystery. Possibly, it took place through interbreeding, as the most recent Neandertal known, from Saint Césaire, exhibits some modern anatomical traits. Similarly, early anatomically modern skulls from Europe often exhibit features reminiscent of Neandertals (see Chapter 10). There seems to have been nothing in the physical or mental makeup of Neandertals to prevent them from leading a "typical" Upper Paleolithic way of life, as in fact the final Neandertals of Western, Central, and Eastern Europe did.[9] Borrowing many ideas and techniques from the Aurignacians, they created their own Upper Paleolithic cultures (see Fig. 9.2). In some respects, they outdid their Auriguanacion contemporaries, as in the use of red ocher, a substance less frequently used by the Aurignaucians than by their late Neandertal neighbors.[10]

A number of scholars have argued for coexistence of the two forms in Southwest Asia as well. While Neandertal skeletons are clearly present at sites such as Kebara and Shanidar caves, skeletons from some older sites have been described as anatomically modern. At Qafzeh, in Israel, for example, 90,000-year-old skeletons are said to show none of the Neandertal hallmarks; although their faces and bodies are large and heavily built by today's standards, they are nonetheless said to be within the range of living peoples. Still, a recent statistical study comparing a number of measurements between Qafzeh, Upper Paleolithic, and Neandertal skulls shows those from Qafzeh to fall in between, though slightly closer to, the Neandertals.[11] Furthermore, an individual from the nearby site of Skuhl, whose skeleton was similar to those from Qafzeh, was part of a population whose continuous range of variation included individuals with markedly Neandertal characteristics. Nor does the idea of two distinctly different but coexisting populations receive any support from cultural remains, inasmuch as people such as those living at Skuhl and Qafzeh were making and using the same Mousterian tools as those at Kebara and Shanidar. Thus, there are no indications of groups with different cultural traditions coexisting

---

[9]Mellars, p. 378.

[10]Bednarik, R. G. (1995). Concept-mediated marking in the Lower Paleolithic. *Current Anthropology, 36,* 606.

[11]Corruccini, R. S. (1992). Metrical reconsideration of the Skhul IV and IX and Border Cave I crania in the context of modern human origins. *American Journal of Physical Anthropology, 87,* 433–445.

Figure 9.2   About 30,000 to 40,000 years ago, the Mousterian-derived Upper Paleolithic industries of the last Neandertal populations in Europe coexisted with the Aurignacian industry, associated with anatomically modern *Homo sapiens.*

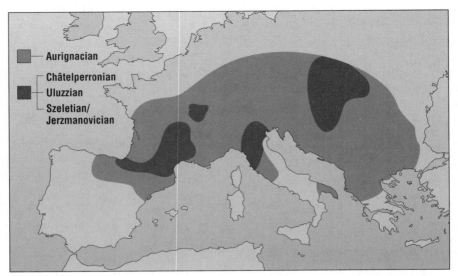

Aurignacian
Châtelperronian
Uluzzian
Szeletian/
Jerzmanovician

in the same region. For that matter, the actual behaviors represented by Middle Paleolithic and early Upper Paleolithic cultures were not significantly different. In Kebara Cave, for example, the Upper Paleolithic people who used the cave continued to live in exactly the same way as their Neandertal predecessors: They procured the same foods, processed them in the same way, used similar hearths, and disposed of their trash in the same way. The only evident difference is that the Neandertals did not bank their fires for warmth with small stones or cobbles as did their Upper Paleolithic successors.[12]

The "Eve" or "Out of Africa" Hypothesis

This alternative to the multiregional hypothesis states that anatomically modern humans are descended from one specific population of *H. sapiens*, replacing not just the Neandertals, but other populations of archaic *H. sapiens* as our ancestors spread out of their original homeland. The idea for this hypothesis came not from fossils, but from a relatively new technique using mitochondrial DNA to reconstruct family trees. Unlike the DNA that determines physical traits, mitochondrial DNA is located outside the cell nucleus in compartments that produce energy needed to keep cells alive. Since the male sperm does not contribute mitochondrial DNA to the fertilized egg, it is inherited only from the mother and is not "rescrambled" with each succeeding generation. Therefore, it should be altered only by mutation. By comparing the mitochondrial DNA of living individuals from diverse geographical populations, anthropologists and molecular biologists seek to determine when and where modern *H. sapiens* originated. As widely reported in the popular press (including a cover story in *Newsweek*), preliminary results suggested that the mitochondrial DNA of all living humans could be traced back to a "Mitochondrial Eve" who lived in Africa (though some argued for Asia) some 200,000 years ago. If so, all other populations of

archaic *H. sapiens*, as well as early *H. erectus*, would have to be ruled out of the ancestry of modern humans.

Although a number of scholars have interpreted fossils from Africa as exhibiting the transition from *H. erectus* through archaic to anatomically modern *sapiens* on that continent, this by itself offers no confirmation of the "Out of Africa" hypothesis. After all, proponents of the multiregional model also argue that the transition took place here, as in other parts of the Old World. If, however, anatomically modern fossils could be shown to be significantly older in Africa than elsewhere, this would bolster the argument for an African homeland for modern humanity. To date, the strongest candidates for such fossils consist of a skull from Border Cave and fragments of jaws of at least 10 people from a cave at the Klasies River mouth. Both sites are in South Africa. Unfortunately, the Border Cave skull is not adequately dated, nor is it as similar to modern African skulls as is often claimed.[13] The Klasies River material is well dated to between 120,000 and 90,000 years ago, but is too fragmentary (they were cut and burned anciently, suggesting cannibalism) to permit categorical statements as to its modernity. Although one mandible displays a well-developed chin, this feature occasionally shows up in fossils of archaic *sapiens* (for example, a Neandertal mandible from La Ferrassie, France). Certainly, the remains are not inconsistent with the sort of wide variation just discussed for Southwest Asia.

It is true that the people of Klasies River were culturally precocious. For one thing, they are the first people we know of to augment resources of the land with those from the sea; their gathering of shellfish led to the buildup of middens comparable to those left by later Upper Paleolithic peoples. Their technology was also advanced in the common production of blades—long parallel-sided flakes of a sort not commonly made in Europe until some 40,000 years ago. By 70,000 years ago, the people at Klasies River were blunting the backs of blades, much as later Europeans did, for hafting in composite tools. To some researchers, these signs of cultural "advancement" would seem to be indicative of anatomically modern status. The fallacy of such argument, however, is revealed by the

[12]Bar-Yosef, O., Vandermeesch, B., Arensburg, B., Belfer-Cohen, A., Goldberg, P., Laville, H., Meignen, L., Rak, Y., Speth, J. D., Tchernov, E., Tillier, A.-M., & Weiner, S. (1992). The excavations in Kebara Cave, Mt. Carmel. *Current Anthropology, 33,* 534.

[13]Corruccini, p. 436.

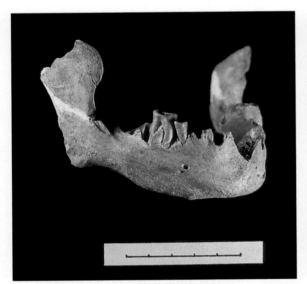
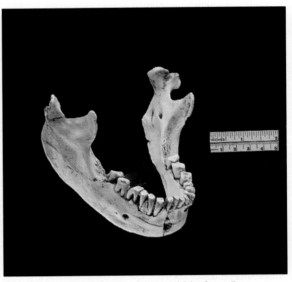

A mandible from the Klasies River in South Africa (left) is compared with a Neandertal mandible from La Ferrassie in France (right). Because of its chin, the South African fossil has been called "modern," yet the La Ferrassie jaw shows that even Neandertals sometimes had chins.

Even older than the blades from the Klasies River mouth are these, from a site in Kenya. Struck from preshaped cores, they are about 240,000 years old, predating any known or possible fossils of anatomically modern humans.

evidence from Europe and Southwest Asia that the cognitive abilities of archaic and modern *H. sapiens* were the same.

The fossil evidence presents other problems for the "Out of Africa" hypothesis as well. For one thing, we would expect an early replacement of archaic *sapiens* in Southwest Asia as more anatomically modern humans moved up out of Africa, but, as we have already seen, we have no clear evidence for such a replacement. Nor is such evidence available for East Asia, where evidence for continuity from regional *H. erectus* through archaic to anatomical *H. sapiens* populations is as good as, if not better than, the evidence for such continuity in Africa. Consistent with this, the archaeological record of East Asia, though distinctly different from Europe, Africa, and western Asia, shows the same kind of continuity as do the fossils.[14] There is no sign of invasion by people possessing a superior, or even different, technology, as an "Out of Africa" scenario would require.

Given the problems in reconciling the "Out of Africa" hypothesis with the archaeological and fossil records, one may ask, what about the DNA analysis that gave birth to the hypothesis? In 1992, serious flaws were discovered in the analysis of mitochondrial DNA. Similarly, studies of the human Y chromosome that have been said to confirm the "Out of Africa" hypothesis are seriously flawed. Just as mitochondrial DNA is passed exclusively from mother to daughter, so is the Y chromosome passed from father to son. Unfortunately, the samples used for Y chromosome analysis are inadequate and involve unwarranted assumptions.[15] Still, analyses do consistently show Africans to have at least twice as much genetic variation as people from other continents, implying a longer human presence in Africa. On the other hand, this may reflect the longer presence of the genus *Homo*, as opposed to the species *sapiens*, on that continent. Another criticism of DNA analyses is that they have interpreted genetic distances from the perspective of a branching model of evolution, ignoring other interpretations that could give rise to

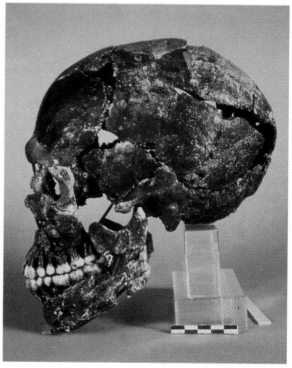

Showing a strikingly modern appearance, this *H. sapiens* skull from Qafzeh, Israel, is 90,000 years old. Measurements taken on the skull, however, fall slightly closer to those of the Neandertals than they do those of anatomically modern Upper Paleolithic people.

similar patterns of variation. The genetic distinctiveness of Africa, for example, could reflect a larger effective population size and less intermixing. For the rest of humanity, a low-level of genetic differentiation may as easily imply high levels of gene flow as recent divergence.[16]

In short, with the possible exception of the European Neandertals (and even that is arguable), it is definitely premature to read out of the modern human ancestry all populations of archaic *sapiens* save those of Africa. We shall return to this problem in the next chapter, but at the moment, the evidence seems to favor a multiregional emergence of anatomically modern humans. Still, the debate is by no means resolved.

[14]Pope, G. C. (1992). Craniofacial evidence for the origin of modern humans in China. *Yearbook of Physical Anthropology, 35,* 291.

[15]Marks, J. (1996). Just when you thought molecular anthropology was safe … *Anthropology Newsletter 37* (3), 19.

[16]Relethford, J. H., & Harpending, H. C. (1994). Craniometric variation, genetic theory, and modern human origins. *American Journal of Physical Anthropology, 95,* 265.

CHAPTER SUMMARY

At various sites in Europe, Africa, and East Asia, a number of fossils have been found that date between about 400,000 and 200,000 years ago and which show a mixture of traits characteristic of both *H. erectus* and *H. sapiens*. They are indicative of evolution from the older into the younger species. Their culture was much like that of *H. erectus*, until about 200,000 years ago, when they developed a new technique of tool manufacture know as the Levalloisian.

By 125,000 years ago, populations of archaic *H. sapiens* lived in all parts of the inhabited world. Although some populations of this species, most notably the Neandertals of Europe and western Asia, survived until at least 35,000 years ago, others had by then evolved into anatomically modern humans.

The brains of archaic *H. sapiens* were no different in size and organization than our own, although their skulls retained some primitive characteristics. With a larger brain, they were able to utilize culture as a means of environmental adaptation to a far greater extent than any of their predecessors; they were capable of an advanced technology and sophisticated conceptual thought.

The cultures of archaic *H. sapiens* are known as Middle Paleolithic, and the best known is the Mousterian of Europe, northern Africa, and western Asia. Mousterian tools included hand axes, flakes, scrapers, borers, wood shavers, and spears. Flake tools were lighter and smaller than those of the Levalloisian. Mousterian tools increased the availability and quality of food, shelter, and clothing. Archaeological evidence indicates that Mousterian peoples buried their dead, cared for the disabled, and made a number of objects for purely symbolic purposes.

All populations of archaic *H. sapiens* are easily derivable from earlier populations of *H. erectus* from the same regions. With the possible exception of the Neandertals, all populations of archaic *H. sapiens* could be ancestral to more modern populations in the same regions. An alternative hypothesis is that the transition from archaic to anatomically modern *H. sapiens* took place in one specific population, probably in Africa. From here, people spread to other regions, replacing older populations as they did so.

SUGGESTED READINGS

Ciochon, R. L., & Fleagle, J. G. (Eds.). (1993). *The human evolution source book*. Englewood Cliffs, NJ: Prentice-Hall.

Two parts of this book contain articles on the evolution of *Homo sapiens* and the Neandertal problem and modern human origins. The debate between proponents of the "Out of Africa" and multiregional hypotheses are well covered, and the editors' introduction to the two sections places the articles in context.

Shreeve, J. (1995). *The Neandertal enigma: Solving the mystery of modern human origins*. New York: Morrow.

Shreeve is a science writer who has written extensively about human evolution. This book is engagingly written and covers most of the major issues in the Neandertal-Modern debate.

Trinkaus, E., & Shipman, P. (1992). *The Neandertals: Changing the image of mankind*. New York: Alfred A. Knopf.

The senior author (Trinkaus) of this book is a long-time specialist on the Neandertals. Emminently readable, the book chronicles the changing interpretations of these fossils since the first recognized find in 1856. This is an excellent source for finding out what is known about the Neandertals.

CHAPTER
10

HOMO SAPIENS AND THE UPPER PALEOLITHIC

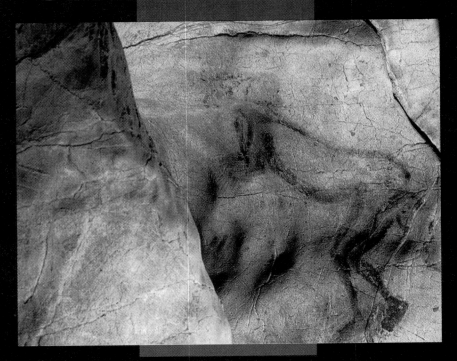

THE INTELLECTUAL CAPABILITIES OF UPPER PALEOLITHIC PEOPLES, WHOSE SKELETONS DIFFER IN NO SIGNIFICANT WAY FROM OUR OWN, ARE SUGGESTED BY THIS FAMOUS PAINTING FROM THE FRENCH CAVE OF THE TROIS FRERES (THREE BROTHERS). DEPICTED IS A HUMAN WHO IS NOT JUST DRESSED AS AN ANIMAL, BUT HAS BECOME PART ANIMAL. SUCH PARTIAL OR EVEN COMPLETE TRANSFORMATION IS A SENSATION WELL-DOCUMENTED ON THE PART OF INDIVIDUALS WHO ENTER TRANCE, A PRACTICE COMMON IN HUMAN SOCIETIES AS PEOPLE SEEK CONTACT WITH SUPERNATURAL BEINGS AND FORCES.

CHAPTER PREVIEW

When Did Anatomically Modern Forms of *Homo sapiens* Appear?

Although some fossils as much as 100,000 years old from Africa and Southwest Asia have been interpreted as essentially modern in appearance, there is now reason to question this. Fossils of *Homo sapiens* that are unequivocally modern in their anatomy were present certainly by 45,000 years ago.

What Was the Culture of Upper Paleolithic Peoples Like?

Upper Paleolithic cultures generally include a greater diversity of tools than before, and techniques of toolmaking previously used to limited degrees came into widespread use. These include the making of blades, pressure flaking, and the use of chisel-like tools called burins to fashion implements of bone and antler. In Europe, spear hunting was improved by invention of the spear-thrower, while in Africa the bow and arrow were invented. Bow hunting spread to Europe by about 12,000 years ago, the end of the Old and the beginning of the Middle Stone Age, or Mesolithic. Technological improvements in the Mesolithic included the invention of ground stone axes and adzes for woodworking as well as widespread use of a variety of composite tools made by inserting microlithic blades into handles of wood, bone, or antler.

What Were the Consequences of the New Upper Paleolithic and Mesolithic Technologies?

First Upper Paleolithic and then Mesolithic technologies improved peoples' abilities to adapt through the medium of culture. This resulted in increased regionalism, as people refined their adaptations to local conditions, and further population caused "spillover" into new regions, most dramatically Australia and the Americas. Biological consequences included final reduction of the human face to modern proportions, and the new hunting technologies led to reduction of body size and mass, especially in men.

Although populations of archaic and anatomically modern *Homo sapiens* seem to have coexisted for a time in Europe, by 30,000 years ago anatomically modern peoples with Upper ("late") Paleolithic cultures had the world to themselves. The remains of these ancient peoples who looked so much like us were first discovered in 1868 at Les Eyzies in France in a rock shelter called Cro-Magnon, and so European remains from the Upper Paleolithic are often referred to as **Cro-Magnons.** Between 1872 and 1902, the fossils of 13 other specimens were unearthed in the caves of the Cote d'Azur near the Italian Riviera. Since then, various other Cro-Magnon skeletons have been recovered from various parts of Europe.

The original Cro-Magnon skull differs very little from modern European skulls.

UPPER PALEOLITHIC PEOPLES: THE FIRST MODERN HUMANS

The Cro-Magnons have suffered their share of idealization on the part of physical anthropologists; at one time they were made to look like Greek gods, in contrast to the Neandertals, who supposedly stood just a step ahead of the ape. The idea found its way into popular culture, as in a best-selling novel of the 1970s, *The Clan of the Cave Bear.* In this book, the heroine is portrayed as a tall, slender, blonde-haired, blue-eyed beauty. As more Upper Paleolithic remains have been found, in various parts of Africa and Asia as well as Europe, more physical variability has been shown, as is to be expected from any human population. Therefore, it is hardly surprising to find specimens that exhibit distinct features. In some ways, such as in the size of the brain, in the narrow nasal openings, and in the high, broad forehead, the European Cro-Magnons resembled modern Europeans. But their faces, for example, were shorter and broader than those of modern Europeans, and their brow ridges were a bit more prominent.

Cro-Magnons: The first anatomically modern Europeans, of Upper Paleolithic times.

Generally speaking, Upper Paleolithic people in all parts of the world evolved a modern-looking face; the full-sized brain had already been achieved by archaic *H. sapiens,* no doubt as a consequence of increased reliance on cultural adaptation. Ultimately, this emphasis on cultural adaptation led to the development of more complex tool kits. The modernization of the face of Upper Paleolithic peoples is the result of a reduction in the size of the teeth, and eventually the jaw, as specialized tools increasingly took over the cutting, softening, and clamping functions once performed by the front teeth. The cooking of food (which began with *H. erectus*) had already favored a reduction in size of the teeth and muscles involved in chewing; consequently, the jaws reduced in size, accompanied by loss of robust sites for muscle attachment and features like brow ridges that buttress the skull from the stresses and strains imposed by massive jaw muscles.

Technological improvements also reduced the intensity of selective pressures favoring especially massive, robust bodies. With more emphasis on elongate tools with greater mechanical advantages, more effective techniques of hafting, and a switch from thrusting to throwing spears, there was a marked reduction in overall muscularity. Moreover, the skeletons of Upper Paleolithic peoples show far less evidence of trauma than do those of archaic *H. sapiens,* whose bones almost always show evidence of injury.

Upper Paleolithic peoples also tended to live longer than their archaic predecessors. Furthermore, the prolonged period of development characteristic of the human species today, which allows people to learn so much before they are responsible for themselves as adults, was associated with the appearance of anatomically modern peoples. Perhaps both have something to do with the burst of creativity that was a part of Upper Paleolithic culture. Being too old for most day-to-day subsistence activities, but able to recall events beyond the experience of younger adults, elders could have spent more time passing on a greater store of wisdom to youngsters who were capable of absorbing it all.

cessors did. What made this possible were new techniques of core preparation that allowed more intensive production of highly standardized blades. To make these, the toolmaker formed a cylindrical core, struck the blade off near the edge of the core, and repeated this procedure, going around the core in one direction until finishing near its center (Fig. 10.1). The procedure is analogous to peeling long leaves off an artichoke. With this **blade technique**, an Upper Paleolithic flint knapper could get 75 feet of working edge from a 2-pound core; his Mousterian counterpart could get only 6 feet from the same-sized core.

Other efficient techniques of tool manufacture also came into common use at this time. One such

Upper Paleolithic Tools

The typical Upper Paleolithic tool was the blade, a flint flake at least twice as long as it is wide. Although Middle Paleolithic toolmakers, especially in Africa, also made blades, they did not do so to the extent that their Upper Paleolithic suc-

Blade technique: A technique of stone tool manufacture by which long, parallel-sided flakes are struck off the edges of a specially prepared core.

Figure 10.1   During the Upper Paleolithic, a new technique was used to manufacture blades. The stone is broken to create a striking platform, then vertical pieces are flaked off the side of the flint, forming sharp-edged tools.

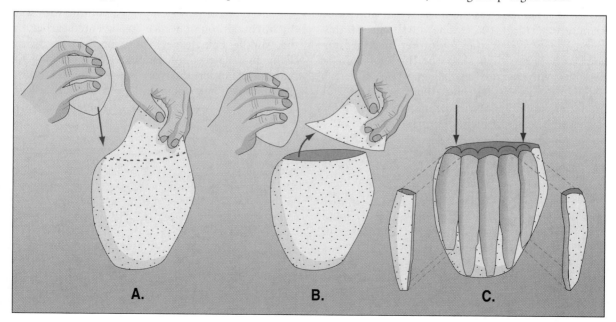

Anthropology Applied

STONE TOOLS FOR MODERN SURGEONS

In 1975, Don Crabtree, then at the Idaho State University Museum, underwent heart surgery; in 1980, an unnamed patient in Boulder, Colorado, underwent eye surgery; and in 1986, David Pokotylo of the Museum of Anthropology at the University of British Columbia underwent reconstructive surgery on his hand. What these operations had in common was that the scalpels used were not of surgical steel. Instead, they were made of obsidian (a naturally occurring volcanic "glass") by the same technique used by Upper Paleolithic people to make blades. In all three cases, the scalpels were handmade by archaeologists who specialized in the study of ancient stone tool technology: Crabtree himself, Payson Sheets at the University of Colorado, and Pokotylo with his colleague Len McFarlane (who hafted the blades) of the Museum of Anthropology.

The reason for the use of scalpels modeled on ancient stone tools, rather than modern steel, or even diamond scalpels, is because the obsidian is superior in almost every way: It is 210 to 1050 times sharper than surgical steel, 100 to 500 times sharper than a razor blade, and three times sharper than a diamond blade (which costs many times more and cannot be made with more than 3mm of cutting edge). Obsidian blades are easier to cut with and do less damage in the process (under a microscope, incisions made with the sharpest steel blades show torn ragged edges and are littered with bits of displaced flesh).* As a consequence, the surgeon has better control over what she or he is doing and the incisions heal faster with less scarring and pain.

In order to develop and market obsidian scalpels, Sheets has formed a corporation in partnership with Boulder, Colorado, eye surgeon Dr. Firmon Hardenbergh. So far, they have developed a means of producing cores of uniform size from molten glass, as well as a machine to detach blades from the cores. Once this equipment is tested and refined, they hope to go into production for the surgical supply trade.

*Sheets, P. D. (1987). Dawn of a New Stone Age in eye surgery. In R. J. Sharer & W. Ashmore (Eds.), *Archaeology: Discovering our past* (p. 231). Palo Alto, CA: Mayfield.

---

method was **pressure-flaking,** in which a bone, antler, or wooden tool was used to press rather than strike off small flakes as the final step in stone tool manufacture (Fig. 10.2). The advantage of this technique was that the toolmaker had greater control over the final shape of the tool than is possible with percussion-flaking. The so-called Solutrean laurel leaf blades found in Spain and France are examples of this technique. The longest of these blades is 13 inches long and only about a quarter of an inch thick. Pressure-flaking also provided great precision in retouching cutting edges for extra sharpness.

Another common Upper Paleolithic tool was the **burin,** although it, too, was invented earlier, in the Middle Paleolithic. These implements, with their chisel-like edges, facilitated the working of bone, horn, antler, and ivory into such useful things as fishhooks, harpoons, and eyed needles, all of

Figure 10.2   Two methods used for pressure flaking.

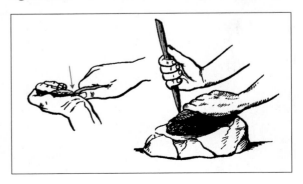

Pressure-flaking: A technique of stone tool manufacture in which a bone, antler, or wooden tool is used to press, rather than strike off, small flakes from a piece of flint or similar stone.

Burins: Stone tools with chisel-like edges used for working bone and antler

Shown here is one of the "Solutrean laurel leaf" bifaces from Europe. Such fine flint work requires a high degree of skill.

which made life easier for *H. sapiens*, especially in northern regions. The spear-thrower also appeared at the time. Spear-throwers are wooden devices, one end of which is gripped in the hunter's hand, while the other end has a hole or hook in or against which the end of the spear is placed (see Fig. 10.3, lower right). It is held so as to effectively extend the length of the hunter's arm, thereby increasing the velocity of the spear when thrown. The spear and spear-thrower when used together make for more efficient hunting than does the use of the spear alone. With handheld spears, hunters had to get close to their quarry to make the kill, and since many of the animals they hunted were quite large and fierce, this was a dangerous business. The need to approach closely, and the improbability of an instant kill, exposed the spear hunter to considerable risk. But with the spear-thrower, the effective killing distance was increased; experiments indicate that the effective killing distance of a spear when used with a spear-thrower is between 18 and 27 meters.[1]

A further improvement of hunting techniques came with the invention of the bow and arrow,

which appeared first in Africa, but not until the end of the Upper Paleolithic in Europe. The greatest advantage of the bow is that it increases the distance between hunter and prey; beyond 18 to 27 meters, the accuracy and penetration of a spear thrown with a spear-thrower is quite poor, whereas even a poor bow will shoot an arrow farther, with greater accuracy and penetrating power. A good bow is effective even at 91 meters. Thus, hunters were able to maintain a safe distance between themselves and dangerous prey, dramatically decreasing their chances of being seriously injured by an animal fighting for its life.

These changes in hunting weaponry had important consequences for human biology. Spear hunting, particularly where large, fierce animals are the prey as they were in Upper Paleolithic Europe, demands strength, power, and overall robusticity on the part of the hunter. Without them, the hunter is poorly equipped to withstand the rigors of close-quarter killing. A high nutritional price must be paid however, for large, powerful, and robust bodies, but in severe cold climates such as that of Upper Paleolithic Europe, adequate nutritional resources cannot always be relied upon. Thus it is not surprising that when Europeans at the end of the Upper Paleolithic began to use bows and arrows to hunt game that was at the same time somewhat

[1]Frayer, D. W. (1981). Body size, weapon use, and natural selection in the European Upper Paleolithic and Mesolithic. *American Anthropologist, 83,* 58.

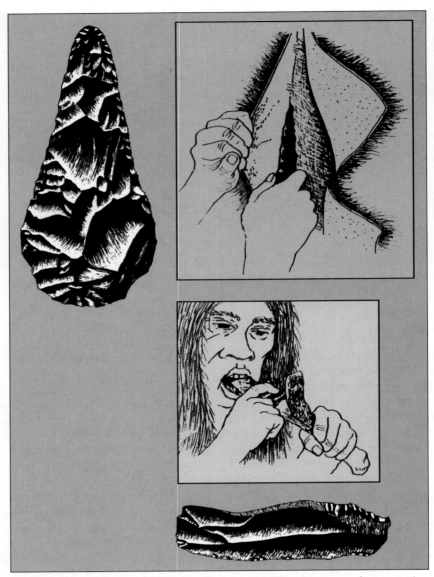

Figure 10.3 This figure, which continues on the following pages, shows a variety of tools commonly found in Upper Paleolithic tool kits, along with an artist's reconstruction of the way they were used.

smaller and less aggressive, the men underwent a further reduction in body size and robusticity. With the personal danger to the hunters reduced, natural selection favored reduced body size as a form of nutritional conservation.[2]

The invention of the bow did more than just improve hunting techniques. Long before anyone

²Ibid.

thought of beating swords into plowshares, some genius discovered that bows could be used not just for killing, but to make music as well. Just when and where this discovery was made we do not know, but we do know that there was music in the lives of Upper Paleolithic peoples, for bone flutes and whistles as much as 30,000 years old have been found. We also know that the musical bow is the oldest of all the stringed instruments, and its

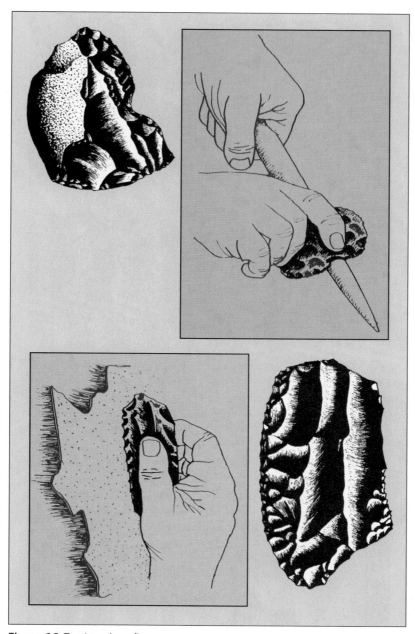

Figure 10.3   (continued)

invention ultimately made possible the development of all of the stringed instruments with which
we are familiar today.

Upper Paleolithic peoples not only had better tools but also a greater diversity of types than
earlier peoples. The highly developed Upper
Paleolithic kit included tools for use during dif-

ferent seasons, and regional variation in tool kits
was greater than ever before (see Fig. 10.3 for
some examples of Upper Paleolithic tools). Thus,
it is really impossible to speak of an Upper
Paleolithic culture, even in a relatively small pe-
ripheral region like Europe; instead, one must
make note of the many different traditions that

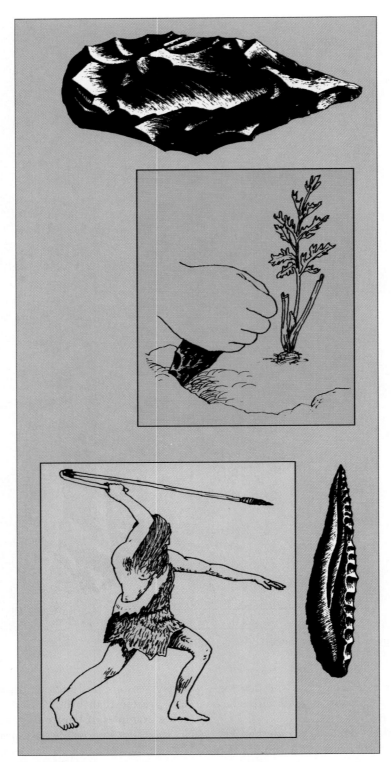

Figure 10.3   (continued)

made it possible for people to adapt ever more specifically to the various environments in which they were living. Just how proficient (and even wasteful) people had become at securing a livelihood is indicated by boneyards containing thousands of skeletons. At Solutré in France, for example, Upper Paleolithic hunters killed 10,000 horses; at Predmost in the Czech Republic, they were responsible for the deaths of 1000 mammoths. The favored game of European hunters, however, was reindeer, which they killed in even greater numbers.

Upper Paleolithic Art

Although the creativity of Upper Paleolithic peoples is evident in the tools and weapons they made, it is nowhere more evident than in their outburst of artistic expression. But just as many of the distinctive tools that were commonly used in Upper Paleolithic times first appear in the Middle Paleolithic, so too does art. In Africa, for example, the earliest figurative pictures are associated with Middle Paleolithic materials in a cave in Namibia. Both engravings and paintings are known from many rock shelters and outcrops in southern Africa, where they continued to be made by Bushman peoples up until about 100 years ago. Scenes shown feature both humans and animals, depicted with extraordinary skill, often in association with geometric and other abstract motifs.

Because this rock art tradition continued unbroken into historic times, it has been possible to discover what this art means. There is a close connection between the art and shamanism, and many scenes depict visions seen in a state of trance. Distortions in the art, usually of human figures, represent sensations felt by individuals in a state of trance, while the geometric designs depict illusions that originate in the central nervous system in

In South Africa, rock art, like these engravings and paintings from Namibia, depict things seen by dancers while in states of trance. The beginnings of this art predate the famous cave paintings of Europe.

altered states of consciousness. These **entoptic phenomena** are luminous grids, dots, zigzags, and other designs that seem to shimmer, pulsate, rotate, and expand, and are seen as one enters a state of trance (sufferers of migraines experience similar hallucinations). The animals depicted in this art, often with startling realism, are not the ones most often eaten. Rather, they are powerful beasts like the eland, and this power is important to shamans—individuals skilled at manipulating supernatural powers and spirits for human benefit—who try to harness it for their rainmaking and other rituals.

Rock art in Australia, too, goes back at least 45,000 years, with the earliest examples consisting entirely of entoptic motifs. But the Upper Paleolithic art that is most famous—largely because most students of prehistoric art are themselves of European background—is that of Europe. The earliest of this art took the form of sculpture and engravings often portraying such animals as reindeer, horses, bears, and ibexes, but there are also numerous portrayals of voluptuous women with exaggerated sexual and reproductive characteristics. Many appear to be pregnant, and some are shown in birthing postures. These so-called Venus figures have been found at sites from southwestern France to as far east as Siberia. Made of stone, ivory, antler, or baked clay, they differ little in style from place to place, testifying to the sharing

Entoptic phenomena: Bright pulsating geometric forms that are generated by the central nervous system and "seen" in states of trance.

Upper Paleolithic art was quite varied: a carved antler spear-thrower ornamented by two headless ibexes (from Enlene Cave, France); a female Venus figurine of yellow steatite (from a cave at Liguria, Italy); and one of the sandstone lamps by which artists worked in caves (from Lascaux Cave, France).

of ideas over vast distances. Although some have interpreted the Venuses as objects associated with a fertility cult, others suggest that they may have been exchanged to cement alliances between groups.

Most spectacular are the paintings on the walls of 200 or so caves in southern France and northern Spain, the oldest of which date from about 30,000 years ago. Most common are visually accurate portrayals of Ice Age mammals, including bison, bulls, horses, mammoths, and stags, often painted one on top of another. Although well represented in other media, humans are not commonly portrayed in cave paintings, nor are scenes or depictions of events at all common. Instead, the animals are usually abstracted from nature and rendered two-dimensionally without regard to the confirmations of the surfaces they are on—no small achievement for these early "artists." Sometimes,

though, the artists made use of bulges and other features of the rock to impart a more three-dimensional feeling. Often, the paintings are in hard-to-get-at places, while suitable surfaces in more accessible places remain untouched. In some caves, the lamps by which the artists worked have been found; these are spoon-shaped objects of sandstone in which animal fat was burned. Experimentation has shown that such lamps would have provided adequate illumination over several hours.

The techniques used by Upper Paleolithic peoples to create their cave paintings have recently been unraveled through the experimental work of Michel Lorblanchet. Interestingly, they turn out to be the same ones used by native rock painters in Australia. Lorblanchet's experiments are described in the following Original Study by science writer Roger Lewin.

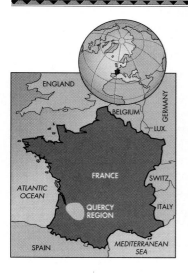

Original Study
Paleolithic Paint Job[3]

Lorblanchet's recent bid to re-create one of the most important Ice Age images in Europe was an affair of the heart as much as the head. "I tried to abandon my skin of a modern citizen, tried to experience the feeling of the artist, to enter the dialogue between the rock and the man," he explains. Every day for a week in the fall of 1990 he drove the 20 miles from his home in the medieval village of Cajarc into the hills above the river Lot. There, in a small, practically inaccessible cave, he transformed himself into an Upper Paleolithic painter. And not just any Upper Paleolithic painter, but the one who 18,400 years ago crafted the dotted horses inside the famous cave of Pech Merle.

You can still see the original horses in Pech Merle's vast underground geologic splendor. You enter through a narrow passageway and soon find yourself gazing across a grand cavern to where the painting seems to hang in the gloom. "Outside, the landscape is very different from the one the Upper Paleolithic people saw," says Lorblanchet. "But in here, the landscape is the same as it was more than 18,000 years ago. You see what the Upper Paleolithic people experienced." No matter where you look in this cavern, the eye is drawn back to the panel of horses.

The two horses face away from each other, rumps slightly overlapping, their outlines sketched in black. The animal on the right seems to come alive as it merges with a crook in the edge of the panel, the perfect natural shape for a horse's head. But the impression of naturalism quickly fades as the eye falls on the painting's dark dots. There are more than 200 of them,

This spotted horse in the French cave of Pech Merle was painted by an Upper Paleolithic artist.

deliberately distributed within and below the bodies and arcing around the right-hand horse's head and mane. More cryptic still are a smattering of red dots and half-circles and the floating outline of a fish. The surrealism is completed by six disembodied human hands stenciled above and below the animals.

Lorblanchet began thinking about re-creating the horses after a research trip to Australia over a decade ago. Not only is Australia a treasure trove of rock art, but its aboriginal people are still creating it. "In Queensland I learned how people painted by spitting pigment onto the rock," he recalls. "They spat paint and used their hand, a piece of cloth, or a feather as a screen to create different lines and other effects. Elsewhere in Australia people used chewed twigs as paintbrushes, but in Queensland the spitting technique worked best." The rock surfaces there were too uneven for extensive brushwork, he adds—just as they are in Quercy.

When Lorblanchet returned home he looked at the Quercy paintings with a new eye. Sure enough, he began seeing the telltale signs of spit-painting—lines with edges that were sharply demarcated on one side and fuzzy on the other, as if they had been airbrushed—instead of the brushstrokes he and others had assumed were there. Could you produce lines that were crisp on both edges with the same technique, he wondered, and perhaps dots too? Archeologists had long recognized that hand stencils, which are common in prehistoric art, were produced by spitting paint around a hand held to the wall. But no one had thought that entire animal images could be created this way. Before he could test his ideas, however, Lorblanchet had to find a suitable rock face—the original horses were painted on a roughly vertical panel 13 feet across and 6 feet high. With the help of a speleologist, he eventually found a rock face in a remote cave high in the hills and set to work.

Following the aboriginal practices he had witnessed, Lorblanchet first made a light outline sketch of the horses with a charred stick. Then he prepared black pigment for the painting. "My intention had been to use manganese dioxide, as the Pech Merle painter did," says Lorblanchet, referring to one of the minerals ground up for paint by the early artists. "But I was advised that manganese is somewhat toxic, so I used wood charcoal instead." (Charcoal was used as pigment by Paleolithic painters in other caves, so Lorblanchet felt he could justify his concession to safety.) To turn the charcoal into paint, Lorblanchet ground it with a limestone block, put the powder in his mouth, and diluted it to the right consistency with saliva and water. For red pigment he used ocher from the local iron-rich clay.

He started with the dark mane of the right-hand horse. "I spat a series of dots and fused them together to represent tufts of hair," he says, unself-consciously reproducing the spitting action as he talks. "Then I painted the horse's back by blowing the pigment below my hand held so"—he holds his hand flat against the rock with his thumb tucked in to form a straight line—"and used it like a stencil to produce a sharp upper edge and a diffused lower edge. You get an illusion of the animal's rounded flank this way."

He experimented as he went. "You see the angular rump?" he says, pointing to the original painting. "I reproduced that by holding my hand perpendicular to the rock, with my palm slightly bent, and I spat along the edge formed by my hand and the rock." He found he could produce sharp lines, such as those in the tail and in the upper hind leg, by spitting into the gap between parallel hands. The belly demanded more ingenuity; he spat paint into a V-shape formed by his two splayed hands, rubbed it into a curved swath to shape the belly's outline, then finger-painted short protruding lines to suggest the animals' shaggy hair. Neatly outlined dots, he found, could not be made by blowing a thin jet of charcoal onto the wall. He had to spit pigment through a hole made in an animal skin. "I spent seven hours a day for a week," he says. "Puff . . . puff . . . puff. . . . It was exhausting, particularly because there was carbon monoxide in the cave. But you experience something special, painting like that. You feel you are breathing the image onto the rock—projecting your spirit from the deepest part of your body onto the rock surface."

Was that what the Paleolithic painter felt when creating this image? "Yes, I know it doesn't sound very scientific," Lorblanchet says of his highly personal style of investigation, "but the intellectual games of the structuralists haven't got us very far, have they? Studying rock art shouldn't be an intellectual game. It is about understanding humanity. That's why I believe the experimental approach is valid in this case."

[3]Lewin, R. (1993). Paleolithic paint job. *Discover, 14* (7), 67–69.

Hypotheses to account for the early European cave art are difficult because they so often depend on conjectural and subjective interpretations. Some have argued that it is art for art's sake, but if that is so, why were animals so often painted over one another, and why were they so often placed in inaccessible places? The latter might suggest that they were for ceremonial purposes and that the caves served as religious sanctuaries. One suggestion is that the animals were drawn to ensure success in the hunt, another that their depiction was seen as a way to promote fertility and increase the size of the herds on which humans depended. Some support for this comes from a major reassessment of the art of Altimira Cave in northern Spain. Here, the art shows a pervasive concern for the sexual reproduction of the bison.[4] In cave art generally, though, the animals painted bear little relationship to those most frequently hunted. Furthermore, there are few depictions of animals being hunted or killed, nor are there depictions of animals copulating or with exaggerated sexual parts as there are in the Venus figures. Another suggestion is that rites by which youngsters were initiated into adulthood took place in the painted galleries. In support of

[4]Halverson, J. (1989). Review of *Altimira revisited and other essays on early art. American Antiquity, 54,* 883.

this idea, footprints, most of which are small, have been found in the clay floors of several caves, and in one, they even circle a modeled clay bison. The animals painted, so this argument goes, may have had to do with knowledge being transmitted from the elders to the youths. Furthermore, the transmission of information might be implied by countless so-called signs, apparently abstract designs that accompany much Upper Paleolithic art. Some have interpreted these as tallies of animals killed, or a reckoning of time according to a lunar calendar.

These abstract designs, including ones such as the spots on the Pech Merle horses, suggest yet another possibility. For the most part, these are just like the entoptic designs seen by subjects in experiments dealing with altered states of consciousness, and which are so consistently present in the rock art of southern Africa. Furthermore, the rock art of southern Africa shows the same painting of new images over older ones, as well as the same sort of fixation on large, powerful animals, as opposed to the ones most often eaten. Thus, the cave art of Europe may well represent the same depictions of trance experiences, painted after the fact. Consistent with this, the caves themselves are conducive to the sort of sensory distortion that can induce trance.

Artistic expression, whatever its purpose may have been, was not confined to rock surfaces and

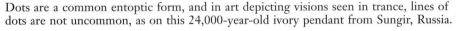

Dots are a common entoptic form, and in art depicting visions seen in trance, lines of dots are not uncommon, as on this 24,000-year-old ivory pendant from Sungir, Russia.

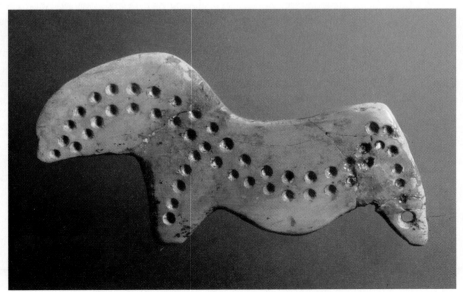

portable objects alone. Upper Paleolithic peoples also ornamented their bodies, with necklaces of perforated animal teeth, shells, beads of bone, stone, and ivory; rings; bracelets; and anklets. Clothing, too, was adorned with beads. This should alert us to the probability that quite a lot of art was executed in perishable materials—wood carving, paintings on bark or animal skins, and the like. Thus, the rarity or absence of Upper Paleolithic art in some parts of the inhabited world may be more apparent than real, as people elsewhere worked with materials unlikely to survive so long in the archeological record.

Other Aspects of Upper Paleolithic Culture

Upper Paleolithic peoples lived not only in caves and rock shelters, but also in structures built out in the open. In the Ukraine, for example, the remains have been found of sizeable settlements, in which huts were built on frameworks of intricately stacked mammoth bones. Where the ground was frozen, cobblestones were heated and placed in the earth to

sink in, thereby providing sturdy, dry floors. Their hearths, no longer shallow depressions or flat surfaces that radiated back little heat, were instead stone-lined pits that conserved heat for extended periods and made for more efficient cooking. For the outdoors, they had the same sort of tailored clothing worn in historical times by the natives of Siberia, Alaska, and Canada. And they engaged in long-distance trade, as indicated, for example, by the presence of sea shells and Baltic amber at sites several hundred kilometers from the sources of these materials. Although Middle Paleolithic peoples made use of rare and distant materials, they did not do so with the regularity seen in the Upper Paleolithic.

The Spread of Upper Paleolithic Peoples

Such was the effectiveness of their cultures that Upper Paleolithic peoples were able to expand into regions previously uninhabited by their archaic forebears. Colonization of Siberia began about 42,000 years ago, although it took something like 10,000 years before they reached the northeastern part of that region. Much earlier, by 60,000 years ago,

Reconstruction of an Upper Paleolithic hut with walls of interlocked mammoth mandibles.

people managed to get to Australia and New Guinea. To do this, they had to use some kind of watercraft to make the difficult crossing of at least 90 kilometers of water that separated Australia and New Guinea (then a single land mass) from the Asian continent throughout Paleolithic times. Once in Australia, these people created some of the world's earliest sophisticated rock art some 10,000 to 15,000 years earlier than the more famous European cave paintings. Other evidence for sophisticated ritual activity in early Australia is provided by 26,000-year-old cremation burials associated with red ocher. It may be that this pigment had more than symbolic value; for example, its iron salts have antiseptic and deodorizing properties, and there are recorded instances in which red ocher is associated with prolonging life and is used medicinally to treat particular conditions or infections. One historically known native Australian society is reported to use ocher to heal wounds, scars, and burns, and a person with internal pain is covered with the substance and placed in the sun to promote sweating. What is especially interesting in view of the impressive accomplishments of native Australians is that the tools used by these people are remarkably similar to those of the Eurasian Middle Paleolithic. Clearly, simplicity of tool kits does not bespeak absence of sophisticated intellectual capabilities.

To get to the Americas, voyages of the sort undertaken by the first Australians were not neces-sary. With much of the world's water supply taken up by the great continental glaciers, there was a worldwide lowering of sea levels, causing an emergence of land joining Siberia to Alaska. With expanding populations in Asia, brought about by increasingly effective cultural adaptations, it was only a matter of time before human populations began to spread gradually eastward over this dry land. The precise timing of their first arrival is still debated, but securely dated remains from Meadowcraft Rockshelter in southwestern Pennsylvania indicate that populations had spread as far as the eastern United States by 15,000 years ago, if not earlier. Moreover, people seem to have gotten as far south as central Chile, where remains of huts have been found at Monte Verde and reliably dated to about 13,000 years ago.

Although the earliest technologies in the Americas remain poorly known, they gave rise in North America, about 12,000 years ago, to the distinctive fluted spear points of **Paleoindian** hunters of big game, such as mammoths, caribou, and now

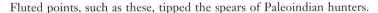

Paleoindian: Inhabitants of North America around 12,000 years ago, who hunted big game such as mammoths with spears tipped with distinctive fluted points.

Fluted points, such as these, tipped the spears of Paleoindian hunters.

extinct forms of bison. Fluted points are finely made, with large channel flakes removed from one or both surfaces. They are found from the Atlantic seaboard to the Pacific coast, and from Alaska down into Panama. So efficient were the hunters who made these points that they may have hastened the extinction of the mammoth and other large Pleistocene mammals. By driving large numbers of animals over cliffs, they killed many more than they could possibly use, thus wasting huge amounts of meat.

Where Did Upper Paleolithic Peoples Come From?

As noted in Chapter 9, we cannot be certain whether the transition from archaic to anatomically modern *H. sapiens* took place in one specific population or was the result of in situ evolution on the part of populations living in Africa and Asia between 100,000 and 40,000 years ago. At the moment, though, the odds seem to favor the latter hypothesis. Even in Europe, where the argument

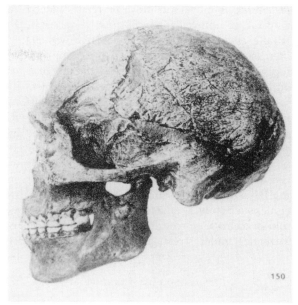

The bulging area on the back of this Upper Paleolithic skull from Predmostí in the Czech Republic, along with its still prominent brow ridges, are reminiscent of the earlier Neandertals.

Paleoindians, like their Upper Paleolithic contemporaries in Eurasia, were such accomplished hunters that they, too, could kill more animals than could possibly be used at one time. These bones are the remains of some 200 bison that Paleoindian hunters stampeded over a cliff 8500 years ago.

for replacement of archaic by modern *sapiens* has been most strongly made, the most recent Neandertals display modern features, whereas the most ancient moderns show what appear to be Neandertal holdovers. For example, the Saint Césaire skull has the high forehead and chin of moderns. Similarly, a late Neandertal from Vindija, northern Croatia, shows a thinning of brow ridges towards their outer margins. Conversely, anatomically modern skulls from Brno, Mladec, and Predmosti, in the Czech Republic, retain heavy brow ridges and Neandertal-like muscle attachments on their backs.[5] Of course, these features could all be the result of interbreeding between two populations that overlapped in time, rather than simple evolution from one into the other. They do not, however, fit with the idea of the complete extinction of the older population.

Looking at the larger picture, what we see in all regions of the Old World, since the time of

[5]Bednarik, R. G. (1995). Concept-mediated marking in the Lower Paleolithic. *Current Anthropology, 36,* 627; Minugh-Purvis, N. (1992). The inhabitants of Ice Age Europe. *Expedition, 34* (3), 33–34.

H. erectus, is more and more emphasis placed on cultural, as opposed to biological, adaptation. To handle environmental stress, reliance was placed increasingly on the development of appropriate tools, clothes, shelter, use of fire, and so forth, as opposed to alteration of the human organism itself. This was true whether human populations lived in hot or cold, wet or dry, forest or grassland areas. Since culture is learned and not carried by genes, it is ultimately based on what might loosely be called "brain power" or, more formally, **cognitive capacity.** While this includes intelligence, in the IQ sense, it is broader than that, for it also includes such skills as educability, concept formation, self-awareness, self-evaluation, reliability of performance under stress, attention span, sensitivity

Cognitive capacity: A broad concept including intelligence, educability, concept formation, self-awareness, self-evaluation, attention span, sensitivity in discrimination, and creativity.

in discrimination, and creativity.

The major thrust in the evolution of the genus *Homo*, then, has been toward improved cognitive capacity through the evolution of the brain regardless of the environmental and climatic differences between the regions in which populations of the genus lived. Hence, there has been a certain similarity of selective pressures in all regions. In addition, this evolution of all populations of the genus *Homo* would have been helped along by a certain amount of gene flow between populations. In an evolving species, genes having survival value anywhere tend to spread from one population to another. In the case of the human species, these would be whatever genes happen to relate to cognitive capacity.

It is impossible to know just how much gene flow took place between ancient human populations, but that some took place is consistent with the sudden appearance of novel traits in one region later than their appearance elsewhere. For example, Upper Paleolithic remains from North Africa exhibit the kind of midfacial flatness previously seen only in East Asian fossils; similarly, various Cro-Magnon fossils from Europe show

These Upper Paleolithic skulls from China (left) and Africa (right) are easily derivable from earlier archaic *sapiens* skulls in the same regions.

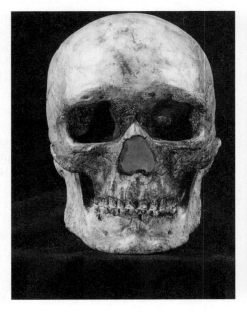
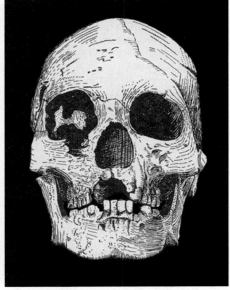

the short upper jaws, horizontally oriented cheek bones, and rectangular eye orbits previously seen in East Asians. Conversely, the round orbits, large frontal sinuses, and thin cranial bones seen in some archaic *sapiens* skulls from China represent the first appearance there of traits that have greater antiquity in the West.[6] What appears to be happening, then, is that genes from the East are being introduced into Western gene pools and vice versa. Not only is such gene flow consistent with the remarkable tendency historically known humans have to "swap genes" between populations, even in the face of cultural barriers to gene flow, it is also consistent with the tendency of other primates to produce hybrids when two subspecies (and sometimes even species) come into contact.[7] Moreover, without such gene flow multiregional evolution inevitably would have resulted in the appearance of multiple species of modern humans, something that clearly has *not* happened. In fact, the low level of genetic differentiation among modern humans can be explained easily as a consequence of high levels of gene flow.[8]

THE MESOLITHIC ERA

By 12,000 years ago, glacial conditions in the world were moderating, causing changes in human habitats. Throughout the world, sea levels were on the rise, ultimately flooding many areas that had been above sea level during periods of glaciation, such as the Bering Strait, parts of the North Sea, and an extensive area that had joined Indonesia to Southeast Asia. In northern regions, milder climates brought about marked changes as tundras were ultimately replaced by hardwood forests. In the process, the herd animals upon which northern Paleolithic peoples had depended for food, clothing, and shelter disappeared from

many areas. Some, like the reindeer and musk ox, moved to colder climates; others, like the mammoths, died out completely. Thus, the northerners especially were forced to adapt to new conditions. In the new forests, animals were more solitary in their habits and so not as easy to hunt as they had been, and large, cooperative hunts were no longer productive. However, plant food was more abundant than before, and there were new and abundant sources of fish and other food around lake shores, bays, and rivers. Hence, human populations developed new and ingenious ways to catch and kill animals, while at the same time they devoted more energy to fishing and the collection of wild plant foods. This new way of life marks the end of the Paleolithic and the start of the **Mesolithic,** or **Middle Stone Age.** In a sense, it marks a return to more typical hominine subsistence patterns.

Mesolithic Tools and Weapons

New technologies were developed for the changed postglacial environment (Fig. 10.4). Ground stone tools, shaped and sharpened by grinding the tool against sandstone (often using sand as an additional abrasive), made effective axes and adzes. Such implements, though they do take longer to make, are less prone to breakage, given heavy-duty usage, than are those made of chipped stone. Thus, they were helpful in clearing forest areas and in the woodwork needed for the creation of dugout canoes and skin-covered boats. Although some kind of water craft had been developed early enough to get humans to Australia by 60,000 years ago, boats become prominent only in Mesolithic sites, indicating that human foraging for food frequently took place on the water as well as the land. Thus, it was possible to make use of deep water resources as well as those of coastal areas.

Mesolithic, or **Middle Stone Age:** Began about 12,000 years ago.

---

[6]Pope, G. C. (1992). Craniofacial evidence for the origin of modern humans in China. *Yearbook of Physical Anthropology, 35,* 287–288.

[7]Simons, E. L. (1989). Human origins. *Science, 245,* 1349.

[8]Relethford, J. H., & Harpending, H. C. (1994). Craniometric variation, genetic theory, and modern human origins. *American Journal of Physical Anthropology, 95,* 265.

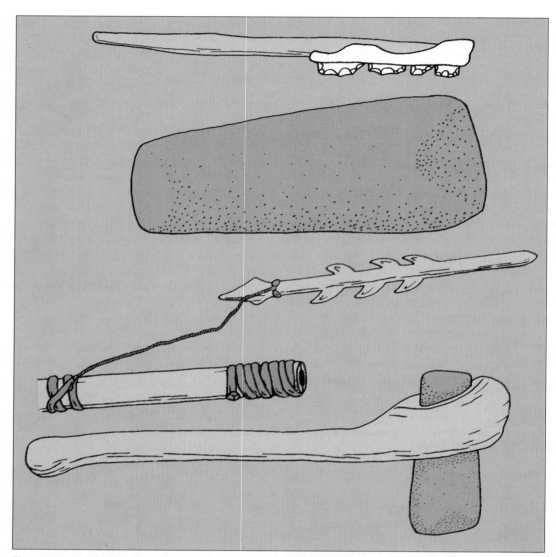

Figure 10.4   The drawing above shows a Mesolithic tool consisting of a wooden or bone handle with microliths set into it. Below is a bone tool of a somewhat earlier date, fitted out for service as a harpoon. The ground stone ax at the bottom has a smooth stone blade set in a wooden handle that gives increased leverage.

The characteristic Mesolithic tool was the **microlith,** a small but hard, sharp blade. Although a microlithic tradition existed in Zaire by about 40,000 years ago,[9] such tools did not become com-

Microlith: A small flint blade widespread in the Mesolithic, several of which were hafted together in wooden handles to make tools.

[9]Bednarik, p. 606.

mon elsewhere until the Mesolithic. Microliths could be mass-produced because they were small, easy to make, and could be of materials other than flint. Also, they could be attached to arrow shafts by using melted resin as a binder. Thus, the bow and arrow with the microlith arrowhead became the deadliest and most common weapon of the Mesolithic.

The reliance of Mesolithic peoples on microliths provided them with an important advantage over their Upper Paleolithic forebearers: The small size of the microlith enabled them to devise a wider array of composite tools made out of stone and wood or bone (see Fig. 10.4, top). Thus, they could make sickles, harpoons, arrows, and daggers by fitting microliths into grooves in wood or bone handles. Later experimentation with these forms led to more sophisticated tools and weapons.

It is possible that the Mesolithic was a more sedentary period for humans than earlier eras. Dwellings from this period seem more substantial, an indication of permanency. Indeed, this is a logical development: Most hunting cultures, and especially those depending on herd animals, are nomadic. To be successful, one must follow the game. This is not necessary for peoples subsisting on a diet of seafood and plants, as the location of shore and vegetation remains relatively constant.

Cultural Diversity in the Mesolithic

In the warmer parts of the world, the collection of wild plant foods had been more of an equal partner in subsistence activities in the Upper Paleolithic than had been the case in the colder north. Hence, in areas like Southwest Asia, the Mesolithic represents less of a changed way of life than was true in Europe. Here, the important **Natufian culture** flourished.

Natufian culture: A Mesolithic culture of Israel, Lebanon, and western Syria, between about 12,500 and 10,200 years ago.

The Natufians were a people who lived between 12,500 and 10,200 years ago at the eastern end of the Mediterranean Sea in caves, rock shelters, and small villages with stone- and mud-walled houses. Nearby, their dead were buried in communal cemeteries, usually in shallow pits without grave goods or decorations. A small shrine is known from one of their villages, a 10,500-year-old settlement at Jericho. Basin-shaped depressions in the rocks found outside homes at Natufian sites are thought to have been storage pits. Plastered storage pits beneath the floors of the houses were also found, indicating that the Natufians were the earliest Mesolithic people known to have stored crops. Certain tools found among Natufian remains bear evidence that they were used to cut grain. These Mesolithic sickles, for that is what they were, consisted of small stone blades set in straight handles of wood or bone.

In the Americas, cultures comparable to Mesolithic cultures of the Old World developed, but here they are referred to as **Archaic cultures.** Outside of the Arctic, microlithic tools are not prominent in them, as they are in parts of the Old World, but ground stone tools such as axes, adzes, gouges, plummets, and spear-thrower weights are common. Archaic cultures were widespread in the Americas; one of the most dramatic was the **Maritime archaic,** which developed about 7000 years ago around the Gulf of St. Lawrence. These people developed an elaborate assortment of bone and ground slate tools with which they hunted a wide variety of sea mammals, including whales; fish, including swordfish; and sea birds. To get some of these, they regularly paddled their dugout canoes far off shore. They also developed

Archaic cultures: Term used to refer to Mesolithic cultures in the Americas.

Maritime archaic culture: An archaic culture of northeastern North America, centered on the Gulf of St. Lawrence, which emphasized the utilization of marine resources.

At Nuliak, Labrador, maritime archaic peoples lived in large, long houses with stone foundations. One such foundation is shown here before excavation.

the first elaborate burial cult in North America, involving the use of red ocher ("red paint") and the placement of finely made grave goods with the deceased.

MAJOR PALEOLITHIC AND MESOLITHIC TRENDS

Certain trends stand out from the information anthropologists have gathered about the Old and Middle Stone ages. These are general progressions that occurred from one culture to the next in most parts of the world.

One trend was toward increasingly more sophisticated, varied, and specialized tool kits. Tools became progressively lighter and smaller, resulting in the conservation of raw materials and a better ratio between length of cutting edge and weight of stone. Tools became specialized according to region and function. Instead of crude, all-purpose tools, more effective particularized devices were made to deal more effectively

with the differing conditions of savanna, forest, and shore.

This more efficient tool technology enabled human populations to increase and spill over into more diverse environments; it also was responsible for the loss of heavy physical features, favoring instead decreased size and weight of face and teeth, the development of larger and more complex brains, and ultimately a reduction in body size and robusticity. This dependence on intelligence rather than bulk provided the key for peoples' increased reliance on cultural rather than physical adaptation. As the brain became modernized, conceptual thought developed, as evidenced by symbolic artifacts and signs of magico-religious ceremonies.

By the Upper Paleolithic, the amount of sexual dimorphism, too, was greatly reduced, as size differences between men and women were relatively slight compared with what they were in *Australopithecus, Homo habilis,* or even *Homo erectus.* This has important implications for gender relations. As noted in earlier chapters, among primates marked sexual dimorphism is associated with male dominance over females. Lack of sexual dimorphism, by contrast, correlates with a lack of such dominance. In evolving humans, it appears that a loss of male dominance went hand in hand with the ever-increasing importance of cooperative relationships.

Through Paleolithic times, at least in the colder parts of the world, there appeared a trend toward the importance of and proficiency in hunting. People's intelligence enabled them to develop tools that exceeded other animals' physical equipment, as well as the improved social organization and cooperation so important for survival and population growth. This trend was reversed during the Mesolithic, when hunting lost its preeminence and the gathering of wild plants and seafood became increasingly important.

As human populations grew and spread, regionalism also became more marked. Tool assemblages developed in different ways at different times in different areas. General differences appeared between north and south, east and west. Although there are some indications of cultural contact and intercommunication, such as the development of long-distance trade in the Upper Paleolithic, regionalism was a dominant characteristic of Paleolithic and Mesolithic times. The persistence of regionalism is probably due in large part to the need to adapt to differing environments. Paleolithic peoples eventually spread over all the continents of the world, including Australia and the Americas, and as they did so, changes in climate and environment called for new kinds of adaptations. Thus Paleolithic and Mesolithic tool kits had to be altered to meet the requirements of many varying locations. In forest environments, people needed strong axes for working wood; on the open savanna and plains, they used the bow and arrow to hunt the game they could not stalk closely; the people in settlements that grew up around lakes and along rivers and coasts developed harpoons and hooks; in the subarctic regions they needed tools to work the heavy skins of seals and caribou; in the grasslands they needed tools for harvesting grain and separating the usable part from the chaff. The fact that culture is first and foremost an adaptive mechanism meant that it was of necessity a regional thing.

CHAPTER SUMMARY

The Cro-Magnons and the other anatomically modern peoples that held exclusive sway in the world after 30,000 years ago, in addition to a full-sized brain, possessed a physical appearance somewhat similar to our own. The modernization of the face of Upper Paleolithic peoples is a result of a reduction in the size of the teeth and the muscles involved in chewing as a consequence of the fact that teeth were no longer being used as tools. Similarly, bodies became somewhat less massive and robust as improved technology reduced the need for brute strength.

The emphasis in evolution of the genus *Homo* in all parts of the world has been toward increasing cognitive capacity through development of the brain. This progression took place regardless of environmental or climatic conditions under which the genus lived. In addition, evolution of the genus *Homo* undoubtedly was aided by gene flow between populations. Lack of much genetic differentiation between human populations today bespeaks high levels of gene flow between populations in the past.

Upper Paleolithic cultures evolved out of the Middle Paleolithic cultures of Africa and Asia. The typical Upper Paleolithic tool was the blade. The blade technique of toolmaking saved much more flint than Middle Paleolithic methods. Other efficient Upper Paleolithic toolmaking techniques were pressure-flaking, and using chisel-like stones called burins to fashion bone, antler horn, and ivory into tools. The cultural adaptation of Upper Paleolithic peoples became specific; they developed different tools for different seasons. There is no one Upper Paleolithic culture, as different environments produced different cultures. Northern Upper Paleolithic cultures supported themselves by the hunting of large herd animals. Upper Paleolithic cultures are the earliest in which pictorial art is common.

The ending of the glacial period caused great physical changes in human habitats. Sea levels were raised, vegetation changed, and herd animals disappeared from many areas. The European Mesolithic period marked a return to more typical hominine ways of subsistence, as big game hunters returned to more of a balance between hunting and gathering. Increased reliance on seafood and plants made the Mesolithic a more sedentary period for people. Ground stone tools, including axes and adzes, answered postglacial needs for new technologies. The characteristic Mesolithic tool in the Old World was made with microliths, small, hard, sharp flint blades that could be mass-produced and hafted with others to produce implements like sickles. Widespread reliance on the bow and arrow to hunt generally smaller, less aggressive animals resulted in a reduction of the size and robusticity of men, at least in Europe.

Three trends emerged from the Paleolithic and Mesolithic periods. First was a trend toward more sophisticated, varied, and specialized tool kits. This trend enabled people to increase their population and spread to new environments. It also was adaptive, leading to decreased size and weight of face and teeth, the development of larger, more complex brains, and ultimately a reduction in body size, mass, and degree of sexual dimorphism. Second was a trend toward the importance of and proficiency in hunting. The importance of hunting was somewhat reversed during the Mesolithic period, as the hunting of large game became less important than smaller game and the gathering of plants and seafood. Third was a trend toward regionalism, as people's technology and life habits increasingly reflected their association with a particular environment.

SUGGESTED READINGS

Campbell, B. G., & Loy, J. D. (1995). *Humankind emerging* (7th ed.). New York: HarperCollins.

Adapted in part from Time-Life's *Emergence of Man* and *Life Nature Library*, this is a richly illustrated, up-to-date account of the Paleolithic. In it, Campbell integrates paleontological and archaeological data with ethnographic data on modern food foragers to present a rich picture of evolving Paleolithic ways of life.

Pfeiffer, J. E. (1985). *The creative explosion*. Ithaca, NY: Cornell University Press.

A fascinating and readable discussion of the origins of art and religion. Its main drawback is its focus on European art.

Prideaux, T. et al. (1973). *Cro-Magnon man*. New York: Time-Life.

This beautifully illustrated volume in the *Time-Life Emergence of Man* series covers the period between 40,000 and 10,000 years ago. A whole chapter is devoted to "The Subtle Mind of Cro-Magnon."

IV

Human Biological and Cultural Evolution Since the Old Stone Age

In the Upper Paleolithic, by 30,000 years ago, anatomically modern varieties of humans, with cultures comparable to those known for recent food-foraging peoples, had sole possession of the inhabited parts of the world. The story of human evolution in the Paleolithic is one of a close interrelation between developing culture and developing humanity. The critical importance of culture as the human adaptive mechanism seems to have imposed selective pressures favoring a better brain, and a better brain, in turn, made possible improved cultural adaptation. Indeed, it seems fair to say that modern humans look the way they do today because cultural adaptation came to play such an important role in the survival of our ancient ancestors. Because cultural adaptation worked so well, human populations were able to grow, probably rather slowly, with a consequent expansion into previously uninhabited parts of the world. And this, too, affected cultural adaptation, as adjustments were made to meet new conditions.

Although food foraging served humans well for hundreds of thousands of years in the Paleolithic, far-reaching changes began to take place in some parts of the world as much as 11,000 years ago. This second major cultural revolution consisted of the emergence of food production, the subject of Chapter 11. Eventually, most of the world's people became food producers, even though food foraging remained a satisfactory way of life for some. At the present time, no more than a quarter of a million people—less than 0.0005 percent of a world population of more than 5 billion—remain food foragers. Just as the emergence of food foraging was followed by modifications and improvements leading to regional variants of this pattern, so the advent of food production opened the way for new cultural variants based upon it. Chapter 12 discusses the result: further cultural diversity, out of which developed civilization, the basis of modern life.

In spite of the increasing effectiveness of culture as the primary mechanism by which humans adapt to diverse environments, our species has continued to evolve biologically. In the course of their movement into other parts of the world, humans had already developed considerable biological variation from one population to another. On top of this, populations of food producers were exposed to selective pressures of a different sort than those affecting food foragers, thereby inducing further changes in human gene pools. Such changes continue to affect the human species today, even though it remains the same species now as it was at the end of the Paleolithic. Chapter 13 discusses how the variation to be seen in *Homo sapiens* today came into existence as the result of forces acting to alter the frequencies of alleles in human gene pools and why such variation probably has nothing to do with intelligence. The chapter concludes with a look at forces apparently active today to produce further changes in those same gene pools.

CHAPTER
11
CULTIVATION AND DOMESTICATION

BEGINNING ABOUT 11,000 YEARS AGO, SOME OF THE WORLD'S PEOPLE EMBARKED ON A NEW WAY OF LIFE BASED ON FOOD PRODUCTION. THIS INCLUDED NEW ATTITUDES TOWARD THE EARTH AND FORCES OF NATURE, REFLECTED IN MONUMENTAL CONSTRUCTION. ONE OF THESE STRUCTURES IS STONEHENGE, THE FAMOUS CEREMONIAL AND ASTRONOMICAL CENTER IN ENGLAND, WHICH DATES BACK TO ABOUT 2500 B.C.

CHAPTER PREVIEW

When and Where Did the Change from Food Foraging to Food Production Begin?

Centers of early plant and animal domestication exist in Africa, China, Mesoamerica, North and South America, as well as Southwest and Southeast Asia. From these places, food production spread to most other parts of the world. It began at different times in these different places; for example, it began about 10,300 years ago in Southwest Asia, but sometime after 8800 but before 5000 years ago in Southeast Asia.

Why Did the Change Take Place?

Since food production by and large requires more work than hunting and gathering, is not necessarily a more secure means of subsistence, and because it requires people to eat more of the foods that food foragers eat only when they have no other choice, it can be assumed that people probably did not become food producers through choice. Of various theories that have been proposed, the most likely is that food production came about as a consequence of a chance convergence of separate natural events and cultural developments.

What Were the Consequences of the Change to Food Production?

Although food production generally provides less leisure time than food foraging, it does permit some reallocation of the workload. Some people can produce enough food to allow others to spend more time at other tasks, and so a number of technological developments, such as weaving and pottery making, generally accompany food production. In addition, it makes possible a more sedentary way of life in villages, with more substantial housing. Finally, the new modes of work and resource allocation require new ways of organizing people, generally into lineages, clans, and common-interest associations.

Throughout the Paleolithic, people depended exclusively on wild sources of food for their survival. In cold northern regions, they came to rely primarily on the hunting of herds of mammoth, bison, horses, and especially reindeer. Elsewhere, they hunted, fished, or gathered whatever nature provided. There is no evidence in Paleolithic remains to indicate that livestock was kept or plants cultivated. Paleolithic people followed wild herds and gathered wild plant foods, relying on their wits and muscles to acquire what nature provided. Whenever favored sources of food became scarce, as sometimes happened, people adjusted by increasing the variety of food eaten and incorporating less-favored food into their diets.

About 12,000 years ago, the subsistence practices of some people began to change in ways that were to transform radically their ways of life, although no one involved had any way of knowing it at the time. Not until these changes were well advanced could people become aware that their mode of subsistence differed from that of other cultures—that they had become farmers, rather than food foragers.[1] This change in the means of obtaining food had important implications for human development, for it meant that by taking matters into their own hands, people could become more sedentary. Moreover, by reorganizing the workload, some of them could be freed from the food quest to devote their energies to other sorts of tasks. With good reason, the **Neolithic period,** when this change took place, has been called a revolutionary one in human history. This period, and the changes that took place within it, are the subjects of this chapter.

Neolithic period: The New Stone Age, which began about 11,000 years ago in Southwest Asia.

---

[1]Rindos, D. (1984). *The origins of agriculture: An evolutionary perspective* (p. 99). Orlando: Academic Press.

In spite of all the innovations that have happened since, it remains a fact that all of the crops we rely on today were "invented" by Neolithic farmers.

THE MESOLITHIC ROOTS OF FARMING AND PASTORALISM

The Mesolithic may be viewed either as the final stage of the Paleolithic (sometimes called the Epipaleolithic) or as the beginning of the Neolithic. Fixed as having begun around 12,000 years ago, people during this period turned increasingly toward abundant food supplies to be found in the rivers, lakes, and oceans. These waterways were teeming with aquatic life because of the rising seas brought about by warmer temperatures and melting glaciers. In addition, people gathered a broad spectrum of plant foods on land and hunted a variety of birds and smaller mammals. Generally, this new way of life offered more secure supplies of food and therefore an increased margin of survival. In some parts of the world, people started living in larger and more sedentary groups, now cooperating with others outside the sphere of family or hunting band. They became settled village dwellers, and some of these settlements were shortly to expand into the first farming villages, towns, and (ultimately) cities.

THE NEOLITHIC REVOLUTION

The Neolithic, or New Stone Age, was characterized by the transition from foraging for food to dependence upon domesticated plants and animals. It was by no means a smooth or rapid transition; in fact, it spread over many centuries and was a direct outgrowth of the preceding Mesolithic. Where to draw the line between the two is not always clear.

The term *New Stone Age* is derived from the polished stone tools that are characteristic of this period. But more important than the presence of these tools is the transition from a hunting, gathering, and fishing economy to one based on food production, representing a major change in the subsistence practices of early peoples. One of the first regions to undergo this transition, and certainly the most intensively studied, was Southwest Asia. The remains of domesticated plants and animals are known from parts of Israel, Jordan, Syria, Turkey, Iraq, and Iran, all before 8000 years ago.

Domestication: What Is It?

Domestication is an evolutionary process whereby humans modify, either intentionally or unintentionally, the genetic makeup of a population of plants or animals, sometimes to the extent that members of the population are unable to survive and/or reproduce without human assistance. As such, it constitutes a special case of a kind of relationship between different species frequently seen in the natural world, as in the case of one species that has come to depend for its protection and reproductive success on some other that feeds upon it. In the case of plants, for instance, there are numerous species that rely on some type of animal—in some cases birds, in others mammals, and in yet others, insects—for protection and dispersal of their seeds. The important thing is that both parties benefit from the arrangement; reliance on animals for seed dispersal ensures that the latter will be carried farther afield than would otherwise be possible, thereby cutting down on competition for sun and nutrients between young and old plants and reducing the likelihood that any diseases or parasites harbored by one will be transmitted to the others. Added vigor is apt to come to plants that are freed from the need to provide themselves with built-in defensive mechanisms such as thorns, toxins, or chemical compounds that make them taste bad. This enhanced vigor may be translated into larger and more tasty edible parts to attract the animals that feed upon them, thereby cementing the relationship between the protected and protector.

Evidence of Early Plant Domestication

The characteristics of plants under human domestication that set them apart from their wild ancestors, and have made them attractive to those who eat them, include increased size, at least of edible

Domestication: An evolutionary process whereby humans modify, either intentionally or unintentionally, the genetic makeup of a population of plants or animals, sometimes to the extent that members of the population are unable to survive and/or reproduce without human assistance.

parts; reduction or loss of natural means of seed dispersal; reduction or loss of protective devices such as husks or distasteful chemical compounds; and loss of delayed seed germination (important to wild plants for survival in times of drought or other adverse conditions of temporary duration), along with simultaneous ripening of the seed or fruit. Many of these characteristics can be seen in plant remains from archaeological sites; thus, paleobotanists can often tell the fossil of a wild plant species from a domesticated one, for example, by studying the seed of cereal grasses, such as barley, wheat, and maize (corn). Wild cereals have a very fragile stem, whereas domesticated ones have a tough stem. Under natural conditions, plants with fragile stems scatter their seed for themselves, while those with tough stems do not. The structural change from a soft to a tough stem in early domesticated plants involves a genetic change, undoubtedly the result of what Darwin referred to as **unconscious selection:** the preservation of valued individuals and the destruction of less valued ones, with no thought as to long-range consequences.[2]

Unconscious selection: The preservation of valued representatives of a plant or animal species and the destruction of less-valued ones, with no thought as to the long-range consequences.

---

[2]Ibid., p. 86.

When the grain stalks were harvested, their soft stem would shatter at the touch of sickle or flail, and many of their seeds would be lost. Inevitably, most of the seeds that people harvested would have been taken from the tough plants. Early domesticators probably also tended to select seed from plants having few husks or none at all—eventually breeding them out—because husking prior to pounding the grains into meal or flour was much too time-consuming. Size of plants is another good indicator of the presence of domestication. For example, the large ear of corn we know today is a far cry from the tiny ears (about an inch long) characteristic of early corn. In fact, the ear of corn may have arisen as a simple gene mutation transformed male tassel spikes of the wild grass, Teosinte, into small and primitive versions of the female corn ear.[3] Small and primitive though these were (an entire ear contained less nourishment than a single kernel of modern corn), they were radically different in structure from the ears of Teosinte.

Evidence of Early Animal Domestication

Domestication also produced changes in the skeletal structure of some animals. For example, the horns of wild goats and sheep differ from those of their domesticated counterparts (domesticated female sheep have none). Another structural change that occurred

[3]Gould, S. J. (1991). *The flamingo's smile: Reflections in natural history* (p. 368). New York: Norton.

Wild wheat kernels from a site in Syria (left) are compared with those of a domestic variety grown in Greece 2000 or 3000 years later (right). Increased size of edible parts is a common feature of domestication.

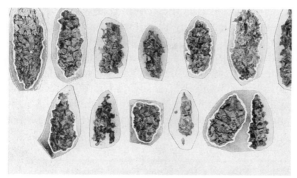

Cobs of 7000-year-old maize (corn) from the Tehuacan Valley in Mexico.

in domestication involves the size of the animal or its parts. For example, certain teeth of domesticated pigs are smaller than those of wild ones.

A study of age and sex ratios of butchered animals at a site may indicate whether or not animal domestication was practiced. Investigators have assumed that if the age and/or sex ratios at the site differ from those in wild herds, the imbalances are due to conscious selection. For example, at the site of Zawi Chemi Shanidar, in northern Iraq, about 50 percent of the sheep killed were under one year of age. Evidently, the occupants of Zawi Chemi Shanidar were slaughtering the young males for food and saving the females for breeding. Although this does not prove that the sheep were fully domesticated, such herd management does suggest a first step in the domestication process.

In Peru, the prominence of bones of newborn llamas at archaeological sites (up to 72 percent at some), dating to around 6300 years ago, is probably indicative of at least incipient domestication. Such high mortality rates for newborn animals are uncommon in wild herds, but are common where animals are penned up. Under confined conditions, a buildup of mud and filth harbors bacteria that cause diarrhea and enterotoxemia, both of which are fatal to newborn animals.

Beginnings of Domestication

Over the past 30 years, a good deal of information has accumulated about the beginnings of domestication, primarily in Southwest Asia as well as Central and South America. We still do not have all the answers about how and why it took place.

Nonetheless, some observations of general validity can be made that help us to understand how the switch to food production may have taken place.

The first of these observations is that the switch to food production was not the result of such discoveries that seeds, if planted, grow into plants. Food foragers are far from ignorant about the forces of nature and are perfectly aware of the role of seeds in plant growth, that plants grow better under certain conditions than others, and so forth. In fact, they frequently put their knowledge to work so as to manage actively the resources on which they depend. For example, Indians living in the northern part of Canada's Alberta province put to use a sophisticated knowledge of the effects of fire to create local environments of their own design. Similarly, Indians in California used fire to perpetuate oak woodland savanna, to promote hunting and the collection of acorns. And in northern Australia, runoff channels of creeks were deliberately altered so as to flood extensive tracts of land, converting them into fields of wild grain. Food foragers do not remain as such through ignorance, but through choice.

A second observation is that a switch from food foraging to food production does not free people from hard work. The available ethnographic data indicate just the opposite—that farmers, by and large, work far longer hours than do most food foragers. Furthermore, it is clear that early farming required people not only to work longer hours but also to eat more "third choice" food. Typically, food foragers divide potentially edible food resources into first, second, and third choice categories; third choice foods are eaten only by necessity, when there is no other option. And in Southwest Asia and Mexico, at least, the plants that were brought under domestication were clearly third choice plants.

A final observation is that food production is not necessarily a more secure means of subsistence than food foraging. Seed crops in particular, of the sort domesticated in Southwest Asia, Mexico, and Peru, are highly productive but very unstable due to low species diversity. Without constant human attention, their productivity suffers.

From all of this, it is little wonder that food foragers do not necessarily regard farming and animal husbandry as superior to hunting, gathering, and fishing. Thus, there are some people in the world who have remained food foragers down into the

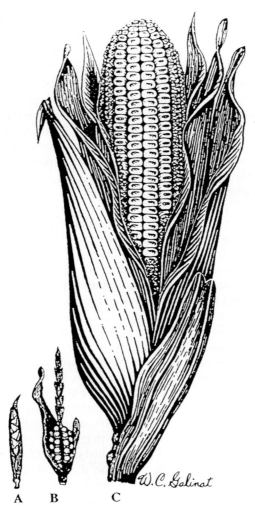

Teosinte (A), compared to the 5500-year-old maize (B) and modern maize (C). The wild grass from which maize originated, teosinte is far less productive than maize and doesn't taste very good. Like most plants that were domesticated, it was not a first- or even second-choice food for foraging people.

1990s, although it has become increasingly difficult for them, as food-producing peoples have deprived them of more and more of the land base necessary for their way of life. But as long as existing practices worked well, there was no felt need to abandon them. After all, their traditional way of life gave them all the food they needed and an eminently satisfactory way of living in small, intimate groups. Free from tedious routine, their lives were often more exciting than those of farmers. Food could be hunted, gathered, or fished for as needed, but in

most environments they could relax when they had enough to eat. Why raise crops by back-breaking work, when the whole family could camp under a tree bearing tasty and nutritious nuts? Farming brings with it a whole new system of human relationships that offers no easily understood advantages and disturbs an age-old balance between humans and nature as well as the people who live together.

Why Humans Became Food Producers

In view of what has been said so far, we may well ask: Why did any human group abandon food foraging in favor of food production?

Several theories have been proposed to account for this change in human subsistence practices. One older theory, championed by V. Gordon Childe, is the desiccation, or oasis, theory based on climatic determinism. Its proponents advanced the idea that the glacial cover over Europe and Asia caused a southern shift in rain patterns from Europe to northern Africa and Southwest Asia. When the glaciers retreated northward, so did the rain patterns. As a result, northern Africa and Southwest Asia became dryer, and people were forced to congregate at oases for water. Because of the scarcity of wild animals in such an environment, people were driven by necessity to collect the wild grasses and seeds growing around the oases. Eventually they had to cultivate the grasses to provide enough food for the community. According to this theory, animal domestication began because the oases attracted hungry animals, such as wild goats, sheep, and also cattle, which came to graze on the stubble of the grain fields. People, finding these animals too thin to kill for food, began to fatten them up.

In spite of its initial popularity, evidence in support of the oasis theory was not immediately forthcoming. Moreover, as systematic fieldwork into the origins of domestication began in the late 1940s, other theories gained favor. One of the pioneers in this work was Robert Braidwood of the University of Chicago, who proposed what is sometimes called the "hilly flanks" theory. Contrary to Childe, Braidwood argued that plants and animals were domesticated by people living in the hill country surrounding the fertile crescent (Fig. 11.1). They had reached the point in their evolutionary development where they were beginning to "settle in"—

V. GORDON CHILDE
(1892–1957)

This distinguished Australian, once the private secretary to the premier of New South Wales, later became an eminent British archaeologist. His knowledge of the archaeological sequences of Europe and the Middle East was unsurpassed, as seen in two of the most popular and influential descriptions of prehistory ever written: *Man Makes Himself* in 1936 and *What Happened in History*. In these, he described two great "revolutions" that added measurably to the capacity of humans to survive the Neolithic and urban revolutions. The first of these transformed food foragers into farmers and brought with it a drastic reordering of society; populations increased, a cooperative group spirit arose, trade began on a large scale, and new religions arose to ensure the success of crops. This set the stage for the urban revolution, which transformed society from one of egalitarianism with a simple age-sex division of labor into one of social classes and organized political bodies. The result of these ideas was to generate a whole new interest in the evolution of human culture in general.

Figure 11.1 In Southwest Asia, early domestication of plants began in the Jordan River Valley and spread from there. Early animal domestication began in the Zagros Mountains and the hills of northern Iraq, spreading to other regions from there.

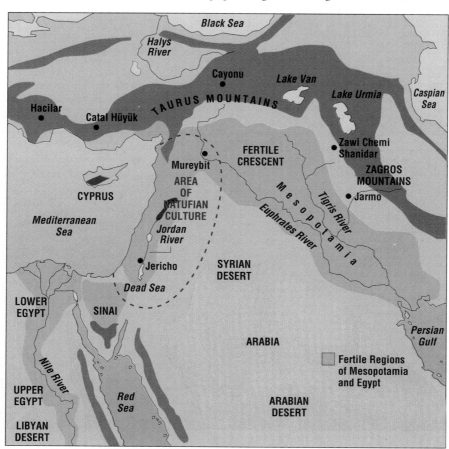

that is, become more sedentary—a consequence of which was that they could become intimately familiar with the plants and animals around their settlements. Given the human capacity and enthusiasm for experimentation, it was inevitable that they would have experimented with grasses and animals, bringing them under domestication. Problems with this theory include the ethnocentric notion that nonsedentary food foragers are not intimately familiar with the plants and animals on which they rely for survival, and its projection onto all human cultures of the great value Western culture places on experimentation and innovation for its own sake. In short, the theory was culture-bound, strongly reflecting the notions of progress in which people in the Western world had such faith in the period following World War II.

Yet another theory, which became popular in the 1960s, is one in which population growth played a key role. In Southwest Asia, so this theory goes, people adapted to the cool, dry conditions of the last glacial period by developing a mixed pattern of resource utilization: They hunted such animals as were available, harvested wild cereal grasses, gathered nuts, and collected a wide variety of birds, turtles, snails, crabs, and mussels. They did so well that their populations grew, requiring the development of new ways of providing sufficient food. The result, especially in marginal situations where wild foods were least abundant, was to improve productivity through the domestication of plants and animals.

Just as there are problems with Braidwood's theory, so are there problems with this one. The most serious is that it requires an intentional decision on the part of the people involved to become producers of domestic crops, whereas, as we have already seen, domestication does not require intentional design. Furthermore, prior to domestication, people could have had no way of knowing that plants and animals could be so radically transformed as to permit a food-producing way of life (even today, the long-term outcome of plant breeding cannot be predicted). Finally, even if people had wanted to become producers of their own food, there is no way such a decision could have had an immediate and perceptible effect; in fact, a complete switch to food production took a few

Today, deliberate attempts to create new varieties of plants take place in many a greenhouse, experiment station, or lab. But when first begun, the creation of domestic plants was not deliberate; rather, it was the unforeseen outcome of traditional food foraging activities.

hundred years to accomplish. Although this may seem a relatively short period of time compared with the 200,000 or 300,000 years since the appearance of *H. sapiens*, it was still too long to have made any difference to people faced with immediate food shortages. Under such conditions, the usual response among food foragers is to make use of a wider variety of foods than before, which acts as a brake on domestication by diverting attention from potential domesticates, while alleviating the immediate problem.

Another theory, in accord with the evidence as we now know it, but also more in accord with the role played by chance both in evolution (Chapter 3) and in cultural innovation, takes us back to some of the ideas of Childe, who, as it turns out, guessed what the environmental circumstances were, even though he did not fully understand the process.[4] We now know that the earliest plant domestication took place around the margins of evaporating lakes in the Jordan River Valley (Fig. 11.1) by 10,300 years ago, as a consequence of a chance convergence of separate natural events and cultural de-

[4]McCorriston, J., & Hole, F. (1991). The ecology of seasonal stress and the origins of agriculture in the Near East. *American Anthropologist, 93,* 46–69.

velopments. The people responsible were the Natufians, whose culture we looked at briefly in the preceding chapter. These people lived at a time of dramatically changing climates in the region. With the end of the last glaciation, climates not only became significantly warmer, but markedly seasonal as well. Between 12,000 and 6,000 years ago, the lands east of the Mediterranean experienced the most extreme seasonality in their history, with summer aridity significantly longer and more pronounced than today. As a consequence of increased evaporation, many shallow lakes dried up, leaving just three in the Jordan Valley. At the same time, the region's plant cover changed dramatically. Those plants best adapted to environmental instability and seasonal aridity were annuals, including wild cereal grains and legumes (plants that fix nitrogen in the soil, including peas, lentils, chickpeas, and bitter vetch). Such plants can evolve very quickly under unstable conditions, since they complete their life cycle in a single year. Moreover, they store their reproductive abilities for the next wet season in abundant seeds, which can remain dormant for prolonged periods.

The Natufians, who lived where these conditions were especially severe, adapted by modifying their subsistence practices in two ways: They

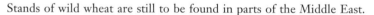

Stands of wild wheat are still to be found in parts of the Middle East.

probably regularly fired the landscape to promote browsing for red deer and grazing for gazelles, the main focus of their hunting activities, and they placed greater emphasis on the collection of wild seeds from the increasingly abundant annual plants that could be effectively stored to see people through the dry season. The importance of stored foods, coupled with the scarcity of reliable water sources, promoted more sedentary living patterns, reflected in the substantial villages of late Natufian times. The greater importance of seeds in Natufian subsistence was made possible by the fact that they already possessed sickles for harvesting grain and grinding stones for processing seeds. The grinding stones were used originally to process a variety of wild foods, while the sickles may originally have served to procure nonfood plants such as sedges or reeds used to make baskets and mats (Natufian sites yielding large numbers of sickles tend to be located near coastal marshes and swamps).[5] Thus, these implements were not invented to enable people to became farmers, even though they turned out to be useful for that purpose.

The use of sickles to harvest grain turned out to have important consequences, again unexpected, for the Natufians. In the course of harvesting, it was inevitable that many easily dispersed seeds would be "lost" at the harvest site, whereas those from plants that did not readily scatter their seeds would mostly be carried back to where people processed and stored them.[6] Genetic mutations against easy dispersal would inevitably arise in the wild stocks, but would be at a competitive disadvantage compared with variants that could readily disperse their seeds. Moreover, the rate of this and other mutations potentially useful to human consumers might have been unknowingly increased by the periodic firing carried out to promote the deer and gazelle herds, for heat is known to be an effective mutagenic agent, and fire can drastically and quickly change gene frequencies. In any event, with seeds

for nondispersing variants being carried back to settlements, it was inevitable that some lost seeds would germinate and grow there on dump heaps and other disturbed sites (latrines, areas cleared of trees, or burned over). As it turns out, many of the plants that became domesticated were colonizers that do particularly well in disturbed habitats. Moreover, with people becoming increasingly sedentary, disturbed habitats became more extensive as resources in proximity to settlements were depleted over time, thus variants of plants particularly susceptible to human manipulation had more and more opportunity to flourish where people were living and where they would inevitably attract attention. Under such circumstances, it was inevitable that people sooner or later would begin actively to promote their growth, even by deliberately sowing them, especially as people otherwise had to travel farther afield to procure the resources that were depleted near their villages. An inevitable consequence of increased human manipulation would be the appearance of other mutant strains of particular benefit. For example, barley, which in its wild state can be tremendously productive but difficult to harvest and process, had developed the tougher stems that make it easier to harvest by 9000 years ago; by 8000 years ago "naked" barley, which is easier to process, was common, and by 7500 years ago six-row barley, which is more productive than the original two-row, was widespread. Sooner or later, people realized that they could play a more active role in the process by deliberately trying to breed more useful strains. With this, domestication may be said to have shifted from a process that was unintentional to one that was intentional.

The development of animal domestication in Southwest Asia seems to have proceeded along somewhat similar lines but in the hilly country of northern Iraq and the Zagros mountains of Iran (Fig. 11.1). Here were to be found large herds of wild sheep and goats, as well as much in the way of environmental diversity. From the low, alluvial plains of the valley of the Tigris and Euphrates rivers, for example, travel to the north or east takes one into the high country through three other zones: first steppeland, then oak and pistachio woodlands, and, finally, high plateau country with grass, scrub, or desert vegetation. Valleys that run

[5]Olszewski, D. I. (1991). Comment. *Current Anthropology, 32,* 43.
[6]Blumer, M. A., & Byrne, R. (1991). The ecological genetics and domestication and the origins of agriculture. *Current Anthropology, 32,* 30.

at right angles to the mountain ranges afford relatively easy access between these zones. Today, a number of pastoral peoples in the region practice a pattern of **transhumance,** in which they graze their herds of sheep and goats on the low steppelands in the winter, moving to high pastures on the plateaus in the summer.

Moving 12,000 years backward in time to the Mesolithic, we find that the region was inhabited by peoples whose subsistence pattern, like that of the Natufians, was one of food foraging. Different plants were found in different ecological zones, and, because of the difference in altitude, plant foods matured at different times in different zones. The animals hunted for meat and hides by these people included several species, among them bear, fox, boar, and wolf. Most notable, though, were the hoofed animals: deer, gazelles, wild goats, and wild sheep. Their bones are far more common in hu-

Transhumance: Among pastoralists, the grazing of sheep and goats in the low steppelands in the winter, moving to high pastures on the plateaus in the summer.

man refuse piles than those of other animals. This is significant, for most of these animals are naturally transhumant in the region, moving back and forth from low winter pastures to high summer pastures. People followed these animals in their seasonal migrations, making use along the way of other wild foods in the zones through which they passed: dates in the lowlands; acorns, almonds, and pistachios higher up; apples and pears higher still; wild grains maturing at different times in different zones; woodland animals in the forested zone between summer and winter grazing land. All in all, it was a rich, varied fare.

There was in hunting, then, a concentration on hoofed animals, including wild sheep and goats, which provided meat and hides. At first, animals of all ages and sexes were hunted. But, beginning about 11,000 years ago, the percentage of immature sheep eaten, for example, increased to about 50 percent of the total. At the same time, the percentage frequency of female animals decreased. Apparently, people were learning that they could increase yields by sparing the females for breeding, while feasting on ram lambs. This marks the beginning of human management of sheep. As this management of flocks became more and more efficient, sheep were increasingly shielded from the

Although sheep and goats were first valued for their meat, hides, and sinew, the changes wrought by domestication made them useful for other purposes as well. This impression, from a 4500-year-old seal, shows a goat being milked.

effects of natural selection. Eventually, they were introduced into areas outside their natural habitat. For example, sheep and goats were kept by farmers at ancient Jericho, in the Jordan River Valley, 8000 years ago (by which time farming, too, had spread from its original homeland far to the north into Turkey and far to the east into the Zagros Mountains). As a consequence of this human intervention, variants that usually were not successful in the wild were able to survive and reproduce. Although variants that were perceived as being of immediate advantage would have attracted peoples' attention, they did not arise out of need, but independent of it at random, as mutations do. In such a way did those features characteristic of domestic sheep, such as greater fat and meat production, excess wool (Fig. 11.2), and so on, begin to develop. By 9000 years ago, the bones of domestic sheep had become distinguishable from those of wild sheep.

In sum, the domesticators of plants and animals sought only to increase to the maximum extent the food sources available to them. They were not aware of the revolutionary consequences their actions were to have. But as the process continued, the productivity of the domestic species increased, relative to wild species. Thus they became increasingly more important to subsistence, resulting in further intensification of interest in, and management of, the domesticates. Inevitably, the result would be further increases in productivity.

Other Centers of Domestication

In addition to Southwest Asia, the domestication of plants and, in some cases, animals took place independently in Southeast Asia, parts of the Americas (southern Mexico, Peru, the Amazon Basin of South America, and eastern North America), and possibly northern China and Africa (Fig. 11.3). In Southeast Asia, domestication took place sometime between 8800 and 5000 years ago. Plant remains, none of them showing any detectable differences from wild strains, have been found in Spirit Cave in northern Thailand in levels dating back as many as 10,000 years. The oldest domestic plant so far identified is rice, in pottery dated to sometime before 5000 years ago.

Figure 11.2 The domestication of sheep resulted in evolutionary changes that created more wool. Drawing A shows a section, as seen through a microscope, of skin of wild sheep, showing the arrangement of primary (hair) and secondary (wool) follicles. Drawing B shows a section of similarly enlarged skin of domestic sheep, showing the changed relationship and the change in the size of follicles that accompanied the development of wool.

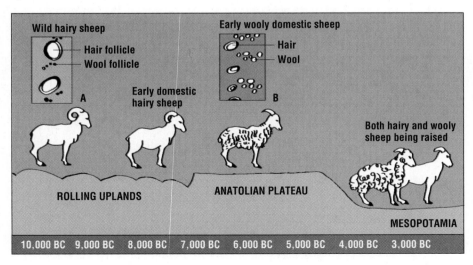

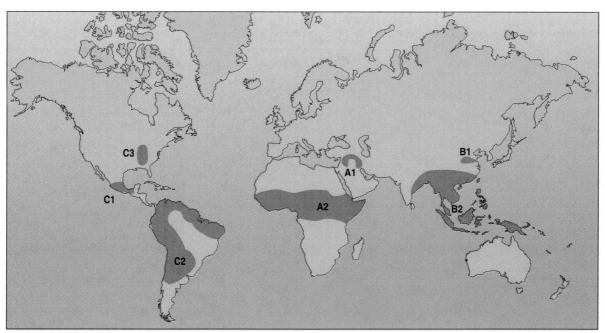

Figure 11.3   Early plant and animal domestication took place in such widely scattered areas as Southwest Asia (A1), Central Africa (A2), China (B1), Southeast Asia (B2), Mesoamerica (C1), South America (C2), and North America (C3). Crops originating in China include foxtail millet, soy, and mung beans; crops originating elsewhere are discussed in the text.

In addition to rice, Southeast Asians domesticated root crops, most notably yams and taro. Root crop farming, or **vegeculture,** typically involves the growing of many different species together in a single field. Because this approximates the complexity of the natural vegetation, vegeculture tends to be more stable than seed crop cultivation.

In the Americas, the domestication of plants did not take place as early as in Southwest and Southeast Asia. In Mexico, for example, it began no earlier than 7000 years ago, and perhaps no more than about 5600 years ago.[7] In spite of their

late start, however, native Americans ultimately domesticated more than three hundred food crops, including two of the four most important ones in the world today: potatoes and maize (the other two are wheat and rice). In fact, 60 percent of the crops grown in the world today were invented by American Indians, who not only remain the developers of the world's largest array of nutritious foods, but also the primary contributors to the world's varied cuisines.[8] After all, where would Italian cuisine be without tomatoes? Thai cooking without the peanut? Northern European cooking without the potato? Or Chinese cooking without the sweet potato (the daily food for peasants but also used to make noodles rivaling in popularity those made of wheat)? Small wonder American Indians have been called the world's greatest farmers.[9]

Vegeculture: The cultivation of domesticated root crops, such as yams and taro.

---

[7]Fritz, G. J. (1994). Are the first American farmers getting younger? *Current Anthropology, 35,* 305–309; Piperno, D. R., & Fritz, G. J. (1994). On the emergence of agriculture in the New World. *Current Anthropology, 35,* 637–643.

[8]Weatherford, J. (1988). *Indian givers: How the Indians of the Americas transformed the world* (pp. 71, 115). New York: Fawcett Columbine.

[9]Ibid., p. 95.

Archaeological evidence for the beginning of farming in Mexico comes from the highland valleys of Oaxaca, Puebla, and Tamaulipas. In the Tehuacan Valley of Puebla, for example, crops such as maize, beans, and squash gradually came to make up a greater percentage of the food eaten (see Fig. 11.4). Like the hill country of Southwest Asia, the Tehuacan Valley is environmentally diverse, and the people living there had a cyclical pattern of hunting and gathering that made use of the resources of different environmental zones. In the course of their seasonal movements, people carried the wild precursors of future domesticates out of their native habitat, exposing them to different selective pressures. Under such circumstances, potentially useful (to humans) variants that did not do well in the native habitat would, by chance, do well in novel settings, again (as in Southwest Asia) attracting human attention.

Figure 11.4 Tehuacan Valley subsistence trends show that dependence on horticulture came about gradually, over a prolonged period of time.

CULTIGENS		PERCENTAGE			BC
		Hunting	Horti-culture	Wild plant use	
Squash Chili Amaranth Avocado	Cotton Maize Beans Gourd Sapote	29%		31%	1000
					1500
					2000
Squash Chili Amaranth Avocado	Maize Beans Gourd Sapote	25%		50%	2500
					3000
Squash Chili Amaranth Avocado	Maize Beans Gourd Sapote	34%		52%	3500
					4000
					4500
					5000
Squash Chili Amaranth Avocado		54%		40%	5500
					6000
					6500

The change to food production also took place in South America, earliest in the highlands of Peru, again an environmentally diverse region. While a number of crops first grown in Mexico eventually came to be grown here, there was more of an emphasis on root crops, the best known being potatoes (of which about 3000 varieties were grown, versus the mere 250 now grown in North America), sweet potatoes, and manioc. South Americans domesticated guinea pigs, llamas, alpacas, and ducks, whereas the Mexicans never did much with domestic livestock. They limited themselves to dogs, turkeys, and bees.

Although the Native Americans living north of Mexico ultimately adopted several crops, such as maize and beans, from their southern neighbors, this occurred after developing some indigenous domesticates themselves. These included local varieties of squash and sunflower (today, grown widely in Russia as a reliable source of edible oil). Other native crops such as lambsquarter and sumpweed reverted to the wild as more useful foods appeared from Mexico.

Considering all the separate innovations of domestic plants, it is interesting to note that in all cases people developed the same categories of foods. Everywhere, starchy grains are accompanied by one or more legumes: wheat and barley with peas, chickpeas, bitter vetch, and lentils in Southwest Asia or maize with various kinds of beans in Mexico, for example. The starchy grains are the core of the diet and are eaten at every meal in the form of bread, some sort of food "wrapper" (like a tortilla), or gruel or thickening agent in a stew along with one or more legumes. Being rather bland, these sources of carbohydrates and proteins are invariably combined with flavor-giving substances that help the food go down. In Mexico, for example, the flavor enhancer par excellence is the chili pepper, but in other cuisines, it may be a bit of meat, dairy product, mushrooms, or whatever. Anthropologist Sidney Mintz refers to this as the core-fringe-legume pattern (CFLP), noting that only recently has it been upset by the worldwide spread of processed sugars and high-fat foods.[10]

[10]Mintz, S. (1996). A taste of history. In W. A. Haviland & R. J. Gordon (Eds.), *Talking about people* (2nd ed., pp. 81–82). Mountain View, CA: Mayfield.

Domestic plants were useful for purposes other than food alone. This illustration from a 16th-century Aztec manuscript shows a woman threatening her child with punishment by being exposed to smoke from chili peppers. Chili smoke was also used as a kind of chemical weapon in warfare.

The Spread of Food Production

Although population growth and the need to feed more people cannot explain the origin of the food-producing way of life, it does have a lot to do with its subsequent spread. As already noted, domestication inevitably leads to higher yields, and higher yields make it possible to feed more people. In addition, farmers have available a variety of foods that are soft enough to be fed to infants, which food foragers usually do not. Hence, farmers do not need to nurse their children so intensively, nor for so many years. In humans, prolonged nursing, so long as it involves frequent stimulation of the nipple by the infant, has a dampening effect on ovulation. As a result, women in food-foraging societies are less likely to become fertile as soon after childbirth as they are in food-producing societies. Coupled with this, too many children to care for at once interferes with the foraging activities of women in hunting, gathering, and fishing societies. Among farmers, however, numerous children are frequently seen as assets, to help out with the many household chores. Small wonder, then, that a sharp upsurge in the birth rate commonly follows a switch from food foraging to farming.

Paradoxically, while domestication increases productivity, so does it increase instability. This is so because those varieties with the highest yields become the focus of human attention, while other varieties are less valued and ultimately ignored. As a result, farmers become dependent on a rather narrow range of resources, compared with the wide range utilized by food foragers. Modern agriculturists, for example, rely on about 20 crops, versus the more than 100 species regarded as edible by the Bushmen of Africa's Kalahari Desert. This dependence upon fewer varieties means that when a crop fails, for whatever reason, farmers have less to fall back on than do food foragers. Furthermore, the likelihood of failure is increased by the common farming practice of planting crops together in one locality, so that a disease contracted by one plant can easily spread to others. Moreover, by relying on seeds from the most productive plants of a species to establish next year's crop, farmers favor genetic uniformity over diversity. The result is that if some virus, bacterium, or fungus is able to destroy one plant, it will likely destroy them all. This is what happened in the famous Irish potato famine of 1845–1846, which sent waves of Irish immigrants to the United States.

The Irish potato famine illustrates how the combination of increased productivity and vulnerability may contribute to the geographical spread of farming. Time and time again in the past, population growth followed by crop failures has triggered movements of people from one place to another, where they have reestablished the subsistence practices with which they were familiar. Thus, once farming came into existence, it was more or less guaranteed that it would spread to neighboring regions (see Fig. 11.5). From Southwest Asia, for instance, it spread to southeastern Europe by 8000 years ago, reaching central Europe and the Netherlands by 4000 years ago, and England between 4000 and 3000 years ago. From Southwest Asia, it also spread westward in North Africa and eastward to India. Here, crops domesticated in the West met those spreading from Southeast Asia, some of which spread farther west. Facilitating this east-west diffusion was the fact that localities shared the same seasonal variations in day length and more or less the same diseases, temperature, and rainfall.

In sub-Saharan Africa, a similar spread occurred, accounting for the modern distribution of speakers of Bantu languages. Crops including sorghum (so valuable today it is grown on all continents in hot, dry areas), pearl millet, watermelon, black-eyed peas, African yams, oil palms, and kola nuts (source of modern cola drinks) were first domesticated in West Africa, but began spreading east by 5000 years ago. Between 3000 and 2000 years ago Bantu speakers with their crops reached the east coast, and a few centuries later, reached the Great Fish River, 500 miles east of Capetown. Being adapted to summer rains, African crops spread no farther, for the Cape has a Mediterranean climate with winter rains.

In some instances, farming appears to have been adopted by food foragers from food-producing neighbors. By way of illustration, a crisis developed on the coast of Peru some 4500 years ago as continental uplift caused lowering of the water table and destruction of marine habitats at a time of growing population; the result was an increasing shortage of the wild food resources on which people depended. Their response was to begin growing along the edges of rivers many of the domestic plants that their highland neighbors to the east had begun to cultivate a few thousand years earlier. Here, then, farming appears to have been a subsistence practice of last resort, which a food-foraging people took up only because they had no real choice.

CULTURE OF NEOLITHIC SETTLEMENTS

A number of Neolithic settlements have been excavated, particularly in Southwest Asia. The structures, artifacts, and food debris found at these sites have revealed much about the daily activities of their former inhabitants as they pursued the business of making a living.

Figure 11.5 Population growth has a tendency to follow increases in farming yields. Inevitably, this results in too large a population to be fed when crops fail, as they periodically do. The result is an outward migration of people to other regions.

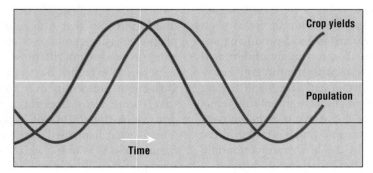

In coastal Peru, the earliest domesticates were the non-edible bottle gourd (like the one shown here) and cotton. They were used to make nets and floats to catch fish, which was an important source of food.

Earliest Full-Fledged Farming Settlements

Dated to between 10,000 and 9000 years ago, the earliest known sites containing domesticated plants and animals are found in Southwest Asia. These sites occur in a region extending from the Jordan Valley northward across the Taurus mountains into Turkey, and eastward across the flanks of the Taurus Mountains into northeastern Iran, and southward into Iraq and Iran along the hilly flanks of the Zagros Mountains. The sites contain evidence of domesticated barley, wheat, peas, chickpeas, bitter vetch, lentils, flax, goats, sheep, dogs, and pigs.

These sites are generally the remains of small village farming communities—small clusters of houses built of mud, each with its own storage pit and clay oven. Their occupants continued to use stone tools of Mesolithic type, plus a few new types of use in farming. Probably the people born into these communities spent their lives in them in a common effort to make their crops grow and their animals prosper. At the same time, they participated in long-distance trade networks. Obsidian found at Jarmo, Iraq, for instance, was imported from 300 miles away.

Jericho: An Early Farming Community

At the Neolithic settlement that later grew to become the biblical city of Jericho, excavation has revealed the remains of a sizable farming community occupied as early as 10,350 years ago. Located in the Jordan River Valley, what made the site attractive was the presence of a bounteous spring and the rich soils of an Ice Age lake that had dried up some 3000 years earlier. Here, crops could be grown almost continuously, since the fertility of the soil was regularly renewed by flood-borne deposits orig-

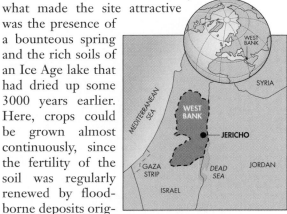

inating in the Judean Highlands, to the west. To protect their settlement against these floods and associated mudflows, the people of Jericho built massive walls of stone around it.[11] Within these walls, an estimated 400 to 900 people lived in houses of mud brick with plastered floors arranged around courtyards. In addition to these houses, a stone tower that would have taken 100 people 104 days to build was located inside one corner of the wall, near the spring. A staircase inside it probably led to a mud brick building on top. Nearby were mud brick storage facilities as well as peculiar structures of possible ceremonial significance. A village cemetery also reflects the sedentary life of these early people; nomadic groups, with few exceptions, rarely buried their dead in a single central location.

Evidence of domestic plants and animals is scant at Jericho. However, indirect evidence in the form of harvesting tools and milling equipment has been uncovered at the site, and wheat, barley, and other domestic plants are known from sites of similar age in the region. We do know that the people of Jericho were keeping sheep and goats by 8000 years ago, although some hunting still went on. Some of the meat from wild animals may have been

[11]Bar-Yosef, O. (1986). The walls of Jericho: An alternative interpretation. *Current Anthropology, 27,* 160.

Neolithic farming communities, such as Jericho in the Jordan River Valley, were made possible by the result of the domestication of plants and animals. Jericho was surrounded by a stone wall as protection against floods. The wall included a tower (left). People lived in substantial houses (right).

supplied by food-foraging peoples whose campsites have been found everywhere in the desert of the Arabian peninsula. Close contacts between these people and the farmers of Jericho and other villages are indicated by common features in art, ritual, use of prestige goods, and burial practices. Other evidence of trade consists of obsidian and turquoise from Sinai as well as marine shells from the coast, all discovered inside the walls of Jericho.

Neolithic Technology

Early harvesting tools were made of wood or bone with serrated flints inserted. Later tools continued to be made by chipping and flaking stone, but during the Neolithic period, stone that was too hard to be chipped was ground and polished for tools (Fig. 11.6). People developed scythes, forks, hoes, and plows to replace their simple digging sticks. Pestles and mortars were used for preparation of grain. Plows were later redesigned when domesticated cattle became available for use as draft animals, after 8000 years ago.

Pottery

In addition to the domestication of plants and animals, one of the characteristics of the Neolithic period is the extensive manufacture and use of pottery. In food-foraging societies, most people are involved in the food quest. In food-producing societies, even though people have to work as long—if not longer—at subsistence activities than food foragers, the whole community need not be involved in the food quest. Hard work on the part of those producing the food may free other members of the society to devote their energies to other craft specialties. One such craft is pottery making, and different forms of pottery were created for transporting and storing food, artifacts, and other material possessions. Because pottery vessels are impervious to damage by insects, rodents, and dampness, they could be used for storing small grain, seeds, and other materials. Moreover, food can be boiled in pottery vessels directly over the fire rather than by such ancient techniques as dropping stones heated directly in the fire into the food being cooked. Pottery is also used for pipes, ladles,

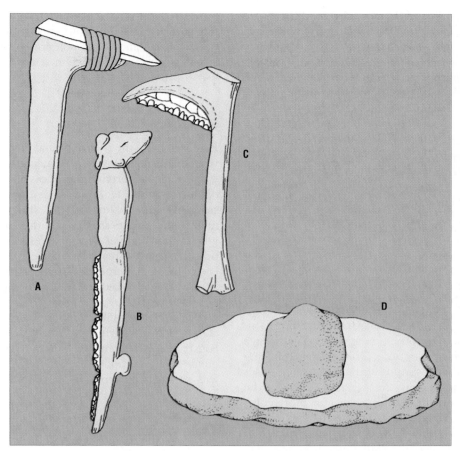

Figure 11.6 In Southwest Asia, many tools fabricated by Neolithic peoples made use of flint microliths in bone or wood handles, as had been done in the Mesolithic, but some tools were made of ground and polished stone.

In the Middle East, the first domestic animals (aside from dogs) were sheep and goats. Pigs, however, followed not long afterward. This pottery vessel in the shape of a pig, found at a site in Turkey, was made about 5600 B.C.

lamps, and other objects, and some cultures used large vessels for burial of the dead. Significantly, pottery containers remain important for much of humanity today.

Widespread use of pottery, which is manufactured of clay and fired, is a good, though not foolproof, indication of a sedentary community. It is found in abundance in all but a few of the earliest Neolithic settlements. At ancient Jericho, for example, the earliest Neolithic people lacked pottery. Its fragility and weight make it impractical for use by nomads and hunters, who use baskets and hide containers. Nevertheless, there are some modern nomads who make and use pottery, just as there are farmers who lack it. In fact, food foragers in Japan were making pottery by 13,000 years ago, long before it was being made in Southwest Asia.

The manufacture of pottery is a difficult art and requires a high degree of technological sophistication. To make a useful vessel requires a knowledge of clay and the techniques of firing or baking. Neolithic pots, for example, are often coarse and ill-made because of improper clay mixture or faulty firing technique.

Pottery is decorated in various ways. For example, designs can be engraved on the vessel before firing, or special rims, legs, bases, and other details may be made separately and fastened to the finished pot. Painting is the most common form of pottery decoration, and there are literally thousands of painted designs found among the pottery remains of ancient cultures.

Housing

Food production and the new sedentary lifestyle engendered another technological development—house building. Permanent housing is of limited interest to food foragers who usually have to move from time to time. Cave shelters, pits dug in the earth, and simple lean-tos made of hides and tree limbs keep the weather out. In the Neolithic, however, dwellings became more complex in design and more diverse in type. Some, like Swiss Lake Dwellings, were constructed of wood, housed several families per building, had doors, and contained beds, tables, and other furniture. More elaborate shelters were made of stone, sun-dried brick, or branches plastered together with mud or clay.

Although permanent housing frequently accompanies food production, there is archaeological evidence that one can have substantial houses without food production. For example, at Mureybit, in Southwest Asia, storage pits and year-round occupation of stone houses indicate that its occupants had definitely settled down between 10,200 and 9500 years ago. Yet the remains and artifacts indicate that the occupants were food foragers, not farmers.

Clothing

During the Neolithic, for the first time in human history, clothing was made of woven textiles. The raw materials and technology necessary for the production of clothing came from three sources: flax and cotton from farming, wool from domesticated sheep, and the spindle for spinning and the loom for weaving from the inventive human mind.

Social Structure

Evidence of all the economic and technological developments listed thus far has enabled archaeologists to draw certain inferences concerning the organization of Neolithic society. The general absence of elaborate buildings in all but a few settlements may suggest that neither religion nor government was yet a formally established institution able to wield real social power. Although there is evidence of ceremonial activity, little evidence of a centrally organized and directed religious life has been found. Burials, for example, show a marked absence of patterning; variation seems to have been common. Since early Neolithic graves were rarely constructed of, or covered by, stone slabs and rarely included grave goods, it is believed that no person had attained the superior social status that would have required an elaborate funeral. The smallness of most villages suggests that the inhabitants knew each other well, so that most of their relationships were probably highly personal ones, charged with emotional significance.

The general picture that emerges is one of an egalitarian society with little division of labor and probably little development of new and more specialized social roles. Villages seem to have been made up of several households, each providing for its own needs. The organizational needs of society beyond the household level were probably met by kinship groups and common-interest associations.

Neolithic Culture in the New World

Outside of Mesoamerica (southern Mexico and northern Central America) and Peru, hunting, fishing, and the gathering of wild plant foods remained important elements in the economy of Neolithic peoples in the New World. Apparently, most American Indians never experienced a complete change from a food-foraging to a food-producing mode of life, even though maize and other domestic crops were cultivated just about everywhere that climate permitted. Farming developed independently of Europe and Asia, and the crops differed because of different natural conditions and cultural traits.

The Neolithic developed later in the New World than in the Old. For example, Neolithic agricultural villages were common in Southwest Asia between 9000 to 8000 years ago, but similar villages did not appear in the New World until about 4500 years ago, in Mesoamerica and Peru. Moreover, pottery, which arose in the Old World shortly after plant and animal domestication, did not develop in the New World until about 4500 years ago. Neither the potter's wheel nor the loom and spindle were used by early Neolithic people in the New World. Both pottery and textiles were manufactured by manual means, and evidence of the loom and spindle does not appear in the New World until 3000 years ago. None of these indicate any "backwardness" on the part of New World peoples, who, as we have already seen, were highly sophisticated farmers and plant breeders. Rather, older practices continued to be satisfactory for relatively long periods of time.

THE NEOLITHIC AND HUMAN BIOLOGY

Although we tend to think of the invention of food production in terms of its cultural impact; it obviously had a biological impact as well. From studies of human skeletons from Neolithic burials, physical anthropologists have found evidence for a somewhat lessened mechanical stress on peoples' bodies and teeth. Although there are exceptions, the teeth of Neolithic peoples show less wear, their bones are less robust, and osteoarthritis (the result

Textiles like this one, produced in Peru sometime between 500 and 200 B.C., remain unsurpassed anywhere in the world, even though weaving began later in the Americas than in some parts of the Old World.

of stressed joint surfaces) is not as marked as in the skeletons of Paleolithic and Mesolithic peoples. On the other hand, there is clear evidence for a marked deterioration in health and mortality. Anthropologist Anna Roosevelt sums up our knowledge of this in the following Original Study.

Original Study
History of Mortality and Physiological Stress[12]

Although there is a relative lack of evidence for the Paleolithic stage, enough skeletons have been studied that it seems clear that seasonal and periodic physiological stress regularly affected most prehistoric hunting-gathering populations, as evidenced by the presence of enamel hypoplasias [horizontal linear defects in tooth enamel] and Harris lines [horizontal lines near the ends of long bones]. What also seems clear is that severe and chronic stress, with high frequency of hypoplasias, infectious disease lesions, pathologies related to iron-deficiency anemia, and high mortality rates, is not characteristic of these early populations. There is no evidence of frequent, severe malnutrition, and so the diet must have been adequate in calories and other nutrients most of the time. During the Mesolithic, the proportion of starch in the diet rose, to judge from the increased occurrence of certain dental diseases, but not enough to create an impoverished diet. At this time, diets seem to have been made up of a rather large number of foods, so that the failure of one food source would not be catastrophic. There is a possible slight tendency for Paleolithic people to be healthier and

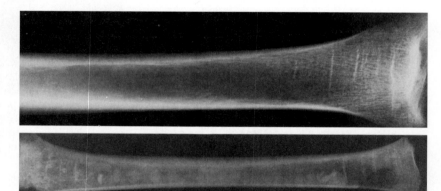

Harris lines near the ends of these youthful thigh bones, found in a prehistoric farming community in Arizona, are indicative of recovery after growth arrest, caused by famine or severe disease.

Enamel hypoplasias such as those shown on these teeth are indicative of arrested growth caused by severe disease or famine. The teeth are from an adult who lived in an ancient farming community in Arizona.

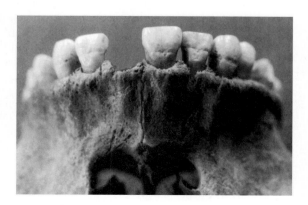

taller than Mesolithic people, but there is no apparent trend toward increasing physiological stress during the Mesolithic. Thus, it seems that both hunter-gatherers and incipient agriculturalists regularly underwent population pressure, but only to a moderate degree.

During the periods when effective agriculture first comes into use there seems to be a temporary upturn in health and survival rates in a few regions: Europe, North America, and the Eastern Mediterranean. At this stage, wild foods are still consumed periodically and a variety of plants are cultivated, suggesting the availability of adequate amounts of different nutrients. Based on the increasing frequency of tooth disease related to high carbohydrate consumption, it seems that cultivated plants probably increased the storable calorie supply, removing for a time any seasonal or periodic problems in food supply. In most regions, however, the development of agriculture seems not to have had this effect, and there seems to have been a slight increase in physiological stress.

Stress, however, does not seem to have become *common* and widespread until after the development of high degrees of sedentism, population density, and reliance on intensive agriculture. At this stage in all regions the incidence of physiological stress increases greatly, and average mortality rates increase appreciably. Most of these agricultural populations have high frequencies of porotic hyperostosis and cribra orbitalia [bone deformities indicative of chronic iron-deficiency anemia] and there is a substantial increase in the number and severity of enamel hypoplasias and pathologies associated with infectious disease. Stature in many populations appears to have been considerably lower than would be expected if genetically determined height maxima had been reached, which suggests that the growth arrests documented by pathologies were causing stunting. Accompanying these indicators of poor health and nourishment, there is a universal drop in the occurrence of Harris lines, suggesting a poor rate of full recovery from the stress. Incidence of carbohydrate-related tooth disease increases, apparently because subsistence by this time is characterized by a heavy emphasis on a few starchy food crops. Populations seem to have grown beyond the point at which wild food resources could be a meaningful dietary supplement, and even domestic animal resources were commonly reserved for farm labor and transport rather than for diet supplementation.

It seems that a large proportion of most sedentary prehistoric populations under intensive agriculture underwent chronic and life-threatening malnutrition and disease, especially during infancy and childhood. The causes of the nutritional stress are likely to have been the poverty of the staple crops in most nutrients except calories, periodic famines caused by the instability of the agricultural system, and chronic lack of food due to both population growth and economic expropriation by elites. The increases in infectious disease probably reflect both a poorer diet and increased interpersonal contact in crowded settlements, and it is, in turn, likely to have aggravated nutritional problems.

[12]Roosevelt, A. C. (1984). Population, health, and the evolution of subsistence: Conclusions from the conference. In M. N. Cohen & G. J. Armelagos (Eds.), *Paleopathology and the origins of agriculture* (pp. 572–574). Orlando: Academic Press.

For the most part, the crops on which Neolithic peoples came to depend were selected for their higher productivity and storability, rather than their nutritional value. Moreover, their nutritional shortcomings would have been exacerbated by their susceptibility to periodic failure, as already noted, particularly as populations grew in size. Thus, the worsened health and mortality of Neolithic peoples is not surprising. Some researchers have gone so far as to assert that the switch from food foraging to food production was the worst mistake that humans ever made!

Another key contributor to the increased incidence of disease and mortality was probably the new mode of life in Neolithic communities. Sedentary life in fixed villages brings with it sanitation problems that do not exist for small groups of people who move about from one campsite to another. Moreover, airborne diseases are more easily transmitted in such villages. Another factor, too, may have been close association between humans and their domestic animals, a situation conducive to the transmission of some animal diseases to humans. Smallpox, chicken pox, and in fact all the infectious diseases of childhood that were not overcome by medical science until the latter half of the twentieth century seem to have been transmitted to humans through their close association with domestic animals.

Another example of the biological impact of food production on human biology is that of the

The chicken pox from which this child suffers is a direct consequence of the domestication of animals thousands of years earlier. Close and continuing contact with domestic stock allowed for the transfer of many animal diseases to humans.

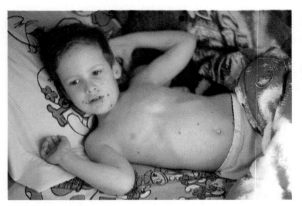

abnormal hemoglobin responsible for sickle-cell anemia, discussed in Chapter 3. Other abnormal hemoglobins are associated with the spread of farming from Southwest Asia westward around the Mediterranean and also with the spread of farming in Southeast Asia. In all these regions, changes in human gene pools took place as a biological response to malaria, which had become a problem as a result of farming practices.

Higher mortality rates in Neolithic villages seem to have been offset by increased fertility, for population growth accelerated dramatically at precisely the moment that health and mortality worsened. The factors responsible for this increased natality have already been discussed earlier in this chapter.

THE NEOLITHIC AND THE IDEA OF PROGRESS

One of the more deeply held biases of Western culture is that human history is basically a record of steady progress over time. The transition from food foraging to food production is generally viewed as a great step upward on a supposed "ladder of progress." To be sure, farming allowed people to increase the size of their populations, to live together in substantial sedentary communities, and to reorganize the workload in ways that permitted craft specialization. If one chooses to regard this as "progress," that is fine—Progress is, after all, whatever it is defined as and different cultures hold different views of this.

Whatever the benefits of food production, however, a substantial price was paid. As anthropologists Mark Cohen and George Armelagos put it:

> Taken as a whole, indicators fairly clearly suggest an overall decline in the quality—and probably the length—of human life associated with the adoption of agriculture. This decline was offset in some regions, but not in others, by a decline in physical demands on the body. The studies support recent ethnographic statements and theoretical arguments about the relatively good health and nutrition of hunter-gatherers. They also suggest that

hunter-gatherers were relatively well buffered against episodic stress. These data call in question simplistic popular ideas about human progress. They also call in question models of human population growth that are based on assumed progressive increases in life expectancy. The data suggest that the well documented expansion of early farming populations was accomplished in spite of general diminution of both and child and adult life expectancy rather than being fueled by increased survivorship.[13]

Rather than imposing ethnocentric notions of progress on the archaeological record, it is best to view the advent of food production as but one more factor contributing to the diversification of cultures, something that had begun in the Paleolithic. While some societies continued to practice hunting, gathering, and fishing, others became **horticultural**—small communities of gardeners working with simple hand tools and using neither irrigation nor the plow. Horticulturists typically cultivate different varieties of crops in small gardens they have cleared by hand. Some horticultural societies, however, became **agricultural.** Technologically more complex than the horticulturalists, agriculturalists often employ irrigation, fertilizers, and the wooden or metal plow pulled by two harnessed draft animals, such as oxen or water buffalo, to produce food on larger plots of land. The distinction between horticulturalist and agriculturalist is not always an easy one to make. For example, the Hopi Indians of the North American Southwest traditionally employed irrigation in their farming, while at the same time used simple hand tools.

Some societies became specialized **pastoralists** in environments that were too dry or too grassy for effective horticulture or agriculture. For example, the Russian steppes, with their heavy grass cover, were not suitable to farming without a plow, but they were ideal for herding. Thus, a number of peoples living in the arid grasslands and deserts that stretch from North Africa into Central Asia kept large herds of domestic animals, relying on their neighbors for plant foods. Finally, some societies went on to develop civilizations—the subject of the next chapter.

[13]Cohen, M. N., & Armelagos, G. J. (1984). Paleopathology and the origins of agriculture: Editors' summation. *Paleopathology and the origins of agriculture* (p. 594). Orlando: Academic Press.

Horticulture: Cultivation of crops carried out with hand tools, such as digging sticks or hoes.

Agriculture: Intensive farming of large plots of land, employing fertilizers, plows, and/or extensive irrigation.

Pastoralists: People who rely on herds of domestic animals for their subsistence.

CHAPTER SUMMARY

Throughout the Paleolithic, people were strictly food foragers moving from place to place as the food supply became exhausted. The change to food production, which (in Southwest Asia) began about 10,300 years ago, meant that people could become more sedentary and reorganize the workload, freeing some people from the food quest to pursue other tasks. From the end of the Mesolithic, human groups became larger and more permanent as people turned to animal breeding and crop growing.

A domesticated plant or animal is one that has become genetically modified as an intended or unintended consequence of human manipulation.

Analysis of plant and animal remains at a site will usually indicate whether its occupants were food producers. Wild cereal grasses, for example, usually have fragile stems, whereas cultivated ones have tough stems. Domesticated plants can also be identified because their edible parts are usually larger than those of their wild counterparts. Domestication produces skeletal changes in some animals. The horns of wild goats and sheep, for example, differ from those of domesticated ones. Age and sex imbalances in herd animals may also indicate manipulation by human domesticators.

Several theories have been proposed to account for the changes in the subsistence patterns of early humans. One theory, the "oasis" or "desccation" theory, is based on climatic determination. Domestication began because the oasis attracted hungry animals, which were domesticated instead of killed by early humans. Although once popular, this theory fell out of favor as systematic studies of the origins of domestication were begun in the late 1940s. One alternative idea was that domestication began in the hilly flanks of the fertile crescent because culture was ready for it. This somewhat culture-bound idea was replaced by theories, popular in the 1960s, that saw domestication as a response to population growth. However, this would require a deliberate decision on the part of people who could have had no knowledge of the long-range consequences of domestication. The most probable theory is that domestication came about as a consequence of a chance convergence of separate natural events and cultural developments. This happened independently and at somewhat different times in Southwest and Southeast Asia, highland Mexico and Peru, South America's Amazon forest, eastern North America, China, and Africa. In all cases, however, people developed food complexes based on starchy grains, which were consumed with protein containing legumes and some other flavor enhancers.

Two major consequences of domestication are that crops become more productive but also more vulnerable. This combination periodically causes populations to outstrip food supplies, whereupon people are apt to move into new regions. In this way, farming has often spread from one region to another, as into Europe from Southwest Asia. Sometimes, food foragers will adopt the cultivation of crops from neighboring peoples in response to the shortage of wild foods, as happened in ancient Peru.

Among the earliest known sites containing domesticated plants and animals, about 10,000 to 9000 years old, are those of Southwest Asia. These sites were mostly small villages of mud huts with individual storage pits and clay ovens. There is evidence not only of cultivation and domestication but also of trade. At ancient Jericho, remains of tools, houses, and clothing indicate the oasis was occupied by Neolithic people as early as 10,350 years ago. At its height, Neolithic Jericho had a population of 400 to 900 people. Similar villages developed independently in Mexico and Peru by about 4500 years ago.

During the Neolithic, stone that was too hard to be chipped was ground and polished for tools. People developed scythes, forks, hoes, and plows to replace simple digging sticks. The Neolithic was also characterized by the extensive manufacture and use of pottery. The widespread use of pottery is a good indicator of a sedentary community; it is found in all but a few of the earliest Neolithic settlements. The manufacture of pottery requires a knowledge of clay and the techniques of firing or baking. Neolithic pottery is often coarse. Other technological developments that accompanied food production and the sedentary life were the building of permanent houses and the weaving of textiles.

Archaeologists have been able to draw some inferences concerning the social structure of Neolithic society. No evidence has been found indicating that religion or government was yet a centrally organized institution. Society was probably egalitarian, with little division of labor and little development of specialized social roles.

The development of food production had biological, as well as cultural, consequences. New diets, living arrangements, and farming practices led to increased incidence of disease and higher mortality rates. Increased fertility of women seems to have more than offset mortality.

SUGGESTED READINGS

Childe, V. G. (1951). *Man makes himself.* New York: New American Library.

In this classic, originally published in 1936, Childe presented his concept of the "Neolithic Revolution." He places special emphasis on the technological inventions that helped transform humans from food gatherers to food producers.

Coe, S. D. (1994). *America's first cuisines.* Austin: University of Texas Press.

Writing in an easily accessible style, Coe discusses some of the more important crops grown by Native Americans and explores their early history and domestication. Following this she describes how these foods were prepared, served and preserved by the Aztec, Maya, and Incas.

MacNeish, R. S. (1992). *The origins of agriculture and settled life.* Norman: University of Oklahoma Press.

MacNeish's work in Mexico is responsible for much of our knowledge of the beginning of food production in the New World. In this book, he reviews the evidence from around the world in order to develop general laws about the development of agriculture and evolution of settled life.

Rindos, D. (1984). *The origins of agriculture: An evolutionary perspective.* Orlando: Academic Press.

This is the most important book on agricultural origins to appear in recent times. After identifying the weaknesses of existing theories, Rindos presents his own evolutionary theory of agricultural origins.

Wernick, R. et al. (1973). *The monument builders.* New York: Time-Life.

This volume of the *Time-Life Emergence of Man* series deals with the spread of the Neolithic to Europe and the emergence of distinctive patterns there of this way of life. Like all volumes in this series, it is richly illustrated and contains a useful bibliography.

Zohary, D., & Hopf, M. (1993). *Domestication of plants in the Old World* (2nd ed.). Oxford: Clarendon Press.

This book deals with the origin and spread of domestic plants in western Asia, Europe, and the Nile Valley. Included is a species-by-species discussion of the various crops, an inventory of remains from archaeological sites, and a conclusion summarizing present knowledge.

THE RISE OF CITIES
AND
CIVILIZATION

ONE OF THE LARGEST CITIES OF THE ANCIENT WORLD WAS
TEOTIHUACAN IN CENTRAL MEXICO. AT ITS HEIGHT, JUST BEFORE
ITS VIOLENT END IN THE EIGHTH CENTURY A.D., A POPULATION OF
125,000 PEOPLE MAY HAVE LIVED THERE. THIS PHOTO LOOKS
SOUTH DOWN THE CITY'S PRINCIPAL AVENUE, AN URBAN AXIS
UNEQUALLED IN ITS SCALE UNTIL CONSTRUCTION OF SUCH MODERN
DAY AVENUES AS THE CHAMPS ELYSEE IN PARIS.

CHAPTER PREVIEW

When and Where Did the World's First Cities First Develop?

Cities—urban settlements with well-defined nuclei, populations that are large, dense, and diversified both economically and socially—are characteristic of civilizations that developed initially in China, the Indus and Nile Valleys, Mesopotamia, Mesoamerica, and Peru. The world's oldest cities were those of Mesopotamia, but one of the world's largest was located in Mesoamerica.

What Changes in Culture Accompanied the Rise of Cities?

Four basic culture changes mark the transition from Neolithic village life to that in civilized urban centers. These are agricultural innovation, as new farming methods were developed; diversification of labor, as more people were freed from food production to pursue a variety of full-time craft specialties; the emergence of centralized governments to deal with the new problems of urban life; and the emergence of social classes as people were ranked according to the work they did or the position of the families into which they were born.

Why Did Civilizations Develop in the First Place?

A number of theories have been proposed to explain why civilizations develop. Most of them emphasize the interrelation of people and what they do on the one hand and their environment on the other. For example, some civilizations may have developed as populations grew, causing competition for space and scarce resources, which necessitated the development of centralized authority to control resources and organize warfare. Some civilizations, though, appear to have developed as a result of certain beliefs and values that brought people together into large, heavily populated centers, again necessitating centralized authority to manage the problems—of which there are many—of living in such a way. Thus, it may be that civilizations arose in different places for somewhat different reasons.

A walk down a street of a busy North American city brings us in contact with numerous activities that are essential to the well-being of North American society. The sidewalks are crowded with people going to and from offices and stores. The traffic of cars, taxis, and trucks is heavy, sometimes almost at a standstill. In a brief two-block stretch, there may be a department store, shops selling clothing, appliances, or books, a restaurant, a newsstand, a gasoline station, and a movie theater. Perhaps there will also be a museum, a police station, a school, a hospital, or a church. That is quite a number of services and specialized skills to find in such a small area.

Each of these services or places of business is dependent on others. A butcher shop, for instance, depends on slaughterhouses and beef ranches. A clothing store depends on designers, farmers who produce cotton and wool, and workers who manufacture synthetic fibers. Restaurants depend on refrigerated trucking and vegetable and dairy farmers. Hospitals depend on a great variety of other institutions to meet their more complex needs. All institutions, finally, depend on the public utilities—the telephone, gas, and electric companies. Although interdependence is not immediately apparent to the passerby, it is an important aspect of modern cities.

The interdependence of goods and services in a big city is what makes so many products readily available to people. For example, refrigerated air transport makes it possible to buy fresh California artichokes on the East Coast. This same interdependence, however, has undesirable effects if one service stops functioning, for example, because of strikes or bad weather. Thus, every so often, major North American cities have had to do without services as vital as newspapers, subways, schools, and trash removal. The question is not so much "Why does this happen?" but rather "Why doesn't it happen more often, and why does the city continue to function as well as it does when one of its services stops?" The answer is that services are not only interdependent, but they are also adaptable. When one breaks down, others take over its functions. During a long newspaper strike in New York City in the 1960s, for example, several new magazines were launched, and television expanded its coverage of news and events.

On the surface, city life seems so orderly that we take it for granted; but a moment's pause reminds us that the intricate fabric of city life did not always exist, and the goods that are so accessible to us were once simply not available.

WHAT CIVILIZATION MEANS

This complicated system of goods and services available in such a small space is a mark of civilization itself. The history of civilization is intimately bound up with the history of cities. This does not mean that civilization is to be equated with modern industrial cities or with present-day North American society. People as diverse as the ancient preindustrial Aztecs and the industrial North Americans of today are included in the term *civilization*, but each represents a very different kind. It was with the development of the earliest preindustrial cities, however, that civilization first developed (Fig. 12.1). In fact, the word comes from the Latin *civis*, which refers to one who is an inhabitant of a city, and *civitas*, which refers to the community in which one dwells. The word *civilization* contains the idea of "citification," or "the coming-to-be of cities."

Today, the term **civilization** has a very specific meaning in anthropology; it refers to societies in which one finds large numbers of people living in cities, who are socially stratified and are governed by centrally organized political systems called states. We shall elaborate on all of these points in the course of this chapter.

The world's first cities sprang up in some parts of the world as Neolithic villages of the sort discussed in Chapter 11 grew into towns, some of which in turn grew into cities. This happened first in Mesopotamia (in modern-day Iraq), then in Egypt and the Indus Valley, between 6000 and

Civilization: A type of society marked by the presence of cities, social classes, and the state.

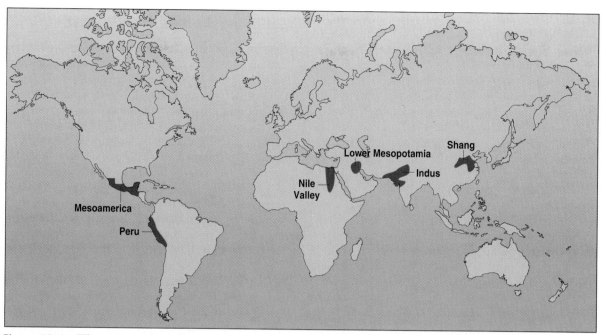

Figure 12.1   The major early civilizations sprang from Neolithic villages in various parts of the world. Those of North and South America developed wholly independently of those in Africa and Asia; Chinese civilization may well have developed independently of Southwest Asian (including the Nile and Indus) civilizations.

4500 years ago. The inhabitants of Sumer, in southern Mesopotamia, developed the world's first civilization about 5000 years ago. In China, civilization was under way by 4100 years ago. Independent of these developments in the Old World, the first cities appeared in Mesoamerica and Peru between 3000 and 2000 years ago.

What characterized these first cities? Why are they called the birthplaces of civilization? The first characteristic of cities—and of civilization—is their large size and population. But the first cities were far more than expanded Neolithic villages. The changes that took place in the transition from village to city were so great that the emergence of urban living is considered by some to be one of the great "revolutions" in human culture. The following case study gives us a glimpse of one of the world's ancient cities, how it was studied by archaeologists, and how it may have grown from a smaller farming community.

TIKAL: A CASE STUDY

The ancient city of Tikal, one of the largest lowland Maya centers in existence, is situated about 200 miles by air from Guatemala City. Tikal was built on a broad limestone terrace in a rain forest setting. Here the Maya settled in the last millennium B.C., and their civilization flourished until about A.D. 869.

At its height, Tikal covered about 120.5 square kilometers, and its nucleus, or "epicenter,"

was the Great Plaza, a large, paved area surrounded by about 300 major structures and thousands of houses. Starting from a small, dispersed population, the population of Tikal swelled to large proportions. By A.D. 600, the density of Tikal was on the order of 600 to 700 persons per square kilometer, six times that of the surrounding regions.

From 1956 through the 1960s, Tikal and the surrounding region were intensively explored under the joint auspices of the University Museum of the University of Pennsylvania and the Guatemalan government. Until 1959, the Tikal Project had investigated only the major temple and palace structures found in the vicinity of the Great Plaza, at the site's epicenter. It became evident, however, that in order to gain a balanced view of Tikal's development and composition, considerable attention would have to be devoted to hundreds of small mounds, thought to be the remains of dwellings, which surround the larger buildings. Just as one cannot get a realistic view of Washington, D.C., by looking at its monumental public buildings alone, so one cannot obtain a realistic view of Tikal without examining the full range of ruins in the area.

It became evident that a long-range program of excavation of small structures, most of which were probably houses, was necessary at Tikal. Such a program would provide some basis for an estimate of the city's population size and density; this information is critical to test the traditional assumption that the Maya could not have sustained large concentrations of population because their subsistence patterns were not adequate. Extensive excavation would also provide a sound basis for a reconstruction of the everyday life of the Maya, previously known almost entirely through a study of ceremonial remains. Moreover, the excavation might shed light on the social organization of the Maya. For example, differences in house construction and in the quality and quantity of associated remains might suggest social class differences; or features of house distribution might indicate the existence of extended families or other types of kin groups. The excavation of both large and small structures could reveal the variations in architecture and associated artifacts and burials; such variations might reflect the social structure of the total population of Tikal.

Surveying the Site

Six square kilometers surrounding the Great Plaza had already been extensively surveyed by mapping crews by the time the first excavations of small structures were undertaken. For this mapping, aerial photography was worthless because the tree canopy in this area is often 100 feet above the ground and obscures all but the tallest temples; many of the small ruins are practically invisible even to the observer on the ground. The only way to explore the region is on foot. Once a ruin is found, it is not easy to mark its exact location. Even after 4 years of careful mapping, the limits of the site still had not been revealed. Ancient Tikal was far larger than the 6 square kilometers so far surveyed. More time and money were required to continue surveying the area in order to define the city's boundaries. To simplify this problem, straight survey trails oriented toward the four cardinal directions, with the Great Plaza as the center point, were cut through the forest, measured, and staked by government surveyors. The distribution of ruins was plotted, using the trails as reference points, and the overall size of Tikal was estimated.

The area selected for the first small structure excavation was surveyed in 1957 while it was still covered by forest. A map was drawn, and 2 years later the first excavations were undertaken. Six structures, two plazas, and a platform were investigated. The original plan was to strip each of the structures to bedrock in order to obtain every bit of information possible. Three obstacles prevented this, however. First was the discovery of new structures not visible before excavation; second, the structures turned out to be much more complex architecturally than anyone had expected; and, finally, the enormous quantity of artifacts found then had to be washed and cataloged, a time-consuming process. Consequently, not every structure was completely excavated, and some remained uninvestigated.

Evidence from the Excavation

Following this initial work, more than 100 additional small structures were excavated in different parts of the site in order to ensure that a representative sample was investigated. Numerous test

The buildings shown here make up the civic and ceremonial heart of Tikal. In the foreground are the palaces where the city's rulers lived and carried out their administrative tasks. Beyond are the temples erected over the tombs of past kings.

pits were sunk in various other small structure groups to supplement the information gained from more extensive excavations.

Excavation at Tikal revealed evidence of trade in nonperishable items. Granite, quartzite, hematite, pyrite, jade, slate, and obsidian were all imported, either as raw materials or finished products. Marine materials came from Atlantic and Pacific coastal areas. Tikal itself is located on a source of abundant flint, which may have been exported in the form of raw material and finished objects. The site also happens to be located between two river systems to the east and west, and so may have been on a major overland trade route between the two. There is indirect evidence that trade went on in perishable goods such as textiles, feathers, salt, and cacao. We can safely conclude that there were full-time traders among the Tikal Maya.

In the realm of technology, specialized woodworking, pottery, obsidian, and shell workshops have been found. The skillful stone carving displayed by carved monuments suggests that this was done by occupational specialists. The complex Maya calendar required astronomers, and in order to control the large population, estimated to

This painting from Cacaxtla in southern Mexico shows a deity with the typical backpack of a Maya merchant.

Carved monuments like this were commissioned by Tikal's rulers to commemorate important events in their reigns. Portrayed on this one is a king who ruled between A.D. 768 and A.D. 790 or a bit later. Such skilled stone carving could only have been accomplished by a specialist. (For a translation of the inscription, on the monument's left, see Figure 12.3.)

have been at least 50,000 people, there must have been some form of bureaucratic organization. We do know that the government was headed by a hereditary ruling dynasty. Although we do not have direct evidence, there are clues to the existence of textile workers, dental workers, makers of bark cloth "paper," and other occupational specialists.

The religion of the Tikal Maya probably developed as a means to cope with the uncertainties of agriculture. When people are faced with problems unsolvable by technological or organizational means, they resort to manipulation of magic and the supernatural. Soils at Tikal are thin, and there is no water except that which can be collected in ponds. Rain is abundant in season, but its onset tends to be unreliable. Once the wet season arrives,

there may be dry spells of varying duration that can seriously affect crop productivity. Or there may be too much rain, so that crops rot in the fields. Other risks include storm damage, locust plagues, and incursions of wild animals. To this day, the native inhabitants of the region display great concern about these risks involved in agriculture over which they have no direct control.

The Maya priesthood devoted much of its time to calendrical matters; the priests tried not only to placate the deities in times of drought but also to propitiate them in times of plenty. They determined the most auspicious time to plant crops and were concerned with other agricultural matters. The dependence of the population in and around Tikal upon their priesthood to manipulate supernatural beings and forces in their behalf, in order that their crops would not fail, tended to keep them in or near the city in spite of the fact that a slash-and-burn method of agriculture, which was probably the prevailing method early in Tikal's history, requires the constant shifting of plots and consequently tended to disperse the population over large areas.

As the population increased, land for agriculture became scarcer, and the Maya were forced to find new methods of food production that could sustain the dense population concentrated at Tikal. To slash-and-burn agriculture as their main form of subsistence, they added the planting and tending of fruit trees and other crops that could be grown around their houses in soils enriched by human waste. Along with increased reliance on household gardening went the construction of artificially raised fields in areas that were flooded each rainy season. In these fields, crops could be intensively cultivated year after year, so long as they were carefully maintained. As these changes were taking place, a class of artisans, craftspeople, and other occupational specialists emerged to serve the needs first of religion, then of an elite consisting of the priesthood and a ruling dynasty. The arts flourished, and numerous temples, public buildings, and houses were built.

For several hundred years, Tikal was able to sustain its ever-growing population. Then the pressure for food and land reached a critical point, and population growth was halted. This event is marked archaeologically by a pullback from prime land, by the advent of nutritional problems as evidenced by the bones from burials, and by the construction of a system of ditches and embankments that probably served in the defense of the city and as a means of regulating commerce by limiting its accessibility. In other words, a period of readjustment set in, which must have been directed by an already strong central authority. Activities then continued as before, but without further population growth for another 250 years or so.

CITIES AND CULTURAL CHANGE

If someone who grew up in a small village of Maine, Wyoming, or Mississippi were to move to Chicago, Detroit, or Los Angeles, that person would experience a number of marked changes in his or her way of life. Some of the same changes in daily life would have been felt 5000 years ago by a Neolithic village dweller upon moving into one of the world's first cities in Mesopotamia. Of course, the differences would be less extreme today. In the twentieth century, every North American village, however small, is part of civilization; back when cities first developed, they were civilization, and the villages for the most part represented a continuation of Neolithic life.

Four basic culture changes mark the transition from Neolithic village life to life in the first urban centers.

This clay tablet map of farmland outside of the Mesopotamian city of Nippur dates to 1300 B.C. Shown are irrigation canals separating the various fields, each of which is identified with the name of the owner.

Agricultural Innovation

The first culture change characteristic of life in cities—hence, of civilization itself—was change in farming methods. The ancient Sumerians, for example, built an extensive system of dikes, canals, and reservoirs to irrigate their farmlands. With such a system, they could control water resources at will; water could be held and then run off into the fields as necessary. Irrigation was an important factor affecting an increase of crop yields. Because farming could now be carried on independently of the seasons, more crops could be harvested in one year. On the other hand, this intensification of agriculture did not necessarily mean that people ate better than before. Under centralized governments, intensification was generally carried out with less regard for human health than when such governments did not exist.[1]

The ancient Maya who lived at Tikal developed systems of tree cultivation and constructed raised fields in seasonally flooded swamplands to supplement their earlier slash-and-burn farming. The resultant increase in crop yields provided for a higher population density. Increased crop yields, resulting from agricultural innovations such as those of the ancient Maya and Sumerians, were undoubtedly a factor contributing to the high population densities of all civilized societies.

[1]Roosevelt, A. C. (1984). Population, health, and the evolution of subsistence: Conclusions from the conference. In M. N. Cohen & G. J. Armelagos (Eds.), *Paleopathology and the origins of agriculture* (p. 568). Orlando: Academic Press.

One technique of agricultural intensification used by the Maya reclaimed swampland by excavating canals between plots of land to drain excess water. The system shown here served until ca. A.D. 200, by which time rising water levels made further use impossible.

Diversification of Labor

The second culture change characteristic of civilization is diversification of labor. In a Neolithic village that possessed neither irrigation nor plow farming, the members of every family were primarily concerned with the raising of crops. The high crop yields made possible by new farming methods and the increased population freed more and more people from farming. For the first time, a sizable number of people were available to pursue nonagricultural activities on a full-time basis. In the early cities, some people still farmed, but a large number of the inhabitants were skilled workers or craftspeople.

Ancient public records indicate there was a considerable variety of such skilled workers. For example, an early Mesopotamian document from the city of Lagash lists the artisans, craftspeople, and others paid from crop surpluses stored in the temple granaries. Among them were coppersmiths, silversmiths, sculptors, merchants, potters, tanners, engravers, butchers, carpenters, spinners, barbers, cabinet makers, bakers, clerks, and brewers. At the ancient Maya city of Tikal we have evidence for traders, potters, woodworkers, obsidian workers, and sculptors, and perhaps textile workers, dental workers, shell workers, and paper makers.

With specialization came the expertise that led to the invention of new and novel ways of making and doing things. In the Old World, civilization ushered in what archaeologists often refer to as the **Bronze Age,** a period marked by the production of tools and ornaments of this metal. Metals were in great demand for the manufacture of farmers' and artisans' tools, as well as for weapons. Copper, tin (the raw materials from which bronze is made), and eventually iron were separated from their ores, then smelted, purified, and cast to make plows, swords, axes, and shields. In wars over border disputes or to extend a state's territory, stone knives, spears, and slings could not stand up against bronze spears, arrowheads, swords, or armor.

Bronze Age: In the Old World, the period marked by the production of tools and ornaments of bronze; began about 3000 B.C. in Southwest Asia.

Anthropology Applied

ECONOMIC DEVELOPMENT AND TROPICAL FORESTS

Prime targets for development in the world today, in the eyes of governments and private corporations alike, are vast tracts of tropical forests. On a global basis, forests are being rapidly cleared for lumber and fuel, as well as to make way for farms, ranches, mines, and other forms of economic development. The world's largest uninterrupted tracts are the forests of the Amazon and Orinoco watersheds of South America, which are being destroyed at about the rate of 4 percent a year. Just what the rate is for the world as a whole no one is quite sure, but it is clearly accelerating. And already there are signs of trouble, as extensive tracts of once-lush growth have been converted to semidesert. What happens is that essential nutrients are lost, either through erosion (which increases by several orders of magnitude under deforestation), or by leaching too deeply, as soils are exposed to the direct force of the heavy tropical rains.

The problem is that developers, until recently, have lacked reliable models by which the long-term impact of their actions might be assessed. Such a model now exists, thanks to the efforts of archaeologists unraveling the mystery of how the ancient Maya, in a tropical rain forest setting, carried out large-scale urban construction and sustained huge numbers of people successfully for two millennia. The key to the Maya success was their implementation of sophisticated practices to reduce regionwide processes of nutrient loss, deterioration of soil structure, destabilization of water flows, soil erosion, and loss of productive components of their environment.* These included construction of terraces, canals, and raised fields, the fertility of which was maintained through mulching with water plants and the addition of organic wastes. Coupled with all this, crops were planted in such a way as to produce complex patterns of foliage distribution, canopy heights, and nutrient demands. Far different from "modern" monocrop agriculture, this reduced the impact on the soils of intensive farming, while making maximum use of nutrients and enhancing their cycling in the system.

In Mexico, where population growth has threatened the country's ability to provide sufficient food for its people, archaeologists and agriculturalists are already cooperating to apply our knowledge of ancient Maya techniques to the problems of modern food production in the tropics. Application of these techniques in other tropical forested countries, like Brazil, could do much to alleviate food shortages.

*Rice, D. S., & Rice, P. M. (1984). Lessons from the Maya. *Latin American Research Review*, 19 (3), 24–28.

The native civilizations of the Americas also made use of metals—in South America, for tools as well as ceremonial and ornamental objects, but in Mesoamerica, for ceremonial and ornamental objects alone. Why people like the Aztecs and Maya continued to rely on stone for their everyday tools has puzzled those who assume that metal is inherently superior. The answer, however, is simple: The availability of obsidian (a glass formed by volcanic activity), its extreme sharpness (many times sharper

Bronze tools and weapons were more durable than their stone counterparts, which were more easily broken. The bronze sword (below) comes from Mycaenae, Greece, dating to about 1200 B.C. The ear pendant from Greece of about the same age is a fine example of the artistry that became possible with the introduction of bronze.

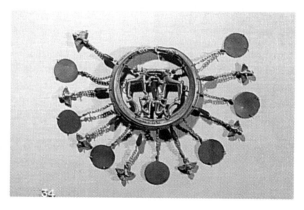

Aztec spears tipped and edged with obsidian blades are shown in this sixteenth-century drawing of a battle with their Spanish conquerors. Though superior to steel for piercing, cutting, and slashing, the brittleness of obsidian placed the Aztecs at a disadvantage when faced with Spanish swords.

than the finest steel), and the ease with which it could be worked made it perfectly suited to their needs. With obsidian, these people made tools with the sharpest cutting edges ever made.

In order to procure the raw materials needed for their technologies, extensive trade systems were developed by the early civilizations. Extensive trade agreements were maintained with distant peoples, not only to secure basic raw materials but to provide luxury items as well.

Boats gave greater access to trade centers; they could easily carry back to cities large loads of imports at less cost than if they had been brought back overland. A one-way trip from Egypt to the northern city of Byblos in Phoenicia took only four to eight days by rowboat. With a sailboat, it took even less.

Egyptian pharaohs sent expeditions to the Sinai Peninsula for copper; to Nubia for gold; to Arabia for spices and perfumes; to Asia for lapis lazuli (a blue semiprecious stone) and other jewels; to Lebanon for cedar, wine, and funerary oils; and to central Africa for ivory, ebony, ostrich feathers, leopard skins, cattle, and slaves.

With technological innovation, along with increased contact with foreign peoples through trade, came new knowledge. It was within the early civilizations that sciences such as geometry and astronomy were first developed. Geometry was used by the Egyptians for such purposes as measuring the area of a field or staking off an accurate right angle at the corner of a building.

Astronomy grew out of the need to know when to plant and harvest crops or to hold religious observances and to find exact bearings on voyages. Astronomy and mathematics were used to devise calendars. The Maya calculated that the solar year was 365 days (actually, it is 365¼ days), accurately predicted the appearances of the planet Venus as morning and evening "star," and were able to predict eclipses. As one scholar comments: "Maya science, in its representation of numbers and its empirical base is in many respects superior to the science of their European contemporaries."[2]

Central Government

The third culture change characteristic of civilization is the emergence of a governing elite, a strong central authority required to deal with the many problems arising within the new cities, owing to their size and complexity. The new governing elite saw that different interest groups, such as farmers, craftsmen, or moneylenders, provided the services that were expected of them and did not infringe on each other's rights. It ensured that the city was safe from its enemies by constructing walls and raising an army. It levied taxes and appointed tax collectors so that construction workers, the army, and other public expenses could be paid. It saw that merchants, carpenters, or farmers who made legal claims received justice. It guaranteed safety for the lives and property of ordinary people and assured that any harm done one person by another would be justly handled. In addition, surplus food had to be stored for times of scarcity, and public works such as extensive irrigation systems had to be supervised by competent, disinterested individuals. The mechanisms of government served all these functions.

[2]Frake, C. O. (1992). Lessons of the Mayan sky: A perspective from medieval Europe. In A. F. Aveni (Ed.), *The sky in Mayan literature* (p. 287). New York: Oxford University Press.

Among the occupational specialists in ancient civilizations were astronomers. This structure, at the ancient Maya city of Chichén Itzá in Mexico, was built as an observatory.

Evidence of Centralized Authority

Evidence of a centralized authority in ancient civilizations comes from such sources as law codes, temple records, and royal chronicles. Excavation of the city structures themselves provides further evidence. For example, archaeologists believe that the cities of Mohenjodaro and Harappa in the Indus Valley were governed by a centralized authority because they show definite signs of city planning. They are both more than 3 miles long; their main streets are laid out in a rectangular grid pattern; and both contain citywide drainage systems.

Monumental buildings and temples, palaces, and large sculptures are usually found in civilizations. The Maya city of Tikal contained more than 300 major structures, including temples, ball courts, and "palaces" (residences of the aristocracy). The Pyramid of the Sun in the pre-Aztec city of Teotihuacan is 700 feet long and more than 200 feet high. Its interior is filled by more than 1 million cubic yards of sun-dried bricks. The tomb of the Egyptian pharaoh Cheops, known as the Great Pyramid, is 755 feet long and 481 feet high.

It contains over 2 million stone blocks, each with an average weight of 2.5 tons. The Greek historian Herodotus reports that it took 100,000 men 20 years to build this tomb. Such gigantic structures could be built only because the considerable manpower, engineering skills, and raw materials necessary for their construction could be harnessed by a powerful central authority.

Another indicator of the existence of centralized authority is writing, or some form of recorded information (Fig. 12.2). In the Old World, early governments found it useful to keep records of state affairs, such as accounts of their food surplus, tribute records, and other business receipts. The earliest documents appear to be just such records—lists of vegetables and animals bought and sold, tax lists, and storehouse inventories. Being able to record information was an extremely important invention, because governments could keep records of their assets instead of simply relying upon the memory of administrators.

Prior to 5000 years ago, records consisted of pictures drawn or carved on stone, bone, or shell to commemorate a notable event, such as a hunt, a military victory, or the deed of some king. The earliest "picture-writing"—called pictographs—functioned much like historical paintings or newspaper photos.

The figures in such pictures gradually became simplified and generalized and stood for ideas of things, rather than for the things themselves. Thus, a royal palace could be represented by a simple stick drawing of a house with a crown placed above it. This representation of the idea of a palace is called an ideogram. In the older pictographic "writing," it would have been necessary to draw a likeness of an actual palace in order to convey the message effectively. Ideographic writing was faster, simpler, and more flexible than the pictographic system. Over the centuries the ideograms became more simplified and, although their meaning was clear to their users, they looked less and less like the natural objects they had originally depicted.

In Mesopotamia, about 6000 years ago, a new writing technique emerged, which used a stylus to make wedge-shaped markings on a tablet of damp clay. Originally, each marking stood for a word. Since most words in this language were monosyllabic, the markings came, in time, to stand for syllables. There were about 600 signs, half of them ideograms, the others functioning either as ideograms or as syllables.

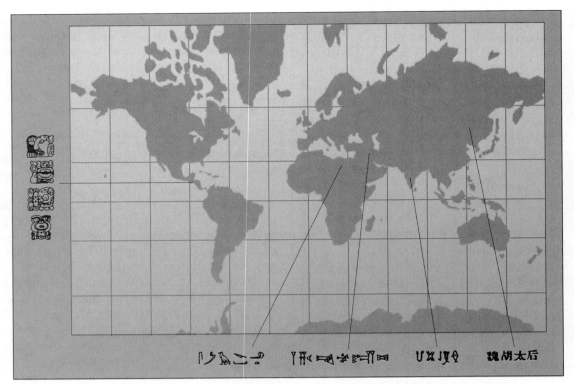

Figure 12.2 The impermanence of spoken words contrasts with the relative permanence of written records. In all of human history, writing has been independently invented no more than five times.

In the New World, systems of writing came into use among various Mesoamerican peoples, but the most sophisticated was that of the Maya. Their hieroglyphic system had less to do with keeping track of state belongings than with "dynastic bombast." Maya lords glorified themselves by recording their dynastic genealogies, important conquests, and royal marriages by using grandiose titles to refer to themselves and by associating their actions with important astrological events (Fig. 12.3). Often, the latter involved complicated mathematical calculations.

The Earliest Governments

The government organization of the earliest cities was typically headed by a king and his special advisers. In addition, there were sometimes councils of lesser advisers. Formal laws were enacted and courts sat in judgment over the claims of rival litigants or the criminal charges brought by the government against an individual.

Of the many ancient kings known, one stands out as truly remarkable for the efficient government organization and highly developed legal system that characterized his reign. This is Hammurabi, the Babylonian king who lived sometime between 1950 and 1700 B.C. He promulgated a set of laws for his kingdom, known as the Code of Hammurabi, which is important because of its thorough detail and standardization. It prescribes the correct form for legal procedures and determines penalties for perjury, false accusation, and injustice done by judges. It contains laws applying to property rights, loans and debts, family rights, and damages paid for malpractice by a physician. There are fixed rates to be charged in various trades and branches of commerce. The poor,

	The day 13 Ahau Eighteenth day of the month, Cumku,
	End of the seventeenth katun. The completion of its period.
	(Part of the ruler's name?) Chitam
	In the dynastic line, lord of Tikal, From Yax Moch Xoc (an early Tikal king)
	The ninth plus twenty, In the count of the rulers
	(Successor to ?) His lord father,
	Yax Kin Caan Chac (A probable title,)
	In the dynastic line, lord of Tikal, In his fourth katun (period of 20 tuns, or 360 day years)
	The leader (batab) Sixteen days plus one period of twenty days,
	Plus two tuns (back to), The day 11 Kan,
	Twelfth day of the month of the parrot, Kayab, He took the throne,
	At the place of leadership, He who scatters blessings.

women, children, and slaves are protected against injustice. The Code was publicly displayed on huge stone slabs so that no one accused could plead ignorance. Even the poorest citizen was supposed to know his or her rights.

Some civilizations flourished under a ruler with extraordinary governing abilities, such as Hammurabi. Other civilizations possessed a widespread governing bureaucracy that was efficient at every level, such as the government of the Inca civilization.

The Inca empire of Peru reached its zenith in the sixteenth century A.D., just before the arrival of the Spanish. In the mid-1400s, the Inca kingdom probably did not extend more than 20 miles beyond the modern-day city of Cuzco, which was then its center. Within a 30-year period, in the late 1400s, the Inca kingdom enlarged a thousand times its original size. By A.D. 1525, it stretched 2500 miles from north to south and 500 miles from east to west, making it at the time the greatest empire on the face of the earth. Its population numbered in the millions, composed of people of various ethnic groups. In the achievements of its governmental and political systems, Inca civilization surpassed every other civilization of the New World and most of those of the Old World. At the head of the government was the emperor, regarded as semidivine, followed by the royal family, the aristocracy, imperial administrators, the lower nobility, and the masses of artisans, craftspeople, and farmers.

The empire was divided into four administrative regions, further subdivided into provinces, and so on down to villages and families. Planting, irrigation, and harvesting were closely supervised by government agricultural experts and tax officials. Teams of professional relay runners could carry messages up to 250 miles in a single day over a network of roads and bridges that remains impressive even today. The Inca are unusual in that

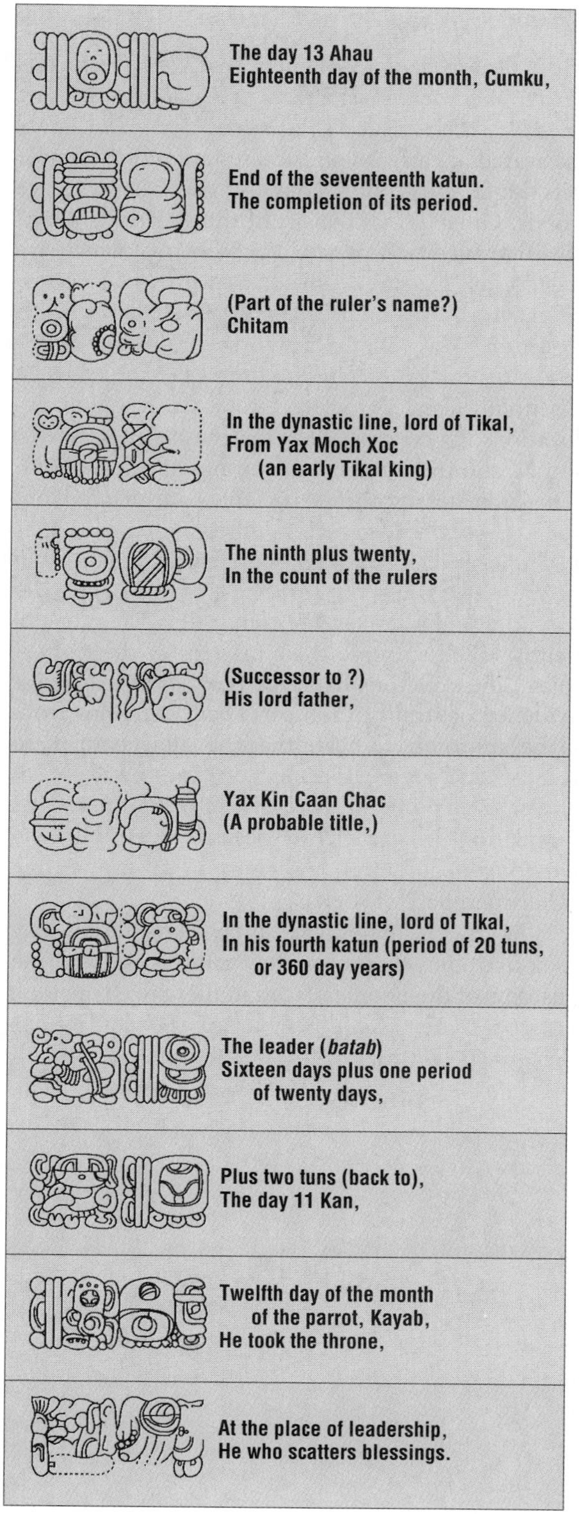

Figure 12.3 Translation of the text on the monument shown on page 288 gives some indication of the importance of dynastic genealogy to Maya rulers. The "scattering" mentioned may refer to bloodletting as part of the ceremonies associated with the end of one 20-year period, or Katun, and the beginning of the next.

they had no writing that we know about; public records and historical chronicles were kept in the form of an ingenious system of colored beads, knots, and ropes.

Social Stratification

The rise of large, economically diversified populations presided over by centralized governing authorities brought with it the fourth culture change characteristic of civilization: social stratification, or the emergence of social classes. Thus, we note that symbols of special status and privilege appeared in the ancient cities of Mesopotamia, and people were ranked according to the kind of work they did or the family into which they were born.

People who stood at or near the head of government were the earliest holders of high status. Although economic specialists of one sort or another—metal workers, tanners, traders, or the like—generally outranked farmers, such specialization did not necessarily bring with it high status. Rather, people engaged in economic activity were either of the lower class or outcasts.[3] The exception was those merchants who were in a position to buy their way into some kind of higher class status. With time, the possession of wealth, and the influence it could buy, became in itself a requisite for high status.

[3]Sjoberg, G. (1960). *The preindustrial city* (p. 325). New York: Free Press.

Evidence of Social Stratification

How do archaeologists know that there were different social classes in ancient civilizations? One way they are revealed is by burial customs. Graves excavated at early Neolithic sites are mostly simple pits dug in the ground, containing few, if any, grave goods. Grave goods consist of things such as utensils, figurines, and personal possessions, which are placed in the grave in order that the dead person might use them in the afterlife. The lack of much variation between burials in terms of the wealth implied by grave goods in Neolithic sites indicates an essentially classless society. Graves excavated in civilizations, by contrast, vary widely in size, mode of burial, and the number and variety of grave goods. This indicates a stratified society—one divided into social classes. The graves of important persons contain not only a great variety of artifacts made from precious materials, but sometimes, as in some early Egyptian burials, even the remains of servants evidently killed to serve their masters in their afterlives. The skeletons from the burials may also give evidence of stratification. At Tikal, skeletons from elaborate tombs indicate that the subjects of these tombs had longer life expectancy, ate better food, and enjoyed better health than the bulk of that city's population. In stratified societies, the elite usually live longer, eat better, and enjoy an easier life than other members of society.

As an example of what upper-class burials may look like, and what more they can tell us about the customs of the people placed in them, we may look at a spectacular tomb from one of the civilizations that preceded that of the Incas in Peru.

Original Study

Finding the Tomb of a Moche Priestess[4]

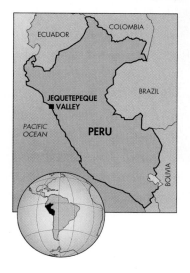

The Moche kingdom flourished on the north coast of Peru between A.D. 100 and 800. Although the Moche had no writing system, they left a vivid artistic record of their beliefs and activities on beautifully modeled and painted ceramic vessels. Because of the realism and detail of these depictions we are able to reconstruct various aspects of Moche society such as religious ceremonies and mythology, as well as activities like hunting, weaving, and combat rarely preserved in the archaeological record.

During the past 20 years we have developed a major photographic archive of Moche art at the University of California, Los Angeles, which serves as an important resource for the study of their culture. Our goal has been to reconstruct aspects of Moche culture by combining systematic studies of their art with archaeological fieldwork in Peru. Our analyses of sites, including residential compounds, palaces, temples, and cemeteries, and the artifacts associated with them have allowed us to document archaeologically some of the complex scenes illustrated in Moche art, and to understand aspects of their culture that are not portrayed in the art.

During the past ten years our research has focused on the Jequetepeque Valley, located in the northern portion of the territory occupied by the Moche. In this region we have undertaken several lines of research, concentrating our efforts on the relationship between Moche ceremonial activities and socioeconomic organization. In June 1991, UCLA began excavations at San José de Moro, a major ceremonial center in the lower Jequetepeque Valley. It was clear from its various ceramic styles that the site had a long history of occupation and thus would be ideal for answering questions about the cultural sequence of the region. Moreover, the quantity and variation in monumental construction at the site strongly suggested that it had served as a major ceremonial center through most of its occupation and thus could provide us with good insights about the nature of Moche ceremonial activity.

During our first field season we excavated three complex late Moche tombs—each consisting of a room-sized burial chamber made of mud bricks. The tomb chambers had originally been roofed with large wooden beams. The principal occupant of each tomb was lying face up in an extended position, with the remains of complete llamas, humans, or both, at their feet. In two of the tombs the principal occupants were flanked by other individuals. Hundreds of ceramic vessels and metal objects, including ceremonial knives, lance points, sandals, cups, masks, and jewelry, had been placed in the tombs as offerings.

The most elaborate of the three tombs was that of a high-status adult female. It is the richest Moche female burial ever scientifically excavated and clearly demonstrates that in Moche society extraordinary wealth and power were not the exclusive domain of males. The tomb chamber was approximately 7½ by 14 feet. The walls, which were made of mud brick, had niches—six on each side and four at the head of the tomb—in which ceramic

A silver-copper alloy mask (left) was found near the priestess's skull. Her body (right) was covered with hammered-metal arms and legs.

vessels and parts of llamas had been placed. Additional ceramic vessels had been stacked on the floor of the tomb chamber.

Some of the artifacts associated with this burial provide clear evidence that the Moche were involved in long-distance trade and that their elite expended a great deal of effort to obtain precious materials. Included among the offerings were three imported ceramic vessels—a plate of Cajamarca style, which must have been brought to San José de Moro from the highland area located more than 70 miles to the east, and two exotic ceramic bottles of Nieveria style, a type of pottery that was made in the area of Lima, more than 350 miles to the south. Two other kinds of materials associated with the tomb provide further evidence of long-distance trade. Over the woman's chest and hands were *Spondylus princeps* shells that had been brought from Ecuador to the north, and around her neck were cylindrical beads of lapis lazuli that had been brought from Chile to the south.

The most remarkable aspect of this woman's tomb, however, was that the objects buried with her allow us to identify her as a specific priestess who is depicted in Moche art. This priestess was first identified in the Moche Archive at UCLA in 1975, at which time she was given the name "Figure C." Five years later, Anne Marie Hocquenghem and Patricia Lyon convincingly demonstrated that this individual was female. She was one of the principal participants in the "Sacrifice Ceremony," an event depicted in Moche art where prisoners of war were sacrificed and their blood ritually consumed in tall ceremonial goblets.

Figure C is always depicted with her hair in wrapped braids that hang across her chest, and wearing a long dress-like garment. Also characteristic of Figure C is her headdress, which is unique in having two prominent tassels. The tomb of the woman at San José de Moro contained an identical headdress with two huge tassels made of a silver copper alloy.

In one corner of the tomb was a large blackware ceramic basin containing cups and a tall goblet. An identical blackware basin with cups in it is shown associated with Figure C in a famous mural at the site of Pañamarca,

The Moche Sacrifice Ceremony

The Sacrifice Ceremony, an event at which prisoners of war are sacrificed and their blood ritually consumed, is a common iconographic theme in Moche art. One of the better known representations of this ceremony appears on a stirrup spout bottle. The scene, center, shows four principal figures and attendants. Below them are bound captives having their throats slashed. During recent excavations at San José de Moro and at Sipán, the remains of several people who participated in this ceremony have been identified. Figure C, a priestess, was discovered at San José de Moro, while Figure A, a warrior-priest, and Figure B, a bird-warrior, were excavated at Sipán.

A goblet, recovered during the excavation of the priestess's tomb at San José de Moro, is decorated with a scene of anthropomorphic war clubs and shields drinking the blood of captives from tall goblets. A similar goblet is being passed between Figure A and Figure B in the drawing below.

Silver-copper alloy tassels worn by the principal occupant of the tomb allowed her to be identified as the priestess depicted in the Sacrifice Ceremony. The tassels are identical to those worn by Figure C in both the drawing below and the Pañamarca mural, bottom.

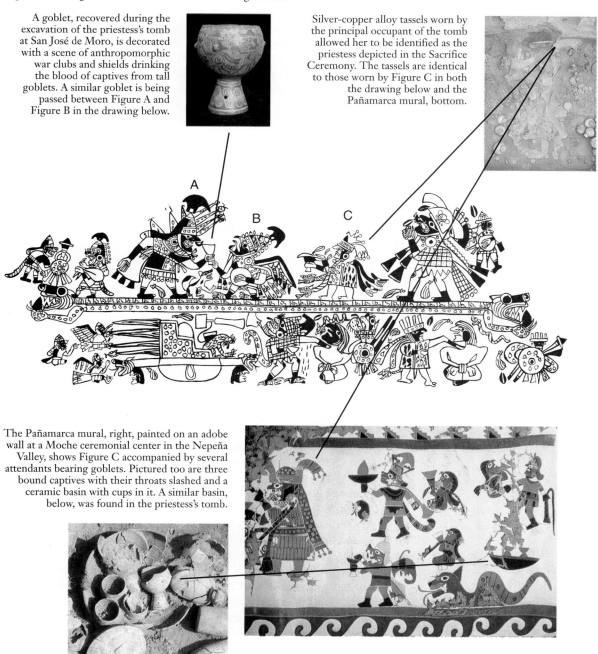

The Pañamarca mural, right, painted on an adobe wall at a Moche ceremonial center in the Nepeña Valley, shows Figure C accompanied by several attendants bearing goblets. Pictured too are three bound captives with their throats slashed and a ceramic basin with cups in it. A similar basin, below, was found in the priestess's tomb.

a ceremonial center located in the Nepeña Valley. Furthermore, the tall gob-let contained in the ceramic basin was of the type used in the Sacrifice Ceremony. It is decorated with a scene of anthropomorphized clubs and shields drinking blood from similar goblets. The tall goblet is a prominent feature in all depictions of the Sacrifice Ceremony, and it is often seen being presented by Figure C. Finding the tall goblet in her grave thus supports her identification as Figure C.

The tomb of Figure C at San José de Moro has profound implications for Moche studies. Excavations by Walter Alva at Sipán, located in a valley to the north of San José de Moro, have revealed the tombs of two other participants, Figure A and Figure B, in the Sacrifice Ceremony. The richest of these tombs is that of the Lord of Sipán, Figure A. He was buried with his characteristic crescent-shaped headdress, crescent-shaped nose orna-ment, large circular ear ornaments, and warrior's backflap, and was holding a rattle like that shown in representations of Figure A. The occupant of another tomb appears to be Figure B, a bird warrior who is frequently shown as companion to Figure A. He was found wearing a headdress adorned with an owl. Although no grave of Figure C has yet been excava-ted at Sipán, it seems likely that someone who performed this role was also buried at that site.

How do the tombs at Sipán relate to the tomb of Figure C at San José de Moro? First, it should be noted that the two tombs at Sipán date to approximately A.D. 300, and those at San José de Moro at least 250 years later—sometime after A.D. 550. Clearly, the Sacrifice Ceremony had a long duration in Moche culture, with individuals consistently dressing in traditional garments and headdresses to perform the roles of specific members of the priesthood.

The Sacrifice Ceremony was also widespread geographically. The Pañamarca mural, which clearly depicts this ceremony, was found in the Nepeña Valley, in the southern part of the Moche kingdom. San José de Moro is more than 150 miles to the north of Pañamarca, and Sipán is an-other 40 miles further north. Moreover, in the 1960s rich tombs contain-ing artifacts with Sacrifice Ceremony iconography were looted from the site of Loma Negra in the Piura Valley, more than 300 miles north of Pañamarca.

The four sites where evidence of the Sacrifice Ceremony has been found have certain characteristics in common. Each is located on an elevat-ed area that rises naturally above the intensively cultivated valley floor and is near, but not immediately adjacent to, a river. Each was a major ceremo-nial complex, with multiple pyramids that for centuries served as staging areas for religious activities. Perhaps each of the other river valleys that made up the Moche Kingdom also had a central ceremonial precinct where the Sacrifice Ceremony was enacted.

The fact that the Sacrifice Ceremony was so widespread in both time and space strongly implies that it was part of a state religion, with a priest-hood in each part of the kingdom comprised of individuals who dressed in prescribed ritual attire. When members of the priesthood died, they were buried at the temple where the Sacrifice Ceremony took place, wear-ing their ceremonial paraphernalia and accompanied by the objects they had used to perform the ritual. Subsequently, other men and women were

chosen to replace them, to dress like them, and to perform the same ceremonial role.

The careful excavation of the tomb of Figure C at San José de Moro has
provided important new insights into the nature of Moche religious practices.
As our excavations continue at this remarkable site, we expect to find additional archaeological evidence that will refine and improve upon these insights.

[4]Donnan, C. B., & Castillo, L. J. (1992). Finding the tomb of a Moche priestess.
Archaeology, 45 (6), 38–42.

In addition to burials, there are three other
ways by which archaeologists may recognize the
stratified nature of ancient civilizations.

1. *The size of dwellings.* In early Neolithic
   sites, dwellings tended to be uniformly
   small in size. In the oldest excavated cities,
   however, some dwellings were notably
   larger than others, well spaced, and located
   together in one district, whereas dwellings
   in other parts of the city were much smaller, sometimes little more than hovels. In
   the city of Eshnunna in Mesopotamia, archaeologists excavated houses that occupied
   an area of 200 meters situated on main
   thoroughfares and huts of only 50 meters

This "palace," which housed members of Tikal's ruling
dynasty, may be compared with the lower-class house
in the next photo.

Lower-class residents of Tikal lived in the same sort of houses in which most Maya
live today.

located along narrow back alleys. The rooms in the larger houses often contained impressive artwork, such as friezes or murals. At Tikal, and other Maya cities, the elite lived in large masonry, multi-roomed houses, mostly in the city's center, while lower-class people lived in small, peripherally scattered houses of one or two rooms, built partly or wholly of pole and thatch materials.

2. *Written documents.* Preserved records of business transactions, royal chronicles, or law codes of a civilization reveal much about the social status of its inhabitants. Babylonian and Assyrian texts reveal three main social classes—aristocrats, commoners, and slaves. The members of each class had different rights and privileges. This stratification was clearly reflected by the law. If an aristocrat put out another's eye, then that person's eye was to be put out, too. Hence, the saying "an eye for an eye…." If the aristocrat broke another's bone, then the first aristocrat's bone was to be broken in return. If the aristocrat put out the eye or broke the bone of a commoner, however, the punishment was to pay a mina of silver. [5]

Even in the absence of written information, people may record much about their society in other ways. As the Original Study demonstrates, the Moche recorded much information about their society in their art. The stratified nature of this ancient society is clearly revealed by the scenes painted on ceramic vessels.

3. *Correspondence.* European documents describing the aboriginal cultures of the New World as seen by early European explorers and adventurers also offer evidence of social stratification. Letters written by the Spanish conquistadors about the Aztec empire indicate that they found a social order divided into three main classes: nobles, commoners, and serfs. The nobles operated outside the lineage system on the basis of land and serfs alloted them by the ruler from conquered peoples. The commoners were divided into lineages, on which they were dependent for land. Within each of these, individual status depended on the degree of descent from the founder; those more closely related to the lineage founder had higher status than those whose kinship was more distant. The third class in Aztec society consisted of serfs bound to the land and porters employed as carriers by merchants. Lowest of this class were the slaves. Some had voluntarily sold themselves into bondage; others were captives taken in war.

Informative though written records may be, they are not without their problems. For example, European explorers did not always understand what they saw; moreover they had their own interests (or those of their sponsors) to look out for and were not above falsifying information to further those interests. These points are of major importance, given the tendency of Western peoples, with their long tradition of literacy, to assume that written documents are reliable. In fact, they are not always reliable and must be checked for accuracy against other sources of information. The same is true of ancient documents written by other people about themselves, for they, too, had their particular agendas. Ancient Maya inscriptions, for example, were often propagandistic in their intent, which was to impress people with particular rulers' importance.

THE MAKING OF CIVILIZATION

From Mesopotamia to China to the South American Andes, we witness the enduring achievements of the human intellect: magnificent palaces built high above ground; sculptures so perfect as to be unrivaled by those of contemporary artists; engineering projects so vast and daring as to awaken in us a sense of wonder. Looking back to the beginnings of history, we can see a point at which humans transform themselves into "civilized" beings; they begin to live in cities and to expand the scope of their achievements at a rapid pace. How is it, then, that humans at a certain moment in history became consummate builders,

---

[5]Moseati, S. (1962). *The face of the ancient Orient* (p. 90). New York: Doubleday.

harnessing mighty rivers so that they could irrigate crops, developing a system whereby their thoughts could be preserved in writing? The fascinating subject of the development of civilization has occupied the minds of philosophers and anthropologists alike for a long time. We do not yet have the answers, but a number of theories have been proposed.

Theories of Civilization's Emergence

Each of the theories sees the appearance of centralized government as the point at which there is no longer any question whether or not a civilization exists. So, the question they pose is: What brought about the appearance of a centralized government? Or, stated another way: What caused the transition from a small, egalitarian farming village to a large urban center in which population density and diversity of labor required a centralized government?

Irrigation Systems

One popular theory concerning the emergence of civilization was given its most forceful statement by Karl Wittfogel,[6] and variants of this theory are still held by some anthropologists. Simply put, the irrigation, or **hydraulic theory,** holds that Neolithic farmers in ancient Mesopotamia and Egypt, and later in the Americas, noticed that the river valleys that were periodically flooded contained better soils than those that were not; but they also noted that violent floods destroyed their planted fields and turned them into swamps. So the farmers built dikes and reservoirs to collect the

---

Hydraulic theory: The theory that sees civilization's emergence as the result of the construction of elaborate irrigation systems, the functioning of which required full-time managers whose control blossomed into the first governing body and elite social class.

---

[6]Wittfogel, K. A. (1957). *Oriental despotism, a comparative study of total power.* New Haven: Yale University Press.

floodwater and save it until it was needed. Then they released it into canals and ran it over the fields. At first, these dikes and canals, built by small groups of neighboring farmers, were very simple. The success of this measure led to larger, more complex irrigation systems, which eventually necessitated the emergence of a group of "specialists"—people whose sole responsibility was managing the irrigation system. The centralized effort to control the irrigation process blossomed into the first governing body and elite social class, and civilization was born.

There are several objections to this theory. One of them is that some of the earliest large-scale irrigation systems we know about anywhere in the world developed in highland New Guinea, where strong centralized governments never emerged. Conversely, actual field studies of ancient Mesopotamian irrigation systems reveal that by the year 2000 B.C., by which time many cities had already flourished, irrigation was still carried out on a small scale, consisting of small canals and diversions of natural waterways. If there were state-managed irrigation, it is argued, such a system would have been far more extensive than excavations show it really was. Moreover, documents indicate that in about 2000 B.C. irrigation was regulated by officials of local temples and not by centralized government. Irrigation systems among the American Indian civilizations of Central and South America began on so small a scale as to suggest they were built and run by families, or, at most, by small groups of local farmers. It can just as well be argued that more extensive irrigation works were a consequence of civilization's development, rather than a cause.

Trade Networks

Some anthropologists argue that trade was a decisive factor in the development of civilizations. In regions of ecological diversity, so the argument goes, trade mechanisms are necessary to procure scarce resources. In Mexico, for example, maize was grown just about everywhere; but chilies were grown in the highlands; cotton and beans were planted at intermediate elevations; certain animals were found only in the river valleys; and salt was found along the coasts.

This theory holds that some form of centralized authority was necessary in order to organize trade for the procurement of these and other commodities. Once procured, some system was necessary in order to redistribute commodities throughout the population. Redistribution, like procurement, must have required a centralized authority, promoting the growth of a centralized government.

While trade may have played an important role in the development of some civilizations, it did not invariably do so. For example, the native peoples of northeastern North America traded widely with each other for at least 6000 years without developing civilizations comparable to those of Mexico or Peru. In the course of this trade, copper from deposits around Lake Superior wound up in such faraway places as New England, as did chert from Labrador and marine shells from the seacoasts of the Gulf of Mexico. Wampum, made on the shores of Long Island Sound, was carried westward, and obsidian from the Yellowstone region has been found in mounds in Ohio.[7]

Environmental and Social Circumscription

In a series of papers, Robert Carneiro[8] has advanced the theory that civilization develops where populations are hemmed in by such things as mountains, seas, or other human populations. As such populations grow, they have no space in which to expand, and so they begin to compete for increasingly scarce resources. Internally, this results in the development of social stratification, in which an elite controls important resources to which lower classes have limited access. Externally, this leads to warfare and conquest, which, to be successful, require elaborate organization under a centralized authority.

Religion

The three theories just summarized exemplify ecological approaches to explaining the development of civilization. Such theories emphasize the inter-

relation between people and what they do on the one hand and their environment on the other. Most recent theories of the emergence of civilization take some such approach. While few anthropologists would deny the importance of the human-environment interrelationship, a growing number of them are dissatisfied with theories that do not take into account the beliefs and values that regulate the interaction between people and their environment.[9]

An example of a theory that does take into account the role of beliefs is one which seeks to explain the emergence of Maya civilization in Mesoamerica.[10] This theory holds that Maya civilization was the result of a process of urbanization that took place at places like Tikal. In the case study on Tikal earlier in this chapter, it is suggested that Maya religion probably developed as a means of coping with the uncertainties of agriculture. In the last millennium B.C., Tikal seems to have been an important religious center. Because of its religious importance, people sought to settle there, with the result that its population grew in size and density. Because this was incompatible with the prevailing slash-and-burn agriculture, which tends to promote dispersed settlement, new subsistence techniques were developed. By chance, these were sufficiently productive to permit further population growth and, by A.D. 600, Tikal had become an urban settlement of at least 50,000 people. Craft specialization also developed, at first in the service of religion but soon in the service of an emerging social elite as well. This social elite was concerned at first with calendrical ritual, but it soon developed into the centralized governing elite needed to control a population growing larger and more diversified in its interests.

Developing craft specialization served as another factor to pull people into Tikal, where their crafts were in demand. It also required further development of trade networks, if only to provide exotic raw materials. More long-distance

[7]Haviland, W. A., & Power, M. W. (1994). *The original Vermonters* (2nd ed.). Hanover, NH: University Press of New England.

[8]Carneiro, R. L. (1970). A theory of the origin of the state. *Science, 169,* 733–738.

[9]Flannery, K. V., & Marcus, J. (1976). Formative Oaxaca and the Zapotec cosmos. *American Scientist, 64,* 374, 375.

[10]Haviland, W. A. (1975). The ancient Maya and the evolution of urban society. *University of Colorado Museum of Anthropology, Miscellaneous Series, 37.*

This mosaic death mask of greenstone, pyrite, and shell was worn by a king of the Maya city of Tikal who died ca. A.D. 527. Obviously the product of skilled craft work, such specialization developed first to serve the needs of religion, but soon served the needs of the emerging elite as well.

trade contacts, of course, brought more contact with outside ideas. In other words, what we seem to have is a complex system with several factors acting upon each other, with religion playing a central role in getting the system started in the first place.

In their search for explanations for civilization's emergence, anthropologists have generally sought to find one theory to explain all cases. Yet, we may have here the cultural equivalent of what biologists call convergent evolution, where somewhat similar forms come about in quite different ways. Thus, a theory that accounts for the rise of civilization in one place may not account for its rise in another.

CIVILIZATION AND STRESS

Living in the context of civilization ourselves, we are inclined to view its development as a great step upward on some sort of ladder of progress. Whatever benefits civilization has brought, though, the cultural changes it represents seem to have produced new sorts of problems. Among them is the problem of waste disposal. Actually, waste disposal probably began to be a problem in settled, farming communities even before the emergence of civilization. But as villages grew into towns and towns grew into cities, the problem became far more serious, as the buildup of waste created optimum environments for such diseases as bubonic plague.

Quite apart from sanitation problems, the rise of towns and cities brought with it a problem of acute, infectious diseases. In a small population, such diseases, including influenza, measles, mumps, polio, rubella, and smallpox, will kill or immunize so high a proportion of the population that the virus cannot continue to propagate. Hence, such diseases, when introduced into small populations, spread immediately to the whole population and then die out. Their continued existence depends upon the presence of large population aggregates, such as towns and cities provide.

In essence, early cities tended to be disease-ridden places, with high death rates. Not until recent times did public health measures reduce the risk of living in cities, and had it not been for a constant influx of rural peoples, they would have been hard pressed to maintain their population size, let alone increase it. One might wonder, then, what would have led people to live in such unhealthy places? The answer is, they were attracted by the same sorts of things that lure people to cities today; they are vibrant, exciting places that also provide people with opportunities not available in rural communities. Of course, their experience in the cities did not always live up to advance expectations, anymore than is true today.

Early cities faced social problems strikingly similar to those found in modern North

Signs of warfare are common in ancient civilizations. China's first emperor wanted his army to remain with him—in the form of 7000 life-sized terra cotta figures of warriors.

America. Dense population, class systems, and a strong centralized government created internal stress. The slaves and the poor saw that the wealthy had all the things that they themselves lacked. It was not just a question of luxury items; the poor did not have enough space in which to live with comfort and dignity.

Evidence of warfare in early civilizations is common. Cities were fortified; documents list many battles, raids, and wars between groups; cylinder seals, paintings, and friezes depict battle scenes, victorious kings, and captured prisoners of war. Increasing population and the accompanying scarcity of good farming land often led to boundary disputes and quarrels over land between civilized states or between tribal peoples and a state. Open warfare often developed. People tended to crowd into walled cities for protection and to be near irrigation systems.

The class system also caused internal stress. As time went on, the rich became richer and the poor poorer. In early civilizations one's place in society was relatively fixed. Wealth was based on free slave labor. For this reason there was little or no impetus for social reform. Records from the Mesopotamian city of Lagash indicate that social unrest due to exploitation of the poor by the rich grew during this period. Members of the upper class received tracts of farmland some 20 times larger than those granted the lower class. An upper-class reformer, Urukaginal, saw the danger and introduced changes to protect the poor from exploitation by the wealthy, thus preserving the stability of the city.

Given the problems associated with civilization, it is perhaps not surprising that a recurring phenomenon is their collapse. Nonetheless, the rise of cities and civilization laid the basis for modern life. It is sobering to note that many of the problems associated with the first civilizations are still with us. Waste disposal, health problems associated with pollution, crowding, social inequities, and warfare continue to be serious problems. Through the study of past civilizations, we now stand a chance of understanding why such problems persist. Such an understanding will be required if the problems are ever to be overcome. It would be nice if the next cultural revolution saw the human species transcending these problems. If this comes about, anthropology, through its comparative study of civilizations, will have played a key role.

CHAPTER SUMMARY

The world's first cities grew out of Neolithic villages between 6000 and 4500 years ago, first in Mesopotamia, then in Egypt and the Indus Valley. Somewhat later, and completely independently, similar changes took place in Mesoamerica and Peru. Four basic culture changes mark the transition from Neolithic village life to life in civilized urban centers. The first culture change is agricultural innovation as new farming methods were developed. For example, the ancient Sumerians built an irrigation system that enabled them to control their water resources and thus increase crop yields.

The second culture change is diversification of labor. With the growth of large populations in cities, some people were freed from agricultural activities to develop skills as artisans and craftspeople. With specialization came the development of new technologies, leading to the beginnings of extensive trade systems. An outgrowth of technological innovation and increased contact with foreign people through trade was new knowledge; within the early civilizations sciences such as geometry and astronomy were first developed.

The third culture change that characterized urban life is the emergence of central government with authority to deal with the complex problems associated with cities. Evidence of a central governing authority comes from such sources as law codes, temple records, and royal chronicles. With the invention of writing, governments could keep records of their transactions and boast of their own glory. Further evidence of centralized government comes from archeological excavations of city structures.

Typically, the first cities were headed by a king and his special advisers. The reign of the Babylonian king Hammurabi, sometime between 1950 and 1700 B.C., is well known for its efficient government organization and the standardization of its legal system. In the New World, in Peru, the Inca empire reached its culmination in the sixteenth century A.D. With a population of several million people, the Inca state, headed by an emperor, possessed a widespread governing bureaucracy that functioned with great efficiency at every level.

The fourth culture change characteristic of civilization is social stratification, or the emergence of social classes. In the early cities of Mesopotamia, symbols of status and privilege appeared for the first time, and individuals were ranked according to the work roles they filled or the position of their families. Archaeologists have been able to verify that social classes existed in ancient civilizations in four ways: by studying burial customs, as well as skeletons, through grave excavations; by noting the size of dwellings in excavated cities; by examining preserved records in writing and art; and by studying the correspondence of Europeans who described the great civilizations they destroyed in the New World.

A number of theories have been proposed to explain why civilizations developed. The irrigation, or hydraulic, theory holds that the effort to build and control an irrigation system required a degree of social organization that eventually led to the formation of a civilization. There are several objections to this theory, however; one might argue that sophisticated irrigation systems were a result of the development of civilization rather than a cause. Another theory suggests that in the multicrop economies of both the Old and the New Worlds, some kind of system was needed to distribute the various food products throughout the population. Such a procedure would have re-

quired a centralized authority, leading to the emergence of a centralized government. A third theory holds that civilization develops where populations are circumscribed by environmental barriers or other societies. As such populations grow, competition for space and scarce resources leads to the development of centralized authority to control resources and organize warfare.

These theories all emphasize the interrelation of people and what they do on the one hand and their environment on the other. A theory that lays greater stress on the beliefs and values that regulate the interaction between people and their environment seeks to explain the emergence of Maya civilization in terms of the role religion may have played in keeping the Maya in and about cities like Tikal.

Sanitation problems in early cities, coupled with large numbers of people living in close proximity, created environments in which infectious diseases were rampant. Early urban centers also faced problems strikingly similar to our own. Dense population, class systems, and a strong centralized government created internal stress. Warfare was a common occurrence; cities were fortified and armies served to protect the state. Nevertheless, a recurrent phenomenon in all civilizations has been their ultimate collapse.

SUGGESTED READINGS

Hamblin, D. J. et al. (1973). *The first cities*. Boston: Little, Brown.

This well-illustrated volume in the Time-Life *Emergence of Man* series deals with the earliest cities in the Middle East and the Indus River Valley. Written for a popular audience, it is a good survey of the data and theories relating to these early civilizations.

Meltzer, D., Fowler, D., & Sabloff, J. (Eds.). (1986). *American archaeology: Past and future*. Washington: Smithsonian Institution Press.

This collection of articles contains one by Henry Wright, "The Evolution of Civilization," an excellent comparative consideration of the subject.

Pfeiffer, J. E. (1977). *The emergence of society*. New York: McGraw-Hill.

This is a comprehensive survey of the origins of food production and the world's first cities. In order to write the book, the author traveled to archaeological sites throughout the world and consulted with numerous investigators. The book is notable for its readability.

Redman, C. E. (1978). *The rise of civilization: From early farmers to urban society in the ancient Near East*. San Francisco: Freeman.

One of the best-documented examples of the rise of urban societies is that of Greater Mesopotamia in the Middle East. This clearly written textbook focuses on that development, presenting the data, discussing interpretations of those data, as well as problems associated with the rise of Mesopotamian civilization.

Sabloff, J. A. (1989). *The cities of ancient Mexico*. New York: Thames and Hudson.

This well written and lavishly illustrated book describes the major cities of the Olmecs, Zapotecs, Maya, Teotihuacanos, Toltecs, and Aztecs. Following the descriptions, Sabloff discusses the question of origins, the problems of archaeological reconstruction, and the basis on which he provides vignettes of life in the ancient cities. The book concludes with a gazetteer of 50 sites in Mesoamerica.

Sabloff, J. A., & Lamberg-Karlovsky, C. C. (Eds.). (1974). *The rise and fall of civilizations: Modern archaeological approaches to ancient cultures*. Menlo Park, CA: Cummings.

The emphasis in this collection of articles is theoretical or methodological rather than purely descriptive. Special emphasis is on Mesopotamia and Mesoamerica, but papers are included on Peru, Egypt, the Indus Valley, China, and Europe.

CHAPTER
13

MODERN HUMAN DIVERSITY

ONE OF THE NOTABLE CHARACTERISTICS OF THE HUMAN SPECIES
TODAY IS ITS GREAT VARIABILITY. HUMAN DIVERSITY HAS LONG
FASCINATED PEOPLE, BUT UNFORTUNATELY, IT ALSO HAS LED TO
DISCRIMINATION AND EVEN BLOODSHED.

CHAPTER PREVIEW

What Are the Causes of Physical Variability in Modern Animals?

In the gene pool of a species like *Homo sapiens*, there are various alleles for any given physical characteristic. When such a species is divided into geographically dispersed populations, as is the human species, forces such as drift and natural selection operate in slightly different ways, causing the store of genetic variability to be unevenly expressed. Thus, for example, genes for dark skin pigmentation are found in high frequency in human populations native to regions of heavy ultraviolet radiation, while genes for light skin pigmentation have a high incidence in populations native to regions of reduced ultraviolet radiation.

Is the Concept of Race Useful for Studying Human Physical Variation?

No. Because races are arbitrarily defined, it is impossible to agree on any specific classification. The problem is compounded by the tendency for "racial" characteristics to occur in gradations from one population to another without sharp breaks. Furthermore, while one characteristic may be distributed in a north-south gradient, another may occur in an east-west gradient. For these and other reasons, most anthropologists have found it most productive to study the distribution and significance of specific characteristics.

Are There Differences in Intelligence from One Population to Another?

Probably not, in spite of the fact that some populations receive lower average scores on IQ tests than others. Even so, many individuals in "low-scoring" populations score higher than some in the "higher-scoring" populations. Part of the problem is that there is no agreement on what intelligence really is, except that it is made up of several different talents and abilities. Certainly, there are genes affecting these, but they may be independently assorted, and their expression is known to be affected significantly by environmental factors.

"**W**hat a piece of work is man," said Hamlet. "How noble in reason, how infinite in faculties, in form and moving how express and admirable, in action how like an angel, in apprehension how like a god: the beauty of the world, the paragon of animals! And yet to me what is this quintessence of dust?"

What people are to each other is the province of anthropology: Physical anthropology reveals what we are; cultural anthropology reveals what we think we are. Our dreams of ourselves are as varied as our languages and our physical bodies. We are the same, but we differ. We speak English or French, our hair is curly or straight, our skin is lightly to heavily pigmented, and in height we range from short to tall. Human genetic variation generally is distributed in such a continuous range, with varying clusters of frequency. The significance we give our variations, the way we perceive them—in fact, whether we perceive them at all—is determined by our culture. For example, in many Polynesian countries, where skin color is not a determinant of social status, people pay little attention to this physical characteristic; in the United States and South Africa, it is one of the first things people do notice.

VARIATION AND EVOLUTION

Many behavioral traits—reading, for instance—are learned or acquired by living in a society; other characteristics, such as blue eyes, are passed on physically by heredity. Environment affects both. A person growing up surrounded by books learns to read. If the culture insists that brown-eyed people watch TV and blue-eyed people read, the brown-eyed people may end up making videotapes while the blue-eyed people are writing books. These skills or tastes are acquired characteristics. Changes in such things within one population but not another are capable of making the two distinct in learned behavioral characteristics within relatively few generations.

Physical Variability

The physical characteristics of both populations and individuals, as we saw in Chapter 3, are a product of the interaction between genes and environ-

ments. Thus, one's genes predispose one to a particular skin color, for example, but the skin color one actually has is strongly affected by environmental factors such as the amount of solar radiation. In this case, phenotypic expression is strongly influenced by environment; in some others, such as one's A–B–O blood type, phenotypic expression closely reflects genotype.

For most characteristics, there are within the gene pool of *Homo sapiens* variant forms of genes, known as alleles. In the color of an eye, the shape of a hand, the texture of skin, many variations can occur. This kind of variability, found in many animal species, signifies a rich potential for new combinations of characteristics in future generations. Such a species is called **polymorphic.** Our blood types, determined by the alleles for A, B, O blood, are an example of a polymorphic trait, which in this case may appear in any of four distinct phenotypic forms. A polymorphic species faced with changing environmental conditions has within its gene pool the possibility of producing individuals with traits appropriate to its altered life. Many may not achieve reproductive success, but those whose physical characteristics enable them to do well in the new environment will usually reproduce, so that their genes will show up more frequently in subsequent generations. Thus, humankind, being polymorphic, has been able to occupy a variety of environments.

A major expansion into new environments was under way by the time *Homo erectus* appeared on the scene (Chapter 8). Populations of this species were living in Africa, Southeast Asia, Europe, and China. Each of these places constitutes a different **faunal region,** which is to say that each possesses its own distinctive assemblage of animal life, not precisely like that of other regions. This differentiation of animal life is the result of selective

---

Polymorphic: A species in the gene pool of which there are alternative forms (alleles) for particular genes.

Faunal region: A geographic region with its own distinctive assemblage of animal life, not precisely like that of other regions.

pressures that, through the Pleistocene, differed from one region to another. For example, the conditions of life were quite different in China, which lies in the temperate zone, than they were in tropical Southeast Asia. Coupled with differing selective pressures were geographical features that restricted or prevented gene flow between populations of different faunal regions.

When a polymorphic species is divided into geographically dispersed populations, it usually is **polytypic;** that is, the store of genetic variability is unevenly expressed. Genetic variants will be expressed in different frequencies in different populations. For example, in the Old World, populations of *H. sapiens* living in the tropics have a higher frequency of genes for dark skin color than do those living in more northerly regions. In blood

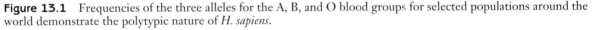

Polytypic: The expression of genetic variants in different frequencies in different populations of a species.

type, *H. sapiens* is polymorphic, with four distinct groups (A, B, O, or AB). In the distribution of these types, the polytypic nature of the species is again revealed. The frequency of the O allele is highest in American Indians, especially among some populations native to South America; the highest frequencies of the allele for type A blood tend to be found among certain European populations (although the highest frequency of all is found among the Blackfoot and Blood Indians of North America); the highest frequencies of the B allele are found in some Asian populations (see Fig. 13.1). We would expect the earlier species, *H. erectus*, with populations in the four faunal regions of the Old World, to have been polytypic. This appears to have been the case, for the fossils from each of the four regions show some differences from those in the others. African *Homo erectus*, for example, had the tall linear body build often seen in some modern African populations, whereas Chinese *erectus*, like the modern Chinese, seems to have been shorter of stature. It seems, then, that the human species has been polytypic since at least the time of *H. erectus*.

Figure 13.1   Frequencies of the three alleles for the A, B, and O blood groups for selected populations around the world demonstrate the polytypic nature of *H. sapiens*.

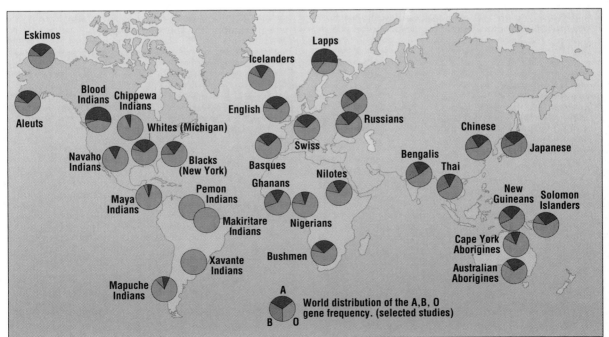

THE MEANING OF RACE

Early anthropologists tried to explore the polytypic nature of the human species by systematically classifying *H. sapiens* into subspecies, or **races,** based on geographic location and phenotypic (physical) features such as skin color, body size, head shape, and hair texture. Such classifications were continually being challenged by the presence of individuals who did not fit the categories, such as light-skinned Africans or dark-skinned "Caucasoids"; to get around the problem, it was assumed that these individuals were hybrids or racial mixtures. Lack of concordance between traits—for example, the fact that long, prominent noses are not only common among Europeans, but have a high frequency in various East African populations as well—was usually explained away in a

Race: A population of a species that differs in the frequency of the variants of some gene or genes from other populations of the same species.

similar manner. The fact is, generalized references to human types such as "Asiatic" or "Mongoloid," "European" or "Caucasoid," and "African" or "Negroid" were at best mere statistical abstractions about populations in which certain physical features appeared in higher frequencies than in other populations; no example of "pure" racial types could be found. These categories turned out to be neither definitive nor particularly helpful. The visible traits were found to occur not in abrupt shifts from population to population, but in a continuum that changed gradually, with few sharp breaks. To compound the problem, one trait might change gradually over a north-south gradient, while another might show a similar change from east to west. Human skin color, for instance, becomes progressively darker as one moves from northern Europe to central Africa, while blood type B becomes progressively more common as one moves from western to eastern Europe. Finally, there were many variations within each group, and those within groups were often greater than those between groups. In Africa, the skin color of someone from the Kalahari Desert might more closely resemble that of a person of East Indian extraction than the darkly pigmented Nilotic Sudanese who was supposed to be of the same race.

The range of variation to be seen within a supposedly single racial category is exemplified by these photos of a Tutsi, among the tallest people on earth, and an Efe pygmy, who are among the shortest.

The Negroid was characterized as having dark skin, thick lips, a broad nose, and tightly curled hair; the Mongoloid, straight hair, a flat face, a flat nose, and spread nostrils; and the Caucasoid, pale skin, a narrow nose, and varied eye color and hair form. The classification then expanded to take in American Indians, Australians, and Polynesians, but even the expanded system failed to account for dramatic differences in appearance among individuals, or even populations, in each racial category; for example, Europeans, Arabs, and East Indians were all lumped together as Caucasoids.

In an attempt to encompass such variations, schemes of racial classification multiplied. In 1926, J. Deniker classified 29 races according to texture of hair, presumably improving upon Roland B. Dixon's 1923 classification based on three indexes of body measures. Hair texture and body build were the characteristics used for another set of racial categories proposed in 1930. By 1947, Earnest Hooton had proposed three new composite races resulting from the interbreeding of "primary" races. Despite these classificatory attempts on the part of Western anthropologists, no definitive grouping of distinct, discontinuous biological groups was found for modern humanity.

A turning point is represented by the publication in 1950 of a book called *Races* by Carleton Coon, Stanley Garn, and Joseph Birdsell. Like their predecessors, they too tried to classify modern humans into a number of racial groups—30 in this case—but they rejected a trait-list approach.

Instead, they recognized races as populations that owed certain common characteristics to environmental, primarily climatic, adaptation, which continued to change in response to evolutionary forces such as gene flow and altered selective pressures. While this book certainly had its weaknesses, it represented a significant departure from previous attempts at racial classification and was influential in paving the way for our more recent understanding of human variation.

Race as a Biological Concept

To understand why the racial approach to human variation has been so unproductive, we must first understand the race concept in strictly biological terms. Briefly, a race may be defined as a population of a species that differs in the frequency of different variants of some gene or genes from other populations of the same species. Simple and straightforward though such a definition may seem, there are three important things to note about it. First, it is arbitrary; there is no agreement on how many genetic differences it takes to make a race. For some who are interested in the topic, different frequencies in the variants of one gene are sufficient; for others, differences in frequencies involving several genes were necessary. The number of genes and precisely which ones are the more important for defining races are still open to debate.

The arbitrariness of racial classification is well illustrated by the following Original Study.

Original Study
Race Without Color[1]

Science often violates simple common sense. Our eyes tell us that the Earth is flat, that the sun revolves around the Earth, and that we humans are not animals. But we now ignore that evidence of our senses. We have learned that our planet is in fact round and revolves around the sun, and that humans are slightly modified chimpanzees. The reality of human races is another commonsense "truth" destined to follow the flat Earth into oblivion.

The commonsense view of races goes somewhat as follows. All native Swedes differ from all native Nigerians in appearance: there is no Swede whom you would mistake for a Nigerian, and vice versa. Swedes have lighter skin than Nigerians do. They also generally have blond or light brown hair, while Nigerians have very dark hair. Nigerians usually have more tightly coiled hair than Swedes do, dark eyes as opposed to eyes that are blue or gray, and fuller lips and broader noses.

In addition, other Europeans look much more like Swedes than like Nigerians, while other peoples of sub-Saharan Africa—except perhaps the Khoisan peoples of southern Africa—look much more like Nigerians than like Swedes. Yes, skin color does get darker in Europe toward the Mediterranean, but it is still lighter than the skin of sub-Saharan Africans. In Europe, very dark or curly hair becomes more common outside Scandinavia, but European hair is still not as tightly coiled as in Africa. Since it's easy then to distinguish almost any native European from any native sub-Saharan African, we recognize Europeans and sub-Saharan Africans as distinct races, which we name for their skin colors: whites and blacks, respectively.

What could be more objective?

As it turns out, this seemingly unassailable reasoning is not objective. There are many different, equally valid procedures for defining races, and those different procedures yield very different classifications. One such procedure would group Italians and Greeks with most African blacks. It would classify Xhosas—the South African "black" group to which President Nelson Mandela belongs—with Swedes rather than Nigerians. Another equally valid procedure would place Swedes with Fulani (a Nigerian "black" group) and not with Italians, who would again be grouped with most other African blacks. Still another procedure would keep Swedes and Italians separate from all African blacks but would throw the Swedes and Italians into the same race as New Guineans and American Indians. Faced with such differing classifications, many anthropologists today conclude that one cannot recognize any human races at all.

If we were just arguing about races of nonhuman animals, essentially the same uncertainties of classification would arise. But the debates would remain polite and would never attract attention outside the halls of academia. Classification of humans is different "only" in that it shapes our views of other peoples, fosters our subconscious differentiation between "us" and "them," and is invoked to justify political and socioeconomic discrimination. On this basis, many anthropologists therefore argue that even if one *could* classify humans into races, one should not.

To understand how such uncertainties in classification arise, let's steer clear of humans for a moment and instead focus on warblers and lions, about which we can easily remain dispassionate. Biologists begin by classifying living creatures into species. A species is a group of populations whose individual members would, if given the opportunity, interbreed with individuals of other populations of that group. But they would not interbreed with individuals of other species that are similarly defined. Thus all human populations, no matter how different they look, belong to the same species because they do interbreed and have interbred whenever they have encountered each other. Gorillas and humans, however, belong to two different species because—to the best of our knowledge—they have never interbred despite their coexisting in close proximity for millions of years.

We know that different populations classified together in the human species are visibly different. The same proves true for most other animal and plant species as well, whenever biologists look carefully. For example, consider one of the most familiar species of bird in North America, the yellow-rumped warbler. Breeding males of eastern and western North America can be distinguished at a glance by their throat color: white in the east, yellow in the west. Hence they are classified into two different races, or subspecies (alternative words with identical meanings), termed the myrtle and Audubon races, respectively. The white-throated eastern birds differ from the yellow-throated western birds in other characteristics as well, such as in voice and habitat preference. But where the two races meet, in western Canada, white-throated birds do indeed interbreed with yellow-throated birds. That's why we consider myrtle warblers and Audubon warblers as races of the same species rather than different species.

Racial classification of these birds is easy. Throat color, voice, and habitat preference all vary geographically in yellow-rumped warblers, but the variation of those three traits is "concordant"—that is, voice differences or habitat differences lead to the same racial classification as differences in throat color because the same populations that differ in throat color also differ in voice and habitat.

Racial classification of many other species, though, presents problems of concordance. For instance, a Pacific island bird species called the golden whistler varies from one island to the next. Some populations consist of big birds, some of small birds; some have black-winged males, others green-winged males; some have yellow-breasted females, others gray-breasted females; many other characteristics vary as well. But, unfortunately for humans like me who study these birds, those characteristics don't vary concordantly. Islands with green-winged males can have either yellow-breasted or gray-breasted females, and green-winged males are big on some islands but small on other islands. As a result, if you classified golden whistlers into races based on single traits, you would get entirely different classifications depending on which trait you chose.

Classification of these birds also presents problems of "hierarchy." Some of the golden whistler races recognized by ornithologists are wildly different from all the other races, but some are very similar to one another. They can therefore be grouped into a hierarchy of distinctness. You start by establishing the most distinct population as a race separate from all other populations. You then separate the most distinct of the remaining populations. You continue by grouping similar populations, and separating distinct populations or groups of populations as races or groups of races. The problem is that the extent to which you continue the racial classification is arbitrary, and it's a decision about which taxonomists disagree passionately. Some taxonomists, the "splitters," like to recognize many different races, partly for the egotistical motive of getting credit for having named a race. Other taxonomists, the "lumpers," prefer to recognize few races. Which type of taxonomist you are is a matter of personal preference.

How does that variability of traits by which we classify races come about in the first place? Some traits vary because of natural selection: that is, one form of the trait is advantageous for survival in one area, another form in a different area. For example, northern hares and weasels develop white fur in the winter, but southern ones retain brown fur year-round. The white winter fur is selected in the north for camouflage against the snow, while any animal unfortunate enough to turn white in the snowless southern states would stand out from afar against the brown ground and would be picked off by predators.

Other traits vary geographically because of sexual selection, meaning that those traits serve as arbitrary signals by which individuals of one sex attract mates of the opposite sex while intimidating rivals. Adult male lions, for instance, have a mane, but lionesses and young males don't. The adult male's mane signals to lionesses that he is sexually mature, and signals to young male rivals that he is a dangerous and experienced adversary. The length and color of a lion's mane vary among populations, being shorter and blacker in Indian lions than in African lions. Indian lions and lionesses evidently find short black manes sexy or intimidating; African lions don't.

Finally, some geographically variable traits have no known effect on survival and are invisible to rivals and to prospective sex partners. They merely reflect mutations that happened to arise and spread in one area. They could equally well have arisen and spread elsewhere—they just didn't.

Nothing that I've said about geographic variation in animals is likely to get me branded a racist. We don't attribute higher IQ or social status to black-winged whistlers than to green-winged whistlers. But now let's consider geographic variation in humans. We'll start with invisible traits, about which it's easy to remain dispassionate.

Many geographically variable human traits evolved by natural selection to adapt humans to particular climates or environments—just as the winter color of a hare or weasel did. Good examples are the mutations that people in tropical parts of the Old World evolved to help them survive malaria, the leading infectious disease of the old-world tropics. One such mutation is the sickle-cell gene, so-called because the red blood cells of people with that mutation tend to assume a sickle shape. People bearing the gene are more resistant to malaria than people without it. Not surprisingly, the gene is absent from northern Europe, where malaria is nonexistent, but it's common in tropical Africa, where malaria is widespread. Up to 40 percent of Africans in such areas carry the sickle-cell gene. It's also common in the malaria-ridden Arabian Peninsula and southern India, and rare or absent in the southernmost parts of South Africa, among the Xhosas, who live mostly beyond the tropical geographic range of malaria.

The geographic range of human malaria is much wider than the range of the sickle-cell gene. As it happens, other antimalarial genes take over the protective function of the sickle-cell gene in malarial Southeast Asia and New Guinea and in Italy, Greece, and other warm parts of the Mediterranean basin. Thus human races, if defined by antimalarial genes would be very different from human races as traditionally defined by traits such as skin color. As classified by antimalarial genes (or their absence), Swedes are grouped with Xhosas but not with Italians or Greeks. Most other peoples usually viewed as African blacks are grouped with Arabia's "whites" and are kept separate from the "black" Xhosas.

Antimalarial genes exemplify the many features of our body chemistry that vary geographically under the influence of natural selection. Another such feature is the enzyme lactase, which enables us to digest the milk sugar lactose. Infant humans, like infants of almost all other mammal species, possess lactase and drink milk. Until about 6,000 years ago most humans, like all other mammal species, lost the lactase enzyme on reaching the age of weaning. The obvious reason is that it was unnecessary—no human or other mammal drank milk as an adult. Beginning around 4000

B.C., however, fresh milk obtained from domestic mammals became a major food for adults of a few human populations. Natural selection caused individuals in these populations to retain lactase into adulthood. Among such peoples are northern and central Europeans, Arabians, north Indians, and several milk-drinking black African peoples, such as the Fulani of West Africa. Adult lactase is much less common in southern European populations and in most other African black populations, as well as in all populations of east Asians, aboriginal Australians, and American Indians.

Once again races defined by body chemistry don't match races defined by skin color. Swedes belong with Fulani in the "lactase-positive race," while most African "blacks," Japanese, and American Indians belong in the "lactase-negative race."

Not all the effects of natural selection are as invisible as lactase and sickle cells. Environmental pressures have also produced more noticeable differences among peoples, particularly in body shapes. Among the tallest and most long-limbed peoples in the world are the Nilotic peoples, such as the Dinkas, who live in the hot, dry areas of East Africa. At the opposite extreme in body shape are the Inuit, or Eskimo, who have compact bodies and relatively short arms and legs. The reasons have to do with heat loss. The greater the surface area of a warm body, the more body heat that's lost, since heat loss is directly proportional to surface area. For people of a given weight, a long-limbed, tall shape maximizes surface area, while a compact, short-limbed shape minimizes it. Dinkas and Inuit have opposite problems of heat balance: the former usually need desperately to get rid of body heat, while the latter need desperately to conserve it. Thus natural selection molded their body shapes oppositely, based on their contrasting climates.

Other visible traits that vary geographically among humans evolved by means of sexual selection. We all know that we find some individuals of the opposite sex more attractive than other individuals. We also know that in sizing up sex appeal, we pay more attention to certain parts of a prospective sex partner's body than to other parts. Men tend to be inordinately interested in women's breasts and much less concerned with women's toenails. Women, in turn, tend to be turned on by the shape of a man's buttocks or the details of a man's beard and body hair, if any, but not by the size of his feet.

But all those determinants of sex appeal vary geographically. Khoisan and Andaman Island women tend to have much larger buttocks than most other women. Nipple color and breast shape and size also vary geographically among women. European men are rather hairy by world standards, while Southeast Asian men tend to have very sparse beards and body hair.

What's the function of these traits that differ so markedly between men and women? They certainly don't aid survival: it's not the case that orange nipples help Khoisan women escape lions, while darker nipples help European women survive cold winters. Instead, these varying traits play a crucial role in sexual selection. Women with very large buttocks are a turn-on, or at least acceptable, to Khoisan and Andaman men but look freakish to many men from other parts of the world. Bearded and hairy men readily find mates in Europe but fare worse in Southeast Asia. The geographic variation of these traits, however, is as arbitrary as the geographic variation in the color of a lion's mane.

There is a third possible explanation for the function of geographically variable human traits, besides survival or sexual selection—namely, no function at all. A good example is provided by fingerprints, whose complex pattern of arches, loops, and whorls is determined genetically. Fingerprints also vary geographically: for example, Europeans' fingerprints tend to have many loops, while aboriginal Australians' fingerprints tend to have many whorls.

If we classify human populations by their fingerprints, most Europeans and black Africans would sort out together in one race, Jews and some Indonesians in another, and aboriginal Australians in still another. But those geographic variations in fingerprint patterns possess no known function whatsoever. They play no role in survival: whorls aren't especially suitable for grabbing kangaroos, nor do loops help bar mitzvah candidates hold on to the pointer for the Torah. They also play no role in sexual selection: while you've undoubtedly noticed whether your mate is bearded or has brown nipples, you surely haven't the faintest idea whether his or her fingerprints have more loops than whorls. Instead it's purely a matter of chance that whorls became common in aboriginal Australians, and loops among Jews. Our rhesus factor blood groups and numerous other human traits fall into the same category of genetic characteristics whose geographic variation serves no function.

Fingerprints' patterns of loops, whorls, and arches are genetically determined. Grouping together people on this basis would place most Europeans, sub-Saharan Africans, and east Asians together as "loops," Australian aborigines and the people of Mongolia together as "whorls," and Central Europeans and the Bushmen of southern Africa together as "arches."

[1]Diamond, J. (1994). Race without color. *Discover, 15* (11), 83–88.

After arbitrariness, the second thing to note about the biological definition of race is that it does not mean that any one race has exclusive possession of any particular variant of any gene or genes. In human terms, the frequency of the allele for blood group O may be high in one population and low in another, but it is present in both. Races are genetically "open," meaning that gene flow takes place between them. Because they are genetically "open," they are apt to be impermanent and subject to reamalgamation. Thus, one can easily see the fallacy of any attempt to identify "pure" races; if gene flow cannot take place between two populations, either directly or indirectly through intermediate populations, then they are not races, but are separate species.

The third thing to note about the biological definition of race is that individuals of one race will not necessarily be distinguishable from those of another. In fact, as we have just noted with respect to humans, the differences between individuals within a population may be greater than the differences between populations. As the science writer James Shreeve puts it, "most of what separates me genetically from a typical African or Eskimo also separates me from another average American of European ancestry."[2] This follows from the genetic "openness" of races; no one race has an exclusive claim to any particular gene or allele.

[2]Shreeve, J. (1994). Terms of estrangement. *Discover, 15* (11), 60.

The "openness" of races to gene flow is illustrated by this picture of an Asian and African-American couple with their children.

The Concept of Human Races

As a device for understanding polytypic variation in humans, the biological race concept has serious drawbacks. One is that the category is arbitrary to begin with, which makes agreement on any given classification difficult, if not impossible. For example, if one researcher emphasizes skin color, while another emphasizes blood group differences, it is unlikely that they will classify people in the same way. Perhaps if the human species were divided into a number of relatively discrete breeding populations, this would not be such a problem, but even this is open to debate. What has happened, though, is that human populations have grown in the course of human evolution, and with this growth have come increased opportunities for contact and gene flow between populations. Since the advent of food production, the process has accelerated as higher birth rates and periodic food shortages have prompted the movement of farmers from their homelands to other places (see Chapter 11). Thus, differences between human populations today are probably less clear-cut than back in the days of *H. erectus* or even archaic *H. sapiens*.

If this is not enough of a problem, things are complicated even more because humans are so complicated genetically. Thus, the genetic underpinnings of the phenotypic traits upon which traditional racial classifications are usually based are poorly understood. To compound the problem, "race" exists as a cultural, as well as a biological, category. In various different ways, cultures define religious, linguistic, and ethnic groups as races, thereby confusing linguistic and behavioral traits with physical traits. For example, in many Central and South American countries, people are commonly classified as "Indian," "Mestizo" (mixed), or "Ladino" (of Spanish descent). But in spite of the biological connotations of these terms, the criteria used for assigning individuals to these categories consist of such things as whether they wear shoes, sandals, or go barefoot; speak Spanish or some Indian language; live in a thatched hut or a European-style house; and so forth. Thus, an Indian, by speaking Spanish, wearing Western-style clothes, and living in a house in a non-Indian neighborhood, ceases to be an Indian, no matter how many "Indian genes" he or she may possess.

This sort of confusion of nonbiological characteristics with what are spoken of as biological

These pictures of individuals from China and the Andaman Islands, both in Asia, reveal the absurdity of lumping all Asians in a single category.

categories is by no means limited to Central and South American societies. To one degree or another, such confusion is found in most Western societies, including those of Europe and North America. Take, for example, the racial categories used by the U.S. Census Bureau: White, Black, American Indian, Asian, and Pacific Islander are large catch-all categories that include diverse people (Asian, for example, includes such different people as Chinese and East Indians—to which Indians, at least, take exception), whereas Eskimo (a term these people find offensive) and Aleut are far more restrictive. Presently under consideration are the addition of slots for native Hawaiians, Middle Easterners, and people who consider themselves multiracial. To compound the confusion, inclusion in one or another of these categories is usually based on self-identification. In short, what we are dealing with here are social rather than biological categories.

To make matters even worse, this confusion of social with biological factors is frequently combined with attitudes that are then taken as excuses to exclude whole categories of people from certain roles or positions in society. In the United States, for example, it has frequently been asserted that "Blacks are born with rhythm," which somehow is thought to give them a "natural affinity" for jazz, "soul music," rap, and similar forms of musical ex-

pression. The corollary of this is that African Americans are unsuited "by nature" for symphonic music. Hence, until recently, one did not find an African American at the head of any major symphony orchestra in the United States, even though African American conductors such as James de Priest, Paul Freeman, and Dean Dixon made distinguished careers for themselves in Canada and Europe.

One of the prime examples of the evil consequences of misconstruction of race occurred when the Nazis declared the superiority of the "Aryan race" (which is really a linguistic grouping and not a race at all), and the inferiority of the gypsy and Jewish "races" (really ethnic/religious categories), and then used this distinction as an excuse to exclude Gypsies and Jews from life altogether. Tragically, such programs of extermination of one group by another continue to occur in many parts of the world today, including parts of South America, Africa, Europe, and Asia. "Holocausts" are by no means things of the past, nor are Gypsies and Jews their only victims. The well-meant vow "never again" contrasts with the reality of "frequently again."

Considering all the problems, confusion, and evil consequences, it is small wonder that there has been much debate not just about how many human races there may be, but about what "race" is

Far from being a thing of the past, genocide continues to occur in the world today, as this picture from Rwanda vividly illustrates.

and is not. Often forgotten is the fact that a race, even if it can be defined, is the result of the operation of evolutionary processes. Because it is these processes rather than racial categories themselves in which we are really interested, most anthropologists have abandoned the race concept as being of no particular utility. Instead, they prefer to study the distribution and significance of specific, genetically based characteristics, or else the characteristics of small breeding populations that are, after all, the smallest units in which evolutionary change occurs.

Some Physical Variables

In spite of all the debate about the reality of human races, human biological variation is a fact of life, and physical anthropologists have learned a great deal about it. Much of it seems related to climatic adaptation. For example, a correlation has been noted between body build and climate. Generally, people native to regions with cold climates tend to have greater body bulk (not to be equated with fat) relative to their extremities (arms and legs) than do people native to regions with hot climates, who tend to be long and slender. Interestingly, these differences show up as early as the time of *Homo erectus*, as already noted. Anthropologists generally argue that such differences of body build represent a climatic adaptation; certain body builds are better suited to particular living conditions than others. A person with larger body bulk and shorter extremities may suffer more from summer heat than someone whose extremities are long and whose body is slender. But they will conserve needed body heat under cold conditions. The reason is that a bulky body tends to conserve more heat than a less bulky one, since it has less surface relative to volume. People living in hot, open country, by contrast, benefit from a body build that can get rid of excess heat quickly so as to keep from overheating; for this, long extremities and a slender body, which increase surface area relative to volume, are advantageous.

Studies of body build and climatic adaptation are complicated by the intervening effects on physique of diet, since dietary differences will cause variation in body build. Another complicating factor is clothing. For example, Inuit peoples (the proper name for "Eskimos") live in a region where it is cold much of the year. To cope with this, they long ago developed efficient clothing to keep the body warm. Because of this, the Inuit are provided with what amount to artificial tropical environments inside their clothing. In spite of such considerations, it remains true that in northerly regions of the world, bulky body builds predominate, whereas the reverse is true in the tropics.

Anthropologists have also studied such body features as nose, eye shape, and hair textures in relation to climate. A wide flaring nose, for example, is common in populations living in tropical forests; here the air is warm and damp, and so the warming and humidifying functions of the nose are secondary. Longer, more prominent noses, common among cold dwellers, are helpful in humidifying and warming cold air before it reaches the lungs. They are also useful in cleaning and humidifying dry, dusty air in hot climates as well, which is why long prominent noses are not restricted to places like Europe. Coon, Garn, and Birdsell once proposed that the "Mongoloid face," common in populations native to East and Central Asia, as well as arctic North America, exhibits features adapted to life in very cold environments. The **epicanthic eye fold,** which reduces eye exposure to the cold to a minimum, a flat facial profile, and extensive fatty deposits may help to protect the face against frostbite. Although experimental studies have failed to sustain the frostbite hypothesis, it is true that a flat facial profile generally goes with a round head. A significant percentage of body heat may be lost from the head; however, a round head, having less surface area relative to volume, loses less heat than a longer, more elliptical head. As one would predict from this, long-headed populations are generally found in hotter climates; round-headed ones are more common in cold climate areas.

The epicanthic eye fold is common among peoples native to eastern Asia.

Skin Color: A Case Study in Adaptation

In the United States, race is most commonly equated with skin color. Perhaps this is inevitable, since it is such an obvious physical trait. Skin color is subject to great variation, and there are at least four main factors associated with it: transparency or thickness of the skin, a copper-colored pigment called carotene, reflected color from the blood vessels, and the amount of **melanin** found in a given

Epicanthic eye fold: A fold of skin at the inner corner of the eye that covers the true corner of the eye; common in Asiatic populations.

Melanin: The chemical responsible for dark skin pigmentation that helps protect against damage from ultraviolet radiation.

area of skin. Exposure to sunlight increases the amount of melanin and, hence, the skin darkens. Melanin is known to protect skin against damaging ultraviolet solar radiation;[3] consequently, darkly pigmented peoples are less susceptible to skin cancers and sunburning than are those whose skin has less melanin. They also seem to be less susceptible to photo-destruction of certain vitamins. Since the highest concentration of dark-skinned people tends to be found in the tropical regions of the world, it appears that natural selection has favored heavily pigmented skin as a protection against the strong solar radiation of equatorial latitudes, where ultraviolet radiation is most intense. Because skin cancers generally do not develop until later in life, they are unlikely to have interfered with the reproductive success of lightly pigmented individuals in the tropics, and so are unlikely to have been the agent of selection. On the other hand, severe sunburn, which is especially dangerous to infants, causes the body to overheat and interferes with its ability to sweat, by which it might rid itself of excess heat. Furthermore, it makes one susceptible to other kinds of infection. In addition to all this, decomposition of folate, a vitamin sensitive to heavy doses of ultraviolet radiation, can cause anemia, spontaneous abortion, and infertility.[4]

While dark skin pigmentation has enjoyed a selective advantage in the tropics, the opposite is true in northern latitudes, where skins have generally been lightly pigmented. This lack of heavy amounts of melanin enables the weak ultraviolet radiation of northern latitudes to penetrate the skin and stimulate formation of vitamin D. Dark pigmentation interferes with this. Without access to external sources of vitamin D, once provided by

[3]Neer, R. M. (1975). The evolutionary significance of vitamin D, skin pigment, and ultraviolet light. *American Journal of Physical Anthropology, 43,* 409–416.

[4]Branda, R. F., & Eatoil, J. W. (1978). Skin color and photolysis: An evolutionary hypothesis. *Science, 201,* 625–626.

These photos of people from Spain, Scandinavia, Senegal, and Indonesia illustrate the range of variation in human skin color. Generally, the closer to the equator populations live, the darker the skin color.

cod liver oil but now more often provided in vitamin D fortified milk, individuals incapable of synthesizing enough of this vitamin in their own bodies were selected against, for they contracted rickets, a disease that seriously deforms children's bones. At its worst, rickets prevents children from reaching reproductive age; at the least, it interferes with a woman's ability to give birth if she does reach reproductive age (see Fig. 13.2).

Given what we know about the adaptive significance of human skin color, and the fact that, until 700,000 years ago, hominines were exclusively creatures of the tropics, it is likely that lightly pigmented skins are a recent development in human history. Darkly pigmented skins likely are quite ancient. Consistent with this, the enzyme tyrosinase, which converts the amino acid tyrosine into the compound that forms melanin, is present in lightly pigmented peoples in sufficient quantity to make them very "black." The reason it does not is that they have genes that inactivate or inhibit it.[5] Human skin is more liberally endowed with sweat glands than is the skin of other mammals; in combination with our lack of much in the way of body hair, this makes for effective elimination of excess body heat in a hot climate. This would have been especially advan-

[5]Wills, C. (1994). The skin we're in. *Discover, 15* (11), 79.

Figure 13.2 The outline of a normal pelvic inlet (A) is compared with that of a woman with rickets (B), which would interfere with her capacity to give birth. Rickets is caused by a deficiency of vitamin D. In the absence of artificial sources of the vitamin among people living in northern latitudes, lightly pigmented people are least likely to contract rickets.

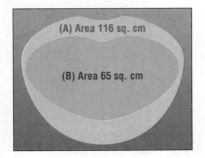

(A) Area 116 sq. cm

(B) Area 65 sq. cm

tageous to early hominines on the savanna, who could have avoided confrontations with carnivorous animals by carrying out most of their activities in the heat of the day. For the most part, carnivores rest then, being active from dusk until early morning. Without much hair to cover early hominine bodies, selection would have favored dark skins; hence all humans appear to have had a "Black" ancestry, no matter how "White" some of them may be today.

One should not conclude that, because it is newer, lightly pigmented skin is better, or more highly evolved, than heavily pigmented skin. The latter is clearly more highly evolved to the conditions of life in the tropics, although with protective clothing, hats, and sunscreen lotions, lightly pigmented peoples can survive there. Conversely, the availability of supplementary sources of vitamin D allows heavily pigmented peoples to do well away from the tropics. In both cases, culture has rendered skin color differences largely irrelevant.

The inheritance of skin color is not well understood, except that several genes (rather than variants of a single gene), each with its own variants, must be involved. Nevertheless, its geographical distribution, with few exceptions, tends to be continuous, like that of other human traits (see Fig. 13.3). The exceptions have to do with the movement of certain populations from their original homelands to other regions, and/or the practice of selective mating. For example, there have been repeated invasions of the Indian subcontinent by peoples from the north, who were then incorporated into the Hindu caste system. Still today, the higher the caste, the lighter its skin color. This skin color gradient is maintained by strict in-group marriage rules. In the United States, statistical studies have shown that there has been a similar trend among African Americans, with African-American women of higher status choosing to marry lighter-skinned males, reflecting the culture's emphasis on light skin as a status symbol. It is possible that the "Black pride" movement, which places positive value on features common among those of West African descent, such as dark skins, tightly curled hair, and broad flat noses, is leading to a reversal of this cultural selection factor.

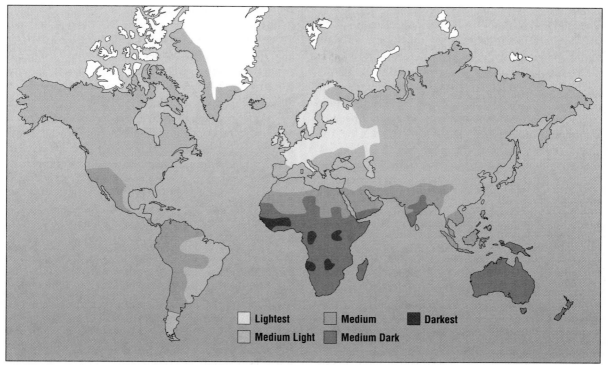

Figure 13.3   This map illustrates the distribution of human skin color before 1492.

THE SOCIAL SIGNIFICANCE OF RACE: RACISM

Scientific facts do not seem to change what people think about race. **Racism** can be viewed solely as a social problem, although at times it has been used by politicians as a purportedly "scientific" tool. It is an emotional phenomenon best explained in terms of collective psychology. Racial conflict results from long-suppressed resentments and hostilities. The racist responds to social stereotypes, not to known scientific facts.

Racism: A doctrine of racial superiority by which one group asserts its superiority over another.

Race and Behavior

The assumption that there are behavioral differences among human races remains an issue of contemporary society, not easily argued away. Throughout history, certain "races" have been attributed certain characteristics, which assume a variety of names—"national character," "spirit," "temperament"—all of them vague and standing for a number of concepts totally unrelated to the biological concept of race. Common myths involve the "coldness" of the Scandinavians or the "martial" character of the Germanics or the "indolent" nature of Africans. These generalizations serve to characterize a people unjustly; German citizens do not necessarily advocate genocide, nor do Africans necessarily hate to work. The term *race* has a precise biological meaning, but in popular usage, as we have already seen, the term often acquires a meaning unrelated to that given by scientists, often with disastrous results.

To date, no innate behavioral characteristic can be attributed to any group of people that the non-scientist would most probably term a "race" that cannot be explained in terms of cultural practices. If the Chinese happen to be especially successful mathematicians, it can probably be explained in terms of emphasis within their culture on abstract concepts, learned ways of perceiving the universe, and their philosophies. If African Americans are not as well represented in managerial positions as their fellow citizens, it is because for a long time they were given neither the necessary training nor the opportunity (nor is the problem fully rectified today). The list could go on, and all such differences or characteristics can be explained in terms of culture.

Similarly, high crime rates among certain groups can be explained with reference to culture and not biology. Individuals alienated and demoralized by poverty, injustice, and inequality of opportunity tend to display what the dominant members of society regard as antisocial behavior more frequently than those who are culturally well integrated. For example, American Indians, when they have been equipped and allowed to compete on an equal footing with other North Americans, have not suffered from the high rate of alcoholism and criminal behavior exhibited by Indians living under conditions of poverty whether on or off reservations.

Race and Intelligence

A question frequently asked by those unfamiliar with the deficiencies of the race concept is whether some races are inherently more intelligent than others. Intelligence tests carried on in the United States by European American investigators among people of European and African descent have often shown that European Americans attain higher scores. During World War I, a series of tests known as Alpha and Beta IQ tests were regularly given to draftees. The results showed that the average score attained by European Americans was higher than that obtained by African Americans. Even though many African Americans scored higher than some European Americans, and some African Americans scored higher than most European Americans (African Americans from the north, for instance,

score better on average than southern Whites), many people took this as proof of the intellectual superiority of "White people." But all the tests really showed was that, on the average, European Americans outperformed African Americans in certain social situations. The tests did not measure "intelligence" per se, but the ability, conditioned by culture, of certain individuals to respond to certain socially conditioned problems. These tests had been conceived by European Americans for comparable middle-class European Americans. While people of color coming from similar backgrounds generally did well (Chinese and Japanese Americans, for example, generally outperform "Whites"), European Americans as well as people of color coming from other backgrounds to meet the challenge of these tests were clearly at a disadvantage. It would be unrealistic to expect individuals unfamiliar with European American middle-class values and linguistic behavior to respond to a problem based on a familiarity with these.

Many large-scale intelligence tests continue to be administered in the United States. Notable among these are several series in which environmental factors are held constant. Where this is done, African and European Americans tend to score equally well.[6] Nor is this surprising; since genes assort themselves independently of one another, there is no reason to suppose that whatever alleles may be associated with intelligence are likely to be concordant with the ones for skin pigmentation. Intelligence tests, however, have increasingly become the subject of controversy. There are many psychologists as well as anthropologists who believe that their use is overdone. Intelligence tests, they say, are of limited use, since they are applicable only to particular cultural circumstances. Only when these circumstances are carefully met can any meaningful generalizations be derived from the use of tests.

Notwithstanding the foregoing, there continue to be some who insist that there are significant differences in intelligence between human populations. The latest proponents of this view are the psychologist Richard Herrnstein and Charles

[6]Sanday, P. R. (1975). On the causes of IQ differences between groups and implications for social policy. In M. F. A. Montagu (Ed.), *Race and IQ* (pp. 232–238). New York: Oxford.

On one IQ test designed to be "fair" to both "Black" and "White" American students, they are asked to identify either of two famous dead scientists, Albert Einstein or George Washington Carver. Unfortunately, Carver is a mostly "White" person's "Black" hero, so a "White" is more likely to identify either than is a "Black" (see Mark Cohen, 1995, "Anthropology and Race: The Bell Curve Phenomenon," *General Anthropology* 2(1), p. 3).

Murray, a social scientist who is a fellow of the American Enterprise Institute, a conservative think tank. Their argument, in a lengthy book called *The Bell Curve*, is that a well-documented 15-point difference in IQ exists between African and European Americans, with the latter scoring higher, though not quite as high as Asian Americans. Furthermore, these differences are mostly determined by genetic factors and are therefore immutable.

Herrnstein and Murray's book has been justly criticized on many grounds, including violation of all sorts of rules of statistics and their practice of utilizing studies, no matter how flawed, that appear to support their thesis while ignoring or barely mentioning those that contradict it. But does this mean that they are wrong? On purely theoretical grounds, could we not suppose that, just as we see a spectrum of inherited variations in physical traits—skin color, hair texture, height, or whatever—might there not be similar variation in innate intellectual potential of different populations? It is likely that just as there are genes affecting the development of such things as blue eyes, curly hair, or heavily pigmented skin, there are others affecting the development of intelligence. Of course, even if genes affecting intelligence do exist, we would still need to ask why their distribution should be any more concordant with those for skin color than with ones that determine whether one has A, B, or O blood, normal or abnormal (antimalarial) hemoglobin, whether one can digest raw milk, or whatever.

From a number of studies it is now clear that there is indeed an appreciable degree of hereditary control of intelligence. First, there is a general tendency for those pairs of individuals who are most genetically similar (identical twins) to be most similar in intelligence, even when reared in different environments. Furthermore, the scores on IQ tests of biological parents and their children are correlated and tend to be similar, while foster parents and their foster children show little of this tendency.

Equally clear are the effects of environment on intelligence. For example, in the early 1900s, new immigrants to the United States, many of whom were Jews, scored lower on IQ tests that U.S. born "Whites." Today, the descendents of those Jewish immigrants score 10 points higher on average than "Whites." In fact, IQ scores of all groups have risen some 15 points in the last 40 years, some faster than others. The gap between African and European Americans, for example, is narrower today than in the past. Nor is this surprising, for there are studies showing impressive IQ scores for African-American children from poor backgrounds who have been adopted into affluent and intellectual homes. It is now known that disadvantaged children adopted into affluent and stable families can boost their IQs by 20 points. It is also well known that IQ scores rise with the amount of schooling the test-takers have.[7] More such cases could be cited, but these suffice to make the point: The assertion that IQ is fixed and immutable is clearly false. Just as millions of people overcome deficiencies of vision that are far more heritable than *anyone* claims intelligence to be, so may enriched education increase intelligence.

Intelligence: What Is It?

A question that must now be asked is: What do we mean by the term *intelligence?* The answer, to some, is that which is measured by IQ tests. Unfortunately, there is no general agreement as to what abilities or talents actually make up the trait of intelligence, even though there are some psychologists who insist that it is a single quantifiable thing. Many more psychologists believe intelligence to be the product of the interaction of different sorts of cognitive abilities: verbal, mathematical-logical, spatial, linguistic, musical, bodily kinesthetic, social, and personal.[8] Each may

be thought of as a particular kind of intelligence, unrelated to the others. This being so, they must be independently inherited (to the degree they are inherited), just as height, blood type, skin color, and so forth are independently inherited. Thus, the various abilities that constitute "intelligence" may be independently distributed as are, for example, the previously discussed skin color and blood type (compare Fig. 13.3 and 13.4).

The next question is: If we are not exactly sure what IQ tests are measuring, how can we be sure of the validity of such tests—that is, can we be sure an IQ test measures what it is supposed to measure? The answer, of course, is that we cannot be sure. But even at best, an IQ test measures performance (something that one does) rather than genetic disposition (something that lies within the individual). Reflected in one's performance are one's past experiences and present motivational state, as well as one's innate ability. In sum, it is fair to say that an IQ test is not a reliable measure of innate intelligence.

Attempts to prove the existence of significant differences in intelligence between human populations have been going on as long as people have been talking about race. But in spite of all, the hypothesis remains unproven. Nor is it ever likely to be proven, in view of what we saw in Chapter 10 as the major thrust in the evolution of the genus *Homo.* Over the past 2.5 million years, in all populations of this genus, the emphasis has been on cultural adaptation—actively inventing solutions to the problems of existence, rather than passively relying on biological adaptation. Thus, we would expect a comparable degree of intelligence in all present-day human populations. But even if this were not the case, it would mean only that "dull" and "bright" people are to be found in all human populations, though in different frequencies. Thus, geniuses can and do appear in any population, regardless of what that population's "average" intelligence may be. The fact of the matter is that the only way to be sure that individual human beings develop their innate abilities and skills, whatever they may be, to the fullest is to make sure they have access to the necessary resources and the opportunity to do so. This certainly cannot be accomplished if whole populations are assumed at the outset to be inferior.

[7]Jacoby, R., & Glauberman, N. (Eds.). (1995). *The bell curve debate* (pp. 7, 55–56, 59). New York: Random House.
[8]Ibid., pp. 9, 121.

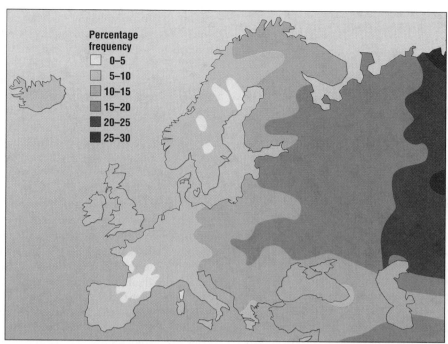

Figure 13.4   The east-west gradient in the frequency of Type B blood (shown above) in Europe contrasts with the north-south gradient in skin color (shown in Figure 13.3). Whatever genes are involved in the various abilities lumped together as "intelligence" must be independently assorted as well.

These winners of the Nobel Peace Prize—Nelson Mandela (Xhosa African), Rigoberta Menchu (Maya Indian), and Daw Aung San Suu Kyi (Burmese Asian)—illustrate the point that individuals of exceptional ability can and do appear in any human population.

CONTINUING HUMAN BIOLOGICAL EVOLUTION

In the course of their evolution, humans in all parts of the world have come to rely on cultural rather than biological adaptation for their survival. Nevertheless, as they spread beyond their tropical homeland into other parts of the world, they did develop considerable physical variation from one population to another. The forces responsible for this include genetic drift and biological adaptation to differing climates.

Although much of this physical variation can still be seen in human populations today, the increasing effectiveness of cultural adaptation has often reduced its importance. For instance, the consumption of cod liver oil or vitamin D–fortified milk has canceled out the selective advantage of lightly pigmented skins in northern peoples. At the same time, culture has also imposed its own selective pressures, as we have seen in preceding chapters. Just as the invention of the spear-thrower was followed by a reduction in overall muscularity, or just as the transition to food production was followed by worsened health and mortality, cultural practices today are affecting the human organism in important, often surprising, ways.

The probability of alterations in human biological makeup induced by culture raises a number of important questions. By trying to eliminate genetic variants for balanced polymorphic traits, such as the sickle-cell trait discussed in Chapter 3, are we also removing alleles that have survival value? Are we weakening the gene pool by allowing people with hereditary diseases and defects to reproduce? Are we reducing chances for genetic variation by trying to control population size?

We are not sure of the answers to all of these questions. If we are able to wipe out sickle-cell anemia, we also may be able to wipe out malaria; thus, we would have eliminated the condition that made the sickle-cell trait advantageous. On the other hand, antimalarial campaigns have had at most limited success, as the disease afflicts some 270 million people around the world. Moreover, as a consequence of global warming, the disease is spreading (with a number of others) into more northerly regions. Over the next century, an average temperature increase of 3 degrees Celsius could result in 50

million to 80 million new malaria cases per year.[9] Nor is it strictly true that medical science is weakening the gene pool by letting those with disorders for which there may be a genetic predisposition, such as diabetes, reproduce. In the present environment, where medication is easily available, such people are as fit as anyone else. However, if such people are denied access to the needed medication, their biological fitness is lost and they die out. In fact, one's financial status affects one's access to medication, and so, however unintentional it may be, one's biological fitness in North American society may be decided by one's financial status.

The effects of culture in enabling individuals to reproduce even though they suffer from genetic disorders are familiar. Perhaps less familiar are the cases in which medical technology selects against some individuals by removing them from the reproducing population. One example can be seen in South Africa. About 1 percent of South Africans of Dutch descent have a gene which, in its dominant form, causes porphyria, a disorder that renders the skin of its victims sensitive to light and causes skin abrasions. If these Afrikaners remain in a rural environment, they suffer only minor skin abrasions as a result of their condition. However, the allele renders them particularly sensitive to modern medical treatment, such as they might receive in a large urban center like Johannesburg. If they are treated for some problem totally unrelated to porphyria, with barbiturates or similar drugs, they suffer acute attacks and often die. In a quiet rural environment where medical services are less readily accessible, the Afrikaners with this peculiar condition are able to live normal lives; it is only in an urban context, where they are more likely to receive medical attention, that they suffer physical impairment or loss of life.

Another example of culture acting as an agent of biological selection has to do with lactose tolerance: the ability to assimilate **lactose,** the

Lactose: The primary constituent of fresh milk.

[9]Stone, R. (1995). If the mercury soars, so may health hazards. *Science, 267,* 958.

primary constituent of fresh milk. This ability depends on the presence of a particular enzyme, **lactase,** in the small intestine. Failure to retain lactase into adulthood, although it is a recessive trait, is characteristic of most human populations, especially Asian, native Australian, and many (but not all) African populations. Hence, only 10 to 30 percent of Americans of African descent, and 0 to 30 percent of adult Orientals, retain lactase into adulthood, and so are lactose tolerant.[10] By contrast, lactase retention and lactose tolerance are normal for more than 80 percent of adults of northern European descent. Eastern Europeans, Arabs, and some East Africans are closer to northern Europeans in lactase retention than they are to Asians and other Africans. Generally speaking, a high retention of lactase is found in populations with a long tradition of fresh milk as an important dietary item. In such populations, selection has in the past favored those individuals with the ability to assimilate lactose, selecting out those without this ability.

In developing countries, milk supplements are used in the treatment of acute protein-calorie malnutrition. Tube-fed diets of milk are used in connection with other medical procedures. Quite apart from medical practices, powdered milk has long been a staple of economic aid to other countries. Such practices in fact discriminate against the members of populations in which lactase is not commonly retained into adulthood. At the least, those individuals who are not lactose tolerant will fail to utilize the nutritive value of milk; frequently they will suffer diarrhea, abdominal cramping, and even bone degeneration, with serious results. In fact, the shipping of powdered milk to victims of South American earthquakes in the 1960s caused many deaths among them.

─────◖◗═══◖◗─────

Lactase: An enzyme in the small intestine that enables humans to assimilate lactose.

─────◖◗═══◖◗─────

[10]Harrison, G. G. (1975). Primary adult lactase deficiency: A problem in anthropological genetics. *American Anthropologist, 77,* 815–819.

In recent years, there has been considerable concern about human activities that have an adverse effect on the earth's ozone layer. A major contributor to the ozone layer's deterioration is the use of chloroflurocarbons in aerosol sprays, refrigeration, and air conditioning, and the manufacture of styrofoam. Since the ozone layer screens out some of the sun's ultraviolet rays, its continued deterioration will expose humans to increased ultraviolet radiation. As we saw earlier in this chapter, some ultraviolet radiation is necessary for the production of vitamin D, but excessive amounts lead, among other things, to an increased incidence of skin cancers. Hence a rising incidence of skin cancers can be predicted as the ozone layer continues to deteriorate. Although a ban on the use of chloroflurocarbons in aerosol sprays was imposed some years ago, the destruction of the ozone layer continued about twice as fast as scientists had predicted it would, even without the ban. Subsequently, an international treaty further limiting the use of chloroflurocarbons was negotiated, but the effect of this is merely to slow down, rather than halt, further deterioration. In fact, the ozone hole over Antarctica in October 1994 was the severest recorded in 35 years. Most immediately affected by the consequent increase in ultraviolet radiation will be the world's lightly pigmented peoples, but ultimately, all will be affected.

Ozone depletion is merely one of a host of problems confronted by humans today that ultimately have an impact on human gene pools. In view of the consequences for human biology of such seemingly benign innovations as dairying or (as discussed in Chapter 11) farming, we may wonder about many recent practices; for example, the effects of increased exposure to radiation through increased use of X rays, exposure to fallout from nuclear accidents and bomb tests, increased production of radioactive wastes, and the like. To be sure, we are constantly reassured by the experts that we are protected by adequate safety regulations, but one is not reassured by discoveries, such as the one announced by the National Academy of Sciences in 1989, that what were accepted as safe levels of radiation were in fact too high, or the earlier discovery that the supposedly safe treatment of sinus disorders in the 1940s by massive doses of x-ray radiation produced a bumper crop of thyroid cancers in the late 1960s. But it is not just increased

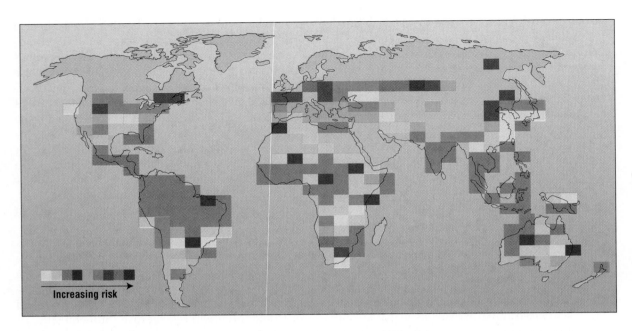

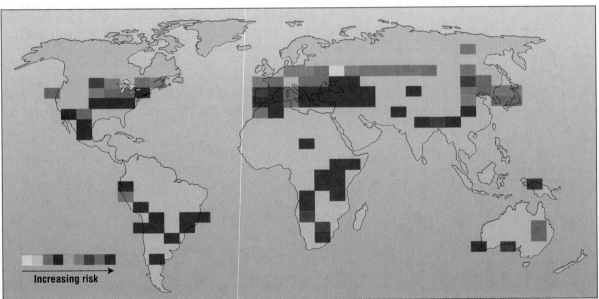

Figure 13.5 These computer models show the predicted spread of the most virulent malarial parasite northward in response to global warming. Below is the change in malaria risk from now to 2055, above is 2055. Darker areas indicate elevated risk.

exposure to radiation that we confront, but increased exposure to other known mutagenic agents, including a wide variety of chemicals, such as pesticides. In spite of repeated assertions regarding their safety, there have been tens of thou-

sands of cases of poisonings in the U.S. alone (probably more in third-world countries, where controls are even less effective than in the United States and where substances banned from the United States are routinely used) and thousands of

Anthropology Applied

STUDYING THE EMERGENCE OF NEW DISEASES*

A source of major concern in the world today is the recent appearance and spread of a host of new and lethal diseases, of which perhaps the best known is AIDS. But there are others—like ebola, which causes victims to hemorrhage to death, blood pouring from every orifice; invasive Streptococcus A, which consumes victims' flesh, dengue fever, Legionnaire's disease and Lyme disease. What has sparked the appearance and spread of these and other new diseases has been a considerable mystery, but one theory is that some are the result of human activities. In particular, the intrusion of people into new ecological settings, such as the rain forest, along with construction of roads allows viruses and other infectious microbes to spread rapidly to large numbers of people.

To test this theory anthropologist Carol Jenkins, whose specialty is medical anthropology, obtained a grant from the MacArthur Foundation in 1993. From her base at the Papua New Guinea Institute of Medical Research, she is following what happens to the health of local people in the wake of a massive logging operation, begun in 1993. From this should come a better understanding of how disease organisms spread from animal hosts to humans. Since most

of the "new" viruses that have suddenly afflicted humans are in fact old ones that have been present in animals like monkeys, rodents, and insects, it appears that something new has enabled them to jump from their animal hosts to humans. Large scale habitat disturbance is an obvious candidate, but this needs to be confirmed and the process understood. So far, only a circumstantial case can be made, by looking back after a disease outbreak. The work of Jenkins and her team is unique, in that she was able to get baseline health data on local people before their environment was disturbed. Thus, she is in a position to follow events as they unfold.

It will be some time before conclusions can be drawn from Jenkins's study. Its importance is obvious: In an era when more and more tropical diseases are spreading beyond the tropics, we need a fuller understanding of how viruses interact with their hosts if we are to devise effective preventive and therapeutic strategies to deal with them.

*Gibbons, A. (1993). Where are new diseases born? *Science, 261*, 680–681.

The impact of such modern practices as crop dusting, which spreads toxic substances and upsets the ecology, is bound to change human gene pools in ways that are not yet known.

cases of cancer related to the manufacture and use of pesticides. All this on top of the several million birds killed each year (many of which would otherwise have been happily gobbling down bugs and other pests), serious fish kills, honey bee kills (bees are needed for the efficient pollination of many crops), and the like. In all, pesticides alone (never mind other agricultural chemicals) are responsible for an estimated $8 *billion* worth of environmental and public health damage in the United States each year.[11]

It is not that the experts who assure us of the safety of such things are deliberately misleading us (although there are cases of that, too, one notorious example being the case of asbestos. As early as 1902 it was included in a list of dusts known to be hazardous, by 1933 it was well documented as a cause of lung cancer, yet in the 1960s, corporate executives denied ever hearing of the dangers). For the most part, experts are convinced of the valid-

ity of what they say; the difficulty is that serious problems, such as those having to do with radiation or exposure to various chemicals, have a way of not being apparent until years or even decades later. By then, of course, serious financial interests are at stake.

What is clear, then, is that cultural practices, probably as never before, are currently having an impact on human gene pools. Unquestionably, this is deleterious to those individuals who suffer the effects of negative selection, whose misery and death are the price paid for many of the material benefits of civilization we enjoy today. It remains to be seen just what the long-term effects on the human species as a whole will be. If the promise of "genetic engineering" offers hope of alleviating some of the misery and death that result from our own practices, it also raises the spectre of removing genetic variants that might turn out to be of future adaptive value, or that might turn out to make us immediately susceptible to new problems that we do not even know about today.

[11]Pimentel, D. (1991). Response. *Science, 252,* 358.

CHAPTER SUMMARY

In humans, most behavioral attitudes are culturally learned or acquired. Other characteristics are determined by an interaction between genes and environment. The gene pools of populations contain various alternative alleles. When the environment changes, their gene pool gives them the possibility of the appropriate physical alteration to meet the change.

When a polymorphic species is separated into different faunal regions, it is usually polytypic; that is, populations differ in the frequency with which genetic variability is expressed. It appears that the human species has been polytypic at least since the time of *Homo erectus*.

Early anthropologists classified *Homo sapiens* into subspecies, or races, based on geographical location and such phenotypic features as skin color, body size, head shape, and hair texture. The presence of atypical individuals and the nonconcordance of traits continually challenged these racial classifications. No examples of "pure" racial types could be found. The visible traits were found to occur in a worldwide continuum. No definite grouping of distinct, discontinuous biological groups has been found in modern humans.

A biological race is a population of a species that differs in the frequency of genetic variants from other populations of the same species. Three observations need to be made concerning this biological definition: (1) It is arbitrary; (2) it does not mean that any one race has exclusive possession of any particular allele(s); and (3) individuals of one race will not necessarily be distinguishable from those of another. As a means for understanding human variation, the concept of race has several limitations. First, race is an arbitrary category, making agreement on any particular classification difficult; second, humans are so complex genetically that often the genetic basis of traits on which racial studies are based is itself poorly understood; and finally, race exists as a cultural as well as a biological category. Most anthropologists now view the race concept as useless for an understanding of human variation, preferring to study the distribution and significance of specific, genetically based charac-

teristics, or else the characteristics of small breeding populations.

Physical anthropologists have determined that much of human physical variation appears related to climatic adaptation. People native to cold climates tend to have greater body bulk relative to their extremities than individuals who live in hot climates; the latter tend to be long and slender. Studies involving body build and climate are complicated by such other factors as the effects on physique of diet and of clothing.

In the United States, race is commonly thought of in terms of skin color. Subject to tremendous variation, skin color is a function of four factors: transparency or thickness of the skin, distribution of blood vessels, and amount of carotene and melanin in a given area of skin. Exposure to sunlight increases the amount of melanin, darkening the skin. Natural selection has favored heavily pigmented skin as protection against the strong solar radiation of equatorial latitudes. In northern latitudes, natural selection has favored relatively depigmented skins, which can utilize relatively weak solar radiation in the production of vitamin D. Selective mating, as well as geographical location, plays a part in skin color distribution.

Racism can be viewed solely as a social problem. It is an emotional phenomenon best explained in terms of collective psychology. The racist individual reacts on the basis of social stereotypes and not established scientific facts.

Many people have assumed that there are behavioral differences among human races. The innate behavioral characteristics attributed by these people to race can be explained in terms of enculturation rather than biology. Those intelligence tests that have been interpreted to indicate that European Americans are intellectually superior to African Americans are designed by European Americans for European Americans from similar backgrounds. It is not realistic to expect individuals who are not familiar with European American middle-class values to respond to items based on knowledge of these values. African and European Americans both, if they come from different types of backgrounds, are thus at a disadvantage. At the present, it is not possible to separate the inherited components of intelligence from those that are culturally acquired. Furthermore, there is still no agreement on what intelligence really is, but it is made up probably of several different talents and abilities.

Although the human species has come to rely on cultural rather than biological adaptation for survival, human gene pools still continue to change in response to external factors. Many of these changes are brought about by cultural prac-tices; for example, the shipment of powdered milk to human populations which are low in the frequency of the allele for lactase retention into adulthood may contribute to the death of large numbers of people. Those who survive are most likely to be those with the allele for lactase retention. Unquestionably, this kind of selection is deleterious to those individuals who are "selected out" in this way. Just what the long-term effects will be on the human species as a whole remains to be seen.

SUGGESTED READINGS

Brace, C. L., & Montagu, A. (1977). *Human evolution* (2nd ed.). New York: Macmillan.

Part 3 of this textbook serves as a good introduction to the nonracial approach to human variation.

Brues, A. M. (1977). *People and races.* New York: Macmillan.

This is a book about the physical differences that distinguish populations of geographically different ancestry. It does not take for granted a background in genetics or any other special field; everything necessary to understand the subject beyond a high school level is here.

Jacoby, R., & Glauberman, N. (Eds.). (1995). *The bell curve debate.* New York: Random House.

This is a collection of articles by a wide variety of authors including biologists, anthropologists, psychologists, mathematicians, essayists, and others critically examining the claims and issues raised in the widely read and much discussed book *The Bell Curve.* Included are pieces written to address many of the same issues as they were raised by earlier writers. For anyone who hopes to understand the "race and intelligence" debate, this book is a must.

Marks, J. (1995). *Human biodiversity: Genes, race and history.* Hawthorne, NY: Aldine de Gruyter.

In this book, Marks shows how genetics has undermined the fundamental assumptions of racial taxonomy. In addition to its presentation of the nature of human biodiversity, the book also deals with the history of cultural attitudes towards "race" and diversity.

Molnar, S. (1992). *Human variation: Races, types, and ethnic groups* (3rd ed.). Englewood Cliffs, NJ: Prentice-Hall.

Key questions examined here are: How does biological diversity relate to the classical racial divisions? Are these divisions useful in the study of our species? How would human environmental relationships affect humanity's future?

V

CULTURE AND SURVIVAL
COMMUNICATING, RAISING CHILDREN, AND STAYING ALIVE

CHAPTER 14
THE NATURE OF CULTURE

CHAPTER 15
LANGUAGE AND COMMUNICATION

CHAPTER 16
GROWING UP HUMAN

CHAPTER 17
PATTERNS OF SUBSISTENCE

CHAPTER 18
ECONOMIC SYSTEMS

All living creatures, be they great or small, fierce or timid, active or inactive, face a common fundamental problem—survival. Simply put, unless they adapt themselves to some available environment, they cannot survive. Adaptation requires the development of behaviors that will help an organism use the environment to its advantage—to find food and sustenance, avoid hazards, and (if the species is to survive) reproduce. In turn, organisms need to have the biological equipment that allows development of appropriate patterns of behavior. For the hundreds of millions of years of life on earth, biological adaptation has been the primary means by which the problem of survival has been solved. This is accomplished as organisms of a particular kind, whose biological equipment is best suited to a particular way of life, produce more offspring than those whose equipment is not. In this way, advantageous characteristics become more common in succeeding generations, while less advantageous ones become less common.

By about 2.5 million years ago, long after the human and ape lines of evolution had diverged, a new means of dealing with the problems of existence came into being. Early members of the genus *Homo* began to rely increasingly on what their minds could invent, rather than on what their bodies were capable of doing. Although the human species has not freed itself entirely, even today, from the forces of biological adaptation, it has come to rely primarily on culture—a body of learned traditions that, in essence, tells people how to live—as the medium through which the problems of human existence are solved. The consequences of this are profound. As the evolving genus *Homo* unconsciously came to rely more on cultural as opposed to biological solutions to its problems, its chances of survival improved. For example, when this genus added scavenging to its subsistence activities some 2.5 million years ago, the resources available to it increased substantially. Moreover, the tools and techniques that made this new way of life possible made our ancient ancestors somewhat less vulnerable to predators than they had been before. Thus life became a bit easier, and with humans, as with other animals, this generally makes for easier reproduction; and with more offspring surviving than before, populations grow. As the archaeological record clearly shows, a slow but steady population growth followed the addition of scavenging to hominine foraging practices.

Among most mammals, population growth frequently leads to the dispersal of fringe populations into regions previously uninhabited by a species. There they find new environments, to which they must adapt or face extinction. This pattern of dispersal seems to have been followed by the evolving human species, for soon after the emergence of scavenging and gathering, humans began to spread geographically, inhabiting new and even harsh environments. As they did so, they devised cultural rather than biological solutions to their new problems of existence. Thus, as they spread into colder regions of the world, humans devised forms of clothing and shelter that, coupled with the use of fire, enabled them to overcome the cold.

As the medium through which humans handle the problems of existence, culture—the subject of Chapter 14—is basic to human survival. It cannot do its job, though, unless it deals successfully with certain basic problems. Because culture is learned and not inherited biologically, its transmission from one person to another, and from one generation to the next, depends on an effective system of communication that must be far more complex than that of any other animal. Thus, a first requirement for any culture is providing a means of communication among individuals. All cultures do this through some form of language, the subject of Chapter 15.

In human societies each generation must learn its culture anew. The learning process itself is thus crucial to a culture's survival. A second requirement of culture, then, is the development of reliable means by which individuals learn the behavior expected of them as members of their community, and how children learn appears to be as important as what they learn. Since to a large extent adult personality is the product of life experiences, the ways children are raised and educated play a major part in the shaping of their later selves: The ability of individuals to function properly as adults depends, to a degree, upon how effectively their personalities have been shaped to fit their culture. As we see in Chapter 16, findings have emerged from anthropological investigations into these areas which have implications for human behavior that go beyond anthropology.

Important as effective communication and eduction are for the survival of a culture, they are of no avail unless the culture is able to satisfy the basic needs of the individuals who live by its rules. A third requirement of culture, therefore, is the ability to provide its members with food, water, and protection from the elements. Chapter 17 discusses the ways in which cultures handle people's basic needs and the ways societies adapt through culture to the environment. Since this leads to the production, distribution, and consumption of goods—the subject matter of economic anthropology—we conclude this section with a chapter (Chapter 18) on economic systems.

THE NATURE OF CULTURE

An example of the power of culture may be seen in international boundaries. Though such boundaries in fact exist only in the imagination, they are made real by a complex political ritual that includes elaborate signposts, people wearing special uniforms with obscure insignia, gates, and an implicit aura of risk.

CHAPTER PREVIEW

What Is Culture?

Culture consists of the abstract values, beliefs, and perceptions of the world that lie behind people's behavior and which are reflected in their behavior. These are shared by members of a society, and when acted upon, they produce behavior considered acceptable within that society. Cultures are learned, largely through the medium of language, rather than inherited biologically, and the parts of a culture function as an integrated whole.

How Is Culture Studied?

Anthropologists, like children, learn about a culture by experiencing it and talking about it with those who live by its rules. Of course, anthropologists have less time to learn, but are more systematic in the way they learn. Through careful observation and discussion with informants who are particularly knowledgeable in the ways of their culture, the anthropologist abstracts a set of rules in order to explain how people behave in a particular society.

Why Do Cultures Exist?

People maintain cultures to deal with problems or matters that concern them. To survive, a culture must satisfy the basic needs of those who live by its rules, provide for its own continuity, and provide an orderly existence for the members of a society. In doing so, a culture must strike a balance between the self-interests of individuals and the needs of society as a whole. And finally, a culture must have the capacity to change in order to adapt to new circumstances or to altered perceptions of existing circumstances.

Students of anthropology are bound to find themselves studying a seemingly endless variety of human societies, each with its own distinctive system of politics, economics, and religion. Yet for all this variation, these societies have one thing in common. Each is a collection of people cooperating to ensure their collective survival and well-being. In order for this to work, some degree of predictable behavior is required of each individual within the society, because group living and cooperation are impossible unless individuals know how others are likely to behave in any given situation. In humans, it is culture that sets the limits of behavior and guides it along predictable paths.

THE CONCEPT OF CULTURE

The **culture** concept was first developed by anthropologists toward the end of the nineteenth century. The first clear and comprehensive definition was that of the British anthropologist Sir Edward Burnett Tylor. Writing in 1871, Tylor defined culture as "that complex whole which includes knowledge, belief, art, law, morals, custom and any other capabilities and habits acquired by man as a member of society." Since Tylor's time, definitions of culture have proliferated, so that by the early 1950s, North American anthropologists A. L. Kroeber and Clyde Kluckhohn were able to collect over a hundred definitions of culture from the literature. Recent definitions tend to distinguish more clearly between actual behavior on the one hand and the abstract values, beliefs, and perceptions of the world that lie behind that behavior on the other. To put it another way, culture is not observable behavior, but rather the shared ideals, values, and beliefs that people use to interpret experience and generate behavior and which are reflected in their behavior. An

Culture: A set of rules or standards shared by members of a society, which when acted upon by the members produce behavior that falls within a range of variation the members consider proper and acceptable.

acceptable modern definition of culture, then, runs as follows: Culture is a set of rules or standards that, when acted upon by the members of a society, produce behavior that falls within a range of variance the members consider proper and acceptable.

CHARACTERISTICS OF CULTURE

Through the comparative study of many different cultures, anthropologists have arrived at an understanding of the basic characteristics that all cultures share. A careful study of these helps us to see the importance and the function of culture itself.

Culture Is Shared

Culture is a set of shared ideals, values, and standards of behavior; it is the common denominator that makes the actions of individuals intelligible to the group. Because they share a common culture, people can predict how others are most likely to behave in a given circumstance and react accordingly. A group of people from different cultures, stranded over a period of time on a desert island, might appear to become a society of sorts. They would have a common interest—survival—and would develop techniques for living and working together. Each of the members of this group, however, would retain his or her own identity and cultural background, and the group would disintegrate without further ado as soon as its members were rescued from the island. The group would have been merely an aggregate in time and not a cultural entity. **Society** may be defined as a group of people occupying a specific locality who are dependent on each other for survival and who share a common culture. The way in which these people depend upon each other can be seen in such things as their economic systems and their family relationships; moreover, members of a society are held together by a sense of group identity. The relationships that hold a society together are known as its **social structure.**

Culture and society are two closely related concepts, and anthropologists study both. Obviously, there can be no culture without a society, just as there can be no society without individuals.

Conversely, there are no known human societies that do not exhibit culture. Some other species of animals, however, do lead a social existence. Ants and bees, for example, instinctively cooperate in a manner that clearly indicates a degree of social organization, yet this instinctual behavior is not a culture. One can, therefore, have a society (but not a *human* society) without a culture, even though one cannot have a culture without a society. Whether or not there exist animals other than humans that are capable of culture is a question that will be dealt with shortly.

While a culture is shared by members of a society, it is important to realize that each person's version of culture is not identical. Beyond such individual variation, however, there is bound to be some further variation within a given culture. At the very least, in any human society, there is some difference between the roles of men and women. This stems from the fact that women give birth but men do not, and that there are obvious differences between male and female anatomy. What every culture does is give meaning to these differences by explaining them and specifying what is to be done about them. Every culture as well specifies how the two kinds of people resulting from the differences should relate to one another and to the world at large. Since each culture does this in its own way, there is tremendous variation from one society to another. Anthropologists use the term **gender** to refer to the cultural elaborations and meanings assigned to the biological differentiation between the sexes. Thus, though one's sex is biologically determined, one's sexual identity or gender is culturally constructed.

The distinction between sex, which is biological, and gender, which is cultural, is an important

⊏⊐∘∘⊏⊐━━⊏⊐∘∘⊏⊐

Society: A group of people who occupy a specific locality and who share common cultural traditions.

Social structure: The relationships of groups within a society that hold it together.

Gender: The elaborations and meanings assigned by cultures to the biological differentiation of the sexes.

⊏⊐∘∘⊏⊐━━⊏⊐∘∘⊏⊐

one. Presumably, gender differences are as old as human culture—about 2.5 million years—and arose from the biological differences between early human males and females. Back then, males were about twice the size of females, as they are today among such related species as gorillas, orangutans, and baboons. As humans evolved, however, the biological differences between the two sexes were radically reduced. Thus, apart from differences directly related to reproduction, whatever biological basis there once was for gender role differences has largely disappeared. Nevertheless, cultures have maintained some differentiation of gender roles ever since, although these are far greater in some societies than others. Paradoxically, gender differences were far more extreme in late nineteenth- and early twentieth-century Western (European and European-derived) societies than they are among most historically known food-foraging peoples whose ways of life, though not unchanged, are more like those of the late Stone Age ancestors of Western peoples. In other words, differences between the behavior of men and women in North

In all human societies, children's play is used both consciously and unconsciously to teach gender roles.

American and Western societies today, which are thought by many to be rooted in human biology, are not so rooted at all. Rather, they appear to have been recently elaborated in the course of history.

In addition to cultural variation along the lines of sex, there will also be some related to age variation. In any society, children are not expected to behave as adults, and the reverse is equally true. Besides age and sex variation, there may be variation among subgroups in societies. These may be occupational groups, where there is a complex division of labor, or social classes in a stratified society, or ethnic groups in some other societies. When such groups exist within a society, each functioning by its own distinctive standards of behavior while at the same time sharing some standards in common, we speak of **subcultures.** The word *subculture*, it should be noted, carries no connotation of lesser status relative to the word *cultural*.

One example of a subculture in the United States can be seen in the Amish.[1] The old-order Amish originated in Austria and Moravia during the Reformation; today members of this order number about 60,000 and live mainly in Pennsylvania, Ohio, and Indiana. They are pacifistic, agrarian people, whose lives focus on their religious beliefs. They value simplicity, hard work, and a high degree of neighborly cooperation. They dress in a distinctive, plain garb, and even today rely on the horse for transportation as well as agricultural work. They mingle as little as possible with non-Amish.

The goal of Amish education is to teach reading, writing, and arithmetic and to instill Amish values in their children. They reject "worldly" knowledge and the idea of schools producing good citizens for the state. The Amish insist that their children attend school near home and that teachers be committed to Amish values. Their nonconformity to many standards of the larger culture has

---

Subculture: A distinctive set of standards and behavior patterns by which a group within a larger society operates.

---

[1]Hostetler, J., & Huntington, G. (1971). *Children in Amish society.* New York: Holt, Rinehart and Winston.

The Amish people have maintained a distinctive agrarian way of life in the midst of industrialized North American society. By maintaining their own schools to instill Amish values in their children, prohibiting mechanized vehicles and equipment, and dressing in their distinctive plain clothing, they proclaim their own special identity.

caused frequent conflict with state authorities, as well as legal and personal harassment. The Amish have resisted all attempts to force their children to attend regular public schools. Some compromise has been necessary, and "vocational training" has been introduced beyond the elementary school level to fulfill state requirements. The Amish have succeeded in gaining control of their schools and maintaining their way of life, but they are a beleaguered, defensive culture, more distrustful than ever of the larger culture around them.

The experience of the Amish is one example of the way a subculture may be dealt with by the larger culture within which it functions. Different as they are, the Amish actually practice many values that citizens of the United States respect in the

The difficulties of making pluralistic societies work is illustrated by the continuing tragedy of Bosnia. Here, a long tradition of different people living together peacefully was overwhelmed by the passions of nationalism.

abstract: thrift, hard work, independence, a close family life. The degree of tolerance accorded to them is also due in part to the fact that the Amish are "white" Europeans. American Indian subcultures have been treated differently by "whites," who came as conquerors and who defined Indian values as "savage." For more than 400 years, Europeans and their descendants in what is now the United States have generally accepted the notion that the Indian cultures were destined to disappear and have done what they could to speed the process along. Yet they are still very much with us, even if in altered form.

Implicit in the discussion thus far is the fact that subcultures may develop in different ways. On the one hand, Amish subculture emerged as the product of the way these people have communicated and interacted in pursuit of their common goals, within the wider society. On the other hand, American Indian subcultures are the result of once independent cultures having been forcibly brought under the control of the United States. Although

Pluralistic societies: Societies in which there exists a diversity of cultural patterns.

all have undergone change as a result, many of them have remained different enough from European-American culture so that it is difficult to decide whether they remain as distinct cultures rather than as subcultures. In this sense, "culture" and "subculture" represent opposite ends of a continuum, with no clear dividing line in the "gray area" between them.

Raised here is the issue of so-called **pluralistic societies** in which cultural variation is especially marked and few standards, if any, are held in common. Plural societies are, in effect, multicultural and could not have existed before the first politically centralized states arose a mere 5,000 years ago. With the rise of the state, it became possible to bring about the political unification of two or more formerly independent societies, each with its own culture, thereby creating what amounts to a higher order social entity that transcends the theoretical one culture–one society linkage. Plural societies are characterized by a particular problem: The groups within them, by virtue of their high degree of cultural variation, are all essentially operating by different sets of rules. This can create problems, given the fact that social living demands predictable behavior. In a culturally plural society, it may become difficult for the members of any one subgroup to comprehend the different standards by which the others operate. At the least, this can lead to major misunderstandings, as in the following case reported in the *Wall Street Journal* of May 13, 1983:

> SALT LAKE CITY—Police called it a cross-cultural misunderstanding. When the man showed up to buy the Shetland pony advertised for sale, the owner asked what he intended to do with the animal.
>
> "For my son's birthday," he replied, and the deal was closed.
>
> The buyer thereupon clubbed the pony to death with a two-by-four, dumped the carcass in his pickup truck and drove away. The horrified seller called the police, who tracked down the buyer. At his house they found a birthday party in progress. The pony was trussed and roasting in a luau pit.
>
> We don't ride horses, we eat them, explained the buyer, a recent immigrant from Tonga.

The difficulty members of one subgroup within a pluralistic society may have understanding the standards by which members of others operate, unfortunately, can go far beyond mere misunderstanding, in which case violence and bloodshed may result. Many cases might be cited, but one that we shall look at in some detail in a later chapter (Chapter 27) is Guatemala, where a government distrustful of its Indian population unleashed a reign of terror against it.

In every culture, there are persons whose idiosyncratic behavior has earned them the descriptions "eccentric," "crazy," or "odd." Such persons are looked upon with disapproval by their societies, and if their behavior becomes too idiosyncratic, they are sooner or later excluded from participating in the activities of the group. Such exclusion acts to keep what is defined as deviant behavior outside the group. On the other hand, what is regarded as deviant in one society may not be in another. In many Native American societies, for example, individuals were permitted to assume for life the role normally associated with people of the opposite sex. Thus, a man could dress as a woman and engage in what were conventionally defined as "female" activities; conversely, women could achieve renown in activities normally in the masculine domain. In effect, four different gender

In the United States, for a man to dress as a woman has been regarded traditionally as abnormal behavior, but in some other cultures, such behavior is regarded as perfectly normal. Not only does culture define what is abnormal as well as normal, but such definitions may change over time, as in the case of women in the United States who often wear men's clothing without being regarded as at all odd.

identities were available: masculine men, feminine men, feminine women, and masculine women. Furthermore, masculine women and feminine men were not merely accepted, but were highly respected.

Because individuals who share a culture tend to marry within their societies and thus to share certain physical characteristics, some people mistakenly believe that there is a direct relationship between culture and race. Research has shown that racial characteristics represent biological adaptations to climate and have nothing to do with differences in intelligence or cultural superiority. Some African Americans have argued that they have more in common with "black" Africans than they do with light-skinned North Americans. Yet

Anthropology Applied
NEW HOUSES FOR APACHE INDIANS

The United States, in common with the other industrialized countries of the world, has within it a number of more or less separate subcultures. Those who live by the standards of one particular subculture have their closest relationships with one another, receiving constant reassurance that their perceptions of the world are the only correct ones, and taking it for granted that the whole culture is as they see it. As a consequence, members of one subcultural group frequently have trouble understanding the needs and aspirations of other such groups. For this reason anthropologists, with their special understanding of cultural differences, are frequently employed as go-betweens in situations requiring interaction between peoples of differing cultural traditions.

As an example, George S. Esber, Jr., while still a graduate student in anthropology, was hired to work with architects and a band of Apache Indians in designing a new community for the Apaches.* Although architects began with an awareness that cross-cultural differences in the use of space exist, they had no idea of how to get relevant information from the Indians. For their part, the Apaches had no explicit awareness of their needs, for these were based on unconscious patterns of behavior. Moreover, the idea that patterns of behavior could be acted out unconsciously was an alien idea to them.

Esber's task was to persuade the architects to hold back on their planning long enough for him to gather, through fieldwork and review of written records, the kind of data from which Apache housing needs could be abstracted. At the same time, he had to overcome Apache anxieties over an outsider coming into their midst to learn about matters as personal as their daily lives. With these things accomplished, Esber was able to identify and successfully communicate to the architects features of Apache life with important implications for community design. At the same time, discussions of findings with the Apaches themselves enhanced awareness of their own unique needs.

As a result of Esber's work in 1981, the Apaches were able to move into houses that had been designed with *their* participation, for *their* specific needs. Among other things, the Indians' need to ease into a social situation, rather than to jump right in, was recognized. Apache etiquette requires that all people be in full view of each other, so each can assess from a distance the behavior of others, in order to act appropriately with them. This requires a large, open living space. At the same time, hosts must be able to offer food to guests as a prelude to further social interaction. Thus, cooking and dining areas cannot be separated from living space. Nor can standard middle-class Anglo kitchen equipment be installed; the need for handling large quantities of food requires large pots and pans, for which extra-large sinks and cupboards are necessary. In such ways were the new houses made to accommodate long-standing native traditions.

*See Esber, G. (1987). Designing Apache houses with Apaches. In R. M. Wulff & S. J. Fiske (Eds.), *Anthropological praxis: Translating knowledge into action*. Boulder, CO: Westview.

---

if they suddenly had to live in a traditional Bantu society, they would find themselves lacking the cultural knowledge to be successful members of this group. The culture they share with "white" North Americans is more significant than the physical traits they share with the Bantu.

Culture Is Learned

All culture is learned rather than biologically inherited, prompting the anthropologist Ralph Linton to refer to it as humanity's "social heredity." One learns one's culture by growing up with it, and the process whereby culture is transmitted from one generation to the next is called **enculturation.**

Most animals eat and drink whenever the urge arises. Humans, however, do most of their eating and drinking at certain culturally prescribed times and feel hungry as those times approach. These eating times vary from culture to culture. Similarly,

Enculturation: The process by which a society's culture is transmitted from one generation to the next.

a North American's idea of a comfortable way to sleep will vary greatly from that of a Japanese. The need to sleep is determined by biology; the way it is satisfied is cultural.

Through enculturation one learns the socially appropriate way of satisfying one's biologically determined needs. It is important to distinguish between the needs themselves, which are not learned, and the learned ways in which they are satisfied. The biological needs of humans are the same as those of other animals: food, shelter, companionship, self-defense, and sexual gratification. Each culture determines in its own way how these needs will be met.

Not all learned behavior is cultural. A pigeon may learn tricks, but this behavior is reflexive, the result of conditioning by repeated training, not the product of enculturation. On the other hand, learned behavior is exhibited to one degree or another by most, if not all, mammals. Moreover, several species may be said to have culture, in that local populations share patterns of behavior that, just like humans, each generation learns from the one before and that differ from one population to another. Elizabeth Marshall Thomas, for example, has described a distinctive pattern of behavior among lions of southern Africa's Kalahari Desert that each generation passed on to the next, by which the lions avoided confrontation with the region's native people, even though both preyed upon the same animals.[2] She has shown as well how the culture of the lions changed over the past thirty years in response to new circumstances.

Among nonhuman primates, examples of cultural behavior are particularly evident. A chimpanzee, for example, will take a twig, strip it of all leaves, and smooth it down in order to fashion a tool for extracting termites from their nest. Such toolmaking, which juveniles learn from their elders, is unquestionably a form of cultural behavior once thought to be exclusively human. In Japan, macaques that learned the advantages of washing sweet potatoes before eating them passed the practice on to the next generation. And so it goes; what is interesting is that within any given primate species, the culture of one population often differs from that of others, just as it does among humans.

In spite of our knowledge that apes and monkeys are much like us in terms of self-awareness, intelligence, and the importance of social bonds, we have yet to come to grips with the moral implications of this knowledge. Thus, we still subject them to behavior that, were a human the victim, could only be described as torture.

Beyond this, we have discovered both in captivity and in the wild that primates in general and apes in particular

possess a near-human intelligence generally, including the use of sounds in representational ways, a rich awareness of the aims and objectives of others, the ability to engage in tactical deception, and the ability to use symbols in communication with humans and each other.[3]

Given the degree of biological similarity between apes and humans (discussed in Chapter 4) it should come as no surprise to find that they are like us in other ways as well. In all respects the differences between apes and humans are differences of degree, rather than kind (although the degree *does* make a difference). All of this knowledge has come as something of a shock, as it contradicts a belief deeply embedded in Western cultures: that there

[2]Thomas, E. M. (1994). *The tribe of the tiger* (pp. 109–186). New York: Simon & Schuster.

[3]Reynolds, V. (1994). Primates in the field, primates in the lab. *Anthropology Today, 10*(2), 4.

LESLIE A. WHITE
(1900–1975)

Leslie White was a major theoretician in North American anthropology who saw culture as consisting of three essential components, which he referred to as techno-economic, the social, and the ideological. White defined the techno-economic aspect of a culture as the way in which members of the culture deal with their environment, and it is this aspect that then determines the social and ideological aspects of the culture. Although he acknowledged the importance of symbols, White considered the manner in which culture harnessed energy to be the most significant factor in its development. Hence in his "culturological" approach, he saw culture (in this case, technology) determining culture, and extracultural phenomena were deemed irrelevant. In *The Evolution of Culture* (1959), White stated his basic law of evolution: Culture evolves in proportion to the amount of energy harnessed on the part of each individual, or to the increased efficiency with which that energy is put to work. In other words, culture develops in direct response to technological "progress." A problem with White's position is his equation of "evolution" with "progress," the latter being a concept invented by Europeans (and European Americans) in the eighteenth century to rationalize the transformation taking place in their societies with the advent of the Industrial Revolution. In this respect, his theories were heavily culture-bound. On the other hand, he did alert anthropologists to the importance that technological changes may have for the rest of culture.

---

is supposed to be a deep and unbridgeable gap between humans and animals. It has not been easy to overcome this bias, and indeed, we still have not fully come to grips with the moral implications with respect to the way we treat primates in research laboratories.

Culture Is Based on Symbols

When anthropologist Leslie White observed that all human behavior originates in the use of symbols, he expressed an opinion shared by all anthropologists. Art, religion, and money involve the use of symbols. We are all familiar with the fervor and devotion that religion can elicit from a believer. A Christian cross, an Islamic crescent, a Jewish Star of David, or any object of worship may bring to mind centuries of struggle and persecution or may stand for a whole philosophy or creed. The most important symbolic aspect of culture is language—the substitution of words for objects.

Through language humans are able to transmit culture from one generation to another. In particular, language makes it possible to learn from cumulative, shared experience.[4] Without it, one could not inform others about events to which the others were not a party. We shall consider the important relationship between language and culture in greater detail in Chapter 15.

Culture Is Integrated

For purposes of comparison and analysis, anthropologists customarily break a culture down into many seemingly discrete parts, even though such distinctions are arbitrary. The anthropologist who examines one aspect of a culture invariably finds it necessary to examine others as well. This tendency for all aspects of a culture to function as an interrelated whole is called **integration.**

The integration of the economic, political, and social aspects of a culture can be illustrated by the Kapauku Papuans, a mountain people of western

Integration: The tendency for all aspects of a culture to function as an interrelated whole.

[4]Goodenough, W. H. (1990). Evolution of the human capacity for beliefs. *American Anthropologist, 92,* 605.

A. R. RADCLIFFE–BROWN
(1881–1955)

The British anthropologist A. R. Radcliffe–Brown was the originator of what has come to be known as the structural–functionalist school of thought. He and his followers maintained that each custom and belief of a society has a specific function that serves to perpetuate the structure of that society—its ordered arrangement of parts—so that the society's continued existence is possible. The job of the anthropologist, therefore, was to study the ways in which customs and beliefs function to solve the problem of maintaining the system. From such studies should emerge universal laws of human behavior.

The value of the structural–functionalist approach is that it caused anthropologists to analyze societies and their cultures as systems and to examine the interconnections between their various parts. It also gave a new dimension to comparative studies, as present-day societies were compared in terms of structural–functional similarities and differences rather than their presumed historical connections. Radcliffe–Brown's universal laws have not emerged, however, and the questions remain: Why do particular customs arise in the first place, and how do cultures change? To answer these questions, other approaches are necessary.

New Guinea studied in 1955 by the North American anthropologist Leopold Pospisil.[5] The Kapauku economy relies on plant cultivation, along with pig breeding, hunting, and fishing. Although plant cultivation provides most of the people's food, it is through pig breeding that men achieve political power and positions of legal authority.

Among the Kapauku, pig breeding is a complex business. Raising lots of pigs, obviously, requires lots of food to feed them. This consists primarily of sweet potatoes, grown in garden plots. Since Kapauku culture defines some essential gardening activities as women's work, they can be performed only by women. Furthermore, pigs must be cared for by women. So, to raise lots of pigs, a man has to have lots of women in the household. The way he gets them is by marrying them. In Kapauku society, multiple wives (polygyny) are not only permitted, they are highly desired. For each wife, however, a man must pay a bride price, which can be

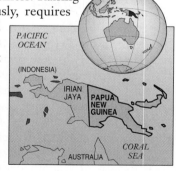

PACIFIC OCEAN

(INDONESIA)

IRIAN JAYA

PAPUA NEW GUINEA

AUSTRALIA

CORAL SEA

expensive. Furthermore, wives have to be compensated for their care of pigs. Put simply, it takes pigs, by which wealth is measured, to get wives, which are necessary to raise pigs in the first place. Needless to say, this requires considerable entrepreneurship. It is this ability that produces leaders in Kapauku society.

The interrelatedness of the various parts of Kapauku culture is even more complex than this. For example, one condition conducive to polygyny is a surplus of adult women. In the Kapauku case, warfare is endemic, regarded as a necessary evil. By the rules of Kapauku warfare, men get killed but women do not. This system works to promote the kind of imbalance of sexes that facilitates polygyny. Polygyny also tends to work best if wives come to live in their husband's village, rather than the other way around, which is the case among the Kapauku. Thus, the men of a village are "blood" relatives of one another. Given this, a patrilineal (descent reckoned through men) emphasis in Kapauku culture is not unexpected.

These examples by no means exhaust the interrelationships to be found in Kapauku culture. For example, both patrilineality and endemic warfare tend to promote male dominance, and so it is not surprising to find that positions of leadership in Kapauku society are held exclusively by men, who appropriate the products of women's labor in order to play their political games. Assertions to the

[5]Pospisil, L. (1963). *The Kapauku Papuans of West New Guinea.* New York: Holt, Rinehart and Winston.

contrary notwithstanding, male dominance is by no means characteristic of all human societies. Rather, as in the Kapauku case, it arises only under particular sets of circumstances which, if changed, will alter the way in which men and women relate to one another.

From what has been said so far, one might suppose that the various parts of a culture must operate in perfect harmony at all times. The analogy would be that of a machine: All parts must be compatible and complementary or it won't run. Try putting diesel fuel in the tank of a car that runs on gasoline and you have a problem; one part of the system is no longer compatible with the rest. To a degree, this is true of all cultures. A change in one part of a culture usually will affect other parts, sometimes in rather dramatic ways. This point, to which we will return later in this chapter, is of particular importance today as diverse agents seek to introduce changes of all sorts into societies all around the world.

At the same time that we must recognize that a degree of harmony is necessary in any properly functioning culture, we should not assume that complete harmony is required. Because no two individuals experience the enculturation process in precisely the same way, no two individuals perceive their culture in exactly the same way, and so there is always some potential for change in any culture. So we should speak, instead, of a strain to consistency in culture. So long as the parts are reasonably consistent, a culture will operate reasonably well. If, however, that strain to consistency breaks down, a situation of cultural crisis ensues.

STUDYING CULTURE IN THE FIELD

Armed, now, with some understanding of what culture is, the question arises: How does an anthropologist study culture in the field? Culture, being

Describing another culture is like trying to describe a new game. The people in this picture may look as though they are playing baseball, but they are playing cricket. To describe cricket in the language of baseball would be at best a caricature of the game as the British know it. The problem in anthropology is how to describe another culture for an audience unfamiliar with it, so that the description is not a caricature.

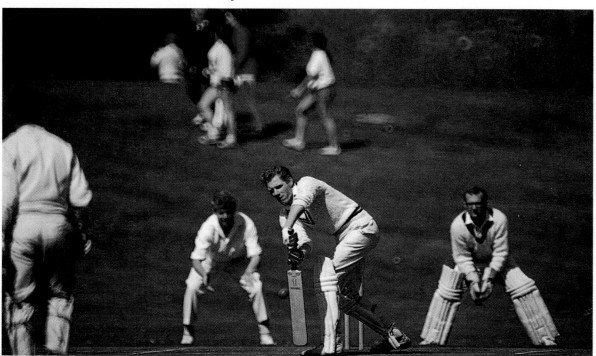

BRONISLAW MALINOWSKI

(1884–1942)

The Polish-born Bronislaw Malinowski argued that people everywhere share certain biological and psychological needs and that the ultimate function of all cultural institutions is to fulfill those needs. Everyone, for example, needs to feel secure in relation to the physical universe. Therefore, when science and technology are inadequate to explain certain natural phenomena—such as eclipses or earthquakes—people develop religion and magic to account for those phenomena and to restore a feeling of security. The nature of the institution, according to Malinowski, is determined by its function.

Malinowski outlined three fundamental levels of needs which he claimed had to be resolved by all cultures:

1. A culture must provide for biological needs, such as the need for food and procreation.
2. A culture must provide for instrumental needs, such as the need for law and education.
3. A culture must provide for integrative needs, such as religion and art.

If anthropologists could analyze the ways in which a culture fills these needs for its members, Malinowski believed that they could also deduce the origin of cultural traits. Although this belief was never justified, the quality of data called for by Malinowski's approach set new standards for ethnographic fieldwork. He himself showed the way with his work in the Trobriand Islands between 1915 and 1918. Never before had such in-depth work been done, nor had such insights been gained into the workings of another culture. Such was the quality of Malinowski's Trobriand research that, with it, ethnography can be said to have come of age as a scientific enterprise.

---

a set of rules or standards, cannot itself be directly observed; only actual behavior is observable. What the anthropologist must do is to abstract a set of rules from what is seen and heard in order to explain social behavior, much as a linguist, from the way people speak a language, tries to develop a set of rules to account for the ways those speakers combine sounds into meaningful phrases.

To pursue this further, consider the following discussion of exogamy—marriage outside one's own group—among the Trobriand Islanders, as described by Bronislaw Malinowski.

If you were to inquire into the matter among the Trobrianders, you would find that . . . the natives show horror at the idea of violating the rules of exogamy and that they believe that sores, diseases, even death might follow clan incest. [But] from the viewpoint of the native libertine, *suvasova* (the breach of exogamy) is indeed a specially interesting and spicy form of erotic experience. Most of my informants would not only admit but did actually boast about having committed this offense.[6]

Malinowski himself determined that although such breaches did occasionally occur, they were much less frequent than gossip would have it. Had Malinowski relied solely on what the Trobrianders told him, his description of their culture would have been inaccurate. The same sort of discrepancy between cultural ideals and the way people really do behave can be found in any culture. In Chapter 1 we saw another example from contemporary North America in our discussion of the Garbage Project.

From these examples, it is obvious that an anthropologist must be cautious, if a realistic description of a culture is to be given. To play it safe, data drawn in three different ways ought to be

[6]Malinowski, B. (1922). *Argonauts of the Western Pacific.* New York: Dutton.

considered. First, the people's own understanding of the rules they share—that is, their notion of the way their society *ought* to be—must be examined. Second, the extent to which people believe they are observing those rules—that is, how they think they actually do behave—needs to be examined. Third, the behavior that can be directly observed should be considered—in the example of the Trobrianders, whether or not the rule of *suvasova* is actually violated. As we see here, and as we saw in our discussion of the Garbage Project, the way people think they *should* behave, the way in which they think they *do* behave, and the way in which they *actually* behave may be three distinctly dif-ferent things. By carefully evaluating these ele-ments, the anthropologist can draw up a set of rules that may explain the acceptable behavior within a culture.

Of course, the anthropologist is only human. It is difficult to completely cast aside one's own personal feelings and biases, which have been shaped by one's own culture. Yet it is important to make every effort to do just this, for otherwise one may seriously misinterpret what one sees. As a case in point, we may see how the male bias of the European culture from which Malinowski came caused him to miss important things in his pio-neering study of the Trobriand Islanders.

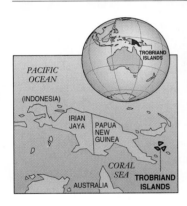

Original Study

The Importance of Trobriand Women[7]

Walking into a village at the beginning of fieldwork is entering a world with-out cultural guideposts. The task of learning values that others live by is never easy. The rigors of fieldwork involve listening and watching, learning a new language of speech and actions, and most of all, letting go of one's own cultural assumptions in order to understand the meanings others give to work, power, death, family, and friends. As my fieldwork in the Trobriand Islands of Papua New Guinea was no exception, I wrestled doggedly with each of these problems. Doing research in the Trobriand Islands created one additional obstacle. I was working in the footsteps of a celebrated anthro-pological ancestor, Bronislaw Kasper Malinowski. . . .

In 1971, before my first trip to the Trobriands, I thought I understood many things about Trobriand customs and beliefs from having read Malinowski's exhaustive writings. Once there, however, I found that I had much more to discover about what I thought I already knew. For many months I worked with these discordant realities, always conscious of Malinowski's shadow, his words, his explanations. Although I found significant differences in areas of importance, I gradually came to understand how he reached cer-tain conclusions. The answers we both received from informants were not so dissimilar, and I could actually trace how Malinowski had analyzed what his informants told him in a way that made sense and was scientifically sig-nificant—given what anthropologists generally then recognized about such societies. Sixty years separate our fieldwork, and any comparison of our stud-ies illustrates not so much Malinowski's mistaken interpretations but the de-velopments in anthropological knowledge and inquiry from his time to mine.

This important point has been forgotten by those anthropologists who today argue that ethnographic writing can never be more than a kind of fictional account of an author's experiences. Although Malinowski and I were in the Trobriands at vastly different historical moments and there also are many

In the Trobriand Islands, women's wealth consists of skirts and banana leaves, large quantities of which must be given away upon the death of a relative.

areas in which our analyses differ, a large part of what we learned in the field was similar. From the vantage point that time gives to me, I can illustrate how our differences, even those that are major, came to be. Taken together, our two studies profoundly exemplify the scientific basis that underlies the collection of ethnographic data. Like all such data, however, whether researched in a laboratory or a village, the more we learn about a subject, the more we can refine and revise earlier assumptions. This is the way all sciences create their own historical developments. Therefore, the lack of agreement between Malinowski's ethnography and mine must not be taken as an adversarial attack against an opponent. Nor should it be read as an example of the writing of ethnography as "fiction" or "partial truths." Each of our differences can be traced historically within the discipline of anthropology.

My most significant point of departure from Malinowski's analyses was the attention I gave to women's productive work. In my original research plans, women were not the central focus of study, but on the first day I took up residence in a village I was taken by them to watch a distribution of their own wealth—bundles of banana leaves and banana fiber skirts—which they exchanged with other women in commemoration of someone who had recently died. Watching that event forced me to take women's economic roles more seriously than I would have from reading Malinowski's studies. Although Malinowski noted the high status of Trobriand women, he attributed their importance to the fact that Trobrianders reckon descent through women, thereby giving them genealogical significance in a matrilineal society. Yet he never considered that this significance was underwritten by women's own wealth because he did not systematically investigate the women's productive activities. Although in his field notes he mentions Trobriand women making these seemingly useless banana bundles to be exchanged at a death, his published work only deals with men's wealth.

My taking seriously the importance of women's wealth not only brought women as the neglected half of society clearly into the ethnographic picture but also forced me to revise many of Malinowski's assumptions about Trobriand men. For example, Trobriand kinship as described by Malinowski has always been a subject of debate among anthropologists. For Malinowski, the basic relationships within a Trobriand family were guided by the matrilineal principle of "mother-right" and "father-love." A father was called "stranger" and had little authority over his own children. A woman's brother was the commanding figure and exercised control over his sister's sons because they were members of his matrilineage rather than their father's matrilineage.

According to Malinowski, this matrilineal drama was played out biologically by the Trobrianders' belief that a man has no role as genitor. A man's wife is thought to become pregnant when an ancestral spirit enters her body and causes conception. Even after a child is born, Malinowski reported, it is the woman's brother who presents a harvest of yams to his sister so that her child will be fed with food from its own matrilineage, rather than its father's matrilineage. In this way, Malinowski conceptualized matrilineality as an institution in which the father of a child, as a member of a *different* matrilineage, was excluded not only from participating in procreation but also from giving any objects of lasting value to his children, thus provisioning them only with love.

In my study of Trobriand women and men, a different configuration of matrilineal descent emerged. A Trobriand father is not a "stranger" in Malinowski's definition, nor is he a powerless figure as the third party to the relationship between a woman and her brother. The father is one of the most important persons in his child's life, and remains so even after his child grows up and marries. Even a father's procreative importance is incorporated into his child's growth and development. A Trobriand man gives his child many opportunities to gain things from his matrilineage, thereby adding to the available resources that he or she can draw upon. At the same time, this giving creates obligations on the part of a man's children toward him that last even beyond his death. Therefore, the roles that men and their children play in each other's lives are worked out through extensive cycles of exchanges, which define the strength of their relationships to each other and eventually benefit the other members of both their matrilineages. Central to these exchanges are women and their wealth.

That Malinowski never gave equal time to the women's side of things, given the deep significance of their role in societal and political life, is not surprising. Only recently have anthropologists begun to understand the importance of taking women's work seriously. In some cultures, such as the Middle East or among Australian aborigines, it is extremely difficult for ethnographers to cross the culturally bounded ritual worlds that separate women from men. In the past, however, both women and men ethnographers generally analyzed the societies they studied from a male perspective. The "women's point of view" was largely ignored in the study of gender roles, since anthropologists generally perceived women as living in the shadows of men—occupying the private rather than the public sectors of society, rearing children rather than engaging in economic or political pursuits.

[7]Weiner, A. B. (1988). *The Trobrianders of Papua New Guinea* (pp. 4–7). New York: Holt, Rinehart and Winston.

CULTURE AND ADAPTATION

In the course of their evolution humans, like all animals, have been continually faced with the problem of adapting to their environment. The term **adaptation** refers to a natural (rather than willful) process by which organisms achieve a beneficial adjustment to an available environment, and the results of that process—the possession of characteristics that permit organisms to overcome the hazards and secure the resources that they need in the particular environments in which they live. With the exception of humans, organisms have generally adapted as natural selection has provided them with advantageous anatomical and physiological characteristics. For example, a body covering of hair, coupled with certain other physiological mechanisms, protects mammals from extremes of temperature; specialized teeth help them to procure the kinds of food they need; and so on. Humans, however, have come to depend more and more on cultural adaptation. For example, biology has not provided them with built-in fur coats to protect them in cold climates, but it has provided them with the ability to make their own coats, build fires, and erect shelters to protect themselves against the cold. More than this, culture enables people to utilize a wide diversity of environments. By manipulating environments through cultural means, people have been able to move into the Arctic, the Sahara, and have even gotten to the

Adaptation: A process by which organisms achieve beneficial adjustment to an available environment and the results of that process; the characteristics of organisms that fit them to the particular set of conditions of the environment in which they are generally found.

moon. Through culture the human species has secured not just its survival but its expansion as well.

This is not to say that everything that humans do they do *because* it is adaptive to a particular environment. For one thing, people do not just react to an environment as given; rather, they react to it as they perceive it, and different groups of people may perceive the same environment in radically different ways. They also react to things other than the environment: their own biological natures, for one, and their beliefs, attitudes, and the consequences of their own behavior, for others. All of these things present them with problems, and people maintain cultures to deal with problems or matters that concern them. To be sure, their cultures must produce behavior that is generally adaptive, or at least not maladaptive, but this is not the same as saying that cultural practices necessarily arise because they are adaptive in a given environment. The fact is, current utility of a custom is an unreliable guide to its origin.

A further complication is the relativity of any given adaptation: What is adaptive in one context may be seriously maladaptive in another. For example, the sanitation practices of food-foraging peoples—their toilet habits and methods of garbage disposal—are appropriate to contexts of low population levels and some degree of residential mobility. These same practices, however, become serious health hazards in the context of large, fully sedentary populations. Similarly, behavior that is adaptive in the short run may be maladaptive over the long run. Thus, the development of irrigation in ancient Mesopotamia (modern-day Iraq) made it possible over the short run to increase food production, but over the long run it favored the gradual accumulation of salts in the soils. This, in turn, contributed to the collapse of civilization there after 2000 B.C. Similarly, the "development" of prime farmland today in places like the eastern United States for purposes other than food production makes us increasingly dependent on food raised in marginal environments. High yields are presently possible through the application of expensive technology, but continuing loss of topsoil, increasing salinity of soils through evaporation of irrigation waters, and silting of irrigation works, not to mention impending shortages of water and fossil fuels, make continuing high yields over the long term unlikely.

Functions of Culture

A culture cannot survive if it does not successfully deal with basic problems. A culture must provide for the production and distribution of goods and services considered necessary for life. It must provide for biological continuity through the reproduction of its members. It must enculturate new members so that they can become functioning adults. It must maintain order among its members, as well as between them and outsiders. It must motivate its members to survive and engage in those activities necessary for survival. Finally, it must be able to change, if it is to remain adaptive under changed conditions.

Culture and Change

All cultures change over time, although not always as rapidly or as massively as many are doing today. Changes take place in response to such events as environmental crises, intrusion of outsiders, or modification of behavior and values within the culture. In North American culture, clothing fashions change frequently. In the past few decades it has become culturally permissible for men and women alike to bare more of their bodies not just in swimming but in dress as well. Along with this has come greater permissiveness about the body in photographs and movies. Finally, the sexual attitudes and practices of North Americans have become less restrictive. Obviously these changes are interrelated, reflecting an underlying change in attitudes toward cultural rules regarding sex.

Although cultures must be able to change to remain adaptive, culture change can also bring unexpected and often disastrous results. A case in point are the droughts that periodically afflict

What is adaptive at one time may not be at another. In the United States, the principal source of fruits, vegetables, and fiber is the Central Valley of California, where irrigation works have made the desert bloom. As happened in ancient Mesopotamia, evaporation concentrates salts in the water, but here pollution is made even worse by the use of chemical fertilizers. These poisons are now accumulating in the soil and threaten to make the valley a desert again.

many peoples living in Africa just south of the Sahara Desert. Native to this region are a number of pastoral nomadic peoples, whose lives are centered on cattle and other livestock, which are herded from place to place as required for pasturage and water. For thousands of years these people have been able to conduct their business, efficiently utilizing vast areas of arid lands in ways that allowed them to survive severe droughts many times in the past. Unfortunately for them, their nomadic lifestyle, which makes it difficult to impose controls upon them and takes them across international boundaries at will, makes them a source of annoyance to the governments of the postcolonial states of the region. Seeing nomads as a challenge to their authority, these governments have made every effort to convert them into sedentary villagers. Overgrazing has resulted from this loss of mobility, and the problem has been compounded by government efforts to involve the pastoralists in a market economy by encouraging them to raise many more animals than required for their own needs in order to have a surplus to sell. The resultant devastation, where there had previously been no significant overgrazing or erosion, now makes droughts far more disastrous than they would otherwise be, placing the former nomads' very existence in jeopardy.

Clothing fashions change frequently in the United States, as illustrated by these photos of men's bathing suits.

CULTURE, SOCIETY, AND THE INDIVIDUAL

Ultimately, a society is no more than a union of individuals, all of whom have their own special needs and interests. If a society is to survive, it must succeed in balancing the self-interest of its members against the demands of the society as a whole. To accomplish this, a society offers rewards for adherence to its cultural standards. In most cases, these rewards assume the form of social acceptance. In contemporary North American society, a man who holds a good job, is faithful to his wife, and goes to church, for example, may be elected "Model Citizen" by his neighbors. In order to ensure the survival of the group, each person must learn to postpone certain immediate satisfactions. Yet the needs of the individual cannot be suppressed too far, lest levels of stress become too much to bear. Hence, a delicate balance always exists between an individual's personal interests and the demands made upon each person by the group. Take, for example, the matter of sex, which, like anything that people do (no matter how basic), is shaped by culture. Sex is important in any society, for it helps to strengthen cooperative bonds between men and women, as well as to ensure the perpetuation of the society itself. Yet sex can be disruptive to social living; if who has sexual access to whom is not clearly spelled out, competition for sexual privileges can destroy the cooperative bonds on which human survival depends. Uncontrolled sexual activity, too, can result in reproductive rates that cause a society's population to outstrip its resources. Hence, as it shapes sexual behavior, every culture must balance the needs of society against the need for sufficient individual gratification, lest frustration build up to the point of being disruptive in itself. Of course, cultures vary widely in the way they go about this, ranging all the way from the quite restrictive approach of British and U.S. society in the late nineteenth and early twentieth centuries, which specified no sex out of wedlock, to practices among the Canela (who live in eastern Brazil) that guarantee that, sooner or later, everyone in a given village has had sex with everyone of the opposite sex, with the exception of close relatives. But permissive though

The power of ethnocentrism—the belief that one's own ways are best—is illustrated by the recent debate over health care in the United States. In spite of repeated assertions that the United States system is "the best in the world," objective measures of infant mortality, life expectancy, and access to health care show that such assertions are false.

the latter situation may sound, there are nonetheless strict rules as to how the system operates.[8]

Not just in sex, but in all things, cultures must strike a balance between the needs of individuals and those of society. When those of society take precedence, then people experience excessive stress. Symptomatic of this are increased levels of mental illness and behavior regarded as antisocial: violence, crime, abuse of alcohol and other drugs, suicide, or simply alienation. If not corrected, the situation can result in cultural breakdown. But just as problems develop if the needs of society take precedence over those of the individual, so also do they develop if the balance is upset in the other direction.

EVALUATION OF CULTURE

We have knowledge of diverse cultural solutions to the problems of human existence. The question often arises: Which is best? In the nineteenth century,

[8]Crocker, W. A., & Crocker, J. (1994). *The Canela, bonding through kinship, ritual and sex* (pp. 143–171). Fort Worth: Harcourt Brace.

Europeans (and European Americans) had no doubts about the answer—they saw their civilization as the peak of human development. At the same time, though, anthropologists were intrigued to find that all cultures with which they had any familiarity saw themselves as the best of all possible worlds. Commonly, this was reflected in a name for the society which, roughly translated, meant "we human beings" as opposed to "you subhumans." We now know that any culture that is functioning adequately regards itself as the best, a view reflecting the phenomenon known as **ethnocentrism.** Hence, the nineteenth-century Europeans and European Americans were merely displaying their own ethnocentrism.

Anthropologists have been actively engaged in the fight against ethnocentrism ever since they started to live among so-called "savage" peoples

Ethnocentrism: The belief that one's own culture is superior to all others.

and discovered that they were just as human as anyone else. As a consequence, anthropologists began to examine each culture on its own terms, asking whether or not the culture satisfied the needs and expectations of the people themselves. If a people practiced human sacrifice, for example, they asked whether or not the taking of human life was acceptable according to native values. The idea that one must suspend judgment on other peoples' practices in order to understand them in their own cultural terms is called **cultural relativism.** Only through such an approach can one gain an undistorted view of another peoples' ways, as well as insights into the practices of one's own society.

Take, for example, the sixteenth-century Aztec practice of sacrificing humans for ritual purposes. Few (if any) North Americans today would condone such practices, but by suspending judgment one can get beneath the surface and understand how it functioned to reassure the populace that the Aztec state was healthy and that the sun would remain in the heavens. Beyond this, one can understand how the death penalty functions in the same way in the United States today. Numerous studies by a variety of social scientists have clearly shown that the death penalty does not deter violent crime any more than Aztec sacrifice really provided sustenance for the sun. Rather, capital punishment is an institutionalized magical response to perceived disorder. As anthropologists Anthony Parades and Elizabeth D. Purdum point out: Capital punishment "reassures many that society is not out of control after all, that the majesty of the law reigns and that God is indeed in his heaven."[9]

Essential though cultural relativism is as a research tool, it does not require suspension of judgment forever, or that we must defend the right of

One sign that a culture is not adequately satisfying the needs and expectations of those who live by its rules is a high incidence of crime and delinquency. It is, therefore, sobering to note that the United States has a higher percent of its population in prison than any other country in the world, yet still has insufficient space to hold all those convicted of crimes.

any people to engage in any practice, no matter how reprehensible. All that is necessary is that we avoid *premature* judgments until we have a proper understanding of the culture in which we are interested. Then, and only then, may the anthropologist adapt a critical stance. As David Maybury-Lewis emphasizes: "one does not avoid making judgments, but rather postpones them in order to make informed judgments later."[10]

If anthropologists avoid the "anything goes" position of cultural relativism pushed to absurdity, they must nonetheless avoid the pitfall of judging the practices of other cultures in terms of ethnocentric criteria. A still useful formula for this was devised more than 40 years ago by the anthropologist Walter Goldschmidt.[11] In his view the important question to ask is: How well does a given culture satisfy the physical and psychological needs

---

Cultural relativism: The thesis that one must suspend judgment on other peoples' practices in order to understand them in their own cultural terms.

---

[9]Parades, J. A., & Purdum, E. D. (1990). Bye, bye Ted . . . *Anthropology Today, 6*(2), 9.

[10]Maybury-Lewis, D. H. (1993). A special sort of pleading. In W. A. Haviland & R. J. Gordon (Eds.), *Talking about people* (p. 18). Mountain View, CA: Mayfield.

[11]Bodley, J. H. (1990). *Victims of progress* (3rd ed.) (p. 138). Mountain View, CA: Mayfield.

of those whose behavior it guides? Specific indicators are to be found in the nutritional status and general physical and mental health of its population, the incidence of crime and delinquency, the demographic structure, stability and tranquility of domestic life, and the group's relationship to its resource base. The culture of a people who experience high rates of malnutrition, crime, delinquency, suicide, emotional disorders and despair, and environmental degradation may be said to be operating less well than that of another people who exhibit few such problems. In a well-working culture, people "can be proud, jealous, and pugnacious, and live a very satisfactory life without feeling '*angst*,' 'alienation,' 'anomie,' 'depression,' or any of the other pervasive ills of our own inhuman and civilized way of living."[12] It is when people feel helpless to effect their own lives in their own societies, when traditional ways of coping no longer seem to work, that the symptoms of cultural breakdown become prominent.

A culture is essentially a system to ensure the continued well-being of a group of people; therefore, it may be termed successful so long as it secures the survival of a society in a way that its members find reasonably fulfilling. What complicates matters is that any society is made up of groups with different interests, raising the possibility that some peoples' may be served better than others'. Therefore, a culture that is quite fulfilling for one group within a society may be less so for another. For this reason, the anthropologist must always ask: Whose needs, and whose survival, is best served by the culture in question? Only by looking at the overall situation can a reasonably objective judgment be made as to how well a culture is working.

---

[12]Fox, R. (1968). *Encounter with anthropology.* (p. 290). New York: Dell.

CHAPTER SUMMARY

Culture, to the anthropologist, is a set of rules or standards that, when acted upon by the members of a society, produce behavior that falls within a range of variance the members consider proper and acceptable.

All cultures share certain basic characteristics; study of these sheds light on the nature and function of culture itself. Culture is a set of shared ideals, values, and standards of behavior. It cannot exist without society: a group of people occupying a specific locality who are dependent on each other for survival. Society is held together by relationships determined by social structure or social organization. Culture cannot exist without society, although one can have society, as do creatures like ants and bees, without culture. All is not uniformity within a culture, partly because there is some difference between male and female roles in any human society. Anthropologists use the term *gender* to refer to the elaborations or meanings cultures assign to the biological differences between men and women. Age variation is also universal, and in some cultures there is other subcultural variation as well. A subculture shares certain overarching assumptions of the larger culture, while observing a set of rules that is distinctively different. One example of a subculture in the United States is that of the Amish. Pluralistic societies are those in which cultural variation is particularly marked. They are characterized by a number of groups operating under different sets of rules.

In addition to being shared, all cultures are learned. Individual members of a society learn the accepted norms of social behavior through the process of enculturation. Another characteristic is that culture is based on symbols. It is transmitted through the communication of ideas, emotions, and desires expressed in language. Finally, culture is integrated, so that all aspects of a culture function as an integrated whole. In a properly functioning culture, though, total harmony of all elements is approximated, rather than completely achieved.

The job of the anthropologist is to abstract a set of rules from what he or she observes in order to explain the social behavior of people. To arrive at a realistic description of a culture free from personal and cultural biases, the anthropologist must (1) examine a people's notion of the way their society ought to function; (2) determine how a people think they behave; and (3) compare these with how a people actually do behave. The anthropologist must also be as free as possible of the biases of his or her own culture.

Cultural adaptation has enabled humans, in the course of evolution, to survive and expand in a variety of environments. Sometimes, though, what is adaptive in one set of circumstances, or over the short run, is maladaptive in another set of circumstances, or over the long run.

To survive, a culture must satisfy the basic biological needs of its members, provide for their continuity, and maintain order among its members and between its members as well as outsiders.

All cultures change over time, sometimes because the environment they must cope with has changed, sometimes as the result of the intrusion of outsiders, or because values within the culture have undergone modification. Although cultures must change to adapt to new circumstances, sometimes the unforeseen consequences of change are disastrous for a society.

A society must strike a balance between the self-interest of individuals and the needs of the group. If one or the other becomes paramount, the result may be cultural breakdown.

Ethnocentrism is the belief that one's own culture is superior to all others. To avoid making ethnocentric judgments, anthropologists adopt the approach of cultural relativism, which requires that each culture be examined in its own terms, according to its own standards. The least biased measure of a culture's success, however, employs criteria indicative of its effectiveness at securing the survival of a society in a way that its members see as being reasonably fulfilling.

SUGGESTED READINGS

Brown, D. E. (1991). *Human universals*. New York: McGraw–Hill.

The message of this book is that we should not let our fascination with the diversity of cultural practices interfere with the study of human universals: those things that all cultures share in spite of their differences. Important though the differences are, the universals have special relevance for our understanding of the nature of all humanity and raise issues that transcend the boundaries of biological and social science, as well as the humanities.

Gamst, F. C., & Norbeck, E. (1976). *Ideas of culture: Sources and uses*. New York: Holt, Rinehart and Winston.

This is a book of selected writings, with editorial comments, about the culture concept. From these selections one can see how the concept has grown, as well as how it has given rise to narrow specializations within the field of anthropology.

Goodenough, W. H. (1970). *Description and comparison in cultural anthropology*. Chicago: Aldine.

The major question to which Goodenough addresses himself is how the anthropologist is to avoid ethnocentric bias when studying culture. His approach relies on models of descriptive linguistics. A large part of the book is concerned with kinship and terminology, with a discussion of the problems of a universal definition of marriage and the family. This is a particularly lucid discussion of culture, its relation to society, and the problem of individual variance.

Keesing, R. M. (1976). *Cultural anthropology: A contemporary perspective*. New York: Holt, Rinehart and Winston.

This book approaches anthropology by tackling the important problems of cultural anthropology, discussing them through ethnographic examples and theoretical considerations. In the process the author takes a critical stance toward conventional anthropological thinking and practice.

Linton, R. (1963). *The study of man: An introduction*. New York: Appleton.

Linton wrote this book in 1936 with the intention of providing a general survey of the field of anthropology. His study of social structure is still illuminating today. This book is regarded as a classic and is an important source historically.

CHAPTER
15

LANGUAGE AND COMMUNICATION

ALTHOUGH HUMANS RELY PRIMARILY ON LANGUAGE FOR
COMMUNICATION, IT IS BY NO MEANS THE ONLY SYSTEM USED.
THESE CHILDREN ARE COMMUNICATING QUITE A LOT THROUGH
THEIR FACIAL EXPRESSIONS ALONE.

CHAPTER PREVIEW

What Is Language?

Language is a system of sounds or gestures that, when put together according to certain rules, results in meanings that are intelligible to all speakers. Although humans rely primarily on language to communicate with one another, it is not their sole means of communication. Language is embedded in a gesture–call system that consists of paralanguage—extralinguistic noises that accompany language—and kinesics—body motions that are used to convey messages.

How Is Language Related to Culture?

Languages are spoken by people, who are members of societies, which have their own distinctive cultures. Social variables, such as class, gender, and status of the speaker, will influence people's use of language. Moreover, people communicate what is meaningful to them, and what is or is not meaningful is defined by their particular culture. In fact, our use of language affects, and is affected by, our culture.

How Did Language Begin?

Many theories have been proposed to account for the origin of language, several of them quite far-fetched. One theory held by anthropologists today is that human language began as a system of gestures with rudimentary syntax. As such, it represents an outgrowth of abilities possessed as well by the great apes. A key factor in its elaboration may have been the importance of planning ahead for future contingencies on the part of our ancient ancestors. Since speech, like gestures, is a product of muscular movements, spoken language may have emerged as the muscles of the mouth and vocal tract were favored, so that people could use their hands for other things as they talked and could communicate with others without having to be in full view to do so.

All normal humans have the ability to talk, and in many societies they may spend a considerable part of each day doing so. Indeed, **language** is so much a part of our lives that it permeates everything we do, and everything we do permeates language. There is no doubt that our ability to speak, whether it is through sounds or gestures (sign languages, such as the American Sign Language used by the hearing impaired, are fully developed languages in their own right), rests squarely upon our biological organization. We are "programmed" to speak, although only in a general sort of way. Beyond the cries of babies, which are not learned but which do communicate, humans must learn how to speak. We must be taught to speak a particular language, and any normal child from anywhere in the world readily learns whatever language is spoken where she or he happens to be reared.

Language is a system for the communication, in **symbols,** of any kind of information. In the sense that nonhuman animals also communicate certain kinds of information systematically, we may speak of animal language. "Symbol" in our definition, however, means any kind of sound or gesture to which cultural tradition has given meaning as standing for something, and not one that has a natural or self-evident meaning, which we call a **signal.** A tear is a signal of crying, and crying is a signal of some kind of emotional or physical state; the word *crying,* however, is a symbol, a group of sounds to which we have learned to assign the meaning of a particular action and which we can use to communicate that meaning whether or not anyone around us is actually crying.

At the moment language experts are not cer-

This example of animal communication shows a young polar bear in a submissive posture to the dog.

tain how much credit to give to animals, such as dolphins, or chimpanzees, for the ability to use symbols as well as signals, even though these animals and many others have been found to communicate in remarkable ways. Several apes have been taught American Sign Language, with results such as those noted in the Original Study for Chapter 4. Even among Vervet monkeys, calls are not mere indexes of degree of arousal or fear. As primatologist Allison Jolly notes:

> They mean something in the outside world; they include which direction to look in or where to run. There is an audience effect: calls are given when there is someone appropriate to listen . . . monkey calls are far more than involuntary expressions of emotion.[1]

What are the implications of this for our understanding of the nature and evolution of language? No final answer will be evident until we have a better understanding of animal communication than we now have. What we can be sure of is that animal communication cannot be dismissed as a set of simple reflexes or fixed action patterns, even though debate continues over just how human and animal communication relate to one another.[2] The

---

Language: A system of communication using sounds or gestures that are put together in meaningful ways according to a set of rules.

Symbols: Sounds or gestures that stand for meanings among a group of people.

Signal: A sound or gesture that has a natural or self-evident meaning.

---

[1]Jolly, A. (1991). Thinking like a vervet. *Science, 251,* 574.

[2]Armstrong, D. F., Stokoe, W. C., & Wilcox, S. E. (1993). Signs of the origin of syntax. *Current Anthropology, 34,* 349–368; Burling, R. (1993). Primate calls, human language, and nonverbal communication. *Current Anthropology, 34,* 25–53.

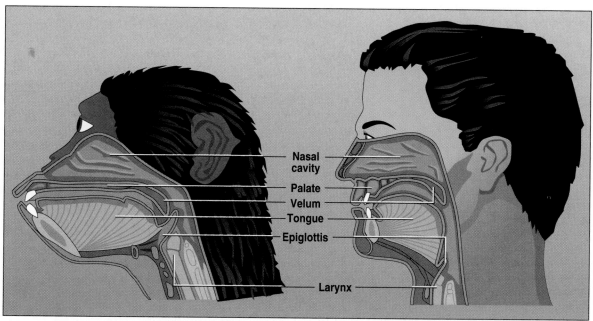

Figure 15.1 The price humans pay for spoken language is an increased risk of choking to death, caused by a lower position of larynx and epiglottis.

fact is that human culture as we know it is ultimately dependent on a system of communication far more complex than that of any other animal. The reason for this is the sheer amount of what must be learned by each individual from other individuals in order to control the knowledge and rules for behavior necessary for full participation in his or her society. Of course, learning can and does take place in the absence of language by observation and imitation, guided by a limited number of signs or symbols. All known cultures, however, are so rich in content that they require systems of communication that not only can give precise labels to various classes of phenomena, but also permit people to think and talk about their own and others' experiences, in the past and future as well as the present. The central and most highly developed human system of communication is language. So important to us is spoken language that we have paid a significant price for it: To be able to speak as we do, our vocal-respiratory tract has been modified in such a way (Fig. 15.1) as to greatly increase both our chances of choking to death and having impacted teeth, the latter condition gener-

ally being fatal until the nineteenth century. Knowledge of the workings of language, then, is essential to a full understanding of culture.

THE NATURE OF LANGUAGE

Any human language—English, Chinese, Swahili, or whatever—is obviously a means of transmitting information and sharing with others both cultural and individual experiences. Because we tend to take language for granted, it is perhaps not so obvious that language is also a system that enables us to translate our concerns, beliefs, and perceptions into symbols that can be understood and interpreted by others. In spoken language, this is done by taking a few sounds—no language uses more than about 50—and developing rules for putting them together in meaningful ways. Sign languages, such as American Sign Language, do the same thing, but with gestures, rather than sounds. The many languages presently in existence all over the world—more than 4,000 different ones—may well

For the linguist studying another language in the field, the tape recorder has become an indispensable tool.

astound and mystify us by their great variety and complexity; but this should not blind us to the fact that all languages, as far back as we can trace them, are organized in the same basic way.

The roots of **linguistics**—the modern scientific study of language—go back a long way, to the works of ancient grammarians in India more than 2,000 years ago. With the age of exploration and discovery, the scientific study of language was given impetus by the accumulation of facts: the collection of sounds, words, and sentences from all sorts of different languages, chiefly those encountered in exotic lands by European explorers, invaders, and missionaries. The great contribution of the nineteenth century was the discovery of system, regularity, and relationships in the data and the tenta-

tive formulation of some laws and regular principles. In the twentieth century, while we are still collecting data, we have made considerable progress in the reasoning process, testing and working from new and improved theories. Insofar as theories and facts of language are verifiable by independent researchers looking at the same materials, there may now be said to be a science of linguistics.

The Sound and Shape of Language

How can an anthropologist, a missionary, a social worker, or a health-care provider approach and make sense of a language that has not already been analyzed and described or for which there are no immediately available materials? There are hundreds of such languages in the world; fortunately, some fairly efficient methods have been developed to help with the task. It is a painstaking process to unravel a language, but it is ultimately rewarding and often even fascinating for its own sake.

Linguistics: The modern scientific study of all aspects of language.

TABLE 15.1 Phonetic Vowel Symbols (Sapir System)*

i (Fr. *fini*)	$ü$ (Fr. *lune*)	$ɨ$	$u̇$ (Swed. *hus*)	$ï$	u (Ger. *gut*)
ι (Eng. *bit*)	$ü̈$ (Ger. *Mütze*)	ι	$v̇$	$ï$	v (Eng. *put*)
e (Fr. *été*)	$ö$ (Fr. *peu*)	—	$ȯ$	α (Eng. *but*)	o (Ger. *so*)
ε (Eng. *men*)	$ɔ̈$ (Ger. *Götter*)	—	$ɔ̇$	a (Ger. *Mann*)	ɔ (Ger. *Volk*)
—	$ω̈$ (Fr. *peur*)		$ω̇$	—	ω (Eng. *law*)
$ä$ (Eng. *man*)	—	$à$ (Fr. *patte*)	—	—	—

*The symbol ə is used for an "indeterminate" vowel.
SOURCE: G. L. Trager. (1972). *Language and languages* (p. 304). San Francisco: Chandler Publishing Company.

For a spoken language, the process requires first a trained ear and a thorough understanding of the way speech sounds are produced. Otherwise, it will be extremely difficult to write out or make intelligent use of any data. To satisfy this preliminary requirement, most people need special training in **phonetics,** or the systematic study of the production, transmission, and reception of speech sounds.

Phonology

In order to analyze and describe any new language, an inventory of all of its sounds and an accurate way of writing them are needed. Some sounds of other languages may be very much like the sounds of English, others (like the "clicks" in various South African languages) may be sounds that English speakers have never consciously produced; but since all people have the same vocal equipment, we are all able, with practice, to reproduce all the sounds that anyone else makes. Once we have knowledge of all of the possible sounds in a lan-

Phonetics: The study of the production, transmission, and reception of speech sounds.

Phonemes: In linguistics, the smallest classes of sound that make a difference in meaning.

guage, we can study the patterns these sounds take as they are used to form words. From this, we discover the underlying rules that tell us which combinations of sounds are permissible in the language and which are not.

The first step in studying any particular language, once a number of utterances have been collected, is to isolate the **phonemes,** or the smallest classes of sound that make a difference in meaning. This isolation and analysis may be done by a process called the minimal-pair test: The linguist tries to find two short words that appear to be exactly alike except for one sound, such as *bit* and *pit* in English. If the substitution of [b] for [p] in this minimal pair makes a difference in meaning, which it does in English, then those two sounds have been identified as distinct phonemes of the language and will require two different symbols to record. If, however, the linguist finds two different pronunciations, as when "butter" is pronounced "budder," and then finds that there is no difference in their meaning for a native speaker, the sounds represented will be considered variants of the same phoneme. In such cases for economy of representation only one of the two symbols will be used to record that sound wherever it is found. For greater accuracy and to avoid confusion with the various sounds of one's language, the symbols of a phonetic alphabet, such as was developed by Edward Sapir for the American Anthropological Association (Table 15.1), can be used to distinguish between the sounds of most languages in a way comprehensible to anyone who knows the system.

Morphology

The process of making and studying an inventory of sounds may, of course, be a long task; concurrently, the linguist may begin to work out all groups or combinations of sounds that seem to have meaning. These are called **morphemes** and they are the smallest units that have meaning in the language (unlike phonemes which, while making a difference in meaning, have no meaning by themselves). They may consist of words or parts of words. A field linguist can abstract morphemes and their meanings from speakers of a language by means of pointing or gesturing to elicit words and their meanings, but the ideal situation is to have an informant, a person who knows enough of a common second language, so that approximate translations can be made more efficiently and confidently. It is pointless to write down data without any suggestion of meaning for them. *Cat* and *dog* would, of course, turn out to be morphemes, or meaningful combinations of phonemes, in English. By pointing to two of either of them, the linguist could elicit *cats* and *dogs*. This indicates that there is another unit that carries meaning, an *-s*, that may be added to the original morpheme to mean "plural." When the linguist finds that this *-s* cannot occur in the language unattached, it will be identified as a **bound morpheme**; because *dog* and *cat* can occur unattached to anything, they are called **free morphemes.** Because the sound represented in writing as *s* is actually different in the two words (*s* in *cats* and *z* in *dogs*), the linguist will conclude that the sounds *s* and *z* are two varieties of the same morpheme (even though they may be two different phonemes), occurring in different contexts but with no difference in meaning.

Grammar and Syntax

The next step is to put morphemes together to form phrases or sentences. This process is known as identifying the syntactic units of the language, or the way morphemes are put together into larger chains or strings that have meaning. One way to do this is to use a method called **frame substitution.** By proceeding slowly at first and relying on

pointing or gestures, the field linguist can elicit such strings as *my cat, your cat* or *her cat,* and *I see your cat, she sees my cat.* This begins to establish the rules or principles of phrase and sentence making, the **syntax** of the language.

Further success of this sort of linguistic study depends greatly on individual ingenuity, tact, logic, and experience with language. A language may make extensive use of kinds of utterances that are not found at all in English and which an English-speaking linguist may not, therefore, even think of requesting. Furthermore, certain speakers may pretend not to be able to say (or may truly not be able to say) certain things considered by their culture to be impolite, taboo, or inappropriate for mention to outsiders. It may even be unacceptable to point, in which case the linguist will have to devise roundabout ways of eliciting words for objects.

The **grammar** of the language will ultimately consist of all observations about its morphemes and syntax. Further work may include the establishment, by means of substitution frames, of all the **form classes** of the language: that is, the parts of speech or categories of words that work the same

---

Morphemes: In linguistics, the smallest units of sound that carry a meaning.

Bound morpheme: A sound that can occur in a language only in combination with other sounds, as *s* in English to signify the plural.

Free morphemes: Morphemes that can occur unattached in a language; for example, *dog* and *cat* are free morphemes in English.

Frame substitution: A method used to identify the syntactic units of language. For example, a category called "nouns" may be established as anything that will fit the substitution frame "I see a ——."

Syntax: In linguistics, the rules or principles of phrase and sentence making.

Grammar: The entire formal structure of a language consisting of all observations about the morphemes and syntax.

Form classes: The parts of speech or categories of words that work the same way in any sentence.

Humans talk, while much communication among other primates is done through gestures. Still, humans have not abandoned gestural communication altogether, as we see here.

way in any sentence. For example, we may establish a category we call "nouns," defined as anything that will fit the substitution frame "I see a——." We simply make the frame, try out a number of words in it, and have a native speaker indicate "yes" or "no" for whether the words work. In English, the words *house* and *cat* will fit this frame and will be said to belong to the same form class, but the word *think* will not. Another possible substitution frame for nouns might be "The —— died," in which the word *cat* will fit, but not the word *house*. Thus we can identify subclasses of our nouns: In this case, what we can call "animate" or "inanimate" subclasses. The same procedure may be followed for all the words of the language, using as many different frames as necessary, until we have a lexicon, or dictionary, that accurately describes the possible uses of all the words in the language.

One of the strengths of modern descriptive linguistics is the objectivity of its methods. A descriptive linguist will not approach a language with the idea that it must have nouns, verbs, prepositions, or any other of the form classes identifiable in English. The linguist instead sees what turns up in the language and makes an attempt to describe it in terms of its own inner workings. For convenience, morphemes that behave approximately like English nouns and verbs may be labeled as such,

but if it is thought that the terms are misleading, the linguist may instead call them "x-words" and "y-words," or "form class A" and "form class B."

THE GESTURE–CALL SYSTEM

Efficient though languages are at naming and talking about things, all are deficient to some degree in communicating certain kinds of information that people need to know in order to understand what is being said. For this reason, human language is always embedded within a gesture–call system of a type that we share with monkeys and apes. The various sounds and gestures of this system serve to "key" speech, providing listeners with the appropriate frame for interpreting what a speaker is saying. Through it, we learn such things as the age and sex of the speaker, as well as his or her individual identity if it is someone we already know. Moreover, subtle messages about emotions and intentions are conveyed: Is the speaker happy, sad, enthusiastic, tired, or in some other emotional state? Is he or she requesting information, denying something, reporting factually, or lying? Very little of this information is conveyed by spoken language alone. In English, for example, at least 90

Shown here are different gender signals sent by men and women in North America. While women tend to hold their arms and legs together, men hold theirs apart.

percent of emotional information is transmitted not by the words spoken, but by "body language" and tone of voice. One (but not the only) reason why English has become the *lingua franca* of business is because of the ease with which deception can be carried out in its written form. Not all languages are as rich in mechanisms of evasion or impoverished in mechanisms for truth,[3] but none communicates peoples' emotions and intentions as effectively as the gesture–call system.

As something that we have inherited from our primate ancestors, many sounds and gestures of our gesture–call system are subject to greater genetic determination than language. This accounts for the universality of various cries and facial expressions, as well as for the great difficulty people have in bluffing or especially lying through gesture–calls. The system is not entirely immune to

Kinesics: A system of notating and analyzing postures, facial expressions, and body motions that convey messages.

[3]Elgin, S. H. (1994). I am not scowling fiercely as I write this. *Anthropology Newsletter, 35,* 44.

deliberate control, but it is less subject to control than is spoken language.

Kinesics

The gestural component of the gesture–call system consists of postures, facial expressions, and bodily motions that convey messages. The method for notating and analyzing this "body language" is known as **kinesics**. Kinesic messages may be communicated directly, as in the case of gestures. For example, in North America scratching one's scalp, biting one's lip, or knitting one's brows are ways of conveying doubt. A more complex example is afforded by the gender signals sent by North American men and women. Although there is some regional and class variation, women when standing generally bring their legs together, at times to the point that the upper legs cross, either in a full leg cross with feet still together, the outer sides of the feet parallel to one another, or in standing knee over knee. The pelvis is rolled slightly forward. The upper arms are held close to the body, and in movement, the entire body from neck to ankle is presented as a moving whole. Men, by contrast, hold their legs apart, with the upper legs at a 10 or 15 degree angle. Their pelvis is carried in a

There is a great deal of similarity around the world in such basic expressions as smiling, laughing, crying, and anger, as one can see from the expressions of these children from Asia, Africa, and South America. Basic expressions like these are part of the human inheritance from their primate ancestry.

slightly rolled-back position. The arms are held out at 10 to 15 degrees from the body, and they are moved independently of the body. Finally, a man may subtly wag his hips with a slight right and left presentation, with a movement involving a twist at the base of the rib cage and at the ankles.

Such gender markers should not be mistaken for invitations to sexual activity. Rather, they are conventions inscribed on the body through imitation and subtle training. In any culture, as little girls grow up, they imitate their mothers or other older women; little boys do the same with their fathers or other older men. In North American culture, by the time individuals become adults, they have acquired a host of gender markers that intrude into every moment of their lives, so much so that they are literally at a loss if they do not know the sex of someone with whom they must interact. This is easily verified, as the philosopher Marilyn Frye suggests:

> To discover the differences in how you greet a woman and how you greet a man, for instance, just observe yourself, paying attention to the following sorts of things: frequency and duration of eye contact, frequency and type of touch, . . . physical distance maintained between bodies, how and whether you smile . . . , whether your body dips into a shadow curtsey or bow. That I

have two repertoires for handling introductions to people was vividly confirmed for me when a student introduced me to his friend, Pat, and I really could not tell what sex Pat was. For a moment I was stopped cold, completely incapable of action. I felt myself helplessly caught between two paths—the one I would take if Pat were female and the one I would take if Pat were male. Of course the paralysis does not last. One is rescued by one's ingenuity and good will: one can invent a way to behave as one says, "How do you do?" to a human being. But the habitual ways are not for humans: they are one way for women and another for men.[4]

Often, kinesic messages complement spoken messages, such as by nodding the head while affirming something verbally. Other examples include punching the palm of the hand for emphasis, raising the head and brows when asking a question, or using the hands to illustrate what is being discussed. Such gestures are rather like bound morphemes—they have meaning but do not stand alone, except in particular situations, such as a nodded response to a question.

[4]Frye, M. (1983). Sexism. In Marilyn Frye (Ed.), *The politics of reality* (p. 20). New York: The Crossing Press.

Learned gestures to which different cultures assign different meanings are known as conventional gestures. An example is this sign, which in North America means "OK." In Brazil, it is an obscene gesture.

Although little scientific notice was taken of "body language" prior to the 1950s, there has since been a great deal of research, particularly among North Americans. Cross-cultural research has shown, however, that there is a good deal of similarity around the world in such basic facial expressions as smiling, laughing, crying, and the facial expressions of anger. Such smirks, frowns, and so forth we have inherited from our primate ancestry, require little learning, and are harder to "fake" than conventional gestures. There is great similarity, too, in the routine for greeting over a distance around the world. Europeans, Balinese, Papuans, Samoans, Bushmen, and at least some South American Indians all smile and nod, and if the individuals are especially friendly, they will raise their eyebrows with a rapid movement, keeping them raised for a fraction of a second. By doing so, they signal a readiness for contact. The Japanese, however, suppress the eyebrow flash, regarding it as indecent, which goes to show that there are important differences, as well as similarities, cross-culturally. This can be seen in gestural expressions for "yes" and "no." In North America, one nods the head for "yes" and shakes it for "no." The people of Sri Lanka, also, will nod to answer "yes" to a factual question, but if asked to do something, a slow sideways movement of the head means "yes." In Greece, the nodded head means "yes," but "no" is indicated by jerking the head back so as to lift the face; at the same time, the eyes are often closed and the eyebrows lifted. Body movements and gestures such as these, which vary cross-culturally and have to be learned, are known as *conventional gestures.*

Paralanguage

The second component of the gesture–call system is **paralanguage,** consisting of cries and other sounds that are not part of language, but always accompany it. The importance of paralanguage is suggested by the remark: "It's not so much *what* was said as *how* it was said." Recent studies have shown, for example, that subliminal messages communicated by seemingly minor differences in phraseology, tempo, length of answers, and the like are far more important in courtroom proceedings than even the most perceptive trial lawyer may have realized. Among other things, how a witness gives testimony alters the reception it gets from jurors and bears on the witness' credibility where inconsistencies exist in testimony.[5]

Paralanguage: The extralinguistic noises that accompany language, for example, those of crying or laughing.

[5]O'Barr, W. M., & Conley, J. M. (1993). When a juror watches a lawyer. In W. A. Haviland & R. J. Gordon (Eds.), *Talking about people* (pp. 44–47). Mountain View, CA: Mayfield.

Voice Qualities

While it is not always easy for the linguist to distinguish between the sounds of language and paralinguistic noises, two different kinds of the latter have been identified. The first has to do with **voice qualities,** which operate as the background characteristics of a speaker's voice. These involve pitch range (from low to high pitched); lip control (from closed to open); glottis control (sharp to smooth transitions in pitch); articulation control (forceful or relaxed speech); rhythm control (smooth or jerky setting off of portions of vocal activity); resonance (from resonant to thin); and tempo (an increase or decrease from the norm).

Voice qualities are capable of communicating much about the state of being of the person who is speaking, quite apart from what is being said. An obvious example of this is slurred speech, which may indicate that the speaker is intoxicated. Or, if someone says rather languidly, coupled with a restricted pitch range, that she or he is delighted with something, it probably indicates that the person is not delighted at all. The same thing said more rapidly, with increasing pitch, might indicate that the speaker genuinely is excited about the matter. While the speaker's state of being is affected by his or her anatomical and physiological status, it is also markedly affected by the individual's overall self-image in the given situation. If an individual is made to feel anxious by being crowded in some way, or by some aspects of the social situation, for example, this anxiety will probably be conveyed by certain voice qualities.

Voice qualities: In paralanguage, the background characteristics of a speaker's voice.

Vocalizations: Identifiable paralinguistic noises that are turned on and off at perceivable and relatively short intervals.

Vocal characterizers: In paralanguage, sound productions such as laughing or crying that humans "speak through."

Vocalizations

The second kind of paralinguistic noises consists of **vocalizations.** Rather than being background characteristics, these are actual identifiable noises that, unlike voice qualities, are turned on and off at perceivable and relatively short intervals. They are, nonetheless, separate from language sounds. One category of vocalizations is **vocal characterizers:** the sounds of laughing or crying, yelling or whispering, yawning or belching, and the like. Many combine sounds with gestures. One "talks through" vocal characterizers, and they are generally indicative of the speaker's attitude. Yawning while speaking to someone, for example, may indicate an attitude of boredom on the part of the speaker. Breaking—an intermittent tensing and relaxing of the vocal musculature producing a tremulousness while speaking—may indicate great emotion on the part of the speaker.

Another category of vocalizations consists of **vocal qualifiers.** These are of briefer duration than vocal characterizers, limited generally to the space of a single intonation, rather than over whole phrases. They modify utterances in terms of intensity—loud versus soft; pitch—high versus low; and extent—drawl versus clipping. These indicate the speaker's attitude to specific phrases such as "get out." The third category consists of **vocal segregates.** Sometimes called "*oh oh* expressions," these are somewhat like the actual sounds of language, but they don't appear in the kinds of sequences that can be called words. Examples of vocal segregates besides *oh oh* that are familiar to English-speaking peoples are such substitutes for language as *shh*, *uh-uh*, or *uh-huh*. Unlike paralinguistic sounds such as sobs, giggles and screams, "*oh oh* expressions" are conventional, learned, and far more variable from culture to culture.

Vocal qualifiers: In paralanguage, sound productions of brief duration that modify utterances in terms of intensity.

Vocal segregates: In paralanguage, sound productions that are similar to the sounds of language, but do not appear in sequences that can properly be called words.

LINGUISTIC CHANGE

In our discussion of the sound and shape of language, we looked briefly at the internal organization of language—its phonology, morphology, syntax, and grammar. It is the descriptive approach to language that is concerned with registering and explaining all the features of any particular language at any one time in its history. Descriptive linguistics concentrates, for example, on the way modern French or Spanish functions now, as if they were separate systems, consistent within themselves, without any reference to historical reasons for their development. Yet languages, like the rest of culture, have histories. The Latin *ille* ("that") is identifiable as the origin of both French *le* ("the") and Spanish *el* ("the"), even though the descriptive linguist treats *le* and *el* only as they function in the modern language, where the meaning "that" is no longer relevant and very few native speakers are aware that they are speaking modern derivatives of Latin. Historical linguistics, by contrast, investigates relationships between earlier and later forms of the same language, antecedents in older languages for developments in modern ones, and questions of relationships between older languages. Historical linguists, for example, attempt to identify and explain the development of early medieval spoken Latin into later medieval French and Spanish by investigating both natural change in the original language and the influence of contacts with invaders from the north. There is no conflict between historical and descriptive linguists, the two approaches being recognized as interdependent. Even a modern language is constantly changing; consider, for example, the changed meaning of the word "gay" in English, which today is used to refer to homosexual and lesbian persons. Its meaning in the title of the 1942 play *Our Hearts Were Young and Gay* illustrates the word's different usage as recently as that time. Such changes take place according to principles that can be established only historically.

Historical linguists have achieved considerable success in working out the genealogical relationships between different languages, and these are reflected in schemes of classification. For example, English is one of a number of languages classified

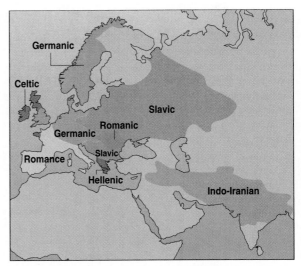

Figure 15.2 The Indo-European Languages.

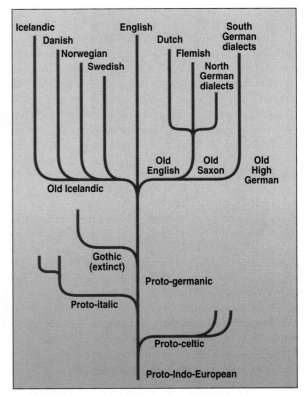

Figure 15.3 English is one of a group of languages in the Germanic subgroup of the Indo-European family. This diagram shows its relationship to other languages in the same subgroup. The root was proto-Indo-European, a language spoken by a people who spread westward over Europe, bringing with them both their customs and their language.

in the Indo-European **language family** (see Fig. 15.2). This family is subdivided into some eleven subgroups, which reflect the fact that there has been a long period of **linguistic divergence** from an ancient unified language (referred to as Proto–Indo-European) into separate "daughter" languages. English is one of a number of languages in the Germanic subgroup (see Fig. 15.3); all are more closely related to one another than they are to the languages of other subgroups of the Indo-European family. So it is that, in spite of the differences between them, the languages of one subgroup show certain features in common when compared to those of another. As an illustration, the word for *father* in the Germanic languages always starts with an *f* or closely related *v* sound (Dutch *vader*; German *Vater*; Gothic *Fadar*). Among the Romance languages, by contrast, the comparable word always starts with a *p*: French *père*, Spanish and Italian *padre*, all derived from the Latin *pater*. The original Indo-European word for *father* was *p'tēr*; so in this case, the Romance languages have retained the earlier pronunciation, whereas the Germanic languages have diverged. Thus many words that begin with *p* in the Romance languages, like Latin *piscis* and *pes*, become words like English *fish* and *foot* in the Germanic languages.

Historical linguists have been successful in describing the changes that have taken place as languages have diverged from more ancient parent languages. They have also developed means of estimating when certain migrations, invasions, and contacts of peoples have taken place, on the basis of linguistic similarities and differences. The con-

cept of linguistic divergence, for example, is used to guess at the time at which one group of speakers of a language separated from another group. A more complicated technique, known as **glottochronology,** was developed by Morris Swadesh and Robert Lees in the early 1950s to try to date the divergence of related languages, such as Latin and Greek, from an earlier common language. The technique is based on the assumption that changes in a language's **core vocabulary**—pronouns, lower numerals, and names for parts of the body and natural objects—change at a more or less constant rate. By applying a logarithmic formula to two related core vocabularies, one should be able to determine how many years the languages have been separated. Although not as precise as this might suggest, glottochronology provides a useful way of estimating when languages may have separated.

While many of the changes that have taken place in the course of linguistic divergence are well known, their causes are not. One force for linguistic change is borrowing by one language from another, something that languages readily do when in a position to do so; but if borrowing were the sole force for change, linguistic differences would be expected to become less pronounced through time. Through the study of modern languages in their cultural settings one can begin to understand the forces for change. One such force is novelty. There seems to be a human tendency to admire the person who invents a new and clever idiom, a fresh and useful word, or a particularly stylish pronunciation, so long as these do not seriously interfere with communication. Indeed, in linguistic matters, complexity tends to be admired, while simplicity seems dull. Hence, about as fast as a language may be simplified, purged of needlessly complex constructions or phrases, new ones will arise.

Group membership also plays a role in linguistic change. Part of this is functional: Professions, sects, or other groups in a society often have need of special vocabularies to be able to communicate effectively about their special interests. Beyond this, special vocabularies may serve as labeling devices; those who use such vocabularies are set off as a group from those who do not. Here, we have the paradox of language acting to *prevent* communication, in this case between members of different groups. Such linguistic barriers serve to create a strong sense of group identity.

Language family: A group of languages that are ultimately descended from a single ancestral language.

Linguistic divergence: The development of different languages from a single ancestral language.

Glottochronology: In linguistics, a method of dating divergence in branches of language families.

Core vocabulary: In language, pronouns, lower numerals, and names for body parts and natural objects.

When a military officer speaks of "incontinent ordnance" and "collateral damage," a physician of "exsanguination," a dentist of the "oral cavity," or an anthropologist of "the structural implications of matrilateral cross-cousin marriage," they express, in part at least, their membership in a profession and their command of its language. For insiders, professional terminology reinforces their sense of belonging to a select "in-group"; to outsiders it often seems an unneeded and pretentious use of "bafflegab" where perfectly adequate and simple words would do as well. Whether needed or not, professional terminology does serve to differentiate language and to set the speech of one group apart from that of others. Therefore, it is a force for stylistic divergence.

Phonological differences between groups may be regarded in the same light as vocabulary differences. In a class-structured society, for example, members of the upper class may try to keep their pronunciation distinct from that of lower classes. An example of a different sort is afforded by coastal communities in the state of Maine, in particular, though it may be seen to varying degrees elsewhere along the New England coast. In the past, people in these communities developed a regional dialect with a style of pronunciation quite distinct from the styles of "inlanders." More recently, as outsiders have moved into these coastal communities, either as summer people or as permanent residents, the traditional coastal style has come to identify those who adhere to traditional coastal values, as opposed to those who do not.

One other far-reaching force for linguistic change is **linguistic nationalism,** an attempt by whole countries to proclaim their independence by purging their vocabularies of "foreign" terms. This phenomenon is particularly characteristic of the former colonial countries in Africa and Asia today.

⊂━━◦◦▭━━━▭◦◦━━⊃

Linguistic nationalism: The attempt by nations to proclaim independence by purging their languages of foreign terms.

Ethnolinguistics: The study of the relation between language and culture.

⊂━━◦◦▭━━━▭◦◦━━⊃

It is by no means limited to those former colonies, however, as one can see by periodic French attempts to purge their language of such Americanisms as *le hamburger.* Also in the category of linguistic nationalism are revivals of languages long out of common use, such as Gaelic and Hebrew.

LANGUAGE IN ITS CULTURAL SETTING

Rewarding though it is to analyze language as a system in which linguistic variables dependent upon other linguistic phenomena operate, it is important to remember that languages are spoken by people, who are members of societies, each of which has its own distinctive culture. Individuals tend to vary in the ways they use language, and as the preceding discussion suggests, social variables such as class and status of the speaker will also influence their use of language. Moreover, people choose words and sentences to communicate meaning, and what is meaningful in one culture may not be so in another. The fact is that our use of language affects, and is affected by, the rest of our culture.

The whole question of the relationships between language and other aspects of culture is the province of **ethnolinguistics,** an outgrowth of both ethnology and descriptive linguistics, which has become almost a separate field of inquiry. Ethnolinguistics is concerned with every aspect of the structure and use of language that has anything to do with society, culture, and human behavior.

Language and Thought

An important ethnolinguistic concern of the 1930s and 1940s was whether language might indeed determine other aspects of culture. Do we see and react differently to the colors blue and green, with different cultural symbolism for the two different colors, only because our language has different names for these two neighboring parts of the unbroken color spectrum? When anthropologists noticed that some cultures lump together blue and green with one name, they began to wonder about this question. The American linguist Edward Sapir

Anthropology Applied
LANGUAGE RENEWAL AMONG THE NORTHERN UTE

On April 10, 1984, the Northern Ute tribe became the first community of American Indians in the United States to affirm the right of its members to regain and maintain fluency in their ancestral language, as well as their right to use it as a means of communication throughout their lives. Like many other Native Americans, these people had experienced a decline in fluency in their native tongue, as they were forced to interact more and more intensively with outsiders who spoke only English. Once the on-reservation boarding school was closed in 1953, Ute children had to attend schools where teachers and most other students were ignorant of the Ute language. Outside the classroom, children and adults alike were increasingly bombarded by English as they sought employment off reservation, traded in non-Indian communities, or were exposed to television and other popular media. By the late 1960s, although Ute language fluency was still highly valued, many members of the community could no longer speak it.

Alarmed by this situation, the group of Ute parents and educators that supervises federally funded tutorial services to Indian students decided that action needed to be taken, lest their native language be lost altogether. With the assistance of other community leaders, they launched discussions into what might be done about the situation, inviting anthropologist William L. Leap to join in these discussions. Previously, Leap had worked on language education with other tribes, and he was subsequently hired by the Utes to assist them in their efforts at linguistic renewal. One result of his work was the official statement of policy, by the tribe's governing body, just noted.

Leap began work for the Northern Utes in 1978, and his first task was to carry out a first-ever reservationwide language survey.* This found, among other things, that inability to speak Ute did not automatically imply loss of skill; evidently, many nonspeakers retained a "passive fluency" in the language and could understand it, even though they could not speak it. Furthermore (and quite contrary to expectations), children who were still able to speak Ute had fewer problems with English in school than did nonspeakers.

Over the next few years, Leap helped set up a Ute language renewal program within the tribe's Division of Education, wrote several grants to provide funding, led staff training workshops in linguistic transcription and grammatical analysis, provided technical assistance in designing a practical writing system for the language, and supervised data-gathering sessions with already fluent speakers of the language. With the establishment in 1980 of an in-school program to provide developmental Ute and English instruction to Indian and other interested children, he became staff linguist. In this capacity he helped train the language teachers (all of whom were Ute and none of whom had degrees in education); carried out research that resulted in numerous technical reports, publications, and in-service workshops; helped prepare a practical Ute language handbook for home use so that parents and grandparents might enrich the children's language learning experience; prepared the preliminary text for the tribe's statement of policy on language; and helped persuade the governing body into acceptance. By 1984, not only did this policy become "official," but also several (not just one) language development projects were in place on the reservation, all monitored and coordinated by a tribally sanctioned language and culture committee. Supported by both tribal and federal funds, these involved the participation of persons with varying degrees of familiarity with the language. Although literacy was not a goal, down-to-earth needs resulted in development of practical writing systems, and a number of people in fact became literate in Ute. One important reason for all this success was the involvement of the Ute people in all stages of development; not only did these projects originate in response to their own expressed needs, they were also active participants in all discussions and made decisions at each stage of activities, participating not just as individuals, but as members of family, kin, community, and band.

*See Leap, W. L. (1987). Tribally controlled culture change: The Northern Ute language renewal project. In R. M. Wulff & S. J. Fiske (Eds.), *Anthropological praxis: Translating knowledge into action.* Boulder, CO: Westview.

first formulated the problem, and his student, Benjamin Lee Whorf, drawing on his experience with the language of the Hopi Indians, developed a full-fledged theory, sometimes called the **Sapir-Whorf hypothesis.** Whorf proposed that a language is not simply an encoding process for voicing our ideas and needs but is rather a shaping force, which, by providing habitual grooves of expression that predispose people to see the world in a certain way, guides their thinking and behavior. The problem is a little like the old question of the chicken or the egg, and some later formulations of Whorf's theory about which came first, thinking and behavior or language, have since been criticized as both logically unsound and not amenable to any experimentation or proof. Its primary value is that it focused attention on the relationships between language and the rest of culture.

The opposite point of view is that language reflects reality. In this view, language mirrors cultural reality, and as the latter changes, so, too, will language. Some support for this is provided by studies of blue-green color terms. It has been shown that eye pigmentation acts to filter out the shorter wavelengths of solar radiation. Color vision is thus limited through a reduced sensitivity to blue and confusion between the short visible wavelengths. The effect shows up in color-naming behavior, where green may be identified with blue, blue with black, or both green and blue with black. The severity of visual limitation, as well as the extent of lumping of color terms, depends on the density of eye pigmentation characteristic of the people in a given society.

These findings do not mean that language merely reflects reality, any more than thinking and behavior are determined by language. Rather, as anthropologist Peter Woolfson points out:

> Reality should be the same for us all. Our nervous systems, however, are being

The ability of language to influence the way we think is illustrated by the bland phrase "collateral damage," by which the military in the 1991 Gulf War referred to civilian casualties from raids on Iraqi cities.

bombarded by a continual flow of sensations of different kinds, intensities, and durations. It is obvious that all of these sensations do not reach our consciousness; some kind of filtering system reduces them to manageable propositions. The Whorfian hypothesis suggests that the filtering system is one's language. Our language, in effect, provides us with a special pair of glasses that heightens certain perceptions and dims others. Thus, while all sensations are received by the nervous system, only some are brought to the level of consciousness.[6]

Sapir-Whorf hypothesis: The hypothesis, proposed by the linguist B. L. Whorf, which states that language, by providing habitual grooves of expression, predisposes people to see the world in a certain way and so guides their thinking and behavior.

[6]Woolfson, P. (1972). Language, thought, and culture. In V. P. Clark, P. A. Escholz, & Alfred F. Rosa (Eds.), *Language* (p. 4). New York: St. Martin's.

So important are cattle to the Nuer of southern Sudan that they have more than 400 names to describe them.

Linguists have found that although language is generally flexible and adaptable, once a terminology is established, it tends to perpetuate itself and to reflect and reveal the social structure and the common perceptions and concerns of a group. For example, English is richly endowed with words having to do with war, the tactics of war, and the hierarchy of officers and fighting men. It is rich, too, in militaristic metaphors, as when we speak of "conquering" space, "fighting" the "battle" of the budget, carrying out a "war" on poverty, making a "killing" on the stockmarket, "shooting down" an argument, or "bombing" an exam, to mention just a few. An observer from an entirely different and perhaps warless culture could understand a great deal about the importance of warfare in our lives, as well as how we go about conducting it, simply from what we have found necessary to name and how we talk. Similarly, anthropologists have noted that the language of the Nuer, a nomadic people of southern Sudan, is rich in words and expressions having to do with cattle; not only are more than 400 words used to describe cattle, but also Nuer boys actually take their names from them. Thus, by studying the language we can determine the importance of cattle to Nuer culture, attitudes to cattle, and the whole etiquette of human and cattle relationships. A people's language does not, however, prevent them from thinking in new and novel ways. If this leads to important changes in common perceptions and concerns, then language can be expected to change accordingly.

Kinship Terms

In the same connection, anthropologists have paid considerable attention to the way people name their relatives in various societies, as we will see in Chapter 21. In English we have terms to identify brother, sister, mother, father, grandmother, grandfather, granddaughter, grandson, niece, nephew, mother-in-law, father-in-law, sister-in-law, and brother-in-law. Some people also distinguish first and second cousin and greataunt and great-uncle. Is this the only possible system for naming relatives and identifying relationships? Obviously not. We could have separate terms, as some cultures do, for younger brother and older brother, for mother's sister and father's sister, and so on. What we can describe in English with a phrase, if pressed to do so, other languages make explicit from the outset, and vice versa: A number of languages use the same word to denote both a brother and a cousin, and a mother's sister may also be called by the same term as one's mother.

What do kinship terms reveal? From them, we can gain a good idea of how the family is structured, what relationships are considered especially important, and sometimes what attitudes toward relationships may prevail. Caution is required, however, in drawing conclusions from kinship terms. Just because we do not distinguish linguistically in English between our mother's parents and our father's parents (both are simply grandmother and grandfather), does that mean that we do not know which is which? Certainly not. Nevertheless, nonanthropologists, when confronted with a kinship system in which the same term is applied to father's brother as to father, frequently make the mistake of assuming that "these people don't know who their own father is."

Language and Gender

Throughout history, human beings have handled the relationship between men and women in many different ways, and here again language can be revealing. In English-speaking societies, for example, men and women use the language in different ways, revealing a deep-seated bias against women, as the following Original Study demonstrates.

Original Study
Sexism and the English Language[7]

There are many ways that women talk that make sense and are effective in conversations with women but [that make women] appear powerless and self-deprecating in conversations with men. One such pattern is that many women seem to apologize all the time. An apology is a move that frames the apologizer as one-down. This might seem obvious. But the following example shows that an apparent apology may not be intended in that spirit at all.

A teacher was having trouble with a student widely known to be incorrigible. Finally, she sent the boy to the principal's office. Later the principal approached her in the teachers' lounge and told her the student had been suspended. The teacher replied, "I'm sorry," and the principal reassured her, "It's not your fault." The teacher was taken aback by the principal's reassurance, because it had not occurred to her that the student's suspension might be her fault until he said it. To her, "I'm sorry" did not mean "I apologize"; it meant "I'm sorry to hear that." "I'm sorry" was intended to establish a connection to the principal by implying, "I know you must feel bad about this; I do too." She was framing herself as connected to him by similar feelings. By interpreting her words of shared feeling as an apology, the principal introduced the notion that she might be at fault, and framed himself as one-up, in a position to absolve her of guilt.

The continuation of this story indicates that these different points of view may be associated with gender. When this teacher told her grown daughter about the incident, the daughter agreed that the principal's reaction had been strange. But when she told her son and husband, they upbraided her for apologizing when she had not been at fault. They too interpreted "I'm sorry" as apology.

There are several dynamics that make women appear to apologize too much. For one thing, women may be more likely to apologize because they do not instinctively balk at risking a one-down position. This is not to say that they relish it, just that it is less likely to set off automatic alarms in their heads. But another factor is that women are heard as apologizing when they do not intend to do so. Women frequently say "I'm sorry" to express sympathy and concern, not apology.

This confusion is rooted in the double meaning of the word *sorry*. This double meaning is highlighted in the following anecdote. A twelve-year-old Japanese girl living in the United States was writing a letter of condolence to her grandmother in Japan because her grandfather had died. The girl was writing in Japanese, but she was more accustomed to English. She began in the appropriate way: "I'm so sorry that Grandfather died." But then she stopped and looked at what she had written. "That doesn't sound right," she said to her mother. "I didn't kill him." Because she was writing in a language that was not second nature to her, this girl realized that an expression most people use automatically had a different meaning when interpreted literally. "I'm sorry," used figuratively to express regret, could be interpreted literally to mean "I apologize."

The difference between ritual and literal uses of language is also at play in the following example. A businesswoman named Beverly returned from an out-of-town trip to find a phone message on her answering machine from her division head. The message explained that he had found an enormous number of errors in a report written by her assistant. He told her that he had indicated the errors, returned the report to the assistant, and arranged for the deadline to be extended while she typed in the corrections. Beverly was surprised, since she had read and approved the report before leaving on vacation, but she said, "I'm sorry"—and was offended when he said, "I'm not blaming anyone." This seemed to imply that he *was* blaming her, since he introduced the idea.

Beverly asked her assistant to show her the lengthy corrected report and became angry when she saw that half the pages had "errors" marked, but few were actually errors. Nearly all involved punctuation, and most were matters of stylistic preference, such as adding commas after brief introductory phrases or before the conjunction *and*. In a large number of cases, she felt that her division head had introduced punctuation errors into sentences that were grammatically correct as they stood.

Later that day she encountered the division head at an office party and announced as soon as she saw him that she was angry at him and told him why. She realized by his reaction that she had offended his sensibilities by raising the matter in front of someone else. She immediately apologized for having blurted out her anger rather than expressing it more diplomatically, and she later visited him in his office to apologize again. She was sure that if she apologized for having confronted him in the wrong way at the wrong time, he would counterapologize for having overcorrected the report and for going directly to the assistant instead of through her. Instead, he generously said, "I accept your apology," and affably changed the subject to office politics.

Now accepting an apology is arguably quite rude. From the point of view of connection, an apology should be matched. And from the perspective of status, an apology should be deflected. In this view, a person who apologizes takes a one-down position, and accepting the apology preserves that asymmetry, whereas deflecting the apology restores balance. Although she felt immediately uncomfortable, Beverly did not realize until after she had left the office, all smiles and goodwill, that not only had her division head rudely accepted her apology, but he had not offered a balancing one.

Women's and men's differential awareness of status may have been the cause of Beverly's problem in a more fundamental way too. She felt quite friendly with her division head; she liked him; she had come to think of him as a friend. For her, as for many women, being friends means downplaying if not obliterating status differences. When she blurted out her anger, she was not thinking of herself as upbraiding a superior in front of others. To the extent that he remained aware of the difference in their status despite their friendly relationship, to accept her criticism would have amounted to public humiliation. Had she focused on their status differences rather than their friendship, she would not have approached him as she did. She would not, for example, have taken that tack with the company president.

Nowhere is the conflict between femininity and authority more crucial than with women in politics. The characteristics of a good man and a good candidate are the same, but a woman has to choose between coming across as a strong leader or a good woman. If a man appears forceful, logical, direct, masterful, and powerful, he enhances his value as a man. If a woman appears forceful, logical, direct, masterful, or powerful, she risks undercutting her value as a woman.

As Robin Lakoff shows in *Language and Woman's Place*, language comes at women from two angles: the words they speak and the words spoken about them. If I wrote, "After delivering the acceptance speech, the candidate fainted," you would know I was talking about a woman. Men do not faint; they pass out. And these terms have vastly different connotations that both reflect and affect our images of women and men. *Fainting* conjures up a frail figure crumpling into a man's rescuing arms, the back of her hand pressed to her forehead—probably for little reason, maybe just for dramatic effect. *Passing out* suggests a straightforward fall to the floor.

An article in *Newsweek* during the 1984 presidential campaign quoted a Reagan aide who called [Vice Presidential candidate] Ferraro "a nasty woman" who would "claw Ronald Reagan's eyes out." Never mind the nastiness of the remark and of the newsmagazine's using it to open its article. Applied to a man, *nasty* would be so tame as to seem harmless. Furthermore, men don't claw; they punch and sock, with correspondingly more forceful results. The verb *claw* both reflects and reinforces the stereotypical metaphor of women as cats. Each time someone uses an expression associated with this metaphor, it reinforces it, suggesting a general "cattiness" in women's character.

Even when seeming to praise Ferraro, the article used terms drenched in gender. She was credited with "a striking gift for tart political rhetoric, needling Ronald Reagan on the fairness issue and twitting the Reagan-Bush campaign for its reluctance to let Bush debate her." If we reversed subject and object, *needling* and *twitting* would not sound like praise for Reagan's verbal ability—or any man's. (I will refrain from commenting on the connotations of *tart*, assuming the word's double meaning was at least consciously unintended.)

In his book *The Language of Politics*, Michael Geis gives several examples of words used to describe Ferraro that undercut her. One headline called her "spunky," another "feisty." As Geis observes, *spunky* and *feisty* are used only for creatures that are small and lacking in real power; they could be said of a Pekingese but not a Great Dane, perhaps of Mickey Rooney but not of John Wayne—in other words, of any average-sized woman, but not of an average-sized man.

I am sure that the journalists who wrote these descriptions of Ferraro came to praise her, not to bury her. Perhaps they felt they were choosing snappy, eye-catching phrases. But their words trivialized the vice presidential candidate, highlighting, even if unintentionally, the incongruity between her images as a woman and as a political leader. When we think we are using language, our language is using us.

It is not that journalists, other writers, or everyday speakers are deliberately, or even unintentionally, "sexists" in their use of language. The important point is that gender distinctions are built into language. The words available to us to describe women and men are not the same words. And, most damaging of all, through language, our images and attitudes are buttressed and shaped. Simply by understanding and using the words of our language, we all absorb and pass on different, asymmetrical assumptions about men and women.

Body language is eloquent, too. Political candidates necessarily circulate photographs of their families. In the typical family photograph, the candidate looks straight out at the camera, while his wife gazes up at him. This leads the viewer's eye to the candidate as the center of interest. In a well-publicized family photograph, Ferraro was looking up at her husband and he was looking straight out. It is an appealing photo, which shows her as a good woman, but makes him the inappropriate center of interest, just as his

The body language shown in this 1993 photo of Senator Robert Dole and First Lady Hillary Rodham Clinton speaks volumes about gender relations in the United States. The senator's discomfort in the presence of Mrs. Clinton's confident assertiveness is obvious.

finances became the center of interest in candidate Ferraro's financial disclosure. Had the family photograph shown Ferraro looking straight out, with her husband gazing adoringly at her, it would not have been an effective campaign photo, because she would have looked like a domineering wife with a namby-pamby for a husband.

Ironically, it is probably more difficult for a woman to hold a position of authority in a relatively fluid society like that of the United States than in more rigidly hierarchical ones. An American woman who owned and edited an English-language magazine in Athens told me that when Greeks came to the magazine to do business, as soon as they realized that she was the boss, they focused their attention on her. But if her male assistant editor was in the room, Americans were irresistibly drawn to address themselves to him. It seems that Greeks' sensitivity to the publisher's status overrode their awareness of her gender, but Americans, who are less intimidated by status than Greeks, could not rise above their awareness of gender.

[7]Tannen, D. (1990). *You just don't understand: Women and men in conversation* (pp. 231–234; 241–244). New York: William Morrow.

Social Dialects

In our previous discussion of linguistic change, phonological and vocabulary differences between groups were noted as important forces for linguistic change. Varying forms of a language that are similar enough to be mutually intelligible are known as **dialects,** and the study of dialects is a concern of **sociolinguistics.** Technically, all dialects are languages—there is nothing partial or sublinguistic about them—and the point at which two different dialects become distinctly different languages is roughly the point at which speakers of one are almost totally unable to communicate with speakers of the other. Boundaries may be

Dialects: Varying forms of a language that reflect particular regions or social classes and that are similar enough to be mutually intelligible.

Sociolinguistics: The study of the structure and use of language as it relates to its social setting.

psychological, geographical, social, or economic, and they are not always very clear. Frequently, there is a transitional territory, or perhaps a buffer zone, where features of both are found and understood, as between central and southern China. The fact is that if you learn the Chinese of Beijing, you cannot communicate with the waiter in your local Chinese restaurant who comes from Canton or Hong Kong, although both languages—or dialects—are conventionally called Chinese.

A classic example of the kind of dialect that may set one group apart from others within a single society is one spoken by many inner-city African Americans. Educator Dorothy Seymour provides the following example:

> "Cmon, man, les git goin'!" called the boy to his companion. "Dat bell ringin'. It say, 'Git in rat now!' " He dashed into the school yard.
>
> "Aw, f'get you," replied the other. "Whe' Richuh? Whe' da' muvvah? He be goin' to schoo'."
>
> "He in de' now, man!" was the answer as they went through the door.

In the classroom they made for their desks and opened their books. The name of the story they tried to read was "Come." It went:

—Come, Bill, come
—Come with me.
—Come and see this.
—See what is here.

The first boy poked the second. "Wha' da' wor'?"

"Da' wor' *is*, you dope."

"*Is?* Ain't no wor' *is*. You jivin' me? Wha' da' wor' mean?"

"Ah dunno. Jus' *is*."[8]

Unfortunately, there is a widespread perception among middle-class whites and African Americans alike that this dialect is somehow substandard or defective, which it is not. Rather, it is a highly structured mode of speech, capable of expressing anything its speakers care to express, often in extremely creative ways (as in "rapping"). Many of its distinctive features stem from retention of sound patterns, grammatical devices, and even words of the West African languages spoken by the ancestors of today's African Americans. Compared to the richness of Black English, the Standard English dialect lacks certain sounds; contains some sounds that are unnecessary for which others may serve just as well; doubles and drawls some of its vowel sounds in sequences that are unusual and difficult to imitate; lacks a method of forming an important tense (the habitual); requires too many ways of indicating tense, plurality, and gender; and does not mark negatives in such a way as to make a strong negative statement.

Because their dialect differs so much from Standard English and has been stigmatized so often, speakers of Black English frequently find themselves at a disadvantage outside of their own communities. In schools, for example, African-American children may be seen by teachers as deficient in verbal skills and may even be diagnosed—quite wrongly—as "learning impaired." The great challenge for the schools is to find ways of teaching these children how to use Standard English in

Because they are culture-bound, standardized tests devised by people from one subcultural background usually fail to measure what they are supposed to when administered to those from another background.

those situations where it is to their advantage to do so, without denigrating or affecting their ability to use the dialect of their own community. Martin Luther King, Jr., was particularly skilled at switching back and forth between the two dialects, depending on the situation in which he was speaking. Less consciously, we all do the same sort of thing when we switch from formality to informality in our speech, depending upon where we are and to whom we are talking. The process of changing from one level of language to another as the situation demands, whether from one language to another or from one dialect of a language to another, is known as **code switching,** and it has been the subject of a number of sociolinguistic studies.

THE ORIGINS OF LANGUAGE

A realization of the central importance of language for human culture leads inevitably to speculation

Code switching: The process of changing from one level of language to another.

[8]Seymour, D. Z. (1986). Black children, black speech. In P. Escholz, A. Rosa, & V. Clark (Eds.), *Language Awareness* (4th ed.) (p. 74). New York: St. Martin's Press.

The importance of code switching is illustrated by Haitian President Aristide's difficulties with United States officials during his period of exile. Though effective in communicating with Haitians, his rhetorical style, laced with proverb and metaphor and relying on ambiguity and indirectness, was easily misunderstood by North Americans. By contrast, Lt. General Cédras, like other members of the Haitian elite, having spent considerable time abroad, was skilled at switching from rhetorical devices effective in Haiti to those more familiar to North Americans.

about how language might have started in the first place. The question of the origin of language has long been a popular subject, and some reasonable and many not so reasonable ideas have been proposed: Exclamations became words, sounds in nature were imitated, or people simply got together and assigned sounds to objects and actions. The main trouble with past ideas is that there was so little in the way of evidence that attempts to explain language origins often amounted to little more than wild speculation. The result was a reaction against such speculation, exemplified by the ban imposed in 1866 by the Société de Linguistique de Paris against papers on linguistic origins. Now there is more evidence to work with—better knowledge of primate brains, new studies of primate communication, more information on the development of linguistic competence in children, more human fossils that can be used to reconstruct tentatively what ancient brains and

vocal tracts were like, and a better understanding of early hominine ways of life. We still cannot prove how and when human language developed, but we can speculate much less wildly than was once the case.

Attempts to teach other primates to talk like humans have not been wholly successful. In one famous experiment in communication that went on for seven years, for example, the chimpanzee Viki learned to voice only a very few words, like "up," "mama," and "papa." This inability to speak is not the result of any obvious sensory or perceptual deficit, and apes can in fact produce many of the sounds used in speech. Evidently, their failure to speak has to do with either a lack of motor control mechanisms to produce articulation of speech or the virtually complete preoccupation of the vocal apparatus for expressing emotional states.

Better results have been achieved through nonvocal methods. Chimpanzees and gorillas in

Owing to our common ancestry, some of the gestures that humans use are shared with other primates.

the wild make a variety of vocalizations, but these are often emotional, rather than propositional. In this sense, they are equivalent to human paralanguage. Much of their communication takes place by kinesic means—the use of specific gestures and postures. Indeed, some of these, such as grimacing, kissing, and embracing, are in universal use today among humans, as well as apes. Recognizing the importance of gestural communication to apes, psychologists Allen and Beatrice Gardner began teaching the American Sign Language, used by the deaf, to their young chimpanzee Washoe, the first of several who have since learned to sign. (See the Original Study in Chapter 4.) With vocabularies of more than 400 signs, chimps have shown themselves to be able to transfer each sign from its original referent to other appropriate objects and even pictures of objects. Their vocabularies include verbs, adjectives, and words like "sorry" and "please"; furthermore, they can string signs together properly to produce original sentences, even inflecting their signs to indicate person, place, and instrument. More impressive still, Washoe has been observed spontaneously teaching her adopted offspring Loulis how to sign by deliberately manipu-

lating his hand. For five years, humans have refrained from signing when in sight of Loulis, over which time he learned no fewer than 50 signs. Today, Loulis and Washoe live with three other signing chimpanzees, all of whom are shown by remote videotaping to use signs to communicate among themselves when no humans are present.

Other chimpanzees have been taught to communicate by other means. One named Sarah learned to converse by means of pictographs—designs such as squares and triangles—on brightly colored plastic chips. Each pictograph stands for a noun or a verb. Sarah can also produce new sentences of her own. Another chimpanzee, Lana, learned to converse by means of a computer with a keyboard somewhat like that of a typewriter, but with symbols rather than letters. One of the most adept with this system is a pygmy chimpanzee named Kanzi who, rather than being taught by a human, learned it as an infant from its mother and soon went on to surpass the mother's abilities.

Chimps have not been the only subjects of ape language experiments. Gorillas and orangutans have also been taught American Sign Language with results that replicate those obtained with chimps. As a consequence, there is now a growing consensus that all of the great apes can develop language skills at least to the level of a two- to three-year-old human.[9] Not only are comprehension skills similar, but so is acquisition order: What and Where, What-to-do and Who, as well as How questions are acquired in that order by both apes and humans. Like humans, apes are capable of referring to events removed in time and space, a phenomenon known as **displacement** and one of the distinctive features of human language.

In view of apes' demonstrated abilities in the use of sign language, it is not surprising that a number of anthropologists, psychologists, and other linguists have shown new interest in an old hypothesis, that human language began as a gestural, rather than vocal, system. Certainly, the potential to communicate through gestures must have been as well developed among the earliest hominines as it is among today's apes, since they share it as a consequence of a common ancestry that predates the divergence of our own line of evolution. Moreover, the bipedalism of our earliest ancestors would have enabled them to use their hands more freely to gesture. Now, manual signing and gesturing are skilled activities in which hand preference plays a major role, and evidence for the pronounced "handedness" found only among humans is provided by the external configuration of the brain of *Homo habilis*, as well as by the stone tools made by this hominine. Furthermore, among modern children learning American Sign Language, hand preference appears in signing *before* it does in object manipulation. Thus, not only is it likely that *Homo habilis* used gestures to communicate, but this may have played a role in the development of the manual dexterity involved in early stone toolmaking.

One of the most difficult problems for students dealing with the origin of language is the origin of syntax, necessary to enable our ancestors to articulate and communicate complex thought. Here, a look at the physical nature of gestures is helpful,

for in fact, they can be construed not just as words, but as sentences. This can be illustrated with the modern gesture meaning *seize:* The hand begins fully open or slightly bent, the elbow is slightly flexed and the upper arm rotates at the shoulder to bring the forearm and hand across the body until the moving hand closes around the upright forefinger of the other hand. What we have here is not just the word *seize*, but a complete transitive sentence with a verb and a direct object, or in semantic terms, an agent, an action, and a patient.[10] In this case, there is a clear relation between the sign and what is signified, suggesting that syntax could have its origin in signs that mimic the things they represent.

Another problem involves the shift from manual gestures to spoken language. Two things to keep in mind here are that (1) the manual signs of a sign language are typically accompanied by facial gestures, and (2) just as a sign is the outcome of a particular motor act, so is speech the outcome of a series of motor acts, in this case concentrated in the mouth and throat. In other words, *all* language, signed or spoken, can be analyzed as gesture. Furthermore, research on hearing-impaired users of American Sign Language suggests that areas of the brain critical for speech may be critical to signing as well. Thus, continuity exists between gestural and spoken language, and the latter could have emerged from the former through increasing emphasis on finely controlled movements of the mouth and throat, a scenario consistent with the appearance of neurological structures underlying language in the earliest representatives of the genus *Homo* and steady enlargement of the human brain *before* the alteration of the vocal tract took place that allows us to speak the way we do.

The advantage of spoken over gestural language to a species increasingly dependent on tool use for survival is obvious. To talk with your hands, you must stop whatever else you are doing with them; speech does not interfere with that. Other

---

Displacement: The ability to refer to things and events removed in time and space.

[9]Miles, H. L. W. (1993). Language and the orangutan: The old person of the forest. In P. Cavalieri & P. Singer (Eds.), *The great ape project* (p. 46). New York: St. Martin's Press.

[10]Armstrong, D. F., Stokoe, W. C., & Wilcox, S. E. (Eds.) (1994). Signs of the origin of syntax. *Current Anthropology, 35*, 355.

benefits include being able to talk in the dark, past opaque objects, or among speakers whose attention is diverted. Just when the changeover to spoken language took place is not known, though all would agree that spoken languages are at least as old as anatomically modern *Homo sapiens*. There is, however, no anatomical evidence to support arguments that Neandertals and other representatives of archaic *H. sapiens* were incapable of speech. Perhaps its emergence began with *Homo erectus*, the first hominine to live in regions with cold climates. The ability to plan ahead for changes in seasonal conditions crucial to survival under such conditions would not have been possible without use of a grammatically structured language, whether it be gestural or vocal. We do know that *H. erectus*, having the use of fire, would not have had to cease all activity when darkness fell. We also know that the vocal tract and brain of *H. erectus* were intermediate between that of *H. sapiens* and earlier *Australopithecus*. It may be that the changeover from gestural to spoken language was a driving force in these evolutionary changes.

The once popular search for a truly primitive language spoken by a living people that might show the processes of language just beginning or developing has now been abandoned. The reason is that there is no such thing as a primitive language in the world today, or even in the recent past. So far, all human languages that have been described and studied, even among people with something approximating a Stone Age technology, are highly developed, complex, and capable of expressing infinite meanings. The truth is that people have been talking in this world for an extremely long time, and every known language, wherever it is, now has a long history and has developed subtleties and complexities that do not permit any label of "primitivism." What a language may or may not express is not a measure of its age, but of its speakers' way of life, reflecting what they want or need to share and communicate with others.

CHAPTER SUMMARY

Anthropologists need to understand the workings of language, because it is through language that people in every society are able to share their experiences, concerns, and beliefs, over the past and in the present, and to communicate these to the next generation. Language makes communication of infinite meanings possible by employing a few sounds or gestures that, when put together according to certain rules, result in meanings that are intelligible to all speakers.

Linguistics is the modern scientific study of all aspects of language. Phonetics focuses on the production, transmission, and reception of speech sounds, or phonemes. Phonology studies the sound patterns of language in order to extract the rules that govern the way sounds are combined. Morphology is concerned with the smallest units of meaningful combinations of sounds—morphemes—in a language. Syntax refers to the principles according to which phrases and sentences are built. The entire formal structure of a language, consisting of all observations about its morphemes and syntax, constitutes the grammar of a language.

Human language is embedded in a gesture–call system inherited from our primate ancestors that serves to "key" speech, providing the appropriate frame for interpreting linguistic form. The gestural component of this system consists of body motions used to convey messages; the system of notating and recording these motions is known as kinesics. The call component is represented by paralanguage, consisting of extralinguistic noises involving various voice qualities and vocalizations.

Descriptive linguistics registers and explains the features of a language at a particular time in its history. Historical linguistics investigates relationships between earlier and later forms of the same language. A major concern of historical linguists is to identify the forces behind the changes that have taken place in languages in the course of linguistic divergence. Historical linguistics also provides a means of roughly dating certain migrations, invasions, and contacts of people.

Ethnolinguistics deals with language as it relates to society, the rest of culture, and human behavior. Some linguists, following Benjamin Lee

Whorf, have proposed that language shapes the way people think and behave. Others have argued that language reflects reality. Although linguists find language flexible and adaptable, they have found that once a terminology is established, it tends to perpetuate itself and to reflect much about the speakers' beliefs and social relationships. Kinship terms, for example, help reveal how a family is structured, what relationships are considered close or distant, and what attitudes toward relationships are held. Similarly, gender language reveals how the men and women in a society relate to one another.

A social dialect is the language of a group of people within a larger one, all of whom may speak more or less the same language. Sociolinguists are concerned with whether dialect differences reflect cultural differences. They also study code switching—the process of changing from one level of language to another as the situation demands—for much the same reason.

One theory of language origins is that early hominines, by developing potentials exhibited also by apes and monkeys, with their hands freed by their bipedalism, began using gestures as a tool to communicate and implement intentions within a social setting. With the movement of *Homo erectus* out of the tropics, the need to plan for future needs in order to survive seasons of cold temperatures required the grammar and syntax necessary to communicate information about events removed in time and space. By the time archaic *Homo sapiens* appeared, emphasis on finely controlled movements of the mouth and throat had probably given rise to spoken language.

For some time linguists searched for a truly primitive language spoken by some living group that would reveal language in its very early state. This search has been abandoned. All languages that have been studied, including those of people with supposedly "primitive" cultures, are complex, sophisticated, and able to express a wide range of experiences. What a language is capable of expressing is anything its speakers wish to talk about and has nothing to do with its age.

SUGGESTED READINGS

Birdwhistell, R. L. (1970). *Kinesics and context: Essays in body motion communication.* Philadelphia: University of Pennsylvania Press.

Because kinesics was first delineated as an area for anthropological research by Birdwhistell, this book is particularly appropriate for those who wish to know more about the phenomenon.

Crane, L. B., Yeager, E., & Whitman, R. L. (1981). *An introduction to linguistics.* Boston: Little, Brown.

This book gives balanced coverage to all subfields of linguistics, including topics traditionally ignored in textbooks.

Eastman, C. M. (1990). *Aspects of language and culture* (2nd ed.). Novato, CA: Chandler and Sharp.

The bulk of this book is devoted to the subjects of worldview, ethnography of communication, nonverbal behavior, animal communication, discourse pragmatics, conversational analysis, semiotics, and ethnicity. A single chapter deals with linguistics as a field tool.

Hickerson, N. P. (1980). *Linguistic anthropology.* New York: Holt, Rinehart and Winston.

This text includes a description and explanation of what anthropological linguistics is all about, written for beginning students.

Lehmann, W. P. (1973). *Historical linguistics, An introduction* (2nd ed.). New York: Holt, Rinehart and Winston.

In recent years, historical linguistics has tended to be overshadowed by descriptive linguistics. Historical linguistics, however, remains an active and changing field, and this book is a good introduction to it.

Gardner, R. A., Gardner, B. T., & Van Cantfort, T. E. (Eds.). (1989). *Teaching sign language to chimpanzees.* Albany, NY: State University of New York Press.

In ten jargon-free chapters, easily accessible to the interested layperson as well as professionals, the methods and results of the Gardners and their students are laid out in great detail. Psychologists and anthropologists who reviewed the book agree that it represents a milestone in ape language research and should be read by all interested in the evolution of human behavior.

Trager, G. L. (1964). Paralanguage: A first approximation. In Dell Hymes (Ed.), *Language in culture and society* (p. 274–279). New York: Harper & Row.

The author was the pioneer in paralinguistic research, and in this article he discusses what paralanguage is and why and how it should be studied.

CHAPTER
16

GROWING UP HUMAN

AMONG THE JU/'HOANSI OF NAMIBIA, CHILDREN ARE GENERALLY INDULGED, ARE NOT TREATED IN AUTHORITARIAN WAYS, AND SPEND MUCH TIME IN NONCOMPETITIVE PLAY IN GROUPS INCLUDING BOTH SEXES AND VARIOUS AGES. IN SOME OTHER SOCIETIES, CHILDREN GROW UP IN QUITE DIFFERENT WAYS. SUCH DIFFERENCES IN CHILD-REARING PRACTICES, AND THEIR POSSIBLE EFFECTS ON ADULT PERSONALITIES, HAVE LONG BEEN OF INTEREST TO ANTHROPOLOGISTS.

CHAPTER PREVIEW

What Is Enculturation?

Enculturation is the process by which culture is passed from one generation to the next. It begins soon after birth, as self-awareness—the ability to perceive oneself as an object in time and space and to judge one's own actions—starts to develop. For self-awareness to function, the individual must be provided with a behavioral environment. This begins as one learns about a world of objects other than self, and these are always perceived in terms that are specified by the culture in which one grows up. One is at the same time provided with spatial, temporal, and normative orientations.

What Is the Effect of Enculturation on Adult Personality?

Studies have shown that there is some kind of nonrandom relationship between enculturation and personality development, although it is also clear that each individual begins with certain broad potentials and limitations that are genetically inherited. In some cultures certain child-rearing practices seem to promote the development of compliant personalities, while in others different practices seem to promote more independent, self-reliant personalities.

Are Different Personalities Characteristic of Different Cultures?

Although cultures vary a great deal in terms of the personality traits that are looked upon with admiration or disapproval, it is difficult to characterize cultures in terms of particular personalities. Of the several attempts that have been made, the concept of modal personality is the most satisfactory. This recognizes that in any human society there will be a range of individual personalities, with some more "typical" than others.

Do Cultures Differ in What They Regard as Abnormal Personalities?

A normal personality may be thought of as one that approximates the modal personality of a particular culture. Since modal personalities may differ from one culture to another, and since cultures may differ in the range of variation they will accept, it is clear that abnormal personality is a relative concept. A particular personality regarded as abnormal in one culture may not be so regarded in another.

A chimpanzee mother with three of her offspring. The basic primate child-rearing unit consists of a mother and her offspring; to this humans have added an adult male. In some societies, this is the mother's husband; in others, it is her brother.

In 1690 John Locke presented his *tabula rasa* theory in his book *An Essay Concerning Human Understanding*. This notion held that the newborn human was like a blank slate, and what the individual became in life was written on the slate by his or her life experiences. The implication is that all individuals are biologically identical at birth in their potential for personality development and that their adult personalities are exclusively the products of their postnatal experiences, which will differ from culture to culture. Stated in these terms, the theory is not acceptable, for we know now that each person is born with unique inherited tendencies that will help determine his or her adult personality. It is also known, however, that genetic inheritance sets certain broad potentials and limitations and that life experiences, particularly in the early years, are critically important in the shaping of individual personalities. Since different cultures handle the raising and education of children in different ways, these practices and their effects on personalities are important subjects of anthropological inquiry. Such studies gave rise to the subfield of psychological anthropology and are the subjects of the present chapter.

THE SELF AND ITS BEHAVIORAL ENVIRONMENT

Since culture is created and learned rather than biologically inherited, all societies must somehow ensure that culture is adequately transmitted from one generation to the next. This process of transmission is known as **enculturation,** and it begins

Enculturation: The process by which a society's culture is transmitted from one generation to the next.

soon after birth. The first agents of encultura-tion in all societies are the members of the house-hold into which a person is born. At first, the most important member of this household is the new-born's mother, but other members of the house-hold soon come to play roles in the process. Just who these others are depends on how households are structured in the particular society (Chapter 20). In the United States, they ideally include the father or stepfather and the child's siblings. In other societies, the father may have little contact with his children in their early years; indeed, there are societies where men do not even live with the mothers of their children. In such instances, broth-ers of the child's mother usually have important re-sponsibilities toward their nieces and nephews. In many societies, grandparents, other wives of the fa-ther, brothers of the father, or sisters of the mother, not to mention their children, are also likely to be key players in the enculturation process.

As the young person matures, individuals out-side the household are brought into the process. These usually include other kin and certainly the individual's peers. The latter may be included in-formally in the form of play groups or formally in age associations, where children actually teach other children. In some societies, such as the United States, professionals are brought into the process of enculturation to provide formal in-struction. In many societies, however, children are allowed to learn through observation and partici-pation, at their own speed.

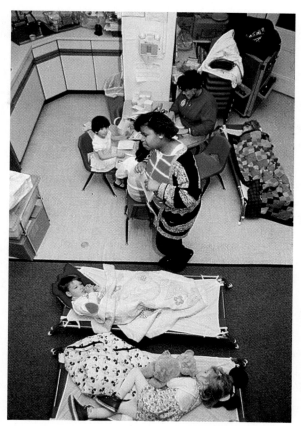

In traditional societies around the world, adults from outside a child's household frequently assist the parents in looking after the child. In the United States, day-care centers may serve this purpose, but to be successful they must approximate conditions in traditional societies: They should be located in the child's neighborhood and personnel should be stable. If personnel are not from the child's neighborhood and there is high turnover, children who spend 8 to 10 hours in such a center may come to have difficulty forming social bonds.

The Self

Enculturation begins with the development of **self-awareness**—the ability to identify oneself as an object, to react to oneself, and to appraise or evaluate oneself. People do not have this ability at birth, even though it is essential for existence in human societies. It is self-awareness that permits

Self-awareness: The ability to identify oneself as an object, to react to oneself, and to appraise oneself.

one to assume responsibility for one's conduct, to learn how to react to others, and to assume a va-riety of roles. An important aspect of self-aware-ness is the attachment of positive value to the self. Without this, individuals cannot be motivated to act to their advantage rather than disadvantage; self-identification by itself is not sufficient for this.

Self-awareness does not come all at once. In modern North American society, for example, self and nonself are not clearly distinguished until about 2 years of age. This development of self-awareness in North American children, however, may lag somewhat behind other cultures, since self–awareness develops in concert with neuromotor development, which is known to proceed at a slower rate in infants from North America than in infants in many, perhaps even most, non-Western societies. The reasons for this are not yet clear, although the amount of human contact and stimulation that infants receive seems to play an important role. For example, at 15 weeks of age, the home-reared infant in North America is in contact with its mother about 20 percent of the time, on the average. At the same age, infants in the traditional Ju/'hoansi society of southern Africa's Kalahari Desert are in close contact with their mothers about 70 percent of the time. Moreover, their contacts are not usually limited to their mothers; they include numerous other adults and children of virtually all ages. In the United States and Canada, something approximating these same conditions is now being provided by day-care centers. So long as their personnel remains stable and is recruited from the same neighborhood as the child, these centers should have a positive effect on the cognitive and social development of the very young children enrolled in them.

In the development of self-awareness, *perception*—a kind of vague awareness of one's existence—precedes *conception*, or more specific knowledge of the interrelated needs, attitudes, concerns, and interests that define what one is. This involves a cultural definition of self, with language playing a crucial role. Consistent with this, in all cultures individuals master personal and possessive pronouns at an early age. Personal names, too, are important devices for self-identification in all cultures. As infancy gives way to early childhood, the "I" or "me" is increasingly separated from the environment.

The Behavioral Environment

In order for self-awareness to emerge and function, basic orientations are necessary to structure the psychological field in which the self is prepared to act. Thus, each individual must learn about a world of objects other than self. The basis of this world of other-than-self is what we would think of as the physical environment of things. The physical environment, though, is organized culturally and mediated symbolically through language. To put it another way, the world around us is perceived through cultural glasses. Those attributes of the environment that are culturally significant are singled out for attention and labeled; those that are not may be ignored or lumped together in broad categories. Culture, however, also *explains* the perceived environment. This is important because it provides the individual with an orderly, rather than chaotic, universe within which to act. Behind this lies a powerful psychological drive to reduce uncertainty, the product of a universal human need for a balanced and integrated perspective on the relevant universe. When confronted with ambiguity and uncertainty, people invariably strive to clarify and give structure to the situation; they do this in ways that their particular culture tells them are appropriate. The greater the lack of structure and certainty, the greater individual suggestibility and persuadability tend to be. Thus, we should not be surprised to find that explanations of the universe are never entirely objective in nature.

The behavioral environment in which the self acts involves more than object orientation alone. Action requires spatial orientation, or the ability to get from one object, or place, to another. In all societies, names and significant features of places are important means of discriminating and representing points of reference for spatial orientation. Individuals must know where they have been and will be in order to get from one place to another. They also need to maintain a sense of self-continuity, so that past actions are connected with those in the present and future. Hence, temporal orientation is also part of the behavioral environment. Just as the perceived environment is organized in cultural terms, so, too, are time and space.

A final aspect of the behavioral environment is the normative orientation. Values, ideals, and standards, which are purely cultural in origin, are as much a part of the individual's behavioral environment as are trees, rivers, and mountains. Without them one would have nothing by which to judge either one's own actions or those of others. In short, the self-appraisal aspect of self-awareness could not be made functional.

Like any aspect of culture, conceptions of the self vary considerably from one society to another. The Penobscot Indians, who at one time relied on fishing, hunting, and the gathering of wild plants

The Ituri forest, in the geographical heart of Africa, is viewed in two very different ways by the people who live there. Mbuti foragers view it with affection; like a benevolent parent, it provides them with all they ask in the way of sustenance, protection, and security. Village-dwelling farmers, by contrast, view the forest with a mixture of fear, hostility, and mistrust—something they must constantly struggle to control.

(food foraging) for subsistence and whose descendants still live today in the woodlands of northeastern North America, serve as an example.[1]

The Penobscot

When first encountered by Europeans, the Penobscot conceived of each individual as being made up of two parts—the body and a "vital self." The latter was dependent on the body, yet was able to have "out of body" experiences—that is, to disengage itself from the body and travel about for short periods of time, to perform overt acts, and to in-

teract with other "selves." It was activity on the part of the vital self that was thought to occur in dreams or in states of trance. So long as the vital self returned to the body before the passage of too much time, the individual remained in good health; if, however, the vital self was prevented from returning to the body, then the individual sickened and died. Along with this dual nature of the self went a potential for every individual to work magic. Theoretically, it was possible to send one's own vital self out to work mischief on others, just as it was possible for others to lure one's vital self away from the body, resulting in sickness and eventual death.

To many people today, the traditional Penobscot concept of self may seem strange. The British colonists of New England regarded such

[1]Speck, F. G. (1920). Penobscot shamanism. *Memoirs of the American Anthropological Association, 6,* 239–288.

ideas as false and steeped in superstition, even though their own concept of self at the time was similarly supernaturalistic. To the Indians their concept made sense, for it adequately accounted for their experience, regardless of its rightness or wrongness in any objective sense. Furthermore, the Penobscot view of self is relevant for anyone who wishes to understand Penobscot behavior in the days when the British and French first tried to settle in North America. For one thing, it was responsible for an undercurrent of suspicion and distrust of strangers, as well as the individual secretiveness that characterized Penobscot society at the time. This propensity for individual secretiveness made it difficult for a potentially malevolent stranger to gain control of an individual's vital self. Also, the belief that dreams are real experiences, rather than expressions of unconscious desires, could impose burdens of guilt and anxiety on individuals who dreamed of doing things not accepted as proper. Finally, individuals indulged in acts that would strike many people today as quite mad. A case in point is a Penobscot Indian who spent the night literally fighting for his life with a fallen tree. To the Indian, this was a metamorphosed magician who was out to get him, and it would have been madness *not* to try to overcome his adversary.

The behavioral environment in which the Penobscot self operated consisted of a flat world, surrounded on all sides by salt water. They could actually see the latter downstream, where the Penobscot River met the sea. The river itself was the spatial reference point and the main artery for canoe travel in the region. The largest of a number of watercourses, it flowed through forests abounding with game. Like humans, each animal was also composed of a body and a vital self. Along with the animals were various quasi-human supernatural beings that inhabited bodies of water and mountains or roamed freely through the forest. One of these, *Gluskabe*, created the all-important Penobscot River by deceiving a greedy giant frog that had monopolized the world's water supply. Gluskabe was also responsible for a number of other natural features of the world, often as a by-product of punishment for such transgressions of the moral code. Individuals had to be concerned about their behavior vis-à-vis both animals and

these quasi-human beings or they, too, would come to various kinds of grief. Hence, these supernaturals not only "explained" many otherwise unexplainable natural phenomena to the Penobscot but were also important in structuring the Penobscot moral order. To the Penobscot, all of this was quite believable; the lone hunter, for example, off for extended periods in the forest, could hear in the night what sounded like the cry of *Pskedemus*, the swamp woman. And a Penobscot accepted as fact that his or her vital self routinely traveled about while the body slept, interacting with various of these supernatural beings.

Penobscot concepts of the self and behavioral environment have changed considerably since the seventeenth century, though no less so than those of the descendants of the early Europeans who first came to New England. Both groups may now be said to hold modern beliefs about the nature of their selves and the world they live in. The old beliefs were associated with **patterns of affect**—how people *feel* about themselves and others—which differed considerably in Indian and European cultures. This is significant, for as the Chinese-born anthropologist Francis Hsu has pointed out, patterns of affect are likely to persist over thousands of years, even in the face of far-reaching changes in all other aspects of culture.[2] A failure to understand this point seems to be at least partially responsible for the generally negative attitude, on the part of many non-Indians, to claims for a variety of aboriginal rights on the part of Native Americans like the Penobscot. Because the changes that have taken place in the external trappings (clothing, housing, transport, etc.) of Native-American cultures have so bedazzled non-natives, the latter fail to realize how many of the less visible, but absolutely basic elements of native culture have persisted even into the 1990s.

Patterns of affect: How people feel about themselves and others.

[2]Hsu, F. L. K. (1977). Role, affect, and anthropology. *American Anthropologist, 79*, 807.

MARGARET MEAD

(1901–1978)

Although all of the natural and social sciences are able to look back and pay homage to certain "founding fathers," anthropologists take pride in the fact that they have a number of "founding mothers." One is Margaret Mead, who was encouraged by her teacher, Franz Boas, to pursue a career in anthropology at a time when most other academic disciplines rarely accepted women into their ranks. In 1925, she set out for Samoa in order to test the theory (widely accepted at the time) that the biological changes of adolescence could not be accomplished without a great deal of stress, both social and psychological. In her book *Coming of Age in Samoa: a Psychological Study of Primitive Youth for Western Civilization*, she concluded that adolescence does not have to be a time of stress and strain, but that cultural conditions may make it so. Published in 1928, this book is generally credited as marking the beginning of the field of culture and personality.

Pioneering works are never without their faults, and *Coming of Age* is no exception. For one thing, it is not clear that her time in the field (9 months) was sufficient for Mead to understand fully the nuances of native speech and body language necessary to comprehend the innermost feelings of her informants. Furthermore, her sample of Samoan adolescents was a mere 50, half of whom had not yet passed puberty. That she exaggerated her findings is suggested by her dismissal of those girls who did not fit her ideal as "deviant" and by inconsistencies with data collected elsewhere in Polynesia. But despite its faults, Mead's book stands as a landmark for several reasons: Not only was it a deliberate test of a Western psychological hypothesis, it also showed psychologists the value of modifying intelligence tests to be appropriate for the population under study; furthermore, by emphasizing the lesson to be drawn for Mead's own society, it laid the groundwork for the popularization of anthropology and advanced the cause of applied anthropology.

PERSONALITY

In the process of enculturation we have seen that each individual is introduced to the concepts of self and the behavioral environment characteristic of his or her culture. The result is that a kind of cognitive or mental map of the operating world is built up, in terms of which the individual will think and act. It is each individual's "map" of how to run the "maze" of life. This cognitive map is an integrated, dynamic system of perceptual assemblages, including the self and its behavioral environment. When we speak of an individual's **personality**, we are generalizing about that individual's cognitive map over time. Hence, personalities are products of enculturation, as experienced by individuals, each with

Personality: The distinctive way a person thinks, feels, and behaves.

his or her distinctive genetic makeup. "Personality" does not lend itself to a formal definition, but for our purposes we may take it as the distinctive way a person thinks, feels, and behaves.

The Development of Personality

Although *what* one learns is important to personality development, most anthropologists assume that *how* one learns is no less important. With the psychoanalytic theorists, anthropologists view adult personality as having been strongly influenced by early childhood experiences. Indeed, many anthropologists have been strongly attracted by Freudian psychoanalytic theory, but with a critical eye. Psychoanalytic literature tends to be long on concepts, speculation, and clinical data, but short on less culture-bound studies. Anthropologists, for their part, are most interested in studies that seek to prove, modify, or at least shed light on the role of early childhood experiences on personality. For example, the traditional ideal in

Western societies has been for men to be tough, aggressive, assertive, dominant, self-reliant, and achievement oriented, whereas women have been expected to be passive, obedient, compliant, loyal, and caring. To many, these personality differences between the sexes seem so "natural" that they must be biologically grounded and therefore inescapable, unchangeable, and universal. But are they? Have anthropologists identified any psychological or personality characteristics that universally differentiate men and women?

As Margaret Mead's pioneering studies suggested and subsequent cross-cultural studies have confirmed, there are no absolute personality differences between men and women. Among the Arapesh of New Guinea it is not just the women, but the men, too, who are gentle and nonaggressive, while among the Mundugamor (also of New Guinea), both sexes are angry and aggressive. In yet another New Guinea society, the Tchambuli, it is the men who decorate themselves, are vain, and are interested in art, theater, and petty gossip, whereas the women are unadorned, brisk, and efficient in such practical tasks as raising children, fishing, and marketing. Although each culture has different expectations for male-female behavior, the criteria of differentiation in one may bear no relation to those in another and may in fact be poles apart. Thus, there is no inevitability to the physical, political, and economic dominance that men have traditionally exerted over women in Western societies, and other arrangements are possible.

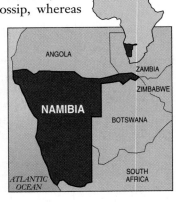

To understand the importance of child-rearing practices for the development of gender-related personality characteristics, we may look briefly at how children grow up among the Ju/'hoansi (pronounced zhutwasi), a people native to the Kalahari Desert of Namibia and Botswana. The Ju/'hoansi are one of a number of people traditionally referred to as Bushmen, who once were widespread through much of southern Africa. In recent times,

anthropologists have referred to these people as the San, thinking the word *Bushman* to be insulting. Unfortunately *San*, a Nama word, has highly pejorative associations. Moreover, anthropologists misunderstood the derivation of the word *Bushman*, which comes from the Dutch *Bossiesman*, meaning "bandit" or "outlaw." This designation the people earned for their refusal to submit to colonial domination, and so to refer to them as Bushman honors their long and valiant, if costly, record of resistance to colonialization. Moreover, *Bushman* is the term they themselves find acceptable as a generic word covering all groups.[3]

Traditionally food foragers, in the past two decades many Ju/'hoansi have adopted a more sedentary lifestyle, tending small herds of goats and planting gardens for their livelihood.[4] Among those who forage for a living, dominance and aggressiveness are not tolerated in either sex, men are as mild-mannered as the women, and women are as energetic and self-reliant as the men. In the villages, by contrast, men and women exhibit personality characteristics approximating those that have traditionally been thought of as typically masculine and feminine in Western societies. Among the food foragers, children of both sexes receive lengthy, intensive care from their mothers, whose attention is not diverted by the birth of new offspring until after the passage of many years. This is not to say that they are constantly with their children, for they are not; when they go gathering wild plant foods in the bush, they do not always take their offspring with them. At such times, the children will be supervised by their fathers or other adults of the community, one-third to one-half of whom are always to be found in camp on any given day. Because these include men as well as women, children are as much habituated to the male as to the female presence.

[3]Gordon, R. J. (1992). *The Bushman myth* (p. 6). Boulder, CO: Westview; Griffin, B. (1994). CHAGS 7. *Anthropology Newsletter, 35*, (1), p. 13; Lewis-Williams, D., Dowson, T., & Deacon, J. (1993). Rock art and changing perceptions of Southern Africa's past: Ezeljagdspoort reviewed. *Antiquity, 67*, 273.

[4]Draper, P. (1975). !Kung women: Contrasts in sexual egalitarianism in foraging and sedentary contexts. In R. Reiter (Ed.), *Toward an anthropology of women* (p. 77–109). New York: Monthly Review Press.

Fathers, too, spend much time with their off-spring, interacting with them in nonauthoritarian ways. Although they may correct their children's behavior, so may women who neither defer to male authority, nor use the threat of paternal anger. Thus, among Ju/'hoansi foragers, no one grows up to respect or fear male authority any more than that of women. In fact, instead of being punished, a child who misbehaves will simply be removed and redirected to some other more inoffensive activity. Nor are boys or girls assigned tasks to do; both sexes do equally little work, instead spending much of their time in play groups that include members of both sexes of widely different ages. Thus, Ju/'hoansi children have few experiences that set one sex apart from another. While older ones do amuse and monitor younger ones, this is done spontaneously rather than as an assigned chore,

In traditional Ju/'hoansi society, children are shown great indulgence by adults of both sexes and do not grow up to fear or respect one sex more than the other.

and the burden does not fall any more heavily on girls than boys.

Among the sedentary villagers, women spend much of their time in and around the home preparing food and attending to other domestic chores, as well as tending the children. The work of men, by contrast, requires them to spend many hours outside the household. As a result, children are less habituated to their presence. This remoteness, coupled with their more extensive knowledge of the outside world, tends to enhance their influence within the household.

Within village households, sex role typing begins early as girls, as soon as they are old enough, are expected to attend to many of the needs of their younger siblings, thereby allowing the mother more time to attend to her other domestic tasks. This not only shapes but also limits the behavior of girls, who cannot range as widely or explore as freely and independently as they could without little brothers and sisters in tow. They must stay close to home, be more careful, more obedient, and more sensitive to the wishes of others than they otherwise might be. Boys, by contrast, have little to do with the handling of infants, and when they are assigned work, it generally takes them away from the household. Thus, the space that girls occupy becomes restricted and they are trained in behaviors that promote passivity and nurturance, whereas boys begin to become the distant, controlling figures they will be as adults.

From this comparison, we may begin to understand how a society's economy helps structure the way a child is brought up, and how this, in turn, influences the adult personality. It also shows that there are alternatives to the ways that children are raised in Western societies and that by changing the conditions in which our children grow up, we might make it significantly easier than it has been for men and women to interact on an equal basis. Thus, child rearing emerges as not only an anthropological problem, but a practical one as well.

Dependence Training

Although Margaret Mead compared sex and temperament in three different societies in the early 1930s, most cross-cultural studies of the effects of child rearing on personality have been carried out

The White Man's Bad Medicine, by American Indian artist Jerome Tiger (1941–1967). In the 1950s, in an effort to end its special relationship with the American Indians, the federal government terminated its establishment of, and aid to, some Indian reservations. This termination policy led many Indians to relocate to urban areas. As a people whose definition of self springs from the group into which they were born, separation from family and kin led many to severe depression and related problems.

more recently by John and Beatrice Whiting and Irvin L. Child, or their associates. Their work has demonstrated a number of apparent regularities. For example, it is possible to distinguish at a broad level of generalization between two different patterns of child rearing, which we may label for convenience "dependence training" and "independence training."[5]

Dependence training promotes compliance in the performance of assigned tasks and favors

<hr />

Dependence training: Child-rearing practices that foster compliance in the performance of assigned tasks and dependence on the domestic group, rather than reliance on oneself.

<hr />

[5]Wolf, E. (1966). *Peasants* (pp. 69–70). Englewood Cliffs, NJ: Prentice-Hall.

keeping individuals within the group. This pattern is typically associated with extended families, which consist of several husband-wife-children units within the same household, and which are most apt to be found in societies in which the economy is based on subsistence farming. Such families are important, for they provide the large labor force necessary to till the soil, tend whatever flocks are kept, and carry out other part-time economic pursuits considered necessary for existence. Such large families, however, have built into them certain tensions that are potentially disruptive. For example, one of the adults typically makes the important family decisions, which must be followed by all other family members. In addition, the in-marrying spouses—husbands or wives—must subordinate themselves to the will of the group, which may not be easy for them. Dependence training helps to keep these potential problems under control, involving both supportive and punitive aspects. On the supportive side, indulgence is shown

to young children, particularly in the form of prolonged oral gratification. Nursing continues for
several years and is virtually on demand. This may
be interpreted as rewarding the child for seeking
support within the family, the main agent in meeting the child's needs. Also on the supportive side,
children at a relatively early age are assigned a
number of child-care and domestic tasks, all of
which make significant and obvious contributions
to the family's welfare. Thus, family members all
actively work to help and support one another. On
the punitive side, behavior that is interpreted by
the adults as aggressive or sexual is apt to be actively discouraged. Moreover, the adults tend to be
quite insistent on overall obedience, which is seen
as rendering the individual subordinate to the
group. This combination of encouragement and
discouragement ideally produces individuals who
are obedient, supportive, noncompetitive, generally responsible, and who will stay within the fold
and not do anything potentially disruptive. Indeed,
their very definition of "self" comes from their affiliation with a group, rather than from the mere
fact of their individual existence.

Independence Training

By contrast, **independence training** emphasizes
individual independence, self-reliance, and personal achievement. It is typically associated with
societies in which nuclear families, consisting of a
husband, wife, and their offspring, are independent rather than a part of some larger household
group. Independence training is particularly characteristic of industrial societies such as that of the
United States, where self-reliance and personal
achievement, especially on the part of men, are
important traits for survival. Again, this pattern of
training involves both encouragement and discouragement. On the negative side, little empha-

Independence training: Child-rearing practices that
promote independence, self-reliance, and personal
achievement on the part of the child.

sis is placed on prolonged oral gratification, and
feeding is prompted more by schedule than demand. In the United States, for example, people
like to establish a schedule as soon as possible, and
it is not long before they start feeding infants baby
food, and even try to get them to feed themselves.
Many parents are delighted if they can prop their
infants up in the crib or playpen so that they can
hold their own bottles. Moreover, as soon after
birth as possible, children are given their own private space, away from their parents. In fact, infants
do not receive the amount of attention they often
do in nonindustrialized societies. In the United
States a mother may be very affectionate with her
15-week-old infant during the 20 percent of the
time she is in contact with it, but for the other 80
percent of the time the infant is more or less on
its own. Collective responsibility is not encouraged
in children; they are not given responsible tasks to
perform until later in childhood, and these are
generally few in number. Furthermore, their contribution to the welfare of the family is often not
immediately apparent to the children, to whom the
tasks appear arbitrary as a result. Indeed, they
are often encouraged to perform tasks for pay,
rather than for the purpose of contributing to the
family's welfare.

Displays of aggression and sexuality are encouraged, or at least tolerated to a greater degree
than where dependence training is the rule. In
schools, and even in the family, competition is emphasized. In the United States, people have gone
to the extreme of turning the biological functions
of infancy—eating, sleeping, crying, and elimination—into contests between parents and offspring.
In schools, considerable resources are devoted to
competitive sports, but competition is fostered
within the classroom as well: overtly through such
devices as spelling bees and competition for prizes
and covertly through such devices as grading on a
curve. The latter practice, widely utilized especially for heavily enrolled courses on some college
campuses, condemns some students to failure, irrespective of how well they actually do, so long as
most of the class does better. This puts students
in competition with each other, for one soon
learns that one's own chances for a decent grade
depend, as much as anything, on other members
of the class not doing well themselves. If the stakes
are high, students may devote considerable effort

In North American society, independence training pits individuals against one another through games and other forms of competition.

to placing obstacles in the way of classmates, so that they are prevented from performing well. Thus, by the time one has grown up in U.S. society, regardless of what one may think about it, one has received a clear message: Success is something that comes at someone else's expense. As anthropologist Colin Turnbull observed: "Even the team spirit, so loudly touted" in school athletics (or out of school in Little League baseball and the like) "is merely a more efficient way, through limited cooperation, to 'beat' a greater number of people more efficiently."[6]

Independence training generally encourages individuals to seek help and attention, rather than to give it, and to try to exert individual dominance. Such qualities are useful in societies with social structures that emphasize personal achievement and where individuals are expected to look out for their own interests.

[6]Turnbull, C. M. (1983). *The human cycle* (p. 74). New York: Simon & Schuster.

Combined Dependence/Independence Training

In actuality, dependence and independence training represent polar positions along a continuum, and actual situations may partake of elements of both. In food-foraging societies, for example, child-rearing practices combine elements of both. "Share and share alike" is the prevailing ethic, while competitive behavior, which can interfere with the cooperation on which all else depends, is discouraged. Thus, infants receive much in the way of positive, affectionate attention from adults, along with prolonged oral gratification. This, as well as low pressure for compliance and a lack of emphasis on competition, encourages individuals to be more supportive of one another than is often the case in modern industrial societies. At the same time, personal achievement and independence are encouraged, for those individuals most capable of self-reliance are apt to be the most successful in the food quest.

In the United States the argument has sometimes been made (not by anthropologists) that "permissive" child rearing produces irresponsible adults. Since the practices of food foragers seem to be about as "permissive" as they can get, and yet socially responsible adults are produced, it is worth taking a closer look at how this is achieved. In the following Original Study, we see how children grow up among the Mbuti, hunters and gatherers who live in Zaire's Ituri forest.

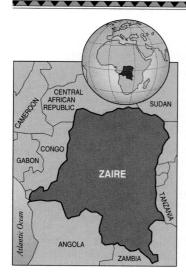

Original Study
Growing Up Among the Mbuti[7]

In the first three years of life every Mbuti alive experiences almost total security. The infant is breastfed for those three years, and is allowed almost every freedom. Regardless of gender, the infant learns to have absolute trust in both male and female parents. If anything, the father is just another kind of mother, for in the second year the father formally introduces the child to its first solid food. There used to be a beautiful ritual in which the mother presented the child to the father in the middle of the camp, where all important statements are made (anyone speaking from the middle of the camp must be listened to). The father took the child and held it to his breast, and the child would try to suckle, crying *"ema, ema,"* or "mother." The father would shake his head, and say "no, father . . . *eba,"* but like a mother (the Mbuti said), then give the child its first solid food.

At three the child ventures out into the world on its own and enters the *bopi,* what we might call a playground, a tiny camp perhaps a hundred yards from the main camp, often on the edge of a stream. The *bopi* were indeed playgrounds, and often very noisy ones, full of fun and high spirits. But they were also rigorous training grounds for eventual economic responsibility. On entry to the *bopi,* for one thing, the child discovers the importance of age as a structural principle, and the relative unimportance of gender and biological kinship. The *bopi* is the private world of the children. Younger youths may occasionally venture in, but if adults or elders try, as they sometimes do when angry at having their afternoon snooze interrupted, they invariably get driven out, taunted, and ridiculed. Children, among the Mbuti, have rights, but they also learn that they have responsibilities. Before the hunt sets out each day it is the children, sometimes the younger youths, who light the hunting fire.

Ritual among the Mbuti is often so informal and apparently casual that it may pass unnoticed at first. Yet insofar as ritual involves symbolic acts that represent unspoken, perhaps even unthought, concepts or ideals, or invoke other states of being, alternative frames of mind and reference, then Mbuti life is full of ritual. The hunting fire is one of the more obvious of such rituals. Early in the morning children would take firebrands from the *bopi,* where they always lit their own fire with embers from their family hearths, and set off on the trail by which the hunt was to leave that day (the direction of each day's hunt was always settled by discussion the night before). Just a short distance from the camp they lit a fire at the base of a large tree, and covered it with special leaves that made it give off a column of

Among traditional Ju/'hoansi as among the Mbuti, education into social consciousness begins literally at the mother's breast. Nursed virtually on demand for the first few years of life, an infant learns to have absolute trust in his or her parents.

dense smoke. Hunters leaving the camp, both men and women, and such youths and children as were going with them, had to pass by this fire. Some did so casually, without stopping or looking, but passing through the smoke. Others reached into the smoke with their hands as they passed, rubbing the smoke into their bodies. A few always stopped, for a moment, and let the smoke envelop them, only then almost dreamily moving off.

And indeed it *was* a form of intoxication, for the smoke invoked the spirit of the forest, and by passing through it the hunters sought to fill themselves with that spirit, not so much to make the hunt successful as to minimize the sacrilege of killing. Yet they, the hunters, could not light the fire themselves. After all, they were already contaminated by death. Even youths, who daily joined the hunt at the edges, catching any game that escaped the nets, by hand, if they could, were not pure enough to invoke the spirit of forestness. But young children were uncontaminated, as yet untainted by contact with the original sin of the Mbuti. It was their responsibility to light the fire, and if it was not lit then the hunt would not take place, or as the Mbuti put it, the hunt *could* not take place.

In this way even the children in Mbuti society, at the first of the four age levels that dominate Mbuti social structure, are given very real social responsibility and see themselves as a part of that structure, by virtue of their purity. After all, they have just been born from the source of all purity, the forest itself. By the same reasoning, the elders, who are about to return to that ultimate source of all being, through death, are at least closer to purity than the adults, who are daily contaminated by killing. Elders no longer go on the hunt. So, like the children, the elders have important sacred ritual responsibilities in the Mbuti division of labor by age. In the *bopi* the children play, but they have no "games" in the strict sense of the word. Levi-Strauss has perceptively compared games with rituals, suggesting that whereas in a game the players start theoretically equal but end up unequal, in a ritual just the reverse takes place. All are equalized. Mbuti children could be seen every day playing in the *bopi*, but not once did I see a game, not one activity that smacked of any kind of competition, except perhaps that competition that it is necessary for us all to feel from time to time, competition with our own private and personal inadequacies. One such pastime (rather than game) was tree climbing. A dozen or so children would climb up a young sapling. Reaching the top, their weight brought the sapling bending down until it almost touched the ground. Then all the children leapt off together, shrieking as the young tree sprang upright again with a rush. Sometimes one child, male or female, might stay on a little too long, either out of fear, or out of bravado, or from sheer carelessness or bad timing. Whatever the reason, it was a lesson most children only needed to be taught once, for the result was that you got flung upward with the tree, and were lucky to escape with no more than a few bruises and a very bad fright.

Other pastimes taught the children the rules of hunting and gathering. Frequently elders, who stayed in camp when the hunt went off, called the children into the main camp and enacted a mock hunt with them there. Stretching a discarded piece of net across the camp, they pretended to be animals, showing the children how to drive them into the nets. And, of course, the children played house, learning the patterns of cooperation that would be necessary for them later in life. They also learned the prime lesson of egality, other than for purposes of division of labor making no distinction between male and female, this nuclear family or that. All in the *bopi* were *apua'i* to each other, and so they would remain throughout their lives. At every age level—childhood, youth, adulthood, or old age—everyone of that level is *apua'i* to all the others. Only adults sometimes (but so rarely that I think it was only done as a kind of joke, or possibly insult) made the distinction that the Bira do, using *apua'i* for male and *amua'i* for female. Male or female, for the Mbuti, if you are the same age you are *apua'i*, and that means that you share everything equally, regardless of kinship or gender.

Sometime before the age of puberty boys or girls, whenever they feel ready, move back into the main camp from the *bopi* and join the youths. This is when they must assume new responsibilities, which for the youths are primarily political. Already, in the *bopi*, the children become involved in disputes, and are sometimes instrumental in settling them by ridicule, for nothing hurts an adult more than being ridiculed publicly by children. The art of reason, however, is something they learn from the youths, and it is the youths who apply the art of reason to the settlement of disputes.

When puberty comes it separates them, for the first time in their experience, from each other as *apua'i*. Very plainly girls are different from boys. When a girl has her first menstrual period the whole camp celebrates with the wild *elima* festival, in which the girl, and some of her chosen girl friends, are the center of all attention, living together in a special *elima* house. Male youths sit outside the *elima* house and wait for the girls to come out, usually in the afternoon, for the *elima* singing. They sing in antiphony, the girls leading, the boys responding. Boys come from neighboring territories all around, for this is a time of courtship. But there are always eligible youths within the camp as well, and the *elima* girl may well choose girls from other territories to come and join her, so there is more than enough excuse for every youth to carry on several flirtations, legitimate or illegitimate. I have known even first cousins to flirt with each other, but learned to be prudent enough not to pull out my kinship charts and point this out—well, not in public anyway.

The *elima* is more than a premarital festival, more than a joint initiation of youth into adulthood, and more than a rite of passage through puberty, though it is all those things. It is a public recognition of the opposition of male and female, and every *elima* is used to highlight the *potential* for conflict that lies in that opposition. As at other times of crisis, at puberty, a time of change and uncertainty, the Mbuti bring all the major forms of conflict out into the open. And the one that evidently most concerns them is the male/female opposition.

The adults begin to play a special form of "tug of war" that is clearly a ritual rather than a game. All the men are on one side, the women on the other. At first it looks like a game, but quickly it becomes clear that the objective is for *neither* side to win. As soon as the women begin to win, one of them will leave the end of the line and run around to join the men, assuming a deep male voice and in other ways ridiculing manhood. Then, as the men begin to win, a male will similarly join the women, making fun of womanhood as he does so. Each adult on changing sides attempts to outdo all the others in ridiculing the opposite sex. Finally, when nearly all have switched sides, and sexes, the ritual battle between the genders simply collapses into hysterical laughter, the contestants letting go of the rope, falling onto the ground, and rolling over with mirth. Neither side wins, both are equalized very nicely, and each learns the essential lesson, that there should be *no* contest.

[7]Turnbull, C. M. (1983). *Mbuti pygmies: Change and adaptation* (pp. 39–47). New York: CBS College Publishing.

It must be recognized that no particular system of child rearing is inherently better or worse than any other; what matters is whether the system is functional or dysfunctional in the context of a particular society. If compliant adults who are accepting of authority are required, then independence training will not work well in that society. Nor will dependence training serve very well a society in which adults are expected to be independent, self-reliant, and questioning of authority. Sometimes, however, inconsistencies develop, and here we may look again at the situation in North America. As we have seen, independence training generally tends to be stressed in the United States, where people often speak in glowing terms of the worth of personal independence, the dignity of the individual, and so on. Their pronouncements, however, do not always suit their actions. In spite

Yanomami men display their fierceness. While flamboyant, belligerent personalities are especially compatible with the Yanomami ideal that men should be fierce, some are quiet and retiring.

of the professed desire for personal independence, and emphasis on competition, there seems to be a strong underlying desire for compliance. This is reflected, for example, in decisions handed down over the past two decades or so by the Supreme Court, which, as observers of the Court have noted, often have favored the rights of authority over those of individuals. It is reflected, too, by the fate of "whistle-blowers" in government bureaus, who, if they don't lose their jobs, are often shunted to one side and passed by when the rewards are handed out. In business as well as in government, there is a tendency for the rewards to be given to those who go along with the system, while criticism, no matter how constructive, is a risky business. In both corporate and government bureaucracies, the ability to please, not shake up the system, is what is required for success. Yet, in spite of pressures for compliance, which would be most effectively served by dependence training, people in the United States continue to raise their children to be independent, and then wonder why they so often refuse to behave in ways adults would have them behave.

GROUP PERSONALITY

From studies such as those reviewed here, it is clear that personality, child-rearing practices, and other aspects of culture are interrelated in some kind of nonrandom way. Whiting and Child have argued that the child-rearing practices of a society originate in basic customs surrounding nourishment, shelter, and protection, and that these child-rearing practices in turn produce particular kinds of adult personalities.[8] The trouble is that correlations do not prove cause and effect. We are still left with the fact that, however logical it may seem, such a causal chain remains an unproven hypothesis.

The existence of a close, if not causal, relationship between child-rearing practices and personality, coupled with variation in child-rearing practices from one society to another, have led to a number of attempts to characterize whole societies in terms of particular kinds of personalities. Common sense suggests that personalities appropriate for one culture may be less appropriate for some others; for example, an egocentric, aggressive personality would be out of place where cooperation and sharing are the keys to success. Or, in the context of traditional Penobscot Indian culture, which we examined briefly earlier in this chapter, an open and extroverted personality would seem inappropriate, given its inconsistency with the prevailing conception of the self. Unfortunately, common sense, like conventional wisdom in general, isn't always true. The question is worth asking: Can we describe a group personality without falling into stereotyping? The answer appears to be a qualified yes; in an abstract way, we may speak of a generalized "cultural personality" for a society, so long as we do not expect to find a uniformity of personalities within that society. Put another way, each individual develops certain personality characteristics that, from common experience, resemble those of other people. Yet, because each individual is exposed to unique experiences, may react to common experiences in novel ways, and brings to these experiences a unique (except for the case of identical twins) genetic potential, each also acquires distinct personality traits. Because individual personalities differ, the organization of diversity is important to all cultures.

As an example of the fact that individual personalities in traditional societies are far from uniform, consider the case of the Yanomami, who live in the forests of northern Brazil and southern Venezuela. Among them, individual men strive to achieve a reputation for fierceness and aggressiveness that they are willing to defend at the risk of serious personal injury and death. And yet there are men among the Yanomami who are quiet and somewhat retiring. In any gathering of

[8]Whiting, J. W. M., & Child, I. L. (1953). *Child training and personality: A cross-cultural study.* New Haven, CT: Yale University Press.

RUTH FULTON BENEDICT

(1887–1947)

Ruth Benedict came late to anthropology; upon her graduation from Vassar College, she taught high school English, published poetry, and tried her hand at social work. In anthropology, she developed the idea that culture was a projection of the personality of those who created it. In her most famous book, *Patterns of Culture* (1934), she compared the cultures of three peoples—the Kwakiutl of western Canada, the Zuni of the southwestern United States, and the Dobuans of Melanesia. She held that each was comparable to a great work of art, with an internal coherence and consistency of its own. Seeing the Kwakiutl as egocentric, individualistic, and ecstatic in their rituals, she labeled their cultural configuration "Dionysian"; the Zuni, whom she saw as living by the golden mean, wanting no part of excess or disruptive psychological states, and distrusting of individualism, she characterized as "Apollonian." The Dobuans, whose culture seemed to her magic-ridden, with everyone fearing and hating everyone else, she characterized as "paranoid."

Although *Patterns of Culture* still enjoys popularity in some nonanthropological circles, anthropologists have long since abandoned its approach as impressionistic and not susceptible to replication. To compound the problem, Benedict's characterizations of cultures are misleading (the supposedly "Apollonian" Zunis, for example, indulge in such seemingly "Dionysian" practices as sword swallowing and walking over hot coals), and the use of such value-laden terms as "paranoid" prejudices others toward it. Nonetheless, the book did have an enormous and valuable influence in focusing attention on the problem of the interrelation between culture and personality and in popularizing the reality of cultural variation.

---

these people, the quiet ones are all too easily overlooked by outsiders, when so many others are in the front row pushing and demanding attention. Not only do traditional societies include a range of personalities, but some of those personalities may differ in no important way from those of some individuals in U.S. society. As Ruth Landes observed, an Ojibwa Indian shaman she knew at Emo, Ontario, displayed the same "cold, moralistic, driven personality" as did the late President Nixon.[9]

Modal Personality

Any fruitful approach to the problem of group personality must recognize that each individual is unique to a degree in both inheritance and life experiences and that we should expect a range of personality types in any society. In addition, personality traits that may be regarded as appropri-

ate in men may not be so regarded in women, and vice versa. Given all this, we may focus our attention on the **modal personality** of a group, defined as the personality typical of a culturally bounded population, as indicated by the central tendency of a defined frequency distribution. Modal personality is a statistical concept, and, as such, it opens up for investigation the questions of how societies organize diversity and how diversity relates to culture change. Such questions are easily overlooked if one associates one particular type of personality with one particular culture, as older approaches (like that of Ruth Benedict, described in the box above) tended to

<hr>

Modal personality: The personality typical of a society as indicated by the central tendency of a defined frequency distribution.

---

[9]Landes, R. (1982). Comment. *Current Anthropology, 23,* 401.

do. At the same time, modal personalities of different groups can be compared.

Data on modal personality are best gathered by means of psychological tests administered to a sample of the population in question. Those most often used include the Rorschach, or "ink-blot" test, and the Thematic Apperception Test (TAT). The latter consists of pictures, which the individual tested is asked to explain or interpret. Other sorts of projective tests have been used also, all have in common a purposeful ambiguity, so that the individual tested has to structure the situation before responding. The idea is that one's personality is projected into the ambiguous situation. Along with the use of such tests, observations recording the frequency of certain behaviors, the collection and analysis of life histories and dreams, and the analysis of oral literature are helpful in eliciting data on modal personality.

While having much to recommend it, the concept of modal personality as a means of dealing with group personality nevertheless presents certain difficulties. One of these is the complexity of the measurement techniques themselves, which may be difficult to carry out in the field. For one thing, an adequate representative sample of subjects is necessary. The problem here is twofold: making sure that the sample is genuinely representative and having the time and personnel necessary to administer the tests, conduct interviews, and so on, all of which can be lengthy proceedings. Also, the tests themselves constitute a problem, for those devised in one cultural setting may not be appropriate in another. This is more of a problem with the TAT than with some other tests, although different pictures have been devised for other cultures. Still, to minimize any hidden cultural bias, it is best not to rely on projective tests alone. In addition to all this, there are often language problems, which may lead to misinterpretation. Furthermore, the field investigator may be in conflict with cultural values. A people like the Penobscot, whose concept of self we surveyed earlier, would not take kindly to revealing their dreams to strangers. Finally, there is the question of what is being measured. Just what, for example, is aggression? Does everyone define it the same way? Is it a legitimate entity, or does it involve other variables?

National Character

No discussion of group personality would be complete without a consideration of national character, which popular thought too often ascribes to the citizens of many different countries. Henry Miller epitomizes this view when he says, "Madmen are logical—as are the French," suggesting that Frenchmen, in general, are overly rational. A Parisian, on the other hand, might view North Americans as maudlin and unsophisticated. Similarly, we all have in mind some image, perhaps not well defined, of the "typical" Russian or Japanese or Englishman. Essentially, these are simply stereotypes. We might ask, however, if these stereotypes have any basis in fact. Is there, in reality, such a thing as national character?

Some anthropologists have thought that the answer may be yes. Accordingly, national character studies were begun that sought to discover basic personality traits shared by the majority of the peoples of modern countries. Along with this went an emphasis on child-rearing practices and education as the factors theoretically responsible for such characteristics. Margaret Mead, Ruth Benedict, Weston LaBarre, and Geoffrey Gorer conducted pioneering studies of national character, using relatively small samples of informants. During World War II, techniques were developed for studying "culture at a distance" through the analysis of newspapers, books, photographs, and interviews with expatriates from the country in question. By investigating memories of childhood and cultural attitudes, and by examining graphic material for the appearance of recurrent themes and values, researchers attempted to portray national character.

The Japanese

At the height of World War II, Geoffrey Gorer attempted to determine the underlying reasons for the "contrast between the all-pervasive gentleness of family life in Japan, which has charmed nearly every visitor, and the overwhelming brutality and sadism of the Japanese at War." Strongly under the influence of Sigmund Freud, Gorer sought his causes in the toilet-training practices of the Japanese, which he believed were severe and threatening. He suggested that because Japanese infants were forced to control their sphincters before they had acquired the necessary muscular or neurological development, they grew up filled with repressed rage. As adults, the Japanese were able to express this rage in their ruthlessness in war.[10]

In the midst of war Gorer was not able to do fieldwork in Japan. After the war was over, though, the toilet-training hypothesis was tested, at which time it was found that the severity of Japanese toilet training was a myth. Children were not subject to severe threats of punishment. Nor were all Japanese soldiers brutal and sadistic in war; some were, but then so were some North Americans. Also, the participation of many Japanese in postwar peace movements in the Far East hardly conformed to the wartime image of brutality.

Gorer's study, along with others by Benedict and LaBarre, was most important, not in revealing the importance of Japanese sphincters on the national character, but in pointing out the dangers of

generalizing from insufficient evidence and employing simplistic individual psychology to explain complex social phenomena.

Objections to National Character Studies

Critics of national character theories have emphasized the tendency for such work to be based on unscientific and overgeneralized data. The concept of modal personality has a certain statistical validity, they argue, but to generalize the qualities of a complex country on the basis of such limited data is to lend insufficient recognition to the countless individuals who vary from the generalization. Further, such studies tend to be highly subjective; for example, the tendency during the late 1930s and 1940s for anthropologists to characterize the German people as aggressive paranoids was a reflection of wartime hostilities rather than scientific objectivity. Finally, it has been pointed out that occupational and social status tends to cut across national boundaries. A French farmer may have less in common with a French factory worker than he does with a German farmer.

[10]Gorer, G. (1943). Themes in Japanese Culture. *Transactions of the New York Academy of Sciences*, Series II, 5.

The core values of Chinese culture promote the integration of the individual into a larger group. By contrast, the core values of Anglo-American culture promote the separation of the individual from the group.

An alternative approach to national character—one that allows for the fact that not all personalities will conform to cultural ideals—is that of anthropologist Francis Hsu. His approach has been to study the **core values** of a country's culture and related personality traits. The Chinese, he suggests, value kin ties and cooperation above all else. To them, mutual dependence is the very essence of personal relationships and has been for thousands of years. Compliance and subordination of one's will to that of family and kin transcend all else, while self-reliance is neither promoted nor a source of pride. Following the 1949 revolution, Mao Tse-Tung sought to expand the sphere of affect to the country as a whole, with himself as the "father" of all citizens.

Perhaps the core value held in highest esteem by North Americans of European descent is that of "rugged individualism," at least for men (only recently has this become recognized as a valid ideal for women). Each individual alone is supposed to be able to achieve anything he or she likes, given a willingness to work hard enough. From their earliest years, individuals are subjected to relentless pressures to excel and, as we have already noted, competition and winning are seen as crucial to this. Undoubtedly, this contributes to the "restlessness" and "drivenness" of North American society, and to the degree that it motivates individuals to work hard and to go where the economy needs them, it fits well with the needs of an industrial society. Thus, while the individual in Chinese society is firmly bound into a larger group to which he or she has lifelong obligations, North Americans are isolated from all other kin except spouses, and even here there is a lessened commitment to marriages.[11] More young couples are living together

———◦◦◦———◦◦◦———

Core values: Those values especially promoted by a particular culture.

———◦◦◦———◦◦◦———

[11]This and most of the following observations on North American culture are drawn from Natadecha-Sponsal, P. (1993). The young, the rich and the famous: Individualism as an American cultural value. In P. R. DeVita & J. D. Armstrong (Eds.), *Distant mirrors: America as a foreign culture* (pp. 46–53). Belmont, CA: Wadsworth.

without either marriage or future plans for marriage. When couples do marry, prenuptial agreements are made to protect their assets, and roughly 50 percent of marriages end in divorce. Even parents and children have no legal obligations to one another, once the latter have reached the age of majority. Indeed, many North American parents seem to "lose" their children in their teenage years. Relations with nonkin tend to remain at an abbreviated and superficial level.

NORMAL AND ABNORMAL PERSONALITY

The concept of modal personality holds that a range of personalities will exist in any society. The modal personality itself may be thought of as normal for that society, but may in fact be shared by less than half the population. What of those personalities that differ from the norm? The Dobuans of New Guinea and certain Plains Indians furnish examples of normal and abnormal behavior strikingly different from that of nonnative North Americans.

The individual man in Dobu whom the other villagers considered neurotic and thoroughly disoriented was a man who was naturally friendly and found activity an end in itself. He was a pleasant fellow who did not seek to overthrow his peers or to punish them. He worked for anyone who asked him, and he was tireless in carrying out their commands. In any other Dobuan, this would have been scandalous behavior, but in him it was regarded as merely silly. The village treated him in a kindly fashion, not taking advantage of him, nor making sport of or ridiculing him, but he was definitely regarded as one who stood outside the normal conventions of behavior.

Among many North American Indians, a man, compelled by supernatural spirits, could assume women's attire and perform woman's work; he could even marry another man, although not all men who assumed a woman's identity were homosexuals, nor did all homosexuals behave in this way (most Indian societies allowed individuals ways to engage in homosexual behavior without altering their gender status). Under this institution of the "two-spirit," an individual would find himself living in a dramatically different manner from most men; yet, although the two-spirit was rare among Indians, it was *not* looked upon as deviant behavior.[12] Quite the contrary, for the two-spirit was often sought out as a curer, artist, matchmaker, and companion of warriors, because of the great spiritual power he was thought to possess.

In Western societies like the United States, behavior like that of the Indian two-spirits has traditionally been regarded as deviant. If a man dresses as a woman, it is still widely regarded as a cause for concern and is likely to lead to psychiatric intervention. Nor have jobs traditionally filled by women been seen as desirable for men. By contrast, women are much more free to wear masculine-style clothing and to assume jobs traditionally held by men, even though others may consider them "unfeminine." What lies behind this are traditional values (jobs customarily associated with men have been more highly valued than those associated with women) and a pattern of child rearing that creates problems of gender identity for both sexes, although of a different sort for each sex.

Nancy Chodorow, a sociologist with a strong background in anthropology, has argued that in U.S. society, girls have traditionally been raised by women, usually their mothers, and most still are. Thus, feminine role models are constantly available and easily understandable. Very early, girls begin to do the things that women do, gradually and continuously acquiring the identity deemed appropriate for their sex. Once they enter school, however, they learn that women are not all-powerful and prestigious, that it is men who generally run things and are portrayed as the ones who have most advanced human progress. As a consequence, a girl finds that the feminine identity, which has become so easy for her, is less valued. Under the circumstances, she is bound to feel a certain resentment towards it.

Boys have a different problem; like girls they, too, begin their lives in a feminine world. With adult men out of the house working, not only is a male model rarely present, but also it is the mother who seems to be all-powerful. Under these condi-

Shown here is the famous Zuni Indian Two-Spirit We'wha, who once had the experience of meeting President Grover Cleveland. For a man to dress as a woman and assume a feminine identity was not regarded as abnormal by the Zuni; in fact such individuals were considered special in that they bridged the gap between the purely feminine and purely masculine. In European-American society, by contrast, behavior like that of the Indian Two-Spirit has traditionally been defined as abnormal.

tions, boys begin to develop a feminine identity with its expected compliant personality. Formerly, boys were even dressed as girls (dresses for little boys were not dropped from the Sears catalog until 1940) until they reached the age thought proper to "graduate" into less feminine attire. Once out of the house and in school, boys learn that they must switch from a female to male identity; in a sense, they must renounce femininity and prove

---

[12]Although the European term *berdache* has been widely used in the literature, it carries a pejorative connotation and so has been abandoned for the term "two-spirit" favored by Native Americans. See Jacobs, S. E. (1994). Native American two-spirits. *Anthropology Newsletter, 35*(8), 7.

their maleness, in a way that girls do not have to prove their femaleness. Generally speaking, the more distant a boy's father is (or other male companion of his mother), the greater the boy's insecurity in his male identity and the greater his compulsion to be seen as really masculine. To do this, he must strive all the harder to be aggressive and assert his dominance, particularly over women.

Nancy Chodorow sums up the consequences of this situation as follows:

> Sex-role ideology and socialization for these roles seem to ensure that neither boys nor girls can attain both stable identity and meaningful roles. The tragedy of woman's socialization is not that she is left unclear, as is the man, about her basic sexual identity. This identity is ascribed to her, and she does not need to prove to herself or to society that she has earned it or continues to have it. Her problem is that this identity is clearly devalued in the society in which she lives. This does not mean that women too should be required to compete for identity, to be assertive and to need to achieve—to "do" like men. Nor does it suggest that it is not crucial for everyone, men and women alike, to have a stable sexual identity. But until male "identity" does not depend upon men's proving themselves, their "doing" will be a reaction to insecurity, not a creative exercise of their humanity, and woman's "being," far from being an easy and positive acceptance of self, will be a resignation to inferiority. And as long as women must live through their children, and men do not genuinely contribute to socialization and provide easily accessible role models, women will continue to bring up sons whose sexual identity depends upon devaluing femininity inside and outside themselves, and daughters who must accept this devalued position and resign themselves to producing more men who will perpetuate the system that devalues them. [13]

What this example shows us is how a culture may itself actually induce certain kinds of psychological conflicts, with important consequences for the entire society. Although the conditions under which children are raised in U.S. society are now changing, there is a long way to go before the conflicts described become things of the past. Still, what has seemed to be "normal" in the past could become "abnormal" in the future.

The standards that define normal behavior for any culture are determined by that culture itself. Consider attitudes towards individuals who enter into altered states of consciousness. Among the Melemchi of Nepal, to effect a cure, the healer must call the gods into his body, to let them speak through him.[14] To do this, he must ride into their world. Through drumming and chanting, sometimes accompanied by use of hallucinogenic drugs and intoxicants, he enters an altered state of consciousness, or trance. This allows him to see and communicate with the gods. To outsiders, what is happening is that the curer is hallucinating: seeing visions, smelling odors, hearing sounds, and experiencing bodily sensations that seem real, but are not seen, smelled, heard, or felt by others who are present but who have not entered into trance. In modern North American society, behavior like that of the Melemchi curer is generally regarded as deviant, and the practice of entering altered states is apt to be seen as a sign of mental instability or even unlawful activity if it involves the use of hallucinogenic substances.

The negative attitude of North American culture to the contrary notwithstanding, there is nothing abnormal per se about the ability to enter trancelike states and experience a wide range of hallucinations. There is good evidence that chimpanzees, baboons, other monkeys, cats, dogs, and other animals hallucinate, and that the ability is a function of the mammalian, not just human, nervous system.[15] Thus, the ability to enter altered states and experience visions and other sensations appears to predate the appearance of *Homo sapiens*, and it is not surprising that the ability to enter trance is a human universal. Although some societies try to suppress the practice of trancing, the

[13]Chodorow, N. (1971). Being and doing: A cross-cultural examination of the socialization of males and females. In V. Gornick & B. K. Moran (Eds.), *Women in sexist society* (p. 193). New York: Basic Books.

[14]Womack, M. (1994). Program 5: Psychological anthropology. *Faces of Culture*. Fountain Valley, CA: Coast Telecourses, Inc.

[15]Lewis-Williams, D., & Dowson, T. A. (1988). Signs of all times: Entoptic phenomena in Upper Paleolithic art. *Current Anthropology, 29*, 202.

Although the ability to enter trance is a consequence of having a normal human nervous system, some societies like that of the United States define entering trance as abnormal, while many others accept it as normal. Among the Ju/'hoansi of Namibia, men enter trance in a dance, accompanied by the rhythmic clapping and singing of women. By entering trance, these men are able to summon supernatural power to heal, bring rain, and control animals.

vast majority (like the Melemchi) accept it and shape it to their own ends. One study, for example, found that as many as 437 out of a sample of 488 historically known societies had some form of *institutionalized* altered states of consciousness.[16]

Does this suggest that "normalcy" is a meaningless concept as it is applied to personality? Within the context of a given culture, the concept of normal personality is quite meaningful. A. I. Hallowell, a major figure in the development of psychological anthropology, somewhat ironically observed that it is normal to share the delusions traditionally accepted by one's society. Abnormality involves the development of a delusional system not sanctioned by the culture. The individual who is disturbed because he or she cannot adequately measure up to the norms of society, and yet be happy, may be termed neurotic. When one's delusional system is so different from that of one's

society that it in no way reflects its norms, the individual may be termed psychotic.

Culturally induced conflicts not only can, if severe enough, produce psychosis but also can determine the form of the psychosis. In a culture that encourages aggressiveness and suspicion, the madman is that individual who is passive and trusting. In a culture that encourages passivity and trust, the madman is that individual who is aggressive and suspicious. Just as each society establishes its own norms, each individual is unique in his or her perceptions. Many anthropologists see the only meaningful criterion for personality evaluation as the correlation between personality and social conformity.

While it is true that culture defines what is and is not normal behavior, the situation is complicated by findings suggesting that major categories of mental disorders may be universal types of human affliction. Take, for example, the case of schizophrenia, probably the most common of all psychoses, found in all cultures, although in many forms. Individuals afflicted by schizophrenia experience distortions of reality that impair their ability

[16]Lewis-Williams, D., & Dowson, T. A. (1993). On vision and power in the Neolithic: Evidence from the decorated monuments. *Current Anthropology, 34,* 55.

Anthropology Applied
ANTHROPOLOGISTS AND MENTAL HEALTH

One consequence of "development" in the newly emerged states of Africa, Asia, and Central and South America is a rising incidence of mental disturbances among their people. Similarly, mental health problems abound among ethnic minorities living within industrialized countries. Unfortunately, orthodox approaches to mental health have not been successful at dealing with these problems, for a number of reasons. For one, different ethnic groups have different attitudes towards mental disorders than do medical practitioners (who are, after all, products of Western culture). For another, the diverse conditions under which different ethnic groups live produce culturally patterned health conditions, including culture-bound syndromes not recognized by the orthodox medical profession. Among Puerto Ricans, for example, a widely held belief is that spirits are active in the world and that they influence human behavior. Thus, for someone with a psychiatric problem, it makes sense to go to a native spiritist for help, rather than to a psychiatrist. In a Puerto Rican community, going to a spiritist is "normal." Not only does the client not understand the symbols of psychiatry, but also to go to a psychiatrist implies that he or she is "crazy" and requires restraint or removal from the community.

Although practitioners of Western medicine have traditionally regarded spiritists and other folk healers as "ignorant," if not "charlatans," efforts were begun in the 1950s to experiment with community-based treatment in which psychiatrists cooperated with traditional healers. Since then, this approach has gained widespread acceptance in many parts of the world, as when (in 1977) the World Health Organization advocated cooperation between health professionals and native specialists (including herbalists and midwives). As a consequence, many anthropologists have found work as cultural brokers, studying the cultural system of the client population and explaining it to health professionals, while at the same time explaining the world of the psychiatrists to folk healers and the client population.

To cite one example, as a part of the Miami Community Mental Health Program, a field team led by an anthropologist was set up to work with the Puerto Rican community of Dade County.* Like other ethnic communities in the area, it was characterized by low incomes, high rents, and a plethora of health (including mental health) problems, yet health facilities and social service agencies were underutilized. Working in the community, the team successfully built up support networks among the Puerto Ricans, involving extended families, churches, clubs, and spiritists. At the same time, they gathered information about the community, which was provided to appropriate social service agencies. At the Dade County Hospital, team members acted as brokers between the psychiatric personnel and their Puerto Rican clients, and a training program was implemented for the mental health staff.

*See Willigan, J. V. (1986). *Applied anthropology* (pp. 128–129; 133–139). South Hadley, MA: Bergin and Garvey.

---

to function adequately, and so they withdraw from the social world into their own psychological shell, from which they do not emerge. Although environmental factors play a role, there is evidence that schizophrenia is caused by a biochemical disorder for which there is an inherited tendency. One of its more severe forms is paranoid schizophrenia. Those suffering from it fear and mistrust almost everyone; they hear voices that whisper dreadful things to them, and they are convinced that someone is "out to get them." Acting on this conviction, they engage in bizarre types of behavior, which leads to their removal from society, usually to a mental institution.

A precise image of paranoid schizophrenia is one of the so-called **ethnic psychoses** known as *Windigo*. Such psychoses involve symptoms of mental disorder specific to particular ethnic groups (Table 16.1). Windigo psychosis is limited to northern Algonkian Indian groups such as the Chippewa, Cree, and Ojibwa. In their traditional

Ethnic psychoses: Mental disorders specific to particular ethnic groups.

TABLE 16.1   Ethnic Psychoses and Other Culture-Bound Psychological Disorders

NAME OF DISORDER	CULTURE	DESCRIPTION
Amok	Malaya (also observed in Java, Philippines, Africa, and Tierra del Fuego)	A disorder characterized by sudden, wild outbursts of homicidal aggression in which the afflicted person may kill or injure others. The rage disorder is usually found in males who are rather withdrawn, quiet, and inoffensive prior to the onset of the disorder. Stress, sleep deprivation, extreme heat, and alcohol are among the conditions thought to precipitate the disorder. Several stages have been observed: Typically in the first stage the person becomes more withdrawn; then a period of brooding follows in which a loss of reality contact is evident. Ideas of persecution and anger predominate. Finally, a phase of automatism, or *amok*, occurs, in which the person jumps up, yells, grabs a knife, and stabs people or objects within reach. Exhaustion and depression usually follow, with amnesia for the rage.
Anorexia nervosa	Western countries	A disorder occurring most frequently among young women in which a preoccupation with thinness produces a refusal to eat. This condition can result in death.
Latah	Malay	A fear reaction often occurring in middle-aged women of low intelligence who are subservient and self-effacing. The disorder is precipitated by the word *snake* or by tickling. It is characterized by *echolalia* (repetition of the words and sentences of others). The disturbed individual may also react with negativism and the compulsive use of obscene language.
Koro	Southeast Asia (particularly Malay Archipelago)	A fear reaction or anxiety state in which the person fears that his penis will withdraw into his abdomen and he will die. This reaction may appear after sexual overindulgence or excessive masturbation. The anxiety is typically very intense and of sudden onset. The condition is "treated" by having the penis held firmly by the patient or by family members or friends. Often the penis is clamped to a wooden box.
Windigo	Algonkian Indians of Canada and northern United States	A fear reaction in which a hunter becomes anxious and agitated, convinced that he is bewitched. Fears center around his being turned into a cannibal by the power of a monster with an insatiable craving for human flesh.
Kitsunetsuki	Japan	A disorder in which victims believe that they are possessed by foxes and are said to change their facial expressions to resemble foxes. Entire families are often possessed and banned by the community. This reaction occurs in rural areas of Japan where people are relatively uneducated.
Pibloktoq and other arctic hysterias	Circumpolar peoples from Lapland eastward across Siberia, northern Alaska, and Canada to Greenland	A disorder brought on by fright, which is followed by a short period of bizarre behavior; victim may tear clothes off, jump in water or fire, roll in snow, try to walk on the ceiling, throw things, thrash about, and "speak in tongues." Outburst followed by return to normal behavior.

Based on Carson, R. C., Butcher, J. N., & Coleman, J. C. (1990). (8th ed.) (p. 85). Glenview, IL: Scott, Foresman.

belief systems, these northern Indians recognized the existence of cannibalistic monsters called Windigos. Individuals afflicted by the psychosis developed the delusion that falling under control of these monsters, they themselves were being transformed into Windigos, with a craving for human flesh. At the same time, they saw people around them turning into various edible animals—fat, juicy beavers, for instance. Although there are no known instances where sufferers of Windigo psychosis actually ate another human being, they nonetheless developed an acute fear of doing so. Furthermore, other members of their group genuinely feared that they might.

At first, Windigo psychosis seems quite different from Western clinical cases of paranoid schizophrenia, but a closer look suggests otherwise; the disorder was merely being expressed in ways compatible with traditional northern Algonkian culture. Ideas of persecution, instead of being directed toward other humans, are directed toward supernatural beings (the Windigo monsters); can-

nibalistic panic replaces homosexual panic, and the like. The northern Algonkian Indian, like the Westerner, expresses his or her problem in terms compatible with the appropriate view of the self and its behavioral environment. The northern Algonkian, though, was removed from society, not by being committed to a mental institution, but by being killed.

Windigo behavior has seemed exotic and dramatic to the Westerner. Yet, the imagery and symbolism that a psychotic person has to draw upon is that which his or her culture has to offer, and in northern Algonkian culture, these involve myths in which cannibal giants figure prominently. By contrast, the delusions of Irish schizophrenics draw upon the images and symbols of Irish Catholicism, and feature Virgin and Savior motifs. Anglo Americans, on the other hand, tend toward secular or electromagnetic persecution delusions. The underlying structure of the mental disorder is the same in all cases, but its expression is culturally specific.

CHAPTER SUMMARY

Enculturation, the process by which culture is passed from one generation to the next, begins soon after birth. Its first agents are the members of an individual's household, but later, in some societies, this role is assumed by professionals. For enculturation to proceed, individuals must possess self-awareness, or the ability to perceive themselves as objects in time and space and to judge their own actions. A major facet of self-awareness is a positive view of the self, which motivates persons to act to their advantage rather than disadvantage.

Several requirements involving one's behavioral environment need to be met in order for emerging self-awareness to function. The individual first needs to learn about a world of objects other than self; this environment is perceived in terms compatible with the values of the culture into which one is born. Also required is a sense of both spatial and temporal orientation. Finally, the growing individual needs a normative orientation, or an understanding of the values, ideals, and standards that constitute the behavioral environment.

Personality is a product of enculturation and refers to the distinctive ways a person thinks, feels, and behaves. With the psychoanalysts, most anthropologists believe that adult personality is shaped by early childhood experiences. A prime goal of anthropologists has been to produce objective studies that test this theory. Cross-cultural studies of gender-related personality characteristics, for example, show that there are no absolute personality differences between men and women. Instead, a society's economy helps structure the way children are brought up, which in turn influences their adult personalities.

Anthropologists John and Beatrice Whiting and Irvin Child, on the basis of cross-cultural studies, have established the interrelation of personality, child-rearing practices, and other aspects of culture. Dependence training is usually associated with traditional farming societies; it tries to ensure that members of society willingly and routinely work for the benefit of the group, performing the jobs assigned to them. At the opposite extreme, independence training, typical of societies characterized by independent nuclear families, puts a premium on self-reliance and independent behavior. Although a society may emphasize one sort of behavior over the other, it may not emphasize it to the same degree in both sexes. Whiting and Child believe that child-rearing practices have their roots in a society's customs surrounding the meeting of the basic physical needs of its members; these practices, in turn, develop particular kinds of adult personalities.

Anthropologists early on began to work on the problem of whether it is possible to delineate a group personality without falling into stereotyping. Each culture chooses, from the vast array of possibilities, those traits that it sees as normative or ideal. Individuals who conform to these traits are rewarded; the rest are not. The modal personality of a group is the personality typical of a culturally bounded population, as indicated by the central tendency of a defined frequency distribution. As a statistical concept, it opens up for investigation how societies organize the diverse personalities of their members, some of which conform more than others to the modal "type."

National character studies have focused on the modal characteristics of modern countries. They have then attempted to determine the child-rearing practices and education that shape such a personality. Investigators during World War II interviewed foreign-born nationals and analyzed other sources in an effort to depict national character. Many anthropologists believe that national character theories are based on unscientific and overgeneralized data. Others have chosen to focus on the core values promoted in particular societies, while recognizing that success in instilling these values in individuals may vary considerably.

What defines normal behavior in any culture is determined by the culture itself, and what may be acceptable, or even admirable, in one may not be in another. Abnormality involves developing a delusional system not accepted by culture. Culturally induced conflicts not only can produce psychological disturbance but can determine the form of the disturbance as well. Similarly, mental disorders that have a biological cause, like schizophrenia, will be expressed in terms of symptoms specific to the culture of the individual who is afflicted.

SUGGESTED READINGS

Barnouw, V. (1985). *Culture and personality* (4th ed.). Homewood, IL: Dorsey Press.

A revision of a well-respected text designed to introduce students to psychological anthropology.

Hunt, R. C. (Ed.). (1967). *Personalities and cultures: Readings in psychological anthropology*. Garden City, NY: Natural History Press.

The 18 articles included in this book focus on various aspects of culture and personality. Attention is given to psychological and sociocultural variables and the relationships between them.

Norbeck, E., Williams, D. P., & McCord, W. (Eds.) (1968). *The study of personality: An interdisciplinary appraisal*. New York: Holt, Rinehart and Winston.

The volume contains addresses given at Rice University in 1966. Its objective is to review and appraise knowledge and theories concerning personality in several scholarly fields (psychology, anthropology, sociology, philosophy of science, and so forth). It also discusses factors that influence the formation of personality, and the personalities of social and psychiatric deviates.

Wallace, A. F. C. (1970). *Culture and personality* (2nd ed.). New York: Random House.

The logical and methodological foundations of culture and personality as a science form the basis of this book. The study is guided by the assumptions that anthropology should develop a scientific theory about culture and that a theory pretending to explain or predict cultural phenomena must reckon with noncultural phenomena (such as personality) as well.

Whiting, J. W. M., & Child, I. (1953). *Child training and personality: A cross-cultural study*. New Haven, CT: Yale University Press.

How culture is integrated through the medium of personality processes is the main concern of this study. It covers both the influence of culture on personality and personality on culture. It is oriented toward testing general hypotheses about human behavior in any and all societies, rather than toward a detailed analysis of a particular society.

CHAPTER 17

PATTERNS OF SUBSISTENCE

A WOMAN PICKS FRESH VEGETABLES IN KENYA. THE BASIC

BUSINESS OF CULTURE IS SECURING THE SURVIVAL OF THOSE

WHO LIVE BY ITS RULES, AND SO THE STUDY OF

SUBSISTENCE IS AN IMPORTANT ASPECT OF

ANTHROPOLOGICAL STUDY.

CHAPTER PREVIEW

What Is Adaptation?

Adaptation refers to the process of interaction between changes an organism makes in its environment and changes the environment makes in the organism. This kind of two-way adjustment is necessary for the survival of all life-forms, including human beings.

How Do Humans Adapt?

Humans adapt through the medium of culture, as they develop ways of doing things that are compatible with the resources they have available to them and within the limitations of the environment in which they live. In a particular region, people living in similar environments tend to borrow from one another customs that seem to work well in those environments. Once achieved, adaptations may be remarkably stable for long periods of time, even thousands of years.

What Sorts of Adaptations Have Humans Achieved Through the Ages?

Food foraging is the oldest and most universal type of human adaptation. To it we owe such important elements of social organization as the sexual division of labor, food sharing, and a home base as the center of daily activity and where food sharing is accomplished. Quite different adaptations, involving farming and animal husbandry, began to develop in some parts of the world between 9,000 and 11,000 years ago. Horticulture—the cultivation of domestic plants by means of simple hand tools— made possible more permanent settlements and a reorganization of the division of labor. Under pastoralism—reliance on raising herds of domestic animals—nomadism continued, but new modes of interaction with other peoples were developed. Urbanism began to develop as early as 5,000 years ago in some places, as intensive agriculture produced sufficient food to support full-time specialists of various sorts. With this went a further transformation of the social fabric.

Several times today you will interrupt your activities to eat or drink. You may take this for granted, but if you went totally without food for as long as a day, you would begin to feel the symptoms of hunger: weakness, fatigue, headache. After a month of starvation, your body would probably never repair the damage. A mere week to ten days without water would be enough to kill you.

All living beings, and people are no exception, must satisfy certain basic needs in order to stay alive. Among these needs are food, water, and shelter. Humans may not live by bread alone, but nobody can live long without any bread at all; and no creature could long survive if its relations with its environment were random and chaotic. Living beings must have regular access to a supply of food and water and a reliable means of obtaining and using it. A lion might die if all its prey disappeared, if its teeth and claws grew soft, or if its digestive system failed. Although people face these same sorts of problems, they have an overwhelming advantage over other creatures: People have culture. If our meat supply dwindles, we can turn to some vegetable, like the soybean, and process it to taste like meat. When our tools fail, we replace them or invent better ones. Even when our stomachs are incapable of digesting food, we can predigest food by boiling or pureeing. We are, however, subject to the same needs and pressures as all living creatures, and it is important to understand human behavior from this point of view. The crucial concept that underlies such a perspective is **adaptation,** that is, how humans manage to deal with the contingencies of daily life. Dealing with these contingencies is the basic business of all cultures.

---◦◦◦---◦◦◦---

Adaptation: A process by which organisms achieve a beneficial adjustment to an available environment, and the results of that process; the characteristics of organisms that fit them to the particular set of conditions of the environment in which they are generally found.

Horticulture: Cultivation of crops using hand tools such as digging sticks or hoes.

---◦◦◦---◦◦◦---

ADAPTATION

The process of adaptation establishes a moving balance between the needs of a population and the potential of its environment. One illustration of this process can be seen in the Tsembaga, New Guinea, highlanders who support themselves chiefly through **horticulture**—the cultivation of crops carried out with simple hand tools.[1] Although they also raise pigs, they eat them only under conditions of illness, injury, warfare, or celebration. At such times the pigs are sacrificed to ancestor spirits, and their flesh is ritually consumed by those people involved in the crisis. (This guarantees a supply of high-quality protein when it is most needed.)

In precolonial times the Tsembaga and their neighbors were bound together in a unique cycle of pig sacrifices that served to mark the end of hostilities between groups. Frequent hostilities were set off by a number of ecological pressures, in which

pigs were a significant factor. Since very few pigs were normally slaughtered and their food requirements were great, they could very quickly literally eat a local group out of house and home. The need to expand food production in order to support the prestigious but hungry pigs put a strain on the land best suited for farming. Therefore, when one group had driven another off its land, hostilities ended, and the new residents celebrated their victory with a pig festival. Many pigs were slaughtered, and the pork was widely shared among allied groups. Even without hostilities, festivals were held whenever the pig population became unmanageable, every 5 to 10 years, depending on the groups' success at farming. Thus the cycle of fighting and feasting kept the balance among humans, land, and animals.

[1]Rappaport, R. A. (1969). Ritual regulation of environmental relations among a New Guinea people. In A. P. Vayda (Ed.), *Environment and cultural behavior* (pp. 181–201). Garden City, NY: Natural History Press.

In New Guinea, pig populations are controlled by consumption at pig feasts, which also ensure access to high-quality protein at periodic intervals.

etative cover. This was conducive to the breeding of mosquitos that carry the parasite causing falciparum malaria. When transmitted to humans, the parasites live in the red blood cells and cause a disease that is always debilitating and very often fatal. Individuals who received the gene for the sickle-cell trait from only one parent, however, while receiving one "normal" gene from the other, turned out to have a specific natural defense against the parasite. The gene's presence caused only some of the cells to take on a sickle shape; when those cells circulated through the spleen, which routinely screens out all damaged or worn red blood cells, the infected cells and the parasites along with them were destroyed. Since these individuals did not succumb to malaria, they were favored by selection, and the sickling trait became more and more frequent in the population. Thus, while people changed their environment, their environment also changed them.

The case of sickle-cell anemia is a neat illustration of the relativity of any adaptation. In malarial areas, the gene responsible for this condition is adaptive for human populations, even though some individuals suffer as a result of its presence. In nonmalarial regions, however, it is highly maladaptive, for it confers no advantage at all on human populations living under such conditions, at the same time that some individuals die as a result of its presence.

The term *adaptation* also refers to the process of interaction between changes an organism makes in its environment and changes the environment makes in the organism. The spread of the gene for sickle-cell anemia is a case in point. Long ago, in the Old World tropics somewhere west of India, a genetic mutation appeared in human populations, causing the manufacture of red blood cells that take on a sickle shape under conditions of low oxygen pressure. Since persons who receive a gene for this trait from each parent usually develop severe anemia and die in childhood, selective pressure was exerted against the spread of this gene in the local gene pool.

Then slash-and-burn horticulture was introduced into this tropical region, creating a change in the natural environment by removal—through cutting (slashing) and burning—of the natural veg-

The Unit of Adaptation

The unit of adaptation includes both organisms and environment. Organisms exist as members of populations; populations, in turn, must have the flexibility to cope with variability and change within the environment. In biological terms, this means that different organisms within the population have somewhat differing genetic endowments. In cultural terms, it means that there is variation among individual skills, knowledge, and personalities. Organisms and environments form interacting systems. People might as easily be farmers as fisherfolk; but we do not expect to find farmers north of the Arctic Circle or people who fish for a living in the Sahara Desert.

We might consider the example of a group of lakeside fisherfolk. The people live off fish, which,

in turn, live off smaller organisms. Those animals, in turn, consume green plants; plants liberate minerals from water and mud, and, with energy from sunlight, transform them into proteins and carbohydrates. Dead plant and animal matter is decomposed by bacteria, and chemicals are returned to the soil and water. Some energy escapes from this system in the form of heat. Evaporation and rainfall constantly recirculate the water. People add chemicals to the system in the form of their wastes, and, if they are judicious, they may help to regulate the balance of animals and plants.

Some anthropologists have borrowed the ecologists' concept of **ecosystem.** An ecosystem is composed of both the physical environment and the organisms living within it. The system is bound by the activities of the organisms, as well as by such physical processes as erosion and evaporation.

Human ecologists are generally concerned with detailed microstudies of particular human ecosystems; they emphasize that all aspects of human culture must be considered, not just the most obvious technological ones. The Tsembaga's attitude toward pigs and the cycle of sacrifices have important economic functions; we see them in this way, but the Tsembaga do not. They are motivated by their belief in the power and needs of their ancestral spirits. Although the pigs are consumed *by* the living, they are sacrificed *for* ancestors. Human ecosystems must often be interpreted in cultural terms.

Evolutionary Adaptation

Adaptation must also be understood from a historical point of view. In order for organisms to fit into an ecosystem, they must have the potential to adjust to or become a part of it. The Comanche, whose history began in the harsh, arid country of southern Idaho, provide a good example.[2] In their original home they subsisted on wild plants, small animals, and occasionally larger game. Their material equipment was simple and limited to what could be transported by their women. The size of their groups was restricted, and what little social power could develop was in the hands of the shaman, who was a combination of medicine man and spiritual guide.

[2]Wallace, E., & Hoebel, E. A. (1952). *The Comanches.* Norman: University of Oklahoma Press.

At some point in their nomadic history, the Comanche moved onto the Great Plains, where buffalo were abundant and the Indians' potential as hunters could be fully developed. As larger groups could be supported by the new food supply, the need arose for a more complex political organization. Hunting ability thus became a means to acquire political power.

Eventually the Comanche acquired horses and guns from "Whites," which greatly enhanced their hunting prowess, and the great hunting chiefs became more powerful. The Comanche became raiders in order to get horses, which they did not breed for themselves, and their hunting chiefs evolved into war chiefs. The once "poor" and peaceful hunter-gatherers of the Great Basin became wealthy and warlike, dominating the Southwest from the borders of New Spain (Mexico) in the south to those of New France (Louisiana) and the fledgling United States in the east and north. In moving from one environment to another, and in evolving from one way of life to a second, the Comanche were able to capitalize on existing cultural capabilities to flourish in their new situation.

Sometimes societies that have developed independently find similar solutions to similar problems. For example, another group that moved onto the Great Plains and took up a form of Plains Indian culture, similar in many ways to that of the Comanche, were the Cheyenne. Yet their cultural background was quite different; formerly, they were settled farmers with social, political, and religious institutions quite unlike those of the Comanche back in their ancestral homeland. This kind of development of similar cultural adaptations to similar environmental conditions by peoples whose ancestral cultures were quite different is called **convergent evolution.** What is especially interesting about this case is that it involves a switch from a farming to a food-foraging

Ecosystem: A system, or a functioning whole, composed of both the physical environment and the organisms living within it.

Convergent evolution: In cultural evolution, the development of similar adaptations to similar environmental conditions by peoples whose ancestral cultures were quite different.

Shown here are Indians of the North American plains hunting bison they have driven into the Missouri River. Plains Indians such as the Cheyenne, Comanche, Crow, and Sioux developed similar cultures, as they had to adapt to similar environmental conditions (for a map of Native American culture areas, see Figure 17.1).

way of life. Contrary to Western notions of "progress," change in subsistence practices does not inevitably go from dependence on wild food to farming; it may go the other way as well.

Somewhat similar to the phenomenon of convergent evolution is **parallel evolution,** the difference being that similar adaptations are achieved by peoples whose ancestral cultures were already somewhat similar. For example, the development of farming in Southwest Asia and Mesoamerica took place independently, as people in both places, whose ways of life were already alike, went on to become dependent on a narrow range of plant foods which themselves depended upon human intervention for their protection and reproductive success.

It is important to recognize that stability as well as change is involved in evolutionary adaptation, and that once a satisfactory adaptation is achieved, too much in the way of change may cause

Parallel evolution: In cultural evolution, the development of similar adaptations to similar environmental conditions by peoples whose ancestral cultures were similar.

it to break down. Thus, episodes of major change may be followed by long periods of relative stability. For example, by 3500 B.C., a way of life had evolved in northwestern New England and southern Quebec that was well attuned to the environmental conditions of the times.[3] Since those conditions remained more or less the same over the next 5,000 years or so, it is understandable that people's lifeways remained so as well. This is not to say that change was entirely absent, for it was not. ("Stable" does not mean "static.") From time to time people refined and enhanced their ways of

To say that a society is stable is not to say that it is changeless. These Western Abenakis are descendants of people who maintained a stable way of life for 5,000 years, even though they frequently incorporated new elements into their culture. Even today, 400 years after first contact with Europeans, many traditional values and practices endure.

[3]Haviland, W. A. & Power, M. (1994). *The original Vermonters* (revised and expanded ed.). Hanover, NH: University Press of New England.

life, for example, when hunting methods were improved as the bow and arrow replaced spears used with spear throwers; when cooking was improved by the substitution of pottery vessels for containers made from animal hide, wood, or bark; when transport was improved by the replacement of heavy and cumbersome dugouts by sturdy, yet lightweight birchbark canoes; or when people began to supplement the products of hunting, gathering, and fishing with limited cultivation of corn, beans, and squash. In spite of these changes, however, the native peoples of the region still basically retained the unique structure of their culture, and tended toward a balance with their resource base, well into the seventeenth century, when the culture began to adjust to pressures associated with European invasions of North America. Such long-term stability by no means implies "stagnation," "backwardness," or "failure to progress"; rather, it is indicative of success. Had this culture not effectively satisfied people's physical and psychological needs, it never would have endured as it did for thousands of years.

Culture Areas

The aboriginal **culture area** of the Great Plains (Fig. 17.1) was a geographic region in which there existed a number of societies with similar ways of life. Thirty-one politically independent peoples (including the aforementioned Cheyenne and Comanche) faced a common environment, in which the buffalo was the most obvious and practical source of food as well as material for clothing and shelter. Living close by each other, they were able to share new inventions and discoveries. They reached a common and shared adaptation to a particular ecological zone.

The Indians of the Great Plains were, at the time of contact with Europeans, invariably buffalo

---

Culture area: A geographic region in which a number of different societies follow similar patterns of life.

Culture type: The view of a culture in terms of the relation of its particular technology to the environment exploited by that technology.

---

hunters, dependent upon this animal for food, clothing, shelter, and bone tools. Each nation was organized into a number of warrior societies, and prestige came from hunting and fighting skills. Their camps were typically arranged in a distinctive circular pattern. Many religious rituals, such as the Sun Dance, were practiced throughout the plains region.

Sometimes geographic regions are not uniform in climate and topography, and so new discoveries do not always spread from one group to another. Moreover, within a culture area, there are variations between local environments, and these favor variations in adaptation. The Great Basin of the western United States—an area embracing the states of Nevada and Utah, with adjacent portions of California, Oregon, Wyoming, and Idaho—is a good example.[4] The Great Basin Shoshone Indians were divided into a northern and a western group, both primarily nomadic hunters and gatherers. In the north, a relative abundance of game animals provided for the maintenance of larger populations, requiring a great deal of cooperation among local groups. The western Shoshone, on the other hand, were almost entirely dependent upon the gathering of wild plants for their subsistence, and as these varied considerably in their seasonal and local availability, the western Shoshone were forced to cover vast distances in search of food. Under such conditions, it was most efficient to travel in groups of but a few families, only occasionally coming together with other groups, and not always with the same ones.

The Shoshone were not the only inhabitants of the Great Basin. To the south lived the closely related Paiutes. They, too, were hunter-gatherers living under the same environmental conditions as the Shoshone, but the Paiute managed their food resources more actively by diverting small streams to irrigate wild crops. They did not plant and cultivate these, but they were able to secure higher yields than their northern neighbors. Hence, their populations were larger than those of the Shoshone, and they led a less nomadic existence.

In order to deal with variations within a given region, Julian Steward proposed the concept of **culture type,** a culture considered in terms of a

[4]Steward, J. H. (1972). *Theory of culture change: The methodology of multilinear evolution.* Urbana: University of Illinois Press.

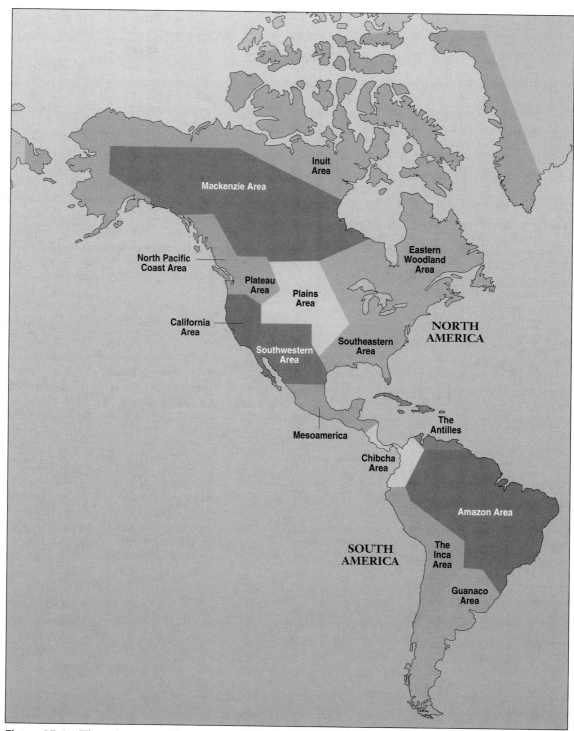

Figure 17.1   The culture-area concept was developed by North American anthropologists in the early part of the twentieth century. This map shows culture areas that have been defined for the Americas. Within each colored area there is an overall similarity of native cultures, which is not as apparent when the native cultures of one area are compared with those of another.

JULIAN H. STEWARD

(1902–1972)

This North American anthropologist developed an approach that he called **cultural ecology**—that is, the interaction between specific cultures with their environments. Initially, Steward was struck by a number of similarities in the development of urban civilizations in both Peru and Mesoamerica, noting that certain developments were paralleled in the urban civilizations of the Old World. He identified the constants and abstracted from this his laws of cultural development. Steward proposed three fundamental procedures for cultural ecology:

1. The interrelationship of a culture's technology and its environment must be analyzed. How effectively does the culture take advantage of available resources to provide food and housing for its members?

2. The pattern of behavior associated with a culture's technology must be analyzed. How do members of the culture perform the work that is necessary for their survival?

3. The relation between those behavior patterns and the rest of the cultural system must be determined. How does the work they do to survive affect the people's attitudes and outlooks? How is their survival behavior linked to their social activities and their personal relationships?

---

particular technology and its relationship with those environmental features with which that technology is equipped to deal. The example of the Great Plains shows how technology helps decide just which environmental features will be useful. Those same prairies that once supported buffalo hunters now support grain farmers. The Indians were prevented from farming the plains not for environmental reasons, nor for lack of knowledge about farming, since some of them, like the Cheyenne, had been farmers before they moved onto the plains. They did not farm because the buffalo herds provided abundant food without farming, and because farming would have been difficult without the steel-tipped plow that was needed to break up the compacted prairie sod. The farming potential of the Great Plains was simply not a relevant feature of the environment, given the available resources and technology before the coming of the Europeans.

Culture Core

Environment and technology are not the only factors that determine a society's way of subsistence; social and political organization also affect the application of technology to the problem of staying alive. In order to understand the rise of irrigation agriculture in the great centers of ancient civilization, such as China, Mesopotamia, and Mesoamerica, it is important to note not only the technological and environmental factors that made possible the building of large-scale irrigation works but also the social and political organization needed to mobilize the many workers necessary to build and maintain the systems. One must examine the monarchies and priesthoods that organized the work and decided where the water would be used and how the agricultural products of this joint venture would be distributed.

Those features of a culture that play a part in the society's way of making its living are called its **culture core**. This includes the society's productive techniques and its knowledge of the resources available to it. It encompasses the patterns of labor involved in applying those techniques to the

---

Cultural ecology: The study of the interaction of specific human cultures with their environment.

Culture core: The features of a culture that play a part in matters relating to the society's way of making a living.

local environment. For example, do people work every day for a fixed number of hours, or is most work concentrated during certain times of the year? The culture core also includes other aspects of culture that bear on the production and distribution of food. An example of the way ideology can indirectly affect subsistence can be seen in a number of cultures where religion may lead to failure to utilize foods that are both locally available and nutritionally valuable. One reported example of this is the taboo that some Inuit of the Canadian Arctic follow, which forbids the hunting of seals in the summer. It has been said that if land game fails, a whole group will starve, even though seals are available to them.[5]

A number of anthropologists, known as **ethnoscientists,** are attempting to understand the principles behind folk ideologies and the way those principles usually help keep a people alive. The Tsembaga, for example, avoid certain low-lying, marshy areas, because they believe those areas are inhabited by red spirits who punish trespassers. Western science, by contrast, interprets those areas as the home of mosquitos and the "punishment" as malaria. Whatever Westerners may think of the Tsembaga's belief in red spirits, it is a perfectly useful and reasonable one; it keeps them away from marshy areas just as surely as does a belief in malaria. If we want to understand why people in other cultures behave the way they do, we must understand their system of thought from their point of view as well as our own. Not all such beliefs are as easy to translate into our terms as are those of the Tsembaga red spirits.

THE FOOD-FORAGING WAY OF LIFE

At the present time, perhaps a quarter of a million people—less than 0.00005 percent of a world population of more than five billion—support themselves chiefly through hunting, fishing, and the gathering of wild plant foods. Yet, before the domestication of plants and animals, which began a mere 10,000 years ago, all people supported themselves through some combination of wild plant collection, hunting, and fishing. Of all the people who have *ever* lived, 90 percent have been food foragers, and it was as food foragers that we became truly human, acquiring the basic habits of dealing with one another and with the world around us that still guide the behavior of individuals, communities, and nations. Thus, if we would know who we are and how we came to be, if we would understand the relationship between environment and culture, and if we would comprehend the institutions of the food-producing societies that have arisen since the development of farming and animal husbandry, we should turn first to the oldest and most universal of fully human lifestyles, the food-foraging adaptation. The beginnings of this we examined in Chapter 3.

When food foragers had the world to themselves 10,000 years ago, they had their pick of the best environments. These have long since been appropriated by farming and, more recently, by industrial societies. Today, most food foragers are to be found only in the world's marginal areas—frozen Arctic tundra, deserts, and inaccessible forests. These habitats, although they may not support large or dense agricultural societies, provide a good living for food-foraging peoples.

Until recently it was assumed that a food-foraging life in these areas was difficult and that one had to work hard just to stay alive. Behind this view lies the Western notion of progress, which, although widely accepted as being a fact of nature, is actually nothing more than a culturally conditioned bias. This predisposes us to see what is new as generally preferable to what is old, and to read human history as a more or less steady climb up an evolutionary ladder of progress. Thus, if food foraging as a way of life is much older than industrial civilization (which it is) the latter must be intrinsically better than the former. Hence, food-foraging societies are referred to as "primitive," "backward," or "undeveloped," by which labels economists, politicians, and other members of industrial or would-be industrial societies express their disapproval. In reality, food-foraging societies

---

Ethnoscientists: Anthropologists who seek to understand the principles behind folk ideologies and the way these ideologies help a people survive.

---

[5]Malefijt, A. D. (1969). *Religion and culture: An introduction to anthropology of religion* (pp. 326–327). London: Macmillan.

Human groups (including food foragers) do not exist in isolation except occasionally, and even then not for long. The bicycle this Bushman of southern Africa is riding is indicative of his links with the wider world. For 2,000 years, Bushmen have been interacting regularly with farmers and pastoralists, and much of the ivory used for the pianos so widely sought in nineteenth-century North America came from the Bushmen.

are highly developed, but in a way quite different from industrial societies.

Detailed studies have revealed that life in food-foraging societies is far from being "solitary, poor, nasty, brutish, and short," as the philosopher Thomas Hobbes asserted more than 300 years ago. Rather, their diets are well balanced and ample, and they are less likely to experience severe famine than are farmers. While their material comforts are limited, so are their desires. On the other hand, they have plenty of leisure time in which to concentrate on family ties, social life, and spiritual development. The Ju/'hoansi, a Bushman people of southern Africa's Kalahari Desert (see Chapter 16)—scarcely what one would call a "lush" environment—obtain a diet that surpasses internationally recommended levels of nutrients in an average workweek of about 20 hours. If one adds to this the time spent making and repairing equipment, the total rises to just over 23 hours, while the equivalent of our "housework" adds another 19 hours. The grand total, just over 42 hours (44.5 for men, 40.1 for women), is still less than the time spent on the job (currently 41 hours for manufacturing jobs, just under 44 hours for "white collar" jobs), and on maintenance

tasks and housework in North America today.[6] Their lives are rich in human warmth and aesthetic experience, displaying a balance of work and love, ritual, and play that many of us might envy. Small wonder that some anthropologists have gone so far as to label this "the original affluent society." The Ju/'hoansi are not exceptional among food foragers today; one can only wonder about the level of affluence achieved by their ancient counterparts who lived in lusher environments with more secure and plentiful supplies of food.

All modern food foragers have had some degree of interaction with neighbors whose ways of life often differ radically from their own. Bushmen people like the Ju/'hoansi, for example, have interacted for at least 2,000 years with Bantu farmers who kept cattle and sheep. Likewise, the Mbuti of Zaire's Ituri rain forest (see the Original Study in Chapter 16) live in a complex patron-client relationship with their neighbors, Bantu- and Sudanic-speaking peoples who are farmers. They exchange

[6]Cashdan, E. (1989). Hunters and gatherers: Economic behavior in bands. In S. Plattner, (Ed.) *Economic anthropology* (pp. 23–24). Stanford, CA: Stanford University Press.

Food foraging has by no means disappeared even in industrial societies like that of the United States. Some do it occasionally for pleasure, as the author and his brother-in-law are shown doing in the top photo—gathering wild mussels. Some, like commercial fishers, forage full-time, as do many homeless people in order to survive.

meat and other products of the forest for farm produce and manufactured goods. During part of the year, they live in their patron's village and are incorporated into his kin group, even to the point of allowing him to initiate their sons.

Although some modern food foragers, like the Mbuti, have continued to maintain traditional ways while adapting to neighbors and traders, various others have reverted to this way of life after giving up other modes of subsistence. Some, like the Cheyenne of the Great Plains, were once farmers, while others, like some of the Bushmen of southern Africa, have at times been farmers, at others pastoral nomads. Nor are such reversions things of the past. In the 1980s, when a world economic recession led to the abandonment of many sheep stations in the Australian "outback," a number of aboriginal peoples returned to a food-foraging way of life, thereby emancipating themselves from a dependency on the government into which they had been forced.

An important point that emerges from the preceding discussion is this: People in the world today who subsist by hunting, fishing, and gathering wild plants are not following an ancient way of life because they do not know any better; they are doing it through deliberate choice. In many cases, they find such satisfaction in living the way they do that they often go to great lengths to avoid adopting other ways of life. Beyond this, foraging constitutes a rational response to particular ecological, economic, and sociopolitical realities. Moreover, for at least 2,000 years, there has been a need for specialist "commercial" hunter-gatherers to supply the wild forest commodities that have helped feed east-west trade since ancient times.[7]

Characteristics of the Food-Foraging Life

Food foragers are by definition people who do not farm or practice animal husbandry. Hence, they must accommodate their places of residence to naturally available food sources, requiring that they move about a great deal. Such movement is not aimless wandering, but is done within a fixed territory or home range. Some, like the Ju/'hoansi who depend on the reliable and highly drought-resistant Mongongo nut, may keep to fairly fixed annual routes and cover only a restricted territory. Others, such as the Great Basin Shoshone, must cover a wider territory; their course is determined

[7]Stiles, D. (1992). The hunter-gatherer "Revisionist" debate. *Anthropology Today, 8* (2), p. 15.

by the local availability of the erratically productive pine nut. A crucial factor in this mobility is the availability of water. The distance between the food supply and water must not be so great that more energy is required to fetch water than can be obtained from the food.

Another characteristic of the food-foraging adaptation is the small size of local groups, which usually include fewer than 100 people. Although no completely satisfactory explanation of group size has yet been offered, it seems certain that both ecological and social factors are involved. Among those suggested are the **carrying capacity** of the land, the number of people who can be supported by the available resources at a given level of food-getting techniques, and the **density of social relations,** roughly the number and intensity of interactions between camp members. More people means a higher social density, which, in turn, means more opportunities for conflict.

Both carrying capacity and social density are complex variables. Carrying capacity involves not only the immediate presence of food and water but also the tools and work necessary to secure them, as well as short- and long-term fluctuations in their availability. Social density involves not only the number of people and their interactions but also the circumstances and quality of those interactions and the mechanisms for regulating them. A mob of a hundred angry strangers has a different social density than the same number of neighbors enjoying themselves at a block party.

Among food-foraging populations, social density seems to be in a constant state of flux, as people spend more or less time away from camp and as they move to other camps, either on visits or more permanently. Among the Ju/'hoansi, for example, exhaustion of local food resources, conflict within the group, or the desire to visit friends or

relatives living elsewhere cause people to leave one group for another. As Richard Lee notes: "Ju love to go visiting, and the practice acts as a safety valve when tempers get frayed. In fact, the Ju usually move, not when their food is exhausted, but rather when only their patience is exhausted."[8] If a camp has so many children as to create a burden for the working adults, some young families may be encouraged to join others where there are fewer children. Conversely, groups with few children may actively recruit families with young children in order to ensure the group's survival. Redistribution of people, then, is an important mechanism for regulating social density, as well as for assuring that the size and composition of local groups are suited to local variations in resources. Thus, cultural adaptations serve to help transcend the limitations of the physical environment.

In addition to seasonal or local adjustments, long-term adjustments to resources must be made. Most food-foraging populations seem to stabilize at numbers well below the carrying capacity of their land. In fact, the home ranges of most food foragers can support from three to five times as many people as they typically do. In the long run, it may be more adaptive for a group to keep its numbers low, rather than to expand indefinitely and risk being cut down by a sudden and unexpected natural reduction in food resources. The population density of food-foraging groups rarely exceeds one person per square mile, a very low density; their resources could support greater numbers.

Just how food-foraging peoples regulate population size has been understood only recently. Typically, such peoples nurse their infants several times each hour over a period of as many as 4 or 5 years. The constant stimulation of the mother's nipple is known to suppress the level of hormones that promote ovulation, making conception unlikely, especially if their work keeps the mothers physically active and they do not have large stores of body fat to draw on for energy.[9] By prolonging nursing over several years, women give birth only at widely spaced intervals, and the total number of offspring remains low.

Carrying capacity: The number of people who can be supported by the available resources at a given level of technology.

Density of social relations: Roughly, the number and intensity of interactions among the members of a camp or other residential unit.

---

[8]Lee, R. (1993). *The Dobe Ju/'hoansi* (p. 65). Fort Worth: Harcourt Brace.
[9]Ellison, P. T. (1990). Human ovarian function and reproductive ecology: New hypotheses. *American Anthropologist, 92,* 933–952.

Frequent nursing of children over as many as 4 or 5 years acts to suppress ovulation among food foragers like Bushmen. As a consequence, women give birth to relatively few offspring, at widely spaced intervals.

The Impact of Food Foraging on Human Society

Although much has been written on the theoretical importance of hunting in shaping the supposedly competitive and aggressive nature of the human species, most anthropologists are unconvinced by these arguments. The fact is that most known food-foraging peoples are remarkably unaggressive and place more emphasis on cooperation than they do on competition. It does seem likely, however, that three crucial elements of human social organization did develop along with food foraging. The first of these is the sexual division of labor. Some form of division of labor by sex, however modified, has been observed in all human societies, and is probably as old as human culture (see Chapter 7). There is some tendency in contemporary Western

society to do away with such division, as we shall see in the next chapter. One may ask what the implications are for future cooperative relationships between men and women, a problem we will discuss further in Chapters 19 and 20.

Subsistence and Sex Roles

The hunting and butchering of large game as well as the processing of hard or tough raw materials are almost universally masculine occupations. Women's work, by contrast, usually consists of gathering and processing a variety of vegetal foods, as well as various other domestic chores. Historically, this pattern appears to have its origin in an earlier era, in which males, who were twice the size of females, got meat by scavenging from the carcasses of dead animals, butchered it with stone tools, and shared it with females (see Chapter 3). The latter, for their part, gathered wild plant foods, probably utilizing digging sticks and carrying devices made of soft, perishable materials. As the hunting of live animals replaced scavenging as a source of meat, and the biological differences between the sexes were reduced to minor proportions, the essence of the original division of labor was maintained nonetheless.

Among food foragers today, the work of women is no less arduous than that of men. Ju/'hoansi women, for example, may walk as many as 12 miles a day 2 or 3 times a week to gather food, carrying not only their children, but on the return home, anywhere from 15 to 33 pounds of food. Still, they don't have to travel quite so far afield as do men on the hunt, nor is their work usually quite so dangerous. Finally, their tasks require less rapid mobility, do not require complete and undivided attention, and are readily resumed after interruption. All of this is compatible with those biological differences that do remain between the sexes. Certainly women who are pregnant or have infants to nurse cannot as easily travel long distances in pursuit of game as can men. In addition to wide-ranging mobility, the successful hunter must also be able to mobilize rapidly high bursts of energy. Although some women can certainly run faster than some men, it is a fact that in general men can run faster than women, even when the latter are not pregnant or encumbered with infants. Because human females must be able to give birth to infants with relatively large heads, their pelvic

Food foragers like the Ju/'hoansi have a division of labor in which women gather and prepare "bush" food, but hunting is usually done by men.

structure differs from that of human males to a greater degree than among most other species of mammals. As a consequence, the human female is not as well equipped as the human male where rapid and prolonged mobility are required.

To say that differing sex roles among food foragers is compatible with the biological differences between men and women is *not* to say that it is biologically determined. Among the Indians of the Great Plains of North America, for example, there are numerous reported cases of women who gained fame as hunters and warriors, both regarded as men's activities. There is even one case of a Gros Ventre girl captured by the Crow who became one of their chiefs, so accomplished was she at what were considered to be masculine pursuits. Conversely, any young man for whom masculine pursuits seemed uncongenial could assume the dress and demeanor of women, providing he had the necessary skills to achieve success in feminine activities. Although sexual preferences might enter into the decision to assume a feminine identity, not all such individuals were homosexuals, nor did all homosexuals assume a woman's role. Clearly, sexual preference was of lesser importance than oc-

cupation and appearance. In fact, the sexual division of labor is nowhere near as rigid among food foragers as it is in most other types of society. Thus, Ju/'hoansi men willingly and without embarrassment, as the occasion demands, will gather wild plant foods, build huts, and collect water, even though all are regarded as women's work.

The nature of women's work in food-foraging societies is such that it can be done while taking care of children. It can also be done in company with other women, which somewhat helps alleviate the monotony of the work. In the past, the gender biases of their culture caused European and North American anthropologists to underestimate the contribution made by the food-gathering activities of women to the survival of their group. We now know that most modern food foragers obtain 60 to 70 percent of their diets from plant foods, with perhaps some fish and shellfish provided by women (the exceptions are food foragers living in the far north, where plant foods are not available for much of the year).

Although women in food-foraging societies may spend some time each day gathering plant food, men do not spend all or even the greatest

Among traditional Ju/'hoansi, the camp is a place where individuals of all ages and both sexes mingle freely, sharing food and companionship.

part of their time in hunting. The amount of energy expended in hunting, especially in hot climates, is often greater than the energy return from the kill. Too much time spent at hunting might actually be counterproductive. Energy itself is derived primarily from plant carbohydrates, and it is the woman gatherer who brings in the bulk of the calories. A certain amount of meat in the diet, though, guarantees high-quality protein that is less easily obtained from plant sources, for meat contains exactly the right balance of all of the amino acids (the building blocks of protein) that are required by the human body. No one plant food does this by itself, and in order to get by without meat, one must hit on exactly the right combination of plants to provide the essential amino acids in the right proportions.

Food Sharing

A second key feature of human social organization associated with food foraging is the sharing of food between adults, something that is very rare among nonhuman primates. It is easy enough to see why sharing takes place, with women supplying one kind of food and men another. Among the Ju/'hoansi, women have control over the food that they collect, and can share it with whomever they choose. Men, by contrast, are constrained by rules that specify how much meat is to be distributed and to whom. Thus, a hunter has little effective control over the meat he brings into camp. For the individual hunter, meat sharing is really a way of storing it for the future; his generosity, obligatory though it might be, gives him a claim on the future kills of other hunters. As a cultural trait, food sharing has the obvious survival value of distributing resources needed for subsistence.

Although carnivorous animals often share food, the few examples of food sharing among nonhuman primate adults all involve groups of male chimpanzees cooperating in a hunt and later sharing the spoils, frequently with adult females as well as juveniles. What this suggests is that the origins of food sharing and the division of labor are related to a shift in food habits from infrequent to more frequent meat eating, which seems to have occurred with the appearance of the earliest members of the genus *Homo* some 2.5 million years ago.

A final distinctive feature of the food-foraging economy is the importance of the camp as the center of daily activity and the place where food sharing actually occurs. Among nonhuman primates, and probably among human ancestors until they controlled the use of fire, activities tend to be divided between feeding areas and sleeping areas, and the latter tend to be shifted each evening. Historically known food-foraging people, however, live in camps of some permanence, ranging from the dry-season camps of the Ju/'hoansi that serve for the entire winter to the dry-season camps of the Hadza of Tanzania, oriented to the hunt and serving for several days or at most a week or two. Moreover, human camps are more than sleeping areas; people are in and out all day, eating, working, and socializing in camps to a greater extent than any other primates.

Cultural Adaptations and Material Technology

The mobility of food-foraging groups may depend on the availability of water, as in the case of the Ju/'hoansi; of pine nuts, as in the Shoshone example; or of game animals, as among the Hadza. Hunting styles and equipment may also play a role in determining population size and movement. Some Mbuti hunt with nets. This requires the cooperation of 7 to 30 families; consequently, their camps are relatively large. The camps of those Mbuti who hunt with bow and arrow number from 3 to 6 families. Too many archers in the same locale means that each must travel a great distance daily to keep out of another's way. Only during midsummer do the archers collect into larger camps for religious ceremonies, matrimonial arrangements, and social exchange. At this time the bowmen turn to communal hunts. Without nets they are less effective than their neighbors, and it is only when the net-hunters are widely dispersed in the pursuit of honey that the archers can come together.

Egalitarian Society

An important characteristic of the food-foraging society is its egalitarianism. Food foragers are usually highly mobile and, lacking animal or mechanical means of transportation, they must be able to travel without many encumbrances, especially on food-getting expeditions. The average weight of one's personal belongings among the Ju/'hoansi, for example, is just under 25 pounds. The material goods of food foragers must be limited to the barest essentials, which include implements that serve for hunting, gathering, fishing, building, and making tools, cooking utensils, traps, and nets. There is little chance for the accumulation of luxuries or surplus goods, and the fact that no one owns significantly more than another helps to limit status differences. Age and sex are usually the only sources of important status differences.

It is important to realize that status differences by themselves do not imply any necessary inequality, a point that has all too often been misunderstood, especially where relations between men and women are concerned. In traditional food-foraging societies, nothing necessitated special deference of women to men. To be sure, women may be excluded from some rituals in which males participate, but the reverse is also true. Moreover, the fruits of women's labor are not controlled by men, but by the women themselves. Nor do women sacrifice their autonomy even in societies in which male hunting, rather than female gathering, brings in the bulk of the food. Such was the case, for example, among the Montagnais and Naskapi people of Labrador. Theirs was a society in which the hunt was of overwhelming importance. For their part, women manufactured clothing and other necessities, but provided much less of the food than is usual among food foragers. Although it is no longer the case, women as well as men could be shamans. Nevertheless, women were excluded from ritual feasts having to do with hunting, but then, so were men excluded from ritual feasts held by women. Basically, each sex carried out its own activities, with neither meddling in those of the other. Early missionaries to the Montagnais and Naskapi lamented that men had no inclination to make their wives obey them, and worked long and hard to convince the Indians that civilization required men to impose their authority on women. But after 300 years of trying, they have still achieved only limited success.

Food foragers make no attempt to accumulate surplus foodstuffs, often an important source of status in agrarian societies. To say that they do not accumulate food surpluses, however, is not to say that they live constantly on the verge of starvation. Their environment is their storehouse, and, except in the coldest climates (where a surplus must be put by to see people through the lean season), or in times of acute ecological disaster, there is always some food to be found in a group's territory. Because food resources are typically distributed equally throughout the group (share and share alike is the order of the day), no one achieves the wealth or status that hoarding might bring. In such a society, wealth is a sign of deviance rather than a desirable characteristic.

The food forager's concept of territory contributes as much to social equality as it does to the equal distribution of resources. Most groups have home ranges, which they utilize and within which access to resources is open to all members: What is available to one is available to all. If a Mbuti hunter discovers a honey tree, he has first rights; but when he has taken his share, others have a turn. In the unlikely possibility that he does not take advantage of his discovery, others will. No one owns the tree; the system is first come, first served. Therefore, knowledge of the existence of food resources circulates quickly throughout the entire group.

Families move easily from one group to another, settling in any group where they have a previous kinship tie. The composition of groups is always shifting. This loose attitude toward group membership promotes the widest access to resources and, at the same time, is a device that maintains a balance between populations and resources.

The food-forager pattern of generalized exchange, or sharing without any expectation of direct return, also serves the ends of resource distribution and social equality. A Ju/'hoansi man or woman spends as much as two-thirds of his or her day visiting others or receiving guests; during this time, many exchanges of gifts take place. To refuse to share—to hoard—would be morally wrong. By sharing whatever is at hand, the Ju/'hoansi achieve social leveling and assure their right to share in the windfalls of others.

FOOD-PRODUCING SOCIETY

As we saw in Chapter 3, it was toolmaking that allowed humans to become meat eaters as well as consumers of plant foods. The next truly momentous event in human history was the domestication of plants and animals (Fig. 11.3). The transition from food forager to food producer (the available evidence suggests this change began 9,000 to 11,000 years ago) has been termed revolutionary. By changing the way they provided for their subsistence, people changed the very nature of human society itself.

Just why this change came about is one of the important questions in anthropology; since food production usually requires more work than food foraging, is more monotonous, is often a less secure means of subsistence, and requires people to eat more of the foods that food foragers eat only when they have no other choice, it can be assumed that people probably did not become food producers through choice. Initially, it appears that food production came about as a largely unintended by-product of existing food management practices. By chance, these promoted the development of new varieties of particular plants and animals, which came to take on increasing importance for peoples' subsistence. Subsequently, many populations adopted farming out of necessity in situations where population growth outstripped peoples' ability to sustain themselves through food foraging. For them, food production became a subsistence option of last resort.

The Settled Life of Farmers

Whatever the causes, one of the most significant correlates of this new way of life was the development of permanent settlements, in which families of farmers lived together. Unlike food foragers, who stay close to their food by moving around, farmers stay close to their food by staying near their gardens. The task of food production lent itself to a different kind of social organization; the hard work of some members of the group could provide food for all, thus freeing certain people to devote their time to inventing and manufacturing the equipment needed for a new sedentary way of life. Harvesting and digging tools, pottery for storage and cooking, clothing made of woven textiles, and housing made of stone, wood, or sun-dried bricks were some of the results of this combination of new sedentary living conditions and altered division of labor.

The transition also brought important changes in social structure. At first, social relations were egalitarian and hardly different from those that prevailed among food foragers. As settlements grew, however, and large numbers of people began to share the same important resources, such as land and water, society became more elaborately structured. Multifamily kinship groups such as lineages, to which people belong by virtue of descent from a common ancestor, but which do not commonly play a large part in the social order of food foragers, were probably the organizing units; as will be discussed in Chapter 21, they provide a convenient way to handle the distinctive problems of land use and ownership that arise in food-producing societies.

Humans adapted to this new settled life in a number of ways. For example, some societies became horticultural—small communities of gardeners working with simple hand tools and using neither irrigation nor the plow. Horticulturists typically cultivate several varieties of crops together in small gardens they have cleared by hand. Because a given garden plot is typically used for only a few years before being abandoned in favor of a new plot, horticulture may be said to constitute an *extensive* form of agriculture. Production is for subsistence, rather than to produce a surplus for sale; however, the politics of horticultural communities commonly involves periodic feasts, in the course of which substantial amounts of produce and other gifts are given away in order to gain prestige. Such prestige is the basis for the political power of leaders, who play important roles in production, exchange, and resource allocation.

One of the most widespread forms of horticulture, especially in the tropics, is slash-and-burn, or **swidden farming.** Unfortunately, widespread use of fire in connection with the clearing of vast tracts of Amazon forest for cattle raising and other development schemes has led many people to see slash-and-burn farming in a negative light. In fact, it is an ecologically sophisticated and sustainable way of raising food, especially in the tropics, when carried out under the right conditions: low population densities and adequate amounts of land. Only when pursued in the absence of these conditions does the practice lead to environmental degradation and destruction. Properly carried out, swidden farming mimics the diversity of the natural ecosystem; moreover, by growing several different crops together in the same field they become less vulnerable to pests and plant diseases than if single crops are grown by themselves. Not

While it supports larger and more sedentary populations than food foraging, farming generally requires longer and more monotonous work.

Swidden farming: An extensive form of horticulture in which the natural vegetation is cut, the slash is subsequently burned, and crops then planted amongst the ashes.

This swidden plot in Chiapas, Mexico, shows what such gardens look like after slash has been burned, but before the crops have begun to grow. Although it looks destructive, if properly carried out, swidden farming is an ecologically sound way of growing crops in the tropics.

only is the system ecologically sound, but it also is far more energy efficient than farming as carried out in developed countries like the United States, which requires the input of more energy than comes out of the system. By contrast, for every unit of energy expended, slash-and-burn farming produces between 10 and 20 units in return. A good example of just how such a system works is provided by the Mekranoti Kayapo Indians of Brazil's Amazon forest.

Original Study
Gardens of the Mekranoti Kayapo[10]

The planting of a Mekranoti garden always follows the same sequence. First, men clear the forest and then burn the debris. In the ashes, both men and women plant sweet potatoes, manioc, bananas, corn, pumpkins, papaya, sugar cane, pineapple, cotton, tobacco, and annatto, whose seeds yield achiote, the red dye used for painting ornaments and people's bodies. Since the Mekranoti don't bother with weeding, the forest gradually invades the garden. After the second year, only manioc, sweet potatoes, and bananas remain. And after three years or so there is usually nothing left but bananas. Except for a few tree species that require hundreds of years to grow, the area will look like the original forest twenty-five or thirty years later.

This gardening technique, known as slash-and-burn agriculture, is one of the most common in the world. The early settlers in North America adopted the method from the surrounding Indians, although it had been used in an earlier period in Europe as well. At one time critics condemned the technique as wasteful and ecologically destructive, but today we know that, especially in the humid tropics, slash-and-burn agriculture may be one of the best gardening techniques possible.

Anthropologists were among the first to note the possibly disastrous consequences of U.S.-style agriculture in the tropics. Continuous high temperatures encourage the growth of the microorganisms that cause rot, so organic matter quickly breaks down into simple minerals. The heavy rains dissolve these valuable nutrients and carry them deep into the soils, out of the reach of plants. The tropical forest maintains its richness because the heavy foliage shades the earth, cooling it and inhibiting the growth of the decomposers. A good deal of the rain is captured by leaves before ever reaching the ground. When a tree falls in the forest, and begins to rot, other plants quickly absorb the nutrients that are released. With open-field agriculture, the sun heats the earth, the decomposers multiply, and the rains quickly leach the soils of their nutrients. In a few years a lush forest, if cleared for open one-crop agriculture, can be transformed into a barren wasteland.

Slash-and-burn agriculture is less of a problem than open-field agriculture. A few months after planting, banana and papaya trees shade the soil, just as the larger forest trees do. The mixing of different kinds of plants in the same area means that minerals can be absorbed as soon as they are released—corn picks up nutrients very fast, while manioc is slow. Also, the small and temporary clearings mean that the forest can quickly reinvade its lost territory.

Because decomposers need moisture as well as warmth, the long Mekranoti dry season could alter this whole picture of soil ecology. But soil samples from recently burned Mekranoti fields and the adjacent forest floor showed that, as in most of the humid tropics, the high fertility of the Indians' garden plots comes from the trees that are burned there, not from the soil, as in temperate climes.

Getting a good burn is a tricky operation. Perhaps for this reason its timing was left to the more experienced and knowledgable members of the community. If the burn is too early, the rains will leach out the minerals in the ash before planting time. If too late, the debris will be too wet to burn properly. Then, insects and weeds that could plague the plants will not die and few minerals will be released into the soil. If the winds are too weak, the burn will not cover the entire plot. If they are too strong, the fire can get out of hand. In the past, the Mekranoti accidently burned down villages several times because of fires that spread too fast.

Ronaldo remembered an incident when a garden fire caught some of the houses in the village. Fearing the flames would spread from one rooftop to the next until the entire village circle was ablaze, the Indians ran inside their homes and gathered their belongings to set them in the center of the village plaza. In the past, this reaction made good sense. Constructions were simpler, and people had fewer belongings to lose. Since moves were frequent anyway, destroying a village in smoke was not very serious. A fire could even get rid of insect pests that infest villages after many years. But this time people were more concerned. Ronaldo finally persuaded some of the Indians to chop down some of the houses next to the burning structures and the village was saved.

Shortly after the burning of the garden plots and the clearing away of some of the charred debris, people began the long job of planting, which took up all of September and lasted into October. Tàkàkngo returned in time to help Kaxti and his wife with their garden. Although he could not walk well enough to work, Kaxti could accompany his wife, Nhàkkamro, to the garden and take care of their children, while she did most of the planting.

In the center of the circular garden plot the women dug holes and threw in a few pieces of sweet potatoes. After covering the tubers with dirt they usually asked a male—one of their husbands or anyone else who happened to be nearby—to stomp on the mound and make a ritual noise resembling a Bronx cheer. This magic would ensure a large crop, I was told. Forming a large ring around the sweet potatoes, the Indians rapidly thrust pieces of manioc stems into the ground, one after the other.

When grown, the manioc stems form a dense barrier to the sweet potato patch, and some of the plants must be cut down to gain entrance. Outside of the ring of manioc, the women plant yams, cotton, sugar cane, and annatto. Banana stalks and papaya trees, planted by simply throwing the seeds on the ground, form the outermost circle. The Indians also plant corn, pumpkins, watermelons, and pineapple throughout the garden. These grow rapidly and are harvested long before the manioc matures. The garden appears to change magically from corn and pumpkins to sweet potatoes and manioc without replanting.

Mekranoti gardens grew well. A few Indians complained now and then about a peccary that had eaten a watermelon they were looking forward to eating, or that had reduced their corn harvest. Capybara, large rodents usually found near the river banks, were known for their love of sugar cane, but in general the animals seemed to leave the crops alone. Even the leaf-cutting ants that are problems in other areas did not bother the Mekranoti. Occasionally a neighbor who had not planted a new garden would make off with a prized first-year crop, such as pumpkin, watermelon, or pineapple. But even these thefts were rare. In general, the Mekranoti could depend on harvesting whatever they planted.

Eventually, I wanted to calculate the productivity of Mekranoti gardens. Agronomists knew very little about slash-and-burn agriculture. They were accustomed to experiments in which a field was given over to one crop only, and in which the harvest happened all at once. Here, the plants were all mixed together, and people harvested piecemeal whenever they needed something. The manioc could stay in the ground, growing for several years before it was dug up.

I began measuring off areas of gardens to count how many manioc plants, ears of corn, or pumpkins were found there. The women thought it strange to see me struggling through the tangle of plants to measure off areas, 10 meters by 10 meters, placing string along the borders, and then counting what was inside. Sometimes I asked a woman to dig up all of the sweet potatoes within the marked-off area. The requests were bizarre, but the women cooperated just the same, holding on to the ends of the measuring tapes, or sending their children to help. For some plants, like bananas, I simply counted the number of clumps of stalks in the garden, and the number of banana bunches I could see growing in various clumps. By watching how long it took the bananas to grow, from the time I could see them until they were harvested, I could calculate a garden's total banana yield per year.

After returning from the field, I was able to combine the time allocation data with the garden productivities to get an idea of how hard the Mekranoti need to work to survive. The data showed that for every hour of gardening one Mekranoti adult produces almost 18,000 kilocalories of food. (As a basis for comparison, people in the United States consume approximately 3,000 kilocalories of food per day.) As insurance against bad years, and in case they receive visitors from other villages, they grow far more produce than they need. But even so, they don't need to work very hard to survive. A look at the average amount of time adults spend on different tasks every week shows just how easygoing life in horticultural societies can be:

- 8.5 hours Gardening
- 6.0 hours Hunting
- 1.5 hours Fishing
- 1.0 hour Gathering wild foods
- 33.5 hours All other jobs

Altogether, the Mekranoti need to work less than 51 hours a week, and this includes getting to and from work, cooking, repairing broken tools, and all of the other things we normally don't count as part of our work week.

[10]Adapted from Werner, D. (1990). *Amazon journey* (pp. 105–112). Englewood Cliffs, NJ: Prentice-Hall.

Technologically more complex than the horticulturists are intensive agriculturalists, whose practices usually result in far more modification of the landscape and ecology than do those of horticulturists. Employed are such techniques as irrigation, fertilizers, and the wooden or metal plow pulled by harnessed draft animals, or in the "developed" countries of the world, tractors, to produce food on larger plots of land. Such farmers are able to grow sufficient food to provide not just for their own needs, but for those of full-time specialists of various sorts as well. This surplus may be sold for cash, or it may be coerced out of the farmers through taxes, or rent paid to owners of the land. These landowners and other specialists typically reside in substantial towns or cities, where political power is centralized in the hands of a socially elite class of people. The distinction between horticulturist and intensive agriculturalist is not always an easy one to make. For example, the Hopi Indians of the North American Southwest traditionally employed irrigation in their farming, while at the same time using simple hand tools. Moreover, they produced for their own immediate needs and lived in towns without centralized political government.

As food producers, people have developed several major crop complexes: two adapted to seasonal uplands and two to tropical wetlands. In the dry uplands of Southwest Asia, for example, they time their agricultural activities with the rhythm of the changing seasons, cultivating wheat, barley, flax, rye, and millet. In the tropical wetlands of Southeast Asia, rice and tubers such as yams and taro are cultivated. In the Americas, people have adapted to environments similar to those of the Old World, but have cultivated different plants. Maize, beans, squash, and the potato are some of the crops grown in drier areas, whereas manioc is extensively grown in the tropical wetlands.

Horticulture: The Gururumba

A good example of a horticultural society that has adapted to its environment successfully is the Gururumba, a people numbering somewhat over 1,000 who live in six villages spread over 30 square miles in the Upper Asaro Valley of New Guinea. Because of the elevation, the climate is cool and damp, and the area receives about 100 inches of rain a year.[11]

Each Gururumba village has a number of gardens separated by fences; several small families may have plots inside each fenced area. Every adult is involved in food production, with a strict division of labor according to sex. Men plant and tend sugarcane, bananas, taro, and yams, while women cultivate sweet potatoes and a variety of green vegetables. A family's social prestige is partially based on the neatness and productivity of its garden. Crops are rotated, but fertilizers are not used. Each gardener maintains more than one plot and uses different soils and different ecological zones for different crops; thus, the gardens are ready for harvesting at different times of the year, assuring a constant food supply. Since rainfall is plentiful, the Gururumba do not irrigate their gardens, and although some

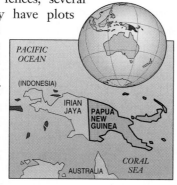

plots are planted on slopes with angles of 45 degrees, terracing is not practiced. Simple hand tools, such as digging sticks made of wood or ground stone, are used by the men to break the soil.

Like many such societies in New Guinea and Melanesia (the islands nearby), Gururumba society is knit together through a complex system of gift exchange, in which men lavish gifts on one another and so accumulate a host of debtors. The more a man gives away, the more is owed him, and hence the more prestige he has. For this reason every man keeps two gardens, one with crops to fulfill his everyday needs and one with "prestige" crops for his exchange needs. Although the crops planted in the latter gardens are not special, particular care is given to this garden to assure crops of the finest quality. A man anticipates a major occasion when he will have to give a feast, such as a daughter's wedding or a son's initiation, by planting his prestige garden a year in advance.

The second major feature of the Gururumba subsistence pattern, also common throughout this culture area, is the keeping of pigs. Pigs are raised not primarily for food but as gift-exchange items to raise social prestige. Every five to seven years, a huge pig feast, called an *idzi namo* ("pig flute") is held. Hundreds of pigs are killed, cooked, and distributed, simultaneously abolishing old obligations and creating new ones for the clan that gives the feast. As was the case among the Tsembaga whom we discussed earlier in this chapter, the pig feast helps the Gururumba get rid of a pig population that has grown too large to continue feeding; it also provides occasional animal protein in their diet.

Pastoralism: The Bakhtiari

One of the more striking examples of human adaptation to the environment is the **pastoralist,** who lives in societies in which animal husbandry is

---

[11]Most of the following information is taken from Newman, P. L. (1965). *Knowing the Gururumba*. New York: Holt, Rinehart and Winston.

Pastoralist: Member of a society in which animal husbandry is regarded as the ideal way of making a living, and in which movement of all or part of the society is considered a normal and natural way of life.

viewed as the ideal way of making a living and in which movement of all or part of the society is considered a normal and natural part of life. This cultural aspect is vitally important, for while all pastoral nomads are dependent to some degree on nearby farmers for some of their supplies, and in some cases they earn more from nonpastoral sources than from their own herds, the concept of nomadic pastoralism remains central to their own identities. These societies are built around a pastoral economic specialization, but imbued with values far beyond just doing a job. This distinguishes them from American ranchers, who likewise have a pastoral economic specialization but identify culturally with a larger society.[12] It also sets them apart from food foragers, migrant farm workers, corporate executives, or others who are nomadic without being pastoralists.

Pastoralism is an effective way of living in arid grasslands and deserts, such as those that stretch eastward from the dry country of North Africa through the Arabian Desert, across the plateau of Iran and into Turkestan and Mongolia. In Africa and Southwest Asia alone, more than 21,000 people follow a pastoral nomadic way of life. One group of people living in this belt of arid lands is the Bakhtiari, a fiercely independent people who live in the south Zagros mountains of western Iran, where they tend herds of goats and fat-tailed sheep.[13] Although some of the Bakhtiari own horses and most own donkeys, these are used only for transport; the animals around which these people's lives revolve are the sheep and goat.

The harsh, bleak environment dominates the lives of these people: It determines when and where they move their flocks, the clothes they wear, the food they eat, and even their dispositions— they have been called "mountain bears" by Iranian townspeople. In the Zagros are ridges that reach altitudes of 12,000 to 14,000 feet. Their steep, rocky trails and escarpments challenge the hardiest and ablest

climbers; jagged peaks, deep chasms, and watercourses with thunderous torrents also make living and traveling hazardous.

The pastoral life of the Bakhtiari revolves around two seasonal migrations to find better grazing lands for the flocks. Twice yearly the people move: in the fall, from their *sardsir*, or summer quarters in the mountains, and in the spring, from their *garmsir*, or winter quarters in the lowlands. In the fall, before the harsh winter comes to the mountains, the nomads load their tents and other belongings on donkeys and drive their flocks down to the warm plains that border Iraq in the west; grazing land here is excellent and well watered in the winter. In the spring, when the low-lying pastures dry up, the Bakhtiari return to the mountain valleys, where a new crop of grass is sprouting. For this trek, they split into five groups, each containing about 5,000 individuals and 50,000 animals.

The return trip north is the more dangerous because the mountain snows are melting and the gorges are full of turbulent, ice-cold water rushing down from the mountain peaks. This long trek is further impeded by the kids that are born in the spring, just before migration. Where the water courses are not very deep, the nomads ford them. Deeper channels, including one river that is a half-mile wide, are crossed with the help of inflatable goatskin rafts, on which are placed infants, the elderly and infirm, and lambs and kids; the rafts are then pushed by the men swimming alongside in the icy water. If they work from dawn to dusk, the nomads can get all of the people and animals across the river in five days. Not surprisingly, dozens of sheep are drowned each day at the river crossing.

In the mountain passes, where a biting wind numbs the skin and brings tears to the eyes, the Bakhtiari must make their way through slippery unmelted snow. Climbing the steep escarpments is dangerous, and the stronger men must often carry their own children and the newborn kids on their

[12]Barfield, T. J. (1984, Spring). Introduction. *Cultural Survival Quarterly, 8*, 2.

[13]Material on the Bakhtiari is drawn mainly from Barth, F. (1960). Nomadism in the mountain and plateau areas of south west Asia. *The problems of the arid zone* (pp. 341–355). UNESCO; Coon, C. S. (1958). *Caravan: The story of the Middle East* (2nd ed.). Chap. 13. New York: Holt, Rinehart and Winston; Salzman, P. C. (1967). Political organization among nomadic peoples. Proceedings of the American Philosophical Society, *111*, 115–131.

Among pastoral nomads like the Bakhtiari, a major event in people's lives is the annual movement of their livestock from lowland to mountain pastures and back, according to the seasons.

shoulders as they make their way over the ice and snow to the lush mountain valley that is their goal. During each migration the people may cover as many as 200 miles, and the trek can take weeks, because the flocks travel slowly and require constant attention. The nomads have fixed routes and a somewhat definite itinerary; generally, they know where they should be and when they should be there. On the drive the men and boys herd the sheep and goats, while the women and children ride the donkeys along with the tents and other equipment.

When they reach their destination, the Bakhtiari live in black tents of goathair cloth woven by the women. The tents have sloping tops and vertical sides, held up by wooden poles. Inside, the furnishings are sparse: rugs woven by the women or heavy felt pads cover the floor. Against one side of the tent are blankets; containers made of goatskin, copper utensils, clay jugs, and bags of

grain line the opposite side. Bakhtiari tents provide an excellent example of adaptation to a changing environment. The goathair cloth retains heat and repels water during the winter and keeps out heat during the summer. These portable homes are very easy to erect, take down, and transport.

Sheep and goats are central to Bakhtiari subsistence. The animals provide milk, cheese, butter, meat, hides, and wool, which is woven into clothes, tents, storage bags, and other essentials by the women or sold in towns. The people also engage in very limited horticulture; they own lands that contain orchards, and the fruit is consumed by the nomads or sold to townspeople. The division of labor is according to sex. The men, who take great pride in their marksmanship and horsemanship, engage in a limited amount of hunting on horseback, but their chief task is the tending of the flocks. The women cook, sew, weave, care for the children, and carry fuel and water.

The Bakhtiari have their own system of justice, including laws and a penal code. They are governed by tribal leaders, or *khans*, men who are elected or inherit their office. Because of the prominent roles played by men in both economic and political affairs, the world of the pastoral nomad is very much a man's world. Thus, women typically occupy subordinate positions *vis-à-vis* men, even though elderly women may eventually gain a good deal of power. Most of the *khans* grew wealthy when oil was discovered in their homeland around the start of the twentieth century, and many of them are well educated, having attended Iranian or foreign universities. Despite this, and although some of them own houses in cities, the *khans* spend much of their lives among their people.

Intensive Agriculture and Nonindustrial Cities

With the intensification of agriculture, some farming communities grew into cities, in which individuals who had previously been engaged in farming were freed to specialize in other activities. Thus, such craft specialists as carpenters, blacksmiths, sculptors, basketmakers, and stonecutters contribute to the vibrant, diversified life of the city.

Unlike horticulturalists and pastoralists, city dwellers are only indirectly concerned with adapting to their natural environment. Far more

One form of intensive agriculture, the *chinampa*, was perfected in ancient Mexico. This picture is of a modern *chinampa* garden on the gulf coast of Mexico.

important is the need to adapt to living and getting along with their fellow urbanites. To an important degree, this is true as well for the farmers who provide the city dwellers with their food. Under the political control of an urban elite, much of what they do is governed by economic forces over which they have little, if any, control. Urbanization brings with it a new social order: Marked inequality develops as society becomes stratified and people are ranked according to their gender, the kind of work they do, or the family into which they are born. As social institutions cease to operate in simple, face-to-face groups of relatives, friends, and acquaintances, they become more formal and bureaucratic, with specialized political institutions.

With urbanization came a sharp increase in the tempo of human cultural evolution. Writing was invented, trade intensified and expanded, the wheel and the sail were invented, and metallurgy and other crafts were developed. In many early cities, monumental buildings, such as royal palaces and temples, were built by thousands of men, often slaves taken in war; these feats of engineering still amaze modern architects and engineers. The inhabitants of these buildings—the ruling class composed of nobles and priests—formed a central government that dictated social and religious rules; in turn, the rules were carried out by the merchants, soldiers, artisans, farmers, and other citizens.

Aztec City Life

The Aztec empire, which flourished in Mexico in the sixteenth century, is a good example of a highly developed urban society among non-Western peoples.[14] The capital city of the empire, Tenochtitlán (modern-day Mexico City), was located in a fertile valley 7,000 feet above sea level. Its population, along with that of its sister city, Tlatelolco, was about 200,000 in 1519, when Cortes first saw it.

[14]Most of the following information is taken from Berdan, F. F. (1982). *The Aztecs of Central Mexico.* New York: Holt, Rinehart and Winston.

Model of the center of Tenochtitlán, the Aztec capital city.

This makes it five times more populous than the city of London at the same time. The Aztec metropolis sat on an island in the middle of a salt lake, which has since dried up, and two aqueducts brought in fresh water from springs on the mainland. A 10-mile dike rimmed the eastern end of the city to ward off floodwaters originating in the neighboring lakes during the rainy season.

As in the early cities of Southwest Asia, the foundation of Aztec society was intensive agriculture. Corn was the principal crop. Each family, allotted a plot of land by its lineage, cultivated any of a number of crops, including beans, squash, gourds, peppers, tomatoes, cotton, and tobacco. Unlike Old World societies, however, only a few animals were domesticated; these included dogs and turkeys (both for eating). Many of the plots in which crops were grown around Tenochtitlán were actually constructed artificially in the shallow waters of the surrounding lake. Canals between these *chinampas* not only facilitated transport, but were also a source of water plants used for heavy mulching. In addition, muck rich in fish feces was periodically dredged from the canals and spread over the gardens to maintain their fertility. Incredibly productive and sustainable, *chinampas* can be found even today at Xochimilco, on the outskirts of Mexico City.

Aztec agricultural success provided for an increasingly large population and the diversification

of labor. Skilled artisans, such as sculptors, silversmiths, stone workers, potters, weavers, feather workers, and painters were able to make good livings by pursuing these crafts exclusively. Since religion was central to the operation of the Aztec social order, these craftspeople were continuously engaged in the manufacture of religious

artifacts, clothing, and decorations for buildings and temples. Other nonagricultural specialists included some of the warriors, the traveling merchants or *pochteca*, the priests, and the government bureaucracy of nobles.

As specialization increased, both among individuals and cities of the Aztec empire, the market became an extremely important economic and social institution. In addition to the daily markets in each city, there were larger markets in the various cities, held at different times of year. Buyers and sellers traveled to these from the far reaches of the empire. The market at Tlatelolco, Tenochtitlán's sister city, was so huge that the Spanish compared it to those of Rome and Constantinople.

Anthropology Applied

AGRICULTURAL DEVELOPMENT AND THE ANTHROPOLOGIST

High up in the Andes mountains of South America, at an elevation of two miles above sea level, lies the vast, intermontane plain known as the Bolivian Altiplano. On this plain, not far from where the modern countries of Bolivia, Chile, and Peru meet, is Lake Titicaca, the world's highest navigable body of water. A kilometer or so from this lake's south end stands the elaborate, monumental architecture of Tiwanaku, one of the most impressive archaeological sites in the region that, 500 years ago, constituted the southern quarter of the Inca empire. Today, the region is a bleak and barren landscape, where some 20,000 Aymara Indians have a hard time producing enough food for their own survival.

Whereas we once thought it to be strictly a ceremonial center with a small resident population, to which pilgrimages were made periodically from vast distances, we now know that Tiwanaku was a major city, inhabited during its Classic Period (A.D. 375 to 725) by between 20,000 and 40,000 people. Another 200,000 or so people inhabited the surrounding Titicaca basin, all under the political control of Tiwanaku, a true imperial city that controlled a vast empire centuries before the Incas were anything but a relatively insignificant people living in the mountains some distance north of Tiwanaku. Its political control stretched beyond the Altiplano into northern Chile and southern Peru, where administrative centers, satellite cities, and even colonies were established.

To support the huge population of the Altiplano, Tiwanaku carried out massive land reclamation, constructing an extensive system of raised and ridged fields in which hardy crops could be intensively grown. These fields have been studied by anthropologist Alan Kolata of the University of Chicago. Built up to a height of 3 to 5 feet, the constituent materials of cobblestones, clay, gravel, and topsoil were carefully layered to prevent the buildup of crop-killing salt that leaches into the ground. Between the fields ran canals that filled with groundwater (the water table here is only a few feet beneath the surface). These 5-foot-wide trenches were oriented to soak up the maximum amount of solar heat during the day, acting as a kind of solar sump. One reason Altiplano agriculture today is difficult is because of periodic frost; as much as 90 percent of a harvest can be lost as a result. In Tiwanaku times, however, the heat stored in the canals radiated over the fields' surface, raising the ambient temperatures as much as 2 or 3 degrees Celsius, which is more than enough to prevent frost. In addition, the canals functioned as fertilizer factories. Organic sediments that settled in the canals could be scooped out at the end of each growing season and dumped on the fields, thereby renewing their fertility.

Having figured out how the system worked, in 1988, Kolata began to put his knowledge to work in the service of the Aymara farmers living in the region today.* In selected communities, Kolata has secured the cooperation of native farmers by guaranteeing a harvest, even if their experimental fields fail. Planting onions, beets, and potatoes, they have increased their yields significantly; not only do they get up to twice as many potatoes per plant, for instance, but also the potatoes are bigger and of better quality. Moreover, the farmers do not have to use scarce funds for fertilizer, since canal muck is free, and they are not causing pollution through use of chemical fertilizers.

By reintroducing an ancient technology that was lost following disintegration of the Tiwanaku empire a thousand years ago, Kolata is now improving the quality of life for many Aymara Indians, reversing the poor harvests that have driven many men from the Altiplano to valleys south and east, where coca is grown to be turned into cocaine. Given its success, Kolata predicts that by the end of 1990s, the ancient raised-field technology will be widely used not just in Bolivia, but in many other parts of South and Central America for which it is suitable.

*Living on Earth (1992, August 28). National Public Radio.

At the Aztec markets barter was the primary means of exchange. For some purposes, however, cacao beans and cotton cloaks were used as a kind of currency. In addition to its obvious economic use, the market served social functions: People went there not only to buy or to sell but to meet other people and to hear the latest news. A law actually required that each person go to market at least once within a specified number of days; this ensured that the citizenry was kept informed

The modern industrial city is a very recent human development, although its roots lie in the so-called preindustrial city. The widespread belief that so-called preindustrial cities are things of the past and that industrial cities are things of the future is based upon culture-bound assumptions, rather than established facts.

of all important news. The other major economic institution, trade networks between the Aztec capital and other cities, brought goods such as chocolate, vanilla beans, and pineapples into Tenochtitlán.

The Aztec social order was stratified into three main classes: nobles, commoners, and serfs. The nobles, among whom gender inequality was most marked, operated outside the lineage system on the basis of land and serfs allotted them by the ruler, from conquered peoples. The commoners were divided into lineages, on which they were dependent for land. Within each of these, individual status depended on the degree of descent from the founder: Those more closely related to the lineage founder had higher status than those whose kinship was more distant. The third class in Aztec society consisted of serfs bound to the land and porters employed as carriers by merchants. Lowest of this class were the slaves. Some had voluntarily sold themselves into bondage; others were captives taken in war.

The Aztecs were governed by a semidivine king, who was chosen by a council of nobles, priests, and leaders from among candidates of royal lineage. Although the king was an absolute monarch, the councilors advised him on affairs of state. A vast number of government officials oversaw various functions, such as the maintenance of the tax system, the courts of justice, management of government storehouses, and control of military training.

The typical Aztec city was rectangular and reflected the way the land was divided among the lineages. In the center was a large plaza containing the temple and the house of the city's ruler. At Tenochtitlán, with a total area of about 20 square miles, a huge temple and two lavish palaces stood in the central plaza, also called the Sacred Precinct. Surrounding this area were other ceremonial buildings belonging to each lineage.

As in a modern city, housing in Tenochtitlán ranged from squalid to magnificent. On the outskirts of the city, on *chinampas*, were the farmers' huts, built of wooden posts, thatched straw, and wattle smeared with mud. In the city proper were the houses of the middle class—graceful, multiroomed, single- and two-story stone and mortar buildings, each of which surrounded a flower-filled patio and rested on a stone platform for protection against floods. It is estimated that there were about 60,000 houses in Tenochtitlán. The focal points of the city were the *teocallis*, or pyramidal temples, at which religious ceremonies, including human sacrifice, were held. The 100-foot-high double temple dedicated to the war god and the rain god was made of stone and featured a steep staircase that led to a platform with an altar, a chamber containing shrines, and an antechamber for the priests.

The palace of the emperor Moctezuma boasted numerous rooms for attendants and concubines, a menagerie, hanging gardens, and a swimming pool. Since Tenochtitlán sat in the middle of a lake, it was unfortified and connected to the mainland by three causeways. Communication among different parts of the city was easy, and one could travel either by land or by water. A series of canals, with footpaths running beside them, ran throughout the city. The Spaniards who came to this city reported that thousands of canoes plied the canals, carrying passengers and cargo around the city; these Europeans were so impressed by the communication network that they called Tenochtitlán the Venice of the New World.

Preindustrial cities: The kinds of urban settlements that are characteristic of nonindustrial civilizations.

NONINDUSTRIAL CITIES IN THE MODERN WORLD

Tenochtitlán is a good example of the kind of urban settlement that was characteristic of most ancient, nonindustrial civilizations. Commonly termed **preindustrial cities,** they are all too easily considered things of the past or as little more than stages in some sort of inevitable progression toward the kinds of industrial cities one finds today in places like Europe and North America. This essentially ethnocentric view obscures the fact that "preindustrial" cities are far from uncommon in the world today—especially in the so-called "underdeveloped" countries. Furthermore, industrial cities have not yet come close to demonstrating that they have the long-term viability shown by nonindustrial cities, which in some parts of the world have been around for not just hundreds but thousands of years.

CHAPTER SUMMARY

In order to meet their requirements for food, water, and shelter, people must adjust their behavior to suit their environment. This adjustment, which involves both change and stability, is a part of adaptation. Adaptation means that there is a moving balance between a society's needs and its environmental potential. Adaptation also refers to the interaction between an organism and its environment, with each causing changes in the other. Adaptation is a continuing process, and it is essential for survival. An ecosystem is bound by the activities of organisms and by physical forces such as erosion. Human ecosystems must be considered in terms of all aspects of culture.

To fit into an ecosystem an organism must be able to adapt or become a part of it. Once such a fit is achieved, stability may serve the organism's interest more than change.

A culture area is a geographical region in which various societies follow similar patterns of life. Since geographical regions are not always uniform in climate and topography, new discoveries do not always spread to every group. Environmental variation also favors variation in technology, since needs may be quite different from area to area.

Julian Steward used the concept of culture type to explain variations within geographical regions. In this view a culture is considered in terms of a particular technology and of the particular environmental features with which that technology is best suited to deal.

The social and political organizations of a society are other factors that influence how technology is to be used to ensure survival. Those features of a culture that play a part in the way the society makes a living are its culture core. Anthropologists can trace direct relationships between types of culture cores and types of environments.

The food-foraging way of life, the oldest and most universal type of human adaptation, requires that people move their residence according to changing food sources. For as yet unknown ecological and social factors, local group size is kept small. One explanation contends that small sizes fit land capacity to sustain the groups. Another states that the fewer the people, the less the chance of social conflict. The primary mechanism for regulation of population size among food foragers is frequent stimulation of the female nipple, which prevents ovulation, as infants nurse several times an hour over several years.

Three important elements of human social organization probably developed along with scavenging and hunting for meat. These are a sexual division of labor, food sharing, and the camp as the center of daily activity and the place where food sharing takes place.

A characteristic of food-foraging societies is their egalitarianism. Since this way of life requires mobility, people accumulate only the material goods necessary for survival, so that status differences are limited to those based on age and sex. Status differences associated with sex, however, do not imply subordination of women to men. Food resources are distributed equally throughout the groups; thus no individual can achieve the wealth or status that hoarding might bring.

The reason for the transition from food foraging to food production, which began about 11,000 to 9,000 years ago, was likely the unforeseen result of increased management of wild food resources. One correlate of the food-producing revolution was the development of permanent settlements, as people practiced simple horticulture using simple hand tools. One common form of horticulture is slash-and-burn, or swidden, farming. Intensive agriculture, a more complex activity, requires irrigation, fertilizers, and draft animals. Pastoralism is a means of subsistence that relies on raising herds of domesticated animals, such as cattle, sheep, and goats. Pastoralists are usually nomads, moving to different pastures as required for grass and water.

Cities developed as intensified agriculture techniques created a surplus, freeing individuals to specialize full-time in other activities. Social structure becomes increasingly stratified with the development of cities, and people are ranked according to gender, the work they do, and the family into which they are born. Social relationships grow more formal and centralized political institutions are formed.

One should not conclude that there is inevitability to the sequence from food foraging, through horticultural/pastoral, to intensive agricultural nonindustrial urban, and then industrial societies, even though these did appear in that order. Where older adaptations continue to prevail, it is because conditions are such that they continue to work so well and provide such satisfaction that the people who maintain them prefer them to the alternatives of which they are aware. It is not because of any "backwardness" or ignorance. Modern food forager, horticultural, pastoral, nonindustrial, and industrial urban societies are all highly evolved adaptations, each in its own particular way.

SUGGESTED READINGS

Bates, D. G., & Plog, F. (1991). *Human adaptive strategies*. New York: McGraw-Hill.

This book takes an ecological approach to understanding human cultural diversity. A chapter each is devoted to hunting and gathering, horticultural, pastoral, intensive agricultural, and industrial societies, with a final chapter devoted to change and development. Theoretical issues are made easy to grasp through use of readable ethnographic cases.

Lustig-Arecco, V. (1975). *Technology: Strategies for survival*. New York: Holt, Rinehart and Winston.

Although the early anthropologists devoted a good deal of attention to technology, the subject fell into neglect early in the twentieth century. This is one of the few recent studies of the subject. The author's particular interest is the technoeconomic adaptation of hunters, pastoralists, and farmers.

Oswalt, W. H. (1972). *Habitat and technology*. New York: Holt, Rinehart and Winston.

The author develops a taxonomy that permits precise cross-cultural comparisons of the complexity of manufactures. The research is based on a systematic analysis of the known manufactures of non-Western peoples. Shelters, tools, clothing, implements, and cultivated foodstuffs are considered.

Schrire, C. (Ed.). (1984). *Past and present in hunter gatherer studies*. Orlando: Academic Press.

This collection of papers demolishes many myths (including several held by anthropologists) about food-foraging societies. Especially recommended is the editor's introduction, "Wild Surmises on Savage Thoughts."

Vayda, A. (Ed.). (1969). *Environment and cultural behavior: Ecological studies in cultural anthropology*. Garden City, NY: Natural History Press.

The focus of the studies collected here is the interrelationship between cultural behavior and environmental phenomena. The writers attempt to make cultural behavior intelligible by relating it to the material world in which it develops. This volume includes articles concerning population, divination, ritual, warfare, food production, climate, and diseases.

CHAPTER
18

ECONOMIC SYSTEMS

THE FUNDAMENTAL CHARACTERISTIC OF THE MARKET IN NON-WESTERN
SOCIETIES IS THAT IT ALWAYS MEANS A LITERAL MARKET *PLACE*,
WHERE ACTUAL GOODS ARE EXCHANGED. AT THIS MARKET IN
GUATEMALA CITY, PEOPLE EXCHANGE ITEMS THEY HAVE PRODUCED
FOR THINGS THEY NEED BUT CAN GET ONLY FROM OTHERS.

CHAPTER PREVIEW

How Do Anthropologists Study Economic Systems?

Anthropologists study the means by which goods are produced, distributed, and consumed in the context of the total culture of particular societies. Although they have borrowed theories and concepts from economists, most anthropologists believe that principles derived from the study of Western market economies have limited applicability to economic systems where people do not produce and exchange goods for profit.

How Do the Economies of Nonindustrial Peoples Work?

In non-Western, nonindustrial societies there is always a division of labor by age and sex, with some additional craft specialization. Land and other valuable resources are usually controlled by groups of relatives, such as bands or lineages, and individual ownership is rare. Production takes place in the quantity and at the time required, and most goods are consumed by the group that produces them. Leveling mechanisms ensure that no one accumulates significantly more goods than anyone else.

How and Why Are Goods Exchanged in Nonindustrial Societies?

Nonindustrial peoples exchange goods through the processes of reciprocity, redistribution, and market exchange. Reciprocity involves the exchange of goods and services of roughly equivalent value, and it is often undertaken for ritual purposes or in order to gain prestige. Redistribution requires some sort of government and/or religious elite to collect and then reallocate resources, in the form of either goods or services. Market exchange, which in nonindustrial societies means going to a specific place for direct exchange of goods, also serves as entertainment and as a means of exchanging important information. The latter are frequently primary motivating forces bringing people into the marketplace.

An economic system may be defined as one by which goods are produced, distributed, and consumed. Since a people, in pursuing a particular means of subsistence, necessarily produces, distributes, and consumes things, it is obvious that our earlier discussion of patterns of subsistence (Chapter 17) involved us with economic matters. Now we will look at aspects of economic systems—specifically systems of production, exchange, and redistribution—that require more discussion.

ECONOMIC ANTHROPOLOGY

It is perhaps in the study of the economies of non-literate peoples that we are most apt to fall prey to interpreting anthropological data in terms of our own technologies, our own values of work and property, and our own determination of what is rational. Take, for example, the following statement from a respected textbook in economics: "In all societies, the prevailing reality of life has been the inadequacy of output to fill the wants and needs of the people."[1] What this ethnocentric assertion fails to realize is that in many societies people's wants are maintained at levels that can be fully and continuously satisfied without jeopardizing the environment. In such societies, things are produced in the quantity and at the time required, and to do more than this makes no sense at all. No matter how hard people may work when hard work is called for, at other times they will have available hours, days, or even weeks on end to devote to "unproductive" (in the economic sense) activities. To Western observers, such people are apt to appear lazy (Fig. 18.1); "instead of disciplined workers, they are reluctant and untrained laborers."[2] If the people are hunters and gatherers, even the hard work is likely to be misinterpreted. In Western culture hunting is defined as a "sport"; hence, the men in food-foraging societies are often perceived as spending virtually all of their time in "recreational pursuits," while the women are seen as working themselves to the bone.

[1]Heilbroner, R. L., & Thurow, L. C. (1981). *The economic problem* (6th ed.) (p. 327). Englewood Cliffs, NJ: Prentice-Hall.
[2]Heilbroner, R. L., & Thurow, L. C. (1981). *The economic problem* (6th ed.) (p. 609). Englewood Cliffs, NJ: Prentice-Hall.

```
The Chief Registrar of Natives,              N.A.D. Form No 54/_____
NAIROBI.

        COMPLAINT OF DESERTION OF REGISTERED NATIVE.

Native's Certificate No. _____   Name _____
The above native deserted from my employ _____
                                                   (date)

He was engaged on _____ on _____ days verbal contract
                      (date)              _____ months written contract

at _____
                      (place)                (Contract No.)

      I wish to prosecute him for this offence and hereby agree to appear as
a witness or to produce evidence if and when called upon.

                                   _____
                                        Signature of Employer

Address _____
        _____
Date    _____
```

Figure 18.1   People with industrial economies frequently misunderstand the work ethic in so-called "tribal" societies. Thus the British, in colonial Kenya, thought it necessary to teach natives "the dignity of labor," and made it a crime for a tribal person to quit work without authorization.

Consider yam production among the Trobriand Islanders, who inhabit a group of coral atolls that lie north of New Guinea's eastern end.[3] Trobriand men spend a great deal of their time and energy raising yams, not for themselves or their own households, but to give others, normally their sisters and married daughters. The purpose of this yam production is not to provision the households of those to whom they are given, as most of what people eat they grow for themselves in gardens in which they plant taro, sweet potatoes, tapioca, greens, beans, and squash, as well as breadfruit and banana trees. The reason for a man to give yams to a woman is to show his support for her husband and to enhance his own influence. Once received by the woman, they are loaded into her husband's yam house, symbolizing his worth as a man of power and influence in his community. Some of these yams he may use to purchase a variety of things, including armshells, shell necklaces and earrings, betel nuts, pigs, chickens, locally produced goods such as wooden bowls, combs, floor mats, lime pots, or even magic spells. Some he must use to discharge obligations, as in the presentation of yams to the relatives of his daughter's husband when she marries, or the payments that must be made following the death of a member of his lineage (an organized group of relatives descended, in this case through women, from a common ancestor). Finally, any man who aspires to high status and power is expected to show his worth by organizing a yam competition, in the course of which huge quantities of yams are given away to invited guests. As anthropologist Annette Weiner explains: "A yam house, then, is like a bank account; when full, a man is wealthy and powerful. Until yams are cooked or they rot, they may circulate as limited currency. That is why, once harvested, the usage of yams for daily food is avoided as much as possible."[4]

By giving yams to his sister or daughter, a man not only expresses his confidence in the woman's husband, he also makes the latter indebted to him. Although the recipient rewards the gardener and his helpers by throwing a feast, at which they are fed cooked yams, taro and—what everyone especially

Trobriand Island men devote a great deal of time and energy to raising yams, not for themselves, but to give to others. These yams, which have been raised by men related through marriage to a chief, are about to be loaded into the chief's yam house.

To understand how the schedule of wants or demands of a given society is balanced against the supply of goods and services available, it is necessary to introduce a noneconomic variable—the anthropological variable of culture. In any given economic system, economic processes cannot be interpreted without culturally defining the demands and understanding the conventions that dictate how and when they are satisfied. The fact is, the economic sphere of behavior is *not* separate from the social, religious, and political spheres, free to follow its own purely economic logic. To be sure, economic behavior and institutions can be analyzed in purely economic terms, but to do so is to ignore crucial noneconomic considerations.

[3]Weiner, A. B. (1988). *The Trobrianders of Papua New Guinea.* New York: Holt, Rinehart and Winston.

[4]Weiner, A. B. (1988). *The Trobrianders of Papua New Guinea* (p. 86). New York: Holt, Rinehart and Winston.

looks forward to—ample pieces of pork, this in no way pays off the debt. Nor does the gift of a stone axe blade (another valuable in the Trobriand system), which may reward an especially good harvest. The debt can be repaid only in women's wealth, which consists of bundles of banana leaves and skirts made of the same material which have been dyed red. Although the bundles are of no utilitarian value, extensive labor is invested in their production, and large quantities of them, along with skirts, are regarded as essential in paying off all the members of other lineages who were close to a recently deceased relative in life and who assisted with the funeral. At the same time, the wealth and vitality of the dead person's lineage is measured by the quality and quantity of the bundles and skirts so distributed. Because a man has received yams from his wife's brother, he is obligated to provide her with yams with which she can purchase the necessary bundles and skirts, over and above those she herself has produced, in order to help with payments following the death of a member of her lineage. Because deaths are unpredictable, and can occur at any time, a man must have yams available for his wife when she needs them. This, and the fact that she may require all of his yams, acts as an effective check on a man's wealth.

Like people the world over, the Trobriand Islanders assign meanings to objects that make them worth far more than their cost in labor or the materials of which they are made. Yams, for example, establish long-term relationships that lead to other advantages, such as access to land, protection, assistance, and other kinds of wealth. Thus, yam exchanges are as much social and political as they are economic transactions. Banana leaf bundles and skirts are symbolic of the political state of lineages and of their immortality. In their distribution, which is related to rituals associated with death, we see how men in Trobriand society are ultimately dependent on women and their valuables. So important are these matters to the Trobrianders that even in the face of Western money, education, religion, and law, these people remain as committed today as in the past to yam cultivation and the production of women's wealth. Looked at in terms of Western economics, this appears to make little sense, but looked at in terms of Trobriand values and concerns, it makes a great deal of sense.

RESOURCES

In every society there are customs and rules governing the kinds of work that are done, who does the work, who controls the resources and tools, and how the work is accomplished. Raw materials, labor, and technology are the productive resources that a social group may use to produce desired goods and services. The rules surrounding the use of these are embedded in the culture and determine the way the economy operates.

Patterns of Labor

In every human society, there has always been a division of labor by both sex and age categories; such division is an elaboration of patterns found among all higher primates. What the former does is to increase the chances that the learning of necessary skills will be more efficient, since only half the adult repertoire needs to be learned by any one individual. The latter provides sufficient time for those skills to be developed.

Sexual Division of Labor

The sexual division of labor in human societies of all sorts has been studied extensively by anthropologists, and we discussed some aspects of it in the preceding chapter, as well as in Chapter 7. Whether men or women do a particular job varies from group to group, but much work has been set apart as the work of either one sex or the other. For example, we have seen that the tasks most often regarded as "women's work" tend to be those that can be carried out near home and that are easily resumed after interruption. The tasks most often regarded as "men's work" tend to be those that require physical strength, rapid mobilization of high bursts of energy, frequent travel at some distance from home, and assumption of high levels of risk and danger. There are, however, plenty of exceptions, as in those societies where women regularly carry burdensome loads or put in long hours of hard work cultivating crops in the fields. In some societies, women perform almost three-quarters of all work, and there are even societies where women serve as warriors. In the nineteenth-century

Often, work that is considered inappropriate for men (or for women) in one society is performed by them in another. Here a Chinese man sews and Guajiro women carry heavy loads.

kingdom of Dahomey, in West Africa, thousands served in the armed forces of the Dahomean king and, in the eyes of some observers, were better fighters than their male counterparts. There are also references to women warriors in ancient Ireland, archaeological evidence exists of their presence among the Vikings, and among the Abkhasians of Georgia, women were trained in weaponry until quite recently. Clearly, the sexual division of labor cannot be explained simply as a consequence of male strength, expendability, or female reproductive biology.

Instead of looking for biological imperatives to explain the sexual division of labor, a more productive strategy is to examine the kinds of work done by men and women in the context of specific societies, to see how it relates to other cultural and historical factors. What we find are three different configurations, one featuring flexibility and sexual integration, another rigid segregation by sex, and a third featuring elements of the other two.[5] The flexible/integrated pattern is exemplified by people like the Ju/'hoansi (whose practices we examined in Chapters 16 and 17), and is seen most often among food foragers and subsistence farmers.

In such societies, up to 35 percent of activities are performed by both sexes with approximately equal participation, while those tasks deemed appropriate for one sex may be performed by the other, without loss of face, as the situation warrants. Where these practices prevail, boys and girls grow up in much the same way, learn to value cooperation over competition, and become equally habituated to adult men and women, who interact with one another on a relatively equal basis.

Sexually segregated societies are those in which almost all work is rigidly defined as either masculine or feminine, so that men and women rarely engage in joint efforts of any kind. In such societies, it is inconceivable that someone would even think of doing something considered to be the work of the opposite sex. This pattern is frequently seen in pastoral nomadic, intensive agricultural, and industrial societies, in which men's work keeps them outside the home for much of the time. Thus, boys and girls alike are raised primarily by women, who encourage compliance in their charges. At some point, however, boys must undergo a role reversal to become like men who are supposed to be tough, aggressive, and competitive, and to do this, they must prove their masculinity in ways that women do not have to prove their feminine identity. Commonly, this involves assertions of male superiority, and hence authority, over

[5]Sanday, P. R. (1981). *Female power and male dominance: On the origins of sexual inequality* (pp. 79–80). Cambridge: Cambridge University Press.

In nonindustrial societies, households produce much of what they consume. Among the Maya, men work in the fields to produce food for the household; women prepare the food and take care of other chores that can be performed in or near the house.

women. Historically, sexually segregated societies have often imposed their control on those featuring sexual integration, upsetting the egalitarian nature of the latter.

In the third, or dual-sex configuration, men and women carry out their work separately, as in sexually segregated societies, but the relationship between them is one of balanced complementarity, rather than inequality. Although competition is a prevailing ethic, each sex manages its own affairs, and the interests of both men and women are represented at all levels. Thus, as in sexually integrated societies, neither sex exerts dominance over the other. The dual-sex orientation may be seen among certain Native American peoples whose economies were based upon subsistence farming, as well as among several West African kingdoms, including that of the aforementioned Dahomeans.

Age Division of Labor

A division of labor according to age is also typical of human societies. Among the Ju/'hoansi, for example, children are not expected to contribute significantly to subsistence until they reach their late teens. Their equivalent of "retirement" comes somewhere around the age of 60. Elderly people, while they will usually do some foraging for themselves, are not expected to contribute much food. On the other hand, older men and women alike play an essential role in spiritual matters; being freed from food taboos and other restrictions that apply to younger adults, they may handle ritual substances considered dangerous to those still involved with hunting or having children. By virtue of their old age, they also remember things that happened far in the past. They are repositories of accumulated wisdom—the "libraries" of a nonliterate people—and are able to suggest solutions to problems that younger adults have never before faced. Thus, they are far from being unproductive members of society.

In many nonindustrial societies, not just older people but children as well may make a greater contribution to the economy in terms of work and responsibility than is common in modern North America. For instance, in Maya communities in southern Mexico and Guatemala, young children not only look after their younger brothers and sisters but also help with housework as well. Girls begin to make a substantial contribution to the work of the household by the age of 7 or 8, and by the

Iqbal Masih, the Pakistani youth who raised the world's consciousness over the abuse of child labor, was murdered in 1994. Even in Western countries, child labor plays a major economic role.

time they are 11, are constantly busy grinding corn, making tortillas, fetching wood and water, sweeping the house, and so forth. Boys have less to do, but are given small tasks, such as bringing in the chickens or playing with a baby; by the time they are 12, however, they are carrying toasted tortillas to the men out working in the fields and returning with loads of corn.[6]

Similar situations are not unknown in industrial societies. In Naples, Italy, children play a significant role in the economy. At a very young age, girls begin to take on responsibilities for housework, freeing the labor of their mothers and older sisters who can then earn money for the household. Nor is it long before they are apprenticed out to neighbors and kin, from whom they learn

the skills that enable them, by age 14, to enter a small factory or workshop. The wages earned are typically turned over to a girl's mother. Boys, too, are apprenticed out at an early age, though they may achieve more freedom from adult control by becoming involved in various street activities that are not available to girls.[7]

Cooperation

Cooperative work groups can be found everywhere in nonliterate as well as literate and in nonindustrial as well as industrial societies. Often, if the effort involves the whole community, there is a festive spirit to the work. Jomo Kenyatta, the anthropologist who became a respected statesman and "father" of an independent Kenya, described the time of enjoyment after a day's labor in his country:

> If a stranger happens to pass by, he will have no idea that these people who are singing and dancing have completed their day's work. This is why most Europeans have erred by not realizing that the African in his own environment does not count hours or work by the movement of the clock, but works with good spirit and enthusiasm to complete the tasks before him.[8]

Among the Ju/'hoansi, women go out to gather wild plant foods about three times a week. Although they may go out alone, they more often go out in groups, talking loudly as they go. This not only turns what might otherwise seem a monotonous task into a social occasion, it also causes large animals—potential sources of danger—to move elsewhere.

In most human societies, the basic unit within which cooperation takes place is the household. It is a unit of production and consumption at one and the same time; only in industrial societies have these two things been separated. The Maya farmer, for example, unlike his North American counterpart, but like peasant and subsistence farmers everywhere, is not so much running a commercial

[6]Vogt, E. Z. (1990). *The Zinacantecos of Mexico, a modern Maya way of life* (2nd ed.) (pp. 83–87). Fort Worth: Holt, Rinehart and Winston.

[7]Goddard, V. (1993). Child labor in Naples. In W. A. Haviland & R. J. Gordon (Eds.), *Talking about people* (pp. 105–109). Mountain View, CA: Mayfield.

[8]Herskovits, M. (1952). *Economic anthropology: A study in comparative economics* (2nd ed.) (p. 103). New York: Knopf.

In industrial societies, people do not have unrestricted access to the means of production, nor do they generally produce directly for their own consumption. Instead, they work for strangers, often at monotonous tasks done in a depersonalized setting. Such conditions contribute to alienation, a major problem in industrial societies.

enterprise as he is a household. He is motivated by a desire to provide for the welfare of his own family; each family, as an economic unit, works as a group for its own good. Cooperative work may be undertaken outside of the household, however, for other reasons, though not always voluntarily. It may be part of fulfilling duties to in-laws, or it may be performed for political officials or priests, by command. Thus, institutions of family, kinship, religion, and the state all may act as organizing elements that define the nature and condition of each worker's cooperative obligations.

Craft Specialization

In nonindustrial societies, where division of labor occurs along lines of age and sex, each person in the society has knowledge and competence in all aspects of work appropriate to his or her age and sex. In modern industrial societies, by contrast, there exists a greater diversity of more specialized tasks to be performed, and no individual can even begin to have knowledge of all those appropriate for his or her age and sex. Yet even in nonindustrial societies, there is some specialization of craft. This is often minimal in food-foraging societies,

but even here the arrow points of one man may be in some demand because of his particular skill at making them. Among people who produce their own food, there is apt to be more in the way of specialization. In the Trobriand Islands, for example, if one wanted stone to make axe blades, one had to travel some distance to a particular island where the appropriate kind of stone was quarried; clay pots, on the other hand, were made by people living on yet another island.

An example of specialization can be seen among the Afar people of Ethiopia's Danakil depression. Afar men are miners of salt, which since ancient times has been widely traded in East Africa. It is mined from the crust of an extensive salt plain in the north part of the depression, and to get it is a risky and difficult business. L. M. Nesbitt, the first European to traverse successfully the depression, labeled it "the hell-hole of creation."[9] The heat is extreme during the day, with shade temperatures between 140° and 156° F not unusual. Shade is not to be found on the salt plain, however, unless a shelter of salt blocks is built. Nor is there food or water for man or beast. To add to the

[9]Nesbitt, L. M. (1935). *Hell-hole of creation*. New York: Knopf.

difficulty, until recently the Muslim Afars and the Christian Tegreans, highlanders who also mine salt, were mortal enemies.

Successful mining, then, requires skill at planning and organization, as well as physical strength and the will to work under the most trying conditions.[10] Pack animals to carry the salt have to be fed in advance, for to carry sufficient fodder for them interferes with their ability to carry out salt. Food and water must be carried for the miners, who usually number 30 to 40 per group. Travel is planned to take place at night to avoid the intense heat of day. In the past, measures to protect against attack had to be taken. Finally, timing is critical; a party has to get back to sources of food and water before their own supplies are too long exhausted and before their animals are unable to continue farther.

Control of Land

All societies have regulations that determine the way valuable land resources will be allocated. Food foragers must determine who can hunt game and gather plants and where these activities take place. Horticulturists must decide how their farmland is to be acquired, worked, and passed on. Pastoralists require a system that determines rights to watering places and grazing land, as well as the right of access to land over which they move their herds. Full-time or intensive agriculturalists must have some means of determining title to land and access to water supplies for irrigation purposes. In industrialized Western societies, a system of private ownership of land and rights to natural resources generally prevails. Although elaborate laws have been established to regulate the buying, owning, and selling of land and water resources, if individuals wish to reallocate valuable farmland, for instance, for another purpose, they are generally able to do so.

In nonindustrial societies, land is often controlled by kinship groups such as the lineage (discussed in Chapter 21) or band, rather than by individuals. For example, among the Ju/'hoansi, each band of anywhere from 10 to 30 people lives on

roughly 250 square miles of land, which they consider to be their territory—their own country. These territories are defined not in terms of boundaries, but rather in terms of waterholes that are located within them. The land is said to be "owned" by those who have lived the longest in the band, usually a group of brothers and sisters or cousins. Their ownership, however, is more symbolic than real. They cannot sell (or buy) land, but their permission must be asked by outsiders to enter the territory. To refuse such permission, though, would be unthinkable.

The practice of defining territories on the basis of core features, be they waterholes (as among the Ju/'hoansi), distinctive features of the landscape where ancestral spirits are thought to dwell (as among Australian aborigines), watercourses (as among Indians of the northeastern United States), or whatever, is typical of food foragers. Territorial boundaries are left vaguely defined. The adaptive value of this is clear; the size of band territories, as well as the size of the bands themselves, can adjust to keep in balance with availability of resources in any given place. Such adjustment would be more difficult under a system of individual ownership of clearly bounded land.

Among some west African farmers, a feudal system of land ownership prevails, by which all land belongs to the head chief. He allocates it to various subchiefs, who in turn distribute it to lineages; lineage leaders then assign individual plots to each farmer. Just as in medieval Europe, these African people owe allegiance to the subchiefs (or nobles) and the principal chief (or king). The people who work the land must pay taxes and fight for the king when necessary. The people, in a sense, "own" the land and transmit their ownership to their heirs. No one, however, can give away, sell, or otherwise dispose of a plot of land without approval from the elder of the lineage. When an individual no longer needs the land that has been allocated, the lineage head rescinds title to it and reallocates it to someone else in the lineage. The important operative principle here is that the system extends the right of the individual to use land for a certain period of time, but the land is not "owned" outright. This serves to maintain the integrity of valuable farmland as such, preventing its loss through subdivision and conversion to other uses.

[10]Mesghinua, H. M. (1966). Salt mining in Enderta. *Journal of Ethiopian Studies, 4*(2); O'Mahoney, K. (1970). The salt trade. *Journal of Ethiopian Studies, 8*(2).

Among the Ju/'hoansi, game "belongs" to the man whose arrow killed it. But because arrows are freely loaned or given, the man who "owns" the kill may not even have been present on the hunt.

Technology

All societies have some means of creating and allocating the tools and other artifacts used in the production of goods and passed on to succeeding generations. The number and kinds of tools a society uses—which, together with knowledge about how to make and use them constitute its **technology**—are related to the lifestyles of its members. Food foragers and pastoral nomads, who are frequently on the move, are apt to have fewer and simpler tools than the more sedentary farmer, in part because a great number of complex tools would decrease their mobility.

Food foragers make and use a variety of tools, many of which are ingenious in their effectiveness. Some of these they make for their own individual use, but codes of generosity are such that a person may not refuse giving or loaning what is requested. Thus, tools may be given or loaned to others in exchange for the products resulting from their use.

Technology: Tools and other material equipment, together with the knowledge of how to make and use them.

For example, a Ju/'hoansi who gives his arrow to another hunter has a right to a share in any animals that the hunter may kill. Game is considered to "belong" to the man whose arrow killed it.

Among horticulturists, the axe, machete, and digging stick or hoe are the primary tools. Since these are relatively easy to produce, every person can make them. Although the maker has first rights to their use, when that person is not using them, any member of the family may ask to use them and usually is granted permission to do so. To refuse would cause the tool owner to be treated with scorn for this singular lack of concern for others. If another relative helps raise the crop that is traded for a particular tool, that relative becomes part owner of the implement, and it may not be traded or given away without his or her permission.

In sedentary communities, which farming makes possible, tools and other productive goods become more complex and more difficult and costlier to make. Where this happens, individual ownership in them usually becomes more absolute, as do the conditions under which persons may borrow and use such equipment. It is easy to replace a knife lost by a relative during palm cultivation, but much more difficult to replace an iron plow or a power-driven threshing machine. Rights to the ownership of complex tools are more rigidly applied;

generally the person who has supplied the funds for the purchase of a complex piece of machinery is considered the sole owner and may decide how and by whom it will be used.

Leveling Mechanisms

In spite of the increased opportunities that exist in sedentary farming communities for people to accumulate belongings, limits on property acquisition may be as prominent in them as among nomadic peoples. In such communities, social obligations compel people to divest themselves of wealth, and no one is permitted to accumulate too much more than others. Greater wealth simply brings greater obligation to give. Anthropologists refer to such obligations as **leveling mechanisms**.

Leveling mechanisms are found in communities where property must not be allowed to threaten a more or less egalitarian social order, as in many Maya villages and towns in the highlands of Mexico and Guatemala. In these communities, cargo systems function to siphon off any excess wealth that people may accumulate. A cargo system is a civil-religious hierarchy, which, on a revolving basis, combines most of the civic and ceremonial offices of a community. All offices are open to all men, and eventually virtually every man has at least one term in office, each term lasting for one year. The scale is pyramidal, which is to say that more offices exist at the lower levels with progressively fewer at the top. For example, in a community of about 8,000 people, there may be four levels of offices with 32 on the lowest level, 12 on the next one up, 6 on the next, and 2 at the top. Offices at the lower level include those for the performance of various menial chores, such as sweeping and carrying messages. The higher offices are those of councilmen, judges, mayors, and ceremonial positions. These positions are regarded as burdens, for which one receives no pay. Instead,

Leveling mechanism: A societal obligation compelling a family to distribute goods so that no one accumulates more wealth than anyone else.

the officeholder is expected to pay for the food, liquor, music, fireworks, or whatever is required for community festivals or for banquets associated with the transmission of office. For some cargos, the cost is as much as a man can earn in four years. After holding a cargo position, a man usually returns to normal life for a period of time, during which he may accumulate sufficient resources to campaign for a higher office. Each male citizen of the community is socially obligated to serve in the system at least once, and social pressure drives individuals who have once again accumulated excess wealth to apply for higher offices in order to raise their social status. Ideally, while some individuals gain appreciably more prestige than others in their community, no one has appreciably more wealth in a material sense than anyone else. In actuality, the ideal is not always achieved, in which case service in the cargo system functions to legitimize wealth differences, thereby preventing disruptive envy.

In addition to equalizing (or legitimizing) wealth, the cargo system accomplishes other things as well. Through its system of offices, it ensures that necessary services within the community are performed. It also keeps goods in circulation, rather than remaining idle. Members are also pressured into investing their resources in their own community, rather than elsewhere. At the same time, the costs of office require participants to produce and sell a surplus or seek work outside the community in order to secure sufficient funds, thereby benefitting outside interests. To the degree that outsiders are able to control the goods and wages required by cargo holders, the basic function of the system may be subverted to serve as a means by which wealth and labor may be drawn *out* of the community.

DISTRIBUTION AND EXCHANGE

In the money economy of industrial societies, there is a two-step process between labor and consumption. The money received for labor must be translated into something else before it is directly consumable. In societies with no such medium of exchange, the rewards for labor are usually direct. The workers in a family group consume what they harvest; they eat what the hunter or gatherer brings

Ju/'hoansi cutting up meat, which will be shared by others in the camp. The food distribution practices of such food foragers constitute an example of generalized reciprocity.

home; they use the tools that they themselves make. But even where there is no formal medium of exchange, some distribution of goods takes place. Karl Polanyi, an economist, classified the cultural systems of distributing material goods into three modes: reciprocity, redistribution, and market exchange.[11]

Reciprocity

Reciprocity refers to a transaction between two parties, whereby goods and services of roughly equivalent value are exchanged. This may involve gift giving, but in non-Western societies, pure altruism in gift giving is as rare as it is in the United

---

Reciprocity: The exchange of goods and services, of approximately equal value, between two parties.

---

[11]Polanyi, K. (1968). The economy as instituted process. In E. E. LeClair, Jr., & H. K. Schneider (Eds.), *Economic anthropology: Readings in theory and analysis* (pp. 127–138). New York: Holt, Rinehart and Winston.

States or any other Western society. The overriding motive is to fulfill social obligations and perhaps gain a bit of prestige in the process. It might be best compared in North American society to someone who gives a party. He or she may go to great lengths to impress others by the excellence of the food and drink served, not to mention the quality of wit and conversation of those in attendance. The expectation is that, sooner or later, he or she will be invited to similar parties by some, although perhaps not all, of the guests.

Social customs dictate the nature and occasion of exchange. When an animal is killed by a group of hunters in Australia, the meat is divided among the families of the hunters and other relatives. Each person in the camp gets a share, the size depending on the nature of the person's kinship tie to the hunters. The least desirable parts may be kept by the hunters themselves. When a kangaroo is killed, for example, the left hind leg goes to the brother of the hunter, the tail to his father's brother's son, the loins and the fat to his father-in-law, the ribs to his mother-in-law, the forelegs to his father's younger sister, the head to his wife, and the entrails and the blood to the hunter. If there were arguments over the apportionment, it would be because the principles of distribution were not being followed properly. The hunter and his family would seem to fare badly according to this arrangement, but they have their turn when another man makes a kill. The giving and receiving is obligatory, as is the particularity of the distribution. Such sharing of food reinforces community bonds and ensures that everyone eats. It might also be viewed as a way of saving perishable goods. By giving away part of his kill, the hunter gets a social IOU for a similar amount of food in the future. It is a little bit like putting money in a time-deposit savings account.

The food distribution practices just described for Australian hunters constitute an example of **generalized reciprocity**. This may be defined as exchange in which the value of what is given is not calculated, nor is the time of repayment specified. Gift giving, in the altruistic sense, also falls in this category. Most commonly, generalized reciprocity occurs among close kin or people who otherwise have very close ties with one another. Typically, participants will deny that the exchanges are economic, couching them explicitly in terms of kinship and friendship obligations.

Balanced reciprocity differs in that it is not part of a long-term process. The giving and receiving, as well as the time involved, are more specific; one has a direct obligation to reciprocate promptly in equal value in order for the social relationship to continue. Examples of balanced reciprocity in North American society would include such practices as trading baseball cards or buying drinks when one's turn comes at a gathering of friends or associates. Examples from a non-Western society include those related by anthropologist Robert Lowie in his classic account of the

---

Crow Indians.[12] A woman skilled in the tanning of buffalo hides might offer her services to a neighbor who needed a new cover for her tepee. It took an expert to design a tepee cover, which required from 14 to 20 skins. The designer might need as many as 20 collaborators, whom she instructed in the sewing together of the skins and whom the tepee owner might remunerate with a feast. The designer herself would be given some kind of property by the tepee owner. In another example from the Crow, Lowie relates that if a married woman brought her brother a present of food, he might reciprocate with a present of 10 arrows for her husband, which rated as the equivalent of a horse.

Giving, receiving, and sharing as so far described constitute a form of social security or insurance. A family contributes to others when they have the means and can count on receiving from others in time of need. A leveling mechanism is at work in the process of generalized or balanced reciprocity, promoting an egalitarian distribution of wealth over the long run.

Negative reciprocity is a third form of exchange, in which the giver tries to get the better of the deal. The parties involved have opposed interests, usually are members of different communities, and are not closely related. The ultimate form of negative reciprocity is to take something by force. Less extreme forms involve the use of guile and deception, or at the least hard bargaining. Among the Navajo, according to the anthropologist Clyde Kluckhohn, "to deceive when trading with foreign peoples is morally accepted."[13]

Barter and Trade

Exchange that takes place within a group of people generally takes the form of generalized or balanced reciprocity. When it takes place between two groups, there is apt to be at least a potential for hostility and competition. Therefore, such exchange may well be in the form of negative reciprocity, unless some sort of arrangement has been made to ensure at least an approach to balance. Barter is one form of negative reciprocity by which

---

Generalized reciprocity: A mode of exchange in which the value of the gift is not calculated, nor is the time of repayment specified.

Balanced reciprocity: A mode of exchange in which the giving and the receiving are specific as to the value of the goods and the time of their delivery.

Negative reciprocity: A form of exchange in which the giver tries to get the better of the exchange.

---

[12]Lowie, R. (1956). *Crow indians* (original ed. 1935) (p. 75). New York: Holt, Rinehart and Winston.

[13]Kluckhohn, C. Quoted in Sahlins, M. (1972). *Stone Age economics* (p. 200). Chicago: Aldine.

scarce items from one group are exchanged for desirable goods from another group. Relative value is calculated, and despite an outward show of indifference, sharp trading is more the rule, when compared to the more balanced nature of exchanges within a group.

An arrangement that combined elements of balanced reciprocity as well as barter existed between the Kota, in India, and three neighboring peoples who traded their surplus goods and certain services with the Kota. The Kota were the musicians and artisans for the region. They exchanged iron tools with the other three groups and provided the music essential for ceremonial occasions. The Toda furnished to the Kota ghee (a kind of butter) for certain ceremonies and buffalo for funerals; relations between the two peoples were amicable. The Badaga were agricultural and traded their grain for music and tools. Between the Kota and Badaga there was a feeling of great competition, which sometimes led to one-sided trading practices; it was usually the Kota who procured the advantage. The forest-dwelling Kurumba, who were renowned as sorcerers, had honey, canes, and occasionally fruits to offer, but their main contribution was protection against the supernatural. The Kota feared the Kurumba, and the Kurumba took advantage of this in their trade dealings, so that they always got more than they gave. Thus there was great latent hostility between these two peoples.

Silent trade is a specialized form of barter in which no verbal communication takes place. In fact, it may involve no actual face-to-face contact at all. Such cases have often characterized the dealings between food-foraging peoples and their food-producing neighbors, as the former have supplied over the past 2,000 or so years various commodities in demand in the world economy. A classic description of such trade is the following:

> The forest people creep through the lianas to the trading place, and leave a neat pile of jungle products, such as wax, cam-

phor, monkeys' gall bladders, birds' nests for Chinese soup. They creep back a certain distance, and wait in a safe place. The partners to the exchange, who are usually agriculturalists with a more elaborate and extensive set of material possessions but who cannot be bothered stumbling through the jungle after wax when they have someone else to do it for them, discover the little pile, and lay down beside it what they consider its equivalent in metal cutting tools, cheap cloth, bananas, and the like. They too discreetly retire. The shy folk then reappear, inspect the two piles, and if they are satisfied, take the second one away. Then the opposite group comes back and takes pile number one, and the exchange is completed. If the forest people are dissatisfied, they can retire once more, and if the other people want to increase their offering they may, time and again, until everyone is happy.[14]

The reasons for silent trade can only be postulated, but in some situations trade may be silent for lack of a common language. More often it may serve to control situations of distrust so as to keep relations peaceful. In a very real sense, good relations are maintained by preventing relations. Another possibility, which does not exclude the others, is that it makes exchange possible where problems of status might make verbal communication unthinkable. In any event, it provides for the exchange of goods between groups in spite of potential barriers.

The Kula Ring

Although we tend to think of trade as something undertaken for purely practical purposes, in order to gain access to necessary goods and services, not all trade is motivated by economic considerations. A classic case of this is the Kula ring (also referred to as the Kula), a Trobriand interisland trading system in which prestige items are ceremoniously exchanged. Bronislaw Malinowski first described the Kula in 1920, and it is still going strong today.[15]

Silent trade: A form of barter in which no verbal communication takes place.

[14]Coon, C. S. (1948). *A reader in general anthropology* (p. 594). New York: Holt, Rinehart and Winston.

[15]Weiner, A. B. (1988). *The Trobrianders of Papua New Guinea* (pp. 139–157). New York: Holt, Rinehart and Winston.

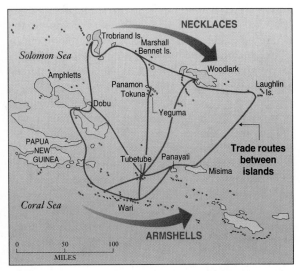

Figure 18.2 The ceremonial trading of necklaces and armshells in the Kula ring encourages trade throughout Melanesia.

The valuables consist of red shell necklaces, which always circulate in a clockwise direction, and ornate white armshells, which move in the opposite direction (Fig. 18.2). These objects are ranked according to their size, color, how finely polished they are, and their particular histories. Such is the fame of some that, when they appear in a village, they create a sensation. No one man holds these valuables for very long, at most perhaps 10 years. To hold on to an armshell or necklace too long risks disrupting the "path" that it must follow, as it is passed from one partner to another.

Although men on Kula voyages may use the opportunity to trade for other things, this is not the reason for such voyages, nor is the Kula necessary for trade to take place. In fact, overseas trade is regularly undertaken without the exchange of shell valuables. Instead, Trobriand men seek to create history through their Kula exchanges. By circulating armshells and necklaces that accumulate the histories of their travels and names of those who have possessed them, men proclaim their individual fame and talent, gaining considerable influence for themselves in the process. Although the idea is to match the size and value of one shell for another, men draw on all their negotiating skills, material resources, and magical expertise to gain access to the strongest partners and most valuable shells; thus, an element of negative reciprocity

These photos show Kula valuables and a canoe used for Kula voyages.

From their coral atolls, men periodically set sail in their canoes in order to exchange shell valuables with their Kula partners, who live on far distant islands. These voyages take men away from their homes for weeks, even months, at a time, and may expose them to various hardships along the way.

enters in as a man may divert shells from their proper "paths" or entice others to compete for whatever necklaces and armshells he may have to offer. But ultimately success is limited, for while a man may keep a shell for 5 or 10 years, sooner or later it must be passed on to others.

The Kula is an elaborate complex of ceremony, political relationships, economic exchange, travel, magic, and social integration. To see it only in its economic aspects is to misunderstand it completely. The Kula demonstrates once more how inseparable economic matters are from the rest of culture, and shows that economics is not a realm unto itself. This is just as true in modern industrial societies as it is in Trobriand society; when the United States stopped trading with Cuba, Haiti, and Serbia, for instance, it was for political rather than economic reasons. Indeed, economic embargoes are becoming increasingly popular as a political weapon wielded by both governments and special interest groups. On a less political note, we may also recognize that retail activity in the United States peaks in December, for a combination of religious and social, rather than purely economic, reasons.

In the United States, the progressive income tax acts to redistribute wealth from more wealthy to less wealthy people. Some, like House Republican leader Dick Armey of Texas, object to this and argue for a flat tax. Yet, by favoring accumulation of wealth by the already wealthy, this, too, would act as an agent of redistribution, as taxes invariably do.

Redistribution

In societies where there is a sufficient surplus to support some sort of government, income will flow into the public coffers in the form of gifts, taxes, and the spoils of war; then it will be distributed again. The chief, king, or whoever the agent of redistribution may be has three motives in disposing of this income: The first is to maintain a position of superiority by a display of wealth; the second is to assure those who support the agent an adequate standard of living; and the third is to establish alliances outside of the agent's territory.

The administration of the Inca empire in Peru was one of the most efficient the world has ever known, both in the collection of taxes and methods of control.[16] A census was kept of the population and resources. Tributes in goods and, more important, in services were levied. Each craft specialist had to produce a specific quota of goods from materials supplied by overseers. Forced labor

might be used for agricultural work or work in the mines. Forced labor was also employed in a program of public works, which included a remarkable system of roads and bridges throughout the mountainous terrain, aqueducts that guaranteed a supply of water, and storehouses that held surplus food for use in times of famine. Careful accounts were kept of income and expenditures. A governmental bureaucracy had the responsibility for seeing that production was maintained and that commodities were distributed according to the regulations set forth by the ruling powers.

Through the activities of the government, **redistribution** took place. The ruling class lived in

Redistribution: A form of exchange in which goods flow into a central place, where they are sorted, counted, and reallocated.

[16]Mason, J. A. (1957). *The ancient civilizations of Peru*. Baltimore, MD: Penguin.

The giving of gifts at a potlatch on the Northwest Coast of North America. Among these Native Americans, one gains prestige by giving away valuables at the potlatch.

great luxury, but goods were redistributed to the common people when necessary. Redistribution is a pattern of distribution by which the exchange is not between individuals or between groups, but, rather, by which a proportion of the products of labor is funneled into one source and is parceled out again as directed by a central administration. Commonly, it involves an element of coercion. Taxes are a form of redistribution in the United States; people pay taxes to the government, some of which support the government itself, while the rest is redistributed either in the form of cash, as in the case of welfare payments and government loans or subsidies to business, or in the form of services, as in the case of food and drug inspection, construction of highways, support of the military, and the like. With the growth of the federal deficit since 1980, more and more wealth in the United States is increasingly being redistributed from middle-income taxpayers to wealthy holders of government securities. For a process of redistribution to be possible, a society must have a centralized system of political organization, as well as an economic surplus over and above people's immediate needs.

Distribution of Wealth

In societies in which people devote most of their time to subsistence activities, gradations of wealth are small, kept that way through leveling mechanisms and systems of reciprocity, that serve to distribute in a fairly equitable fashion what little wealth exists.

Display for social prestige, what economist Thorstein Veblen called **conspicuous consumption,** is a strong motivating force for the distribution of wealth in societies where some substantial surplus is produced. It has, of course, long been recognized that conspicuous consumption plays a prominent role in Western societies, as individuals compete with one another for prestige. Indeed, many North Americans spend much of their lives

Conspicuous consumption: A term coined by Thorstein Veblen to describe the display of wealth for social prestige.

trying to impress others, requiring the display of items symbolic of prestigious positions in life. The ultimate in prestigious statuses is that of someone who doesn't have to work for a living, and here lies the irony: People may work long and hard in order to acquire the things that will make it appear as if they belong to a nonworking class of society. This all fits very nicely into an economy based on consumer wants:

> In an expanding economy based on consumer wants, every effort must be made to place the standard of living in the center of public and private consideration, and every effort must therefore be lent to remove material and psychological impediments to consumption. Hence, rather than feelings of restraint, feelings of letting-go must be in the ascendant, and the institutions support-

ing restraint must recede into the background and give way to their opposite.[17]

A form of conspicuous consumption may occur in nonindustrial societies, as illustrated by the lavish feasts given by Big Men in many societies of Papua New Guinea. In the course of these feasts, food and various other items of wealth, laboriously accumulated over several preceding months, are all given away to others. To Western observers, such grandiose displays are apt to be seen as extremely wasteful, but to the people involved, these giveaways accomplish important social and political goals, as the following analysis demonstrates.

[17]Henry, J. (1974). A theory for an anthropological analysis of American culture. In J. G. Jorgensen & M. Truzzi (Eds.), *Anthropology and American life* (p. 14). Englewood Cliffs, NJ: Prentice-Hall.

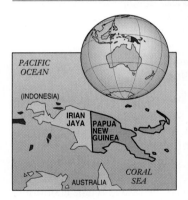

Original Study
Prestige Economics in Papua New Guinea[18]

The average Enga patrilineage group [people who trace their descent back through men to a particular male ancestor] numbers about 33 and . . . [constitutes a] . . . close knit extended family . . . . At the next level, however, is the Enga subclan, a [larger-order patrilineal descent] group numbering about 90 members that owns a sacred dance ground and a sacred grove of trees. Members of a subclan are required to pool wealth for bride payments whenever any of their members marries and in support of one of their members who is striving to become a Big Man. A subclan is in competition with other subclans for prestige, which affects its members' ability to obtain wives and their desirability as partners in regional alliances. An individual householder is motivated to contribute to his subclan's political and economic activities, therefore, because his immediate family's self-interest is intimately bound with that of the subclan.

The Enga subclan is a unit approximately the size of the largest corporate kin groups in societies occupying the less densely populated highland fringe of New Guinea, such as the Tsembaga [see Chapter 17]. But the Enga are organized into a still higher level grouping [also based on patrilineal descent], the clan, which averages about 350 members and is the ultimate owner and defender of the territory of the clan, from which all clan members ultimately derive their subsistence. Clans own carefully defined territories and defend them both in battle and on ceremonial occasions. They are led by Big Men who speak for their clans in interclan relations and who work within their clans to mobilize the separate households for military, political, and ceremonial action.

Like the subclan, the clan is an arena for dramatic public activities. The clan owns a main dance ground and an ancestral cult house. At these ceremonial centers, public gatherings take place that emphasize the unity of the group as against other clans. Sackschewsky . . . sees this as an essential tactic to overcome the fierce independence of Enga households, where "each man makes his own decisions." Such familistic independence creates problems for Big Men, who encourage interfamily unity in the effort to enhance the strength of their own clans in a fiercely competitive and dangerous social environment.

Let us imagine the problems faced by the members of an Enga clan. They are trying to make an adequate subsistence from small amounts of intensely utilized land. Surrounding them is a world of enemies ready to drive them from their land and seize it at the first sign of weakness. They must attempt to neutralize this external threat by several means: (1) by maintaining a large, unified group, they show strength in numbers, making others afraid to attack them; (2) by collaborating in the accumulation of food and wealth to be generously given away at ceremonies, they make themselves attractive as feasting partners; and (3) by being strong and wealthy, they become attractive as allies for defensive purposes, turning their neighbors either into friends or into outnumbered enemies. These three goals can be achieved only if each member of a clan is willing to fight on behalf of other members, to avoid fighting within the clan (even though it is with his clan members that a man is most directly in competition for land, since they are his most immediate neighbors), and to give up a share of his precious household accumulation of food and wealth objects in order that his Big Man may host an impressive feast.

This dependence of the household on the economic and political success of the clan is the basis of the Big Man's power. A Big Man is a local leader who motivates his followers to act in concert. He does not hold office and has no ultimate institutional power, so he must lead by pleading and bullyragging. His personal characteristics make him a leader . . . : He is usually a good speaker, convincing to his listeners; he has an excellent memory for kinship relations and for past transactions in societies where there is no writing; he is a peacemaker whenever possible, arranging compensatory payments and fines in order to avoid direct violent retribution from groups who feel they have been injured; and, when all else fails, he leads his followers into battle.

Of great importance in this system is the exchange of brides between patrilineal groups, for which payments of food, especially pigs, and wealth objects are required. An individual's political position—which affects his access to land, pigs, and other necessities—depends on alliances formed via his own marriage and those of his close kin. A Big Man, skilled as a negotiator and extremely knowledgeable about the delicate web of alliances created across the generations by a myriad of previous marriages and wealth payments, can help a group to marry well and maintain its competitive edge. By arranging his own marriages, of course, the Big Man cannot only increase the number of alliances in which he is personally involved, but he can also bring more women, which is to say, more production of sweet potatoes and pigs, under his control. Hence, as he strengthens his group, he does not neglect his own personal power, as measured by his control of women, pigs, and wealth objects. His efforts both public and personal come together most visibly when he succeeds in hosting a feast.

Among the most dramatic economic institutions on earth, the Melanesian feasts have fascinated economic anthropologists. The Big Man works for months, painfully acquiring food and wealth from his reluctant followers, only to present them in spectacular accumulations—as *gifts* to his allies. But the generosity has an edge, as the Kawelka Big Man Ongka put it: "I have won. I have knocked you down by giving so much . . . ." And the Big Man expects that his turn will come to be hosted by his allies, when they will be morally bound to return his gift with an equivalent or larger one. The "conspicuous consumption" and underlying competitiveness of these displays of generosity have been regarded as so similar to philanthropy in our own economy as to seem to close the gap between "primitive" and "modern" economies.

But the Big Man feast must be understood in context. Similar to the famous potlatch of the northwest coast of North America, these feasts do not exist merely as arenas for grandiose men to flaunt their ambition. As analyzed for the northwest coast, the competitive feast is the most dramatic event in a complex of interactions that maintain what Newman . . . calls "the intergroup collectivity." We must remember that, beyond the Enga clan, there is no group that can guarantee the rights of the individual, in the sense that the modern state does for us. Beyond the clan are only allies, strangers, and enemies. Many of them covet the desirable lands of other clans, and, if they sense weakness, they will strike. Small groups—weak in numbers and vulnerable to attack—must seek to swell their numbers and to attract allies in other clans. Thus an individual family's access to the means of subsistence depends on the success of its clan in the political arena, ultimately in the size of fighting force that can be mounted from within the clan and recruited from allied clans.

In the absence of courts and constitutions regulating intergroup relations, the Big Men assume central importance. It is they who maintain and advertise their group's attractiveness as allies (hence the bragging and showmanship that accompany Big Man feasts), who mediate disputes to avoid the dangerous extremity of homicidal violence, who remember old alliances and initiate new ones. Despite the public competitiveness between Big Men as they attempt to humiliate one another with generosity, over time they develop relationships of a predictable, even trustworthy, nature with other Big Men, lending intergroup stability in an unstable world.

A good example of this stabilizing effect is seen in the *Te* cycle, a series of competitive exchanges that link many Central Enga clans. Starting at one end of the chain, initiatory gifts of pigs, salt, and other valuables are given as individual exchanges from one partner to the next down the chain of clans. Big Men do not have to be directly involved, since such individual exchanges follow personal lines of alliance. But because the gifts are flowing in one direction down the chain of clans, after a time the giving clans begin to demand repayment. As this signal passes through the system, individuals amass pigs for larger feasts at the opposite, or receiving end, of the chain. These larger interclan ceremonies are full of oratory and display that serve to advertise the size and wealth of individual clans. Over a period of months a series of large gifting ceremonies move back up the chain of clans toward the beginning. The emphasis on prestige in these ceremonies is certainly gratifying to the participants, but it serves larger purposes: to maintain peace by substituting competitive feasting for open warfare, to establish and reinforce alliances, and to advertise a clan's attractiveness as an ally and fearsomeness as an enemy.

The central points to note from this example are the following:

1. The high population density of the Enga . . . implies two related developments: First, there is little wild forest left and virtually no supply of wild foods for the diet; and, second, the best horticultural land is fully occupied and in permanent use. These two primary consequences of population growth have further implications.

2. One is an intensive mode of food production that does not rely so much on regeneration of natural soil fertility through fallowing as upon mounding and the addition of green manure to soils. Because of the Enga's reliance on pigs, these fields must support not only the human population but also that of the pigs, who consume as much garden produce as humans do. The labor costs of pigs therefore include both producing their food and building fences to control their predation of gardens. Although the Enga populations are able to provide their basic nutritional needs in this manner, other highland groups with similar economies do show some signs of malnutrition, suggesting that overall production is not much more than adequate.

3. Furthermore, with land scarce, warfare shows a clear emphasis on territorial expansion and displacement. In response to this basic threat to their livelihood, families participate, albeit somewhat reluctantly, in the political activities of the lineage and clan. Although these activities often appear belligerent and can lead to warfare by deflecting hostilities outside the clan or local alliance of clans, it remains true that they have the primary function of preventing violence and stabilizing access to land.

The three major paths for creating alliances are marriage exchanges, sharing of food at feasts (commensality), and an intricate web of debt and credit established through exchanges of food and wealth objects. All of these together constitute the prestige economies for which such groups are famous. Crucial junctures in the prestige economy are occupied by Big Men, who earn their status by personally managing the complex alliances that provide a degree of security to otherwise vulnerable groups of closely related kin.

[18]Johnson, A. (1989). Horticulturists: Economic behavior in tribes. In S. Plattner (Ed.), *Economic anthropology* (pp. 63–67). Stanford, CA: Stanford University Press.

In the case of these Big Man feasts, a surplus is created for the express purpose of gaining prestige through a display of wealth and generous giving of gifts. But, unlike conspicuous consumption in Western societies, the emphasis is not on the hoarding of goods that would make them unavailable to others. Instead, the emphasis is on giving away, or at least getting rid of one's wealth goods. Thus, these feasts serve as a leveling mechanism, preventing some individuals from accumulating too much wealth at the expense of other members of society.

The Chicago Commodities Exchange, where people are buying and selling, even though no goods are physically present.

Market Exchange

To an economist, **market exchange** involves the buying and selling of goods and services, with prices set by powers of supply and demand. Loyalties and values are not supposed to play a role, but they often do. Just where the buying and selling takes place is largely irrelevant, and so we must distinguish between market *exchange* and the mar-

⊏━━━◦◦◦━━━◦◦◦━━━⊐

Market exchange: The buying and selling of goods and services, with prices set by powers of supply and demand.

⊏━━━◦◦◦━━━◦◦◦━━━⊐

ket *place*. Although some of our market transactions do take place in a specific identifiable location—much of the trade in cotton, for example, takes place in the New Orleans Cotton Exchange—it is also quite possible for a North American to buy and sell goods without ever being on the same side of the continent. When people talk about a market in today's world, the particular place where something is sold is often not important at all. For example, think of the way people speak of a "market" for certain types of automobiles or for mouthwash.

Until well into the twentieth century, market exchange typically was carried out in specific places, as it still is in much of the non-Western world. In peasant or agrarian societies, market places overseen by a centralized political authority

In non-Western societies, the market is an important focus of social as well as economic activity, as typified by this market in Guatemala.

provide the opportunity for farmers living in rural regions to exchange some of their livestock and produce for needed items manufactured in factories or the workshops of craft specialists living (usually) in towns and cities. Thus, some sort of complex division of labor as well as centralized political organization is necessary for the appearance of markets. In the marketplace, land, labor, and occupations are not bought and sold as they are through the Western market economy. In other words, what happens in the marketplace has little to do with the price of land, the amount paid for labor, or the cost of services. The market is local, specific, and contained. Prices are apt to be set on the basis of face-to-face bargaining (buy cheap and sell dear is the order of the day), rather than by faceless "market forces" wholly removed from the transaction itself. Nor need some form of money be involved; instead, goods may be directly exchanged through some form of reciprocity between the specific individuals involved.

In non-Western societies, marketplaces have much of the excitement of a fair; they are vibrant places where one's senses are assaulted by a host of colorful sights, sounds, and smells. Indeed, many of the large urban and suburban malls built in the United States and other industrialized countries

over the past few decades have tried to recreate, though in a more contrived manner, some of the interest and excitement of more traditional marketplaces. In the latter, noneconomic activities may even overshadow the economic. Social relationships are as important there as anywhere else. As anthropologist Stuart Plattner observes, the marketplace is where friendships are made, love affairs begun, and marriages arranged.[19] Dancers and musicians may perform, and the end of the day may be marked by drinking, dancing, and fighting. At the market, too, people gather to hear news. In ancient Mexico, under the Aztecs, people were required by law to go to market at specific intervals in order to keep informed. Government officials held court and settled judicial disputes there. Thus, the market is a gathering place where people renew friendships, see relatives, gossip, and keep up with the world, at the same time procuring needed goods that they cannot produce for themselves.

Although there have been marketplaces without money of any sort, there is no question that money

[19]Plattner, S. (1989). Markets and market places. In S. Plattner (Ed.), *Economic anthropology* (p. 171). Stanford, CA: Stanford University Press.

Figure 18.3   Marketplace structure and function may range from formal to informal and from economic to festive, as this diagram suggests.

facilitates trade. **Money** may be defined as something used to make payments for other things as well as to measure their value. Its critical attributes are durability, portability, divisibility, recognizability, and fungibility (the quality that any item of money can be used in place of any other item of the same value, as when four "quarters" are substituted for a dollar bill). The wide range of things that have been used as money in one or another society includes salt, shells, stones, beads, feathers, fur, bones, teeth, and of course metals, from iron to gold and silver. Among the Aztecs of Mexico, both cacao beans and cotton cloaks served as money. The beans could be used to purchase merchandise and labor, though usually as a supplement to barter; if the value of the items exchanged was not equal, cacao beans could be used to make up the difference. Cotton cloaks represented a higher

<hr>

Money: Anything used to make payments for other things (goods or labor) as well as to measure their value; may be special purpose or multipurpose.

<hr>

denomination in the monetary system, with 65 to 300 beans equivalent to one cloak, depending on the latter's quality. Cloaks could be used to obtain credit, to purchase land, as restitution for theft, and to ransom slaves, whose value in any case was measured in terms of cloaks. Interestingly, counterfeiting was not unknown to the Aztecs, as unscrupulous people sometimes carefully peeled back the outer skin of cacao beans and removed the contents, for which packed earth was then substituted!

Among the Tiv of West Africa, brass rods might be exchanged for cattle, with the seller then using the rods to purchase slaves (the economic value of the cattle being converted into the rods and then reconverted into slaves). In both the Aztec and Tiv cases, the money in question is (or was) only used for special purposes. To a Tiv, the idea of exchanging a brass rod for subsistence foods is repugnant, and most market exchanges involve direct barter. Special-purpose monies usually have more moral restrictions on their use than do general-purpose monies, which can be used to purchase just about anything. Even here, however, there are limits. For example, in the United States it is considered immoral, as well as illegal, to exchange

Anthropology Applied
THE ANTHROPOLOGIST AS BUSINESS CONSULTANT

When people hear of anthropologists working for and sometimes running private sector businesses ranging from major financial institutions to consulting firms for major corporations, their reaction is usually one of surprise. In the public mind, anthropologists are supposed to work in exotic, faraway places like remote islands, deep forests, hostile deserts, or arctic wastes—not in the world of business. After all, when anthropology makes the pages of the *New York Times*, is it not to report the "discovery" of a "last surviving Stone Age tribe," the uncovering of some ancient "lost city," or the recovery of bones of some remote human ancestor, usually in some out-of-the-way part of the world?

As we saw in the first chapter of this book, anthropologists have had a long-standing interest in their own culture, and large numbers of them, as applied anthropologists, are putting their expertise to work in attempts to find solutions to problems of various sorts. Since 1972, the number of anthropologists going into business has grown fivefold. One example is Steve Barnett, holder of a Ph.D. in anthropology from the University of Chicago, who in the 1980s headed the Cultural Analysis group at Planmetrics, a Chicago-based consulting firm. His job was to solve problems concerning consumer behavior, and his clients were some of the country's largest corporations. Another example is the work of Peter Reynolds and Sunny Baker, cofounders of the Seattle consulting firm Corporate Anthropology Group. They have been called upon by companies desiring a change in their corporate culture. Reynolds and Baker's clients include such firms as Microsoft, CAE Systems, and Rohm; in fact, demand for anthropologists is particularly strong in Silicon Valley, where job-hopping and rapid changes can be a source of corporate instability.

What anthropologists have to offer the corporate world are skills in analyzing everyday life that other social and behavioral scientists do not have. For example, instead of using the polling techniques market researchers prefer, Barnett relied on participant observation. Thus when Kimberly-Clark hired him to help with the redesign of disposable diapers, he recorded on videotape 200 hours of diaper changing at a day-care center, which he then analyzed as if it were a ritual in some other culture. From this, he could develop meaningful categories by which to understand the diaper-changing process. Similar techniques were used in studies of dishwashing and dusting for Procter and Gamble. Unlike interviews and questionnaires, the techniques traditionally used in ethnographic fieldwork are less likely to be tinged by politics, personal biases, and *post hoc* rationalization. As John Seely Brown, director of Xerox Corporation's Palo Alto Research Center, points out, anthropologists can deliver "dramatic improvements in productivity. To get these, companies have to go beyond industrial psychology and reengineer the business process. They have to work from the bottom up. And anthropology is the field most attuned to that."*

Stimulating though it may be, the life of an anthropologist working for business may not always be easy. Managers may be inclined to "tune out" when anthropologists start talking about values. For another, the anthropologist must always keep in mind the welfare of those being studied, be they corporate employees or potential consumers, so that their best interests are not ignored or violated by those paying for the services of the anthropologist. This, though, is no different from the problems faced by ethnographers in more traditional settings, who must always be on guard that their findings not be used by governments or other powerful organizations in ways that are harmful to those they study.

*Garza, C. E. (1991, September). Studying the natives on the shop floor. *Business Week*, 74.

See also Lewin, T. (1986, May). Casting an anthropological eye on American consumers. *New York Times*, p. 6F; and Sinolop, S. (1991). What's an anthropologist doing in my office? In A. Podofsky & P. J. Brown (Eds.), *Applying anthropology* (pp. 34–35). Mountain View, CA: Mayfield.

money for sexual and political favors, even though infractions of these constraints occur.

In the United States, as part of a reaction to the increasingly "face-to-faceless" nature of the modern economic system, there has been something of a revival and proliferation of "flea markets" (Fig. 18.3), where anyone, for a small fee, may display and sell handicrafts, secondhand items, farm produce, and paintings in a face-to-face setting. There is excitement in the search for bargains and an opportunity for haggling. A carnival atmosphere prevails, with eating, laughing, and conversation, and items may even be bartered without any cash passing hands. These flea markets, or farmers' markets, are similar to the marketplaces of non-Western societies.

Flea markets also raise the issue of the distinction between the informal and formal sectors of the market economy. The **informal economy** may be defined as the system by which producers of goods and services provide marketable commodities that for various reasons escape enumeration, regulation, or other type of public monitoring or auditing. The enterprises may encompass just about anything: market gardening, making and selling beer or other alcoholic beverages, doing repair or construction work, begging, selling things on the street, performing ritual services, lending money, dealing drugs, picking pockets, and gambling, to mention just a few. The sort of "off the books" activities involved have been known for a long time, but have generally been dismissed by economists as aberrant and therefore more of an annoyance than anything of importance. It is also difficult for them to track; yet, in many countries of the world, the informal economy is, in fact, more important than the formal economy. In many parts of the world, large numbers of under- and unemployed peoples who have only limited access to the formal sector in effect improvise various means of

---

Informal economy: The production of marketable commodities that for various reasons escape enumeration, regulation, or any other sort of public monitoring or auditing.

"getting by" on scant resources. At the same time, more affluent members of society may evade various regulations in order to maximize returns and/or to vent their frustrations at their perceived loss of self determination in the face of increasing government regulation.

ECONOMICS, CULTURE, AND THE WORLD OF BUSINESS

At the start of this chapter, we noted that it is perhaps in the study of the economies of nonliterate peoples that we are most apt to fall prey to our own ethnocentric biases. The misunderstandings that result from our failure to overcome these biases are of major importance to us in the modern world in at least two ways. For one, they encourage development schemes in those countries that, by Western economic standards, are regarded as "underdeveloped" (a comfortably ethnocentric term) that all too often result in poverty, poor health, discontent, and a host of other ills. In northeastern Brazil, for example, development of large-scale plantations in order to grow sisal for export to the United States took over numerous small farms on which peasants grew food in order to feed themselves. With this, peasants joined the ranks of the unemployed. Being unable to earn enough money to satisfy their minimal nutritional needs, peasants saw the incidence of malnutrition rise dramatically. Similarly, development projects in Africa, designed to bring about changes in local hydrology, vegetation, and settlement patterns—and even programs aimed at reducing certain diseases—have frequently led directly to *increased* disease rates.[20] Fortunately, there is now a growing awareness on the part of development officials that future projects are unlikely to succeed without the expertise of anthropologically trained people.

Achieving an understanding of the economic systems of other peoples that is not bound by the hopes and expectations of one's own culture

---

[20]Bodley, J. H. (1990). *Victims of progress* (3rd ed.) (p. 141). Mountain View, CA: Mayfield.

In Africa, much of the farming is the job of women, like this Kenyan. Failure to accept this cultural fact is one reason development schemes have so often failed in Africa, as outside experts design projects that usually assume that men are the farmers.

has also become a matter of import for corporate executives in today's world. At least, recognition of how embedded such systems are within the cultures of which they are parts could avoid problems of the sort experienced by a large New York City–based cosmetics manufacturer. About to release an ad in Italy featuring a model holding some flowers, it was discovered that the flowers were the kind traditionally given at Italian funerals. Along the same lines, the Chevrolet Nova did not sell well in Spanish-speaking countries because in Spanish "No Va" means "No Go." Anthropologists Edward and Mildred Hall describe another case of the same sort:

> José Ybarra and Sir Edmund Jones are at the same party and it is important for them to establish a cordial relationship for business reasons. Each is trying to be warm and friendly, yet they will part with mutual distrust and their business transaction will probably fall through. José, in Latin fashion, moved closer and closer to Sir Edmund

as they spoke, and this movement was miscommunicated as pushiness to Sir Edmund, who kept backing away from this intimacy, and this was miscommunicated to José as coldness.[21]

Where the so-called underdeveloped countries of Africa, Asia, South and Central America are involved, the chances for cross-cultural misunderstandings increase dramatically. The executives of major corporations realize their dependency on these countries for raw materials, they are increasingly inclined to manufacture their products in them, and they see their best potential for market expansion as lying outside of North America and Europe. That is why business recruiters on college campuses in the United States are on the lookout for job candidates with the kind of understanding of the world that anthropology provides.

[21]Hall, E. T., & Hall, M. R. (1986). The sounds of silence. In E. Angeloni (Ed.), *Anthropology 86/87* (p. 65). Guilford, CT: Dushkin.

CHAPTER SUMMARY

An economic system is the means by which goods are produced, distributed, and consumed. The study of the economics of nonliterate, nonindustrial societies can be undertaken only in the context of the total culture of each society. Each society solves the problem of getting its living by allocating raw materials, land, labor, and technology, and distributing goods according to its own priorities.

The work people do is a major productive resource, and the allotment of work is always governed by rules according to sex and age. Only a few broad generalizations can be made covering the kinds of work performed by men and women. Instead of looking for biological imperatives to explain the sexual division of labor, a more productive strategy is to examine the kinds of work done by men and women in the context of specific societies to see how it relates to other cultural and historical factors. The cooperation of many people working together is a typical feature of both nonliterate and literate societies. Specialization of craft is important even in societies with a very simple technology.

All societies regulate the way that the valuable resources of land will be allocated. In nonindustrial societies, individual ownership of land is rare; generally land is controlled by kinship groups, such as the lineage or band. This system provides for greater flexibility of land use, since the size of the band territories, or of the bands themselves, can be adjusted according to availability of resources in any particular place. The technology of a people, in the form of the tools they use, is related to their mode of subsistence. In food-foraging societies, codes of generosity promote free access to tools, even though these may have been made by individuals for their own use. In sedentary, farming communities, there is greater opportunity to accumulate material belongings, and inequalities of wealth may develop. In many such communities, though, a relatively egalitarian social order may be maintained through the operation of leveling mechanisms.

Nonliterate people consume most of what they produce themselves, but they do exchange goods.

The processes of distribution that may be distinguished are reciprocity, redistribution, and market exchange. Reciprocity is a transaction between individuals or groups, involving the exchange of goods and services of roughly equivalent value. Usually it is prescribed by ritual and ceremony.

Barter and trade take place between groups. There are elements of reciprocity in trading exchanges, but there is a greater calculation of the relative value of goods exchanged. Barter is one form of negative reciprocity, by which scarce goods from one group are exchanged for desirable goods from another group. Silent trade, which need not involve face-to-face contact, is a specialized form of barter in which no verbal communication takes place. It is one means by which the potential dangers of negative reciprocity may be controlled. A classic example of exchange between groups that partook of both reciprocity and sharp trading was the Kula ring of the Trobriand Islanders.

Strong centralized political organization is necessary for redistribution to take place. The government assesses each citizen a tax or tribute, uses the proceeds to support the governmental and religious elite, and redistributes the rest, usually in the form of public services. The collection of taxes and delivery of government services and subsidies in the United States are forms of redistribution.

Display for social prestige is a motivating force in societies where there is some surplus of goods produced. In the United States, goods that are accumulated for display generally remain in the hands of those who accumulated them, whereas in other societies they are generally given away; the prestige comes from publicly divesting oneself of valuables.

Exchange in the marketplace serves to distribute goods in a region. In nonindustrial societies, the marketplace is usually a specific site where produce, livestock, and material items produced by the people are exchanged. It also functions as a social gathering place and a news medium. Although market exchanges may take place without money through bartering and other forms of reciprocity, some form of money at least for special transactions makes market exchange more efficient.

In market economies, the informal sector may become more important than the formal sector, as large numbers of under- and unemployed people with marginal access to the formal economy seek to survive. The informal economy consists of those economic activities that escape official scrutiny and regulation.

The anthropological approach to economics has taken on new importance in today's world of international development and commerce. Without it, development schemes in the Third World are prone to failure, and international trade is handicapped as a result of cross-cultural misunderstandings.

SUGGESTED READINGS

Dalton, G. (1971).   *Traditional tribal and peasant economies: An introductory survey of economic anthropology.* Reading, MA: Addison-Wesley.

This is just what the title says it is, by a major specialist in economic anthropology.

Leclair, E. E., Jr., & Schneider, H. K. (Eds.). (1968). *Economic anthropology: Readings in theory and analysis.* New York: Holt, Rinehart and Winston.

A selection of significant writings in economic anthropology from the preceding 50 years. In the first section are theoretical papers covering major points of view, and in the second are case materials selected to show the practical application of the various theoretical positions.

Nash, M. (1966). *Primitive and peasant economic systems.* San Francisco: Chandler.

This book studies the problems of economic anthropology, especially the dynamics of social and economic change in terms of primitive and peasant economic systems. The book is heavily theoretical, but draws on the author's fieldwork in Guatemala, Mexico, and Burma.

Plattner, S. (Ed.) (1989). *Economic anthropology.* Stanford, CA: Stanford University Press.

This is the first comprehensive text in economic anthropology to appear since the 1970s. Twelve scholars in the field contributed chapters on a variety of issues ranging from economic behavior in foraging, horticultural, "preindustrial" state, peasant, and industrial societies; to sex roles, common-property resources, informal economics in industrial societies, and mass-marketing in urban areas.

VI

THE FORMATION OF GROUPS
SOLVING THE PROBLEM OF COOPERATION

CHAPTER 19
SEX AND MARRIAGE

CHAPTER 20
FAMILY AND HOUSEHOLD

CHAPTER 21
KINSHIP AND DESCENT

CHAPTER 22
GROUPING BY SEX, AGE, COMMON INTEREST, AND CLASS

One of the really important things to emerge from anthropological study is the realization of just how fundamental cooperation is to human survival. Through cooperation, all known humans handle even the most basic problems of existence, the need for food and protection—not only from the elements but also from predatory animals and even each other. To some extent, this is true not only for humans, but for monkeys and apes as well. Baboons, for example, protect themselves against predators by traveling in large troops that include males as well as females with their young. Owing to their much larger size and far more formidable canine teeth, the males are a more credible threat to predators than are the females. Within the troop, females provide themselves and their infants with protection against harassment from other baboons by forming friendships with particular males. Among humans, males still usually bear primary responsibility for their group's defense, even though the anatomical and physiological differences between the sexes have been reduced to relatively minor proportions compared to what we see in most monkeys and apes. Moreover, women are potentially as capable of fighting as are men, and in some societies women do bear arms. But what sets humans apart from other primates even more is some form of cooperation in subsistence activities on a regular basis. At the least, this takes the form of the sexual division of labor as seen among food-foraging-peoples. Such cooperation is not customary among nonhuman primates; adult chimpanzees, for example, may cooperate to get meat and share it when they get it, but they don't get meat very often, and they don't normally share other kinds of food the way humans regularly do.

Just as cooperation seems to be basic to human nature, so the organization of groups is basic to effective cooperation. Humans form many kinds of groups, and each is geared to solving different kinds of problems with which people must cope. Social groups are important to humans also because they give identity and support to their members. The basic building block of human societies is the household, within which economic production, consumption, inheritance, child rearing, and shelter are organized and carried out. Usually, the core of the household consists of some form of family, a group of relatives that stems from the parent-child bond and the interdependence of men and women. Although it may be structured in many different ways, the family, however structured, provides for economic cooperation between men and women, while furnishing at the same time the kind of setting within which child rearing may take place. Another problem faced by all human societies is the need to control sexual activity, which is the function of marriage. Given the inevitable connection between sexual activity and the production of children, who must then be nurtured, a close interconnection between marriage and family is to be expected.

Many different marriage and family patterns exist the world over, but all societies have some form of marriage and most (but not all) have some form of family organization. As we shall see in Chapters 19 and 20, the forms of family and marriage organization are to a large extent shaped by the specific kinds of problems people must solve in particular situations.

The solutions to some organizational challenges are beyond the scope of family and household. These include such matters as defense, allocation of resources, and provision of work forces for tasks too large to be undertaken by a family. Some societies develop formal political systems to perform these functions. Nonindustrial societies frequently meet these challenges through kinship groups, which we discuss in Chapter 21. These large, cohesive groups of individuals base their loyalty to one another on descent from a common ancestor or their relationship to a living individual. In societies where a great number of people are linked by kinship, these groups serve the important function of precisely defining the social roles of their members. In this way they reduce the potential for tension that might arise from the sudden and unexpected behavior of an individual. They also provide their members with material security and moral support through religious and ceremonial activities.

Other important forms of human social groups are the subjects of Chapter 22. Where kinship ties do not provide for all of the organizational needs of a society, grouping by age and/or sex is one force that may be used to create social groups. In North America, as well as in many non-Western countries, today and in the past, the organization of persons by age is common. In many areas of the world, too, social groups based on the common interests of their members serve a vital function. In industrializing countries, they may help to ease the transition of rural individuals into the urban setting. Finally, groups based on social rank are characteristic of the world's civilizations, past and present. Such groups are referred to as social classes, and they are always ranked high versus low relative to one another. Class structure involves inequalities between classes and frequently is the means by which one group may dominate large numbers of other people. To the extent that social class membership cuts across lines of kinship, residence, age, or other group membership, it may work to counteract tendencies for a society to fragment into discrete special interest groups. Paradoxically, it does so in a way which is itself divisive, in that class distinctions systematically deprive people of equal access to important resources. Thus, class conflict has been a recurrent phenomenon in class-structured societies, in spite of the existence of political and religious institutions that function to perpetuate the status quo.

SEX AND MARRIAGE

A MASAI WEDDING CEREMONY. IN ALL SOCIETIES, MARRIAGE
ESTABLISHES A CONTINUING SEXUAL RELATIONSHIP BETWEEN A
MAN AND A WOMAN, BACKED BY LEGAL, ECONOMIC, AND SOCIAL
FORCES. THUS, UNLIKE MATING (WHICH IS BIOLOGICAL),
MARRIAGE IS DISTINCTIVELY CULTURAL.

CHAPTER PREVIEW

What Is Marriage?

Marriage is a transaction and resulting contract in which a woman and a man are recognized by society as having a continuing claim to the right of sexual access to one another, and in which the woman involved is eligible to bear children. Although in many societies, husbands and wives live together as members of the same household, this is not true in all societies. And though most marriages around the world tend to be to a single spouse, most societies permit, and regard as most desirable, marriage of a single individual to multiple spouses.

What Is the Difference Between Marriage and Mating?

All animals, including humans, mate—that is, they form a sexual bond with individuals of the opposite sex. In some species, the bond lasts for life, but in some others, it lasts no longer than a single sex act. Thus, some animals mate with a single individual of the opposite sex, while others mate with several. Only marriage, however, is backed by social, legal, and economic forces. Consequently, while mating is biological, marriage is cultural.

Why Is Marriage Universal?

A problem universal to all human societies is the need to control sexual relations so that they not introduce a disruptive, combative influence into society. Because the problem it deals with is universal, it follows that marriage should be universal. The specific form marriage takes is related to who has rights to offspring that normally result from sexual intercourse, as well as how property is distributed.

Among the Trobriand Islanders, whose yam exchanges and Kula voyages we examined in Chapter 18, children who have reached the age of 7 or 8 years begin playing erotic games with each other and imitating adult seductive attitudes. Within another 4 or 5 years they begin to pursue sexual partners in earnest, changing partners often, experimenting sexually first with one, and then another. By the time the youngsters are in their mid-teens, meetings between lovers take up most of the night, and affairs between them are apt to last for several months. Ultimately, lovers begin to meet the same partner again and again, rejecting the advances of others. When the couple is ready, they appear together one morning outside the young man's house, as a way of announcing their intention to be married.

For young Trobrianders, attracting sexual partners is an important business, and they spend a great deal of time making themselves look as attractive and seductive as possible. Youthful conversations during the day are loaded with sexual innuendos, and magical spells as well as small gifts are employed to entice a prospective sex partner to the beach at night or to the house in which boys sleep apart from their parents. Because girls, too, sleep apart from their parents, youths and adolescents have considerable freedom in arranging their love affairs. Boys and girls play this game as equals, with neither sex being more dominant than the other.

To attract lovers, young Trobriand Islanders must look as attractive and seductive as possible. The young men shown here have decorated themselves with Johnson's Baby Powder, while the young girl's beauty has been enhanced by decorations given by her father.

As anthropologist Annette Weiner points out, all of this sexual activity is not a frivolous, adolescent pastime. Attracting lovers:

> is the first step toward entering the adult world of strategies, where the line between influencing others while not allowing others to gain control of oneself must be carefully learned . . . . Sexual liaisons give adolescents the time and occasion to experiment with all the possibilities and problems that adults face in creating relationships with those who are not relatives. Individual wills may clash, and the achievement of one's desire takes patience, hard work, and determination. The adolescent world of lovemaking has its own dangers and disillusionments. Young people, to the degree they are capable, must learn to be both careful and fearless.[1]

The Trobriand attitude towards adolescent sexuality stands in marked contrast to that of North American society. Theoretically, North Americans are not supposed to have sexual relations outside of wedlock, although as is well known, there is a considerable discrepancy between theory and practice. Nonetheless, premarital sexual activity in North American society cannot be conducted with the openness and approval that characterizes the Trobriand situation. As a consequence, it is not subject to the kind of social pressures from the community at large that prepare traditional Trobriand youths for the adult world after marriage.

CONTROL OF SEXUAL RELATIONS

One distinctively human characteristic is the ability for the human female, like the human male, to engage in sexual relations at any time she wants to or whenever her culture deems it appropriate. While this ability to perform at any time when provided with the appropriate cue is not unusual on the part of male mammals in general, it is not usual on the part of females. Although female primates, whose offspring are weaned but who have not yet become pregnant again, are likely to engage in sexual activity around the time of ovulation (approximately once a month), they are otherwise little interested in such activity. Only the human female may be willing to engage in sex at any point in her cycle, or even when she is pregnant. In some societies, intercourse during pregnancy is thought to promote the growth of the fetus. Among Trobriand Islanders, for example, a child's identity is thought to come from its mother, but it is the father's job to build up and nurture the child, which he begins to do before birth through frequent intercourse with its mother.

On the basis of clues from the behavior of other primates, anthropologists have speculated about the evolutionary significance of this human female sexuality. The best current explanation is that it arose as a side effect of persistent bipedal locomotion in early hominines.[2] The energetic requirements of this form of locomotion are such that endurance is impossible without a hormone output that is significantly greater than that of other primates. These hormones catalyze the steady release of muscular energy that is required for endurance; at the same time, they make us the "sexiest" of all primates. This is not to say that either men or women are simply at the mercy of their hormones where sex is concerned, for in the human species, both males and females have voluntary control over sex. People engage in it when it suits them to do so and when it is deemed appropriate.

Although developed as an accidental by-product of something else, a common phenomenon in evolution, the ability of females as well as males to engage in sex at any time would have been advantageous to early hominines to the extent that it acted, not alone but with other factors, to tie members of both sexes more firmly to the social groups so crucial to their survival. At the same time that sexual activity can reinforce group ties, however, it can also be disruptive. This stems from the common primate characteristic of male dominance. On the average, males are bigger and more muscular

[1]Weiner, A. B. (1988). *The Trobrianders of Papua New Guinea* (p. 71). New York: Holt, Rinehart and Winston.

[2]Spuhler, J. N. (1979). Continuities and discontinuities in anthropoid-hominid behavioral evolution: Bipedal locomotion and sexual reception. In N. A. Chagnon & W. Irons (Eds.), *Evolutionary biology and human social behavior* (pp. 454–461). North Scituate, MA: Duxbury Press.

than females, although this differentiation has become drastically reduced in modern *Homo sapiens* compared to the earliest hominines. Among other primates, the males' larger size allows them to try to dominate females when the latter are at the height of their sexuality; this trait can be seen among baboons, gorillas, and, though less obviously, chimpanzees (significantly, the size difference between male and female chimpanzees is not as great as among baboons or gorillas, but it is still substantially greater than among modern humans). With early hominine females potentially ready for sexual intercourse at any time, dominant males may have attempted to monopolize females; an added inducement could have been the prowess of the female at food gathering. (In food-foraging societies, the bulk of the food is usually provided by the gathering activities of women.) In any event, a tendency to monopolize females would introduce the kind of competitive, combative element into hominine groupings that one sees among many other primate species—one that cannot be allowed to disrupt harmonious social relationships. The solution to this problem is to bring sexual activity under cultural control. Thus, just as a culture tells people what, when, and how they should eat, so does it tell them when, where, how, and with whom they should have sex.

Attempts by males to dominate females may introduce a competitive, combative element into social relations. Among gorillas, male silverbacks maintain absolute breeding rights over females in their group. All other adult males must acknowledge this dominance or leave the group and attempt to lure females from other groups.

Rules of Sexual Access

We find that everywhere societies have cultural rules that seek to control sexual relations. In the United States and Canada, the official ideology has been that all sexual activity outside of wedlock is taboo. One is supposed to establish a family, which is done through marriage. With this, a person establishes a continuing claim to the right of sexual access to another person. Actually very few known societies—only about 5 percent—prohibit all sexual involvement outside of marriage, and even North American society has become less restrictive. Among other peoples, as we have already seen, things are often done quite differently. As a further example, we may look at the Nayar peoples of India.[3]

The Nayar constitute a landowning, warrior caste (rather than an independent society) from southwest India. Among them, estates are held by corporations of sorts, which are made up of kinsmen related in the female line. These kinsmen all live together in a large household, with the eldest male serving as manager.

Three transactions that take place among the Nayar are of interest to us here. The first occurs shortly before a girl undergoes her first menstruation. It involves a ceremony that joins together in a temporary union the girl with a young man. This union, which may or may not involve sexual relations, lasts for a few days and then breaks up. There is no further obligation on the part of either individual, although the woman and her future children will probably mourn for the man when he dies. What this transaction does is to establish the girl's eligibility for sexual activity with men who

---

[3]My interpretation of the Nayar follows Goodenough, W. H. (1970). *Description and comparison in cultural anthropology* (pp. 6–11). Chicago: Aldine.

are approved by her household. With this, she is officially an adult.

The second transaction takes place when a girl enters into a continuing sexual liaison with an approved man. This is a formal relationship, which requires the man to present her with gifts three times each year until such time as the relationship may be terminated. In return, the man may spend the nights with her. In spite of continuing sexual privileges, however, the man has no obligation to support his sex partner economically, nor is her home regarded as his home. In fact, she may have such an arrangement with more than one man at the same time. Regardless of how many men are involved with a single woman, this second Nayar transaction, which is their version of marriage, clearly specifies who has sexual access to whom, so as to avoid conflict. We may define **marriage** as a transaction and resulting contract in which a woman and man are recognized by society as having a continuing claim to the right of sexual access to one another and in which the woman involved is eligible to bear children. Thus defined, marriage is universal, presumably because the problems with which it deals are universal. As the Nayar case demonstrates, however, marriage need not have anything to do with beginning a new family or even establishing a cooperative economic relationship between people of opposite sexes.

In the absence of effective birth control devices, the usual outcome of sexual activity is that, sooner or later, the woman becomes pregnant. When this happens among the Nayar, some man must formally acknowledge paternity. This is done by his making gifts to the woman and the midwife. Though he may continue to take much interest in the child, he has no further obligations, for the education and support of the child are the responsibility of the child's mother's brothers, with whom the child and its mother live. What we have in this third transaction is one that establishes the legitimacy of the child. In this sense, it is the counterpart of the registration of birth in North American culture, in which motherhood and fatherhood are spelled out. In Western societies generally, the father is supposed to be the mother's husband, but in numerous other societies, there is no such necessity.

Before leaving the Nayar, it is important to note that there is nothing here comparable to the family as we know it in North America. The group that forms the household does not include **affinal kin,** or those individuals joined by a **conjugal bond** established by marriage. As will be seen in Chapter 20, a household doesn't have to be a family as we know it. Among the Nayar the household is composed wholly of what we often call "blood" relatives, which are technically known as **consanguineal kin.** Sexual relations are with those who are not consanguineal kin, and so live in other households. And this brings us to another human universal, the incest taboo.

The Incest Taboo

A cultural rule that has long fascinated anthropologists as well as other students of human behavior is the **incest taboo,** which prohibits sexual relations at least between parents and children of opposite sex and usually siblings as well. Thought to be universal, save for a few exceptions involving siblings, it has become something of a challenge for anthropologists to explain both this supposed universality, as well as why incest should commonly be regarded as such a loathsome thing.

Marriage: A transaction and resulting contract in which a woman and a man are recognized by society as having a continuing claim to the right of sexual access to one another, and in which the woman involved is eligible to bear children.

Affinal kin: Relatives by marriage.

Conjugal bond: The bond between a man and a woman who are married.

Consanguineal kin: Relatives by birth; that is, "blood" relatives.

Incest taboo: The prohibition of sexual relations between specified individuals, usually parent–child and sibling relations at a minimum.

Many explanations have been given. Of those that have gained some popularity at one time or another, the simplest and least satisfactory is based on "human nature"—that is, some instinctive horror of incest. It has been documented that human beings raised together have less sexual attraction for one another, but by itself this "familiarity breeds contempt" argument may simply substitute the result for the cause. The incest taboo ensures that children and their parents, who are constantly in intimate contact, avoid regarding one another as sexual objects. Besides this, if there were an instinctive horror of incest, we would be hard pressed to account for the far from rare violations of the incest taboo, such as occur in North American society (an estimated 10–14 percent of children under 18 years of age in the United States have been involved in incestuous relations[4]) or for cases of institutionalized incest, such as that which required the head of the Inca empire in Peru to marry his own sister.

Various psychological explanations of the incest taboo have been advanced at one time or another. Sigmund Freud tried to account for it in his psychoanalytic theory of the unconscious. According to him, the son desires the mother (familiarity breeds attempt), creating a rivalry with the father. (Freud called this the Oedipus complex.) He must suppress these feelings or earn the wrath of the father, who is far more powerful than he. Similarly, the attraction of the daughter to the father, or the Electra complex, places her in rivalry with her mother. From this, we might expect a same-sex bias in the case of intrafamily homicides—mother versus daughter or son versus father—but in fact no such bias exists. Some psychologists have argued that young children can be emotionally scarred by sexual experiences, which they may interpret as violent and frightening acts of aggression. The incest taboo thus protects children against sexual advances by older members of the family. A closely related theory is that the incest taboo helps prevent girls who are socially and emotionally too young for motherhood from becoming pregnant.

Early students of genetics argued that the incest taboo precluded the harmful effects of in-

breeding. While this is so, it is also true that as with domestic animals, inbreeding can increase desired characteristics as well as detrimental ones. Furthermore, undesirable effects will show up sooner than would otherwise be the case, so that whatever genes are responsible for them are quickly eliminated from the population. On the other hand, preference for a genetically different mate does tend to maintain a higher level of genetic diversity within a population, and in evolution this generally works to a species' advantage. Without genetic diversity a species cannot adapt biologically to a changed environment when and if this becomes necessary.

A truly convincing explanation of the incest taboo has yet to be advanced. Certainly, there are persistent hints that it may be a cultural elaboration of an underlying biological tendency toward avoidance of inbreeding. Studies of animal behavior have shown such a tendency to be common among those species that are relatively large, long-lived, slow to mature, and intelligent. Humans qualify for membership in this group on all counts. So do a number of other primates, including those most closely related to humans—chimpanzees. Although they exhibit few sexual inhibitions, chimpanzees do tend to avoid inbreeding between siblings and between females and their male offspring. This suggests that the tendency for human children to look for sex partners outside the group in which they have been raised is not just the result of a cultural taboo after all. Support for this might seem to come from studies that show that children raised together on an Israeli kibbutz, although not required or even encouraged to do so, almost invariably marry outside their group. In this case, however, appearances seem to be deceiving. For one thing, there is hardly a kibbutz without a report of heterosexual relationships between adolescents who have grown up together since infancy.[5] As for actual marriage, most Israeli youths leave the kibbutz in their late teens for service in the armed forces. Thus, they are away from the kibbutz precisely when they are most ready to consider marriage. Consequently, those most available as potential spouses are from other parts of

---

[4]Whelehan, P. (1985). Review of *Incest, A biosocial view. American Anthropologist, 87*, 678.

[5]Leavitt, G. C. (1990). Sociobiological explanations of incest avoidance: A critical review of evidential claims. *American Anthropologist, 92*, 973.

Although children raised together on an Israeli kibbutz rarely marry one another, it is not because of any instinctive desire to avoid mating with people who are close. Rather, they marry outside their group because service in the army takes them out of their kibbutz, where they meet new people, precisely when they are most likely to begin thinking about marriage.

the country. An even greater challenge to the "biological avoidance" theory, however, is raised by detailed census records made in Roman Egypt that conclusively demonstrate that brother-sister marriages were not only common, but preferred by ordinary members of the farming class.[6] Moreover, anthropologist Nancy Thornhill found that in a sample of 129 societies only 57 had specific rules against parent-child or sibling incest, whereas 114 had explicit rules to control activity with cousins, in-laws, or both.[7]

If indeed there is a biological basis for inbreeding avoidance among humans, it is far from being completely effective in its operation. Nor is its mechanism understood. Moreover, it still leaves us with these questions: Why do some societies have an explicit taboo while others do not? And why do some societies not only condone certain kinds of incest, but also even favor them?

Endogamy and Exogamy

Whatever its cause, the utility of the incest taboo can be seen by examining its effects on social structure. Closely related to prohibitions against incest are rules against **endogamy,** or marriage within a particular group of individuals (cousins and in-laws, for example). If the group is defined as one's immediate family alone, then societies generally prohibit, or at least discourage, endogamy and

[6]Leavitt, G. C. (1990). Sociobiological explanations of incest avoidance: A critical review of evidential claims. *American Anthropologist, 92,* 982.

[7]Thornhill, N. (1993). Quoted in W. A. Haviland & R. J. Gordon (Eds.), *Talking about people* (p. 127). Mountain View, CA: Mayfield.

Endogamy: Marriage within a particular group or category of individuals.

CLAUDE LÉVI-STRAUSS
(b. 1908)

Claude Lévi-Strauss is the leading exponent of French structuralism, which sees culture as a surface representation of underlying mental structures that have been affected by a group's physical and social environment as well as its history. Thus, cultures may vary considerably, even though the structure of the human thought processes responsible for them is the same for all people, everywhere.

Human thought processes are structured, according to Lévi-Strauss, into contrastive pairs of polar opposites, such as light versus dark, good versus evil, nature versus culture, raw versus cooked. The ultimate contrastive pair is that of "self" versus "others," which is necessary for true symbolic communication to take place and upon which culture depends. Communication is a reciprocal exchange, which is extended to include goods and marital partners. Hence, the incest taboo stems from this fundamental contrastive pair of "self" versus "others." From this universal taboo are built the many and varied marriage rules that have been described by ethnographers.

practice **exogamy,** or marriage outside the group. On the other hand, a society that practices exogamy at one level may practice endogamy at another. Among the Trobriand Islanders, for example, each individual has to marry outside of his or her own clan and lineage (exogamy). However, since eligible sex partners are to be found within one's own community, village endogamy, though not obligatory, is commonly practiced. What is interesting is the wide variety that exists from one society to another in the relatives that are or are not covered by rules of exogamy. In Europe, for example, the Catholic Church has long had a prohibition on marriages to first cousins and in the nineteenth century such marriages were illegal in most of the United States. In numerous other societies, however, first cousins are preferred spouses.

Sir Edward Tylor long ago advanced the proposition that alternatives to inbreeding were either "marrying out or being killed out."[8] Our ancestors, he suggested, discovered the advantage of intermarriage to create bonds of friendship. Claude Lévi-Strauss elaborated on this premise. He saw exogamy as the basis of a distinction between early hominine life in isolated endogamous groups and the life of *Homo sapiens* in a supportive society with an accumulating culture. Alliances with other groups, established and strengthened by marriage ties, make possible a sharing of culture. Building on Lévi-Strauss's work, anthropologist Yehudi Cohen suggests that exogamy was an important means of promoting trade between groups, thereby ensuring access to needed goods and resources not otherwise available. Noting that incest taboos necessitating exogamy are generally most widely extended in the least complex of human societies, but do not extend beyond parents and siblings in industrialized societies, he argues that as formal governments and other institutions have come to control trade, the need for extended taboos has been removed. Indeed, he suggests that this may have reached the point where the incest taboo is becoming obsolete altogether.

In a roundabout way, exogamy also helps to explain some exceptions to the incest taboo, such as that of obligatory brother and sister marriage within the royal families of ancient Egypt, the Inca empire, and Hawaii. Members of these royal families were considered semidivine, and their very sacredness kept them from marrying mere mortals.

Exogamy: Marriage outside the group.

[8]Quoted in Roger M. Keesing (1976). *Cultural anthropology: A contemporary perspective* (p. 286). New York: Holt, Rinehart and Winston.

In the United States, as in most Western countries, monogamy is the only legally recognized form of marriage. Nevertheless, about 50 percent of all marriages end in divorce, and most divorced people remarry at least once. Thus, serial monogamy is far from uncommon.

The brother and sister married so as *not* to share their godliness, thereby maintaining the "purity" of the royal line, not to mention control of royal property. By the same token, in Roman Egypt, where property was inherited by women as well as men, and where there was a particularly tight relationship between land and people, brother-sister marriages among the farming class acted to prevent fragmentation of a family's holdings.

The Distinction Between Marriage and Mating

Having defined marriage in terms of sexual access, it is important at this point to make clear the distinction between systems of marriage and mating. All animals, including humans, mate; some for life and some not, some with a single individual of the opposite sex, and some with several. Only marriage, however, is backed by legal, economic, and social forces. Even among the Nayar, where marriage seems to involve little else than a sexual relationship, a woman's husband is legally obligated to provide her with gifts at specified intervals. Nor

may a woman legally have sex with a man to whom she is not married. Thus, while mating is biological, marriage is cultural.

The distinction between marriage and mating may be seen by looking at practices in North American society, in which **monogamy**—the taking of a single spouse—is the only legally recognized form of marriage. Not only are other forms not legally sanctioned, but also systems of inheritance, by which property and wealth are transferred from one generation to the next, are predicated upon the institution of monogamous marriage. Mating patterns, by contrast, are frequently *not* monogamous. Not only is adultery far from rare in the United States and Canada, but it has also become increasingly acceptable for individuals of the opposite sex—particularly young people who have not yet married—to live together outside of wedlock. None of these arrangements, however, is

Monogamy: Marriage in which an individual has a single spouse.

Anthropology Applied
ANTHROPOLOGY AND AIDS

In North America, the 1960s and 1970s were a time of social ferment involving, among other things, significant changes in sexual values and practices. With this revolution developed new lifestyles including sexual experimentation with different partners as well as with different techniques. Inevitably, these changes were reflected in the health problems of sexually active individuals; in particular, the incidence of sexually transmitted diseases of all kinds has skyrocketed. Among these is acquired immune-deficiency syndrome, or AIDS, which can be transmitted through intravenous drug use and blood transfusions as well as through sexual intercourse. In the United States, AIDS was unknown prior to the late 1970s; since then, it has become probably the most serious menace to public health in the twentieth century. By the beginning of 1992, more than one million people in the United States were infected with the AIDS virus. Since then, many more have become so.

Worldwide, AIDS is spread primarily through heterosexual transmission, and in the United States today, transmission among heterosexuals is rising. During its first decade in the United States, AIDS predominantly affected the gay (homosexual and bisexual) male population. Although at one point, it showed a decline in this population, it has since been on the increase again. In San Francisco's gay community, the first cases appeared in 1979, and by 1980, it was evident that a major epidemic was underway. As part of a concerted effort to deal with this situation, a group at the University of California–San Francisco began a team effort to learn more about the disease, and implement efforts at prevention and health education based on current knowledge of AIDS. Included on the team was E. Michael Gorman, a medical anthropologist with training in epidemiology and infectious disease and who had extensive experience working with the city's gay population on health-related issues. Data gathered by the team included information on demography, medical history, sexual history, social factors, alcohol and drug usage, and sexual contacts. Gaining information on history posed a particular challenge, requiring knowledge of and sensitivity not only to various aspects of gay male sexual behavior, but also the cultural themes of gay subcultures.

As Gorman points out, the participation of a medical anthropologist and the use of anthropological methodologies were of great relevance in many respects.

> Epidemiological inquiry focuses primarily on the determinants of disease in human population. In this context, anthropological knowledge assisted in the more precise definition of the epidemiological variables of interest: person, time, and place. Specific knowledge of the population at risk and familiarity with the cultural context also aided in the process of investigating the epidemic. Experience with the community and understanding of its mores and history likewise facilitated the research process and brought community needs such as health education, risk reduction information, and prevention generally to the attention of the investigators.*

No less important than the research is prevention, for in the absence of either cure or vaccine, neither of which is on the horizon, the only effective way to deal with AIDS is through education and the development of risk reduction strategies. Here, the input of anthropologists is especially valuable in designing and implementing prevention programs tailored (as they must be) to the concerns of particular high-risk populations, each of which has its distinctive subculture. Finally, anthropologists are highly qualified to act as culture brokers, clarifying issues and positions to both public health officials and the communities they seek to serve.

*Gorman, E. M. (1989). The AIDS epidemic in San Francisco: Epidemiological and anthropological perspectives. In A. Podolefsky & P. J. Brown (Eds.), *Applying anthropology, An introductory reader* (pp. 197–198). Mountain View, CA: Mayfield.

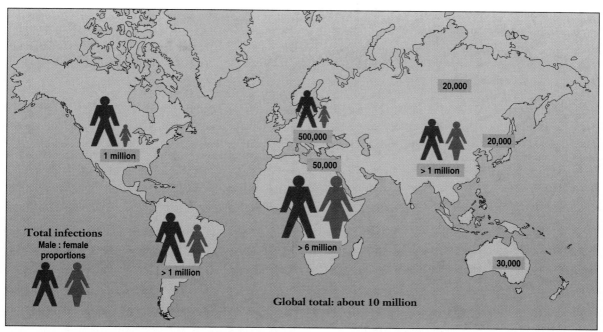

Figure 19.1   Estimated global distribution of adult HIV infections, early 1992.

legally sanctioned. Even married couples who do not engage in sexual activity outside of wedlock frequently mate with more than one individual of the opposite sex; this follows from the fact that over 50 percent of first marriages in the United States end in divorce, and most divorced people ultimately remarry.

Among primates in general, monogamous mating patterns are not common. Although some smaller species of South American monkeys, a few island-dwelling populations of leaf-eating Old World monkeys, and all of the smaller apes (gibbons and siamangs) do mate for life with a single individual of the opposite sex, none of these is closely related to human beings. Nor do "monogamous" primates ever display the degree of anatomical differences between males and females that is characteristic of our closest primate relatives or

Family: A residential kin group composed of a woman, her dependent children, and at least one adult male joined through marriage or blood relationship.

that were characteristic of our own ancient ancestors. This all suggests that it is not likely that the human species began its career as one with monogamous mating patterns. Certainly, one cannot say (as some have tried to assert) that the human species is, by nature, monogamous in its mating behavior.

Marriage and the Family

Although, as we saw in our discussion of the Nayar, marriage does not have to result in the formation of a new family, it can easily serve this purpose, in addition to its main function of indicating who has continuing sexual access to whom. This is precisely what is done in most human societies. Consequently, some mention of family organization—otherwise discussed in Chapter 20—is necessary before we can proceed further with our discussion of marriage. If we were to define the family in terms with which we are familiar, as requiring fathers, mothers, and children, then we would have to say that people like the Nayar (who, as we shall see in Chapter 20, do not constitute a unique case) do not have families. We can, however, define the **family** in a less ethnocentric way as a group composed of a woman and her dependent children and at least one adult male joined through marriage or blood relationship.[9] The Nayar family is a **consanguine** one, consisting as it does of women with their brothers and the dependent offspring of the women. In such societies, men and women get married, but do not live together as members of a single household. Rather, they spend their lives in the households in which they grew up, with the men "commuting" for sexual activity with their wives. Economic cooperation between men and women takes place between sisters and brothers, rather than husbands and wives.

Conjugal, as opposed to consanguine families, are formed on the basis of marital ties between husband and wife. Minimally, a conjugal family consists of a married couple with their dependent children, otherwise known as the **nuclear family;** other forms of conjugal families are polygynous and polyandrous families, which may be thought of as aggregates of nuclear families with one spouse in common. A polygynous family includes the multiple wives of a single husband, while a polyandrous family includes the multiple husbands of a single wife. Both are often lumped together under the heading of polygamous families.

FORMS OF MARRIAGE

Monogamy is the form of marriage with which North Americans are most familiar. It is also the most common, but for economic rather than moral reasons. In many polygynous societies, a man must be fairly wealthy to be able to afford **polygyny,** or

---

Consanguine family: A family consisting of related women, their brothers, and the offspring of the women.

Nuclear family: A family unit consisting of husband, wife, and dependent children.

Polygyny: The marriage custom of a man having several wives at the same time; a form of polygamy.

---

marriage to more than one wife. Among the Kapauku of western New Guinea,[10] the ideal is to have as many wives as possible, and a woman actually urges her husband to spend money on acquiring additional wives. She even has the legal right to divorce him if she can prove that he has money for bride price and refuses to remarry. As we saw in Chapter 14, wives are desirable because they work in the fields and care for pigs, by which wealth is measured, but not all men are wealthy enough to afford bride price for multiple wives.

Among the Turkana, a pastoral nomadic people of northern Kenya, the number of animals at a family's disposal is directly related to the number of adult women available to care for them. The more wives a man has, the more women there are to look after the livestock, and so the more substantial the family's holdings can be. Thus, it is not uncommon for a man's existing wife to search actively for another woman to marry her husband. Again, however, a substantial bride price is involved in marriage, and only men of wealth and prominence can afford large numbers of wives.

Although monogamy may be the most common form of marriage around the world, it is not the most preferred. That distinction goes to polygyny, which is favored by about 80 to 85 percent of the world's societies. Even in the United States, an estimated 50,000 people in the Rocky Mountain states live in households made up of a man with two or more wives. In spite of its illegality, regional law enforcement officials have adopted a "live and let live" attitude toward polygyny. Nor are those involved in such marriages uneducated. One woman—a lawyer and one of nine co-wives—expresses her attitude as follows:

> I see it as the ideal way for a woman to have a career and children. In our family, the women can help each other care for the children. Women in monogamous relationships don't have that luxury. As I see it, if this lifestyle didn't already exist, it would have to be invented to accommodate career women.[11]

---

[9]Goodenough, W. H. (1970). *Description and comparison in cultural anthropology* (p. 19). Chicago: Aldine.

[10]Pospisil, L. (1963). *The Kapauku Papuans of West New Guinea.* New York: Holt, Rinehart and Winston.

[11]Johnson, D. (1993). Polygamists emerge from secrecy, seeking not just peace but respect. In W. A. Haviland & R. J. Gordon (Eds.), *Talking about people* (pp. 129–131). Mountain View, CA: Mayfield.

Shown here are the members of a polygynous family in northern Kenya with some of the dwellings that make up their household compound.

Polygyny is particularly common in societies that support themselves by growing crops, and the bulk of the farm work is done by women. Under these conditions, women are valued both as workers as well as child bearers. Because the labor of wives in polygynous households generates wealth and little support is required from husbands, the wives' bargaining position within the household is a strong one. Often, they have considerable freedom of movement and some economic independence from sale of crops. Commonly, each wife within the household lives with her children in her own dwelling, apart from her co-wives and husband, who occupy other houses within some sort of larger household compound (note that the terms "house" and "household" need not be synonymous; a household may consist of several houses together, as here). Because of this residential autonomy, fathers are usually remote from their sons, who grow up among women. As noted in Chapter 16, this setting is conducive to the development of aggressiveness in adult males, who must prove their masculinity. As a consequence, a high value is often placed on military glory, and one reason for

going to war is to capture women, who may then become a warrior's co-wives. This wealth-increasing pattern is found in its fullest elaboration in sub-Saharan Africa, though it is known elsewhere as well (the Kapauku are a case in point). Moreover, it is still intact in the world today, as its wealth-generating properties at the household level have made it an economically productive system.[12]

In societies practicing wealth-generating polygyny most men and women do enter into polygynous marriages, although some are able to do this earlier in life than others. By contrast, in societies in which men are more heavily involved in productive work, generally only a small minority of marriages are polygynous. Under these circumstances, women are more dependent on men for support so that they are valued as child bearers more than for the work they do. This makes them especially vulnerable if they prove incapable of bearing children, which is one reason a man may seek another wife. Another reason for a man to take

[12]White, D. R. (1988). Rethinking polygyny: Co-wives, codes and cultural systems. *Current Anthropology, 29,* 529–572.

on secondary wives is to demonstrate his high position in society. But where most productive work is done by men, they must work exceptionally hard to support more than one wife, and few actually do so. Usually, it is the exceptional hunter, or a shaman ("medicine man") in a food-foraging society or a particularly wealthy man in an agricultural or pastoral society who is most apt to practice polygyny. When he does, it is usually of the sororal type, in which the women he marries are sisters. Having already lived together before marriage, they continue to do so with their husband, instead of occupying separate dwellings of their own.

Although monogamy and polygyny are the most common forms of marriage in the world today, other forms do occur, however rarely. **Polyandry,** the marriage of one woman to several men at the same time, is known in only a few societies, perhaps in part because a man's life expectancy is shorter than a woman's, and male infant mortality is high, so a surplus of men in a society is unlikely. Another reason is that it limits a man's descendants more than any other pattern. Fewer than a dozen societies are known to have favored polyandry, but they involve people as widely separated from one another as the eastern Inuit (Eskimos), Marquesan Islanders of Polynesia, and Tibetans. In Tibet, where inheritance is in the male line and arable land is limited, the marriage of brothers to a single woman averted the danger of constantly subdividing farmlands among all the sons of any one landholder.

Group marriage, in which several men and women have sexual access to one another, also occurs but rarely. Even in recent communal groups, among young people seeking alternatives to modern marriage forms, group marriage seems to be a transitory phenomenon, despite the publicity it has sometimes received.

Polyandry: The marriage custom of a woman having several husbands at one time; a form of polygamy.

Group marriage: Marriage in which several men and women have sexual access to one another.

The Levirate and the Sororate

If a husband dies, leaving a wife and children, it is often the custom that the wife marry one of the brothers of the dead man. This custom, called the **levirate,** not only provides social security for the widow and her children but also is a way for the husband's family to maintain their rights over her sexuality and her future children: It acts to preserve relationships previously established. When a man marries the sister of his dead wife, it is called the **sororate;** in essence, a family of "wife givers" supplies one of "wife takers" with another spouse to take the place of the one who died. In societies that have the levirate and sororate, the relationship between the two families is maintained even after the death of a spouse; and in such societies, an adequate supply of brothers and sisters is generally ensured by the structure of the kinship system (discussed in Chapter 21), in which individuals whom North Americans would call "cousins" are classified as brothers and sisters.

Serial Monogamy

A form of marriage that is becoming increasingly common in North American society today is **serial monogamy,** in which the man or the woman marries a series of partners in succession. Currently, more than 50 percent of first marriages end in divorce, and some experts project that two-thirds of recent marriages will not last.[13] Upon dissolution, the children of each marriage usually remain with the mother. This pattern is an outgrowth

---

Levirate: A marriage custom according to which a widow marries a brother of her dead husband.

Sororate: A marriage custom according to which a widower marries his dead wife's sister.

Serial monogamy: A marriage form in which a man or a woman marries or lives with a series of partners in succession.

---

[13]Stacey, J. (1990). *Brave new families* (pp. 15; 286, n. 46). New York: Basic Books.

Although the standards by which feminine beauty is judged have changed, the great emphasis Western cultures continue to place on it is illustrated by the use of Vanna White as a prop to turn letters on "Wheel of Fortune." The photo of Lillie Langtry (1852–1929) represents an earlier standard of beauty.

of one first described by sociologists and anthropologists among West Indians and lower-class urban African Americans in the United States. Early in life, women begin to bear children by men who are not married to them. In order to support themselves and their children, the women must look for work outside of the household, but to do so, they must seek help from other kin, most commonly the children's maternal grandmother. As a consequence, households are frequently headed by women (about 32 percent in the West Indies). After a number of years, however, an unmarried woman usually does marry a man, who may or may not be the father of some or all of her children. Under conditions of poverty, where this pattern has been most common, women are driven to seek this male support, owing to the difficulties of supporting themselves and their children, while at the same time fulfilling their domestic obligations.

In the United States, with the rise of live-in premarital arrangements between couples, the increasing necessity for women to seek work outside the home, and rising divorce rates, a similar pattern is becoming more common among middle-class whites. In 90 percent of divorce cases, women assume responsibility for any children; furthermore, of all children born in the United States today, fully

25 percent are born out of wedlock. Frequently isolated from kin or other assistance, women in single-parent households (which now outnumber nuclear family households) commonly find it difficult to cope. Within a year following divorce, the standard of living for women drops some 73 percent, whereas that of men *increases* by about 42 percent.[14] To be sure, fathers of children are usually expected to provide child support, but in 50 percent of the cases of children born out of wedlock, paternity cannot be established. Furthermore, failure of fathers to live up to their obligations is far from rare. One solution for unmarried women is to marry (often, to remarry), in order to get the assistance of another adult.

Choice of Spouse

The Western egalitarian ideal that an individual should be free to marry whomever he or she chooses is an unusual arrangement, certainly not one that is universally embraced. However

[14]Weitzman, L. J. (1985). *The divorce revolution: The unexpected social and economic consequences for women and children in America* (p. 338). New York: The Free Press.

Marriage is a means of creating alliances between groups of people—the relatives of the bride and those of the groom. Since such alliances have important economic and political implications, the decision cannot be left in the hands of the two young and inexperienced people. At the left is shown a Moroccan bride, whose marriage has been arranged between her parents and those of the groom. The picture on the right was taken at the wedding of Prince Charles and Lady Diana in England.

desirable such an ideal may be in the abstract, it is fraught with difficulties, certainly contributing to the apparent instability of marital relationships in modern North American society. Part of the problem is the great emphasis that the culture places on the importance of youth and glamour—especially on the part of women—for romantic love. Female youth and beauty are perhaps most glaringly exploited by the women's fashion, cosmetics, and beauty industries, but movies, TV, and the recorded music business have generally not lagged far behind; nor do advertisements for cigarettes, hard and soft drinks, beer, automobiles, and a host of other products that make liberal use of young, glamorous women. As anthropologist Jules Henry once observed, "even men's wear and toiletries could not be marketed as efficiently without an adoring, pretty woman (well under thirty-five years of age) looking at a man wearing a stylish shirt or sniffing at a man wearing a deodorant."[15] By no means are all North Americans taken in by this, but it does tend to nudge people in such a way that marriages may all too easily be based on trivial and transient characteristics. In no other part of the

world are such chances taken with something as momentous as marriage.

In many societies, marriage and the establishment of a family are considered far too important to be left to the whims of young people. The marriage of two individuals who are expected to spend their whole lives together and raise their children together is incidental to the more serious matter of making allies of two families by means of the marriage bond. Marriage involves a transfer of rights between families, including rights to property and rights over the children, as well as sexual rights. Thus, marriages tend to be arranged for the economic and political advantage of the family unit.

Arranged marriages, needless to say, are not commonplace in North American society, but they do occur. Among ethnic minorities, they may serve to preserve traditional values that people fear might otherwise be lost. Among families of wealth and power, marriages may be arranged by segregating their children in private schools and carefully steering them toward "proper" marriages. A careful reading of announced engagements in the society pages of the *New York Times* provides clear evidence of such family alliances. The following Original Study illustrates how marriages may be arranged in societies where such practices are commonplace.

[15]Henry, J. (1966). The metaphysic of youth, beauty, and romantic love. In S. Farber & R. Wilson (Eds.), *The challenge to women.* New York: Basic Books.

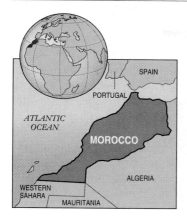

Original Study

Engagement and Marriage in a Moroccan Village[16]

Marriages in Sidi Embarek are all arranged by the parents of the couple in-volved, although the parties on occasion may make suggestions, or veto those of their parents. The author heard an older woman describe, with ob-vious glee, how she had foiled her parents' plans for her. The prospective groom's family sent a donkey bearing baskets full of ripe grapes and a large sack of *henna* (a cosmetic made of powdered leaves, used to color hair red in the U.S.) as a gift. To show her disapproval, Fatna dumped all the grapes on the ground, sprinkled the *henna* over them, and set the chickens loose in the mess—and ran away to hide. When her parents found her, they chained her ankles together so she could not run far, and went ahead with the wed-ding plans. But Fatna was not about to be subdued, and a girl friend helped her remove the chain from one ankle. She put this over her shoulder and ran off to a nearby French farm where she knew some Moroccan workers, and they interceded with the owner. He let her stay, and when her parents came for her persuaded them to delay the marriage. According to Fatna, she was fourteen at the time, and she did not marry (and then it was some-one else) for another several years.

Legally, a girl now has the right to refuse the match and is asked if she agrees to it during the engagement ceremony, but the legal prerogative does not always match the reality of the situation. If a girl fears a beating, or lack of further support from her family, she will agree publicly to the marriage, whatever her personal preferences (which are just beginning to be impor-tant in village marriages). Traditionally, marriage is an alliance between two families. It was said to often be of the patrilateral parallel cousin type, in which a boy married his father's brother's daughter, which had the effect of keeping jointly owned property in the same patrilineal family. Since the fam-ilies involved were related and may even have lived together as an extended family, it also meant that it was easier to assess both the types of relation-ships being entered into and the characters of the actors. Data collected in Sidi Embarek, however, show that in only three of twenty-four cases did per-sons related by blood (not only parallel cousins) marry, while in the other twenty-one marriages the partners were unrelated. While this was not a ran-dom or representatively selected sample, it does indicate that marriage of-ten occurs between unrelated couples.

Since marriage is mainly an alliance between two families, the partners do not have expectations of Western-style "love" (although movies and magazines are beginning to arouse such expectations), but rather work as a partnership with the object of raising a family. In this context arranged marriages are not resented, as many Western observers suspect, but rather accepted as the most sensible way to go about the matter. Even if a girl and boy in the village decide they want to marry, the decision is probably based on only a few meet-ings, since the sexes do not usually mix and in rural Morocco there is nothing like the custom of dating. Parents have more experience in life and more knowl-edge of the families which may be involved, so they are the logical agents.

The age at marriage of village girls is considerably higher than was that of their mothers. Many women recall that they had barely reached puberty when they were married ("I hardly had any breasts yet"), were afraid of their husbands, and ran away several times before finally settling down. There is now a Moroccan law setting the minimum age at marriage for girls as sixteen years and boys as eighteen, but this can easily be circumvented (an agreement with the proper official, or a change in the birth certificate) and is thus unlikely to be the cause of the higher age at marriage, now usually seventeen or eighteen for girls and the early or mid-twenties for boys. Unmarried teenage girls are still seen as a threat to the family honor, and in other rural regions of Morocco (e.g., the Southeast, near the Sahara) may still be married when they are eleven or twelve years old. The higher age at marriage in Sidi Embarek is probably due to the general lack of agriculturally based extended families living as a single household unit that could absorb and support the new couple. Marriages now usually do not occur until the male has a job with which he can support his new family, and when the job is not involved with family agriculture (and given the general shortage of jobs available), he is usually in his twenties before he can afford to be married. Thus age at marriage is higher, and most girls approve of this (although some of the boys get impatient). However, girls are still regarded as likely to be old maids if they are not married by the time they are twenty.

It is the male's family which selects the wife for its son and makes the first overtures to her family. The first sign the girl has of her impending marriage (it is improper for a father and daughter to discuss such things) is a visit paid to her home by a few female members of the groom's family, including his mother. While the males of the groom's family are important in selecting with which family they desire further ties, since they are men they can play little part in personally assessing the worthiness of the proposed bride. The women of the family are given this task, both because they can interact with her face-to-face, and because they will be more accurate judges of her housekeeping skills. In fact, household skills and honor are highly correlated; one would not expect to find an honorable girl a sloppy housekeeper, and a messy house suggests also a looseness in a woman's moral character. In this way, even if the women have been overruled initially by the men in the choice of the bride, they still have the opportunity to influence the decision in their favor.

If the groom's family is pleased with the reputation, demeanor (very shy and retiring), and household skills of the potential bride, males of the two families discuss the bride price (*sdaq* in Morocco, *mahr* in classical Arabic and in the Middle East). This sum is included in the marriage contract, and may either be given as a large lump sum to the family of the bride, or given only in part at the marriage with the other portion to be paid only in case of divorce or death of the husband. In either case, the bride price contributes to the stability of the marriage. A man considers seriously before divorcing a woman when it means he will have to pay her family additional money. Even if he has paid the total amount initially, he must still raise the bride price for another wife, for men seldom live as bachelors. Usually his family contributes to the bride price, and their hesitance to invest any further money leads them to put pressure on him to sustain his current marriage.

The inflation of bride prices in recent years is a problem for many bachelors and has also contributed to the rising age at marriage. The family of a country girl in 1972 demanded $100.00 or $200.00, while that of a city girl asked between $700.00 and $1,000.00 (village girls fell in between), in a country where the per capita income was then $80.00 a year. Divorcees and widows are much more easily attainable; their price fell within the $20.00 to $40.00 range (and did not require a large wedding celebration either), but usually only a man who has in some way lost his first wife will marry a woman who is not a virgin.

The Moroccan case also refutes (once again) those who suggest that a bride price involves the "selling" of a daughter. The money is paid to the bride's father, but it is used to buy jewelry for the bride or household furnishings for the new couple, and to finance the elaborate and costly wedding celebration. Guests do bring gifts, but these are usually something personal for the bride (such as a slip or nightgown) or cash, and are not large enough to furnish a house. The bride's father may manage to retain some of the money (for this reason some prospective grooms attempt to provide the furnishings themselves rather than giving cash to the bride's family to do so, confident that in this way they can be more economical), but not a great deal in any case. Rather, he is expected to contribute a similar sum as a dowry, to be used for the celebration, the bride's garments, and household furnishings.

If a bride price is agreed upon by the two families, there are exchanges of gifts and meals between them and a contract is prepared. The legal part of the ceremony of signing the marriage contract in rural Morocco (literally, "they do the paper") is considered as part of the engagement, but is actually also the only legal part of the marriage. If one decides afterwards to break the "engagement," one must obtain a divorce. The marriage is usually not consummated until months or even years later at a marriage ceremony (which is purely secular and consists of several days of celebration and feasting), but it is legally binding from the signing of the contract at the engagement.

The signature of the contract is done at home in the presence of a judge or his assistant and attended by members of each family. The bride is present but is spoken for by her father (or other male relative) except when asked if she agrees to the marriage. Otherwise she maintains a demure silence, her eyes cast down.

[16]Davis, S. S. (n.d.). *Patience and power, Women's lives in a Moroccan village* (pp. 26–30). Cambridge, MA: Schenkman.

Cousin Marriage

In the Original Study, mention was made of **patrilateral parallel cousin marriage** (Fig. 19.2), in which a man marries his father's brother's daughter (a parallel cousin is the child of father's brother or mother's sister). Although not obligatory, such marriages have been favored historically among Arabs, the ancient Israelites, and also in ancient Greece and traditional China. All of these societies

are hierarchical in nature—that is, some people have more property than others—and although male

Patrilateral parallel cousin marriage: Marriage of a man to his father's brother's daughter, or a woman to her father's brother's son (i.e., to a parallel cousin on the paternal side).

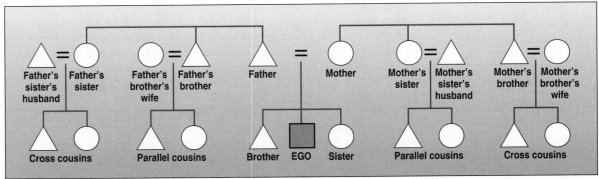

Figure 19.2 Anthropologists use diagrams of this sort to illustrate kinship relationships. Shown in this one is the distinction between cross and parallel cousins. In such diagrams, males are always shown as triangles, females as circles, marital ties by a =, sibling relationships as a horizontal line, and parent–child relationships as a vertical line. Terms are given from the perspective of the individual labeled *ego*, who can be female or male.

On the day that her marriage is announced, the Trobriand bride must give up the provocative miniskirts she has worn until then in favor of longer skirts, the first of which are provided by the groom's sister. This announces that her days of sexual freedom are gone.

dominance and descent are emphasized, property of interest to men is inherited by daughters as well as sons. Thus, when a man marries his father's brother's daughter (or, from the woman's point of view, her father's brother's son), property is retained within the single male line of descent. In these societies, generally speaking, the greater the property, the more this form of parallel cousin marriage is apt to occur.

Matrilateral cross cousin marriage (Fig. 19.2)—that is, of a man to his mother's brother's daughter, or a woman to her father's sister's son (a cross cousin is the child of mother's brother or father's sister)—is a preferred form of marriage in a variety of societies ranging from food foragers (Australian aborigines, for example) to intensive agriculturists (as among various peoples of South India). Among food-foraging peoples, who inherit relatively little in the way of property from adults, such marriages help establish and maintain ties of solidarity between social groups. In agricultural societies, on the other hand, the transmission of property is once again an important determinant.

Matrilateral cross cousin marriage: Marriage of a woman to her father's sister's son, or a man to his mother's brother's daughter (his cross cousin on the maternal side, her cross cousin on the paternal side).

In societies in which descent is traced exclusively in the female line, for instance, property and important rights usually pass from a man to his sister's son; under cross cousin marriage, sister's son is at the same time the man's daughter's husband.

Marriage Exchanges

In the Trobriand Islands, when a young couple decides to get married, they sit in public on the veranda of the young man's adolescent retreat, where all may see them. Here they remain until the bride's mother brings the couple cooked yams, which they then eat together, making their marriage official. This is followed a day later by the presentation of three long skirts to the bride by the husband's sister, a symbol of the fact that the sexual freedom of adolescence is now over for the newly wed woman. This is followed up by a large presentation of uncooked yams by the bride's father and her mother's brother, who represent both her lineage and that of her father. Meanwhile, the groom's father and mother's brother—representing his father's and his own lineages—collect such valuables as stone axe blades, clay pots, money, and the occasional Kula shell to present to the young wife's maternal kin and father. After the first year of the marriage, during which the bride's mother continues to provide the couple's meals of cooked yams, each of the young husband's relatives who provided valuables for his father and mother's brother to present to the bride's relatives will receive yams from her maternal relatives and father. All of this gift giving back and forth between the lineages to which the husband and wife belong, as well as those of their fathers, serves to bind the four parties together in a way that people respect, honor the marriage, and create obligations on the part of the woman's kin to take care of her husband in the future.

As among the Trobriand Islanders, marriages in many human societies are formalized by some sort of economic exchange. Among the Trobrianders, this takes the form of a gift exchange, as described earlier. Far more common is **bride price**, sometimes called bride wealth. This involves payments of money or other valuables to a bride's parents or other close kin. This usually happens in societies where the bride will become a member of

the household in which her husband grew up; it is they who will benefit from her labor, as well as the offspring she produces. Thus, her family must be compensated for their loss. Other forms of compensation are an exchange of women between families—my son will marry your daughter if your son will marry my daughter—or **bride service,** a period of time during which the groom works for the bride's family. In a number of societies more or less restricted to the western, southern, and eastern margins of Eurasia, in which the economy is based on intensive agriculture, women often bring a **dowry** with them at marriage. A form of dowry in the United States is the custom of the bride's family paying the wedding expenses. In effect, a dowry is a woman's share of parental property which, instead of passing to her upon her parents' death, is distributed to her at the time of her marriage. This is not to say that she retains control of this property after marriage: in a number of European countries, for example, a woman's property falls exclusively under the control of her husband. Having benefitted by what she has brought to the marriage, however, he is obligated to look out for her future well-being, even after his death. Thus, one of the functions of dowry is to ensure a woman's support in widowhood (or after divorce), an important consideration in a society where men carry out the bulk of productive work, and women are valued for their reproductive potential, but not the work they do. In such societies, women incapable of bearing children are especially vulnerable, but the dowry they bring with them at marriage helps protect them against desertion. Another function of dowry is to reflect the economic status of the woman in societies where differences in wealth are important. Thus, the property that a woman brings with her at marriage demonstrates that the man is marrying a woman whose standing is on a par with

Bride price: Compensation paid by the groom or his family to the bride's family upon marriage.

Bride service: A designated period of time after marriage during which the groom works for the bride's family.

Dowry: Payment of a woman's inheritance at the time of her marriage, either to her or to her husband.

In some societies, when a woman marries, she receives her share of the family inheritance (her dowry), which she brings to her new family (unlike bride price, which passes from the groom's family to the bride's family). Shown here are Slovakian women carrying the objects of a woman's dowry.

his own. It also permits women, with the aid of their parents and kin, to compete through dowry for desirable (that is, wealthy) husbands.

Relationships Modeled on Marriage

As we have seen, marriage, although defined in terms of a continuing sexual relationship between individuals of opposite sex, always involves various other nonsexual rights and obligations as well. In some societies, however, marriagelike arrangements may occur between individuals of the same sex. Although not marriage in the technical sense of our definition, they are clearly modeled on marriage and represent legal fictions designed to deal with problems for which ordinary marriage offers no satisfactory solution. Such is the case with woman/woman marriage, a practice sanctioned in many societies of sub-Saharan Africa, although in none does it involve more than a small minority of all women.

Although details differ from one society to another, woman/woman marriages among the Nandi of western Kenya may be taken as reasonably representative of such practices in Africa.[17] The Nandi are a pastoral people who also do considerable farming. Control of most significant property and the primary means of production—live-

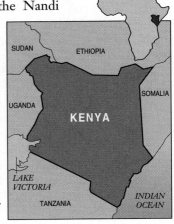

stock and land—is exclusively in the hands of men and may be transmitted only to their male heirs,

[17]The following is based on Obler, R. S. (1980). Is the female husband a man? Woman/woman marriage among the Nandi of Kenya. *Ethnology, 19,* 69–88.

usually their sons. Since polygyny is the preferred form of marriage, a man's property is normally divided equally among his wives for their sons to inherit. Within the household, each wife has her own house in which she lives with her children, but all are under the authority of the woman's husband, who is a remote and aloof figure within the household. In such situations, the position of a woman who bears no sons is difficult; not only does she not help perpetuate her husband's male line—a major concern among the Nandi—but she also has no one to inherit the proper share of her husband's property.

To get around these problems, a woman of advanced age to whom no sons have been born may become a female husband by marrying a young woman. The purpose of this arrangement is for the wife to provide the male heirs that her female husband could not. To accomplish this, the woman's wife enters into a sexual relationship with a man other than her female husband's; usually it is one of his male relatives. No other obligations exist between this woman and her male sex partner, and it is her female husband who is recognized as the social and legal father of any children born under these conditions.

In keeping with her role as female husband, this woman is expected to abandon her female gender identity and, ideally, dress and behave as a man. In practice, the ideal is not completely achieved, for the habits of a lifetime are difficult to reverse. Generally, it is in the context of domestic activities, which are most highly symbolic of female identity, that female husbands most completely assume a male identity.

For the individuals who are parties to woman/woman marriages, there are several advantages. By assuming male identity, a barren or sonless woman raises her status considerably and even achieves near equality with men, who otherwise occupy a far more favored position in Nandi society than do women. A woman who marries a female husband is usually one who is unable to make a good marriage, often because she has lost face as a consequence of premarital pregnancy. By marrying a female husband, she, too, raises her status, and secures legitimacy for her children. Moreover, a female husband is usually less harsh and demanding, spends more time with her, and allows her a greater say in decision making than does a male

husband. The one thing she may not do is engage in sexual activity with her marriage partner; in fact, female husbands are expected to abandon sexual activity altogether, even with their male husbands, to whom they remain married even though the woman now has her own wife.

Divorce

Like marriage, divorce in non-Western societies is a matter of great concern to the families of the couple. Since marriage is less often a religious than it is an economic matter, divorce arrangements can be made for a variety of reasons and with varying degrees of difficulty.

Among the Gusii of Kenya, sterility or impotence were grounds for a divorce. Among the Chenchu of Hyderabad and the Caribou Indians of Canada, divorce was discouraged after children were born, and a couple were usually urged by their families to adjust their differences. By contrast, in the southwestern United States, a Hopi woman might divorce her husband at any time merely by placing his belongings outside the door to indicate he was no longer welcome. Divorce was fairly common among the Yahgan, who lived at the southernmost tip of South America, and was seen as justified if the husband was considered cruel or failed as a provider.

Divorce in these societies seems familiar and even sensible and in one way or another, the children are taken care of. An adult unmarried woman is almost unheard of in most non-Western societies; a divorced woman will soon remarry. In many societies, economic considerations are often the strongest motivation to marry. On the island of New Guinea, a man does not marry because of sexual needs, which he can readily satisfy out of wedlock, but because he needs a woman to make pots and cook his meals, to fabricate nets and weed his plantings. A man without a wife among the Australian aborigines is in an unsatisfactory position, since he has no one to supply him regularly with food or firewood.

It is of interest to note that divorce rates in Western societies are low when compared to those in some societies, notably matrilineal societies such as that of the Hopi. Yet they are high enough to cause many North Americans to worry about the

In Europe, where both men and women inherit family wealth, the "marriage" of women to the Church as nuns passed wealth that might otherwise have gone to husbands and offspring to the Church instead.

that we have already mentioned, on which marriages may all too easily be based. Beyond this, marriage is supposed to involve an enduring supportive, intimate bond between a man and woman, full of affection and love. In this relationship, people are supposed to find escape from the pressures of the competitive workaday world, as well as from the legal and social constraints that affect their behavior outside the family. Yet, in a society in which people are brought up to seek individual gratification, where this often is seen to come through competition at someone else's expense (see Chapter 16) and in which women have traditionally been expected to be submissive to men, it should not come as a surprise to find that the reality of marriage does not always live up to the ideal. Harsh treatment and neglect of spouses—usually wives by husbands—in the United States is neither new nor rare; furthermore, people are more tolerant of violence directed against spouses and children than they are against outsiders. As anthropologists Jane Collier, Michelle Rosaldo, and Sylvia Yanagisako have observed: "A smaller percentage of homicides involving family members are prosecuted than those involving strangers. We are faced with the irony that in our society the place where nurturance and noncontingent [unconditional] affection are supposed to be located is simultaneously the place where violence is most tolerated."[18] What has happened in recent years is that people have become less inclined to moral censure of those—women especially—who seek escape from unsatisfactory marriages. No longer are people as willing to "stick it out at all costs," no matter how intolerable the situation may be. Thus, divorce is increasingly exercised as a sensible reaction to marriages that don't work.

[18]Collier, J., Rosaldo, M. Z., & Yanagisako, S. (1982). Is there a family? New anthropological views. In B. Thorne & M. Yalom (Eds.), *Rethinking the family: Some feminist problems* (p. 36). New York: Longman.

future of marriage and the family in the contemporary world. Undoubtedly, the causes of divorce in the United States are many and varied. Among them are the trivial and transient characteristics

CHAPTER SUMMARY

Among primates, the human female is unique in her ability to engage in sexual behavior whenever she wants to or whenever her culture tells her it is appropriate, irrespective of whether or not she is fertile. While such activity may reinforce social bonds between men and women, it can also be disruptive, so that in every society there are rules that govern sexual access. The near universality of the incest taboo, which forbids sexual relations between parents and their children and usually between siblings, has long interested anthropologists, but a truly convincing explanation of the taboo has yet to be advanced. Related to incest are the practices of endogamy and exogamy. Endogamy is marriage within a group of individuals; exogamy is marriage outside the group. If the group is limited to the immediate family, all societies can be said to prohibit endogamy and practice exogamy. At the same time, societies that practice exogamy at one level may practice endogamy at another. Community endogamy, for example, is a relatively common practice. In a few societies, royal families are known to have practiced endogamy rather than exogamy among siblings, in order to preserve intact the purity of the royal line.

Although defined in terms of a continuing sexual relationship between a man and woman, marriage should not be confused with mating. Although mating takes place within marriage, it often takes place outside of it as well. Unlike mating, marriage is backed by social, legal, and economic forces. In some societies, new families are formed through marriage, but this is not true for all societies.

Monogamy, or the taking of a single spouse, is the most common form of marriage, primarily for economic reasons. A man must have a certain amount of wealth to be able to afford polygyny, or marriage to more than one wife at the same time. On the other hand, in societies where most of the productive work is done by women, polygyny may serve as a means of generating wealth for a household. Although few marriages in a given society may be polygynous, it is regarded as an appropriate, and even preferred, form of marriage in the majority of the world's societies. Since few communities have a surplus of men, polyandry, or the custom of a woman having several husbands, is uncommon. Also rare is group marriage, in which several men and several women have sexual access to one another. The levirate ensures the security of a woman by providing that a widow marry her husband's brother; the sororate provides that a widower marry his wife's sister.

Serial monogamy is a form in which a man or woman marries a series of partners. In recent decades, this pattern has become increasingly common among middle-class North Americans as individuals divorce and remarry.

In the United States and many of the other industrialized countries of the West, marriages are often based on an ideal of romantic love, in which youthful beauty is emphasized. In no other parts of the world would marriages based on such trivial and transitory characteristics be expected to work. In non-Western societies economic considerations are of major concern in arranging marriages. Love follows rather than precedes marriage. The family arranges marriages in societies in which it is the most powerful social institution. Marriage serves to bind two families as allies.

Preferred marriage partners in many societies are particular cross cousins (mother's brother's daughter if a man; father's sister's son if a woman) or less commonly, parallel cousins on the paternal side (father's brother's son or daughter). Cross cousin marriage is a means of establishing and maintaining solidarity between groups. Marriage to a paternal parallel cousin serves to retain property within a single male line of descent.

In many human societies, marriages are formalized by some sort of economic exchange. Sometimes this takes the form of reciprocal gift exchange between the bride's and groom's relatives. More common is bride price, the payment of money or other valuables from the groom's to the bride's kin; this is characteristic of societies in which the women will work and bear children for the husband's family. An alternative arrangement is for families to exchange daughters. Bride service occurs when the groom is expected to work for a period of time for the bride's family. Dowry is the payment of a woman's inheritance at the time of marriage to her or her husband; its purpose is to ensure support for women in societies where most productive work is done by men and women are valued for their reproductive potential alone.

In some societies, arrangements exist between individuals that are modeled on marriage. An example is woman/woman marriage, as practiced in many African societies. Such arrangements provide a socially approved way to deal with problems for which conventional marriage offers no satisfactory solution.

Divorce is possible in all societies, though reasons for divorce as well as its frequency vary widely from one society to another. In the United States, factors contributing to the breakup of marriages include the trivial and transitory characteristics on which many marriages are based, and the difficulty of establishing a supportive, intimate bond in a society in which people are brought up to seek individual gratification, often through competition at someone else's expense, and in which women have traditionally been expected to be submissive to men.

SUGGESTED READINGS

duToit, B. M. (1991). *Human sexuality: Cross cultural readings.* New York: McGraw-Hill.

Of the numerous texts that deal with most aspects of human sexuality, this is the only one that gives adequate recognition to the fact that most peoples in the world do things differently than they are done by North Americans. This reader deals cross-culturally with such topics as menstrual cycle, pair bonding, sexuality, pregnancy and childbirth, childhood, puberty, birth control, sexually transmitted diseases, sex roles, and the climacteric.

Goodenough, W. H. (1970). *Description and comparison in cultural anthropology.* Chicago: Aldine.

The book illustrates the difficulties anthropologists confront in describing and comparing social organization cross-culturally. The author begins with an examination of marriage and family, clarifying these and related concepts in important ways.

Goody, J. (1976). *Production and reproduction: A comparative study of the domestic domain.* Cambridge: Cambridge University Press.

This book is especially good in its discussion of the interrelationship between marriage, property, and inheritance. Although cross–cultural in its approach, the book will fascinate readers with its many insights into the history of marriage in the Western world.

Mair, L. (1971). *Marriage.* Baltimore: Penguin.

Mair traces the evolution of marriage and such alternative relationships as surrogates and protectors. Commenting on marriage as an institution and drawing her examples from tribal cultures, Mair deals with the function, rules, symbolic rituals, and economic factors of marriage. She also cites the inferior status of women and discusses the self-determining behavior of "serious free women" as an important factor in social change.

CHAPTER
20
FAMILY AND HOUSEHOLD

A MARRIED COUPLE AND THEIR CHILDREN ON THEIR WAY TO GO

FISHING. ONE OF THE BASIC FUNCTIONS OF FAMILIES IS

RAISING CHILDREN.

CHAPTER PREVIEW

What Is the Family?

The human family is a group composed of a woman, her dependent children, and at least one adult male joined through marriage or blood relationship. The family may take many forms, ranging all the way from a single married couple with their children, as in North American society, to a large group composed of several brothers and sisters with the sisters' children, as in southwest India among the Nayar. The particular form taken by the family is related to particular social, historical, and ecological circumstances.

What Is the Difference Between Family and Household?

Households are task-oriented residential units within which economic production, consumption, inheritance, child rearing, and shelter are organized and carried out. In the vast majority of human societies, households either consist of families, or else their core members constitute families, even though some members of the household may not be relatives of the family around which it is built. In some societies, although households are present, families are not. Furthermore, in some societies where families are present, they may be less important in people's thinking than the households of which they are parts.

What Are Some of the Problems of Family and Household Organization?

Although families and households exist to solve in various ways problems with which all peoples must deal, the different forms that they may take are all accompanied by their own characteristic problems. Where families and households are small and relatively independent, as they are in North American society, individuals are isolated from the aid and support of kin and must fend for themselves in many situations. By contrast, families that include several adults within the same large household must find ways of controlling various kinds of tensions that invariably exist between their members.

The nuclear family, consisting of a married couple and dependent offspring, is held up as the ideal in the United States.

The family, long regarded by North Americans as a critically necessary, core social institution, today has become a matter for controversy and discussion. Women going outside the home to take jobs rather than staying home with children, young couples living together without the formality of marriage, soaring divorce rates, and increasing numbers of households headed by a single parent have raised questions about the functions of the family in North American society and its ability to survive in a period of rapid social change. Evidence of the widespread interest in these questions can be seen in the convening, in 1980, of a White House Conference on Families. Since then, scarcely a political campaign for national office has passed without frequent reference to what candidates like to think are "traditional family values."

Does the family, as presently constituted in North America, offer the best environment for bringing up children? Does it impose an inferior status on the woman, confined and isolated in the home, performing household and child-raising chores? Does the man, locked into an authoritarian role, suffer unduly in his personal development from bearing the primary responsibility for sup-

port of the family? Are there adequate substitutes for people who have no family to care for them, such as old people and orphans? If the family as people in the United States know it today is found wanting, what are the alternatives?

Historical and cross-cultural studies of the family offer as many different family patterns as the fertile human imagination can invent. The one considered "normal" or "natural" to most North Americans —a discrete and independent living unit consisting of the nuclear family (Fig. 20.1)—is in fact no more normal or natural than any other and cannot be used as the standard against which other forms should be measured. Neither universal, nor even common among human societies, the independent nuclear family emerged only recently in human history. Its roots go back to a series of regulations imposed by the Roman Catholic Church in the fourth century A.D. that prohibited close marriages, discouraged adoption, and condemned polygyny, concubinage, divorce, and remarriage (all of which had previously been perfectly respectable, as the Old Testament of the Bible, among other sources, makes clear). Not only did this strengthen the conjugal tie between a single

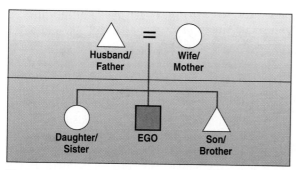

Figure 20.1 This diagram shows the relationships in a nuclear family, like those found in North American society.

POSTQVAM CONSVMATI SVNT DIES OCTO VT CIRCVCIDERET PVER VOCATV E NOM ÉI IHES.LVCE.II.C.
ELONGAVI FVGIENS Z MANSI INSOLITVDINE . PS . XXXXXV . C

SVRGE ACCIPE PVERVM Z MATREM EI Z FVGE INEGIP TVM .MACEI.II.C.

The Holy Family of Christianity. Mary's husband Joseph was her father's brother's son, and was himself the product of a leviratic marriage. Even though both kinds of marriage were considered proper in the early days of Christianity, they were not allowed by the Church after the fourth century.

concubinage, divorce, remarriage, and discouraging adoption, the Church removed the means by which people overcame these odds and made sure that they would have male heirs. The result of all this was to facilitate the transfer of property from families to the Church, which rapidly became the largest landowner in most European countries, a position it has retained to this day. By insinuating itself into the very fabric of domestic life, of heirship, and marriage, the Church gained tremendous control over the grass roots of society, enriching itself in the process.[1]

With the industrialization of Europe and North America, the nuclear family became further isolated from other kin. One reason for this is that industrial economies require a mobile labor force; people must be prepared to move to where the jobs are, something that is most easily done without excess kin in tow. Another reason is that the family came to be seen as a kind of refuge from a public world that people saw as threatening to their sense of privacy and self-determination.[2] Within the family, relationships were supposed to be enduring and noncontingent, entailing love and affection, based upon cooperation, and governed by feeling and morality. Outside the family, where people sold their work and negotiated contracts, relationships increasingly were seen as competitive, temporary, and contingent upon performance, requiring buttressing by law and legal sanction. Such views were most widely held in the late nineteenth and early twentieth centuries, and in the United States, independent nuclear family households reached their highest frequency around 1950, when 60 percent of all households conformed to this model.[3] Since then, things have changed, and a mere 26 percent of U.S. households now conform to the independent nuclear family ideal. More are now headed by divorced, separated, and never-married individuals. Increasingly large numbers of people have found more intimacy and emotional support in relationships

[1]Goody, J. (1983). *The development of the family and marriage in Europe* (pp. 44–46). Cambridge: Cambridge University Press.

[2]Collier, J., Rosaldo, M. Z., & Yanagisako, S. (1982). Is there a family? New anthropological views. In B. Thorne & M. Yalom (Eds.), *Rethinking the family: Some feminist problems* (pp. 34–35). New York: Longman.

[3]Stacey, J. (1990). *Brave new families* (pp. 5, 10). New York: Basic Books.

man and woman, at the expense of consanguineal or "blood" ties, it also ensured that large numbers of people would be left with no male heirs. It is a biological fact that 20 percent of all couples will have only daughters and another 20 percent will have no children at all. By eliminating polygyny,

outside the family, thereby becoming less inclined to tolerate the harsh treatment and neglect of children and spouses, especially wives, that has been all too common within families. (In the United States, some two million women experience abuse from the men in their families, and at least an equal number of children are also abused.)

The family as it has emerged in Europe and North America, then, is the product of particular historical and social circumstances; where these have differed, so have family forms. Thus, how men and women in other societies live together must be studied, not as bizarre and exotic forms of human behavior, but as logical outcomes of peo-ples' experience living in particular times, places, and social situations.

FAMILY AND SOCIETY

Although many North Americans continue to think of families as standing in opposition to the rest of society, the truth is that they are affected by, and in turn affect, the values and structure of the society in which they are embedded. For a closer look at this, we may take a more detailed look at the rise and fall of nuclear families in the United States.

Original Study
The Ephemeral Modern Family[4]

Now that the "modern" [i.e., independent nuclear] family system has almost exited from its historical stage, we can perceive how peculiar, ephemeral, and internally contradictory was this once-revolutionary gender and kinship order. Historians place the emergence of the modern [North] American family among white middle-class people in the late eighteenth century; they depict its flowering in the nineteenth century and chart its decline in the second half of the twentieth. Thus, for white Americans, the history of modern families traverses the same historical trajectory as that of modern industrial society. What was modern about upper-middle-class family life in the half century after the American Revolution was the appearance of social arrangements governing gender and kinship relationships that contrasted sharply with those of "traditional," or premodern, patriarchal corporate units.

The premodern family among white Colonial Americans, an institution some scholars characterize as "the Godly family," was the constitutive element of Colonial society. This integrated economic, social, and political unit explicitly subordinated individual to corporate family interests and women and children to the authority of the household's patriarchal head. Decisions regarding the timing and crafting of premodern marriages served not the emotional needs of individuals but the economic, religious, and social purposes of larger kin groups, as these were interpreted by patriarchs who controlled access to land, property, and craft skills. Nostalgic images of "traditional" families rarely recall their instability or diversity. Death visited Colonial homes so frequently that second marriages and blended households composed of stepkin were commonplace. With female submission thought to be divinely prescribed, conjugal love was a fortuitous bonus, not a prerequisite of such marriages. Similarly the doctrine of innate depravity demanded authoritarian parenting to break the will and save the souls of obstinate children, a project that required extensive paternal involvement in child rearing. Few boundaries between family and work impeded such patriarchal supervision, or segregated the sexes who labored at their arduous and interdependent tasks in close proximity. Boundaries between public and private life were equally permeable. Communities regulated proper family conduct, intervening actively to enforce disciplinary codes, and parents exchanged their children as apprentices and servants.

Four radical innovations differentiate modern from premodern family life among white Americans: (1) Family work and productive work became separated, rendering women's work invisible as they and their children became economically dependent on the earnings of men. (2) Love and companionship became the ideal purposes of marriages that were to be freely contracted by individuals. (3) A doctrine of privacy emerged that attempted to withdraw middle-class family relationships from public scrutiny. (4) Women devoted increased attention to nurturing fewer and fewer children as mothering came to be exalted as both a natural and demanding vocation.

The rise of the modern American family accompanied the rise of industrial capitalist society, with its revolutionary social, spatial, and temporal reorganization of work and domestic life. The core premises and practices of the new family regime were far more contradictory than those of the premodern family order. Coding work as masculine and home as feminine modern economic arrangements deepened the segregation of the sexes by extracting men from, and consigning white married women to, an increasingly privatized domestic domain. The institutionalized subordination of these wives to their husbands persisted; indeed, as factory production supplanted domestic industry, wives became increasingly dependent on their spouse's earnings. The doctrine of separate gender spheres governing the modern family order in the nineteenth century was so potent that few married women among even the poorest of native white families dared to venture outside their homes in search of income.

The proper sphere of working-class married white women also was confined to the home. Yet few working-class families approximated the modern family ideal before well into the twentieth century. Enduring conditions of poverty, squalor, disease, and duress rivaling those in industrializing England, most immigrant and native white working-class families in nineteenth-century America depended on supplementary income. Income from women's out work, child labor, lodgers, and the earnings of employed unmarried sons and daughters supplemented the meager and unreliable wages paid to working men. Not until the post–World War II era did substantial numbers of working-class households achieve the "modern family" pattern.

If the doctrine of separate, and unequal, gender spheres limited women's domain and rendered their work invisible, it also enhanced their capacity to formulate potent moral and political challenges to patriarchy. Men ceded the domains of child rearing and virtue to "moral" mothers who made these responsibilities the basis for expanding their social influence and political rights. This and the radical ideologies of individualism, democracy, and conjugal love, which infused modern family culture, would lead ultimately to its undoing. It is no accident, historians suggest, that the first wave of American feminism accompanied the rise of the modern family.

With rearview vision one glimpses the structural fragility of the modern family system, particularly its premise of enduring voluntary commitment. For modern marriages, unlike their predecessors, were properly affairs not of the purse but of the heart. A romantic "until death do us part" commitment volunteered by two young adults acting largely independent of the needs, interests, or wishes of their kin was the vulnerable linchpin of the modern family order. It seems rather remarkable, looking back, that during the first century of the modern family's cultural ascendancy, death did part the vast majority of married couples. But an ideology of conjugal love and companionship implies access to divorce as a safety valve for failures of youthful judgment or the vagaries of adult affective development. Thus, a statistical omen of the internal instability of this form of marriage lies in the unprecedented rise of divorce rates that accompanied the spread of the modern family. Despite severe legal and social restrictions, divorce rates began to climb at least as early as the 1840s. They have continued their ascent ever since, until by the middle of the 1970s divorce outstripped death as a source of marital dissolution. A crucial component of the modern family system, divorce would ultimately prove to be its Achilles' heel.

For a century, as the cultural significance of the modern family grew, the productive and even the reproductive work performed within its domain contracted. By the end of the "modern" industrial era in the 1950s, virtually all productive work had left the home. While advances in longevity stretched enduring marriages to unprecedented lengths, the full-time homemaker's province had been pared to the chores of housework, consumption, and the cultivation of a declining number of progeny during a shortened span of years.

Those Americans, like myself, who came of age at that historic moment were encouraged to absorb a particularly distorted impression of the normalcy and timelessness of the modern family system. The decade between the late 1940s and the late 1950s represents an aberrant period in the history of this aberrant form of family life. Fueled in part, as historian Elaine May has suggested, by the apocalyptic Cold War sensibilities of the post–World War II nuclear age, the nation indulged in what would prove to be a last-gasp orgy of modern nuclear family domesticity. Three-fifths of American households conformed to the celebrated breadwinner–fulltime homemaker modern form in 1950, as substantial sectors of working-class men began at long last to secure access to a family wage. A few years later Walt Disney opened the nation's first family theme park in southern California, designed to please and profit from the socially conservative fantasies of such increasingly prosperous families.

The aberrant fifties temporarily reversed the century's steady decline in birth rates. The average age of first-time visitors to the conjugal altar also dropped to record lows. Higher percentages of Americans were marrying than ever before or since, and even the majority of white working-class families achieved coveted homeownership status. It was during this time that Talcott Parsons provided family sociology with its most influential theoretical elaboration of the modern American family, of how its nuclear household structure and complementary division of roles into female "expressive" and male "instrumental" domains was sociologically adaptive to the functional demands of an industrial society. Rare are the generations, or even the sociologists, who perceive the historical idiosyncrasies of the normal cultural arrangements of their time.

The postwar baby boom was to make the behaviors and beliefs of that decade's offspring disproportionately significant for the rest of their lives. The media, the market, and all social and political institutions would follow their development with heightened interest. Thus, a peculiar period in U.S. family history came to set the terms for the waves of rebellion against, and nostalgia for, the passing modern family and gender order that have become such prominent and disruptive features of the American political landscape. The world's first generation of childhood television viewers grew up, as I did, inundated by such weekly paeans to the male breadwinner nuclear household and modern family ideology as *Father Knows Best, Leave It to Beaver,* and *Ozzie and Harriet.* Because unusual numbers of us later pushed women's biological "clock" to its reproductive limits, many now find ourselves parenting (or choosing not to) in the less innocent age of *Thirtysomething, Kate and Allie,* and *Who's the Boss?* For beneath the sentimental gloss that the fifties enameled onto its domestic customs, forces undermining the modern family of the 1950s accelerated while those sustaining it eroded. In the midst of profamily pageantry, nonfamily households proliferated. As the decade drew to a close, the nation entered what C. Wright Mills, with characteristic prescience, termed its "postmodern period." The emergent postindustrial economy shifted employment from heavy industries to nonunionized clerical, service, and new industrial sectors. Employers found themselves irresistibly attracted to the nonunionized, cheaper labor of women and, thus, increasingly to that of married women and mothers.

One glimpses the ironies of class and gender history here. For decades industrial unions struggled heroically for a socially recognized male breadwinner wage that would allow the working class to participate in the modern gender order. These struggles, however, contributed to the cheapening of female labor that helped gradually to undermine the modern family regime. Escalating consumption standards, the expansion of mass collegiate coeducation, and the persistence of high divorce rates then gave more and more women ample cause to invest a portion of their identities in the "instrumental" sphere of paid labor. Thus, middle-class women began to abandon their confinement in the modern family just as working-class women were approaching its access ramps. The former did so, however, only after the wives of working-class men had pioneered the twentieth-century revolution in women's paid work. Entering employment during the catastrophic 1930s, participating in defense industries in the 1940s, and raising their family incomes to middle-class standards by returning to the labor force rapidly after child rearing in the 1950s, working-class women quietly modeled and normalized the postmodern family standard of employment for married mothers. Whereas in 1950 the less a man earned, the more likely his wife was to be employed, by 1968 wives of middle-income men were the most likely to be in the labor force.

[4]Stacey, J. (1990). *Brave new families* (pp. 6–11). New York: Basic Books.

FUNCTIONS OF THE FAMILY

Among humans, reliance on group living for survival is a basic characteristic. They have inherited this from their primate ancestors, though they have developed it in their own distinctively human ways.

Even among monkeys and apes, group living requires the participation of adults of both sexes. Among those species which, like us, have taken up life on the ground, as well as among those species most closely related to us, adult males are normally much larger and stronger than females, and their teeth are usually more efficient for fighting. Thus,

A female baboon with her infant and male friend. Baboon males are protective of their female friends, even though they are not always the fathers of their friends' infants. Thus shielded from danger and harassment from other troop members, females are able to give their infants the attention they require to survive.

they are essential for the group's defense. Moreover, the close and prolonged relationship between infants and their mothers, without which the infants cannot survive, renders the adult primate female less well suited than the males to handle defense.

Nurturance of Children

Taking care of the young is primarily the job of the adult primate female. Primate babies are born relatively helpless, and remain dependent upon their mothers for a longer time than any other animals (a chimpanzee, for example, cannot survive without its mother until it reaches the age of 4 or even 5). This dependence is not only for food and physical care, but, as a number of studies have shown, primate infants deprived of normal maternal attention will not grow and develop normally, if they survive at all. The protective presence of adult males shields the mothers from both danger and harassment from other troop members, allowing them to give their infants the attention they require.

Among humans, the sexual division of labor has been developed beyond that of other primates.

Until the recent advent of synthetic infant formulas, human females have more often than not been occupied much of their adult lives with child rearing. And human infants need no less active "mothering" than do the young of other primates. For one thing, they are even more helpless at birth, and for another, the period of infant dependency is longer in humans. Besides all this, studies have shown that human infants, no less than other primates, need more than just food and physical care if they are to develop normally. But among humans, unlike other primates, all this "mothering" does not have to be provided by the infant's biological mother. Not only may other women provide the child with much of the attention it needs, but so may men. In many societies children may be handled and fondled as much by men as by women, and in some societies men are more nurturant to children than are women.

In all human societies, even though women may be the primary providers of child care, they have other responsibilities as well. While several of the economic activities that they have traditionally engaged in have been compatible with their child-rearing role and have not placed their offspring at risk, this cannot be said of all of their

Chapter 19, a family is a residential group composed of a woman, her dependent children, and at least one male joined through marriage or consanguineal ("blood") relationship.

Well suited though it may be for the task, we should not suppose that the family is the only unit capable of providing these conditions. In fact, other arrangements are possible, as on the Israeli kibbutz where groups of children are raised by paired teams of male and female specialists. In many food-foraging societies (the Ju/'hoansi and Mbuti, discussed in Chapters 16 and 17, are good examples), all adult members of a community share in the responsibilities of child care. Thus, when parents go off to hunt or to collect plants and herbs, they may leave their children behind, secure in the knowledge that they will be looked after by whatever adults remain in the camp. Yet another arrangement may be seen among the Mundurucu, a horticultural people of South America's Amazon forest. Their children live in houses with their mothers, apart from all men until the age of 13, whereupon the boys leave their mothers' houses to go live with the men of the village. Because Mundurucu men and women do not live together as members of discrete residential units, it cannot be said that families are present in their society.

One alternative to the family as a child-rearing unit is the Israeli kibbutz. Here, children of a kibbutz are shown on their playground.

activities. As a case in point, the common combination of child care with food preparation, especially if cooking is done over an open fire, creates a potentially hazardous situation for children. With the mother (or other caregiver) distracted by some other task, the child may all too easily receive a severe burn or bad cut, with serious consequences. The economic activities of women have generally complemented those of men, even though in some societies individuals may perform tasks normally assigned to the opposite sex, as the occasion dictates. Thus, men and women could share the results of their labors on a regular basis, as was discussed in Chapters 17 and 18.

An effective way both to facilitate economic cooperation between the sexes while at the same time providing for a close bond between mother and child is through the establishment of residential groups that include adults of both sexes. The differing nature of male and female roles, as these are defined by different cultures, requires a child to have an adult of the same sex available to serve as a proper model for the appropriate adult role. The presence of adult men and women in the same residential group provides for this. As defined in

FAMILY AND HOUSEHOLD

Although it is often stated that some form of family is present in all human societies, the Mundurucu case just cited demonstrates otherwise. In Mundurucu villages, the men all live together in a single house with all boys over the age of 13; women live with others of their sex as well as younger boys in two or three houses grouped around that of the men. As among the Nayar (discussed in Chapter 19), married

A celebration at the palace in the Yoruba city of Oyo, Nigeria. As is usual in societies in which royal households are found, that of the Yoruba includes many individuals not related to the ruler, as well as the royal family itself.

men and women are members of separate households, meeting periodically for sexual activity.

Although the family is not universally present in human societies, the **household,** defined as the basic residential unit within which economic production, consumption, inheritance, child rearing, and shelter are organized and carried out, is universally present. Among the Mundurucu, the men's house constitutes one household, and the women's houses constitute others. Although in this case, as in many, each house is in effect a household, there are a number of societies in which households are made up of two or more houses together, as we shall see later in this chapter.

In many human societies, most households in fact constitute families, although other sorts of

households may be present as well (single-parent households, for example, in the United States and many Caribbean countries). Often, a household may consist of a family along with some more distant relatives of family members. Or, coresidents may be unrelated, as in the case of service personnel in an elaborate royal household, apprentices in the household of craft specialists, or low status clients of rich and powerful patrons. In such societies, even though people may think in terms of households rather than families, it is the latter around which the households are built. Thus, even though the family is not universal, in the vast majority of human societies, the basic core of the household is the family.

Household: The basic residential unit in which economic production, consumption, inheritance, child rearing, and shelter are organized and carried out; may or may not be synonymous with family.

Conjugal family: A family consisting of one (or more) man married to one (or more) woman, and their offspring.

FORM OF THE FAMILY

As suggested earlier in this chapter, the family may take any one of a number of forms in response to particular social, historical, and ecological circumstances. At the outset, a distinction must be made between **conjugal families,** which are formed on the basis of marital ties, and consanguine families, which are not. As defined in Chapter 19, consanguine families consist of related women, their brothers, and the women's offspring. Such families are not common; the classic case is the Nayar household group. The Nayar are not unique, however, and consanguine families are found elsewhere, for example, among the Tory Islanders, a Roman Catholic, Gaelic-speaking fisher folk living off the coast of Ireland. These people do not marry until they are in their late 20s or early 30s, by which time there is tremendous resistance to breaking up existing household arrangements. The Tory Islanders look at it this way: "Oh well, you get married at that age, it's too late to break up arrangements that you have already known for a long time. . . . You know, I have my sisters and brothers to look after, why should I leave home to go live with a husband? After all, he's got his sisters and his brothers looking after him."[5] Because the community numbers only a few hundred people, husbands and wives are within easy commuting distance of one another.

The Nuclear Family

The form of conjugal family most familiar to most North Americans is the independent nuclear family, which in spite of its precipitous decline is still widely regarded as the standard in the United States and Canada. In these countries it is not considered desirable for young people to live with their parents beyond a certain age, nor is it considered a moral responsibility for a couple to take their aged parents into their home when the old people are no longer able to care for themselves. For this there are retirement communities and nursing homes, and to take aged parents into one's own home is commonly regarded as not only an economic burden, but also as a threat to the privacy and independence of the household.

The nuclear family is also apt to be prominent in societies such as the Inuit, which live in harsh environments. In the winter the Inuit husband and wife, with their children, roam the vast Arctic wilderness in search of food. The husband hunts and makes shelters. The wife cooks, cares

for the children, and makes and keeps the clothing in good repair. One of her chores is to chew her husband's boots to soften the leather for the next day, so that he can resume his search for game. The wife and her children could not survive without the husband, and life for a man is unimaginable without a wife.

Certain parallels can be drawn between the nuclear family in industrial societies and families living under especially harsh environmental conditions. In both cases, the family is an independent unit that must be prepared to fend for itself; this creates a strong dependence of individual members on one another. There is minimal help from outside in the event of emergencies or catastrophes. When their usefulness is at an end, the elderly are cared for only if it is feasible. In the event of death of the mother or father, life becomes precarious for the child. Yet this form of family is well adapted to a life that requires a high degree of geographical mobility. For the Inuit, this mobility permits the hunt for food; for North Americans, it is the hunt for jobs and improved social status that requires a mobile form of family unit.

Not even among the Inuit, however, is the nuclear family as isolated from other kin as it has become among most nonnative North Americans. When Inuit families are off by themselves, it is regarded as a matter of temporary expediency; most of the time, they are found in groups of at least a few families together with members of one having relatives in all of the others.[6] Families cooperate with one another on a daily basis, sharing food and other resources, looking out for each other's children, and sometimes even eating together. The sense of shared responsibility for each other's children,

---

[5]Fox, R. (1981, December 3). Interview for Coast Telecourses, Inc., Los Angeles.

[6]Graburn, N. H. H. (1969). *Eskimos without igloos: Social and economic development in Sugluk* (pp. 56–58). Boston: Little, Brown.

Among the Inuit, nuclear families such as the one shown here are the norm, although they are not as isolated from other kin as are nuclear families in the United States.

and general welfare, in Inuit multifamily groups contrasts with families in the United States, which are basically "on their own." Here the state has assigned sole responsibility to the family for child care and the welfare of its members, with relatively little assistance from outside.[7] To be sure, families can and often do help one another out, but they are under no obligation to do so. In fact, once children reach the age of majority, parents have no further legal obligation to them, nor do the children to their parents. When families do have difficulty fulfilling their assigned functions—as is increasingly the case—even though it be through no fault of their own, less support is available to them from the community at large than in most of the world's "stateless" societies, including that of the Inuit.

The Extended Family

In North America, nuclear families have not always had the degree of independence that they came to have with the rise of industrialism. In an earlier,

more agrarian era, the small nuclear family commonly was part of a larger **extended family.** This kind of family, in part conjugal and in part consanguine, might include grandparents, mother and father, brothers and sisters, perhaps an uncle and aunt, and a cousin or two. All these people, some related by blood and some by marriage, lived and worked together. Because members of the younger generation brought their spouses to live in the family, extended families, like consanguine families, had continuity through time. As older members died off, new members were born into the family.

In the United States, such families have survived, until recently, in some communities, as along the Maine coast.[8] There they developed in response to a unique economy featuring a mix of farming and seafaring, coupled with an ideal of self-sufficiency. Because family farms were incapable of providing

Extended family: A collection of nuclear families, related by ties of blood, that live together in one household.

[7]Collier, J., Rosaldo, M. Z., & Yanagisako, S. (1982). Is there a family? Some new anthropological views. In B. Thorne & M. Yalom (Eds.), *Rethinking the family: Some feminist problems* (pp. 28–29). New York: Longman.

[8]Haviland, W. A. (1973, Fall). Farming, seafaring and bilocal residence on the coast of Maine. *Man in the Northeast, 6,* 31–44.

Extended families like this one are still found in parts of rural North America.

self-sufficiency, seafaring was taken up as an economic alternative. Seagoing commerce, however, was periodically afflicted by depression, and so family farming remained important as a cushion against economic hard times. The need for a sufficient labor pool to tend the farm, while at the same time furnishing officers, crew, or (frequently) both for locally owned vessels, was satisfied by the practice of a couple, when they married, settling on the farm of either the bride's or the groom's parents. Thus, most people spent their lives cooperating on a day-

to-day basis in economic activities with close relatives, all of whom lived together (even if in separate houses) on the same farm.

The Maya of Guatemala and southern Mexico also live in extended family households.[9] In many of their communities, sons bring their wives to live in houses built on the edges of a small open plaza, on one edge of which their father's house already

[9]Vogt, E. Z. (1990). *The Zinacantecos of Mexico, A modern Maya way of life* (2nd ed.) (pp. 30–34). Fort Worth: Holt, Rinehart and Winston.

Members of modern Maya extended families carry out various activities on the household plaza; here, for example, women weave and family members interact with outsiders.

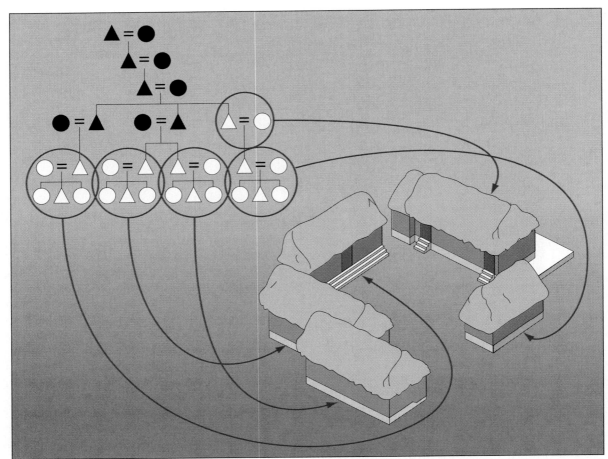

Figure 20.2   This diagram shows the living arrangements and relationships in a patrilocal extended family. Deceased household members are blacked out.

stands (Fig. 20.2). Numerous household activities take place out on this plaza; here women may weave, men may receive guests, and children play together. The head of the family is the sons' father, who makes most of the important decisions. All members of the family work together for the common good and deal with outsiders as a single unit.

Extended families living together in single households were important social units among the Hopi Indians of Arizona.[10] Ideally, the head of the household was an old woman; her married daughters, their husbands, and their children lived with her. The women of the household owned land, but

it was tilled by the men (usually their husbands). When extra help was needed during the harvest, for example, other male relatives, friends, or persons designated by local religious organizations formed work groups and turned the hard work into a festive occasion. The women performed household tasks, such as the making of pottery, together.

The 1960s saw a number of attempts on the part of young people in the United States to reinvent a form of extended family living. Their families were groups of unrelated nuclear families that held property in common and lived together. It is further noteworthy that the lifestyle of these modern families often emphasized the kinds of cooperative ties found in the rural North American extended family of old, which provided a labor pool

[10]Forde, C. D. (1950). *Habitat, economy and society* (pp. 225–245). New York: E. P. Dutton.

This old photo shows members of a Hopi Indian matrilocal extended family in front of their house. Traditionally, women who were sisters and daughters, with their husbands, lived in adjacent rooms of a single tenement.

for the many tasks required for economic survival. In some of them the members even reverted to old traditional gender roles; the women took care of the child rearing and household chores, while the men took care of those tasks that took people outside of the household itself.

Residence Patterns

Where some form of conjugal or extended family is the norm, family exogamy requires that either the husband or wife, if not both, must move to a new household upon marriage. There are five common patterns of residence that a newly married couple may adopt:

1. As just described for the Maya, a woman may go to live with her husband in the household in which he grew up, which is known as **patrilocal residence.**
2. As among the Hopi, the man may leave the family in which he grew up to live with his wife in her parents' household, which is called **matrilocal residence.**
3. As in the case of extended families on the coast of Maine, a married couple may have the option of choosing whether to live matrilocally

or patrilocally, an arrangement that is labeled **ambilocal residence.**

4. As in most of modern North America, a married couple may form a household in an independent location, an arrangement referred to as **neolocal residence.**
5. The final pattern, to which we will return later for an example, is far less common than any of the others; this is **avunculocal residence,** in which a married couple goes to live with the groom's mother's brother.

There are variations of these patterns, but they need not concern us here.

Why do postmarital patterns of residence differ so from one society to another? Briefly, the prime determinants of residence are ecological circumstances, although other factors enter in as well. If these make the role of the man predominant in subsistence, patrilocal residence is a likely result. This is even more likely if in addition men own property that can be accumulated, if polygyny is customary, if warfare is prominent enough to make cooperation among men especially important, and if there is elaborate political organization in which men wield authority. These conditions are most often found together in societies that rely on animal husbandry and/or intensive agriculture for their subsistence. Where patrilocal residence is customary, it is often the case that the bride must move to a different band or community. In such

Patrilocal residence: A residence pattern in which a married couple lives in the locality associated with the husband's father's relatives.

Matrilocal residence: A residence pattern in which a married couple lives in the locality associated with the wife's relatives.

Ambilocal residence: A pattern in which a married couple may choose either matrilocal or patrilocal residence.

Neolocal residence: A pattern in which a married couple may establish their household in a location apart from either the husband's or the wife's relatives.

Avunculocal residence: Residence of a married couple with the husband's mother's brother.

cases, her parents' family is not only losing the services of a useful family member, they are losing her potential offspring as well. Hence, some kind of compensation to her family, most commonly bride price, is usual.

Matrilocal residence is a likely result if ecological circumstances make the role of the woman predominant in subsistence. It is found most often in horticultural societies, where political organization is relatively uncentralized, and where cooperation among women is important. Under matrilocal residence, men usually do not move very far from the family in which they were raised, and so they are available to help out there from time to time. Therefore, marriage usually does not involve compensation to the groom's family.

Ambilocal residence is particularly well suited to situations where economic cooperation of more people than are available in the nuclear family is needed, but where resources are limited in some way. Because one can join either the bride's or the groom's family, family membership is flexible, and one can go where the resources look best or where one's labor is most needed. This was once the situation on the peninsulas and islands along the coast of Maine, where extended family households were based upon ambilocal residence. The same pattern of residence is particularly common among food-foraging peoples, as among the Mbuti of Africa's Ituri forest. Typically, a Mbuti marries someone from another band, so that each individual has in-laws who live elsewhere. Thus, if foraging is bad in their part of the forest, there is somewhere else to go where food may be more readily available. Ambilocality greatly enhances the Mbutis' opportunity to find food. It also provides a place to go if a dispute breaks out with someone in the band in which one is currently living. Consequently, Mbuti camps are constantly changing their composition as people split off to go live with their in-laws, while others are joining from other groups. For a people like food foragers, who find their food in nature and who maintain an egalitarian social order, ambilocal residence can be a crucial factor in both survival and conflict resolution.

Neolocal residence occurs where the independence of the nuclear family is emphasized. In industrial societies like the United States, where most economic activity occurs outside rather than inside the family and where it is important for in-

This Trobriand Island chief, shown in front of his house, will be succeeded by his sister's son. Hence, men who will become chiefs live avunculocally.

dividuals to be able to move where jobs are to be found, neolocal residence is better suited than any of the other patterns.

Avunculocal residence is favored by the same factors that promote patrilocal residence, but only in societies in which descent through women is deemed crucial for the transmission of important rights and property. Such is the case among the people of the Trobriand Islands, where each individual is a member from birth of a group of relatives, all of whom trace their descent back through their mother, their mother's mother, and so on to the one woman from whom all others are descended. Each of these descent groups holds property, consisting of hamlet sites, bush and garden lands and, in some cases, beach fronts, to which members have rights of access. These properties are controlled each generation by a chief or other

In extended families such as this one, tensions may arise between the married couples, as younger individuals must defer to older ones.

leader who inherits these rights and obligations, but because descent is traced exclusively through women, these cannot be inherited by a man from his father. Thus, succession to positions of leadership passes from a man to his sister's son. For this reason, a man who is in line to take over control of his descent group's assets will take his wife to live with the one he will succeed—his mother's brother. This enables him to observe how the older man takes care of his hamlet's affairs, as well as to learn the oral traditions and magic that he will need to be an effective leader.

Although Trobriand leaders and chiefs live avunculocally, most married couples in this society live patrilocally. This allows sons to fulfill their obligations to their fathers, who helped build up and nurture them when they were small; in return, the sons will inherit personal property such as clay pots and valuable stone axe blades from their fathers. This also gives men access to land controlled by their fathers' descent groups in addition to their own, enabling them to improve their own economic and political position in Trobriand society. In short, here, as in any human society, practical considerations play a central role in determining where people will live following marriage.

PROBLEMS OF FAMILY AND HOUSEHOLD ORGANIZATION

Effective though the family may be at organizing economic production, consumption, inheritance, and child rearing, at the household level, relationships within the family inevitably involve a certain amount of conflict and tension, even though they may involve a great deal of warmth and affection. The potential for conflict is always there, however, and must be dealt with so families do not become dysfunctional. Different forms of families are associated with different sorts of tensions, and the means employed to manage these tensions differ accordingly.

Polygamous Families

A major source of tension within polygamous families is the potential for conflict that exists between the multiple spouses of the one individual to whom they are married. For example, under polygyny (the most common form of polygamy), the several wives of a man must be able to get along with a minimum of bickering and jealousy. One way to handle this is through sororal polygyny, or marriage to women who are sisters. Presumably, women who have grown up together can get along as co-wives of a man more easily than can women who grew up in different households and have never had to live together before. Another mechanism is to provide each wife with a separate apartment or house within a household compound, perhaps requiring the husband to adhere to a system of rotation for sleeping purposes. The latter at least prevents the husband from playing obvious favorites among his wives. Although polygyny can be difficult for the women involved, this is not always the case (recall the comments of the women in polygynous marriages in the Rocky Mountains discussed in the previous chapter). In some polygynous societies, women enjoy considerable economic autonomy, and in societies where women's work is hard and boring, polygyny can provide a means of sharing the work load and alleviating boredom through sociability.

Extended Families

Extended families, too, no matter how well they may work, have their own potential areas of stress. Decision making in such families usually rests with an older individual, and other family members must defer to the elder's decisions. Among a group of siblings, an older one usually has the authority. Then there is the problem of in-marrying spouses, who must adjust their ways to conform to the expectations of the family into which they have come to live. To combat these problems, cultures rely on various techniques to enforce harmony, including such things as dependence training and the concept of "face" or "honor." Dependence training, discussed in Chapter 16, is typically associated with extended family organization, raising people who are more inclined to be compliant and accept their lot in life than are individuals who have been raised to be independent. One of the many problems faced by young people in North American society who have experimented with extended family living is that they have generally been raised to be independent, making it hard to defer to the wishes of others when they are in disagreement.

The concept of "face" may constitute a particularly potent check on the power of senior members of extended families. Among pastoral nomads of North Africa, for example, young men can escape from ill treatment of a father or older brother by leaving the patrilocal extended family to join the household of his maternal relatives, in-laws, or even an unrelated family willing to take him in.[11] Because men lose face if their sons or brothers flee in this way, they are generally at pains to control their behavior in order to prevent this from happening. Women, who are the in-marrying spouses, may also return to their natal families if they are mistreated in their husbands' families. A woman who does this exposes her husband and his family to scolding by her kin, again causing loss of face.

Effective though such techniques may be in societies that stress the importance of the group over the individual, and where loss of face is to be avoided at almost any cost, not all conflict may be avoided. When all else fails to restore harmony, siblings may be forced to demand their share of family assets in order to set up separate households, and in this way, new families may come into being. Divorce, too, may be possible, although the ease with which this may be accomplished varies considerably from one society to another. In societies that practice matrilocal residence, divorce rates tend to be high, reflecting the ease with which unsatisfactory marriages may be terminated. In some (not all) societies with patrilocal residence, by contrast, divorce may be all but impossible, at least for women (the in-marrying spouses). This was the case in traditional China, for example, where women were raised to be cast out of their families.[12] When they married, they exchanged their dependence on fathers and brothers for absolute dependence on husbands, and later in life, sons. Without divorce as an option to protect themselves against ill treatment, women went to great lengths to develop the strongest bond possible between themselves and their sons in order that the latter would rise to their mothers' defense when necessary. So single minded were many women in developing such relationships with their

[11]Abu-Lughod, L. (1988). *Veiled sentiments: Honor and poetry in a Bedouin society* (pp. 99–103). Berkeley: University of California Press.

[12]Wolf, M. (1972). *Women and the family in rural Taiwan* (pp. 32–35). Stanford: Stanford University Press.

Some young North Americans have attempted to recreate the extended family in the formation of communes. These attempts sometimes run into trouble as young people cope with stress associated with extended family organization for which they are unprepared.

sons that they often made life miserable for their daughters-in-law, who were seen as competitors for their sons' affections.

Nuclear Families

Just as extended families have built into them particular sources of stress and tensions, so, too, do nuclear families, especially in modern industrial societies where the family has lost one of its chief reasons for being: its economic function as a basic unit of production. Instead of staying within the fold, working with and for each other, one or both adults must seek work outside of the family. Furthermore, their work may keep them away for prolonged periods of time. If both spouses are employed

(as is increasingly the case since couples find it ever more difficult to maintain their desired standard of living on a single income), the requirement for workers to go where their jobs take them may pull the husband and wife in different directions. On top of all this, neolocal residence tends to isolate husbands and wives from both sets of kin. Because clearly established patterns of responsibility no longer exist between husbands and wives, couples must work these out for themselves. Two things make this difficult, one being the traditional dependence of women on men that has for so long been a feature of Western society. In spite of recent changes in the direction of greater equality between men and women, all too often the partners to a marriage do not come to it as equals. The other problem is the great emphasis North American society places on the pursuit of individual gratification through competition, often at someone else's expense. The problem is especially acute if the husband and wife grew up in households with widely divergent outlooks on life and ways of doing things. Furthermore, being isolated from their kin, there is no one on hand to help stabilize the new marriage; for that matter, intervention of kin would likely be regarded as interference.

Isolation from kin also means that a young mother-to-be must face pregnancy and childbirth without the aid and support of female kin with whom she already has a relationship and who have been through pregnancy and childbirth themselves. Instead, she must turn for advice and guidance to physicians (who are more often men than women), books, and friends and neighbors who themselves are likely to be inexperienced. The problem continues through motherhood, with the absence of experienced women within the family, as well as a clear model for child rearing. Therefore, reliance on physicians, books, and mostly inexperienced friends for advice and support continues. The problems are exacerbated, for families differ widely in the ways in which they deal with their children. In the competitive society of the United States, the children themselves recognize this and often use such differences against their parents to their own ends.

A further problem connected with the raising of children confronts the woman who has devoted herself entirely to this task: What will she do when the children are gone? One answer to this, of

In the United States, single mothers who are heads of households are often placed in no-win situations: If they work to support the household, they are seen as unfit mothers; if they stay home with the children, they are labelled "deadbeats."

course, is to pursue some sort of career, but this, too, may present problems. She may have a husband with traditional values who thinks "a woman's place is in the home." Or it may be difficult to begin a career in middle age. To begin a career earlier, though, may involve difficult choices: Should she have her career at the expense of having children, or should she have both simultaneously? If the latter, there are not likely to be kin available to look after the children, as there would be in an extended family, and so arrangements must be made with people who are non–kin. And, of course, all of these thorny decisions must be made without the aid and support of kin.

The impermanence of the nuclear family itself may constitute a problem in the form of anxieties over old age. Once the children are gone, who will care for the parents in their old age? In North American society, there is no *requirement* for the children to do so. The problem does not arise in an extended family, where one is cared for from womb to tomb.

Female-Headed Households

In North America, as increasing numbers of adults have sought escape from dysfunctional nuclear families through divorces and as young adults have become more sexually active outside of wedlock, there has been a dramatic rise in the incidence of single-parent households headed by women. By the 1990s, there were twice as many households in the United States headed by divorced, separated, and never-married individuals as there were occupied by supposedly "normal" nuclear families.[13] In the vast majority of cases, as we saw in Chapter 19, children remain with their mother, who then faces the problem of having to provide for them as well as for herself. In the case of divorces, fathers are usually required to pay child support, but they are not always able or willing to do this, and when they are the amount is often not sufficient to pay for all the food, clothes, and medical care that are needed, as well as the cost of child care allowing the woman to seek income-producing work outside the house in order to support herself. One of the problems here is that support payments determined in court are based not so much by the needs of the woman and her children as by her "earning potential" which, if she has been true to middle-class values by staying at home rather than going out to earn money, is seen as low given that she has not brought income into the family. What is ignored, of course, is the fact that her unpaid work at home contributed to her husband's ability to pursue a financially rewarding career, but since she is not paid for her work at home, no value is set on it.

As in the case of working women who remain with their husbands, kin may not be available to look after the single mother's children, and so outside help must be sought and (usually) paid for, thereupon making it even more difficult for the woman to support herself adequately. To compound the problem, women frequently lack the skills necessary to secure other than menial and low-paying jobs, not having acquired such skills earlier in order to raise children. Even when they do have skills, women are not paid as much as are men who hold the same jobs. Not surprisingly, as the number of female-headed households has

[13]Stacey, J. (1990). *Brave new families* (pp. 5, 15). New York: Basic Books.

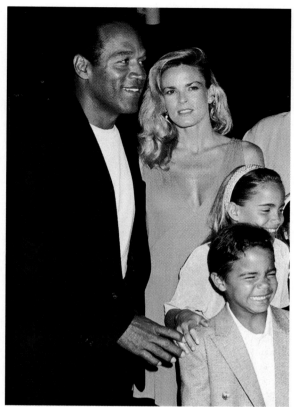

In North America, families are widely believed to be places of refuge from the rough-and-tumble outside world. Yet, domestic violence is far from rare, and women and children are its usual victims. Shown here is O. J. Simpson and his wife Nicole, whom he was tried and acquitted of murdering.

increased, so has the number of women (and, of course, their children) who live below the poverty line. Over one third of all female-headed households in the United States now fall into this category, and one quarter of all children are poor (Fig. 20.3). Moreover, these women and children are the ones most severely affected by cutbacks that have been made in social welfare programs since 1980. Even before Ronald Reagan was inaugurated president, the purchasing power of women was declining, and since then, the programs that were of most assistance to women and children are the ones that have suffered the deepest cuts. One reason for this is a flawed assumption that is nonetheless entrenched in public policy: That the poverty seen in so many female-headed households is caused by the supposedly deviant nature of such households. This is alleged to be caused in part by women wanting to go outside the home to earn money instead of finding husbands to support them so that they can stay home and bring up the children. Women have participated in the labor force throughout U.S. history, whereas only a limited proportion of the population ever possessed the resources to be "proper," nonworking "ladies."[14] Far from being "pathological," female-headed households are in fact a rational response to economic constraints in

[14]Mullings, L. (1989). Gender and the application of anthropological knowledge to public policy in the United States. In Morgen, S. (Ed.), *Gender and anthropology* (pp. 362–365). Washington: American Anthropological Association.

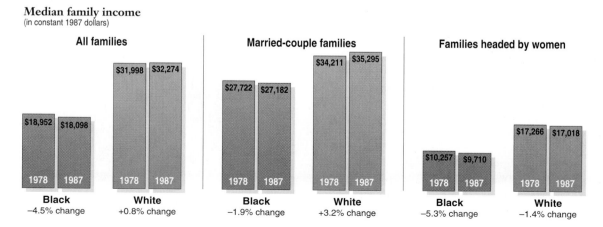

Figure 20.3 Median family income: Married-couple families and female-headed families compared. Source: Center on Budget and Policy Priorities, based on Bureau of the Census data.

Anthropology Applied
DEALING WITH INFANT MORTALITY

In 1979 Dr. Margaret Boone, an anthropologist who now works as a social science analyst with the program evaluation and methodology division of the U.S. government's General Accounting Office, began a residency on the staff of Washington, D.C.'s only public hospital. Her task was to gain an understanding of the sociocultural basis of poor maternal and infant health among inner-city African Americans—something about which little was known at the time—and to communicate that understanding to the relevant public and private agencies, as well as to a wider public. As Dr. Boone put it:

> The problem was death—the highest infant death rate in the United States. In Washington, D.C., babies were dying in their first years of life at the highest rate for any large American city, and nobody could figure out why.[*]

In Washington, as in the rest of the United States, infant mortality is mainly an African-American health problem because of the large and increasing number of disadvantaged African-American women; African-American infants die at almost twice the rate of White infants. In the hospital in which Boone worked, the population served was overwhelmingly poor and Black.

For the next year and a half, Boone worked intensively reviewing medical, birth, and death records; carrying out statistical analyses; and interviewing women whose infants had died, as well as nurses, physicians, social workers, and administrators. As she points out, no matter how important the records review and statistical analyses were (and they were important), her basic understanding of reproduction in the inner-city African-American community came from the daily experience working in the "community center" for birth and death, which was the hospital—classic anthropological participant observation.

What Boone found out was that infant death and miscarriage are associated with absence of prenatal care, smoking, the consumption of alcohol, psychological distress during pregnancy and hospitalization, evidence of violence, ineffective contraception, rapid childbearing in the teens (average age at first pregnancy was 18), and the use of several harmful drugs together (contrary to everyone's expectations, heroin abuse was less important a factor than alcohol abuse, and drug abuse in general was no higher among women whose infants died than among those whose infants did not). Cultural factors found to be important include a belief in a birth for every death, a high value placed on children, a value on gestation without necessarily any causal or sequential understanding of the children it will produce, a lack of planning ability, distrust of both men and women, and a separation of men's roles from the process of family formation (indeed, three quarters of the women in Boone's study were unmarried at the time of delivery). Of course, some of these factors were already known to be related to infant mortality, but many were not.

As a consequence of Boone's work, there have been important changes in policies and programs relating to infant mortality. It is now widely recognized that the problem goes beyond mere medicine, and that medical solutions have gone about as far as they can go. Only by dealing with the social and cultural factors connected to impoverished African-American health in the inner city will further progress be made, and new service delivery systems are slowly emerging to reflect this fact.

[*]Boone, M. S. (1987). Practicing sociomedicine: Redefining the problem of infant mortality in Washington, D.C. In R. M. Wulff & S. J. Fiske (Eds.), *Anthropological praxis: Translating knowledge into action* (p. 56). Boulder, CO: Westview Press.

a society that defines gender roles in such a way that puts women at a disadvantage.

Single-parent households headed by women are neither new, nor are they restricted to industrialized societies like the United States. They have been known and studied for a long time in the countries of the Caribbean basin, where men have historically been exploited as a cheap source of labor on plantations. Under such conditions, men have no power and few economic rewards; hence they are tenuously attached at best to any particular household. These are held together by women, who as producers of subsistence foods, provide the means of economic survival for households. Similar female-headed households are becoming increasingly common in other "underdeveloped" countries, too, as development projects increasingly restrict the ability of women to earn a living wage (reasons for this are discussed in Chapters 15 and 16). Thus, women constitute the majority of the poor, the underprivileged, and the economically and socially disadvantaged in most of the world's societies, just as is coming to be the case in the United States. In "underdeveloped" countries, the situation has been made worse by "reforms" required by the International Monetary Fund (IMF) in order to renegotiate payment of foreign debts. Cutbacks in government education, health, and social programs for debt service have their most direct (and negative) impact on women and children, at the same time that further development designed to increase foreign exchange (for debt repayment and the financing of further industrialization) also comes at the expense of women and children. Meanwhile, the prices people must pay for basic necessities of life increase (to cut down on unfavorable balances of trade). If

a women is *lucky*, the wage she earns to buy bread for herself and her children remains constant, even if low, while the price she must pay for that bread continues to rise.

At the start of this chapter we posed a number of questions relating in one way or another to the effectiveness of the family, as it is known today in North America, in meeting human needs. From what we have just discussed, it is obvious that neolocal nuclear families impose considerable anxiety and stress upon the individuals in such families. Deprived of the security and multiplicity of emotional ties to be found in polygamous, extended, or consanguine families, if something goes wrong, it is potentially more devastating to the individuals involved. On the other hand, it is also obvious that alternative forms of family and household organization come complete with their own distinctive stresses and strains. Which of the alternatives is preferable? One must answer it depends on what problems one wishes to overcome and what price one is willing to pay.

In the United States, it is clear that the problems inherent in the "traditional" nuclear family have led to a marked decline in the percentage of households occupied by such families. At the same time, the conditions that gave rise to these families in the first place have changed. So far, no single family structure or ideology has arisen to supplant the nuclear family, nor can we predict which (if any) of the alternatives will gain preeminence in the future. The only thing of which we can be certain is that family and household arrangements, not just in the United States but throughout the world, will continue to evolve, as they always have, as the conditions to which they are sensitive change.

CHAPTER SUMMARY

Dependence on group living for survival is a basic human characteristic. Nurturance of children has traditionally been the job of the adult female, although men may also play a role, and in some societies men are even more involved with their children than are women. In addition to at least some child

care, women also carry out other economic tasks that complement those of men. The presence of adults of both sexes in a residential group is advantageous in that it provides the child with an adult model of the same sex, from whom can be learned the gender-appropriate role as defined in that society.

A definition of the family that avoids Western ethnocentrism sees it as a group composed of a woman and her dependent children, with at least one adult male joined through marriage or blood relationship. In most human societies, families either constitute households, or else households are built around them. Although families are not universally present in human societies, households are. Households are defined as the basic residential units in which economic production, consumption, inheritance, child rearing, and shelter are organized and carried out.

Far from being a stable, unchanging entity, the family may take any one of a number of forms in response to particular social, historical, and ecological circumstances. Conjugal families are those formed on the basis of marital ties. The smallest conjugal unit of mother, father, and their dependent children is called the nuclear family. Contrasting with the conjugal is the consanguine family, consisting of women, their brothers, and the dependent children of the women. The nuclear family, which became the ideal in North American society, is also found in societies that live in harsh environments, such as the Inuit. In industrial societies as well as societies that exist in particularly harsh environments, the nuclear family must be able to look after itself. The result is that individual members are strongly dependent on very few people. This form of family is well suited to the mobility required in food-foraging groups and in industrial societies as well, where frequent job changes necessitate family mobility. Among food foragers, however, the nuclear family is not as isolated from other kin as in modern industrial society.

Characteristic of many nonindustrial societies is the large extended, or conjugal-consanguineal, family. Ideally, some of an extended family's members are related by blood, others are related by marriage, and all live and work together as members of a single household. Conjugal or extended families are based upon five basic residence patterns: patrilocal, matrilocal, ambilocal, neolocal, and avunculocal.

Different forms of family organization are accompanied by their own distinctive problems. In polygamous families there is the potential for conflict among the several spouses of the one individual to whom they are married. One way to ameliorate this problem is through sororal polygyny. In extended families, the matter of decision making may be the source of stress, resting as it does with an older individual whose views may not coincide with those of the younger family members. In-marrying spouses in particular may have trouble complying with the demands of the family in which they must now live.

In neolocal, nuclear families, individuals are isolated from the aid and support of kin, and so husbands and wives must work out their own solutions to the problems of living together and having children. The problems are especially difficult in North American society, owing to the inequality that still persists between men and women, the great emphasis placed on individualism and competition, and an absence of clearly understood patterns of responsibility between husbands and wives, as well as a clear model for child rearing.

In North America, an alternative to the independent nuclear family, which is now twice as common, is the single-parent household, usually headed by a woman. Female-headed households are also common in underdeveloped countries. Because the women in such households are hard pressed to provide adequately for themselves as well as for their children, more and more women in the United States and abroad find themselves sinking into poverty.

SUGGESTED READINGS

Fox, R. (1968). *Kinship and marriage in an anthropological perspective*. Baltimore: Penguin.

Fox's book is a good introduction to older, orthodox theories about the family.

Goody, J. (1983). *The development of the family and marriage in Europe*. Cambridge: Cambridge University Press.

A historical study, which shows how the nature of the family changed in Europe in response to regulations introduced by the Catholic Church in order to weaken the power of kin groups and gain access to property. Explains how European patterns of kinship and marriage came to differ from those of the ancient circum-Mediterranean world and those that succeeded them in the Middle East and North Africa.

Netting, R. M., Wilk, R. R., & Arnould, E. J. (Eds.). (1984). *Households: Comparative and historical studies of the domestic group*. Berkeley, CA: University of California Press.

This collection of essays by 20 anthropologists and historians focuses on how and why households vary within and between societies, and over time within single societies.

Stacey, J. (1990). *Brave new families: Stories of domestic conflict in late twentieth-century America*. New York: Basic Books.

Written by a sociologist, this book takes an anthropological approach to understanding the changes affecting family structure in the United States. Stacey's conclusion is that "the family" is *not* here to stay, nor should we wish otherwise. For all the difficulties attendant on "the family's demise," alternative arrangements do open up hopeful possibilities for the future.

Thorne, B., & Yalom, M. (Eds.). (1982). *Rethinking the family: Some feminist questions*. New York: Longman.

As anthropologists have paid more attention to how institutions and practices work from a woman's perspective, they have had to reexamine existing assumptions about families in human societies. The 12 original essays in this volume, by scholars in the fields of economics, history, law, literature, philosophy, psychology, and sociology as well as anthropology, examine such topics as the idea of the monolithic family; the sexual division of labor and inequality; motherhood; parenting; mental illness; and relations between family, class, and state. Especially recommended is the essay: "Is There a Family? New Anthropological Views."

KINSHIP AND DESCENT

In Papua New Guinea, members of a clan participate in putting on a feast for members of other clans. Because members of a clan are all blood relatives of one another, all are obliged to contribute to the feast. In many human societies, kin groups, like clans, are important organizational units.

CHAPTER PREVIEW

What Are Descent Groups?

A descent group is a kind of kinship group in which being a lineal descendant of a particular real or mythical ancestor is a criterion of membership. Descent may be reckoned exclusively through men, exclusively through women, or through either at the discretion of the individual. In some cases, two different means of reckoning descent are used at the same time, to assign individuals to different groups for different purposes.

What Functions Do Descent Groups Serve?

Descent groups of various kinds—lineages, clans, phratries, and moieties—are convenient devices for solving a number of problems that commonly confront human societies: how to maintain the integrity of resources that cannot be divided without being destroyed; provide work forces for tasks that require a labor pool larger than households can provide; and allow members of one sovereign local group to claim support and protection from members of another. Not all societies have descent groups; in many food-foraging and industrial societies, some of these problems are often handled by the kindred, a group of people with a living relative in common. The kindred, however, does not exist in perpetuity, as does the descent group, nor is its membership as clearly and explicitly defined. Hence, it is generally a weaker unit than the descent group.

How Do Descent Groups Evolve?

Descent groups arise from extended family organization, so long as there are problems of organization that such groups help to solve. This is most apt to happen in food-producing, as opposed to food-foraging, societies. First to develop are localized lineages, followed by larger, dispersed groups such as clans and phratries. With the passage of time, kinship terminology itself is affected by and adjusts to the kinds of descent or other kinship groups that are important in a society.

All societies have found some form of family and/or household organization a convenient way to deal with problems faced by all human groups: how to facilitate economic cooperation between the sexes, how to provide a proper setting within which child rearing may take place, and how to regulate sexual activity. Efficient and flexible though family and household organization may be in rising to challenges connected with such problems, the fact is that many societies confront problems that are beyond the ability of family and household organization to deal with. For one, there is often a need for some means by which members of one sovereign local group can claim support and protection from individuals in another. This can be important for defense against natural or human-made disasters; if people have the right of entry into local groups other than their own, they are able to secure protection or critical resources when their own group cannot provide them. For another, there frequently is a need for a way to share rights in some means of production that cannot be divided without its destruction. This is often the case in horticultural societies, where division of land is impractical beyond a certain point. It can be avoided if ownership of land is vested in a corporate group that exists in perpetuity. Finally, there is often a need for some means of providing cooperative work forces for tasks that require more participants than can be provided by households alone.

There are many ways to deal with these sorts of problems. One is through the development of a formal political system, with personnel to make and enforce laws, keep the peace, allocate resources, and perform other regulatory and societal functions. A more common way in nonindustrial societies—especially horticultural and pastoral societies—is through the development of kinship groups.

DESCENT GROUPS

A common way of organizing a society along kinship lines is by creating what anthropologists call descent groups. A **descent group** is any publicly recognized social entity in which being a lineal descendant of a particular real or mythical ancestor is a criterion of membership. Members of a descent group trace their connections back to a common ancestor through a chain of parent-child links. In this feature, we may have an answer to why descent groups are found in so many human societies. They appear to stem from the parent-child bond, which is built upon as the basis for a structured social group. This is a convenient thing to seize upon, and the addition of a few nonburdensome obligations and avoidances acts as a kind of "glue" to help hold the group together.

To operate most efficiently, membership in a descent group ought to be clearly defined. Otherwise, membership overlaps and it is not always clear where one's primary loyalty belongs. There are a number of means by which membership can be restricted. It can be done on the basis of where you live; for example, if your parents live patrilocally, you might automatically be assigned to your father's descent group. Another way is through choice; each individual might be presented with a number of options, among which he or she may choose. This, though, introduces a possibility of competition and conflict as groups vie for members, and may cause problems. The most common way to restrict membership is by making sex jurally relevant. Instead of tracing membership back to the common ancestor, sometimes through men and sometimes through women, one does it exclusively through one sex. In this way, each individual is automatically assigned to his or her mother's or father's group and that group only.

Unilineal Descent

Unilineal descent (sometimes called unilateral descent) establishes descent-group membership ex-

Descent group: Any publicly recognized social entity such that being a lineal descendant of a particular real or mythical ancestor is a criterion of membership.

Unilineal descent: Descent that establishes group membership exclusively through either the mother's or the father's line.

On this altar, King Yax-Pac of the ancient Maya city of Copan portrays himself and his predecessors, thereby tracing his descent back to the founder of the dynasty. In many human societies, such genealogical connections are used to define each individual's rights, privileges, and obligations.

clusively through the male or the female line. In non-Western societies, unilineal descent groups are quite common. The individual is assigned at birth to membership in a specific descent group, which may be traced either by **matrilineal descent,** through the female line, or by **patrilineal descent,** through the male line, depending on the society. In patrilineal societies the males are far more important than the females, for it is they who are considered to be responsible for the perpetuation of the group. In matrilineal societies, this responsibility falls on the female members of the group, whose importance is thereby enhanced.

There seems to be a close relation between the descent system and the economy of a society.

Matrilineal descent: Descent traced exclusively through the female line for purposes of group membership.

Patrilineal descent: Descent traced exclusively through the male line for purposes of group membership.

Generally, patrilineal descent predominates where the man is the breadwinner, as among pastoralists and intensive agriculturalists, where male labor is a prime factor. Matrilineal descent is important mainly among horticulturists with societies in which women are the breadwinners. Numerous matrilineal societies are found in South Asia, one of the cradles of food production in the Old World. Matrilineal systems exist as well in India, Sri Lanka, Indonesia, Sumatra, Tibet, South China, and many Indonesian islands. They were also prominent in parts of aboriginal North America and still are in parts of Africa.

It is now recognized that in all societies, the kin of both mother and father are important components of the social structure. Just because descent may be reckoned patrilineally, for example, does not mean that maternal relatives are necessarily unimportant. It simply means that, for purposes of *group membership,* the mother's relatives are being excluded. Similarly, under matrilineal descent, the father's relatives are being excluded for purposes of group membership. By way of example, we have already seen in the two preceding

LEWIS HENRY MORGAN

(1818–1881)

This major theoretician of nineteenth-century North American anthropology has been regarded as the founder of kinship studies. In *Systems of Consanguinity and Affinity of the Human Family* (1871), he classified and compared the kinship systems of peoples around the world in an attempt to prove the Asiatic origin of American Indians. In doing so, he developed the idea that the human family had evolved through a series of evolutionary stages, from primitive promiscuity on the one hand to the monogamous, patriarchal family on the other. Although subsequent work showed Morgan to be wrong about this and a number of other things, his work showed the potential value of studying the distribution of different kinship systems in order to frame hypotheses of a developmental or historical nature and, by noting the connection between terminology and behavior, showed the value of kinship for sociological study. Besides his contributions to kinship and evolutionary studies, he produced an ethnography of the Iroquois, which still stands as a major source of information.

---

chapters how important paternal relatives are among the matrilineal Trobriand Islanders. Although children belong to their mother's descent groups, fathers play an important role in nurturing and building them up. Upon marriage, the bride's and groom's paternal relatives contribute to the exchange of gifts that takes place, and throughout life, a man may expect his paternal kin to assist him in improving his economic and political position in society. Eventually, sons may expect to inherit personal property from their fathers.

Patrilineal Descent and Organization

Patrilineal descent (sometimes called agnatic or male descent) is the more widespread of the two systems of unilineal descent. The male members of a patrilineal descent group trace through other males their descent from a common ancestor (Fig. 21.1). Brothers and sisters belong to the descent group of their father's father, their father, their father's siblings, and their father's brother's children. A man's son and daughter also trace their descent

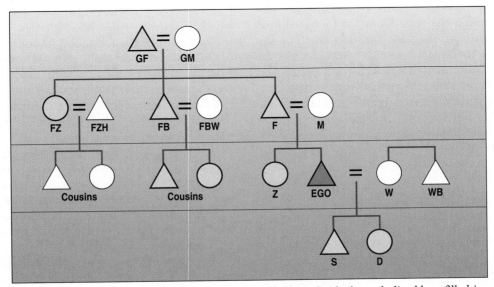

Figure 21.1 How patrilineal descent is traced. Only the individuals symbolized by a filled-in circle or triangle are in the same descent group as ego. The abbreviation F stands for father, B for brother, H for husband, S for son, M for mother, Z for sister, D for daughter, and W for wife.

back through the male line to their common ancestor. In the typical patrilineal group, the responsibility for training the children rests with the father or his elder brother. A woman belongs to the same descent group as her father and his brothers, but her children cannot trace their descent through them. A person's paternal aunt's children, for example, trace their descent through the patrilineal group of her husband.

TRADITIONAL CHINA: A PATRILINEAL SOCIETY. Up until World War II, rural Chinese society was strongly patrilineal. Since then, there have been considerable changes, although vestiges of the old system persist to varying degrees in different regions. Traditionally, the basic unit for economic cooperation was the large extended family, typically including aged parents, their sons, their sons' wives and sons' children.[1] Residence, therefore, was patrilocal, as defined in Chapter 20. As in most patrilocal societies, then, children grew up in a household dominated by their father and his male relatives. The father himself was a source of discipline, from whom a child would maintain a respectful social distance. Often, the father's brother and his sons were members of the same household. Thus, one's paternal uncle was rather like a second father and was treated with obedience and respect, while his sons were like one's own brothers. Accordingly, the kinship term applied to one's own father was extended to father's brother, as the term for one's brother was extended to father's brother's sons. When families became too large and unwieldy, as frequently happened, one or more sons would move elsewhere to establish their own separate households; when one did so, however, the tie to his natal household remained strong.

Important though family membership was for each individual, it was the *tsu* that was regarded as the primary social unit. Each *tsu* consisted of men who traced their ancestry back through the male line to a common ancestor, usually within about five generations. Although a woman belonged to the *tsu* of her father, for all practical purposes she was absorbed by that of her husband, with whom she went to live upon marriage. Nonetheless, members of her natal *tsu* retained some interest in

her after her departure. Her mother, for example, would come to assist her in the birth of her children, and her brother or some other male relative would look after her interests, perhaps even intervening if the woman was badly treated by her husband or other members of his family.

The function of the *tsu* was to assist its members economically and to come together on ceremonial occasions such as weddings, funerals, or to make offerings to the ancestors. Recently deceased ancestors, up to about three generations back, were given offerings of food and paper money on the anniversaries of their births and deaths, while more distant ancestors were collectively worshipped five times a year. Each *tsu* maintained its own place for storage of ancestral tablets, on which the names of all members were recorded. In addition to its economic and ritual functions, the *tsu* also functioned as a legal body, passing judgment on errant members.

Just as families periodically split up into new ones, so would the larger descent groups periodically splinter along the lines of its main family branches. Causes included disputes among brothers over management of land holdings or suspicion of unfair division of profits. When such separation occurred, a representative of the new *tsu* would return periodically to the ancestral temple in order to pay respect to the ancestors and record recent births and deaths in the official genealogy. Ultimately, though the tie to the old *tsu* would still be recognized, a copy of the old genealogy would be made and brought home to the younger *tsu*, following which only its births and deaths would be recorded. In this way, over many centuries, a whole hierarchy of descent groups developed, with all persons having the same surname considering themselves to be members of a great patrilineal clan. With this went surname exogamy, which is still widely practiced today even though clan members no longer carry on ceremonial activities together.

The patrilineal system reached throughout rural Chinese social relations. Children owed obedience and respect to their fathers and older patrilineal relatives in life and had to marry whomever their parents chose for them. It was the duty of sons to care for their parents when they became old and helpless, and even after death, sons had ceremonial obligations to them. Inheritance passed from fathers to sons, with an extra share going to

[1]Most of the following is from Hsiaotung, F. (1939). *Peasant life in China*. London: Kegan, Paul, Trench and Truber.

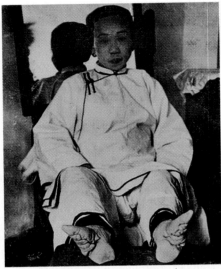

In patrilineal and other societies that promote the dominance of men over women, this practice some-times goes to the extreme of inflicting physical, as well as social, disabilities on women. In the nine-teenth century, Chinese women had their feet tightly bound, while in North America, women were often tightly corseted. The result in both cases was actual physical impairment.

the eldest, since he ordinarily made the greater contribution to the household and had the greater responsibility to his parents after their deaths. Women, by contrast, had no claims on their families' heritable property. Once married, a woman was in effect cast off by her own patrilineal kin (even though they might continue to take an interest in her) in order to produce children for her husband's family and *tsu*.

As the preceding suggests, a patrilineal society is very much a man's world; no matter how valued they may be, women inevitably find themselves in a difficult position. Far from resigning themselves to a subordinate position, however, they actively manipulate the system to their own advantage as best they are able. How they may do so can be seen by looking more closely at the way women relate to one another in traditional Chinese society.

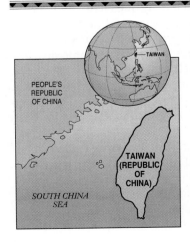

Original Study
Coping as a Woman in a Man's World[2]

Women in rural Taiwan do not live their lives in the walled courtyards of their husbands' households. If they did, they might be as powerless as their stereotype. It is in their relations in the outside world (and for women in rural Taiwan that world consists almost entirely of the village) that women develop sufficient backing to maintain some independence under their powerful mothers-in-law. A successful venture into the men's world is no small feat when one recalls that the men of a village were born there and are often related to one another, whereas the women are unlikely to have either the ties of childhood or the ties of kinship to unite them. All the same, shared interests, and common problems of women are reflected in every village in a loosely knit society that can when needed be called on to exercise considerable influence.

Women carry on as many of their activities as possible outside the house. They wash clothes on the riverbank, clean and pare vegetables at a communal pump, mend under a tree that is a known meetingplace, and stop to rest on a bench or group of stones with other women. There is a continual moving back and forth between kitchens, and conversations are carried on from open doorways through the long, hot afternoons of summer. The shy young girl who enters the village as a bride is examined as frankly and suspiciously by the women as an animal that is up for sale. If she is deferential to her elders, does not criticize or compare her new world unfavorably with the one she has left, the older residents will gradually accept her presence on the edge of their conversations and stop changing the topic to general subjects when she brings the family laundry to scrub on the rocks near them. As the young bride meets other girls in her position, she makes allies for the future, but she must also develop relationships with the older women. She learns to use considerable discretion in making and receiving confidences, for a girl who gossips freely about the affairs of her husband's household may find herself always on the outside of the group, or worse yet, accused of snobbery. I described in *The House of Lim* the plight of Lim Chui-ieng, who had little village backing in her troubles with her husband and his family as a result of her arrogance toward the women's community. In Peihotien the young wife of the storekeeper's son suffered a similar lack of support. Warned by her husband's parents not to be too "easy" with the other villagers lest they try to buy things on credit, she obeyed to the point of being considered unfriendly by the women of the village. When she began to have serious troubles with her husband and eventually his family, there was no one in the village she could turn to for solace, advice, and most important, peacemaking.

Once a young bride has established herself as a member of the women's community, she has also established for herself a certain amount of protection. If the members of her husband's family step beyond the limits of propriety in their treatment of her—such as refusing to allow her to return to her natal home for her brother's wedding or beating her without serious justification—she can complain to a woman friend, preferably older, while they are washing vegetables at the communal pump. The story will quickly spread to the other women, and one of them will take it upon herself to check the facts with another member of the girl's household. For a few days the matter will be thoroughly discussed whenever a few women gather. In a young wife's first few years in the community, she can expect to have her mother-in-law's side of any disagreement given fuller weight than her own—her mother-in-law has, after all, been a part of the community a lot longer. However, the discussion itself will serve to curb many offenses. Even if the older woman knows that public opinion is falling to her side, she will be somewhat more judicious about refusing her daughter-in-law's next request. Still, the daughter-in-law who hopes to make use of the village forum to depose her mother-in-law or at least gain herself special privilege will discover just how important the prerogatives of age and length of residence are. Although the women can serve as a powerful protective force for their defenseless younger members, they are also a very conservative force in the village.

Taiwanese women can and do make use of their collective power to lose face for their menfolk in order to influence decisions that are ostensibly not theirs to make. Although young women may have little or no influence over their husbands and would not dare express an unsolicited opinion (and perhaps not even a solicited one) to their fathers-in-law, older women who have raised their sons properly retain considerable influence over their sons' actions, even in activities exclusive to men. Further, older women who have displayed years of good judgment are regularly consulted by their husbands about major as well as minor economic and social projects. But even men who think themselves free to ignore the opinions of their women are never free of their own concept, face. It is much easier to lose face than to have face. We once asked a male friend in Peihotien just what "having face" amounted to. He replied, "When no one is talking about a family, you can say it has face." This is precisely where women wield their power. When a man behaves in a way that they consider wrong, they talk about him—not only among themselves, but to their sons and husbands. No one "tells him how to mind his own business," but it becomes abundantly clear that he is losing face and by continuing in this manner may bring shame to the family of his ancestors and descendants. Few men will risk that.

The rules that a Taiwanese man must learn and obey to be a successful member of his society are well developed, clear, and relatively easy to stay within. A Taiwanese woman must also learn the rules, but if she is to be a successful woman, she must learn not to stay within them, but to appear to stay within them; to manipulate them, but not to appear to be manipulating them; to teach them to her children, but not to depend on her children for her protection. A truly successful Taiwanese woman is a rugged individualist who has learned to depend largely on herself while appearing to lean on her father, her husband, and her son. The contrast between the terrified young bride and the loud, confident, often lewd old woman who has outlived her mother-in-law and her husband reflects the tests met and passed by not strictly following the rules and by making purposeful use of those who must. The Chinese male's conception of women as "narrow-hearted" and socially inept may well be his vague recognition of this facet of women's power and technique.

[2]Wolf, M. (1972). *Women and the family in rural Taiwan* (pp. 37–41). Stanford: Stanford University Press.

Matrilineal Descent and Organization

In one respect, matrilineal descent is the opposite of patrilineal: It is reckoned through the female line (Fig. 21.2). The matrilineal pattern differs from the patrilineal, however, in that descent does not automatically confer authority. Thus, while patrilineal societies are patriarchal, matrilineal societies are not matriarchal. Although descent passes through the female line, and women may have considerable power, they do not hold exclusive authority in the descent group: They share it with men. These are the brothers, rather than the husbands, of the women through whom descent is reckoned. Apparently, the adaptive purpose of the matrilineal system is to provide continuous female solidarity within the female work group. Matrilineal systems are usually found in farming societies in which women perform much of the productive work. Because women's work is regarded as so important to the society, matrilineal descent prevails.

In the matrilineal system, brothers and sisters belong to the descent group of the mother's mother, the mother, the mother's siblings, and the mother's sister's children. Males belong to the

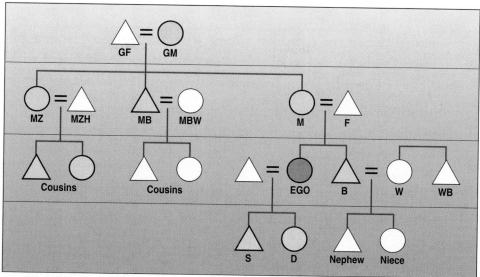

Figure 21.2 This diagram, which traces descent matrilineally, can be compared with that in Figure 21.1, showing patrilineal descent. The two patterns are virtually mirror images. Note that a man cannot transmit descent to his own children.

same descent group as their mother and sister, but their children cannot trace their descent through them. For example, the children of a man's maternal uncle are considered members of the uncle's wife's matrilineal descent group. Similarly, a man's own children belong to his wife's, but not his, descent group.

Although not true of all matrilineal systems a common feature is the weakness of the tie between husband and wife. The wife's brother, and not the husband/father, distributes goods, organizes work, settles disputes, administers inheritance and succession rules, and supervises rituals. The husband has legal authority not in his own household but in that of his sister. Furthermore, his property and status are inherited by his sister's son, rather than his own. Thus, brothers and sisters maintain lifelong ties with one another, whereas marital ties are easily severed. In matrilineal societies, unsatisfactory marriages are more easily ended than in patrilineal societies.

THE HOPI: A MATRILINEAL SOCIETY.   In northeastern Arizona are the villages, or pueblos, of the Hopi Indians, a farming people whose ancestors have lived in the region for at least 2,000 years. Their society is divided into a number of named

clans, based strictly on matrilineal descent.[3] Each individual is assigned from birth to the clan of his or her mother, and so important is this affiliation that, in a very real sense, a person has no identity apart from it. Two or more clans together constitute larger, supraclan units, or phratries, of which there are nine in Hopi society. Within each of these, member clans are expected to support one another and to observe strict exogamy. Because members of all nine phratries can be found living in any given pueblo, marriage partners can always be found in one's home community. This same dispersal of membership provides individuals with rights of entry into villages other than their own.

Although clans are the major units in Hopi thinking, the functional units consist of subclans, or lineages, of which there are several per village. Each is headed by a senior woman—usually the eldest, although it is her brother or maternal uncle who keeps the sacred "medicine bundle" and plays an active role in running lineage affairs. The woman, however, is not a mere figurehead; she may act as mediator to help resolve disputes between

[3]Most of the following is from Connelly, J. C. (1979). Hopi social organization. In A. Ortiz (Ed.), *Handbook of North American Indians: Vol. 9. Southwest* (pp. 539–553). Washington: Smithsonian Institution.

Among the Hopi Indians, a man grows crops that are owned by women of the lineage to which the land belongs. This lineage is that of the man's wife; he himself belongs to the lineage of his mother and sisters.

members of the group; nor does she yield any authority to her brother or uncle. Although these men have the right to offer her advice and criticism, they are equally obligated to listen to what she has to say. Most female authority, however, is exerted within the household, and here men clearly take second place. These households consist of the women of the lineage with their husbands and unmarried sons, all of whom used to live in sets of adjacent rooms in single large tenements. Nowadays, nuclear families often live (frequently with a maternal relative or two) in separate houses, but pickup trucks enable related households to maintain close contacts and to cooperate as before.

Lineages function as landholding corporations, allocating land for the support of member households. These lands are farmed by "outsiders," the husbands of the women whose lineage owns the land, and it is to these women that the harvest belongs. Thus, Hopi men spend their lives laboring for alien lineages (their wives'), in return for which they are given food and shelter (by their wives). Although sons learn from their fathers how to farm, a man has no real authority over his son (the two belong to different lineages). Thus, when parents have difficulty with an unruly child, it is the mother's brother who is called upon to mete out punishment. Male loyalties are therefore divided, between their wives' households on the one hand, and their sisters' on the other. If at any time, a man is perceived as being an unsatisfactory husband, his wife has merely to place his belongings outside the door, and the marriage is over.

In addition to their economic and legal functions, lineages play a role in Hopi ceremonial activities. Although membership in the associations that actually perform ceremonies is open to all who have the proper qualifications for membership, they are all owned and managed by clans, and in each village, a leading lineage acts as its clan's representative. Owned by this lineage is a special house in which the clan's religious paraphernalia is stored and cared for by the "clan mother." Together with her brother, the clan's "Big Uncle," she helps manage ceremonial activity. While most of the associations that do the actual performing are controlled by men, women still have vital roles to play. For example, they provide the cornmeal, symbolic of natural and spiritual life, that is a necessary ingredient in virtually all ceremonies.

Anthropology Applied

FEDERAL RECOGNITION FOR NATIVE AMERICANS

In 1981, the Washington (D.C.) Association of Professional Anthropologists bestowed its first annual Praxis Award on James Wherry,* for his use of anthropological knowledge to win federal recognition for the Houlton Band of Maliseet Indians in Maine. The Praxis Award is an international competition open to all projects, programs, or activities that illustrate the translation of anthropological knowledge into action. As a consequence of their recognition, the Houlton Band became eligible to receive services and contracts from the Bureau of Indian Affairs and Indian Health Services and to share in the settlement of the Maine Indian Land Claim, with which they could purchase land to be held in trust for them. With these arrangements, they were transformed from a poor and powerless minority into a semi-sovereign people with the means to establish their own land base and a broad range of programs controlled by themselves.

The Houlton Band is one of over 150 Native American communities that were forgotten or overlooked by the federal government over the past 200 years, owing to drastic depopulation, forced removals, and other dislocations in the regions in which they lived. Under the U.S. Constitution, Indians are a federal responsibility, but without official recognition, native communities are unable to gain access to government health, education, and other services that derive from treaty obligations of the United States towards Indian "tribes." As a result, unrecognized

Indians are poorer, less well educated, and subject to more serious health problems than are those in recognized "tribes." Most unrecognized groups are landless, and some have disintegrated through lack of protection by the federal government.

In 1978, federal regulations were adopted by which unrecognized Native American communities could petition for acknowledgment, and more than 100 petitions are now pending. To secure recognition, communities must provide extensive ethnohistorical, genealogical, and ethnographic information on their origins, development, and present social and political organization. Genealogical data are especially important, for genealogies of all present "tribal" members are required. Moreover, traditional communities often were structured on the basis of kinship and descent, and recurring marriages between families have been an important means by which community organization has been perpetuated and identity maintained. Since the gathering of such data has long been an anthropological specialty, Native American communities commonly turn to anthropologists like James Wherry to assist in meeting the criteria required for recognition.

*James Wherry now serves as socioeconomic development specialist of the Mashantucket Pequot Tribe, a Native American community in Connecticut that won federal recognition in 1983.

Prior to the imposition by the U.S. government in 1936 of a different system, each Hopi pueblo was politically autonomous, with its own chief and village council. Here again, however, descent-group organization made itself felt, for the council was made up of men who inherited their positions through their clans. Moreover, the powers of the chief and his council were limited; the chief's major job was to maintain harmony between his village and the spiritual world, and whatever authority he and his council wielded was directed at coordination of community effort, not enforcement of unilateral decrees. Decisions were made on the basis of consensus, and women's views had to be considered as well as those of men. Once

again, although positions of authority were held by men, women had considerable control over their decisions in a behind-the-scene way. These men, after all, lived in households that were controlled by women, and their position within them depended largely on how well they got along with the senior women. Outside the household, refusal to play their part in the performance of ceremonies gave women the power of the veto. Small wonder, then, that Hopi men readily admit that "women usually get their way."[4]

[4]Schlegel, A. (1977). Male and female in Hopi thought and action. In A. Schlegel (Ed.), *Sexual stratification* (p. 254). New York: Columbia University Press.

Double Descent

Double descent, or double unilineal descent, in which descent is reckoned both patrilineally and matrilineally at the same time, is very rare. In this system descent is matrilineal for some purposes and patrilineal for others. Generally, where double descent is reckoned, the matrilineal and patrilineal groups take action in different spheres of society.

For example, among the Yakö of eastern Nigeria, property is divided into patrilineal line possessions and matrilineal line possessions.[5] The patrilineage owns perpetual productive resources, such as land, whereas the matrilineage owns consumable property, such as livestock. The legally weaker matrilineal line is somewhat more important in religious matters than the patrilineal line. Through double descent, a Yakö might inherit grazing lands from the father's patrilineal group and certain ritual privileges from the mother's matrilineal line.

Ambilineal Descent

Unilineal descent provides an easy way of restricting descent group membership to avoid problems of divided loyalty and the like. A number of societies, many of them in the Pacific and in Southeast Asia, accomplish the same thing in other ways, though perhaps not as neatly. The resultant descent groups are known as ambilineal, nonunilineal, or cognatic. **Ambilineal descent** provides a measure of flexibility not normally found under unilineal descent; each individual has the option of

---

Double descent: A system according to which descent is reckoned matrilineally for some purposes and patrilineally for others.

Ambilineal descent: Descent in which the individual may affiliate with either the mother's or the father's descent group.

---

[5]Forde, C. D. (1968). Double descent among the Yako. In P. Bohannan & J. Middleton (Eds.), *Kinship and social organization* (pp. 179–191). Garden City, NY: Natural History Press.

affiliating with either the mother's or the father's descent group. In many of these societies an individual is allowed to belong to only one group at any one time, regardless of how many groups he or she may be eligible to join. Thus, the society may be divided into the same sorts of discrete and separate groups of kin as in a patrilineal or matrilineal society. There are other cognatic societies, however, such as the Samoans of the South Pacific or the Bella Coola and the southern branch of the Kwakiutl of the Pacific Northwest coast of North America, which allow overlapping membership in a number of descent groups. As anthropologist George Murdock observed, too great a range of individual choice interferes with the orderly functioning of any kin-oriented society:

> An individual's plural membership almost inevitably becomes segregated into one primary membership, which is strongly activated by residence, and one or more secondary memberships in which participation is only partial or occasional.[6]

AMBILINEAL DESCENT AMONG NEW YORK CITY JEWS.   For an example of ambilineal organization we might easily turn to a traditional, non-Western society, as we have for patrilineal and matrilineal organization. Instead, we shall turn to contemporary North American society, in order to dispel the common (but false) notion that descent groups are necessarily incompatible in structure and function with the demands of modern, industrial society. In fact, large corporate descent groups that hold assets in common and exist in perpetuity are to be found in New York City, as well as in every other large city in the United States where a substantial Jewish population of eastern European background is to be found.[7] Furthermore, these descent groups are not survivals of an old eastern European, descent-based organization. Rather, they represent a social innovation designed to restructure and preserve the traditionally close affective family ties of the old eastern European Jewish culture in the face of continuing emigration

[6]Murdock, G. P. (1960). Cognatic forms of social organization. In G. P. Murdock (Ed.), *Social structure in Southeast Asia* (p. 11). Chicago: Quadrangle Books.

[7]Mitchell, W. E. (1978). *Mishpokhe: A study of New York City Jewish family clubs.* The Hague: Mouton.

This photo shows three generations of a Jewish family. Close family ties have always been important in eastern European Jewish culture. To maintain such ties in the United States, the descendants of eastern European Jews developed ambilineal descent groups.

to the United States, subsequent dispersal from New York City, and the development of significant social and even temperamental differences among their descendants. The earliest of these descent groups did not develop until the end of the first decade of the 1900s, some 40 years after the immigration of eastern European Jews began in earnest. Although some groups have disbanded, they generally have remained alive and vital right down to the present day.

The original Jewish descent groups in New York City are known as *family circles*. The potential members of a family circle consist of all living descendants, with their spouses, of an ancestral pair. In actuality, not all who are eligible actually join, so there is an element of voluntarism. But eligibility is explicitly determined by descent, using both male and female links, without set order, to establish the connection with the ancestral pair. Thus, individuals are normally eligible for membership in more than one group. To activate one's membership, one simply pays the required dues, attends meetings, and participates in the affairs of the group. Individuals can, and frequently do, belong at the same time to two or three groups for which they are eligible. Each family circle bears a name, usually including the surname of the male ancestor, each has elected officers, and each meets regularly throughout the year. The family circle as a corporation holds funds in common, and some

hold title to burial plots for the use of members. Originally, they functioned as mutual aid societies and maintained family solidarity. Now, as the mutual aid functions have been taken over by outside agencies, the promotion of solidarity has become their primary goal. It will be interesting to see if reduced government funding for these agencies leads to a resurgence of the mutual aid function of family circles.

In the years just prior to World War II, an interesting variant of the ambilineal descent group developed among younger-generation descendants of east European Jewish immigrants. Being more assimilated into North American culture, some of them sought to separate themselves somewhat from members of older generations, who were perceived as being a bit old-fashioned. Yet, they still wished to maintain the traditional Jewish ethic of family solidarity. The result was the *cousins club*, which consists of a group of first cousins, who themselves share a common ancestry, their spouses, and their descendants. Excluded are parents and grandparents of the cousins, with their older views and lifestyles. Ambilineal descent remains the primary organizing principle, but it has been modified by a generational principle. Otherwise, cousins clubs are organized and function in many of the same ways as family circles.

FORMS AND FUNCTIONS OF DESCENT GROUPS

Descent groups with restricted membership, regardless of how descent is reckoned, are usually more than mere groups of relatives providing warmth and a sense of belonging; in nonindustrial societies they are tightly organized working units providing security and services in the course of what can be a difficult, uncertain life. The tasks performed by descent groups are manifold. Besides acting as economic units providing mutual aid to their members, they may act to support the aged and infirm or help in the case of marriage or death. Often, they play a role in determining whom an individual may or may not marry. The descent group may also act as a repository of religious traditions. Ancestor worship, for example, is a powerful force acting to reinforce group solidarity.

Lineage

A **lineage** is a corporate descent group composed of consanguineal kin who trace descent genealogically through known links back to a common ancestor. The term is usually employed where some form of unilineal descent is the rule, but there are similar ambilineal groups, such as the Jewish family circles just discussed.

The lineage is ancestor oriented; membership in the group is recognized only if relationship to a common ancestor can be traced and proved. In many societies an individual has no legal or political status except as a member of a lineage. Since "citizenship" is derived from lineage membership and legal status depends on it, political and religious power are thus derived from it as well. Important religious and magical powers, such as those associated with the cults of gods and ancestors, may also be bound to the lineage.

The lineage, like General Motors or IBM, is a corporate group. Because it endures after the death of members as new members are continually being born into it, it has a perpetual existence that enables it to take corporate actions, such as owning property, organizing productive activities, distributing goods and labor power, assigning status, and regulating relations with other groups. The lineage is a strong, effective base of social organization.

A common feature of lineages is that they are exogamous. This means that members of a lineage must find their marriage partners in other lineages. One advantage of lineage exogamy is that potential sexual competition within the group is curbed, promoting the group's solidarity. Lineage exogamy also means that each marriage is more than an arrangement between two individuals; it amounts as well to a new alliance between lineages, which helps to maintain them as components of larger social systems. Finally, lineage exogamy maintains open communication within a society, promoting the diffusion of knowledge from one lineage to another.

Lineage: A corporate descent group whose members trace their genealogical links to a common ancestor.

Clan

In the course of time, as generation succeeds generation and new members are born into the lineage, its membership may become too large to be manageable or too much for the lineage's resources to support. When this happens, **fission** will take place; that is, the lineage will split up into new, smaller lineages. When fission occurs, it is usual for the members of the new lineages to continue to recognize their ultimate relationship to one another. The result of this process is the appearance of a second kind of descent group, the **clan.** The term *clan*, and its close relative, the term *sib*, have been used differently by different anthropologists, and a certain amount of confusion exists as to their meaning. The clan (or sib) will here be defined as a noncorporate descent group in which each member assumes descent from a common ancestor (who may be real or fictive), but is unable to trace the actual genealogical links back to that ancestor. This stems from the great genealogical depth of the clan, whose founding ancestor lived so far in the past that the links must be assumed rather than known in detail. A clan differs from a lineage in another respect: It lacks the residential unity that is generally—though not invariably—characteristic of the core members of a lineage. As with the lineage, descent may be patrilineal, matrilineal, or ambilineal.

Because clan membership is dispersed rather than localized, it usually does not hold tangible property corporately. Instead, it tends to be more a unit for ceremonial matters. Only on special occasions will the membership gather together for specific purposes. Clans, however, may handle important integrative functions. Like lineages, they may regulate marriage through exogamy. Because of their dispersed membership, they give individuals the right of entry into local groups other than their

Fission: The splitting of a descent group into two or more new descent groups.

Clan: A noncorporate descent group with each member claiming descent from a common ancestor without actually knowing the genealogical links to that ancestor.

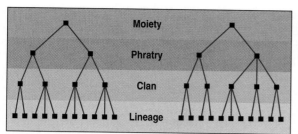

Figure 21.3 This diagram shows how lineages, clans, phratries, and moieties form an organizational hierarchy. Each moiety is subdivided into phratries, each phratry is subdivided into clans, and each clan is subdivided into lineages.

own. One is usually expected to give protection and hospitality to other members of one's own clan. Hence, these can be expected in any local group that includes people who belong to one's own clan.

Clans, lacking the residential unity of lineages, frequently depend on symbols—of animals, plants, natural forces, and objects—to provide members with solidarity and a ready means of identification. These symbols, called totems, are often associated with the clan's mythical origin and provide clan members with a means of reinforcing the awareness of their common descent. The word *totem* comes from the Ojibwa American Indian word *ototeman,* meaning "he is a relative of mine." **Totemism** was defined by the British anthropologist A. R. Radcliffe-Brown as a set of "customs and beliefs by which there is set up a special system of relations between the society and the plants, animals, and other natural objects that are important in the social life."[8] Hopi Indian matriclans, for example, bear such totemic names as Bear, Bluebird, Butterfly, Lizard, Spider, and Snake.

Totemism is a changing concept that varies from clan to clan. A kind of diluted Totemism may be found in modern North American society, where baseball and football teams are given the names of such powerful wild animals as bears,

Totemism: The belief that people are related to particular animals, plants, or natural objects by virtue of descent from common ancestral spirits.

[8]Radcliffe-Brown, A. R. (1931). Social organization of Australian tribes. *Oceania Monographs, 1,* 29.

tigers, and wildcats. This extends to the Democratic Party's donkey and the Republican Party's elephant, to the Elks, the Lions, and other fraternal and social organizations. Our animal emblems, however, do not involve the same notions of descent and strong sense of kinship, nor are they associated with the various ritual observances associated with clan totems.

Phratries and Moieties

Other kinds of descent groups are phratries and moieties (Fig. 21.3). A **phratry,** like those of the Hopi that we have already discussed, is a unilineal descent group composed of at least two clans that supposedly share a common ancestry, whether or not they really do. Like individuals of the clan, members of the phratry are unable to trace accurately their descent links to a common ancestor, though they believe such an ancestor existed.

If the entire society is divided into two and only two major descent groups, be they equivalent to clans or phratries, or at an even more all-inclusive level, each group is called a **moiety** (after the French word for "half"). Members of the moiety believe themselves to share a common ancestor, but are unable to prove it through definite genealogical links. As a rule, the feeling of kinship among members of lineages and clans is stronger than that felt among members of phratries and moieties. This may be due to the larger size and more diffuse nature of the latter groups.

Bilateral Kinship and the Kindred

Important though descent groups are in many societies, they are not found in all societies, nor are they the only kinds of nonfamilial kinship groups to be found. Bilateral kinship, a characteristic of

Phratry: A unilineal descent group composed of two or more clans that claim to be of common ancestry. If there are only two such groups, each is a moiety.

Moiety: Each group that results from a division of a society into two halves on the basis of descent.

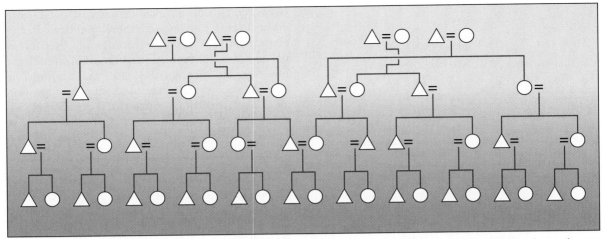

Figure 21.4   The kinship pattern of the kindred. These people are related, not to a common ancestor, but rather to a living relative, here the sister and brother shown at the center of the bottom row.

Western society as well as a number of food-foraging societies, affiliates a person with other close relatives through both sexes; in other words, the individual traces descent through both parents, all four grandparents, and so forth, recognizing multiple ancestors. Theoretically, one is associated equally with all consanguineal relatives on both the mother's and father's sides of the family. Thus, this principle relates an individual lineally to all eight great-grandparents and laterally to all third and fourth cousins. Since such a huge group is too big to be socially practical, the group is usually reduced to a small circle of paternal and maternal relatives, called the **kindred.** The kindred may be defined as a group of people closely related to one living individual through both parents. Since the kindred is laterally rather than lineally organized—that is, ego, or the focal person from whom the degree of each relationship is reckoned, is the center of the group (Fig. 21.4)—it really is not a descent group, even though it occurs in societies with bilateral descent. North Americans are all familiar with the kindred; those who belong are simply called relatives. It includes the relatives on both sides of the

family who are seen on important occasions, such as family reunions and funerals. Most people in the United States can identify the members of their kindred up to grandparents and first and second cousins. The limits of the kindred, however, are variable and indefinite; no one can ever be absolutely certain which relatives to invite to every important function and which to exclude. Inevitably, situations arise that require some debate about whether or not to invite particular, usually distant, relatives. The kindred is thus not clearly bounded, lacking the discreteness of the unilineal or ambilineal descent group. (It is also temporary, lasting only as long as the function it has been assembled to attend.)

Because of its bilateral structure, a kindred is never the same for any two persons except siblings (brothers and sisters). Thus, no two people (except siblings) belong to the same kindred. The kindred of ego's first cousin on the father's side, for example, includes not only father's sister (or brother), as does ego's, but father's sister's (or brother's) spouse as well as consanguineal relatives of the latter. As for the kindreds of ego's parents, these will range lineally to grandparents and laterally to cousins too distant for ego to know, and the same is true of ego's aunts and uncles. Thus, the kindred is not composed of people with an ancestor in common, but with a living relative in common—ego. Furthermore, as ego goes through life, the kindreds with which he or she is affiliated will change. When one is young, one belongs to the kindreds

Kindred: A group of consanguineal kin linked by their relationship to one living individual; includes both maternal and paternal kin.

Members of the groom's personal kindred shown here are his new wife, father, mother, two brothers, sister-in-law, aunt, and niece.

of one's parents; ultimately, one finds oneself belonging to the kindreds of sons and daughters as well as nieces and nephews. Thus, because of its vagueness, temporary nature, and changing affiliation, the kindred cannot function as a group except in relation to ego. Unlike descent groups, it is not self-perpetuating—it ceases with ego's death. It has no constant leader, nor can it easily hold, administer, or pass on property. In most cases, it cannot organize work, nor can it easily administer justice or assign status. It can, however, be turned to for aid. In non-Western societies, for example, raiding or trading parties may be composed of kindred groups. The group is assembled, does what it was organized to do, shares the results, then disbands. It can also act as a ceremonial group for rites of passage: initiation ceremonies and the like. Thus, kindreds assemble only for specific purposes. Finally, they can also regulate marriage through exogamy.

Kindreds are frequently found in industrial societies such as that of the United States, where mobility weakens contact with relatives. Individuality is emphasized in such societies, and strong kinship organization is usually not as important as it is among non-Western peoples. On the other hand, the bilateral kindred may also be found in societies where kinship ties are important, and in some instances, they even occur alongside descent groups.

Evolution of the Descent Group

Just as different types of families occur in different societies, so do different kinds of nonfamilial kin groups. Descent groups, for example, are not a common feature of food-foraging societies, where marriage acts as the social mechanism for integrating individuals within communities. In horticultural, pastoral, or many intensive agricultural societies, however, the descent group usually provides the structural framework upon which the fabric of the society rests.

It is generally agreed that lineages arise from extended family organization, so long as there are problems of organization that such groups help solve. All that is required, really, is that as members of existing extended families find it necessary to split off and establish new households elsewhere, they not move too far away, that the core members of such related families (men in patrilocal, women in matrilocal, members of both sexes in ambilocal extended families) explicitly acknowledge their descent from a common ancestor, and that they continue to participate in common activities in an organized way. As this proceeds, lineages will develop, and these may with time give rise to clans and ultimately phratries.

Another way that clans may arise is as legal fictions to bring about the integration of otherwise

Iroquoian clans were a legal fiction that allowed people to travel back and forth between villages of the "Five Nations" in what is now New York state. This portrait, done in 1710, shows a member of the Mohawk Nation. Behind him stands a bear, which represents his clan.

autonomous units. The five Iroquoian Indian nations of what now is New York state, for example, developed clans by simply behaving as if lineages of the same name in different villages were related. Thus, their members became fictitious brothers and sisters. By this device, members of, say, a "Turtle" lineage in one village could travel to another and be welcomed in and hosted by members of another "Turtle" lineage. In this way, the "Five Nations" achieved a wider unity than had previously existed.

As larger, dispersed descent groups develop, the conditions that gave rise to extended families and lineages may change. For example, economic diversity and the availability of alternative occupations among which individuals may choose may conflict with the residential unity of extended families and (usually) lineages. Or, lineages may lose their economic bases if control of resources is taken over by developing political institutions. In such circumstances, lineages would be expected to disappear as important organizational units. Clans, however, might survive, if they continued to provide an important integrative function. In this sense, the Jewish family circles and cousins clubs that we discussed earlier have become essentially clanlike in their function. This helps explain their continued strength and vitality in the United States today: They perform an integrative function among kin who are geographically dispersed as well as socially diverse, but in a way that does not conflict with the mobility that is characteristic of North American society.

In societies where the small domestic units—nuclear families or single-parent households—are of primary importance, bilateral descent and kindred organization are apt to be the result. This can be seen in modern industrial societies, newly emerging societies in the "underdeveloped" world, and many food-foraging societies throughout the world.

KINSHIP TERMINOLOGY AND KINSHIP GROUPS

Any system of organizing people who are relatives into different kinds of groups, whether they are descent-based or ego-oriented, is bound to have an important effect upon the ways in which relatives are labelled in any given society. The kinship terminologies of other peoples are far from being the arbitrary and even capricious ways of labelling relatives that Westerners all too often assume they are. Rather, they reflect the positions individuals occupy within their society. In particular, kinship terminology is affected by, and adjusts to, the kinds of kinship groups that exist in a society. There are, however, other factors at work as well in each system of kinship terminology, which help differentiate one kin from another. These factors may be sex, generational differences, or genealogical differences. In the various systems of kinship terminology, any one of these factors may be emphasized at the expense of others, and sometimes they are qualified by distinguishing younger from older individuals in a particular category, or by emphasizing the sex of the person referring to a particular relative. But regardless of the factors emphasized, all kinship terminologies accomplish two important tasks: First, they classify similar kinds of persons into single specific categories; second, they separate different kinds of persons into distinct categories. Generally, two or more kin are merged under the same term when similarity of status exists between the individuals. These similarities are then emphasized by the application of one term to both individuals.

Six different systems of kinship terminology result from the application of the above principles: the Eskimo, Hawaiian, Iroquois, Crow, Omaha, and Sudanese or Descriptive systems, each identified according to the way cousins are classified.

Eskimo System

Eskimo kinship terminology, comparatively rare among all the systems of the world, is the one used by Anglo-Americans as well as by a number of food-foraging peoples (including the Inuit, once called Eskimos; hence the name). The Eskimo or lineal system emphasizes the nuclear family by specifically identifying mother, father, brother, and sister, while lumping together all other relatives into a few gross categories (Fig. 21.5). For example, one's father is distinguished from one's father's brother (uncle); but one's father's brother is not distinguished from the mother's brother (both are called "uncle"). Mother's sister and father's sister are treated similarly, both being called "aunt." In addition, one calls all the sons and daughters of aunts and uncles cousin, thereby making a generational distinction but without indicating the side of the family to which they belong, or even their sex.

Unlike other terminologies, the Eskimo system provides separate and distinct terms for each member of the nuclear family. This is probably because the Eskimo system is generally found in societies where the dominant kin group is the bilateral kindred, in which only the members of the immediate family are important in day-to-day affairs. This is especially true of modern North American society, in which the family is independent, living apart from, and not directly involved with, other kin except on ceremonial occasions. Thus, people in the United States distinguish between their closest kin (parents and siblings), but lump together (as aunts, uncles, cousins) other kin on both sides of the family.

Hawaiian System

The **Hawaiian system** of kinship terminology, common (as its name implies) in Hawaii and other Malayo-Polynesian-speaking areas, but found elsewhere as well, is the least complex system, in that

Eskimo system: System of kinship terminology, also called lineal system, which emphasizes the nuclear family by specifically identifying mother, father, brother, and sister, while lumping together all other relatives into broad categories such as "uncle," "aunt," and "cousin."

Hawaiian system: A mode of kinship reckoning in which all relatives of the same sex and generation are referred to by the same term.

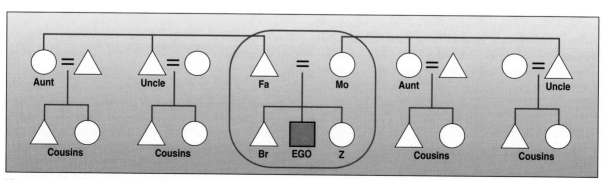

Figure 21.5 The Eskimo system of kinship terminology emphasizes the nuclear family (surrounded by the red line). Ego's father and mother are distinguished from ego's aunts and uncles, and siblings from cousins.

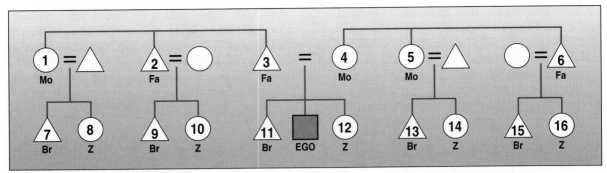

Figure 21.6   The Hawaiian kinship system. The men numbered 2 and 6 are called by the same term as father (3) by ego; the women numbered 1 and 5 are called by the same term as mother (4). All cousins of ego's own generation (7–16) are considered brothers and sisters.

it uses the fewest terms. The Hawaiian system is also called the generational system, since all relatives of the same generation and sex are referred to by the same term (Fig. 21.6). For example, in one's parents' generation, the term used to refer to one's father is used as well for father's brother and mother's brother. Similarly, one's mother, her sister, and one's father's sister are all lumped together under a single term. In ego's generation, male and female cousins are distinguished by sex and are equated with brothers and sisters.

The Hawaiian system reflects the absence of strong unilineal descent and is usually associated with ambilineal descent. Because ambilineal rules allow one the option of tracing one's ancestry back through either side of the family, and members on both the father's and the mother's side are looked upon as being more or less equal, a certain degree of similarity is created among the father's and the mother's siblings. Thus, they are all simultaneously recognized as being similar relations and are merged together under a single term appropriate for their sex. In like manner, the children of the mother's and father's siblings are related to oneself in the same way as one's brother and sister are. Thus, they are ruled out as potential marriage partners.

Iroquois System

In the **Iroquois system** of kinship terminology, one's father and father's brother are referred to by a single term, as are one's mother and mother's sister; however, one's father's sister and mother's brother are given separate terms (Fig. 21.7). In one's own generation, brothers, sisters, and parallel cousins (offspring of parental siblings of the same sex, that is, the children of mother's sister or father's brother) of the same sex are referred to by the same terms, which is logical enough considering that they are the offspring of people who are classified in the same category as ego's actual mother and father. Cross cousins (offspring of parental siblings of opposite sex, that is, the children of mother's brother or father's sister) are distinguished by terms that set them apart from all other kin. In fact, cross cousins are often preferred as spouses, for marriage to them reaffirms alliances between related lineages.

Iroquois terminology, named for the Iroquoian Indians of northeastern North America who employ such terminology, is in fact very widespread and is usually found with unilineal descent groups. It was, for example, the terminology in use until recently in rural Chinese society.

━━━━oo━━━━oo━━━━

Iroquois system: System of kinship terminology wherein one's father and father's brother are referred to by a single term, as are one's mother and mother's sister, but one's father's sister and mother's brother are given separate terms; parallel cousins are classified with brothers and sisters, while cross cousins are classified separately, but (unlike Crow and Omaha kinships) not equated with relatives of some other generation.

━━━━oo━━━━oo━━━━

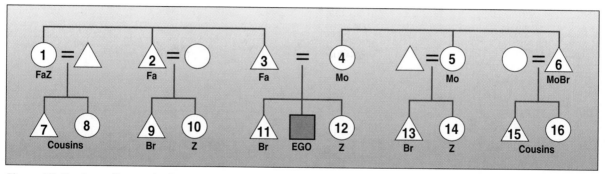

Figure 21.7 According to the Iroquois system of kinship terminology, father's brother (2) is called by the same term as father (3); mother's sister (5) is called by the same term as mother (4) ; but the people 1 and 6 have separate terms for themselves. Those people numbered 9-14 are all considered siblings, but 7, 8, 15, and 16 are cousins.

Crow System

In the preceding systems of terminology some relatives were grouped under common terms, while others of the same generation were separated and given different labels or terms. In the Crow system, another variable enters the picture: The system ignores the distinction that occurs between generations among certain kin.

The **Crow system** (named for the Crow Indians of Montana), found in many parts of the world, is the one used by the Hopi Indians, who were discussed earlier in this chapter. Associated with strong matrilineal descent organization, it

Crow system: A mode of kinship classification usually associated with matrilineal descent in which father's sister and father's sister's daughter are called by the same term, mother and mother's sister are merged under another, while father and father's brother are merged under a third. Parallel cousins are equated with brothers and sisters.

In matrilineal societies with Crow kinship, sisters remain close to one another throughout their lives. Such a people are the Hopi, in whose traditional housing sisters lived in adjacent rooms. Under these circumstances, there is very little to differentiate between one's mother and her sister, or between one's own siblings and the children of mother's sister. Mother's brother and his children, however, live elsewhere.

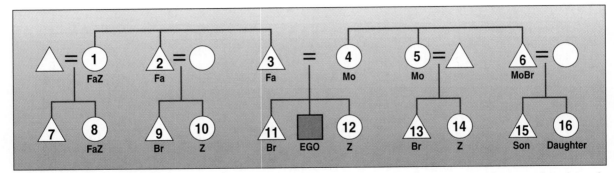

Figure 21.8   The Crow system is the obverse of the Omaha system, shown in Figure 21.9. Those numbered 4 and 5 are merged under a single term, as are 2 and 3. Ego's parallel cousins (9, 10, 13, 14) are considered siblings, while mother's brother's children are equated with the children of a male ego and his brother.

groups differently the relations on the father's side and mother's side (Fig. 21.8). Cross cousins on the father's side are equated with relatives on the parental generation, while those on the mother's side are equated with the generation of ego's children. Otherwise, the system is much like Iroquois terminology.

To those unfamiliar with it, the Crow system seems terribly complex and illogical. Why does it exist? In societies like that of the Hopi, where individual identity is dependent on descent group affiliation, and descent is matrilineal, it makes sense to merge father's sister, her daughter, and even her mother together under a single term, regardless of generation. These are women through whom descent is traced in the lineage that sired ego, just as a male ego's own children, along with those of his mother's brother, were sired by men of ego's own lineage. Thus, it makes perfectly good sense for ego to equate his maternal cross cousins with the generation of his own children.

Omaha System

The **Omaha system** (named for the Omaha Indians of Nebraska) is the patrilineal equivalent

Omaha system: The patrilineal equivalent of the Crow system; the line of mother's patrilineal kin is equated across generations.

of the matrilineal Crow system. Thus, one's mother and one's mother's sister are designated by a single term, one's father and father's brother are merged together under another, while one's parallel cousins are merged with brothers and sisters (Fig. 21.9). Cross cousins on the maternal side are raised a generation, while those on the paternal side are equated with the generation of ego's children. Thus, children born of women from one patrilineage, for the men of another, are lowered by one generation.

Sudanese or Descriptive System

The **Sudanese** or **descriptive system** is found among the peoples of southern Sudan in Africa—hence the name Sudanese. Otherwise, it is found among few of the world's societies, although it has come to replace Iroquois terminology among rural Chinese. In this system, one's mother's brother is distinguished from one's father's brother, who is distinguished from one's father; one's mother's sister is distinguished from one's

Sudanese or **descriptive system:** System of kinship terminology wherein one's father, father's brother, and mother's brother are distinguished from one another, as are mother, mother's sister, and father's sister; cross and parallel cousins are distinguished from each other as well as from siblings.

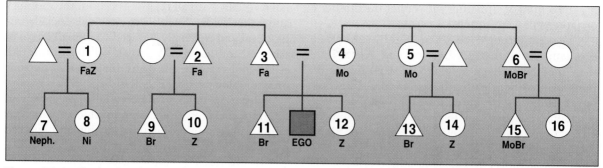

Figure 21.9   In the Omaha system, 2 is called by the same term as father (3); 5 is called by the same term as mother (4); but 1 and 6 have separate terms. In ego's generation 9–14 are all considered siblings, but 7 and 8 are equated with the generation of ego's children, while 15 and 16 are equated with the generation of ego's parents.

mother, as well as from one's father's sister. Each cousin is distinguished from all others, as well as from siblings. It is therefore more precise than any of the other systems (including that used by Anglo-Americans), which may be one reason it is so rare. In few societies are all one's aunts, uncles, cousins, and siblings treated differently from one another.

CHAPTER SUMMARY

In nonindustrial societies, kinship groups commonly deal with problems that cannot be handled by families and households alone, such as problems involving defense, the allocation of property, or the pooling of other resources. As societies become larger and more complex, formal political systems take over many of these matters.

A common form of kinship group is the descent group, which has as its criterion of membership descent from a common ancestor through a series of parent-child links. Unilineal descent establishes kin group membership exclusively through the male or female line. Matrilineal descent is traced through the female line; patrilineal, through the male.

The descent system is closely tied to the economic base of a society. Generally, patrilineal descent predominates where the male is the breadwinner, matrilineal where the female is the breadwinner. Anthropologists now recognize that in all societies the kin of both mother and father are important elements in the social structure, regardless of how descent group membership is defined.

The male members of a patrilineage trace their descent from a common male ancestor. A female belongs to the same descent group as her father and his brother; but her children cannot trace their descent through him. Typically, authority over the children lies with the father or his elder brother. The requirement for younger men to defer to older men and for women to defer to men as well as to the women of a household into which they marry are common sources of tension in a patrilineal society.

In one respect, matrilineal is the opposite of patrilineal descent, with descent being traced through the female line. Unlike the patrilineal pattern, which confers authority on men, matrilineal descent does not necessarily confer authority on women, although they usually have more of a say in the making of decisions than they do in patrilineal societies. The matrilineal system is common in societies in which women perform much of the productive work. This system may be a source of family tension, since the husband's authority is not in his own household but in that of his sister. This, and the ease with which unsatisfactory marriages may be ended, often results in higher divorce rates in matrilineal than in patrilineal societies.

Double descent is matrilineal for some purposes and patrilineal for others. Ambilineal descent provides a measure of flexibility in that an individual has the option of affiliating with either the mother's or father's descent group.

Descent groups are often highly structured economic units that provide aid and security to their members. They may also be repositories of religious tradition, with group solidarity enhanced by worship of a common ancestor. A lineage is a corporate descent group made up of consanguineal kin who are able to trace their genealogical links to a common ancestor. Since lineages are commonly exogamous, sexual competition within the group is largely avoided. In addition, marriage of a member of the group represents an alliance of two lineages. Lineage exogamy also serves to maintain open communication within a society and fosters the exchange of information among lineages.

Fission is the splitting up of a large lineage group into new, smaller ones, with the original lineage becoming a clan. Clan members claim descent from a common ancestor but without actually knowing the genealogical links to that ancestor. Unlike lineages, clan residence is usually dispersed rather than localized. In the absence of residential unity, clan identification is often reinforced by totems, usually symbols from nature, that remind members of their common ancestry. A phratry or moiety is a unilineal descent group of two or more clans that supposedly share a common ancestry.

Bilateral kinship, characteristic of Western, modernizing, and many food-foraging societies, is traced through both parents simultaneously and recognizes several ancestors. An individual is affil-iated equally with all relatives on both the mother's and father's sides. Such a large group is socially impractical and is usually reduced to a small circle of paternal and maternal relatives called the kindred. A kindred is never the same for any two persons except siblings.

Different types of descent systems appear in different societies. In societies in which the nuclear family is paramount, bilateral kinship and kindred organization are likely to prevail.

In any society cultural rules dictate the way kinship relationships are defined. Factors such as sex, generational, or genealogical differences help distinguish one kin from another. The Hawaiian system is the simplest kinship system. All relatives of the same generation and sex are referred to by the same term. The Eskimo system, used by Anglo-Americans, emphasizes the nuclear family and merges all other relatives in a given generation into a few large, generally undifferentiated categories. In the Iroquois system, a single term is used for an individual's father and father's brother, another for one's mother and mother's sister. Parallel cousins are equated with brothers and sisters but distinguished from cross cousins. The same is true in the Omaha and Crow systems, except that in them cross cousins are equated with relatives of other generations. The relatively rare Sudanese or Descriptive system treats all one's aunts, uncles, cousins, and siblings as different from one another.

SUGGESTED READINGS

Fox, R. (1968). *Kinship and marriage in an anthropological perspective*. Baltimore: Penguin.

An excellent introduction to the concepts of kinship and marriage, outlining some of the methods of analysis used in the anthropological treatment of kinship and marriage. Updates Radcliffe-Brown's *African Systems of Kinship and Marriage* and features a perspective focused on kinship groups and social organization.

Goodenough, W. H. (1970). *Description and comparison in cultural anthropology*. Chicago: Aldine.

This is an important contribution to the study of social organization, which confronts the problem of describing kinship organization—kindred and clan, sibling and cousin—in such a way that meaningful cross-cultural comparisons can be made.

Keesing, R. M. (1975). *Kin groups and social structure*. New York: Holt, Rinehart and Winston.

This is a high-level introduction to kinship theory suitable for advanced undergraduate students. A strong point of the work is the attention given to nonunilineal, as well as unilineal, systems.

Schusky, E. L. (1975). *Variation in kinship*. New York: Holt, Rinehart and Winston.

This book is an introduction to kinship, descent, and residence for the beginner. A reliance on a case-study approach leads the reader from basic data to generalizations, a strategy that helps remove some of the abstraction students of kinship organization sometimes find confusing.

Schusky, E. L. (1983). *Manual for kinship analysis* (2nd ed.). Lanham, MD: University Press of America.

A useful book that discusses the elements of kinship, diagramming, systems classification, and descent, with specific examples.

GROUPING BY SEX, AGE, COMMON INTEREST, AND CLASS

THESE BOY SCOUTS FROM SAN ANTONIO, TEXAS, EXEMPLIFY THE PHENOMENA OF GROUPING BY SEX, AGE, AND COMMON INTEREST, SOME OF THE MEANS BY WHICH PEOPLE MAY BE ORGANIZED INTO GROUPS WITHOUT RECOURSE TO KINSHIP OR DESCENT.

CHAPTER PREVIEW

What Principles, Besides Kinship and Marriage, Are Used to Organize People Within Societies?

Grouping by sex, age, common interest, and position within a ranked hierarchy (class stratification) all may be used to deal with problems not conveniently handled by marriage, the family and/or household, descent group, or kindred. In addition, stratification is a means by which certain groups within society secure preferential treatment for themselves at the expense of other groups.

What Is Age Grading?

Age grading—the formation of groups on the basis of age—is a means of organizing people that is widely used in human societies, including those of Europe and North America. In industrial societies, or nonindustrial societies in which populations are relatively large, age grades may be broken down into age sets—groups of people of approximately the same age who move as groups through the series of age grades.

What Are Common-Interest Associations?

Common-interest associations are formed to deal with specific problems. They acquire their members through an act of joining on the part of individuals. This act may range all the way from fully voluntary to compulsory. Common-interest associations have been a feature of human societies since the advent of the first farming villages several thousand years ago, but have become especially prominent in modern industrial or industrializing societies.

What Is Social Stratification?

Stratification is the division of society into two or more classes of people who do not share equally in basic resources, influence, or prestige. Such class structure is characteristic of all of the world's societies in which one finds large and heterogeneous populations with centralized political control. Among others, these include the ancient civilizations of the Middle East, Asia, Mexico, and Peru, as well as modern industrial societies, including the United States.

Social organization based on kinship and marriage has received an extraordinary amount of attention from anthropologists, and the subject usually is quite prominent in anthropological writing. There are several reasons for this: In one way or another, kinship and marriage operate as organizing principles in all societies, and in the small stateless societies so often studied by anthropologists, they are usually the most important organizational principles. There is, too, a certain fascination in the almost mathematical way in which kinship systems at least appear to work. To the unwary, all this attention to kinship and marriage may convey the impression that these are the only principles of social organization that matter. Yet it is obvious from the case of modern industrial societies that other principles of social organization not only exist but also may be quite important. Those that we will examine in this chapter are grouping by sex, age, common interest, and class (stratification).

GROUPING BY SEX

As we have seen in preceding chapters, some division of labor by sex is characteristic of all human societies. Although in some—the Ju/'hoansi, for example (Chapter 17)—many tasks undertaken by men and women may be shared, and people may perform work normally assigned to the opposite

sex without loss of face, in some other societies, men and women are rigidly segregated in what they do. For instance, among the Mohawk, Oneida, Onondaga, Cayuga, and Seneca Indians of New York—the famous Five Nations Iroquois—society was divided into two parts consisting of sedentary women on the one hand and nomadic men on the other. Living in villages were the women, who were "blood" relatives of one another, and whose job it was to grow the corn, beans, and squash on which the Iroquois relied for subsistence. Although houses and the palisades that protected villages were built by men, who also helped women to clear their fields, the most important of men's work was pursued at some distance from their villages. This consisted of hunting, fishing, trading, warring, and engaging in diplomacy. As a consequence, men were transients in the villages, being present for only brief periods of time.

Although masculine activities were considered to be more prestigious than those of women, the latter were regarded by all as the sustainers of life. Moreover, women headed the longhouses (dwellings occupied by matrilocal extended families), descent and inheritance passed through women, and ceremonial life centered on the activities of women. Although men held all positions of leadership outside of households, on the councils of the villages, tribes, and the League of Five Nations, it was the women of their lineages who nominated them for these positions and who held the power of the veto over them. Thus, male leadership was balanced by female authority. Overall,

Among the Iroquoians of New York, society was divided into sedentary women whose work was carried out in or near the village, and nomadic men, whose work was carried out away from the village. This pattern still holds today, as men leave their villages for extended periods to do much of the high steel work in the cities of North America.

the phrase "separate but equal" accurately describes relations between the sexes in Five Nations Iroquoian society, with members of neither sex being dominant nor submissive to the other. Related to this seems to have been a low incidence of rape, at least among the Five Nations. Widely commented upon by outside observers in the nineteenth century was an apparent absence of rape within Iroquoian communities. On the other hand, earlier Jesuit missionaries do record its occurrence in association with the violence directed at peoples outside of the League of Five Nations, over whom the league wished to impose its dominance.

Although Iroquoian men were often absent from the village, when present they ate and slept with women. Among the Mundurucu, discussed briefly in Chapter 20, men not only work apart from women, but eat and sleep separately as well. All men after reaching the age of 13 live in a large house of their own, while women with their young children occupy two or three houses grouped around that of the men. For all intents and purposes, men associate with men, and women with women. The relation between the sexes, rather than being harmonious, is one of opposition. According to Mundurucu belief, sex roles were once reversed, and women ruled over men, controlling the sacred trumpets that are the symbols of power representing the generative capacities of women. But because women could not hunt, they could not supply the meat demanded by the ancient spirits contained within the trumpets, enabling the men to take the trumpets from the women, establishing their dominance in the process. Ever since, the trumpets have been kept carefully guarded and hidden in the men's house, and no woman can see them under penalty of gang rape. Thus, Mundurucu men express fear and envy towards women, whom they seek to control by force. For their part, the women neither like nor accept a submissive status, and even though men occupy all formal positions of political and religious leadership, women are autonomous in the economic realm.

Although there are important differences, there are nonetheless interesting similarities between Mundurucu beliefs and those of traditional European (including European-American) culture. The idea of rule by men replacing an earlier state of matriarchy (rule by women), for example, was held by many nineteenth-century intellectuals.

Moreover, the idea that men may use force in order to control women is deeply embedded in both Judaic and Christian traditions (and even today, in spite of changing attitudes, one out of three women in the United States is sexually assaulted at some time in her life). A major difference between Mundurucu and traditional European society is that, in the latter, women have not had control of their own economic activities. Although this is now changing, there is still a considerable distance to go before women in North America and other Western countries achieve economic parity with men.

AGE GROUPING

Age grouping is so familiar and so important that it and sex have sometimes been called the only universal factors in the determination of one's position in society. In North American society today, one's first friends generally are children one's own age. Together they are sent off to school, where together they remain until their late teens. At specified ages they are finally allowed to do things reserved for adults, such as driving a car, voting, and drinking alcoholic beverages, and (if they are males) are required to go off to war if called upon to do so. Ultimately, North Americans retire from their jobs at some specified age and, more and more, live out the final years of their lives in "retirement communities," segregated from the rest of society. North Americans are "teenagers," "middle-aged," "senior citizens," whether they like it or not and for no other reason than their age.

The pervasiveness of age grouping in North American society is further illustrated by its effects on the Jewish descent groups that we discussed in Chapter 21. Until the mid-1930s, these always took on a more or less conventional ambilineal structure, which united relatives of all generations from the very old to the very young, with no age restrictions. By the late 1930s, however, younger generations of Jews of eastern European background were becoming assimilated into North American culture to such a degree that some of them began to form new descent groups that deliberately excluded any kin of the parental and grandparental generations. In these new cousins

Age grading in modern North American society is exemplified by the educational system, which specifies that at 6 years of age all children must enter the first grade.

clubs, as they are called, descendants of the cousins are eligible for membership, but not until they reach legal majority or are married, whichever comes first. Here again, these newer descent groups contrast with the older family circles, in which membership can be activated at any age, no matter how young.

Age classification also plays a significant role in non-Western societies, where at least a distinction is made between the immature, mature, and older people whose physical powers are waning. Old age often has profound significance, bringing with it the period of greatest respect (for women it may mean the first social equality with men); rarely are the elderly shunted aside or abandoned. Even the Inuit, who are frequently portrayed as a people who quite literally abandon their aged relatives, do so only in truly desperate circumstances, where the physical survival of the group is at stake. In all nonliterate societies, the elders are the repositories of accumulated wisdom; they are the "living libraries" for their people. To cast them aside would be analogous to closing down all the archives and libraries in a modern industrial state.

In the United States people rely on the written word, rather than on their elders, for long-term memory. Moreover, people have become so accustomed to rapid change that they tend to assume that the experiences of their grandparents and others of their generation are of little relevance to them in "today's world." Indeed, retirement from earning a living implies that one has nothing further to offer society and that one should stay out of the way of those who are younger. "The symbolism of the traditional gold watch is all too plain: you should have made your money by now, and your time has run out. The watch will merely tick off the hours that remain between the end of adulthood and death."[1] What makes the status of the elderly even more problematic is the fact that they now constitute so large a part of the overall population. Thus, the achievement of old age seems less of an accomplishment than it once did and so commands less respect. Furthermore, they begin to be seen as not just unproductive, but as a serious economic burden. The ultimate irony is that in the

[1]Turnbull, C. M. (1983). *The human cycle* (p. 229). New York: Simon & Schuster.

In many societies it is common for children of the same age to play, eat, and learn together, like these Masai boys, who are coming together for the first time to receive instruction for their initiation into an age grade.

United States all of the ingenuity of modern science is used to keep alive the bodies of individuals who, in virtually every other way, have been shunted aside by society.

In the institutionalization of age, cultural rather than biological factors are of prime importance in determining social status. All human societies recognize a number of life stages; precisely how they are defined will vary from one culture to another. Out of this recognition they establish patterns of activity, attitudes, prohibitions, and obligations. In some instances, these are designed to help the transition from one age to another, to teach needed skills, or to lend economic assistance. Often they are taken as the basis for the formation of organized groups.

propriate age, and so one is included, without question, in the particular age grade. Such situations do exist, among the East African Tiriki, for example, whose system we will examine shortly. Sometimes, though, one has to buy one's way into the age grade for which one is eligible. By way of illustration, among some of the Indians of the North American plains, boys had to purchase the appropriate costumes, dances, and songs for age-grade membership. In societies where entrance fees are expensive, not all people eligible for membership in a particular age grade may actually be able to join.

Entry into and transfer out of age grades may be accomplished individually, either by a biological distinction, such as puberty, or by a socially recognized status, such as marriage or childbirth. Whereas age-grade members may have much in

Institutions of Age Grouping

An organized class of people with membership on the basis of age is known as an **age grade.** Theoretically speaking, membership in an age grade ought to be automatic: One reaches the ap-

Age grade: An organized category of people based on age; every individual passes through a series of such categories in the course of a lifetime.

common, engage in similar activities, cooperate with one another, and share the same orientation and aspirations, their membership may not be entirely parallel with physiological age. A specific time is often ritually established for moving from a younger to an older grade. Although members of senior groups commonly expect deference from and acknowledge certain responsibilities to their juniors, this does not necessarily mean that one grade is "better" or "worse" or even more important than another. There can be standardized competition (opposition) between age grades, as between first-year students and sophomores on U.S. college campuses. One can, comparably, accept the realities of being a teenager without feeling the need to "prove anything."

In some societies, age grades are subdivided into **age sets**. An age set is a group of persons initiated into an age grade who will move through the system together. For example, among the Tiriki of East Africa, the age group consisting of those initiated into an age grade over a 15-year period amounts to an age set. Age sets, unlike age grades, do not cease to exist after a specified number of years; the members of an age set usually remain closely associated throughout their lives or at least through much of their lives.

A certain amount of controversy has arisen over the relative strength, cohesiveness, and stability that go into an age grouping. The age-set notion implies strong feelings of loyalty and mutual support. Because such groups may possess property, songs, shield designs, and rituals and are internally organized for collective decision making and leadership, a distinction is called for between them and simple age grades. We may also distinguish between transitory age grades—which initially concern younger men (sometimes women, too), but become less important and disintegrate as the members grow older—and the comprehensive systems that affect people through the whole of their lives.

⊂⊃○⊂———⊃○⊂⊃

Age sets: Groups of persons initiated into age grades at the same time and who move through the series of categories together.

⊂⊃○⊂———⊃○⊂⊃

Age Grouping in African Societies

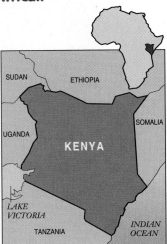

While age is used as a criterion for group membership in many parts of the world, its most varied and elaborate use is found in Africa south of the Sahara. An example may be seen among the Tiriki, one of several pastoral nomadic groups who live in Kenya.[2] In this society, each boy born over a 15-year period becomes a member of a particular age set then open for membership. There are seven such named age sets, only one of which is open for membership at a time; when membership in one is closed, the next one is open for a fifteen-year period, and so on until the passage of 105 years (7x15), when the first once again takes in new "recruits."

Members of Tiriki age sets remain together for life, as they move through four age grades: advancement occurs at 15-year intervals, at the same time that one age set closes and another opens for membership. Each age grade has its own particular duties and responsibilities. The first, or "Warrior" age grade, traditionally served as guardians of the country, and members gained renown through fighting. Since colonial times, however, this traditional function has been lost with cessation of warfare, and members of this age grade now find excitement and adventure by leaving their community for extended employment or study elsewhere.

The next age grade, the "Elder Warriors," traditionally had few specialized tasks, but the members learned skills they would need later on by assuming an increasing share of administrative activities. For example, they would chair the post-funeral gatherings held to settle property claims after someone's death. Elder Warriors were also

[2]Sangree, W. H. (1965). The Bantu Tiriki of Western Kenya. In J. Gibbs, Jr. (Ed.), *Peoples of Africa* (pp. 69–72). New York: Holt, Rinehart and Winston.

the ones who served as envoys between elders of different communities. Nowadays, Elder Warriors hold nearly all of the administrative and executive roles opened up by the creation and growth of a centralized Tiriki administrative bureaucracy.

"Judicial Elders," the third age grade, traditionally handled most tasks connected with the administration and settlement of local disputes. Today, they still serve as the local judiciary body. Members of the "Ritual Elders," the senior age grade, presided over the priestly functions of ancestral shrine observances on the household level, at subclan meetings, at semiannual community appeals, and at rites of initiation into the various age grades. They were also credited with access to special magical powers. With the decline of ancestor worship over the past several decades, many of these traditional functions have been lost and no new ones have arisen to take their places. Nonetheless, Ritual Elders continue to hold the most important positions in the initiation ceremonies, and their powers as sorcerers and expungers of witchcraft are still recognized.

COMMON-INTEREST ASSOCIATIONS

The proliferation of **common-interest associations,** whether out of individual predilection or community need, is a theme intimately associated with world urbanization and its attendant social upheavals; the fondness of people in modern societies for joining all sorts of organizations is incontestably related to these societies' complexity. This "fondness for joining" poses a major threat to the inviolability of age and kinship grouping. Individuals are often separated from their brothers, sisters, or age mates; they obviously cannot obtain their help in learning to cope with life in a new and bewildering environment, in learning a new language or mannerisms necessary for the

---

Common-interest associations: Associations not based on age, kinship, marriage, or territory that result from an act of joining.

---

change from village to city, if they are not present. But such functions must somehow be met. Because common-interest associations are by nature quite flexible, they are increasingly, both in the cities and in traditional villages, filling this gap in the social structure. Common-interest associations are not, however, restricted to modernizing societies alone. They are also found in many traditional societies, and there is reason to believe that they may have arisen with the emergence of the first horticultural villages. Furthermore, those in traditional societies may be just as complex and highly organized as those of the United States and Canada.

Common-interest associations have often been referred to in the anthropological literature as voluntary associations, but this term is misleading. The act of joining may range from being fully voluntary to being required by law. For example, in the United States, under the draft laws one became a member of the armed forces without choosing to join. It is not compulsory to join a labor union, but unless one does, one cannot work in a union shop. What is really meant by the term *voluntary association* are those associations not based on sex, age, kinship, marriage, or territory that result from an act of joining. The act may often be voluntary, but it does not have to be.

Kinds of Common-Interest Associations

The diversity of common-interest associations is astonishing. In the United States, they include such diverse entities as women's clubs of all sorts, street gangs, Kiwanis, Rotary, PTA, political parties, labor unions—the list could go on and on. Their goals may include the pursuit of friendship, recreation, the expression and distinction of rank, as well as governing and the pursuit or defense of economic interests. Traditionally, associations have served for the preservation of tribal songs, history, language, and moral beliefs; the Tribal Unions of West Africa, for example, continue to serve this purpose. Similar organizations, often operating clandestinely, have kept traditions alive among North American Indians, who are undergoing a resurgence of ethnic pride despite generations of schooling designed to stamp out tribal identity. Another significant force in the formation of associations may

The diversity of common-interest associations is astounding. Shown here are a spokeswoman for an adoptive parents' group and a bikers' organization.

be some supernatural experience common to all members; the Crow Indian Tobacco Society, the secret associations of the Kwakiutl Indians of British Columbia with their cycles of rituals known only to initiates, and the Kachina cults of the Hopi Indians are well-known examples. Among other traditional forms of association are military, occupational, political, and entertainment groups that parallel such familiar groups as the American Legion, labor unions, block associations, college fraternities and sororities, not to mention "co-ops" of every kind.

Such organizations are frequently exclusive, but a prevailing characteristic is their concern for the general well-being of an entire village or group of villages. The rain that falls as a result of the work of Hopi rainmakers nourishes the crops of members and nonmembers alike.

Men's and Women's Associations

For many years, women's contributions to common-interest associations were asserted by social scientists to be less significant than men's because men's associations attracted more notice around the world than did women's. Heinrich Schurtz's theory, published in 1902, that underlying the differentiation between kinship and associational groups is a profound difference in the psychology of the sexes, was widely accepted for years. Schurtz

In many contemporary societies, common-interest associations arise to help protect and perpetuate the cultural and human rights of particular ethnic groups within multi-ethnic states. One example is the American Indian Movement whose founder, Dennis Banks, is shown here in Washington at the termination of the 1994 Walk for Justice for Native People.

Common-interest associations are not limited to modern industrial societies. This 1832 picture shows a Mandan Indian Bull Dance. The Bulls were one of several common-interest groups that were concerned with both social and military affairs.

regarded women as eminently unsocial beings who preferred to remain in kinship groups based on sexual relations and the reproductive function rather than form units on the basis of commonly held interests. Men, on the other hand, were said to view sexual relations as isolated episodes, an attitude that fostered the purely social factor that makes "birds of a feather flock together."

In the past two decades, scholars of both sexes have shown this kind of thinking to be culture bound. In some societies women have not formed associations to the extent that men have because the demands of raising a family and their daily activities have not permitted it and because men have not always encouraged them to do so. Given the plethora of women's clubs of all kinds in the United States for several generations, however, one wonders how this belief in women as unsocial beings survived as long as it did. Earlier in this country's history, of course, when women were

homebound in rural situations, with no near neighbors, they had little chance to participate in common-interest associations. Moreover, some functions of men's associations—like military duties—are often culturally defined as purely for men or repugnant to women. In a number of the world's traditional societies, however, the opportunities for female sociability are so great that there may be little need for women's associations. Among the Indians of northeastern North America (including the Five Nations Iroquois discussed earlier), the men spent extended periods away in the woods hunting, either by themselves or with a single companion. The women, by contrast, spent most of their time in and around their villages, in close, everyday contact with the other women of the group. Not only were there many people to talk to but there also was always someone available to help with whatever tasks required assistance.

Still, as cross-cultural research makes clear, women do play important roles in associations of their own and even in those in which men predominate. Among the Crow Indians, women participated even in the secret Tobacco Society, as well as in their own exclusive groups. Throughout Africa, women's social clubs complement the men's and are concerned with educating women, with crafts, and with charitable activities. In Sierra Leone, where once-simple dancing societies have developed under urban conditions into complex organizations with a set of new objectives, the dancing *compin* consists of young women as well as men, who together perform plays based on traditional music and dancing, raising money for various mutual-benefit causes. The Kpelle of Liberia maintain initiation or "bush" schools for both young men and women; women also alternate with men in ritual supremacy of a chiefdom. The cycle of instruction and rule (4 years for males, 3 for females) that marks these periods derives from the Kpelle's association of the number four with maleness and three with femaleness, rather than from a notion of male superiority.

Women's rights organizations, consciousness-raising groups, and professional organizations for women are examples of some of the associations arising directly or indirectly out of today's social climate. These groups cover the entire range of association forming, from simple friendship and support groups to political, guildlike, and economic (the publication of magazines, and groups designed to influence advertising) associations on a national scale. If an unresolved point does exist in the matter of women's participation, it is in determining why women are excluded from associations in some societies, while in others their participation is essentially equal with that of men.

The importance of common-interest associations in areas of rapid social change is considerable. Increasingly, such organizations assume the roles and functions formerly held by kinship or age groups; in many areas they hold the key both to individual adaptation to new circumstances and to group survival. Where once groups were organized to preserve traditional ways and structure against the intrusion of the modern world, urban associations accept the reality of such intrusions and help their members to cope both socially and economically. Members may turn to associations for support and sympathy while unemployed or sick; the groups may also provide education or socialization. An important need met by many of these associations is economic survival; to achieve such ends they may help raise capital, regulate prices, discourage competition, and organize cooperative activities.

Always the keynote of these groups is adaptation. As Kenneth Little observes, adaptation implies not only the modification of institutions but also the development of new ones to meet the demands of an industrial economy and urban way of life.[3] Modern urbanism involves the rapid diffusion of entirely new ideas, habits, and technical procedures, as well as a considerable reconstruction of social relationships as a consequence of new technical roles and groups created. Age-old conventions yield to necessity, as women and young people in general gain new status in the urban economy. Women's participation, especially in associations with mixed membership, involves them in new kinds of social relationships with men, including companionship and the chance to choose a spouse by oneself. Young persons on the whole become leaders for their less Westernized counterparts. Even in rural areas, such associations thrive, reflecting the increasing consciousness of the outer world. With an irony implicit in many former colonial situations, the European contact that so frequently shattered permanent age and kinship groups has, partly through the influence of education, helped remove restrictions in association membership both in age and sex.

SOCIAL STRATIFICATION

The study of social stratification involves the examination of distinctions that strike us as unfair and even outrageous, but social stratification is a common and powerful phenomenon in some of the world's societies. Civilizations, in particular, with their large and heterogeneous populations, are invariably stratified.

[3]Little, K. (1964). The role of voluntary associations in West African urbanization. In Pierre Van den Berghe (Ed.), *Africa: Social problems of change and conflict.* San Francisco: Chandler.

Basically, a **stratified society** is one that is divided into two or more categories of people who are ranked high and low relative to one another. When the people in one such group or stratum are compared with those in another, marked differences in privileges, rewards, restrictions, and obligations become apparent. Members of low-ranked groups will tend to have fewer privileges than those in high-ranked groups. In addition, they tend not to be rewarded to the same degree, and are denied equal access to basic resources. Their restrictions and obligations, too, are usually more onerous, although members of high-ranked groups will usually have their own distinctive restrictions and obligations to meet. In short, social stratification amounts to institutionalized inequality. Without ranking—high versus low—there is no stratification; social differences without this do not constitute stratification.

Stratified societies stand in sharp contrast to **egalitarian societies.** As we saw in Chapter 17, societies of food-foraging peoples are characteristically egalitarian, although there are some exceptions. In such societies there are as many valued positions as there are people capable of filling them. Hence, individuals' positions in society depend pretty much on their own abilities alone. A poor hunter may become a good hunter if he has the ability; he is not excluded from such a prestigious position because he comes from a group of poor hunters. Poor hunters do not constitute a social stratum. Furthermore, they have as much right to the resources of their society as any other of its members. No one can deny a poor hunter a fair share of food, the right to be heard when important decisions are to be made, or anything else to which a man is entitled.

Despite their close association, the clothing worn by these two individuals and the way they interact clearly indicate that they are of different social classes.

Class and Caste

A **social class** may be defined as a set of families that show equal or nearly equal prestige according to the system of evaluation.[4] The qualification "nearly equal" is important, for there may be a certain amount of inequality even within a given class; for example, low-ranking individuals in an upper class may not seem much different from the

---

Stratified society: The division of society into two or more categories of people who do not share equally in the basic resources that support life, influence, and prestige.

Egalitarian societies: Social systems in which as many valued positions exist as there are persons capable of filling them.

Social class: A set of families that enjoy equal or nearly equal prestige according to the system of evaluation.

---

[4]Barber, B. (1957). *Social stratification* (p. 73). New York: Harcourt.

Anthropology Applied

ANTHROPOLOGISTS AND SOCIAL IMPACT ASSESSMENT

A kind of policy research frequently done by anthropologists is the social impact assessment, which entails collection of data about a community or neighborhood for use by planners of development projects. Specifically, such assessments seek to determine the effect of a project by determining how and upon whom its impact will fall, and whether the impact is likely to be positive or negative. In the United States, any project requiring a federal permit or license, or using federal funds, by law must be preceded by a social impact assessment, as part of the environmental review process. Examples of such projects include highway construction, urban renewal, water diversion schemes, and land reclamation. Often, projects of these sorts are sited so that their impact falls most heavily on neighborhoods or communities inhabited by people in low socioeconomic strata, sometimes because the projects are seen as ways of improving the lives of poor people, and sometimes because the poor people are seen as having less political power to block proposals that others conceive to be (sometimes rightly, sometimes wrongly) in "the public interest."

As an illustration of this kind of work, anthropologist Sue Ellen Jacobs was hired to carry out a social impact assessment of a water diversion project in New Mexico planned by the Bureau of Land Reclamation in cooperation with the Bureau of Indian Affairs. This would have involved construction of a diversion dam and extensive canal system for irrigation on the Rio Grande River. Affected by this would be 22 communities inhabited primarily by Hispanic Americans, as well as two Indian Pueblos. In the region, unemployment was high (19.1 percent in June 1970), and the project was seen as a way of promoting a perceived trend to urbanism (which theoretically would be associated with industrial development), while bringing new land into production for intensive agriculture. What the planners failed to take into account was the fact that both the Hispanic and Indian populations were heavily committed to farming for household consumption, with some surpluses raised for the market, using a system of irrigation canals established as many as 300 years ago. This system is

maintained by elected supervisors who know the communities as well as the requirements of the land and crops, water laws, and ditch management skills. Such individuals can allocate water equitably in times of scarcity and can prevent and resolve conflict in the realm of water and land use, as well as community life beyond the ditches. Under the proposed project, this system would be given up in favor of one in which fewer people would control larger tracts of land, and water allocation would be in the hands of a government technocrat. One of the strongest measures of local government would be lost.

Not surprisingly, Jacobs discovered widespread community opposition to this project, and it was her report that helped convince Congress that any positive impact was far outweighed by negative effects. According to anthropologist John Van Willigen:

> One of the major objections to the construction of the project is that it would result in the obliteration of the three-hundred-year-old irrigation system structures. Project planners did not seem to recognize the antiquity and cultural significance of the traditional irrigation system. These were referred to as "temporary diversion structures." The fact that the old dams associated with the ditches were attached to local descent groups was simply not recognized by the official documents.*

Other negative effects, besides loss of local control, were problems associated with population growth and relocation, loss of fishing and other river-related resources, and new health hazards, including increased threat of drowning, breeding of insects, and airborne dust. Finally, physical transformation of the communities' life space was seen likely to result in changes in the context of the informal processes of enculturation that go on within the communities.

*Van Willigen, J. (1986). *Applied anthropology* (p. 169). South Hadley, MA: Bergin and Garvey.

---

highest-ranking members of a lower class. Yet there will be marked differences when the classes are compared as wholes with one another. The point here is that class distinctions will not be clear-cut and obvious in societies like those of North America, where

there is a continuous range of differential privileges, for example, from virtually none to several. Such a continuum can be divided up into classes in a variety of ways. If fine distinctions are made, then many classes may be recognized. If, however, only

"Outcast" groups like India's untouchables are a common feature of stratified societies; the United States, for example, has in recent years seen the growth of a castelike underclass.

a few gross distinctions are made, then only a few classes will be recognized. Thus, some speak of North American society as divided into three classes: lower, middle, and upper. Others speak of several classes: lower-lower, middle-lower, upper-lower, lower-middle, and so forth.

A **caste** is a special kind of social class in which membership is fairly fixed or impermeable. Castes are strongly endogamous, and offspring are automatically members of their parents' caste. The classic case is the caste system of India. Coupled with strict endogamy and membership by descent in Indian castes is an association of particular castes with specific occupations and customs, such as food habits and styles of dress, along with rituals involving notions of purity and impurity. The literally thousands of castes are organized into a hierarchy of four named groups, at the top of which are the priests or *Brahmins*, the bearers of universal order and values, and of highest ritual purity. Below them are the powerful—though less pure—warriors. Dominant at the local level, besides fulfilling warrior functions, they control all village lands. Furnishing services to the landowners, and owning the tools of their trade, are two lower-ranking landless caste groups of artisans and laborers. At the bottom of the system, owning neither land nor the tools of their trade, are the out-

---

Caste: A special form of social class in which membership is determined by birth and remains fixed for life.

---

casts or "untouchables." These most impure of all people constitute a large pool of labor at the beck and call of those controlling economic and political affairs, the landholding warrior caste.

Although some argue that the term *caste* should be restricted to the Indian situation, others find this much too narrow a usage, since castelike situations are known elsewhere in the world. In South Africa, for example, although the situation is now changing, blacks were traditionally relegated to a low-ranking stratum in society, were until recently barred by law from marrying nonblacks, and could not hold property except to a limited degree in specified "black homelands." Most blacks still perform menial jobs for whites, but even the small cadres of "middle class" blacks that existed were until recently prohibited from living where whites do, or even swimming in the same water, or holding the hand of someone who is white. All of this brings to mind the concepts of ritual purity and pollution so basic to the Indian caste system. In South Africa, whites feared pollution of their purity through improper contact with blacks.

In India and South Africa, untouchables and blacks have comprised categories of landless or near-landless people who made up a body of mobile laborers available to those in political control. A similar mobile labor force of landless men at the disposal of the state emerged in China as many as 2,200 years ago (caste, in India, is at least as old). Paradoxically, at the very same time that South Africa is trying to change its system, a similar caste-like "underclass" has emerged in U.S. society, as automation has reduced the need for unskilled workers and "downsizing" has taken place. Its members consist of unemployed, unemployable, or drastically underemployed people who own little if any property, and who live "out on the streets" or—at best—in urban or rural slums. Lacking both economic and political power, they have no access to the kinds of educational facilities that would enable them or their children to improve their lot. Rather than providing a pool of cheap labor for the state, this new underclass serves the economy by ensuring a significant incidence of permanent unemployment, thereby making the employed feel less secure in their jobs. As a consequence, the employed are apt to be less demanding of wages and benefits from their employers.

India, South Africa, China, and the United States are all very different countries, in different parts of the world, with different ideologies and yet, a similar phenomenon has emerged, or is emerging, in each. Is there something about the structure of socially stratified states that sooner or later produces some sort of exploitable, impoverished outcast group? The answer to this is clearly unknown, but the question deserves the attention of anthropologists and other social scientists.

The basis of social class structure is role differentiation. Some role differentiation, of course, exists in any society, at least along the lines of sex and age. Furthermore, any necessary role will always be valued to some degree. In a food-foraging society, the role of "good hunter" will be valued. The fact that one man may already play that role does not, however, prevent another man from playing it, too, in an egalitarian society. Therefore, role differentiation by itself is not sufficient for stratification. Two more ingredients are necessary: formalized evaluation of roles involving attitudes such as like–dislike, or admiration–revulsion, and restricted access to the more highly valued ones. Obviously, the greater the diversity of roles in a society, the more complex evaluation and restriction can become. Since great role diversity is most characteristic of civilizations, it is not surprising that they provide the greatest opportunities for stratification. Furthermore, the large size and heterogeneity of populations in civilizations create a need for ways of classifying people into a manageable number of social categories. Small wonder, then, that social stratification is one of the defining characteristics of a true civilization.

Social classes are manifest in several ways. One is through **verbal evaluation**—what people say about others in their own society. For this, anything can be singled out for attention and spoken of favorably or unfavorably: political, military, religious, economic, or professional roles; wealth and property; kinship; personal qualities; community activity; and a host of other things. Different cultures do this differently, and what may be spoken of favorably in one may be spoken of unfavorably in another and ignored in a third. Furthermore, cultural values may change, so that something regarded favorably at one time may not be so at another. This is one reason why a researcher may be misled by verbal evaluation, for what people say may not correspond completely with reality.

Social classes are also manifest through patterns of association: not just who interacts with whom, but in what context, and how those who are interacting treat one another. In Western society, informal, friendly relations take place mostly within one's own class. Relations with members of other classes tend to be less informal and occur in the context of specific situations. For example, a corporation executive and a janitor normally are members of different social classes. They may have frequent contact with one another, but it occurs in the setting of the corporation offices and usually requires certain stereotyped behavior patterns.

A third way social classes are manifest is through **symbolic indicators.** Included here are activities and possessions indicative of class. For example, in North American society, occupation (a garbage collector has different class status than a physician); wealth (rich people generally are in a higher social class than poor people); dress ("white collar" versus "blue collar"); form of recreation (upper-class people are expected to play golf rather than shoot pool down at the pool hall—but they can shoot pool at home or in a club); residential location (upper-class people do not ordinarily live in slums); kind of car; and so on. The fact is that

---

Verbal evaluation: The way people in a stratified society evaluate other members of their own society.

Symbolic indicators: In a stratified society, activities and possessions that are indicative of social class.

Symbolic indicators of class or caste standing include factors of lifestyle as illustrated here by ways of enjoying oneself on a hot day.

there are all sorts of status symbols indicative of class position, including such things as the number of bathrooms in one's house. At the same time, symbolic indicators may be cruder reflections of class position than verbal indicators or patterns of association. One reason is that access to wealth may not be wholly restricted to upper classes, so that individuals can buy symbols suggestive of upper-class status, whether or not this really is their status. To take an extreme example, the head of an organized crime ring may display more of the symbols of high-class status than may some members of old, established upper-class families. For that matter, someone from an upper class may deliberately choose a simpler lifestyle than would be expected. Instead of driving a Mercedes, he or she may drive a beat-up Volkswagen.

Symbolic indicators involve factors of lifestyle, but differences in life chances may also signal differences in class standing. Life is apt to be less physically hard for members of an upper class as opposed to a lower class. This will show up in a tendency for lower infant mortality and longer life expectancy for the upper class. One may also see a tendency to greater physical stature and robustness on the part of upper-class people, the result of better diet and less physical hardship.

Mobility

In all stratified societies there is at least some **mobility,** which helps to ease the strains that exist in any system of inequality. Even in the Indian caste system, with its guiding ideology that pretends that all arrangements within it are static, there is a surprising amount of flexibility and mobility, not all of it associated with the recent changes that "modernization" has brought to India. As a rather dramatic case in point, in the state of Rajasthan, those who own and control most land and who are wealthy and politically powerful, are not of warrior caste, as one would expect, but are of the lowest caste. Their tenants and laborers, by contrast, are Brahmins. Thus, the group that is ritually superior to all others finds itself in the same social position as untouchables, whereas the landowners who are the Brahmins' ritual inferiors are superior in all other ways. Meanwhile, a group of leatherworkers in the untouchable category, who have gained political power in India's new democracy, are trying to better their position by claiming that they are Brahmins who were tricked in the past into doing defiling work. Although individuals cannot move up or down the caste hierarchy, whole groups can move up or down depending on claims they are able to make for higher status and how well they can manipulate others into acknowledging their claims. Interestingly, the people at the bottom of India's caste system have not traditionally questioned the validity of the system itself, so much as their particular position within it.

Mobility: The ability to change one's class position.

In the United States, the ability to "move up" in the system of stratification is increasingly dependent upon access to higher education.

Societies that permit a great deal in the way of mobility are referred to as **open class societies.** Even here, however, mobility is apt to be more limited than one might suppose. In the United States, in spite of its "rags to riches" ideology, most mobility involves a move up or down only a notch, although if this continues over several generations, it may add up to a major change. Generally, the culture makes much of those relatively rare examples of great upward mobility that are consistent with its cultural values, doing its best to ignore the numerous cases of little upward, not to mention downward, mobility.

The degree of mobility in a stratified society is related to the prevailing kind of family organization. In societies where the extended family is the usual form, mobility is apt to be difficult because each individual is strongly tied to the large family group. Hence, for a person to move up to a higher social class, his or her family must move up as well. Mobility is easier for independent nuclear families in which the individual is closely tied to fewer persons. Moreover, under neolocal residence, individuals normally leave the family into which they were born. So it is, then, that through careful marriage, occupational success, and by disassociating one's self from a lower-class family in which one was raised, all of which are made possible by residential mobility, one can more easily "move up" in society.

Gender Stratification

Closely associated with class and caste stratification is the related phenomenon of gender stratification. For instance, in our earlier discussion of sex as an organizing principle, we saw that in some (but not all) societies, men and women may be regarded

Open class societies: Stratified societies that permit a great deal of social mobility.

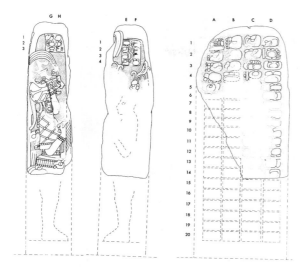

At the ancient Maya city of Tikal, in Central America, one reflection of gender stratification is the rarity of portrayals of women, compared to men, in the city's public art. The woman shown in this drawing was sculpted on the side of a stone monument only because of her status as mother of the king portrayed on the monument's front (and wife of the king's father, shown on the stone's other side).

as unequal, with the former outranking the latter. Generally speaking, sexual inequality is characteristic of societies that are stratified in other ways as well; thus women have historically occupied a position of inferiority to men in the class-structured societies of the Western world. Nevertheless, sexual inequality may sometimes be seen in societies that are not otherwise stratified; in such instances, men and women are always physically as well as conceptually separated from one another. On the other hand, as the Iroquoian case cited earlier in this chapter demonstrates, not all societies in which men and women are separated exhibit gender stratification.

The rise of gender stratification often seems to be associated with the development of strongly centralized states. For example, among the Maya of Central America the basic social unit in the past as today was the complementary gender pair. On the household level, men raise the crops and bring in the other raw materials, which the women transform into food, textiles, and other cultural objects. The same complementarity existed in public ritual and politics, but in the last century B.C. at the Maya

city of Tikal, things began to change. With the development of strong dynastic rule by men, women began to be excluded from favored places for burial, their graves were not as richly stocked with grave goods as were those of important men, they all but disappeared from public art and were rarely mentioned in inscriptions. When women were portrayed or mentioned, it was because of their relationship to a particular male ruler. Clearly, women came to hold a lesser place in Maya society than did men, although gender stratification was not nearly as marked at the "grass roots" of society as it was among the elite. When the Tikal state collapsed, as it did in the ninth century A.D., the relationship of equality between men and women returned to what it had been eight or nine centuries before.[5]

Development of Stratification

Because social stratification of any kind tends to make life oppressive for large segments of a population, the lower classes are usually placated by means of religion, which promises them a better existence in the hereafter. If they have this to look forward to, they are more likely to accept the "here and now." In India, for example, belief in reincarnation and the existence of an incorruptible supernatural power that assigns people to a particular caste position as a reward or punishment for the deeds and misdeeds of past lives justifies one's position in this life. If, however, one performs the duties appropriate to one's caste in this lifetime, then one can expect to be reborn into a higher caste in a future existence. Truly exemplary performance of one's duties may even release one from the cycle of rebirth, to be reunited with the divinity from which all existence springs. In the minds of orthodox Hindus, then, one's caste position is something one earns (an achieved status), rather than the accident of birth (ascribed) that it appears to outside observers. Thus, while the caste system explicitly recognizes inequality between people, it is underlain with an implicit assumption of ultimate equality. This contrasts with the situation in the United

[5]Haviland, W. A. (1993, November). The rise of sexist society: Death and gender at Tikal, Guatemala. Paper presented at the 92nd Annual Meeting of the American Anthropological Association, Washington, D.C.

The high status of the two Maya kings shown in this painting from a pottery vessel is revealed by their jewelry, elaborate headdresses, and the fact that they sit on thrones. Among these people, stratification arose as certain lineages monopolized important offices.

States, where the equality of all people is proclaimed at the same time that various groups are clearly regarded as unequal.

In considering the origin of social stratification, we must reckon with such common tendencies as the desire for prestige, either for oneself or one's group. Although the impulse need not result inevitably in the ranking of individuals or groups relative to one another, it sometimes may. Among the Iroquois and Hopi Indians, the Sherente and Ugandan peoples, the superiority of some kinship lineages over others is recognized in electing chiefs, performing sacred rituals, and other special tasks, whether or not membership entails any economic advantages.

This sort of situation could easily develop into full-fledged stratification. Just such a development may have taken place among the Maya of Central America.[6] These people began as horticulturists with a relatively egalitarian, kinship-based organization. In the last centuries B.C., elaborate rituals developed as a way of dealing with the very serious

[6]Haviland, W. A. (1975). The ancient Maya and the evolution of urban society. *University of Colorado Museum of Anthropology Miscellaneous Series, 37*; and Haviland, W. A., & Moholy-Nagy, H. (1992). Distinguishing the high and mighty from the hoi polloi at Tikal, Guatemala. In A. F. Chase & D. Z. Chase (Eds.), *Mesoamerican elites: An archaeological assessment*. Norman: University of Oklahoma Press.

In South Africa, stratification emerged as conquerors excluded the conquered from positions of importance and restricted their access to basic resources. Shown here is the black township outside the capital of Namibia, until recently ruled from South Africa.

problems of agriculture, such as uncertain rains, vulnerability of crops to a variety of pests, and periodic devastation from hurricanes. As this took place, a full-time priesthood arose, along with some craft specialization in the service of religion. Out of the priesthood developed, in the last century B.C., the hereditary ruling dynasties mentioned earlier. In this developmental process, certain lineages seem to have monopolized the important civic and ceremonial positions and so came to be ranked above other lineages, forming the basis of an upper class.

Just as lineages may come to be ranked differentially relative to one another, so may ethnic groups. In South Africa, for example, the whites came as conquerors, establishing a social order by which they could maintain their favored position. Even without conquest, though, ethnic differences often are a factor in the definition of social classes and castes, as members of North American society have experienced through the racial stereotyping that leads to social and economic disadvantages.

Sometimes, rather than providing the basis for stratification, ethnicity comes to serve as a metaphor for what began as nothing more than distinctions of class. A dramatic example of this can be found in the African state of Rwanda where what began simply as distinctions of class have come to be seen as if they involved differences in ethnicity. Ultimately, they were magnified to the point that the whole country erupted in a bloodbath, illustrating how class systems have built into them the seeds of their own destruction. In Rwanda, this happened through an intersection of class differences with the interests of particular common-interest associations.

Original Study
Genocide in Rwanda[7]

The genocide in Rwanda is a crime, perpetrated by a known group of individuals associated with two extremist parties, the National Republican Movement for Development of Democracy (MRND) and the Coalition for the Defense of the Republic (CDR). The first targets were members of opposition parties, journalists and human rights activists, both Hutu and Tutsi. As the killing spread to the rural areas, it has become a programme of genocide specifically targeted at the Tutsi, who before the killing represented about ten percent of Rwanda's seven million people. Over 200,000 have died so far [June 1994], and the killing continues.

A crime requires motive, means, and opportunity. The motive of those responsible was to continue to monopolize power and to seek a "final solution" to the political opposition, both civilian and armed. Attempts by President Juvenal Habyarimana to stall on the implementation of agreements for power sharing were not succeeding, owing to domestic and international pressure.

The primary means for perpetuating genocide is mobilization of the militias that had been established by the MRND and CDR since late 1971. Use of the civil administration to encourage ordinary people to participate in killings is a supplementary strategy. Army units, especially from the Presidential Guard, and death squads have also helped direct the killings, especially in the towns. Radio broadcasts have been used to incite the population.

The genocide against rural Tutsi in Rwanda is particularly traumatic because the killers are largely people from the same community as their victims. People are murdered by their neighbors, their schoolteachers, their local shopkeepers. Such mass mobilization of killers was necessary because of the particular nature of Rwandese society.

In Rwanda, under Belgian colonial rule, an indigenous system of stratification was distorted by defining class differences as if they were ethnic differences and destroying traditional patterns of reciprocity between classes. As a consequence, the stage was set for the outbreaks of violence that have plagued the country ever since the end of colonial rule.

Rwanda has long been known as a true nation in Africa, containing three groups: Twa, Hutu and Tutsi. German and Belgian colonists characterized them as respectively aboriginal Pygmies, Bantu peasants and Nilo-Hamitic aristocrats. The truth is that they were three different strata of the same group, differentiated by occupational and political status. There is some analogy with the Indian caste system, though individuals could and did move with difficulty between the categories; and the Twa are victims of some of the worst discrimination in Africa.

The reciprocity in Hutu-Tutsi relations that had diluted the latter's dominance in pre-colonial days was destroyed by Belgian rule. Instead a rigid system of tribute and exploitation was imposed, creating deep grievances that underlie today's violence. In the northwest, formerly an autonomous region of Hutu kingdoms, the Belgians dismantled the pre-colonial political system, and imposed Tutsi overlords. The modern Hutu extremists—the late President Habyarimana and his clan—derive from this area.

The differences in physical stature between the groups have been widely exaggerated: it is rarely possible to tell whether an *individual* is a Twa, Hutu or Tutsi from his or her height. Speaking the same language, sharing the same culture and religion, living in the same places, they are in no sense "tribes," nor even distinct "ethnic groups."

Two things enable one to identify an individual as Twa, Hutu or Tutsi: knowledge of the person's ancestry, and the possession of an identity card which, since 1926, has by law specified which group he or she belongs to. The latter is a legacy of Belgian rule: those with ten or more cows were classified as Tutsi, those with less as Hutu—and a tiny minority as those recognized as Twa has their status as an ethnographic curiosity confirmed in perpetuity. But checking every identity card is time-consuming, and the killings needed to be carried out rapidly to be successful, so those planning the killing needed to mobilize militiamen from every community in the country, who knew every Tutsi family personally. In 1991, the government began to implement a system known as "Nyumba Kumi" (literally "ten houses")—one man from every ten houses was mobilized and armed. Such are the logistical challenges facing those who contemplate genocide.

The killers were able to practice their methods on various occasions since 1990, killing perhaps 3,000 people, mainly Tutsi. This is well-documented in the 1993 report of an international human rights commission.

The opportunity was provided by a conjunction of circumstances, which allowed the hardliners to confuse the international community for sufficiently long to be able to perpetuate the crime with extraordinarily little international response. The sowing of confusion was the key to the killers' success. Because President Habyarimana himself was the first casualty, his acolytes were able to present themselves as victims of the plot, rather than the perpetrators. The deaths of ten Belgians serving on the UN force focused international attention on the plight of foreigners. The renewed offensive by the Rwandan Patriotic Front (RPF)—motivated in part by the desire to rescue Tutsi civilians from the militias—enabled the government to speak of aggression and the need for a ceasefire. But above all, the killers portrayed the situation as one of uncontrollable spontaneous ethnic violence.

Prompt international condemnation of the coup in Burundi in October 1993 prevented political extremists from seizing and holding on to power. The absence of such condemnation in Rwanda last month [May 1994] allowed the killers to carry out their task undisturbed. This was largely because the crime of genocide was misdiagnosed as a spontaneous ethnic violence. The Secretary General of the United Nations, Boutros Boutros-Ghali, spoke in late April of "Hutus killing Tutsi and Tutsi killing Hutus" and proposed sending troops to bring about a ceasefire between the (Tutsi-dominated) RPF and the (Hutu-dominated) army. This was precisely what the militias wanted: a chance to stop the RPF advance so they could complete the genocide of unarmed Tutsi away from the battle lines.

[7]de Waal, A. (1994). Genocide in Rwanda. *Anthropology Today, 10*(3), 1–2.

Although the cost is great—social classes do, after all, make life oppressive for large numbers of people—classes may nevertheless perform an integrative function in society. By cutting across some or all lines of kinship, residence, occupation, and age group, depending on the particular society, they counteract potential tendencies for society to fragment into discrete entities. In India diverse tribal groups were incorporated into the larger society by certification of their leaders as warriors and marriage of their women to Brahmins. The problem is that stratification, by its very nature, provides a means by which one, usually small group of people may dominate and make life miserable for large numbers of others, as in the case of Rwanda or South Africa, where 4.5 million whites dominated 25 million non-whites. In India a succession of conquerors was able to move as warriors into the caste hierarchy near its top. In any system of stratification, those who dominate proclaim their supposedly "superior" status, which they try to convert into respect, or at least acquiescence, on the part of the lower classes. In this they are generally aided by a religious ideology that asserts that the social order is divinely fixed and therefore unquestionable. Thus, they hope that members of the lower classes will thereby "know their places" and so not contest their domination by the "chosen elite." If, however, this domination is contested, the elite usually have the power of the state to back them up in their privileged positions.

CHAPTER SUMMARY

Grouping by sex separates men and women to varying degrees in different societies; in some, they may be together much of the time, while in others, they may spend much of their time apart, even to the extreme of eating and sleeping separately. Although women are perceived by men to be their inferiors in some sexually segregated societies, in others they are perceived as equals.

Age grouping is another form of association that may augment or replace kinship grouping. An age grade is a category of persons, usually of the same sex, organized on the basis of age. Age grades in some societies are broken up into age sets, which include individuals who are initiated into an age grade at the same time and move together through a series of life stages. A specific time is often ritually established for moving from a younger to an older age grade.

The most varied use of grouping by age is found in African societies south of the Sahara. Among the Tiriki of East Africa, for example, seven named age sets pass through four successive age grades. Each age set embraces a 15-year age span, and so opens to accept new initiates every 105 years. In principle, the system resembles our college classes, where (say) the "Class of 1990" (an age set) will move through the four age grades: first year, sophomore, junior, senior.

Common-interest associations are linked with rapid social change and urbanization. They are increasingly assuming the roles formerly played by kinship or age groups. In urban areas they help new arrivals cope with the changes demanded by the move from the village to the city. Common-interest associations are also seen in traditional societies, and their roots are probably found in the first horticultural villages. Membership may range from voluntary to legally compulsory.

For a long time social scientists mistakenly viewed women's contributions to common-interest associations as less important than men's, largely because of culture-bound assumptions. A question that remains is why women are barred from associations in some societies, while in others they participate on an equal basis with men.

A stratified society is one that is divided into two or more categories of people who do not share equally in basic resources, influence, or prestige. This form contrasts with the egalitarian society, in which as many valued positions exist as there are persons capable of filling them. Societies may be stratified in various ways, as by gender, age, social class, or caste. Members of a class enjoy equal or nearly equal access to basic resources and prestige (according to the way the latter is defined). Class differences are not always clear-cut and obvious. Where fine distinctions are made in privileges, the result is a multiplicity of classes. In societies where only gross distinctions are made, only a few social classes may be recognized.

Caste is a special form of social class in which membership is determined by birth and fixed for life. Endogamy is particularly marked within castes, and children automatically belong to their parents' caste. Social class structure is based on role differentiation, although this by itself is not sufficient for stratification. Also necessary are formalized positive and negative attitudes toward roles and restricted access to the more valued ones.

Social classes are given expression in several ways. One is through verbal evaluation, or what people say about other people in their society. Another is through patterns of association—who interacts with whom, how, and in what context. Social classes are also manifest through symbolic indicators: activities and possessions indicative of class position. Finally, they are reflected by differences in life chances, as high-status people generally live longer and in better health than people of low status.

Mobility is present to a greater or lesser extent in all stratified societies. Open class societies are those in which mobility is easiest. In most cases, however, the move is limited to one rung up or down the social ladder. The degree of mobility is related to the type of family organization that prevails in a society. Where the extended family is the norm, mobility tends to be severely limited. The independent nuclear family provides a situation in which mobility is easier.

Social stratification can be based on many criteria, such as wealth, legal status, birth, personal qualities, and ideology. A rigidly stratified society in which mobility is limited normally makes life particularly oppressive for large segments of a population.

SUGGESTED READINGS

Bernardi, B. (1985). *Age class systems; Social institutions and policies based on age*. New York: Cambridge University Press.

A cross-cultural analysis of age as a device for organizing society and seeing to the distribution and rotation of power.

Bradfield, R. M. (1973). *A natural history of associations*. New York: International Universities Press.

This two-volume work is the first major anthropological study of common-interest associations since 1902. It attempts to provide a comprehensive theory of the origin of associations and their role in kin-based societies.

Hammond, D. (1972). *Associations*. Reading, MA: Addison-Wesley Modular Publications.

This is a brief, first-rate review of anthropological thinking and the literature on common-interest associations and age groups.

Lenski, G. E. (1966). *Power and privilege: A theory of social stratification*. New York: McGraw-Hill.

Who gets what and why is explained by the distributive process and systems of social stratification in industrial nations: the United States, Russia, Sweden, and Britain. Using a broadly comparative approach, the author makes heavy use of anthropological and historical material, as well as the usual sociological materials on modern industrial societies. The basic approach is theoretical and analytical; the book builds on certain postulates about the nature of humans and society, seeking to develop in a systematic manner an explanation of a variety of patterns of stratification. The theory presented is a synthesis of the two dominant theoretical traditions of the past and present, currently represented in both Marxian and functionalist theory.

Sanday, P. R. (1981). *Female power and male dominance: On the origins of sexual inequality*. Cambridge: Cambridge University Press.

In this cross-cultural study, Sanday reveals the various ways that male-female relations are organized in human societies, demonstrating that male dominance is not inherent in those relations. Rather, it appears to emerge in situations of stress, as a result of such things as chronic food shortages, migration, and colonial domination.

VII
THE SEARCH FOR ORDER
SOLVING THE PROBLEM OF DISORDER

It is an irony of human life that something as fundamental to our existence as cooperation should contain within it the seeds of its own destruction. It is nonetheless true that the groups that people form to take care of important organizational needs do not just facilitate cooperation among the members of those groups, they also create conditions that may lead to the disruption of society. A case in point is the escalating gang violence seen in many North American cities. The attitude that "my group is better than your group" is not confined to any one of the world's cultures, and it not infrequently takes the form of a sense of rivalry between groups: descent group against descent group, men against women, age grade against age grade, social class against social class, and so forth. Still, such rivalry does not have to be disruptive; it may indeed function to ensure that the members of groups perform their jobs well so as not to "lose face" or be subject to ridicule. Rivalry can, however, become a serious problem if it develops into conflict.

Social living inevitably entails a certain amount of friction—not just between groups, but between individual members of groups as well. Thus, any society can count on some degree of disruptive behavior on the part of some of its members, at some time or other. On the other hand, no one can know precisely when such outbursts will occur or what form they will take. Not only does this uncertainty go against the predictability that social life demands; it also goes against the deep-seated psychological need on the part of each individual for structure and certainty, which we discussed in Chapter 16. Therefore, every society must have means by which conflicts can be resolved and breakdown of the social order prevented. Social control and political systems, which have as their primary function the maintenance of the social order, are the subjects of Chapter 23.

Religion and politics may seem like strange bedfellows, but both exist to do the same thing: to protect society against the unexpected and unwanted. Effective though a culture may be in equipping, organizing, and controlling a society to provide for the needs of its members, there are always certain problems that defy solution through existing technological or organizational means. The response of every culture is to devise a set of rituals, with a set of beliefs to explain them, aimed at solving these problems through the manipulation of supernatural beings and powers. In short, religion and magic exist to transform the uncertainties of life into certainties. At the same time, they may serve as powerful integrative forces through commonly held values, beliefs, and practices. Also important is religion's rationalization of the existing social order, which thereby becomes a moral order as well. Thus, there is a link between religion and magic on the one hand, and political organization and social control on the other. Religion and the supernatural are, then, appropriate subjects for discussion in Chapter 24 of this section on the search for order.

Like religion and the supernatural, the arts also contribute to human well-being, helping give shape and significance to life. The relationship between art and religion goes even deeper than this, though, for much of what we call art has come into being in the service of religion: myths to explain ritual practices, objects to portray important deities, music and dances for ceremonial use, pictorial art to record religious experiences and/or to serve as objects of supernatural power in their own right, and the like. In a very real sense, music, dance, and any other form of art, like magic, exploit psychological predispositions so as to enchant other people and cause them to perceive social reality in a way favorable to the interests of the enchanter. And like religion, art of any kind expresses the human search for order, in that some essentially formless raw material is given form by the artist. Accordingly, a chapter on the arts (Chapter 25) follows that on religion, concluding this section.

CHAPTER
23

POLITICAL ORGANIZATION AND SOCIAL CONTROL

POLITICAL ORGANIZATION IN HUMAN SOCIETIES TAKES MANY FORMS, OF WHICH THE STATE IS BUT ONE. ONE REASON STATES GENERALLY DO NOT LAST VERY LONG IS THAT THEY ARE OFTEN CONTROLLED BY MEMBERS OF ONE NATIONALITY WHO TRY TO REPRESS (OR EVEN EXTERMINATE) OTHER NATIONALITIES WITHIN THE STATE, AS SERBS ARE ATTEMPTING IN MUCH OF BOSNIA.

CHAPTER PREVIEW

What Is Political Organization?

Political organization refers to the means by which a society maintains order internally and manages its affairs with other societies externally. Such organization may be relatively uncentralized and informal, as in bands and tribes, or centralized and formal, as in chiefdoms and states.

How Is Order Maintained Within a Society?

Social controls may be internalized—"built into" individuals—or externalized, in the form of sanctions. Built-in controls rely on such deterrents as personal shame and fear of supernatural punishment. Negative sanctions, by contrast, rely on actions taken by other members of society toward behavior that is specifically approved or disapproved. Positive sanctions encourage approved behavior, while negative sanctions discourage behavior that is disapproved. Negative sanctions that are formalized and enforced by an authorized political body are called laws. Consequently, we may say that laws are sanctions, but not all sanctions are laws. Similarly, societies do not maintain order through law alone.

How Is Order Maintained Between Societies?

Just as the threatened or actual use of force may be employed to maintain order within a society, so may it be used to manage affairs among bands, lineages, clans, or whatever the largest autonomous political units may be. Not all societies, however, rely on force, because there are some that do not practice warfare as we know it. Such societies generally have a view of themselves and their place in the world that is quite different from those characteristic of centrally organized states.

How Do Political Systems Obtain People's Allegiance?

No form of political organization can function without the loyalty and support of those it governs. To a greater or lesser extent, political organizations the world over use religion to legitimize their power. In uncentralized systems loyalty and cooperation are freely given because everyone participates in making decisions. Centralized systems, by contrast, rely more heavily on force and coercion, although in the long run these may lessen the effectiveness of the system.

Louis XIV proclaimed, "I am the state." With this sweeping statement, the king declared absolute rule over France; he held himself to be the law, the lawmaker, the courts, the judge, jailer, and executioner—the seat of all political power in France.

Louis took a great deal of responsibility on his royal shoulders; had he actually performed each of these functions, he would have done the work of thousands of people, the number required to keep the machinery of a large political organization such as a state running. As a form of political organization, the seventeenth-century French state was not much different from those that exist in modern times. All large states require elaborate, centralized structures, involving hierarchies of executives, legislators, and judges who initiate, pass, and enforce laws for large numbers of people.

Such complex structures, however, have not always been in existence: The oldest European states, for instance, aren't much older than the United States, and many are in fact younger. Even today there are societies that depend on far less formal means of organization. In some societies, flexible and informal kinship systems with leaders who lack real power prevail. Problems, such as homicide and theft, are perceived as serious "family quarrels," rather than affairs that affect the entire community. Between these two polarities of political organization lies a world of variety, including societies with chiefs, Big Men, or charismatic leaders, and segmented tribal societies with multicentric authority systems. Such disparity prompts the question, what is political organization?

The term *political organization* refers to the way power is distributed and embedded in society, whether it is in organizing a giraffe hunt or raising an army. Political organization has to do with the way power is used in the coordination and regulation of behavior, in such a way that order is maintained. Government, on the other hand, consists of an administrative system having specialized personnel that may or may not form a part of the political organization, depending on the complexity of the society. Some form of political organization exists in all societies, but it is not always a government.

KINDS OF POLITICAL SYSTEMS

Political organization is the means through which a society maintains social order and reduces social disorder. It assumes a variety of forms among the peoples of the world, but scholars have simplified this complex subject by identifying four basic kinds of political systems: bands, tribes, chiefdoms, and states. The first two are uncentralized systems; the latter two are centralized.

Uncentralized Political Systems

Until recently, many non-Western peoples have had neither chiefs with established rights and duties nor any fixed form of government, as the citizens of modern states understand the term. Instead, marriage and kinship form the principal means of social organization among such peoples. The economies of these societies are of a subsistence type, and populations are typically quite small. Leaders do not have real power to force compliance with the society's customs or laws, but if individual members do not conform, they may be made the target of scorn, gossip, or ostracism. Important decisions are usually made in a democratic manner by a consensus of adults, often including women as well as men; dissenting members may decide to act with the majority, or they may choose to adopt some other course of action if they are willing to risk the social consequences. This form of political organization provides great flexibility, which in many situations confers an adaptive advantage.

Band Organization

The **band** is a small group of politically independent, though related, households and is the least complicated form of political organization. Bands are usually found among food foragers and other

Band: A small group of related households occupying a particular region, that come together periodically on an ad hoc basis, but which do not yield their sovereignty to the larger collective.

Toma, a Ju/'hoansi headman known to many North Americans through the documentary film, *The Hunters*.

nomadic societies in which people are organized into politically autonomous extended family groups that usually camp together, although the members of such families may frequently split up into smaller groups for periods of time to forage for food or visit other relatives. Bands are thus kin groups, composed of men and/or women who are related (or assumed to be), with their spouses and unmarried children; the closeness of the group is indicated by the fact that most marriages are between members of the same band. Bands may be characterized as associations of related families who occupy a common (often vaguely defined) territory and who live there together, so long as environmental and subsistence circumstances are favorable. The band is probably the oldest form of political organization, since all humans were once food foragers, and remained so until the development of farming and pastoralism over the last 10,000 years.

Since bands are small in size, numbering at most a few hundred people, there is no real need for formal, centralized political systems. In egalitarian groups, where everyone is related to—and knows on a personal basis—everyone else with whom dealings are required and where most everyone values "getting along" with the natural order of life, there is reduced potential for conflicts to develop in the first place. Many of those that do arise are settled informally through gossip, ridicule, direct negotiation, or mediation. In the latter instances, the emphasis is on achieving a solution considered "just" by most parties concerned, rather than conforming to some abstract law or rule. Where all else fails, disgruntled individuals have the option of leaving the band to live in another in which they have relatives. Decisions affecting a band are made with the participation of all its adult members, with an emphasis on achieving consensus, rather than a simple majority. Leaders become such by virtue of their abilities and serve in that capacity only as long as they retain the confidence of the community. Thus, they have neither a guaranteed hold on their position for a specified length of time, nor the power to force people to abide by their decisions. People will follow them only as long as they consider it to be in their best interests, and a leader who exceeds what people are willing to accept quickly loses followers.

An example of the informal nature of leadership in the band is found among the Ju/'hoansi Bushmen of the Kalahari Desert, whom we met in Chapters 16 and 17. Each Ju/'hoansi band is composed of a group of families who live together, linked to one another and to the headman or, less often, headwoman, through kinship. Although each band has rights to the territory it occupies and the resources within it, two or more bands may range over the same territory. The head, called the *kxau*, or "owner," is the focal point for the band's theoretical ownership of the territory. The headman or woman does not really own the land or resources, but symbolically personifies the rights of band members to them. If the head leaves a territory to live elsewhere, he or she ceases to be head, as people turn to someone else to lead them.

The head coordinates the band's movements when resources are no longer adequate for subsistence in a particular territory. This leader's chief duty is to plan when and where the group will move; when the move does take place, his or her position is at the head of the line. The leader chooses the site for the new settlement and has the first choice of a spot for his or her own fire. There are no other rewards or duties. For example, a headman does not organize hunting parties, trading expeditions, the making of artifacts, or gift giving; nor does he make marriage arrangements. Instead, individuals instigate their own activities. The head man or woman is not a judge and does not punish other band members. Wrongdoers are judged and regulated by public opinion, usually expressed by gossip among band members. A prime technique for resolving disputes, or even avoiding them in the first place, is mobility. Those unable to get along with others of their group simply move to another to which kinship ties give them rights of entry.

Tribal Organization

The second type of uncentralized or multicentric authority system is the **tribe,** a word that, unfortunately, is used in different ways by different people. Among the general public, it is used commonly to label any people who are not organized into states, irrespective of whether or not they constitute what anthropologists would call bands, tribes,

Tribe: A group of nominally independent communities occupying a specific region, sharing a common language and culture, which are integrated by some unifying factor.

or chiefdoms. Sometimes, the term is even applied to non-Western peoples who in fact had strongly centralized states (the Aztecs, for example), a practice no more warranted than calling the Chinese people a tribe. Historically, the term was coined by Europeans in order to contrast people whom they regarded as inferior with supposedly superior, "civilized" Europeans. The word is still often used in a derogatory way, as when political unrest in many parts of the world is blamed on "tribalism," which it is not (usually, these conflicts are the direct consequence of the creation of multinational states, which makes it possible for a governing elite of one nationality to exploit others for their own benefit).[1] To complicate matters, the term *tribe* also has a distinct legal meaning in the United States, as it refers to a centralized political organization imposed upon Native American communities that traditionally were organized in a variety of ways—some as bands, some as tribes (in the anthropological sense), and some as chiefdoms.

So what, then, do anthropologists have in mind when they speak of tribal organization? To them, a tribal system is one in which separate bands or villages are integrated by factors such as clans that unite people in separate communities, or age grades, or associations that cross-cut kinship or territorial boundaries. In such cases people sacrifice a degree of household autonomy to some larger order group in return for greater security against attacks by enemies or starvation. Typically, though not invariably, a tribe has an economy based on some form of farming or herding. Since these methods of production usually yield more food than those of the food-foraging band, tribal membership is usually larger than band membership. Compared to bands, where population densities are usually less than one person per square mile, tribal population densities always exceed one person per square mile and may be as high as 250 persons per square mile. Greater population density in tribes than in bands brings a new set of problems to be solved, as opportunities for bickering, begging, adultery, and theft increase markedly, especially among people living in sedentary villages.

[1]Whitehead, N. L., & Ferguson, R. B. (1993, November). Deceptive stereotypes about tribal warfare (p. A48). *Chronicle of Higher Education; Nov. 10, 1993;* and Van Den Berghe, P. L. (1992). The modern state: Nation builder or nation killer? *International Journal of Group Tensions, 92*(3), 199–200.

The Navajo Indians do not view government as something fixed and all-powerful, and their leadership is not vested in a central authority. Shown here is Navajo Tribal Council Delegate David John.

Each tribe consists of one or more small autonomous local communities, which may then form alliances with one another for various purposes. As in the band, political organization in the tribe is informal and temporary. Whenever a situation requiring political integration of all or several groups within the tribe arises—perhaps for defense, to carry out a raid, to pool resources in times of scarcity, or to capitalize on a windfall that must be distributed quickly lest it spoil—they join to deal with the situation in a cooperative manner. When the problem is satisfactorily solved, each group then returns to its autonomous state.

Leadership among tribes is also informal. Among the Navajo Indians, for example, the individual did not view government as something fixed and all-powerful, and leadership was not vested in a central authority. A local leader was a man respected for his age, integrity, and wisdom. His advice was therefore sought frequently, but he had no formal means of control and could not force any decision on those who asked for his help. Group decisions were made on the basis of public consensus, although the most influential man usually played a key role in reaching a decision. Among the social mechanisms that induced members to abide by group decisions were withdrawal of cooperation, gossip, criticism, and the belief that disease was caused by antisocial actions.

Another example of tribal leadership is afforded by the Melanesian Big Man. Such men are leaders of localized descent groups or of a territorial group. The Big Man combines a small amount of interest in his tribe's welfare with a great deal of self-interested cunning and calculation for his own personal gain. His authority is personal; he does not come to office nor is he elected. His status is the result of acts that raise him above most other tribe members and attract to him a band of loyal followers.

Typical of this form of political organization are the Kapauku of west New Guinea. Among them, the Big Man is called the *tonowi*, or "rich one." To achieve this status, one must be male, wealthy, generous, and eloquent; physical bravery and skills in dealing with the supernatural are also frequent characteristics of a *tonowi*, but they are not essential. The *tonowi* functions as the headman of the village unit.

Kapauku culture places a high value on wealth, so it is not surprising that a wealthy individual is considered to be a successful and admirable man. Yet the possession of

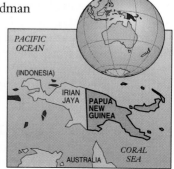

This Big Man from New Guinea is wearing his "official" regalia.

to learn the *tonowi*'s business wisdom, and given a loan to get a wife when they leave; in return, they act as messengers and bodyguards. Even after they leave his household, these men are tied to the *tonowi* by bonds of affection and gratitude. Political support also comes from the *tonowi*'s kinsmen, whose relationship brings with it varying obligations.

The *tonowi* functions as a leader in a wide variety of situations. He represents his group in dealing with outsiders and other villages; he acts as negotiator and judge when disputes break out among his followers. Leopold Pospisil, who studied the Kapauku, notes:

> The multiple functions of a *tonowi* are not limited to the political and legal fields only. His word also carries weight in economic and social matters. He is especially influential in determining proper dates for pig feasts and pig markets, in inducing specific individuals to become co-sponsors at feasts, in sponsoring communal dance expeditions to other villages, and in initiating large projects, such as extensive drainage ditches and main fences or bridges, the completion of which requires a joint effort of the whole community.[2]

The *tonowi*'s wealth comes from his success at pig breeding (as we discussed in Chapter 14), for pigs are the focus of the entire Kapauku economy. Like all kinds of cultivation and domestication, raising pigs requires a combination of strength, skill, and luck. It is not uncommon for a *tonowi* to lose his fortune rapidly, due to bad management or bad luck with his pigs. Thus the political structure of the Kapauku shifts frequently; as one man loses wealth and consequently power, another gains it and becomes a *tonowi*. These changes confer a degree of flexibility on the political organization, and prevent any one *tonowi* from holding political power for too long a time.

Kinship Organization

In many tribal societies (as among the Kapauku) the organizing unit and seat of political authority is the clan, an association of people who believe

wealth must be coupled with the trait of generosity, which in this society means not gift giving but willingness to make loans. Wealthy men who refuse to lend money to other villagers may be ostracized, ridiculed, and, in extreme cases, actually executed by a group of warriors. This social pressure ensures that economic wealth is rarely hoarded, but is distributed throughout the group.

It is through the loans he makes that the *tonowi* acquires his political power. Other villagers comply with his requests because they are in his debt (often without paying interest), and they do not want to have to repay their loans. Those who have not yet borrowed from the *tonowi* may wish to do so in the future, and so they, too, want to keep his goodwill.

Other sources of support for the *tonowi* are apprentices whom he has taken into his household for training. They are fed, housed, given a chance

[2]Pospisil, L. (1963). *The Kapauku Papuans of West New Guinea* (pp. 51–52). New York: Holt, Rinehart and Winston.

themselves to share a common ancestry. Within the clan, elders or headmen are responsible for regulating the affairs of members and represent their clan in relations with other clans. As a group, the elders of all the clans may form a council that acts within the community or for the community in dealings with outsiders. Because clan members usually do not all live together in one community, clan organization facilitates joint action with members of other communities when necessary.

Another form of tribal kinship bond that provides political organization is the **segmentary lineage system.** This system is similar in operation to the clan, but it is less extensive and is a relatively rare form of political organization. The economy of the segmentary tribe is generally just above subsistence level. Production is small-scale, and the tribe has a labor pool just large enough to provide necessities. Since each lineage in the tribe produces the same goods, none depends on another for goods or services. Political organization among segmentary lineage societies is usually informal: There are neither political offices nor chiefs, although older tribal members may exercise some personal authority. In his classic study of segmentary lineage organization, Marshall Sahlins describes how this works among the Nuer.[3] According to Sahlins, segmentation is the normal process of tribal growth. It is also the social means of temporary unification of a fragmented tribal society to join in particular action. The segmentary lineage may be viewed as a substitute for the fixed political structure, which a tribe cannot maintain.

Among the Nuer, who number some 200,000 people living in the swampland and savanna of East Africa (the southern Sudan), there are at least 20 clans. Each is patrilineal and is segmented into maximal lineages; each of these is in turn segmented into major lineages, which are segmented into minor lineages, which in turn are segmented

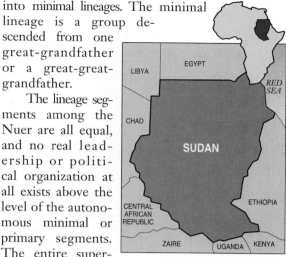

into minimal lineages. The minimal lineage is a group descended from one great-grandfather or a great-great-grandfather.

The lineage segments among the Nuer are all equal, and no real leadership or political organization at all exists above the level of the autonomous minimal or primary segments. The entire superstructure of the lineage is nothing more than an alliance, active only during conflicts between any of the minimal segments. In any serious dispute between members of different minimal lineage segments, members of all other segments take the side of the contestant to whom they are most closely related, and the issue is then joined between the higher-order lineages involved. Such a system of political organization is known as complementary or balanced opposition.

Disputes among the Nuer are frequent, and under the segmentary lineage system, they can lead to widespread feuds. This possible source of social disruption is minimized by the actions of the "leopard-skin chief," or holder of a ritual office of conciliation. The leopard-skin chief has no political power and is looked on as standing outside the lineage network. All he can do is try to persuade feuding lineages to accept payment in "blood cattle" rather than taking another life. His mediation gives each side the chance to back down gracefully before too many people are killed; but if the participants are for some reason unwilling to compromise, the leopard-skin chief has no authority to enforce a settlement.

Age-Grade Organization

Age-grade systems provide a tribal society with the means of political integration beyond the kin group. Under this system, youths are initiated into an age grade, following which they pass as sets from one age grade to another at appropriate ages. Age grades and sets cut across territorial and kin

---

Segmentary lineage system: A form of political organization in which a larger group is broken up into clans, which are divided into lineages.

---

[3]Sahlins, M. (1961). The segmentary lineage: An organization of predatory expansion. *American Anthropologist, 63*, 322–343.

Among the Nuer, the leopard-skin chief tries to settle disputes between lineages.

groupings and so may be important means of political organization. This was the case with the Tiriki of East Africa, whose age grades and sets we examined in Chapter 22. Among them, the Warrior age grade guarded the country, while Judicial Elders resolved disputes. Between these two age grades were Elder Warriors, who were in a sense understudies to the Judicial Elders. The oldest age grade, the Ritual Elders, advised on matters involving the well-being of all the Tiriki people. Thus, political affairs of the tribe were in the hands of the age grades and their officers.

Association Organization

Common-interest associations that function as politically integrative systems within tribes are found in many areas of the world, including Africa, Melanesia, and India. A good example of association organization functioned during the nineteenth

century among the plains Indians of the United States, such as the Cheyenne, whom we will discuss later in this chapter. The basic territorial and political unit of the Cheyenne was the band, but seven military societies, or warriors' clubs, were common to the entire tribe; the clubs functioned in several areas. A boy might be invited to join one of these societies when he achieved warrior status, whereupon he became familiar with the society's particular insignia, songs, and rituals. In addition to their military functions, the warriors' societies also had ceremonial and social functions.

The Cheyenne warriors' routine daily tasks consisted of overseeing movements in the camp, protecting a moving column, and enforcing rules against individual hunting when the whole tribe was on a buffalo hunt. In addition, each warrior society had its own repertoire of dances that the members performed on special ceremonial occasions. Since identical military societies bearing identical names existed in each Cheyenne band, the societies thus served to integrate the entire tribe for military and political purposes.[4]

Centralized Political Systems

In bands and tribes, authority is uncentralized, and each group is economically and politically autonomous. Political organization is vested in kinship, age, and common-interest groups. Populations are small and relatively homogeneous, with people engaged for the most part in the same sorts of activities throughout their lives. As a society's social life becomes more complex, however, as population rises and technology becomes more complex, as specialization of labor and trade networks produce surpluses of goods, the opportunity for some individuals or groups to exercise control increases. In such societies, political authority and power are concentrated in a single individual—the chief—or in a body of individuals—the state. The state is a form of organization found in societies in which each individual must interact on a regular basis with large numbers of people with diversified interests, who are neither kin nor close acquaintances.

[4]Hoebel, E. A. (1960). *The Cheyennes: Indians of the Great Plains.* New York: Holt, Rinehart and Winston.

Chiefdoms

A **chiefdom** is a regional polity in which two or more local groups are organized under a single ruling individual—the chief—who is at the head of a ranked hierarchy of people. An individual's status in such a polity is determined by closeness of one's relationship to the chief. Those closest are officially superior and receive deferential treatment from those in lower ranks.

The office of the chief is usually hereditary, passing from a man to his own or his sister's son, depending on how descent is reckoned. Unlike the headmen in bands and lineages, the chief is generally a true authority figure, and his authority serves to unite his people in all affairs and at all times. For example, a chief can distribute land among his community and recruit members into his military service. In chiefdoms, there is a recognized hierarchy consisting of major and minor authorities who control major and minor subdivisions of the chiefdom. Such an arrangement is, in effect, a chain of command, linking leaders at every level. It serves to bind tribal groups in the heartland to the chief's headquarters, whether it is a mud and dung hut or a marble palace.

On the economic level, a chief controls the economic activities of his people. Chiefdoms are typically redistributive systems; the chief has control over surplus goods and perhaps even the labor force of his community. Thus, he may demand a quota of rice from farmers, which he will redistribute to the entire community. Similarly, he may recruit laborers to build irrigation works, a palace, or a temple.

The chief may also amass a great amount of personal wealth and pass it on to his heirs. Land, cattle, and luxury goods produced by specialists can be collected by the chief and become part of his power base. Moreover, high-ranking families of the chiefdom may engage in the same practice and use their possessions as evidence of status.

An example of this form of political organization may be seen among the Kpelle of Liberia, in West Africa.[5] Among them is a class of paramount chiefs, each of whom presides over one of the Kpelle chiefdoms (each of which is now a district of the Liberian state). The paramount chiefs' traditional tasks are hearing disputes, preserving order, seeing to the upkeep of trails, and maintaining "medicines." In addition, they are now salaried officials of the Liberian government, mediating between it and their own people. Other rewards received by a paramount chief include a commission on taxes collected within his chiefdom, a commission for laborers furnished for the rubber plantations, a portion of court fees collected, a stipulated amount of rice from each household, and gifts brought by people who come to request favors and intercessions. In keeping with his exalted station in life, a paramount chief has at his disposal uniformed messengers, a literate clerk, and the symbols of wealth: many wives, embroidered gowns, and freedom from manual labor.

In a ranked hierarchy, beneath each paramount chief are several lesser chiefs; one for each district within the chiefdom, one for each town within a district, and one for each quarter of all but the smallest towns. Each acts as a kind of lieutenant for his chief of the next higher rank and serves as well as a liaison between him and those of lower rank. Unlike paramount or district chiefs, who are comparatively remote, town and quarter chiefs are readily accessible to people at the local level.

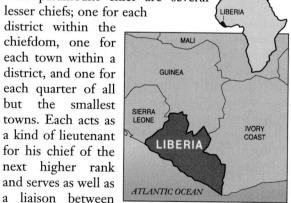

Stable though the Kpelle political system may be today, traditionally chiefdoms in all parts of the world have been highly unstable. This happens as lesser chiefs try to take power from higher-ranking chiefs, or as paramount chiefs vie with one

---

Chiefdom: A regional polity in which two or more local groups are organized under a single chief, who is at the head of a ranked hierarchy of people.

---

[5]Gibbs, Jr., J. L. (1965). The Kpelle of Liberia. In J. L. Gibbs, Jr. (Ed.), *Peoples of Africa* (pp. 216–218). New York: Holt, Rinehart and Winston.

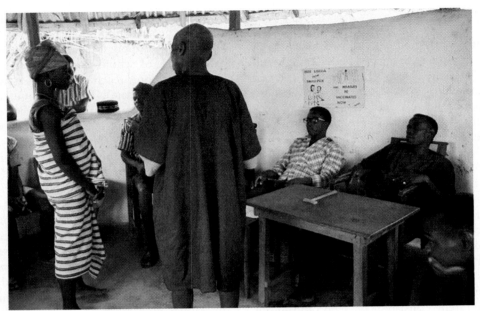

A Kpelle town chief settles a dispute.

another for supreme power. In precolonial Hawaii, for example, war was the way to gain territory and maintain power; great chiefs set out to conquer one another in an effort to become paramount chief of all the islands. When one chief conquered another, the loser and all his nobles were dispossessed of all property and were lucky if they escaped alive. The new chief then appointed his own supporters to positions of political power. As a consequence, there was very little continuity of governmental or religious administration.

State Systems

The **state,** the most formal of political organizations, is (like stratification) one of the hallmarks of civilization. In the state, political power is centralized in a government, which may legitimately use force to regulate the affairs of its citizens, as well as its relations with other states. As anthropologist Bruce Knauft observes:

〜〜〜oo〜〜〜oo〜〜〜

State: In anthropology, a centralized political system with the power to coerce.

〜〜〜oo〜〜〜oo〜〜〜

It is likely . . . that coercion and violence as systematic means of organizational constraint developed especially with the increasing socioeconomic complexity and potential for political hierarchy afforded by substantial food surplus and food production."[6]

Associated with increased food production is increased population. Together, these lead to a filling in of the landscape, improvements such as irrigation and terracing, carefully managed rotation cycles, intensive competition for clearly demarcated lands, and rural populations large enough to support market systems and a specialized urban sector. Under such conditions, corporate groups that stress exclusive membership proliferate, ethnic differentiation and ethnocentrism become more pronounced, and the potential for social conflict increases dramatically. Given these circumstances, the institutions of the state, which minimally involve a bureaucracy, a military, and (usually) an official religion, provide a means by which numerous and diverse groups can be made to function together as an integrated whole.

Although their guiding ideology pretends that they are permanent and stable, the fact is that, since

[6]Knauft, B. M. (1991). Violence and sociality in human evolution. *Current Anthropology, 32,* 391.

their appearance some 5,000 years ago, states have been anything but permanent. Whatever stability they have achieved has been short term at best; over the long term, they show a clear tendency to instability and transience. Nowhere have states even begun to show the staying power exhibited by more uncentralized political systems, the longest-lasting social forms invented by humans.

An important distinction to make at this point is between **nation** and state. Today, there are roughly 181 states in the world, most of which did not exist before the end of World War II. By contrast, there are probably about 5,000 nations in the world today. "What makes each a nation is that its people share a language, culture, territorial base, and political organization and history."[7] Today, states commonly have living within their boundaries people of more than one nation; for example, the Yanomami are but one of many nations within the state of Brazil (other Yanomami live within the state of Venezuela). Rarely do state and nation coincide, as they do, for example, in the case of Finland, Iceland, Japan, Somalia, or Swaziland. By contrast, some 73 percent of the world's states are multinational.[8]

An important aspect of the state is its delegation of authority to maintain order within and outside its borders. Police, foreign ministries, war ministries, and other bureaucracies function to control and punish disruptive acts of crime, terror, and rebellion. By such agencies authority in the state is asserted impersonally and in a consistent, predictable manner.

Western forms of government, like that of the United States, of course, are state governments, and their organization and workings are

⊂◦◦⊏⊃◦◦⊏

Nation: Communities of people who see themselves as "one people" on the basis of common ancestry, history, society, institutions, ideology, language, territory, and (often) religion.

⊂◦◦⊏⊃◦◦⊏

Reflecting the state's ability to force people to abide by its decisions are institutions to administer force, like police.

undoubtedly familiar to most everyone. An example of a not-so-familiar state is afforded by the Swazi of Swaziland (one of the world's few true nation-states), a Bantu-speaking people who live in southeast Africa.[9] They are primarily farmers, but cattle raising is more highly valued than farming: The ritual, wealth, and power

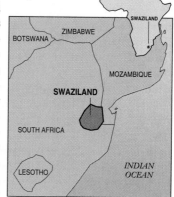

of their authority system are all intricately linked with cattle. In addition to farming and cattle raising, there is some specialization of labor; certain people become specialists in ritual,

[7]Clay, J. W. (1993). What's a nation? In W. A. Haviland & R. J. Gordon (Eds.), *Talking about people* (p. 221). Mountain View, CA: Mayfield.

[8]Van Den Berghe, P. L. (1992). The modern state: Nation builder or nation killer? *International Journal of Group Tensions, 92*(3), 193.

[9]Kuper, H. (1965). The Swazi of Swaziland. In J. L. Gibbs, Jr. (Ed.), *Peoples of Africa* (pp. 479–512). New York: Holt, Rinehart and Winston.

smithing, woodcarving, and pottery. Their goods and services are traded, although the Swazi do not have elaborate markets.

The Swazi authority system is characterized by a highly developed dual monarchy, a hereditary aristocracy, and elaborate rituals of kinship, as well as by statewide age sets. The king and his mother are the central figures of all national activity, linking all the people of the Swazi state: They preside over higher courts, summon national gatherings, control age classes, allocate land, disburse national wealth, take precedence in ritual, and help organize important social events.

Advising the king are the senior princes, who are usually his uncles and half-brothers. Between the king and the princes are two specially created *tinsila*, or "blood brothers," who are chosen from certain common clans. These men are his shields, protecting him from evildoers and serving him in intimate personal situations. In addition, the king is guided by two *tindvuna*, or counselors, one civil and one military. The people of the state make their opinions known through two councils: the *liqoqo*, or privy council, composed of senior princes, and the *libanda*, or council of state, composed of chiefs and headmen and open to all adult males of the state. The *liqoqo* may advise the king, make decisions, and execute them. For example, they may rule on such questions as land, education, traditional ritual, court procedure, and transport.

Government extends from the smallest local unit—the homestead—upward to the central administration. The head of a homestead has legal and administrative powers; he is responsible for the crimes of those under him, controls their property, and speaks for them before his superiors. On the district level, political organization is similar to that of the central government. The relationship between a district chief, however, and his subjects is personal and familiar; he knows all the families in his district. The main check on any autocratic tendencies he may exhibit rests in his subjects' ability to transfer their allegiance to a more responsive chief. Swazi officials hold their positions for life and are dismissed only for treason or witchcraft. Incompetence, drunkeness, and stupidity are frowned upon, but they are not considered to be sufficient grounds for dismissal.

Political Leadership and Gender

Irrespective of cultural configuration or type of political organization, women rarely hold important positions of political leadership. Furthermore, when they do occupy publicly recognized offices, their power and authority rarely exceed those of men. Nevertheless, there have been exceptions, including Corazon Aquino, Sirimavo Badaranaike, Benazir Bhutto, Gro Harlem Brundtland, Indira Gandhi, Golda Meir, and Margaret Thatcher, who do or have headed governments of the Philippines, Sri Lanka, Pakistan, Norway, India, Israel, and Great Britain, respectively. Historically, one might cite the occasional "squaw sachems" (woman chiefs), mentioned in early accounts of New England Indians, or powerful queens such as Elizabeth I of England or Catherine the Great of Russia. When women do hold high office, it is often because of their relationship to men. Thus, a queen is either the wife of a reigning monarch or the daughter of a king who died without a male heir to succeed him. Moreover, women in focal positions frequently must adopt many of the characteristics of temperament normally deemed appropriate for men in their societies. In her role as prime minister, Margaret Thatcher, for instance, displayed the toughness and assertiveness that, in Western societies, have long been considered to be desirable masculine qualities, rather than the nurturance and compliance that Westerners have traditionally expected of women.

In spite of their rarity in formal positions of political leadership, there are a number of societies in which women regularly enjoy as much political power as men. In band societies, it is common for them to have as much of a say in public affairs as men, even though the latter more often than not are the nominal leaders of their groups. Among the Iroquoian nations of New York State (discussed in Chapter 22), all positions of leadership above the household level were, without exception, filled by men. Thus they held all positions on the village and tribal councils, as well as on the great council of the League of Five Nations. However, they were completely beholden to women, for only the latter could appoint men to high office. Moreover, women actively lobbied the men on the councils and could remove someone from office whenever it suited them to do so.

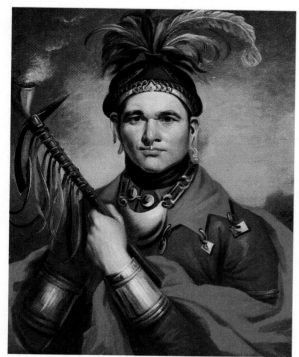

This Seneca chief, Cornplanter, participated in three treaties with the United States in the late eighteenth century. Although Iroquoian chiefs were always men, they served strictly at the pleasure of women, whose position in society was equal to that of men.

As the above cases make clear, low visibility of women in politics does not necessarily exclude them from the realm of social control or mean that men have more power in political affairs. Sometimes, though, women may play more visible roles, as in the dual-sex systems of west Africa. Among the Igbo of Nigeria, in each political unit, separate political institutions for men and women gave each sex their own autonomous spheres of authority, as well as an area of shared responsibility.[10] At the head of each was a male *obi*, considered the head of government though in fact he presided over the male community, and a female *omu*, the acknowledged mother of the whole community, but who in practice was concerned with the female section of the community. Unlike a queen (though both she and the *obi* were crowned), the *omu* was neither wife of the *obi*, nor the daughter of the previous one.

[10]Okonjo, K. (1976). The dual-sex political system in operation: Igbo women and community politics in midwestern Nigeria. In N. Hafkin & E. Bay (Eds.), *Women in Africa*. Stanford, CA: Stanford University Press.

Just as the *obi* had a council of dignitaries to advise him and act as a check against any arbitrary exercise of power, so was the *omu* served by a council of women, in equal number to the *obi*'s male councilors. The duties of the *omu* and her councilors involved such things as establishing rules and regulations for the community market (marketing was a woman's activity) and hearing cases involving women brought to her from throughout the town or village. If such cases also involved men, then she and her council would cooperate with the *obi* and his council. Widows also went to the *omu* for the final rites required to end their period of mourning for dead husbands. Since the *omu* represented all women, she had to be responsive to her constituency and would seek their approval and cooperation in all major decisions.

In addition to the *omu* and her council, the women's government included a representative body of women chosen from each quarter or section of the village or town, on the basis of their ability to think logically and speak well. In addition, political pressure groups of women acted at the village or lineage level to stop quarrels and prevent wars. There were two types of groups, one consisting of women born into a community, most of whom lived elsewhere since villages were exogamous and residence was patrilocal. The other consisted of women who had married into their communities. Its duties included helping companion wives in times of illness and stress, as well as meting out discipline to lazy or recalcitrant husbands.

In the Igbo system, then, women managed their own affairs, and their interests were represented at all levels of government. Moreover, they had the right to enforce their decisions and rules by recourse to sanctions similar to those employed by men. Included were strikes, boycotts, and "sitting on a man" or woman. Political scientist Judith Van Allen describes the latter:

To "sit on" or "make war on" a man involved gathering at his compound, sometimes late at night, dancing, singing scurrilous songs which detailed the women's grievances against him and often called his manhood into question, banging on his hut with the pestles women used for pounding yams, and perhaps demolishing his hut or plastering it with mud and roughing him up a bit. A man might be sanctioned in this way for mistreating his wife, for violating the women's market rules, or for letting his cows eat the women's crops. The women would stay at his hut throughout the day, and late into the night if necessary, until he repented and promised to mend his ways. . . . Although this could hardly have been a pleasant experience for the offending man, it was considered legitimate and no man would consider intervening.[11]

Given the high visibility of women in the Igbo political system, it is surprising to learn that when the British imposed colonial rule upon these people, they failed to recognize the autonomy and power possessed by those women, because the British were blinded by their Victorian values, which then were at their height. To them, a woman's mind was not strong enough for such supposedly masculine subjects as science, business, and politics; her place was clearly in the home. Hence, it was inconceivable that women might play important roles in politics. As a consequence, the British introduced "reforms" that destroyed women's traditional forms of autonomy and power, without providing alternative forms in exchange. Far from enhancing the status of women, as Westerners like to think their influence does, in this case, women lost their equality and became subordinate to men. Nor is the Igbo situation unusual in this regard. Historically, in state-organized societies, women have usually been subordinate to men. Hence, when states impose their control on societies in which the sexes are equal to one another, the situation almost invariably changes to one in which women become subordinate to men.

POLITICAL ORGANIZATION AND SOCIAL CONTROL

Whatever form the political organization of a society may take, and whatever else it may do, it is always involved in one way or another with social control. Always it seeks to ensure that people behave in acceptable ways and defines the proper action to take when they do not. In the case of chiefdoms and states, some sort of centralized authority has the power to regulate the affairs of society. In bands and tribes, however, people behave generally as they are expected to, without the direct intervention of any centralized political authority. To a large degree, gossip, criticism, fear of supernatural forces, and the like serve as effective deterrents to antisocial behavior.

As an example of how such seemingly informal considerations serve to keep people in line, we may look at the Wape people of Papua New Guinea, who believe that the ghosts of dead ancestors roam lineage lands, protecting them from trespassers and helping their hunting descendants by driving game their way.[12] These ghosts also punish those who have wronged them or their descendants by preventing hunters from finding game or causing them to miss their shots, thereby depriving people of much needed meat. Nowadays, the Wape hunt with shotguns, which are purchased by the community for the use of one man, whose job it is to hunt for all the others. The cartridges used in the hunt, however, are invariably supplied by individual members of the community. Not always is the gunman successful; if he shoots and misses, it is because the owner of the fired shell, or some close relative, has quarreled or wronged another person whose ghost relative is securing revenge by causing the hunter to miss. Or, if the gunman cannot even find game, it is because vengeful ghosts have chased the animals away. As a proxy hunter for the villagers, the gunman is potentially subject to ghostly sanctions in response to collective wrongs on the part of those for whom he hunts.

For the Wape, then, successful hunting depends upon avoiding quarrels and maintaining tranquility within the community to avoid

---

[11]Van Allen, J. (1979). Sitting on a man: Colonialism and the lost political institutions of Igbo women. In S. Tiffany (Ed.), *Women in society* (p. 169). St. Albans, VT: Eden Press.

[12]Mitchell, W. E. (1973, December). A new weapon stirs up old ghosts. *Natural History Magazine*, pp. 77–84.

antagonizing anybody's ghost ancestors. Unfortunately, complete peace and tranquility are impossible to achieve in any human community, and the Wape are no exception. Thus, when hunting is poor, the gunman must discover what quarrels and wrongs have taken place within his village in order to identify the proper ancestral ghosts to appeal to for renewed success. Usually, this is done in a special meeting, in which confessions of wrongdoing may be forthcoming. If not, questioning accusations are bandied about until resolution occurs, but even if there is no resolution, the meeting must end amicably in order to create no new antagonisms. Thus, everyone's behavior comes under public scrutiny, reminding everyone of what is expected of them and encouraging everyone to avoid acts that will cast them in an unfavorable light.

Internalized Controls

The Wape concern about ancestral ghosts is a good example of internalized controls—beliefs that are so thoroughly ingrained that each person becomes personally responsible for his or her own good conduct. Examples of this can also be found in North American society; for instance, people refrain from committing incest not so much from fear of legal punishment as from a sense of deep disgust at the thought of the act and the shame they would feel in performing it. Obviously, not all members of North American society feel this disgust, or there would not be such a high incidence of incest, especially between fathers and daughters, but then, no deterrent to misbehavior is ever 100 percent effective. Built-in or internalized controls rely on such deterrents as the fear of supernatural punishment—ancestral ghosts sabotaging the hunting, for example—and magical retaliation. The individual expects to be punished, even though no one in the community may be aware of the wrongdoing.

Externalized Controls

Because internalized controls are not wholly sufficient even in bands and tribes, every society develops customs designed to encourage conformity to social norms. These institutions are referred to

Awards such as Olympic medals are examples of positive sanctions, by which societies promote behavior deemed appropriate.

as **sanctions;** they are externalized social controls. According to A. R. Radcliffe-Brown, "a sanction is a reaction on the part of a society or of a considerable number of its members to a mode of behavior which is thereby approved (positive sanctions) or disapproved (negative sanctions)."[13] Sanctions may also be either formal or informal and may vary significantly within a given society.

Sanctions operate within social groups of all sizes. Moreover, they need not be enacted into law

Sanctions: Externalized social controls designed to encourage conformity to social norms.

[13]Radcliffe-Brown, A. R. (1952). *Structure and function in primitive society* (p. 205). New York: Free Press.

Negative sanctions may involve some form of regulated combat, seen here as armed dancers near Mount Hagen in New Guinea demand redress in the case of murder.

in order to play a significant role in social control: "they include not only the organized sanctions of the law but also the gossip of neighbors or the customs regulating norms of production that are spontaneously generated among workers on the factory floor. In small scale communities . . . informal sanctions may become more drastic than the penalties provided for in the legal code."[14] If, however, a sanction is to be effective, it cannot be arbitrary. Quite the opposite: Sanctions must be consistently applied, and their existence must be generally known by the members of the society.

Social sanctions may be categorized as either positive or negative. Positive sanctions consist of incentives to conformity such as awards, titles, and recognition by one's neighbors. Negative sanctions consist of threats such as imprisonment, corporal punishment, or ostracism from the community for violation of social norms. One example of a negative sanction discussed earlier is the Igbo practice of "sitting on a man." If some individuals are not convinced of the advantages of social conformity, they are still likely to be more willing to go along with society's rules than to accept the consequences of not doing so.

Sanctions may also be categorized as either formal or informal, depending on whether or not a legal statute is involved. In the United States the man who wears tennis shorts to a church service may be subject to a variety of informal sanctions, ranging from the glances of the minister to the chuckling of other parishioners. If, however, he were to show up without any trousers at all, he would be subject to the formal negative sanction of arrest for indecent exposure. Only in the second instance would he have been guilty of breaking the **law.**

Formal sanctions, like laws, are always organized, because they attempt to regulate precisely and explicitly people's behavior. Other examples of organized sanctions include, on the positive side, such things as military decorations and monetary rewards. On the negative side are loss of face, exclusion from social life and its privileges, seizure

Law: Formal negative sanctions.

[14]Epstein, A. L. (1968). Sanctions. *International Encyclopedia of Social Sciences* (Vol. 14, p. 3).

of property, imprisonment, and even bodily mutilation or death.

Informal sanctions are diffuse in nature, involving spontaneous expressions of approval or disapproval by members of the group or community. They are, nonetheless, very effective in enforcing a large number of seemingly unimportant customs. Because most people want to be accepted, they are willing to acquiesce to the rules that govern dress, eating, conversation, even in the absence of actual laws.

As an example of how informal sanctions work, we may examine them in the context of power relationships among the Bedouins of Egypt's western desert. The example is of special interest, for it shows how sanctions not only act to control people's behavior, but also to keep them in their places in a hierarchical society.

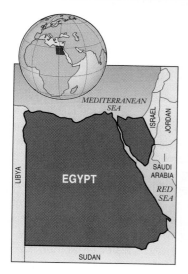

Original Study

Limits on Power in Bedouin Society[15]

Where individuals value their independence and believe in equality, those who exercise authority over others enjoy a precarious status. In Bedouin society, social precedence or power depends not on force but on demonstration of the moral virtues that win respect from others. Persons in positions of power are said to have social standing (*gíma*), which is recognized by the respect paid them. To win the respect of others, in particular dependents, such persons must adhere to the ideals of honor, provide for and protect their dependents, and be fair, taking no undue advantage of their positions. They must assert their authority gingerly lest it so compromise their dependents' autonomy that it provoke rebellion and be exposed as a sham.

Because those in authority are expected to treat their dependents, even children, with some respect, they must draw as little attention as possible to the inequality of their relationships. Euphemisms that obscure the nature of such relationships abound. For example, Sa'ádi [free tribes] individuals do not like to call Mrábit [client tribes] associates Mrábtín in their presence. My host corrected me once when I referred to his shepherds by the technical word for shepherd, saying, "We prefer to call them 'people of the sheep' [*hal il-ghanam*]. It sounds nicer." The use of fictive kin terms serves the same function of masking relations of inequality, as for example in the case of patrons and clients.

Those in authority are also expected to respect their dependents' dignity by minimizing open assertion of their power over them. Because the provider's position requires dependents, he risks losing his power base if he alienates them. When a superior publicly orders, insults, or beats a dependent, he invites the rebellion that would undermine his position. Such moments are fraught with tension, as the dependent might feel the need to respond to a public humiliation to preserve his dignity or honor. Indeed, refusal to comply with an unreasonable order, or an order given in a compromising way, reflects well on the dependent and undercuts the authority of the person who gave it.

Tyranny is never tolerated for long. Most dependents wield sanctions that check the power of their providers. Anyone can appeal to a mediator to intervene on his or her behalf, and more radical solutions are open to all but young children. Clients can simply leave an unreasonable patron and attach themselves to a new one. Young men can always escape the tyranny of a father or paternal uncle by leaving to join maternal relatives or, if they have them, affines, or even to become clients to some other family. For the last twenty years or so, young men could go to Libya to find work.

Younger brothers commonly get out from under difficult elder brothers by splitting off from them, demanding their share of the patrimony and setting up separate households. The dynamic is clear in the case of four brothers who constituted the core of the camp in which I lived. Two had split off and lived in separate households. Another two still shared property, herds, and expenses. While I was there, tensions began to develop. Although the elder brother was more important in the community at large, and the younger brother was slightly irresponsible and less intelligent, for the most part they worked various enterprises jointly and without friction. The younger brother deferred to his older brother and usually executed his decisions.

But one day the tensions surfaced. The elder brother came home at midday in a bad mood only to find that no one had prepared him lunch. He went to one of his wives and scolded her for not having prepared any lunch, asserting that his children had complained that they were hungry. He accused her of trying to starve his children and threatened to beat her. His younger brother tried to intervene, but the elder brother then turned on him, calling him names. Accusing him of being lazy (because he had failed to follow through on a promise involving the care of the sheep that day), he then asked why the younger brother let his wife get away with sitting in her room when there was plenty of work to be done around the household. Then he went off toward his other wife carrying a big stick and yelling.

The younger brother was furious and set off to get their mother. The matriarch, accompanied by another of her sons, arrived and conferred at length with the quarreling men. The younger son wished to split off from his elder brother's household; the other brother scolded him for being so sensitive about a few words, reminding him that this was his elder brother, from whom even a beating should not matter. His mother disapproved of splitting up the households. Eventually everyone calmed down. But it is likely that a few more incidents such as that will eventually lead the younger brother to demand a separate household.

Even a woman can resist a tyrannical husband by leaving for her natal home "angry" (*mughtáẓa*). This is the approved response to abuse, and it forces the husband or his representatives to face the scolding of the woman's kin and, sometimes, to appease her with gifts. Women have less recourse against tyrannical fathers or guardians, but various informal means to resist the imposition of unwanted decisions do exist. As a last resort there is always suicide, and I heard of a number of both young men and women who committed suicide in desperate resistance to their fathers' decisions, especially regarding marriage. One old woman's tale illustrates the extent to which force can be resisted, even by women. Náfla reminisced:

> My first marriage was to my paternal cousin [*ibn 'amm*]. He was from the same camp. One day the men came over to our tent. I saw the tent full of men and wondered why. I heard they were coming to ask for my hand [*yukhultú fiyya*]. I went and stood at the edge of the tent and called out, "If you're planning to do anything, stop. I don't want it." Well, they went ahead anyway, and every day I would cry and say that I did not want to marry him. I was young, perhaps fourteen.

When they began drumming and singing, everyone assured me that it was in celebration of another cousin's wedding, so I sang and danced along with them. This went on for days. Then on the day of the wedding my aunt and another relative caught me in the tent and suddenly closed it and took out the washbasin. They wanted to bathe me. I screamed. I screamed and screamed; every time they held a pitcher of water to wash me with, I knocked it out of their hands.

His relatives came with camels and dragged me into the litter and took me to his tent. I screamed and screamed when he came into the tent in the afternoon [for the defloration]. Then at night, I hid among the blankets. Look as they might, they couldn't find me. My father was furious. After a few days he insisted I had to stay in my tent with my husband. As soon as he left, I ran off and hid behind the tent in which the groom's sister stayed. I made her promise not to tell anyone I was there and slept there.

But they made me go back. That night, my father stood guard nearby with his gun. Every time I started to leave the tent, he would take a puff on his cigarette so I could see that he was still there. Finally I rolled myself up in the straw mat. When the groom came, he looked and looked but could not find me.

Finally I went back to my family's household. I pretended to be possessed. I tensed my body, rolled my eyes, and everyone rushed about, brought me incense and prayed for me. They brought the healer [or holyman, *fḡih*], who blamed the unwanted marriage. Then they decided that perhaps I was too young and that I should not be forced to return to my husband. I came out of the seizure, and they were so grateful that they forced my husband's family to grant a divorce. My family returned the bride-price, and I stayed at home.

Náfla could not oppose her father's decision directly, but she was nevertheless able to resist his will through indirect means. Like other options for resistance by dependents unfairly treated, abused, or humiliated publicly, her rebellion served as a check on her father's and, perhaps, more important, her paternal uncle's power.

Supernatural sanctions, which seem to be associated with the weak and with dependents, provide the final check on abuse of authority. Supernatural retribution is believed to follow when the saintly lineages of Mrábtín are mistreated, their curses causing death or the downfall of the offender's lineage. In one Bedouin tale, when a woman denied food to two young girls, she fell ill, and blood appeared on food she cooked—a punishment for mistreating the helpless. Possession, as Náfla's tale illustrates, may also be a form of resistance . . . .

All these sanctions serve to check the abuse of power by eminent persons who have the resources to be autonomous and to control those who are dependent upon them. At the same time, moreover, figures of authority are vulnerable to their dependents because their positions rest on the respect these people are willing to give them.

[15]Abu-Lughod, L. (1986). *Veiled sentiments: Honor and poetry in a Bedouin society* (pp. 99–103). Berkeley, CA: University of California Press.

Another agent of social control in societies, whether or not they possess centralized political systems, may be witchcraft. An individual would naturally hesitate to offend one's neighbor, when that neighbor might retaliate by resorting to black magic. Similarly, individuals may not wish to be accused of practicing witchcraft themselves, and so they will behave with greater circumspection. Among the Azande of the Sudan, people who think they have been bewitched may consult an oracle who, after performing the appropriate mystical rites, may then establish or confirm the identity of the offending witch.[16] Confronted with this evidence, the "witch" will usually agree to cooperate in order to avoid any additional trouble. Should the victim die, the relatives of the deceased may choose to make magic against the witch, ultimately accepting the death of some villager both as evidence of guilt and the efficacy of their magic. For the Azande, witchcraft provides not only a sanction against antisocial behavior but also a means of dealing with natural hostilities and death. No one wishes to be thought of as a witch, and surely no one wishes to be victimized by one. By institutionalizing their emotional responses, the Azande successfully maintain social order. (For more on witchcraft, see Chapter 24.)

Another important social control that is likely to be internalized is the religious sanction. Just as a devout Christian may avoid sinning for fear of hell, so may other worshippers tend to behave in a manner intended not to offend their powerful supernatural beings. The threat of punishment—either in this life or in the next—by gods, ancestral spirits, or ghosts is a strong incentive for proper behavior. In some societies, it is believed that ancestral spirits are very much concerned with the maintenance of good relations among the living members of their lineage. Death or illness in the lineage may be explained by reference to some violation of tradition or custom. Religious sanctions may thus serve not only to regulate behavior but to explain unexplainable phenomena as well.

[16]Evans-Pritchard, E. E. (1937). *Witchcraft, oracles and magic among the Azande*. London: Oxford University Press.

SOCIAL CONTROL THROUGH LAW

Among the Inuit of northern Canada, all offenses are considered to involve disputes between individuals; thus, they must be settled between the disputants themselves. One way they may do so is through a song duel, in which they heap insults upon one another in songs specially composed for the occasion. Although "society" does not intervene, its interests are represented by spectators, whose applause determines the outcome. If, however, social harmony cannot be restored—and that, rather than assigning and punishing guilt, is the goal—one or the other disputant may move to another band. Among the Inuit, the alternative to peaceful settlement is to leave the group. Ultimately, there is no binding legal authority.

In Western society, on the other hand, someone who commits an offense against another person is subject to a series of complex legal proceedings. In criminal cases the primary concern is to assign and punish guilt, rather than to help out the victim. The offender will be arrested by the police; tried before a judge and, perhaps, a jury; and, if the crime is serious enough, may be fined, imprisoned, or even executed. Rarely is there restitution or compensation for the victim. Throughout this chain of events, the accused party is dealt with by presumably disinterested police, judges, jurors, and jailers, who may have no personal acquaintance whatsoever with the plaintiff or the defendant. How strange this all seems from the standpoint of traditional Inuit culture! Clearly, the two systems operate under distinctly different assumptions.

Definition of Law

Once two Inuit settle a dispute by engaging in a song contest, the affair is considered closed; no further action is expected. Would we choose to describe the outcome of such a contest as a legal decision? If every law is a sanction, but not every sanction is a law, how are we to distinguish between social sanctions in general and those to which we will apply the label "law"?

The definition of law has been a lively point of contention among anthropologists in the twentieth

In Western society, someone who commits an offense against someone else is subject to a series of complex proceedings, in which the emphasis is on assigning and punishing guilt. In non-Western societies, by contrast, the emphasis is often on finding a solution that both parties can live with.

century. In 1926, Bronislaw Malinowski argued that the rules of law are distinguished from the rules of custom in that "they are regarded as the obligation of one person and the rightful claim of another, sanctioned not by mere psychological motive, but by a definite social machinery of binding force based . . . upon mutual dependence."[17] An example of one rule of custom in contemporary North American society might be seen in the dictate that guests at a dinner party should repay the person who gave the party with entertainment in the future. A host or hostess who does not receive

a return invitation may feel cheated of something thought to be owed, but there is no legal claim against the ungrateful guest for the $22.67 spent on food. If, however, an individual was cheated of the same sum by the grocer when shopping, the law could be invoked. Although Malinowski's definition introduced several important elements of law, his failure to distinguish adequately between legal and nonlegal sanctions left the problem of formulating a workable definition of law in the hands of later anthropologists.

An important pioneer in the anthropological study of law was E. Adamson Hoebel, according to whom "a social norm is legal if its neglect or infraction is regularly met, in threat or in fact, by the application of physical force by an individual or group possessing the socially recognized privilege of so acting."[18] In stressing the legitimate use of physical coercion, Hoebel deemphasized the traditional association of law with a centralized court system. Although judge and jury are fundamental features of Western jurisprudence, they are not the universal backbone of human law. Some anthropologists have proposed that a precise definition of law is an impossible—and perhaps even undesirable—undertaking. When we speak of "the law," are we not inclined to fall back on our familiar Western conception of rules enacted by an authorized legislative body and enforced by the judicial mechanisms of the state? Can any concept of law be applied to such societies as the Nuer or the Inuit, for whom the notion of a centralized judiciary is virtually meaningless? How shall we categorize duels, song contests, and other socially condoned forms of self-help, which seem to meet some but not all of the criteria of law?

Ultimately, it is always of greatest value to consider each case within its cultural context. Nonetheless, a working definition of law is useful for purposes of discussion and cross-cultural comparison, and for this, law is adequately characterized as formal negative sanctions.

---

[17]Malinowski, B. (1951). *Crime and custom in savage society* (p. 55). London: Routledge.

[18]Hoebel, E. A. (1954). *The law of primitive man: A study in comparative legal dynamics* (p. 28). Cambridge, MA: Harvard University Press.

Anthropology Applied

AFRICAN PUBLIC DEFENDER AND LEGAL AID TRAINING EXCHANGE

After three decades of economic, political, and social disaster in Africa, issues of development, government, culture change, and empowerment are being seriously rethought in many countries on that continent. To aid in this process, University of Vermont anthropologist Robert J. Gordon together with personnel from the Vermont Office of the Defender General and a sociologist with expertise in the areas of criminology and civil rights have developed an exchange program designed to provide training in legal aid and public defense for personnel from Ethiopia, Tanzania, Uganda, and Zambia.* With funds provided by the U.S. Information Agency, 15 Africans from these four countries were brought in early 1995 to Vermont for an introduction to the history and operation of the United States' legal system, field visits to courts, police and prisons, as well as briefings and visits to legal aid, civil rights, consumer protection, and public interest groups; all to emphasize the different modes and philosophies of providing legal aid and public defender services. The State of Vermont was chosen as the primary site for the program not only because its public defender system is one of the most successful in the United States, but also because of its similarities with many African countries: It is predominantly a poor, rural state which must deal with the problem of domination by larger and more powerful neighbors. But to ensure broader exposure to public defender and legal aid systems in the United States,

participants made field visits to Portland, Maine (a medium-sized city) and Brooklyn, New York.

What makes this program unique is its anthropological component. Unlike most such programs, it avoided unidirectional teaching from "established authorities" to "inexperienced students." Instead, it recognized the professional stature of the Africans, who were dealt with as colleagues, from whom U.S. participants could also learn. Inevitably, conventional workshop techniques were necessary for purposes of orientation. But the key element was for the Africans to do an evaluation of the Vermont Public Defender System. To prepare for this, a workshop was held on "Participatory Rapid Assessment," a research technique developed by the University of Sussex and used with great success in India. By drawing on techniques that have been developed and used successfully in other parts of the world, and structuring the program so that power relations among participants were balanced and symmetrical, rather than asymmetrical and hierarchical, an atmosphere was created that fostered not only effective learning, but continued collaborative work as well.

*Proposal to U.S. Information Agency to Undertake an African Public Defender and Legal Aid Training Exchange, submitted by the University of Vermont and Office of the Defender General of Vermont.

Functions of Law

In *The Law of Primitive Man* (1954), Hoebel writes of a time when the notion that private property should be generously shared was a fundamental precept of Cheyenne Indian life. Subsequently, however, some men assumed the privilege of borrowing other men's horses without bothering to obtain permission. When Wolf Lies Down complained of such unauthorized borrowing to the members of the Elk Soldier Society, the Elk Soldiers not only had his horse returned to him but also secured an award for damages from the

offender. The Elk Soldiers then announced that, to avoid such difficulties in the future, horses were no longer to be borrowed without permission. Furthermore, they declared their intention of retrieving any such property and administering a whipping to anyone who resisted their efforts to return improperly borrowed goods.

The case of Wolf Lies Down and the Elk Soldier Society illustrates three basic functions of law. First, it defines relationships among the members of society, determining proper behavior under specified circumstances. Knowledge of the law permits each person to know his or her rights and duties in respect to every other member of society. Second, law allocates the authority to employ coercion in the enforcement of sanctions. In societies with centralized political systems, such authority is generally vested in the government and its judiciary system. In societies that lack centralized political control, the authority to employ force may be allocated directly to the injured party. Third, law functions to redefine social relations and to ensure social flexibility. As new situations arise, law must determine whether old rules and assumptions retain their validity and to what extent they must be altered. Law, if it is to operate efficiently, must allow room for change.

In actual practice, law is rarely the smooth and well-integrated system described above. In any given society, various legal sanctions may apply at various levels. Because the people in a society are usually members of numerous subgroups, they are subject to the various dictates of these diverse groups. Each individual Kapauku is, simultaneously, a member of a family, a household, a sublineage, and a confederacy, and is subject to all the laws of each. In some cases it may be impossible for an individual to submit to contradictory legal indications:

> In one of the confederacy's lineages, incestuous relations between members of the same clan were punished by execution of the culprits, and in another by severe beating, in the third constituent lineage such a relationship was not punishable and . . . was not regarded as incest at all. In one of the sublineages, it became even a preferred type of marriage.[19]

Furthermore, the power to employ sanctions may vary from level to level within a given society. The head of a Kapauku household may punish a member of his household by means of slapping or beating, but the authority to confiscate property is vested exclusively in the headman of the lineage. Analogous distinctions exist in the United States between municipal, state, and federal jurisdictions. The complexity of legal jurisdiction within each society makes any easy generalization about law difficult.

Crime

As we have observed, an important function of sanctions, legal or otherwise, is to discourage the breach of social norms. A person contemplating theft is aware of the possibility of being captured and punished. Yet, even in the face of severe sanctions, individuals in every society sometimes violate the norms and subject themselves to the consequences of their behavior. What is the nature of crime in non-Western societies?

In Western society, a clear distinction can be made between offenses against the state and offenses against an individual. *Black's Law Dictionary* tells us:

> The distinction between a crime and a tort or civil injury is that the former is a breach and violation of the public right and of duties due to the whole community considered as such, and in its social and aggregate capacity; whereas the latter is an infringement or privation of the civil rights of individuals merely.[20]

Thus, a reckless driver who crashes into another car may be guilty of a crime in endangering public safety. The same driver may also be guilty of a tort in causing damages to the other car and can be sued for their costs by the other driver.

In many non-Western societies, however, there is no conception of a central state. Consequently, all offenses are viewed as offenses against individuals, rendering the distinction between crime and tort of no value. Indeed, a dispute between individuals may seriously disrupt the social order, especially in small groups where the number of disputants, though small in absolute numbers, may be a large percentage of the total population. Although the Inuit have no effective domestic or economic unit beyond the family, a dispute between two people will interfere with the ability of members of separate families to come to one another's aid when necessary and is consequently a matter of wider social concern. The goal of judicial proceedings in most cases is to restore social harmony instead of punishing an offender. In distinguishing between offenses of concern to the

[19]Pospisil, L. (1971). *Anthropology of law: A comparative theory* (p. 36). New York: Harper & Row.

[20]Black, H. C. (1968). *Black's law dictionary.* St. Paul, MN: West.

community as a whole and those of concern only to a few individuals, we may refer to offenses as public or private, rather than distinguishing between criminal and civil law. In this way we may avoid values and assumptions that are irrelevant to a discussion of non-Western systems of law.

Disputes are settled in either of two ways. On the one hand, disputing parties may, by means of argument and compromise, voluntarily arrive at a mutually satisfactory agreement. This form of settlement is referred to as **negotiation** or, if it involves the assistance of an unbiased third party, **mediation.** In bands and tribes a third-party mediator has no coercive power and so cannot force disputants to abide by such a decision, but as a person who commands great personal respect, the mediator may frequently effect a settlement through these judgments.

In chiefdoms and states, an authorized third party may issue a binding decision, which the disputing parties will be compelled to respect. This process is referred to as **adjudication.** The difference between mediation and adjudication is basically a difference in authorization. In a dispute settled by adjudication, the disputing parties present their positions as convincingly as they can, but they do not participate in the ultimate decision making.

Although the adjudication process is not universally characteristic, every society employs some form of negotiation in the settlement of disputes. Often negotiation acts as a prerequisite or an alternative to adjudication. For example, in the resolution of U.S. labor disputes, striking workers may first negotiate with management, often with the mediation of a third party. If the state decides that the strike constitutes a threat to the public welfare, the disputing parties may be forced to submit to adjudication. In this case, the responsibility for resolving the dispute is transferred to a presumably impartial judge.

The work of the judge is difficult and complex. Not only must the evidence that is presented be sifted through but the judge must also consider a wide range of norms, values, and earlier rulings in order to arrive at a decision that is intended to be considered just not only by the disputing parties but by the public and other judges as well. In most band and tribal societies a greater value is placed on reconciling disputing parties and resuming harmony than on administering awards and punishments. Thus, "tribal courts may . . . work in ways more akin to Western marriage conciliators, lawyers, arbitrators, and industrial conciliators than to Western judges in court."[21]

In many societies judgment is thought to be made by incorruptible supernatural, or at least nonhuman, powers, through a trial by ordeal. Among the Kpelle of Liberia, for example, where guilt is in doubt, an ordeal operator licensed by the government may apply a hot knife to the leg of a suspect. If the leg is burned, the suspect is guilty; if not, innocence is assumed. But the operator does not merely heat the knife and apply it. After massaging the suspect's legs and, after it has been determined that the knife is hot enough, the operator then strokes his own leg with it, without being burned, demonstrating that the innocent will escape injury. The knife is then applied to the suspect. What has been done up to this point—consciously or unconsciously—is to read the suspect's nonverbal cues: gestures, the degree of muscular tension, amount of perspiration, and so forth. From this the operator is able to judge whether or not the accused is showing so much anxiety as to indicate probable guilt; in effect, there has been carried out a psychological stress evaluation. As the knife is applied it is manipulated so as to either burn or not burn the suspect, once this judgment has been made. This manipulation is easily done by controlling how long the knife is in the fire, as well as by the pressure and angle at which it is pressed against the leg.[22]

Negotiation: The use of direct argument and compromise by the parties to a dispute to arrive voluntarily at a mutually satisfactory agreement.

Mediation: Settlement of a dispute through negotiation assisted by an unbiased third party.

Adjudication: Mediation, with the ultimate decision made by an unbiased third party.

---

[21]Gluckman, M. (1975). *The judicial process among the Barotse of northern Rhodesia.* New York: Free Press.

[22]Gibbs, Jr., J. L. (1983). Interview, *Faces of Culture:* Program 18. Fountain Valley, CA: Coast Telecourses.

Two means of psychological evaluation: a Kpelle trial by ordeal and a Western polygraph ("lie detector").

Similar to this is the use of the lie detector (polygraph) in the United States, although the guiding ideology is scientific rather than supernaturalistic. Nevertheless, an incorruptible nonhuman agency is thought to establish who is lying and who is not, whereas in reality the polygraph operator cannot simply "read" the needles of the machine. What he or she must do is judge whether or not they are registering a high level of anxiety brought on by the testing situation, as opposed to the stress of guilt. Thus, the polygraph operator has much in common with the Kpelle ordeal operator.

POLITICAL ORGANIZATION AND EXTERNAL AFFAIRS

Although the regulation of internal affairs is an important function of any political system, it is by no means the sole function. Another is the management of external or international affairs—relations not just between states, but between different bands, lineages, clans, or whatever the largest autonomous political unit may be. And just as the threatened or actual use of force may be used to maintain order within a society, so may it be used in the conduct of external affairs.

War

One of the responsibilities of the state is the organization and execution of the activities of war.

Throughout the last few thousand years of history, people have engaged in a seemingly endless chain of wars and intergroup hostilities. Why do wars occur? Is the need to wage war an instinctive feature of the human personality? What are the alternatives to violence as a means of settling disputes between societies?

War is not a universal phenomenon, for in various parts of the world there are societies in which warfare as we know it is not practiced. Examples include people as diverse as the Bushmen of southern Africa, the Arapesh of New Guinea, and the Hopi of North America. Among those societies where warfare is practiced, levels of violence may differ dramatically. Of warfare in New Guinea, for example, the anthropologist Robert Gordon notes:

> It's slightly more civilized than the violence of warfare which we practice insofar as it's strictly between two groups. And as an outsider, you can go up and interview people and talk to them while they're fighting and the arrows will miss you. It's quite safe and you can take photographs. Now, of course, the problem with modern warfare is precisely that it kills indiscriminately and you can't do much research on it, but at the same time, you can learn a lot talking to these people about the dynamics of how violence escalates into full-blown warfare.[23]

[23]Gordon, R. J. (1981, December). Interview for Coast Telecourses, Los Angeles.

In Iraq, as in many countries of the world, war has become commonplace as governments controlled by one ethnic group seek to impose their control over other previously autonomous ethnic groups in order to gain access to their resources and labor. Shown here are Kurdish guerrillas, who have been fighting Iraqi attempts to destroy the Kurds as a people.

There is ample reason to suppose that war has become a problem only in the last 10,000 years, since the invention of food-production techniques, and especially since the invention of centralized states. It has reached crisis proportions in the last 200 years, with the invention of modern weaponry and increased direction of violence against civilian populations. In contemporary warfare, we have reached the point where casualties not just among civilians, but among *children* outnumber those among soldiers. Thus, war is not so much an age-old problem as it is a relatively recent one. Among food foragers, with their uncentralized political systems, although violence emerges sporadically, warfare is unknown. Because territorial boundaries and membership among food-foraging bands are usually fluid and loosely defined, a man who hunts with one band today may hunt with a neighboring band tomorrow. Warfare is further rendered impractical by the systematic interchange of women among food-foraging groups—it is likely that someone in each band will have a sister, a brother, or a cousin in a neighboring band. Moreover, absence of a food surplus does not permit prolonged combat. Where populations are small, food surpluses absent, property ownership minimal, and no state organization exists, the likelihood of organized violence by one group against another is virtually nonexistent.[24]

Although there are peaceful farmers, despite the traditional view of the farmer as a gentle tiller of the soil, it is among such people, along with pastoralists, that warfare becomes prominent. One reason for this may be that food-producing peoples are far more prone to population growth than are food foragers, whose numbers are generally maintained well below carrying capacity. This population growth, if unchecked, can lead to resource depletion, one solution to which may be to seize the resources of some other people. In addition, the commitment to a fixed piece of land inherent in farming makes such societies somewhat less fluid in their membership than among people who are food foragers. In those societies that are rigidly matrilocal or patrilocal, each new generation is

[24]Knauft, B. (1991). Violence and sociality in human evolution. *Current Anthropology, 32,* 391–409.

bound to the same territory, no matter how small it may be or how large the group trying to live within it.

The availability of virgin land may not serve as a sufficient detriment to the outbreak of war. Among slash-and-burn horticulturists, for example, competition for land cleared of virgin forest frequently leads to hostility and armed conflict. The centralization of political control and the possession of valuable property among farming people provide many more stimuli for warfare. It is among such peoples, especially those organized into states, that the violence of warfare is most apt to result in indiscriminate killing. This development has reached its peak in modern states. Indeed, much (but not all) of the warfare that has been observed in stateless societies has been induced by states, as a reaction to colonial expansion.[25]

Another difference between food-gathering and food-producing populations lies in their different **worldviews.** As a general rule, food foragers tend to conceive of themselves as a part of the natural world and in some sort of balance with it. This is reflected in their attitudes toward the animals they kill. Western Abenaki hunters, for example, thought that animals, like humans, were composed of both a body and vital self. Although Abenakis hunted and killed animals to sustain their own lives, they clearly recognized that animals were entitled to proper respect. Thus, when beaver, muskrat, or waterfowl were killed, one could not just toss their bones into the nearest garbage pit. Proper respect required that their bones be returned to the water, with a request that the species be continued. Such attitudes may be referred to as a naturalistic worldview.

The Abenakis' respect for nature contrasts sharply with the kind of worldview prevalent among farmers and pastoralists, who do not find

Worldviews: The conceptions, explicit and implicit, of a society or an individual of the limits and workings of its world.

[25]Whitehead, N. L., & Ferguson, R. B. (1995, November). Deceptive stereotypes about tribal warfare. *Chronicle of Higher Education*, p. A48.

their food in nature but impose their dominance upon it to produce food for themselves. The attitude that nature exists only to be used by humans may be referred to as an exploitative worldview. With such an outlook, it is a small step from dominating the rest of nature to dominating other societies for the benefit of one's own. The exploitative worldview, prevalent among food-producing peoples, is an important contributor to intersocietal warfare.

A comparison between the Western Abenakis and their Iroquoian neighbors to the west is instructive. Among the Abenakis warfare was essentially a defensive activity. These food foragers, with their naturalistic worldview, believed that one could not operate in someone else's territory, since one did not control the necessary supernatural powers. Furthermore, operating far below carrying capacity, they had no need to prey upon the resources of others. The Iroquois, by contrast, were slash-and-burn horticulturists who engaged in predatory warfare. Archaeological evidence indicates that significant environmental degradation took place around their settlements, suggesting overutilization of resources. Although the Iroquois went to war in order to replace men lost in previous battles, the main motive was to achieve dominance by making their victims acknowledge Iroquoian superiority. The relation between victim and victor, however, was one of subjection, rather than outright subordination. The payment of tribute purchased "protection" from the Iroquois, no doubt helping to offset the depletion of resources near the village of the would-be protectors. The price of protection went further than this, though; it included constant and public ceremonial deference to the Iroquois, free passage for their war parties through the subjugated group's country, and the contribution of young men to Iroquoian war parties.

A comparison between the Iroquois and Europeans is also instructive. Sometime in the sixteenth century, five Iroquoian nations—the Mohawks, Oneidas, Onondagas, Cayugas, and Senecas—determined to bring to an end warfare among themselves by the simple device of directing their predatory activities against outsiders, rather than each other. In this way the famous League of the Iroquois came into being. Similarly, in the year 1095, Pope Urban II launched the

Crusades with a speech in which he urged European barons to bring to an end their ceaseless wars against each other by directing their hostilities outwards, against the Turks and Arabs. In that same speech he also alluded to the economic benefits to be realized by seizing the resources of the infidels. Although rationalized as a "holy war," the Crusades clearly were motivated by more than religious ideology.

Although the Europeans never did "liberate" the Holy Land, at least some of them did benefit from the booty obtained in battle, lending credence to the idea that people could live better than they had before by locating and seizing the resources of others. Thus, the state formation that took place in Europe in the centuries after 1000 A.D. was followed by colonial expansion into other parts of the world. Proceeding in concert with this growth and outward expansion was the development of the technology and organization of warfare.

The idea that warfare is an acceptable way to bring about economic benefits is still a part of the European cultural tradition, as the following from a quite serious letter that appeared in New Hampshire's largest daily newspaper a few years ago illustrates: "If a war is necessary to stabilize the economy, then we shall have a war. It affects the everyday lives of most of us so little that we need hardly acknowledge the fact that it is going on. Surely the sacrifice of a son, husband or father by a hundred or so of our citizens every week is not that overwhelming. They will forget their losses in time."[26] Certainly, we would like to think that this kind of attitude is not widespread in the United States, and perhaps it is not, but we do not know this for a fact. Nor do we really know the extent to which it is or is not held by members of those segments of U.S. society that tend to be influential in the setting of public policy. These are obviously important questions, and we need to find out more about them.

As the preceding examples show, the causes of warfare are complex; economic, political, and ideological factors are all involved. With the emergence of states (not just in Europe, but in other parts of the world as well) has come a dramatic increase in the scale of warfare. Perhaps this is not surprising, given the state's acceptance of force as a legitimate tool to use in the regulation of human affairs and its ability to organize large numbers of people. In the modern world, we are as far (and

[26]Quoted in MacNeil, R. (1982). *The right place at the right time* (p. 263). Boston: Little, Brown.

Shown here are U.S. soldiers in Haiti, where intervention to restore President Aristide to power fortunately turned out to be relatively peaceful. Since World War II, no state has gone to war as often as the United States.

probably farther) from the elimination of war as humanity ever has been, a fact reflected in the 120-odd shooting wars going in the early 1990s. Moreover, value systems would seem to be as crucial as any element in the continued existence of warfare.

POLITICAL SYSTEMS AND THE QUESTION OF LEGITIMACY

Whatever form the political system of a society may take, and however it may go about its business, it must always find some way to obtain the people's allegiance. In uncentralized systems, in which every adult participates in the making of all decisions, loyalty and cooperation are freely given, since each person is considered to be a part of the political system. As the group grows larger, however, and the organization becomes more formal, the problems of obtaining and keeping public support become greater.

In centralized political systems increased reliance is placed upon coercion as a means of social control. This, however, tends to lessen the effectiveness of a political system. For example, the staff needed to apply force must often be large and may itself grow to be a political power. The emphasis on force may also create resentment on the part of those to whom it is applied and so lessens cooperation. Thus, police states are generally short-lived; most societies choose less extreme forms of social coercion.

Also basic to the political process is the concept of legitimacy, or the right of political leaders to rule. Like force, legitimacy is a form of support for a political system; unlike force, legitimacy is based on the values a particular society believes most important. For example, among the Kapauku the legitimacy of the *tonowi*'s power comes from his wealth; the kings of Hawaii and England and France, before their revolutions, were thought to have a divine right to rule; the head of the Dahomey state of west Africa acquires legitimacy through his age, as he is always the oldest living male.

Legitimacy grants the right to hold, use, and allocate power. Power based on legitimacy may be distinguished from power based on force alone:

Obedience to the former results from the belief that obedience is "right"; compliance to power based on force is the result of fear of the deprivation of liberty, physical well-being, life, material property. Thus, power based on legitimacy is symbolic and depends not upon any intrinsic value, but upon the positive expectations of those who recognize and accede to it. If the expectations are not met regularly (if the head of state fails to deliver "economic prosperity" or the leader is continuously unsuccessful in preventing horse or camel theft), the legitimacy of the recognized power figure is minimized and may collapse altogether.

RELIGION AND POLITICS

Religion is intricately connected with politics. Religious beliefs may influence laws: Acts that people believe to be sinful, such as sodomy and incest, are often illegal as well. Frequently it is religion that legitimizes the political order.

In both industrial and nonindustrial societies, belief in the supernatural is important and is reflected in people's governments. The effect of religion on politics is perhaps best exemplified in medieval Europe. Holy wars were fought over the smallest matter; labor was mobilized to build immense cathedrals in honor of the Virgin Mary and other saints; kings and queens ruled by "divine right," pledged allegiance to the pope, and asked his blessing in all important ventures, were they marital or martial. In the pre-Columbian Americas the Aztec state was a religious state, or theocracy, which thrived in spite of more or less constant warfare carried out to procure captives for human sacrifices to assuage or please the gods. In Peru the Inca emperor proclaimed absolute authority based on the proposition that he was descended from the sun god. Modern Iran has been proclaimed an "Islamic republic" and its first head of state was the most holy of all Shiite Moslem holy men. In the United States the Declaration of Independence, which is an expression of the social and political beliefs of the country, stresses a belief in a supreme being. The document states that "all men are created [by God] equal," a tenet that gave rise to American democracy, because it implied that

In the United States, in spite of an official separation of church and state, the president is always sworn in over a Christian Bible.

all people should participate in governing themselves. The fact that the president of the United States takes the oath of office by swearing on the Bible is another instance of the use of religion to legitimize political power, as is the phrase: "one nation, under God" in the Pledge of Allegiance.

On U.S. coins is the phrase "In God We Trust," many meetings of government bodies begin with a prayer or invocation, and the phrase "so help me God" is routinely used in legal proceedings. In spite of an official separation of church and state, religious legitimization of government lingers on.

CHAPTER SUMMARY

Political organization and social control are about the ways in which power is distributed and embedded in society. Through political organization societies maintain social order, manage public affairs, and reduce social disorder. No group can live together without persuading or coercing its members to conform to agreed-upon rules of conduct. To properly understand the political organization of a society, one needs to view it in the light of its ecological, social, and ideological context.

Four basic types of political systems may be identified. In order of complexity, these range from uncentralized bands and tribes to centralized chiefdoms and states. The band, characteristic of food-foraging and some other nomadic societies, is an

association of politically independent but related families or households occupying a common territory. Political organization in bands is democratic, and informal social control is exerted by public opinion in the form of gossip and ridicule. Band leaders are older men, or sometimes women, whose personal authority lasts only as long as members believe they are leading well and making the right decisions.

The tribe is composed of separate bands or other social units that are tied together by such unifying factors as descent, age grading, or common interest. With an economy usually based on farming or herding, the population of the tribe is larger than that of the band, although family units within the tribe are still relatively autonomous and egalitarian. As in the band, political organization is transitory, and leaders have no formal means of maintaining authority.

Many tribal societies vest political authority in the clan, an association of people who consider themselves to be descended from a common ancestor. A group of elders or headmen regulate the affairs of members and represent their group in relations with other clans. Another variant of authority in tribes in Melanesia is the Big Man, who builds up his wealth and political power until he must be reckoned with as a leader. The segmentary lineage system, similar in operation to the clan, is a rare form of tribal organization based on kinship bonds.

Tribal age-grade systems cut across territorial and kin groupings. Leadership is vested in men in the group who were initiated into the age grade at the same time and passed as a set from one age grade to another until reaching the proper age to become elders. Common-interest associations wield political authority in some tribes. A boy joins one club or another when he reaches warrior status. These organizations administer the affairs of the tribe.

As societies include larger numbers of people and become more heterogeneous socially, politically, and economically, leadership becomes more centralized. Chiefdoms are ranked societies in which every member has a position in the hierarchy. Status is determined by the individual's position in a descent group and distance of relationship to the chief. Power is concentrated in a single chief whose true authority serves to unite his community in all matters. The chief may accumulate great personal wealth, which enhances his power base and which he may pass on to his heirs.

The most centralized of political organizations is the state. It has a central power that can legitimately use force to administer a rigid code of laws and to maintain order, even beyond its borders. A large bureaucracy functions to uphold the authority of the central power. The state is found only in societies with numerous diverse groups. Typically, it is a stratified society, in which economic functions and wealth are distributed unequally. Although thought of as being stable and permanent, it is, in fact, inherently unstable and transitory. States differ from nations, which are communities of people who see themselves as "one people" with a common culture, but who may or may not have a centralized form of political organization.

Historically women have rarely held important positions of political leadership, and when they have, it has sometimes been for lack of a qualified man to hold the position. Nonetheless, in a number of societies, women have enjoyed political equality with men, as among the Iroquoian tribes of New York State. Among them, all men held office at the pleasure of women, who not only appointed them but could remove them as well. Among the Igbo of midwestern Nigeria, women held positions in an administrative hierarchy that paralleled and balanced that of the men. Under centralized political systems, women are most apt to be subordinate to men, and when states impose their control on societies marked by sexual egalitarianism, the relationship changes to one in which men dominate women.

There are two kinds of social controls, internalized and externalized. Internalized controls are self-imposed by guilty individuals. These built-in controls, which include morality, rely on such deterrents as personal shame, fear of divine punishment, or magical retaliation. Although bands and tribes rely heavily on them, internalized controls are generally insufficient by themselves. Every society develops externalized controls, called sanctions. Positive sanctions, in the form of rewards or recognition by one's neighbors, are the position a society, or a number of its members, takes toward behavior that is approved; negative sanctions, such as threat of imprisonment, corporal punishment, or "loss of face," reflect societal reactions to behavior that is disapproved.

Sanctions may also be classified as either formal, including actual laws, or informal, involving norms but not legal statutes. Formal sanctions are organized and reward or punish behavior through a rigidly regulated social procedure. Informal sanctions are diffuse, involving immediate reactions of approval or disapproval by individual community members to one of their compatriot's behavior. Other important agents of social control are witchcraft beliefs and religious sanctions.

Sanctions serve to formalize conformity to group norms, including actual law, and to maintain each social faction in a community in its "proper" place. An adequate working definition of law is that it consists of formal negative sanctions.

Law serves several basic functions. First, it defines relationships among the members of a society and thereby dictates proper behavior under different circumstances. Second, law allocates authority to employ coercion in the enforcement of sanctions. In centralized political systems this authority rests with the government and court system. Uncentralized societies may give this authority directly to the injured party. Third, law redefines social relations and aids its own efficient operation by ensuring that there is room for change.

Western societies clearly distinguish offenses against the state, called crimes, from offenses against an individual, called torts. Uncentralized societies may view all offenses as against individuals. One way to understand the nature of law is to analyze individual dispute cases against their own cultural background. A dispute may be settled in two ways, negotiation and adjudication. All societies use negotiation to settle individual disputes. In negotiation the parties to the dispute themselves reach an agreement, with or without the help of a third party. In adjudication, not found in some societies, an authorized third party issues a binding decision. The disputing parties present their petitions, but play no part in the decision making.

In addition to regulating internal affairs, political systems also attempt to regulate external affairs, or relations between politically autonomous units. In doing so they may resort to the threat or use of force.

War is not a universal phenomenon, since there are societies that do not practice warfare as we know it. Usually these are stateless societies that have some kind of naturalistic worldview, an attitude that until recently had become nearly extinguished in modern industrial societies.

A major problem faced by any form of political organization is obtaining and maintaining people's loyalty and support. Reliance on force and coercion in the long run usually tends to lessen the effectiveness of a political system. A basic instrument of political implementation is legitimacy, or the right of political leaders to exercise authority. Power based on legitimacy stems from the belief of a society's members that obedience is "right," and therefore from the positive expectations of those who obey. It may be distinguished from compliance based on force, which stems from fear, and thus from negative expectations.

Religion is so intricately woven into the life of the people in both industrial and nonindustrial countries that its presence is inevitably felt in the political sphere. To a greater or lesser extent, most governments use religion to legitimize political power.

SUGGESTED READINGS

Cohen, R., & Middleton, J. (Eds.) (1967). *Comparative political systems.* Garden City, NY: Natural History Press.

The editors have selected some 20 studies in the politics of nonindustrial societies by well-known scholars such as Lévi-Strauss, S. F. Nadel, Marshall Sahlins, and S. N. Eisenstadt.

Fried, M. (1967). *The evolution of political society: An essay in political anthropology.* New York: Random House.

The author attempts to trace the evolution of political society through a study of simple, egalitarian societies. The character of the state and the means whereby this form of organization takes shape are considered in terms of pristine and secondary states, formed because preexisting states supplied the stimuli or models for organization.

Gordon, R. J., & Meggitt, M. J. (1985). *Law and order in the New Guinea highlands.* Hanover, NH: University Press of New England.

This ethnographic study of the resurgence of tribal fighting among the Mae-Enga addresses two issues of major importance in today's world: the changing nature of law and order in the Third World and the nature of violence in human societies.

Johnson, A. W., & Earle, T. (1987). *The evolution of human societies, from foraging group to agrarian state.* Stanford, CA: Stanford University Press.

Although written as a synthesis of economic and ecological anthropology, this is also a book on the evolution of political organization in human societies. Proceeding from family level organization up through states, the authors discuss nine levels of organization, illustrating each with specific case studies, and specifying the conditions that give rise to each level.

Nader, L. (Ed.) (1980). *No access to law: Alternatives to the American judicial system.* New York: Academic Press.

This is an eye-opening study of how consumer complaints are resolved in our society. After 10 years of study, Nader found repeated and documented offenses by business that cannot be handled by present complaint mechanisms, either in or out of court. The high cost exacted includes a terrible sense of apathy and loss of faith in the system itself.

Whitehead, N., & Ferguson, R. B. (Eds.) (1992). *War in the tribal zone.* Santa Fe: School of American Research Press.

The central point of this book is that both the transformation and intensification of war, as well as the formation of tribes, result from complex interaction in the "tribal zone" that begins where centralized authority makes contact with stateless people it does not rule. In such zones, newly introduced plants, animals, diseases, and technologies often spread widely, even before colonizers appear. These and other changes disrupt existing social and political relationships, fostering new alliances and creating new kinds of conflicts.

CHAPTER
24
RELIGION AND THE SUPERNATURAL

RITUAL IS RELIGION IN ACTION, AND TRANCE, DANCE, AND SACRIFICE ARE FREQUENTLY PARTS OF RITUAL. SHOWN HERE IS A TRANCE DANCE AROUND A SACRIFICE IN A HINDU TEMPLE IN FIJI.

CHAPTER PREVIEW

What Is Religion?

Religion may be regarded as the beliefs and patterns of behavior by which humans try to deal with what they view as important problems that cannot be solved through the application of known technology or techniques of organization. To overcome these limitations, people turn to the manipulation of supernatural beings and powers.

What Are Religion's Identifying Features?

Religion consists of various rituals—prayers, songs, dances, offerings, and sacrifices— through which people try to manipulate supernatural beings and powers to their advantage. These beings and powers may consist of gods and goddesses, ancestral and other spirits, or impersonal powers, either by themselves or in various combinations. In all societies there are certain individuals especially skilled at dealing with these beings and powers, who assist other members of society in their ritual activities. A body of myths rationalizes or "explains" the system in a manner consistent with people's experience in the world in which they live.

What Functions Does Religion Serve?

Whether or not a particular religion accomplishes what people believe it does, all religions serve a number of important psychological and social functions. They reduce anxiety by explaining the unknown and making it understandable, as well as provide comfort in the belief that supernatural aid is available in times of crisis. They sanction a wide range of human conduct by providing notions of right and wrong, setting precedents for acceptable behavior, and transferring the burden of decision making from individuals to supernatural powers. Through ritual, religion may be used to enhance the learning of oral traditions. Finally, religion plays an important role in maintaining social solidarity.

According to their origin myth, the Tewa Indians of New Mexico emerged from a lake far to the north of where they now live. Once on dry land, they divided into two groups, the Summer People and the Winter People, and migrated south along the Rio Grande. During their travels they made 12 stops before finally being reunited into a single community.

For the Tewa all existence is divided into six categories, three human and three supernatural. Each of the human categories, which are arranged in a hierarchy, is matched by a spiritual category, so that when people die, they immediately pass into their proper spiritual role. Not only are the supernatural categories identified with human categories; they also correspond to divisions in the natural world.

To those of some other religious persuasion, such beliefs may seem, at best, irrational and arbitrary, but in fact they are neither. Alfonso Ortiz, an anthropologist who is also a Tewa, points out that his native religion is not only logical and socially functional, it is the very model of Tewa society.[1] These people have a society that is divided into two independent moieties, each having its own economy, rituals, and authority. The individual is introduced into one of these moieties (which in this case are *not* based on kinship), and his or her membership is regularly reinforced through a series of life-cycle rituals that correspond to the stops on the mythical tribal journey down the Rio Grande. The rites of birth and death are shared by the whole community; other rites differ in the two moieties. The highest status of the human hierarchy belongs to the priests, who also help integrate this divided society; they mediate not only between the human and spiritual world but between the two moieties as well.

Tewa religion enters into virtually every aspect of Tewa life and society. It is the basis of the

[1]Ortiz, A. (1969). *The Tewa world* (p. 43). Chicago: University of Chicago Press.

simultaneously dualistic/unified worldview of the individual Tewa. It provides numerous points of mediation through which the two moieties can continue to exist together as a single community. It sanctifies the community by linking its origin with the realm of the supernatural, and it offers divine sanction to those "rites of passage" that soften life's major transitions. In providing an afterworld that is the mirror image of human society, it answers the question of death in a manner that reinforces social structure. In short, Tewa religion, by weaving all elements of Tewa experience into a single pattern, gives a solid foundation to the stability and continuity of their society.

All religions fulfill numerous social and psychological needs. Some of these—the need to confront and explain death, for example—appear to be universal; indeed, we know of no group of people anywhere on the face of the earth who, at any time over the past 100,000 years, have been without religion. Unbound by time, religion gives meaning to individual and group life, drawing power from "the time of the gods in the Beginning," and offering continuity of existence beyond death. It can provide the path by which people transcend their arduous earthly existence and attain, if only momentarily, spiritual selfhood. The social functions of religion are no less important than the psychological functions. A traditional religion reinforces group norms, provides moral sanctions for individual conduct, and furnishes the substratum of common purpose and values upon which the equilibrium of the community depends.

In the nineteenth century the European intellectual tradition gave rise to the idea that science would ultimately destroy religion by showing people the irrationality of their myths and rituals. Indeed, many still believe that as scientific explanations replace those of religion, the latter should wither. An opposite tendency has occurred, however; not only do traditional, "main line" religions continue to attract new adherents, but there has been a strong resurgence of fundamentalist religions. Examples include the Islamic fundamentalism of the Shiite Muslims in Iran and, in the United States, the Christian fundamentalism of Jerry Falwell, Pat Robertson, and others, with its marked anti–science bias. Moreover, interest in astrology and occultism continues to be strong in North

America, and there are new religious options, such as sects derived from Eastern religions.

Science, far from destroying religion, may have contributed to the creation of a veritable religious boom. In the United States, religion is worth billions of tax–free dollars each year, and some religious leaders even flaunt luxurious lifestyles as proof that they enjoy God's favor. Science has fostered this religious boom by removing many traditional psychological props, while at the same time creating, in its technological applications, a host of new problems—threat of nuclear catastrophe, health threats from pollution, fear of loss of economic security, and fear of loneliness in a society that isolates us from our kin and that places impediments in the way of establishing deep and lasting friendships, to list a few with which people must contend. In the face of these new anxieties, religion offers social and psychological support.

The continuing strength of religion in the face of Western rationalism clearly reveals that it is a powerful and dynamic force in society. Although anthropologists are not qualified to pass judgment on the metaphysical truth of any particular religion, they can show how each religion embodies a number of "truths" about humans and society.

THE ANTHROPOLOGICAL APPROACH TO RELIGION

Anthropologist Anthony F. C. Wallace has defined **religion** as "a set of rituals, rationalized by myth, which mobilizes supernatural powers for the purpose of achieving or preventing transformations of state in man and nature."[2] What lies behind this definition is a recognition that people, when they cannot "fix" serious problems that cause them anxiety through technological or organizational means, try to do so through the manipulation of supernatural beings and powers. This requires ritual, which Wallace sees as the primary phenomenon of religion, or "religion in action." Its major function is to reduce anxiety and keep confidence high, all of which serves to keep people in some

[2]Wallace, A. F. C. (1966). *Religion: An anthropological view* (p. 107). New York: Random House.

Far from causing the death of religion, the growth of scientific knowledge, by producing new anxieties and raising new questions about human existence, may have contributed to the continuing practice of religion in modern life. North Americans continue to participate in traditional religions, such as Judaism (top), as well as imported sects, such as the new Vrindaban (middle), and evangelism (bottom).

Religion: A set of rituals, rationalized by myth, which mobilizes supernatural powers for the purpose of achieving or preventing transformations of state in people and nature.

The people of Bali believe in the existence of three worlds: an upper one inhabited by the gods, a middle one inhabited by people, and a lower one inhabited by demons. Elaborate rituals are the means by which the people keep the inhabitants of all three worlds in balance.

sort of shape to cope with reality. It is this that gives religion survival value.

Religion, then, may be regarded as the beliefs and patterns of behavior by which people try to control the area of the universe that is otherwise beyond their control. Since no known culture, including those of modern industrial societies, has achieved complete certainty in controlling the universe, religion is a part of all known cultures. There is, however, considerable variability here. At one end of the human spectrum are food-foraging peoples, whose technological ability to manipulate their environment is limited, and who tend to see themselves more as part, rather than masters, of nature. This is what we referred to in Chapter 23 as a naturalistic worldview. Among food foragers religion is apt to be inseparable from the rest of daily life. It also mirrors and confirms the egalitarian nature of social relations in their societies, in that individuals do not plead for aid to high-ranking deities in the way that members of stratified societies do. At the other end of the human spectrum is Western civilization, with its ideological commitment to overcoming problems through technological and organizational skills. Here religion is less a part of daily activities and is restricted to more specific occasions. Moreover, with its hi-

erarchy of supernatural beings—for instance, God, the angels, and saints of Christianity—it reflects and confirms the stratified nature of the society in which it is embedded. Even so, there is variation. Religious activity may be less prominent in the lives of social elites, who see themselves as more in control of their own destinies, than it is to peasants or members of lower classes. Among the latter, religion may afford some compensation for a dependent status in society. On the other hand, religion is still important to elite members of society, in that it rationalizes the system in such a way that less advantaged people are not as likely to question the existing social order as they might otherwise be. After all, if there is hope for a better existence after death, then one may be more willing to tolerate the difficulties of this life. Thus, religious beliefs serve to influence and perpetuate conceptions, if not actual relations, between different classes of people.

THE PRACTICE OF RELIGION

Much of the value of religion comes from the activities called for by its practice. Participation in religious ceremonies may bring a sense of personal transcendence, a wave of reassurance, security, and even ecstasy, or a feeling of closeness to fellow participants. Although the rituals and practices of religions vary considerably, even those rites that seem to us most bizarrely exotic can be shown to serve the same basic social and psychological functions.

Supernatural Beings and Powers

One of the hallmarks of religion is a belief in supernatural beings and forces. In attempting to control by religious means what cannot be controlled in other ways, humans turn to prayer, sacrifice, and other religious rituals. This presupposes a world of supernatural beings that have an interest in human affairs and to whom one may turn for aid. For convenience we may divide these beings into three categories: major deities (gods and goddesses), ancestral spirits, and other sorts of spirit beings. Although the variety of deities and spirits recognized by the world's cultures is tremendous, certain generalizations about them are possible.

Gods and Goddesses

Gods and goddesses are the great and more remote beings. They are usually seen as controlling the universe, or, if several are recognized, each has charge of a particular part of the universe. Such was the case of the gods and goddesses of ancient Greece: Zeus was lord of the sky, Poseidon was ruler of the sea, and Hades was lord of the underworld and ruler of the dead. Besides these three brothers, there were a host of other deities, female as well as male, each similarly concerned with specific aspects of life and the universe. **Pantheons,** or collections of gods and goddesses such as those of the Greeks, are common in non-Western states as well. Since states have commonly grown through conquest, their pantheons often have developed as local deities of conquered peoples were incorporated into the official state pantheon. Although creators of the present world may be included, this is not always the case; the Greeks, to cite one exam-

ple, did not include them. Another frequent though not invariable feature of pantheons is the presence of a supreme deity, who may be all but totally ignored by humans. The Aztecs of Mexico, for instance, recognized a supreme pair, to whom they paid little attention. After all, being so remote, they were unlikely to be interested in human affairs. The sensible thing, then, was to focus attention on those deities who were less remote and therefore more directly concerned in human matters.

Whether a people recognize gods, goddesses, or both has to do with how men and women relate to one another in everyday life. Generally speaking, in societies in which women are subordinate to men, the godhead is defined in exclusively masculine terms. Such societies are mainly those with economies based on the herding of animals or intensive agriculture carried out by men, who as fathers, are distant and controlling figures to their children. Goddesses, by contrast, are apt to be most prominent in societies in which women make a major contribution to the economy, enjoy relative equality with men, and in which men are more involved in their children's lives. Such societies are most often those that depend upon farming, much or all of which is done by women. As an illustration, the early Hebrews, like other pastoral nomadic tribes of the Middle East, described their god in masculine, authoritarian terms. By contrast, goddesses played central roles in religious ritual and the popular consciousness of the agricultural peoples of the region. Associated with these goddesses were concepts of light, love, fertility, and procreation. Around 1300 B.C., the Hebrew tribes entered the land of Canaan and began to practice agriculture, requiring them to establish a new kind of relationship with the soil. As they became dependent upon rainfall and on the rotation of the seasons for crops and concerned about fertility (as the Canaanites already were), they adopted many of the Canaanite goddess cults. Although diametrically opposed to the original Hebrew cult, belief in the Canaanite goddesses catered to the human desire for security by seeking to control the forces of fertility in the interest of people's well-being.

Later on, when the Israelite tribes sought national unity in the face of a military threat by the Philistines, and they strengthened their identity as a "chosen people," the goddess cults lost out

Pantheon: The several gods and goddesses of a people.

The patriarchal nature of Western society is expressed in its theology, in which a masculine God gives life to the first man, as depicted here on the ceiling of the Sistine Chapel. Only after this is the first woman created, from the first man.

to followers of the old, masculine tribal god. This ancient masculine-authoritarian concept of god has been perpetuated down to the present, not just in the Judaic tradition, but also by Christians and Muslims, whose religions stem from the old Hebrew religion. As a consequence, this masculine-authoritarian model has played an important role in perpetuating a relationship between men and women in which the latter traditionally have been expected to submit to the "rule" of men at every level of Jewish, Christian, and Islamic society.

Ancestral Spirits

A belief in ancestral spirits is consistent with the widespread notion that human beings are made up of two parts, a body and some kind of vital spirit. For example, the Penobscot Indians, whom we met in Chapter 16, maintained that each person had a vital spirit that could even detach itself and travel apart from the body, while the latter remained inert. Given such a concept, the idea of the spirit being freed by death from the body and having a continued existence seems logical.

Ancestral spirits are frequently seen as retaining an active interest and even membership in society. In the last chapter, for instance, we saw how ghost ancestors of the Wape acted to provide or withhold meat from their living descendants. Like living persons, ancestral spirits may be benevolent or malevolent, but one is never sure what their behavior will be. The same feeling of uncertainty—how will they react to what I have done?—may be displayed toward ancestral spirits that tends to be displayed to those of a senior generation who hold authority over the individual. Beyond this, ancestral spirits closely resemble living humans in appetites, feelings, emotions, and behavior. Thus, they reflect and reinforce social reality.

A belief in ancestral spirits of one sort or another is found in many parts of the world. In several African societies, however, the concept is highly elaborated. Here one frequently finds ancestral spirits behaving just like humans. They are able to feel hot, cold, and pain, and they may be capable of dying a second death by drowning or burning. They may even participate in family and lineage affairs, and seats will be provided for them,

These faces were carved into a rock along the Connecticut River by native Indians to depict spirit beings that they saw here while in states of trance.

even though the spirits are invisible. If they are annoyed, they may send sickness or even death. Eventually, they are reborn as new members of their lineage, and in societies that hold such beliefs, there is a need to observe infants closely in order to determine just who it is that has been reborn.

Deceased ancestors were also important in the patrilineal society of traditional China. For the gift of life, a boy was forever indebted to his parents, owing them obedience, deference, and a comfortable old age. Even after their death, he had to provide for them in the spirit world, offering food, money, and incense to them on the anniversaries of their births and deaths. In addition, collective worship of all lineage ancestors was carried out periodically throughout the year. Even the birth of sons was regarded as an obligation to the ancestors, as this ensured that the latter's needs would continue to be met even after their sons' own death. To satisfy the needs of ancestors for descendants (and a man's own need to be respectable in a culture that demanded that he satisfy his ancestors' needs) a man would even marry a girl who had been adopted into his family as an infant, in order to be raised as a dutiful wife for him, even when this arrangement went against the wishes of both parties. Furthermore, a man would readily force his daughter to marry a man against her will.

In fact, a woman was raised to be cast out by her natal family, and yet might not find acceptance in her husband's family for years. Not until after death, when her soul was carried in a tablet and placed in the shrine of her husband's family, was she an official member of it. As a consequence, once a son was born to her, a woman worked long and hard to establish the strongest possible tie between herself and her son to ensure that she would be looked after in life.

Strong beliefs in ancestral spirits are particularly appropriate in a society of descent-based groups with their associated ancestor orientation. More than this, though, they provide a strong sense of continuity in which past, present, and future are all linked.

Animism

One of the most widespread beliefs about supernatural beings is **animism,** which sees nature as animated by all sorts of spirits. In reality, the term

Animism: A belief in spirit beings, which are thought to animate nature.

SIR EDWARD B. TYLOR
(1832–1917)

The concept of animism was first brought to the attention of anthropologists by the British scholar Sir Edward B. Tylor. Though not university-educated himself, Tylor was the first person to hold a chair in anthropology at a British university, with his appointment first as lecturer, then reader, and finally (in 1895) professor at Oxford. His interest in anthropology developed as a consequence of travels that took him as a young man to the United States (where he visited an Indian Pueblo), Cuba, and Mexico, where he was especially impressed by the achievements of the ancient Aztec and the contemporary blend of Indian and Spanish culture.

Tylor's numerous publications ranged over such diverse topics as the possible historical connection between the games of pachisi and patolli (played in India and ancient Mexico), the origin of games of Cat's Cradle, and the structural connections between post-marital residence, descent, and certain other customs such as in-law avoidance and the couvade (the confinement of a child's father following birth). It was also Tylor who formulated the first widely accepted definition of culture (see Chapter 14). The considerable attention paid to religious concepts and practices in his writings stemmed from a lifelong commitment to combat the idea, still widely held in his time, that so-called savage people had degenerated more than civilized people from an original state of grace. To Tylor, "savages" were intellectuals just like anyone else, grappling with their problems, but handicapped (as was Tylor in his intellectual life) by limited information.

---

masks a wide range of variation. Animals and plants, like humans, may all have their individual spirits, as may springs, mountains, or other natural features. So, too, may stones, weapons, ornaments, and so on. In addition, the woods may be full of a variety of unattached or free-ranging spirits. The various spirits involved are a highly diverse lot. Generally speaking, though, they are less remote from people than gods and goddesses and are more involved in daily affairs. They may be benevolent, malevolent, or neutral. They may also be awesome, terrifying, lovable, or mischievous. Since they may be pleased or irritated by human actions, people are obliged to be concerned with them.

Animism is typical of those who see themselves as being a part of nature rather than superior to it. This takes in most food foragers, as well as those food-producing peoples who recognize little difference between a human life and that of any growing thing. Among them, gods and goddesses are relatively unimportant, but the woods are full of all sorts of spirits. (For a good example, see the discussion of the Penobscot behavioral environment in Chapter 16.) Gods and goddesses, if they exist at all, may be seen as having created the world and perhaps making it fit to live in; but it is spirits to whom one turns for curing, who help or hinder the shaman, and whom the ordinary hunter may meet when off in the woods.

Animatism

While supernatural power is often thought of as being vested in supernatural beings, it does not have to be. The Melanesians, for example, think of *mana* as a force inherent in all objects. It is not in itself physical, but it can reveal itself physically. A warrior's success in fighting is not attributed to his own strength but to the *mana* contained in an amulet that hangs around his neck. Similarly, a farmer may know a great deal about horticulture, soil conditioning, and the correct time for sowing and harvesting, but nevertheless depend upon *mana* for a successful crop, often building a simple altar to this power at the end of the field. If the crop is good, it is a sign that the farmer has in some way appropriated the necessary *mana*. Far from being a personalized force, *mana* is abstract in the extreme, a power lying always just beyond reach of the senses. As R. H. Codrington described it, "virtue, prestige, authority, good fortune, influence, sanctity, luck are all words which, under certain conditions, give something near the meaning. . . . *Mana* sometimes means a more than natural virtue or power attaching to some person or thing."[3] This concept of impersonal power was also widespread among North American Indians. The Iroquois called it *orenda;* to the Sioux it was *wakonda;* to the Algonquians, *manitu.* Though found on every continent, the concept is not necessarily universal, however.

R. R. Marett called this concept of impersonal power **animatism.** The two concepts, animatism (which is inanimate) and animism (a belief in spirit beings), are not mutually exclusive. They are often found in the same culture, as in Melanesia, and also in the Indian societies mentioned above.

People trying to comprehend beliefs in the supernatural beings and powers recognized by others frequently ask how such beliefs are maintained. In part, the answer is through manifestations of power. By this is meant that, given a belief in animatism and/or the powers of supernatural beings, then one is predisposed to see what appear to be results of the application of such powers. For example, if a Melanesian warrior is convinced of his power because he possesses the necessary *mana,* and he is successful, he may very well interpret this success as proof of the power of *mana.* "After all, I would have lost had I not possessed it, wouldn't I?" Beyond this, because of his confidence in his *mana,* he may be willing to take more chances in his fighting, and this could indeed mean the difference between success and failure.

Failures, of course, do occur, but they can be explained. Perhaps one's prayer was not answered because a deity or spirit was still angry about some past insult. Or perhaps our Melanesian warrior lost his battle—the obvious explanation is that he was not as successful in bringing *mana* to bear as he

Animatism: A belief that the world is animated by impersonal supernatural powers.

[3]Quoted by Leinhardt, G. (1960). Religion. In H. Shapiro (Ed.), *Man, culture, and society* (p. 368). New York: Oxford University Press.

thought, or else his opponent had more of it. In any case, humans generally emphasize successes over failures, and long after many of the latter have been forgotten, tales will probably still be told of striking cases of the workings of supernatural powers.

Another feature that tends to perpetuate beliefs in supernatural beings is that they have attributes with which people are familiar. Allowing for the fact that supernatural beings are in a sense larger than life, they are generally conceived of as living the way people do and are interested in the same sorts of things. For example, the Penobscot Indians believed in a quasi-human being called Gluskabe. Like ordinary mortals, Gluskabe traveled about in a canoe, used snowshoes, lived in a wigwam, and made stone arrowheads. The gods and goddesses of the ancient Greeks had all the familiar human lusts and jealousies. Such features serve to make supernatural beings believable.

The role of mythology in maintaining beliefs should not be overlooked. Myths, which are discussed in some detail in Chapter 25, are explanatory narratives that rationalize religious beliefs and practices. To European Americans, the word *myth* immediately conjures up the idea of a story about imaginary events, but the people responsible for a particular myth usually do not see it that way. To them myths are true stories, analogous to historical documents in modern North American culture. Even so, myths exist even in literate societies, as in the case of the Judaic and Christian account of creation, as contained in the Book of Genesis. Myths invariably are full of accounts of the doings of various supernatural beings, and so serve to reinforce beliefs in them.

Religious Specialists

Priests and Priestesses

In all human societies there exist individuals whose job it is to guide and supplement the religious practices of others. Such individuals are highly skilled at contacting and influencing supernatural beings and manipulating supernatural forces. Their qualification for this is that they have undergone special training. In addition, they may display certain

An evangelist heals a follower. Such faith healers in the United States and elsewhere correspond in every respect to our definition of the shaman; hence, shamanism is by no means absent in modern industrial societies.

distinctive personality traits that particularly suit them for their jobs. In societies with the resources to support full-time occupational specialists, the role of guiding religious practices and influencing the supernaturals belongs to the **priest** or **priestess.** He or she is the socially initiated, ceremonially inducted member of a recognized religious organization, with a rank and function that belongs to him or her as the tenant of an office held before by others. The sources of power are the society and the institution in which the priest or priestess functions. The priest, if not the priestess, is a familiar figure in Western societies; he is the priest,

Priest or Priestess: A full-time religious specialist.

minister, pastor, rector, rabbi, or whatever the official title may be in some organized religion. With their god defined in masculine, authoritarian terms, it was not surprising that the most important religious positions in the Judaic, Christian, and Islamic religions have traditionally been filled by men. Only in societies in which women make a major contribution to the economy, and which recognizes goddesses as well as gods, are female religious specialists likely to be found.

Shamans

Societies that lack full-time occupational specialization have existed far longer than those in which one finds such specialization, and in them there have always been individuals who have acquired religious power individually, usually in solitude and isolation, when the Great Spirit, the

Power, the Great Mystery, or whatever is revealed to them. These persons become the recipients of certain special gifts, such as healing or divination; when they return to society they are frequently given another kind of religious role, that of the **shaman.**

In the United States millions of people have learned something about shamans through their reading of the popular autobiography of Black Elk, a traditional Sioux Indian "medicine man," or Carlos Castaneda's apparently fictional accounts of his experiences with Don Juan, the Yaqui Indian shaman. Few of them may realize, however, that the faith healers and many other evangelists in their own societies conform in every respect to our definition of the shaman. Thus, one should not get the idea that shamans are not to be found in modern, industrial societies, for they are. Furthermore, they may become more common, given current high levels of interest in the occult and supernatural in the United States.

Typically, one becomes a shaman by passing through stages commonly set forth in many myths. These stages are often thought to involve torture and violent dismemberment of the body; scraping away of the flesh until the body is reduced to a skeleton; substitution of the viscera and renewal of the blood; a period spent in a nether region, or land of the dead, during which the shaman is taught by the souls of dead shamans and other spirit beings; and an ascent to a sky realm. Among the Crow Indians, for example, any man could become a shaman, since there was no ecclesiastical organization that handed down laws for the guidance of the religious consciousness. The search for shamanistic visions was pursued by most adult Crow males, who would engage in bodily deprivation, even self-torture, to induce such visions. Not all seekers were granted a vision, but failure carried no social stigma. While those who claimed

Shaman: A part-time religious specialist who has unique power acquired through his or her own initiative; such individuals are thought to possess exceptional abilities to deal with supernatural beings and powers.

supernatural vision would be expected to manifest some special power in battle or wealth, it was the sincerity of the seeker that carried the essential truth of the experience. Many of the elements of shamanism, such as transvestism, trance states, and speaking in undecipherable languages, can just as easily be regarded as abnormalities, and it has been frequently pointed out that those regarded as specially gifted in some societies would be outcasts or worse in others. The position of shaman can provide a socially approved role for what in other circumstances might be unstable personalities.

The shaman is essentially a religious entrepreneur, who acts on behalf of some human client, often to effect a cure or foretell some future event. To do so, the shaman intervenes to influence or impose his or her will on supernatural powers. The shaman can be contrasted with the priest or priestess, whose "clients" are the deities. Priests and priestesses frequently tell people what to do; the shaman tells supernaturals what to do. In return for services rendered, the shaman may collect a fee—fresh meat, yams, a favorite possession. In some cases, the added prestige, authority, and social power attached to the status of shaman are reward enough.

When a shaman acts for a client, he or she may put on something of a show—one in which the basic drama is heightened by a sense of danger. Frequently, the shaman must enter a trancelike state, in which he or she will experience the sensation of traveling to the spirit world, being able to see and interact there with spirit beings. (For more on trance, see Chapters 16 and 25.) What the shaman tries to do is to impose his or her will upon these spirits, an inherently dangerous contest, considering the superhuman powers that spirits are usually thought to possess. One example of this is afforded by the trance dances of the Ju/'hoansi Bushmen of Africa's Kalahari Desert. Among these people shamans constitute, on average, about half the men and a third of the older women in any group. The most common reasons for their going into trance are to bring rain, control animals, and—as in the present example—to heal the sick (always an important activity of shamans, wherever they are found).

Ju/'hoansi healers, when entering trance, are assisted by others among the trance dancers.

Original Study

Healing Among the Ju/'hoansi of the Kalahari[4]

One way the spirits affect humans is by shooting them with invisible arrows carrying disease, death, or misfortune. If the arrows can be warded off, illness will not take hold. If illness has already penetrated, the arrows must be removed to enable the sick person to recover. An ancestral spirit may exercise this power against the living if a person is not being treated well by others. If people argue with her frequently, if her husband shows how little he values her by carrying on blatant affairs, or if people refuse to cooperate or share with her, the spirit may conclude that no one cares whether or not she remains alive and may "take her into the sky."

Interceding with the spirits and drawing out their invisible arrows is the task of [Ju/'hoansi] healers, men and women who possess the powerful healing force called *n/um* [the Ju/'hoansi equivalent of *mana*]. N/um generally remains dormant in a healer until an effort is made to activate it. Although an occasional healer can accomplish this through solo singing or instrumental playing, the usual way of activating n/um is through the medicinal curing ceremony or trance dance. To the sound of undulating melodies sung by women, healers dance around and around the fire, sometimes for hours. The music, the strenuous dancing, the smoke, the heat of the fire, and the healers' intense concentration cause their n/um to heat up. When it comes to a boil, trance is achieved.

At this moment the n/um becomes available as a powerful healing force, to serve the entire community. In trance, a healer lays hands on and ritually cures everyone sitting around the fire. His hands flutter lightly beside each person's head or chest or wherever illness is evident; his body trembles; his breathing becomes deep and coarse; and he becomes coated with a thick sweat—also considered to be imbued with power. Whatever "badness" is discovered in the person is drawn into the healer's own body and met by the n/um coursing up his spinal column. The healer gives a mounting cry that culminates in a soul-wrenching shriek as the illness is catapulted out of his body and into the air.

While in trance, many healers see various gods and spirits sitting just outside the circle of firelight, enjoying the spectacle of the dance. Sometimes the spirits are recognizable—departed relatives and friends—at other times they are "just people." Whoever these beings are, healers in trance usually blame them for whatever misfortune is being experienced by the community. They are barraged by hurled objects, shouted at, and aggressively warned not to take any of the living back with them to the village of the spirits.

To cure a very serious illness, the most experienced healers may be called upon, for only they have enough knowledge to undertake the dangerous spiritual exploration that may be necessary to effect a cure. When they are in a trance, their souls are said to leave their bodies and to travel to the spirit world to discover the cause of the illness or the problem. An ancestral spirit or a god is usually found responsible and asked to reconsider. If the healer is persuasive and the spirit agrees, the sick person recovers. If the spirit is elusive or unsympathetic, a cure is not achieved. The healer may go to the principal god, but even this does not always work. As one healer put it, "Sometimes, when you speak with God, he says, 'I want this person to die and won't help you make him better.' At other times, God helps; the next morning, someone who has been lying on the ground, seriously ill, gets up and walks again."

These journeys are considered dangerous because while the healer's soul is absent his body is in half-death. Akin to loss of consciousness, this state has been observed and verified by medical and scientific investigators. The power of other healers' n/um is all that is thought to protect the healer in this state from actual death. He receives lavish attention and care—his body is vigorously massaged, his skin is rubbed with sweat, and hands are laid on him. Only when consciousness returns—the signal that his soul has been reunited with his body—do the other healers cease their efforts.

[4]Shostak, M. (1983). *Nisa: The life and words of a !Kung woman* (pp. 291–293). New York: Vintage.

In many human societies trancing is accompanied by sleight-of-hand tricks and ventriloquism. Among Arctic peoples, for example, a shaman may summon spirits in the dark and produce all sorts of flapping noises and strange voices to impress the audiences. To some Western observers, this kind of trickery is regarded as evidence of the fraudulent nature of shamanism; but is this so? The truth is that shamans know perfectly well that they are pulling the wool over people's eyes with their tricks. On the other hand, virtually everyone who has studied them agrees that shamans really believe in their power to deal with supernatural powers and spirits. It is this power that gives them the right as well as the ability to fool people in minor technical matters. In short, the shaman regards his or her ability to perform tricks as proof of superior powers.

The importance of shamanism in a society should not be underestimated. For the individual members of society, it promotes, through the drama of the performance, a feeling of ecstasy and release of tension. It provides psychological assurance, through the manipulation of supernatural powers and spirits otherwise beyond human control, of such things as invulnerability from attack, success at love, or the return of health. In fact, a frequent reason for a shamanistic performance is to cure illness. Although the treatment may not be medically effective, the state of mind induced in the patient may be critical to his or her recovery.

What shamanism does for society is to provide a focal point of attention. This is not without danger to the shaman. Someone with so much skill and power has the ability to work evil as well as good and so is potentially dangerous. Too much nonsuccess on the part of a shaman may be interpreted as evidence of malpractice, resulting in his or her banishment or death. The shaman may also help maintain social control through the ability to detect and punish evildoers.

The benefits of shamanism for the shaman are that it provides prestige and perhaps even wealth. It may also be therapeutic, in that it provides an approved outlet for the outbreaks of what otherwise might seem an unstable personality. An individual who is psychologically unstable (and not all shamans are) may actually get better by becoming intensely involved with the problems of others. In this respect, shamanism is a bit like self-analysis. Finally, shamanism is a good outlet for the self-expression of those who might be described as being endowed with an "artistic temperament."

Anthropology Applied

RECONCILING MODERN MEDICINE WITH TRADITIONAL BELIEFS IN SWAZILAND

Although the biomedical germ theory is generally accepted in Western societies today, this is not the case in many other societies around the world. In southern Africa's Swaziland, for example, all types of illnesses are generally thought to be caused by sorcery, or by loss of ancestral protection. Even where the effectiveness of Western medicine is recognized, the ultimate question remains: Why was the disease sent in the first place? Thus, for the treatment of disease, the Swazi have traditionally relied upon herbalists, diviner mediums through whom ancestor spirits are thought to work, and Christian faith healers. Unfortunately, such individuals have usually been regarded as quacks and charlatans by the medical establishment, even though the herbal medicines used by traditional healers are effective in several ways, and the reassurance provided patient and family alike through rituals that reduce stress and anxiety plays an important role in the patient's recovery. In a country where there is one traditional healer for every 110 people, but only one physician for every 10,000, the potential benefit of cooperation between physicians and healers seems self-evident. Nevertheless, it was unrecognized until proposed by anthropologist Edward C. Green.*

Green, who is now senior research associate with a private firm, went to Swaziland in 1981 as a researcher for a Rural Water-Borne Disease Control Project, funded by the U.S. Agency for International Development. Assigned the task of finding out about knowledge, attitudes, and practices related to water and sanitation, and aware of the serious deficiencies of conventional surveys that rely on precoded questionnaires (see Chapter 1), Green used instead the traditional anthropological techniques of open-ended interviews with key informants, along with participant observation. The key informants were traditional healers, patients, and rural health motivators (individuals chosen by their communities to receive eight weeks of training in preventive health care in regional clinics). Without such work, it would have been impossible to design and interpret a reliable survey instrument, but the added payoff was that Green learned a great deal about Swazi theories of disease

and its treatment. Disposed at the outset to recognize the positive value of many traditional practices, he was able to see as well how cooperation with physicians might be achieved. For example, traditional healers already recognized the utility of Western medicines for the treatment of diseases not indigenous to Africa, and traditional medicines were routinely given to children through inhalation and a kind of vaccination. Thus, nontraditional medicines and vaccinations might be accepted, if presented in traditional terms.

Realizing the suspicion that existed on both sides, Green and his Swazi associate Lydia Makhubu (a chemist who had studied the properties of native medicines) recommended to the Minister of Health a cooperative project focused on a problem of concern to health professionals and native healers alike: infant diarrheal diseases. These had recently become a health problem of high concern to the general public; healers wanted a means of preventing such diseases, and a means of treatment existed—oral rehydration therapy—that was compatible with traditional treatments for diarrhea (herbal preparations taken orally over a period of time). Packets of oral rehydration salts, along with instructions as to their use, were provided healers in a pilot project with positive results. This helped convince health professionals of the benefits of cooperation, while at the same time, the distribution of packets to the healers was seen by them as a gesture of trust and cooperation on the part of the Ministry of Health. Since then, further steps at cooperation have been taken. What this demonstrates is the importance of finding how to work in ways that are compatible with existing belief systems. To directly challenge traditional beliefs, as all too often happens, does little more than create stress, confusion, and resentment.

*Green, E. C. (1987). The planning of health education strategies in Swaziland and The integration of modern and traditional health sectors in Swaziland. In R. M. Wulff & S. J. Fiske (Eds.), *Anthropological praxis: Translating knowledge into action* (pp. 15–25; 87–97). Boulder, CO: Westview.

Rites of Passage

In one of anthropology's classic works, Arnold Van Gennep analyzed the rites of passage that help individuals through the crucial crises of their lives, such as birth, puberty, marriage, parenthood, advancement to a higher class, occupational specialization, and death.[5] He found it useful to divide ceremonies for all of these life crises into three stages: **separation, transition,** and **incorporation.** The individual would first be ritually removed from the society as a whole, then isolated for a period, and finally incorporated back into society in his or her new status.

Van Gennep described the male initiation rites of Australian aborigines. When the time for the initiation is decided by the elders, the boys are taken from the village, while the women cry and make a ritual show of resistance. At a place distant from the camp, groups of men from many villages gather. The elders sing and dance, while the initiates act as though they are dead. The climax of this part of the ritual is a bodily operation, such as circumcision or the

Rites of passage are commonly associated with the transition to adulthood, as here among the Xavante of Brazil. The formal separation and reincorporation of the individuals into society remove the ambiguity that otherwise might characterize the transition.

Rituals and Ceremonies

Although not all rituals are religious in nature (graduation ceremonies in North America, for example), those which are play a crucial role in religious activity. Religious ritual is the means through which persons relate to the sacred; it is religion in action. Not only is ritual the means by which the social bonds of a group are reinforced and tensions relieved; it is also one way that many important events are celebrated and crises, such as death, made less socially disruptive and less difficult for individuals to bear. Anthropologists have classified several different types of ritual, among them **rites of passage,** which pertain to stages in the life cycle of the individual, and **rites of intensification,** which take place during a crisis in the life of the group, serving to bind individuals together.

Rites of passage: Rituals, often religious in nature, marking important stages in the lives of individuals, such as birth, marriage, and death.

Rites of intensification: Religious rituals that take place during a real or potential crisis for a group.

Separation: In rites of passage, the ritual removal of the individual from society.

Transition: In rites of passage, the isolation of the individual following separation and prior to incorporation.

Incorporation: In rites of passage, reincorporation of the individual into society in his or her new status.

[5]Van Gennep, A. (1960). *The rites of passage.* Chicago: University of Chicago Press.

knocking out of a tooth. Anthropologist A. P. Elkin says:

> This is partly a continuation of the drama of death. The tooth-knocking, circumcision or other symbolical act "killed" the novice; after this he does not return to the general camp and normally may not be seen by any woman. He is dead to the ordinary life of the tribe.[6]

The novice may be shown secret ceremonies and receive some instruction during this period, but the most significant element is his complete removal from society. In the course of these Australian puberty rites, the initiate must learn the tribal lore that all adult men are expected to know; he is given, in effect, a "cram course." The trauma of the occasion is a pedagogical technique that ensures that he will learn and remember everything; in a nonliterate society the perpetuation of cultural traditions requires no less, and so effective teaching methods are necessary.

On his return to society the novice is welcomed with ceremonies, as though he had returned from the dead. This alerts the society at large to the individual's new status—that he can be expected to act in certain ways and in return people must act in the appropriate ways toward him. The individual's new rights and duties are thus clearly defined. He is spared, for example, the problems of "American teenage," a time when an individual is neither adult nor child, but a person whose status is ill defined.

In the Australian case just cited, boys are prepared not just for adulthood, but for *manhood*. In their society, for example, fortitude is considered an important masculine virtue, and the pain of tooth-knocking and circumcision helps instill this in initiates. Similarly, female initiation rites help prepare Mende girls in West Africa for womanhood. After they have begun to menstruate, they are removed from society to spend weeks, or even months, in seclusion. There, they discard the clothes of childhood, smear their bodies with white clay and dress in brief skirts and many strands of beads. Shortly after their seclusion, they undergo surgery in which their clitoris and part of the labia

minora are excised, something that they believe enhances their procreative potential. Until their return to society, they are trained in the moral and practical responsibilities of potential childbearers by experienced women in the Sande association, an organization to which the initiates will belong once their training has ended. This training is not all harsh, however, for it is accompanied by a good deal of singing, dancing, and storytelling, and the initiates are very well fed. Thus, they acquire both a positive image of womanhood and a strong sense of sisterhood. Once their training is complete, a medicine made by brewing leaves in water is used for a ritual washing, removing the magical protection that has shielded them during the period of their confinement.

Mende women emerge from their initiation, then, as women in knowledgeable control of their sexuality, eligible for marriage and childbearing. The pain and danger of the surgery, which was endured in the context of intense social support from other women, serves as a metaphor for childbirth which, when it happens, may well take place in the same place of seclusion, again with the support of Sande women. It has also been suggested that, symbolically, excision of the clitoris (the feminine version of the male penis) removed sexual ambiguity.[7] Once done, a woman *knows* she is all woman. Thus, we have symbolic expression of gender as something important in people's cultural lives.

In the case just cited, the anthropological commitment to cultural relativism permits an understanding of the practice of cliterecdomy (removal of the clitoris) in the female initiation rites of the Mende. But as discussed earlier in this book (see Chapter 14), cultural relativism does not preclude the anthropologist from being critical of a given practice. In this case, removal of the clitoris (like male circumcision) is a form of genital mutilation—one that is particularly dangerous. Some form of genital mutilation, ranging from the removal of the clitoris to the removal of the entire external female genitalia including the partial closing of the vaginal opening (surgically opened for intercourse and closed again after giving birth until intercourse is again desired by the male), affects an estimated 80 million women in the world today

[6]Elkin, A. P. (1964). *The Australian aborigines.* Garden City, NY: Doubleday.

[7]MacCormack, C. P. (1977). Biological events and cultural control. *Signs, 3*, 98.

Queen Elizabeth II of England presides at the launching of a ship. Magic plays an important part in British ship-launching ceremonies, involving symbolic classification of the ship, the reincarnating power of the ship's name, and the relationship between women and ships. All play an important role in how sailors, including their officers, believe and act.

and is particularly widespread in Africa, where it occurs in 28 countries.[8] The custom is found also among groups in the Middle East and Far East. Quite apart from the pain involved and the effect of the operation on a woman's future sexual satisfaction, significant numbers of young women die from excessive bleeding, shock, infection, or (later on) when giving birth as scar tissue tears. As a consequence, the practice has been widely condemned in recent years, and committees to end such practices have been set up in 22 African countries.

Rites of Intensification

Rites of intensification are those rituals that mark occasions of crisis in the life of the group, rather than an individual. Whatever the precise nature of the crisis—a severe lack of rain that threatens crops in the fields, the sudden appearance of an enemy war party, the onset of an epidemic, or some other event that disturbs everyone—mass ceremonies are performed to allay the danger to the group. What this does is to unite people in a common effort in such a way that fear and confusion yield to collective action and a degree of optimism. The balance

in the relations of all concerned, which has been upset, is restored to normal.

While the death of an individual might be regarded as the ultimate crisis in the life of that individual, it is, as well, a crisis for the entire group, particularly if the group is small. A member of the group has been removed, and so its equilibrium has been upset. The survivors, therefore, must readjust and restore balance. At the same time, they need to reconcile themselves to the loss of someone to whom they were emotionally tied. Funerary ceremonies, then, can be regarded as rites of intensification that permit the living to express in nondisruptive ways their upset over the death, while providing for social readjustment. A frequent feature of such ceremonies is an ambivalence towards the dead person. For example, one of the parts of the funerary rites of certain Melanesians was the eating of the flesh of the dead person. This ritual cannibalism, witnessed by anthropologist Bronislaw Malinowski, was performed with "extreme repugnance and dread and usually followed by a violent vomiting fit. At the same time it is felt to be a supreme act of reverence, love and devotion."[9] This custom, and the emotions accompanying it, clearly reveal the

[8]Armstrong, S. (1991, February). Female circumcision: Fighting a cruel tradition. *New Scientist*, p. 42.

[9]Malinowski, B. (1954). *Magic, science and religion* (p. 50). Garden City, NY: Doubleday.

What these two pictures have in common is that both are examples of institutionalized magical responses to concerns harbored by many in their societies. In "death penalty" states, executing criminals does no more to deter violent crimes than human sacrifice among the Aztecs did to keep the sun in the sky.

ambiguous attitude toward death: On the one hand, there is the desire to maintain the tie to the dead person, and on the other hand, one feels disgust and fear at the transformation wrought by death. According to Malinowski, funeral ceremonies provide an approved collective means by which individuals may express these feelings, while at the same time maintaining social cohesiveness and preventing disruption of society.

The performance of rites of intensification does not have to be limited to times of overt crisis. In regions where the seasons differ enough so that human activities must change accordingly, they will take the form of annual ceremonies. These are particularly common among horticultural and agricultural people, with their planting, first-fruit, and harvest ceremonies. These are critical times in the lives of people in such societies, and the ceremonies express a reverent attitude toward the forces of generation and fertility in nature, on which people's very existence depends. If all goes well, as it often does at such times, participation in a happy situation reinforces group involvement. It also serves as a kind of dress rehearsal for serious crisis situations; it promotes a habit of reliance on supernatural forces through ritual activity, which can be easily activated under stressful circumstances when it is important not to give way to fear and despair.

RELIGION, MAGIC, AND WITCHCRAFT

Among the most fascinating of ritual practices is application of the belief that supernatural powers can be compelled to act in certain ways for good or evil purposes by recourse to certain specified formulas. This is a classical anthropological notion of magic. Many societies have magical rituals to ensure good crops, the replenishment of game, the fertility of domestic animals, and the avoidance or cure of illness in humans. Although Western peoples today, in seeking to objectify and demythologize their world, have often tried to suppress the existence of these fantastic notions in their own consciousness, they continue to be fascinated by them. Not only are books and films about demonic possession and witchcraft avidly devoured and discussed, but by 1967 (after some 40 years of poor sales) sales of Ouija boards in the United States passed the two million mark. Thirty years ago about 100 newspapers carried horoscope columns, but by 1970, 1,200 of a total of 1,750 daily newspapers regularly carried such columns. Anthropologist Lauren Kendall notes that "Many witches, wizards, druids, Cabalists, and shamans . . . practice modern magic in contemporary England and the United States, where their ranks are comfortably reckoned in the tens of thousands."

Furthermore, "The usual magician is ordinary, generally middle class, and often highly intelligent—a noticeable number of them have something to do with computers."[10] Although it is certainly true that non-Western and peasant peoples tend to endow their world quite freely with magical properties, so do many highly educated Western peoples.

In the nineteenth century Sir James George Frazer, author of one of the most widely read anthropological books of all time, *The Golden Bough*, made a strong distinction between religion and magic. Religion he saw as "a propitiation or conciliation of powers superior to man which are believed to direct and control the course of nature and human life."[11] Magic, on the other hand, he saw as an attempt to manipulate certain perceived "laws" of nature. The magician never doubts that the same causes will always produce the same effects. Thus, Frazer saw magic as a sort of pseudoscience, differing from modern science only in its misconception of the nature of the particular laws that govern the succession of events.

Useful though Frazer's characterization of magic has been, anthropologists no longer accept his distinction between it and religion. Far from being separate, magical procedures frequently are part of religious rituals, and both magic and religion deal directly with the supernatural. In fact, Frazer's distinction seems to be no more than a bias of Western culture, in which magic is regarded as quite separate from religion.

Frazer did make a useful distinction between two fundamental principles of magic. The first principle, that "like produces like," he called **imitative magic**. In Burma, for example, a rejected lover might engage a sorcerer to make an image of his would-be love. If this image were tossed into water, to the accompaniment of certain charms, the hapless girl would go mad. Thus, the girl would suffer a fate similar to that of her image.

Frazer's second principle was that of **contagious magic**—the concept that things or persons that have once been in contact can afterward influence one another. The most common example of contagious magic is the permanent relationship between an individual and any part of his or her body, such as hair, fingernails, or teeth. Frazer cites the Basutos of southern Africa, who were careful to conceal their extracted teeth, because these might fall into the hands of certain mythical beings who could harm the owner of the tooth by working magic on it. Related to this is the custom, in Western societies, of treasuring things that have been touched by special people.

Witchcraft

In Salem, Massachusetts, two hundred suspected witches were arrested in 1692; of these, 19 were hanged and one other was hounded to death. Despite the awarding of damages to descendants of some of the victims 19 years later, not until 1957 were the last of the Salem witches exonerated by the Massachusetts legislature. Although many North Americans suppose that **witchcraft** is something that belongs to a less-enlightened past, in fact, it is alive in the United States today. Indeed, starting in the 1960s, witchcraft began to undergo a boom in this country. North Americans are by no means alone in this; for example, as the Ibibio of Nigeria have become increasingly exposed to modern education and scientific training, their reliance on witchcraft as an explanation for misfortune has increased.[12] Furthermore, it is often the younger, more educated members of Ibibio society who accuse others of "bewitching" them. Frequently, the accused are older, more traditional

Imitative magic: Magic based on the principle that like produces like.

Contagious magic: Magic based on the principle that things once in contact can influence one another after separation.

Witchcraft: An explanation of misfortune based on the belief that certain individuals possess an innate, psychic power capable of causing harm, including sickness and death.

[10]Kendall, L. (1990). In the company of witches. *Natural History*, 10(90), 92.

[11]Frazer, J. G. (1931). Magic and religion. In V. F. Calverton (Ed.), *The making of man: An outline of anthropology* (p. 693). New York: Modern Library.

[12]Offiong, D. (1985). Witchcraft among the Ibibio of Nigeria. In A. C. Lehmann & J. E. Myers (Eds.), *Magic, witchcraft and religion* (pp. 152–165). Palo Alto, CA: Mayfield.

In North America, interest in and practice of witchcraft have grown significantly over the past 20 years, often among highly educated segments of society. Contrary to popular belief, witchcraft is *not* concerned exclusively, or even primarily, with working evil.

members of society; thus, we have an expression of the intergenerational hostility that often exists in fast-changing traditional societies.

Ibibio Witchcraft

Among the Ibibio, as among most peoples of sub-Saharan Africa, witchcraft beliefs are highly developed and are of long standing. A rat that eats up a person's crops is not really a rat, but a witch who changed into one; if a young, enterprising man cannot get a job or fails an exam, he has been bewitched; if someone's money is wasted away, if they become sick, if they are bitten by a snake or struck by lightning, the reason is always the same: It is witchcraft. Indeed, virtually all misfortune, illness, or death is attributed to the malevolent activity of some witch. Their modern knowledge of such things as the role played by microorganisms

in disease has little impact; after all, it says nothing about why these were sent to the afflicted individual. Although Ibibio religious beliefs provide alternative explanations for misfortune, they carry negative connotations and do not elicit nearly as much sympathy from others. Thus, if evil befalls a person, witchcraft is a far more satisfying explanation than something like "filial disobedience" or violation of some taboo.

Who are these Ibibio witches? They are thought to be those, male or female, who have within them a special substance acquired from some other established witch. This substance is made up of red, white, and black threads, needles, and other ingredients, and one gets it by swallowing it. From it comes a special power that causes harm, up to and including death, irrespective of whether its possessor intends to cause harm or not. The power is purely psychic, and witches do not

perform rites, nor make use of "bad medicine." It gives them the ability to change into animals, to travel any distance at incredible speed to get at their victims, whom they may torture or kill by transferring the victim's soul into an animal, which is then eaten.

To identify a witch, one looks for any person whose behavior is out of the ordinary. Specifically, some combination of the following may cause one to be labeled a witch: not being fond of greeting people; living alone in a place apart from others; charging too high a price for something; enjoying adultery or committing incest; walking about at night; not showing sufficient grief upon the death of a relative or other member of the community; taking improper care of one's parents, children, or wives; hard-heartedness. Witches are apt to look and act mean and to be socially disruptive people in the sense that their behavior too far exceeds the range of variance considered acceptable.

Neither the Ibibio in particular nor Africans in general are alone in attributing most malevolent happenings to witchcraft. Similar beliefs can be found in any human society, including—as already noted—that of the United States. As among the Ibibio, the powers (however they may be gained) are generally considered to be innate and uncontrollable; they result in activities that are the antithesis of proper behavior, and persons displaying undesirable characteristics of personality (however these may be defined) are generally the ones accused of being witches. The Ibibio make a distinction between "black witches"—those whose acts are especially diabolical and destructive—and "white witches," whose witchcraft is relatively benign, even though their powers are thought to be greater than those of their black counterparts. This exemplifies a common distinction between what Lucy Mair, a British anthropologist, has dubbed "nightmare witches" and "everyday witches."[13] The nightmare witch is the very embodiment of a society's conception of evil, a being that flouts the rules of sexual behavior and disregards every other standard of decency. Nightmare witches, being almost literally the product of dreams and repressed fantasies, have much in common wherever they appear: The modern Navajo and the ancient Roman, for example, like the Ibibio, conceived of witches who could turn themselves into animals and gather to feast on their victims. Everyday witches are often the nonconformists of a community, who are morose, who eat alone, who are arrogant and unfriendly, but who otherwise cause little trouble. Such witches may be dangerous when offended and retaliate by causing sickness, death, crop failure, cattle disease, or any number of lesser ills; people thought to be witches are usually treated very courteously.

The Functions of Witchcraft

Why witchcraft? We might better ask, why not? As Mair aptly observed, in a world where there are few proven techniques for dealing with everyday crises, especially sickness, a belief in witches is not foolish; it is indispensable. No one wants to resign oneself to illness, and if the malady is caused by a witch's hex, then magical countermeasures should cure it. Not only does the idea of personalized evil answer the problem of unmerited suffering, it also provides an explanation for many of those happenings for which no cause can be discovered. Witchcraft, then, cannot be refuted. Even if we could convince a person that his or her illness was due to natural causes, the victim would still ask, as the Ibibio do: Why me? Why now? There is no room for pure chance in such a view; everything must be assigned a cause or meaning. Witchcraft provides the explanation, and in so doing, also provides both the basis and the means for taking counteraction.

Nor is witchcraft always malevolent; even during the Spanish Inquisition, church officials recognized a benevolent or "white" variety. The positive functions of even malevolent witchcraft may be seen in many African societies in which sickness and death are regarded as caused by witches. The ensuing search for the perpetrator of the misfortune becomes, in effect, a communal probe into social behavior.

A witch-hunt is, in fact, a systematic investigation, through a public hearing, into all social relationships involving the victim of the sickness or death. Was her husband unfaithful, her son lacking in the performance of his duties; were her friends uncooperative or was she herself any of these things? Accusations are reciprocal, and before long just about every unsocial or hostile act that has occurred in that society since the last outbreak of witchcraft (sickness or death) is brought into the open.[14]

Through such periodic public scrutiny of everyone's behavior, people are reminded of what their society regards as both strengths and weaknesses of character. This encourages individuals to suppress as best they can those traits of personality that are looked upon with disapproval, for if they do not, they may at some time be accused of being a witch. A belief in witchcraft thus serves a function of social control.

Psychological Functions of Witchcraft Among the Navajo

Several types of witchcraft are distinguished among the Navajo. Witchery encompasses the practices of witches, who are said to meet at night to practice

[13]Mair, L. (1969). *Witchcraft* (p. 37). New York: McGraw-Hill.

[14]Turnbull, C. M. (1983). *The human cycle* (p. 181). New York: Simon & Schuster.

cannibalism and kill people at a distance. Sorcery is distinguished from witchery only by the methods used by the sorcerer, who casts spells on individuals, using the victim's fingernails, hair, or discarded clothing. Wizardry is not distinguished so much by its effects as by its manner of working; wizards kill by injecting a cursed substance, such as a tooth from a corpse, into the victim's body.

Whether or not a particular illness results from witchcraft is determined by **divination,** a magical procedure by which the identity of the witch is also learned. Once a person is charged with witchcraft, he or she is publicly interrogated, possibly even tortured, until there is a confession. It is believed that the witch's own curse will turn against the witch once this happens, so it is expected that the witch will die within a year. Some confessed witches have been allowed to live in exile.

According to Clyde Kluckhohn, Navajo witchcraft served to channel anxieties, tensions, and frustrations that were caused by the pressures from Anglo Americans.[15] The rigid rules of decorum among the Navajo allow little means of expression of hostility, except through accusations of witchcraft. Such accusations funnel pent-up negative emotions against individuals, without upsetting the wider society. Another function of accusations of witchcraft is that they permit the direct expression of hostile feelings against people to whom one would ordinarily be unable to express anger or enmity. On a more positive note, individuals strive to behave in ways that will prevent their being accused of witchcraft. Since excessive wealth is believed to result from witchcraft, individuals are encouraged to redistribute their assets among friends and relatives, thereby leveling economic differences. Similarly, because it is believed that uncared-for elders will turn into witches, people are strongly motivated to take care of aged relatives. And because leaders are thought to be witches, people are

Divination: A magical procedure by which the cause of a particular event, such as illness, may be determined or the future foretold.

[15]Kluckhohn, C. (1944). Navajo witchcraft. *Papers of the Peabody Museum of American Archaeology and Ethnology,* 22(2).

understandably reluctant to go against their wishes, lest they suffer supernatural retribution.

What analyses such as these demonstrate is that witchcraft, in spite of its often negative image, frequently functions in a positive way to manage tensions within a society. Nonetheless, things may get out of hand, particularly in crisis situations, when widespread accusations may cause great suffering. This certainly was the case in the Salem witch trials, but even this pales in comparison to the something like half a million individuals executed as witches in Europe from the fifteenth through seventeenth century. This was a time of profound change in European society, marked by a good deal of political and religious conflict. At such times, it is all too easy to search out scapegoats on whom to place the blame for what are believed to be undesirable changes.

THE FUNCTIONS OF RELIGION

Just as a belief in witchcraft may serve a variety of psychological and social functions, so, too, do religious beliefs and practices in general. Here we may summarize these functions in a somewhat more systematic way. One psychological function is to provide an orderly model of the universe, the importance of which for orderly human behavior is discussed in Chapter 16. Beyond this, by explaining the unknown and making it understandable, the fears and anxieties of individuals are reduced. As we have seen, the explanations usually assume the existence of various sorts of supernatural beings and powers, which may potentially be appealed to or manipulated by people. This being so, a means is provided for dealing with crises: Divine aid is, theoretically, available when all else fails.

A social function of religion is to sanction a wide range of conduct. In this context, religion plays a role in social control, which, as we saw in Chapter 23, does not rely on law alone. This is done through notions of right and wrong. If one does the right thing, one earns the approval of whatever supernatural powers are recognized by a particular culture. If, on the other hand, one does the wrong thing, one may suffer retribution through supernatural agencies. In short, by deliberately *raising* people's feelings of guilt and anxiety,

Though religion may serve many positive functions, formally organized religions have often been responsible for a great deal of human misery, as in the fighting between Catholics and Protestants in Northern Ireland.

religion helps keep them in line. Religion does more than this, though; it sets precedents for acceptable behavior. We have already noted the connection between myths and religion. Usually, myths are full of tales of various supernatural beings, which in various ways illustrate the society's ethical code in action. So it is that Gluskabe, the Penobscot culture hero, is portrayed in the Penobscot myths as tricking and punishing those who mock others, lie, are greedy, or go in for extremes of behavior. Moreover, the specific situations serve as precedents for human behavior in similar circumstances. The Old and New Testaments of the Bible are rich in the same sort of material. Related to this, by the models it presents and the morals it espouses, religion serves to justify and perpetuate a particular social order. Thus, in the Jewish, Christian, and Islamic traditions, a masculine, authoritarian godhead along with a creation story in which a woman is seen responsible for a fall from grace serves to justify a social order in which men have exercised control over women.

There is a psychological function tied up in this. The moral code of a society, since it is held to be divinely fixed, lifts the burden of responsibility for one's conduct from the shoulders of the individual members of society, at least in important situations. It can be a tremendous relief to individuals to know that the responsibility for the way things are rests with the gods, rather than with themselves.

Another social function of religion is its role in the maintenance of social solidarity. In our discussion of the shaman we saw how such individuals provide focal points of interest, thus supplying one ingredient of assistance in maintaining the unity of the group. In addition, common participation in rituals, coupled with a basic uniformity of beliefs, helps to bind people together and reinforce their identification with their group. Particularly effective may be their participation together in rituals, when the atmosphere is charged with emotion. The exalted feelings people may experience in such circumstances serve as a positive reinforcement in that they "feel good" as a result. Here, once again, we find religion providing psychological assurance, while providing for the needs of society.

One other area in which religion serves a social function is education. In our discussion of rites of passage, we noted that Australian puberty rites served as a kind of cram course in tribal lore. By providing a memorable occasion, initiation rites can serve to enhance learning and so help ensure the perpetuation of a nonliterate culture. And as we saw in the case of female initiation rites among the Mende, they can serve to ensure that individuals have the knowledge they will need to fulfill their adult roles in society. Education may also be served by rites of intensification. Frequently such rites involve dramas that portray matters of cultural importance. For example, among a food-foraging people dances may imitate the movement of game and techniques of hunting. Among farmers a fixed round of ceremonies may emphasize the steps necessary for good crops. What this does is to help preserve knowledge that is of importance to a people's material well-being.

These members of a Melanesian cargo cult are carrying mock rifles made of bamboo.

RELIGION AND CULTURE CHANGE

Although the subject of culture change is taken up in Chapter 26, no anthropological consideration of religion is complete without some mention of revitalization movements. In 1931, at Buka in the Solomon Islands, a native religious cult suddenly emerged, its prophets predicting that a deluge would soon engulf all whites. This would be followed by the arrival of a ship laden with European goods. The believers were to construct a storehouse for the goods and to prepare themselves to repulse the colonial police. Because the ship would arrive only after the natives had used up all their own supplies, they ceased working in the fields. Although the leaders of the cult were arrested, the movement continued for some years.

This was not an isolated instance. Such "cargo cults"—and many other movements that have promised the resurrection of the dead, the destruction or enslavement of Europeans, and the coming of utopian riches—have sporadically appeared throughout Melanesia ever since the beginning of this century. Since these cults are widely separated in space and time, their similarities are apparently the result of similarities in social conditions. In these areas the traditional cultures of the indigenous peoples have been uprooted. Europeans, or European-influenced natives, hold all political and economic power. Natives are employed in unloading and distributing Western-made goods, but have no practical knowledge of how to attain these goods. When cold reality offers no hope from the daily frustrations of cultural deterioration and economic deprivation, religion offers the solution.

Revitalization Movements

From the 1890 Ghost Dance of many North American Indians to the Mau Mau of Kenya to the "cargo cults" of Melanesia, extreme and sometimes violent religious reactions to European domination are so common that anthropologists have sought to formulate their underlying causes and general characteristics. Yet **revitalization movements,** as they are now called, are by no means restricted to

Revitalization movements: Social movements, often of a religious nature, with the purpose of totally reforming a society.

In the United States, Mormonism is an example of a revitalization movement that was enormously successful in gaining acceptance in the wider society. By contrast, the Branch Davidians so antagonized elements of "mainstream" society that a confrontation occurred, ending with the mass immolation of many cult members.

the colonial world, and in the United States alone hundreds of such movements have arisen. Among the more widely known are Mormonism, which began in the nineteenth century, the more recent Unification Church of the Reverend Sun Myung Moon, and the Branch Davidians whose "prophet" was David Koresh. As these three examples suggest, revitalization movements show a great deal of diversity, and some have been much more successful than others.

A revitalization movement is a deliberate effort by members of a society to construct a more satisfying culture. The emphasis in this definition is on the reformation not just of the religious sphere of activity, but of the entire cultural system. Such a drastic solution is attempted when a group's anxiety and frustration have become so intense that the only way to reduce the stress is to overturn the entire social system and replace it with a new one.

Anthropologist Anthony Wallace has outlined a sequence common to all expressions of the revitalization process.[16] First is the normal state of society, in which stress is not too great and there exist sufficient cultural means of satisfying needs. Under certain conditions, such as domination by a more powerful group or severe economic depres-

[16]Wallace, A. F. C. (1970). *Culture and personality* (2nd ed.) (pp. 191–196). New York: Random House.

sion, stress and frustration will be steadily amplified; this ushers in the second phase, or the period of increased individual stress. If there are no significant adaptive changes, a period of cultural distortion follows, in which stress becomes so chronic that socially approved methods of releasing tension begin to break down. This steady deterioration of the culture may be checked by a period of revitalization, during which a dynamic cult or religious movement grips a sizable proportion of the population. Often the movement will be so out of touch with reality that it is doomed to failure from the beginning. This was the case with the Ghost Dance, as practiced by the Sioux Indians, which was supposed to make the participants impervious to the bullets of the white men's guns. This was the case also with the Branch Davidians, where the suspicions of government authorities led to an assault on the cult's compound. In reaction, cult members committed mass suicide by deliberately immolating themselves in their headquarters. More rarely, a movement may tap long-dormant adaptive forces underlying a culture, and a long-lasting religion may result. Such was the case with Mormonism. Indeed, revitalization movements lie at the root of all known religions, Judaism, Christianity, and Islam included. We shall return to revitalization movements in Chapter 26.

CHAPTER SUMMARY

Religion is a part of all cultures. It consists of beliefs and behavior patterns by which people try to control the area of the universe that is otherwise beyond their control. Among food-foraging peoples religion is a basic ingredient of everyday life. As societies become more complex, religion is less a part of daily activities and tends to be restricted to particular occasions.

Religion is characterized by a belief in supernatural beings and forces. Through prayer, sacrifice, and other religious rituals, people appeal to the supernatural world for aid. Supernatural beings may be grouped into three categories: major deities (gods and goddesses), ancestral spirits, and other sorts of spirit beings. Gods and goddesses are the great but remote beings. They are usually thought of as controlling the universe or a specific part of it. Whether people recognize gods, goddesses, or both has to do with how men and women relate to one another in everyday life. Animism is a belief in spirit beings other than ancestors who are believed to animate all of nature. These spirit beings are closer to humans than gods and goddesses and are intimately concerned with human activities. Animism is typical of peoples who see themselves as a part of nature rather than as superior to it. A belief in ancestral spirits is based on the idea that human beings are made up of a body and soul. At death the spirit is freed from the body and continues to participate in human affairs. Belief in ancestral spirits is particularly characteristic of descent-based groups with their associated ancestor orientation. Animatism may be found with animism in the same culture. Animatism is a force or power directed to a successful outcome, which may make itself manifest in any object.

Beliefs in supernatural beings and powers are maintained, first, through what are interpreted as manifestations of power. Second, they are perpetuated because supernatural beings possess attributes with which people are familiar. Finally, myths serve to rationalize religious beliefs and practices.

All human societies have specialists—priests and priestesses and/or shamans—to guide religious practices and to intervene with the supernatural world. Shamanism, with its often dramatic ritual, promotes a release of tension among individuals in a society. The shaman provides a focal point of attention for society and can help maintain social control. The benefits of shamanism for the shaman are prestige, sometimes wealth, and an outlet for artistic self-expression.

Religious rituals are religion in action. Through ritual acts, social bonds are reinforced. Times of life crises are occasions for ritual. Arnold Van Gennep divided such rites of passage into rites of separation, transition, and incorporation. Rites of intensification are rituals to mark occasions of crisis in the life of the group rather than the individual. They serve to unite people, allay fear of the crisis, and prompt collective action. Funerary ceremonies are rites of intensification that provide for social readjustment after the loss of the deceased. Rites of intensification may also involve annual ceremonies to seek favorable conditions surrounding such critical activities as planting and harvesting.

Ritual practices of peasant and non-Western peoples are often an expression of the belief that supernatural powers can be made to act in certain ways through the use of certain prescribed formulas. This is the classic anthropological notion of magic. Sir James Frazer differentiated two principles of magic—"like produces like," or imitative magic, and the law of contagion.

Witchcraft functions as an effective way for people to explain away personal misfortune without having to shoulder any of the blame themselves. Even malevolent witchcraft may function positively in the realm of social control. It may also provide an outlet for feelings of hostility and frustration without disturbing the norms of the larger group.

Religion (including magic and witchcraft) serves several important social functions. First, it sanctions a wide range of conduct by providing notions of right and wrong. Second, it sets precedents for acceptable behavior and helps perpetuate an existing social order. Third, religion serves to lift the burden of decision making from individuals and places responsibility with the gods. Fourth, religion plays a large role in maintaining social solidarity. Finally, religion serves education. Ritual ceremonies enhance learning of tribal lore and so help ensure the perpetuation of a nonliterate culture.

Domination by Western society has been the cause of certain religious manifestations in non-Western societies. In the islands of Melanesia, cargo cults have appeared spontaneously at different times since the beginning of the century. Anthony Wallace has interpreted religious reformations as revitalization movements in which an attempt is made, sometimes successfully, to change the society. He argues that all religions stem from revitalization movements.

SUGGESTED READINGS

Kalwet, H. (1988). *Dreamtime and inner space: The world of the shaman*. New York: Random House.

Written by an ethnopsychologist, this book surveys the practices and paranormal experiences of healers and shamans from Africa, the Americas, Asia, and Australia.

Lehmann, A. C., & Myers, J. E. (Eds.) (1993). *Magic, witchcraft and religion: An anthropological study of the supernatural* (3rd ed.). Mountain View, CA: Mayfield.

An anthology of readings, cross-cultural in scope, and covering traditional as well as nontraditional themes. Well represented are both "tribal" and "modern" religions. A good way to discover the relevance and vitality of anthropological approaches to the supernatural.

Malinowski, B. (1954). *Magic, science and religion, and other essays*. Garden City, NY: Doubleday.

The articles collected here provide a discussion of the Trobriand Islanders as illustrative of conceptual and theoretical knowledge of humankind. The author covers such diversified topics as religion, life, death, character of "primitive" cults, magic, faith, and myth.

Norbeck, E. (1974). *Religion in human life: Anthropological views*. New York: Holt, Rinehart and Winston.

The author presents a comprehensive view of religion based on twin themes: the description of religious events, rituals, and states of mind and the nature of anthropological aims, views, procedures, and interpretations.

Wallace, A. F. C. (1966). *Religion: An anthropological view*. New York: Random House.

This is a classic textbook treatment of religion by an anthropologist who has specialized in the study of revitalization movements.

CHAPTER
25
THE ARTS

NO KNOWN HUMAN CULTURE IS WITHOUT SOME FORM OF ART, EVEN
THOUGH THAT ART MAY BE APPLIED TO PURELY UTILITARIAN OBJECTS.
SNEAKER ART, HERE BEING DISPLAYED IN CHICAGO, IS ONE EXPRESSION
OF THE UNIVERSAL URGE FOR ARTISTIC CREATION.

CHAPTER PREVIEW

What Is Art?

Art is the creative use of the human imagination to interpret, understand, and enjoy life. Although the idea of art serving nonuseful, nonpractical purposes seems firmly entrenched in the thinking of modern Western peoples, in other cultures art often serves what are regarded as important, practical purposes.

Why Do Anthropologists Study Art?

Anthropologists have found that art reflects the cultural values and concerns of a people. This is especially true of the verbal arts—myths, legends, and tales. From these the anthropologist may learn how a people order their universe, and may discover much about a people's history as well. Also, music and the visual arts may provide insights into a people's worldview and, through distributional studies, may suggest things about a people's history.

What Are the Functions of the Arts?

Aside from adding enjoyment to everyday life, the various arts serve a number of functions. Myths, for example, set standards for orderly behavior, and the verbal arts generally transmit and preserve a culture's customs and values. Songs, too, may do this, within the restrictions imposed by musical form. And any form of art, to the degree that it is characteristic of a particular society, may contribute to the cohesiveness or solidarity of that society.

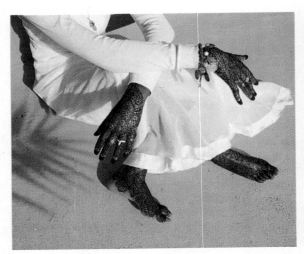

Perhaps the oldest means of artistic expression is body decoration. Shown here is a Moroccan woman whose hands and feet are dyed with henna (to celebrate a royal wedding) and a tattooed Asian man.

In the United States, the arts are often seen as something of a frill, something to be engaged in apart from more productive pursuits for one's personal enjoyment, to provide pleasure for others, or both. This attitude becomes apparent whenever public funds are in short supply; on the local level, for example, in battles over school budgets, art programs are often the first to be cut. Unlike sports, which usually are supported over the arts because they are perceived as providing skills thought to be essential to success in a competitive world, the arts are seen as nonessential, pleasurable, and worthwhile, but expensive and with little practical payoff. On the national level, fiscal conservatives labor to cut back funds for the arts, on the premise that they lack the practical importance of defense, economic, or other governmental activities. Indeed, artists and their supporters are seen as something of an elite, subsidized at the expense of hard-working "practical" people. Yet one might ask: Why in recent years has the National Endowment for the Arts so often been the center of such hot political controversy? If art really is such an unimportant, diversionary activity, why has so much legislative time and energy been devoted to often bitter fights to impose controls on the kinds of work in which artists may engage?

The fact is that artistic behavior is far from unimportant and is as basic to human beings as talking. Just as speech is used to communicate feelings, to make statements so, too, is artistic expression. Moreover, it is not just a special category of persons called "artists" who do this; for example, all human beings adorn their bodies in certain ways and in so doing, make a statement about who they are, both as individuals and members of social groups of various sorts. Similarly, all people tell stories, in which they express their values, their hopes, and their concerns and which reveal much about themselves and the nature of the world as they see it. In short, all peoples engage in artistic behavior, as they use their imagination creatively to interpret, understand, and even enjoy life. Far from being a luxury to be afforded or appreciated by a minority of aesthetes or escapists, art is a necessary kind of social behavior in which every normal and active human being participates.

The idea of art serving nonuseful, nonpractical purposes seems firmly entrenched in the thinking of modern Western peoples. Today, for example, the objects from the tomb of the young Egyptian king Tut-ankh-amen are on display in a museum, where they may be seen and admired as the exquisite works of art they are. They were made, however, to be hidden away from human eyes, where they were to guarantee the eternal life of the king and protect him from evil forces that might enter his body and gain control over it. Or, we may listen to the singing of a sea chantey purely for aesthetic pleasure, as a form of entertainment.

Much of the world's art is created for functional rather than aesthetic purposes. Shown here are examples of art to be used to cure sickness (a Navajo sand painting), to express cultural identity (the Mardi Gras costume of one of New Orleans' "Black Indians"), and for political purposes (graffiti from Katatura, Namibia).

In fact, in the days of sail, sea chanteys served very useful and practical purposes. They set the appropriate rhythm for the performance of specific shipboard tasks, and the same qualities that make them pleasurable to listen to today served to relieve the boredom of those tasks. Such links between art and other aspects are common in human societies around the world. Because art, like any aspect of culture, is inextricably intertwined with everything else that people do, it affords us glimpses into other aspects of peoples' lives, including their values and worldview.

To people today, the making of exquisite objects of gold and precious stones to place in a tomb might seem like throwing them away. Yet, something of the same sort happens when a Navajo Indian creates an intricate sand painting as part of

a ritual act, only to destroy it once the ritual is over. Johann Sebastian Bach was doing the very same thing when, almost 300 years ago, he composed his cantatas to be used in church services. These were "throw away" music, to be discarded after the services for which they were written. That many of them are still performed today is something of an accident, for Bach was not composing them for posterity. In many human societies the "doing" of art is often of greater importance than the final product itself.

Whether a particular work of art is intended to be appreciated purely as such or to serve some practical purpose, as in the examples just noted, it will in every case require the same special combination of the symbolic representation of form and the expression of feeling that constitutes the creative imagination. Insofar as the creative use of the human ability to symbolize is universal and both expresses and is shaped by cultural values and concerns, it is an important subject for anthropological study.

As an activity or kind of behavior that contributes to well-being and helps give shape and significance to life, art must be at the same time related to, yet differentiated from, religion. The dividing line between the two is not distinct: It is not easy to say, for example, precisely where art stops and religion begins in an elaborate ceremony involving ornamentation, masks, costumes, songs, dances, and effigies. And like magic, music, dance, and other arts may be used as a form of "enchantment" to exploit the innate or psychological biases of some other person or group so as to cause them to perceive social reality in a way favorable to the interests of the "enchanter." Indeed, the arts may be used to manipulate a seemingly inexhaustible list of human passions, including desire, terror, wonder, cupidity, fantasy, and vanity.[1]

Although the distinction is not always easy to make, one is often made between secular and religious art. In what is called purely secular art, whether it is light or serious, our imaginations are free to roam without any ulterior motives—creating and recreating patterns, plots, rhythms, and feelings at leisure and without any thought of consequence or aftermath. In religious art, on the other hand, the imagination is working still, but the whole activity is somehow aimed at assuring our well-being through manipulation and acknowledgment of forces beyond ourselves. At any rate, whether categorized as secular or religious, art of all varieties can be expected to reflect the values and concerns of the people who create and enjoy it; the nature of the things reflected and expressed in art is the concern of the anthropologist.

THE ANTHROPOLOGICAL STUDY OF ART

In approaching art as a cultural phenomenon, the anthropologist has the pleasant task of cataloguing, photographing, recording, and describing all

---

[1]Gell, A. (1988). Technology and magic. *Anthropology Today,* *4*(2), 7.

possible forms of imaginative activity in any particular culture. There is an enormous variety of forms and modes of artistic expression in the world. Because people everywhere continue to create and develop in new directions, there is no foreseeable point of diminishing returns in the interesting process of collecting and describing the world's ornaments, body decorations, variations in clothing, blanket, and rug designs, pottery and basket styles, architectural embellishments, monuments, ceremonial masks, legends, work songs, dances, and other art forms. The process of collecting, however, must eventually lead to some kind of analysis and generalizations about relationships between art and the rest of culture.

A good way to begin a study of this problem of the relationships between art and culture is to examine critically some of the generalizations that have already been made about specific arts. Since it is impossible to cover all forms of art in the space of a single chapter, we shall concentrate on just a few: verbal arts, music, and pictorial art. We shall start with the verbal arts, for we have already touched upon them in our earlier discussions of religion (Chapter 24) and worldview (Chapters 16 and 23).

VERBAL ARTS

The term **folklore** was coined in the nineteenth century to denote the unwritten stories, beliefs, and customs of European peasantry, as opposed to the traditions of the literate elite. The subsequent study of folklore, **folkloristics,** has become a discipline allied to but somewhat independent of anthropology, working on cross-cultural comparisons of themes, motifs, and structures, from a literary as well as ethnological point of view. Many linguists

---

Folklore: A nineteenth-century term first used to refer to the traditional oral stories and sayings of the European peasant and later extended to those traditions preserved orally in all societies.

Folkloristics: The study of folklore (as linguistics is the study of language).

and anthropologists prefer to speak of the oral traditions and verbal arts of a culture rather than its folklore and folktales, recognizing that creative verbal expression takes many forms and that the implied distinction between folk and "fine" art is a projection of the attitude of European (and European-derived) cultures onto others.

The verbal arts include narrative, drama, poetry, incantations, proverbs, riddles, word games, and even naming procedures, compliments, and insults, when these take structured and special forms. The narrative seems to be one of the easiest kinds of verbal arts to record or collect. Perhaps because it is also the most publishable, with popular appeal in North American culture, it has received the most study and attention. Generally, narratives have been divided into three basic and recurring categories: myth, legend, and tale.

Myth

The word *myth*, in popular usage, refers to something that is widely believed to be true, but probably is not. Actually, a true **myth** is basically

religious, in that it provides a rationale for religious beliefs and practices. Its subject matter is the ultimates of human existence: where we and the things in our world came from, why we are here, and where we are going. As was noted in Chapter 24, the myth has an explanatory function: It depicts and describes an orderly universe, which sets the stage for orderly behavior. Below is a typical origin myth traditional with the Western Abenaki of northwestern New England and southern Quebec.

In the beginning, *Tabaldak*, "The Owner," created all living things but one—the spirit being who was to accomplish the final transformation of the earth. Man and woman *Tabaldak* made out of a piece of stone, but he did not like the result, their hearts being cold and hard. This being so, he broke them up and tried again, this time using living wood, and from them came all later Abenakis. Like

Myth: A sacred narrative explaining how the world came to be in its present form.

Among the Inuit, the artist does not impose his or her will on the medium, but rather seeks to help what is already there to emerge from hiding.

the trees from which the wood came, these people were rooted in the earth and (like trees when being blown by the wind) could dance gracefully. The one living thing not created by *Tabaldak* was *Odziózo*, "He Makes Himself from Something." This being seems to have created himself out of dust, but since he was more transformer than creator, he was not able to accomplish it all at once. At first, he managed only his head, body, and arms; the legs came later, growing slowly as legs do on a tadpole. Not waiting until his legs were grown, he set out to change the shape of the earth. He dragged his body about with his hands, gouging channels that became the rivers. To make the mountains, he piled dirt up with his hands. Once his legs grew, *Odziózo's* task was made easier; by merely extending his legs, he made the tributaries of the main streams.

Anthropologist Gordon Day has described *Odziózo's* last act of landscape transformation as follows:

> It was *Odziózo* who laid out the river channels and lake basins and shaped the hills and mountains. Just how long he took is a subject which Abenakis, only recently deceased, used to discuss over their campfires. At last he was finished, and like Jehovah in Genesis, he surveyed his handiwork and found it was good. The last work he made was Lake Champlain and this he found especially good. It was his masterpiece. He liked it so much that he climbed onto a rock in Burlington Bay and changed himself into stone so that he could better sit there and enjoy the spectacle through the ages. He still likes it, because he is still there and used to be given offerings of tobacco as long as Abenakis went this way by canoe, a practice which continued until about 1940. The rock is also called *Odziózo*, since it is the Transformer himself.[2]

Such a myth, insofar as it is believed, accepted, and perpetuated in a culture, may be said to express a part of the worldview of a people: the unexpressed but implicit conceptions of their place in nature

and of the limits and workings of their world. (This concept we discussed in Chapters 16 and 23.) Extrapolating from the details of the Abenaki myth, we might arrive at the conclusion that these people recognized a kinship among all living things; after all, they were all part of the same creation, and humans were even made from living wood. Moreover, an attempt to make them of nonliving stone was not satisfactory. This idea of a closeness between all living things led the Abenaki to show special respect to the animals that they hunted in order to sustain their own lives. For example, when one killed a beaver, muskrat, or waterfowl, one could not unceremoniously toss the bones into the nearest garbage pit. Proper respect demanded that the bones be returned to the water, with a request that their kind be continued. Similarly, before eating meat, an offering of grease was placed on the fire to thank *Tabaldak*. More generally, waste was to be avoided, so as not to offend the animals. Failure to respect the rights of the animals would result in their no longer being willing to sacrifice their lives so that people might live.

In transforming himself into stone in order to enjoy his work for all eternity, *Odziózo* may be seen as setting an example for people: They should see the beauty in things as they are and not seek to alter what is already good. To question the goodness of existing reality would be to call into question the judgment of an important deity. It is characteristic of an explanatory myth, such as this one, that the unknown will be simplified and explained in terms of the known. This myth accounts in terms of human experience for the existence of rivers, mountains, lakes, and other features of the landscape, as well as for humans and all other living things. It also serves to sanction particular attitudes and behaviors. It is a product of creative imagination, and it is a work of art, as well as a potentially religious statement.

One aspect of mythology that has attracted a good deal of interest over the years is the similarity of certain themes in the stories of peoples living in separate parts of the world. One of these themes is the myth of matriarchy, or one-time rule by women. In a number of societies, stories tell about a time when women ruled over men. Eventually, so these stories go, men were forced to rise up and assert their dominance over women in order to combat their tyranny or incompetence (or both). In the

[2]Day, G. M. (1994). Quoted in W. A. Haviland & M. W. Power (Eds.), *The original Vermonters: Native inhabitants, past and present* (rev. and exp. ed.) (p. 193). Hanover, NH: University Press of New England.

To Native American peoples, the earth is viewed as the source of all life, a concept reflected in this picture by Hopi artist Waldo Nootzka. In it, corn—the fruit of the earth—represents fertility.

nineteenth century, a number of eminent scholars interpreted such myths as evidence for an early stage of matriarchy in the evolution of human culture, an idea that has recently been revived by some feminists. Although a number of societies are known in which the two sexes relate to one another as equals (Western Abenaki society was one), never have anthropologists found one in which women rule over or dominate men. The interesting thing about myths of matriarchy is that they are generally found in societies in which men dominate women, while at the same time the latter have considerable autonomy.[3] Under such conditions, male dominance is insecure, and a rationale is needed to justify it. Thus, myths of men overthrowing women

and taking control mirror an existing paradoxical relationship between the two sexes.

The analysis and interpretation of myths has been carried to great lengths, becoming a field of study almost unto itself. It is certain that myth making is an extremely important kind of human creativity, and the study of the myth-making process and its results can give some valuable clues to the way people perceive and think about their world. The dangers and problems of interpretation, however, are great. Several questions arise. Are myths literally believed or perhaps accepted symbolically or emotionally as a different kind of truth? To what extent do myths actually determine or reflect human behavior? Can an outsider discover the meaning that a myth has in its own culture? How do we account for contradictory myths in the same culture? New myths arise and old ones die. Is it then the content or the structure of the myth that is important? All of these questions deserve, and are currently receiving, serious consideration.

Legend

Less problematical, but perhaps more complex than myth, is the legend. **Legends** are stories told as true, set in the post-creation world. An example of a modern urban legend in the United States is one often told by President Ronald Reagan, about an African-American woman on welfare in Chicago. Supposedly, her ability to collect something like 103 welfare checks under different names enabled her to live lavishly. Although proven to be false, the story was told as if true (by the President even after he was informed that it was not true), as all legends are. This particular legend illustrates a number of features all such narratives share: They cannot be attributed to any known author, they always exist in multiple versions, but in spite of variation, they are told with sufficient detail to be plausible, and they tell us

[3]Sanday, P. R. (1981). *Female power and male dominance: On the origins of sexual inequality* (p. 181). Cambridge: Cambridge University Press.

Legends: Stories told as true, set in the post-creation world.

something about the societies in which they are found. In this case, we learn something about the existence of racism in U.S. society (the story is told by whites, who identify the woman as an African American), social policy (the existence of government policies to help the poor), and attitudes towards the poor (distrust, if not dislike).

As this illustration shows, legends (no more than myths) are not confined to nonliterate, nonindustrialized societies. Commonly, legends consist of pseudo-historical narratives that account for the deeds of heroes, the movements of peoples, and the establishment of local customs, typically with a mixture of realism and the supernatural or extraordinary. As stories, they are not necessarily believed or disbelieved, but they usually serve to entertain as well as to instruct and to inspire or bolster pride in family, tribe, or nation.

To a degree, in literate states such as the United States, the function of legends has been taken over by history. Yet much of what passes for history, to paraphrase one historian, consists of the legends we develop to make ourselves feel better about who we are.[4] The trouble is that history does not always tell people what they want to hear about themselves or, conversely, it tells them things that they would prefer not to hear. By projecting their culture's hopes and expectations onto the record of the past, they seize upon and even exaggerate some past events, while ignoring or giving scant attention to others. Although this often takes place unconsciously, so strong is the motivation to transform history into legend that states have often gone so far as to deliberately rewrite it, as when the Aztecs in the reign of their fifteenth-century king Itzcoatl rewrote their history in a way befitting their position of dominance in ancient Mexico. An example from the colonial past of the United States may be seen in the deliberate "slanting" (and in some cases destruction) of written documents by the Puritan authorities of colonial New England, so that their policies toward Indians might be seen in the most favorable light.[5] In modern times, the Soviet Union was particularly well-known for similar practices. Historians, in their attempts to separate fact from fiction, frequently incur the wrath

of people who will not willingly abandon what they wish to believe is true, whether or not it really is.

Long legends, sometimes in poetry or in rhythmic prose, are known as **epics.** In parts of West and Central Africa there are remarkably elaborate and formalized recitations of extremely long legends, lasting several hours, and even days. These long narratives have been described as veritable encyclopedias of the most diverse aspects of a culture, with direct and indirect statements about history, institutions, relationships, values, and ideas. Epics are typically found in nonliterate societies with a form of state political organization; they serve to transmit and preserve a culture's legal and political precedents and practices. The Mwindo epic of the Nyanga people, the Lianja epic of the Mongo, and the Kambili epic of the Mande, for example, have been the subject of extensive and rewarding study by French, British, and American anthropologists in the last several years.

Legends may incorporate mythological details, especially when they make appeal to the supernatural, and are therefore not always clearly distinct from myth. The legend about Mwindo follows him through the earth, the atmosphere, the underworld, and the remote sky, and gives a complete picture of the Nyanga people's view of the organization and limits of the world. Legends may also incorporate proverbs and incidental tales and thus be related to other forms of verbal art as well. A recitation of the legend of Kambili, for example, has been said to include as many as 150 proverbs.

Below is an example of a short legend that instructs, traditional with the Western Abenakis of northwestern New England and southern Quebec.

This is a story of a lonesome little boy who used to wander down to the riverbank at Odanak or downhill toward the two swamps. He used to hear someone call his name but when he got to the swamp pond, there was no one to be seen or heard. But when he went back, he heard his name

Epics: Long oral narratives, sometimes in poetry or rhythmic prose, recounting the glorious events in the life of a real or legendary person.

[4]Stoler, M. (1982). To tell the truth. *Vermont Visions, 82*(3), 3.
[5]Jennings, F. (1976). *The invasion of America* (p. 182). New York: Norton.

The telling of legends and tales is no less important in the education of children in the United States than it is on the Ivory Coast of Africa.

called again. As he was sitting by the marshy bank waiting, an old man came and asked him why he was waiting. When the boy told him, the old man said that the same thing happened long ago. What he heard was the Swamp Creature and pointed out the big tussocks of grass where it hid; having called out it would sink down behind them. The old man said: "It just wants to drown you. If you go out there you will sink in the mud. You better go home!"[6]

The moral of this story is quite simple: Swamps are dangerous places; stay away from them. When told well, the story is a lot more effective in keeping children away from swamps than just telling them, "Don't go near swamps."

For the anthropologist a major significance of the secular and apparently realistic portions of legends, whether long or short, is in the clues they provide to what constitutes approved or model ethical behavior in a culture. The subject matter of legends is essentially problem solving, and the content is likely to include combat, warfare, confrontations, and physical and psychological trials of many kinds. Certain questions may be answered explicitly or implicitly. Does the culture justify homicide? What kinds of behavior are considered to be brave or cowardly? What is the etiquette of combat or warfare? Is there a concept of altruism

or self-sacrifice? Here again, however, there are pitfalls in the process of interpreting art in relation to life. It is always possible that certain kinds of behavior are acceptable or even admirable, with the distance or objectivity afforded by art, but are not at all so approved in daily life. In European-American culture, murderers, charlatans, and rakes have sometimes become popular "heroes" and the subjects of legends; North Americans would object, however, to the inference of an outsider that they necessarily approved or wanted to emulate the morality of Billy the Kid or Jesse James.

Tale

The term **tale** is a nonspecific label for a third category of creative narratives, those that are purely secular, nonhistorical, and recognized as fiction for entertainment, though they may draw a moral or teach a practical lesson, as well. Consider this brief summary of a tale from Ghana, known as "Father, Son, and Donkey":

A father and his son farmed their corn, sold it, and spent part of the profit on a

[6]Day, G. M. (1972). Quoted in the film *Prehistoric life in the Champlain Valley*, by Thomas C. Vogelman and others. Burlington, VT: Department of Anthropology, University of Vermont.

Tale: A creative narrative recognized as fiction for entertainment.

donkey. When the hot season came, they harvested their yams and prepared to take them to storage, using their donkey. The father mounted the donkey and they all three proceeded on their way until they met some people. "What? You lazy man!" the people said to the father. "You let your young son walk barefoot on this hot ground while you ride on a donkey? For shame!" The father yielded his place to the son, and they proceeded until they came to an old woman. "What? You useless boy!" said the old woman. "You ride on the donkey and let your poor father walk barefoot on this hot ground? For shame!" The son dismounted, and both father and son walked on the road, leading the donkey behind them until they came to an old man. "What? You foolish people!" said the old man. "You have a donkey and you walk barefoot on the hot ground instead of riding?" And so it goes. Listen: When you are doing something and other people come along, just keep on doing what you like.

This is precisely the kind of tale that is of special interest in traditional folklore studies. It is an internationally popular "numbskull" tale; versions of it have been recorded in India, the Middle East, the Balkans, Italy, Spain, England, and the United States, as well as in West Africa. It is classified or catalogued as exhibiting a basic **motif** or story situation—father and son trying to please everyone—one of the many thousands that have been found to recur in world folktales. In spite of variations in detail, every version will be found to have about the same basic structure in the sequence of events, sometimes called the syntax of the tale; a peasant father and son work together, a beast of burden is purchased, the three set out on a short excursion, the father rides and is criticized, the son rides and is criticized, both walk and are criticized, and a conclusion is drawn.

Motif: A story situation in a folktale.

Tales of this sort with an international distribution sometimes raise more problems than they solve: Which one is the original? What is the path of its diffusion? Could it be sheer coincidence that different cultures have come up with the same motif and syntax, or could it be a case of independent invention with similar tales developing in similar situations in response to like causes? A surprisingly large number of motifs in European and African tales are traceable to ancient sources in India. Is this good evidence of a spread of culture from a "cradle" of civilization, or is it an example of diffusion of tales in contiguous areas? There are, of course, purely local tales, as well as tales with a wide distribution. Within any particular culture it will probably be found possible to categorize local types of tales: animal, human experience, trickster, dilemma, ghost, moral, scatological, nonsense, and so on. In West Africa there is a remarkable prevalence of animal stories, for example, with such creatures as the spider, the rabbit, and the hyena as the protagonists. Many were carried to the slave-holding areas of the Americas; the Uncle Remus stories about Br'er Rabbit, Br'er Fox, and other animals may be a survival of this tradition.

The significance of tales for the anthropologist rests partly in this matter of their distribution. They provide evidence for either cultural contacts or cultural isolation, and for limits of influence and cultural cohesion. It has been debated for decades now, for example, to what extent the culture of West Africa was transmitted to the southeast United States. So far as folktales are concerned, one school of folklorists has always found and insisted on European origins; another school, somewhat more recently, points to African prototypes. The anthropologist is interested, however, in more than these questions of distribution. Like legends, tales very often illustrate local solutions to universal human ethical problems, and in some sense they state a moral philosophy. The anthropologist sees that whether the tale of the father, the son, and the donkey originated in West Africa or arrived there from Europe or the Middle East, the very fact that it is told in West Africa suggests that it states something valid for that culture. The tale's lesson of a necessary degree of self-confidence in the face of arbitrary social criticism

The "little songs" of the Awlad 'Ali Bedouins punctuate conversations carried out while performing everyday chores, like making bread, as these young women are doing. Through these "little songs," they are able to express what otherwise are taboo topics.

is therefore something that can be read into the culture's values and beliefs.

Other Verbal Arts

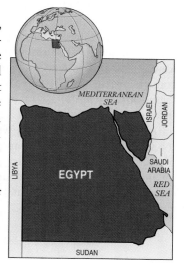

Myths, legends, and tales, prominent as they are in anthropological studies, turn out to be no more important than the other verbal arts in many cultures. In the culture of the Awlad 'Ali Bedouins of Egypt's western desert, for example, poetry is a lively and active verbal art, especially as a vehicle for personal expression and private communication. Among these people, there are two forms of poetry, one being the elaborately structured and heroic poems chanted or recited by men only on ceremonial occasions and in specific public contexts. The other is the *ghinnáwa*, or "little songs" that punctuate everyday conversations. Simple in structure, these deal with personal matters and feelings more appropriate to informal social situations and are regarded by older men as the unimportant productions of women and youths. In spite of this official devaluation in the male-dominated society of the Bedouins, however, they play a vital part in people's daily lives. In their "little songs" individuals are shielded from the consequences of making statements and expressing sentiments that contravene the moral system. Paradoxically, in sharing these "immoral" sentiments only with intimates and veiling them in impersonal traditional formulas, those who recite them demonstrate that they have a certain control, which actually enhances their moral standing.

As is often true of folklore in general, the "little songs" of the Awlad 'Ali provide a sanctioned outlet for thoughts or opinions that are otherwise taboo. Disaster jokes are an example of this in contemporary North American society. As anthropologist Lila Abu-Lughod points out:

> What may be peculiar to Awlad ʻAli is that their discourse of rebellion is both culturally elaborated and sanctioned. Although poetry refers to personal life, it is not individual, spontaneous, idiosyncratic, or unofficial but public, conventional, and formulaic—a highly developed art. More important, this poetic discourse of defiance is not condemned, or even just tolerated, as well it might be given all the constraints of time and place and form that bind it. Poetry is a privileged discourse in Awlad ʻAli society. Like other Arabs, and perhaps like many oral cultures, the Bedouins cherish poetry and other verbal arts. . . . They are drawn to *ghinnáwas*, and at the same time they consider them risqué, against religion, and slightly improper. . . . This ambivalence about poetry is significant, and it makes sense only in terms of the cultural meaning of opposition. Because ordinary discourse is informed by the values of honor and modesty, the moral correlates of the ideology that upholds the Awlad ʻAli social and political system, we would expect the antistructural poetic discourse, with its contradictory messages, to be informed by an opposing set of values. This is not the case. Poetry as a discourse of defiance of the system symbolizes freedom—the ultimate value of the system and the essential entailment of the honor code.[7]

In all cultures the words of songs constitute a kind of poetry. Poetry and stories recited with gesture, movement, and props become drama. Drama combined with dance, music, and spectacle becomes a public celebration. The more we look at the individual arts, the clearer it becomes that they are often interrelated and interdependent. The verbal arts are, in fact, simply differing manifestations of the same creative imagination that produces music and the other arts.

THE ART OF MUSIC

The study of music in specific cultural settings, beginning in the nineteenth century with the collection of folksongs, has developed into a specialized field, called **ethnomusicology.** Like the study of folktales for their own sake, ethnomusicology is at the same time related to and somewhat independent of anthropology. Nevertheless, it is possible to sort out from the various concerns of the field several concepts that are of interest in general anthropology.

In order to talk intelligently about the verbal arts of a culture, it is, of course, desirable to know as much as possible about the language itself. In order to talk about the music of a culture, it is equally desirable to know the language of music—that is, its conventions. The way to approach a totally unfamiliar kind of musical expression is to learn first how it functions in respect to melody, rhythm, and form.

In general, human music is said to differ from natural music—the songs of birds, wolves, and whales, for example—in being almost everywhere perceived in terms of a repertory of tones at fixed or regular intervals from each other: in other words, a scale. We have made closed systems out of a formless range of possible sounds by dividing the distance between a tone and its first overtone or sympathetic vibration (which always has exactly twice as many vibrations as the basic tone) into a series of measured steps. In the Western or European system, the distance between the basic tone and the first overtone is called the octave; it consists of seven steps—five "whole" tones and two "semitones"—which are named with the letters A through G. The whole tones are further divided into semitones, for a total working scale of 12 tones. Westerners learn at an early age to recognize and imitate this arbitrary system and its conventions, and it comes to sound natural. Yet the overtone series, on which it is partially based, is

Ethnomusicology: The study of a society's music in terms of its cultural setting.

[7]Abu-Lughod, L. (1986). *Veiled sentiments* (pp. 248–252). Berkeley, CA: University of California Press.

the only part of it that can be considered a wholly natural phenomenon.

One of the most common alternatives to the semitonal system is the pentatonic system, which divides the octave into five nearly equidistant tones. In Japan there is a series of different pentatonic scales, in which some semitones are employed. In Java there are scales of both five and seven equal steps, which have no relation to the intervals Europeans and European Americans hear as "natural" in their system. In Arabic and Persian music there are smaller units of a third of a tone (some of which Westerners may accidentally produce on an "out-of-tune" piano), with scales of 17 and 24 steps in the octave. There are even quarter-tone scales in India and subtleties of interval shading that are nearly indistinguishable to a Western ear. Small wonder, then, that even when Westerners can hear what sounds like melody and rhythm in these systems, the total result may sound peculiar to them, or out of tune. The anthropologist needs a very practiced ear to learn to appreciate—perhaps even to tolerate—some of the music heard, and only some of the most skilled folksong collectors have attempted to notate and analyze the music of nonsemitonal systems.

Scale systems and their modifications comprise what is known as **tonality** in music. Tonality determines the possibilities and limits of both melody and harmony. Not much less complex than tonality is the matter of rhythm. Rhythm, whether regular or irregular, is an organizing factor in music, sometimes more important than the melodic line. Traditional European music is rather neatly measured into recurrent patterns of two, three, and four beats, with combinations of weak and strong beats to mark the division and form patterns. Non-European music is likely to move also in patterns of five, seven, or eleven, with complex arrangements of internal beats and sometimes polyrhythms: one instrument or singer going in a pattern of three beats, for example, while another is in a pattern of five or seven. Polyrhythms are

This man carries a West African talking drum under his elbow. Such drums "talk" by copying the distinctive speech patterns of West African languages, which are tonal.

Tonality: In music, scale systems and their modifications.

frequent in the drum music of West Africa, which shows remarkable precision in the overlapping of rhythmic lines. In addition to polyrhythms, non-European music may also contain shifting rhythms: a pattern of three, for example, followed by a pattern of two, or five, with little or no regular recurrence or repetition of any one pattern, though the patterns themselves are fixed and identifiable as units.

Although it is not necessarily the concern of anthropologists to untangle all these complicated technical matters, they will want to know enough to be aware of the degree of skill or artistry involved in a performance and to have some measure of the extent to which people in a culture have learned to practice and respond to this often

To shamans, drums are often more than musical instruments. In many societies, they are a means of communicating with the spirit world, while at the same time helping to induce trance.

important creative activity. Moreover, as with myths, legends, and tales, the distribution of musical forms and instruments can reveal much about cultural contact or isolation.

Functions of Music

Even without concern for technical matters, the anthropologist can profitably investigate the function of music in a society. First, rarely has a culture been reported to be without any kind of music. Bone flutes and whistles as much as 30,000 years old have been found by archaeologists. Nor have historically known food-foraging peoples been without their music. In the Kalahari Desert, for example, a Ju/'hoansi hunter off by himself would play a tune for himself on his bow simply to help while away the time (long before anyone thought of beating swords into plowshares some genius discovered—when and where we do not know—that bows could be used not just to kill, but to make music as well). In northern New England

Abenaki shamans used cedar flutes to call game, lure enemies, and attract women. In addition, a drum over which two rawhide strings were stretched to produce a buzzing sound, thought to represent singing, gave the shaman the power to communicate with the spirit world. But however played and for whatever reason, music (like all art) is an individual creative skill that one can cultivate and be proud of, whether from a sense of accomplishment or the sheer pleasure of performing; and it is a form of social behavior through which there is a communication or sharing of feelings and life experience with other humans. At the same time, because the individual's creativity is constrained by the traditions of his or her particular culture, each society's art is distinctive and helps to define its members' sense of identity.

The social function of music is perhaps most obvious in song. Songs very often express as much as tales the values and concerns of the group, but they do so with the increased formalism that results from the restrictions of closed systems of tonality, rhythm, and musical form. Early investigators of

Anthropology Applied
PROTECTING CULTURAL HERITAGES

In these last years of the twentieth century, the time is long past when the anthropologist could go out and describe small tribal groups in out-of-the-way places that had not been "contaminated" by contact with Westerners. Not only are there few such groups in the world today, but those that do remain face strong pressures to abandon their traditional ways in the name of "progress." All too often, tribal peoples are made to forfeit their indigenous identity and are pressed into a mold that allows them neither the opportunity nor the motivation to rise above the lowest rung of the social ladder. From an autonomous people able to provide for their own needs, with pride and a strong sense of their own identity as a people, they are transformed into a deprived underclass with neither pride nor a sense of their own identity, often despised by more fortunate members of some multinational state in which they live.

The basic right of groups of people to be themselves and not be deprived of their own distinctive cultural identities is and should be our paramount consideration, and will be dealt with in the final two chapters of this book. There are, however, additional reasons to be concerned about the disappearance of the societies with which anthropologists have been so concerned. For one thing, the need for information about them has become steadily more apparent. If we are ever to have a realistic understanding of that elusive thing called human nature, we need reliable data on all humans. There is more to it than this, though; once a tribal society is gone, it is lost to humanity, unless an adequate record of it exists. When this happens, humanity is the poorer for the loss. Hence, anthropologists have in a sense rescued many such societies from oblivion. This not only helps to preserve the human heritage, it may also be important to an ethnic group that, having become Westernized, wishes to rediscover and reassert its past cultural identity. Better yet, of course, is to find ways to prevent the loss of cultural traditions in the first place.

To the Pomo Indians of California, the art of basketmaking has been important for their sense of

who they are since before the coming of European settlers. Recognized for their skilled techniques and aesthetic artistry, Pomo baskets—some of the finest in the world—are prized by both museums and private collectors alike. Nevertheless, the art of Pomo basketmaking was threatened in the 1970s by the impending construction of the Warm Springs Dam–Lake Sonoma Project to the north of San Francisco. The effect of this project would be to wipe out virtually all existing habitat for a particular species of sedge essential for the weaving of Pomo baskets. Accordingly, a coalition of archaeologists, Native Americans, and others with objections to the project brought suit in federal district court. As it happened, the U.S. Army Corps of Engineers had recently hired anthropologist Richard N. Lerner for its San Francisco District Office to advise on sociocultural factors associated with water resources programs in northwestern California. One of Lerner's first tasks, therefore, was to undertake studies of the problem and to find ways to overcome it.[*]

After comprehensive archaeological, ethnographic, and other studies were completed in 1976, Lerner succeeded in having the Pomo basketry materials recognized by the National Register of Historic Places as "historic property," requiring the corps of engineers to find ways of mitigating the adverse impact dam construction would have. The result was a complex ethnobotanical project, developed and implemented by Lerner. Working in concert with Pomo Indians as well as botanists, 48,000 sedge plants were relocated onto nearly three acres of suitable lands downstream from the dam. By the fall of 1983, the sedge was doing well enough to be harvested, and proved to be of excellent quality. Since this initial harvest, groups of weavers have returned each year, and the art of Pomo Indian basketmaking appears to be safe for the time being.

[*]Lerner, R. N. (1987). Preserving plants for Pomos. In R. M. Wulff & S. J. Fiske (Eds.), *Anthropological praxis: Translating knowledge into action* (pp. 212–222). Boulder, CO: Westview.

non-European song were struck by the apparent simplicity of pentatonic scales and a seemingly endless repetition of phrases. They often did not give sufficient credit to the formal function of repetition

in such music, confusing repetition with lack of invention. A great deal of non-European music was dismissed as "primitive" and formless, and typically treated as trivial.

Repetition is, nevertheless, a fact of music, including European music, and a basic formal principle. Consider this little song from Nigeria:

Ijangbon l'o ra,
Ijangbon l'o ra,
Eni r'asho Oshomalo,
Ijangbon l'o ra,

(He buys trouble,
He buys trouble,
He who buys Oshomalo cloth,
He buys trouble.)

Several decades ago, the Oshomalo were cloth sellers in Egba villages who sold on credit, then harassed, intimidated, and even beat their customers to make them pay before the appointed day. The message of the song is simple, and both words and music are the same for three lines out of four; the whole song may be repeated many times at will. What is it that produces this kind of artistic expression and makes it more than primitive trivia? A single Egba undoubtedly improvised the song first, reacting to a personal experience or observation, lingering on one of its elements by repeating it. The repetition gives the observation not emphasis but symbolic form, and therefore a kind of concreteness or permanence. In this concrete form, made memorable and attractive with melody and rhythm, the song was taken up by other Egba, perhaps with some musical refinements or embellishments from more creative members of the group, including clapping or drumming to mark the rhythm. Thus a bit of social commentary was crystallized and preserved even after the situation had passed into history.

Whether the content of songs is didactic, satirical, inspirational, religious, political, or purely emotional, the important thing is that the formless has been given form, and feelings are communicated in a symbolic and memorable way that can be repeated and shared. The group is consequently united and has the sense that their experience, whatever it may be, has shape and meaning.

PICTORIAL ART

To many Europeans and European-Americans, the first thing that springs to mind in connection with the word *art* is some sort of picture, be it a

This stylized painting on a ceremonial shirt represents a bear. Though the art of the northwest coast Indians often portrays actual animals, they are not depicted in a naturalistic style. To identify them, one must be familiar with the conventions of this art.

painting, drawing, sketch, or whatever. And indeed, in many parts of the world, people have been making pictures in one way or another for a very long time—etching them in bone, engraving them in rock, painting them on cave walls and rock faces, carving and painting them on wood, gourds, pots, or painting them on textiles, bark, bark cloth, animal hide, or even their own bodies. As with musical art, some form of pictorial art is a part of every historically known human culture.

As a type of symbolic expression, pictorial art may be representational, imitating closely the forms of nature—or abstract, drawing from natural forms but representing only their basic patterns or arrangements. Actually, the two categories are not mutually exclusive, for even the most naturalistic portrayal is partly abstract to the extent that it generalizes from nature and abstracts patterns of ideal beauty, ugliness, or typical expressions of emotion. But between the most naturalistic and the most schematic or symbolic abstract art lies a continuum. In some of the art produced by Indians of North America's northwest coast, for example, animal figures may be so highly stylized as to be difficult for an outsider to identify. Although abstract, the artist has drawn on nature, even though he or she has exaggerated and deliberately transformed some of its shapes for the purpose of expressing a particular feeling toward them. Because these exaggerations and transformations are done according to the canons of northwest coast Indian culture, their meanings are understood not just by the artist, but by other members of the community as well.

Southern African Rock Art

The rock art of southern Africa, which has been described and studied in considerable detail, especially over the past three decades, is a rich non-Western tradition that helps illustrate different ways of approaching the study of art. This rock art is one of the world's oldest traditions, extending unbroken from at least 27,000 years ago until a mere 100 years ago. It came to an end only with the destruction of the Bushman people responsible for it, at the hands of European colonizers. Those (like the Ju/'hoansi) who have survived in places like Namibia and Botswana, did not themselves produce rock art, but do share the same general belief system which the rock art expresses.

Bushman rock art consists of both paintings and engravings on the faces of rock outcrops as well as on the walls of rock shelters. Depicted are a variety of animals as well as humans in highly sophisticated ways, sometimes in static poses but often in highly animated scenes. Associated with these figures are a variety of abstract signs including dots, zigzags, nested curves, and the like. Until fairly

recently, the significance of these latter signs was not understood by non-Bushmen; equally puzzling was the frequent presence of new pictures painted or engraved directly over existing ones.

In spite of its puzzling aspects, southern African rock art has long been considered worthy of being looked at and admired. The paintings, especially, are generally seen as being quite beautiful and a source of pleasure to view. Consequently, it is not surprising that the earliest approach to the study of the art was the aesthetic, an approach also well developed in the study of European and other Western art. Thus, the art could be studied for its use of pigments: charcoal and specularite for black; silica, china clay, and gypsum for white; and ferric oxide for red and reddish brown hues. These were mixed with fat, blood, and perhaps water and applied to the rough rock with consummate artistry. The economy of line and the way shading is used to mold the contours of animal bodies elicit admiration, as does the rendering of all sorts of realistic details. One of the more popular animals depicted was the eland, shown with such details as the tuft of red hair on its forehead, the black line running along its back, the darkening of its snout, its cloven hoofs, the folds of skin on its shoulders, and the twist of its horns.

Similar anatomical details are shown for humans, including the details of dress, headgear, and body ornamentation, such as leather bands and ostrich eggshell beads. At the same time, human figures appear more as caricatures of what they are, rather than literal depictions; features such as fatness and thinness may be exaggerated, the figures are sometimes elongated, sometimes in positions suggestive of flying across the rock face. Sometimes, too, the feet take on the appearance of a swallow tail or the tail of a fish. Even more puzzling are figures that appear to be part human–part animal (therianthropes).

Another obvious approach to Bushman rock art, the narrative, focuses on *what* it depicts, supplementing the focus of the aesthetic approach on *how* things are depicted. Certainly, aspects of Bushman life are shown, as in several hunting scenes depicting men with bows, arrows, quivers, and hunting bags. Occasional depictions occur showing nets used in the hunt and fish traps. Women are also shown—identifiable by their primary sexual characteristics

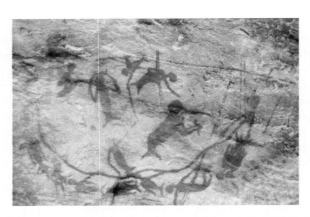

Bushman rock paintings and engravings from southern Africa often depict animals thought to possess great supernatural power. Shamans appear as well: In the painted example at the top, we see rain shamans with swallow tails acting in the spirit realm to protect people from the dangers of storms. Like modern Bushman shamans, several of these hold paired dance sticks. The idea of shamans being transformed into birds, as well as being greatly elongated (note one figure's long, undulating body above the lower row of shamans) is based on sensations experienced in trance. Other undulating lines and dots in the picture are entoptic phenomena.

and the stone-weighted digging sticks they carry, but they are rarely shown gathering food. Considering the importance of food gathered by women in the Bushman diet, this seems rather odd. Of course, it might merely reflect the importance Bushmen attach to the hunt, but the fact is that hunting scenes are not at all common, either. Furthermore, the animals shown in the art are *not* representative of the meat eaten; animals commonly depicted (like the eland) are not eaten. Thus, a narrative approach can lead to a distorted view of Bushman life.

Other scenes portrayed in the art clearly relate to the trance dance, still the most important ritual today among Bushmen (see the Original Study in Chapter 24). This is clearly indicated by the numbers of people shown, the arrangement of hand-clapping women surrounding dancing men

Leonardo da Vinci's *The Last Supper.*

whose bodies are bent forward in the distinctive posture caused by the cramping of abdominal muscles as they go into trance, whose noses are shown bleeding (common today when Bushmen trance), whose arms are stretched behind their backs (modern Bushmen do this to gather more of the supernatural potency, *n/um*), who are wearing dance rattles, and who carry fly whisks (used to extract invisible arrows of sickness). Here is a significant clue to what the rock art is really all about, though we cannot discern this from the narrative and aesthetic approaches alone. For this we need the third, or *interpretive*, approach.

The distinction between the aesthetic, narrative, and interpretive approaches becomes clear if we pause for a moment to consider a famous work of Western art, Leonardo da Vinci's painting, *The Last Supper.*[8] A non-Westerner viewing this mural will see what appear to be 13 ordinary men at a table, apparently enjoying an ordinary meal. Although one of the men appears a bit clumsy, knocking over the salt, and clutches a bag of money, there is nothing else here to indicate that the scene is anything out of the ordinary. Aesthetically, our non-Western observer may admire

[8]This example is drawn from Lewis-Williams, J. D. (1990). *Discovering southern African rock art* (p. 9). Cape Town and Johannesburg: David Philip.

the way the composition fits the space available, the attitudes in which the men are depicted, and the way the artist conveys a sense of movement. As narrative, the painting may be seen as a record of customs, table manners, dress, and architecture. But to know the real meaning of this picture, the viewer must be aware that, in Western culture, spilling the salt is a symbol of impending disaster, and that money symbolizes the root of all evil. But even this is not enough; for a full understanding of this work of art, one must know something of the beliefs of Christianity. To move to the interpretive level, then, requires knowledge of the symbols and beliefs of the people responsible for the art.

Applying the interpretive approach to southern African rock art requires knowledge of two things in particular: Bushman ethnography and the nature of trance. With respect to the latter, a clear understanding comes from a combination of ethnographic data as well as that gained experimentally in laboratories. Because all human beings have essentially the same nervous system, whether they be urban dwellers from the United States, food foragers from southern Africa, horticulturalists from the Amazon forest, or wherever, they all progress through the same three stages when going into trance. In the first stage, one's nervous system generates a variety of luminous,

The zigzags and curves in two of these pictures, drawn by migraine sufferers, are classic entoptic phenomena seen in early stages of trance. The "tunnel" with lattice walls in the third picture is representative of those seen when passing from the second to third stage of trance.

pulsating, revolving, and constantly shifting geometric patterns known as **entoptic phenomena** (anyone who has suffered from migraine headaches will be familiar with these). Typical forms include grids, parallel lines, zigzags, dots, nested curves, and filigrees, often in a spiral pattern. As one goes into deeper trance, the brain tries to "make sense" of these abstract forms, just as it does of sensations received when in an unaltered state of consciousness. This process is known as **construal,** and here differences in culture and experience come into play. Commonly, a Bushman in trance will construe a grid pattern as the markings on the skin of a giraffe, nested curves as a honeycomb (honey is a Bushman delicacy, and the

auditory sensation of buzzing that often accompanies trance promotes the illusion), and dots as *nu/m,* the potency seen only by shamans in trance. Obviously, we would not expect an Inuit or someone

Entoptic phenomena: Bright, pulsating geometric forms that are generated by the central nervous system and "seen" in states of trance.

Construal: In the second stage of trance, the process by which the brain tries to "make sense" of entoptic images.

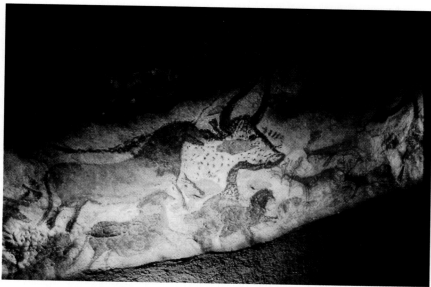

This late Stone Age painting from the Peche-Merle cave in France incorporates dot entoptics over and near the body of a bull, one indication that the artist was painting something that had been seen in a state of trance. An association of rock art with trance experience has been noted in many parts of the world.

from Los Angeles to construe these patterns in the same way.

In the third and deepest stage of trance, subjects cease to be observers of their hallucinations, but seem to become part of them. As this happens, they feel themselves passing into a rotating tunnel or vortex, the sides of which are latticelike, and on which appear images of animals, humans, and monsters of various sorts. In the process, the entoptic forms of the earlier stages become integrated into these **iconic images,** as they are called. In the process, the entoptics may be hard to discern apart from the main image, although sometimes they appear as a kind of background. Iconic images are culture specific; one "sees" the things that one's culture disposes one to see; often, they are things having high emotional content. In the case of Bushmen, they often see the

---

Iconic images: Hallucinations of people, animals, and monsters, "seen" in the deepest stage of trance.

---

eland, an animal thought to be imbued with specially strong potency, particularly for rain making. Given this, one of the things shamans try to do in trance is to "capture" elands—"rain animals"— for purposes of making rain.

From this, we begin to understand why elands are so prominent in the rock art. It also reveals the significance of the zigzags, dots, grids, and so forth which are so often a part of the compositions. Moreover, it leads to an understanding of other puzzling features of the art. For example, sensations in Stage 3 of trance include such things as being stretched out or elongated, weightlessness as in flight or in the water, and difficulty breathing as when under water. Hence we find depictions in the art of humans who appear to be abnormally long, as well as individuals who appear to be swimming or flying. Another well-documented trance phenomenon is the sense of being transformed into some sort of animal. Such sensations are triggered in the deepest stage of trance if the individual sees or thinks of an animal, and the sensation accounts for the part human–part animal therianthropes in the art. Finally, the superpositioning of one work of art over another becomes comprehensible; not only are the visions seen in trance commonly superimposed on one another as they rotate and move, but if the trancer stares at a painting or engraving of an earlier vision, the new one will appear as if projected on the old.

What the interpretive approach makes clear, then, is that the rock art of southern Africa—even in the case of compositions that might otherwise appear to be scenes of everyday life—is intimately connected with the practices and beliefs of shamanism. After shamans came out of trance and reflected on their visions, they then proceeded to paint or engrave their recollections of them on the rock faces. But these were more than records of important visions; they had their own innate power, owing to their supernatural origin. This being so, when the need arose for a new trance experience, it might be held where the old vision was recorded, in order to draw power from it.

With the fuller understanding provided by the interpretive approach, we may now look at the broader significance of what the Bushmen were doing with their art. For this, we turn to the writings of the two South African anthropologists who are the leading authorities on the rock art.

Original Study

Bushman Rock Art and Political Power[9]

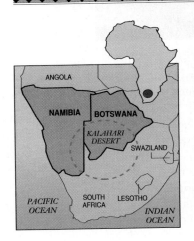

Whatever may be said about Bushman rock art, its images are not the "banal, meaningless artefacts" into which exhibits can so easily transform them. "Meaning" is, of course, an elusive concept. Like all art, the Bushman images did not have a single, one-to-one "meaning" that they unequivocally transmitted from maker to viewer. "Meaning" was historically and complexly constituted; Bushman viewers shared with the makers of the art in the construction of "meaning." Similarly, modern viewers who engage the images will inevitably bring with them their own contribution to their "meaning". If all the original viewers did not "read" the images identically, each viewer having had his or her own socially constituted perspective, how much less likely is it that modern viewers will share identical responses? None the less, some general observations on the art's "meaning" and its role in Bushman communities can be made in the hope that they will challenge the current trivialising stereotypes.

The "ideas which most deeply moved the Bushman mind" were rooted in what our reading of the nineteenth-century accounts suggests was a three-tiered, though not strictly demarcated, view of the cosmos: the level of daily life, the realm above, and the realm below. These levels were mediated by shamans. Amongst the Kalahari groups of the 1950s and 1960s, about half of the men and a third of the women were shamans. Entering an altered state of consciousness during a communal dance or in more solitary circumstances, these shamans were believed to activate a supernatural potency so that they could move between the cosmological levels as they performed such diverse tasks as curing the sick, making rain and controlling animals.

The making of rock art was associated with these shamanistic practices in ways not fully understood. The images comprise: representations of animals that were believed to possess supernatural potency, privileged views of communal dances that show not only what ordinary people saw but also elements, such as potency, that were seen by shamans only; conflicts in the spiritual realm between benign shamans and shamans of illness; rain-animals that shamans killed so that their blood and milk would fall as rain;

therianthropic figures showing the blending of a shaman with a power-animal; geometric images derived from entoptic phenomena (bright pulsating forms "seen" in certain altered states of consciousness); and a range of other fantastic experiences. The images were not, however, simply records of religious experiences. There is reason to believe that at least some of them were reservoirs of potency that could be tapped by trancing shamans. They were not just pictures, but powerful things in themselves that could be implicated in effecting alterations in the shamans' states of consciousness, that is, in facilitating the mediation of the cosmological realms.

Even this brief outline shows that the art can be presented as a challenge to the popular belief that the making of art was, for the Bushmen, an idle pastime. The artists' manipulation of metaphors and symbols was far more complex and subtle than many modern viewers realize. The painted and engraved images explore unknown and unsuspected realms in often idiosyncratic ways. In the past the images were active; today they are made static by being separated from their highly charged ritual, social and conceptual contexts.

The activity of the images, however, extended beyond the generation of religious experience to the negotiation of political power. Especially in the last two hundred years of the Bushmen's occupation of the south-eastern part of the subcontinent, major and escalating changes were taking place. For many hundreds of years the Bushmen had interacted in various and changing ways with Bantu-speaking agropastoralists, but these, for the most part amicable, exchanges were disrupted by colonial expansion. New social relations began to develop. Shamans, who were already being paid with cattle and a share of the crops by the agropastoralists for whom they made rain, found that they had access to new resources. As the colonists shot out the game and the Bushman territories became more and more restricted, relations with the agropastoralists increased in importance, and political and economic struggles developed between competing shamans and between shamans and ordinary people. The "egalitarian" values that militated against development of political power by shamans were eroded.

Rock painting was implicated in these changes. To illustrate the artistic dynamics of, largely, the nineteenth century, we mention three types of painting. One type shows groups of people, some of whom are identifiable by various features as shamans, in which no one is larger or more elaborately painted than another. A second type shows groups of people in which two or three shaman figures are more elaborately and individually depicted. The third type shows an elaborately painted central shaman with sometimes, facial features, surrounded by "lesser" figures. The historical record from parts of the Kalahari combines with these three types of paintings to suggest that the art became a site of struggle. As social circumstances changed, shamans translated their supernatural potency into political power and vied with one another for control of resources that were, in the final decades, increasingly derived from rain-making for agropastoralists.

The artists who made these types of paintings were not merely painting historical events, chronicling social changes. Such an understanding would be related to the close-to-nature stereotype—simple people painting what was happening around them. Rather, the making of each painting was a socio-political intervention that negotiated the artist's (or artists') political status. The art did not simply reflect social relations: In some instances it transformed those relations: In other instances it worked to reproduce them.

Each painting was more than an image of the way things were, or even of the way artists wished they would become. Because the images were themselves charged with the supernatural potency that mediated the levels of the cosmos and made shamanistic activity possible, they exercised a coercive, persuasive influence that was founded in their factuality.

In specific and diverse historical circumstances, the artists invoked this coercive function in their responses to the colonial invasion. Unlike the agropastoralists, the colonists were not intended to be among the viewers of the art, but their threatening presence implicated them in the social production of the art none the less. As the shamans had, for centuries, battled in the spiritual realm with marauding shamans of illness, who often took feline forms, so, the art suggests, did they battle in the spiritual realm with the colonists. The shamans tried to deploy their powers in such a way as to thwart the advance of the colonists. As we know, their efforts were fruitless; the colonists' rifles were, in the end, invincible. At times prosecuting a policy of calculated genocide, at other times mounting ad hoc but nevertheless vicious "retaliatory" commandos, the colonists all but wiped out the Bushman communities south of the Orange River. Many Bushmen, it is true, intermarried with agropastoralists and others went to live with them, but, all in all, the unpalatable truth of the matter is that genocide was the finality.

[9]Adapted from Dowson, T. A., & Lewis-Williams, J. D. (1993, November). Myths, museums, and southern African rock art. *South African Historical Journal, 29,* pp. 52–56.

Although all too often dismissively labelled as "primitive" or "simple," it can be seen from the discussion here that the rock art of southern Africa is anything but primitive or simple. Neither the art itself nor the belief system in which it was embedded can be described as remotely "simple." To understand such art requires a good deal more than simply staring at a picture, but the effort is well worth making.

CHAPTER SUMMARY

Art is the creative use of the human imagination to interpret, understand, and enjoy life. It stems from the uniquely human ability to use symbols to give shape and significance to the physical world for more than just a utilitarian purpose. Anthropologists are concerned with art as a reflection of the cultural values and concerns of people.

Oral traditions denote the unwritten stories, beliefs, and customs of a culture. Verbal arts include narrative, drama, poetry, incantations, proverbs, riddles, and word games. Narratives, which have received the most study, have been divided into three categories: myths, legends, and tales.

Myths are basically sacred narratives that explain how the world came to be how it is. In describing an orderly universe, myths function to set standards for orderly behavior. Legends are stories told as if true that often recount the exploits of heroes, the movements of people, and the establishment of local customs. Epics, which are long legends in poetry or prose, are typically found in nonliterate societies with a form of state political organization. They serve to transmit and preserve a culture's legal and political practices. In literate states, these functions have been taken over to one degree or another by history. Anthropologists are interested in legends because they provide clues as to what constitutes model ethical behavior in a culture. Tales are fictional, secular, nonhistorical narratives that instruct as they entertain. Anthropological interest in tales centers in part on the fact that their distribution provides evidence of cultural contacts or cultural isolation.

The study of music in specific cultural settings has developed into the specialized field of ethnomusicology. Almost everywhere human music is perceived in terms of a scale. Scale systems and their modifications comprise tonality in music. Tonality determines the possibilities and limits of melody and harmony. Rhythm is an organizing factor in music. Traditional European music is measured into recurrent patterns of two, three, and four beats.

The social function of music is most obvious in song. Like tales, songs may express the concerns of the group, but with greater formalism because of the restrictions imposed by closed systems of tonality, rhythm, and musical form.

Pictorial art may be regarded as either representational or abstract, though in truth these categories represent polar ends of a continuum. The rock art of southern Africa illustrates three ways that the study of art may be approached. The aesthetic and narrative approaches focus on *how* and *what* things are depicted. By themselves they reveal little about what the art is all about and may convey a distorted view of the people responsible for it. Only the interpretive approach can reveal the meaning of another people's art. To carry it out, one must have a rich body of ethnography, and often other sets of data, to draw on. The effort is worthwhile, as it may reveal the art to be far more complex than one might otherwise expect. In the case of southern African rock art, it shows how paintings and engravings were actually part of Bushman strategy for negotiating changing power relations as colonists invaded their lands.

SUGGESTED READINGS

Dundes, A. (1980). *Interpreting folk lore.* Bloomington: Indiana University Press.

A collection of articles that assesses the materials folklorists have amassed and classified; seeks to broaden and refine traditional assumptions about the proper subject matter and methods of folklore.

Hannah, J. L. (1988). *Dance, sex and gender.* Chicago: University of Chicago Press.

Like other forms of art, dances are social acts that contribute to the continuation and emergence of culture. One of the oldest—if not the oldest—art forms, dance shares the same instrument, the human body, with sexuality. This book, written for a broad, nonspecialist audience, explicitly examines sexuality and the construction of gender identities as they are played out in the production and visual imagery of dance.

Hatcher, E. P. (1985). *Art as culture: An introduction to the anthropology of art.* New York: University Press of America.

This handy, clearly written book nicely relates the visual arts to other aspects of culture. Topics include "the technological means," "the psychological perspective," "so-cial contexts and social functions," "art as communication," and "the time dimension." Numerous line drawings help the reader to understand the varied forms of art in non-Western societies.

Layton, R. (1991). *The anthropology of art* (2nd ed.). Cambridge, England: Cambridge University Press.

This readable introduction to the diversity of non-Western art deals with questions of aesthetic appreciation, the use of art, and the big question: What *is* art?

Merriam, A. P. (1964). *The anthropology of music.* Chicago: Northwestern University Press.

This book focuses on music as a complex of behavior, which resonates throughout all of culture: social organization, aesthetic activity, economics, and religion.

Otten, C. M. (1971). *Anthropology and art: Readings in cross-cultural aesthetics.* Garden City, NY: Natural History Press.

This is a collection of articles by anthropologists and art historians, with an emphasis on the functional relationships between art and culture.

PART
VIII

CHANGE AND THE FUTURE
SOLVING THE PROBLEM OF ADJUSTING TO CHANGED CONDITIONS

CHAPTER 26
CULTURAL CHANGE

CHAPTER 27
THE FUTURE OF HUMANITY

Without the ability to conceive new ideas and change existing behavior patterns, no human society could survive for very long. Human culture, though never static, is remarkably stable, but it is also resilient and therefore able to adapt to altered circumstances.

Understanding the processes of change, the subject of Chapter 26, is one of the most important and fundamental of anthropological goals. Unfortunately, the task is made difficult by the cultural biases of most modern North Americans, which predispose them to see change as a progressive process leading in a predictable and determined way to where they are now, and even beyond into a future to which they are leading the way. So pervasive is this notion of progress that it motivates the thinking of North Americans in a great many ways of which they are hardly aware. Among other things, it leads them to view cultures not like their own as "backward" and "underdeveloped"; as two well-known economists put it, "we . . . have the feeling that we are encountering in the present the anachronistic counterparts of the static societies of antiquity."[1A] Of course, they are no such thing; as we saw in Chapter 17, no culture is static, and cultures may be very highly developed in quite different ways. A simple analogy with the world of nature may be helpful here. In the course of evolution, single-celled organisms appeared long before vertebrate animals, and land vertebrates like mammals are relative latecomers indeed. Yet, single-celled organisms abound in the world today, not as relics of the past, but as creatures highly adapted to situations for which mammals are totally unsuited. Just because mammals got here late does not mean that a dog is "better" or "more progressive" than an amoeba.

Belief in "progress" and its inevitability has important implications for North Americans as well as others. For people in the United States, it means that change has become necessary for its own sake, for whatever they have today is, by definition, not as good as what they will have tomorrow. Put another way, whatever is old is, by virtue of that fact alone, inadequate and should be gotten rid of, no matter how well it seems to be working. This virtually guarantees the continuing existence of significant levels of dissatisfaction within the United States. For others, the logic runs like this: If the old must inevitably give way to the new, then societies that North Americans perceive as being "old" or "out of the past" must also give way to the new. Since the way of life in the United States is a recent development in human history, the United States must represent the new. "Old" societies must therefore become like that of the United States, or else it is their fate to disappear altogether. What this amounts to is a charter for massive intervention into the lives of others, whether they want this or not; the outcome, more often than not, is the destabilization and even destruction of other societies in the world at large.

[1A]Heilbroner, R. L., & Thurow, L. C. (1981). *The economic problem* (6th ed.) (p. 607). Englewood Cliffs, NJ: Prentice-Hall.

A conscious attempt to identify and eliminate the biases of North American culture allows us to see change in a very different way. It allows us to recognize that, although people can respond deliberately to problems in such a way as to change their culture, much change occurs accidentally. This should not surprise us, though, when we consider that in biological evolution accidents (called mutations) are the ultimate source of all change. The fact is that the historical record, too, is quirky and full of random events. And while it is true that without change, cultures could never adapt to changed conditions, we must recognize that too much in the way of large-scale, continuing change may also place a culture in jeopardy. This is because it conflicts with the social need for predictability, discussed in Chapter 14; the need of individuals for regularity and structure, discussed in Chapter 16; and the need of populations for an adaptive "fit" with their environment, discussed in Chapter 17. Just as a runaway rate of mutation is a threat to the survival of a biological species, so is a runaway rate of change to a human society.

The more anthropologists study change and learn about the various ways people go about solving their problems of existence, the more aware they become of a great paradox of culture. While the basic business of culture is to solve problems, in doing so, inevitably, new problems are created, which themselves demand solutions. Throughout this book we have seen examples of this—the problem of forming groups in order to cooperate in solving the problems of staying alive, the problem of finding ways to overcome the stresses and strains on individuals as a consequence of their membership in groups, as well as the structural problems that are inherent in the division of society into a number of smaller groups, to mention but a few. Every solution to a problem has its price, but so long as culture is able to keep at least a step ahead of the problems, all is reasonably well. This seems to have been the case generally over the past two million years.

When we see all of the problems that face the human species today (Chapter 27), most of them the result of cultural practices, we may wonder if we have not passed some critical threshold where culture has begun to fall a step behind the problems. This is not to say that the future necessarily has to be bleak for the generations that come after us, but it would certainly be irresponsible to project some sort of rosy, science-fiction type of future as inevitable, at least on the basis of present evidence. To prevent the future from being bleak, humans will have to rise to the challenge of changing their behaviors and ideas in order to conquer the large problems that threaten to annihilate them: overpopulation and unequal access to basic resources with their concomitant starvation, poverty, and squalor; environmental pollution and poisoning; and the culture of discontent and bitterness that rises out of the widening economic gap separating industrialized and non-industrialized countries as well as the "haves" from the "have nots" within countries.

CHAPTER
26

CULTURAL CHANGE

THE CAPACITY TO CHANGE HAS ALWAYS BEEN IMPORTANT TO HUMAN CULTURES. PROBABLY AT NO TIME HAS THE PACE OF CHANGE EQUALED THAT OF TODAY, AS TRADITIONAL PEOPLES ALL OVER THE WORLD ARE PRESSURED BY GOVERNMENTS TO CHANGE THEIR WAYS OR BE "RUN OVER" BY "PROGRESS." BUT INDIGENOUS PEOPLES ARE FIGHTING BACK AND GAINING THE WORLD'S ATTENTION. SHOWN HERE IS RIGOBERTA MENCHU, WINNER OF THE 1992 NOBEL PEACE PRIZE IN RECOGNITION OF HER ADVOCACY ON BEHALF OF HER PEOPLE, THE MAYA OF GUATEMALA.

CHAPTER PREVIEW

Why Do Cultures Change?

All cultures change at one time or another for a variety of reasons. Although people may deliberately change their ways in response to some perceived problem, much change is accidental, including the unforeseen outcome of existing events. Or, contact with other peoples may lead to the introduction of "foreign" ideas, bringing about changes in existing values and behavior. This may even involve the massive imposition of foreign ways through conquest of one group by another. Through change, cultures are able to adapt to altered conditions; on the other hand, not all change is adaptive.

How Do Cultures Change?

The mechanisms of change are innovation, diffusion, cultural loss, and acculturation. Innovation occurs when someone within a society discovers something new that is then accepted by other members of the society. Diffusion is the borrowing of something from another group, and cultural loss is the abandonment of an existing practice or trait, with or without replacement. Acculturation is the massive change that occurs with the sort of intensive, firsthand contact that has occurred under colonialism.

What Is Modernization?

Modernization is an ethnocentric term used to refer to a global process of change by which traditional, nonindustrial societies seek to acquire characteristics of industrially "advanced" societies. Although modernization has generally been assumed to be a good thing, and there have been some successes, it has frequently led to the development of a new "culture of discontent," a level of aspirations far exceeding the bounds of an individual's local opportunities. Sometimes it leads to the destruction of cherished customs and values people had no desire to abandon.

Culture is the medium through which the human species solves the problems of existence, as these are perceived by members of the species. Various cultural institutions, such as kinship and marriage, political and economic organization, and religion, mesh together to form an integrated cultural system. Because systems generally work to maintain stability, cultures are often fairly stable and remain so unless either the conditions to which they are adapted, or human perceptions of those conditions, change. Archaeological studies have revealed how elements of a culture may persist for long periods of time. In Chapter 6, for example, we saw how the culture of the native inhabitants of northwestern New England and southern Quebec remained relatively stable over thousands of years.

Although stability may be a striking feature of many cultures, none is ever changeless, as the cultures of food foragers, subsistence farmers, or pastoralists are all too often assumed to be. In a stable society, change may occur gently and gradually, without altering in any fundamental way the underlying logic of the culture. Sometimes, though, the pace of change may increase dramatically, causing a radical cultural alteration in a relatively short period of time. The modern world is full of examples as diverse as the disintegration of the Soviet Union, or what is happening to the native peoples of the Amazon forest as Brazil presses ahead to "develop" this vast region. The causes of change are many and include the unexpected outcome of existing activities. To cite an example from U.S. history, the settlement of what we now call New England by English-speaking people had nothing to do with their culture being "better" or "more advanced" than those of the region's native inhabitants (it was neither, but merely different). Rather, it was the outcome of a series of unrelated events that happened to coincide at a critical moment in time. In England, economic and political developments that drove large numbers of farmers off the land, occurring at a time of population growth, together favored an outward migration of people; that this happened shortly after the European discovery of the Americas was purely a matter of chance. Even at that, attempts to establish British colonies in New England ended in failure, until an epidemic of unprecedented scope resulted in the sudden death of about 90 percent of the native inhabitants of coastal New England. This epidemic did not happen because the British would be unable to settle unless the land were cleared of its original occupants, but rather because the Indians had been in regular contact with European fishermen and fur traders—whose activities were independent of British attempts at colonization—from whom they contracted the disease. For centuries, up to this time, Europeans had been living under conditions that were ideal for the incubation and spread of all sorts of infectious diseases, but the Indians had not. Consequently, the Europeans had developed over time a degree of resistance to them, which Indians lacked altogether. To be sure, the consequences were inevitable, once direct contact between these people occurred; nonetheless, differential immunity did not occur in order to clear the coast of New England for English settlement. And even once those settlements were established, it is unlikely that the colonists would have been able to alienate the remaining natives from their land, had they not come equipped with the political and military techniques for dominating other peoples previously used to impose their control upon the Scots, Irish, and Welsh. In sum, had not a number of otherwise unrelated phenomena come together by chance at just the right moment in time, English might very well not be the language spoken by most North Americans today.

Not just the unexpected outcome of existing activities, but other sorts of accidents, too, may bring about changes if people perceive them to be useful. Of course, people may also respond deliberately to altered conditions, thereby correcting the perceived problem that made the cultural modification seem necessary. Change may also be forced upon one group by another, as happened in colonial New England and as is happening in so much of the world today, in the course of especially intense contact between two societies. Progress and adaptation, on the other hand, are *not* causes of change; the latter is a consequence of it that happens to work well for a population, and the former is a judgment of those consequences in terms of the group's cultural values. Progress is whatever it is defined as.

MECHANISMS OF CHANGE

Innovation

The ultimate source of all change is through innovation: any new practice, tool, or principle that gains widespread acceptance within a group. Those that involve the chance discovery of some new principle we refer to as **primary innovations;** those that result from the deliberate applications of known principles are **secondary innovations.** It is the latter that correspond most closely with Western culture's model of change as predictable and determined, while the former involves accidents of one sort or another.

An example of a primary innovation is the discovery that the firing of clay makes it permanently hard. Presumably, accidental firing of clay took place frequently in ancient cooking fires. An accidental occurrence is of no account, however, unless some application of it is perceived. This first happened about 25,000 years ago, at which time people began making figurines of fired clay. Pottery vessels were not made, however, nor did the practice of making things of fired clay reach southwest Asia; at least if it did, it failed to take root. Not until some time between 7000 and 6500 B.C. did people living in southwest Asia recognize a significant application of fired clay, at which time they began using it to make cheap, durable, easy-to-produce containers and cooking vessels.

As nearly as we can reconstruct it, the development of the earliest known pottery vessels came about in the following way.[1B] By 7000 B.C., cooking areas in southwest Asia included clay-lined basins built into the floor, clay ovens, and hearths, making the accidental firing of clay inevitable.

―――∞∞∞――∞∞∞――

Primary innovation: The chance discovery of some new principle.

Secondary innovation: Something new that results from the deliberate application of known principles.

―――∞∞∞――∞∞∞――

[1B]Amiran, R. (1965). The beginnings of pottery-making in the Near East. In F. R. Matson (Ed.), *Ceramics and man* (pp. 240–247). Viking Fund Publications in Anthropology, *41.*

Two Mayan women fire pottery vessels. The discovery that firing clay vessels makes them virtually indestructible (unless they are dropped or otherwise smashed) probably came about when clay-lined basins next to cooking fires in the Middle East were accidentally fired.

Moreover, people were already familiar with the working of clay, which they used to build houses, line storage pits, and model figurines. For containers, however, they still relied upon baskets and leather bags.

Once the significance of fired clay—the primary innovation—was perceived, then the application of known techniques to it—secondary innovation—became possible. Clay could be modeled in the familiar way into the known shapes of baskets, leather bags, and stone bowls and then fired, either in an open fire or in the same ovens used for cooking food. In fact, the earliest known southwest Asian pottery is imitative of leather and stone containers, and the decoration consists of motifs transferred from basketry, even though they were ill suited to the new medium. Eventually, shapes and decorative techniques more suited to the new technology were developed.

Since men are never the potters in traditional societies unless the craft has become something of a commercial operation, the first pottery was probably made by women. The vessels that they produced were initially handmade, and the earliest kilns were the same ovens that were used for cooking. As people became more adept at making pottery, there were further technological refinements. As an aid in production, the clay could be modeled on a mat or other surface, which the woman could move as work progressed. Hence, she could sit in one place while she worked, without

In the face of the AIDS epidemic sweeping southern Africa, the beliefs of several million Christian Zionists, like the one being baptized here, are highly adaptive in that they militate against the kind of sexual practices that spread the disease. That these practices are adaptive, however, is a consequence of, rather than reason for, their origin.

having to get up to move around the clay. A further refinement was to mount the movable surface on a vertical rotating shaft—an application of a known principle used for drills—which produced the potter's wheel and permitted mass production. Kilns, too, were improved for better circulation of heat by separating the firing chamber from the fire itself. By chance, it happened that these improved kilns produced enough heat to smelt some ores such as copper, tin, gold, silver, and lead. Presumably, this discovery was made by accident—another primary innovation—and the stage was set for the eventual development of the forced-draft furnace out of the earlier pottery kiln.

The accidents responsible for primary innovations are not generated by environmental change or some other "need," nor are they preferentially oriented in an adaptive direction. They are, however, given structure by the cultural context in which they occur. Thus, the outcome of the discovery of fired clay by mobile hunters and gatherers 25,000 years ago was very different from what it was when discovered later on by more sedentary farmers in Southwest Asia, where it set

off a chain reaction as one invention led to another. Indeed, given certain sets of cultural goals, values, and knowledge, particular innovations are almost bound to be made, as illustrated by the case of penicillin. This antibiotic was discovered in 1928 when a mold blew in through the window of Sir Alexander Fleming's lab and landed on a microbial colony of staphylococcus, which it then dissolved. Fleming recognized the importance of this accident, because he had become aware of the need for more than antiseptics and immunization, the mainstays of medicine at the time, to fight infection. Of course, he was not alone in his awareness, nor was the accident involved at all unusual. Any physician who studied medicine in the early part of this century has stories about having to scrub down laboratories when their studies in bacteriology were brought to a halt by molds that persisted in contaminating cultures and killing off the bacteria. To them, it was an annoyance; to Fleming, it was a "magic bullet" to fight infection. Under the circumstances, however, had he not made the discovery, someone else would have before long.

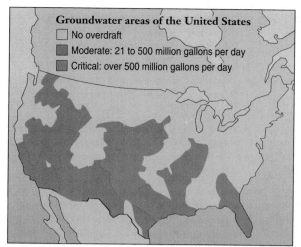

Figure 26.1 Human practices may or may not be adaptive. In the United States, for example, it is not adaptive over the long run to deplete groundwater in regions of fast-growing populations, yet this is being done.

Although a culture's internal dynamics may encourage certain innovative tendencies, they may discourage others or even remain neutral with respect to yet others. Copernicus's discovery of the rotation of the planets around the sun and Mendel's discovery of the basic laws of heredity are instances of genuine creative insights out of step with the established needs, values, and goals of their times and places. In fact, Mendel's work remained obscure until 16 years after his death, when three scientists working independently rediscovered, all in the same year (1900), the same laws of heredity. Thus, in the context of turn-of-the-century Western culture, Mendel's laws were bound to be discovered, even had Mendel himself not hit upon them earlier.

An innovation's consistency with a society's needs, values, and goals is necessary, but not sufficient to assure its acceptance. Force of habit tends to be an obstacle to acceptance; people will generally tend to stick with what they are used to, rather than adopt something new that will require some adjustment on their part. An example of this can be seen in the continued British practice of driving on the left-hand side of the road, rather than on the right. Driving on the left is no more natural than driving on the right, but to someone from Britain it seems so, because of the body reflexes that have developed in the course of driving on the left. In this case the individual's very body has become adjusted to certain patterns of behav-

ior that bypass any presumed "openness" to change. An innovation's chance of acceptance tends to be greater if it is obviously better than the thing or idea it replaces. Beyond this, much may depend on the prestige of the innovator and imitating groups. If the innovator's prestige is high, this will help gain acceptance for the innovation. If it is low, acceptance is less likely, unless the innovator can attract a sponsor who has high prestige.

Diffusion

When the Pilgrims established their colony of New Plymouth in North America, they very likely would have starved to death, had the Indian Squanto not showed them how to grow the native American crops—corn, beans, and squash. The borrowing of cultural elements from one society

One barrier to change is sheer force of habit. Although Western people may learn to use chopsticks for eating, it requires more effort than simply continuing to eat with a fork.

by members of another is known as **diffusion,** and the donor society is, for all intents and purposes, the "inventor" of that element. So common is borrowing that the late Ralph Linton, a North American anthropologist, suggested that borrowing accounts for as much as 90 percent of any culture's content. People are creative about their borrowing, however, picking and choosing from multiple possibilities and sources. Usually their selections are limited to those compatible with the existing culture. In modern-day Guatemala, for example, Maya Indians, who make up over half of that country's population, will adopt Western ways if the value of what they adopt is self-evident and does not conflict with traditional ways and values. The use of metal hoes, shovels, and machetes became standard long ago, for they are superior to stone tools, and yet they are compatible with the cultivation of corn in the traditional way by men using hand tools. Yet certain other "modern" practices, which might appear advantageous to the Maya, tend to be resisted if they are perceived as running counter to Indian tradition. Thus, a young man in one community who tried his hand at truck gardening, using chemical fertilizers and pesticides to grow cash crops with market value only in the city—vegetables never eaten by the Maya—could not secure a "good" woman for a wife (a "good" woman is one who has never had sex with another man, who is skilled at domestic chores, not lazy, and willing to attend to her husband's needs). Upon abandonment of his unorthodox ways, however, he became accepted by his community as a "real man," no longer different from the rest of them and therefore conspicuous (a real "man" is one who will work steadily to provide his household with what they need to live by farming and making charcoal in the traditional ways). Before long, he was well married.[2]

While the tendency toward borrowing is so great as to lead Robert Lowie to comment, "Culture is a thing of shreds and patches," the borrowed traits usually undergo sufficient modifications to

make this wry comment more colorful than critical. Moreover, existing cultural traits may be modified to accommodate a borrowed one. An awareness of the extent of borrowing can be eye opening. Take, for example, the numerous things European Americans have borrowed from American Indians. Domestic plants that were developed ("invented") by the Indians—"Irish" potatoes, avocados, corn, beans, squash, tomatoes, peanuts, manioc, chili peppers, chocolate, and sweet potatoes, to name a few—furnish a major portion of the world's food supply. In fact, American Indians remain the developers of the world's largest array of nutritious foods and the primary contributors to the world's varied cuisine.[3] Among drugs and stimulants, tobacco is the best known, but others include coca in cocaine, ephedra in ephedrine, datura in pain relievers, and cascara in laxatives. Early on, European physicians recognized that Indians had the world's most sophisticated pharmacy, and almost all drugs known today made from plants native to the Americas were used by Indians. More than 200 plants and herbs that they used for medicinal purposes have at some time been included in the *Pharmacopeia of the United States* or in the *National Formulary*. Varieties of cotton developed by Indians supply much of the world's clothing needs, while the woolen poncho, the parka, and moccasins are universally familiar items. Not only has Anglo-American literature been permanently shaped by such works as Longfellow's *Hiawatha* and James Fenimore Cooper's *Leather-stocking Tales*, but also American Indian music has contributed to world music such ultramodern devices as unusual intervals, arbitrary scales, conflicting rhythms, and hypnotic monotony. These borrowings are so well integrated into modern North American culture that few people are aware of their source.

In spite of the obvious importance of diffusion, there are probably more obstacles to accepting an innovation from another culture than there are to accepting one that is "homegrown." In addition to the same obstacles that stand in the way of "homegrown" inventions is the fact that a borrowed one is, by its very nature, "foreign." In the United States, for example, this is one reason why people have been

---

Diffusion: The spread of customs or practices from one culture to another.

---

[2]Reina, R. E. (1966). *The law of the saints* (pp. 65–68). Indianapolis: Bobbs-Merrill.

[3]Weatherford, J. (1988). *Indian givers: How the Indians of the Americas transformed the New World* (p. 115). New York: Ballantine.

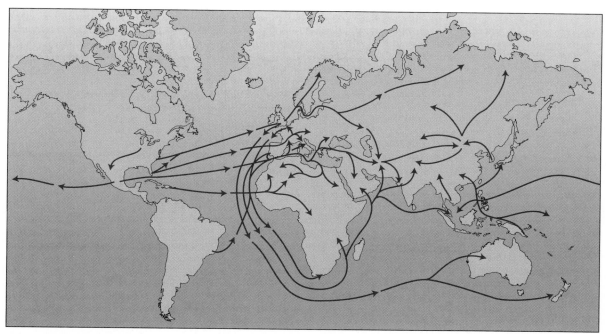

Figure 26.2   The diffusion of tobacco. Having spread from the tropics of the Western hemisphere to much of the rest of North and South America, it rapidly spread after 1492 to the rest of the world.

so reluctant to abandon completely the awkward and cumbersome old English system of weights and measures for the far more logical metric system, which has been adopted by just about everyone else on earth. (The only holdouts besides the United States are South Yemen and Liberia.) Hence, the ethnocentrism of the potential borrowing culture may act as a barrier to acceptance.

Cultural Loss

Most often people tend to think of change as an accumulation of innovations; new things being added to those already there. They do so because this seems so much a part of the way they live. A little reflection, however, leads to the realization that frequently the acceptance of a new innovation leads to the loss of an older one. This sort of replacement is not just a feature of Western civilization. For example, back in biblical times, chariots and carts were in widespread use in the Middle East, but by the sixth century A.D., wheeled vehicles had virtually disappeared from Morocco to Afghanistan. They were replaced by camels, not because of some reversion to the past on the part of the region's inhabitants, but because camels, used as pack animals, worked better. By the sixth century Roman roads

had deteriorated, but camels, so long as they were not used as draft animals, were not bound to them. Not only that, their longevity, endurance, and ability to ford rivers and traverse rough ground without having to build roads in the first place made pack camels admirably suited for the region. Finally there was a saving in labor: A wagon required a man for every two draft animals, whereas a single person can manage from three to six pack camels. Stephen Jay Gould comments:

> We are initially surprised . . . because wheels have come to symbolize in our culture the sine qua non of intelligent exploitation and technological progress. Once invented, their superiority cannot be gainsaid or superseded. Indeed, "reinventing the wheel" has become our standard metaphor for deriding the repetition of such obvious truths. In an earlier era of triumphant social Darwinism, wheels stood as an ineluctable stage of human progress. The "inferior" cultures of Africa slid to defeat; their conquerors rolled to victory. The "advanced" cultures of Mexico and Peru might have repulsed Cortés and Pizarro if only a clever artisan had thought of turning a calendar stone into a cartwheel. The notion that carts could ever

Although the wheel has become a symbol of progress in Western cultures, wheeled transport is not always superior to other forms. Such was the case in pre-Columbian Mexico, where wheels were used on toys but not for transport. The existence of adequate alternatives made wheeled vehicles unnecessary.

be replaced by pack animals strikes us not only as backward but almost sacrilegious.

The success of camels reemphasizes a fundamental theme . . . Adaptation, be it biological or cultural, represents a better fit to specific, local environments, not an inevitable stage in a ladder of progress. Wheels were a formidable invention, and their uses are manifold (potters and millers did not abandon them, even when cartwrights were eclipsed). But camels may work better in some circumstances. Wheels, like wings, fins, and brains, are exquisite devices for certain purposes, not signs of intrinsic superiority.[4]

Often overlooked is another facet of the loss of apparently useful traits: loss without replacement. An example of this is the absence of boats among the inhabitants of the Canary Islands, an archipelago isolated in the stormy seas off the coast of West Africa. The ancestors of these people must have had boats, for without them they could never have transported themselves and their domestic livestock to the islands in the first place. Later, without boats, they had no way to communicate between islands. The cause of this loss of something useful was that the islands contain no stone suitable for making polished stone axes, which in turn limited the islanders' carpentry.[5]

FORCIBLE CHANGE

Innovation, diffusion, and cultural loss all may take place among peoples who are free to decide for themselves what they will or will not accept in the way of change. Not always, however, are people left free to make their own choices; frequently changes that they would not willingly make themselves have been forced upon them by some other group, usually in the course of colonialism and conquest. A direct outcome in many cases is a phenomenon that anthropologists call acculturation.

Acculturation

Acculturation occurs when groups having different cultures come into intensive firsthand contact, resulting in subsequent massive changes in the original culture patterns of one or both groups. It always involves an element of force, either directly, as in the case of conquest, or indirectly, as in the implicit or explicit threat that force will be used if people refuse to make the changes that those in the other group expect them to make. Other variables include degree of cultural difference; circumstances, intensity, frequency, and hostility of contact; relative status of the agents of contact; who is dominant and who is submissive; and whether the nature of the flow is reciprocal or nonreciprocal. It should be emphasized that acculturation and

Acculturation: Major culture changes that people are forced to make as a consequence of intensive, firsthand contact between societies.

[4]Gould, S. J. (1983). *Hen's teeth and horses' toes* (p. 159). New York: Norton.

[5]Coon, C. S. (1954). *The story of man* (p. 174). New York: Knopf.

diffusion are not equivalent terms; one culture can borrow from another without being in the least acculturated.

In the course of acculturation, any one of a number of things may happen. Merger or fusion occurs when two cultures lose their separate identities and form a single culture, as expressed by the "melting pot" ideology of Anglo-American culture in the United States. Sometimes, though, one of the cultures loses its autonomy but retains its identity as a subculture, in the form of a caste, class, or ethnic group; this is typical of conquest or slavery situations, and there are examples in the United States in spite of its melting-pot ideology, as may be seen on any Indian reservation. Today, in virtually all parts of the world, people are faced with the indignity of forced removal from their traditional homelands, as entire communities are uprooted to make way for hydroelectric projects, grazing lands for cattle, mining operations, or the construction of highways. In Brazil's rush to develop the Amazon basin, for instance, whole villages have been relocated to "national parks," where resources are inadequate for so many people, and where former enemies are often forced to live in close proximity.

Extinction is the phenomenon in which so many carriers of a culture die that those who survive become refugees, living among peoples of other cultures. Examples of this may be seen in many parts of the world today; the closest examples are to be found in many parts of South America, again as in Brazil's Amazon basin. One particularly well-documented case occurred in 1968, when hired killers tried to wipe out several Indian groups, including the Cinta-Larga. For this they used arsenic, dynamite, and machine guns from light planes; in the case of the Cinta-Largas, the killers chose a time when an important native ceremony was taking place to attack a village, seen as an obstacle to development. Violence continues to be used in Brazil as a means of dealing with native people. For example, as a conservative estimate, at least 1,500 Yanomami died in the 1980s, often as victims of deliberate massacres, as cattle ranchers and miners poured into north-

ern Brazil. By 1990, 70 percent of the Yanomami's land in Brazil had been unconstitutionally expropriated, their supplies of fish were poisoned by mercury contamination of rivers, and malaria, venereal disease, and tuberculosis were widespread. The Yanomami were dying at the rate of 10 percent a year, and their fertility had dropped off to near zero. Many villages were left with no children or old people, and the survivors awaited their fate with a profound terror of extinction.[6] The usual attitude of the Brazilians to such situations is illustrated by the reaction of their government when two Kayapó Indians and an anthropologist traveled to the United States, where they spoke with members of several congressional committees, as well as officials of the Department of State, the Treasury, and the World Bank about the destruction of their land and way of life caused by internationally financed development projects. All three were charged with violating Brazil's Foreign

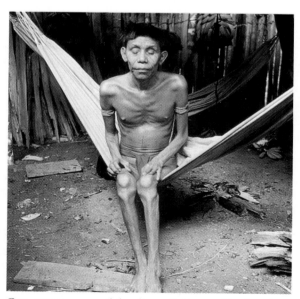

One consequence of the disruption caused by invasion of the Yanomami homeland by miners and other Brazilians is starvation, clearly the plight of the man shown here.

[6]Turner, T. (1991). Major shift in Brazilian Yanomami policy. *Anthropology Newsletter, 32*(5), 1; 46.

Sedition Act. Fortunately, international expressions of outrage at these and other atrocities have brought about positive changes on the part of Brazilian authorities, but whether their recommendations will be sufficient, or will even be acted upon fully, remains to be seen. We will return to this problem later in this chapter.

Genocide

The case of the Brazilian Indians just cited raises the issue of **genocide**—the extermination of one group of people by another, often deliberately and in the name of "progress." Genocide is not new in the world, as we need look no farther than North American history to see. In 1637, for example, a deliberate attempt was made to destroy the Pequot Indians by setting afire their village at Mystic, Connecticut, and then shooting down all those—primarily women and children—who sought to escape being burned alive. To try to ensure that even their very memory would be stamped out, colonial authorities forbad even the mention of the Pequot's name. Several other massacres of Indian peoples occurred thereafter, up until the last one at Wounded Knee, South Dakota, in 1890. Of course, such acts were by no means restricted to North America; one of the most famous nineteenth-century acts of genocide was the extermination of the aboriginal inhabitants of Tasmania, a large island south of Australia. In this case, the use of military force failed to achieve the complete elimination of the Tasmanians, but what the military could not achieve, a missionary could. George Augustus Robinson was able to round up the surviving natives, and at his mission station the deadly combination of psychological depression and European diseases brought about the demise of the last full-blooded Tasmanians in time for Robinson to retire to England a moderately wealthy man.

<hr>

Genocide: The extermination of one people by another, often in the name of "progress," either as a deliberate act or as the accidental outcome of activities carried out by one people with little regard for their impact on others.

<hr>

The most widely known act of genocide in recent history was the attempt of the Nazi Germans to wipe out European Jews and gypsies in the name of racial superiority. Unfortunately, the common practice of referring to this as "*the* holocaust"—as if it were something unique or at least exceptional—tends to blind us to the fact that this thoroughly monstrous act is simply one more example of an all too common phenomenon. From 1945 to 1987, a minimum of 6.8 million, but perhaps as many as 16.3 million people were victims of internal (within state) genocide, as compared to the 3.34 million people who have died in wars between different countries from 1945 to 1980.[7] Moreover, genocide continues to occur in the world today in places like Iraq, where, in 1988, the government began to use poison gas against Kurdish villagers, and (as we will see in Chapter 16) Guatemala, to mention but two cases. If such ugly practices are ever to end, we must gain a better understanding of them than currently exists. Anthropologists are actively engaged in this, carrying out cross-cultural as well as individual case studies. One finding to emerge is the regularity with which religious, economic, and political interests are allied in cases of genocide. In Tasmania, for example, wool growers wanted aborigines off the land so they could have it for their sheep. The government advanced their interests through its military campaigns against the natives, but it was Robinson's missionary work that finally secured Tasmania for the wool interests. In the 1960s and 1970s, the Ju/'hoansi living in Namibia found themselves in a situation remarkably similar to that experienced earlier by the Tasmanians; a combination of religious (Dutch Reformed church), political (Namibia's Department of Nature Conservation), and economic (agricultural/pastoral and touristic) interests brought about the people's confinement to a reserve where disease and apathy caused death rates to outstrip birth rates. Other such cases might be cited; for example, a cooperative relationship among Oblate missions, the Royal Canadian Mounted Police, and the Hudson Bay Company was instrumental in bringing about the demise, in the 1950s, of the Ihalmiut who lived in Canada's

[7]Van Den Berghe, P. (1992). The modern state: Nation builder or nation killer? *International Journal of Group Tensions, 22*(3), 198.

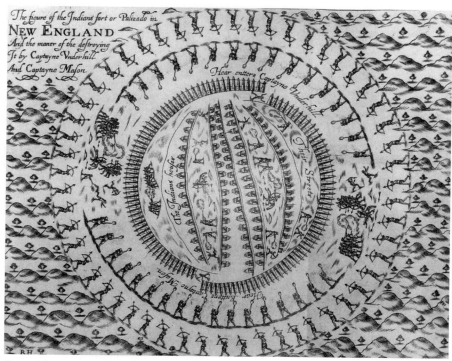

Genocide is not new in the world; this 1638 illustration shows English colonists with their Narragansett allies (the outer ring of bowmen) shooting down Pequot Indian women, children, and unarmed men attempting to flee their homes, which have been set afire.

"Barren Grounds" west of Hudson Bay.[8] The latter case is important, for it clearly illustrates that genocide is not always a deliberate act. It also occurs as the unforeseen outcome of activities carried out with little regard for their impact on other peoples. For the people whose lives are snuffed out, however, it makes no difference whether the genocide is deliberate or not; for them, the outcome is the same.

Directed Change

The most extreme cases of acculturation usually occur as a result of military conquest and displacement of traditional political authority by conquerors who know or care nothing about the culture they control. The indigenous people, unable to resist imposed changes and prevented from carrying out many of their traditional social,

religious, and economic activities, may be forced into new activities that tend to isolate individuals and tear apart the integration of their societies. Such a people are the Ju/'hoansi of Namibia, who were rounded up in the early 1960s and confined to a reserve where they could not possibly provide for their own needs. In this situation, they were provided by the government with rations that were insufficient to meet their nutritional needs. In poor health and prevented from developing meaningful alternatives to traditional activities, the people became argumentative and depressed and, as already noted, their death rate came to exceed that of birth. After a visit to the reserve in 1980, anthropologist Robert J. Gordon commented: "I had never been in a place where one could literally smell death and decay, as in Tsumkwe."[9] In the 1980s, however, the Ju/'hoansi began to take matters into their own hands, returning to

[8]Mowat, F. (1959). *The desperate people.* Boston: Little, Brown.

[9]Gordon, R. J. (1992). *The Bushman myth: The making of a Namibian underclass* (p. 3). Boulder, CO: Westview.

Two examples (out of many) of attempted genocide in the twentieth century: Hitler's Germany against Jews and gypsies, during the 1930s and the 1940s; and Saddam Hussein's Iraq against the Kurds, beginning in the 1980s.

waterholes in the backcountry where, assisted by anthropologists and others concerned with their welfare, they are trying to sustain themselves by raising livestock. Whether this will succeed or not remains to be seen, as there are still many obstacles to success.

One by-product of colonial dealings with indigenous peoples has been the growth of **applied anthropology** and the use of anthropological techniques and knowledge for certain "practical" ends. For example, British anthropology has often

been considered the "handmaiden" of that country's colonial policy, for it typically provided the kind of information of particular use in maintaining effective colonial rule. In the United States,

Applied anthropology: The use of anthropological knowledge and techniques for the purpose of solving "practical" problems, often for a specific "client."

A common agent of change in many nonindustrial societies is the religious missionary. Although they see themselves as bringing enlightenment to indigenous peoples, such missionaries seek to subvert the beliefs that lie at the heart of such cultures and that make life within them meaningful.

FRANZ BOAS
(1858–1942)

Born in Germany, where he studied physics and geography, Franz Boas came to the United States to live in 1888. His interest in anthropology began a few years earlier with a trip to Baffinland, where he met his first so-called primitive people. Thereafter, he and his students came to dominate anthropology in North America through the first three decades of the 1900s. Through meticulous and detailed fieldwork, which set new standards for excellence, Boas and his students were able to expose the shortcomings of the grandiose, culture-bound schemes of cultural evolution which had been proposed by earlier social theorists. His thesis that a culture must be understood according to its own standards and values, rather than those of the investigator, represented a tremendously liberating philosophy in his time. (The photo shows Boas posing as a Kwakiutl hanatsa dancer for a National Museum diorama, 1895.)

the Bureau of American Ethnology was founded toward the end of the nineteenth century, to gather reliable data on which the government might base its Indian policies. At the time, North American anthropologists were convinced of the practical usefulness of their discipline, and many who carried out ethnographic work among Indians devoted a great deal of time, energy, and even money to assisting their informants, whose interests were frequently threatened from outside. In the present century the scope of applied anthropology has broadened. Early on, the applied work of Franz Boas, who almost single-handedly trained a generation of anthropologists in the United States, was instrumental in reforming the country's immigration policies. In the 1930s, anthropologists carried out a number of studies in industrial and other institutional settings in the United States, with avowedly applied goals. With World War II came the first efforts at colonial administration beyond U.S. borders, especially in the Pacific, made by officers trained in anthropology. The rapid recovery of Japan was due in no small measure to the influence of anthropologists in structuring the U.S. occupation. Anthropologists continue to play an active role today in administering the U.S. trust territories in the Pacific.

Today, applied anthropologists are in demand in the field of international development because of their specialized knowledge of social structure,

In the past few decades, Western countries have sent technological "missionaries" to teach people in other places new ways of doing old tasks. Unless they have had anthropological training, however, such "missionaries" are apt to be unaware of the side effects their new ways will have.

value systems, and the functional interrelatedness of cultures targeted for development. The role of the applied anthropologists, however, is far from easy; as anthropologists, they respect the dignity of other peoples and the integrity of their cultures, yet they are being asked for advice on how to change certain aspects of those cultures. If the request comes from the people themselves, that is one thing, but more often than not, the request comes from some outside "expert." Supposedly, the proposed change is for the good of the targeted population, yet they do not always see it that way. Just how far applied anthropologists should go in advising how people—especially ones without the power to resist—can be made to embrace changes that have been proposed for them is a serious ethical question.

In spite of such difficulties, applied anthropology is flourishing today as never before. As the several Anthropology Applied boxes throughout this book illustrate, anthropologists now practice their profession in many different nonacademic settings, both at home and abroad, in a wide variety of ways.

Applied anthropologists work not only abroad but at home as well. Here, an anthropologist, who is a business consultant, advises a car repair business.

REACTIONS TO FORCIBLE CHANGE

The reactions of indigenous peoples to the changes that have been thrust upon them by outsiders have varied considerably. Some have responded by removing themselves to the nearest available forest, desert, or other inhospitable place, in hopes of being left alone. In Brazil, a number of communities once located near the coast took this option a few hundred years ago and were successful until the great push to develop the Amazon forest began in the 1960s. Others, like the Indians of North America, tried to fight back, but were ultimately defeated and reduced to an impoverished underclass in their own land. Sometimes, though, people have managed to keep faith with their own traditions by inventing creative and ingenious ways of expressing them in the face of powerful foreign domination. This blending of indigenous and foreign elements into a new system is known as

syncretism, and a fine illustration of it is the game of cricket as played by the Trobriand Islanders, some of whose practices we looked at in Chapters 18, 19, and 20.

Under British rule, the Trobrianders were introduced by missionaries to the rather staid British game of cricket, to replace the erotic dancing and open sexuality that normally followed the harvest of yams. Traditionally, this was the time when chiefs sought to spread their fame by hosting nights of dancing, in the course of which they provided food for the hundreds of young married people who participated. For two months or so, there

Syncretism: In acculturation, the blending of indigenous and foreign traits to form a new system.

Anthropology Applied
GROWING TREES IN HAITI

When foreigners go to Haiti, one of the things that impresses them is the massive deforestation that has taken place. Since colonial times, this country's population has swelled from fewer than half a million to more than six million—too many people for too little arable land. In their quest for fields, peasants eventually cut down nearly all stands of trees in remote areas. The resultant erosion, coupled with overutilization of crop land, resulted in catastrophic declines in yields, sending many peasants into the capital, Port au Prince, in search of other work. This in turn created a growing demand for construction wood and charcoal in that city, which the rural poor were happy to satisfy by going after the country's few remaining trees. Responding to this crisis, international development organizations unsuccessfully poured millions of dollars into studies of the problem, as well as into reforestation schemes. Not only were very few seedlings planted, but also those that were quickly became forage for the goats of peasants, who were reluctant to devote any of their scarce land holdings to the growing of state-owned trees.

Faced with failure, the U.S. Agency for International Development (AID) in Haiti invited anthropologist Gerald F. Murray to develop an alternative approach to reforestation and subsequently hired him as Project Director. Already familiar with peasant land usage in Haiti, Murray knew that typical reforestation projects, such as the planting of fruit trees by agents of the government for purposes of soil conservation, would not work. To peasants, fruit trees were of little commercial or nutritional value, especially if they were perceived as being state owned. What they needed was a cash crop which was theirs to do with as they wished. Accordingly, what Murray did was to make available, through nongovernmental organizations rather than state agencies, seedlings of leucaena, ocassia, and eucalyptus, fast-growing trees good for charcoal and basic construction material, for

which there was a ready market. Moreover, the trees could be cut in some instances as early as four years after planting and could be grown along borders of fields or even intercropped among other plants, rather than in large unbroken, uncropped stands. Thus, their growth was compatible with continued subsistence farming. Moreover, any potential loss from decreased food production was far offset by income the trees would generate.

The idea that trees were meant to be cut, while heretical to the international development "establishment," was extremely popular with the peasants. As Murray observes, "though it had taken AID two years to decide about the project; it took about twenty minutes with any group of skeptical but economically rational peasants to generate a list of enthusiastic potential tree planters. . . . Cash-flow dialogues and ownership . . . were a far cry from the finger-wagging ecological sermons to which many peasant groups had been subjected on the topic of trees."* When first conceived, the planting of three million trees, on the land of six thousand peasants, was set as the project's four year goal. In fact, by the end of the fourth year, 20 million trees had been planted by 75,000 peasants. Unlike bureaucratically conceived projects, this anthropologically conceived and carried out agroforestry project turned out to be reasonably successful, up until the ouster of President Aristide by the Haitian military. Unfortunately, one of the means by which the military regime asserted its control in rural areas was to wantonly cut down trees. What will happen following the restoration of Aristide to power remains to be seen.

*Murray, G. F. (1989). The domestication of wood in Haiti: A case study in applied evolution. In A. Podolefsky & P. J. Brown (Eds.), *Applying anthropology, An introductory reader* (pp. 151–152). Mountain View, CA: Mayfield.

would be night after night of provocative dancing, accompanied by chanting and shouting full of sexual innuendo, each night ending as couples disappeared off into the bush together. Since no chief wished to be outdone by any other (to be outdone reflected on the strength of one's magic), there was

a strong competitive element to all of this dancing, and fighting sometimes erupted. To the missionaries, cricket seemed a good way to end all of this, in a way that would encourage conformity to "civilized" comportment in dress, religion, and "sportsmanship." The Trobrianders, however, were determined to "rubbish" (throw out) the British game, and turned it into the same kind of distinctly Trobriand event that their dance competitions had once been.[10]

The Trobrianders made cricket their own by adding battle dress and battle magic and by incorporating erotic dancing into the festivities. Instead of inviting dancers each night, chiefs now arrange games of cricket. Pitching has been modified from the British style to one closer to their old way of throwing a spear. Following the game, they hold massive feasts, where wealth is displayed to enhance their prestige. Cricket, in its altered form, has been made to serve traditional systems of prestige and exchange. Neither "primitive" nor passively accepted in its original form, Trobriand cricket was thoughtfully and creatively adapted into a sophisticated activity reflecting the importance of basic indigenous cultural premises. Exuberance and pride are displayed by everyone associated with the game, and the players are as much concerned with conveying the full meaning of who they are as with scoring well. From the sensual dressing in preparation for the game to the team chanting of songs full of sexual metaphors and to erotic chorus-line dancing between the innings, there is little doubt that each player is playing for his own importance, for the fame of his team, and for the hundreds of attractive young women who usually watch the game.

Revitalization movements that attempt to revive traditional ways of the past are not restricted to "underdeveloped" countries; in the United States, the Reverend Pat Robertson is a leader in such a movement.

Revitalization Movements

Another common reaction to forcible change is revitalization, a process already touched upon in Chapter 24. Revitalization may be defined as a deliberate attempt by some members of a society to construct a more satisfactory culture by the rapid acceptance of a pattern of multiple innovations. Once primary ties of culture, social relationships, and activities are broken, and meaningless activity is imposed by force, individuals and groups characteristically react with fantasy, withdrawal, and escape.

Examples of revitalization movements have been common in the history of the United States whenever significant segments of the population have found their conditions in life to be at odds

[10]Weiner, A. B. (1977). Review of Trobriand cricket: An ingenious response to colonialism. *American Anthropologist, 79,* 506.

with the values of "the American Dream." For example, in the nineteenth century, periodic depression and the disillusionment of the decades after the Civil War produced a host of revitalization movements, of which the most successful was that of the Mormons. In the twentieth century, movements repeatedly sprung up in the slums of major cities, as well as in depressed rural areas such as Appalachia. By the 1960s, a number of movements were becoming less inward-looking and more "activist," a good example being the rise of the Black Muslim movement. The 1960s also saw the rise of revitalization movements among the young of middle-class and even upper-class families. In their case, the professed values of peace, equality, and individual freedom were seen to be at odds with the reality of persistent war, poverty, and constraints on individual action imposed by a variety of impersonal institutions. Their reaction to these things was expressed by their use of drugs, in their outlandish or "freaky" clothes, hair styles, music, speech, and in their behavior toward authority and authority figures.

By the 1980s revitalization movements were becoming prominent even among older, more affluent segments of society, as in the rise of the so-called religious right. In these cases, the reaction is not so much against a perceived failure of the American dream as it is against perceived threats to that dream by dissenters and activists within their society, by foreign governments, by new ideas that challenge other ideas that they would like to believe, and by the sheer complexity of modern life.

Clearly, when value systems get out of step with existing realities, for whatever reason, a condition of cultural crisis is likely to build up that may breed some form of reactive movement. Not all suppressed, conquered, or colonized people eventually rebel against established authority, although why they do not is still a debated issue. When they do, however, resistance may take one of several forms, all of which are varieties of revitalization movements. A culture may seek to speed up the acculturation process in order to share more fully in the supposed benefits of the dominant cultures. Melanesian cargo cults of the post–World War II era have generally been of this sort, although earlier ones stressed a revival of traditional ways. Sometimes, a movement tries to reconstitute a destroyed but not forgotten way of life, as did many Plains Indians in the nineteenth century, and as do movements of the "religious right" today. Sometimes, attempts are made by a suppressed pariah group, which has long suffered in an inferior social standing and which has its own special subcultural ideology, to create a new social order; the most familiar examples of this to Western peoples are prophetic Judaism and early Christianity. If the aim of the movement is directed primarily to the ideological system and the attendant social structure of a cultural system from within, it is then called **revolutionary.**

Revolutionary: A revitalization movement from within, directed primarily at the ideological system and the attendant social structure of a culture.

REBELLION AND REVOLUTION

When the scale of discontent within a society reaches a certain level, the possibilities for rebellion and revolution—such as the Iranian Revolution, the Sandinista Revolution in Nicaragua, or the Zapatista uprising in Mexico—are high.

The question of why revolutions come into being, as well as why they frequently fail to live up to the expectations of the people initiating them, is a problem. It is clear, however, that the colonial policies of countries such as England, France, Spain, Portugal, and the United States during the nineteenth and early twentieth centuries have created a worldwide situation in which revolution has become nearly inevitable. In spite of the political independence most colonies have gained since World War II, many of them continue to be exploited by more powerful countries for their natural resources and cheap labor, causing a deep resentment of rulers beholden to foreign powers. Further discontent has been caused by the attempts of the governing elite of newly independent states to assert their control over peoples living within their boundaries who, by virtue of a common ancestry, possession of distinct cultures, persistent occupation of their own territories, and traditions of self-determination, identify themselves as distinct nations and refuse to recognize the sovereignty of what they regard as a foreign government. Thus, in many a former colony, large numbers of people have taken up arms to resist annexation and absorption by imposed state regimes run by people of other nationalities. In their attempts to make their states into nations, governing elites of one nationality endeavor to strip the peoples of other nations within their states of their lands, resources, and sense of identity as a people. The phenomenon is so common as to lead anthropologist Pierre Van Den Berghe to label what modern states refer to as "nation building" as, in fact, "nation killing."[11] One of the most important facts of our time is that the vast majority of the distinct peoples of the world have never consented to rule by the governments of states within which they find themselves living.[12] In many newly emerged

---

[11]Van Den Berghe, P. (1992). The modern state: Nation builder or nation killer? *International Journal of Group Tensions, 22*(3), 191–207.

[12]Nietschmann, B. (1987). The third world war. *Cultural Survival Quarterly, 11*(3), 3.

countries, such peoples feel they have no other option than to fight.

On the basis of an examination of four revolutions of the past—English, American, French, and Bolshevik—the following conditions have been offered as precipitators of rebellion and revolution:

1. Loss of prestige of established authority, often as a result of the failure of foreign policy, financial difficulties, dismissals of popular ministers, or alteration of popular policies.
2. Threat to recent economic improvement. In France and Russia, those sections of the population (professional classes and urban workers) whose economic fortunes had previously taken an upward swing were "radicalized" by unexpected setbacks, such as steeply rising food prices and unemployment.
3. Indecisiveness of government, as exemplified by lack of consistent policy; such governments appear to be controlled by, rather than in control of, events.
4. Loss of support of the intellectual class. Such a loss deprived the prerevolutionary governments of France and Russia of philosophical support, thus leading to their lack of popularity with the literate public.
5. A leader or group of leaders with charisma enough to mobilize a substantial part of the population against the establishment.

Apart from resistance to internal authority, such as in the English, French, and Russian revolutions, many revolutions in modern times have been struggles against an authority imposed on them by outsiders. Such resistance usually takes the form of independence movements that wage campaigns of armed defiance against colonial powers. The Algerian struggle for independence from France and the American Revolution are typical examples. Of the 120 or so armed conflicts in the world today, 98 percent are in the economically poor countries of Africa, Asia, Central and South America, almost all of which were at one time under European colonial domination. Of these wars, 75 percent are between the state and one or more peoples within the state's borders who are seeking to maintain or regain control of their persons, communities, lands, and resources in the face

A leading cause of rebellion and revolution in the world today is the refusal of governing elites to recognize the cultural, economic, and political rights of people of other nationalities over which the state has unilaterally asserted its authority. A recent illustration is the Zapatista uprising in Mexico, in response to continued repressive control by Ladinos (non-Indians).

of what they regard as subjugation by a foreign power.[13]

Not all revolts are truly revolutionary in their consequences. According to Max Gluckman, rebellions:

> "throw the rascals out" and substitute another set, but there is no attempt to alter either the cultural ideology or the form of the social structure. In political revolution, attempts are made to seize the offices of power in order to change social structure, belief systems, and their symbolic representations. Political revolutions are usually turbulent, violent, and not long-lasting. A successful revolution soon moves to re-establish a stable, though changed, social structure; yet it has far-reaching political, social and sometimes economic and cultural consequences.[14]

Not always are revolutions successful about accomplishing what they set out to do. One of the stated goals of the Chinese revolution, for example, was to liberate women from the oppression of a strongly patriarchal society in which a woman owed life-long obedience to some man or other—first her father, later her husband and, after his death, her sons. Although some progress was made, the overall effort has been frustrated by the cultural lens through which the revolutionaries have viewed their work. A tradition of extreme patriarchy extending back at least 22 centuries is not easily overcome and has unconsciously influenced many of the decisions made by China's leaders since 1949. In rural China today, as in the past, a woman's life is still usually determined by her relationship to some man, be it her father, husband, or son, rather than her own efforts or failures. What's more, women are being told more and more that their primary role is as wives and mothers. When they do work outside the house, it is generally at jobs with low pay, low status, and no benefits. Thus in spite of whatever autonomy they may achieve for a while, they become totally dependent in their old age on their sons. What we

see here is that subversion of revolutionary goals, if it occurs, is not necessarily brought about by political opponents. Rather, it may be a consequence of the revolutionaries' own cultural background. In rural China, so long as women marry out, and land is held by families, daughters will always be seen as something of a liability.

It should be pointed out that revolution is a relatively recent phenomenon, occurring only during the last 5,000 years or so. The reason for this is that political rebellion requires a centralized political authority (chiefdom or state) to rebel against, and states (if not chiefdoms) have been in existence for only 5,000 years. Obviously, then, in those societies typified by tribes and bands, and in other nonindustrial societies lacking central authority, there could not have been rebellion or political revolution.

MODERNIZATION

One of the most frequently used terms to describe social and cultural change as these are occurring today is **modernization.** This is most clearly defined as an all-encompassing and global process of cultural and socioeconomic change, whereby developing societies seek to acquire some of the characteristics common to industrial societies. If one looks very closely at this definition, one sees that "becoming modern" really means "becoming like us," ("us" being the United States) with the very clear implication that not being like us is to be antiquated and obsolete. Not only is this ethnocentric, it also fosters the notion that these other societies must be changed to be more like us, irrespective of other considerations. It is unfortunate that the term *modernization* continues to be so widely used. Since we seem to be stuck with it, the best we can do at the moment is to recognize its inappropriateness, even though we continue to use it.

⟨◦◦◦⟩

Modernization: The process of cultural and socioeconomic change, whereby developing societies acquire some of the characteristics of Western industrialized societies.

⟨◦◦◦⟩

---

[13]Nietschmann, B. (1987). The third world war. *Cultural Survival Quarterly, 11*(3), 7.

[14]Hoebel, E. A. (1972). *Anthropology: The study of man* (4th ed.) (p. 667). New York: McGraw-Hill.

Structural differentiation. Whereas most items for daily use were once made at home, as in this quilting party (left), almost everything we use today is the product of specialized production, as are the quilts shown in the linens boutique (right).

The process of modernization may be best understood as consisting of four subprocesses, of which one is technological development. In the course of modernization, traditional knowledge and techniques give way to the application of scientific knowledge and techniques borrowed mainly from the West. Another subprocess is agricultural development, represented by a shift in emphasis from subsistence farming to commercial farming. Instead of raising crops and livestock for their own use, people turn more and more to the production of cash crops, with greater reliance on a cash economy and markets for the sale of farm products and purchase of goods. A third subprocess is industrialization, with a greater emphasis placed on inanimate forms of energy—especially fossil fuels—to power machines. Human and animal power become less important, as do handicrafts in general. The fourth subprocess is urbanization, marked particularly by population movements from rural settlements into cities. Although all four subprocesses are interrelated, there is no fixed order of appearance.

As modernization takes place, other changes are likely to follow. In the political realm, political parties and some sort of electoral machinery frequently appear, along with the development of a bureaucracy. In education, there is an expansion of learning opportunities, literacy increases, and an indigenous educated elite develops. Religion becomes less important in many areas of thought and behavior, as traditional beliefs and practices are undermined. The traditional rights and duties connected with kinship are altered, if not eliminated, especially where distant kin are concerned. Finally, where stratification is a factor, mobility increases as ascribed status becomes less important and achievement counts for more.

Two other features of modernization go hand in hand with those already noted. One, **structural differentiation,** is the division of single traditional roles, which embrace two or more functions, into two or more separate roles, each with a single specialized function. This represents a kind of fragmentation of society, which must be counteracted by new **integrative mechanisms,** if the society is not to disintegrate into a number of discrete units. These new mechanisms take such forms as formal governmental structures, official state ideologies, political parties, legal codes, labor and trade unions, as well as other common-interest associations. All

Structural differentiation: The division of single traditional roles, which embrace two or more functions (for example, political, economic, and religious) into two or more roles, each with a single specialized function.

Integrative mechanisms: Cultural mechanisms that oppose forces for differentiation in a society; in modernizing societies, they include formal governmental structures, official state ideologies, political parties, legal codes, labor and trade unions, and other common-interest associations.

of these cross-cut other societal divisions and so serve to oppose differentiating forces. These two forces, however, are not the only ones in opposition in a situation of modernization; to them must be added a third, the force of **tradition.** This opposes the new forces of both differentiation and integration. On the other hand, the conflict does not have to be total. Traditional ways may on occasion facilitate modernization. For example, rural people may be assisted by traditional kinship ties as they move into cities, if they have relatives already there to whom they may turn for aid. One's relatives, too, may provide the financing that is necessary for business success.

One aspect of modernization, the technological explosion, has made it possible to transport human beings and ideas from one place to another with astounding speed and in great numbers. Formerly independent cultural systems have been brought into contact with others. The cultural differences between New York and Pukapuka are declining, while the differences between fishing people and physicists are increasing. No one knows whether this implies a net gain or net loss in cultural diversity, but the worldwide spread of anything, whether it is DDT or a new idea, should be viewed with at least caution. That human beings and human cultural systems are different is the most exciting thing about them, yet the destruction of diversity is implicit in the worldwide spread of rock-and-roll, socialism, capitalism, or anything else. When a song is forgotten or a ceremony ceases to be performed, a part of the human heritage is destroyed forever.

An examination of three traditional cultures that have felt the impact of modernization or other cultural changes will help to pinpoint some of the problems these cultures have met. The cultures are the Skolt Lapps of Finland, the Shuar Indians of Ecuador, and the Wauja of Brazil.

Tradition: In a modernizing society, old cultural practices, which may oppose new forces of differentiation and integration.

Skolt Lapps and the Snowmobile Revolution

The Skolt Lapps, whose homeland straddles the Arctic Circle in Finland, traditionally supported themselves by fishing and the herding of reindeer.[15] Although they depended on the outside world for certain material goods, the resources crucial for their system were locally available to all. No one was denied access to critical resources, and there was little social and economic differentiation among people. Theirs was basically an egalitarian society.

Of particular importance to the Skolt Lapps was reindeer herding. Indeed, herd management is central to their definition of themselves as a people. These animals were a source of meat, for home consumption or for sale in order to procure outside goods. They were also a source of hides for shoes and clothing, sinews for sewing, and antler and bone for making certain things. Finally, reindeer were used to pull sleds in the winter and as pack animals when there was no snow on the ground. Understandably, the animals were the objects of much attention. The herds were not large, but without a great deal of attention, productivity suffered. Hence, most winter activities centered on reindeer. Men, operating on skis, were closely associated with their herds, intensively from November to January, periodically from January to April.

In the early 1960s these reindeer herders speedily adopted snowmobiles, on the premise that the new machines would make herding physically easier and economically more advantageous. The first machine arrived in Finland in 1962; by 1971 there were 70 operating machines owned by the Skolt Lapps and non-Lapps in the same area.

[15]Pelto, P. J. (1973). *The snowmobile revolution: Technology and social change in the Arctic.* Menlo Park, CA: Cummings.

Although men on skis still carry out some herding activity, their importance and prestige are now diminished. As early as 1967 only four people were still using reindeer sleds for winter travel; most had gotten rid of draft animals. Those who had not converted to snowmobiles felt themselves disadvantaged compared to the rest.

The consequences of this mechanization were extraordinary and far-reaching. The need for snowmobiles, parts and equipment to maintain them, and a steady supply of gasoline created a dependency on the outside world unlike anything that had previously existed. As traditional skills were replaced by snowmobile technology, the ability of the Lapps to determine their own survival without dependence on outsiders, should this be necessary, was lost. Snowmobiles are also expensive, costing several thousand dollars in the Arctic. Maintenance and gasoline expenses must be added to this initial cost. Accordingly, there has been a sharp rise in the need for cash. To get this, men must go outside the Lapp community for wage work more than just occasionally, as had once been the case, or else rely on such sources as government pensions or welfare.

The argument may be made that dependency and the need for cash are prices worth paying for an improved system of reindeer herding; but has it improved? In truth, snowmobiles have contributed in a significant way to a disastrous decline in reindeer herding. By 1971 the average size of the family herd had declined from 50 to 12. Not only is this too small a number to be economically viable, it is too small to maintain at all. The reason is that the animals in such small herds will take the first opportunity to run off to join another larger one. What happened was that the old close, prolonged, and largely peaceful relationship between herdsman and beast changed to a noisy, traumatic relationship. Now, when men appear, it is to come speeding out of the woods on snarling, smelly machines that invariably chase animals, often for long distances. Instead of helping the animals in their winter food quest, helping females with their calves, and protecting them from predators, the appearance of men now means either slaughter or castration. Naturally enough, the reindeer have become suspicious. The result has been actual dedomestication, with reindeer scattering and running off to more inaccessible areas whenever possible. Moreover, there are indications that snowmobile

harassment has adversely affected the number of viable calves added to the herds. What we have here is a classic illustration of the fact that change is not always adaptive.

The cost of mechanized herding—and the decline of the herds—has led many Lapps to abandon it altogether. Now, the majority of males are no longer herders at all. This constitutes a serious economic problem, since few economic alternatives are available. The problem is compounded by the fact that participation in a cash-credit economy means that most people, employed or not, have payments to make. This is more than just an economic problem, for in the traditional culture of this people, being a herder of reindeer is the very essence of manhood. Hence, today's nonherders are not only poor in a way that they could not be in previous times, but they also are in a sense inadequate as "men" quite apart from this.

This economic differentiation with its evaluation of roles has led to the development of a stratified society out of the older egalitarian one. Differences have developed in terms of wealth, and with this, in lifestyles. It is difficult to break into reindeer herding now, for one needs a substantial cash outlay. And herding now requires skills and knowledge that were not a part of traditional culture. Not everyone has these, and those without them are dependent on others if they are to participate. Hence, there is now restricted access to critical resources, where once there had been no such restriction.

The Shuar Solution

Although the Skolt Lapps have not escaped many negative aspects of modernization, the choice to modernize or not was essentially theirs. The Shuar (sometimes called Jivaro) Indians, by contrast, deliberately avoided modernization, until they felt that they had no other option if they were to fend off the same outside forces that elsewhere in the Amazon Basin have resulted in the destruction of whole societies. Threatened with the loss of their land base as Ecuadoran colonists intruded into their territory, the Shuar in 1964 founded a fully independent corporate body, the Shuar Federation, to take control over their own future. Recognized by the government of Ecuador, albeit grudgingly, the federation is officially dedicated to promotion of the social, economic, and moral advancement of its members and to coordination of development with official government agencies. Since its founding, the federation has secured title to over 96,000 hectares of communal land, has established a cattle herd of more than 15,000 head as the people's primary source of income, has taken over control of their own education, using their own language and mostly Shuar teachers, has established their own bilingual broadcasting station and a bilingual newspaper. Obviously, all this

has required enormous changes on the part of the Shuar, but they have been able to maintain a variety of distinctive cultural markers, including their own language, communal land tenure, cooperative production and distribution, a basically egalitarian economy, and kin-based communities that retain maximum autonomy. Thus, for all the changes, they feel they are still Shuar and quite distinct from other Ecuadorans.[16]

What the Shuar case shows us is that Amazonian Indian nations are capable of taking control of their own destinies even in the face of intense outside pressures, if allowed to do so. Unfortunately, until recently, few have had that option. Prior to European invasions of the Amazon, more than 700 distinct groups inhabited the region. By 1900 in Brazil, the number was down to 270, and today something like 180 remain.[17] Many of these survivors find themselves in situations not unlike that of the Yanomami, described earlier in this chapter. Nevertheless, many of these peoples are showing a new resourcefulness in standing up to the forces of destruction arrayed against them, as the following Original Study illustrates.

[16]Bodley, J. H. (1990). *Victims of progress* (3rd ed.) (pp. 160–162). Mountain View, CA: Mayfield.

[17]*Cultural Survival Quarterly, 15*(4), (1991) 38.

Original Study
Wauja Organization in Defense of Their Homeland[18]

An idea is spreading in the rain forests of central Brazil, perhaps even more rapidly than the fires of deforestation: that Indians as a group are politically powerful. Indians living in isolated rainforest villages throughout Amazonia are coming to think of themselves as sharing an identity as Indian people.

In February 1989, the Kayapó and their allies staged a historic peaceful demonstration against a proposed hydroelectric project at Altamira, Brazil. The project, to be funded by the World Bank, would have flooded vast areas of Kayapó land and destroyed most of their rivers for fishing. Outraged that they had not even been consulted, the Kayapó organized themselves and mounted a spectacular media event in protest. Their campaign was so creative and well-executed that the ensuing international outcry caused the World Bank to withdraw its support for the dam project. The success of this initiative at Altamira profoundly changed political reality and expectations for Indian people in Brazil and beyond. The stereotype of Indian as victim was broken.

One example of this legacy is the current effort of the Wauja of the Upper Xingu to reclaim peacefully, under Brazilian law, traditional fishing grounds and a sacred ceremonial site, Kamukuaka. Both are currently being invaded or occupied by ranchers and poachers.

The Kayapo are one of a number of native Amazonian people who have become quite skilled at using techniques borrowed from the industrialized world to assert their own rights.

The Wauja are a community of about 200 relatively traditional Arawak-speaking Indians who live by fishing and swidden horticulture in the Xingu National Park in Northern Mato Grosso. Although during the past generation their economy has become dependent on steel tools, fishhooks, and other manufactured goods, their involvement in the cash economy is still minimal and sporadic, limited mainly to sale of handicrafts.

Like virtually all Indian people, during the early period of contact they suffered horrific population losses due to recurrent epidemics of introduced disease. Unlike most other Indians, however, much of their traditional land was reserved for them under law soon after regular contact began in the 1940s. Despite this measure of protection, an essential part of their traditional territory was left out of the park. This unprotected area includes fishing grounds; agricultural land; and, most important, Kamukuaka, the most sacred Wauja ceremonial site.

When the Wauja first began to understand that only part of their traditional territory fell within park boundaries, they protested to the government Indian agency, FUNAI, saying that the excluded area was essential to their survival as an Indian people. In response to the Wauja's most recent protests on the matter, FUNAI stated that a five-year study is needed before action can be taken.

The Wauja say that if nothing is done, in five years their ancestral land will be overrun and lost to them forever. Ranchers already occupy Kamukuaka, which is situated on the upper Batovi-Tamitatoala River. Atamai, political chief of the Wauja, describes the site as an extraordinary place, a great stone cavern beside a waterfall. At the mouth of the cavern are rock carvings made by ancestors of the Wauja, images of the parts of women that create life. The Wauja say the carvings have power to make living things increase and become abundant.

In addition, the Wauja revere Kamukuaka as the dwelling place of spirits. These spirits are respectfully addressed as kin, and referred to in the Wauja language as *inyākānāu,* "those who teach." The spirits guide the elders, appearing to them in visions and helping them heal the sick and maintain harmony within the village. To honor these spirits, the Wauja and their neighbors the Bacari have performed ceremonies at Kamukuaka for many generations. Wauja elders emphasize their most sacred ceremony, *kawika,* was performed at that place, and can proudly list deceased relatives who played kawika flutes at Kamukuaka. Mayaya, brother of Atamai and ceremonial leader of the Wauja, once sought to express his attachment to Kamukuaka without reducing it to words. An accomplished musician, he softly sang the melody of the sacred flute ceremony, concluding, "therefore that land means everything to us." In Wauja oral tradition, Kamukuaka has existed since the beginning of the world, before human beings were created. Chief Atamai says his late father took his children there before he died and told them the sacred story linked to that place, of how the Sun dwelt in the great stone house when he still walked the earth in human form. Atamai himself has seen the gaping hole in the side of the cavern where, according to the ancestors, the Sun tried to tear the house apart in those ancient times.

Today, the ranchers keep the Wauja out. The ancient ceremonies cannot be performed, and young people know Kamukuaka only through the stories of their elders. Even worse, the Wauja say, is the desecration the ranchers have brought:

> They have turned Kamukuaka into a cattle pasture. There used to be giant trees all around the stone cavern, right up to the waterfall, but the ranchers have ripped them all out, leaving the earth bare and pitiful. They graze cattle there now. Our ceremonial ground is covered with stinking cattle droppings. The whiteman has covered the dust of our ancestors with shit.

The loss of Kamukuaka has had economic consequences for the Wauja as well, since the area along the Batovi near Kamukuaka is the only source for certain essential raw materials, including ceramic pigments, medicinal plants, and shells used in trade.

But Kamukuaka is not the only area where outsiders are invading the Wauja's ancestral land. In 1988 and again in 1989, Atamai complained to government officials that poachers were penetrating deep into Wauja territory and taking commercial quantities of fish to sell in Brazilian towns along the upper Batovi River. The poachers enter Wauja waters in boats filled with heavily armed men, and transport the fish to small trucks waiting at designated locations outside Wauja territory.

Wauja attempts to keep poachers out have led to violent confrontations in which poachers have shot at Wauja fishermen without provocation. Because of poachers, ordinary overnight fishing trips have suddenly become dangerous. Parents now discourage their adolescent boys from going on fishing trips unless accompanied by an elder who can be trusted to handle a threatening situation.

In addition to the physical danger posed by armed invaders, the sheer loss of fish is a serious problem, since the Wauja depend on fish for most of the protein in their diet. The areas currently being invaded by poachers are some of the best traditional fishing grounds. Generations of Wauja have relied on these areas to provide the large numbers of fish needed for ceremonial feasts. As a result of the continuing depredation by poachers, the Wauja say these areas are becoming "fished out." Poaching therefore threatens traditional Wauja economy, which is based in large part on communal sharing and ceremonial redistribution, not private profit and accumulated wealth.

The incident in early 1989, when the chief and other elders were shot at by poachers, was a turning point for the Wauja. That summer they decided the government would not defend their land and resources, and that they would have to do it themselves. They built a new village, Aldeia Batovi, within the park but near the area where the poachers and ranchers were penetrating. Gardens were cleared and planted; three large, traditional houses were built; and several families took up permanent residence there, maintaining contact with the main village at Lake Piyulaga by radio.

In June 1990, this new village was burned to the ground by an employee of a local rancher. The three houses were lost, along with all they contained: tools, stores of food, and medical supplies. Responding to letters of protest from abroad, the Brazilian government tried to minimize this incident, alleging the ranchers merely torched a makeshift campsite the Wauja had used overnight and abandoned. This is not the case. No temporary Wauja campsite has first-year gardens; the village was inhabited. Confrontation was avoided only because the occupants were away attending a ceremony at the main village during the attack.

The Brazilian government insists these incidents were not violent, even though shots were fired and houses burned. The Wauja do not agree. They consider themselves under attack, and blame the escalating violence on faulty demarcation of their territory years ago, when the Xingu National Park was created. To correct the situation, the Wauja say park boundaries must be moved south a distance of 30–40 km, to include critical parts of their traditional territory. The area of land is not large, but it is crucial to the Wauja and to peace in the region. Though it forms the outer margin of their territory, it is at the center of their traditions and their identity as Indian people.

The Wauja have already rebuilt their burned village and renamed it Aldeia Ulupuene. To maintain an increased presence in the area, they are adding an airstrip at the site of the attack. Soon after their village was burned, the Wauja asked the government to survey the land officially outside the park in order to have it included in the park and thereby protected. Officials replied that they lacked funds for such a project. In response, the Wauja, together with members of other indigenous communities, decided to survey the land themselves.

In August, a volunteer force of about 50 men drawn from Kayapó, Kajabi, Soya, Trumai, Yawalapiti, and Wauja communities assembled at the burned village site to survey the land. This in itself is a major achievement by the Wauja, and a credit to the volunteers. In the first half of this century, some of these communities fought pitched battles against each other, and in several well-remembered instances inflicted heavy casualties and took women and children captive. The men in this volunteer group are working close beside traditional enemies of their fathers and grandfathers. That they all are united in a common purpose bespeaks their determination to protect their shared future as Indian people.

The volunteers have begun clearing surveying sightlines and building the airstrip. The project is expected to take three to six months, depending on support from outside sources. Since the new village is six days' journey from the main village by dugout canoe, the Wauja need motorboats to transport people and supplies, as well as food to feed the volunteers.

The Rainforest Foundation, founded in 1988 by Kapapó chief Raoni and rock musician Sting to support Indian-initiated efforts to protect the rain forest, has taken on the Wauja project as a top priority. Olympio Serra, formerly director of the Xingu National Park and now working on the Rainforest Foundation's Brazilian board, Fundação Mata Virgem, reports that 4,000 liters of gasoline and food for the volunteers were shipped to the Wauja the first week of October 1990. These supplies should enable the Wauja to finish the job before the heavy rains arrive in December.

José Carlos Libânio at the Nucleus for Indigenous Rights (NDI) in Brasilia explains that surveying the area is an important step in protecting it for Indian people under Brazilian law. He says the Wauja's legal case, currently under preparation, stands to set a legal precedent on behalf of all Brazilian Indians. To expand the Xingu National Park boundaries, the Wauja's lawyers must challenge an administrative decree that currently prohibits altering existing boundaries of indigenous reserves. This decree works against Indians, denying them redress against boundary decisions made without their knowledge or consent.

Libânio says the Wauja case is strong, and he expects them to win it. However, it will take at least a year for the case to proceed through the Brazilian courts. During that time, the Wauja will need support from the international community. A public information and letter-writing campaign is currently being organized to help create a climate of opinion in Brazil favorable to a just resolution of the Wauja's legal case.

Although all Amazonian Indians are facing serious threats to their survival, the Wauja's case is crucial in several respects. First, their legal case stands to set a major precedent on behalf of all Brazilian Indians. If the Wauja win the right to reclaim traditional territory under law, all Brazilian Indians benefit.

Second, the Wauja campaign for nonviolent, legal reclamation of territory is setting a historical precedent as well. The Wauja have never attacked or killed Brazilian settlers. If they are successful in reclaiming their territory through entirely nonviolent means, it will be a landmark victory for both Indian rights and rainforest conservation.

Third, the Wauja's case presents a unique opportunity simply because they stand a good chance of winning. The Yanomami situation is currently receiving worldwide attention; Survival International rightly calls it one of the great humanitarian campaigns of the late twentieth century. Both in numbers of people affected, and in severity of human rights violations, the Yanomami case outweighs the Wauja case. But the Yanomami campaign faces great odds, and will be very difficult to win. The gold miners are organized and determined; the political situation is complex and entrenched. The suffering of the Yanomami is so intense and unrelenting that it is a public relations problem to maintain enough optimism to keep the international community actively involved.

The Wauja case, on the other hand, is relatively straightforward and easy to win. A win for the Wauja will help the Yanomami as well, because success attracts optimism and support. The Yanomami situation seems almost hopeless, and this is a great part of the problem. If the Wauja create a well-publicized victory for indigenous rights in Brazil, the cause of the Yanomami and other Brazilian Indians will be advanced, just as the Wauja's own cause was advanced by the Kapapó victory at Altamira.

It is difficult to convey to members of an international community that is increasingly mobile and secular how the Wauja, and other people in traditional small-scale societies, are connected to their ancestral lands not only by economic necessity, but by far deeper bonds. The Wauja's land provides far more than food, tools, and shelter. It is the dwelling place of the spirits who guide them, the birthplace of their children, and the resting place of their ancestors. It is the sacred landscape of all their poetry, stories, songs, and prayers; it is their one place upon the earth. Everything needed for human life, everything sacred and precious, flows from that land. If it is ripped away from the Wauja, if they lose it, they lose their future as Indian people, a danger of which they are keenly aware.

[18]Ireland, E. (1991). Neither warriors nor victims, The Wauja peacefully organize to defend their land. *Cultural Survival Quarterly, 15*(1), 54–59.

Modernization and the "Underdeveloped" World

In the examples that we have just examined, we have seen how modernization has affected tribal peoples in otherwise "modern" states. Elsewhere in the so-called Underdeveloped World, whole countries are in the throes of modernization. Throughout Africa, Asia, and South and Central America we are witnessing the widespread removal of economic activities from the family-community setting; the altered structure of the family in the face of the changing labor market; the increased reliance of young children on parents alone for affection, instead of on the extended family; the decline of general parental authority; schools replacing the family as the primary educational unit; the discovery of a generation gap; and many others. The difficulty is that it all happens so fast that traditional societies are unable to adapt themselves to it gradually. Changes that took generations to accomplish in Europe and North America are attempted within the span of a single generation in developing countries. In the process they are fre-

quently faced with the erosion of a number of dearly held values they had no intention of giving up.

Commonly the burden of modernization falls most heavily on women. For example, the commercialization of agriculture often involves land reforms that overlook or ignore traditional land rights of women. At the same time that this reduces their control of, and access to, resources, mechanization of food production and processing drastically reduces their opportunities for employment. As a consequence, they are confined more and more to traditional domestic tasks which, as commercial production becomes people's dominant concern, is increasingly downgraded in value. To top it all off, the domestic workload tends to increase, as men are less available to help out, while tasks such as fuel gathering and water collection are made more difficult as common land and resources come under private ownership, and woodlands are reserved for commercial exploitation. In short, with modernization, women frequently find themselves in an increasingly marginal position. At the same time that their workload increases, the value assigned the work they do declines, as does

In Guatemala, where these bananas are grown, agricultural development has caused increased levels of malnutrition. As in many developing countries, modernization of agriculture has meant the conversion of land from subsistence farming to the raising of crops for export, making it increasingly difficult for people to satisfy their basic nutritional needs.

their relative and absolute health, nutritional, and educational status.

Modernization: Must It Always Be Painful?

Although most anthropologists see the change that is affecting traditional, non-Western peoples caught up in the modern technological world as an ordeal, the more widespread opinion has been that it is a good thing; that however disagreeable the "medicine" may be, it is worth it for the people to become just like "us" (that is, the people of Europe and North America). This view of modernization, unfortunately, is based more on the hopes and expectations of Western culture than it is on reality. There is no doubt that Western peoples would like to see the non-Western world attain the high levels of development seen in Europe and North America, as the Japanese, Taiwanese, and some other Asians, in fact, have done. Overlooked is the stark fact that the standard of living in the Western world is based on a rate of consumption of nonrenewable resources, where far less than 50 percent of the world's population uses a good deal more than 50 percent of these resources. By the early 1970s, for example, the peo-

ple of the United States—less than 5 percent (approximately) of the world's population—were consuming more than 50 percent of all of the world's resources. Figures like this suggest that it is not realistic to expect most peoples of the world to achieve a standard of living comparable to that of the Western world in the near future, if at all. At the very least, the countries of the Western world would have to cut drastically their consumption of resources. So far, they have shown no willingness to do this, and if they did, their living standards would have to change. Yet more and more non-Western people, quite understandably, aspire to a standard of living such as Western countries now enjoy, even though the gap between the rich and poor people of the world is widening rather than narrowing. This has led to the development of what anthropologist Paul Magnarella has called a new "culture of discontent," a level of aspirations that far exceeds the bounds of an individual's local opportunities. No longer satisfied with traditional values, people all over the world are fleeing to the cities to find a "better life," all too often to live out their days in poor, congested, and diseased slums in an attempt to achieve what is usually beyond their reach. Unfortunately, despite all sorts of rosy predictions about a better future, this basic reality remains.

CHAPTER SUMMARY

Although cultures may be remarkably stable, culture change is characteristic to a greater or lesser degree of all cultures. Change is often caused by accidents, including the unexpected outcome of existing events. Another cause is the deliberate attempt of people to solve some perceived problem. Finally, change may be forced upon one group in the course of especially intense contact between two societies. Adaptation and progress are consequences rather than causes of change, although not all changes are necessarily adaptive. Progress is whatever a culture defines it as.

The mechanisms involved in cultural change are innovation, diffusion, cultural loss, and acculturation. The ultimate source of change is through innovation of some new practice, tool, or principle. Other individuals adopt the innovation, and it becomes socially shared. Primary innovations are chance discoveries of new principles, for example, the discovery that the firing of clay makes the material permanently hard. Secondary innovations are improvements made by applying known principles, for example, modeling the clay that is to be fired by known techniques into familiar objects. Primary innovations may prompt rapid culture change and stimulate other inventions. An innovation's chance of being accepted depends on its perceived superiority to the method or object it replaces. Its acceptance is also connected with the prestige of the innovator and imitating groups. Diffusion is the borrowing by one society of a cultural element from another. Cultural loss involves the abandonment of some trait or practice with or without replacement. Anthropologists have given considerable attention to acculturation. It stems from intensive firsthand contact of groups with different cultures and produces major changes in the cultural patterns of one or both groups. The actual or threatened use of force is always a factor in acculturation.

Applied anthropology arose as anthropologists sought to provide colonial administrators with a better understanding of native cultures, so as to avoid serious disruption of them, or as anthropologists tried to help indigenous peoples cope with outside threats to their interests. A serious ethical issue for applied anthropologists is how far they should go in trying to change the ways of other peoples.

Reactions of indigenous peoples to changes that are forced upon them vary considerably. Some have retreated to inaccessible places in hopes of being left alone, while some others have lapsed into apathy. Some, like the Trobriand Islanders, have been able to reassert their traditional culture's values by modifying foreign practices to conform to indigenous values, a phenomenon known as syncretism. If a culture's values get widely out of step with reality, revitalization movements may appear. Some revitalization movements try to speed up the acculturation process in order to get more of the benefits expected from the dominant culture. Others try to reconstitute a gone but not forgotten way of life. In other cases, a pariah group may try to introduce a new social order, based on its ideology. Revolutionary movements try to reform the culture from within. Rebellion differs from revolution, in that the aim is merely to replace one set of officeholders with another.

Modernization refers to a global process of cultural and socioeconomic change by which developing societies seek to acquire characteristics of industrially advanced societies. The process consists of four subprocesses: technological development, agricultural development, industrialization, and urbanization. Other changes follow in the areas of political organization, education, religion, and social organization. Two other accompaniments of modernization are structural differentiation and new forces of social integration. An example of modernization is found in the Skolt Lapps of Finland, whose traditional reindeer-herding economy was nearly destroyed when snowmobiles were adopted to make herding easier. In Ecuador, the Shuar Indians modernized in order to escape the destruction that has been visited upon many other Amazonian peoples. So far they have been successful, and others are mobilizing their resources in an attempt to achieve similar success. Nevertheless, formidable forces are still arrayed against them, and on a worldwide basis, it is probably fair to say that modernization has led to a deterioration, rather than improvement, of peoples' quality of life.

SUGGESTED READINGS

Barnett, H. G. (1953). *Innovation: The basis of cultural change*. New York: McGraw-Hill.

This is the standard work on the subject, widely quoted by virtually everyone who writes about change.

Bodley, J. H. (1990). *Victims of progress* (3rd ed.). Mountain View, CA: Mayfield.

Few North Americans are aware of the devastation that has been unleashed upon indigenous peoples in the name of "progress," nor are they aware that this continues on an unprecedented scale today, or of the extent to which the institutions of their own society contribute to it. For most, this book will be a real eye opener.

Gordon, R. J. (1992). *The Bushman myth: The making of a Namibian underclass*. Boulder, CO: Westview.

This is a remarkably enlightening study of how both Bushman culture and European myths about the Bushman have changed over the past 150 years. Not only does it demolish myths ranging from the "Bushmen as Vermin" stereotype of the colonial era to the child-like innocence of the film *The Gods Must Be Crazy*, but it also shows how these people have been part of the world system since before their first discovery by Europeans. To see how they have managed their interactions with outsiders and how outsiders have manipulated images of the Bushmen for their own economic, political, and social interests is eye opening.

Magnarella, P. J. (1974). *Tradition and change in a Turkish town*. New York: Wiley.

This book, one of the best anthropological community studies of the Middle East, is also an excellent introduction to the phenomenon known as modernization. There are none of the facile generalizations about modernization that one often finds, and the author's view of the phenomenon, which is well documented, is quite different from that which was promoted in the optimistic days of the 1950s.

Stannard, D. E. (1992). *American holocaust*. Oxford: Oxford University Press.

Stannard deals with 500 years of culture change in the Americas related to the contact of European and native cultures. In doing so, he focuses on the phenomenon of genocide, relates it to "the holocaust" of World War II, and demonstrates how deeply rooted the phenomenon is in Western culture and Christianity.

CHAPTER
27
THE FUTURE OF HUMANITY

REFUGEES IN BOSNIA-HERZEGOVINA LOAD A TRUCK WITH THEIR BELONGINGS AS THEY PREPARE TO LEAVE THEIR HOMES. A FLOOD OF REFUGEES IS A RESULT OF EFFORTS BY STATES CONTROLLED BY PEOPLE OF ONE NATIONALITY TO REPRESS THE ATTEMPTS BY PEOPLE OF OTHER NATIONALITIES WITHIN THEIR BORDERS TO RETAIN AND ASSERT THEIR OWN IDENTITIES AND TRADITIONS, AS IS OCCURRING IN ALL PARTS OF THE WORLD.

CHAPTER PREVIEW

What Can Anthropologists Tell Us of the Future?

Anthropologists cannot any more accurately predict future forms of culture than biologists can predict future forms of life or geologists future landforms. They can, though, identify certain trends of which we might otherwise be unaware and anticipate some of the consequences these might have if they continue. They can also shed light on problems already identified by nonanthropologists, by showing how these relate to each other as well as to cultural practices and attitudes of which "experts" in other fields are often unaware. This ability to place problems in their wider context is an anthropological specialty, and it is essential if these problems are ever to be solved.

What Present-Day Trends Are Taking Place in the Evolution of Culture?

One major trend in present-day cultural evolution is toward the worldwide adoption of the products, technology, and practices of the industrialized world. This apparent gravitation toward a homogenized, one-world culture is, however, opposed by another very strong trend for ethnic groups all over the world to reassert their own distinctive identities. A third trend, of which we are just becoming aware, is that the problems created by cultural practices seem to be outstripping the capacity of culture to find solutions to problems.

What Problems Will Have to Be Solved If Humanity Is to Have a Future?

If humanity is to have a future, human cultures will have to find solutions to problems of population growth, food and other resource shortages, pollution, and a growing culture of discontent. One difficulty is that, up to now, there has been a tendency to see these as if they were discrete and unrelated. Thus, attempts to deal with one problem, such as short food supplies, are often at cross-purposes with others, such as an inequitable global system for the distribution of basic resources.
Unless humanity has a more realistic understanding of the "global society" than presently exists, it will not be able to solve the problems that are crucial for its future.

Anthropology is often described by those who know little about it as a backward-looking discipline. The most common stereotype is that anthropologists devote all of their attention to the interpretation of the past and the description of present-day tribal remnants. Yet as we saw in Chapter 1, as well as in the Anthropology Applied boxes for Chapters 12 and 17, not even archaeologists, the anthropologists most prone to looking backward, limit their interests to the past, nor are ethnologists uninterested in their own cultures. Thus, throughout this book we have constantly made comparisons between "us" and "others." Moreover, anthropologists have a special concern with the future and the changes it may bring. Like many members of Western industrialized societies, they wonder what the "postindustrial" society now being predicted will hold. They also wonder what changes the coming years will bring to non-Western cultures. As we saw in the preceding chapter, when non-Western peoples are thrown into contact with Western industrialized peoples, their culture rapidly changes, often for the worse, becoming both less supportive and less adaptive. Since Westerners show no inclination to leave non-Westerners alone, we may ask: How can these threatened cultures adapt to the future?

THE CULTURAL FUTURE OF HUMANITY

Whatever the biological future of the human species, culture remains the mechanism by which people solve their problems of existence. Yet some anthropologists have noted with concern—and interpret as a trend—that the problems of human existence seem to be outstripping culture's ability to find solutions. The main problem seems to be that in solving existing problems, culture inevitably poses new ones. To paraphrase anthropologist Jules Henry, although culture is "for" people, it is also "against" them.[1] As we shall see, this is now posing serious new problems for human beings. What can anthropologists tell us about the culture of the future?

Anthropologists—like evolutionary biologists and geologists—are historical scientists; as such, they can identify and understand the processes that have shaped the past and will shape the future. They cannot, however, tell us precisely what these processes will produce in the way of future cultures, any more than biologists can predict future forms of life or geologists future landforms. The cultural future of humanity, though, will certainly be affected in important ways by decisions that we humans will be making in the future. This being so, if those decisions are to be made intelligently, it behooves us to have a clear understanding of the way things are in the world today. It is here that anthropologists have something vital to offer.

To comprehend anthropology's role in understanding and solving the problems of the future, we must look at certain flaws frequently seen in the enormous body of future-oriented literature that has appeared over the past few decades, not to mention the efforts to plan for the future that have become commonplace on regional, national, and international levels. For one, rarely do futurist writers or planners look more than about 50 years into the future, and the trends they project into it, more often than not, are those of recent history. This predisposes people to think that a trend that seems fine today will always be so, and that it may be projected indefinitely into the future. The danger inherent in this is neatly captured in anthropologist George Cowgill's comment: "It is worth recalling the story of the person who leaped from a very tall building and on being asked how things were going as he passed the 20th floor replied 'Fine, so far.'"[2]

Another flaw is a tendency to treat subjects in isolation, without reference to pertinent trends outside an expert's field of competence. For example, agricultural planning is often predicated upon the assumption that a certain amount of water is available for irrigation, whether or not urban planners or others have designs upon that same water. Thus—as in the southwestern United States, where more of the Colorado River's water has been allocated than actually exists—people may be counting on resources in the future that will not, in fact, be available. One would suppose that this

---

[1]Henry, J. (1965). *Culture against man* (p. 12). New York: Vintage Books.

[2]Cowgill, G. L. (1980). Letter. *Science, 210,* 1305.

would be a cause for concern, but as two well-known futurists put it, "if you find inconsistencies the model is better off without them."[3] These same two authorities, in editing a volume aimed at refuting the somewhat pessimistic projections of *Global 2000* (the first attempt at a coordinated analysis of global resources on the part of the U.S. government), deliberately avoided going into population growth and its implications, because they knew that to do so would lead their contributing authors to disagree with one another.[4] This brings us to yet another common flaw: A tendency to project the hopes and expectations of one's own culture into the future interferes with the scientific objectivity that one ought to bring to the problem.

Against this background, anthropology's contribution to our view of the future is clear. With our holistic perspective, we are specialists at seeing how parts fit together into a larger whole; with our evolutionary perspective, we are able to see short-term trends in longer-term perspective; with more than 100 years of cross-cultural research behind us, we are able to recognize culture-bound assertions when we encounter them; and we are familiar with alternative ways of dealing with a wide variety of problems.

One World Culture

A popular belief since the end of World War II has been that the future world will see the development of a single homogeneous world culture. The idea that such a "one-world culture" is emerging is based largely on the observation that developments in communication, transportation, and trade so link the peoples of the world that they are increasingly wearing the same kinds of clothes, eating the same kinds of food, reading the same kinds of newspapers, watching the same kinds of television programs, and so on. The continuation of such trends, so this thinking goes, should lead North Americans, traveling in the year 2100 to Tierra del Fuego, China, or New Guinea, to find

the inhabitants of these areas living in a manner identical or similar to theirs.

The extent to which such things as Western-style clothing, transistor radios, Coca-Cola, and McDonald's hamburgers have spread to virtually all parts of the world certainly is striking. And, many countries—Japan, for example—have gone a long way toward becoming "Westernized." Moreover, if one looks back over the past 5,000 years of human history, one will see that there has been a clear-cut trend for political units to become larger and more all-encompassing, while becoming at the same time fewer in number. A logical outcome of the continuation of this trend into the future would be the reduction of autonomous political units to a single one, encompassing the entire world. In fact, by extrapolation from this past trend into the future, some anthropologists have gone so far as to predict that the world will become politically integrated, perhaps by the twenty-third century, but no later than the year 4850.[5]

One problem with such a prediction is that it ignores the one thing that all large states, past and present, irrespective of other differences between them, share in common: a tendency to come apart. Not only have the great empires of the past, without exception, broken up into numbers of smaller independent states, but also countries in all parts of the world today are showing a tendency to fragment. The most dramatic illustrations of this in recent years have been the breakup of the Soviet Union into several smaller, independent states, and the attempt of several Yugoslavian republics to regain their independence. It can also be seen in separatist movements such as that of French-speaking peoples in Canada; Basque and Catalonian nationalist movements in Europe; Scottish, Irish, and Welsh nationalist movements in Britain; Tibetan nationalism in China; Kurdish nationalism in Turkey, Iran, and Iraq; Sikh separatism in India; Tamil separatism in Sri Lanka; Igbo separatism in Nigeria; Eritrean and Tigrean secession movements in Ethiopia; Namibian nationalism; and so on—this list is far from exhaustive. Nor is the United States immune, as can be seen from Puerto Rican nationalist movements and Native

[3]Holden, C. (1983). Simon and Kahn versus *Global 2000*. *Science, 221,* 342.

[4]Holden, C. (1983). Simon and Kahn versus *Global 2000*. *Science, 221,* 343

[5]Ember, C. R., & Ember, M. (1985). *Cultural anthropology* (4th ed.) (p. 230). Englewood Cliffs, NJ: Prentice-Hall.

The worldwide spread of such products as Pepsi is taken by some as a sign that a single homogeneous world culture is developing.

American attempts to secure greater political self-determination and autonomy. These examples all involve peoples who consider themselves to be members of distinct nations by virtue of birth and cultural and territorial heritage, over whom peoples of some other ethnic background have tried to assert control. There are an estimated 5,000 such national groups in the world today, as opposed to a mere 181 recognized states (up from fewer than 50 in the 1940s).[6] Although some of these national groups are quite small in population and area—100 or so people living on a few acres—some are quite large. The Karen people of Burma, for example, number some 4.5 to 5 million, making them larger than 48 percent of United Nations member states.

Reactions of these peoples to attempts at annexation and absorption by imposed state regimes controlled by other peoples range all the way from the successful fight for independence from Pakistan on the part of Bangladesh (or the Igbos' unsuccessful fight for independence from Nigeria) to the nonviolence of Scottish and Welsh nationalism. Many struggles for independence have been going on for years, as in the case of Karen resistance to the Burmese invasion of their territory in 1948, the takeover of Kurdistan by Iraq, Iran, and Turkey in 1925, or the Russian takeover of Chechnya in 1864. Even in cases of relative nonviolence, the stresses and strains are obviously there. Similar stresses and strains may even develop in the absence of ethnic differences, as regional interests within a large country come into increasing competition. Again, hints of this may be seen in the United States—for example, in arguments over access to Colorado River water, in attempts by oil- and gas-producing states to get the most out of their resources at the expense of other states ("Let the Bastards Freeze in the Dark" proclaimed bumper stickers in oil- and gas-producing states during the Arab oil embargo of the 1970s) or in the refusal in some states to curb smokestack emissions that cause acid rain, which is destroying resources and endangering the health of people in other states (not to mention other countries, Canada in particular).

Expansionist attempts on the part of existing states to annex all or parts of other states also seem to be running into difficulty, as in the case of the

[6]*Cultural Survival Quarterly, 15*(4), (1991) 38.

One recent example of the tendency for states to fragment is the former Yugoslavia. Shown here is the Croatian capital under attack by Serbs.

Iraqi attempt to take over Kuwait. It is just possible that we are reaching a point at which the old tendency for political units to increase in size, while decreasing in number, is being canceled out by the tendency to fragment into a greater number of smaller units.

The Rise of the Multinational Corporations

The resistance of the world to political integration seems to be offset, at least partially, by the rise of multinational corporations. Because these cut across the boundaries between states, they are a force for global unity in spite of the political differences that divide people. Situations like this are well known to anthropologists, as illustrated by this description of Zuni Indian integrative mechanisms:

> Four or five different planes of systemization crosscut each other and thus preserve for the whole society an integrity that would speedily be lost if the planes merged and thereby inclined to encourage segregation and fission. The clans, the fraternities, the priesthoods, the kivas, in a measure the gaming parties, are all dividing agencies. If they coincided, the rifts in the social struc-

ture would be deep; by countering each other they cause segmentations which produce an almost marvelous complexity, but can never break apart the national entity.[7]

Multinational corporations are not new in the world (the Dutch East India Company is a good example from the seventeenth century), but they were rare until the 1950s. Since then they have become a major force in the world. These modern-day giants are actually clusters of corporations of diverse nationality, joined together by ties of common ownership and responsive to a common management strategy. More and more tightly controlled by a head office in one particular country, these multinationals are able to organize and integrate production across the boundaries of different countries for interests formulated in corporate boardrooms, irrespective of whether these are consistent with the interests of the countries within which they operate. In a sense they are products of the technological revolution, for without sophisticated data-processing equipment, the multinationals could not keep adequate track of their worldwide operations.

[7]Kreober, A. L. (1970). Quoted in Dozier, E. *The Pueblo Indians of North America* (p. 19). New York: Holt, Rinehart and Winston.

Brazil's Grand Carajas iron ore mine is an example of the kind of project favored by states in their drive to develop. Not only does this introduce ecologically unsound technologies, it also commonly has devastating effects on the indigenous people whose land is seized.

So great is the power of multinationals that they are increasingly able to thwart the wishes of governments. Because the information processed by these corporations is kept from flowing in a meaningful way to the population at large, or even to lower levels within the organization, it becomes difficult for governments to get the information they need for informed policy decisions. For example, the U.S. Congress repeatedly expressed its frustration in trying to get from corporations the information that it needed in order to consider what federal energy policies should be. Beyond this, though, the multinationals have shown themselves able to overrule foreign policy decisions, as when they got around a U.S. embargo on pipeline equipment for the Soviet Union in the 1980s. While some might see this as a hopeful augury for the transcendence of national vices and rivalries, it raises the unsettling issue as to whether the global order should be determined by corporations interested only in their own profits.

If the ability of multinational corporations to ignore the wishes of sovereign governments is cause for concern, so is their ability to act in concert with such governments. Here, in fact, is where their worst excesses have taken place. In Brazil, for example, where the situation is hardly unique but is especially well documented, a partnership emerged after the military coup of 1964 between a government anxious to proceed as rapidly as possible with "development" of the Amazon basin and a number of multinational corporations such as ALCOA, Borden, Union Carbide, Swift-Armour, and Volkswagen, to mention only a very few, and also several international lending institutions, such as the Export-Import Bank, the Inter-American Development Bank, and the World Bank.[8] In order to realize their goals, these allies introduced inappropriate technology and ecologically unsound practices into the region, which have converted vast areas into semidesert. Far more shocking, however, has been the practice of uprooting whole human societies because they are seen as obstacles to economic growth. Literally overnight, people are deprived of the means to provide for their own needs and forcibly removed to places where they do not choose to live. Little distinction is made here between Indians and Brazilian small-holders who were brought into the

[8]Davis, S. H. (1982). *Victims of the miracle.* Cambridge: Cambridge University Press.

In so-called "underdeveloped" countries, women have become a source of cheap labor for large corporations, as subsistence farming has given way to mechanized agriculture. Unable to contribute to their families' well-being in any other way, they have no choice but to take on menial jobs for low wages.

region in the first place by a government anxious to alleviate acute land shortages in the northeast. Bad as this is for these Brazilian small-holders, the amount of disease, death, and human suffering unleashed upon the Indians can be described only as massive; in the process, whole peoples have been (and are still being) destroyed with a thoroughness not achieved even by Stalin during his "Great Terror" in the Soviet Union of the 1930s or the Nazis in World War II. Were it not so well documented, it would be beyond belief. This is "culture against people" with a vengeance.

The power of multinational corporations creates problems on the domestic as well as on the international scene. Anthropologist Jules Henry, in his classic study of life in the United States, observed that working for any large corporation—multinational or not—tends to generate "hostility, instability, and fear of being obsolete and unprotected. For most people their job was what they had to do rather than what they wanted to do, . . . taking a job, therefore, meant giving up part of their selves."[9]

Consumers, too, have their problems with big business. After a 10-year intensive study of relations between producers and consumers of prod-

ucts and services, the anthropologist Laura Nader found repeated and documented offenses by business that cannot be handled by present complaint mechanisms, either in or out of court. Viable alternatives to a failed judicial system do not seem to be emerging. Face-to-faceless relations between producers and consumers, among whom there is a grossly unequal distribution of power, exact a high cost: a terrible sense of apathy, even a loss of faith in the system itself.

These problems are exacerbated, and new ones arise in the "sprawling, anonymous, networks" that are the multinational corporations.[10] Not only are corporate decisions made in boardrooms far removed from where other corporate operations take place, but, given their dependence on ever more sophisticated data-processing systems to keep their operations running smoothly, many decisions can be and are being made by computers programmed for given contingencies and strategies. As anthropologist Alvin Wolfe has observed, "a social actor has been created which is much less under the control of men than we expected it to be, much less so than many even think it to be."[11] In the face of

[9]Henry, J. (1965). *Culture against man* (p. 127). New York: Vintage Books.

[10]Pitt, D. (1977). Comment. *Current Anthropology, 18,* 628.
[11]Wolfe, A. W. (1977). The supranational organization of production: An evolutionary perspective. *Current Anthropology, 18,* 619.

such seemingly mindless systems for making decisions in the corporate interest, employees become ever more fearful that, if they ask too much of the corporation, it may simply shift its operations to some other part of the globe where it can find cheaper, more submissive personnel, as has happened with some frequency with respect to labor forces. Indeed, whole communities become fearful that, if they do not acquiesce to corporate interests, local operations may be closed down.

In their never-ending search for cheap labor multinational corporations more and more have come to favor women for low skilled assembly jobs. In third-world countries, as subsistence farming gives way to mechanical agriculture for production of crops for export, women are less able to contribute to their families' survival. Together with devaluation of the worth of domestic work, this places pressure on women to seek jobs outside the household, in order to contribute to its support. Since most women do not have the time or resources to get an education or to develop special job skills, only low-paying jobs are open to them. Corporate officials, for their part, assume that female workers are strictly temporary, and high turnover means that wages can be kept low. Unmarried women are especially favored for employment, for it is assumed that they are free from family responsibilities until they marry, whereupon they will leave the labor force. Thus, the increasing importance of the multinationals in developing countries is contributing to the emergence of a division of labor in which gender segregation is prominent. On top of their housework, women hold low-paying jobs that require little skill; altogether, they may work as many as 15 hours a day. Higher-paying jobs, or at least those that require special skills, are generally held by men, whose workday may be shorter since they do not have additional domestic tasks to perform. Those men who lack special skills—and there are many—are often doomed to lives of unemployment.

In sum, multinational corporations have become a major force in the world today, drawing people more firmly than ever before into a system of relationships that is truly global in scope. While this brings with it potential benefits, it is also clear that it poses serious new problems, which now must be solved.

One World Culture: A Good Idea or Not?

In the abstract, the idea of a single culture for all the world's people is one that has had a degree of popular appeal, in that it might offer fewer chances for the kinds of misunderstandings to develop that, so often in the past few hundred years, have led to wars. Some anthropologists question this, though, in the face of evidence that traditional ways of thinking of oneself and the rest of the world may persist, even in the face of massive changes in other aspects of culture. Indeed, one might argue that the chances for misunderstandings actually increase; an example of this is the Penobscot Indian land-claims case mentioned in Chapter 16. Many non-Indian residents of the State of Maine simply could not comprehend how a people who look and act so much like themselves could not see things as they do.

Some have argued that perhaps a generalized world culture would be desirable in the future, because certain cultures of today may be too specialized to survive in a changed environment. Examples of this situation are sometimes said to abound in modern anthropology. When a traditional culture that is highly adapted to a specific environment—such as that of the Indians of Brazil, who are well adapted to life in a tropical rain forest—meets European-derived culture and the social environment changes suddenly and drastically, the traditional culture often collapses. The reason for this, it is argued, is that its traditions and its political and social organizations are not at all adapted to "modern" ways. Here we have, once again, the ethnocentric notion (discussed in Chapter 26) that "old" cultures are destined to give way to the new. Since this is regarded as inevitable, actions are taken that by their very nature virtually guarantee that the 457 traditional cultures will not survive; it is a classic case of the self-fulfilling prophecy.

A problem with this argument is that, far from being unable to adapt, traditional societies in places like Brazil's Amazon forest usually have been given no chance to work out their own adaptations. It is *not* any laws of nature that cause the collapse of traditional cultures, but rather the political choices of the powerful, their willingness to overpower traditional peoples and their unwillingness to live and let live. That Amazonian

ADVOCACY FOR THE RIGHTS OF INDIGENOUS PEOPLES

Anthropologists are increasingly concerned about the rapid disappearance of the world's remaining indigenous peoples for a number of reasons, foremost among them a basic issue of human rights. In the world today there is a rush to develop those parts of the planet that have so far escaped industrialization or to extract resources regarded as vital to the well-being of "developed" economies. These efforts at development are planned, financed, and carried out by both governments and businesses (generally the huge multinational corporations) as well as international lending institutions. Unfortunately, the rights of native peoples generally have not been incorporated into the programs and concerns of these organizations, even where laws exist that are supposed to protect the rights of such peoples.

For example, the typical pattern for development of Brazil's Amazon basin has been for the government to build roads, along which poor people from other parts of the country are settled. This brings them into conflict with Indians already living there, and who begin to die off in large numbers from diseases contracted from the settlers. Before long, the settlers learn that the soils are not suited for their kind of farming; at the same time, outside logging, mining, and agribusiness interests exert pressure to get them off the land. Ultimately, the poor people wind up living in disease-ridden slums, while the Indians end up decimated by the diseases and violence unleashed upon them by the outsiders. Those who survive are usually relocated to places where resources are inadequate to support them.

In an attempt to do what they can to help indigenous peoples gain title to their lands and avoid exploitation by outsiders, anthropologists in various countries have formed advocacy groups. The major one in the United States is Cultural Survival, Inc., based in Cambridge, Massachusetts. The interest of this organization is not in preserving indigenous cultures in some sort of romantic, pristine condition, so

that they will be there to study or to serve as "living museum exhibits," as it were. Rather, it is to provide the information and support to help endangered groups assess their situation, maintain or even strengthen their sense of self, and adapt to the changing circumstances. It does not regard assimilation of these groups into the "mainstream" societies of states as necessarily desirable; rather, they should be allowed the freedom to make their own decisions about how they wish to live. Instead of designing projects and then imposing them on endangered societies, Cultural Survival prefers to respond to the requests and desires of groups that see a problem and the need to address it. Cultural Survival can suggest ways to help and can activate extensive networks of anthropologists, other indigenous peoples who have already faced similar problems, and those government officials whose support can be critical to success.

Most projects funded or assisted by Cultural Survival have been focused on securing the land rights of indigenous peoples and organizing native federations. It has also identified and funded a number of locally designed experiments in sustainable development, such as the Turkmen Weaving Project, which allows Afghan refugees to make profitable income from traditional rug weaving; the Ikwe Marketing Collective through which Minnesota Indians market wild rice and crafts; or Cultural Survival Enterprises, which has developed and expanded markets for such products as the nuts used in the popular Rainforest Crunch snack food (itself a creation of Cultural Survival). Of major importance was the success of Cultural Survival in getting the World Bank, in 1982, to require as a matter of policy that the rights and autonomy of tribal peoples and minorities be *guaranteed* in any project in which the bank is involved. In spite of such successes, however, much remains to be done to secure the survival of indigenous peoples in all parts of the world.

* * *

Indians can adapt themselves to the modern world if left alone to do so, without losing their own distinctive ethnic and cultural identity, is demonstrated by the Shuar case, noted in the preceding chapter. In Brazil, however, the pressures to "develop" the Amazon are so great that whole groups of people are swept aside, as multinational corporations and agribusiness pursue their own particular interests. People do not have much chance to work out their own adaptations to the modern

This demonstration for indigenous rights symbolizes the increasing success of Ecuadoran Indians in defending their interests.

world if they are transported en masse from their homelands and deprived literally overnight of their means of survival, so that more acreage can be devoted to the raising of beef cattle. Few Brazilians get to eat any of this meat, for the bulk of it is shipped to Europe; nor do many of the profits stay in Brazil, since the major ranches are owned and operated by corporations based elsewhere. The process continues apace, nonetheless.

There is an important issue at stake in such situations, for what has happened is that some of the world's people with the power to do so have defined others—indeed, whole societies—as obsolete. This is surely a dangerous precedent, which if allowed to stand, means that any of the world's people may at some time in the future be declared obsolete by someone else who thinks they have the power to back it up.

Ethnic Resurgence

In spite of the worldwide adoption of such things as Coca-Cola and the "Big Mac," and in spite of

pressure for traditional cultures to disappear, it is clear that cultural differences are still very much with us in the world today. In fact, there is a strengthening tendency for peoples all around the world to resist modernization and in many cases retreat from it. Manifestations of this to which we have already alluded are the separatist movements around the world, the success so far of the Shuar in retaining their own ethnic and cultural identity, and the increasing political activism of Brazilian Indians—indeed, of native peoples everywhere.

During the 1970s indigenous peoples around the world began to organize self-determination movements, culminating in the formation of the World Council of Indigenous Peoples in 1975. This now has official status as a nongovernmental organization of the United Nations, which allows it to present the case of indigenous people before the world community. Leaders of this movement see their own societies as community based, egalitarian, and close to nature and are intent upon maintaining them that way. Further credibility to their cause came from the dedication of 1993 as the Year of Indigenous Peoples.

Sometimes, resistance to modernization takes the form of a fundamentalist reaction, as it did in Iran and as is happening today in Algeria. This photo is of an FIS (Islamic Salvation Front) rally in Algiers.

North Americans often have difficulty adjusting to the fact that not everyone wants to be just like they are. As children, people in the United States are taught to believe that "the American way of life" is one to which all other peoples aspire (and how arrogant they are to appropriate the label "Americans" strictly for themselves), but it is not only people like the Shuar who resist becoming "just like us." There are in the world today whole countries that, having striven to emulate Western ways, have become disenchanted and suddenly backed off. The most striking recent case of such a retreat from modernity is Iran. With the overthrow of the Shah, a policy of deliberate modernization was abandoned in favor of a radical attempt to return to an Islamic republic out of a past "golden age" (mythical though the latter is). A somewhat similar, though far less radical, retreat from modernity seems to be underway in the United States, which, in the 1980s and again in 1994, elected governments dedicated to a return to certain "traditional values" out of its past. To note just one other parallel between the two situations, in the United States, the analogue to the control of the Iranian government by a fundamentalist religious leader is the strong sympathy shown by members of the Republican Party to fundamentalist religious views.[12]

Cultural Pluralism

If a single homogeneous world culture is not necessarily the wave of the future, what is? Some see **cultural pluralism,** in which more than one culture exists in a given society, as the future condition of humanity. Cultural pluralism is the social and political interaction within the same society, or multinational state, of people with different ways of living and thinking. Ideally, it implies the rejection of bigotry, bias, and racism in favor of respect for the cultural traditions of other peoples. In reality, it has rarely worked that way.

Cultural pluralism: Social and political interaction within the same society of people with different ways of living and thinking.

[12]Marsella, J. (1982). Pulling it together: Discussion and comments. In S. Pastner & W. A. Haviland (Eds.), *Confronting the creationists* (pp. 79–80). *Northeastern Anthropological Association, Occasional Proceedings, 1.*

Elements of pluralism are to be found in the United States, in spite of its melting-pot ideology. For example, in New York City there are neighborhoods where Puerto Ricans, with their own distinctive cultural traditions and values, exist side by side with other New Yorkers. Besides living in their own *barrio*, the Puerto Ricans have their own language, music, religion, and food. This particular pluralism, however, may be of a temporary nature, a stage in the process of integration into what is sometimes referred to as "standard American culture." Thus, the Puerto Ricans, in four or five generations, like many Italians, Irish, and east European Jews before them, may also become North Americanized to the point where their lifestyle will be indistinguishable from others around them. On the other hand, some Puerto Ricans, African and Asian Americans, American Indians, Hispanics, and others have strongly resisted abandoning their distinctive cultural identities. Whether this marks the beginning of a trend away from the melting-pot philosophy and toward real pluralism, however, remains to be seen.

Some familiar examples of cultural pluralism may be seen in Switzerland, where Italian, German, and French cultures exist side by side; in Belgium, where the French Walloons and the Flemish have somewhat different cultural heritages; and in Canada, where French- and English-speaking Canadians live in a pluralistic society (but where most native people are not accorded equal recognition). In none of these cases, though, are the cultural differences (save those of native people in Canada) of the magnitude seen in many a non-Western pluralistic society. As an example of one such society—and its attendant problems—we may look at the Central American country of Guatemala.

Guatemalan Cultural Pluralism

Guatemala, like many other pluralistic countries, came into being through conquest. In Guatemala's case, the conquest was about as violent and brutal as it could be, given the technology of the time, as a rough gang of Spanish adventurers led by a man known even then for his cruelty and inhuman treatment of foes defeated a people whose civilization was far older than Spain's. The aim of the conquerors was quite simply to extract as much wealth

In Quebec, French-speaking people have worked hard to secure their own sovereignty, whether within or wholly independent of a pluralistic Canada. At the same time, they have been reluctant to acknowledge the sovereignty of the native people like Mohawks. In 1990, a protest by the Mohawk nation over the taking of some of their land at Oka triggered an attack by the provincial police.

as they could, primarily for themselves but also for Spain, by seizing the riches of those they conquered and by putting the native population to work extracting the gold and silver they hoped to find. Although the treasures did not live up to the expectations of the conquerors (no rich deposits of ore were found) their main interest in their new possession continued to be in whatever they could extract from it that could be turned into wealth for themselves. Over the nearly 500 years since, their *Ladino* descendants have continued to be motivated by the same interests, even after independence from Spain.

Following its conquest, there was never substantial emigration from Spain, or anywhere else in Europe, into Guatemala. The conquerors and their descendants, for their part, wished to restrict the spoils of victory as much as possible to themselves, even though those spoils did not live up to

 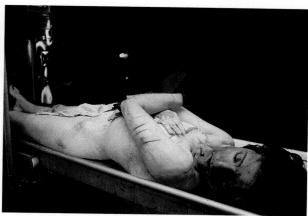

In Guatemala, violence continues to be used by the military and by other groups tolerated by the government to maintain the control of one nationality (*Ladino*) over another (Maya). As the illustration from a 1552 Spanish source shows, there is an eerie similarity to the way the Spanish treated the native people of Guatemala 450 years ago.

advance expectations. There was, in fact, little to attract outsiders to the country. Thus, as in South Africa where blacks have always outnumbered whites, Indians have always outnumbered non-Indians in Guatemala and continue to do so today. And as in South Africa, where (until 1994) whites held all political power, Indians have never been allowed to hold any important political power at all; the apparatus of state, with its instruments of force (the police and army) remained firmly in the hands of the *Ladino* minority. This enabled them to continue exacting tribute and forced labor from Indian communities.

In the nineteenth century, Guatemala's *Ladino* population saw the export of coffee and cotton as a new source of wealth for themselves. For this, they took over huge amounts of Indian lands to create their plantations, at the same time depriving Indians of sufficient land for their own needs. Consequently, the latter had no option but to work for the plantation owners on their enlarged holdings at wages cheap beyond belief. Any reluctance on the part of these native laborers, who were required to carry passbooks showing they had performed the legally required days of labor, was dealt with by brute force.

In the 1940s democratic reforms took place in Guatemala. Although Indians played no role in bringing them about, they benefitted from them; for the first time in more than 400 years native peoples could at least hold municipal offices in their own communities. In the 1950s the Roman Catholic church began to promote agricultural, consumer, and credit cooperatives in rural areas (which, in Guatemala, are predominantly Indian).

With the U.S.-engineered military coup of 1954 this brief interlude, in which the government recognized that Indians had social, economic, and cultural rights, came to an end. As before, the Indians stayed out of politics except within their own villages. And for the most part, they remained aloof from the guerrilla activities that soon arose in reaction to a succession of military regimes. But because the guerrillas operated in the countryside, and because of 400 years of *Ladino* distrust of Indians, these regimes came to regard all rural people, most of whom are Indian, with ever deeper suspicion. Inevitably, the latter were drawn into the conflict.

In 1966, the United States Advisory Mission introduced the use of terror tactics to maintain government control over the countryside.[13] By 1978, this had escalated into a "reign of terror" known as *La Violencia*: Whole villages were razed, inhabitants killed, bodies burnt and otherwise mutilated, by either the army or by unofficial death squads to which the army turned a blind eye. Whether people were or were not guerillas or guerilla sympathizers was largely irrelevant, as repression came to be seen as the most effective way to maintain order. At the height of *La Violencia*

[13]Zur, J. (1994). The psychological impact of impunity. *Anthropology Today, 10*(3), 16.

(between 1981 and 1983) an estimated 15,000 people were "disappeared," at least 90,000 were killed, and many more became refugees, many fleeing to Mexico. In the hardest-hit areas, the population was reduced by almost half, and whole towns—some of which had existed for a thousand years—were destroyed. The overwhelming majority of victims of this violence, which reached genocidal proportions, were Indians.

Although the violence in Guatemala has been the most unrelenting in the Western Hemisphere, it has not gotten much attention from the press. Anthropologists, by contrast, have given it a great deal of attention (and some have lost their lives as a consequence). In the following Original Study, one anthropologist who is also a clinical psychologist analyzes *La Violencia* and its consequences.

Original Study
The Psychological Impact of Impunity[14]

La Violencia was relentless and unavoidable. It comprised two types of violence: the visible and the invisible. Overt violence consisted of burning and bombing villages, a tactic called "Operation Cinders" within the army: it was also referred to as a "clean up" of a group the army portrayed as less than human: the guerilla. Over a short period of time, the *Ladino* led army seems to have conflated stereotypical ideas of the rarely seen guerilla hiding in the mountains with long established attitudes regarding the Indian heartland—that it was remote, Indian, and dangerous—and has particularly targeted Indian villages for destruction.

Visible violence also consisted of public executions and massacres, events which addressed no-one but were an end in themselves, intended to efface completely the identities of individuals and populations. The government made no secret of some of its violent actions: it wanted to terrorize the rural population, which it viewed as subversive.

Invisible forms of violence seemed to aim for completeness and silence on the one hand and brutal suppression on the other. This is revealed with ruthless clarity in atrocities comprising both types of violence: a common example is the dumping of mutilated bodies in public spaces following unwitnessed abductions and secret murders, thus evoking terror in the local population. Corpses were also found in deep gullies, rivers or clandestine graves. Certain liminal places, such as crossroads, river banks and roadsides, became regular dumping grounds.

Anonymity was another controlling mechanism. Whilst some bodies were identified, most were not. Many had been transported from else-where, stripped naked and disfigured. Bodies were frequently described as having been tortured or bearing the signs of torture, including fire or acid burns, stake insertions, flayed skin, mutilated genitals and amputations. Sense organs were a common target of both symbolic and literal assault: ears and tongues were cut out, eyes gouged or burnt out. This was a potent meta-message: all sense is attacked, leaving the population without "sense," without a means to perceive, reason, criticize or, most crucially, name the guilty.

Massacres committed in the villages where I worked were carried out by the civil patrol commanders who were local men. The dead were buried, by the commanders, in shallow graves within the village boundaries. Neither the massacres nor the dead men have ever been mentioned in public since; the commanders threatened witnesses with the same fate should they talk about it. Initially, the commanders' motivation in committing these atrocities was to save their own lives, for the military had given them the choice of kill or be killed. However, the massacres had a hypnotic effect on the survivors, who were also victims of this atrocious piece of theatre, as well as the local perpetrators. The massacres conducted by the commanders under the coercion of the army began a process which the commanders continued themselves in an apparently auto-suggestive fashion: they convinced themselves that they had the right and the strength to make further displays of their violent power and they soon found out that they could do so with impunity.

Punishment of the "guilty" by means of massacres, like the punishment of patrollers who did not obey, was less intended to punish them than to force all villagers to do as the state wished. Villagers were to refrain from involving themselves with the guerillas, the patroller was to cooperate with the patrol system, and the commander was to carry out massacres and do so willingly. The widow was to witness and record the official "truth" on the one hand, but to be silent and to "forget" her own truth, the "real" truth, on the other.

Apart from the forced silence and forgetting, there is also a collective reaction towards repressive acts through collective processes of negation, guilt and complicity. By strengthening these processes, impunity prevents the whole society from elaborating the facts (that is, inhibits reconciliation). This results in distrust and confusion of values.

Psychological After-Effects of Impunity

Whatever the pre-history of *La Violencia,* the deaths and disappearances of "the innocent," and the knowledge that these could resume at any moment without recourse, created a new awareness among survivors of their vulnerability. This was usually accompanied by an increase in affective response, usually fear, horror, guilt and anger. The sense of exposure and vulnerability was heightened after the village massacres by the fact that the killers continued to live in close proximity (the fear was so great that when a clandestine grave was exhumed in Chijtinimit, Chichicastenango, El Quiché, in 1988, not one relative came forward to identify the remains). It was not an anonymous person or crowd who had carried out the killing. In a village of approximately 1,000 people, most of whom are related in one way or another, these men were known and continued to be the authorities in the village. Witnessing the killing of the innocent kin by a known person meant that the murder became an "intimate truth." This differed from the killing of men by an unknown soldier, and from "disappearance" by an anonymous person, particularly if this act was never seen.

Disappearances carried out by the police and the army, the authorities of society on whom people depend, have a quite different effect. In this case, not knowing who the perpetrator was leaves relatives perhaps with an even greater sense of uncertainty about the fate of kin. The question of the fate of the dead and disappeared, together with memories of them, clings tenaciously to the present; the fear of what became of the missing, and of further disappearances, follows the survivor day and night. Such uncertainty also inhibits the ability to mourn, leaving women in a state of liminality, betwixt and between social categories, neither widow nor non-widow. It also leaves survivors, especially women, with an awareness of their own powerlessness; the lack of power stems from the all-embracing might of the powerful which is stabilized in various social strata and supported by the situation of impunity in which they operate. One of the effects of this powerlessness is that people are left without a language to explain what has happened.

While the survivors are unable to describe the ineffable, terror works through an inner voice quoting the outer madness. Collective terror, like any other cultural system, possesses an underlying structure, its own grammar as it were. The calculated unleashing of terror brings about shared denial in a population; knowing what not to know is a major coping response to terror.

Without doubt, one of the purposes of political oppression is to make citizens psychologically repress—that is, not see—the less than democratic aspects of the government they may observe. Denial, although a coping mechanism because the secrecy is internalized, becomes a pervasive way of relating to the world, especially in relation to those perceived to be in authority. The effect is similar to the well-documented effect of serious abuse perpetuated on children within families: children attached to and dependent on their parents usually cannot allow themselves consciously to acknowledge the abuse and may adopt (consciously and/or unconsciously) various processes that interfere with the assessment of reality. Such psychological processes affect perception in the service of internal needs for security resulting in a "failure to recognize" certain aspects of the environment and the self. This can become almost a cognitive style: the inhibition of thought process phenomena (given that one cannot put into words what one sees) and the transition to the area where orders of not-knowing are learnt can become pervasive mechanisms of thinking. The abuse thus interferes with victims' thinking and relationships with themselves, their bodies, with others and with authority. Life in a repressive regime can have similar effects. School children with learning difficulties referred to Kordon and Edelman were identified as suffering from "secret psychopathology": a secret which really never is a secret at all, since there are always hints of what is being hidden. Consequently, an active exclusion of a content which is shown but can never be mentioned is produced. Such problems are not confined to children; when I asked Guatemalans why they hadn't fled when the army requisitioned the local church and began to use it as a torture chamber, many adults told me, "We were doing nothing wrong so we believed that nothing would happen to us." When acquiescing to the silent pact, mechanisms such as censorship may become extreme and even recoil on the self, producing feelings of hostility and guilt with various symptomatic consequences ranging from alcoholism (said to be a way of anaesthetizing one's self temporarily) to somatic symptoms such as headaches, heart ache and other body aches.

Conclusion

Killing with impunity was psychologically shattering not only because of the interference with the assessment of reality but also because people had to construe meaning all over again. Attempts to construct meaning were frustrated not only through the absence of a language with which to make sense of the situation and the distorting effects of employing neologisms, but also because existing concepts, and the vocabulary and grammar used to express them, were distorted through the state's use of rhetoric and the pervasive use of euphemisms. The state's use of euphemisms to hide reality as a part of the cover-up is, in fact, a form of violence, if on the symbolic level. These effects have repercussions for years because the silence is internalized; emotions are suppressed and repressed, partly as a result of state oppression. At some level, people also internalized the army's idea that the victims themselves, and not their killers, were responsible for *La Violencia;* the self-blame that this produced fed into the guilt felt by people who retrospectively judged their own silence—when they saw nothing, said nothing and heard nothing, because they were terrified—as complicity with the perpetrators of violence. Perhaps only giving voice to what they saw and the establishment of the truth, including the identification of the perpetrators, those who gave them their orders, and the intellectual authors of the crimes, will be the only reality test which would enable the relatives of the dead and missing to see who the real culprits were.

[14]Zur, J. (1994). The psychological impact of impunity. *Anthropology Today, 10*(3), 14–16.

In the late 1980s, violence in the Guatemalan countryside lapsed from the acute phase to the merely chronic. Ominously, it began to escalate anew in the early 1990s. Nevertheless, in spite of this and the fear still felt by the Maya Indians, political activism among them is on the rise. And forensic anthropologists, at considerable risk to themselves, are working with local communities to exhume the bodies of victims to help bring the perpetrators to account (see Anthropology Applied in Chapter 1). At the same time, the *Ladino* elite is talking more about the need to forge a true national identity for Guatemala, an ominous development in that such nation building historically, in all parts of the world, in most cases involves attempts to exterminate the culture of peoples belonging to nations other than those who control the government.[15] Even in the 1980s, states were borrowing more money to fight peoples within their boundaries than for all other programs combined. Nearly all debt in Africa, and nearly half of all other debt in "underdeveloped" countries, comes from the purchase of weapons by states to fight people claimed to be citizens by those very same states.[16] So far, the situation in the 1990s is no better.

Of all the world's states, Switzerland is one of the very few where pluralism has worked to the satisfaction of all parties to the arrangement, perhaps because in spite of linguistic differences, they are all heirs to a common European cultural tradition. In Northern Ireland, on the other hand, being heirs to a common tradition has not prevented violence and bloodshed. The more divergent cultural traditions are, the more difficult it appears to be to make pluralism work.

Given this dismal situation, can nothing be done about it? As anthropologists David Maybury-Lewis and Pierre Van Den Berghe point out, we tend to idealize the peace and social order maintained by the unitary state and to exaggerate the

[15]Van Den Berghe, P. (1992). The modern state: Nation builder or nation killer? *International Journal of Group Tensions 22*(3), 194–198.

[16]*Cultural Survival Quarterly, 15*(4), 38.

These pictures show a Chechen woman in front of her home that has been destroyed by a Russian rocket, and federal marshals at Wounded Knee, South Dakota, where U.S. troops laid siege to the Sioux Indian town in 1973. Both exemplify the willingness of states controlled by one nationality to use their armies against people of other nationalities within their borders to promote the interests of the state over those of the other nationality.

danger to this vision presented by allowance of cultural distinctiveness and/or local autonomy to peoples of other nationalities.[17] The sooner we recognize this, the better off we will be. States as cultural constructs are products of human imagination, and there is nothing to prevent our imagining in ways that are more accepting of pluralism. Obviously, this will take a good deal of work, but at least the recognition exists that such things as *group* rights exist. Even though it often fails to act on it, the United Nations General Assembly in its Covenant of Human Rights, passed in 1966, states unequivocally that: "In those states in which ethnic, religious or linguistic minorities exist, persons belonging to such minorities shall not be denied the rights, in community with the other members of their group, to enjoy their own culture, to profess and practice their own religion or to use their own language."[18] Besides education, one of the things that can help make this acknowledged right a reality is the advocacy work on behalf of indigenous peoples engaged in by substantial numbers of anthropologists (see the Anthropology Applied box in this chapter).

[17]Maybury-Lewis, D. (1993, Fall). A new world dilemma: The Indian question in the Americas. *Symbols, 22*; Van Den Berghe, P. (1992). The modern state: Nation builder or nation killer? *International Journal of Group Tensions, 22*(3), 191–192.

[18]Quoted in Bodley, J. H. (1990) *Victims of progress* (3rd ed.) (p. 99). Mountain View, CA: Mayfield.

ETHNOCENTRISM

The major problem associated with cultural pluralism has to do with ethnocentrism, a concept introduced in Chapter 14. In order to function effectively, a culture must instill the idea that its ways are "best," or at least preferable to those of all other cultures. It provides individuals with a sense of pride in and loyalty to their traditions, from which they derive psychological support and which binds them firmly to their group. In societies in which one's self-identification derives from the group, ethnocentrism is essential to a sense of personal worth. The problem with ethnocentrism is that it can all too easily be taken as a charter for manipulating other cultures for the benefit of one's own, even though—as we saw in Chapter 23—it does not have to be taken as such. When it is, however, unrest, hostility, and violence commonly result.

A typical expression of ethnocentrism is provided by President James Monroe's view, expressed in 1817, of Native American rights:

> The hunter state can exist only in the vast uncultivated deserts. It yields to the . . . greater force of civilized population; and of right, it ought to yield, for the earth was given to mankind to support the greater number of which it is capable; and no tribe or people have a right to withhold from the

wants of others, more than is necessary for their support and comfort.[19]

This attitude is, of course, alive in the world today, and the idea that no group has the right to stand in the way of "the greater good for the greater number" is frequently used by governments to justify the development of resources in regions occupied by subsistence farmers, pastoral nomads, or food foragers—irrespective of the wishes of those peoples. But is it the greater good for the greater number? A look at the world as it exists today as a kind of global society, in which all the world's peoples are bound by interdependency, raises serious questions.

Global Apartheid

Apartheid, which was until recently the official policy of the government of South Africa, consists of programs or measures that aim to maintain racial segregation.[20] Structurally, it served to perpetuate the dominance of a "white" minority over a nonwhite majority through the social, economic, political, military, and cultural constitution of society. Nonwhites were denied effective participation in political affairs, were restricted as to where they could live and what they could do, and were denied the right to travel freely. Whites, by contrast, controlled the government including, of course, the military and police. Although there are 4.7 nonwhites for every white, being white and belonging to the upper stratum of society have tended to go together. The richest 20 percent of South Africa took 58 percent of the country's income and enjoyed a high standard of living, while the poorest 40 percent of the population received only 6.2 percent of the national product.

What has South Africa to do with a global society? Structurally, the latter is very similar—almost a mirror image of South Africa's society, even though there is no "official" policy of global apartheid. In the world society about two-thirds

[19]Quoted in Forbes, J. D. (1964). *The Indian in America's past* (p. 103). Englewood Cliffs, NJ: Prentice-Hall.

[20]Material on global apartheid is drawn from Kohler, G. (1992). Global apartheid. Reprinted in W. A. Haviland & R. J. Gordon (Eds.), *Talking about people: Readings in contemporary cultural anthropology* (pp. 283–288). Mountain View, CA: Mayfield.

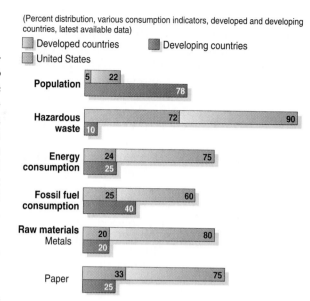

Figure 27.1   Though a minority of the world's population, people in the developed countries consume the most resources and generate the bulk of hazardous wastes.

of the population is nonwhite and one-third white. In the world as a whole, being white and belonging to the upper stratum tend to go together, even though there are some exceptions (Japan and Kuwait, for example). Although this upper, largely white stratum has not been a homogeneous group, being divided until recently into Communist and non-Communist peoples, neither was the upper stratum of South African society, where there has always been friction between the English, who controlled business and industry, and the Afrikaners, who controlled the government and military. In the world today, the poorest 75 percent of the population make do with 30 percent of the world's energy, 25 percent of its metals, 15 percent of its wood, and 40 percent of its food. The greater percentage of these and other resources goes to the richest 25 percent of the population (Fig. 27.1). Life expectancy, as in South Africa, is poorest among nonwhites. Most of the world's weapons of mass destruction are owned by whites: the United States, Russia, France, and Britain. As in South Africa, death and suffering from war and violence are distributed unequally; in the world, the poorest 70 percent of the population suffer more than 90 percent of violent deaths in all categories.

One could go on, but enough has been said to make the point: The parallels between the current world situation and that in South Africa are striking. We may sum up global apartheid as a de facto structure of world society which combines socioeconomic and racial antagonisms and in which (1) a minority of largely white people occupies the pole of affluence, while a majority composed of other races occupies the pole of poverty; (2) social integration of the two groups is made extremely difficult by barriers of complexion, economic position, political boundaries, and other factors; (3) economic development of the two groups is interdependent; and (4) the affluent, largely white minority possesses a disproportionately large share of the world society's political, economic, and military power. Global apartheid is thus a structure of extreme inequality in cultural, racial, social, political, economic, military, and legal terms, as in South African apartheid.

Around the world, condemnation of South African apartheid was close to universal, and even South Africa itself has abolished the system. Since global apartheid is even more severe than the South African version was, we ought to be much more concerned about it than we have been up to now.

PROBLEMS OF STRUCTURAL VIOLENCE

One of the consequences of a system of apartheid, whether it is official or unofficial, on the state level or global level, is a great deal of **structural violence:** violence that is exerted by situations, institutions, and social, political, and economic structures. A classic instance of structural violence is the

⊏⊏⊏○○⊏⊏⊏⊏○○⊏⊏⊏

Structural violence: Violence exerted by situations, institutions, and social, political, and economic structures.

⊏⊏⊏○○⊏⊏⊏⊏○○⊏⊏⊏

In April of 1986 an explosion and fire in the Soviet Union's Chernobyl nuclear power plant released massive amounts of radioactivity into the atmosphere over the USSR and Europe. Fallout from this devastated the reindeer-herding economy of Scandinavian Lapps: a classic example of structural violence.

accident that occurred in April 1986, when radiation released from a nuclear power reactor at Chernobyl, Ukraine, was responsible for numerous deaths and necessitated the relocation of 126,000 people from the surrounding area. People as far away as the Lapps were affected, as fallout contaminated their reindeer herds. And today, almost 10 years later, the incidence of radiation-caused thyroid cancer and damaged immune systems remains high. As far as the victims of this accident are concerned, the effect was violent, even though the cause was not the hostile act of a specific individual. The source of the violence was an anonymous structure, which is what structural violence is all about. In what remains of this chapter, there is not sufficient space to go into all aspects of structural violence, but we can look at some aspects of it that have been of particular concern to anthropologists. They are of concern to other specialists, too, and anthropologists draw on the work of these specialists as well as their own, thereby fulfilling their traditional role as synthesizers (discussed in Chapter 1). Moreover, anthropologists are less apt than other specialists to see these aspects of structural violence as discrete and unrelated. Thus, they have a key contribution to make to our understanding of such modern-day problems as overpopulation, food shortages, pollution, and widespread discontent in the world.

World Hunger

As frequently dramatized by events in Ethiopia and other parts of Africa, a major source of structural violence in the world today is our failure to provide food for all of its people. Not only is Africa losing the capacity to feed itself; by 1980, 52 countries worldwide were producing less food per capita than they were 10 years previously, and in 42 countries, available supplies of food were not adequate to supply the caloric requirements of their populations.[21] One factor that has contributed to this food crisis is a dramatic growth in the world's population.

Population growth is more than a simple addition of people. If it were just that, the addition of 20 people a year to a population of 1,000 would result in that population's being doubled in 50 years; but because the added people beget more people, the doubling time is actually much less than 50 years. Hence, it took the whole of human history and prehistory for the world's population to reach one billion people, which was achieved in 1850. By 1950, world population had reached almost 2.5 billion, representing an annual growth rate of about 0.8 percent. Between 1950 and 1960, the rate of growth had climbed to 1.8 percent (doubling time 39 years), and in the 1960s fluctuated between 1.8 percent and 2 percent (doubling time 35 years at 2 percent). There are now more than five and a half billion people in the world, with growth rates ranging from less than 1 percent (Europe and North America) to as high as 4.9 percent (Fig. 27.2).

The obvious question arising from the burgeoning world population is: Can we produce enough food to feed all of those people? The majority opinion among those in the field of agriculture is that we can do so, although we probably will not be able to in the future, if populations continue to grow as they have. In the 1960s a major effort was launched to expand food production in the poor countries of the world by introducing new high-yield strains of grains. Yet in spite of some dramatic gains from this "green revolution"—India, for example, was able to double its wheat

[21]Bodley, J. H. (1985). *Anthropology and contemporary human problems* (2nd ed.) (p. 114). Palo Alto, CA: Mayfield.

Hunger stalks much of the world as a result of a world food system geared to satisfy an affluent minority in the developed nations of the world.

crop in six years and was on the verge of grain self-sufficiency by 1970—and in spite of the impressive output of North American agriculture, millions of people on the face of the globe continue to face malnutrition and starvation. In the United States, meanwhile, about $85 million worth of *edible* food is thrown out every day (far more food than is sent out for famine relief), and farms are going out of business in record numbers.

The immediate cause of world hunger has less to do with food production than with food distribution. For example, millions of acres in Africa, Asia, and Latin America, which once were devoted to subsistence farming, have been given over to the raising of cash crops for export, to satisfy appetites in the "developed" countries of the world for such things as coffee, tea, chocolate, bananas, and beef. Those who had farmed the land for their own food

Figure 27.2   Population growth rates around the world.

needs are relocated, either to urban areas, where there often is no employment for them, or to other areas that are ecologically unsuited for farming. In Africa such lands are often occupied by pastoral nomads; as these are encroached upon by farmers, insufficient pasturage is left for livestock. The resultant overgrazing, coupled with the clearing of the land for farming, leads to increased loss of both soil and water, with disastrous consequences to nomad and farmer alike. In Brazil, which is highly dependent on outside sources of fossil fuels for its energy needs, millions of acres in the northeast part of the country were taken over for sugar production, which could be used to make alcohol to fuel the vehicles in Rio. The people who were displaced by this were given small holdings in the Amazon, where they are now being uprooted to make way for huge ranches on which beef is raised for export.

One strategy urged upon so-called underdeveloped countries, especially by government officials and development advisors from the United States, is to adopt the practices that have made North American agriculture so incredibly productive. On the face of it, this seems like a good idea; what it overlooks is the fact that it requires investment in expensive seeds and chemicals that neither small farmers nor poor countries can afford.

Intensive agriculture on the U.S. model requires enormous inputs of chemical fertilizers, pesticides, and herbicides, not to mention fossil fuels needed to run all the mechanized equipment. Even where high production lowers costs, the price is likely to be beyond the reach of poor farmers. And there are other problems: Farming U.S.-style is energy inefficient. For every calorie that is produced, at least 8—some say as many as 20—calories go into its production and distribution.[22] By contrast, an Asian wet rice farmer using traditional methods produces 300 calories for each one expended. North American agriculture is wasteful of other resources as well: About 30 pounds of fertile topsoil are ruined for every pound of food produced.[23] In the midwestern United States, about 50 percent of the topsoil has been lost over the past 100 years. Meanwhile, toxic substances from chemical nutrients and pesticides pile up in unexpected places, poisoning ground and surface waters, killing fish, birds, and other useful forms of life, upsetting natural ecological cycles, and causing major public health problems. In spite of its spectacular

[22]Bodley, J. H. (1985). *Anthropology and contemporary human problems* (2nd ed.) (p. 128). Palo Alto, CA: Mayfield.

[23]Chasin, B. H., & Franke, R. W. (1983). U.S. farming: A world model? *Global Reporter, 1*(2), 10.

short-term success, there are serious questions about whether such a profligate system of food production can be sustained over the long run, even in North America.

Pollution

It is ironic that a life-sustaining activity such as food production should constitute a health hazard, but that is precisely what it becomes, as agricultural chemicals poison soils and waters, and food additives (over 2,500 are or have been used) expose people to substances that often turn out to be harmful. This, though, is only a part of a larger problem of environmental pollution. Industrial activities are producing highly toxic waste at unprecedented rates, and emissions from factories are poisoning the air. For example, smokestack gases are clearly implicated in "acid rain," which is causing damage to lakes and forests all over northeastern North America. Air containing water vapor with a high acid content is, of course, harmful to the lungs, but the health hazard is greater than this. As surface and ground waters become more acidic, the solubility of lead, cadmium, mercury, and aluminum increases sharply. The increase of dissolved aluminum, in particular, is becoming truly massive, and aluminum has been found to be associated with senile dementia as well as Alzheimer's and Parkinson's diseases. Today, these rank as major health problems in the United States.

As with world hunger, the structural violence that results from pollution tends to be greatest in the poorer countries of the world, where chemicals banned for use in countries like the United States are still widely used. Moreover, the industrial countries of the world have taken advantage of lax environmental regulations of "underdeveloped" states to get rid of hazardous wastes. For instance, the president of Benin (in West Africa) not long ago signed a contract with a European waste company to dump toxic and low-grade radioactive waste on the lands of his opposition.[24] And as manufacturing shifts from the developed to the less developed countries of the world, a trend also encouraged by fewer safety and environmental regulations to comply with, lethal accidents such as the

[24]*Cultural Survival Quarterly,* 15(4), 5.

A form of structural violence is the misery to which the demand for resources on the part of industrialized countries condemns many people in the nonindustrialized countries of the world. In Bolivia, tin is a primary export. Those who mine it are Quechua Indians, who are paid the equivalent of one U.S. dollar a day. Rarely do they live more than seven years after entering the mines.

one at Chernobyl may be expected to increase. Indeed, development itself seems to be a health hazard; it is well known that indigenous peoples in Africa, the Pacific islands, South America, and elsewhere are relatively free from diabetes, obesity, hypertension, and a variety of circulatory diseases, until they adopt the ways of the developed countries. With this, rates of these "diseases of development" escalate dramatically.

Modern humanity knows the causes of pollution and realizes it is a danger to future survival. Why, then, can humanity not control this evil by which it fouls its own nest? At least part of the answer lies in philosophical and theological traditions. As we saw in Chapter 23, Western industrialized societies accept the biblical assertion that they have dominion over the earth with all that grows and lives on it, which it is their duty to subdue. It is these societies that contribute most to global pollution. One North American, for example, consumes hundreds of times the resources of a single African, with all that implies with respect to waste disposal and environmental degradation.

The exploitative worldview, characteristic of all civilizations, extends to all natural resources (see Fig. 27.3). Only when problems have reached crisis proportions, as in the case of destruction of the earth's protective ozone layer, have Western peoples protected or replaced what greed and acquisitiveness have prompted them to take from the

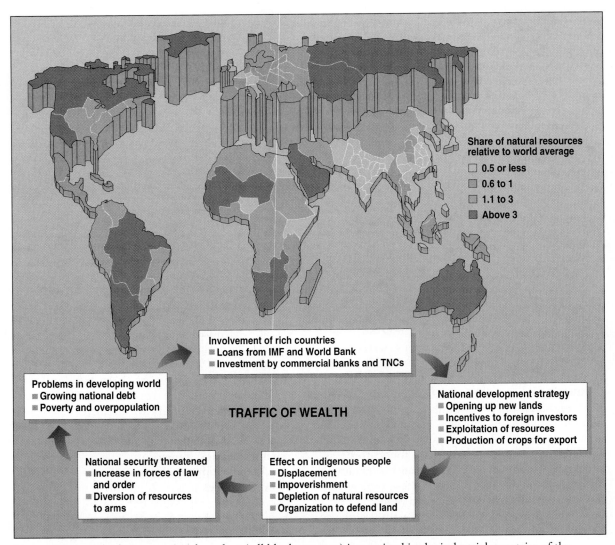

Share of natural resources
relative to world average

☐ 0.5 or less
◻ 0.6 to 1
◻ 1.1 to 3
■ Above 3

Involvement of rich countries
■ Loans from IMF and World Bank
■ Investment by commercial banks and TNCs

Problems in developing world
■ Growing national debt
■ Poverty and overpopulation

TRAFFIC OF WEALTH

National development strategy
■ Opening up new lands
■ Incentives to foreign investors
■ Exploitation of resources
■ Production of crops for export

National security threatened
■ Increase in forces of law
  and order
■ Diversion of resources
  to arms

Effect on indigenous people
■ Displacement
■ Impoverishment
■ Depletion of natural resources
■ Organization to defend land

Figure 27.3   A high gross national product (tall blocks on map) is sustained in the industrial countries of the world by a flow of mineral and land wealth from the lands of indigenous peoples.

environment. In recent years, recognizing the seriousness of the environmental crisis people were creating for themselves, authorities have passed laws against such activities as hunting whales out of existence, dumping toxic wastes into streams and rivers, and poisoning the air with harmful fumes. However, most such laws apply to the more affluent countries of the world—the very ones where levels of consumption drive the forces of exploitation responsible for environmental degradation in the poor countries of the world.

A large part of the problem in this and similar situations is a reluctance to perceive as disadvantageous practices that previously seemed to

work well. What frequently happens is that practices carried out on one particular scale, or that were suited to one particular context, become unsuitable when carried out on another scale or in another context. Because they are trained to look at customs in their broader context, anthropologists would seem to have an important role to play in convincing people that solutions to many problems require changed behavior.

Indigenous peoples, in particular, are apt to stand in awe of natural forces, bestowing on them a special place in their religious system. For example, many people believe that rushing rapids, storms, the mountains, and the jungles possess awesome powers. This is also true of fire, which both warms and destroys. For farmers, the sun, rain, and thunder are important to their existence and are often considered divine. Such worldviews are not foolproof checks to the kind of environmental manipulation that causes severe pollution, but they certainly act as powerful restraining influences.

Population Control

Although the problems we have discussed so far may not be caused by population growth, they are certainly made worse by it. For one thing, it increases the scale of the problems; thus, the waste generated by a small population is far easier to deal with than that generated by a large one. For another, it often nullifies efforts made to solve the problems, as when increased food production is offset by increased numbers of people to be fed. While solving the problem of population growth will not by itself make the other problems go away, it is unlikely that those other problems can be solved unless population growth is arrested.

As our earlier look at population demonstrated, the world's population has grown enormously since the beginning of the industrial age. With the exception of European and North American populations, there was no sign of a significant decline in birth rates prior to 1976. The reason that poor people, in particular, have so many children is simple: Children are the main resource of the poor. They provide a needed pool of labor to work farms and they are the only source of security for the elderly; hence, to have lots of offspring makes sense. Historically, people are apt to limit the size of their families only when they become wealthy enough that money replaces children as their main resource; at that point, children actually *cost* them money. Given this, we can see why birth rates, in spite of some recent decrease, still remain high in the poorer countries of the world. To those who live in poverty, children are seen as the only hope. Nevertheless, since 1976 there have been some encouraging signs, as in China, where there has been a steep decline in birth rates. In South Asia, Africa, and much of Central and South America (again, the poorer countries of the world), birth rates have also declined, but far less dramatically (see Fig. 27.4). In these countries growing populations still make it difficult even to maintain their present per capita

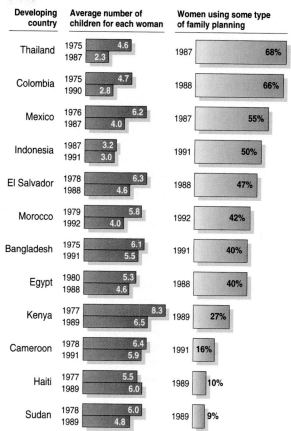

Linking fertility and family planning

The following is based on surveys of over 300,000 women in 44 developing nations. China and India were not included in the studies, which were done in different years.

Developing country	Average number of children for each woman		Women using some type of family planning	
Thailand	1975	4.6	1987	68%
	1987	2.3		
Colombia	1975	4.7	1988	66%
	1990	2.8		
Mexico	1976	6.2	1987	55%
	1987	4.0		
Indonesia	1987	3.2	1991	50%
	1991	3.0		
El Salvador	1978	6.3	1988	47%
	1988	4.6		
Morocco	1979	5.8	1992	42%
	1992	4.0		
Bangladesh	1975	6.1	1991	40%
	1991	5.5		
Egypt	1980	5.3	1988	40%
	1988	4.6		
Kenya	1977	8.3	1989	27%
	1989	6.5		
Cameroon	1978	6.4	1991	16%
	1991	5.9		
Haiti	1977	5.5	1989	10%
	1989	6.0		
Sudan	1978	6.0	1989	9%
	1989	4.8		

Figure 27.4   Although they are still above the level of replacement reproduction, birth rates in some "underdeveloped" countries have shown some decline.

share of food and other resources. Even if, through some miracle, those countries having policies aimed at population control were able to bring about an immediate balance between birth and death rates (**replacement reproduction**), their populations would continue to grow for the next 50 years before the age distribution flattened out and zero growth was achieved.

Replacement reproduction: When birth and death rates are in equilibrium; people produce no more offspring than necessary to replace themselves when they die.

The severity of the problem becomes clear when it is realized that the present world population of more than 5.6 billion people can be sustained only by using up what are actually nonrenewable resources, which is like living off income-producing capital. It works for a time, but once the capital is gone, so is the possibility of even having an income to live on.

Evident though the problem is, efforts to bring about reduced birth rates face enormous cultural and structural obstacles. Some of these, as well as the kinds of new problems that may arise, are well illustrated by China's much publicized policy to promote one-child families. While this has slowed the rate of growth of China's population, it has given rise to some serious new problems. The difficulty stems from a basic contradiction with another policy, to raise agricultural productivity by granting more economic autonomy to rural households, and the continued existence of families, which (as in old China) are strongly patriarchal. Within such families, men are responsible for farm work, perpetuation of the male line of descent is considered essential to everyone's well-being, and postmarital residence is strictly patrilocal. Under these circumstances, the birth of male children is considered essential; without them, the household will not have the workforce it needs and will suffer economically. Furthermore, the parents will have no one to support them, once they are too old for physical labor. Daughters are of little use to them, since they will marry out of the household and can offer little aid to their parents. Since married couples are supposed to have only one child, the birth of a daughter is greeted with dismay, for if the couple tries again for a boy, tremendous pressures will be brought to bear by local officials of the state for the woman to have an abortion, and for her or her husband to undergo sterilization.

Not surprisingly, in the face of all this, female infanticide is on the rise in China, and women who bear daughters are often physically and mentally abused by their husbands and mothers-in-law, sometimes to the point of committing suicide (although the state teaches that men determine the sex of a baby, most rural Chinese believe that the woman is still responsible for the outcome of birth, perhaps through her diet and behavior). Women pay in other ways with their bodies; when a second pregnancy occurs, it is the woman who must have the abortion, and it is usually she who

Illegal immigrants jump a border fence near Tijuana, Mexico. Already, economic refugees are causing several problems for the so-called "developed" countries. As the gap between rich and poor countries grows, as it currently is, the flood of illegal immigration is bound to get worse.

is sterilized (surgical intervention in men in their prime is discouraged, owing to the importance of their labor in agriculture). This leaves the man free to coerce his daughter-bearing wife into a divorce, so that he can try again for a son with a new wife, leaving the old one of no use to anyone and with no son to care for her in old age. In a married woman, one means by which unauthorized pregnancy is prevented is through placement of an intrauterine device (IUD) in her womb. This cannot be removed without official permission, which is hard to get even in the face of compelling medical reasons to do so, since removal is contrary to official policy. Nor is an attached cord for removal provided, all of which has led to proliferation of back alley practitioners who remove IUDs with improvised hooks, often leading to infection and death.

The Culture of Discontent

In spite of the difficulties, stabilization of the world's population appears to be a necessary step if the problems of the future are ever to be solved. Without this, whatever else is done, an inability to provide enough food seems inevitable. Up until about 1950, growth in the world's food supply came almost entirely from expanding the amount of land under cultivation. Since then, it has come increasingly from high-energy inputs in the form of chemical fertilizers upon which new high-yield varieties of crops depend, pesticides and herbicides, as well as fuel to run tractors and other mechanical equipment, including irrigation pumps. The source of almost all this energy is oil, yet while the demand for food is projected to rise until at least the middle of the twenty-first century, oil supplies are diminishing and will surely decline over this same period. Insufficient supplies of food are bound to result in increased structural violence in the form of higher death rates in the "underdeveloped" countries of the world. This will surely have an impact on the "developed" countries, with their relatively stable populations and high standards of living. It is hard to see how such countries could exist peacefully side by side with others experiencing high death rates and abysmally low living standards. Already, the combination of overpopulation and poverty is causing a rising tide of migration from poor to more affluent countries like the United States, with a consequent rise of intolerance, antiforeign feeling, and general social unrest.

Necessary though it may be in solving problems of the future, there is no reason to suppose that birth control will be sufficient by itself. The result would be only to stabilize things as they are. The problem is twofold. Over the past several years, the poor countries of the world have been sold on the idea that they should enjoy a standard of living comparable to that of the rich countries. At the same time, the resources necessary to maintain such a standard of living are running out. As we saw in Chapter 26, this situation has led to the creation of a culture of discontent, whereby people's aspirations far exceed their opportunities. The problem involves not just a case of population growth outstripping food supplies; it is also one of unequal access to decent jobs, housing, sanitation, health care, and adequate police and fire protection. And it is one of steady deterioration of the natural environment as a result of increasing industrialization.

What are required are some dramatic changes in cultural values and motivations, as well as in social institutions. The emphasis on individual self-interest, materialism, and conspicuous production, acquisition, and consumption, which is characteristic of the richer countries of the world, needs to be abandoned in favor of a more human self-image and social ethic, which can be created from values still found in many of the world's non-Western cultures. These include a worldview that sees humanity as a part of the natural world, rather than superior to it. Included, too, is a sense of social responsibility that recognizes that no individual, people, or state has the right to expropriate resources at the expense of others. Finally, there is needed an awareness of the importance of the supportive ties among individuals, such as are seen in kinship or other associations in the traditional societies of the world.

CHAPTER SUMMARY

Since future forms of culture will be shaped by decisions humans have yet to make, they cannot be predicted with any accuracy. Thus, instead of trying to foretell the future, a number of anthropologists are trying for a better understanding of the existing world situation, so that those decisions may be made intelligently. Anthropologists are especially well suited to do this, owing to their experience at seeing things in context, their long-term evolutionary perspective, their ability to recognize culture-bound biases, and their familiarity with cultural alternatives.

However humanity changes biologically, culture remains the chief means by which humans try to solve their problems of existence. Some anthropologists are concerned that there is a trend for the problems to outstrip culture's ability to find solutions. Rapid developments in communication, transportation, and world trade, some believe, will link people together to the point that a single world culture will result. Their thinking is that such a homogenized superculture would offer fewer chances for conflict between peoples than in the past. A number of anthropologists are skeptical of such an argument, in view of the recent tendency for ethnic groups to reassert their own distinctive identities, and in view of the persistence of traditional ways of thinking about oneself and others, even in the face of massive changes in other aspects of culture. Anthropologists are also concerned about the tendency for many of the world's traditional societies to be treated as obsolete when they appear to stand in the way of "development."

Another alternative is for humanity to move in the direction of cultural pluralism, in which more than one culture exists in a society. To work, cultural pluralism must reject bigotry, bias, and racism. Some anthropologists maintain that pluralistic arrangements are the only feasible means for achieving global equilibrium and peace. A problem associated with cultural pluralism is ethnocentrism. All too often, in the name of "nation building," it has led one group to impose its control on others. A common consequence is prolonged, violent, and bloody political upheavals, including genocide.

Adopting a global perspective, a picture emerges that is strikingly similar to South Africa's system of apartheid. It serves to maintain the dominance of a largely white minority over a nonwhite majority, through the social, economic, political, military, and cultural constitution of the "global society."

One consequence of any system of apartheid is a great deal of structural violence exerted by situations, institutions, and social, political, and economic structures. Such violence involves things like overpopulation and food shortages, which anthropologists are actively working to understand and help alleviate. One challenge is to provide food re-sources to keep pace with the burgeoning population. The immediate problem, though, is not so much one of producing enough food as it is a food-distribution system that is geared to the satisfaction of appetites in the "rich" countries of the world, at the expense of those living in poorer countries.

Pollution has become a direct threat to humanity. Western peoples have protected their environments only when some crisis forced them to do so, and even at that their rates of consumption continue to drive environmental degradation in other countries. Western societies have felt no long-term responsibilities toward the earth or its resources and could learn much from those non-Western peoples who see themselves as integral parts of the earth.

Meeting the problems of structural violence that beset the human species today probably can be done only if we are able to reduce the birth rate. Effective birth-control methods are now available. Whether or not these methods are used on a vast enough scale depends on their availability and acceptance. Many of the world's developing countries have policies aimed at controlling population growth, but these sometimes conflict with other policies, giving rise to new kinds of problems. Even if replacement reproduction were immediately achieved their populations would continue to grow.

Solving the problems of the global society depends also on lessening the gap between the living standards of poor and developed countries, which will call for dramatic changes in the values of Western societies with their materialistic, consumer orientation. All people need to see themselves as a part of nature, rather than as superior to it. Also needed are a social responsibility that recognizes that no people has a right to expropriate important resources at the expense of others, and an awareness of the importance of supportive ties between individuals.

SUGGESTED READINGS

Bodley, J. H. (1985). *Anthropology and contemporary human problems* (2nd ed.). Palo Alto, CA: Mayfield.

Anthropologist Bodley examines some of the most serious problems in the world today: overconsumption, resource depletion, hunger and starvation, overpopulation, violence, and war.

Bodley, J. H. (1990). *Victims of progress* (3rd ed.). Mountain View, CA: Mayfield.

Explores the impact of industrial civilization on the indigenous peoples of the world and how the latter are organizing to protect themselves.

Davis, S. H. (1982). *Victims of the miracle*. Cambridge: Cambridge University Press.

An anthropologist looks at Brazil's efforts to develop the Amazon region, the motivations behind those efforts, and their impact on indigenous peoples. Davis pays special attention to the role played by multinational corporations, how they relate to the Brazilian government, and who benefits from it all.

Maybury-Lewis, D. (Ed.) (1982). *The prospects for plural societies*. 1982 Proceedings of the American Ethnological Society.

In 1982, a group of anthropologists met to discuss one of the most crucial issues of our time, the prospects for multiethnic societies. What emerged as the "villain" of the conference was the state; not just particular countries but states as a kind of political structure and the hold that they have over modern thought and political action. Maybury-Lewis confronts this issue in the concluding essay, which by itself makes this volume worth examining.

Miller, M. S. (Ed.) (1993). *State of the peoples: A global human rights report on societies in danger*. Boston: Beacon Press.

This important publication from Cultural Survival, Inc., systematically reports on the situation of indigenous people throughout the world, region by region. Also included are "expert" articles on critical issues affecting such diverse peoples as Bosnians and Bushmen, all sorts of useful maps and charts, and suggested solutions to many challenges facing indigenous peoples. A "must read" for anyone who is in any way concerned with the "New World Disorder."

BIBLIOGRAPHY

Aberle, David F. 1961. "Culture and Socialization" in F. Hsu, ed., *Psychological Anthropology: Approaches to Culture and Personality.* Homewood, Ill.: Dorsey Press, pp. 381–399.

Aberle, David F., Urie Bronfenbrenner, Eckhard H. Hess, Daniel R. Miller, David H. Schneider, and James N. Spuhler. 1963. "The Incest Taboo and the Mating Patterns of Animals" *American Anthropologist,* 65:253–265.

Abu-Lughold, Lila. 1988. *Veiled Sentiments: Honor and Poetry in a Bedouin Society.* Berkeley, Ca.: University of California Press.

Adams, Richard E. W. 1977. *Prehistoric Mesoamerica.* Boston: Little, Brown.

Adams, Robert McC. 1965. *Land Behind Baghdad.* Chicago: University of Chicago Press.

Adams, Robert McC. 1966. *The Evolution of Urban Society.* Chicago: Aldine.

Al-Issa, Ihsan, and Wayne Dennis, eds. 1970. *Cross-cultural Studies of Behavior.* New York: Holt, Rinehart and Winston.

Alland, Alexander, Jr. 1970. *Adaptation in Cultural Evolution: An Approach to Medical Anthropology.* New York: Columbia University Press.

Alland, Alexander, Jr. 1971. *Human Diversity.* New York: Columbia University Press.

Allen, Susan L. 1984. "Media Anthropology: Building a Public Perspective" *Anthropology Newsletter,* 25:6.

Amiran, Ruth. 1965. "The Beginnings of Pottery-Making in the Near East" in Frederick R. Matson, ed., *Ceramics and Man.* Viking Fund Publications in Anthropology, No. 41.

Anderson, Connie M. 1989. "Neanderthal Pelves and Gestational Length" *American Anthropologist,* 91:327–340.

Anonymous. 1983. *Cultural Survival Quarterly,* "Death and Disorder in Guatemala." *Cultural Survival Quarterly,* 7(1).

Anonymous. 1991. *Cultural Survival Quarterly,* 15, No. 4:5.

Anonymous. 1991. *Cultural Survival Quarterly,* 15, No. 4:38.

Arensberg, Conrad M. 1961. "The Community as Object and Sample" *American Anthropologist,* 63:241–264.

Arensberg, Conrad M., and Arthur H. Niehoff. 1964. *Introducing Social Change: A Manual for Americans Overseas.* Chicago: Aldine.

Armstrong, David F., William C. Stokoe, and Sherman E. Wilcox. 1994. "Signs of the Origin of Syntax," *Current Anthropology,* 35:349–368.

Armstrong, Sue. 1991. "Female Circumcision: Fighting a Cruel Tradition," *New Scientist,* 2 Feb.: 42–47.

Ashmore, Wendy, ed. 1981. *Lowland Maya Settlement Patterns.* Albuquerque: University of New Mexico Press.

Balandier, Georges. 1971. *Political Anthropology.* New York: Pantheon.

Banton, Michael. 1968. "Voluntary Association: Anthropological Aspects" *International Encyclopedia of the Social Sciences,* 16:357–362.

Bar-Yosef, O. 1986. "The Walls of Jericho: An Alternative Interpretation" *Current Anthropology,* 27:157–162.

Bar-Yosef, O. B. Vandermeesch, B. Arensburg, A. Belfer-Cohen, P. Goldberg, H. Laville, L. Meignen, Y. Rak, J. D. Speth, E. Tchernov, A-M. Tillier, and S. Weiner. 1992. "The Excavations in Kebara Cave, Mt. Carmel." *Current Anthropology,* 33:497–550.

Barber, Bernard. 1957. *Social Stratification.* New York: Harcourt.

Barfield, Thomas J. 1984. "Introduction" *Cultural Survival Quarterly,* 8:2.

Barnett, H. G. 1953. *Innovation: The Basis of Cultural Change.* New York: McGraw-Hill.

Barnouw, Victor. 1963. *Culture and Personality.* Homewood, Ill.: Dorsey Press.

Barth, Frederick. 1960. "Nomadism in the Mountain and Plateau Areas of South West Asia" *The Problems of the Arid Zone,* UNESCO, pp. 341–355.

Barth, Frederick. 1961. *Nomads of South Persia: The Basseri Tribe of the Khamseh Confederacy.* Boston: Little, Brown (Series in Anthropology).

Barton, R. F. 1919. Ifugao Law. Berkeley: *University of California Publications in American Archaeology and Ethnology,* Vol. XV.

Bascom, William. 1969. *The Yoruba of Southwestern Nigeria.* New York: Holt, Rinehart and Winston.

Bates, Daniel G., and Fred Plog. 1991. *Human Adaptive Strategies.* New York: McGraw-Hill.

Bateson, Gregory. 1958. *Naven.* Stanford, Calif.: Stanford University Press.

Beals, Alan R. 1972. *Gopalpur: A South Indian Village.* New York: Holt, Rinehart and Winston.

Beattie, John. 1964. *Other Cultures: Aims, Methods and Achievements.* New York: Free Press.

Bednarik, Robert G. 1995. "Concept-mediated Marking in the Lower Paleolithic," *Current Anthropology,* 36:605–634.

Beidelman, T. O., ed. 1971. *The Transition of Culture: Essays to E. E. Evans-Pritchard.* London: Tavistock.

Belshaw, Cyril S. 1958. "The Significance of Modern Cults in Melanesian Development" in William Lessa and Evon Z. Vogt, eds., *Reader in Comparative Religion: An Anthropological Approach.* New York: Harper & Row.

Benedict, Ruth. 1959. *Patterns of Culture.* New York: New American Library.

Bennett, John W. 1964. "Myth, Theory and Value in Cultural Anthropology" in E. W. Caint and G. T. Bowles, eds., *Fact and Theory in Social Science.* Syracuse, N.Y.: Syracuse University Press.

Berdan, Frances F. 1982. *The Aztecs of Central Mexico.* New York: Holt, Rinehart and Winston.

Bernal, I. 1969. *The Olmec World.* Berkeley: University of California Press.

Bernard, H. Russell, and Willis E. Sibley. 1975. *Anthropology and Jobs.* Washington, D.C.: American Anthropological Association.

Bernardi, Bernardo. 1985. *Age Class Systems: Social Institutions and Policies Based on Age.* New York: Cambridge University Press.

Bernstein, Basin. 1961. "Social Structure, Language and Learning" *Educational Research*, 3:163–176.

Berreman, Gerald D. 1962. *Behind Many Masks: Ethnography and Impression Management in a Himalayan Village*. Ithaca, N.Y.: Society for Applied Anthropology (Monograph No. 4).

Berreman, Gerald D. 1968. "Caste: The Concept of Caste" *International Encyclopedia of the Social Sciences*, 2:333–338.

Bicchieri, M. G., ed. 1972. *Hunters and Gatherers Today: A Socioeconomic Study of Eleven Such Cultures in the Twentieth Century*. New York: Holt, Rinehart and Winston.

Bidney, David. 1953. *Theoretical Anthropology*. New York: Columbia University Press.

Binford, L. R. 1972. *An Archaeological Perspective*. New York: Seminar Press.

Binford, Lewis R., and Chuan Kun Ho. 1985. "Taphonomy at a Distance: Zhonkoudian, The Cave Home of Beijing Man?", *Current Anthropology*, 26:413–442.

Birdwhistell, Ray. 1970. *Kinesics and Context*. Philadelphia: University of Pennsylvania Press.

Black, Henry Campbell. 1968. *Black's Law Dictionary*. St. Paul, MN: West.

Blumer, Mark A., and Roger Byrne. 1991. "The Ecological Genetics and Domestication and the Origins of Agriculture" *Current Anthropology*, 32:23–54.

Boas, Franz. 1962. *Primitive Art*. Gloucester, Mass.: Peter Smith.

Boas, Franz. 1966. *Race, Language and Culture*. New York: Free Press.

Bodley, John H. 1985. *Anthropology and Contemporary Human Problems*, 2d ed. Palo Alto, Cal.: Mayfield.

Bodley, John H. 1990. *Victims of Progress*. 3d ed. Mountain View, CA: Mayfield.

Bohannan, Paul. 1966. *Social Anthropology*. New York: Holt, Rinehart and Winston.

Bohannan, Paul, ed. 1967. *Law and Warfare: Studies in the Anthropology of Conflict*. Garden City, N.Y.: Natural History Press.

Bohannan, Paul, and George Dalton, eds. 1962. *Markets in Africa*. Evanston, Ill.: Northwestern University Press.

Bohannan, Paul, and John Middleton, eds. 1968. *Kinship and Social Organization*. Garden City, N.Y.: Natural History Press (American Museum Source Books in Anthropology).

Bohannan, Paul, and John Middleton, eds. 1968. *Marriage, Family, and Residence*. Garden City, N.Y.: Natural History Press (American Museum Source Books in Anthropology).

Bolinger, Dwight. 1968. *Aspects of Language*. New York: Harcourt.

Bordes, Francois. 1972. *A Tale of Two Caves*. New York: Harper & Row.

Bornstein, Marc H. 1975. "The Influence of Visual Perception on Culture" *American Anthropologist*, 77(4):774–798.

Brace, C. Loring. 1981. "Tales of the Phylogenetic Woods: The Evolution and Significance of Phylogenetic Trees" *American Journal of Physical Anthropology*, 56:411–429.

Brace, C. Loring, Harry Nelson, and Noel Korn. 1979. *Atlas of Human Evolution*, 2d ed., New York: Holt, Rinehart and Winston.

Brace, C. Loring, Alan S. Ryan, and B. Holly Smith. 1981. "Comment" *Current Anthropology*, 22(4):426–430.

Bradfield, Richard 1973. *A Natural History of Associations*. New York: International Universities Press.

Braidwood, Robert J. 1960. "The Agricultural Revolution" *Scientific American*, 203:130–141.

Braidwood, Robert J. 1975. *Prehistoric Men*, 8th ed. Glenview, Ill.: Scott, Foresman.

Braidwood, Robert J., and Gordon R. Willey. 1962. *Courses Toward Urban Life: Archeological Consideration of Some Cultural Alternatives*. Chicago: Aldine (publications in Anthropology Series, No. 32).

Brain, C. K. 1968. "Who Killed the Swartkrnas Ape-Men?" *South African Museums Association Bulletin*, 9:127–139.

Brain, C. K. 1969. The Contribution of Namib Desert Hottentots to an Understanding of Australopithecine Bone Accumulations. *Scientific Papers of the Namib Desert Research Station* 13.

Branda, Richard F., and John W. Eatoil. 1978. "Skin Color and Photolysis: An Evolutionary Hypothesis" *Science*, 201:625–626.

Brew, John O. 1968. *One Hundred Years of Anthropology*. Cambridge, Mass.: Harvard University Press.

Brinton, Crane. 1953. *The Shaping of the Modern Mind*. New York: Mentor.

Brothwell, D. R., and E. Higgs, eds. 1969. *Science in Archaeology*, rev. ed. London: Thames and Hudson.

Brown, B., A. Walker, C. V. Ward, and R. E. Leakey. 1993. "New *Australopithecus boisei* Calvaria from East Lake Turkana, Kenya," *American Journal of Physical Anthropology*, 91:137–159.

Brown, Donald E. 1991. *Human Universals*. New York: McGraw-Hill.

Brues, Alice M. 1977. *People and Races*. New York: Macmillan.

Bruner, Edward M. 1970. "Medan: The Role of Kinship in an Indonesian City" in William Mangin, ed., *Peasants in Cities: Readings in the Anthropology of Urbanization*. Boston: Houghton Mifflin.

Burling, Robbins. 1969. "Linguistics and Ethnographic Description" *American Anthropologist*, 71:817–827.

Burling, Robbins. 1970. *Man's Many Voices: Language in Its Cultural Context*. New York: Holt, Rinehart and Winston.

Burling, Robbins. 1993. Primate Calls, Human Language and Nonverbal Communication" *Current Anthropology*, 34(11):25–53.

Butzer, K. 1971. *Environment and Anthropology: An Ecological Approach to Prehistory*, 2d ed. Chicago: Aldine.

Byers, D. S., ed. 1967. *The Prehistory of the Tehuacan Valley: Vol. 1. Environment and Subsistence*. Austin: University of Texas Press.

Campbell, Bernard G., and James D. Loy. 1995. *Humankind Emerging*, 7th ed. New York: HarperCollins.

Carmack, Robert. 1983. "Indians and the Guatemalan Revolution" *Cultural Survival Quarterly*, 7(3):52–54.

Carneiro, Robert L. 1961. "Slash and Burn Cultivation among the Kuikuru and Its Implications for Cultural Development in the Amazon Basin" in J. Wilbert, ed., *The Evolution of Horticultural Systems in Native South America: Causes and Consequences*. Caracas: Sociedad de Ciencias Naturales La Salle.

Carneiro, Robert L. 1970. "A Theory of the Origin of the State" *Science*, 169:733–738.

Carpenter, Edmund. 1973. *Eskimo Realities*. New York: Holt, Rinehart and Winston.

Carroll, John B., ed. 1956. *Language, Thought and Reality: Selected Writings of Benjamin Lee Whorf*. New York: Wiley.

Cashdan, Elizabeth. 1989. "Hunters and Gatherers: Economic Behavior in Bands" in *Economic Anthropology*, edited by Stuart Plattner. Stanford, Ca.: Stanford University Press.

Cavalli-Sforza, L. L. 1977. *Elements of Human Genetics*. Menlo Park, Calif.: W. A. Benjamin.

Cavallo, John A. 1990. "Cat in the Human Cradle," *Natural History*, 2/90:54–60.

Chagnon, Napoleon A. 1988. *Yanomamö: The Fierce People*. 3d ed., New York: Holt, Rinehart and Winston.

Chagnon, N. A., and William Irons, eds. 1979. *Evolutionary Biology and Human Social Behavior*. North Scituate, Mass.: Duxbury Press.

Chambers, Robert. 1983. *Rural Development: Putting The Last First*. New York: Longman.

Chang, K. C., ed. 1968. *Settlement Archaeology*. Palo Alto, Calif.: National Press.

Chapple, Eliot D. 1970. *Cultural and Biological Man: Explorations in Behavioral Anthropology*. New York: Holt, Rinehart and Winston.

Chasin, Barbara H., and Richard W. Franke. 1983. "U.S. Farming: A World Model?" *Global Reporter*, 1, No. 2:10.

Childe, V. Gordon. 1951, orig. 1936. *Man Makes Himself*. New York: New American Library.

Childe, V. Gordon. 1954. *What Happened in History*. Baltimore: Penguin.

Chodorow, Nancy. 1971. "Being and Doing: A Cross-Cultural Examination of the Socialization of Males and Females" in *Woman in Sexist Society*, Vivian Gornick and Barbara K. Moran, eds. New York: Basic Books.

Ciochon, Russell L., and John G. Fleagle. 1987. "Ramapithecus and Human Origins" in *Primate Evolution and Human Origins*, ed. Russell L. Ciochon and John G. Fleagle. Hawthorne, NY: Aldine de Gruyter.

Ciochon, Russell L., and John G. Fleagle, eds. 1987. *Primate Evolution and Human Origins*. Hawthorne, N.Y.: Aldine de Gruyter.

Ciochon, Russell L., and John G. Fleagle. 1993. *The Human Evolution Source Book*. Englewood Cliffs, N.J.: Prentice Hall.

Clark, Ella E. 1966. *Indian Legends of the Pacific Northwest*. Berkeley: University of California Press.

Clark, Grahame. 1967. *The Stone Age Hunters*. New York: McGraw-Hill.

Clark, Grahame. 1972. *Starr Carr: A Case Study in Bioarchaeology*. Reading, Mass.: Addison-Wesley.

Clark, J. G. D. 1962. *Prehistoric Europe: The Economic Basis*. Stanford, Calif.: Stanford University Press.

Clark, W. E. LeGros. 1960. *The Antecedents of Man*. Chicago: Quadrangle Books.

Clark, W. E. LeGros. 1966. *History of the Primates*, 5th ed. Chicago: University of Chicago Press.

Clark, W. E. LeGros. 1967. *Man-Apes or Ape-Men? The Story of Discoveries in Africa*. New York: Holt, Rinehart and Winston.

Clarke, Ronald J., and Philip V. Tobias. 1995. "Sterkfontein Member 2 Foot Bones of the Oldest South African Hominid," *Science*, 269:521–524.

Clay, Jason W. 1987. "Genocide in the Age of Enlightenment" *Cultural Survival Quarterly*, 12, No. 3.

Clay, Jason W. 1990. "What's a Nation" *Mother Jones*, 15, No. 7:28.

Clough, S. B., and C. W. Cole. 1952. *Economic History of Europe*, 3d ed. Lexington, Mass.: Heath.

Codere, Helen. 1950. *Fighting with Property*. Seattle: University of Washington Press (American Ethnological Society, Monograph 18).

Coe, William R. 1967. *Tikal: A Handbook of the Ancient Maya Ruins*. Philadelphia: University of Pennsylvania Museum.

Cohen, Mark N. 1977. *The Food Crisis in Prehistory*. New Haven, Conn.: Yale University Press.

Cohen, Mark N. 1995. "Anthropology and Race: The Bell Curve Phenomenon," *General Anthropology*, 2(1):1–4.

Cohen, Mark, and George Armelagos, eds. 1984. *Paleopathology and the Origins of Agriculture*. Orlando, Fla.: Academic Press.

Cohen, Mark N., and George J. Armelagos. 1984. "Paleopathology and the Origins of Agriculture: Editors' Summation," in Cohen and Armelagos, eds. *Paleopathology and the Origins of Agriculture*. Orlando, Fla.: Academic Press.

Cohen, Myron L. 1967. "Variations in Complexity among Chinese Family Groups: The Impact of Modernization" *Transactions of the New York Academy of Sciences*, 295:638–647.

Cohen, Myron L. 1968. "A Case Study of Chinese Family Economy and Development" *Journal of Asian and African Studies*, 3:161–180.

Cohen, Ronald, and John Middleton, eds. 1967. *Comparative Political Systems*. Garden City, N.Y.: Natural History Press.

Cohen, Yehudi. 1968. *Man in Adaptation: The Cultural Present*. Chicago: Aldine.

Cole, Sonia. 1975. *Leakey's Luck: The Life of Louis Seymour Bazett Leakey. 1903–1972*. New York: Harcourt Brace Jovanovich.

Collier, Jane Fishburne, and Sylvia Junko Yanagisako, eds. 1987. *Gender and Kinship: Essays Toward a Unified Analysis*. (Stanford, Ca.: Stanford University Press).

Collier, Jane, Michelle Z. Rosaldo, and Sylvia Yanagisako. 1982. "Is There a Family? New Anthropological Views" in *Rethinking the Family: Some Feminist Problems*. Barrie Thorne and Marilyn Yalom, eds. New York: Longman.

Connelly, John C. 1979. "Hopi Social Organization" in *Handbook of North American Indians Vol. 9*, Southwest, ed. Alfonso Ortiz. Washington: Smithsonian Institution, pp. 539–553.

Constable, George, and the Editors of Time-Life. 1973. *The Neanderthals*. New York: Time-Life.

Cook, S. F. 1972. *Prehistoric Demography*. Reading, Mass.: Addison-Wesley.

Coon, Carleton S. 1948. *A Reader in General Anthropology*. New York: Holt, Rinehart and Winston.

Coon, Carleton S. 1954. "Climate and Race." *Smithsonian Report* for 1953, pp. 277–298.

Coon, Carleton S. 1954. *The Story of Man*. New York: Knopf.

Coon, Carleton S. 1957. *The Seven Caves*. New York: Knopf.

Coon, Carleton S. 1958. *Caravan: The Story of the Middle East*, 2d ed. New York: Holt, Rinehart and Winston.

Coon, Carleton S. 1971. *The Hunting Peoples*. Boston: Little, Brown.

Coon, Carleton S., Stanley N. Garn, and Joseph Birdsell. 1950. *Races: A Study of the Problems of Race Formation in Man*. Springfield, Ill.: Charles C Thomas.

Coppens, Yves, F. Clark Howell, Glyn L. Isaac, and Richard E. F. Leakey, eds. 1976. *Earliest Man and Environments in the Lake Rudolf Basin: Stratigraphy, Paleoecology, and Evolution*. Chicago: University of Chicago Press.

Corruccini, Robert S. 1992. "Metrical Reconsideration of the Skhul IV and IX and Border Cave I Crania in the Context of Modern Human Origins" *American Journal of Physical Anthropology*, 87:433–445.

Cottrell, Fred. 1965. *Energy and Society: The Relation between Energy, Social Changes and Economic Development*. New York: McGraw-Hill.

Cottrell, Leonard. 1963. *The Lost Pharaohs*. New York: Grosset & Dunlap.

Courlander, Harold. 1971. *The Fourth World of the Hopis*. New York: Crown.

Cowgill, George L. 1980. Letter, *Science*, 210:1305.

Cox, Oliver Cromwell. 1959. *Caste, Class and Race: A Study in Dynamics*. New York: Monthly Review Press.

Crane, L. Ben, Edward Yeager, and Randal L. Whitman. 1981. *An Introduction to Linguistics.* Boston: Little, Brown.

Crocker, William A., and Jean Crocker. 1994. *The Canela, Bonding Through Kinship, Ritual and Sex.* Fort Worth, TX.: Harcourt Brace.

Culbert, T. P., ed. 1973. *The Classic Maya Collapse.* Albuquerque: University of New Mexico Press.

Culotta, Elizabeth. 1992. "A New Take on Anthropoid Origins," *Science,* 256: 1516–1517.

Culotta, Elizabeth. 1995. "Asian Hominids Grow Older," *Science,* 270: 1116–1117.

Culotta, Elizabeth. 1995. "New Finds Rekindle Debate Over Anthropoid Origins," *Science,* 268:851.

Culotta, Elizabeth. 1995. "New Hominid Crowds the Field," *Science,* 269:918

Dalton, George, ed. 1967. *Economic Anthropology and Development: Essays on Tribal and Peasant Economics.* New York: Basic Books.

Dalton, George, ed. 1967. *Tribal and Peasant Economics: Readings in Economic Anthropology.* Garden City, N.Y.: Natural History Press.

Dalton, George. 1971. *Traditional Tribal and Peasant Economics: An Introductory Survey of Economic Anthropology.* Reading, Mass.: Addison-Wesley.

Daniel, Glyn. 1970. *The First Civilizations: The Archaeology of Their Origins.* New York: Apollo Editions.

Daniel, Glyn. 1970. *The Origins and Growth of Archaeology.* Baltimore, Md.: Penguin.

Daniel, Glyn. 1975. *A Hundred and Fifty Years of Archaeology.* 2d ed. London: Duckworth.

Darwin, Charles. 1936; orig. 1871. *The Descent of Man and Selection in Relation to Sex.* New York: Random House (Modern Library).

Darwin, Charles. 1967; orig. 1859. *On the Origin of Species.* New York: Atheneum.

Davenport, William. 1959. "Linear Descent and Descent Groups." *American Anthropologist,* 61:557–573.

Davis, Shelton. 1982. *Victims of the Miracle.* Cambridge: Cambridge University Press.

Davis, Susan S., n.d. *Patience, and Power, Women's Lives in a Moroccan Village.* Cambridge, Mass.: Schenkman.

de Laguna, Frederica. 1977. *Voyage to Greenland: A Personal Initiation into Anthropology.* New York: Norton.

de Laguna, Grace A. 1966. *On Existence and the Human World.* New Haven, Conn.: Yale University Press.

de Pelliam, Alison, and Francis D. Burton. 1976. "More on Predatory Behavior in Nonhuman Primates" *Current Anthropology,* 17(3).

de Waal, Alex. 1994. "Genocide in Rwanda," *Anthropology Today,* 10, No. 3:1–2

Dean, M. C., A. D. Beynon, J. F. Thackeray, and G. A. Macho. 1993. "Histological reconstruction of Dental Development and Age at Death of a Juvenile *Paranthropus robustus* Specimen, SK 63, from Swartkrans, South Africa," *American Journal of Physical Anthropology,* 91:401–419.

DeBeer, Sir Gavin R. 1964. *Atlas of Evolution.* London: Nelson.

Deetz, James. 1967. *Invitation to Archaeology.* New York: Doubleday.

Deevy, Edward S., Jr. 1960. "The Human Population" *Scientific American,* 203: 194–204.

Despres, Leo A. 1968. "Cultural Pluralism and the Study of Complex Societies" *Current Anthropology,* 9:3–26.

Devereux, George. 1963. "Institutionalized Homosexuality of the Mohave Indians" in Hendrik M. Ruitenbeck, ed., *The Problem of Homosexuality in Modern Society.* New York: Dutton.

DeVore, Irven, ed. 1965. *Primate Behavior: Field Studies of Monkeys and Apes.* New York: Holt, Rinehart and Winston.

Diamond, Jared. 1994. "How Africa Became Black," *Discover,* 15 (2):72–81.

Diamond, Jared. 1994. "Race Without Color," *Discover,* 15 (11):83–89.

Dixon, J. E., J. R. Cann, and C. Renfrew. 1968. "Obsidian and the Origins of Trade" *Scientific American,* 218:38–46.

Dobyns, Henry F., Paul L. Doughty, and Harold D. Lasswell, eds. 1971. *Peasants, Power, and Applied Social Change.* London: Sage.

Dobzhansky, Theodosius. 1962. *Mankind Evolving.* New Haven, Conn.: Yale University Press.

Donnan, Christopher B., and Luis Jaime Castillo. 1992. "Finding the Tomb of a Moche Priestess," *Archaeology,* 45(6):38–42.

Douglas, Mary. 1958. "Raffia Cloth Distribution in the Lele Economy" *Africa,* 28:109–122.

Dowson, T. A. and J. D. Lewis-Williams. 1993. "Myths, Museums, and Southern African Rock Art," *South African Historical Journal* 29: pp. 44–60.

Dozier, Edward. 1970. *The Pueblo Indians of North America.* New York: Holt, Rinehart and Winston.

Draper, Patricia. 1975. "!Kung Women: Contrasts in Sexual Egalitarianism in Foraging and Sedentary Contexts" in Rayna Reiter, ed., *Toward an Anthropology of Women.* New York: Monthly Review Press.

Driver, Harold. 1964. *Indians of North America.* Chicago: University of Chicago Press.

Dubois, Cora. 1944. *The People of Alor.* Minneapolis: University of Minnesota Press.

Dubos, René. 1968. *So Human an Animal.* New York: Scribner.

Dumond, Don E. 1977. "Science in Archaeology: The Saints Go Marching In" *American Antiquity,* 42(3):330–349.

Duncan, Alexander S., John Kappelman, and Liza J. Shapiro. 1994. "Metatasophalangeal Joint Function and Positional Behavior in *Australopithecus afarensis,*" *American Journal of Physical Anthropology,* 93:67–81.

Dundes, Alan. 1980. *Interpreting Folk Lore.* Bloomington: Indiana University Press.

Durkheim, Emile. 1965. *The Elementary Forms of the Religious Life.* New York: Free Press.

Durkheim, Emile. 1964. *The Division of Labor in Society.* New York: Free Press.

duToit, Brian M. 1991. *Human Sexuality: Cross Cultural Readings.* New York: McGraw-Hill.

Eastman, Carol M. 1990. *Aspects of Language and Culture,* 2d ed. Novato, Ca.: Chandler and Sharp.

Edey, Maitland A., and Donald Johanson. 1989. *Blueprints: Solving the Mystery of Evolution.* Boston: Little, Brown.

Edey, Maitland, and the Editors of Time-Life. 1972. *The Missing Link.* New York: Time-Life.

Edmonson, Munro S. 1971. *Lore: An Introduction to the Science of Folklore.* New York: Holt, Rinehart and Winston.

Edwards, Stephen W. 1978. "Nonutilitarian Activities on the Lower Paleolithic: A Look at the Two Kinds of Evidence" *Current Anthropology,* 19(l):135–137.

Eggan, Fred. 1954. "Social Anthropology and the Method of Controlled Comparison" *American Anthropologist,* 56:743–763.

Ehrlich, Paul R., and Anne H. Ehrlich. 1970. *Population, Resources, Environment.* San Francisco: Freeman.

Eiseley, Loren. 1958. *Darwin's Century: Evolution and the Men Who Discovered It.* New York: Doubleday.

Eisenstadt, S. N. 1956. *From Generation to Generation: Age Groups and Social Structure.* New York: Free Press.

Elgin, Suzette Haden. 1994. "I Am Not Scowling Fiercely As I Write This," *Anthropology Newsletter,* 35, No. 9:44.

Elkin, A. P. 1964. *The Australian Aborigines.* Garden City, N.Y.: Doubleday, Anchor Books.

Ellison, Peter T. 1990. "Human Ovarian Function and Reproductive Ecology: New Hypotheses" *American Anthropologist,* 92:933–952.

Ember, Carol R., and Melvin Ember. 1985. *Cultural Anthropology.* 4th ed. Englewood Cliffs, NJ: Prentice-Hall.

Ember, Melvin, and Carol R. Ember. 1971. "The Conditions Favoring Matrilocal vs. Patrilocal Residence" *American Anthropologist,* 73:571–594.

Epstein, A. 1968. "Sanctions" *International Encyclopedia of the Social Sciences,* Vol. 14.

Erasmus, C. J., and W. Smith. 1967. "Cultural Anthropology in the United States since 1900" *Southwestern Journal of Anthropology,* 23:11–40.

Erasmus, C. J. 1950. "Patolli, Pachisi, and the Limitation of Possibilities" *Southwestern Journal of Anthropology,* 6:369–381.

Ervin-Tripp, Susan. 1973. *Language Acquisition and Communicative Choice.* Stanford, Cal.: Stanford University Press.

Esber, George S. Jr. 1987. "Designing Apache Houses with Apaches", in *Anthropological Praxis: Translating Knowledge into Action,* edited by Robert M. Wulff and Shirley J. Fiske. Boulder Co.: Westview Press.

Evans, William. 1968. *Communication in the Animal World.* New York: Crowell.

Evans-Pritchard, E. E. 1937. *Witchcraft, Oracles, and Magic among the Azande.* London: Oxford University Press.

Evans-Pritchard, E. E. 1968. *The Nuer: A Description of the Modes of Livelihood and Political Institutions of a Nilotic People.* London: Oxford University Press.

Fagan, Brian M. 1992. *People of the Earth,* 7th ed. New York: HarperCollins.

Falk, Dean. 1975. "Comparative Anatomy of the Larynx in Man and the Chimpanzee: Implications for Language in Neanderthal" *American Journal of Physical Anthropology,* 43(1):123–132.

Falk, Dean. 1989. "Ape-like Endocast of 'Ape Man' Taung," *American Journal of Physical Anthropology,* 80:335–339.

Falk, Dean. 1993. "A Good Brain Is Hard to Cool," *Natural History,* 102(8):65.

Falk, Dean. 1993. "Hominid Paleoneurology," in *The Human Evolution Source Book.* Russell L. Ciochon and John G. Fleagle, eds. Englewood Cliffs, N.J.: Prentice Hall.

Farsoun, Samih K. 1970. "Family Structures and Society in Modern Lebanon" in Louise E. Sweet, ed., *Peoples and Cultures of the Middle East,* Vol. 2. Garden City, N.Y.: Natural History Press.

Fedigan, Linda Marie. 1986. "The Changing Role of Women in Models of Human Evolution" *Annual Review of Anthropology,* 15:25–56.

Fei Hsiaotung. 1939. *Peasant Life in China.* London: Kegan, Paul, Trench and Truber.

Firth, Raymond. 1952. *Elements of Social Organization.* London: Watts.

Firth, Raymond. 1957. *Man and Culture: An Evaluation of Bronislaw Malinowski.* London: Routledge.

Firth, Raymond. 1963. *We the Tikopia.* Boston: Beacon Press.

Firth, Raymond, ed. 1967. *Themes in Economic Anthropology.* London: Tavistock.

Fishman, Joshua. 1994. "Putting a New Spin on the Human Birth," *Science,* 264:1082–1083.

Flannery, Kent V. 1973. "The Origins of Agriculture" Bernard J. Siegel, Alan R. Beals, and Stephen A. Tyler, eds., *Annual Review of Anthropology,* Palo Alto, Calif.: Annual Reviews, Inc. 1973, pp. 271–310, vol. 2.

Flannery, Kent V., and Joyce Marcus. 1976. "Formative Oaxaca and the Zapotec Cosmos" *American Scientist,* 64.

Flannery, Kent V., ed. 1976. *The Mesoamerican Village.* New York: Seminar Press.

Fleagle, John G. 1992. "Early Anthropoid Evolution." Paper presented at the 91st Annual Meeting of the American Anthropological Association, Dec.

Forbes, Jack D. 1964. *The Indian in America's Past.* Englewood Cliffs, NJ: Prentice-Hall.

Forde, C. Daryll. 1955. "The Nupe" in Daryll Forde, ed., *Peoples of the Niger-Benue Confluence.* London: International African Institute (Ethnographic Survey of Africa. Western Africa, part 10).

Forde, C. Daryll. 1968. "Double Descent among the Yako" in Paul Bohannan and J. Middleton, eds., *Marriage, Family and Residence.* Garden City, N.Y.: Natural History Press, pp. 179–192.

Forde, C. Daryll. 1963. *Habitat, Economy and Society.* New York: Dutton.

Fortes, Meyer. 1969. *Kinship and the Social Order: The Legacy of Lewis Henry Morgan.* Chicago: Aldine.

Fortes, Meyer, and E. E. Evans-Prichard, eds. 1962; orig. 1940. *African Political Systems.* London: Oxford University Press.

Fortes, Meyer. 1950. "Kinship and Marriage among the Ashanti" in A. R. Radcliffe-Brown and C. Daryll Forde, eds., *African Systems of Kinship and Marriage.* London: Oxford University Press.

Fossey, Dian. 1983. *Gorillas in the Mist.* Burlington, Mass.: Houghton Mifflin.

Foster, G. M. 1955. "Peasant Society and the Image of the Limited Good" *American Anthropologist,* 67:293–315.

Fox, Robin. 1968. *Kinship and Marriage in an Anthropological Perspective.* Baltimore, Md.: Penguin.

Fox, Robin. 1968. *Encounter with Anthropology.* New York: Dell.

Frake, Charles O. 1992. "Lessons of the Mayan Sky," in Anthony F. Aveni, ed., *The Sky in Mayan Literature.* New York: Oxford University Press, pp. 274–291.

Frankfort, Henri. 1968. *The Birth of Civilization in the Near East.* New York: Barnes & Noble.

Fraser, Douglas. 1962. *Primitive Art.* New York: Doubleday.

Fraser, Douglas, ed. 1966. *The Many Faces of Primitive Art: A Critical Anthology.* Englewood Cliffs, N.J.: Prentice-Hall.

Frayer, David W. 1981. "Body Size, Weapon Use, and Natural Selection in the European Upper Paleolithic and Mesolithic" *American Anthropologist,* 83:57–73.

Frazer, Sir James George. 1961 reissue. *The New Golden Bough.* New York: Doubleday, Anchor Books.

Frazer, James G. 1931. "Magic and Religion" in *The Making of Man: An Outline of Anthropology,* ed. V. F. Calverton. New York: Modern Library.

Freeman, J. D. 1960. "The Iban of Western Borneo" in G. P. Murdock, ed., *Social Structure in Southeast Asia.* Chicago: Quadrangle Books.

Freeman, Leslie G. 1992. "Ambrona and Torralba: New Evidence and Interpretation" Paper presented at the 91st Annual Meeting, American Anthropological Association, San Francisco.

Fried, Morton. 1972. *The Study of Anthropology.* New York: Crowell.

Fried, Morton. 1967. *The Evolution of Political Society: An Essay in Political Anthropology.* New York: Random House.

Fried, Morton, Marvin Harris, and Robert Murphy. 1968. *War: The Anthropology of Armed Conflict and Aggression.* Garden City, N.Y.: Natural History Press.

Fried, Morton. 1960. "On the Evolution of Social Stratification and the State" in S. Diamond, ed., in *Culture in History: Essays in Honor of Paul Radin.* New York: Columbia University Press.

Friedl, Ernestine. 1975. *Women and Men: An Anthropologist's View.* New York: Holt, Rinehart and Winston.

Fritz, Gayle J. 1994. "Are the First American Farmers Getting Younger?" *Current Anthropology,* 35:305–309.

Frye, Marilyn. 1983. "Sexism" in *The Politics of Reality.* New York: The Crossing Press.

Gamble, Clive. 1986. *The Paleolithic Settlement of Europe.* Cambridge: Cambridge University Press.

Gamst, Frederick C., and Edward Norbeck. 1976. *Ideas of Culture: Sources and Uses.* New York: Holt, Rinehart and Winston.

Garn, Stanley M. 1970. *Human Races,* 3d ed. Springfield, Ill.: Charles C Thomas.

Geertz, Clifford. 1963. *Agricultural Involution: The Process of Ecological Change in Indonesia.* Berkeley: University of California Press.

Geertz, Clifford. 1968. "Religion: Anthropological Study" *International Encyclopedia of the Social Sciences,* Vol. 13. New York: Macmillan.

Geertz, Clifford. 1984. "Distinguished Lecture: Anti Anti-Relativism" *American Anthropologist,* 86:263–278.

Geertz, Clifford. 1965. "The Impact of the Concept of Culture on the Concept of Man" in John R. Platt, ed., *New Views of Man.* Chicago: University of Chicago Press.

Gelb, Ignace J. 1952. *A Study of Writing.* London: Routledge.

Gell, Alfred. 1988. "Technology and Magic," *Anthropology Today,* 4, No. 2:6–9.

Gellner, Ernest. 1969. *Saints of the Atlas.* Chicago: University of Chicago Press (The Nature of Human Society Series).

Gennep, Arnold Van. 1960. *The Rites of Passage.* Chicago: University of Chicago Press.

Gibbons, Ann. 1992. "Mitochondrial Eve: Wounded, but Not Yet Dead," *Science,* 257:873–875.

Gibbs, James L., Jr. 1965. "The Kpelle of Liberia" in James L. Gibbs, ed., *Peoples of Africa.* New York: Holt, Rinehart and Winston.

Gleason, H. A., Jr. 1966. *An Introduction to Descriptive Linguistics,* rev. ed. New York: Holt, Rinehart and Winston.

Glob, P. 1969. *The Bog People.* London: Faber & Faber.

Gluckman, Max. 1955. *The Judicial Process among the Barotse of Northern Rhodesia.* New York: Free Press.

Goddard, Victoria. 1993. "Child Labor in Naples," in William A. Haviland and Robert J. Gordon, eds., *Talking About People.* Mountain View Ca.: Mayfield: pp. 105–109.

Godlier, Maurice. 1971. "Salt Currency and the Circulation of Commodities among the Baruya of New Guinea" in George Dalton, ed., *Studies in Economic Anthropology.* Washington, D.C.: American Anthropological Association (Anthropological Studies No. 7).

Golden, M., B. Birns, W. Bridger, and A. Moss. 1971. "Social-Class Differentiation in Cognitive Development among Black Preschool Children" *Child Development,* 42:37–45.

Goodall, Jane. 1986. *The Chimpanzees of Gombe: Patterns of Behavior.* Cambridge, Ma.: Belknap Press.

Goodall, Jane. 1990. *Through a Window: My thirty years with the chimpanzees of Gombe.* Boston: Houghton Mifflin.

Goodall-Van Lawick, Jane. 1972. *In the Shadow of Man.* New York: Dell.

Goode, William 1963. *World Revolution and Family Patterns.* New York: Free Press.

Goodenough, Ward. 1956. "Residence Rules" *Southwestern Journal of Anthropology,* 12:22–37.

Goodenough, Ward. 1961. "Comment on Cultural Evolution" *Daedalus,* 90:521–528.

Goodenough, Ward, ed. 1964. *Explorations in Cultural Anthropology: Essays in Honor of George Murdock.* New York: McGraw-Hill.

Goodenough, Ward. 1965. "Rethinking Status" and "Role: Toward a General Model of the Cultural Organization of Social Relationships" in Michael Benton, ed., *The Relevance of Models for Social Anthropology, ASA Monographs 1.* New York: Praeger.

Goodenough, Ward. 1970. *Description and Comparison in Cultural Anthropology.* Chicago: Aldine (Lewis H. Morgan Lecture Series).

Goodenough, Ward H. 1990. "Evolution of the Human Capacity for Beliefs" *American Anthropologist,* 92:601.

Goodman, Morris, Wendy J. Bartez, Kenji Hayasaka, Michael J. Stanhope, Jerry Slightom, and John Czelusniak. 1994. "Molecular Evidence on Primate Phylogeny From DNA Sequences," *American Journal of Physical Anthropology,* 94:3–24.

Goodman, Mary Ellen. 1967. *The Individual and Culture.* Homewood, Ill.: Dorsey Press.

Goody, Jack, ed. 1972. *Developmental Cycle in Domestic Groups.* New York: Cambridge University Press (Papers in Social Anthropology, No. 1).

Goody, Jack. 1976. *Production and Reproduction: A Comparative Study of the Domestic Domain.* Cambridge: Cambridge University Press.

Goody, Jack. 1983. *The Development of the Family and Marriage in Europe.* Cambridge: Cambridge University Press.

Goody, John. 1969. *Comparative Studies in Kinship.* Stanford, Cal.: Stanford University Press.

Gordon, Robert. 1981. Interview for Coast Telecourses, Inc., Los Angeles.

Gordon, Robert. 1990. "The Field Researcher as a Deviant: A Namibian Case Study" in *Truth Be in the Field: Social Science Research in Southern Africa,* edited by Pierre Hugo. Pretoria: University of South Africa.

Gordon, Robert J. 1992. *The Bushman Myth: The Making of a Namibian Underclass.* Boulder, Colo.: Westview.

Gordon, Robert J., and Mervyn J. Meggitt. 1985. *Law and Order in the New Guinea Highlands.* Hanover, N.H.: University Press of New England.

Gorer, Geoffrey. 1943. "Themes in Japanese Culture" *Transactions of the New York Academy of Sciences,* Series II, 5.

Gorman, E. Michael. 1989. "The AIDS Epidemic in San Francisco: Epidemiological and Anthropological Perspectives," in *Applying Anthropology, An Introductory Reader.* Aaron Podolefsky and Peter J. Brown, eds. Mountain View, Co., Mayfield.

Gornick, Vivian, and Barbara K. Moran, eds. 1971. *Woman in Sexist Society.* New York: Basic Books.

Gould, Stephen J. 1981. *The Mismeasure of Man.* New York: W. W. Norton.

Gould, Stephen Jay. 1983. *Hen's Teeth and Horses' Toes.* New York: Norton.

Gould, Stephen J. 1985. *The Flamingo's Smile: Reflections in Natural History.* New York: Norton.

Gould, Stephen J. 1986. "Of Kiwi Eggs and the Liberty Bell" *Natural History*, 95:20–29.

Gould, Stephen Jay. 1989. *Wonderful Life*. New York: Norton.

Gould, Stephen Jay. 1991. *Bully for Brontosaurus*. New York: W. W. Norton.

Graburn, Nelson H. 1969. *Eskimos Without Igloos: Social and Economic Development in Sugluk*. Boston: Little, Brown.

Graburn, Nelson H. 1971. *Readings in Kinship and Social Structure*. New York: Harper & Row.

Graham, Susan Brandt. 1979. "Biology and Human Social Behavior: A Response to van den Berghe and Barash" *American Anthropologist*, 81(2):357–360.

Graves, Paul. 1991. "New Models and Metaphors for the Neanderthal Debate," *Current Anthropology*, 32(5):513–543.

Green, Edward C. 1987. "The Planning of Health Education Strategies in Swaziland" and "The Integration of Modern and Traditional Health Sectors in Swaziland" in *Anthropological praxis: Translating Knowledge into Action*, Robert M. Wulff and Shirley J. Fiske, eds. Boulder, Co.:Westview.

Greenberg, Joseph H. 1968. *Anthropological Linguistics: An Introduction*. New York: Random House.

Greene, John C. 1959. *The Death of Adam*. Ames: Iowa State University Press.

Greenfield, Leonard Owen. 1980. "A Late Divergence Hypothesis" *American Journal of Physical Anthropology*, 52:351–366.

Greenfield, Leonard Owen. 1979. "On the Adaptive Pattern of Ramapithecus" *American Journal of Physical Anthropology*, 50:527–547.

Griffin, Bion. 1994. "CHAGS 7," *Anthropology Newsletter* 35, No. 1: p. 12–14.

Grine, F. E. 1993. "Australopithecine Taxonomy and Phylogeny: Historical Background and Recent Interpretation," in *The Human Evolution Source Book*, Russell L. Ciochon and John G. Fleagle, eds. Englewood Cliffs, N.J.: Prentice Hall.

Gulliver, P. 1968. "Age Differentiation" *International Encyclopedia of the Social Sciences*, 1:157–162.

Gutin, Jo Ann. 1995. "Do Kenya Tools Root Birth of Modern Thought in Africa?" *Science*, 270:1118–1119.

Hafkin, Nancy, and Edna Bay, eds. 1976. *Women in Africa*. Stanford Ca.: Stanford University Press.

Hall, Edward T., and Mildred Reed Hall. 1986. "The Sounds of Silence" in *Anthropology 86/87*, Elvio Angeloni, ed. Guilford, Ct.: Dushkin.

Hall, K. R. L., and Irven DeVore. 1965. "Baboon Social Behavior" in Irven DeVore, ed., *Primate Behavior*. New York: Holt, Rinehart and Winston.

Hallowell, A. Irving. 1955. *Culture and Experience*. Philadelphia: University of Pennsylvania Press.

Halverson, John. 1989. "Review of *Altimira Revisited and Other Essays on Early Art*" *American Antiquity*, 54:883.

Hamblin, Dora Jane, and the Editors of Time-Life. 1973. *The First Cities*. New York: Time-Life.

Hamburg, David A., and Elizabeth R. McGown, eds. 1979. *The Great Apes*. Menlo Park, Calif.: Cummings.

Hammond, Dorothy. 1972. *Associations*. Reading, Mass.: Addison-Wesley (Modular Publications, 14).

Harlow, Harry F. 1962. "Social Deprivation in Monkeys" *Scientific American*, 206:1–10.

Harpending, John H., and Henry C. Harpending. 1995. "Ancient Differences in Population Can Mimic a Recent African Origin of Modern Humans," *Current Anthropology*, 36:667–674.

Harris, Marvin. 1968. *The Rise of Anthropological Theory: A History of Theories of Culture*. New York: Crowell.

Harris, Marvin. 1965. "The Cultural Ecology of India's Sacred Cattle" *Current Anthropology*, 7:51–66.

Harrison, G. A., et al. 1964. *Human Biology: An Introduction to Human Evolution, Variation and Growth*. New York: Oxford.

Harrison, Gail G. 1975. "Primary Adult Lactase Deficiency: A Problem in Anthropological Genetics" *American Anthropologist*, 77:812–835.

Hart, Charles W., Arnold R. Pilling, and Jane Goodale. 1988. *Tiwi of North Australia*. 3d ed. New York: Holt, Rinehart and Winston.

Hatcher, Evelyn Payne. 1985. *Art As Culture: An Introduction to the Anthropology of Art*. New York: University Press of America.

Haviland, W. 1970. "Tikal, Guatemala and Mesoamerican Urbanism" *World Archaeology*, 2:186–198.

Haviland, W. A. 1972. "A New Look at Classic Maya Social Organization at Tikal" *Ceramica de Cultura Maya*, 8:1–16.

Haviland, W. A. 1974. "Farming, Seafaring and Bilocal Residence on the Coast of Maine" *Man in the Northeast*, 6:31–44.

Haviland, W. A. 1975. "The Ancient Maya and the Evolution of Urban Society" *University of Northern Colorado Museum of Anthropology, Miscellaneous Series*, No. 37.

Haviland, W. A. 1983. *Human Evolution and Prehistory*, 2d ed. New York: Holt, Rinehart and Winston.

Haviland, William A. 1991. "Star Wars at Tikal, or Did Caracol Do What the Glyphs Say They Did?" Paper presented at the 90th Annual Meeting of the American Anthropological Association.

Haviland, William A. 1993. "The Rise of Sexist Society: Death and Gender at Tikal, Guatemala," paper presented at the 92nd Annual Meeting of the American Anthropological Association, Washington, D.C.

Haviland, William A., and Hattula Moholy-Nagy. 1992. "Distinguishing the High and Mighty from the Hoi Polloi at Tikal, Guatemala" in *Mesoamerican Elites: An Archaeological Assessment*, ed. Arlen F. and Diane Z. Chase. Norman, Ok.: University of Oklahoma Press.

Haviland, W., and M. W. Power. 1994. *The Original Vermonters: Native Inhabitants, Past and Present*. 2d ed. Hanover, N.H.: University Press of New England.

Hawkins, Gerald S. 1965. *Stonehenge Decoded*. New York: Doubleday.

Hays, H. R. 1965. *From Ape to Angel: An Informal History of Social Anthropology*. New York: Knopf.

Heichel, G. 1976. "Agricultural Production and Energy Resources" *American Scientist*, Vol. 64.

Heilbroner, Robert L. 1972. *The Making of Economic Society*, 4th ed. Englewood Cliffs, N.J.: Prentice-Hall.

Heilbroner, Robert L., and Lester C. Thurow. 1981. *The Economic Problem*, 6th ed. Englewood Cliffs, N.J.: Prentice-Hall.

Helm, June. 1962. "The Ecological Approach in Anthropology" *American Journal of Sociology*, 67:630–649.

Henry, Jules. 1965. *Culture against Man*. New York: Vintage Books.

Henry, Jules. 1966. "The Metaphysic of Youth, Beauty, and Romantic Love" in *The Challenge to Women*, ed. Seymour Farber and Roger Wilson. New York: Basic Books.

Henry, Jules. 1974. "A Theory for an Anthropological Analysis of American Culture," in *Anthropology and American Life*, ed. Joseph G. Jorgensen and Marcello Truzzi. Englewood Cliffs, NJ: Prentice-Hall: p. 14.

Herskovits, Melville J. 1952. *Economic Anthropology: A Study in Comparative Economics*, 2d ed. New York: Knopf.

Herskovits, Melville J. 1964. *Cultural Dynamics*. New York: Knopf.

Hewes, Gordon W. 1973. "Primate Communication and the Gestural Origin of Language" *Current Anthropology*, 14:5–24.

Hickerson, Nancy Parrot. 1980. *Linguistic Anthropology*. New York: Holt, Rinehart and Winston.

Hjelmsiev, Louis. 1970. *Language: An Introduction*. Francis J. Whitfield, trans. Madison: University of Wisconsin Press.

Hodgen, Margaret. 1964. *Early Anthropology in the Sixteenth and Seventeenth Centuries*. Philadelphia: University of Pennsylvania Press.

Hoebel, E. A. 1960. *The Cheyennes: Indians of the Great Plains*. New York: Holt, Rinehart and Winston.

Hoebel, E. A. 1972. *Anthropology: The Study of Man*, 4th ed. New York: McGraw-Hill.

Hoebel, E. A. 1954. *The Law of Primitive Man: A Study in Comparative Legal Dynamics*. Cambridge, Mass.: Harvard University Press; Atheneum. 1968.

Hogbin, Ian. 1964. *A Guadalcanal Society*. New York: Holt, Rinehart and Winston.

Holden, Constance. 1983. "Simon and Kahn versus *Global 2000*," *Science*, 221:342.

Hole, Frank. 1966. "Investigating the Origins of Mesopotamian Civilization" *Science*, 153:605–611.

Holloway, Ralph L. 1980. "The O. H. 7 (Olduvai Gorge, Tanzania) Hominid Partial Brain Endocast Revisited" *American Journal of Physical Anthropology*, 53: 267–274.

Holloway, Ralph L. 1981. "The Indonesian *Homo erectus* Brain Endocast Revisited" *American Journal of Physical Anthropology*, 55:503–521.

Holloway, Ralph L. 1981. "Volumetric and Asymmetry Determinations on Recent Hominid Endocasts: Spy I and II, Djebel Jhroud 1, and the Salb *Homo erectus* specimens, with some Notes on Neanderthal Brain Size" *American Journal of Physical Anthropology*, 55:385–393.

Hostetler, John, and Gertrude Huntington. 1971. *Children in Amish Society*. New York: Holt, Rinehart and Winston.

Howell, F. Clark. 1970. *Early Man*. New York: Time-Life.

Hsiaotung, Fei. 1939. *Peasant Life in China*. London: Kegan, Paul, Trench and Truber.

Hsu, Francis L. 1961. *Psychological Anthropology: Approaches to Culture and Personality*. Homewood, Ill.: Dorsey Press.

Hsu, Francis L. K. 1977. "Role, Affect, and Anthropology" *American Anthropologist*, 79:805–808.

Hsu, Francis L. K. 1979. "The Cultural Problems of the Cultural Anthropologist" *American Anthropologist*, 81:517–532.

Hubert, Henri, and Marcel Mauss. 1964. *Sacrifice*. Chicago: University of Chicago Press.

Hunt, Robert C., ed. 1967. *Personalities and Cultures: Readings in Psychological Anthropology*. Garden City, N.Y.: Natural History Press.

Hymes, Dell. 1964. *Language in Culture and Society: A Reader in Linguistics and Anthropology*. New York: Harper & Row.

Hymes, Dell, ed. 1972. *Reinventing Anthropology*. New York: Pantheon.

Inkeles, Alex. 1966. "The Modernization of Man" in Myron Weiner, ed., *Modernization: The Dynamics of Growth*. New York: Basic Books.

Inkeles, Alex, Eugenia Hanfmann, and Helen Beier. 1961. "Modal Personality and Adjustment to the Soviet Socio-political System" in Bert Kaplan, ed., *Studying Personality Cross-culturally*. New York: Harper & Row.

Inkeles, Alex, and D. J. Levinson. 1954. "National Character: The Study of Modal Personality and Socio-cultural Systems" in G. Lindzey, ed., *Handbook of Social Psychology*. Reading, Mass.: Addison-Wesley.

Ireland, Emilienne. 1991. "Neither Warriors nor Victims, The Wauja Peacefully Organize to Defend Their Land." *Cultural Survival Quarterly*, 15, No. 1 (1991), pp. 54–59.

Jacobs, Sue Ellen. 1994. "Native American Two-spirits" *Anthropology Newsletter*, 35, No. 8: p.7.

Jacoby, Russell, and Naomi Glauberman, eds. 1995. *The Bell Curve*. New York: Random House.

Jennings, Jesse D. 1974. *Prehistory of North America*, 2d ed., New York: McGraw-Hill.

Jennings, Francis. 1976. *The Invasion of America*. New York: Norton.

Johanson, Donald C., and Maitland Edey. 1981. *Lucy, The Beginnings of Humankind*. New York: Simon & Schuster.

Johanson, Donald, and James Shreeve 1989. *Lucy's Child: The Discovery of a Human Ancestor*. New York: Avon.

Johanson, D. C., and T. D. White. 1979. "A Systematic Assessment of Early African Hominids" *Science*, 203:321–330.

John, V. 1971. "Whose Is the Failure?" in C. L. Brace, G. R. Gamble, and J. T. Bond, eds., *Race and Intelligence*. Washington, D.C.: American Anthropological Association (Anthropological Studies No. 8).

Johnson, Allen W., and Timothy Earle. 1987. *The Evolution of Human Societies, from Foraging Group to Agrarian State*. Stanford University Press.

Johnson, Dirk. 1993. "Polygamists Emerge From Secrecy, Seeking Not Just Peace But Respect," in William A. Haviland and Robert J. Gordon, eds., *Talking About People*. Mountain View, Ca.: Mayfield: pp. 129–131.

Jolly, Alison. 1985. "The Evolution of Primate Behavior," *American Scientist*, 73(3):230–239.

Jolly, Allison. 1985. *The Evolution of Primate Behavior*. 2d ed. New York: Macmillan.

Jolly, Allison. 1991. "Thinking Like a Vervet" *Science*, 251(1991):574.

Jolly, C. J. 1970. "The Seed Eaters: A New Model of Hominid Differentiation Based on a Baboon Analogy" *Man*, 5:5–26.

Jolly, Clifford J., and Fred Plog. 1986. *Physical Anthropology and Archaeology*, 4th ed. New York: Knopf.

Jopling, Carol F. 1971. *Art and Aesthetics in Primitive Societies: A Critical Anthology*. New York: Dutton.

Jorgensen, Joseph. 1972. *The Sun Dance Religion*. Chicago: University of Chicago Press.

Joukowsky, Martha A. 1980. *A Complete Field Manual of Archeology: Tools and Techniques of Field Work for Archaeologists*. Englewood Cliffs, N.J.: Prentice-Hall.

Joyce, Christopher. 1991. *Witnesses from the Grave: The Stories Bones Tell*. Boston: Little, Brown.

Kahn, Herman, and Anthony J. Wiener. 1967. *The Year 2000*. New York: Macmillan.

Kaiser, Jocelyn. 1994. "A New Theory of Insect Wing Origins Takes Off," *Science*, 266:363.

Kalwet, Holger. 1988. *Dreamtime and Inner Space: The World of the Shaman.* New York: Random House. 1988.

Kaplan, David. 1968. "The Superorganic: Science or Metaphysics" in Robert Manners and David Kaplan, eds., *Theory in Anthropology: A Sourcebook.* Chicago: Aldine.

Kaplan, David. 1972. *Culture Theory.* Englewood Cliffs, N.J.: Prentice-Hall (Foundations of Modern Anthropology).

Kardiner, Abram. 1939. *The Individual and His Society. The Psycho-dynamics of Primitive Social Organization.* New York: Columbia University Press.

Kardiner, Abram, and Edward Preble. 1961. *They Studied Men.* New York: Mentor.

Kay, Richard F., J. G. M. Theweissen, and Anne D. Yoder. 1992. "Cranial Anatomy of *Ignacius graybullianus* and the Affinities of the Plesiadapiformes," *American Journal of Physical Anthropology,* 89(4): 477–498.

Kay, Richard F. 1981. "The Nut-Crackers—A New Theory of the Adaptations of the Ramapithecinae" *American Journal of Physical Anthropology,* 55:141–151.

Kay, R. F., J. F. Fleagle, and E. L. Simons. 1981. "A Revision of the Oligocene Apes of the Fayum Province, Egypt" *American Journal of Physical Anthropology,* 55:293–322.

Keesing, Roger M. 1975. *Kin Groups and Social Structure.* New York: Holt, Rinehart and Winston.

Keesing, Roger M. 1976. *Cultural Anthropology: A Contemporary Perspective.* New York: Holt, Rinehart and Winston.

Kenyon, Kathleen. 1957. *Digging Up Jericho.* London: Ben.

Kerri, James N. 1976. "Studying Voluntary Associations as Adaptive Mechanisms: A Review of Anthropological Perspectives" *Current Anthropology,* 17(1).

Kessler, Evelyn. 1975. *Women.* New York: Holt, Rinehart and Winston.

Kleinman, Arthur. 1982. "The Failure of Western Medicine" in David Hunter and Phillip Whitten, *Anthropology: Contemporary Perspectives.* Boston: Little, Brown.

Kluckhohn, Clyde. 1944. "Navajo Witchcraft." Cambridge, Mass.: Harvard University Press. (Papers of the Peabody Museum of American Archaeology and Ethnology 22, 2).

Kluckhohn, Clyde. 1970. *Mirror for Man.* Greenwich, Conn.: Fawcett.

Kluckhohn, Clyde. 1994. "Navajo Witchcraft," *Papers of the Peabody Museum of American Archaeology and Ethnology,* 22, No. 2.

Knauft, Bruce M. 1991. "Violence and Sociality in Human Evolution" *Current Anthropology,* 32 (1991):391–428.

Kohler, Gernot. 1978. "Global Apartheid" in *World Order Models Project, Paper 7.* New York: Institute for World Order.

Koufos, G. 1993. "Mandible of Ouranopithecus macedoniensis (Hominidae: Primates) From a New Late Miocene Locality in Macedonia (Greece)," *American Journal of Physical Anthropology,* 91, 225–234.

Krader, Lawrence. 1968. *Formation of the State.* Englewood Cliffs, N.J.: Prentice-Hall (Foundation of Modern Anthropology).

Kroeber, A. L. 1939. "Cultural and Natural Areas of Native North America" *American Archaeology and Ethnology,* Vol. 38. Berkeley, Cal.: University of California Press.

Kroeber, A. 1958. "Totem and Taboo: An Ethnologic Psycho-analysis" in William Lessa and Evon Z. Vogt, eds., *Reader in Comparative Religion: An Anthropological Approach.* New York: Harper & Row.

Kroeber, A. L. 1963. *Anthropology: Cultural Processes and Patterns.* New York: Harcourt.

Kroeber, A. L., and Clyde Kluckhohn. 1952. *Culture: A Critical Review of Concepts and Definitions.* Cambridge, Mass.: Harvard University Press (Papers of the Peabody Museum of American Archaeology and Ethnology, 47).

Kuhn, Thomas. 1968. *The Structure of Scientific Revolutions.* Chicago: University of Chicago Press (International Encyclopedia of Unified Science, 2(27)).

Kummer, Hans. 1971. *Primate Societies: Group Techniques of Ecological Adaptation.* Chicago: Aldine.

Kuper, Hilda. 1965. "The Swazi of Swaziland" in James L. Gibbs, ed., *Peoples of Africa.* New York: Holt, Rinehart and Winston.

Kurath, Gertrude Probosch. 1960. "Panorama of Dance Ethnology" *Current Anthropology,* 1:233–254.

Kushner, Gilbert. 1969. *Anthropology of Complex Societies.* Stanford, Cal.: Stanford University Press.

La Barre, Weston. 1945. "Some Observations of Character Structure in the Orient: The Japanese," *Psychiatry,* Vol. 8.

Lancaster, Jane B. 1975. *Primate Behavior and the Emergence of Human Culture.* New York: Holt, Rinehart and Winston.

Landes, Ruth. 1982. "Comment" *Current Anthropology,* 23:401.

Lanning, Edward P. 1967. *Peru before the Incas.* Englewood Cliffs, N.J.: Prentice-Hall.

Lanternari, Vittorio. 1963. *The Religions of the Oppressed.* New York: Mentor.

Lasker, Gabriel W., and Robert Tyzzer. 1982. *Physical Anthropology,* 3d ed. New York: Holt, Rinehart and Winston.

Laughlin, W. S., and R. H. Osborne, eds. 1967. *Human Variation and Origins.* San Francisco: Freeman.

Laurel Kendall. 1990. "In the Company of Witches" *Natural History,* 10/90, p. 92.

Lévi-Strauss, Claude. 1963. *Structural Anthropology.* New York: Basic Books.

Lévi-Strauss, Claude. 1963. *Totemism.* Boston: Beacon Press.

Lévi-Strauss, Claude. 1966. *The Savage Mind.* Chicago: University of Chicago Press.

Lévi-Strauss, Claude. 1969. *The Elementary Structures of Kinship.* Boston: Beacon Press.

Lévi-Strauss, Claude. 1971. "The Family" in Harry L. Shapiro, ed., *Man, Culture and Society.* London: Oxford University Press, pp. 333–357.

Leach, Edmund. 1961. *Rethinking Anthropology.* London: Athione Press.

Leach, Edmund. 1962. "The Determinants of Differential Cross-cousin Marriage" *Man,* 62:238.

Leach, Edmund. 1962. "On Certain Unconsidered Aspects of Double Descent Systems" *Man,* 214:13–34.

Leach, Edmund. 1965. *Political Systems of Highland Burma.* Boston: Beacon Press.

Leach, Edmund. 1982. *Social Anthropology.* Glasgow: Fontana Paperbacks.

Leacock, Eleanor. 1981. *Myths of Male Dominance: Collected Articles on Women Cross Culturally.* New York: Monthly Review Press.

Leacock, Eleanor. 1981. "Women's Status in Egalitarian Society: Implications for Social Evolution," in *Myths of Male Dominance: Collected Articles on Women Cross Culturally.* New York: Monthly Review Press.

Leakey, L. S. B. 1965. *Olduvai Gorge. 1951–1961, Vol. 1.* London: Cambridge University Press.

Leakey, L. S. B. 1967. "Development of Aggression as a Factor in Early Man and Prehuman Evolution" in C. Clements and D. Lundsley, eds., *Aggression and Defense*. Los Angeles: University of California Press.

Leakey, M. D. 1971. *Olduvai Gorge: Excavations in Beds I and II. 1960–1963*. London and New York: Cambridge University Press.

Leap, William L. 1987. "Tribally Controlled Culture Change: The Northern Ute Language Renewal Project" in: *Anthropological Praxis: Translating Knowledge into Action*, edited by Robert M. Wulff and Shirley J. Fiske. Boulder Co.: Westview.

Leavitt, Gregory C. 1990. "Sociobiological Explanations of Incest Avoidance: A Critical Review of Evidential Claims" *American Anthropologist*, 92:973.

LeClair, Edward, and Harold K. Schneider, eds. 1968. *Economic Anthropology: Readings in Theory and Analysis*. New York: Holt, Rinehart and Winston.

Lee, Richard B. 1993. *The Dobe Ju/'hoansi*. Fort Worth: Harcourt Brace.

Lee, Richard B., and Irven DeVore, eds. 1968. *Man the Hunter*. Chicago: Aldine.

Leeds, Anthony, and Andrew P. Vayda, eds. 1965. *Man, Culture and Animals: The Role of Animals in Human Ecological Adjustments*. Washington, D.C.: American Association for the Advancement of Science.

Lees, Robert. 1953. "The Basis of Glottochronology" *Language*, 29:113–127.

Lehmann, Arthur C., and James E. Myers, eds. 1988. *Magic, Witchcraft and Religion*. 2d ed. Palo Alto, Cal.: Mayfield.

Lehmann, Winifred P. 1973. *Historical Linguistics, An Introduction*, 2d ed. New York: Holt, Rinehart and Winston.

Leinhardt, Godfrey. 1964. *Social Anthropology*. London: Oxford University Press.

Leinhardt, Godfrey. 1971. "Religion" in Harry Shapiro, ed., *Man, Culture and Society*. 2nd ed. London: Oxford University Press.

LeMay, Marjorie. 1975. "The Language Capability of Neanderthal Man" *American Journal of Physical Anthropology*, 43(1):9–14.

Lenski, Gerhard. 1966. *Power and Privilege: A Theory of Social Stratification*. New York: McGraw-Hill.

Leonard, William R., and Michelle Hegman. 1987 "Evolution of P$_3$ Morphology in *Australopithecus afarensis*" *American Journal of Physical Anthropology*, 73:41–63.

Leroi-Gourhan, A. 1968. "The Evolution of Paleolithic Art" *Scientific American*, 218:58ff.

Lett, James. 1987. *The Human Enterprise: A Critical Introduction to Anthropological Theory*. Boulder, Co., Westview.

Levanthes, Louise E. 1987. "The Mysteries of the Bog" *National Geographic*, 171:397–420.

Levine, Robert. 1973. *Culture, Behavior and Personality*. Chicago: Aldine.

Levine, Robert Paul. 1968. *Genetics*. New York: Holt, Rinehart and Winston.

Lewin, Roger. 1983. "Is the Orangutan a Living Fossil?" *Science*, 222:1223.

Lewin, Roger. 1985. "Tooth Enamel Tells a Complex Story" *Science*, 228:707.

Lewin, Roger. 1986. "New Fossil Upsets Human Family" *Science*, 1986, 233:720–721.

Lewin, Roger. 1987. "Debate over Emergence of Human Tooth Pattern" *Science*, 235:749.

Lewin, Roger. 1987. "The Earliest Humans Were More Like Apes" *Science*, 236:106–163.

Lewin, Roger. 1987. "Four Legs Bad, Two Legs Good" *Science*, 235:969–971.

Lewin, Roger. 1988. "Molecular Clocks Turn a Quarter Century" *Science*, 235:969–971.

Lewin, Roger. 1987. "Why Is Ape Tool Use So Confusing?" *Science*, 236:776–777.

Lewin, Roger. 1993. "Paleolithic Paint Job," *Discover*, 14 (7):64–70.

Lewis, I. M. 1976. *Social Anthropology in Perspective*. Harmondsworth, Eng.: Penguin.

Lewis, I. M. 1965. "Problems in the Comparative Study of Unilineal Descent" in Michael Banton, ed., *The Relevance of Models for Social Organization* (A.S.A. Monograph No. 1). London: Tavistock.

Lewis-Williams, J. D. 1990. *Discovering Southern African Rock Art*. Cape Town and Johannesburg: David Philip.

Lewis-Williams, J. D., and T. A. Dowson. 1988. "The Signs of All Times: Entopic Phenomena in Upper Paleolithic Art." *Current Anthropology*, 29(2):201–245.

Lewis-Williams, J. David, and Thomas A. Dowson. 1993. "On Vision and Power in the Neolithic: Evidence from the Decorated Monuments," *Current Anthropology*, 34: p. 55–65.

Lewis-Williams, J. David, Thomas Dowson, and Janette Deacon. 1993. "Rock Art and Changing Perceptions of Southern Africa's past: Ezeljagdspoort Reviewed," *Antiquity*, 67: p. 273–291.

Linton, Ralph. 1936. *The Study of Man: An Introduction*. New York: Appleton.

Little, Kenneth. 1964. "The Role of Voluntary Associations in West African Urbanization" in Pierre van den Berghe, ed., *Africa: Social Problems of Change and Conflict*. San Francisco: Chandler.

Livingstone, Frank B. 1973. "The Distribution of Abnormal Hemoglobin Genes and Their Significance for Human Evolution" in C. Loring Brace and James Metress, eds., *Man in Evolutionary Perspective*. New York: Wiley.

Louckey, James, and Robert Carlsen. 1991. "Massacre in Santiago Atitlán," *Cultural Survival Quarterly*, 15, No. 3, p. 70.

Lounsbury, F. 1964. "The Structural Analysis of Kinship Semantics" in Horace G. Lunt, ed., *Proceedings of the Ninth International Congress of Linguists*. The Hague: Mouton.

Lovejoy, C. Owen. 1981. "Origin of Man" *Science*, 211(4480):341–350.

Lowenstein, Jerold M. 1992. "Genetic Surprises," *Discover*, 13(12), December 1992, p. 82–88.

Lowie, Robert H. 1948. *Social Organization*. New York: Holt, Rinehart and Winston.

Lowie, Robert H. 1956. *Crow Indians*. New York: Holt, Rinehart and Winston.

Lowie, Robert H. 1966. *Culture and Ethnology*. New York: Basic Books.

Lustig-Arecco, Vero. 1975. *Technology: Strategies for Survival*. New York: Holt, Rinehart and Winston.

MacCormack, Carol P. 1977. "Biological Events and Cultural Control" *Signs*. 3 (1977).

MacNeil, Robert. 1982. *The Right Place at the Right Time*. Boston: Little, Brown.

Magnarella, Paul J. 1974. *Tradition and Change in a Turkish Town*. New York: Wiley.

Mair, Lucy. 1969. *Witchcraft*. New York: McGraw-Hill.

Mair, Lucy. 1971. *Marriage*. Baltimore, Md.: Penguin.

Malefijt, Annemarie de Waal. 1969. *Religion and Culture: An Introduction to Anthropology of Religion*. London: Macmillan.

Malefijt, Annemarie de Waal. 1974. *Images of Man*. New York: Knopf.

Malinowski, Bronislaw. 1922. *Argonauts of the Western Pacific*. New York: Dutton.

Malinowski, Bronislaw. 1945. *The Dynamics of Culture Change*. New Haven, Conn.: Yale University Press.

Malinowski, Bronislaw. 1951. *Crime and Custom in Savage Society*. London: Routledge.

Malinowski, Bronislaw. 1954. *Magic, Science and Religion*. Garden City, N.Y.: Doubleday, Anchor Books.

Marano, Lou. 1982. "Windigo Psychosis: The Anatomy of an Emic-Etic Confusion" *Current Anthropology*, 23:385–412.

Marks, Jonathan. 1995. *Human Biodiversity: Genes, Race and History*. Hawthorne, N.Y.: Aldine de Gruyter.

Marsella, Joan. 1982. "Pulling It Together: Discussion and Comments" in *Confronting the Creationists*, ed. Stephen Pastner and William A. Haviland, Northeastern Anthropological Association, Occasional Proceedings, No. 1, pp. 79–80.

Marshack, Alexander. 1972. *The Roots of Civilization: A Study in Prehistoric Cognition; The Origins of Art, Symbol and Notation*. New York: McGraw-Hill.

Marshack, Alexander. 1976. "Some Implications of the Paleolithic Symbolic Evidence for the Origin of Language" *Current Anthropology*, 17(2):274–282.

Marshack, Alexander. 1989. "Evolution of the Human Capacity: The Symbolic Evidence" *Yearbook of Physical Anthropology*, 32:1–34.

Marshall, Lorna. 1961. "Sharing, Talking and Giving: Relief of Social Tensions among !Kung Bushmen" *Africa*, 31:231–249.

Marshall, Mac. 1990. "Two Tales from the Trukese Taproom," in Philip R. De Vita, ed., *The Humbled Anthropologist*. Belmont, Ca.: Wadsworth: pp. 12–17.

Mason, J. Alden. 1957. *The Ancient Civilizations of Peru*. Baltimore, Md.: Penguin.

Matson, Frederick R., ed. 1965. *Ceramics and Man*. New York: Viking Fund Publications in Anthropology No. 41.

Maybury-Lewis, David. 1960. "Parallel Descent and the Apinaye Anomaly" *Southwestern Journal of Anthropology*, 16:191–216.

Maybury-Lewis, David. 1984. *The Prospects for Plural Societies*. 1982 Proceedings of the American Ethnological Society.

Maybury-Lewis, David. 1993. "A New World Dilemma: The Indian Question in the Americas," *Symbols*, Fall: p.17–23.

Maybury-Lewis, David H. P. 1993. "A Special Sort of Pleading" in *Talking About People*, ed. William A. Haviland and Robert J. Gordon. Mountain View, CA.: Mayfield: pp. 16–24.

McCorriston, Joy, and Frank Hole. 1991. "The Ecology of Seasonal Stress and the Origins of Agriculture in the Near East" *American Anthropologist*, 93:46–69.

McFee, Malcolm. 1972. *Modern Blackfeet: Montanans on a Reservation*. New York: Holt, Rinehart and Winston.

McGimsey, Charles R. 1972. *Public Archaeology*. New York: Seminar Press.

McHale, John. 1969. *The Future of the Future*. New York: Braziller.

McHenry, Henry. 1975. "Fossils and the Mosaic Nature of Human Evolution" *Science*, October. 190:424–431.

McHenry, Henry M. 1992. "Body Size and Proportions in Early Hominids" *American Journal of Physical Anthropology*, 87:407–431.

Mead, Margaret. 1928. *Coming of Age in Samoa*. New York: Morrow.

Mead, Margaret. 1970. *Culture and Commitment*. Garden City, N.Y.: Natural History Press. Universe Books.

Mead, Margaret. 1963. *Sex and Temperament in Three Primitive Societies*, 3d ed. New York: Morrow.

Meadows, Donella H., Dennis L. Meadows, Jorgen Randers, and William W. Behrens III. 1974. *The Limits to Growth*. New York: Universe Books.

Melaart, James. 1967. *Catal Hüyük: A Neolithic Town in Anatolia*. London: Thames and Hudson.

Mellars, Paul. 1989. "Major Issues in the Emergence of Modern Humans" *Current Anthropology*, 30:349–385.

Merrell, David J. 1962. *Evolution and Genetics: The Modern Theory of Genetics*. New York: Holt, Rinehart and Winston.

Merriam, Alan. 1964. *The Anthropology of Music*. Chicago: Northwestern University Press.

Mesghinua, Haile Michael. 1966. "Salt Mining in Enderta" *Journal of Ethiopian Studies*, 4(2).

Michaels, Joseph W. 1973. *Dating Methods in Archaeology*. New York: Seminar Press.

Middleton, John, ed. 1970. *From Child to Adult: Studies in the Anthropology of Education*. Garden City, N.Y.: Natural History Press (American Museum Source Books in Anthropology).

Miles, H. Lynn White. 1993. "Language and the Orang-utan: The Old 'Person' of the Forest," in Paola Cavalieri and Peter Singer, eds., *The Great Ape Project*. New York: St. Martin's Press, pp. 42–57.

Millon, René. 1973. *Urbanization of Teotihuacán, Mexico, Vol. 1, Part 1: The Teotihuacán Map*. Austin: University of Texas Press.

Minugh-Purvis, Nancy. 1992. "The Inhabitants of Ice Age Europe," *Expedition*, 34(3):23–36.

Mitchell, William E. 1973. "A New Weapon Stirs Up Old Ghosts" *Natural History Magazine*, December, pp. 77–84.

Mitchell, William E. 1978. *Mishpokhe: A Study of New York City Jewish Family Clubs*. The Hague: Mouton.

Molnar, Stephen. *Human Variation: Races, Types and Ethnic Groups*. 3rd ed. Englewood Cliffs, N.J.: 1992.

Montagu, Ashley. 1963. *Human Heredity*, 2d ed. New York: Signet Books.

Montagu, Ashley. 1964. *The Concept of Race*. London: Macmillan.

Montagu, Ashley. 1964. *Man's Most Dangerous Myth: The Fallacy of Race*, 4th ed. New York: World Publishing.

Montagu, Ashley. 1969. *Man: His First Two Million Years*. New York: Columbia University Press.

Montagu, Ashley. 1975. *Race and IQ*. New York: Oxford University Press.

Morgan, Lewis H., 1877. *Ancient Society*. New York: World Publishing.

Moscati, Sabatino. 1962. *The Face of the Ancient Orient*. New York: Doubleday.

Mowat, Farley. 1959. *The Desperate People*. Boston: Little, Brown.

Mowat, Farley. 1981. *People of the Deer*. Toronto: Bantam Books.

Mullings, Leith. 1989. "Gender and the Application of Anthropological Knowledge to Public Policy in the United States," in *Gender and Anthropology*. Sandra Morgen, ed., Washington: American Anthropological Association: pp. 360–381.

Murdock, George P. 1960. "Cognatic Forms of Social Organization" in G. P. Murdock, ed., *Social Structure in Southeast Asia*. Chicago: Quadrangle Books.

Murdock, George P. 1965. *Social Structure*. New York: Free Press.

Murdock, George P. 1971. "How Culture Changes" in Harry L. Shapiro, ed., *Man, Culture and Society*. 2nd ed. New York: Oxford University Press.

Murphy, Robert. 1971. *The Dialectics of Social Life: Alarms and Excursions in Anthropological Theory*. New York: Basic Books.

Murphy, Robert, and Leonard Kasdan. 1959. "The Structure of Parallel Cousin Marriage" *American Anthropologist*, 61:17–29.

Murray, Gerald F. 1989. "The Domestication of Wood in Haiti: A Case Study in Applied Evolution," in *Applying Anthropology, An Introductory Reader*, Aaron Podolefsky and Peter J. Brown, eds. Mountain View, CA, Mayfield.

Myrdal, Gunnar. 1974. "Challenge to Affluence: The Emergence of an 'Underclass'" in Joseph G. Jorgensen and Marcello Truzzi, eds., *Anthropology and American Life*. Englewood Cliffs, N.J.: Prentice-Hall.

Nader, Laura, ed. 1965. "The Ethnography of Law" *American Anthropologist*, Part II, 67(6).

Nader, Laura, ed. 1969. *Law in Culture and Society*. Chicago: Aldine.

Nader, Laura, ed. 1980. *No Access to Law: Alternatives to the American Judicial System*. New York: Academic Press.

Naroll, Raoul. 1973. "Holocultural Theory Tests" in Raoul Naroll and Frada Naroll, eds., *Main Currents in Cultural Anthropology*. New York: Appleton.

Nash, Manning. 1966. *Primitive and Peasant Economic Systems*. San Francisco: Chandler.

Natadecha-Sponsal, Porance. 1993. "The Young, the Rich and the Famous: Individualism as an American Cultural Value," in Philip R. DeVita and James D. Armstrong, eds., *Distant Mirrors: America as a Foreign Culture*. Belmont, Ca.: Wadsworth: pp. 46–53.

Needham, Rodney, ed. 1971. *Rethinking Kinship and Marriage*. London: Tavistock.

Needham, Rodney. 1972. *Belief, Language and Experience*. Chicago: University of Chicago Press.

Neer, Robert M. 1975. "The Evolutionary Significance of Vitamin D, Skin Pigment and Ultraviolet Light" *American Journal of Physical Anthropology*, 43:409–416.

Nesbitt, L. M. 1935. *Hell-Hole of Creation*. New York: Knopf.

Netting, R. M., R. R. Wilk, and E. J. Arnould, eds. 1984. *Households: Comparative and Historical Studies of the Domestic Group*. Berkeley, Ca.: University of California Press.

Nettl, Bruno. 1956. *Music in Primitive Culture*. Cambridge, Mass.: Harvard University Press.

Newman, Philip L. 1965. *Knowing the Gururumba*. New York: Holt, Rinehart and Winston.

Nietschmann, Bernard. 1978. "The Third World War" *Cultural Survival Quarterly*, 11,(3): pp. 1–16.

Norbeck, Edward. 1974. *Religion in Human Life: Anthropological Views*. New York: Holt, Rinehart and Winston.

Norbeck, Edward, Douglas Price-Williams, and William McCord, eds. 1968. *The Study of Personality: An Interdisciplinary Appraisal*. New York: Holt, Rinehart and Winston.

Nye, E. Ivan, and Felix M. Berardo. 1975. *The Family: Its Structure and Interaction*. New York: Macmillan.

O'Barr, William M., and John M. Conley. 1993. "When a Juror Watches a Lawyer," in *Talking About People*, eds. William A. Haviland and Robert J. Gordon. Mountain View, Ca.: Mayfield: pp. 44–47.

O'Mahoney, Kevin. 1970. "The Salt Trade" *Journal of Ethiopian Studies*, 8(2).

Oakley, Kenneth P. 1964. *Man the Tool-Maker*. Chicago: University of Chicago Press.

Oboler, Regina Smith. 1980. "Is the Female Husband a Man? Woman/Woman Marriage Among the Nandi of Kenya" *Ethnology*, pp. 69–88.

Offiong, Daniel. 1985. "Witchcraft among the Ibibio of Nigeria" in *Magic, Witchcraft and Religion*, ed. Arthur C. Lehmann and James E. Myers. Palo Alto, CA: Mayfield.

Okonjo, Kamene. 1976. "The Dual-Sex Political System in Operation: Igbo Women and Community Politics in Midwestern Nigeria" in *Women in Africa*, ed. Nancy Hafkin and Edna Bay. Stanford, Ca.: Stanford University Press.

Oliver, Douglas Z. 1964. *Invitation to Anthropology*. Garden City, N.Y.: Natural History Press.

Olszewski, Deborah I. 1991. "Comment" *Current Anthropology*, 32:43.

Ortiz, Alfonso. 1969. *The Tewa World*. Chicago: University of Chicago Press.

Oswalt, Wendell H. 1970. *Understanding Our Culture*. New York: Holt, Rinehart and Winston.

Oswalt, Wendell H. 1972. *Habitat and Technology*. New York: Holt, Rinehart and Winston.

Oswalt, Wendell H. 1972. *Other Peoples Other Customs: World Ethnography and Its History*. New York: Holt, Rinehart and Winston.

Otten, Charlotte N. 1971. *Anthropology and Art: Readings in Cross-cultural Aesthetics*. Garden City, N.Y.: Natural History Press (American Museum Sourcebooks in Anthropology).

Ottenberg, Phoebe. 1965. "The Afikpo Ibo of Eastern Nigeria" in James L. Gibbs, ed., *Peoples of Africa*. New York: Holt, Rinehart and Winston.

Otterbein, Keith F. 1971. *The Evolution of War*. New Haven, Conn.: HRAF Press.

Parades, J. Anthony, and Elizabeth D. Purdum. 1990. "Bye, Bye Ted," *Anthropology Today* 6, No. 2, pp. 9–11.

Parker, Seymour, and Hilda Parker. 1979. "The Myth of Male Superiority: Rise and Demise" *American Anthropologist*, 81(2):289–309.

Partridge, William ed. 1984. *Training Manual in Development Anthropology*. Washington, D.C.: American Anthropological Association.

Pastner, Stephen, and William A. Haviland, eds. 1982. "Confronting the Creationists" *Northeastern Anthropological Association Occasional Proceedings*, I.

Patterson, Francine, and Eugene Linden. 1981. *The Education of Koko*. New York: Holt, Rinehart and Winston.

Patterson, Thomas C. 1981. *Archeology: The Evolution of Ancient Societies*. Englewood Cliffs, N.J.: Prentice-Hall.

Peacock, James L. 1986. *The Anthropological Lens: Harsh Light, Soft Focus*. New York: Cambridge University Press.

Pelliam, Alison de, and Francis D. Burton. 1976. "More on Predatory Behavior in Nonhuman Primates" *Current Anthropology*, 17(3):512–513.

Pelto, Pertti J. 1966. *The Nature of Anthropology*. Columbus, Oh.: Merrill (Social Science Perspectives).

Pelto, Pertti J. 1973. *The Snowmobile Revolution: Technology and Social Change in the Arctic*. Menlo Park, Cal.: Cummings.

Penniman, T. K. 1965. *A Hundred Years of Anthropology*. London: Duckworth.

Peters, Charles R. 1979. "Toward an Ecological Model of African Plio-Pleistocene Hominid Adaptations" *American Anthropologist*, 81(2):261–278.

Peterson, Frederick L. 1962. *Ancient Mexico, An Introduction to the Pre-Hispanic Cultures*. New York: Capricorn Books.

Pfeiffer, John E. 1977. *The Emergence of Society*. New York: McGraw-Hill.

Pfeiffer, John E. 1978. *The Emergence of Man*. New York: Harper & Row.

Pfeiffer, John E. 1985. *The Creative Explosion*. Ithaca, NY: Cornell University Press.

Piddocke, Stuart. 1965. "The Potlatch System of the Southern Kwakiutl: A New Perspective" *Southwestern Journal of Anthropology*, 21:244–264.

Piggott, Stuart. 1965. *Ancient Europe.* Chicago: Aldine.

Pilbeam, David. 1986. *Human Origins.* David Skamp Distinguished Lecture in Anthropology, Indiana University.

Pilbeam, David. 1987. "Rethinking Human Origins" in *Primate Evolution and Human Origins.* Hawthorne, N.Y.: Aldine de Gruytar.

Pilbeam, David, and Stephen Jay Gould. 1974. "Size and Scaling in Human Evolution" *Science,* 186:892–901.

Pimentel, David. 1991. "Response" *Science,* 991, 252:358.

Pimentel, David, L. E. Hurd, A. C. Bellotti, M. J. Forster, I. N. Oka, O. D. Sholes, and R. J. Whitman. 1973. "Food Production and the Energy Crisis" *Science,* Vol. 182.

Piperno, Dolores R., and Gayle J. Fritz. 1994. "On the Emergence of Agriculture in the New World," *Current Anthropology,* 35:637–643.

Pitt, David. 1977. "Comment" *Current Anthropology,* 18:628.

Plattner, Stuart. 1989. "Markets and Market Places," in Stuart Plattner, ed. *Economic Anthropology.* Stanford, Ca.: Stanford University: 171–208.

Podplefsky, Aaron, and Peter J. Brown, eds. 1989. *Applying Anthropology, An Introductory Reader.* Mountain View, Ca.: Mayfield.

Polanyi, Karl. 1968. "The Economy as Instituted Process" in E. E. LeClair, Jr., and H. K. Schneider, eds., *Economic Anthropology: Readings in Theory and Analysis.* New York: Holt, Rinehart and Winston.

Pope, Geoffrey G. 1989. "Bamboo and Human Evolution" *Natural History,* 10/89, pp. 48–57.

Pope, Geoffrey G. 1992. "Craniofacial Evidence for the Origin of Modern Humans in China" *Yearbook of Physical Anthropology,* 35:243–298.

Pospisil, Leopold. 1963. *The Kapauku Papuans of West New Guinea.* New York: Holt, Rinehart and Winston.

Pospisil, Leopold. 1971. *Anthropology of Law: A Comparative Theory.* New York: Harper & Row.

Powdermaker, Hortense. 1966. *Stranger and Friend: The Way of an Anthropologist.* New York: Norton.

Power, Margaret G. 1995. "Gombe Revisited: Are Chimpanzees Violent and Hierarchical in the 'Free' State?" *General Anthropology,* 2(1):5–9.

Premack, Ann James, and David Premack. 1972. "Teaching Language to an Ape" *Scientific American,* 277(4):92–99.

Price-Williams, D. R., ed. 1970. *Cross-cultural Studies: Selected Readings.* Baltimore, Md.: Penguin (Penguin Modern Psychology Readings).

Prideaux, Tom, and the Editors of Time-Life. 1973. *Cro-Magnon Man.* New York: Time-Life.

Prins, A. H. 1953. *East African Class Systems.* Gronigen, The Netherlands: J. B. Walters.

Radcliffe-Brown, A. R. 1931. "Social Organization of Australian Tribes" *Oceania Monographs,* No. 1. Melbourne: Macmillan.

Radcliffe-Brown, A. R. 1952. *Structure and Function in Primitive Society.* New York: Free Press.

Radcliffe-Brown, A. R., and C. D. Forde, eds. 1950. *African Systems of Kinship and Marriage.* London: Oxford University Press.

Rappaport, Roy A. 1969. "Ritual Regulation of Environmental Relations among a New Guinea People" in Andrew P. Vayda, ed., *Environment and Cultural Behavior.* Garden City, N.Y.: Natural History Press.

Rappaport, Roy. 1984. *Pigs for the Ancestors,* new enlarged ed. New Haven, Conn.: Yale University Press.

Rappaport, Roy A. 1994. "Commentary," *Anthropology Newsletter,* 35, No. 6:76.

Rathje, William L. 1974. "The Garbage Project: A New Way of Looking at the Problems of Archaeology" *Archaeology,* 27:236–241.

Rathje, William L. 1993. "Rubbish!" in *Talking About People: Readings in Contemporary Cultural Anthropology,* William A. Haviland and Robert J. Gordon, eds. Mountain View, CA: Mayfield Publishing Company.

Read-Martin, Catherine E., and Dwight W. Read. 1975. "Australopithecine Scavenging and Human Evolution: An Approach from Faunal Analysis" *Current Anthropology,* 16(3):359–368.

Read, Catherine E. 1973. "The Role of Faunal Analysis in Reconstructing Human Behavior: A Mousterian Example" paper presented at the meetings of the California Academy of Sciences, Long Beach.

Redfield, Robert, Ralph Linton, and Melville J. Herskovits. 1936. "Memorandum of the Study of Acculturation" *American Anthropologist,* 38:149–152.

Redman, Charles L. 1978. *The Rise of Civilization: From Early Farmers to Urban Society in the Ancient Near East.* San Francisco: Freeman.

Reid, J. J., M. B. Schiffer, and W. L. Rathje. 1975. "Behavioral Archaeology: Four Strategies" *American Anthropologist,* 77:864–869.

Reina, Ruben. 1966. *The Law of the Saints.* Indianapolis: Bobbs-Merrill.

Reiter, Rayna, ed. 1975. *Toward an Anthropology of Women.* New York: Monthly Review Press.

Relethford, John. H., and Henry C. Harpending. 1994. "Craniometric Variation, Genetic Theory, and Modern Human Origins," *American Journal of Physical Anthropology,* 95:249–270.

Renfrew, Colin. 1973. *Before Civilization: The Radiocarbon Revolution and Prehistoric Europe.* London: Jonathan Cape.

Reynolds, Vernon. 1994. "Primates in the Field, Primates in the Lab," *Anthropology Today* 10, No. 2: pp. 3–5.

Rice, Don S., and Prudence M. 1984. "Lessons from the Maya" *Latin American Research Review.* 19 (3):7–34.

Rindos, David. 1984. *The Origins of Agriculture: An Evolutionary Perspective.* Fl.: Academic Press.

Rodman, Hyman. 1968. "Class Culture" *International Encyclopedia of the Social Sciences,* Vol. 15. New York: Macmillan, pp. 332–337.

Rogers, Jeffery. 1994. "Levels of the Genealogical Hierarchy and the Problem of Hominoid Phylogeny," *American Journal of Physical Anthropology,* 94:81–88.

Romer, Alfred S. 1945. *Vertebrate Paleontology.* Chicago: University of Chicago Press.

Roosevelt, Anna Curtenius. 1984. "Population, Health, and the Evolution of Subsistence: Conclusions from the Conference" in Mark N. Cohen and George J. Armelagos, eds., *Paleopathology and the Origins of Agriculture.* Orlando, FL: Academic Press.

Rowe, Timothy. 1988. "New Issues for Phylogenetics" *Science,* 239:1183–1184.

Ruvdo, Maryellen. 1994. "Molecular Evolutionary Processes and Conflicting Gene Trees: The Hominoid Case," *American Journal of Physical Anthropology,* 94:89–113.

Sabloff, Jeremy, and C. C. Lambert-Karlovsky. 1973. *Ancient Civilization and Trade.* Albuquerque: University of New Mexico Press.

Sabloff, Jeremy A. 1989. *The Cities of Ancient Mexico*. New York: Thomas and Hudson.

Sabloff, J. A., and C. C. Lamberg-Karlovsky, eds. 1974. *The Rise and Fall of Civilizations, Modern Archaeological Approaches to Ancient Cultures*. Menlo Park, Calif.: Cummings.

Sahlins, Marshall. 1968. *Tribesmen*. Englewood Cliffs, N.J.: Prentice-Hall (Foundations of Modern Anthropology).

Sahlins, Marshall. 1961. "The Segmentary Lineage: An Organization of Predatory Expansion" *American Anthropologist*, 63:322–343.

Sahlins, Marshall. 1972. *Stone Age Economics*. Chicago: Aldine.

Salthe, Stanley N. 1972. *Evolutionary Biology*. New York: Holt, Rinehart and Winston.

Salzman, Philip C. 1967. "Political Organization among Nomadic Peoples" *Proceedings of the American Philosophical Society*, 3:115–131.

Sanday, Peggy R. 1975. "On the Causes of IQ Differences Between Groups and Implications for Social Policy" in Ashley Montagu, ed., *Race and IQ*. London: Oxford.

Sanday, Peggy Reeves. 1981. *Female Power and Male Dominance: On the Origins of Sexual Inequality*. Cambridge: Cambridge University Press.

Sangree, Walter H. 1965. "The Bantu Tiriki of Western Kenya" in James L. Gibbs, ed., *Peoples of Africa*. New York: Holt, Rinehart and Winston.

Sapir, E. 1917. "Do We Need a Superorganic?" *American Anthropologist*, 19:441–447.

Sapir, E. 1921. *Language*. New York: Harcourt.

Sapir, E. 1924. "Culture, Genuine or Spurious?" *American Journal of Sociology*, 29:401–429.

Savage, Jay M. 1969. *Evolution*, 3d ed. New York: Holt, Rinehart and Winston.

Scaglion, Richard. 1987. "Contemporary Law Development in Papua New Guinea" in *Anthropological Praxis: Translating Knowledge into Action*, edited by Robert M. Wulff and Shirley J. Fiske. Boulder, Co.: Westview Press.

Scarr-Salapatek, S. 1971. "Unknowns in the I.Q. Equation" *Science*, 174: 1223–1228.

Schaller, George B. 1963. *The Mountain Gorilla*. Chicago: Chicago University Press.

Schaller, George B. 1971. *The Year of the Gorilla*. New York: Ballantine.

Scheflen, Albert E. 1972. *Body Language and the Social Order*. Englewood Cliffs, N.J.: Prentice-Hall.

Schepartz, L. A. 1993. "Language and Human Origins," *Yearbook of Physical Anthropology*, 36:91–126.

Scheper-Hughes, Nancy. 1979. *Saints, Scholars and Schizophrenics*. Berkeley: University of California Press.

Schlegel, Alice. 1977. "Male and Female in Hopi Thought and Action" in *Sexual Stratification*, ed. Alice Schlegel. New York: Columbia University Press.

Schrire, Carmel, ed. 1984. *Past and Present in Hunter-Gatherer Studies*. Orlando, Fla.: Academic Press.

Schurtz, Heinrich. 1902. *Alterklassen und Männerbünde*. Berlin: Reimer.

Schusky, Ernest L. 1975. *Variation in Kinship*. New York: Holt, Rinehart and Winston.

Schusky, Ernest L. 1983. *Manual for Kinship Analysis*, 2d ed. Lanham, Md.: University Press of America.

Schwartz, Jeffrey H. 1984. "Hominoid Evolution: A Review and a Reassessment." *Current Anthropology*, 25(5):655–672.

Semenov, S. A. 1964. *Prehistoric Technology*. New York: Barnes & Noble.

Sen, Gita, and Caren Grown. 1987. *Development, Crisis, and Alternative Visions: Third World Women's Perspectives*. New York: Monthly Review Press.

Service, Elman R. 1971. *Primitive Social Organization: An Evolutionary Perspective*, 2nd ed. New York: Random House.

Seymour, Dorothy Z. 1986. "Black Children, Black Speech" in *Language Awareness*, 4th ed., ed. Paul Escholz, Alfred Rosa, and Virginia Clark. New York: St. Martin's Press.

Shapiro, Harry, ed. 1971. *Man, Culture and Society*. 2d ed. New York: Oxford University Press.

Sharer, Robert J., and Wendy Ashmore. 1993. *Archaeology: Discovering Our Past*, 2nd ed. Palo Alto, Calif.: Mayfield.

Sharp, Lauriston. 1952. "Steel Axes for Stone Age Australians" in Edward H. Spicer, ed., *Human Problems in Technological Change*. New York: Russell Sage.

Shaw, Dennis G. 1984. "A Light at the End of the Tunnel: Anthropological Contributions Toward Global Competence" *Anthropology Newsletter*, 25:16.

Sheets, Payson. 1993. "Dawn of a New Stone Age in Eye Surgery" in *Archaeology: Discovering Our Past* 2nd ed., by Robert J. Sharer and Wendy Ashmore. Palo Alto, Ca.: Mayfield.

Shimkin, Dimitri B., Sol Tax, and John W. Morrison, eds. 1978. *Anthropology for the Future*. Urbana, Ill.: Department of Anthropology, University of Illinois, Research Report No. 4.

Shinnie, Margaret. 1970. *Ancient African Kingdoms*. New York: New American Library.

Shostak, Marjorie. 1983. *Nisa: The Life and Words of a !Kung Woman*. New York: Vintage.

Shreeve, James. 1994. "'Lucy', Crucial Early Human Ancestor, Finally Gets a Head," *Science*, 264:34–35.

Shreeve, James. 1995. *The Neandertal Enigma*. New York: Willliam Morrow.

Shuey, A. M. 1966. *The Testing of Negro Intelligence*. New York: Social Science Press.

Sillen, Andrew, and C. K. Brain. 1990. "Old Flame," *Natural History*, 4/90:6–10.

Simons, Elwyn L. 1972. *Primate Evolution*. New York: Macmillan.

Simons, Elwyn L. 1989. "Human Origins" *Science*, 245:1343–1350.

Simons, Elwyn L. 1995. "Skulls and Anterior Teeth of *Catopithecus* (Primates: Anthropoidea) From the Eocene and Anthropoid Origins," *Science*, 268:1885–1888.

Simons, E. L., D. T. Rasmussen, and D. L. Gebo. 1987. "A New Species of Propliopithecus from the Fayum Egypt" *American Journal of Physical Anthropology*, 73:139–147.

Simpson, George G. 1949. *The Meaning of Evolution*. New Haven, Conn.: Yale University Press.

Sjoberg, Gideon. 1960. *The Preindustrial City*. New York: Free Press.

Skelton, Randall R., Henry M. McHenry, and Gerrell M. Drawhorn. 1986. "Phylogenetic Analysis of Early Hominids" *Current Anthropology*, 27:21–43.

Slobin, Dan I. 1971. *Psycholinguistics*. Glenview, Ill.: Scott, Foresman.

Smith, Allan H., and John L. Fisher. 1970. *Anthropology*. Englewood Cliffs, N.J.: Prentice-Hall.

Smith, B. Holly. 1994. "Patterns of Dental Development in *Homo*, *Australopithecus*, *Pan*, and *Gorilla*," *American Journal of Physical Anthropology*, 94:307–325.

Smith, Bruce D. 1977. "Archaeological Inference and Inductive Confirmation" *American Anthropologist*, 79(3):598–617.

Smith, Fred H., and Gail C. Raynard. 1980. "Evolution of the Supraorbital Region in Upper Pleistocene Fossil Hominids from South-Central Europe" *American Journal of Physical Anthropology*, 53:589–610.

Smith, Philip E. L. 1976. *Food Production and Its Consequences*, 2d ed. Menlo Park, Calif.: Cummings.

Smith, Raymond. 1970. "Social Stratification in the Caribbean" in Leonard Plotnicov and Arthur Tudin, eds., *Essays in Comparative Social Stratification*. Pittsburgh: University of Pittsburgh Press.

Smuts, Barbara. 1987. "What Are Friends For?" *Natural History*. 96(2):36–44.

Snowden, Charles T. 1990. "Language Capabilities of Nonhuman Animals" *Yearbook of Physical Anthropology*, 33, 215–243.

Speck, Frank G. 1920. "Penobscot Shamanism" *Memoirs of the American Anthropological Association*, 6:239–288.

Speck, Frank G. 1935. "Penobscot Tales and Religious Beliefs" *Journal of American Folk-Lore*, 48(187):1–107.

Speck, Frank G. 1940. *Penobscot Man*. Philadelphia: University of Pennsylvania Press.

Spencer, Frank, and Fred H. Smith. 1981. "The Significance of Ales Hrdlicka's 'Neanderthal Phase of Man': A Historical and Current Assessment" *American Journal of Physical Anthropology*, 56: 435–459.

Spencer, Herbert, 1896. *Principles of Sociology*. New York: Appleton.

Spiro, Melford E. 1966. "Religion: Problems of Definition and Explanation" in Michael Banton, ed., *Anthropological Approaches to the Study of Religion* (A.S.A. Monographs). London: Tavistock.

Spitz, René A. 1949. "'Hospitalism" *The Psychoanalytic Study of the Child, Vol. 1*. New York: International Universities Press.

Spradley, James P. 1979. *The Ethnographic Interview*. New York: Holt, Rinehart and Winston.

Spradley, James P. 1980. *Participant Observation*. New York: Holt, Rinehart and Winston.

Spuhler, James N. 1979. "Continuities and Discontinuities in Anthropoid-Hominid Behavioral Evolution: Bipedal Locomotion and Sexual Reception" in *Evolutionary Biology and Human Social Behavior*, ed. N. A. Chagnon and William Irons. North Scituate, MA: Duxbury Press.

Stacey, Judith. 1990. *Brave New Families*. New York: Basic Books.

Stahl, Ann Brower. 1984. "Hominid Dietary Selection Before Fire" *Current Anthropology*, 25:151–168.

Stanley, Stephen M. 1979. *Macroevolution*. San Francisco: Freeman.

Stanner, W. E. 1968. "Radcliffe-Brown, A. R." *International Encyclopedia of the Social Sciences*, Vol. 13. New York: Macmillan.

Steward, Julian H. 1972. *Theory of Culture Change: The Methodology of Multilinear Evolution*. Urbana: University of Illinois Press.

Stiles, Daniel. 1979. "Early Acheulian and Developed Oldowan" *Current Anthropology*, 20(l):126–129.

Stiles, Daniel. 1992. "The Hunter-Gatherer 'Revisionist' Debate," *Anthropology Today*, 8, No. 2: pp. 13–17.

Stirton, Ruben Arthur. 1967. *Time, Life, and Man*. New York: Wiley.

Stocker, Terry. 1987. "A Technological Mystery Resolved" *Invention and Technology*, Spring:64.

Stocking, George W., Jr. 1968. *Race, Culture and Evolution: Essays in the History of Anthropology*. New York: Free Press.

Stoler, Mark. 1982. "To Tell the Truth," *Vermont Visions*, 82, No. 3:3.

Straus, W. L., and A. J. E. Cave. 1957. "Pathology and the Posture of Neanderthal Man" *Quarterly Review of Biology*, 32.

Susman, Randall L. 1988. "Hand of *Paranthropus robustus* from Member 1, Swartkrans: Fossil Evidence for Tool Behavior," *Science*, 240:781–784.

Swadesh, Morris. 1959. "Linguistics as an Instrument of Prehistory" *Southwestern Journal of Anthropology*, 15:20–35.

Swartz, Marc J., Victor W. Turner, and Arthur Tuden. 1966. *Political Anthropology*. Chicago: Aldine.

Swisher III, C. C., G. H. Curtis, T. Jacob, A. G. Getty, A. Suprijo, Widiasmoro. 1994. "Age of the Earliest Known Hominids in Java, Indonesia," *Science*, 263:1118–1121.

Tague, Robert G. 1992. "Sexual Dimorphism in the Human Bony Pelvis, with a Consideration of the Neanderthal Pelvis from Kebara Cave, Israel" *American Journal of Physical Anthropology*, 88:1–21.

Tannen, Deborah. 1990. *You Just Don't Understand: Women and Men in Conversation*. New York: William Morrow.

Tattersall, Ian. 1975. *The Evolutionary Significance of Ramapithecus*. Minneapolis: Burgess.

Tax, Sol. 1953. *Penny Capitalism: A Guatemalan Indian Economy*, Smithsonian Institution, Institute of Social Anthropology, Pub. No. 16. Washington, D.C.: Government Printing Office.

Tax, Sol, ed. 1962. *Anthropology Today: Selections*. Chicago: University of Chicago Press.

Tax, Sol, Sam Stanley, and others. 1975. "In Honor of Sol Tax" *Current Anthropology*, 16:507–540.

Templeton, Alan R. 1994. "'Eve': Hypothesis Compatability Versus Hypothesis Testing," *American Anthropologist*, 96:144–147.

Thomas, David H. 1974. *Predicting the Past*. New York: Holt, Rinehart and Winston.

Thomas, David H. 1989. *Archaeology*, 2nd ed. New York: Holt, Rinehart and Winston.

Thomas, Elizabeth Marshall. 1994. *The Tribe of the Tiger*. New York: Simon and Schuster.

Thomas, W. L., ed. 1956. *Man's Role in Changing the Face of the Earth*. Chicago: University of Chicago Press.

Thompson, J. E. S. 1960. *Maya Hieroglyphic Writing: Introduction*. Norman: University of Oklahoma Press.

Thompson, Stith. 1960. *The Folktale*. New York: Holt, Rinehart and Winston.

Thorne, Alan G., and Melford H. Wolpoff. 1981. "Regional Continuity in Australasian Pleistocene Hominid Evolution" *American Journal of Physical Anthropology*, 55:337–349.

Thorne, Barrie, and Marilyn Yalom, eds. 1982. *Rethinking the Family: Some Feminist Problems*. New York: Longman.

Tiffany, Sharon, ed. 1979. *Women in Africa*. St. Albans, Vt.: Eden Press.

Tobias, Philip V. 1980. "The Natural History of the Heliocoidal Occlusal Plane and Its Evolution in Early Homo" *American Journal of Physical Anthropology*, 53:173–187.

Trager, George L. 1964. "Paralanguage: A First Approximation" in Dell Hymes, ed., *Language in Culture and Society*. New York: Harper & Row.

Trinkaus, Erik. 1986. "The Neanderthals and Modern Human Origins" *Annual Review of Anthropology*, 15:197.

Tuden, Arthur. 1970. "Slavery and Stratification among the Ila of Central Africa" in Arthur Tuden and Leonard Plotnicov, eds., *Social Stratification in Africa*. New York: Free Press.

Tumin, Melvin M. 1967. *Social Stratification: The Forms and Functions of Inequality*. Englewood Cliffs, N.J.: Prentice-Hall (Foundations of Modern Sociology).

Turnbull, Colin M. 1961. *The Forest People*. New York: Simon & Schuster.

Turnbull, Colin M. 1972. *The Mountain People*. New York: Simon & Schuster.

Turnbull, Colin M. 1983. *The Human Cycle*. New York: Simon & Schuster.

Turnbull, Colin. 1983. *Mbuti Pygmies: Change and Adaptation*. New York: Holt, Rinehart and Winston.

Turner, Terry. 1991. "Major Shift in Brazilian Yanomami Policy" *Anthropology Newsletter* 32, No. 5: pp. 1 and 46.

Turner, V. W. 1957. *Schism and Continuity in an African Society*. Manchester Eng.: The University Press.

Turner, V. W. 1969. *The Ritual Process*. Chicago: Aldine.

Tylor, Edward Burnett, 1871. *Primitive Culture: Researches into the Development of Mythology, Philosophy, Religion, Language, Art and Customs*. London: Murray.

Tylor, Sir Edward B. 1931. "Animism" in V. F. Calverton, ed., *The Making of Man: An Outline of Anthropology*. New York: Modern Library.

Ucko, Peter J., and Andrée Rosenfeld. 1967. *Paleolithic Cave Art*. New York: McGraw-Hill.

Ucko, P. J., R. Tringham, and G. W. Dimbleby, eds. 1972. *Man, Settlement and Urbanism*. London: Duckworth.

Valentine, Charles A. 1968. *Culture and Poverty*. Chicago: University of Chicago Press.

Van Willigen, John. 1986. *Applied Anthropology, An Introduction*. South Hadley, Ma.: Bergin and Garvey.

Van Den Berghe, Pierre. 1992. "The Modern State: Nation Builder or Nation Killer?," *International Journal of Group Tensions* 22, No. 3:191–207.

Van Gennep, Arnold. 1960. *The Rites of Passage*. Chicago: University of Chicago Press.

Van Allen, Judith. 1979. "Sitting on a Man: Colonialism and the Lost Political Institutions of Igbo Women" in *Women in Society*, ed. Sharon Tiffany. St. Albans, Vt.: Eden Press.

Vansina, Jan. 1965. *Oral Tradition: A Study in Historical Methodology*, H. M. Wright, trans. Chicago: Aldine.

Vayda, Andrew P. 1961. "Expansion and Warfare among Swidden Agriculturalists" *American Anthropologist*, 63:346–358.

Vayda, Andrew, ed. 1969. *Environment and Cultural Behavior: Ecological Studies in Cultural Anthropology*, Garden City, N.Y.: Natural History Press.

Vincent, John. 1979. "On the Special Division of Labor, Population, and the Origins of Agriculture" *Current Anthropology*, 20(2):422–425.

Vogelman, Thomas C., and others. 1972. Film: *Prehistoric Life in the Champlain Valley*. Burlington, Vt.: Department of Anthropology, University of Vermont.

Voget, F. W. 1960. "Man and Culture: An Essay in Changing Anthropological Interpretation" *American Anthropologist*, 62:943–965.

Voget, F. W. 1975. *A History of Ethnology*. New York: Holt, Rinehart and Winston.

Vogt, Evon Z. 1970. *The Zinacantecos of Mexico, A Modern Maya Way of Life*. New York: Holt, Rinehart and Winston, pp. 30–34.

Wagner, Philip L. 1960. *A History of Ethnology*. New York: Holt, Rinehart and Winston.

Wallace, Anthony F. C. 1956. "Revitalization Movements" *American Anthropologist*, 58:264–281.

Wallace, Anthony F. C. 1965, "The Problem of the Psychological Validity of Componential Analysis" *American Anthropologist, Special Publication*, Part 2, 67(5):229–248.

Wallace, Anthony F. C. 1966. *Religion: An Anthropological View*. New York: Random House.

Wallace, Anthony F. C. 1970. *Culture and Personality*, 2d ed. New York: Random House.

Wallace, Ernest, and E. Adamson Hoebel. 1952. *The Comanches*. Norman: University of Oklahoma Press.

Ward, C. V., A. Walker, M. F. Teaford, and I. Odhiambo. 1993. "Partial Skeleton of *Proconsul nyanzae* from Mfangano Island, Kenya," *American Journal of Physical Anthropology*, 90:77–111.

Wardhaugh, Ronald. 1972. *Introduction to Linguistics*. New York: McGraw-Hill.

Washburn, S. L., and Ruth Moore. 1980. *Ape into Human: A Study of Human Evolution*, 2d ed. Boston: Little, Brown.

Weatherford, Jack. 1988. *Indian Givers: How the Indians of the Americas Transformed the World*. New York: Fawcett Columbine.

Weaver, Muriel P. 1972. *The Aztecs, Maya and Their Predecessors*. New York: Seminar Press.

Weiner, J. S. 1955. *The Piltdown Forgery*. Oxford: Oxford University Press.

Weiner, Annette B. 1977. Review of "Trobriand Cricket: An Ingenious Response to Colonialism" *American Anthropologist*, 79:506.

Weiner, Annette. 1988. *The Trobrianders of Papua New Guinea*. New York: Holt, Rinehart and Winston.

Weiner, Myron. 1966. *Modernization: The Dynamics of Growth*. New York: Basic Books.

Weiss, Mark L., and Alan E. Mann. 1990. *Human Biology and Behavior*, 5th ed. Boston: Little, Brown.

Weitzman, Lenore J. 1985. *The Divorce Revolution: The Unexpected Social and Economic Consequences for Women and Children in America*. New York: The Free Press.

Wells, Calvin. 1964. *Bones, Bodies and Disease*. London: Thames and Hudson.

Werner, Dennis. 1990. *Amazon Journey*. Englewood Cliffs, NJ: Prentice Hall.

Wernick, Robert, and the Editors of Time-Life. 1973. *The Monument Builders*. New York: Time-Life.

Westermarck, Edward A. 1926. *A Short History of Marriage*. New York: Macmillan.

Wheeler, Pete. "Human Ancestors Walked Tall, Stayed Cool," *Natural History*, 102 (8), 65–66.

Whelehan, Patricia. 1985. "Review of Incest, a Biosocial View" *American Anthropologist*, 87:678.

White, Douglas R. 1988. "Rethinking Polygyny: Co-Wives, Codes and Cultural Systems" *Current Anthropology*, 29.

White, Edmond, Dale Brown, and the Editors of Time-Life. 1973. *The First Men*. New York: Time-Life.

White, Leslie. 1949. *The Science of Culture: A Study of Man and Civilization*. New York: Farrar, Strauss.

White, Leslie. 1959. *The Evolution of Culture: The Development of Civilization to the Fall of Rome*. New York: McGraw-Hill.

White, Peter. 1976. *The Past Is Human*, 2d ed. New York: Maplinger.

White, Randall. 1992. "The Earliest Images: Ice Age 'Art' in Europe," *Expedition*, 34(3):37–51.

White, Tim D. 1979. "Evolutionary Implications of Pliocene Hominid Footprints" *Science*, 208:175–176.

Whitehead, Neil L., and R. Brian Ferguson. 1993. "Deceptive Stereotypes About Tribal Warfare," *Chronicle of Higher Education*, Nov. 10: p. A48.

Whiting, Beatrice B., ed. 1963. *Six Cultures: Studies of Child Rearing*. New York: Wiley.

Whiting, John W. M., and J. Child. 1953. *Child Training and Personality: A Cross-cultural Study*. New Haven, Conn.: Yale University Press.

Willey, Gordon R. 1971. *An Introduction to American Archaeology, Vol. 2: South America*. Englewood Cliffs, N.J.: Prentice-Hall.

Willey, Gordon R. 1966. *An Introduction to American Archaeology, Vol. 1: North America*. Englewood Cliffs, N.J.: Prentice-Hall.

Wills, Christopher. 1994. "The Skin We're In," *Discover*, 15(11):77–81.

Wilson, A. K., and V. M. Sarich. 1969. "A Molecular Time Scale for Human Evolution" *Proceedings of the National Academy of Science*, 63:1089–1093.

Wingert, Paul. 1962. *Primitive Art: Its Tradition and Styles*. London: Oxford University Press; New York: World. 1965.

Wirsing, Rolf L. 1985. "The Health of Traditional Societies and the Effects of Acculturation" *Current Anthropology*, 26(3):303–322.

Wittfogel, Karl A. 1957. *Oriental Despotism, A Comparative Study of Total Power*. New Haven, Conn.: Yale University Press.

Wolf, Eric. 1959. *Sons of the Shaking Earth*. Chicago: University of Chicago Press.

Wolf, Eric. 1966. *Peasants*. Englewood Cliffs, N.J.: Prentice-Hall (Foundations of Modern Anthropology).

Wolf, Eric. 1982. *Europe and the People without History*. Berkeley: University of California Press.

Wolf, Margery. 1972. *Women and the Family in Rural Taiwan*. Stanford, Ca.: Stanford University Press.

Wolf, Margery. 1985. *Revolution Postponed-Women in Contemporary China*. Stanford Ca.: Stanford University Press.

Wolfe, Alvin W. 1977. "The Supranational Organization of Production: An Evolutionary Perspective." *Current Anthropology*, 18:615–635.

Wolpoff, M. H. 1971. "Interstitial Wear" *American Journal of Physical Anthropology*, 34:205–227.

Wolpoff, M. H. 1977. "Review of Earliest Man in the Lake Rudolf Basin" *American Anthropologist*, 79:708–711.

Wolpoff, Milford H. 1982. "*Ramapithecus* and Hominid Origins" *Current Anthropology*, 23:501–522.

Wolpoff, M.H. 1993. "Evolution in *Homo erectus*: The Question of Stasis" in *The Human Evolution Source Book*, Russell L. Ciochon and John G. Fleagle, eds. Englewood Cliffs, N.J.: Prentice Hall.

Wolpoff, M. H. 1993. "Multiregional Evolution: The Fossil Alternative to Eden" in *The Human Evolution Source Book*, Russell L. Ciochon and John G. Fleagle, eds. Englewood Cliffs, N.J.: Prentice Hall.

Wood, Bernard, Christopher Wood, and Lyle Konigsberg. 1994. "*Paranthropus boisei*: An Example of Evolutionary Stasis?" *American Journal of Physical Anthropology*, 95:117–136.

Woolfson, Peter. 1972. "Language, Thought, and Culture" in Virginia P. Clark, Paul A. Escholz, and Alfred F. Rosa, eds., *Language*. New York: St. Martins.

World Bank. 1982. *Tribal Peoples and Economic Development*. Washington, D.C.: World Bank.

Wright, Robin. 1984. "Towards a New Indian Policy in Brazil" *Cultural Survival Quarterly*, 8,(1).

Wulff, Robert M., and Shirley J. Fiske. 1987. *Anthropological Praxis: Translating Knowledge into Action*. Boulder, Co.: Westview.

Zur, Judith. 1994. "The Psychological Impact and Impunity," *Anthropology Today*, 10, No. 3: p. 16, 12–17.

INDEX

deviant, 350, *350*
field studies of, 354–356
of Kalahari Desert lions, 352
language and, 384–385
learning new patterns of, 366
primate, 99–113
race and, 327–328
religion and, 660–661
in Samoa, 405
Behavioral environment, 402–405
Beijing. *See* Peking
Belfer-Cohen, A., 219n
Bell Curve, The (Herrnstein and Murray), 329
Benedict, Ruth Fulton, 416, *416*, 418
Benyon, A. D., 144n
Berdache, 420n
Berdan, F. F., 455n
Bernardi, B., 599
Berra, T. M., 77
Bible, creation in, 6
Big Man, in Melanesia, 609. *See also* Melanesia
Bilateral kinship, 565–567, *566*
Binford, Lewis R., 212, 213
Biological adaptation, 242, 342
Biological avoidance, of incest, 502–503
Biological selection, evolution and, 332–336
Biology. *See also* Evolution
evolution and, *54*
population in, 62
race and, 315–323
sex and, 347
Biomedical research, primate extinction and, 100
Biostratigraphers, 193
Bipedalism, 132–133
of *Australopithecus*, 139, 143–144
female human sexuality and, 180
heat stress and, 152–155
of humans, 150–156
Birdsell, Joseph, 315, 324
Birdwhistell, R. L., 397
Birth control, 754
Birth rate, among food foragers, 440
Black, Davidson, 186
Black, H. C., 627n
Black English, 391
Black Muslim movement, 712
Black pride movement, 326
Blacks. *See* African Americans
Blade technique, 227
Blood, 58, 60–61
Blood types
alleles for, 312, 313, *313*
east-west gradient in frequency of, *331*
polymorphic traits and, 312
Blumenschine, Robert J., 175
Blumer, M. A., 264n
Boas, Franz, *23*, 405, 709, *709*
Boats. *See* Ships and shipping
Bodley, J. H., 21n, 488n, 719n, 727, 746n, 749n, 757
Body
decoration of, *668*
structure, function, and growth of, 84, 85

Body hair, of humans, 152–155
Body language, 376–378
sexism and, 389–390
Body types
racial classification by, 315
racial variables and, 323
technology and, 226
Bones. *See* Fossils
Boone, Margaret S., 546n
Border Cave skull, 219
Borrowing, cultural diffusion and, 702
Bosnia
refugees in, *728*
social control and, *604*
Botswana, Ju/'hoansi people in, 406. *See also* Ju/'hoansi people
Bound morpheme, 374
Bow and arrow, 229–230
in Mesolithic period, 245
musical bows and, 230–231
Boys. *See also* Men
role models of, 420–421
sexual behavior of, 498–499
Brace, C. L., 339
Brachiate, 92
Bradfield, R. M., 599
Brahmins, in India, 589
Braidwood, Robert, 260
Brain
of *Australopithecus*, 142–143
cognitive capacity and, 242
of Cro-Magnons, 226
heat stress and, *154*, 155
of Neandertals, 209, 216
of primates, 89–90
speech, signing, and, 394
tools, meat, and, 172–178
Brain, C. K., 174, 175, 198
Branch Davidians, *663*
Branda, R. E., 325n
Brazil
Amazon rain forest in, 736–737
development in, *734*, 734–735
genocide in, 705–706
malnutrition in, 488
Wauja people in, 719–724
Breeding, among primates, 104
Br'er Rabbit, 676
Bride price, 517
Bride service, 517
Britain. *See also* England
ship-launching by, *655*
women in Igbo society and, 618
Bronze Age, 290
burial mounds from, 37
Brown, D., 203
Brown, John Seely, 487
Brown, P. J., 487n, 506n, 711n
Brues, A. M., 339
Building, at Tikal, 293. *See also* Construction; Housing
Buka (Solomon Islands), native religious cult in, 662
Bunn, Henry, 173
Bureau of American Ethnology, 709
Burials
English mounds for, 37

Florida sites of, 34–35
of Moche priestess, 297–301, *298, 299*
Neandertal sites of, 215
social stratification and, 296
Burin, 228
Burling, R., 370n
Burning. *See* Slash-and-burn agriculture
Bushmen, 406–407, *407, 438,* 439. *See also* Ju/'hoansi people
rock art of, 683–690, *684, 688–690*
warfare and, 629
Business
anthropologists as consultants to, 487
economics, culture, and, 487, 488–489
language use in, 387
Butcher, J. N., 424n
Byrne, R., 264n

Calendars
astronomy and, 292
dating and, *47*
of Maya, 287, 288
Camp, in food foraging societies, 444
Campbell, B. G., 157, 183, 203, 249, 363
Canaanites, gods of, 643
Canada, monogamy in, 505–507
Cancers
pesticides and, 336
of skin, 325
ultraviolet radiation and, 333
Canela people, 362–363
Cannibalism, ritual, 655–656
Carbon dating. *See* Radiocarbon analysis
Cargo cult, *662,* 713
Caribou Indians, 519
Carneiro, Robert, 304
Carnivores
hominines and, 175
scavenging by, 173
Carrying capacity, 440
Carson, R. C., 424n
Carver, George Washington, *329*
Carvings, of Mousterian peoples, 215
Cashdan, F., 438n
Caste, 587–591, 589. *See also* Social class
Castenada, Carlos, 649
Castillo, L. J., 297n
Catarrhine origins, *123,* 123–125
Catarrhine primates, evolutionary relationships among, *131*
Catopithecus, 122, *123,* 125
fossils of, 124
origins, 123–125
Caucasoid, use of term, 314, 315
Cavalieri, P., 107n, 394n
Cavalli-Sforza, L. L., 77
Cavallo, J. A., 173n
Cave art, 235–239, *687*
Caveman, 208
Cell division, 58–61
Census Bureau, racial categories of, 322
Central America, racial classifications, 321
Central government. *See* Government
Centralized political systems, 612–616
chiefdoms, 613–614
state systems, 614–616
Cercopithecoidea (Old World monkeys), 87

LITERARY CREDITS